AMERICA VOTES 12

A HANDBOOK OF CONTEMPORARY
AMERICAN ELECTION STATISTICS

COMPILED AND EDITED BY
RICHARD M. SCAMMON
and
ALICE V. McGILLIVRAY

1976 [redacted]

ELECTIONS RESEARCH CENTER

CONGRESSIONAL QUARTERLY WASHINGTON 1977

Copies available from: Congressional Quarterly Inc., 1414 22nd St. N.W., Washington, D.C. 20037

Printed in the United States of America

Library of Congress Catalog Card Number: 56-10132
International Standard Book Number: 0-87187-033-9

CONTENTS

Cities will be found in their appropriate state sections.

INTRODUCTION

The twelfth volume of AMERICA VOTES follows the general pattern used in the first eleven handbooks. Users will note a continuation of the state chapter system, including a "profile" sheet, maps, county and ward breakdowns of voting data, time sequence detail in the vote for Congress, and primary election figures. The Congressional figures, as in earlier volumes of AMERICA VOTES, are in the form of a time series, running back to the date of formation of each Congressional District in its present boundaries. Due to the extensive redistricting undertaken after the 1970 Census, there are only 19 districts in which data are at hand for elections prior to the 1972 voting. Both county-by-county and time sequence data are printed in comparable formats and the new processing technique first used in AMERICA VOTES 9 has been continued to make the data as readable as possible.

Attention of AMERICA VOTES 12 users is directed particularly to the note sections at the close of each state chapter. Many special situations develop in the politics of the various states, and these are detailed in the note sections. Distribution of the non-major-party vote, boundary changes, discrepancies or corrections in the canvassed returns — these and similar state peculiarities are listed here.

Users will also note several slight discrepancies in the population data, caused usually by recounting and recapitulation problems after data had been employed to realign local districts. Users should not be taken aback by the few counties (all very small) in which more votes were cast than there were people in the 1970 Census count. Such circumstances are due to changeable residences and employment circumstances or increases in the population since 1970.

Originally the note section was intended to include for each state a source reference as well as comments on special state electoral situations, but this has appeared to be unnecessary. American elections data, organized as they are by the states rather than by Federal authority, come almost entirely from state sources. With a few exceptions, examples of which are North Carolina, Oklahoma, and Virginia, materials come from the Secretary of State, the official responsible in most states for election administration and election reporting. Some Secretaries report their elections voluminously, some in very limited detail, but all states make out at least a minimum type of reporting document.

The special section has been continued in this volume to detail the voting in the 1972 and 1976 Presidential preference primaries and the tables for Presidential voting back to 1948 have been continued. Statistics of voting in New England by larger cities and towns have also been continued for 1976. However, because of the decreasing share of the vote cast in large cities, the AMERICA VOTES coverage of such voting has been cut back to cities of over one million population in which voting data are available by ward or district.

AMERICA VOTES 12 seeks to draw from all these sources the raw material of American elections behavior. From that raw material is built a national reference volume on American politics. To make this reference volume of maximum efficiency in meeting the needs of its users, suggestions as to new materials, together with any corrections of data in this volume, are solicited.

It is encouraging to note here the growing number of individual state studies appearing in the AMERICA VOTES pattern. Data collections now exist for a number of states and work is in progress on still more such undertakings. These are essential studies for those concerned with the politics of the states they cover and their appearance represents a most useful additional source of detailed information on American political behavior.

For AMERICA VOTES 12 as for its predecessors, it would be impossible to list all those to whom acknowledgment is due for aid in bringing this volume to the public. To all who have helped in gathering this material and preparing it for publication must go the gratitude of the Editors and of all those who will use this newest volume in the series AMERICA VOTES.

Richard M. Scammon
Alice V. McGillivray

Washington, D.C.
August, 1977

PREFACE
by
RICHARD M. SCAMMON

The American electorate ended eight years of divided government Nov. 2, 1976, selecting Democrat Jimmy Carter of Georgia as the 39th President and maintaining lopsided Democratic majorities in both houses of Congress.

Carter's victory over President Ford was narrow, achieved by a popular plurality of fewer than two million and an electoral count of only 297-240. The congressional decision was overwhelming, with Democrats keeping their 2-1 advantage in the House and their 62-38 margin over Republicans in the Senate.

The combined result was to restore Democratic leadership at both ends of Pennsylvania Avenue, the first such restoration since John F. Kennedy's election in 1960.

This volume of AMERICA VOTES reports the Presidential voting of 1976, as the first volume in this series reported the Presidential election of 1952. During that period the population of voting age in the United States rose from one hundred million to one hundred fifty million and the popular vote for President increased from 61,550,000 in the first Eisenhower victory to 81,555,000 in last fall's election of Jimmy Carter as President.

Actually, the twenty million increase in gross vote overstates the situation. Had Alaska, Hawaii, and the District of Columbia voted in 1952, the gap would be less. So would it have been lowered if young voters 18, 19, and 20 had voted in 1952 as they did in 1976. And so would it have been narrowed if black voters had had the full franchise in 1952 as they did in 1976.

Whatever the true gap might have been, the changes in voting have been markedly different across the country. Of the eleven states of the Old Confederacy, six more than doubled their vote and Louisiana and Texas came close to doubling. Outside the South only Arizona and Nevada did so.

On the other side of the coin, Nebraska, New York, Rhode Island, and West Virginia cast fewer votes in 1976 than they had 24 years earlier, with New York alone having a drop of nearly 600,000 in its Presidential vote. Three other states came very close to this group, showing only very small increases in their vote from 1952-1976. Where there were losses in total vote, these appear to have come largely with population changes in older cities and in rural areas.

On the urban side, for example, consider these cities of the East and Midwest and their vote in 1976 with their 1952 vote in brackets, both figures in the hundreds of thousands of votes cast: New York 2,145 (3,411); Chicago 1,227 (1,842); Philadelphia 746 (959); Detroit 446 (813); Boston 192 (357); St. Louis 180 (381). From another viewpoint, what is most important to the cities is their political "clout," their relative political influence. In Maryland, for example, Baltimore cast 39% of the Maryland state Presidential vote in 1952; by 1976 this share had fallen to 18%. Similarly, in Detroit, that city's share of the 1952 Michigan vote was 29%; by 1976 it had dropped down to but 12%. In New York city, which more than provided the huge drop-off in New York state's vote between Eisenhower and Carter, the 1952 share of the state vote was 48%, nearly half; by 1976, it had fallen to less than one-third. And the circumstances could be duplicated in many other of the older cities; even though there would be exceptions in the newer communities, and exceptions in parts of the South and West, the pattern of voting equals the pattern of population, and often exceeds it.

But this is not true for the cities alone. In the rush to suburbia, rural America, as well as the older cities, had examples of loss in total votes from 1952 (and Eisenhower) to 1976 (and Carter). Some states could list counties with a 10, 20, or 30 percent drop-off in votes counted in the two elections. Just for one example, in Iowa, the Presidential vote total for 1952 and 1976 increased by only 11,000 votes. But in the nine largest counties of the state, counties with cities of some size, the vote went up 121,000. In the rest of the state, it dropped 110,000.

These long-range changes, taken over the quarter century since the first Eisenhower election, can be seen in somewhat different patterns in more recent comparatives, in the shifting voting totals between the 1972 Nixon-McGovern race and the Carter-Ford contest last year. Between these two contests the Presidential vote rose by some 3,800,000 votes, and most states participated in this increase. Interestingly enough, it was the biggest states which dropped off substantially — California by 500,000 votes, New York by 630,000. Several other states had small decreases in their vote, but in both gross size and percentage loss the greatest decline came in the nation's two largest states.

During this quarter century America had its highest voter turnout figure in Presidential voting in 1960, the year of John Kennedy's election, though the participation rate dropped from that 63% to 54% in the November 1976 voting.

By states the leader in 1976 turnout was Minnesota with a participation of 71.7% of the total voting age population. Closely following were Utah (69.1%) and North Dakota (68.8%). In 1972 the leading states were these three plus South Dakota, perhaps due to the stimulus of Senator McGovern's campaign for the Presidency that year. Back in 1968, Utah was the highest turnout state.

Moving the shifts from those of voter turnout to political persuasion, the pattern from 1972 to 1976 is an inconstant one. Over-all the Democratic gain between the two elections was one of 12.6 percentage points, from 37.5% for Senator McGovern in 1972 to 50.1% for Jimmy Carter in 1976. But changes in the states varied significantly. In seven states the Democratic Presidential percentage rose by double the national average — that is, rose by at least 25 points. In four others (Florida and Louisiana in the South, Oklahoma and West Virginia among the "border states") the double gain figure was nearly met. Every one of the "doubling" high change states was Southern and all had been carried by President Nixon by heavy margins in 1972. In 1968 they were won by either Nixon or AIP candidate George Wallace. The Carter candidacy evidently provided an opportunity to move back to a more traditional political allegiance, not unrelated to the candidate not only being a moderate but also the first non-incumbent Southerner to be nominated for the Presidency by one of the two major political parties since well before the Civil War.

The nature of this shift can also be deduced from the shifting support pattern of the 578 counties carried in 1968 by George Wallace. Of these 578, all save eight were in the South. Those in the Old Confederacy (570) went overwhelmingly for President Nixon's re-election in 1972, with Nixon carrying 564 and six going to Senator McGovern. In 1976 these same 570 Southern counties were carried 505 by Jimmy Carter and 65 by President Ford. This shift of Wallaceites to Carter, and the melding of a heavy pro-Carter black vote was a hallmark of the Carter primary victory and of the general election win as well.

In all, Carter carried ten of the eleven Southern states, losing only Virginia. His margin of 297-240 in the Electoral College (one vote went to non-candidate Ronald Reagan) was made up of a solid 118 to 12 vote in the South (with a popular plurality of 1,725,000), and a strong minority in the rest of the country. In the Electoral College outside the South, President Ford won by 228 to 179, and led in the popular vote (again outside the South) by some 42,000. But in the South the margin in both categories was such as to win the 1976 vote for the Democrats on a complete reversal of the area's political behavior in the two previous campaigns.

This marked shift from 1972 (McGovern) to 1976 (Carter) can also be observed in the pattern of highest percentages of support for the Democratic candidates. In 1972 the best Democratic showing was made in the District of Columbia, as has been the case ever since the District started voting for Presidential electors back in 1964. Next came Massachusetts, the only state carried by Senator McGovern in 1972, and three states in which his vote was 45% or better — Rhode Island, Minnesota, and South Dakota.

In 1976 the District of Columbia remained highest on the Democratic list, a tribute to Carter's heavy black support, with the next highest states being Georgia and Arkansas. Georgia, as might be imagined, registered an especially high jump; in 1972, it was the second highest state in the Union for Nixon, voting for his re-election by 3:1. The 1976 shift was 42 percentage points Democratic, and a 2:1 vote for favorite-son Carter.

For the Republicans, highest Ford states in 1976 were in the West — Utah (highest in the country at 62.4%), Idaho, Nebraska, and Wyoming. In 1972 the highest percentages for Nixon's re-election were in Mississippi (78.2%, highest in the nation), Georgia (75.0%), and Oklahoma (73.7%).

No states did better in 1976 for President Ford than they did for President Nixon in 1972. The size of the shift (12.7 percentage points lower for Ford than for Nixon) almost guaranteed that all states would show some GOP loss and some Democratic gain. Minimum Republican losses (and minimum Democratic gains) in 1976 came in a dozen states in the Middle West and West, plus the two jurisdictions carried by candidate McGovern in 1972 – Massachusetts and the District of Columbia.

For those seeking some guidance to the next Presidential election, it might be noted that three states have polled in both 1972 and 1976 very much as has the whole country. Considering the major party vote for President, Hawaii, Missouri, and Ohio have been within one percentage point or less of the winner's final national figure in both elections. On election night, Ohio is one of the first reporting states, Missouri in the middle, Hawaii a late-comer.

Among the counties of America, the 1976 percentage calculations showed Jimmy Carter's highest support in Banks county, Georgia (87.9%) followed closely by Starr county, Texas (87.2%), Brantley county, Georgia (86.5%) and Duval county, Texas (86.4%). On the Republican side, President Ford's best areas were Jackson county, Kentucky, with 79.8%, another Kentucky county (Owsley) with 77.0%, and Hooker county, Nebraska, with 76.3%. An early uncorrected canvass in Illinois showed one county in that state at over ninety percent for Ford, but this was due to a printing error and credited the Republicans with 20,000 more Presidential votes than they had actually polled.

For 1972, the county leads showed Senator McGovern strongest in Duval county (Texas) with 85.7% and in Shannon county (South Dakota) with 77.3%; on the Republican side, best Nixon county was Glascock county (Georgia) with 93.4%; others over ninety percent Nixon were four in Mississippi, three others in Georgia, and Jackson county (Kentucky).

Should the user of AMERICA VOTES wish to go even further back in this list of "maximum counties," 1968 would show half-a-dozen counties in the deep South at 85%-plus for Wallace, Nixon with top support in Jackson county, Kentucky, and a few rural counties in the Middle West, and Humphrey's top counties in southwestern Texas.

Some years ago there were a number of counties which could lay claim to having been on the winning side in every Presidential election since McKinley defeated Bryan in 1896. That number has been cut back over the years, and 1976 cut it back even a bit more. Only remaining "back to '96" bellwether counties, ready to be tested for their constancy in 1980, are Palo Alto county, Iowa, and Crook county, Oregon. Laramie county, Wyoming, which had been in this special group right up to 1976, was carried by President Ford, leaving only two for the next Presidential race.

Voting for Congress in 1976 provided few party changes of moment. Republicans and Democrats continued in virtually unchanged numbers in both the House and Senate. Though there were a good many shifts in personnel and party, especially in the Senate, these tended to balance off in party changes and to end up reproducing in the 1976 vote just about the same party balance as had the 1974 contests.

In party voting for the House, Democrats continued to hold the substantial lead they developed in 1974 after Watergate. Their 1972 Congressional vote rose from 52% to 57% that year, and went back down to 56% in 1976. The much vaunted Republican drive against the 1974 Democratic freshmen never seemed to get off the ground and the advantage of 1974 was repeated last fall. Nonetheless, fearful Republicans might take solace in the fact that the vote for Republican candidates for the House has never fallen below forty percent in any election in the thirty years since the end of the second World War.

The relationship between Presidential and Congressional voting in 1976 continued to underline the decline of "coat-tailing" and the growth of independent voting and split ticket voting in American election patterns. In the post-war years Republicans have controlled the House for only two of sixteen Congresses, but have had the White House for eight of those same sixteen. Earlier theories of the close relationship between Presidential and Congressional voting have long since gone by the board, and the "two-track" system of voting has evidently become a feature of our electoral life, at least for now.

On comparative voting for President and for the House, studies are available for about one-third of the House seats, for "clean" Congressional districts, those made up of whole and complete counties only. In these CD's, the great majority of Democrats ran ahead of candidate Carter, especially incumbent members. Equally on the

Republican side, the great majority of Republican candidates ran ahead of Ford. In both parties incumbency appeared to be more important than the Presidential nominee, for incumbents did better against their opponents in both parties than did newly nominated candidates. This tells us nothing new, especially in terms of a close national campaign, but it does tend to underline the "new" character of the vote relationship in the diminished importance of "coat-tailing" of the type so notable in the Roosevelt years.

Perhaps the most important aspect of the 1976 voting was in the concretization of the concept of primary nomination. As the figures in this AMERICA VOTES indicate, the participation in the 1976 Presidential primaries rose from the 21,871,000 of the 1972 race to 26,427,000 last year. Taken back to 1952, participation in Presidential primaries has more than doubled. Moreover, the share of delegates to national conventions who are elected by the voters has now risen to over three-quarters. Very likely the number of primary states, which rose sharply from 1952 to 1976, and the share of delegates popularly elected, will rise again in 1980. The old argument over a national primary to nominate Presidential candidates seems now to be over. America *has* a national primary right now.

UNITED STATES

President 1948

	Electoral								Percentage			
		Vote		Total					Total Vote		Major Vote	
State	Rep.	Dem.	Other	Vote	Republican	Democratic	Other	Plurality	Rep.	Dem.	Rep.	Dem.
Alabama			11	214,980	40,930		174,050	130,513 SR	19.0%		100.0%	
Alaska												
Arizona		4		177,065	77,597	95,251	4,217	17,654 D	43.8%	53.8%	44.9%	55.1%
Arkansas		9		242,475	50,959	149,659	41,857	98,700 D	21.0%	61.7%	25.4%	74.6%
California		25		4,021,538	1,895,269	1,913,134	213,135	17,865 D	47.1%	47.6%	49.8%	50.2%
Colorado		6		515,237	239,714	267,288	8,235	27,574 D	46.5%	51.9%	47.3%	52.7%
Connecticut	8			883,518	437,754	423,297	22,467	14,457 R	49.5%	47.9%	50.8%	49.2%
Delaware	3			139,073	69,588	67,813	1,672	1,775 R	50.0%	48.8%	50.6%	49.4%
Florida		8		577,643	194,280	281,988	101,375	87,708 D	33.6%	48.8%	40.8%	59.2%
Georgia		12		418,844	76,691	254,646	87,507	169,511 D	18.3%	60.8%	23.1%	76.9%
Hawaii												
Idaho		4		214,816	101,514	107,370	5,932	5,856 D	47.3%	50.0%	48.6%	51.4%
Illinois		28		3,984,046	1,961,103	1,994,715	28,228	33,612 D	49.2%	50.1%	49.6%	50.4%
Indiana	13			1,656,212	821,079	807,831	27,302	13,248 R	49.6%	48.8%	50.4%	49.6%
Iowa		10		1,038,264	494,018	522,380	21,866	28,362 D	47.6%	50.3%	48.6%	51.4%
Kansas	8			788,819	423,039	351,902	13,878	71,137 R	53.6%	44.6%	54.6%	45.4%
Kentucky		11		822,658	341,210	466,756	14,692	125,546 D	41.5%	56.7%	42.2%	57.8%
Louisiana			10	416,336	72,657	136,344	207,335	67,946 SR	17.5%	32.7%	34.8%	65.2%
Maine	5			264,787	150,234	111,916	2,637	38,318 R	56.7%	42.3%	57.3%	42.7%
Maryland	8			596,748	294,814	286,521	15,413	8,293 R	49.4%	48.0%	50.7%	49.3%
Massachusetts		16		2,107,146	909,370	1,151,788	45,988	242,418 D	43.2%	54.7%	44.1%	55.9%
Michigan	19			2,109,609	1,038,595	1,003,448	67,566	35,147 R	49.2%	47.6%	50.9%	49.1%
Minnesota		11		1,212,226	483,617	692,966	35,643	209,349 D	39.9%	57.2%	41.1%	58.9%
Mississippi			9	192,190	5,043	19,384	167,763	148,154 SR	2.6%	10.1%	20.6%	79.4%
Missouri		15		1,578,628	655,039	917,315	6,274	262,276 D	41.5%	58.1%	41.7%	58.3%
Montana		4		224,278	96,770	119,071	8,437	22,301 D	43.1%	53.1%	44.8%	55.2%
Nebraska	6			488,940	264,774	224,165	1	40,609 R	54.2%	45.8%	54.2%	45.8%
Nevada		3		62,117	29,357	31,291	1,469	1,934 D	47.3%	50.4%	48.4%	51.6%
New Hampshire	4			231,440	121,299	107,995	2,146	13,304 R	52.4%	46.7%	52.9%	47.1%
New Jersey	16			1,949,555	981,124	895,455	72,976	85,669 R	50.3%	45.9%	52.3%	47.7%
New Mexico		4		187,063	80,303	105,464	1,296	25,161 D	42.9%	56.4%	43.2%	56.8%
New York	47			6,177,337	2,841,163	2,780,204	555,970	60,959 R	46.0%	45.0%	50.5%	49.5%
North Carolina		14		791,209	258,572	459,070	73,567	200,498 D	32.7%	58.0%	36.0%	64.0%
North Dakota	4			220,716	115,139	95,812	9,765	19,327 R	52.2%	43.4%	54.6%	45.4%
Ohio		25		2,936,071	1,445,684	1,452,791	37,596	7,107 D	49.2%	49.5%	49.9%	50.1%
Oklahoma		10		721,599	268,817	452,782		183,965 D	37.3%	62.7%	37.3%	62.7%
Oregon	6			524,080	260,904	243,147	20,029	17,757 R	49.8%	46.4%	51.8%	48.2%
Pennsylvania	35			3,735,348	1,902,197	1,752,426	80,725	149,771 R	50.9%	46.9%	52.0%	48.0%
Rhode Island		4		327,702	135,787	188,736	3,179	52,949 D	41.4%	57.6%	41.8%	58.2%
South Carolina			8	142,571	5,386	34,423	102,762	68,184 SR	3.8%	24.1%	13.5%	86.5%
South Dakota	4			250,105	129,651	117,653	2,801	11,998 R	51.8%	47.0%	52.4%	47.6%
Tennessee		11	1	550,283	202,914	270,402	76,967	67,488 D	36.9%	49.1%	42.9%	57.1%
Texas		23		1,249,577	303,467	824,235	121,875	520,768 D	24.3%	66.0%	26.9%	73.1%
Utah		4		276,306	124,402	149,151	2,753	24,749 D	45.0%	54.0%	45.5%	54.5%
Vermont	3			123,382	75,926	45,557	1,899	30,369 R	61.5%	36.9%	62.5%	37.5%
Virginia		11		419,256	172,070	200,786	46,400	28,716 D	41.0%	47.9%	46.1%	53.9%
Washington		8		905,058	386,314	476,165	42,579	89,851 D	42.7%	52.6%	44.8%	55.2%
West Virginia		8		748,750	316,251	429,188	3,311	112,937 D	42.2%	57.3%	42.4%	57.6%
Wisconsin		12		1,276,800	590,959	647,310	38,531	56,351 D	46.3%	50.7%	47.7%	52.3%
Wyoming		3		101,425	47,947	52,354	1,124	4,407 D	47.3%	51.6%	47.8%	52.2%
United States	189	303	39	48,793,826	21,991,291	24,179,345	2,623,190	2,188,054 D	45.1%	49.6%	47.6%	52.4%

President 1948

The electoral votes of Alabama, Louisiana, Mississippi, and South Carolina were cast for the States Rights nominees. In addition, one of the 12 Democratic electors chosen in Tennessee cast his Electoral College vote for the States Rights nominees rather than for the national Democratic candidates.

In Alabama the Democratic electors were pledged to the States Rights candidates. There were no national Democratic electors on the ballot in that state.

The Republican figure in Mississippi includes votes cast for two elector tickets. In New York the Democratic figure includes Liberal votes.

The full list of candidates for President and Vice-President was:

24,179,345	Harry S. Truman and Alben W. Barkley, Democratic.
21,991,291	Thomas E. Dewey and Earl Warren, Republican.
1,176,125	Strom Thurmond and Fielding L. Wright, States Rights.
1,157,326	Henry A. Wallace and Glen H. Taylor, Progressive.
139,572	Norman Thomas and Tucker P. Smith, Socialist.
103,900	Claude A. Watson and Dale H. Learn, Prohibition.
29,241	Edward A. Teichert and Stephen Emery, Socialist Labor.
13,614	Farrell Dobbs and Grace Carlson, Socialist Workers.

In addition, 3,412 scattered votes were reported from various states.

UNITED STATES

President 1952

State	Electoral Vote Rep.	Electoral Vote Dem.	Electoral Vote Other	Total Vote	Republican	Democratic	Other	Plurality	Percentage Total Vote Rep.	Percentage Total Vote Dem.	Percentage Major Vote Rep.	Percentage Major Vote Dem.
Alabama		11		426,120	149,231	275,075	1,814	125,844 D	35.0%	64.6%	35.2%	64.8%
Alaska												
Arizona	4			260,570	152,042	108,528		43,514 R	58.3%	41.7%	58.3%	41.7%
Arkansas		8		404,800	177,155	226,300	1,345	49,145 D	43.8%	55.9%	43.9%	56.1%
California	32			5,141,849	2,897,310	2,197,548	46,991	699,762 R	56.3%	42.7%	56.9%	43.1%
Colorado	6			630,103	379,782	245,504	4,817	134,278 R	60.3%	39.0%	60.7%	39.3%
Connecticut	8			1,096,911	611,012	481,649	4,250	129,363 R	55.7%	43.9%	55.9%	44.1%
Delaware	3			174,025	90,059	83,315	651	6,744 R	51.8%	47.9%	51.9%	48.1%
Florida	10			989,337	544,036	444,950	351	99,086 R	55.0%	45.0%	55.0%	45.0%
Georgia		12		655,785	198,961	456,823	1	257,862 D	30.3%	69.7%	30.3%	69.7%
Hawaii												
Idaho	4			276,254	180,707	95,081	466	85,626 R	65.4%	34.4%	65.5%	34.5%
Illinois	27			4,481,058	2,457,327	2,013,920	9,811	443,407 R	54.8%	44.9%	55.0%	45.0%
Indiana	13			1,955,049	1,136,259	801,530	17,260	334,729 R	58.1%	41.0%	58.6%	41.4%
Iowa	10			1,268,773	808,906	451,513	8,354	357,393 R	63.8%	35.6%	64.2%	35.8%
Kansas	8			896,166	616,302	273,296	6,568	343,006 R	68.8%	30.5%	69.3%	30.7%
Kentucky		10		993,148	495,029	495,729	2,390	700 D	49.8%	49.9%	50.0%	50.0%
Louisiana		10		651,952	306,925	345,027		38,102 D	47.1%	52.9%	47.1%	52.9%
Maine	5			351,786	232,353	118,806	627	113,547 R	66.0%	33.8%	66.2%	33.8%
Maryland	9			902,074	499,424	395,337	7,313	104,087 R	55.4%	43.8%	55.8%	44.2%
Massachusetts	16			2,383,398	1,292,325	1,083,525	7,548	208,800 R	54.2%	45.5%	54.4%	45.6%
Michigan	20			2,798,592	1,551,529	1,230,657	16,406	320,872 R	55.4%	44.0%	55.8%	44.2%
Minnesota	11			1,379,483	763,211	608,458	7,814	154,753 R	55.3%	44.1%	55.6%	44.4%
Mississippi		8		285,532	112,966	172,566		59,600 D	39.6%	60.4%	39.6%	60.4%
Missouri	13			1,892,062	959,429	929,830	2,803	29,599 R	50.7%	49.1%	50.8%	49.2%
Montana	4			265,037	157,394	106,213	1,430	51,181 R	59.4%	40.1%	59.7%	40.3%
Nebraska	6			609,660	421,603	188,057		233,546 R	69.2%	30.8%	69.2%	30.8%
Nevada	3			82,190	50,502	31,688		18,814 R	61.4%	38.6%	61.4%	38.6%
New Hampshire	4			272,950	166,287	106,663		59,624 R	60.9%	39.1%	60.9%	39.1%
New Jersey	16			2,418,554	1,373,613	1,015,902	29,039	357,711 R	56.8%	42.0%	57.5%	42.5%
New Mexico	4			238,608	132,170	105,661	777	26,509 R	55.4%	44.3%	55.6%	44.4%
New York	45			7,128,239	3,952,813	3,104,601	70,825	848,212 R	55.5%	43.6%	56.0%	44.0%
North Carolina		14		1,210,910	558,107	652,803		94,696 D	46.1%	53.9%	46.1%	53.9%
North Dakota	4			270,127	191,712	76,694	1,721	115,018 R	71.0%	28.4%	71.4%	28.6%
Ohio	25			3,700,758	2,100,391	1,600,367		500,024 R	56.8%	43.2%	56.8%	43.2%
Oklahoma	8			948,984	518,045	430,939		87,106 R	54.6%	45.4%	54.6%	45.4%
Oregon	6			695,059	420,815	270,579	3,665	150,236 R	60.5%	38.9%	60.9%	39.1%
Pennsylvania	32			4,580,969	2,415,789	2,146,269	18,911	269,520 R	52.7%	46.9%	53.0%	47.0%
Rhode Island	4			414,498	210,935	203,293	270	7,642 R	50.9%	49.0%	50.9%	49.1%
South Carolina		8		341,087	168,082	173,004	1	4,922 D	49.3%	50.7%	49.3%	50.7%
South Dakota	4			294,283	203,857	90,426		113,431 R	69.3%	30.7%	69.3%	30.7%
Tennessee	11			892,553	446,147	443,710	2,696	2,437 R	50.0%	49.7%	50.1%	49.9%
Texas	24			2,075,946	1,102,878	969,228	3,840	133,650 R	53.1%	46.7%	53.2%	46.8%
Utah	4			329,554	194,190	135,364		58,826 R	58.9%	41.1%	58.9%	41.1%
Vermont	3			153,557	109,717	43,355	485	66,362 R	71.5%	28.2%	71.7%	28.3%
Virginia	12			619,689	349,037	268,677	1,975	80,360 R	56.3%	43.4%	56.5%	43.5%
Washington	9			1,102,708	599,107	492,845	10,756	106,262 R	54.3%	44.7%	54.9%	45.1%
West Virginia		8		873,548	419,970	453,578		33,608 D	48.1%	51.9%	48.1%	51.9%
Wisconsin	12			1,607,370	979,744	622,175	5,451	357,569 R	61.0%	38.7%	61.2%	38.8%
Wyoming	3			129,253	81,049	47,934	270	33,115 R	62.7%	37.1%	62.8%	37.2%
United States	442	89		61,550,918	33,936,234	27,314,992	299,692	6,621,242 R	55.1%	44.4%	55.4%	44.6%

President 1952

The Republican figure in South Carolina includes votes cast for two elector tickets; in Mississippi the Republican total is the vote cast for an Independent elector ticket "pledged to vote for the nominees of the National Republican Party". In New York the Democratic figure includes Liberal votes.

The full list of candidates for President and Vice-President was:

33,936,234	Dwight D. Eisenhower and Richard M. Nixon, Republican.
27,314,992	Adlai E. Stevenson and John J. Sparkman, Democratic.
140,023	Vincent Hallinan and Charlotta Bass, Progressive.
72,949	Stuart Hamblen and Enoch A. Holtwick, Prohibition.
30,267	Eric Hass and Stephen Emery, Socialist Labor.
20,203	Darlington Hoopes and Samuel H. Friedman, Socialist.
10,312	Farrell Dobbs and Myra Tanner Weiss, Socialist Workers.
4,203	Henry B. Krajewski and Frank Jenkins, Poor Man's Party.

In addition, 17,205 votes were cast for various elector tickets filed on behalf of General Douglas MacArthur, including Christian Nationalist (with Jack B. Tenney as candidate for Vice-President), Constitution (with Vivien Kellems), and America First (with Senator Harry Flood Byrd). In California, Missouri, and Texas the MacArthur vote was cast for two elector tickets. 4,530 scattered votes were reported from various states.

UNITED STATES

President 1956

State	Electoral Vote Rep.	Electoral Vote Dem.	Electoral Vote Other	Total Vote	Republican	Democratic	Other	Plurality	Percentage Total Vote Rep.	Percentage Total Vote Dem.	Percentage Major Vote Rep.	Percentage Major Vote Dem.
Alabama		10	1	496,861	195,694	280,844	20,323	85,150 D	39.4%	56.5%	41.1%	58.9%
Alaska												
Arizona	4			290,173	176,990	112,880	303	64,110 R	61.0%	38.9%	61.1%	38.9%
Arkansas		8		406,572	186,287	213,277	7,008	26,990 D	45.8%	52.5%	46.6%	53.4%
California	32			5,466,355	3,027,668	2,420,135	18,552	607,533 R	55.4%	44.3%	55.6%	44.4%
Colorado	6			657,074	394,479	257,997	4,598	136,482 R	60.0%	39.3%	60.5%	39.5%
Connecticut	8			1,117,121	711,837	405,079	205	306,758 R	63.7%	36.3%	63.7%	36.3%
Delaware	3			177,988	98,057	79,421	510	18,636 R	55.1%	44.6%	55.3%	44.7%
Florida	10			1,125,762	643,849	480,371	1,542	163,478 R	57.2%	42.7%	57.3%	42.7%
Georgia		12		669,655	222,778	444,688	2,189	221,910 D	33.3%	66.4%	33.4%	66.6%
Hawaii												
Idaho	4			272,989	166,979	105,868	142	61,111 R	61.2%	38.8%	61.2%	38.8%
Illinois	27			4,407,407	2,623,327	1,775,682	8,398	847,645 R	59.5%	40.3%	59.6%	40.4%
Indiana	13			1,974,607	1,182,811	783,908	7,888	398,903 R	59.9%	39.7%	60.1%	39.9%
Iowa	10			1,234,564	729,187	501,858	3,519	227,329 R	59.1%	40.7%	59.2%	40.8%
Kansas	8			866,243	566,878	296,317	3,048	270,561 R	65.4%	34.2%	65.7%	34.3%
Kentucky	10			1,053,805	572,192	476,453	5,160	95,739 R	54.3%	45.2%	54.6%	45.4%
Louisiana	10			617,544	329,047	243,977	44,520	85,070 R	53.3%	39.5%	57.4%	42.6%
Maine	5			351,706	249,238	102,468		146,770 R	70.9%	29.1%	70.9%	29.1%
Maryland	9			932,827	559,738	372,613	476	187,125 R	60.0%	39.9%	60.0%	40.0%
Massachusetts	16			2,348,506	1,393,197	948,190	7,119	445,007 R	59.3%	40.4%	59.5%	40.5%
Michigan	20			3,080,468	1,713,647	1,359,898	6,923	353,749 R	55.6%	44.1%	55.8%	44.2%
Minnesota	11			1,340,005	719,302	617,525	3,178	101,777 R	53.7%	46.1%	53.8%	46.2%
Mississippi		8		248,104	60,685	144,453	42,966	83,768 D	24.5%	58.2%	29.6%	70.4%
Missouri		13		1,832,562	914,289	918,273		3,984 D	49.9%	50.1%	49.9%	50.1%
Montana	4			271,171	154,933	116,238		38,695 R	57.1%	42.9%	57.1%	42.9%
Nebraska	6			577,137	378,108	199,029		179,079 R	65.5%	34.5%	65.5%	34.5%
Nevada	3			96,689	56,049	40,640		15,409 R	58.0%	42.0%	58.0%	42.0%
New Hampshire	4			266,994	176,519	90,364	111	86,155 R	66.1%	33.8%	66.1%	33.9%
New Jersey	16			2,484,312	1,606,942	850,337	27,033	756,605 R	64.7%	34.2%	65.4%	34.6%
New Mexico	4			253,926	146,788	106,098	1,040	40,690 R	57.8%	41.8%	58.0%	42.0%
New York	45			7,095,971	4,345,506	2,747,944	2,521	1,597,562 R	61.2%	38.4%	61.3%	38.7%
North Carolina		14		1,165,592	575,062	590,530		15,468 D	49.3%	50.7%	49.3%	50.7%
North Dakota	4			253,991	156,766	96,742	483	60,024 R	61.7%	38.1%	61.8%	38.2%
Ohio	25			3,702,265	2,262,610	1,439,655		822,955 R	61.1%	38.9%	61.1%	38.9%
Oklahoma	8			859,350	473,769	385,581		88,188 R	55.1%	44.9%	55.1%	44.9%
Oregon	6			736,132	406,393	329,204	535	77,189 R	55.2%	44.7%	55.2%	44.8%
Pennsylvania	32			4,576,503	2,585,252	1,981,769	9,482	603,483 R	56.5%	43.3%	56.6%	43.4%
Rhode Island	4			387,609	225,819	161,790		64,029 R	58.3%	41.7%	58.3%	41.7%
South Carolina		8		300,583	75,700	136,372	88,511	47,863 D	25.2%	45.4%	35.7%	64.3%
South Dakota	4			293,857	171,569	122,288		49,281 R	58.4%	41.6%	58.4%	41.6%
Tennessee	11			939,404	462,288	456,507	20,609	5,781 R	49.2%	48.6%	50.3%	49.7%
Texas	24			1,955,168	1,080,619	859,958	14,591	220,661 R	55.3%	44.0%	55.7%	44.3%
Utah	4			333,995	215,631	118,364		97,267 R	64.6%	35.4%	64.6%	35.4%
Vermont	3			152,978	110,390	42,549	39	67,841 R	72.2%	27.8%	72.2%	27.8%
Virginia	12			697,978	386,459	267,760	43,759	118,699 R	55.4%	38.4%	59.1%	40.9%
Washington	9			1,150,889	620,430	523,002	7,457	97,428 R	53.9%	45.4%	54.3%	45.7%
West Virginia	8			830,831	449,297	381,534		67,763 R	54.1%	45.9%	54.1%	45.9%
Wisconsin	12			1,550,558	954,844	586,768	8,946	368,076 R	61.6%	37.8%	61.9%	38.1%
Wyoming	3			124,127	74,573	49,554		25,019 R	60.1%	39.9%	60.1%	39.9%
United States	457	73	1	62,026,908	35,590,472	26,022,752	413,684	9,567,720 R	57.4%	42.0%	57.8%	42.2%

President 1956

One of the 11 Democratic electors chosen in Alabama cast his Electoral College vote for Walter B. Jones and Herman Talmadge rather than for the national Democratic candidates.

The Republican figure in Mississippi includes votes cast for two elector tickets. In New York the Democratic figure includes Liberal votes.

The full list of candidates for President and Vice-President was:

35,590,472	Dwight D. Eisenhower and Richard M. Nixon, Republican.
26,022,752	Adlai E. Stevenson and Estes Kefauver, Democratic.
111,178	T. Coleman Andrews and Thomas H. Werdel, States Rights.
44,450	Eric Hass and Georgia Cozzini, Socialist Labor.
41,937	Enoch A. Holtwick and Edwin M. Cooper, Prohibition.
7,797	Farrell Dobbs and Myra Tanner Weiss, Socialist Workers.
2,657	Harry Flood Byrd and William E. Jenner, States Rights.
2,126	Darlington Hoopes and Samuel H. Friedman, Socialist.
1,829	Henry B. Krajewski and Anne Marie Yezo, American Third Party.
8	Gerald L. K. Smith and Charles F. Robertson, Christian Nationalist.

In addition, 196,318 votes were cast in Alabama, Louisiana, Mississippi, and South Carolina for Independent electors or for States Rights elector tickets not officially pledged to any candidate, and 5,384 scattered votes were reported from various states.

UNITED STATES

President 1960

State	Electoral Vote			Total Vote	Republican	Democratic	Other	Plurality	Percentage			
									Total Vote		Major Vote	
	Rep.	Dem.	Other						Rep.	Dem.	Rep.	Dem.
Alabama		5	6	570,225	237,981	324,050	8,194	86,069 D	41.7%	56.8%	42.3%	57.7%
Alaska	3			60,762	30,953	29,809		1,144 R	50.9%	49.1%	50.9%	49.1%
Arizona	4			398,491	221,241	176,781	469	44,460 R	55.5%	44.4%	55.6%	44.4%
Arkansas		8		428,509	184,508	215,049	28,952	30,541 D	43.1%	50.2%	46.2%	53.8%
California	32			6,506,578	3,259,722	3,224,099	22,757	35,623 R	50.1%	49.6%	50.3%	49.7%
Colorado	6			736,236	402,242	330,629	3,365	71,613 R	54.6%	44.9%	54.9%	45.1%
Connecticut		8		1,222,883	565,813	657,055	15	91,242 D	46.3%	53.7%	46.3%	53.7%
Delaware		3		196,683	96,373	99,590	720	3,217 D	49.0%	50.6%	49.2%	50.8%
Florida	10			1,544,176	795,476	748,700		46,776 R	51.5%	48.5%	51.5%	48.5%
Georgia		12		733,349	274,472	458,638	239	184,166 D	37.4%	62.5%	37.4%	62.6%
Hawaii		3		184,705	92,295	92,410		115 D	50.0%	50.0%	50.0%	50.0%
Idaho	4			300,450	161,597	138,853		22,744 R	53.8%	46.2%	53.8%	46.2%
Illinois		27		4,757,409	2,368,988	2,377,846	10,575	8,858 D	49.8%	50.0%	49.9%	50.1%
Indiana	13			2,135,360	1,175,120	952,358	7,882	222,762 R	55.0%	44.6%	55.2%	44.8%
Iowa	10			1,273,810	722,381	550,565	864	171,816 R	56.7%	43.2%	56.7%	43.3%
Kansas	8			928,825	561,474	363,213	4,138	198,261 R	60.4%	39.1%	60.7%	39.3%
Kentucky	10			1,124,462	602,607	521,855		80,752 R	53.6%	46.4%	53.6%	46.4%
Louisiana		10		807,891	230,980	407,339	169,572	176,359 D	28.6%	50.4%	36.2%	63.8%
Maine	5			421,767	240,608	181,159		59,449 R	57.0%	43.0%	57.0%	43.0%
Maryland		9		1,055,349	489,538	565,808	3	76,270 D	46.4%	53.6%	46.4%	53.6%
Massachusetts		16		2,469,480	976,750	1,487,174	5,556	510,424 D	39.6%	60.2%	39.6%	60.4%
Michigan		20		3,318,097	1,620,428	1,687,269	10,400	66,841 D	48.8%	50.9%	49.0%	51.0%
Minnesota		11		1,541,887	757,915	779,933	4,039	22,018 D	49.2%	50.6%	49.3%	50.7%
Mississippi			8	298,171	73,561	108,362	116,248	7,886 U	24.7%	36.3%	40.4%	59.6%
Missouri		13		1,934,422	962,221	972,201		9,980 D	49.7%	50.3%	49.7%	50.3%
Montana	4			277,579	141,841	134,891	847	6,950 R	51.1%	48.6%	51.3%	48.7%
Nebraska	6			613,095	380,553	232,542		148,011 R	62.1%	37.9%	62.1%	37.9%
Nevada		3		107,267	52,387	54,880		2,493 D	48.8%	51.2%	48.8%	51.2%
New Hampshire	4			295,761	157,989	137,772		20,217 R	53.4%	46.6%	53.4%	46.6%
New Jersey		16		2,773,111	1,363,324	1,385,415	24,372	22,091 D	49.2%	50.0%	49.6%	50.4%
New Mexico		4		311,107	153,733	156,027	1,347	2,294 D	49.4%	50.2%	49.6%	50.4%
New York		45		7,291,079	3,446,419	3,830,085	14,575	383,666 D	47.3%	52.5%	47.4%	52.6%
North Carolina		14		1,368,556	655,420	713,136		57,716 D	47.9%	52.1%	47.9%	52.1%
North Dakota	4			278,431	154,310	123,963	158	30,347 R	55.4%	44.5%	55.5%	44.5%
Ohio	25			4,161,859	2,217,611	1,944,248		273,363 R	53.3%	46.7%	53.3%	46.7%
Oklahoma	7		1	903,150	533,039	370,111		162,928 R	59.0%	41.0%	59.0%	41.0%
Oregon	6			776,421	408,060	367,402	959	40,658 R	52.6%	47.3%	52.6%	47.4%
Pennsylvania		32		5,006,541	2,439,956	2,556,282	10,303	116,326 D	48.7%	51.1%	48.8%	51.2%
Rhode Island		4		405,535	147,502	258,032	1	110,530 D	36.4%	63.6%	36.4%	63.6%
South Carolina		8		386,688	188,558	198,129	1	9,571 D	48.8%	51.2%	48.8%	51.2%
South Dakota	4			306,487	178,417	128,070		50,347 R	58.2%	41.8%	58.2%	41.8%
Tennessee	11			1,051,792	556,577	481,453	13,762	75,124 R	52.9%	45.8%	53.6%	46.4%
Texas		24		2,311,084	1,121,310	1,167,567	22,207	46,257 D	48.5%	50.5%	49.0%	51.0%
Utah	4			374,709	205,361	169,248	100	36,113 R	54.8%	45.2%	54.8%	45.2%
Vermont	3			167,324	98,131	69,186	7	28,945 R	58.6%	41.3%	58.6%	41.4%
Virginia	12			771,449	404,521	362,327	4,601	42,194 R	52.4%	47.0%	52.8%	47.2%
Washington	9			1,241,572	629,273	599,298	13,001	29,975 R	50.7%	48.3%	51.2%	48.8%
West Virginia		8		837,781	395,995	441,786		45,791 D	47.3%	52.7%	47.3%	52.7%
Wisconsin	12			1,729,082	895,175	830,805	3,102	64,370 R	51.8%	48.0%	51.9%	48.1%
Wyoming	3			140,782	77,451	63,331		14,120 R	55.0%	45.0%	55.0%	45.0%
United States	219	303	15	68,838,219	34,108,157	34,226,731	503,331	118,574 D	49.5%	49.7%	49.9%	50.1%

President 1960

Senator Harry Flood Byrd received 15 votes for President in the Electoral College; these were the votes of 6 of the 11 Democratic electors in Alabama, all 8 unpledged Democratic electors in Mississippi, and one of the 8 Republican electors in Oklahoma. The Alabama and Mississippi electors also cast 14 votes for Senator Strom Thurmond for Vice-President; the single Oklahoma elector voted for Senator Barry M. Goldwater for Vice-President.

In New York the Democratic figure includes Liberal votes.

The full list of candidates for President and Vice-President was:

34,226,731	John F. Kennedy and Lyndon B. Johnson, Democratic.
34,108,157	Richard M. Nixon and Henry Cabot Lodge, Republican.
47,522	Eric Hass and Georgia Cozzini, Socialist Labor.
46,203	Rutherford L. Decker and E. Harold Munn, Prohibition.
44,977	Orval E. Faubus and John G. Crommelin, National States Rights.
40,165	Farrell Dobbs and Myra Tanner Weiss, Socialist Workers.
18,162	Charles L. Sullivan and Merritt B. Curtis, Constitution.
8,708	J. Bracken Lee and Kent H. Courtney, Conservative.
4,204	C. Benton Coiner and Edward J. Silverman, Conservative.
1,767	Lar Daly and B. M. Miller, Tax Cut.
1,485	Clennon King and Reginald Carter, Independent Afro-American.
1,401	Merritt B. Curtis and B. M. Miller, Constitution.

In addition, 169,572 votes were cast in Louisiana for Independent electors and 116,248 in Mississippi for an unpledged Democratic elector ticket. 539 votes were cast in Michigan for an Independent American ticket and 2,378 scattered votes were reported from various states.

UNITED STATES

President 1964

State	Electoral Vote Rep.	Electoral Vote Dem.	Electoral Vote Other	Total Vote	Republican	Democratic	Other	Plurality	Percentage Total Vote Rep.	Percentage Total Vote Dem.	Percentage Major Vote Rep.	Percentage Major Vote Dem.
Alabama	10			689,818	479,085		210,733	268,353 R	69.5%		100.0%	
Alaska		3		67,259	22,930	44,329		21,399 D	34.1%	65.9%	34.1%	65.9%
Arizona	5			480,770	242,535	237,753	482	4,782 R	50.4%	49.5%	50.5%	49.5%
Arkansas		6		560,426	243,264	314,197	2,965	70,933 D	43.4%	56.1%	43.6%	56.4%
California		40		7,057,586	2,879,108	4,171,877	6,601	1,292,769 D	40.8%	59.1%	40.8%	59.2%
Colorado		6		776,986	296,767	476,024	4,195	179,257 D	38.2%	61.3%	38.4%	61.6%
Connecticut		8		1,218,578	390,996	826,269	1,313	435,273 D	32.1%	67.8%	32.1%	67.9%
Delaware		3		201,320	78,078	122,704	538	44,626 D	38.8%	60.9%	38.9%	61.1%
Florida		14		1,854,481	905,941	948,540		42,599 D	48.9%	51.1%	48.9%	51.1%
Georgia	12			1,139,335	616,584	522,556	195	94,028 R	54.1%	45.9%	54.1%	45.9%
Hawaii		4		207,271	44,022	163,249		119,227 D	21.2%	78.8%	21.2%	78.8%
Idaho		4		292,477	143,557	148,920		5,363 D	49.1%	50.9%	49.1%	50.9%
Illinois		26		4,702,841	1,905,946	2,796,833	62	890,887 D	40.5%	59.5%	40.5%	59.5%
Indiana		13		2,091,606	911,118	1,170,848	9,640	259,730 D	43.6%	56.0%	43.8%	56.2%
Iowa		9		1,184,539	449,148	733,030	2,361	283,822 D	37.9%	61.9%	38.0%	62.0%
Kansas		7		857,901	386,579	464,028	7,294	77,449 D	45.1%	54.1%	45.4%	54.6%
Kentucky		9		1,046,105	372,977	669,659	3,469	296,682 D	35.7%	64.0%	35.8%	64.2%
Louisiana	10			896,293	509,225	387,068		122,157 R	56.8%	43.2%	56.8%	43.2%
Maine		4		380,965	118,701	262,264		143,563 D	31.2%	68.8%	31.2%	68.8%
Maryland		10		1,116,457	385,495	730,912	50	345,417 D	34.5%	65.5%	34.5%	65.5%
Massachusetts		14		2,344,798	549,727	1,786,422	8,649	1,236,695 D	23.4%	76.2%	23.5%	76.5%
Michigan		21		3,203,102	1,060,152	2,136,615	6,335	1,076,463 D	33.1%	66.7%	33.2%	66.8%
Minnesota		10		1,554,462	559,624	991,117	3,721	431,493 D	36.0%	63.8%	36.1%	63.9%
Mississippi	7			409,146	356,528	52,618		303,910 R	87.1%	12.9%	87.1%	12.9%
Missouri		12		1,817,879	653,535	1,164,344		510,809 D	36.0%	64.0%	36.0%	64.0%
Montana		4		278,628	113,032	164,246	1,350	51,214 D	40.6%	58.9%	40.8%	59.2%
Nebraska		5		584,154	276,847	307,307		30,460 D	47.4%	52.6%	47.4%	52.6%
Nevada		3		135,433	56,094	79,339		23,245 D	41.4%	58.6%	41.4%	58.6%
New Hampshire		4		288,093	104,029	184,064		80,035 D	36.1%	63.9%	36.1%	63.9%
New Jersey		17		2,847,663	964,174	1,868,231	15,258	904,057 D	33.9%	65.6%	34.0%	66.0%
New Mexico		4		328,645	132,838	194,015	1,792	61,177 D	40.4%	59.0%	40.6%	59.4%
New York		43		7,166,275	2,243,559	4,913,102	9,614	2,669,543 D	31.3%	68.6%	31.3%	68.7%
North Carolina		13		1,424,983	624,844	800,139		175,295 D	43.8%	56.2%	43.8%	56.2%
North Dakota		4		258,389	108,207	149,784	398	41,577 D	41.9%	58.0%	41.9%	58.1%
Ohio		26		3,969,196	1,470,865	2,498,331		1,027,466 D	37.1%	62.9%	37.1%	62.9%
Oklahoma		8		932,499	412,665	519,834		107,169 D	44.3%	55.7%	44.3%	55.7%
Oregon		6		786,305	282,779	501,017	2,509	218,238 D	36.0%	63.7%	36.1%	63.9%
Pennsylvania		29		4,822,690	1,673,657	3,130,954	18,079	1,457,297 D	34.7%	64.9%	34.8%	65.2%
Rhode Island		4		390,091	74,615	315,463	13	240,848 D	19.1%	80.9%	19.1%	80.9%
South Carolina	8			524,779	309,048	215,723	8	93,325 R	58.9%	41.1%	58.9%	41.1%
South Dakota		4		293,118	130,108	163,010		32,902 D	44.4%	55.6%	44.4%	55.6%
Tennessee		11		1,143,946	508,965	634,947	34	125,982 D	44.5%	55.5%	44.5%	55.5%
Texas		25		2,626,811	958,566	1,663,185	5,060	704,619 D	36.5%	63.3%	36.6%	63.4%
Utah		4		401,413	181,785	219,628		37,843 D	45.3%	54.7%	45.3%	54.7%
Vermont		3		163,089	54,942	108,127	20	53,185 D	33.7%	66.3%	33.7%	66.3%
Virginia		12		1,042,267	481,334	558,038	2,895	76,704 D	46.2%	53.5%	46.3%	53.7%
Washington		9		1,258,556	470,366	779,881	8,309	309,515 D	37.4%	62.0%	37.6%	62.4%
West Virginia		7		792,040	253,953	538,087		284,134 D	32.1%	67.9%	32.1%	67.9%
Wisconsin		12		1,691,815	638,495	1,050,424	2,896	411,929 D	37.7%	62.1%	37.8%	62.2%
Wyoming		3		142,716	61,998	80,718		18,720 D	43.4%	56.6%	43.4%	56.6%
Dist. of Col.		3		198,597	28,801	169,796		140,995 D	14.5%	85.5%	14.5%	85.5%
United States	52	486		70,644,592	27,178,188	43,129,566	336,838	15,951,378 D	38.5%	61.1%	38.7%	61.3%

President 1964

In New York the Democratic figure includes Liberal votes.

The full list of candidates for President and Vice-President was:

43,129,566	Lyndon B. Johnson and Hubert H. Humphrey, Democratic.
27,178,188	Barry M. Goldwater and William E. Miller, Republican.
45,219	Eric Hass and Henning A. Blomen, Socialist Labor.
32,720	Clifton DeBerry and Edward Shaw, Socialist Workers.
23,267	E. Harold Munn and Mark R. Shaw, Prohibition.
6,953	John Kasper and J. B. Stoner, National States Rights.
5,060	Joseph B. Lightburn and T. C. Billings, Constitution.
19	James Hensley and John O. Hopkins, Universal.

In addition, 210,732 votes were cast in Alabama for an unpledged Democratic elector ticket and 12,868 scattered votes were reported from various states.

UNITED STATES

President 1968

State	Electoral Vote Rep.	Electoral Vote Dem.	Electoral Vote AIP	Total Vote	Republican	Democratic	AIP	Other	Plurality	Percentage Total Vote Rep.	Percentage Total Vote Dem.	Percentage Total Vote AIP
Alabama			10	1,049,922	146,923	196,579	691,425	14,995	494,846 A	14.0%	18.7%	65.9%
Alaska	3			83,035	37,600	35,411	10,024		2,189 R	45.3%	42.6%	12.1%
Arizona	5			486,936	266,721	170,514	46,573	3,128	96,207 R	54.8%	35.0%	9.6%
Arkansas			6	619,969	190,759	188,228	240,982		50,223 A	30.8%	30.4%	38.9%
California	40			7,251,587	3,467,664	3,244,318	487,270	52,335	223,346 R	47.8%	44.7%	6.7%
Colorado	6			811,199	409,345	335,174	60,813	5,867	74,171 R	50.5%	41.3%	7.5%
Connecticut		8		1,256,232	556,721	621,561	76,650	1,300	64,840 D	44.3%	49.5%	6.1%
Delaware	3			214,367	96,714	89,194	28,459		7,520 R	45.1%	41.6%	13.3%
Florida	14			2,187,805	886,804	676,794	624,207		210,010 R	40.5%	30.9%	28.5%
Georgia			12	1,250,266	380,111	334,440	535,550	165	155,439 A	30.4%	26.7%	42.8%
Hawaii		4		236,218	91,425	141,324	3,469		49,899 D	38.7%	59.8%	1.5%
Idaho	4			291,183	165,369	89,273	36,541		76,096 R	56.8%	30.7%	12.5%
Illinois	26			4,619,749	2,174,774	2,039,814	390,958	14,203	134,960 R	47.1%	44.2%	8.5%
Indiana	13			2,123,597	1,067,885	806,659	243,108	5,945	261,226 R	50.3%	38.0%	11.4%
Iowa	9			1,167,931	619,106	476,699	66,422	5,704	142,407 R	53.0%	40.8%	5.7%
Kansas	7			872,783	478,674	302,996	88,921	2,192	175,678 R	54.8%	34.7%	10.2%
Kentucky	9			1,055,893	462,411	397,541	193,098	2,843	64,870 R	43.8%	37.6%	18.3%
Louisiana			10	1,097,450	257,535	309,615	530,300		220,685 A	23.5%	28.2%	48.3%
Maine		4		392,936	169,254	217,312	6,370		48,058 D	43.1%	55.3%	1.6%
Maryland		10		1,235,039	517,995	538,310	178,734		20,315 D	41.9%	43.6%	14.5%
Massachusetts		14		2,331,752	766,844	1,469,218	87,088	8,602	702,374 D	32.9%	63.0%	3.7%
Michigan		21		3,306,250	1,370,665	1,593,082	331,968	10,535	222,417 D	41.5%	48.2%	10.0%
Minnesota		10		1,588,506	658,643	857,738	68,931	3,194	199,095 D	41.5%	54.0%	4.3%
Mississippi			7	654,509	88,516	150,644	415,349		264,705 A	13.5%	23.0%	63.5%
Missouri	12			1,809,502	811,932	791,444	206,126		20,488 R	44.9%	43.7%	11.4%
Montana	4			274,404	138,835	114,117	20,015	1,437	24,718 R	50.6%	41.6%	7.3%
Nebraska	5			536,851	321,163	170,784	44,904		150,379 R	59.8%	31.8%	8.4%
Nevada	3			154,218	73,188	60,598	20,432		12,590 R	47.5%	39.3%	13.2%
New Hampshire	4			297,298	154,903	130,589	11,173	633	24,314 R	52.1%	43.9%	3.8%
New Jersey	17			2,875,395	1,325,467	1,264,206	262,187	23,535	61,261 R	46.1%	44.0%	9.1%
New Mexico	4			327,350	169,692	130,081	25,737	1,840	39,611 R	51.8%	39.7%	7.9%
New York		43		6,791,688	3,007,932	3,378,470	358,864	46,422	370,538 D	44.3%	49.7%	5.3%
North Carolina	12		1	1,587,493	627,192	464,113	496,188		131,004 R	39.5%	29.2%	31.3%
North Dakota	4			247,882	138,669	94,769	14,244	200	43,900 R	55.9%	38.2%	5.7%
Ohio	26			3,959,698	1,791,014	1,700,586	467,495	603	90,428 R	45.2%	42.9%	11.8%
Oklahoma	8			943,086	449,697	301,658	191,731		148,039 R	47.7%	32.0%	20.3%
Oregon	6			819,622	408,433	358,866	49,683	2,640	49,567 R	49.8%	43.8%	6.1%
Pennsylvania		29		4,747,928	2,090,017	2,259,405	378,582	19,924	169,388 D	44.0%	47.6%	8.0%
Rhode Island		4		385,000	122,359	246,518	15,678	445	124,159 D	31.8%	64.0%	4.1%
South Carolina	8			666,978	254,062	197,486	215,430		38,632 R	38.1%	29.6%	32.3%
South Dakota	4			281,264	149,841	118,023	13,400		31,818 R	53.3%	42.0%	4.8%
Tennessee	11			1,248,617	472,592	351,233	424,792		47,800 R	37.8%	28.1%	34.0%
Texas		25		3,079,216	1,227,844	1,266,804	584,269	299	38,960 D	39.9%	41.1%	19.0%
Utah	4			422,568	238,728	156,665	26,906	269	82,063 R	56.5%	37.1%	6.4%
Vermont	3			161,404	85,142	70,255	5,104	903	14,887 R	52.8%	43.5%	3.2%
Virginia	12			1,361,491	590,319	442,387	321,833	6,952	147,932 R	43.4%	32.5%	23.6%
Washington		9		1,304,281	588,510	616,037	96,990	2,744	27,527 D	45.1%	47.2%	7.4%
West Virginia		7		754,206	307,555	374,091	72,560		66,536 D	40.8%	49.6%	9.6%
Wisconsin	12			1,691,538	809,997	748,804	127,835	4,902	61,193 R	47.9%	44.3%	7.6%
Wyoming	3			127,205	70,927	45,173	11,105		25,754 R	55.8%	35.5%	8.7%
Dist. of Col.		3		170,578	31,012	139,566			108,554 D	18.2%	81.8%	
United States	301	191	46	73,211,875	31,785,480	31,275,166	9,906,473	244,756	510,314 R	43.4%	42.7%	13.5%

President 1968

In North Carolina one Republican elector voted in the Electoral College for the American Independent candidates for President and Vice-President.

In New York the Democratic figure includes Liberal votes and in Alabama the Democratic vote is the total of the Alabama Independent Democratic and National Democratic Party of Alabama vote. In certain states candidates appeared under variants of the party name used below and in most states the Vice-Presidential candidate of the American Independent party was listed as Marvin Griffin rather than Curtis E. LeMay.

The full list of candidates for President and Vice-President was:

31,785,480	Richard M. Nixon and Spiro T. Agnew, Republican.
31,275,166	Hubert H. Humphrey and Edmund S. Muskie, Democratic.
9,906,473	George C. Wallace and Curtis E. LeMay, American Independent.
52,588	Henning A. Blomen and George S. Taylor, Socialist Labor.
47,133	Dick Gregory, Peace and Freedom, with various Vice-Presidential candidates.
41,388	Fred Halstead and Paul Boutelle, Socialist Workers.
36,563	Eldridge Cleaver, Peace and Freedom, with various Vice-Presidential candidates.
25,552	Eugene J. McCarthy, under various titles and written-in, but without indication of Vice-Presidential candidates.
15,123	E. Harold Munn and Rolland E. Fisher, Prohibition.
1,519	Ventura Chavez and Adelicio Moya, People's Constitutional.
1,075	Charlene Mitchell and Michael Zagarell, Communist.
142	James Hensley and Roscoe B. MacKenna, Universal.
34	Richard K. Troxell and Merle Thayer, Constitution.
17	Kent M. Soeters and James P. Powers, Berkeley Defense Group.

In the vote listed above for Eldridge Cleaver, two states are included (California and Utah) in which only the party Vice-Presidential candidate appeared on the ballot.

In addition to these votes, 12,430 were cast for elector tickets for which there were no formal Presidential or Vice-Presidential candidates, and 11,192 scattered votes were reported from various states.

UNITED STATES

President 1972

State	Electoral Vote Rep.	Electoral Vote Dem.	Electoral Vote Other	Total Vote	Republican	Democratic	Other	Plurality	Percentage Total Vote Rep.	Percentage Total Vote Dem.	Percentage Major Vote Rep.	Percentage Major Vote Dem.
Alabama	9			1,006,111	728,701	256,923	20,487	471,778 R	72.4%	25.5%	73.9%	26.1%
Alaska	3			95,219	55,349	32,967	6,903	22,382 R	58.1%	34.6%	62.7%	37.3%
Arizona	6			622,926	402,812	198,540	21,574	204,272 R	64.7%	31.9%	67.0%	33.0%
Arkansas	6			651,320	448,541	199,892	2,887	248,649 R	68.9%	30.7%	69.2%	30.8%
California	45			8,367,862	4,602,096	3,475,847	289,919	1,126,249 R	55.0%	41.5%	57.0%	43.0%
Colorado	7			953,884	597,189	329,980	26,715	267,209 R	62.6%	34.6%	64.4%	35.6%
Connecticut	8			1,384,277	810,763	555,498	18,016	255,265 R	58.6%	40.1%	59.3%	40.7%
Delaware	3			235,516	140,357	92,283	2,876	48,074 R	59.6%	39.2%	60.3%	39.7%
Florida	17			2,583,283	1,857,759	718,117	7,407	1,139,642 R	71.9%	27.8%	72.1%	27.9%
Georgia	12			1,174,772	881,496	289,529	3,747	591,967 R	75.0%	24.6%	75.3%	24.7%
Hawaii	4			270,274	168,865	101,409		67,456 R	62.5%	37.5%	62.5%	37.5%
Idaho	4			310,379	199,384	80,826	30,169	118,558 R	64.2%	26.0%	71.2%	28.8%
Illinois	26			4,723,236	2,788,179	1,913,472	21,585	874,707 R	59.0%	40.5%	59.3%	40.7%
Indiana	13			2,125,529	1,405,154	708,568	11,807	696,586 R	66.1%	33.3%	66.5%	33.5%
Iowa	8			1,225,944	706,207	496,206	23,531	210,001 R	57.6%	40.5%	58.7%	41.3%
Kansas	7			916,095	619,812	270,287	25,996	349,525 R	67.7%	29.5%	69.6%	30.4%
Kentucky	9			1,067,499	676,446	371,159	19,894	305,287 R	63.4%	34.8%	64.6%	35.4%
Louisiana	10			1,051,491	686,852	298,142	66,497	388,710 R	65.3%	28.4%	69.7%	30.3%
Maine	4			417,042	256,458	160,584		95,874 R	61.5%	38.5%	61.5%	38.5%
Maryland	10			1,353,812	829,305	505,781	18,726	323,524 R	61.3%	37.4%	62.1%	37.9%
Massachusetts		14		2,458,756	1,112,078	1,332,540	14,138	220,462 D	45.2%	54.2%	45.5%	54.5%
Michigan	21			3,489,727	1,961,721	1,459,435	68,571	502,286 R	56.2%	41.8%	57.3%	42.7%
Minnesota	10			1,741,652	898,269	802,346	41,037	95,923 R	51.6%	46.1%	52.8%	47.2%
Mississippi	7			645,963	505,125	126,782	14,056	378,343 R	78.2%	19.6%	79.9%	20.1%
Missouri	12			1,855,803	1,153,852	697,147	4,804	456,705 R	62.2%	37.6%	62.3%	37.7%
Montana	4			317,603	183,976	120,197	13,430	63,779 R	57.9%	37.8%	60.5%	39.5%
Nebraska	5			576,289	406,298	169,991		236,307 R	70.5%	29.5%	70.5%	29.5%
Nevada	3			181,766	115,750	66,016		49,734 R	63.7%	36.3%	63.7%	36.3%
New Hampshire	4			334,055	213,724	116,435	3,896	97,289 R	64.0%	34.9%	64.7%	35.3%
New Jersey	17			2,997,229	1,845,502	1,102,211	49,516	743,291 R	61.6%	36.8%	62.6%	37.4%
New Mexico	4			386,241	235,606	141,084	9,551	94,522 R	61.0%	36.5%	62.5%	37.5%
New York	41			7,165,919	4,192,778	2,951,084	22,057	1,241,694 R	58.5%	41.2%	58.7%	41.3%
North Carolina	13			1,518,612	1,054,889	438,705	25,018	616,184 R	69.5%	28.9%	70.6%	29.4%
North Dakota	3			280,514	174,109	100,384	6,021	73,725 R	62.1%	35.8%	63.4%	36.6%
Ohio	25			4,094,787	2,441,827	1,558,889	94,071	882,938 R	59.6%	38.1%	61.0%	39.0%
Oklahoma	8			1,029,900	759,025	247,147	23,728	511,878 R	73.7%	24.0%	75.4%	24.6%
Oregon	6			927,946	486,686	392,760	48,500	93,926 R	52.4%	42.3%	55.3%	44.7%
Pennsylvania	27			4,592,106	2,714,521	1,796,951	80,634	917,570 R	59.1%	39.1%	60.2%	39.8%
Rhode Island	4			415,808	220,383	194,645	780	25,738 R	53.0%	46.8%	53.1%	46.9%
South Carolina	8			673,960	477,044	186,824	10,092	290,220 R	70.8%	27.7%	71.9%	28.1%
South Dakota	4			307,415	166,476	139,945	994	26,531 R	54.2%	45.5%	54.3%	45.7%
Tennessee	10			1,201 182	813,147	357,293	30,742	455,854 R	67.7%	29.7%	69.5%	30.5%
Texas	26			3,471,281	2,298,896	1,154,289	18,096	1,144,607 R	66.2%	33.3%	66.6%	33.4%
Utah	4			478,476	323,643	126,284	28,549	197,359 R	67.6%	26.4%	71.9%	28.1%
Vermont	3			186,947	117,149	68,174	1,624	48,975 R	62.7%	36.5%	63.2%	36.8%
Virginia	11		1	1,457,019	988,493	438,887	29,639	549,606 R	67.8%	30.1%	69.3%	30.7%
Washington	9			1,470,847	837,135	568,334	65,378	268,801 R	56.9%	38.6%	59.6%	40.4%
West Virginia	6			762,399	484,964	277,435		207,529 R	63.6%	36.4%	63.6%	36.4%
Wisconsin	11			1,852,890	989,430	810,174	53,286	179,256 R	53.4%	43.7%	55.0%	45.0%
Wyoming	3			145,570	100,464	44,358	748	56,106 R	69.0%	30.5%	69.4%	30.6%
Dist. of Col.		3		163,421	35,226	127,627	568	92,401 D	21.6%	78.1%	21.6%	78.4%
United States	520	17	1	77,718,554	47,169,911	29,170,383	1,378,260	17,999,528 R	60.7%	37.5%	61.8%	38.2%

President 1972

In Virginia one Republican elector voted in the Electoral College for the Libertarian candidates for President and Vice-President.

In New York the Republican figures include Conservative votes and the Democratic figures include Liberal votes. In Alabama the Democratic figures include votes cast on the National Democratic Party of Alabama ticket, and in South Carolina include United Citizens Party votes.

In certain states candidates appeared on the ballot under party names other than those used below; for the Socialist Workers party the votes listed for Jenness and Pulley were actually cast for substitute candidates (Reed and DeBerry) or without named candidates in several states.

The Democratic Vice-Presidential candidate originally was Senator Thomas F. Eagleton; on his withdrawal shortly after the party convention, R. Sargent Shriver was named by the Democratic National Committee as candidate.

The full list of candidates for President and Vice-President was:

47,169,911	Richard M. Nixon and Spiro T. Agnew, Republican.
29,170,383	George S. McGovern and R. Sargent Shriver, Democratic.
1,099,482	John G. Schmitz and Thomas J. Anderson, American.
78,756	Benjamin Spock and Julius Hobson, People's.
66,677	Linda Jenness and Andrew Pulley, Socialist Workers.
53,814	Louis Fisher and Genevieve Gunderson, Socialist Labor.
25,595	Gus Hall and Jarvis Tyner, Communist.
13,505	E. Harold Munn and Marshall E. Uncapher, Prohibition.
3,673	John Hospers and Theodora Nathan, Libertarian.
1,743	John V. Mahalchik and Irving Homer, America First.
220	Gabriel Green and Daniel Fry, Universal.

In addition to the above, 34,795 scattered votes were reported from various states.

Vice-President Agnew resigned in October 1973 and Representative Gerald R. Ford of Michigan was nominated by President Nixon to fill the vacancy. In November (Senate) and December (House of Representatives) this action was approved by Congress.

In August 1974 President Nixon resigned and was succeeded by Vice-President Ford. In the same month Nelson A. Rockefeller, former Governor of New York, was nominated to be Vice-President and was confirmed by Congress in December 1974.

UNITED STATES

PRESIDENT 1976

State	Electoral Vote Rep.	Electoral Vote Dem.	Electoral Vote Other	Total Vote	Republican	Democratic	Other	Plurality	Percentage Total Vote Rep.	Percentage Total Vote Dem.	Percentage Major Vote Rep.	Percentage Major Vote Dem.
Alabama		9		1,182,850	504,070	659,170	19,610	155,100 D	42.6%	55.7%	43.3%	56.7%
Alaska	3			123,574	71,555	44,058	7,961	27,497 R	57.9%	35.7%	61.9%	38.1%
Arizona	6			742,719	418,642	295,602	28,475	123,040 R	56.4%	39.8%	58.6%	41.4%
Arkansas		6		767,535	267,903	498,604	1,028	230,701 D	34.9%	65.0%	35.0%	65.0%
California	45			7,867,117	3,882,244	3,742,284	242,589	139,960 R	49.3%	47.6%	50.9%	49.1%
Colorado	7			1,081,554	584,367	460,353	36,834	124,014 R	54.0%	42.6%	55.9%	44.1%
Connecticut	8			1,381,526	719,261	647,895	14,370	71,366 R	52.1%	46.9%	52.6%	47.4%
Delaware		3		235,834	109,831	122,596	3,407	12,765 D	46.6%	52.0%	47.3%	52.7%
Florida		17		3,150,631	1,469,531	1,636,000	45,100	166,469 D	46.6%	51.9%	47.3%	52.7%
Georgia		12		1,467,458	483,743	979,409	4,306	495,666 D	33.0%	66.7%	33.1%	66.9%
Hawaii		4		291,301	140,003	147,375	3,923	7,372 D	48.1%	50.6%	48.7%	51.3%
Idaho	4			344,071	204,151	126,549	13,371	77,602 R	59.3%	36.8%	61.7%	38.3%
Illinois	26			4,718,914	2,364,269	2,271,295	83,350	92,974 R	50.1%	48.1%	51.0%	49.0%
Indiana	13			2,220,362	1,183,958	1,014,714	21,690	169,244 R	53.3%	45.7%	53.8%	46.2%
Iowa	8			1,279,306	632,863	619,931	26,512	12,932 R	49.5%	48.5%	50.5%	49.5%
Kansas	7			957,845	502,752	430,421	24,672	72,331 R	52.5%	44.9%	53.9%	46.1%
Kentucky		9		1,167,142	531,852	615,717	19,573	83,865 D	45.6%	52.8%	46.3%	53.7%
Louisiana		10		1,278,439	587,446	661,365	29,628	73,919 D	46.0%	51.7%	47.0%	53.0%
Maine	4			483,216	236,320	232,279	14,617	4,041 R	48.9%	48.1%	50.4%	49.6%
Maryland		10		1,439,897	672,661	759,612	7,624	86,951 D	46.7%	52.8%	47.0%	53.0%
Massachusetts		14		2,547,558	1,030,276	1,429,475	87,807	399,199 D	40.4%	56.1%	41.9%	58.1%
Michigan	21			3,653,749	1,893,742	1,696,714	63,293	197,028 R	51.8%	46.4%	52.7%	47.3%
Minnesota		10		1,949,931	819,395	1,070,440	60,096	251,045 D	42.0%	54.9%	43.4%	56.6%
Mississippi		7		769,361	366,846	381,309	21,206	14,463 D	47.7%	49.6%	49.0%	51.0%
Missouri		12		1,953,600	927,443	998,387	27,770	70,944 D	47.5%	51.1%	48.2%	51.8%
Montana	4			328,734	173,703	149,259	5,772	24,444 R	52.8%	45.4%	53.8%	46.2%
Nebraska	5			607,668	359,705	233,692	14,271	126,013 R	59.2%	38.5%	60.6%	39.4%
Nevada	3			201,876	101,273	92,479	8,124	8,794 R	50.2%	45.8%	52.3%	47.7%
New Hampshire	4			339,618	185,935	147,635	6,048	38,300 R	54.7%	43.5%	55.7%	44.3%
New Jersey	17			3,014,472	1,509,688	1,444,653	60,131	65,035 R	50.1%	47.9%	51.1%	48.9%
New Mexico	4			418,409	211,419	201,148	5,842	10,271 R	50.5%	48.1%	51.2%	48.8%
New York		41		6,534,170	3,100,791	3,389,558	43,821	288,767 D	47.5%	51.9%	47.8%	52.2%
North Carolina		13		1,678,914	741,960	927,365	9,589	185,405 D	44.2%	55.2%	44.4%	55.6%
North Dakota	3			297,188	153,470	136,078	7,640	17,392 R	51.6%	45.8%	53.0%	47.0%
Ohio		25		4,111,873	2,000,505	2,011,621	99,747	11,116 D	48.7%	48.9%	49.9%	50.1%
Oklahoma	8			1,092,251	545,708	532,442	14,101	13,266 R	50.0%	48.7%	50.6%	49.4%
Oregon	6			1,029,876	492,120	490,407	47,349	1,713 R	47.8%	47.6%	50.1%	49.9%
Pennsylvania		27		4,620,787	2,205,604	2,328,677	86,506	123,073 D	47.7%	50.4%	48.6%	51.4%
Rhode Island		4		411,170	181,249	227,636	2,285	46,387 D	44.1%	55.4%	44.3%	55.7%
South Carolina		8		802,583	346,149	450,807	5,627	104,658 D	43.1%	56.2%	43.4%	56.6%
South Dakota	4			300,678	151,505	147,068	2,105	4,437 R	50.4%	48.9%	50.7%	49.3%
Tennessee		10		1,476,345	633,969	825,879	16,497	191,910 D	42.9%	55.9%	43.4%	56.6%
Texas		26		4,071,884	1,953,300	2,082,319	36,265	129,019 D	48.0%	51.1%	48.4%	51.6%
Utah	4			541,198	337,908	182,110	21,180	155,798 R	62.4%	33.6%	65.0%	35.0%
Vermont	3			187,765	102,085	80,954	4,726	21,131 R	54.4%	43.1%	55.8%	44.2%
Virginia	12			1,697,094	836,554	813,896	46,644	22,658 R	49.3%	48.0%	50.7%	49.3%
Washington	8		1	1,555,534	777,732	717,323	60,479	60,409 R	50.0%	46.1%	52.0%	48.0%
West Virginia		6		750,964	314,760	435,914	290	121,154 D	41.9%	58.0%	41.9%	58.1%
Wisconsin		11		2,104,175	1,004,987	1,040,232	58,956	35,245 D	47.8%	49.4%	49.1%	50.9%
Wyoming	3			156,343	92,717	62,239	1,387	30,478 R	59.3%	39.8%	59.8%	40.2%
Dist. of Col.		3		168,830	27,873	137,818	3,139	109,945 D	16.5%	81.6%	16.8%	83.2%
United States	240	297	1	81,555,889	39,147,793	40,830,763	1,577,333	1,682,970 D	48.0%	50.1%	48.9%	51.1%

President 1976

In Washington, one Republican elector voted in the Electoral College for Ronald Reagan for President and Robert Dole for Vice-President.

In New York the Republican figures include Conservative votes and the Democratic figures include Liberal votes; in Vermont the Democratic figures include votes cast on the Independent Vermonters party ticket.

In a number of states candidates appeared on the ballot with variants of the party designations listed below and in several cases with entirely different party names.

The ballot designations for electors for Eugene J. McCarthy for President varied from state to state, as did the names of Vice-Presidential candidates running with him. In New Jersey, the Maddox Vice-Presidential candidate was Edmund O. Matzal.

The full list of candidates for President and Vice-President was:

40,830,763	Jimmy Carter and Walter F. Mondale, Democratic.
39,147,793	Gerald R. Ford and Robert Dole, Republican.
756,691	Eugene J. McCarthy with various Vice-Presidential candidates, Independent.
173,011	Roger L. MacBride and David D. Bergland, Libertarian.
170,531	Lester G. Maddox and William D. Dyke, American Independent.
160,773	Thomas J. Anderson and Rufus Shackelford, American.
91,314	Peter Camejo and Willie Mae Reid, Socialist Workers.
58,992	Gus Hall and Jarvis Tyner, Communist.
49,024	Margaret Wright and Benjamin Spock, People's.
40,043	Lyndon LaRouche and R. W. Evans, United States Labor.
15,934	Benjamin C. Bubar and Earl F. Dodge, Prohibition.
9,616	Julius Levin and Constance Blomen, Socialist Labor.
6,038	Frank P. Zeidler and J. Q. Brisben, Socialist.
361	Ernest L. Miller and Roy N. Eddy, Restoration.
36	Frank Taylor and Henry Swan, United American.

In addition to these votes, 39,861 scattered write-in votes were reported from various states and 5,108 votes were cast for "None of these Candidates" in Nevada.

1972 PRESIDENTIAL PREFERENCE PRIMARIES

In 1972 twenty states and the District of Columbia held preferential primaries. California, South Dakota and the District of Columbia held slate-type preferential primaries. In the other eighteen states the voter marked his ballot for his preference among the candidates listed and in some states could write in his choice if the candidate he preferred was not on the ballot. In a few states the voter had an additional option for uncommitted or for none of the listed candidates. In Alabama and New York, delegates to the national party conventions were elected in primaries, but neither state provided for a specific expression of Presidential preference by the voter, nor printed on the ballot any indication of the Presidential preference of the candidates for convention delegates.

In each state the vote used is the preferential vote if there was such a vote. In Ohio, where no specific preference vote was authorized, the major candidates ran state-wide at-large blocks of delegate candidates, and the vote given is that for the highest vote winner in each of these blocks. In several states there were both a preference and a delegate vote. In such cases the preference vote is indicated here, even though the delegate contest was controlling in terms of individuals chosen to go to the party national conventions in Miami Beach.

The tables included here give the vote in each state for those candidates on the ballot in ten or more states. Other votes, for ballot candidates or written-in, are included in the general "Other" category.

Republican candidates on the ballot in at least one state were John M. Ashbrook, Paul N. McCloskey, Richard M. Nixon, Patrick Paulsen.

Democratic candidates on the ballot in at least one state were Shirley Chisholm, Edward T. Coll, Walter E. Fauntroy, R. Vance Hartke, Hubert H. Humphrey, Henry M. Jackson, Edward M. Kennedy, John V. Lindsay, Eugene J. McCarthy, George S. McGovern, Wilbur D. Mills, Patsy Mink, Edmund S. Muskie, Terry Sanford, George C. Wallace, Samuel W. Yorty.

CALIFORNIA JUNE 6

Republican 2,058,825 Nixon slate; 224,922 Ashbrook slate; 175 scattered.

Democratic 1,550,652 McGovern slate; 1,375,064 Humphrey slate; 268,551 Wallace (write-in); 157,435 Chisholm slate; 72,701 Muskie slate; 50,745 Yorty slate; 34,203 McCarthy slate; 28,901 Jackson slate; 26,246 Lindsay slate; 20 scattered.

FLORIDA MARCH 14

Republican 360,278 Nixon; 36,617 Ashbrook; 17,312 McCloskey.

Democratic 526,651 Wallace; 234,658 Humphrey; 170,156 Jackson; 112,523 Muskie; 82,386 Lindsay; 78,232 McGovern; 43,989 Chisholm; 5,847 McCarthy; 4,539 Mills; 3,009 Hartke; 2,564 Yorty.

ILLINOIS MARCH 21

Republican No Presidential candidates on the ballot. Write-in votes were 32,550 Nixon; 170 Ashbrook; 47 McCloskey; 802 scattered.

Democratic 766,914 Muskie; 444,260 McCarthy; 7,017 Wallace (write-in); 3,687 McGovern (write-in); 1,476 Humphrey (write-in); 777 Chisholm (write-in); 442 Jackson (write-in); 242 Kennedy (write-in); 118 Lindsay (write-in); 211 scattered.

INDIANA MAY 2

Republican 417,069 Nixon, unopposed.

Democratic 354,244 Humphrey; 309,495 Wallace; 87,719 Muskie.

MARYLAND MAY 16

Republican 99,308 Nixon; 9,223 McCloskey; 6,718 Ashbrook.

Democratic 219,687 Wallace; 151,981 Humphrey; 126,978 McGovern; 17,728 Jackson; 13,584 Yorty; 13,363 Muskie; 12,602 Chisholm; 4,776 Mills; 4,691 McCarthy; 2,168 Lindsay; 573 Mink.

MASSACHUSETTS APRIL 25

Republican 99,150 Nixon; 16,435 McCloskey; 4,864 Ashbrook; 1,690 scattered.

Democratic 325,673 McGovern; 131,709 Muskie; 48,929 Humphrey; 45,807 Wallace; 22,398 Chisholm; 19,441 Mills; 8,736 McCarthy; 8,499 Jackson; 2,348 Kennedy (write-in); 2,107 Lindsay; 874 Hartke; 646 Yorty; 589 Coll; 760 scattered.

MICHIGAN MAY 16

Republican 321,652 Nixon; 9,691 McCloskey; 5,370 Uncommitted; 30 scattered.

Democratic 809,239 Wallace; 425,694 McGovern; 249,798 Humphrey; 44,090 Chisholm; 38,701 Muskie; 10,700 Uncommitted; 6,938 Jackson; 2,862 Hartke; 51 scattered.

NEBRASKA MAY 9

Republican 179,464 Nixon; 9,011 McCloskey; 4,996 Ashbrook; 801 scattered.

Democratic 79,309 McGovern; 65,968 Humphrey; 23,912 Wallace; 6,886 Muskie; 5,276 Jackson; 3,459 Yorty; 3,194 McCarthy; 1,763 Chisholm; 1,244 Lindsay; 377 Mills; 293 Kennedy (write-in); 249 Hartke; 207 scattered.

NEW HAMPSHIRE MARCH 7

Republican 79,239 Nixon; 23,190 McCloskey; 11,362 Ashbrook; 1,211 Paulsen; 2,206 scattered.

Democratic 41,235 Muskie; 33,007 McGovern; 5,401 Yorty; 3,563 Mills (write-in); 2,417 Hartke; 954 Kennedy (write-in); 348 Humphrey (write-in); 280 Coll; 197 Jackson (write-in); 175 Wallace (write-in); 1,277 scattered.

NEW JERSEY JUNE 6

Republican No Presidential candidates on the ballot.

Democratic 51,433 Chisholm; 25,401 Sanford.

NEW MEXICO JUNE 6

Republican 49,067 Nixon; 3,367 McCloskey; 3,035 None of the Names Shown.

Democratic 51,011 McGovern; 44,843 Wallace; 39,768 Humphrey; 6,411 Muskie; 4,236 Jackson; 3,819 None of the Names Shown; 3,205 Chisholm.

NORTH CAROLINA MAY 6

Republican 159,167 Nixon; 8,732 McCloskey.

Democratic 413,518 Wallace; 306,014 Sanford; 61,723 Chisholm; 30,739 Muskie; 9,416 Jackson.

OHIO MAY 2

Republican 692,828 Nixon, unopposed.

Democratic 499,680 Humphrey; 480,320 McGovern; 107,806 Muskie; 98,498 Jackson; 26,026 McCarthy.

OREGON MAY 23

Republican 231,151 Nixon; 29,365 McCloskey; 16,696 Ashbrook; 4,798 scattered.

Democratic 205,328 McGovern; 81,868 Wallace; 51,163 Humphrey; 22,042 Jackson; 12,673 Kennedy; 10,244 Muskie; 8,943 McCarthy; 6,500 Mink; 5,082 Lindsay; 2,975 Chisholm; 1,208 Mills; 618 scattered.

PENNSYLVANIA APRIL 25

Republican No Presidential candidates on the ballot. Write-in votes were 153,886 Nixon; 30,915 scattered. Of the latter, most were for candidates for the Democratic nomination, including 20,472 Wallace.

Democratic 481,900 Humphrey; 292,437 Wallace; 280,861 McGovern; 279,983 Muskie; 38,767 Jackson; 306 Chisholm (write-in); 585 scattered.

RHODE ISLAND MAY 23

Republican 4,953 Nixon; 337 McCloskey; 175 Ashbrook; 146 Uncommitted.

Democratic 15,603 McGovern; 7,838 Muskie; 7,701 Humphrey; 5,802 Wallace; 490 Uncommitted; 245 McCarthy; 138 Jackson; 41 Mills; 6 Yorty.

SOUTH DAKOTA JUNE 6

Republican 52,820 Nixon slate, unopposed.

Democratic 28,017 McGovern slate, unopposed.

TENNESSEE MAY 4

Republican 109,696 Nixon; 2,419 Ashbrook; 2,370 McCloskey; 4 scattered.

Democratic 335,858 Wallace; 78,350 Humphrey; 35,551 McGovern; 18,809 Chisholm; 9,634 Muskie; 5,896 Jackson; 2,543 Mills; 2,267 McCarthy; 1,621 Hartke; 1,476 Lindsay; 692 Yorty; 24 scattered.

WEST VIRGINIA MAY 9

Republican No Presidential candidates on the ballot.

Democratic 246,596 Humphrey; 121,888 Wallace.

WISCONSIN APRIL 4

Republican 277,601 Nixon; 3,651 McCloskey; 2,604 Ashbrook; 2,315 None of the Names Shown; 273 scattered.

Democratic 333,528 McGovern; 248,676 Wallace; 233,748 Humphrey; 115,811 Muskie; 88,068 Jackson; 75,579 Lindsay; 15,543 McCarthy; 9,198 Chisholm; 2,450 None of the Names Shown; 2,349 Yorty; 1,213 Mink; 913 Mills; 766 Hartke; 183 Kennedy (write-in); 559 scattered.

DISTRICT OF COLUMBIA MAY 2

Republican No slates entered.

Democratic 21,217 Fauntroy slate; 8,343 Uncommitted slate.

REPUBLICAN PREFERENCE PRIMARIES

Date	State	Total Vote	Ashbrook	McCloskey	Nixon	Other
March 7	New Hampshire	117,208	11,362	23,190	79,239	3,417
14	Florida	414,207	36,617	17,312	360,278	–
21	Illinois	33,569	170	47	32,550	802
April 4	Wisconsin	286,444	2,604	3,651	277,601	2,588
25	Massachusetts	122,139	4,864	16,435	99,150	1,690
25	Pennsylvania	184,801	–	–	153,886	30,915
May 2	District of Columbia	No Slates Entered				
2	Indiana	417,069	–	–	417,069	–
2	Ohio	692,828	–	–	692,828	–
4	Tennessee	114,489	2,419	2,370	109,696	4
6	North Carolina	167,899	–	8,732	159,167	–
9	Nebraska	194,272	4,996	9,011	179,464	801
9	West Virginia	No Candidates Entered				
16	Maryland	115,249	6,718	9,223	99,308	–
16	Michigan	336,743	–	9,691	321,652	5,400
23	Rhode Island	5,611	175	337	4,953	146
23	Oregon	282,010	16,696	29,365	231,151	4,798
June 6	California	2,283,922	224,922	–	2,058,825	175
6	New Jersey	No Candidates Entered				
6	New Mexico	55,469	–	3,367	49,067	3,035
6	South Dakota	52,820	–	–	52,820	–
		5,876,749	311,543	132,731	5,378,704	53,771

Other vote includes 1,211 Paulsen; 52,559 Uncommitted, None, and scattered.

DEMOCRATIC PREFERENCE PRIMARIES

Date	State	Total Vote	Chisholm	Humphrey	Jackson	McCarthy	McGovern	Muskie	Wallace	Other
March 7	New Hampshire	88,854	–	348	197	–	33,007	41,235	175	13,892
14	Florida	1,264,554	43,989	234,658	170,156	5,847	78,232	112,523	526,651	92,498
21	Illinois	1,225,144	777	1,476	442	444,260	3,687	766,914	7,017	571
April 4	Wisconsin	1,128,584	9,198	233,748	88,068	15,543	333,528	115,811	248,676	84,012
25	Massachusetts	618,516	22,398	48,929	8,499	8,736	325,673	131,709	45,807	26,765
25	Pennsylvania	1,374,839	306	481,900	38,767	–	280,861	279,983	292,437	585
May 2	District of Columbia	29,560	–	–	–	–	–	–	–	29,560
2	Indiana	751,458	–	354,244	–	–	–	87,719	309,495	–
2	Ohio	1,212,330	–	499,680	98,498	26,026	480,320	107,806	–	–
4	Tennessee	492,721	18,809	78,350	5,896	2,267	35,551	9,634	335,858	6,356
6	North Carolina	821,410	61,723	–	9,416	–	–	30,739	413,518	306,014
9	Nebraska	192,137	1,763	65,968	5,276	3,194	79,309	6,886	23,912	5,829
9	West Virginia	368,484	–	246,596	–	–	–	–	121,888	–
16	Maryland	568,131	12,602	151,981	17,728	4,691	126,978	13,363	219,687	21,101
16	Michigan	1,588,073	44,090	249,798	6,938	–	425,694	38,701	809,239	13,613
23	Rhode Island	37,864	–	7,701	138	245	15,603	7,838	5,802	537
23	Oregon	408,644	2,975	51,163	22,042	8,943	205,328	10,244	81,868	26,081
June 6	California	3,564,518	157,435	1,375,064	28,901	34,203	1,550,652	72,701	268,551	77,011
6	New Jersey	76,834	51,433	–	–	–	–	–	–	25,401
6	New Mexico	153,293	3,205	39,768	4,236	–	51,011	6,411	44,843	3,819
6	South Dakota	28,017	–	–	–	–	28,017	–	–	–
		15,993,965	430,703	4,121,372	505,198	553,955	4,053,451	1,840,217	3,755,424	733,645

Other vote includes 331,415 Sanford; 196,406 Lindsay; 79,446 Yorty; 37,401 Mills; 21,217 Fauntroy; 16,693 Kennedy; 11,798 Hartke; 8,286 Mink; 869 Coll; 30,114 Uncommitted, None, and scattered.

1976 PRESIDENTIAL PREFERENCE PRIMARIES

In 1976 twenty-six states and the District of Columbia held preferential primaries. California and South Dakota held slate-type preferential primaries. In the District and the other twenty-four states the voter marked his ballot for his preference among the candidates listed and in some states could write in his choice if the candidate he preferred was not on the ballot. In a few states the voter had an additional option for uncommitted, no preference or none. In Alabama, New York and Texas delegates to the national party conventions were elected in primaries, but none of these states provided for a specific expression of Presidential preference by the voter save by an indication of the Presidential preference of the candidates for convention delegates.

In each state the vote used is the preferential vote if there was such a vote. In Ohio, the vote is for delegates at-large pledged to specific candidates and elected as a group. In several states there were both a preference and a delegate vote. In such cases the preference vote is indicated here, even though the delegate contest was controlling in terms of individuals chosen to go to the party national conventions in Kansas City and New York City.

The tables included here give the major party primary vote in each state for those candidates who were on the ballot in at least ten states or who polled a minimum of one percent of their party's total national Presidential preference vote.

Republican candidates on the ballot in at least one state were Lar Daly, Gerald R. Ford, Tommy Klein and Ronald Reagan.

Democratic candidates on the ballot in at least one state were Frank Ahern, Stanley N. Arnold, Birch Bayh, Lloyd Bentsen, Arthur O. Blessitt, Frank Bona, Edmund G. Brown, Jr., Robert C. Byrd, Jimmy Carter, Frank Church, Billy Joe Clegg, Gertrude W. Donahey, Abram Eisenman, John S. Gonas, Jesse Gray, Fred R. Harris, Hubert H. Humphrey, Henry M. Jackson, Robert L. Kelleher, Edward M. Kennedy, Rick Loewenherz, Frank Lomento, Floyd L. Lunger, Ellen McCormack, Fifi Rockefeller, George Roden, Ray Rollinson, Terry Sanford, Bernard B. Schechter, Milton Shapp, R. Sargent Shriver, Morris K. Udall and George C. Wallace.

ARKANSAS MAY 25

Republican	20,628 Reagan; 11,430 Ford; 483 Uncommitted.
Democratic	314,306 Carter; 83,005 Wallace; 57,152 Uncommitted; 37,783 Udall; 9,554 Jackson. Original uncorrected canvass gave the Uncommitted vote as 57,067.

CALIFORNIA JUNE 8

Republican	1,604,836 Reagan; 845,655 Ford; 20 scattered write-ins.
Democratic	2,013,210 Brown slate; 697,092 Carter slate; 250,581 Church slate; 171,501 Udall slate; 102,292 Wallace slate; 78,595 Uncommitted slate; 38,634 Jackson slate; 29,242 McCormack slate; 16,920 Harris slate; 11,419 Bayh slate; 215 scattered write-ins.
American Independent	3,447 Shea; 2,922 Rarick; 2,447 Watson; 1,719 Procell; 1,523 Goodloe; 7 scattered write-ins.
Peace & Freedom	4,351 Wright; 1,372 Zeidler; 12 scattered write-ins.

FLORIDA MARCH 9

Republican	321,982 Ford; 287,837 Reagan.
Democratic	448,844 Carter; 396,820 Wallace; 310,944 Jackson; 37,626 No Preference; 32,198 Shapp; 27,235 Udall; 8,750 Bayh; 7,889 Blessitt; 7,595 McCormack; 7,084 Shriver; 5,397 Harris; 5,042 Byrd; 4,906 Church.

GEORGIA MAY 4

Republican 128,671 Reagan; 59,801 Ford.

Democratic 419,272 Carter; 57,594 Wallace; 9,755 Udall; 3,628 Byrd; 3,358 Jackson; 2,477 Church; 1,487 Ahern; 1,378 Shriver; 824 Bayh; 699 Harris; 635 McCormack; 351 Eisenman; 277 Bentsen; 263 Bona; 181 Shapp; 153 Roden; 139 Kelleher.

IDAHO MAY 25

Republican 66,743 Reagan; 22,323 Ford; 727 Uncommitted.

Democratic 58,570 Church; 8,818 Carter; 1,700 Humphrey; 1,453 Brown (write-in); 1,115 Wallace; 981 Udall; 964 Uncommitted; 485 Jackson; 319 Harris.

American 409 Rarick; 261 Anderson; 92 Uncommitted.

ILLINOIS MARCH 16

Republican 456,750 Ford; 311,295 Reagan; 7,582 Daly; 266 scattered write-ins.

Democratic 630,915 Carter; 361,798 Wallace; 214,024 Shriver; 98,862 Harris; 6,315 scattered write-ins.

INDIANA MAY 4

Republican 323,779 Reagan; 307,513 Ford.

Democratic 417,480 Carter; 93,121 Wallace; 72,080 Jackson; 31,708 McCormack.

KENTUCKY MAY 25

Republican 67,976 Ford; 62,683 Reagan; 1,781 Uncommitted; 1,088 Klein.

Democratic 181,690 Carter; 51,540 Wallace; 33,262 Udall; 17,061 McCormack; 11,962 Uncommitted; 8,186 Jackson; 2,305 Fifi Rockefeller.

MARYLAND MAY 18

Republican 96,291 Ford; 69,680 Reagan.

Democratic 286,672 Brown; 219,404 Carter; 32,790 Udall; 24,176 Wallace; 13,956 Jackson; 7,907 McCormack; 6,841 Harris.

MASSACHUSETTS MARCH 2

Republican 115,375 Ford; 63,555 Reagan; 6,000 No Preference; 3,519 scattered write-ins.

Democratic 164,393 Jackson; 130,440 Udall; 123,112 Wallace; 101,948 Carter; 55,701 Harris; 53,252 Shriver; 34,963 Bayh; 25,772 McCormack; 21,693 Shapp; 9,804 No Preference; 7,851 Humphrey (write-in); 1,623 Kennedy (write-in); 1,603 Kelleher; 364 Bentsen; 351 Sanford; 2,951 scattered write-ins.

American No candidate names were printed on the ballot; there were 595 write-in votes including 86 for Wallace. In addition there were 98 No Preference votes.

MICHIGAN MAY 18

Republican 690,180 Ford; 364,052 Reagan; 8,473 Uncommitted; 109 scattered write-ins.

Democratic 307,559 Carter; 305,134 Udall; 49,204 Wallace; 15,853 Uncommitted; 10,332 Jackson; 7,623 McCormack; 5,738 Shriver; 4,081 Harris; 3,142 scattered write-ins.

MONTANA JUNE 1

Republican 56,683 Reagan; 31,100 Ford; 1,996 No Preference.

Democratic 63,448 Church; 26,329 Carter; 6,708 Udall; 3,820 No Preference; 3,680 Wallace; 2,856 Jackson.

NEBRASKA MAY 11

Republican 113,493 Reagan; 94,542 Ford; 379 scattered write-ins.

Democratic 67,297 Church; 65,833 Carter; 12,685 Humphrey; 7,199 Kennedy; 6,033 McCormack; 5,567 Wallace; 4,688 Udall; 2,642 Jackson; 811 Harris; 407 Bayh; 384 Shriver; 1,467 scattered write-ins.

NEVADA MAY 25

Republican 31,637 Reagan; 13,747 Ford; 2,365 "None of these Candidates".

Democratic 39,671 Brown; 17,567 Carter; 6,778 Church; 4,603 "None of these Candidates"; 2,490 Wallace; 2,237 Udall; 1,896 Jackson.

NEW HAMPSHIRE FEBRUARY 24

Republican 55,156 Ford; 53,569 Reagan; 2,949 scattered write-ins.

Democratic 23,373 Carter; 18,710 Udall; 12,510 Bayh; 8,863 Harris; 6,743 Shriver; 4,596 Humphrey (write-in); 1,857 Jackson (write-in); 1,061 Wallace (write-in); 1,007 McCormack; 828 Blessitt; 371 Arnold; 174 Clegg; 173 Schechter; 135 Bona; 87 Kelleher; 53 Sanford; 49 Loewenherz; 1,791 scattered write-ins.

NEW JERSEY JUNE 8

Republican 242,122 Ford, unopposed.

Democratic 210,655 Carter; 49,034 Church; 31,820 Jackson; 31,183 Wallace; 21,774 McCormack; 3,935 Lunger; 3,574 Gray; 3,555 Lomento; 3,021 Rollinson; 2,288 Gonas.

NORTH CAROLINA MARCH 23

Republican 101,468 Reagan; 88,897 Ford; 3,362 No Preference.

Democratic 324,437 Carter; 210,166 Wallace; 25,749 Jackson; 22,850 No Preference; 14,032 Udall; 5,923 Harris; 1,675 Bentsen.

OHIO JUNE 8

Republican 516,111 Ford; 419,646 Reagan.

Democratic 593,130 Carter; 240,342 Udall; 157,884 Church; 63,953 Wallace; 43,661 Donahey; 35,404 Jackson.

OREGON MAY 25

Republican 150,181 Ford; 136,691 Reagan; 11,663 scattered write-ins.

Democratic 145,394 Church; 115,310 Carter; 106,812 Brown (write-ins); 22,488 Humphrey; 11,747 Udall; 10,983 Kennedy; 5,797 Wallace; 5,298 Jackson; 3,753 McCormack; 1,344 Harris; 743 Bayh; 2,963 scattered write-ins.

PENNSYLVANIA APRIL 27

Republican 733,472 Ford; 40,510 Reagan (write-in); 22,678 scattered write-ins.

Democratic 511,905 Carter; 340,340 Jackson; 259,166 Udall; 155,902 Wallace; 38,800 McCormack; 32,947 Shapp; 15,320 Bayh; 13,067 Harris; 12,563 Humphrey (write-in); 5,032 scattered write-ins.

Constitutional 1,333 Cunningham; 87 scattered write-ins.

RHODE ISLAND JUNE 1

Republican 9,365 Ford; 4,480 Reagan; 507 Uncommitted.

Democratic 19,035 Uncommitted; 18,237 Carter; 16,423 Church; 2,543 Udall; 2,468 McCormack; 756 Jackson; 507 Wallace; 247 Bayh; 132 Shapp.

SOUTH DAKOTA JUNE 1

Republican 43,068 Reagan slate; 36,976 Ford slate; 4,033 No Preference slate.

Democratic 24,186 Carter slate; 19,510 Udall slate; 7,871 No Preference slate; 4,561 McCormack slate; 1,412 Wallace slate; 573 Harris slate; 558 Jackson slate.

TENNESSEE MAY 25

Republican 120,685 Ford; 118,997 Reagan; 2,756 Uncommitted; 97 scattered write-ins.

Democratic 259,243 Carter; 36,495 Wallace; 12,420 Udall; 8,026 Church; 6,148 Uncommitted; 5,672 Jackson; 1,782 McCormack; 1,628 Harris; 1,556 Brown (write-in); 507 Shapp; 109 Humphrey (write-in); 492 scattered write-ins, including all 424 write-ins in Shelby County.

VERMONT MARCH 2

Republican 27,014 Ford; 4,892 Reagan (write-in); 251 scattered.

Democratic 16,335 Carter; 10,699 Shriver; 4,893 Harris; 3,324 McCormack; 3,463 scattered.

Liberty Union 965 Wright; 150 scattered.

WEST VIRGINIA MAY 11

Republican 88,386 Ford; 67,306 Reagan.

Democratic 331,639 Byrd; 40,938 Wallace.

WISCONSIN APRIL 6

Republican	326,869 Ford; 262,126 Reagan; 2,234 "None of the Names Shown"; 583 scattered write-ins.
Democratic	271,220 Carter; 263,771 Udall; 92,460 Wallace; 47,605 Jackson; 26,982 McCormack; 8,185 Harris; 7,154 "None of the Names Shown"; 5,097 Shriver; 1,730 Bentsen; 1,255 Bayh; 596 Shapp; 14,473 scattered write-ins.
American	No candidate names were printed on the ballot; there were 1,033 write-in votes.

DISTRICT OF COLUMBIA MAY 4

Republican	No Presidential candidates on the ballot.
Democratic	10,521 Carter; 10,149 Uncommitted (Fauntroy slate); 6,999 Udall; 5,161 Uncommitted (Washington slate); 461 Harris.

REPUBLICAN PREFERENCE PRIMARIES

Date		State	Total Vote	Ford	Reagan	Other
February	24	New Hampshire	111,674	55,156	53,569	2,949
March	2	Massachusetts	188,449	115,375	63,555	9,519
	2	Vermont	32,157	27,014	4,892	251
	9	Florida	609,819	321,982	287,837	–
	16	Illinois	775,893	456,750	311,295	7,848
	23	North Carolina	193,727	88,897	101,468	3,362
April	6	Wisconsin	591,812	326,869	262,126	2,817
	27	Pennsylvania	796,660	733,472	40,510	22,678
May	4	District of Columbia	No Primary			
	4	Georgia	188,472	59,801	128,671	–
	4	Indiana	631,292	307,513	323,779	–
	11	Nebraska	208,414	94,542	113,493	379
	11	West Virginia	155,692	88,386	67,306	–
	18	Maryland	165,971	96,291	69,680	–
	18	Michigan	1,062,814	690,180	364,052	8,582
	25	Arkansas	32,541	11,430	20,628	483
	25	Idaho	89,793	22,323	66,743	727
	25	Kentucky	133,528	67,976	62,683	2,869
	25	Nevada	47,749	13,747	31,637	2,365
	25	Oregon	298,535	150,181	136,691	11,663
	25	Tennessee	242,535	120,685	118,997	2,853
June	1	Montana	89,779	31,100	56,683	1,996
	1	Rhode Island	14,352	9,365	4,480	507
	1	South Dakota	84,077	36,976	43,068	4,033
	8	California	2,450,511	845,655	1,604,836	20
	8	New Jersey	242,122	242,122	–	–
	8	Ohio	935,757	516,111	419,646	–
			10,374,125	5,529,899	4,758,325	85,901

Other vote includes 7,582 Daly; 1,088 Klein; 42,514 scattered write-ins; 15,391 No Preference; 14,727 Uncommitted; 2,365 "None of These Candidates"; 2,234 "None of the Names Shown".

DEMOCRATIC PREFERENCE PRIMARIES

Date		State	Total Vote	Bayh	Brown	Byrd	Carter	Church	Harris	Jackson	McCormack	Shriver	Udall	Wallace	Other
February	24	New Hampshire	82,381	12,510	—	—	23,373	—	8,863	1,857	1,007	6,743	18,710	1,061	8,257
March	2	Massachusetts	735,821	34,963	—	—	101,948	—	55,701	164,393	25,772	53,252	130,440	123,112	46,240
	2	Vermont	38,714	—	—	—	16,335	—	4,893	—	3,324	10,699	—	—	3,463
	9	Florida	1,300,330	8,750	—	5,042	448,844	4,906	5,397	310,944	7,595	7,084	27,235	396,820	77,713
	16	Illinois	1,311,914	—	—	—	630,915	—	98,862	—	—	214,024	—	361,798	6,315
	23	North Carolina	604,832	—	—	—	324,437	—	5,923	25,749	—	—	14,032	210,166	24,525
April	6	Wisconsin	740,528	1,255	—	—	271,220	—	8,185	47,605	26,982	5,097	263,771	92,460	23,953
	27	Pennsylvania	1,385,042	15,320	—	—	511,905	—	13,067	340,340	38,800	—	259,166	155,902	50,542
May	4	District of Columbia	33,291	—	—	—	10,521	—	461	—	—	—	6,999	—	15,310
	4	Georgia	502,471	824	—	3,628	419,272	2,477	699	3,358	635	1,378	9,755	57,594	2,851
	4	Indiana	614,389	—	—	—	417,480	—	—	72,080	31,708	—	—	93,121	—
	11	Nebraska	175,013	407	—	—	65,833	67,297	811	2,642	6,033	384	4,688	5,567	21,351
	11	West Virginia	372,577	—	—	331,639	—	—	—	—	—	—	—	40,938	—
	18	Maryland	591,746	—	286,672	—	219,404	—	6,841	13,956	7,907	—	32,790	24,176	—
	18	Michigan	708,666	—	—	—	307,559	—	4,081	10,332	7,623	5,738	305,134	49,204	18,995
	25	Arkansas	501,800	—	—	—	314,306	—	—	9,554	—	—	37,783	83,005	57,152
	25	Idaho	74,405	—	1,453	—	8,818	58,570	319	485	—	—	981	1,115	2,664
	25	Kentucky	306,006	—	—	—	181,690	—	—	8,186	17,061	—	33,262	51,540	14,267
	25	Nevada	75,242	—	39,671	—	17,567	6,778	—	1,896	—	—	2,237	2,490	4,603
	25	Oregon	432,632	743	106,812	—	115,310	145,394	1,344	5,298	3,753	—	11,747	5,797	36,434
	25	Tennessee	334,078	—	1,556	—	259,243	8,026	1,628	5,672	1,782	—	12,420	36,495	7,256
June	1	Montana	106,841	—	—	—	26,329	63,448	—	2,856	—	—	6,708	3,680	3,820
	1	Rhode Island	60,348	247	—	—	18,237	16,423	—	756	2,468	—	2,543	507	19,167
	1	South Dakota	58,671	—	—	—	24,186	—	573	558	4,561	—	19,510	1,412	7,871
	8	California	3,409,701	11,419	2,013,210	—	697,092	250,581	16,920	38,634	29,242	—	171,501	102,292	78,810
	8	New Jersey	360,839	—	—	—	210,655	49,034	—	31,820	21,774	—	—	31,183	16,373
	8	Ohio	1,134,374	—	—	—	593,130	157,884	—	35,404	—	—	240,342	63,953	43,661
			16,052,652	86,438	2,449,374	340,309	6,235,609	830,818	234,568	1,134,375	238,027	304,399	1,611,754	1,995,388	591,593

Other vote includes 88,254 Shapp; 61,992 Humphrey; 43,661 Donahey; 19,805 Kennedy; 8,717 Blessitt; 4,046 Bentsen; 3,935 Lunger; 3,574 Gray; 3,555 Lomento; 3,021 Rollinson; 2,305 Fifi Rockefeller; 2,288 Gonas; 1,829 Kelleher; 1,487 Ahern; 404 Sanford; 398 Bona; 371 Arnold; 351 Eisenman; 174 Clegg; 173 Schechter; 153 Roden; 49 Loewenherz; 205,019 Uncommitted; 81,971 No Preference; 42,304 scattered write-ins; 7,154 "None of the Names Shown"; 4,603 "None of These Candidates".

UNITED STATES

POST ELECTION CHANGES

Following the 1976 elections several changes took place among the Governors and the members of Congress. Summarized below are all such changes up to August 1, 1977.

GOVERNORS

Idaho. Governor Cecil D. Andrus (D) resigned to become Secretary of the Interior; succeeded by Lieutenant-Governor John V. Evans (D). Next election in 1978.

Minnesota. Governor Wendell R. Anderson (D) resigned to be appointed to the vacancy caused by the resignation of Senator Walter F. Mondale (D) on his election to be Vice-President; succeeded by Lieutenant-Governor Rudy Perpich (D). Next election in 1978.

Wisconsin. Governor Patrick J. Lucey (D) resigned to be appointed Ambassador to Mexico; succeeded by Lieutenant-Governor Martin J. Schreiber (D). Next election in 1978.

SENATORS

Minnesota. Senator Walter F. Mondale (D) resigned to become Vice-President; resigning Governor Wendell R. Anderson(D) was appointed to succeed him for the remainder of the term. Next election in 1978.

REPRESENTATIVES

5th Georgia. Representative Andrew Young (D) resigned to be appointed Ambassador to the United Nations; Wyche Fowler (D) was elected in April, 1977 to succeed him.

1st Louisiana. Representative Richard A. Tonry (D) resigned; this vacancy to be filled in an election in late August, 1977.

7th Minnesota. Representative Bob Bergland (D) resigned to become Secretary of Agriculture; Arlan Stangeland (R) was elected in February, 1977 to succeed him.

7th Washington. Representative Brock Adams (D) resigned to become Secretary of Transportation; John E. Cunningham (R) was elected in May, 1977 to succeed him.

ALABAMA

GOVERNOR

George C. Wallace (D). Re-elected 1974 to a four-year term. Previously elected 1970, 1962.

SENATORS

James B. Allen (D). Re-elected 1974 to a six-year term. Previously elected 1968.

John J. Sparkman (D). Re-elected 1972 to a six-year term. Previously elected 1966, 1960, 1954, 1948, and in 1946 to fill out term vacated by the death of Senator John H. Bankhead.

REPRESENTATIVES

1. Jack Edwards (R)
2. William Dickinson (R)
3. Bill Nichols (D)
4. Tom Bevill (D)
5. Ronnie G. Flippo (D)
6. John Buchanan (R)
7. Walter Flowers (D)

POSTWAR VOTE FOR GOVERNOR

Year	Total Vote	Republican Vote	Republican Candidate	Democratic Vote	Democratic Candidate	Other Vote	Rep.-Dem. Plurality	Percentage Total Vote Rep.	Percentage Total Vote Dem.	Percentage Major Vote Rep.	Percentage Major Vote Dem.
1974	598,305	88,381	McCary, Elvin	497,574	Wallace, George C.	12,350	409,193 D	14.8%	83.2%	15.1%	84.9%
1970	854,952	–	–	637,046	Wallace, George C.	217,906	637,046 D	–	74.5%	–	100.0%
1966	848,101	262,943	Martin, James D.	537,505	Wallace, Mrs. Lurleen	47,653	274,562 D	31.0%	63.4%	32.8%	67.2%
1962	315,776	–	–	303,987	Wallace, George C.	11,789	303,987 D	–	96.3%	–	100.0%
1958	270,952	30,415	Longshore, W. L.	239,633	Patterson, John	904	209,218 D	11.2%	88.4%	11.3%	88.7%
1954	333,090	88,688	Abernethy, Tom	244,401	Folsom, James E.	1	155,713 D	26.6%	73.4%	26.6%	73.4%
1950	170,541	15,127	Crowder, John S.	155,414	Persons, Gordon	–	140,287 D	8.9%	91.1%	8.9%	91.1%
1946	197,324	22,362	Ward, Lyman	174,962	Folsom, James E.	–	152,600 D	11.3%	88.7%	11.3%	88.7%

POSTWAR VOTE FOR SENATOR

Year	Total Vote	Republican Vote	Republican Candidate	Democratic Vote	Democratic Candidate	Other Vote	Rep.-Dem. Plurality	Percentage Total Vote Rep.	Percentage Total Vote Dem.	Percentage Major Vote Rep.	Percentage Major Vote Dem.
1974	523,290	–	–	501,541	Allen, James B.	21,749	501,541 D	–	95.8%	–	100.0%
1972	1,051,099	347,523	Blount, Winton M.	654,491	Sparkman, John J.	49,085	306,968 D	33.1%	62.3%	34.7%	65.3%
1968	912,708	201,227	Hooper, Perry	638,774	Allen, James B.	72,707	437,547 D	22.0%	70.0%	24.0%	76.0%
1966	802,608	313,018	Grenier, John	482,138	Sparkman, John J.	7,452	169,120 D	39.0%	60.1%	39.4%	60.6%
1962	397,079	195,134	Martin, James D.	201,937	Hill, Lister	8	6,803 D	49.1%	50.9%	49.1%	50.9%
1960	554,081	164,868	Elgin, Julian	389,196	Sparkman, John J.	17	224,328 D	29.8%	70.2%	29.8%	70.2%
1956	330,191	–	–	330,182	Hill, Lister	9	330,182 D	–	100.0%	–	100.0%
1954	314,459	55,110	Guin, J. Foy	259,348	Sparkman, John J.	1	204,238 D	17.5%	82.5%	17.5%	82.5%
1950	164,011	–	–	125,534	Hill, Lister	38,477	125,534 D	–	76.5%	–	100.0%
1948	220,875	35,341	Parsons, Paul G.	185,534	Sparkman, John J.	–	150,193 D	16.0%	84.0%	16.0%	84.0%
1946s	163,217	–	–	163,217	Sparkman, John J.	–	163,217 D	–	100.0%	–	100.0%

The 1946 election was for a short term to fill a vacancy.

ALABAMA

Districts Established January 19, 1972

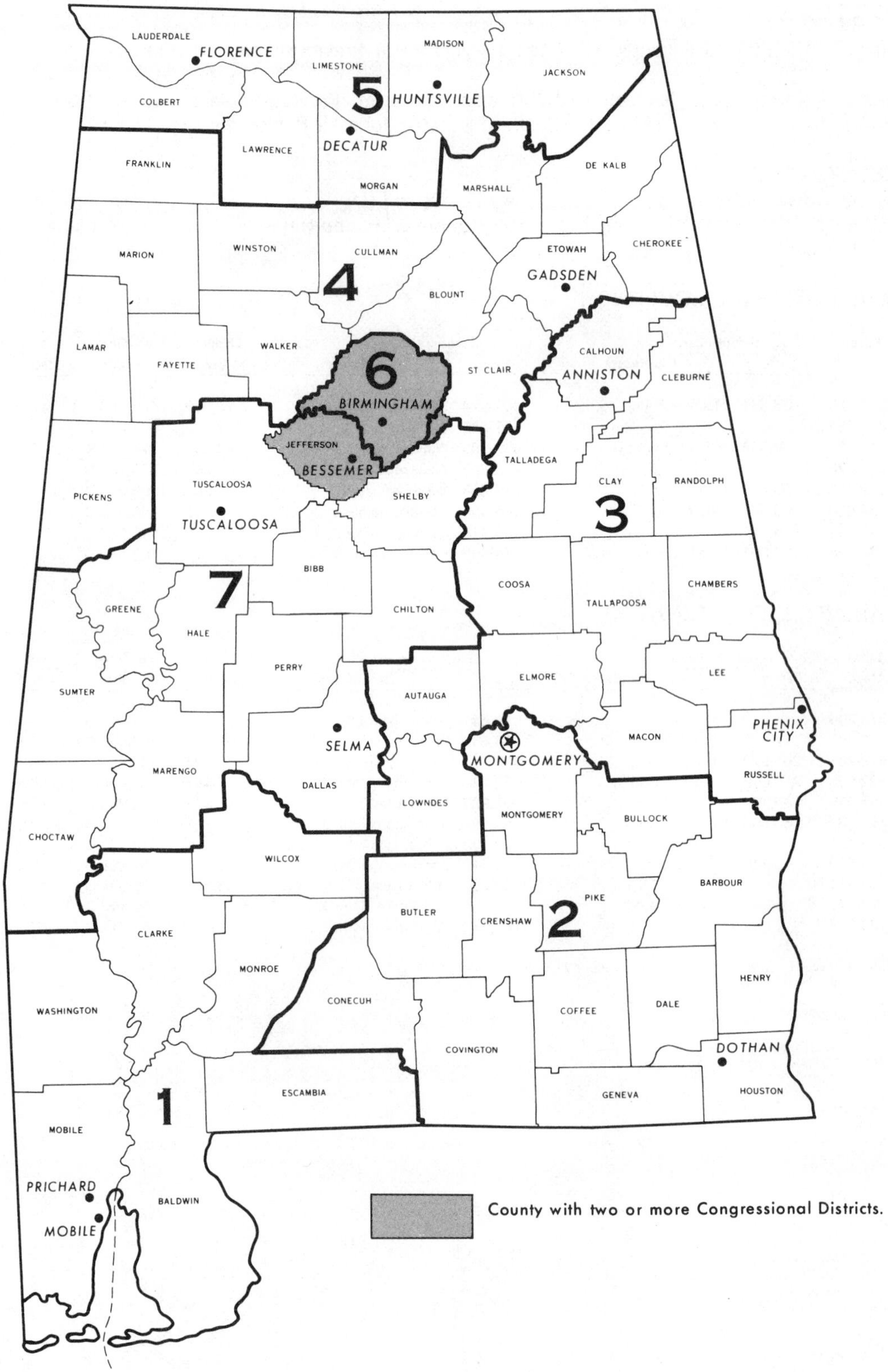

ALABAMA

PRESIDENT 1976

1970 Census Population	County	Total Vote	Republican	Democratic	Other	Rep.-Dem. Plurality	Percentage Total Vote Rep.	Percentage Total Vote Dem.	Percentage Major Vote Rep.	Percentage Major Vote Dem.
24,460	AUTAUGA	9,338	4,512	4,640	186	128 D	48.3%	49.7%	49.3%	50.7%
59,382	BALDWIN	22,967	13,256	9,191	520	4,065 R	57.7%	40.0%	59.1%	40.9%
22,543	BARBOUR	8,690	3,758	4,730	202	972 D	43.2%	54.4%	44.3%	55.7%
13,812	BIBB	4,474	1,591	2,850	33	1,259 D	35.6%	63.7%	35.8%	64.2%
26,853	BLOUNT	10,978	4,233	6,645	100	2,412 D	38.6%	60.5%	38.9%	61.1%
11,824	BULLOCK	5,092	1,482	3,536	74	2,054 D	29.1%	69.4%	29.5%	70.5%
22,007	BUTLER	7,208	2,909	4,271	28	1,362 D	40.4%	59.3%	40.5%	59.5%
103,092	CALHOUN	32,700	11,763	20,466	471	8,703 D	36.0%	62.6%	36.5%	63.5%
36,356	CHAMBERS	11,848	5,488	6,164	196	676 D	46.3%	52.0%	47.1%	52.9%
15,606	CHEROKEE	6,256	1,492	4,668	96	3,176 D	23.8%	74.6%	24.2%	75.8%
25,180	CHILTON	10,385	4,725	5,550	110	825 D	45.5%	53.4%	46.0%	54.0%
16,589	CHOCTAW	6,972	3,033	3,911	28	878 D	43.5%	56.1%	43.7%	56.3%
26,724	CLARKE	9,006	4,126	4,737	143	611 D	45.8%	52.6%	46.6%	53.4%
12,636	CLAY	4,858	1,883	2,946	29	1,063 D	38.8%	60.6%	39.0%	61.0%
10,996	CLEBURNE	3,981	1,436	2,490	55	1,054 D	36.1%	62.5%	36.6%	63.4%
34,872	COFFEE	12,651	4,683	7,844	124	3,161 D	37.0%	62.0%	37.4%	62.6%
49,632	COLBERT	16,842	4,471	11,996	375	7,525 D	26.5%	71.2%	27.2%	72.8%
15,645	CONECUH	4,980	1,812	3,086	82	1,274 D	36.4%	62.0%	37.0%	63.0%
10,662	COOSA	3,766	1,196	2,533	37	1,337 D	31.8%	67.3%	32.1%	67.9%
34,079	COVINGTON	12,224	4,977	7,081	166	2,104 D	40.7%	57.9%	41.3%	58.7%
13,188	CRENSHAW	5,266	1,801	3,372	93	1,571 D	34.2%	64.0%	34.8%	65.2%
52,445	CULLMAN	20,055	6,899	12,961	195	6,062 D	34.4%	64.6%	34.7%	65.3%
52,938	DALE	11,531	4,996	6,346	189	1,350 D	43.3%	55.0%	44.0%	56.0%
55,296	DALLAS	16,361	7,144	8,866	351	1,722 D	43.7%	54.2%	44.6%	55.4%
41,981	DE KALB	16,437	6,597	9,759	81	3,162 D	40.1%	59.4%	40.3%	59.7%
33,535	ELMORE	13,508	6,551	6,646	311	95 D	48.5%	49.2%	49.6%	50.4%
34,906	ESCAMBIA	11,157	4,934	5,957	266	1,023 D	44.2%	53.4%	45.3%	54.7%
94,144	ETOWAH	35,750	10,333	25,020	397	14,687 D	28.9%	70.0%	29.2%	70.8%
16,252	FAYETTE	6,287	2,165	4,076	46	1,911 D	34.4%	64.8%	34.7%	65.3%
23,933	FRANKLIN	9,721	3,345	6,279	97	2,934 D	34.4%	64.6%	34.8%	65.2%
21,924	GENEVA	8,739	2,663	5,983	93	3,320 D	30.5%	68.5%	30.8%	69.2%
10,650	GREENE	3,818	903	2,900	15	1,997 D	23.7%	76.0%	23.7%	76.3%
15,888	HALE	5,394	2,034	3,236	124	1,202 D	37.7%	60.0%	38.6%	61.4%
13,254	HENRY	5,234	2,052	3,144	38	1,092 D	39.2%	60.1%	39.5%	60.5%
56,574	HOUSTON	19,738	10,672	8,787	279	1,885 R	54.1%	44.5%	54.8%	45.2%
39,202	JACKSON	15,325	3,913	10,989	423	7,076 D	25.5%	71.7%	26.3%	73.7%
644,991	JEFFERSON	217,090	113,590	99,531	3,969	14,059 R	52.3%	45.8%	53.3%	46.7%
14,335	LAMAR	5,724	1,739	3,860	125	2,121 D	30.4%	67.4%	31.1%	68.9%
68,111	LAUDERDALE	23,185	7,226	15,549	410	8,323 D	31.2%	67.1%	31.7%	68.3%
27,281	LAWRENCE	8,284	1,415	6,810	59	5,395 D	17.1%	82.2%	17.2%	82.8%
61,268	LEE	18,737	9,884	8,427	426	1,457 R	52.8%	45.0%	54.0%	46.0%
41,699	LIMESTONE	12,000	2,997	8,803	200	5,806 D	25.0%	73.4%	25.4%	74.6%
12,897	LOWNDES	5,462	1,621	3,732	109	2,111 D	29.7%	68.3%	30.3%	69.7%
24,841	MACON	7,449	1,387	5,915	147	4,528 D	18.6%	79.4%	19.0%	81.0%
186,540	MADISON	57,287	20,959	35,497	831	14,538 D	36.6%	62.0%	37.1%	62.9%
23,819	MARENGO	8,755	3,841	4,731	183	890 D	43.9%	54.0%	44.8%	55.2%
23,788	MARION	9,303	3,036	6,244	23	3,208 D	32.6%	67.1%	32.7%	67.3%
54,211	MARSHALL	20,100	6,006	13,696	398	7,690 D	29.9%	68.1%	30.5%	69.5%
317,308	MOBILE	105,876	53,835	50,264	1,777	3,571 R	50.8%	47.5%	51.7%	48.3%
20,883	MONROE	7,263	3,476	3,669	118	193 D	47.9%	50.5%	48.6%	51.4%
167,790	MONTGOMERY	54,733	29,360	24,641	732	4,719 R	53.6%	45.0%	54.4%	45.6%
77,306	MORGAN	25,986	9,058	16,547	381	7,489 D	34.9%	63.7%	35.4%	64.6%
15,388	PERRY	6,683	2,164	4,486	33	2,322 D	32.4%	67.1%	32.5%	67.5%
20,326	PICKENS	6,786	2,969	3,776	41	807 D	43.8%	55.6%	44.0%	56.0%
25,038	PIKE	9,889	4,363	5,387	139	1,024 D	44.1%	54.5%	44.7%	55.3%
18,331	RANDOLPH	6,044	2,286	3,539	219	1,253 D	37.8%	58.6%	39.2%	60.8%
45,394	RUSSELL	12,592	4,150	8,077	365	3,927 D	33.0%	64.1%	33.9%	66.1%
27,956	ST. CLAIR	10,869	4,877	5,653	339	776 D	44.9%	52.0%	46.3%	53.7%
38,037	SHELBY	16,629	9,035	7,197	397	1,838 R	54.3%	43.3%	55.7%	44.3%
16,974	SUMTER	5,689	2,191	3,457	41	1,266 D	38.5%	60.8%	38.8%	61.2%
65,280	TALLADEGA	17,608	6,425	10,577	606	4,152 D	36.5%	60.1%	37.8%	62.2%
33,840	TALLAPOOSA	13,163	5,237	7,614	312	2,377 D	39.8%	57.8%	40.8%	59.2%
116,029	TUSCALOOSA	37,006	16,021	20,275	710	4,254 D	43.3%	54.8%	44.1%	55.9%
56,246	WALKER	23,710	7,389	16,232	89	8,843 D	31.2%	68.5%	31.3%	68.7%
16,241	WASHINGTON	5,670	2,171	3,471	28	1,300 D	38.3%	61.2%	38.5%	61.5%
16,303	WILCOX	5,565	1,824	3,723	18	1,899 D	32.8%	66.9%	32.9%	67.1%
16,654	WINSTON	7,868	3,710	4,134	24	424 D	47.2%	52.5%	47.3%	52.7%
3,444,165	TOTAL	1,182,850	504,070	659,170	19,610	155,100 D	42.6%	55.7%	43.3%	56.7%

ALABAMA

CONGRESS

CD	Year	Total Vote	Republican Vote	Republican Candidate	Democratic Vote	Democratic Candidate	Other Vote	Rep.-Dem. Plurality	Percentage Total Vote Rep.	Percentage Total Vote Dem.	Percentage Major Vote Rep.	Percentage Major Vote Dem.
1	1976	157,170	98,257	EDWARDS, JACK	58,906	DAVENPORT, BILL	7	39,351 R	62.5%	37.5%	62.5%	37.5%
1	1974	102,066	60,710	EDWARDS, JACK	37,718	WILSON, AUGUSTA E.	3,638	22,992 R	59.5%	37.0%	61.7%	38.3%
1	1972	136,710	104,606	EDWARDS, JACK	24,357	MCCRORY, O. W.	7,747	80,249 R	76.5%	17.8%	81.1%	18.9%
2	1976	156,362	90,069	DICKINSON, WILLIAM	66,288	KEAHEY, J. CAROLE	5	23,781 R	57.6%	42.4%	57.6%	42.4%
2	1974	81,818	54,089	DICKINSON, WILLIAM	27,729	CHISLER, CLAIR		26,360 R	66.1%	33.9%	66.1%	33.9%
2	1972	146,508	80,362	DICKINSON, WILLIAM	60,769	REEVES, BEN C.	5,377	19,593 R	54.9%	41.5%	56.9%	43.1%
3	1976	108,048			106,935	NICHOLS, BILL	1,113	106,935 D		99.0%		100.0%
3	1974	66,312			63,582	NICHOLS, BILL	2,730	63,582 D		95.9%		100.0%
3	1972	132,383	27,253	KERR, ROBERT M.	100,045	NICHOLS, BILL	5,085	72,792 D	20.6%	75.6%	21.4%	78.6%
4	1976	176,022	34,531	WILSON, LEONARD	141,490	BEVILL, TOM	1	106,959 D	19.6%	80.4%	19.6%	80.4%
4	1974	78,118			77,925	BEVILL, TOM	193	77,925 D		99.8%		100.0%
4	1972	155,301	46,551	NELSON, ED	108,039	BEVILL, TOM	711	61,488 D	30.0%	69.6%	30.1%	69.9%
5	1976	113,560			113,553	FLIPPO, RONNIE G.	7	113,553 D		100.0%		100.0%
5	1974	56,381			56,375	JONES, ROBERT E.	6	56,375 D		100.0%		100.0%
5	1972	136,553	33,352	SCHRADER, DIETER J.	101,303	JONES, ROBERT E.	1,898	67,951 D	24.4%	74.2%	24.8%	75.2%
8	1970	90,058			76,413	JONES, ROBERT E.	13,645	76,413 D		84.8%		100.0%
8	1968	112,449			85,528	JONES, ROBERT E.	26,921	85,528 D		76.1%		100.0%
8	1966	91,386	25,404	MAYHALL, DONALD G.	65,982	JONES, ROBERT E.		40,578 D	27.8%	72.2%	27.8%	72.2%
8	1964	43,842			43,842	JONES, ROBERT E.		43,842 D		100.0%		100.0%
6	1976	162,518	92,113	BUCHANAN, JOHN	69,384	BAILEY, MEL	1,021	22,729 R	56.7%	42.7%	57.0%	43.0%
6	1974	96,237	54,505	BUCHANAN, JOHN	39,444	MIGLIONICO, NINA	2,288	15,061 R	56.6%	41.0%	58.0%	42.0%
6	1972	153,133	91,499	BUCHANAN, JOHN	54,497	ERDREICH, BEN	7,137	37,002 R	59.8%	35.6%	62.7%	37.3%
7	1976	110,501			110,496	FLOWERS, WALTER	5	110,496 D		100.0%		100.0%
7	1974	80,468			73,203	FLOWERS, WALTER	7,265	73,203 D		91.0%		100.0%
7	1972	112,041			95,060	FLOWERS, WALTER	16,981	95,060 D		84.8%		100.0%

ALABAMA

1976 GENERAL ELECTION

President — Other vote was 9,198 Maddox (Conservative); 6,669 Bubar (Prohibition); 1,954 Hall (Independent); 1,481 MacBride (Libertarian); 99 McCarthy (write-in); 70 Anderson (write-in); 1 Camejo (write-in); 1 LaRouche (write-in); 137 scattered (write-in). State-wide vote total includes write-ins not available by county.

Congress — Other vote was scattered in CD's 1, 2, 4, 5 and 7; Dorsey (NDPA) in CD 6; 1,111 Gardner (Prohibition) and 2 scattered in CD 3.

1976 PRIMARIES

MAY 4 REPUBLICAN

Congress — Unopposed in five CD's. No candidates in CD's 3 and 7. Doug Hale, the unopposed candidate in CD 5, withdrew after the primary and no substitution was made.

MAY 4 DEMOCRATIC

Congress — Unopposed in two CD's. Contested as follows:

CD 2 — 28,549 Floyd Sparkman; 23,283 J. Carole Keahey; 12,465 Jake Watson.
CD 3 — 93,905 Bill Nichols; 8,593 George Wingard.
CD 4 — 90,168 Tom Bevill; 21,335 James E. Folsom, Jr.
CD 5 — 25,895 Ronnie G. Flippo; 22,348 John Eyster; 17,097 Jyles Machen; 14,978 Robert L. Potts; 11,835 Gene McLain; 5,336 Lynn Greer; 4,407 Kyo R. Jhin; 1,348 Judy Wilson; 1,293 Joe Monroe; 929 Donald N. Curbow.
CD 7 — 65,289 Walter Flowers; 27,915 James W. Patton.

MAY 25 DEMOCRATIC RUN-OFF

Congress

CD 2 — 34,600 J. Carole Keahey; 25,949 Floyd Sparkman.
CD 5 — 56,213 Ronnie G. Flippo; 40,305 John Eyster.

ALASKA

GOVERNOR

Jay S. Hammond (R). Elected 1974 to a four-year term.

SENATORS

Mike Gravel (D). Re-elected 1974 to a six-year term. Previously elected 1968.

Ted Stevens (R). Re-elected 1972 to a six-year term. Previously elected 1970 to fill out term vacated by the death of Senator E. L. Bartlett; had been appointed December 1968 to fill this vacancy.

REPRESENTATIVE

At-Large. Don Young (R)

POSTWAR VOTE FOR GOVERNOR

		Republican		Democratic				Percentage			
	Total					Other	Rep.-Dem.	Total Vote		Major Vote	
Year	Vote	Vote	Candidate	Vote	Candidate	Vote	Plurality	Rep.	Dem.	Rep.	Dem.
1974	96,163	45,840	Hammond, Jay S.	45,553	Egan, William A.	4,770	287 R	47.7%	47.4%	50.2%	49.8%
1970	80,779	37,264	Miller, Keith	42,309	Egan, William A.	1,206	5,045 D	46.1%	52.4%	46.8%	53.2%
1966	66,294	33,145	Hickel, Walter J.	32,065	Egan, William A.	1,084	1,080 R	50.0%	48.4%	50.8%	49.2%
1962	56,681	27,054	Stepovich, Mike	29,627	Egan, William A.	–	2,573 D	47.7%	52.3%	47.7%	52.3%
1958	48,968	19,299	Butrovich, John	29,189	Egan, William A.	480	9,890 D	39.4%	59.6%	39.8%	60.2%

POSTWAR VOTE FOR SENATOR

		Republican		Democratic				Percentage			
	Total					Other	Rep.-Dem.	Total Vote		Major Vote	
Year	Vote	Vote	Candidate	Vote	Candidate	Vote	Plurality	Rep.	Dem.	Rep.	Dem.
1974	93,275	38,914	Lewis, C. R.	54,361	Gravel, Mike	–	15,447 D	41.7%	58.3%	41.7%	58.3%
1972	96,007	74,216	Stevens, Ted	21,791	Guess, Gene	–	52,425 R	77.3%	22.7%	77.3%	22.7%
1970s	80,364	47,908	Stevens, Ted	32,456	Kay, Wendell P.	–	15,452 R	59.6%	40.4%	59.6%	40.4%
1968	80,931	30,286	Rasmuson, Elmer	36,527	Gravel, Mike	14,118	6,241 D	37.4%	45.1%	45.3%	54.7%
1966	65,250	15,961	McKinley, Lee L.	49,289	Bartlett, E. L.	–	33,328 D	24.5%	75.5%	24.5%	75.5%
1962	58,181	24,354	Stevens, Ted	33,827	Gruening, Ernest	–	9,473 D	41.9%	58.1%	41.9%	58.1%
1960	59,978	21,937	McKinley, Lee L.	38,041	Bartlett, E. L.	–	16,104 D	36.6%	63.4%	36.6%	63.4%
1958s	49,525	23,462	Stepovich, Mike	26,063	Gruening, Ernest	–	2,601 D	47.4%	52.6%	47.4%	52.6%
1958s	48,837	7,299	Robertson, R. E.	40,939	Bartlett, E. L.	599	33,640 D	14.9%	83.8%	15.1%	84.9%

The two 1958 elections were held to indeterminate terms and the Senate later determined by lot that Senator Gruening would serve four years, Senator Bartlett two. The 1970 election was for a short term to fill a vacancy.

ALASKA

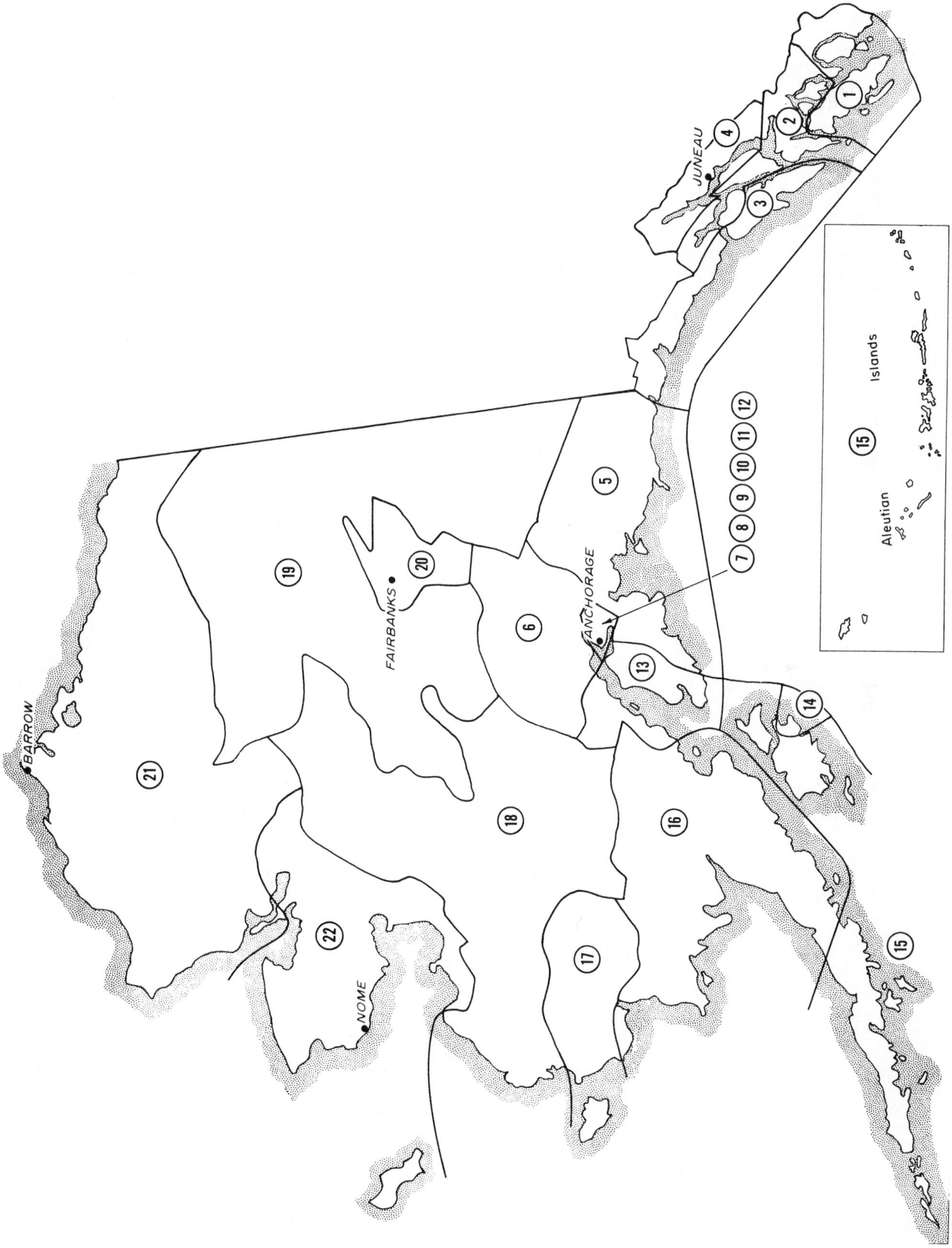
JUNEAU
ANCHORAGE
FAIRBANKS
BARROW
NOME
Aleutian Islands
1
2
3
4
5
6
7
8
9
10
11
12
13
14
15
16
17
18
19
20
21
22

ALASKA

PRESIDENT 1976

1970 Census Population	District	Total Vote	Republican	Democratic	Other	Rep.-Dem. Plurality	Percentage: Total Vote Rep.	Percentage: Total Vote Dem.	Percentage: Major Vote Rep.	Percentage: Major Vote Dem.
	DISTRICT 1	5,216	2,994	1,983	239	1,011 R	57.4%	38.0%	60.2%	39.8%
	DISTRICT 2	2,595	1,423	1,022	150	401 R	54.8%	39.4%	58.2%	41.8%
	DISTRICT 3	3,006	1,710	1,152	144	558 R	56.9%	38.3%	59.7%	40.3%
	DISTRICT 4	8,903	5,252	3,214	437	2,038 R	59.0%	36.1%	62.0%	38.0%
	DISTRICT 5	3,638	2,071	1,307	260	764 R	56.9%	35.9%	61.3%	38.7%
	DISTRICT 6	4,775	2,882	1,486	407	1,396 R	60.4%	31.1%	66.0%	34.0%
	DISTRICT 7	7,444	4,105	2,935	404	1,170 R	55.1%	39.4%	58.3%	41.7%
	DISTRICT 8	9,369	5,412	3,368	589	2,044 R	57.8%	35.9%	61.6%	38.4%
	DISTRICT 9	4,627	2,561	1,726	340	835 R	55.3%	37.3%	59.7%	40.3%
	DISTRICT 10	10,070	6,837	2,839	394	3,998 R	67.9%	28.2%	70.7%	29.3%
	DISTRICT 11	10,834	6,588	3,568	678	3,020 R	60.8%	32.9%	64.9%	35.1%
	DISTRICT 12	9,533	6,381	2,700	452	3,681 R	66.9%	28.3%	70.3%	29.7%
	DISTRICT 13	6,652	4,057	2,099	496	1,958 R	61.0%	31.6%	65.9%	34.1%
	DISTRICT 14	2,382	1,380	856	146	524 R	57.9%	35.9%	61.7%	38.3%
	DISTRICT 15	1,335	746	538	51	208 R	55.9%	40.3%	58.1%	41.9%
	DISTRICT 16	2,033	1,063	876	94	187 R	52.3%	43.1%	54.8%	45.2%
	DISTRICT 17	2,310	1,074	1,149	87	75 D	46.5%	49.7%	48.3%	51.7%
	DISTRICT 18	1,812	942	804	66	138 R	52.0%	44.4%	54.0%	46.0%
	DISTRICT 19	3,610	1,893	1,415	302	478 R	52.4%	39.2%	57.2%	42.8%
	DISTRICT 20	19,096	10,306	6,706	2,084	3,600 R	54.0%	35.1%	60.6%	39.4%
	DISTRICT 21	2,048	749	1,229	70	480 D	36.6%	60.0%	37.9%	62.1%
	DISTRICT 22	2,286	1,129	1,086	71	43 R	49.4%	47.5%	51.0%	49.0%
302,173	TOTAL	123,574	71,555	44,058	7,961	27,497 R	57.9%	35.7%	61.9%	38.1%

ALASKA

CONGRESS

CD	Year	Total Vote	Republican Vote	Republican Candidate	Democratic Vote	Democratic Candidate	Other Vote	Rep.-Dem. Plurality	Percentage Total Vote Rep.	Percentage Total Vote Dem.	Percentage Major Vote Rep.	Percentage Major Vote Dem.
AL	1976	118,208	83,722	YOUNG, DON	34,194	HOPSON, EBEN	292	49,528 R	70.8%	28.9%	71.0%	29.0%
AL	1974	95,921	51,641	YOUNG, DON	44,280	HENSLEY, WILLIAM L.		7,361 R	53.8%	46.2%	53.8%	46.2%
AL	1972	95,401	41,750	YOUNG, DON	53,651	BEGICH, N. J.		11,901 D	43.8%	56.2%	43.8%	56.2%
AL	1970	80,084	35,947	MURKOWSKI, FRANK H.	44,137	BEGICH, N. J.		8,190 D	44.9%	55.1%	44.9%	55.1%
AL	1968	80,362	43,577	POLLOCK, HOWARD W.	36,785	BEGICH, N. J.		6,792 R	54.2%	45.8%	54.2%	45.8%
AL	1966	65,907	34,040	POLLOCK, HOWARD W.	31,867	RIVERS, RALPH J.		2,173 R	51.6%	48.4%	51.6%	48.4%
AL	1964	67,146	32,556	THOMAS, LOWELL	34,590	RIVERS, RALPH J.		2,034 D	48.5%	51.5%	48.5%	51.5%
AL	1962	58,591	26,638	THOMAS, LOWELL	31,953	RIVERS, RALPH J.		5,315 D	45.5%	54.5%	45.5%	54.5%
AL	1960	59,063	25,517	RETTIG, R. L.	33,546	RIVERS, RALPH J.		8,029 D	43.2%	56.8%	43.2%	56.8%
AL	1958	48,647	20,699	BENSON, HENRY A.	27,948	RIVERS, RALPH J.		7,249 D	42.5%	57.5%	42.5%	57.5%
AL	1956	28,266	9,332	GILLAM, BYRON A.	18,934	BARTLETT, E. L.		9,602 D	33.0%	67.0%	33.0%	67.0%
AL	1954	26,999	7,083	DIMOCK, BARBARA D.	19,916	BARTLETT, E. L.		12,833 D	26.2%	73.8%	26.2%	73.8%
AL	1952	25,112	10,893	REEVE, ROBERT C.	14,219	BARTLETT, E. L.		3,326 D	43.4%	56.6%	43.4%	56.6%
AL	1950	18,726	5,138	PETERSON, ALMER J.	13,588	BARTLETT, E. L.		8,450 D	27.4%	72.6%	27.4%	72.6%
AL	1948	22,309	4,789	STOCK, R. H.	17,520	BARTLETT, E. L.		12,731 D	21.5%	78.5%	21.5%	78.5%
AL	1946	16,384	4,868	PETERSON, ALMER J.	11,516	BARTLETT, E. L.		6,648 D	29.7%	70.3%	29.7%	70.3%

ALASKA

1976 GENERAL ELECTION

The election districts in Alaska were established in June 1974 and no population figures are given for these new districts.

President Other vote was 6,785 MacBride (Libertarian) and 1,176 scattered.

Congress Alaska elects a single Representative at-large; the data for the state on the previous page includes the postwar voting for Delegate from 1946 to 1956 and for Representative at-large since statehood. Other vote in 1976 was scattered.

1976 PRIMARIES

AUGUST 24 REPUBLICAN

Congress Unopposed at-large.

AUGUST 24 DEMOCRATIC

Congress Contested as follows:

AL 5,790 Eben Hopson; 4,852 Donald R. Wright; 3,829 Kevin Parnell; 3,075 Allan D. Blume; 2,916 Norman A. Bailey.

ARIZONA

GOVERNOR

Raul H. Castro (D). Elected 1974 to a four-year term.

SENATORS

Dennis DeConcini (D). Elected 1976 to a six-year term.

Barry M. Goldwater (R). Re-elected 1974 to a six-year term. Previously elected 1968, 1958, 1952.

REPRESENTATIVES

1. John J. Rhodes (R)
2. Morris K. Udall (D)
3. Bob Stump (D)
4. Eldon Rudd (R)

POSTWAR VOTE FOR GOVERNOR

								Percentage			
	Total	Republican		Democratic		Other	Rep.-Dem.	Total Vote		Major Vote	
Year	Vote	Vote	Candidate	Vote	Candidate	Vote	Plurality	Rep.	Dem.	Rep.	Dem.
1974	552,202	273,674	Williams, Russell	278,375	Castro, Raul H.	153	4,701 D	49.6%	50.4%	49.6%	50.4%
1970	411,409	209,522	Williams, John R.	201,887	Castro, Raul H.	–	7,635 R	50.9%	49.1%	50.9%	49.1%
1968	483,998	279,923	Williams, John R.	204,075	Goddard, Sam	–	75,848 R	57.8%	42.2%	57.8%	42.2%
1966	378,342	203,438	Williams, John R.	174,904	Goddard, Sam	–	28,534 R	53.8%	46.2%	53.8%	46.2%
1964	473,502	221,404	Kleindienst, Richard	252,098	Goddard, Sam	–	30,694 D	46.8%	53.2%	46.8%	53.2%
1962	365,841	200,578	Fannin, Paul	165,263	Goddard, Sam	–	35,315 R	54.8%	45.2%	54.8%	45.2%
1960	397,107	235,502	Fannin, Paul	161,605	Ackerman, Lee	–	73,897 R	59.3%	40.7%	59.3%	40.7%
1958	290,465	160,136	Fannin, Paul	130,329	Morrison, Robert	–	29,807 R	55.1%	44.9%	55.1%	44.9%
1956	288,592	116,744	Griffen, Horace B.	171,848	McFarland, Ernest W.	–	55,104 D	40.5%	59.5%	40.5%	59.5%
1954	243,970	115,866	Pyle, Howard	128,104	McFarland, Ernest W.	–	12,238 D	47.5%	52.5%	47.5%	52.5%
1952	260,285	156,592	Pyle, Howard	103,693	Haldiman, Joe C.	–	52,899 R	60.2%	39.8%	60.2%	39.8%
1950	195,227	99,109	Pyle, Howard	96,118	Frohmiller, Ana	–	2,991 R	50.8%	49.2%	50.8%	49.2%
1948	175,767	70,419	Brockett, Bruce	104,008	Garvey, Dan E.	1,340	33,589 D	40.1%	59.2%	40.4%	59.6%
1946	122,462	48,867	Brockett, Bruce	73,595	Osborn, Sidney P.	–	24,728 D	39.9%	60.1%	39.9%	60.1%

The term of office for Arizona's Governor was increased from two to four years effective with the 1970 election.

POSTWAR VOTE FOR SENATOR

								Percentage			
	Total	Republican		Democratic		Other	Rep.-Dem.	Total Vote		Major Vote	
Year	Vote	Vote	Candidate	Vote	Candidate	Vote	Plurality	Rep.	Dem.	Rep.	Dem.
1976	741,210	321,236	Steiger, Sam	400,334	DeConcini, Dennis	19,640	79,098 D	43.3%	54.0%	44.5%	55.5%
1974	549,919	320,396	Goldwater, Barry M.	229,523	Marshall, Jonathan	–	90,873 R	58.3%	41.7%	58.3%	41.7%
1970	407,796	228,284	Fannin, Paul	179,512	Grossman, Sam	–	48,772 R	56.0%	44.0%	56.0%	44.0%
1968	479,945	274,607	Goldwater, Barry M.	205,338	Elson, Roy L.	–	69,269 R	57.2%	42.8%	57.2%	42.8%
1964	468,801	241,089	Fannin, Paul	227,712	Elson, Roy L.	–	13,377 R	51.4%	48.6%	51.4%	48.6%
1962	362,605	163,388	Mecham, Evan	199,217	Hayden, Carl	–	35,829 D	45.1%	54.9%	45.1%	54.9%
1958	293,623	164,593	Goldwater, Barry M.	129,030	McFarland, Ernest W.	–	35,563 R	56.1%	43.9%	56.1%	43.9%
1956	278,263	107,447	Jones, Ross F.	170,816	Hayden, Carl	–	63,369 D	38.6%	61.4%	38.6%	61.4%
1952	257,401	132,063	Goldwater, Barry M.	125,338	McFarland, Ernest W.	–	6,725 R	51.3%	48.7%	51.3%	48.7%
1950	185,092	68,846	Brockett, Bruce	116,246	Hayden, Carl	–	47,400 D	37.2%	62.8%	37.2%	62.8%
1946	116,239	35,022	Powers, Ward S.	80,415	McFarland, Ernest W.	802	45,393 D	30.1%	69.2%	30.3%	69.7%

ARIZONA

Districts Established October 21, 1971

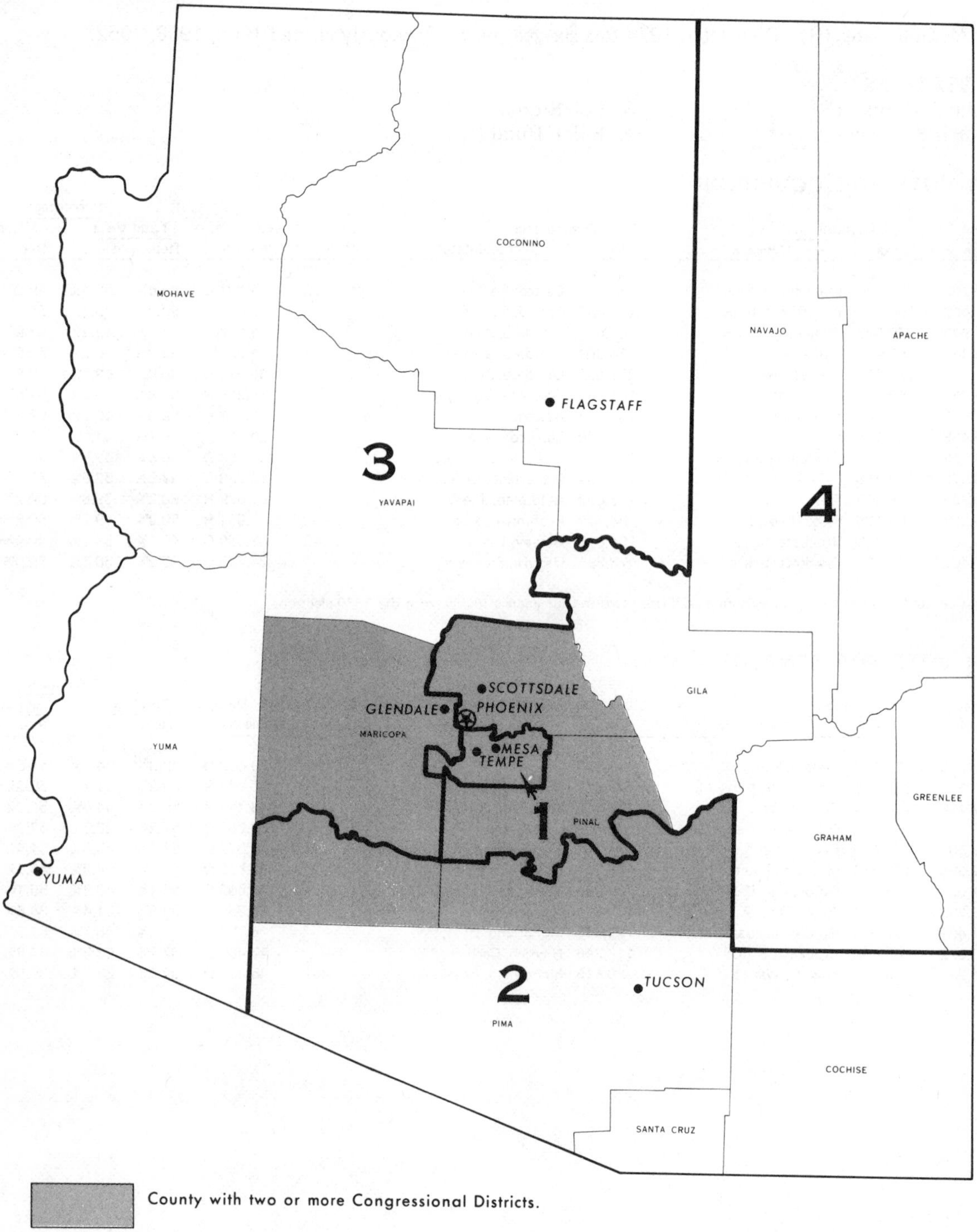

ARIZONA

PRESIDENT 1976

1970 Census Population	County	Total Vote	Republican	Democratic	Other	Rep.-Dem. Plurality	Percentage Total Vote Rep.	Total Vote Dem.	Major Vote Rep.	Major Vote Dem.
32,304	APACHE	10,327	3,447	6,583	297	3,136 D	33.4%	63.7%	34.4%	65.6%
61,910	COCHISE	19,883	9,921	9,281	681	640 R	49.9%	46.7%	51.7%	48.3%
48,326	COCONINO	21,418	11,036	9,450	932	1,586 R	51.5%	44.1%	53.9%	46.1%
29,255	GILA	11,962	5,136	6,440	386	1,304 D	42.9%	53.8%	44.4%	55.6%
16,578	GRAHAM	6,958	3,659	3,050	249	609 R	52.6%	43.8%	54.5%	45.5%
10,330	GREENLEE	4,247	1,532	2,601	114	1,069 D	36.1%	61.2%	37.1%	62.9%
968,487	MARICOPA	418,841	258,262	144,613	15,966	113,649 R	61.7%	34.5%	64.1%	35.9%
25,857	MOHAVE	14,640	7,601	6,504	535	1,097 R	51.9%	44.4%	53.9%	46.1%
47,559	NAVAJO	14,560	6,796	7,323	441	527 D	46.7%	50.3%	48.1%	51.9%
351,667	PIMA	155,061	77,264	71,214	6,583	6,050 R	49.8%	45.9%	52.0%	48.0%
68,579	PINAL	20,604	9,354	10,595	655	1,241 D	45.4%	51.4%	46.9%	53.1%
13,966	SANTA CRUZ	4,738	2,312	2,265	161	47 R	48.8%	47.8%	50.5%	49.5%
36,837	YAVAPAI	21,600	12,998	7,685	917	5,313 R	60.2%	35.6%	62.8%	37.2%
60,827	YUMA	17,880	9,324	7,998	558	1,326 R	52.1%	44.7%	53.8%	46.2%
1,772,482	TOTAL	742,719	418,642	295,602	28,475	123,040 R	56.4%	39.8%	58.6%	41.4%

SENATOR 1976

1970 Census Population	County	Total Vote	Republican	Democratic	Other	Rep.-Dem. Plurality	Percentage Total Vote Rep.	Total Vote Dem.	Major Vote Rep.	Major Vote Dem.
32,304	APACHE	9,903	2,568	6,841	494	4,273 D	25.9%	69.1%	27.3%	72.7%
61,910	COCHISE	19,304	7,692	11,275	337	3,583 D	39.8%	58.4%	40.6%	59.4%
48,326	COCONINO	21,373	8,061	12,750	562	4,689 D	37.7%	59.7%	38.7%	61.3%
29,255	GILA	11,957	4,178	7,593	186	3,415 D	34.9%	63.5%	35.5%	64.5%
16,578	GRAHAM	6,907	3,295	3,507	105	212 D	47.7%	50.8%	48.4%	51.6%
10,330	GREENLEE	4,225	1,145	3,023	57	1,878 D	27.1%	71.6%	27.5%	72.5%
968,487	MARICOPA	419,253	200,395	206,481	12,377	6,086 D	47.8%	49.2%	49.3%	50.7%
25,857	MOHAVE	14,288	7,091	6,959	238	132 R	49.6%	48.7%	50.5%	49.5%
47,559	NAVAJO	14,506	5,574	8,608	324	3,034 D	38.4%	59.3%	39.3%	60.7%
351,667	PIMA	153,452	52,129	97,841	3,482	45,712 D	34.0%	63.8%	34.8%	65.2%
68,579	PINAL	21,749	7,110	14,086	553	6,976 D	32.7%	64.8%	33.5%	66.5%
13,966	SANTA CRUZ	4,633	1,478	3,038	117	1,560 D	31.9%	65.6%	32.7%	67.3%
36,837	YAVAPAI	21,874	12,251	9,182	441	3,069 R	56.0%	42.0%	57.2%	42.8%
60,827	YUMA	17,786	8,269	9,150	367	881 D	46.5%	51.4%	47.5%	52.5%
1,772,482	TOTAL	741,210	321,236	400,334	19,640	79,098 D	43.3%	54.0%	44.5%	55.5%

ARIZONA

CONGRESS

CD	Year	Total Vote	Republican Vote	Republican Candidate	Democratic Vote	Democratic Candidate	Other Vote	Rep.-Dem. Plurality	Percentage Total Vote Rep.	Percentage Total Vote Dem.	Percentage Major Vote Rep.	Percentage Major Vote Dem.
1	1976	168,119	96,397	RHODES, JOHN J.	68,404	FULLINWIDER, PATRICIA	3,318	27,993 R	57.3%	40.7%	58.5%	41.5%
1	1974	124,961	63,847	RHODES, JOHN J.	52,897	FULLINWIDER, PATRICIA	8,217	10,950 R	51.1%	42.3%	54.7%	45.3%
1	1972	140,353	80,453	RHODES, JOHN J.	59,900	POLLOCK, GERALD A.		20,553 R	57.3%	42.7%	57.3%	42.7%
2	1976	182,128	71,765	GUTTERSEN, LAIRD	106,054	UDALL, MORRIS K.	4,309	34,289 D	39.4%	58.2%	40.4%	59.6%
2	1974	136,377	51,886	DOLGAARD, KEITH	84,491	UDALL, MORRIS K.		32,605 D	38.0%	62.0%	38.0%	62.0%
2	1972	153,804	56,188	SAVOIE, GENE	97,616	UDALL, MORRIS K.		41,428 D	36.5%	63.5%	36.5%	63.5%
3	1976	187,165	79,162	KOORY, FRED	88,854	STUMP, BOB	19,149	9,692 D	42.3%	47.5%	47.1%	52.9%
3	1974	139,921	71,497	STEIGER, SAM	68,424	BOSCH, PAT		3,073 R	51.1%	48.9%	51.1%	48.9%
3	1972	143,930	90,710	STEIGER, SAM	53,220	WYCKOFF, TED		37,490 R	63.0%	37.0%	63.0%	37.0%
4	1976	191,590	93,154	RUDD, ELDON	92,435	MASON, TONY	6,001	719 R	48.6%	48.2%	50.2%	49.8%
4	1974	142,564	78,887	CONLAN, JOHN B.	63,677	BROWN, BYRON T.		15,210 R	55.3%	44.7%	55.3%	44.7%
4	1972	155,820	82,511	CONLAN, JOHN B.	73,309	BROWN, JACK E.		9,202 R	53.0%	47.0%	53.0%	47.0%

ARIZONA

1976 GENERAL ELECTION

President Other vote was 19,229 McCarthy (Independent); 7,647 MacBride (Libertarian); 928 Camejo (Socialist Workers); 564 Anderson (write-in); 85 Maddox (write-in); 22 Taylor (write-in).

Senator Other vote was 10,765 Field (Independent); 7,310 Norwitz (Libertarian); 1,565 Feighan (no designation).

Congress Other vote was 2,278 Dodge (Libertarian) and 1,040 Braun (Independent) in CD 1; Emerling (Libertarian) in CD 2; McCune (no designation) in CD 3; Harper (Libertarian) in CD 4.

1976 PRIMARIES

SEPTEMBER 7 REPUBLICAN

Senator 102,843 Sam Steiger; 93,033 John B. Conlan.

Congress Unopposed in CD 2. Contested as follows:

CD 1 37,015 John J. Rhodes; 11,145 Louis E. Stradling.
CD 3 32,756 Fred Koory; 18,964 Don Aldridge.
CD 4 28,004 Eldon Rudd; 22,284 Ernest Garfield; 3,839 Arch DiRoberts.

SEPTEMBER 7 DEMOCRATIC

Senator 121,423 Dennis DeConcini; 71,612 Carolyn Warner; 34,266 Wade Church.

Congress Unopposed in CD 1. Contested as follows:

CD 2 52,509 Morris K. Udall; 14,242 Ruben Romero.
CD 3 17,730 Bob Stump; 14,349 Sid Rosen; 10,626 Tony Gabaldon; 7,352 Joe Eddie Lopez; 6,389 Max Klass.
CD 4 30,648 Tony Mason; 26,700 Craig E. Davids.

SEPTEMBER 7 LIBERTARIAN

Senator Allan Norwitz, unopposed.

Congress Unopposed in all CD's in which candidates were entered.

ARKANSAS

GOVERNOR

David H. Pryor (D). Re-elected 1976 to a two-year term. Previously elected 1974.

SENATORS

Dale Bumpers (D). Elected 1974 to a six-year term.

John L. McClellan (D). Re-elected 1972 to a six-year term. Previously elected 1966, 1960, 1954, 1948, 1942.

REPRESENTATIVES

1. William Alexander (D)
2. Jim Guy Tucker (D)
3. John Hammerschmidt (R)
4. Ray Thornton (D)

POSTWAR VOTE FOR GOVERNOR

Year	Total Vote	Republican Vote	Republican Candidate	Democratic Vote	Democratic Candidate	Other Vote	Rep.-Dem. Plurality	Percentage Total Vote Rep.	Percentage Total Vote Dem.	Percentage Major Vote Rep.	Percentage Major Vote Dem.
1976	726,949	121,716	Griffith, Leon	605,083	Pryor, David H.	150	483,367 D	16.7%	83.2%	16.7%	83.3%
1974	545,974	187,872	Coon, Ken	358,018	Pryor, David H.	84	170,146 D	34.4%	65.6%	34.4%	65.6%
1972	648,069	159,177	Blaylock, Len E.	488,892	Bumpers, Dale	–	329,715 D	24.6%	75.4%	24.6%	75.4%
1970	609,198	197,418	Rockefeller, Winthrop	375,648	Bumpers, Dale	36,132	178,230 D	32.4%	61.7%	34.4%	65.6%
1968	615,595	322,782	Rockefeller, Winthrop	292,813	Crank, Marion	–	29,969 R	52.4%	47.6%	52.4%	47.6%
1966	563,527	306,324	Rockefeller, Winthrop	257,203	Johnson, James D.	–	49,121 R	54.4%	45.6%	54.4%	45.6%
1964	592,113	254,561	Rockefeller, Winthrop	337,489	Faubus, Orval E.	63	82,928 D	43.0%	57.0%	43.0%	57.0%
1962	308,092	82,349	Ricketts, Willis	225,743	Faubus, Orval E.	–	143,394 D	26.7%	73.3%	26.7%	73.3%
1960	421,985	129,921	Britt, Henry M.	292,064	Faubus, Orval E.	–	162,143 D	30.8%	69.2%	30.8%	69.2%
1958	286,886	50,288	Johnson, George W.	236,598	Faubus, Orval E.	–	186,310 D	17.5%	82.5%	17.5%	82.5%
1956	399,012	77,215	Mitchell, Roy	321,797	Faubus, Orval E.	–	244,582 D	19.4%	80.6%	19.4%	80.6%
1954	335,176	127,004	Remmel, Pratt C.	208,121	Faubus, Orval E.	51	81,117 D	37.9%	62.1%	37.9%	62.1%
1952	391,592	49,292	Speck, Jefferson W.	342,292	Cherry, Francis	8	293,000 D	12.6%	87.4%	12.6%	87.4%
1950	317,087	50,309	Speck, Jefferson W.	266,778	McMath, Sidney S.	–	216,469 D	15.9%	84.1%	15.9%	84.1%
1948	249,301	26,500	Black, Charles R.	222,801	McMath, Sidney S.	–	196,301 D	10.6%	89.4%	10.6%	89.4%
1946	152,162	24,133	Mills, W. T.	128,029	Laney, Ben T.	–	103,896 D	15.9%	84.1%	15.9%	84.1%

POSTWAR VOTE FOR SENATOR

Year	Total Vote	Republican Vote	Republican Candidate	Democratic Vote	Democratic Candidate	Other Vote	Rep.-Dem. Plurality	Percentage Total Vote Rep.	Percentage Total Vote Dem.	Percentage Major Vote Rep.	Percentage Major Vote Dem.
1974	543,082	82,026	Jones, John H.	461,056	Bumpers, Dale	–	379,030 D	15.1%	84.9%	15.1%	84.9%
1972	634,636	248,238	Babbitt, Wayne H.	386,398	McClellan, John L.	–	138,160 D	39.1%	60.9%	39.1%	60.9%
1968	591,704	241,739	Bernard, Charles T.	349,965	Fulbright, J. W.	–	108,226 D	40.9%	59.1%	40.9%	59.1%
1966	–	–	–	–	McClellan, John L.	–	–	–	–	–	–
1962	312,880	98,013	Jones, Kenneth	214,867	Fulbright, J. W.	–	116,854 D	31.3%	68.7%	31.3%	68.7%
1960	–	–	–	–	McClellan, John L.	–	–	–	–	–	–
1956	399,695	68,016	Henley, Ben C.	331,679	Fulbright, J. W.	–	263,663 D	17.0%	83.0%	17.0%	83.0%
1954	291,058	–	–	291,058	McClellan, John L.	–	291,058 D	–	100.0%	–	100.0%
1950	302,582	–	–	302,582	Fulbright, J. W.	–	302,582 D	–	100.0%	–	100.0%
1948	216,401	–	–	216,401	McClellan, John L.	–	216,401 D	–	100.0%	–	100.0%

Senator McClellan was re-elected in 1966 and in 1960, but his vote was not canvassed in many counties.

ARKANSAS

Districts Established March 22,1971

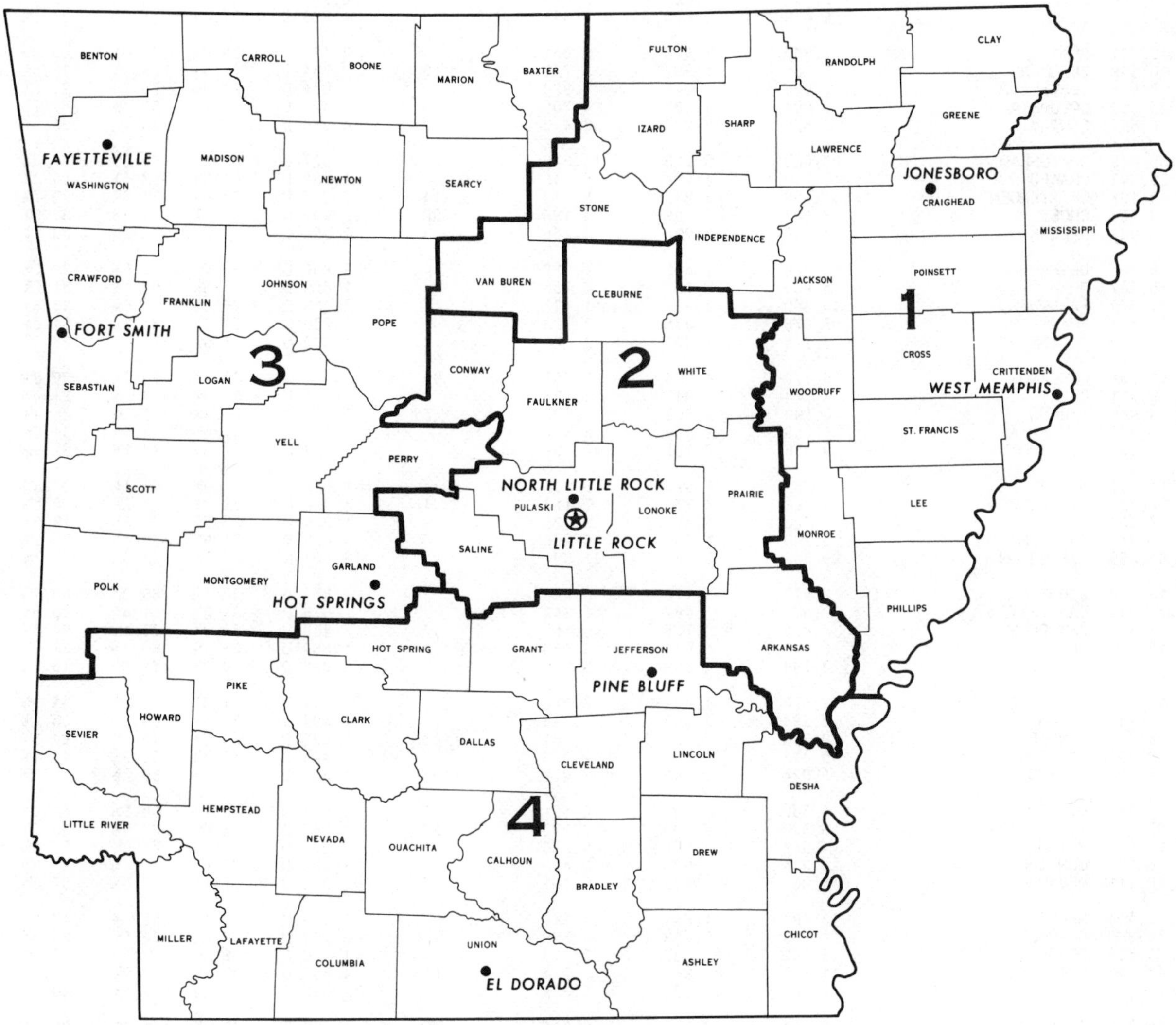

ARKANSAS

PRESIDENT 1976

1970 Census Population	County	Total Vote	Republican	Democratic	Other	Rep.-Dem. Plurality	Percentage Total Vote Rep.	Total Vote Dem.	Major Vote Rep.	Major Vote Dem.
23,347	ARKANSAS	8,120	2,480	5,640		3,160 D	30.5%	69.5%	30.5%	69.5%
24,976	ASHLEY	8,354	3,092	5,253	9	2,161 D	37.0%	62.9%	37.1%	62.9%
15,319	BAXTER	11,651	5,885	5,766		119 R	50.5%	49.5%	50.5%	49.5%
50,476	BENTON	24,017	12,670	11,289	58	1,381 R	52.8%	47.0%	52.9%	47.1%
19,073	BOONE	9,347	3,959	5,388		1,429 D	42.4%	57.6%	42.4%	57.6%
12,778	BRADLEY	4,701	1,134	3,567		2,433 D	24.1%	75.9%	24.1%	75.9%
5,573	CALHOUN	2,514	495	2,014	5	1,519 D	19.7%	80.1%	19.7%	80.3%
12,301	CARROLL	6,650	2,804	3,791	55	987 D	42.2%	57.0%	42.5%	57.5%
18,164	CHICOT	5,495	1,621	3,868	6	2,247 D	29.5%	70.4%	29.5%	70.5%
21,537	CLARK	8,479	1,816	6,641	22	4,825 D	21.4%	78.3%	21.5%	78.5%
18,771	CLAY	7,557	1,893	5,664		3,771 D	25.0%	75.0%	25.0%	75.0%
10,349	CLEBURNE	7,731	1,992	5,726	13	3,734 D	25.8%	74.1%	25.8%	74.2%
6,605	CLEVELAND	2,966	646	2,320		1,674 D	21.8%	78.2%	21.8%	78.2%
25,952	COLUMBIA	9,001	4,287	4,708	6	421 D	47.6%	52.3%	47.7%	52.3%
16,805	CONWAY	8,629	2,177	6,443	9	4,266 D	25.2%	74.7%	25.3%	74.7%
52,068	CRAIGHEAD	20,053	6,213	13,840		7,627 D	31.0%	69.0%	31.0%	69.0%
25,677	CRAWFORD	10,710	4,764	5,946		1,182 D	44.5%	55.5%	44.5%	55.5%
48,106	CRITTENDEN	13,465	5,202	8,249	14	3,047 D	38.6%	61.3%	38.7%	61.3%
19,783	CROSS	6,137	1,909	4,198	30	2,289 D	31.1%	68.4%	31.3%	68.7%
10,022	DALLAS	4,286	1,012	3,266	8	2,254 D	23.6%	76.2%	23.7%	76.3%
18,761	DESHA	5,600	1,372	4,228		2,856 D	24.5%	75.5%	24.5%	75.5%
15,157	DREW	5,480	1,730	3,750		2,020 D	31.6%	68.4%	31.6%	68.4%
31,572	FAULKNER	15,343	3,904	11,423	16	7,519 D	25.4%	74.5%	25.5%	74.5%
11,301	FRANKLIN	5,676	1,973	3,703		1,730 D	34.8%	65.2%	34.8%	65.2%
7,699	FULTON	3,715	1,038	2,670	7	1,632 D	27.9%	71.9%	28.0%	72.0%
54,131	GARLAND	26,170	10,394	15,707	69	5,313 D	39.7%	60.0%	39.8%	60.2%
9,711	GRANT	4,844	1,047	3,797		2,750 D	21.6%	78.4%	21.6%	78.4%
24,765	GREENE	10,192	2,690	7,495	7	4,805 D	26.4%	73.5%	26.4%	73.6%
19,308	HEMPSTEAD	8,256	2,859	5,397		2,538 D	34.6%	65.4%	34.6%	65.4%
21,963	HOT SPRING	9,996	2,187	7,809		5,622 D	21.9%	78.1%	21.9%	78.1%
11,412	HOWARD	4,782	1,575	3,207		1,632 D	32.9%	67.1%	32.9%	67.1%
22,723	INDEPENDENCE	9,998	2,878	7,116	4	4,238 D	28.8%	71.2%	28.8%	71.2%
7,381	IZARD	4,722	1,394	3,328		1,934 D	29.5%	70.5%	29.5%	70.5%
20,452	JACKSON	8,239	1,783	6,456		4,673 D	21.6%	78.4%	21.6%	78.4%
85,329	JEFFERSON	29,035	8,034	21,001		12,967 D	27.7%	72.3%	27.7%	72.3%
13,630	JOHNSON	7,217	2,173	5,044		2,871 D	30.1%	69.9%	30.1%	69.9%
10,018	LAFAYETTE	3,809	1,467	2,342		875 D	38.5%	61.5%	38.5%	61.5%
16,320	LAWRENCE	6,882	1,708	5,167	7	3,459 D	24.8%	75.1%	24.8%	75.2%
18,884	LEE	5,038	1,574	3,463	1	1,889 D	31.2%	68.7%	31.2%	68.8%
12,913	LINCOLN	3,744	699	3,045		2,346 D	18.7%	81.3%	18.7%	81.3%
11,194	LITTLE RIVER	4,573	1,431	3,142		1,711 D	31.3%	68.7%	31.3%	68.7%
16,789	LOGAN	8,294	2,909	5,313	72	2,404 D	35.1%	64.1%	35.4%	64.6%
26,249	LONOKE	10,299	2,522	7,761	16	5,239 D	24.5%	75.4%	24.5%	75.5%
9,453	MADISON	5,428	2,502	2,926		424 D	46.1%	53.9%	46 1%	53.9%
7,000	MARION	5,024	2,045	2,979		934 D	40.7%	59.3%	40.7%	59.3%
33,385	MILLER	11,580	4,737	6,821	22	2,084 D	40.9%	58.9%	41.0%	59.0%
62,060	MISSISSIPPI	16,328	6,009	10,292	27	4,283 D	36.8%	63.0%	36.9%	63.1%
15,657	MONROE	4,848	1,285	3,556	7	2,271 D	26.5%	73.3%	26.5%	73.5%
5,821	MONTGOMERY	3,344	924	2,420		1,496 D	27.6%	72.4%	27.6%	72.4%
10,111	NEVADA	4,269	1,163	3,101	5	1,938 D	27.2%	72.6%	27.3%	72.7%
5,844	NEWTON	3,481	1,641	1,840		199 D	47.1%	52.9%	47.1%	52.9%
30,896	OUACHITA	11,699	2,753	8,946		6,193 D	23.5%	76.5%	23.5%	76.5%
5,634	PERRY	3,142	832	2,310		1,478 D	26.5%	73.5%	26.5%	73.5%
40,046	PHILLIPS	11,117	3,342	7,774	1	4,432 D	30.1%	69.9%	30.1%	69.9%
8,711	PIKE	4,066	1,234	2,822	10	1,588 D	30.3%	69.4%	30.4%	69.6%
26,822	POINSETT	9,566	2,726	6,835	5	4,109 D	28.5%	71.5%	28.5%	71.5%
13,297	POLK	5,966	2,432	3,505	29	1,073 D	40.8%	58.7%	41.0%	59.0%
28,607	POPE	12,732	4,348	8,355	29	4,007 D	34.2%	65.6%	34.2%	65.8%
10,249	PRAIRIE	3,649	813	2,836		2,023 D	22.3%	77.7%	22.3%	77.7%
287,189	PULASKI	101,475	37,690	63,541	244	25,851 D	37.1%	62.6%	37.2%	62.8%
12,645	RANDOLPH	6,122	1,571	4,551		2,980 D	25.7%	74.3%	25.7%	74.3%
30,799	ST. FRANCIS	10,520	3,639	6,851	30	3,212 D	34.6%	65.1%	34.7%	65.3%
36,107	SALINE	16,138	4,123	12,008	7	7,885 D	25.5%	74.4%	25.6%	74.4%
8,207	SCOTT	4,314	1,427	2,880	7	1,453 D	33.1%	66.8%	33.1%	66.9%
7,731	SEARCY	3,834	1,767	2,067		300 D	46.1%	53.9%	46.1%	53.9%

ARKANSAS

PRESIDENT 1976

1970 Census Population	County	Total Vote	Republican	Democratic	Other	Rep.-Dem. Plurality	Percentage Total Vote Rep.	Total Vote Dem.	Major Vote Rep.	Major Vote Dem.
79,237	SEBASTIAN	33,397	17,665	15,698	34	1,967 R	52.9%	47.0%	52.9%	47.1%
11,272	SEVIER	4,877	1,468	3,391	18	1,923 D	30.1%	69.5%	30.2%	69.8%
8,233	SHARP	5,683	2,151	3,532		1,381 D	37.8%	62.2%	37.8%	62.2%
6,838	STONE	3,747	1,014	2,718	15	1,704 D	27.1%	72.5%	27.2%	72.8%
45,428	UNION	16,182	7,918	8,257	7	339 D	48.9%	51.0%	49.0%	51.0%
8,275	VAN BUREN	5,628	1,624	4,004		2,380 D	28.9%	71.1%	28.9%	71.1%
77,370	WASHINGTON	29,834	14,132	15,610	92	1,478 D	47.4%	52.3%	47.5%	52.5%
39,253	WHITE	16,168	4,756	11,412		6,656 D	29.4%	70.6%	29.4%	70.6%
11,566	WOODRUFF	3,893	848	3,040	5	2,192 D	21.8%	78.1%	21.8%	78.2%
14,208	YELL	7,717	1,932	5,785		3,853 D	25.0%	75.0%	25.0%	75.0%
1,923,295	TOTAL	767,535	267,903	498,604	1,028	230,701 D	34.9%	65.0%	35.0%	65.0%

ARKANSAS

GOVERNOR 1976

1970 Census Population	County	Total Vote	Republican	Democratic	Other	Rep.-Dem. Plurality	Percentage Total Vote Rep.	Percentage Total Vote Dem.	Percentage Major Vote Rep.	Percentage Major Vote Dem.
23,347	ARKANSAS	7,870	660	7,210		6,550 D	8.4%	91.6%	8.4%	91.6%
24,976	ASHLEY	7,768	1,157	6,611		5,454 D	14.9%	85.1%	14.9%	85.1%
15,319	BAXTER	11,297	3,365	7,932		4,567 D	29.8%	70.2%	29.8%	70.2%
50,476	BENTON	23,456	7,710	15,746		8,036 D	32.9%	67.1%	32.9%	67.1%
19,073	BOONE	7,853	1,868	5,985		4,117 D	23.8%	76.2%	23.8%	76.2%
12,778	BRADLEY	4,440	377	4,063		3,686 D	8.5%	91.5%	8.5%	91.5%
5,573	CALHOUN	2,303	224	2,079		1,855 D	9.7%	90.3%	9.7%	90.3%
12,301	CARROLL	6,416	1,633	4,783		3,150 D	25.5%	74.5%	25.5%	74.5%
18,164	CHICOT	5,199	590	4,608	1	4,018 D	11.3%	88.6%	11.4%	88.6%
21,537	CLARK	8,265	768	7,497		6,729 D	9.3%	90.7%	9.3%	90.7%
18,771	CLAY	7,252	1,126	6,126		5,000 D	15.5%	84.5%	15.5%	84.5%
10,349	CLEBURNE	7,734	1,038	6,696		5,658 D	13.4%	86.6%	13.4%	86.6%
6,605	CLEVELAND	2,861	251	2,610		2,359 D	8.8%	91.2%	8.8%	91.2%
25,952	COLUMBIA	7,627	1,449	6,178		4,729 D	19.0%	81.0%	19.0%	81.0%
16,805	CONWAY	8,417	849	7,568		6,719 D	10.1%	89.9%	10.1%	89.9%
52,068	CRAIGHEAD	18,083	3,791	14,292		10,501 D	21.0%	79.0%	21.0%	79.0%
25,677	CRAWFORD	10,662	2,745	7,917		5,172 D	25.7%	74.3%	25.7%	74.3%
48,106	CRITTENDEN	11,039	1,525	9,512	2	7,987 D	13.8%	86.2%	13.8%	86.2%
19,783	CROSS	6,074	691	5,381	2	4,690 D	11.4%	88.6%	11.4%	88.6%
10,022	DALLAS	4,098	307	3,791		3,484 D	7.5%	92.5%	7.5%	92.5%
18,761	DESHA	5,025	388	4,637		4,249 D	7.7%	92.3%	7.7%	92.3%
15,157	DREW	5,159	688	4,471		3,783 D	13.3%	86.7%	13.3%	86.7%
31,572	FAULKNER	14,582	2,174	12,408		10,234 D	14.9%	85.1%	14.9%	85.1%
11,301	FRANKLIN	5,762	1,150	4,612		3,462 D	20.0%	80.0%	20.0%	80.0%
7,699	FULTON	3,560	546	3,014		2,468 D	15.3%	84.7%	15.3%	84.7%
54,131	GARLAND	25,173	5,351	19,821	1	14,470 D	21.3%	78.7%	21.3%	78.7%
9,711	GRANT	4,691	442	4,249		3,807 D	9.4%	90.6%	9.4%	90.6%
24,765	GREENE	9,996	1,132	8,864		7,732 D	11.3%	88.7%	11.3%	88.7%
19,308	HEMPSTEAD	8,057	802	7,255		6,453 D	10.0%	90.0%	10.0%	90.0%
21,963	HOT SPRING	9,958	1,053	8,905		7,852 D	10.6%	89.4%	10.6%	89.4%
11,412	HOWARD	4,574	616	3,958		3,342 D	13.5%	86.5%	13.5%	86.5%
22,723	INDEPENDENCE	9,859	1,319	8,540		7,221 D	13.4%	86.6%	13.4%	86.6%
7,381	IZARD	4,628	891	3,737		2,846 D	19.3%	80.7%	19.3%	80.7%
20,452	JACKSON	7,910	590	7,214	106	6,624 D	7.5%	91.2%	7.6%	92.4%
85,329	JEFFERSON	25,835	3,008	22,823	4	19,815 D	11.6%	88.3%	11.6%	88.4%
13,630	JOHNSON	7,320	1,230	6,090		4,860 D	16.8%	83.2%	16.8%	83.2%
10,018	LAFAYETTE	3,416	413	3,003		2,590 D	12.1%	87.9%	12.1%	87.9%
16,320	LAWRENCE	6,853	923	5,930		5,007 D	13.5%	86.5%	13.5%	86.5%
18,884	LEE	4,610	560	4,050		3,490 D	12.1%	87.9%	12.1%	87.9%
12,913	LINCOLN	3,630	235	3,395		3,160 D	6.5%	93.5%	6.5%	93.5%
11,194	LITTLE RIVER	4,426	511	3,915		3,404 D	11.5%	88.5%	11.5%	88.5%
16,789	LOGAN	8,279	1,665	6,614		4,949 D	20.1%	79.9%	20.1%	79.9%
26,249	LONOKE	9,975	928	9,047		8,119 D	9.3%	90.7%	9.3%	90.7%
9,453	MADISON	5,519	1,842	3,677		1,835 D	33.4%	66.6%	33.4%	66.6%
7,000	MARION	5,008	1,216	3,792		2,576 D	24.3%	75.7%	24.3%	75.7%
33,385	MILLER	10,974	1,540	9,434		7,894 D	14.0%	86.0%	14.0%	86.0%
62,060	MISSISSIPPI	15,686	1,853	13,833		11,980 D	11.8%	88.2%	11.8%	88.2%
15,657	MONROE	4,663	456	4,207		3,751 D	9.8%	90.2%	9.8%	90.2%
5,821	MONTGOMERY	3,299	458	2,841		2,383 D	13.9%	86.1%	13.9%	86.1%
10,111	NEVADA	4,151	409	3,742		3,333 D	9.9%	90.1%	9.9%	90.1%
5,844	NEWTON	3,360	1,192	2,168		976 D	35.5%	64.5%	35.5%	64.5%
30,896	OUACHITA	10,495	781	9,714		8,933 D	7.4%	92.6%	7.4%	92.6%
5,634	PERRY	3,071	404	2,667		2,263 D	13.2%	86.8%	13.2%	86.8%
40,046	PHILLIPS	10,956	1,471	9,485		8,014 D	13.4%	86.6%	13.4%	86.6%
8,711	PIKE	3,969	517	3,452		2,935 D	13.0%	87.0%	13.0%	87.0%
26,822	POINSETT	9,194	1,227	7,963	4	6,736 D	13.3%	86.6%	13.4%	86.6%
13,297	POLK	6,011	1,154	4,857		3,703 D	19.2%	80.8%	19.2%	80.8%
28,607	POPE	12,509	1,969	10,539	1	8,570 D	15.7%	84.3%	15.7%	84.3%
10,249	PRAIRIE	3,558	329	3,229		2,900 D	9.2%	90.8%	9.2%	90.8%
287,189	PULASKI	93,440	13,391	80,027	22	66,636 D	14.3%	85.6%	14.3%	85.7%
12,645	RANDOLPH	5,914	832	5,082		4,250 D	14.1%	85.9%	14.1%	85.9%
30,799	ST. FRANCIS	9,814	1,162	8,652		7,490 D	11.8%	88.2%	11.8%	88.2%
36,107	SALINE	16,412	2,066	14,346		12,280 D	12.6%	87.4%	12.6%	87.4%
8,207	SCOTT	4,121	711	3,410		2,699 D	17.3%	82.7%	17.3%	82.7%
7,731	SEARCY	3,707	1,396	2,311		915 D	37.7%	62.3%	37.7%	62.3%

ARKANSAS

GOVERNOR 1976

1970 Census Population	County	Total Vote	Republican	Democratic	Other	Rep.-Dem. Plurality	Percentage Total Vote Rep.	Total Vote Dem.	Major Vote Rep.	Major Vote Dem.
79,237	SEBASTIAN	30,888	8,606	22,276	6	13,670 D	27.9%	72.1%	27.9%	72.1%
11,272	SEVIER	4,709	584	4,124	1	3,540 D	12.4%	87.6%	12.4%	87.6%
8,233	SHARP	5,650	1,329	4,321		2,992 D	23.5%	76.5%	23.5%	76.5%
6,838	STONE	3,652	614	3,038		2,424 D	16.8%	83.2%	16.8%	83.2%
45,428	UNION	14,001	2,967	11,034		8,067 D	21.2%	78.8%	21.2%	78.8%
8,275	VAN BUREN	5,286	839	4,447		3,608 D	15.9%	84.1%	15.9%	84.1%
77,370	WASHINGTON	27,564	8,414	19,150		10,736 D	30.5%	69.5%	30.5%	69.5%
39,253	WHITE	16,024	2,083	13,941		11,858 D	13.0%	87.0%	13.0%	87.0%
11,566	WOODRUFF	3,753	335	3,418		3,083 D	8.9%	91.1%	8.9%	91.1%
14,208	YELL	7,599	830	6,769		5,939 D	10.9%	89.1%	10.9%	89.1%
1,923,295	TOTAL	726,949	121,716	605,083	150	483,367 D	16.7%	83.2%	16.7%	83.3%

ARKANSAS

CONGRESS

CD	Year	Total Vote	Republican Vote	Republican Candidate	Democratic Vote	Democratic Candidate	Other Vote	Rep.-Dem. Plurality	Percentage Total Vote Rep.	Percentage Total Vote Dem.	Percentage Major Vote Rep.	Percentage Major Vote Dem.
1	1976	168,782	52,565	HOLLEMAN, HARLAN	116,217	ALEXANDER, WILLIAM		63,652 D	31.1%	68.9%	31.1%	68.9%
1	1974	115,068	10,821	DAUER, JAMES L.	104,247	ALEXANDER, WILLIAM		93,426 D	9.4%	90.6%	9.4%	90.6%
1	1972					ALEXANDER, WILLIAM						
2	1976	167,607	22,819	KELLY, JAMES J.	144,780	TUCKER, JIM GUY	8	121,961 D	13.6%	86.4%	13.6%	86.4%
2	1974	136,334	56,038	PETTY, JUDY	80,296	MILLS, WILBUR D.		24,258 D	41.1%	58.9%	41.1%	58.9%
2	1972					MILLS, WILBUR D.						
3	1976			HAMMERSCHMIDT, JOHN								
3	1974	172,354	89,324	HAMMERSCHMIDT, JOHN	83,030	CLINTON, BILL		6,294 R	51.8%	48.2%	51.8%	48.2%
3	1972	187,052	144,571	HAMMERSCHMIDT, JOHN	42,481	HATFIELD, GUY W.		102,090 R	77.3%	22.7%	77.3%	22.7%
4	1976					THORNTON, RAY						
4	1974					THORNTON, RAY						
4	1972					THORNTON, RAY						

ARKANSAS

1976 GENERAL ELECTION

President — Other vote was 639 McCarthy (write-in); 389 Anderson (write-in).

Governor — Other vote was Honeycutt (write-in).

Congress — Under present legislation, votes are not tallied in unopposed elections, so no total vote or candidate vote is available for unopposed Congressional elections. Other vote in CD 2 was scattered.

1976 PRIMARIES

MAY 25 REPUBLICAN

Governor — 13,044 Leon Griffith; 9,753 Joseph H. Weston.

Congress — Unopposed in two CD's. No candidate in CD 4. Contested as follows:

CD 2 — 2,895 James J. Kelly; 1,727 Sherman L. Bremmer.

MAY 25 DEMOCRATIC

Governor — 312,865 David H. Pryor; 171,031 Jim Lindsey; 36,832 Frank Lady; 5,233 John H. Chambers.

Congress — Unopposed in two CD's. No candidate in CD 3. Contested as follows:

CD 2 — 64,213 Jim Guy Tucker; 17,536 William P. Clark; 16,035 C. V. Ford; 13,445 Cal Ledbetter; 8,892 Bob McHenry; 3,888 Ed Gran.

CALIFORNIA

GOVERNOR

Edmund G. Brown, Jr. (D). Elected 1974 to a four-year term.

SENATORS

Alan Cranston (D). Re-elected 1974 to a six-year term. Previously elected 1968.

S. I. Hayakawa (R). Elected 1976 to a six-year term.

REPRESENTATIVES

1. Harold T. Johnson (D)
2. Don H. Clausen (R)
3. John E. Moss (D)
4. Robert L. Leggett (D)
5. John Burton (D)
6. Phillip Burton (D)
7. George Miller (D)
8. Ronald V. Dellums (D)
9. Fortney Stark (D)
10. Don Edwards (D)
11. Leo J. Ryan (D)
12. Paul N. McCloskey (R)
13. Norman Y. Mineta (D)
14. John J. McFall (D)
15. B. F. Sisk (D)
16. Leon E. Panetta (D)
17. John Krebs (D)
18. William M. Ketchum (R)
19. Robert J. Lagomarsino (R)
20. Barry M. Goldwater, Jr. (R)
21. James C. Corman (D)
22. Carlos J. Moorhead (R)
23. Anthony C. Beilenson (D)
24. Henry A. Waxman (D)
25. Edward R. Roybal (D)
26. John H. Rousselot (R)
27. Robert K. Dornan (R)
28. Yvonne Brathwaite Burke (D)
29. Augustus Hawkins (D)
30. George E. Danielson (D)
31. Charles H. Wilson (D)
32. Glenn M. Anderson (D)
33. Del Clawson (R)
34. Mark W. Hannaford (D)
35. Jim Lloyd (D)
36. George E. Brown (D)
37. Shirley N. Pettis (R)
38. Jerry M. Patterson (D)
39. Charles E. Wiggins (R)
40. Robert E. Badham (R)
41. Bob Wilson (R)
42. Lionel Van Deerlin (D)
43. Clair W. Burgener (R)

POSTWAR VOTE FOR GOVERNOR

								Percentage			
	Total	Republican		Democratic		Other	Rep.-Dem.	Total Vote		Major Vote	
Year	Vote	Vote	Candidate	Vote	Candidate	Vote	Plurality	Rep.	Dem.	Rep.	Dem.
1974	6,248,070	2,952,954	Flournoy, Houston I.	3,131,648	Brown, Edmund G., Jr.	163,468	178,694 D	47.3%	50.1%	48.5%	51.5%
1970	6,510,072	3,439,664	Reagan, Ronald	2,938,607	Unruh, Jess	131,801	501,057 R	52.8%	45.1%	53.9%	46.1%
1966	6,503,445	3,742,913	Reagan, Ronald	2,749,174	Brown, Edmund G.	11,358	993,739 R	57.6%	42.3%	57.7%	42.3%
1962	5,853,270	2,740,351	Nixon, Richard M.	3,037,109	Brown, Edmund G.	75,810	296,758 D	46.8%	51.9%	47.4%	52.6%
1958	5,255,777	2,110,911	Knowland, William F.	3,140,076	Brown, Edmund G.	4,790	1,029,165 D	40.2%	59.7%	40.2%	59.8%
1954	4,030,368	2,290,519	Knight, Goodwin J.	1,739,368	Graves, Richard P.	481	551,151 R	56.8%	43.2%	56.8%	43.2%
1950	3,796,090	2,461,754	Warren, Earl	1,333,856	Roosevelt, James	480	1,127,898 R	64.8%	35.1%	64.9%	35.1%
1946	2,558,399	2,344,542	Warren, Earl	–	–	213,857	2,344,542 R	91.6%	–	100.0%	–

In 1946 the Republican candidate won both major party nominations.

POSTWAR VOTE FOR SENATOR

								Percentage			
	Total	Republican		Democratic		Other	Rep.-Dem.	Total Vote		Major Vote	
Year	Vote	Vote	Candidate	Vote	Candidate	Vote	Plurality	Rep.	Dem.	Rep.	Dem.
1976	7,472,268	3,748,973	Hayakawa, S. I.	3,502,862	Tunney, John V.	220,433	246,111 R	50.2%	46.9%	51.7%	48.3%
1974	6,102,432	2,210,267	Richardson, H. L.	3,693,160	Cranston, Alan	199,005	1,482,893 D	36.2%	60.5%	37.4%	62.6%
1970	6,492,157	2,877,617	Murphy, George	3,496,558	Tunney, John V.	117,982	618,941 D	44.3%	53.9%	45.1%	54.9%
1968	7,102,465	3,329,148	Rafferty, Max	3,680,352	Cranston, Alan	92,965	351,204 D	46.9%	51.8%	47.5%	52.5%
1964	7,041,821	3,628,555	Murphy, George	3,411,912	Salinger, Pierre	1,354	216,643 R	51.5%	48.5%	51.5%	48.5%
1962	5,647,952	3,180,483	Kuchel, Thomas H.	2,452,839	Richards, Richard	14,630	727,644 R	56.3%	43.4%	56.5%	43.5%
1958	5,135,221	2,204,337	Knight, Goodwin J.	2,927,693	Engle, Clair	3,191	723,356 D	42.9%	57.0%	43.0%	57.0%
1956	5,361,467	2,892,918	Kuchel, Thomas H.	2,445,816	Richards, Richard	22,733	447,102 R	54.0%	45.6%	54.2%	45.8%
1954s	3,929,668	2,090,836	Kuchel, Thomas H.	1,788,071	Yorty, Samuel W.	50,761	302,765 R	53.2%	45.5%	53.9%	46.1%
1952	4,542,548	3,982,448	Knowland, William F.	–	–	560,100	3,982,448 R	87.7%	–	100.0%	–
1950	3,686,315	2,183,454	Nixon, Richard M.	1,502,507	Douglas, Helen	354	680,947 R	59.2%	40.8%	59.2%	40.8%
1946	2,639,465	1,428,067	Knowland, William F.	1,167,161	Rogers, Will	44,237	260,906 R	54.1%	44.2%	55.0%	45.0%

The 1954 election was for a short term to fill a vacancy. In 1952 the Republican candidate won both major party nominations.

CALIFORNIA

Districts Established November 28, 1973

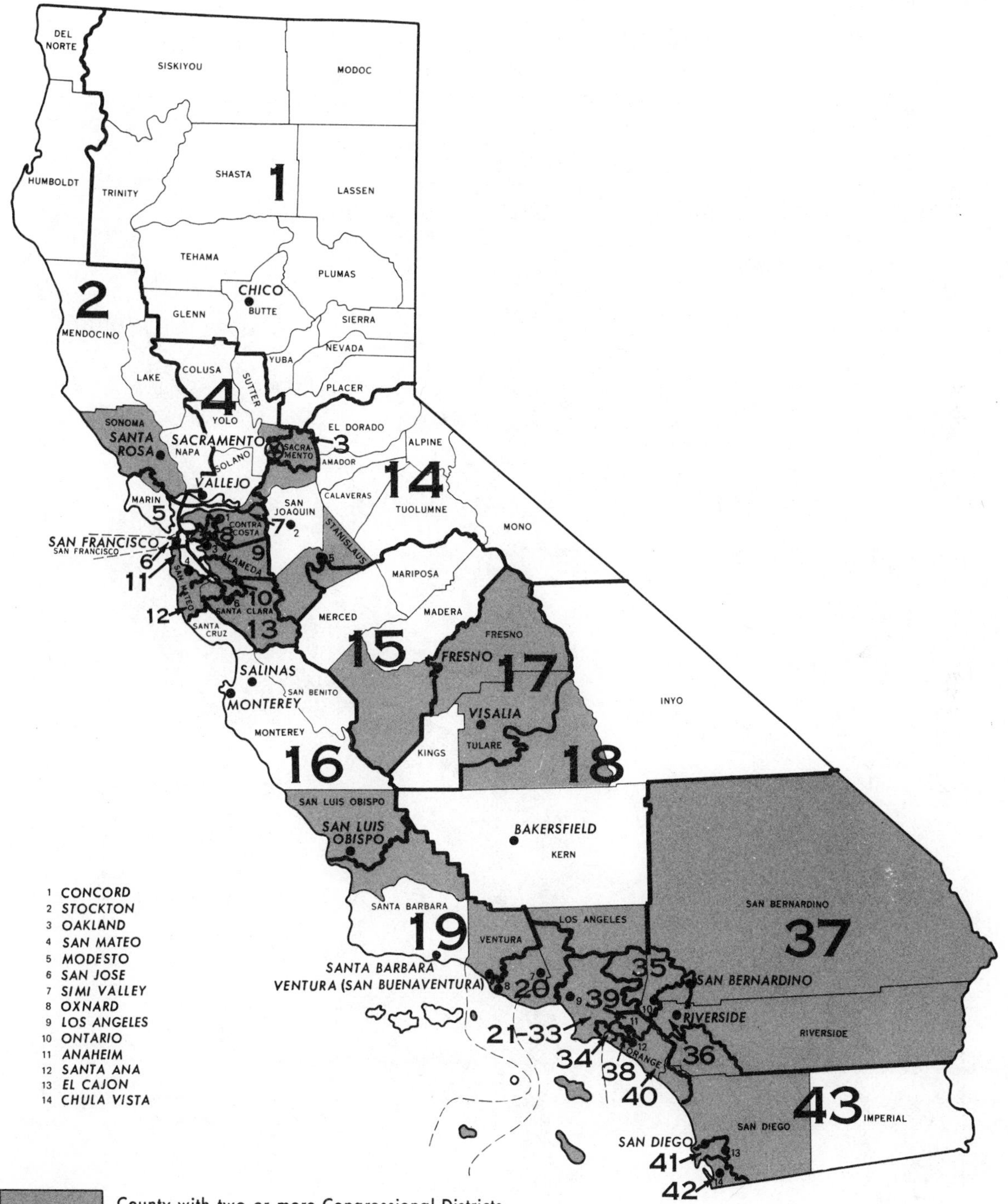

County with two or more Congressional Districts.

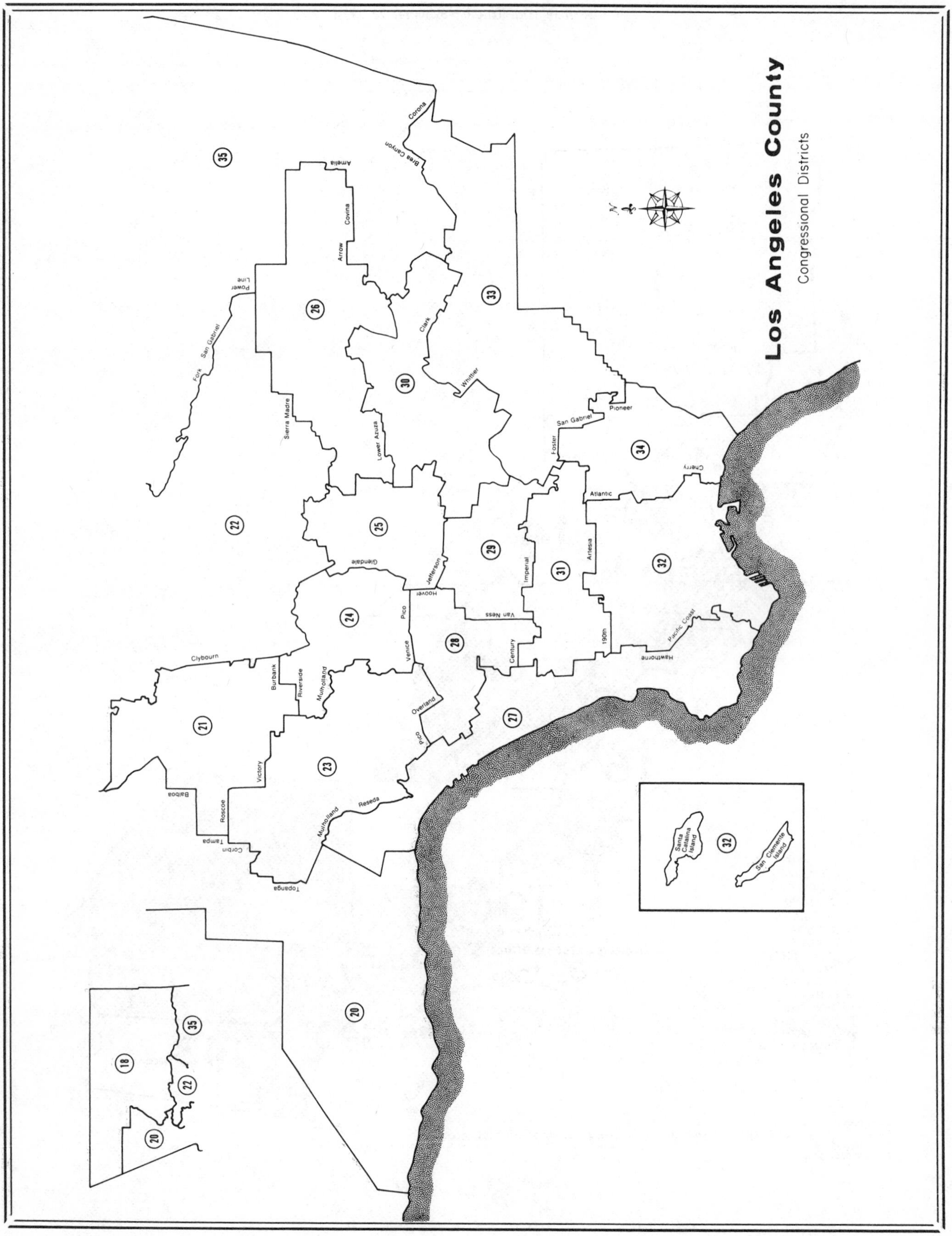
Los Angeles County
Congressional Districts
35
33
26
30
22
25
29
31
34
32
24
28
21
23
27
20
18
Corona
Brea Canyon
Amelia
Covina
Arrow
Power Line
San Gabriel
Fork
Clark
Whittier
Sierra Madre
Lower Azuza
San Gabriel
Foster
Pioneer
Cherry
Atlantic
Glendale
Jefferson
Imperial
Artesia
Hoover
Van Ness
Pico
Venice
Century
190th
Pacific Coast
Hawthorne
Clybourn
Burbank
Riverside
Mulholland
Overland
Pico
Victory
Balboa
Roscoe
Reseda
Mulholland
Tampa
Corbin
Topanga
Santa Catalina Island
San Clemente Island

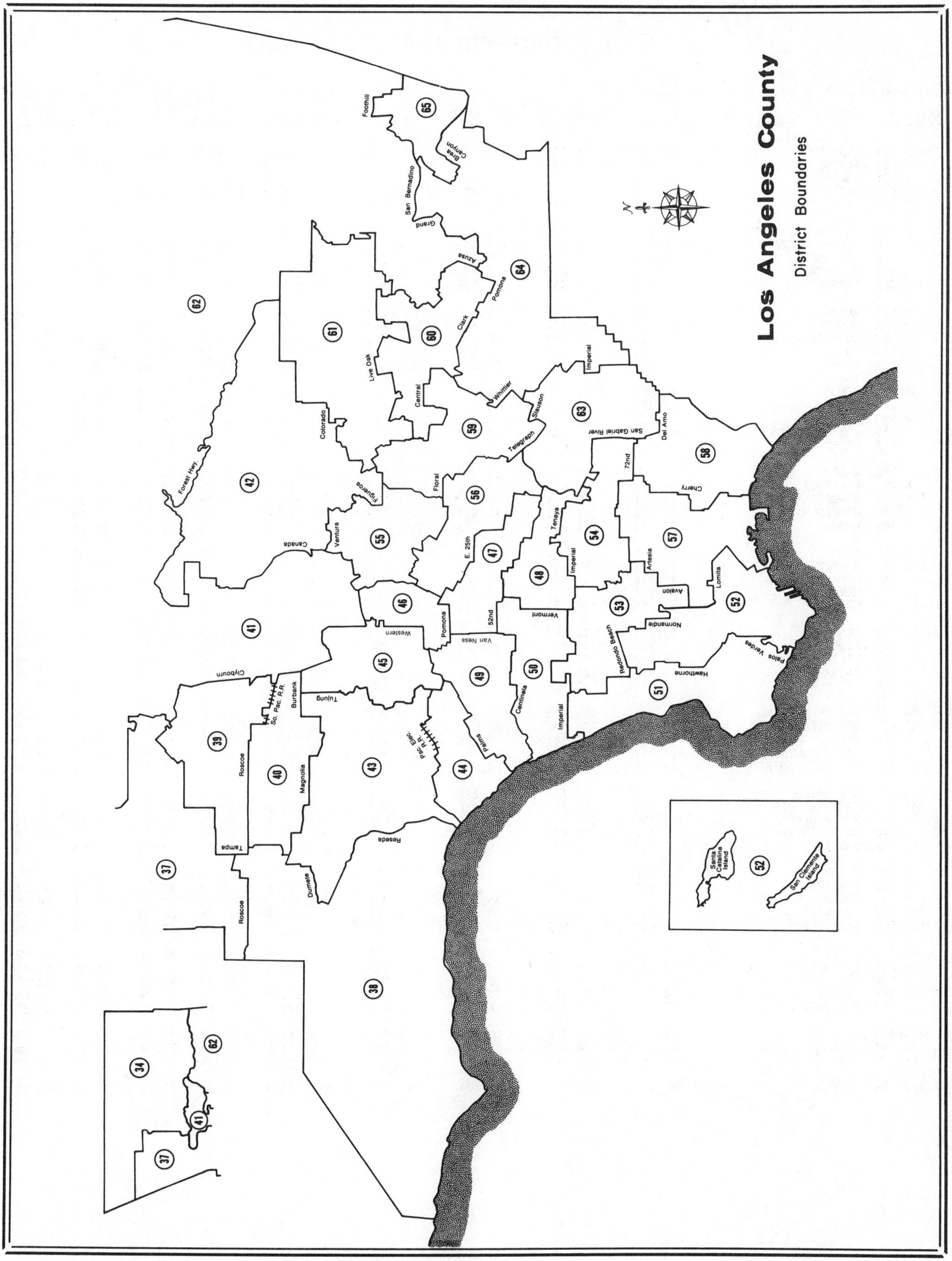
Los Angeles County
District Boundaries
N
Foothill
Brea Canyon
San Bernadino
Grand
Azusa
Pomona
Clark
Live Oak
Central
Whittier
Imperial
Slauson
Colorado
Telegraph
San Gabriel River
Del Amo
72nd
Cherry
Forest Hwy.
Figueroa
Floral
Canada
Ventura
E. 25th
Tenaya
Imperial
Artesia
Lomita
Avalon
Vermont
52nd
Pomona
Western
Van Ness
Normandie
Redondo Beach
Palos Verdes
Hawthorne
Centinela
Imperial
Clybourn
So. Pac. R.R.
Burbank
Tujung
Pac. Elec. R.R.
Palms
Roscoe
Magnolia
Tampa
Reseda
Dumetz
Roscoe
Santa Catalina Island
San Clemente Island
34
37
38
39
40
41
42
43
44
45
46
47
48
49
50
51
52
53
54
55
56
57
58
59
60
61
62
63
64
65

CALIFORNIA

PRESIDENT 1976

1970 Census Population	County	Total Vote	Republican	Democratic	Other	Rep.-Dem. Plurality	Percentage Total Vote Rep.	Total Vote Dem.	Major Vote Rep.	Major Vote Dem.
1,073,184	ALAMEDA	407,681	155,280	235,988	16,413	80,708 D	38.1%	57.9%	39.7%	60.3%
484	ALPINE	447	225	189	33	36 R	50.3%	42.3%	54.3%	45.7%
11,821	AMADOR	8,018	3,699	4,037	282	338 D	46.1%	50.3%	47.8%	52.2%
101,969	BUTTE	54,854	28,400	24,203	2,251	4,197 R	51.8%	44.1%	54.0%	46.0%
13,585	CALAVERAS	7,528	3,695	3,607	226	88 R	49.1%	47.9%	50.6%	49.4%
12,430	COLUSA	5,182	2,733	2,340	109	393 R	52.7%	45.2%	53.9%	46.1%
558,389	CONTRA COSTA	256,534	126,598	123,742	6,194	2,856 R	49.3%	48.2%	50.6%	49.4%
14,580	DEL NORTE	5,478	2,481	2,789	208	308 D	45.3%	50.9%	47.1%	52.9%
43,833	EL DORADO	26,154	12,472	12,763	919	291 D	47.7%	48.8%	49.4%	50.6%
413,053	FRESNO	150,805	72,533	74,958	3,314	2,425 D	48.1%	49.7%	49.2%	50.8%
17,521	GLENN	7,773	4,094	3,501	178	593 R	52.7%	45.0%	53.9%	46.1%
99,692	HUMBOLDT	43,372	18,034	23,500	1,838	5,466 D	41.6%	54.2%	43.4%	56.6%
74,492	IMPERIAL	21,262	10,618	10,244	400	374 R	49.9%	48.2%	50.9%	49.1%
15,571	INYO	6,706	3,905	2,635	166	1,270 R	58.2%	39.3%	59.7%	40.3%
329,162	KERN	110,961	58,023	50,567	2,371	7,456 R	52.3%	45.6%	53.4%	46.6%
64,610	KINGS	16,642	8,263	8,061	318	202 R	49.7%	48.4%	50.6%	49.4%
19,548	LAKE	12,285	5,462	6,374	449	912 D	44.5%	51.9%	46.1%	53.9%
14,960	LASSEN	6,998	3,007	3,801	190	794 D	43.0%	54.3%	44.2%	55.8%
7,032,075	LOS ANGELES	2,459,077	1,174,926	1,221,893	62,258	46,967 D	47.8%	49.7%	49.0%	51.0%
41,519	MADERA	14,892	6,844	7,625	423	781 D	46.0%	51.2%	47.3%	52.7%
206,038	MARIN	101,715	53,425	43,590	4,700	9,835 R	52.5%	42.9%	55.1%	44.9%
6,015	MARIPOSA	4,317	2,012	2,093	212	81 D	46.6%	48.5%	49.0%	51.0%
51,101	MENDOCINO	21,509	9,784	10,653	1,072	869 D	45.5%	49.5%	47.9%	52.1%
104,629	MERCED	32,208	14,842	16,637	729	1,795 D	46.1%	51.7%	47.1%	52.9%
7,469	MODOC	3,744	1,917	1,733	94	184 R	51.2%	46.3%	52.5%	47.5%
4,016	MONO	2,721	1,600	1,025	96	575 R	58.8%	37.7%	61.0%	39.0%
250,071	MONTEREY	80,153	40,896	36,849	2,408	4,047 R	51.0%	46.0%	52.6%	47.4%
79,140	NAPA	40,205	20,839	18,048	1,318	2,791 R	51.8%	44.9%	53.6%	46.4%
26,346	NEVADA	16,881	8,170	7,926	785	244 R	48.4%	47.0%	50.8%	49.2%
1,420,386	ORANGE	657,433	408,632	232,246	16,555	176,386 R	62.2%	35.3%	63.8%	36.2%
77,306	PLACER	40,311	18,154	21,026	1,131	2,872 D	45.0%	52.2%	46.3%	53.7%
11,707	PLUMAS	6,563	2,884	3,429	250	545 D	43.9%	52.2%	45.7%	54.3%
459,074	RIVERSIDE	198,558	97,774	96,228	4,556	1,546 R	49.2%	48.5%	50.4%	49.6%
631,498	SACRAMENTO	275,876	123,110	144,203	8,563	21,093 D	44.6%	52.3%	46.1%	53.9%
18,226	SAN BENITO	6,680	3,398	3,122	160	276 R	50.9%	46.7%	52.1%	47.9%
684,072	SAN BERNARDINO	228,885	113,265	109,636	5,984	3,629 R	49.5%	47.9%	50.8%	49.2%
1,357,854	SAN DIEGO	633,795	353,302	263,654	16,839	89,648 R	55.7%	41.6%	57.3%	42.7%
715,674	SAN FRANCISCO	256,888	103,561	133,733	19,594	30,172 D	40.3%	52.1%	43.6%	56.4%
290,208	SAN JOAQUIN	101,361	50,277	48,733	2,351	1,544 R	49.6%	48.1%	50.8%	49.2%
105,690	SAN LUIS OBISPO	54,298	27,785	24,926	1,587	2,859 R	51.2%	45.9%	52.7%	47.3%
556,234	SAN MATEO	231,741	117,338	102,896	11,507	14,442 R	50.6%	44.4%	53.3%	46.7%
264,324	SANTA BARBARA	119,844	60,922	55,018	3,904	5,904 R	50.8%	45.9%	52.5%	47.5%
1,064,714	SANTA CLARA	443,138	219,188	208,023	15,927	11,165 R	49.5%	46.9%	51.3%	48.7%
123,790	SANTA CRUZ	73,969	31,872	37,772	4,325	5,900 D	43.1%	51.1%	45.8%	54.2%
77,640	SHASTA	37,854	17,273	19,200	1,381	1,927 D	45.6%	50.7%	47.4%	52.6%
2,365	SIERRA	1,576	680	841	55	161 D	43.1%	53.4%	44.7%	55.3%
33,225	SISKIYOU	14,615	7,070	7,060	485	10 R	48.4%	48.3%	50.0%	50.0%
169,941	SOLANO	61,644	26,136	33,682	1,826	7,546 D	42.4%	54.6%	43.7%	56.3%
204,885	SONOMA	105,952	50,555	50,353	5,044	202 R	47.7%	47.5%	50.1%	49.9%
194,506	STANISLAUS	73,465	32,937	38,448	2,080	5,511 D	44.8%	52.3%	46.1%	53.9%
41,935	SUTTER	16,131	8,745	6,966	420	1,779 R	54.2%	43.2%	55.7%	44.3%
29,517	TEHAMA	13,635	6,110	6,990	535	880 D	44.8%	51.3%	46.6%	53.4%
7,615	TRINITY	4,356	1,989	2,172	195	183 D	45.7%	49.9%	47.8%	52.2%
188,322	TULARE	58,441	31,864	25,551	1,026	6,313 R	54.5%	43.7%	55.5%	44.5%
22,169	TUOLUMNE	13,003	6,104	6,492	407	388 D	46.9%	49.9%	48.5%	51.5%
376,430	VENTURA	155,401	82,670	68,529	4,202	14,141 R	53.2%	44.1%	54.7%	45.3%
91,788	YOLO	43,317	18,376	23,533	1,408	5,157 D	42.4%	54.3%	43.8%	56.2%
44,736	YUBA	12,285	5,496	6,451	338	955 D	44.7%	52.5%	46.0%	54.0%
19,953,134	TOTAL	7,867,117	3,882,244	3,742,284	242,589	139,960 R	49.3%	47.6%	50.9%	49.1%

CALIFORNIA

SENATOR 1976

1970 Census Population	County	Total Vote	Republican	Democratic	Other	Rep.-Dem. Plurality	Percentage Total Vote Rep.	Total Vote Dem.	Major Vote Rep.	Major Vote Dem.
1,073,184	ALAMEDA	394,736	150,813	230,545	13,378	79,732 D	38.2%	58.4%	39.5%	60.5%
484	ALPINE	449	241	182	26	59 R	53.7%	40.5%	57.0%	43.0%
11,821	AMADOR	8,041	4,230	3,580	231	650 R	52.6%	44.5%	54.2%	45.8%
101,969	BUTTE	54,464	32,120	19,922	2,422	12,198 R	59.0%	36.6%	61.7%	38.3%
13,585	CALAVERAS	7,261	3,871	3,061	329	810 R	53.3%	42.2%	55.8%	44.2%
12,430	COLUSA	4,975	2,761	2,038	176	723 R	55.5%	41.0%	57.5%	42.5%
558,389	CONTRA COSTA	256,108	129,008	121,195	5,905	7,813 R	50.4%	47.3%	51.6%	48.4%
14,580	DEL NORTE	5,082	2,417	2,409	256	8 R	47.6%	47.4%	50.1%	49.9%
43,833	EL DORADO	26,131	13,982	11,122	1,027	2,860 R	53.5%	42.6%	55.7%	44.3%
413,053	FRESNO	146,944	75,951	66,628	4,365	9,323 R	51.7%	45.3%	53.3%	46.7%
17,521	GLENN	7,814	4,525	3,120	169	1,405 R	57.9%	39.9%	59.2%	40.8%
99,692	HUMBOLDT	42,945	17,787	23,031	2,127	5,244 D	41.4%	53.6%	43.6%	56.4%
74,492	IMPERIAL	20,774	9,390	10,818	566	1,428 D	45.2%	52.1%	46.5%	53.5%
15,571	INYO	6,715	4,097	2,446	172	1,651 R	61.0%	36.4%	62.6%	37.4%
329,162	KERN	108,779	59,740	46,411	2,628	13,329 R	54.9%	42.7%	56.3%	43.7%
64,610	KINGS	16,148	7,979	7,612	557	367 R	49.4%	47.1%	51.2%	48.8%
19,548	LAKE	12,265	6,103	5,801	361	302 R	49.8%	47.3%	51.3%	48.7%
14,960	LASSEN	7,020	2,895	3,781	344	886 D	41.2%	53.9%	43.4%	56.6%
7,032,075	LOS ANGELES	2,108,061	992,752	1,061,839	53,470	69,087 D	47.1%	50.4%	48.3%	51.7%
41,519	MADERA	13,854	6,948	6,234	672	714 R	50.2%	45.0%	52.7%	47.3%
206,038	MARIN	101,214	54,322	43,499	3,393	10,823 R	53.7%	43.0%	55.5%	44.5%
6,015	MARIPOSA	4,311	2,275	1,853	183	422 R	52.8%	43.0%	55.1%	44.9%
51,101	MENDOCINO	21,671	10,174	10,594	903	420 D	46.9%	48.9%	49.0%	51.0%
104,629	MERCED	29,957	13,669	15,217	1,071	1,548 D	45.6%	50.8%	47.3%	52.7%
7,469	MODOC	3,684	1,924	1,627	133	297 R	52.2%	44.2%	54.2%	45.8%
4,016	MONO	2,690	1,638	945	107	693 R	60.9%	35.1%	63.4%	36.6%
250,071	MONTEREY	78,009	43,024	32,750	2,235	10,274 R	55.2%	42.0%	56.8%	43.2%
79,140	NAPA	40,100	20,983	18,088	1,029	2,895 R	52.3%	45.1%	53.7%	46.3%
26,346	NEVADA	16,992	9,643	6,695	654	2,948 R	56.8%	39.4%	59.0%	41.0%
1,420,386	ORANGE	694,285	421,373	255,072	17,840	166,301 R	60.7%	36.7%	62.3%	37.7%
77,306	PLACER	40,482	20,829	18,314	1,339	2,515 R	51.5%	45.2%	53.2%	46.8%
11,707	PLUMAS	6,370	2,973	3,070	327	97 D	46.7%	48.2%	49.2%	50.8%
459,074	RIVERSIDE	198,926	93,426	101,031	4,469	7,605 D	47.0%	50.8%	48.0%	52.0%
631,498	SACRAMENTO	270,511	137,871	123,217	9,423	14,654 R	51.0%	45.5%	52.8%	47.2%
18,226	SAN BENITO	6,308	3,543	2,538	227	1,005 R	56.2%	40.2%	58.3%	41.7%
684,072	SAN BERNARDINO	218,975	106,715	106,116	6,144	599 R	48.7%	48.5%	50.1%	49.9%
1,357,854	SAN DIEGO	629,656	360,722	248,958	19,976	111,764 R	57.3%	39.5%	59.2%	40.8%
715,674	SAN FRANCISCO	247,630	91,924	147,305	8,401	55,381 D	37.1%	59.5%	38.4%	61.6%
290,208	SAN JOAQUIN	98,935	52,465	44,262	2,208	8,203 R	53.0%	44.7%	54.2%	45.8%
105,690	SAN LUIS OBISPO	52,990	27,372	23,614	2,004	3,758 R	51.7%	44.6%	53.7%	46.3%
556,234	SAN MATEO	226,744	112,445	105,541	8,758	6,904 R	49.6%	46.5%	51.6%	48.4%
264,324	SANTA BARBARA	119,348	58,653	56,752	3,943	1,901 R	49.1%	47.6%	50.8%	49.2%
1,064,714	SANTA CLARA	440,477	228,399	198,703	13,375	29,696 R	51.9%	45.1%	53.5%	46.5%
123,790	SANTA CRUZ	73,057	35,628	33,735	3,694	1,893 R	48.8%	46.2%	51.4%	48.6%
77,640	SHASTA	37,491	19,110	16,691	1,690	2,419 R	51.0%	44.5%	53.4%	46.6%
2,365	SIERRA	1,556	739	765	52	26 D	47.5%	49.2%	49.1%	50.9%
33,225	SISKIYOU	14,454	6,933	6,968	553	35 D	48.0%	48.2%	49.9%	50.1%
169,941	SOLANO	60,566	27,529	31,502	1,535	3,973 D	45.5%	52.0%	46.6%	53.4%
204,885	SONOMA	104,705	54,084	46,654	3,967	7,430 R	51.7%	44.6%	53.7%	46.3%
194,506	STANISLAUS	70,636	34,408	33,826	2,402	582 R	48.7%	47.9%	50.4%	49.6%
41,935	SUTTER	15,695	9,586	5,560	549	4,026 R	61.1%	35.4%	63.3%	36.7%
29,517	TEHAMA	13,494	7,420	5,560	514	1,860 R	55.0%	41.2%	57.2%	42.8%
7,615	TRINITY	4,334	2,402	1,698	234	704 R	55.4%	39.2%	58.6%	41.4%
188,322	TULARE	56,221	30,498	23,917	1,806	6,581 R	54.2%	42.5%	56.0%	44.0%
22,169	TUOLUMNE	12,653	6,151	5,863	639	288 R	48.6%	46.3%	51.2%	48.8%
376,430	VENTURA	153,562	84,685	65,254	3,623	19,431 R	55.1%	42.5%	56.5%	43.5%
91,788	YOLO	42,814	19,674	21,703	1,437	2,029 D	46.0%	50.7%	47.5%	52.5%
44,736	YUBA	12,199	6,154	5,630	415	524 R	50.4%	46.2%	52.2%	47.8%
19,953,134	TOTAL	7,472,268	3,748,973	3,502,862	220,433	246,111 R	50.2%	46.9%	51.7%	48.3%

Los Angeles County

PRESIDENT 1976

1970 Census Population	District	Total Vote	Republican	Democratic	Other	Rep.-Dem. Plurality	Percentage Total Vote Rep.	Percentage Total Vote Dem.	Percentage Major Vote Rep.	Percentage Major Vote Dem.
	DISTRICT 34 (PART)	35,466	22,123	12,539	804	9,584 R	62.4%	35.4%	63.8%	36.2%
	DISTRICT 37 (PART)	79,152	46,295	31,066	1,791	15,229 R	58.5%	39.2%	59.8%	40.2%
	DISTRICT 38 (PART)	96,308	55,232	39,246	1,830	15,986 R	57.3%	40.8%	58.5%	41.5%
	DISTRICT 39	80,144	37,733	40,707	1,704	2,974 D	47.1%	50.8%	48.1%	51.9%
	DISTRICT 40	95,948	45,539	48,399	2,010	2,860 D	47.5%	50.4%	48.5%	51.5%
	DISTRICT 41	98,687	60,477	36,306	1,904	24,171 R	61.3%	36.8%	62.5%	37.5%
	DISTRICT 42	108,798	65,984	40,864	1,950	25,120 R	60.6%	37.6%	61.8%	38.2%
	DISTRICT 43	138,157	67,494	68,658	2,005	1,164 D	48.9%	49.7%	49.6%	50.4%
	DISTRICT 44	112,660	47,955	61,892	2,813	13,937 D	42.6%	54.9%	43.7%	56.3%
	DISTRICT 45	110,862	44,962	63,767	2,133	18,805 D	40.6%	57.5%	41.4%	58.6%
	DISTRICT 46	65,295	28,449	35,053	1,793	6,604 D	43.6%	53.7%	44.8%	55.2%
	DISTRICT 47	52,933	10,384	41,683	866	31,299 D	19.6%	78.7%	19.9%	80.1%
	DISTRICT 48	53,456	10,916	41,689	851	30,773 D	20.4%	78.0%	20.8%	79.2%
	DISTRICT 49	92,961	28,361	63,287	1,313	34,926 D	30.5%	68.1%	30.9%	69.1%
	DISTRICT 50	77,073	24,846	51,185	1,042	26,339 D	32.2%	66.4%	32.7%	67.3%
	DISTRICT 51	113,524	73,072	38,150	2,302	34,922 R	64.4%	33.6%	65.7%	34.3%
	DISTRICT 52	78,438	39,977	36,943	1,518	3,034 R	51.0%	47.1%	52.0%	48.0%
	DISTRICT 53	67,195	27,439	38,451	1,305	11,012 D	40.8%	57.2%	41.6%	58.4%
	DISTRICT 54	57,802	15,868	40,921	1,013	25,053 D	27.5%	70.8%	27.9%	72.1%
	DISTRICT 55	56,604	22,572	32,477	1,555	9,905 D	39.9%	57.4%	41.0%	59.0%
	DISTRICT 56	35,824	9,948	25,205	671	15,257 D	27.8%	70.4%	28.3%	71.7%
	DISTRICT 57	75,150	32,464	41,139	1,547	8,675 D	43.2%	54.7%	44.1%	55.9%
	DISTRICT 58	107,779	58,062	47,540	2,177	10,522 R	53.9%	44.1%	55.0%	45.0%
	DISTRICT 59	81,703	36,132	44,194	1,377	8,062 D	44.2%	54.1%	45.0%	55.0%
	DISTRICT 60	58,628	24,233	33,056	1,339	8,823 D	41.3%	56.4%	42.3%	57.7%
	DISTRICT 61	100,681	64,466	34,271	1,944	30,195 R	64.0%	34.0%	65.3%	34.7%
	DISTRICT 62	100,709	58,445	40,260	2,004	18,185 R	58.0%	40.0%	59.2%	40.8%
	DISTRICT 63	86,856	43,529	41,736	1,591	1,793 R	50.1%	48.1%	51.1%	48.9%
	DISTRICT 64	102,369	61,665	39,016	1,688	22,649 R	60.2%	38.1%	61.2%	38.8%
	DISTRICT 65 (PART)	22,629	10,094	12,014	521	1,920 D	44.6%	53.1%	45.7%	54.3%
	SPECIAL BALLOTS	403	210	179	14	31 R	52.1%	44.4%	54.0%	46.0%
7,032,075	TOTAL	2,459,077	1,174,926	1,221,893	62,258	46,967 D	47.8%	49.7%	49.0%	51.0%

Los Angeles County

SENATOR 1976

1970 Census Population	District	Total Vote	Republican	Democratic	Other	Rep.-Dem. Plurality	Percentage Total Vote Rep.	Percentage Total Vote Dem.	Percentage Major Vote Rep.	Percentage Major Vote Dem.
	DISTRICT 34 (PART)	29,300	17,994	10,551	755	7,443 R	61.4%	36.0%	63.0%	37.0%
	DISTRICT 37 (PART)	69,503	41,017	26,562	1,924	14,455 R	59.0%	38.2%	60.7%	39.3%
	DISTRICT 38 (PART)	86,820	47,581	37,273	1,966	10,308 R	54.8%	42.9%	56.1%	43.9%
	DISTRICT 39	71,407	34,823	34,552	2,032	271 R	48.8%	48.4%	50.2%	49.8%
	DISTRICT 40	82,813	38,767	41,936	2,110	3,169 D	46.8%	50.6%	48.0%	52.0%
	DISTRICT 41	82,822	51,060	29,774	1,988	21,286 R	61.7%	35.9%	63.2%	36.8%
	DISTRICT 42	94,393	56,055	36,125	2,213	19,930 R	59.4%	38.3%	60.8%	39.2%
	DISTRICT 43	126,302	48,271	75,957	2,074	27,686 D	38.2%	60.1%	38.9%	61.1%
	DISTRICT 44	99,340	37,641	58,765	2,934	21,124 D	37.9%	59.2%	39.0%	61.0%
	DISTRICT 45	96,329	34,554	59,406	2,369	24,852 D	35.9%	61.7%	36.8%	63.2%
	DISTRICT 46	55,996	24,427	29,751	1,818	5,324 D	43.6%	53.1%	45.1%	54.9%
	DISTRICT 47	42,608	8,327	33,115	1,166	24,788 D	19.5%	77.7%	20.1%	79.9%
	DISTRICT 48	44,379	8,990	34,675	714	25,685 D	20.3%	78.1%	20.6%	79.4%
	DISTRICT 49	80,032	24,034	54,262	1,736	30,228 D	30.0%	67.8%	30.7%	69.3%
	DISTRICT 50	68,253	21,572	45,118	1,563	23,546 D	31.6%	66.1%	32.3%	67.7%
	DISTRICT 51	98,729	60,611	35,888	2,230	24,723 R	61.4%	36.4%	62.8%	37.2%
	DISTRICT 52	67,451	34,998	30,550	1,903	4,448 R	51.9%	45.3%	53.4%	46.6%
	DISTRICT 53	57,943	25,710	30,854	1,379	5,144 D	44.4%	53.2%	45.5%	54.5%
	DISTRICT 54	45,817	13,653	30,777	1,387	17,124 D	29.8%	67.2%	30.7%	69.3%
	DISTRICT 55	47,726	19,993	26,165	1,568	6,172 D	41.9%	54.8%	43.3%	56.7%
	DISTRICT 56	30,037	8,296	20,594	1,147	12,298 D	27.6%	68.6%	28.7%	71.3%
	DISTRICT 57	64,582	28,137	34,392	2,053	6,255 D	43.6%	53.3%	45.0%	55.0%
	DISTRICT 58	93,537	50,922	40,050	2,565	10,872 R	54.4%	42.8%	56.0%	44.0%
	DISTRICT 59	69,087	30,865	36,500	1,722	5,635 D	44.7%	52.8%	45.8%	54.2%
	DISTRICT 60	49,299	22,600	25,250	1,449	2,650 D	45.8%	51.2%	47.2%	52.8%
	DISTRICT 61	84,120	53,360	28,911	1,849	24,449 R	63.4%	34.4%	64.9%	35.1%
	DISTRICT 62	85,113	49,462	33,488	2,163	15,974 R	58.1%	39.3%	59.6%	40.4%
	DISTRICT 63	74,930	37,140	35,959	1,831	1,181 R	49.6%	48.0%	50.8%	49.2%
	DISTRICT 64	89,693	53,018	34,620	2,055	18,398 R	59.1%	38.6%	60.5%	39.5%
	DISTRICT 65 (PART)	19,090	8,712	9,871	507	1,159 D	45.6%	51.7%	46.9%	53.1%
	SPECIAL BALLOTS	327	162	148	17	14 R	49.5%	45.3%	52.3%	47.7%
7,032,075	TOTAL	2,108,061	992,752	1,061,839	53,470	69,087 D	47.1%	50.4%	48.3%	51.7%

CALIFORNIA

CONGRESS

CD	Year	Total Vote	Republican Vote	Republican Candidate	Democratic Vote	Democratic Candidate	Other Vote	Rep.-Dem. Plurality	Percentage Total Vote Rep.	Percentage Total Vote Dem.	Percentage Major Vote Rep.	Percentage Major Vote Dem.
1	1976	217,016	56,539	TAYLOR, JAMES E.	160,477	JOHNSON, HAROLD T.		103,938 D	26.1%	73.9%	26.1%	73.9%
1	1974	160,963			138,082	JOHNSON, HAROLD T.	22,881	138,082 D		85.8%		100.0%
2	1976	216,563	121,290	CLAUSEN, DON H.	88,829	KLEE, OSCAR H	6,444	32,461 R	56.0%	41.0%	57.7%	42.3%
2	1974	180,905	95,929	CLAUSEN, DON H.	77,232	KLEE, OSCAR H.	7,744	18,697 R	53.0%	42.7%	55.4%	44.6%
3	1976	191,854	52,075	MARSH, GEORGE R.	139,779	MOSS, JOHN E.		87,704 D	27.1%	72.9%	27.1%	72.9%
3	1974	168,846	46,712	LENCI, IVALDO	122,134	MOSS, JOHN E.		75,422 D	27.7%	72.3%	27.7%	72.3%
4	1976	162,368	75,193	DEHR, ALBERT	75,844	LEGGETT, ROBERT L.	11,331	651 D	46.3%	46.7%	49.8%	50.2%
4	1974	101,152			101,152	LEGGETT, ROBERT L.		101,152 D		100.0%		100.0%
5	1976	167,754	64,008	FANNING, BRANWELL	103,746	BURTON, JOHN		39,738 D	38.2%	61.8%	38.2%	61.8%
5	1974	149,260	56,274	CAYLOR, THOMAS	88,909	BURTON, JOHN	4,077	32,635 D	37.7%	59.6%	38.8%	61.2%
6	1976	130,916	35,359	SPINOSA, TOM	86,493	BURTON, PHILLIP	9,064	51,134 D	27.0%	66.1%	29.0%	71.0%
6	1974	120,248	26,260	SPINOSA, TOM	85,712	BURTON, PHILLIP	8,276	59,452 D	21.8%	71.3%	23.5%	76.5%
7	1976	196,816	45,863	VICKERS, ROBERT L.	147,064	MILLER, GEORGE	3,889	101,201 D	23.3%	74.7%	23.8%	76.2%
7	1974	149,379	66,325	FERNANDEZ, GARY	83,054	MILLER, GEORGE		16,729 D	44.4%	55.6%	44.4%	55.6%
8	1976	197,012	68,374	BRECK, PHILIP S.	122,342	DELLUMS, RONALD V.	6,296	53,968 D	34.7%	62.1%	35.9%	64.1%
8	1974	167,865	66,386	REDDEN, JACK	95,041	DELLUMS, RONALD V.	6,438	28,655 D	39.5%	56.6%	41.1%	58.9%
9	1976	164,391	44,607	MILLS, JAMES K.	116,398	STARK, FORTNEY	3,386	71,791 D	27.1%	70.8%	27.7%	72.3%
9	1974	130,957	38,521	ADAMS, EDSON	92,436	STARK, FORTNEY		53,915 D	29.4%	70.6%	29.4%	70.6%
10	1976	155,443	38,088	SMITH, HERB	111,992	EDWARDS, DON	5,363	73,904 D	24.5%	72.0%	25.4%	74.6%
10	1974	114,266	26,288	ENRIGHT, JOHN M.	87,978	EDWARDS, DON		61,690 D	23.0%	77.0%	23.0%	77.0%
11	1976	176,194	62,435	JONES, BOB	107,618	RYAN, LEO J.	6,141	45,183 D	35.4%	61.1%	36.7%	63.3%
11	1974	140,356	29,861	MERDINGER, BRAINARD G.	106,429	RYAN, LEO J.	4,066	76,568 D	21.3%	75.8%	21.9%	78.1%
12	1976	196,857	130,332	MCCLOSKEY, PAUL N.	61,526	HARRIS, DAVID	4,999	68,806 R	66.2%	31.3%	67.9%	32.1%
12	1974	150,075	103,692	MCCLOSKEY, PAUL N.	46,383	GILLMOR, GARY G.		57,309 R	69.1%	30.9%	69.1%	30.9%
13	1976	202,611	63,130	KONNYU, ERNEST L.	135,291	MINETA, NORMAN Y.	4,190	72,161 D	31.2%	66.8%	31.8%	68.2%
13	1974	150,099	63,573	MILIAS, GEORGE W.	78,858	MINETA, NORMAN Y.	7,668	15,285 D	42.4%	52.5%	44.6%	55.4%
14	1976	169,959	46,674	BLAIN, ROGER A.	123,285	MCFALL, JOHN J.		76,611 D	27.5%	72.5%	27.5%	72.5%
14	1974	144,078	34,775	GIBSON, CHARLES M.	102,180	MCFALL, JOHN J.	7,123	67,405 D	24.1%	70.9%	25.4%	74.6%
15	1976	128,435	35,700	HARNER, CAROL O.	92,735	SISK, B. F.		57,035 D	27.8%	72.2%	27.8%	72.2%
15	1974	112,336	31,439	HARNER, CAROL O.	80,897	SISK, B. F.		49,458 D	28.0%	72.0%	28.0%	72.0%
16	1976	195,705	91,160	TALCOTT, BURT L.	104,545	PANETTA, LEON E.		13,385 D	46.6%	53.4%	46.6%	53.4%
16	1974	155,113	76,356	TALCOTT, BURT L.	74,168	CAMACHO, JULIAN	4,589	2,188 R	49.2%	47.8%	50.7%	49.3%
17	1976	158,168	54,270	ANDREAS, HENRY J.	103,898	KREBS, JOHN		49,628 D	34.3%	65.7%	34.3%	65.7%
17	1974	128,487	61,812	MATHIAS, ROBERT B.	66,675	KREBS, JOHN		4,863 D	48.1%	51.9%	48.1%	51.9%
18	1976	158,341	101,658	KETCHUM, WILLIAM M.	56,683	CLOSE, DEAN		44,975 R	64.2%	35.8%	64.2%	35.8%
18	1974	128,383	67,650	KETCHUM, WILLIAM M.	60,733	SEIELSTAD, GEORGE A.		6,917 R	52.7%	47.3%	52.7%	47.3%
19	1976	192,923	124,201	LAGOMARSINO, ROBERT J.	68,722	SISSON, DON		55,479 R	64.4%	35.6%	64.4%	35.6%
19	1974	149,718	84,249	LAGOMARSINO, ROBERT J.	65,469	LOEBL, JAMES D.		18,780 R	56.3%	43.7%	56.3%	43.7%
20	1976	217,351	146,158	GOLDWATER, BARRY M., JR.	71,193	CORMAN, PATTI L.		74,965 R	67.2%	32.8%	67.2%	32.8%
20	1974	160,736	98,410	GOLDWATER, BARRY M., JR.	62,326	MATHEWS, ARLINE		36,084 R	61.2%	38.8%	61.2%	38.8%
21	1976	153,109	44,094	HOGAN, ERWIN	101,837	CORMAN, JAMES C.	7,178	57,743 D	28.8%	66.5%	30.2%	69.8%
21	1974	120,957	32,038	NADELL, MEL	88,915	CORMAN, JAMES C.	4	56,877 D	26.5%	73.5%	26.5%	73.5%
22	1976	183,312	114,769	MOORHEAD, CARLOS J.	68,543	SALLEY, ROBERT L.		46,226 R	62.6%	37.4%	62.6%	37.4%
22	1974	146,332	81,641	MOORHEAD, CARLOS J.	64,691	HALLIN, RICHARD		16,950 R	55.8%	44.2%	55.8%	44.2%
23	1976	217,053	86,434	BARTMAN, THOMAS F.	130,619	BEILENSON, ANTHONY C.		44,185 D	39.8%	60.2%	39.8%	60.2%
23	1974	170,902	48,826	ROBERTS, JACK E.	122,076	REES, THOMAS M.		73,250 D	28.6%	71.4%	28.6%	71.4%
24	1976	159,774	51,478	SIMMONS, DAVID I.	108,296	WAXMAN, HENRY A.		56,818 D	32.2%	67.8%	32.2%	67.8%
24	1974	136,722	45,128	GRAHAM, ELLIOTT S.	87,521	WAXMAN, HENRY A.	4,073	42,393 D	33.0%	64.0%	34.0%	66.0%
25	1976	80,625	17,737	MADRID, JIM	57,966	ROYBAL, EDWARD R.	4,922	40,229 D	22.0%	71.9%	23.4%	76.6%
25	1974	45,163			45,059	ROYBAL, EDWARD R.	104	45,059 D		99.8%		100.0%
26	1976	171,712	112,619	ROUSSELOT, JOHN H.	59,093	LATTA, BRUCE		53,526 R	65.6%	34.4%	65.6%	34.4%
26	1974	140,420	82,735	ROUSSELOT, JOHN H.	57,685	CONFORTI, PAUL A.		25,050 R	58.9%	41.1%	58.9%	41.1%
27	1976	209,611	114,623	DORNAN, ROBERT K.	94,988	FAMILIAN, GARY		19,635 R	54.7%	45.3%	54.7%	45.3%
27	1974	160,605	102,663	BELL, ALPHONZO E.	52,236	DALESSIO, JOHN	5,706	50,427 R	63.9%	32.5%	66.3%	33.7%
28	1976	142,915	28,303	SKINNER, EDWARD S.	114,612	BURKE, YVONNE BRATHWAITE		86,309 D	19.8%	80.2%	19.8%	80.2%
28	1974	110,629	21,957	NEDDY, TOM	88,655	BURKE, YVONNE BRATHWAITE	17	66,698 D	19.8%	80.1%	19.9%	80.1%

CALIFORNIA

CONGRESS

CD	Year	Total Vote	Republican Vote	Republican Candidate	Democratic Vote	Democratic Candidate	Other Vote	Rep.-Dem. Plurality	Percentage Total Vote Rep.	Percentage Total Vote Dem.	Percentage Major Vote Rep.	Percentage Major Vote Dem.
29	1976	96,602	10,852	GERMONPREZ, MICHAEL D.	82,515	HAWKINS, AUGUSTUS	3,235	71,663 D	11.2%	85.4%	11.6%	88.4%
29	1974	47,204			47,204	HAWKINS, AUGUSTUS		47,204 D		100.0%		100.0%
30	1976	111,270	28,503	COUCH, HARRY	82,767	DANIELSON, GEORGE E.		54,264 D	25.6%	74.4%	25.6%	74.4%
30	1974	90,711	23,383	PEREZ, JOHN J.	67,328	DANIELSON, GEORGE E.		43,945 D	25.8%	74.2%	25.8%	74.2%
31	1976	83,155			83,155	WILSON, CHARLES H.		83,155 D		100.0%		100.0%
31	1974	87,058	23,359	HODGES, NORMAN A.	61,322	WILSON, CHARLES H.	2,377	37,963 D	26.8%	70.4%	27.6%	72.4%
32	1976	127,428	35,394	YOUNG, CLIFFORD O.	92,034	ANDERSON, GLENN M.		56,640 D	27.8%	72.2%	27.8%	72.2%
32	1974	96,265			84,428	ANDERSON, GLENN M.	11,837	84,428 D		87.7%		100.0%
33	1976	173,205	95,398	CLAWSON, DEL	77,807	SNYDER, TED		17,591 R	55.1%	44.9%	55.1%	44.9%
33	1974	135,688	72,471	CLAWSON, DEL	58,492	WHITE, ROBERT E.	4,725	13,979 R	53.4%	43.1%	55.3%	44.7%
34	1976	199,191	98,147	LUNGREN, DANIEL E.	100,988	HANNAFORD, MARK W.	56	2,841 D	49.3%	50.7%	49.3%	50.7%
34	1974	163,003	75,426	BOND, BILL	81,151	HANNAFORD, MARK W.	6,426	5,725 D	46.3%	49.8%	48.2%	51.8%
35	1976	164,237	76,765	BRUTOCAO, LOUIS	87,472	LLOYD, JIM		10,707 D	46.7%	53.3%	46.7%	53.3%
35	1974	123,071	61,168	VEYSEY, VICTOR V.	61,903	LLOYD, JIM		735 D	49.7%	50.3%	49.7%	50.3%
36	1976	147,556	49,368	CARNER, GRANT	90,830	BROWN, GEORGE E.	7,358	41,462 D	33.5%	61.6%	35.2%	64.8%
36	1974	111,415	35,938	OSGOOD, JIM	69,766	BROWN, GEORGE E.	5,711	33,828 D	32.3%	62.6%	34.0%	66.0%
37	1976	188,007	133,634	PETTIS, SHIRLEY N.	49,021	NILSON, DOUGLAS C.	5,352	84,613 R	71.1%	26.1%	73.2%	26.8%
37	1974	142,202	89,849	PETTIS, JERRY L.	46,783	VINCENT, BOBBY RAY	5,570	43,066 R	63.2%	32.9%	65.8%	34.2%
38	1976	162,409	59,092	COMBS, JAMES	103,317	PATTERSON, JERRY M.		44,225 D	36.4%	63.6%	36.4%	63.6%
38	1974	126,461	52,207	REHMANN, DAVID	68,335	PATTERSON, JERRY M.	5,919	16,128 D	41.3%	54.0%	43.3%	56.7%
39	1976	209,402	122,657	WIGGINS, CHARLES E.	86,745	FARRIS, WILLIAM E.		35,912 R	58.6%	41.4%	58.6%	41.4%
39	1974	161,446	89,220	WIGGINS, CHARLES E.	65,170	FARRIS, WILLIAM E.	7,056	24,050 R	55.3%	40.4%	57.8%	42.2%
40	1976	250,644	148,512	BADHAM, ROBERT E.	102,132	HALL, VIVIAN		46,380 R	59.3%	40.7%	59.3%	40.7%
40	1974	183,797	116,449	HINSHAW, ANDREW J.	56,850	WILSON, RODERICK J.	10,498	59,599 R	63.4%	30.9%	67.2%	32.8%
41	1976	223,374	128,784	WILSON, BOB	94,590	GOLDEN, KING		34,194 R	57.7%	42.3%	57.7%	42.3%
41	1974	173,886	94,709	WILSON, BOB	74,823	O CONNOR, COLLEEN M.	4,354	19,886 R	54.5%	43.0%	55.9%	44.1%
42	1976	135,627	32,565	MARDEN, WES	103,062	VAN DEERLIN, LIONEL		70,497 D	24.0%	76.0%	24.0%	76.0%
42	1974	101,014	30,435	MARDEN, WES	70,579	VAN DEERLIN, LIONEL		40,144 D	30.1%	69.9%	30.1%	69.9%
43	1976	267,051	173,576	BURGENER, CLAIR W.	93,475	KELLY, PAT		80,101 R	65.0%	35.0%	65.0%	35.0%
43	1974	191,007	115,275	BURGENER, CLAIR W.	75,629	BANDES, BILL	103	39,646 R	60.4%	39.6%	60.4%	39.6%

CALIFORNIA

1976 GENERAL ELECTION

President — Other vote was 58,412 McCarthy (write-in); 56,388 MacBride (Independent); 51,098 Maddox (American Independent); 41,731 Wright (Peace and Freedom); 17,259 Camejo (Independent); 12,766 Hall (Independent); 4,565 Anderson (write-in); 222 Levin (write-in); 34 Bubar (write-in); 26 Miller (write-in); 14 Taylor (write-in); 74 scattered (write-in).

Senator — Other vote was 104,383 Wald (Peace and Freedom); 82,739 McCoy (American Independent); 31,629 Musa (Independent); 907 Kinsky (write-in); 457 Bodle (write-in); 160 Bills (write-in); 158 Cross (write-in).

Congress — Other vote was Stanley (American Independent) in CD 7; Kaiser (American Independent) in CD 10; Kudrovzeff (American Independent) in CD 11; Cooney (American Independent) in CD 12; Herrell (American Independent) in CD 13; Pasley (American Independent) in CD 36; Wahl (American Independent) in CD 37; Allred (Peace and Freedom) in CD 2; Sargis (Peace and Freedom) in CD 9; Hill (Peace and Freedom) in CD 21; Seals (Peace and Freedom) in CD 25; Leburg (Independent) in CD 29; scattered in CD 34; 11,279 Sheedy (write-in) and 52 scattered in CD 4; 6,570 Siegel (Peace and Freedom) and 2,494 Heaps (American Independent) in CD 6; 6,238 Evans (Peace and Freedom) and 58 scattered in CD 8.

LOS ANGELES COUNTY

Assembly District lines were redrawn prior to the 1974 elections and 1970 population figures are omitted.

President — Special ballots include new resident and overseas votes. Other vote was 15,164 MacBride (Independent); 13,799 McCarthy (write-in); 13,441 Maddox (American Independent); 11,232 Wright (Peace and Freedom); 3,781 Hall (Independent); 3,757 Camejo (Independent); 1,030 Anderson (write-in); 37 Levin (write-in); 4 Bubar (write-in); 13 scattered. Write-in votes are included in the total but are not available by assembly district.

Senator — Special ballots include new resident and overseas votes. Other vote was 26,129 Wald (Peace and Freedom); 19,489 McCoy (American Independent); 7,569 Musa (Independent); 283 scattered. Write-in votes are included in the total but are not available by assembly district.

1976 PRIMARIES

JUNE 8 REPUBLICAN

Senator — 886,743 S. I. Hayakawa; 614,240 Robert H. Finch; 532,969 Alphonzo E. Bell; 197,252 John L. Harmer; 28,573 Walter Hollywood; 17,954 Clyde F. Tracy; 15,211 James A. Ware; 10,438 Henry Hill; 10,076 Michael A. Hirt; 6,318 Hannibal C. Burchette; 13 scattered.

Congress — Unopposed in thirty-one CD's. Contested as follows:

CD 4 — 12,139 Albert Dehr; 9,897 Harvey Taylor; 9,546 Laurence G. Wegienka.
CD 6 — 15,174 Tom Spinosa; 3,202 Thomas C. Sanders.
CD 13 — 30,347 Ernest L. Konnyu; 18,446 Grant P. Jones; 59 scattered.
CD 21 — 14,200 Erwin Hogan; 7,280 Steve Fox; 7,120 Amy W. Fixler; 6,879 Mark M. Dickerson.
CD 23 — 25,897 Thomas F. Bartman; 9,285 Patricia A. Gallucci; 8,441 Rick Nelson; 4,087 Charonne Wali.
CD 24 — 18,105 David I. Simmons; 11,948 Jerry Fogel; 4,970 Albert M. Karsa.
CD 27 — 24,957 Robert K. Dornan; 17,911 Joe Blatchford; 15,909 Michael C. Donaldson; 6,935 Robert A. Welbourn; 5,609 Dennis O'Block; 1,266 Gary L. Symonds.
CD 30 — 11,254 Harry Couch; 7,824 Diane Condon.
CD 31 — No candidates appeared on the ballot; there were 236 write-in votes for Jerry Saavedra. Mr. Saavedra withdrew and no substitution was made.
CD 34 — 30,619 Daniel E. Lungren; 22,866 Bill Bond; 9,078 Art Jacobson.
CD 38 — 23,404 James Combs; 21,612 David H. Paynter.

CALIFORNIA

CD 40 — 36,954 Robert E. Badham; 35,591 John G. Schmitz; 19,128 Thomas J. Mauro; 7,666 Andrew J. Hinshaw; 6,632 Harry Jeffrey; 4,346 Alicia H. Cooper; 2,966 W. F. Davenport; 1,958 Michael P. Clancey; 580 Dale Davis; 2 scattered.

JUNE 8 DEMOCRATIC

Senator — 1,774,879 John V. Tunney; 1,210,637 Tom Hayden; 73,142 Bob Wallach; 54,220 Lois T. Bodle; 53,843 Frank L. Thomas; 46,977 Howard L. Gifford; 29,511 Ronald L. Williams; 28,583 Les Craven; 28,108 Milliard F. Slover; 25 scattered.

Congress — Unopposed in twenty CD's. Contested as follows:

CD 1 — 70,199 Harold T. Johnson; 18,348 Marion W. Steele.
CD 2 — 33,731 Oscar H. Klee; 21,709 Douglas H. Bosco; 21,145 Gerald Hill; 13,105 Jim Brown; 6,331 May Chote.
CD 6 — 58,971 Phillip Burton; 12,520 Mary Anne Bouey.
CD 11 — 53,382 Leo J. Ryan; 21,331 John J. McGuire; 17 scattered.
CD 12 — 32,620 David Harris; 22,060 Norman J. Shaskey.
CD 14 — 52,999 John J. McFall; 11,098 Norma Lowry.
CD 16 — 34,556 Leon E. Panetta; 19,250 John R. Bakalian; 12,374 Robert B. Morton.
CD 18 — 42,954 Dean Close; 13,901 Santi Tafarella.
CD 20 — 32,905 Patti L. Corman; 22,760 Charles L. Lindsay; 14,408 James H. Gilmartin.
CD 22 — 21,161 Robert L. Salley; 20,363 Stanley M. Sapiro; 13,384 H. Starr Pak.
CD 23 — 61,153 Anthony C. Beilenson; 22,077 Wallace Albertson; 10,255 Noel S. Horwin; 5,085 Martin M. Altman; 4,174 Robert Brown; 3,145 Julius Shulman.
CD 24 — 59,822 Henry A. Waxman; 14,305 Chris Musun.
CD 25 — 36,479 Edward R. Roybal; 5,896 Michael P. Rives.
CD 26 — No candidates appeared on the ballot; there were 1,499 write-in votes for Bruce Latta; 898 George H. Donnelly; 132 Jean Valentine; 107 Patrick Kidd; 45 Harry Paylides.
CD 27 — 27,013 Gary Familian; 21,524 Dave Horner; 12,637 Jack Shaffer; 7,152 Robyn J. Hickey; 4,276 Shirley Smith; 2,270 Tom Pezzuti; 1,398 David P. Helgevold; 1,103 George Soen.
CD 29 — 46,715 Augustus Hawkins; 4,976 Jay B. Price; 4,137 Oliver W. Wilson; 3,584 Joe Taylor.
CD 31 — 34,979 Charles H. Wilson; 12,386 Joseph Rice; 8,706 Saul E. Lankster.
CD 32 — 50,583 Glenn M. Anderson; 8,501 Albert Landers.
CD 33 — 45,030 Ted Snyder; 10,176 Philip Megdal; 9,506 Merl T. Doty.
CD 39 — 34,626 William E. Farris; 25,542 Dickran Boranian.
CD 40 — 30,094 Vivian Hall; 14,223 Roderick J. Wilson; 12,853 George H. Margolis; 5,987 John B. Schoonover.
CD 41 — 16,341 King Golden; 13,670 Dan Finnigan; 13,279 Gordon Gastil; 10,400 Arnold L. Flick; 8,153 Louisa A. Desmond; 7,462 Joseph J. Trento; 3,381 Stephan R. Jones; 3,055 Hank Roloff.
CD 43 — 47,219 Pat Kelly; 25,608 H. Lee Stout.

JUNE 8 AMERICAN INDEPENDENT

Senator — Jack McCoy, unopposed.

Congress — Unopposed in all CD's in which candidates were entered.

JUNE 8 PEACE AND FREEDOM

Senator — David Wald, unopposed.

Congress — Unopposed in all CD's in which candidates were entered.

COLORADO

GOVERNOR

Richard D. Lamm (D). Elected 1974 to a four-year term.

SENATORS

Gary W. Hart (D). Elected 1974 to a six-year term.

Floyd K. Haskell (D). Elected 1972 to a six-year term.

REPRESENTATIVES

1. Patricia Schroeder (D)
2. Timothy E. Wirth (D)
3. Frank E. Evans (D)
4. James P. Johnson (R)
5. William L. Armstrong (R)

POSTWAR VOTE FOR GOVERNOR

Year	Total Vote	Republican Vote	Republican Candidate	Democratic Vote	Democratic Candidate	Other Vote	Rep.-Dem. Plurality	Percentage Total Vote Rep.	Percentage Total Vote Dem.	Percentage Major Vote Rep.	Percentage Major Vote Dem.
1974	828,968	378,698	Vanderhoof, John D.	441,408	Lamm, Richard D.	8,862	62,710 D	45.7%	53.2%	46.2%	53.8%
1970	668,496	350,690	Love, John A.	302,432	Hogan, Mark	15,374	48,258 R	52.5%	45.2%	53.7%	46.3%
1966	660,063	356,730	Love, John A.	287,132	Knous, Robert L.	16,201	69,598 R	54.0%	43.5%	55.4%	44.6%
1962	616,481	349,342	Love, John A.	262,890	McNichols, Stephen	4,249	86,452 R	56.7%	42.6%	57.1%	42.9%
1958	549,808	228,643	Burch, Palmer L.	321,165	McNichols, Stephen	–	92,522 D	41.6%	58.4%	41.6%	58.4%
1956	645,233	313,950	Brotzman, Donald G.	331,283	McNichols, Stephen	–	17,333 D	48.7%	51.3%	48.7%	51.3%
1954	489,540	227,335	Brotzman, Donald G.	262,205	Johnson, Ed C.	–	34,870 D	46.4%	53.6%	46.4%	53.6%
1952	613,034	349,924	Thornton, Dan	260,044	Metzger, John W.	3,066	89,880 R	57.1%	42.4%	57.4%	42.6%
1950	450,994	236,472	Thornton, Dan	212,976	Johnson, Walter	1,546	23,496 R	52.4%	47.2%	52.6%	47.4%
1948	501,680	168,928	Hamil, David A.	332,752	Knous, William Lee	–	163,824 D	33.7%	66.3%	33.7%	66.3%
1946	335,087	160,483	Lavington, Leon E.	174,604	Knous, William Lee	–	14,121 D	47.9%	52.1%	47.9%	52.1%

The term of office of Colorado's Governor was increased from two to four years effective with the 1958 election.

POSTWAR VOTE FOR SENATOR

Year	Total Vote	Republican Vote	Republican Candidate	Democratic Vote	Democratic Candidate	Other Vote	Rep.-Dem. Plurality	Percentage Total Vote Rep.	Percentage Total Vote Dem.	Percentage Major Vote Rep.	Percentage Major Vote Dem.
1974	824,166	325,508	Dominick, Peter H.	471,691	Hart, Gary W.	26,967	146,183 D	39.5%	57.2%	40.8%	59.2%
1972	926,093	447,957	Allott, Gordon	457,545	Haskell, Floyd K.	20,591	9,588 D	48.4%	49.4%	49.5%	50.5%
1968	785,536	459,952	Dominick, Peter H.	325,584	McNichols, Stephen	–	134,368 R	58.6%	41.4%	58.6%	41.4%
1966	634,898	368,307	Allott, Gordon	266,259	Romer, Roy	332	102,048 R	58.0%	41.9%	58.0%	42.0%
1962	613,444	328,655	Dominick, Peter H.	279,586	Carroll, John A.	5,203	49,069 R	53.6%	45.6%	54.0%	46.0%
1960	727,633	389,428	Allott, Gordon	334,854	Knous, Robert L.	3,351	54,574 R	53.5%	46.0%	53.8%	46.2%
1956	636,974	317,102	Thornton, Dan	319,872	Carroll, John A.	–	2,770 D	49.8%	50.2%	49.8%	50.2%
1954	484,188	248,502	Allott, Gordon	235,686	Carroll, John A.	–	12,816 R	51.3%	48.7%	51.3%	48.7%
1950	450,176	239,734	Millikin, Eugene D.	210,442	Carroll, John A.	–	29,292 R	53.3%	46.7%	53.3%	46.7%
1948	510,121	165,069	Nicholson, W. F.	340,719	Johnson, Ed C.	4,333	175,650 D	32.4%	66.8%	32.6%	67.4%

COLORADO

Districts Established May 11, 1972

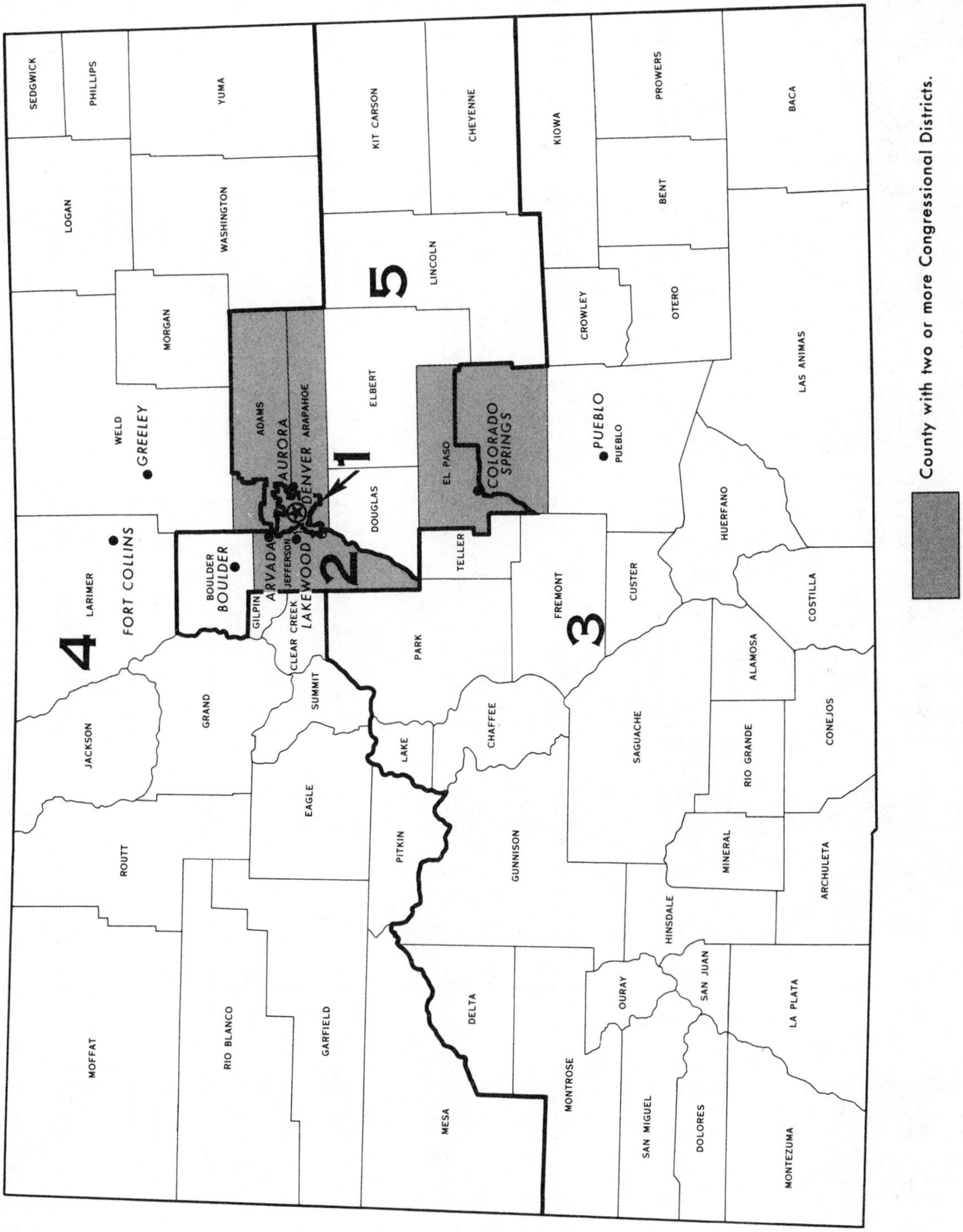

COLORADO

PRESIDENT 1976

1970 Census Population	County	Total Vote	Republican	Democratic	Other	Rep.-Dem. Plurality	Percentage Total Vote Rep.	Percentage Total Vote Dem.	Percentage Major Vote Rep.	Percentage Major Vote Dem.
185,789	ADAMS	78,127	35,392	40,551	2,184	5,159 D	45.3%	51.9%	46.6%	53.4%
11,422	ALAMOSA	4,862	2,599	2,052	211	547 R	53.5%	42.2%	55.9%	44.1%
162,142	ARAPAHOE	99,526	63,154	33,685	2,687	29,469 R	63.5%	33.8%	65.2%	34.8%
2,733	ARCHULETA	1,432	768	632	32	136 R	53.6%	44.1%	54.9%	45.1%
5,674	BACA	2,507	1,303	1,164	40	139 R	52.0%	46.4%	52.8%	47.2%
6,493	BENT	2,480	1,156	1,268	56	112 D	46.6%	51.1%	47.7%	52.3%
131,889	BOULDER	81,300	42,830	33,284	5,186	9,546 R	52.7%	40.9%	56.3%	43.7%
10,162	CHAFFEE	5,162	2,925	2,064	173	861 R	56.7%	40.0%	58.6%	41.4%
2,396	CHEYENNE	1,271	610	625	36	15 D	48.0%	49.2%	49.4%	50.6%
4,819	CLEAR CREEK	2,669	1,477	1,069	123	408 R	55.3%	40.1%	58.0%	42.0%
7,846	CONEJOS	3,194	1,426	1,698	70	272 D	44.6%	53.2%	45.6%	54.4%
3,091	COSTILLA	1,454	392	1,033	29	641 D	27.0%	71.0%	27.5%	72.5%
3,086	CROWLEY	1,519	834	667	18	167 R	54.9%	43.9%	55.6%	44.4%
1,120	CUSTER	791	491	259	41	232 R	62.1%	32.7%	65.5%	34.5%
15,286	DELTA	8,483	4,980	3,232	271	1,748 R	58.7%	38.1%	60.6%	39.4%
514,678	DENVER	226,773	105,960	112,229	8,584	6,269 D	46.7%	49.5%	48.6%	51.4%
1,641	DOLORES	752	343	374	35	31 D	45.6%	49.7%	47.8%	52.2%
8,407	DOUGLAS	7,757	5,078	2,459	220	2,619 R	65.5%	31.7%	67.4%	32.6%
7,498	EAGLE	4,618	2,963	1,502	153	1,461 R	64.2%	32.5%	66.4%	33.6%
3,903	ELBERT	2,428	1,279	1,068	81	211 R	52.7%	44.0%	54.5%	45.5%
235,972	EL PASO	86,168	50,929	32,911	2,328	18,018 R	59.1%	38.2%	60.7%	39.3%
21,942	FREMONT	10,769	5,647	4,886	236	761 R	52.4%	45.4%	53.6%	46.4%
14,821	GARFIELD	7,871	4,699	2,852	320	1,847 R	59.7%	36.2%	62.2%	37.8%
1,272	GILPIN	1,095	451	563	81	112 D	41.2%	51.4%	44.5%	55.5%
4,107	GRAND	2,760	1,703	910	147	793 R	61.7%	33.0%	65.2%	34.8%
7,578	GUNNISON	4,150	2,568	1,250	332	1,318 R	61.9%	30.1%	67.3%	32.7%
202	HINSDALE	284	189	83	12	106 R	66.5%	29.2%	69.5%	30.5%
6,590	HUERFANO	3,165	1,182	1,932	51	750 D	37.3%	61.0%	38.0%	62.0%
1,811	JACKSON	748	455	279	14	176 R	60.8%	37.3%	62.0%	38.0%
233,031	JEFFERSON	144,102	87,080	52,782	4,240	34,298 R	60.4%	36.6%	62.3%	37.7%
2,029	KIOWA	1,137	598	529	10	69 R	52.6%	46.5%	53.1%	46.9%
7,530	KIT CARSON	3,621	1,888	1,647	86	241 R	52.1%	45.5%	53.4%	46.6%
8,282	LAKE	3,279	1,575	1,549	155	26 R	48.0%	47.2%	50.4%	49.6%
19,199	LA PLATA	10,573	6,228	3,843	502	2,385 R	58.9%	36.3%	61.8%	38.2%
89,900	LARIMER	53,009	32,169	19,005	1,835	13,164 R	60.7%	35.9%	62.9%	37.1%
15,744	LAS ANIMAS	7,175	2,615	4,459	101	1,844 D	36.4%	62.1%	37.0%	63.0%
4,836	LINCOLN	2,387	1,276	1,059	52	217 R	53.5%	44.4%	54.6%	45.4%
18,852	LOGAN	7,988	4,256	3,543	189	713 R	53.3%	44.4%	54.6%	45.4%
54,374	MESA	27,419	17,924	8,807	688	9,117 R	65.4%	32.1%	67.1%	32.9%
786	MINERAL	423	235	167	21	68 R	55.6%	39.5%	58.5%	41.5%
6,525	MOFFAT	3,775	2,099	1,451	225	648 R	55.6%	38.4%	59.1%	40.9%
12,952	MONTEZUMA	5,190	3,002	1,993	195	1,009 R	57.8%	38.4%	60.1%	39.9%
18,366	MONTROSE	8,300	4,838	3,164	298	1,674 R	58.3%	38.1%	60.5%	39.5%
20,105	MORGAN	8,631	4,603	3,798	230	805 R	53.3%	44.0%	54.8%	45.2%
23,523	OTERO	8,920	4,597	4,118	205	479 R	51.5%	46.2%	52.7%	47.3%
1,546	OURAY	1,032	645	333	54	312 R	62.5%	32.3%	66.0%	34.0%
2,185	PARK	1,872	1,034	741	97	293 R	55.2%	39.6%	58.3%	41.7%
4,131	PHILLIPS	2,373	1,142	1,173	58	31 D	48.1%	49.4%	49.3%	50.7%
6,185	PITKIN	5,512	2,955	2,194	363	761 R	53.6%	39.8%	57.4%	42.6%
13,258	PROWERS	5,592	2,578	2,861	153	283 D	46.1%	51.2%	47.4%	52.6%
118,238	PUEBLO	45,157	18,518	25,841	798	7,323 D	41.0%	57.2%	41.7%	58.3%
4,842	RIO BLANCO	2,141	1,439	627	75	812 R	67.2%	29.3%	69.7%	30.3%
10,494	RIO GRANDE	4,212	2,627	1,475	110	1,152 R	62.4%	35.0%	64.0%	36.0%
6,592	ROUTT	5,213	2,822	2,130	261	692 R	54.1%	40.9%	57.0%	43.0%
3,827	SAGUACHE	2,210	1,094	1,059	57	35 R	49.5%	47.9%	50.8%	49.2%
831	SAN JUAN	411	221	167	23	54 R	53.8%	40.6%	57.0%	43.0%
1,949	SAN MIGUEL	1,419	622	674	123	52 D	43.8%	47.5%	48.0%	52.0%
3,405	SEDGWICK	1,700	902	773	25	129 R	53.1%	45.5%	53.9%	46.1%
2,665	SUMMIT	3,142	1,826	1,087	229	739 R	58.1%	34.6%	62.7%	37.3%
3,316	TELLER	2,521	1,410	986	125	424 R	55.9%	39.1%	58.8%	41.2%
5,550	WASHINGTON	2,767	1,440	1,211	116	229 R	52.0%	43.8%	54.3%	45.7%
89,297	WELD	39,732	21,976	16,501	1,255	5,475 R	55.3%	41.5%	57.1%	42.9%
8,544	YUMA	4,504	2,350	2,025	129	325 R	52.2%	45.0%	53.7%	46.3%
2,207,259	TOTAL	1,081,554	584,367	460,353	36,834	124,014 R	54.0%	42.6%	55.9%	44.1%

COLORADO

CONGRESS

CD	Year	Total Vote	Republican Vote	Republican Candidate	Democratic Vote	Democratic Candidate	Other Vote	Rep.-Dem. Plurality	Percentage Total Vote Rep.	Percentage Total Vote Dem.	Percentage Major Vote Rep.	Percentage Major Vote Dem.
1	1976	193,610	89,384	FRIEDMAN, DON	103,037	SCHROEDER, PATRICIA	1,189	13,653 D	46.2%	53.2%	46.5%	53.5%
1	1974	161,734	66,046	SOUTHWORTH, FRANK	94,583	SCHROEDER, PATRICIA	1,105	28,537 D	40.8%	58.5%	41.1%	58.9%
1	1972	197,495	93,733	MCKEVITT, JAMES D.	101,832	SCHROEDER, PATRICIA	1,930	8,099 D	47.5%	51.6%	47.9%	52.1%
2	1976	240,272	118,936	SCOTT, ED	121,336	WIRTH, TIMOTHY E.		2,400 D	49.5%	50.5%	49.5%	50.5%
2	1974	180,500	86,720	BROTZMAN, DONALD G.	93,728	WIRTH, TIMOTHY E.	52	7,008 D	48.0%	51.9%	48.1%	51.9%
2	1972	199,983	132,562	BROTZMAN, DONALD G.	66,817	BRUSH, FRANCIS W.	604	65,745 R	66.3%	33.4%	66.5%	33.5%
3	1976	175,184	82,269	TAKAKI, MELVIN H.	89,308	EVANS, FRANK E.	3,607	7,039 D	47.0%	51.0%	47.9%	52.1%
3	1974	135,081	38,688	RECORDS, E. KEITH	96,393	EVANS, FRANK E.		57,705 D	28.6%	71.4%	28.6%	71.4%
3	1972	162,067	54,556	BRADY, CHUCK	107,511	FVANS, FRANK E.		52,955 D	33.7%	66.3%	33.7%	66.3%
4	1976	222,328	119,408	JOHNSON, JAMES P.	78,355	OGDEN, DAN	24,565	41,053 R	53.7%	35.2%	60.4%	39.6%
4	1974	159,434	82,608	JOHNSON, JAMES P.	76,826	CARROLL, JOHN		5,782 R	51.8%	48.2%	51.8%	48.2%
4	1972	186,145	94,994	JOHNSON, JAMES P.	91,151	MERSON, ALAN		3,843 R	51.0%	49.0%	51.0%	49.0%
5	1976	190,851	126,784	ARMSTRONG, WILLIAM L.	64,067	HORES, DOROTHY		62,717 R	66.4%	33.6%	66.4%	33.6%
5	1974	147,794	85,326	ARMSTRONG, WILLIAM L.	56,888	GALLOWAY, BEN	5,580	28,438 R	57.7%	38.5%	60.0%	40.0%
5	1972	167,190	104,214	ARMSTRONG, WILLIAM L.	60,948	JOHNSON, BYRON L.	2,028	43,266 R	62.3%	36.5%	63.1%	36.9%

COLORADO

1976 GENERAL ELECTION

President — Original uncorrected canvass gave the state-wide vote as follows: 284,278 Ford (Republican); 460,801 Carter (Democratic); 26,047 McCarthy (Independent); 5,338 MacBride (Libertarian); 2,886 Bubar (Prohibition); 1,122 Camejo (Socialist Workers); 565 LaRouche (U.S. Labor); 403 Hall (Communist). Write-in votes are from original canvass. Amendments were made in the following counties: Boulder, Las Animas, Moffat, Montrose and Saguache. Other vote was 26,107 McCarthy (Independent); 5,330 MacBride (Libertarian); 2,882 Bubar (Prohibition); 1,126 Camejo (Socialist Workers); 567 LaRouche (U.S. Labor); 403 Hall (Communist); 397 Anderson (write-in); 14 Levin (write-in); 6 Miller (write-in); 2 scattered.

Governor — The 1974 vote in the Postwar Vote for Governor table is a correction of earlier data published in AMERICA VOTES 11 (earlier figures were 378,907 Republican; 441,199 Democratic).

Congress — The 1974 vote in both CD's 3 and 4 is a correction of earlier data published in AMERICA VOTES 11 (earlier figures in CD 3 were 43,298 Republican; 91,783 Democratic and in CD 4 were 82,982 Republican; 76,452 Democratic). In 1976 the original uncorrected canvass gave the vote in CD 3 as 82,315 Republican; 89,320 Democratic and 3,615 Other, and the vote in CD 4 as 119,458 Republican; 76,995 Democratic. Other vote in 1976 was as follows:

CD 1 — 681 Schenk (Socialist Workers); 508 Meyers (U.S. Labor).
CD 3 — 2,426 Archer (Raza Unida); 1,181 Olshaw (Independent).
CD 4 — 20,398 Davis (Independent); 4,167 Thiel (Independent).

1976 PRIMARIES

SEPTEMBER 14 REPUBLICAN

Congress — Unopposed in three CD's. Contested as follows:

CD 1 — 13,751 Don Friedman; 6,391 John Gonce.
CD 2 — 17,020 Ed Scott; 7,526 Bob Dugan.

SEPTEMBER 14 DEMOCRATIC

Congress — Unopposed in four CD's. Contested as follows:

CD 3 — 30,200 Frank E. Evans; 9,697 William J. Gradishar.

CONNECTICUT

GOVERNOR

Ella T. Grasso (D). Elected 1974 to a four-year term.

SENATORS

Abraham A. Ribicoff (D). Re-elected 1974 to a six-year term. Previously elected 1968, 1962.

Lowell P. Weicker (R). Re-elected 1976 to a six-year term. Previously elected 1970.

REPRESENTATIVES

1. William R. Cotter (D)
2. Christopher J. Dodd (D)
3. Robert N. Giaimo (D)
4. Stewart B. McKinney (R)
5. Ronald A. Sarasin (R)
6. Anthony T. Moffett (D)

POSTWAR VOTE FOR GOVERNOR

								Percentage			
	Total	Republican		Democratic		Other	Rep.-Dem.	Total Vote		Major Vote	
Year	Vote	Vote	Candidate	Vote	Candidate	Vote	Plurality	Rep.	Dem.	Rep.	Dem.
1974	1,102,773	440,169	Steele, Robert H.	643,490	Grasso, Ella T.	19,114	203,321 D	39.9%	58.4%	40.6%	59.4%
1970	1,082,797	582,160	Meskill, Thomas J.	500,561	Daddario, Emilio	76	81,599 R	53.8%	46.2%	53.8%	46.2%
1966	1,008,557	446,536	Gengras, E. Clayton	561,599	Dempsey, John N.	422	115,063 D	44.3%	55.7%	44.3%	55.7%
1962	1,031,902	482,852	Alsop, John	549,027	Dempsey, John N.	23	66,175 D	46.8%	53.2%	46.8%	53.2%
1958	974,509	360,644	Zeller, Fred R.	607,012	Ribicoff, Abraham A.	6,853	246,368 D	37.0%	62.3%	37.3%	62.7%
1954	936,753	460,528	Lodge, John D.	463,643	Ribicoff, Abraham A.	12,582	3,115 D	49.2%	49.5%	49.8%	50.2%
1950	878,735	436,418	Lodge, John D.	419,404	Bowles, Chester	22,913	17,014 R	49.7%	47.7%	51.0%	49.0%
1948	875,170	429,071	Shannon, James C.	431,296	Bowles, Chester	14,803	2,225 D	49.0%	49.3%	49.9%	50.1%
1946	683,831	371,852	McConaughy, J. L.	276,335	Snow, Wilbert	35,644	95,517 R	54.4%	40.4%	57.4%	42.6%

The term of office of Connecticut's Governor was increased from two to four years effective with the 1950 election.

POSTWAR VOTE FOR SENATOR

								Percentage			
	Total	Republican		Democratic		Other	Rep.-Dem.	Total Vote		Major Vote	
Year	Vote	Vote	Candidate	Vote	Candidate	Vote	Plurality	Rep.	Dem.	Rep.	Dem.
1976	1,361,666	785,683	Weicker, Lowell P.	561,018	Schaffer, Gloria	14,965	224,665 R	57.7%	41.2%	58.3%	41.7%
1974	1,084,918	372,055	Brannen, James H.	690,820	Ribicoff, Abraham A.	22,043	318,765 D	34.3%	63.7%	35.0%	65.0%
1970	1,089,353	454,721	Weicker, Lowell P.	368,111	Duffey, Joseph D.	266,521	86,610 R	41.7%	33.8%	55.3%	44.7%
1968	1,206,537	551,455	May, Edwin H.	655,043	Ribicoff, Abraham A.	39	103,588 D	45.7%	54.3%	45.7%	54.3%
1964	1,208,163	426,939	Lodge, John D.	781,008	Dodd, Thomas J.	216	354,069 D	35.3%	64.6%	35.3%	64.7%
1962	1,029,301	501,694	Seely-Brown, Horace	527,522	Ribicoff, Abraham A.	85	25,828 D	48.7%	51.3%	48.7%	51.3%
1958	965,463	410,622	Purtell, William A.	554,841	Dodd, Thomas J.	–	144,219 D	42.5%	57.5%	42.5%	57.5%
1956	1,113,819	610,829	Bush, Prescott	479,460	Dodd, Thomas J.	23,530	131,369 R	54.8%	43.0%	56.0%	44.0%
1952	1,093,467	573,854	Purtell, William A.	485,066	Benton, William	34,547	88,788 R	52.5%	44.4%	54.2%	45.8%
1952s	1,093,268	559,465	Bush, Prescott	530,505	Ribicoff, Abraham A.	3,298	28,960 R	51.2%	48.5%	51.3%	48.7%
1950	877,827	409,053	Talbot, Joseph E.	453,646	McMahon, Brien	15,128	44,593 D	46.6%	51.7%	47.4%	52.6%
1950s	877,135	430,311	Bush, Prescott	431,413	Benton, William	15,411	1,102 D	49.1%	49.2%	49.9%	50.1%
1946	682,921	381,328	Baldwin, Raymond	276,424	Tone, Joseph M.	25,169	104,904 R	55.8%	40.5%	58.0%	42.0%

One each of the 1952 and 1950 elections was for a short term to fill a vacancy.

CONNECTICUT

Districts Established July 18, 1972

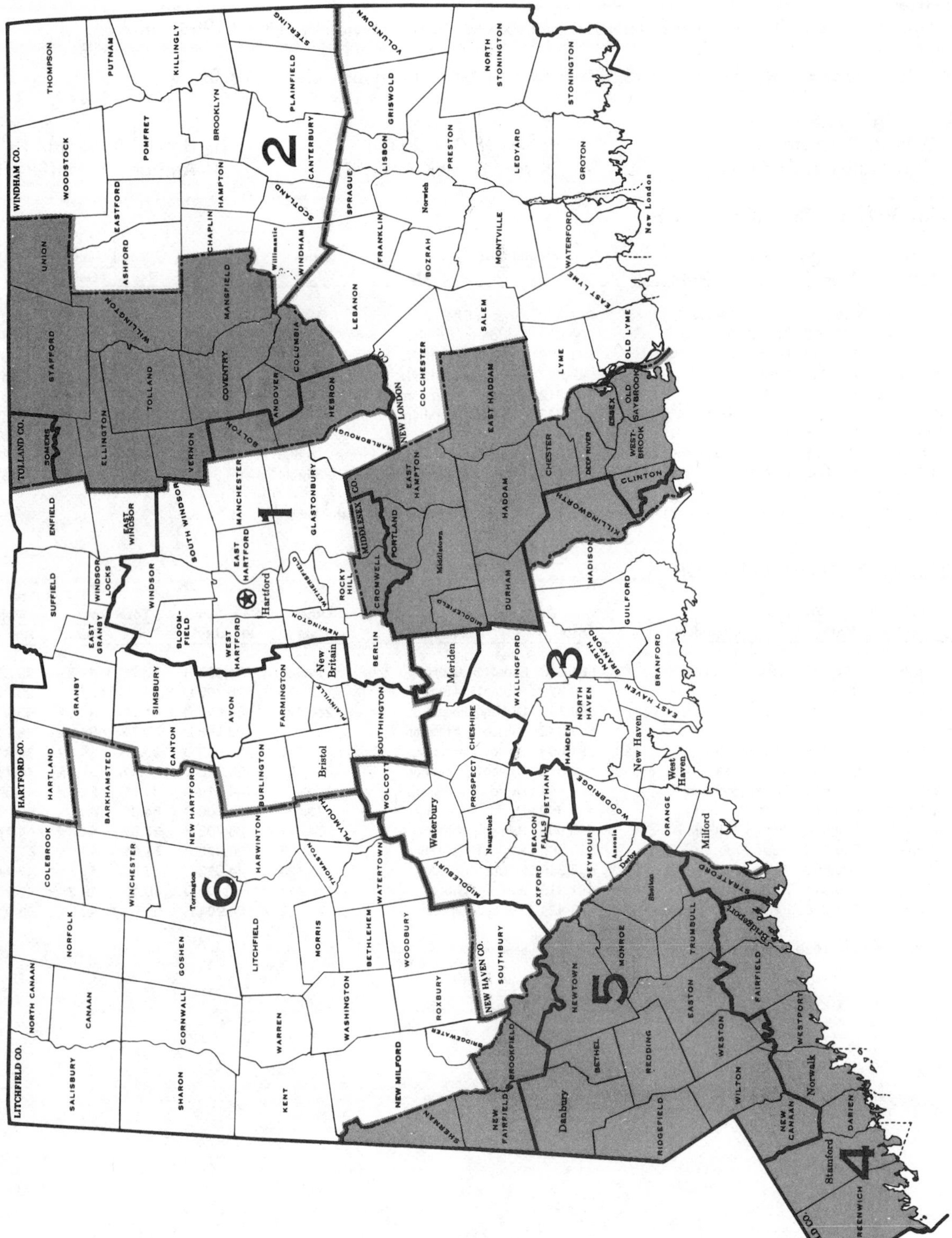

CONNECTICUT

PRESIDENT 1976

1970 Census Population	County	Total Vote	Republican	Democratic	Other	Rep.-Dem. Plurality	Percentage Total Vote Rep.	Total Vote Dem.	Major Vote Rep.	Major Vote Dem.
792,814	FAIRFIELD	360,224	209,458	148,353	2,413	61,105 R	58.1%	41.2%	58.5%	41.5%
816,737	HARTFORD	368,494	175,064	191,257	2,173	16,193 D	47.5%	51.9%	47.8%	52.2%
144,091	LITCHFIELD	73,583	40,705	32,419	459	8,286 R	55.3%	44.1%	55.7%	44.3%
115,018	MIDDLESEX	60,550	31,115	29,097	338	2,018 R	51.4%	48.1%	51.7%	48.3%
744,948	NEW HAVEN	334,189	174,342	157,402	2,445	16,940 R	52.2%	47.1%	52.6%	47.4%
230,654	NEW LONDON	93,720	47,231	45,908	581	1,323 R	50.4%	49.0%	50.7%	49.3%
103,440	TOLLAND	47,024	23,703	23,079	242	624 R	50.4%	49.1%	50.7%	49.3%
84,515	WINDHAM	38,262	17,643	20,380	239	2,737 D	46.1%	53.3%	46.4%	53.6%
3,032,217	TOTAL	1,381,526	719,261	647,895	14,370	71,366 R	52.1%	46.9%	52.6%	47.4%

SENATOR 1976

1970 Census Population	County	Total Vote	Republican	Democratic	Other	Rep.-Dem. Plurality	Percentage Total Vote Rep.	Total Vote Dem.	Major Vote Rep.	Major Vote Dem.
792,814	FAIRFIELD	354,677	218,877	131,125	4,675	87,752 R	61.7%	37.0%	62.5%	37.5%
816,737	HARTFORD	365,853	203,057	159,822	2,974	43,235 R	55.5%	43.7%	56.0%	44.0%
144,091	LITCHFIELD	72,891	43,429	28,842	620	14,587 R	59.6%	39.6%	60.1%	39.9%
115,018	MIDDLESEX	60,382	35,117	24,682	583	10,435 R	58.2%	40.9%	58.7%	41.3%
744,948	NEW HAVEN	330,914	188,924	137,262	4,728	51,662 R	57.1%	41.5%	57.9%	42.1%
230,654	NEW LONDON	92,324	49,992	41,592	740	8,400 R	54.1%	45.1%	54.6%	45.4%
103,440	TOLLAND	46,900	26,878	19,649	373	7,229 R	57.3%	41.9%	57.8%	42.2%
84,515	WINDHAM	37,725	19,409	18,044	272	1,365 R	51.4%	47.8%	51.8%	48.2%
3,032,217	TOTAL	1,361,666	785,683	561,018	14,965	224,665 R	57.7%	41.2%	58.3%	41.7%

CONNECTICUT

PRESIDENT 1976

1970 Census Population	City/Town	Total Vote	Republican	Democratic	Other	Rep.-Dem. Plurality	Percentage Total Vote Rep.	Total Vote Dem.	Major Vote Rep.	Major Vote Dem.
21,160	ANSONIA	8,888	4,539	4,293	56	246 R	51.1%	48.3%	51.4%	48.6%
20,444	BRANFORD	11,465	6,487	4,886	92	1,601 R	56.6%	42.6%	57.0%	43.0%
156,542	BRIDGEPORT	47,551	20,824	26,330	397	5,506 D	43.8%	55.4%	44.2%	55.8%
55,487	BRISTOL	24,654	11,151	13,330	173	2,179 D	45.2%	54.1%	45.5%	54.5%
50,781	DANBURY	22,322	11,777	10,379	166	1,398 R	52.8%	46.5%	53.2%	46.8%
20,411	DARIEN	10,812	7,992	2,784	36	5,208 R	73.9%	25.7%	74.2%	25.8%
57,583	EAST HARTFORD	24,409	10,178	14,052	179	3,874 D	41.7%	57.6%	42.0%	58.0%
25,120	EAST HAVEN	10,693	5,633	4,974	86	659 R	52.7%	46.5%	53.1%	46.9%
46,189	ENFIELD	18,291	7,344	10,845	102	3,501 D	40.2%	59.3%	40.4%	59.6%
56,487	FAIRFIELD TOWN	30,009	17,916	11,895	198	6,021 R	59.7%	39.6%	60.1%	39.9%
20,651	GLASTONBURY	12,664	7,634	4,952	78	2,682 R	60.3%	39.1%	60.7%	39.3%
59,755	GREENWICH	31,312	20,725	10,400	187	10,325 R	66.2%	33.2%	66.6%	33.4%
38,244	GROTON	11,891	6,432	5,386	73	1,046 R	54.1%	45.3%	54.4%	45.6%
49,357	HAMDEN	26,492	15,051	11,259	182	3,792 R	56.8%	42.5%	57.2%	42.8%
158,017	HARTFORD CITY	42,146	11,473	30,355	318	18,882 D	27.2%	72.0%	27.4%	72.6%
47,994	MANCHESTER	24,577	12,728	11,690	159	1,038 R	51.8%	47.6%	52.1%	47.9%
55,959	MERIDEN	24,608	11,785	12,656	167	871 D	47.9%	51.4%	48.2%	51.8%
36,924	MIDDLETOWN	17,047	6,954	9,981	112	3,027 D	40.8%	58.5%	41.1%	58.9%
50,858	MILFORD	22,216	12,927	9,147	142	3,780 R	58.2%	41.2%	58.6%	41.4%
23,034	NAUGATUCK	11,033	5,587	5,343	103	244 R	50.6%	48.4%	51.1%	48.9%
83,441	NEW BRITAIN	31,061	12,101	18,737	223	6,636 D	39.0%	60.3%	39.2%	60.8%
137,707	NEW HAVEN CITY	45,169	17,321	27,581	267	10,260 D	38.3%	61.1%	38.6%	61.4%
26,037	NEWINGTON	14,621	7,349	7,173	99	176 R	50.3%	49.1%	50.6%	49.4%
31,630	NEW LONDON CITY	10,510	4,519	5,897	94	1,378 D	43.0%	56.1%	43.4%	56.6%
22,194	NORTH HAVEN	11,755	7,005	4,671	79	2,334 R	59.6%	39.7%	60.0%	40.0%
79,113	NORWALK	32,150	18,176	13,724	250	4,452 R	56.5%	42.7%	57.0%	43.0%
41,739	NORWICH	14,744	6,649	8,001	94	1,352 D	45.1%	54.3%	45.4%	54.6%
27,165	SHELTON	13,090	8,056	4,938	96	3,118 R	61.5%	37.7%	62.0%	38.0%
30,946	SOUTHINGTON	14,725	7,347	7,295	83	52 R	49.9%	49.5%	50.2%	49.8%
108,798	STAMFORD	46,390	25,422	20,666	302	4,756 R	54.8%	44.5%	55.2%	44.8%
49,775	STRATFORD	24,981	13,908	10,885	188	3,023 R	55.7%	43.6%	56.1%	43.9%
31,952	TORRINGTON	15,388	7,231	8,057	100	826 D	47.0%	52.4%	47.3%	52.7%
31,394	TRUMBULL	16,586	10,277	6,194	115	4,083 R	62.0%	37.3%	62.4%	37.6%
27,237	VERNON	12,190	6,259	5,895	36	364 R	51.3%	48.4%	51.5%	48.5%
35,714	WALLINGFORD	16,388	8,492	7,802	94	690 R	51.8%	47.6%	52.1%	47.9%
108,033	WATERBURY	43,010	19,663	22,834	513	3,171 D	45.7%	53.1%	46.3%	53.7%
68,031	WEST HARTFORD	39,884	22,264	17,447	173	4,817 R	55.8%	43.7%	56.1%	43.9%
52,851	WEST HAVEN	24,209	12,267	11,758	184	509 R	50.7%	48.6%	51.1%	48.9%
27,414	WESTPORT	14,774	8,677	6,053	44	2,624 R	58.7%	41.0%	58.9%	41.1%
26,662	WETHERSFIELD	15,553	8,597	6,889	67	1,708 R	55.3%	44.3%	55.5%	44.5%
22,502	WINDSOR	12,503	6,184	6,249	70	65 D	49.5%	50.0%	49.7%	50.3%

CONNECTICUT

SENATOR 1976

1970 Census Population	City/Town	Total Vote	Republican	Democratic	Other	Rep.-Dem. Plurality	Percentage Total Vote Rep.	Percentage Total Vote Dem.	Percentage Major Vote Rep.	Percentage Major Vote Dem.
21,160	ANSONIA	8,771	4,968	3,712	91	1,256 R	56.6%	42.3%	57.2%	42.8%
20,444	BRANFORD	11,368	6,764	4,444	160	2,320 R	59.5%	39.1%	60.3%	39.7%
156,542	BRIDGEPORT	47,714	23,134	24,054	526	920 D	48.5%	50.4%	49.0%	51.0%
55,487	BRISTOL	24,544	13,338	10,958	248	2,380 R	54.3%	44.6%	54.9%	45.1%
50,781	DANBURY	21,937	12,117	9,602	218	2,515 R	55.2%	43.8%	55.8%	44.2%
20,411	DARIEN	10,425	7,695	2,582	148	5,113 R	73.8%	24.8%	74.9%	25.1%
57,583	EAST HARTFORD	24,369	12,340	11,822	207	518 R	50.6%	48.5%	51.1%	48.9%
25,120	EAST HAVEN	10,606	5,926	4,495	185	1,431 R	55.9%	42.4%	56.9%	43.1%
46,189	ENFIELD	18,227	9,223	8,863	141	360 R	50.6%	48.6%	51.0%	49.0%
56,487	FAIRFIELD TOWN	29,641	19,815	9,470	356	10,345 R	66.8%	31.9%	67.7%	32.3%
20,651	GLASTONBURY	12,624	8,180	4,298	146	3,882 R	64.8%	34.0%	65.6%	34.4%
59,755	GREENWICH	30,750	20,374	9,880	496	10,494 R	66.3%	32.1%	67.3%	32.7%
38,244	GROTON	11,693	6,658	4,952	83	1,706 R	56.9%	42.4%	57.3%	42.7%
49,357	HAMDEN	26,192	16,388	9,360	444	7,028 R	62.6%	35.7%	63.6%	36.4%
158,017	HARTFORD CITY	41,112	15,113	25,725	274	10,612 D	36.8%	62.6%	37.0%	63.0%
47,994	MANCHESTER	24,108	14,119	9,786	203	4,333 R	58.6%	40.6%	59.1%	40.9%
55,959	MERIDEN	24,540	13,766	10,498	276	3,268 R	56.1%	42.8%	56.7%	43.3%
36,924	MIDDLETOWN	17,002	8,608	8,254	140	354 R	50.6%	48.5%	51.0%	49.0%
50,858	MILFORD	21,981	13,797	7,873	311	5,924 R	62.8%	35.8%	63.7%	36.3%
23,034	NAUGATUCK	10,903	6,060	4,737	106	1,323 R	55.6%	43.4%	56.1%	43.9%
83,441	NEW BRITAIN	30,650	15,164	15,236	250	72 D	49.5%	49.7%	49.9%	50.1%
137,707	NEW HAVEN CITY	44,457	19,827	24,110	520	4,283 D	44.6%	54.2%	45.1%	54.9%
26,037	NEWINGTON	14,555	8,674	5,741	140	2,933 R	59.6%	39.4%	60.2%	39.8%
31,630	NEW LONDON CITY	10,299	4,825	5,378	96	553 D	46.8%	52.2%	47.3%	52.7%
22,194	NORTH HAVEN	11,687	7,465	4,016	206	3,449 R	63.9%	34.4%	65.0%	35.0%
79,113	NORWALK	31,550	18,725	12,375	450	6,350 R	59.4%	39.2%	60.2%	39.8%
41,739	NORWICH	14,358	7,212	7,057	89	155 R	50.2%	49.2%	50.5%	49.5%
27,165	SHELTON	13,038	8,486	4,365	187	4,121 R	65.1%	33.5%	66.0%	34.0%
30,946	SOUTHINGTON	14,666	8,392	6,160	114	2,232 R	57.2%	42.0%	57.7%	42.3%
108,798	STAMFORD	45,140	26,349	18,120	671	8,229 R	58.4%	40.1%	59.3%	40.7%
49,775	STRATFORD	24,627	14,856	9,434	337	5,422 R	60.3%	38.3%	61.2%	38.8%
31,952	TORRINGTON	15,339	8,044	7,194	101	850 R	52.4%	46.9%	52.8%	47.2%
31,394	TRUMBULL	16,373	10,973	5,193	207	5,780 R	67.0%	31.7%	67.9%	32.1%
27,237	VERNON	12,196	6,891	5,219	86	1,672 R	56.5%	42.8%	56.9%	43.1%
35,714	WALLINGFORD	16,216	9,443	6,553	220	2,890 R	58.2%	40.4%	59.0%	41.0%
108,033	WATERBURY	42,702	21,740	20,280	682	1,460 R	50.9%	47.5%	51.7%	48.3%
68,031	WEST HARTFORD	39,856	25,211	14,341	304	10,870 R	63.3%	36.0%	63.7%	36.3%
52,851	WEST HAVEN	23,853	12,685	10,824	344	1,861 R	53.2%	45.4%	54.0%	46.0%
27,414	WESTPORT	14,474	9,939	4,401	134	5,538 R	68.7%	30.4%	69.3%	30.7%
26,662	WETHERSFIELD	15,499	9,800	5,564	135	4,236 R	63.2%	35.9%	63.8%	36.2%
22,502	WINDSOR	12,465	7,131	5,238	96	1,893 R	57.2%	42.0%	57.7%	42.3%

CONNECTICUT

CONGRESS

CD	Year	Total Vote	Republican Vote	Republican Candidate	Democratic Vote	Democratic Candidate	Other Vote	Rep.-Dem. Plurality	Percentage Total Vote Rep.	Percentage Total Vote Dem.	Percentage Major Vote Rep.	Percentage Major Vote Dem.
1	1976	225,076	94,106	DI FAZIO, LUCIEN	128,479	COTTER, WILLIAM R.	2,491	34,373 D	41.8%	57.1%	42.3%	57.7%
1	1974	186,772	67,080	BUCKLEY, F. MAC	117,038	COTTER, WILLIAM R.	2,654	49,958 D	35.9%	62.7%	36.4%	63.6%
1	1972	229,682	96,188	RITTENBAND, RICHARD M.	130,701	COTTER, WILLIAM R.	2,793	34,513 D	41.9%	56.9%	42.4%	57.6%
2	1976	219,308	74,743	JACKSON, RICHARD M.	142,684	DODD, CHRISTOPHER J.	1,881	67,941 D	34.1%	65.1%	34.4%	65.6%
2	1974	176,949	69,380	HELLIER, SAMUEL B.	104,436	DODD, CHRISTOPHER J.	3,133	35,056 D	39.2%	59.0%	39.9%	60.1%
2	1972	215,512	142,094	STEELE, ROBERT H.	73,400	HILSMAN, ROGER	18	68,694 R	65.9%	34.1%	65.9%	34.1%
3	1976	222,643	96,714	PUCCIANO, JOHN G.	121,623	GIAIMO, ROBERT N.	4,306	24,909 D	43.4%	54.6%	44.3%	55.7%
3	1974	175,507	55,177	ALTHAM, JAMES	114,316	GIAIMO, ROBERT N.	6,014	59,139 D	31.4%	65.1%	32.6%	67.4%
3	1972	227,561	106,313	POVINELLI, HENRY A.	121,217	GIAIMO, ROBERT N.	31	14,904 D	46.7%	53.3%	46.7%	53.3%
4	1976	207,058	126,314	MCKINNEY, STEWART B.	76,722	PETERSON, GEOFFREY	4,022	49,592 R	61.0%	37.1%	62.2%	37.8%
4	1974	157,235	83,630	MCKINNEY, STEWART B.	71,047	KELLIS, JAMES G.	2,558	12,583 R	53.2%	45.2%	54.1%	45.9%
4	1972	215,433	135,883	MCKINNEY, STEWART B.	79,515	MCLOUGHLIN, JAMES P.	35	56,368 R	63.1%	36.9%	63.1%	36.9%
5	1976	236,087	157,009	SARASIN, RONALD A.	77,308	ADANTI, MICHAEL J.	1,770	79,701 R	66.5%	32.7%	67.0%	33.0%
5	1974	188,489	94,998	SARASIN, RONALD A.	90,407	RATCHFORD, WILLIAM	3,084	4,591 R	50.4%	48.0%	51.2%	48.8%
5	1972	229,731	117,578	SARASIN, RONALD A.	112,142	MONAGAN, JOHN S.	11	5,436 R	51.2%	48.8%	51.2%	48.8%
6	1976	238,300	102,364	UPSON, THOMAS F.	134,914	MOFFETT, ANTHONY T.	1,022	32,550 D	43.0%	56.6%	43.1%	56.9%
6	1974	193,581	69,942	PISCOPO, PATSY J.	122,785	MOFFETT, ANTHONY T.	854	52,843 D	36.1%	63.4%	36.3%	63.7%
6	1972	233,082	92,783	WALSH, JOHN F.	140,290	GRASSO, ELLA T.	9	47,507 D	39.8%	60.2%	39.8%	60.2%

CONNECTICUT

1976 GENERAL ELECTION

In addition to the county-by-county figures, 1976 data are presented for selected Connecticut communities. Since not all jurisdictions of the state are listed in this special tabulation, state-wide totals are shown only with the county-by-county statistics.

President — Other vote was 7,101 Maddox (George Wallace Party); 3,759 McCarthy (write-in); 1,789 LaRouche (U.S. Labor); 209 MacBride (write-in); 186 Hall (write-in); 155 Anderson (write-in); 42 Camejo (write-in); 5 Zeidler (write-in); 1 Levin (write-in); 1 Wright (write-in); 1,122 scattered. State-wide other vote total includes 5,480 write-in votes not available by county without overcounting votes for named electors. The overcount of write-in names was 10,309.

Senator — Other vote was 14,407 Barnabei (George Wallace Party); 558 scattered.

Congress — Other vote was as follows:

CD 1	1,326 Burke (George Wallace Party); 1,110 McDonough (U.S. Labor); 55 scattered.
CD 2	1,857 Discepolo (Independent); 24 scattered.
CD 3	2,947 Fishman (Communist); 1,339 Cossette (George Wallace Party); 20 scattered.
CD 4	3,318 Cunningham (George Wallace Party); 679 Solymossy (Conservative); 25 scattered.
CD 5	1,743 Kozak (George Wallace Party); 27 scattered.
CD 6	1,004 Marietta (Independent); 18 scattered.

1976 PRIMARIES

Party conventions nominate Connecticut candidates, subject to a system of "challenge" primaries. Any candidate who receives more than 20 percent of the convention vote is entitled to challenge the endorsed candidate in a primary. There was one such primary in 1976.

SEPTEMBER 4 DEMOCRATIC

Congress

CD 4 — 8,896 Geoffrey G. Peterson; 7,666 Charles B. Tisdale.

DELAWARE

GOVERNOR

Pierre duPont (R). Elected 1976 to a four-year term.

SENATORS

Joseph R. Biden (D). Elected 1972 to a six-year term.

William V. Roth (R). Re-elected 1976 to a six-year term. Previously elected 1970.

REPRESENTATIVE

At-Large. Thomas B. Evans (R)

POSTWAR VOTE FOR GOVERNOR

	Total	Republican		Democratic		Other	Rep.-Dem.	Percentage			
								Total Vote		Major Vote	
Year	Vote	Vote	Candidate	Vote	Candidate	Vote	Plurality	Rep.	Dem.	Rep.	Dem.
1976	229,563	130,531	duPont, Pierre	97,480	Tribbitt, Sherman W.	1,552	33,051 R	56.9%	42.5%	57.2%	42.8%
1972	228,722	109,583	Peterson, Russell W.	117,274	Tribbitt, Sherman W.	1,865	7,691 D	47.9%	51.3%	48.3%	51.7%
1968	206,834	104,474	Peterson, Russell W.	102,360	Terry, Charles L.	–	2,114 R	50.5%	49.5%	50.5%	49.5%
1964	200,171	97,374	Buckson, David P.	102,797	Terry, Charles L.	–	5,423 D	48.6%	51.4%	48.6%	51.4%
1960	194,835	94,043	Rollins, John W.	100,792	Carvel, Elbert N.	–	6,749 D	48.3%	51.7%	48.3%	51.7%
1956	177,012	91,965	Boggs, J. Caleb	85,047	McConnell, J. H. T.	–	6,918 R	52.0%	48.0%	52.0%	48.0%
1952	170,749	88,977	Boggs, J. Caleb	81,772	Carvel, Elbert N.	–	7,205 R	52.1%	47.9%	52.1%	47.9%
1948	140,335	64,996	George, Hyland P.	75,339	Carvel, Elbert N.	–	10,343 D	46.3%	53.7%	46.3%	53.7%

POSTWAR VOTE FOR SENATOR

	Total	Republican		Democratic		Other	Rep.-Dem.	Percentage			
								Total Vote		Major Vote	
Year	Vote	Vote	Candidate	Vote	Candidate	Vote	Plurality	Rep.	Dem.	Rep.	Dem.
1976	224,859	125,502	Roth, William V.	98,055	Maloney, Thomas C.	1,302	27,447 R	55.8%	43.6%	56.1%	43.9%
1972	229,828	12,844	Boggs, J. Caleb	116,006	Biden, Joseph R.	978	3,162 D	49.1%	50.5%	49.3%	50.7%
1970	161,439	94,979	Roth, William V.	64,740	Zimmerman, Jacob	1,720	30,239 R	58.8%	40.1%	59.5%	40.5%
1966	164,549	97,268	Boggs, J. Caleb	67,281	Tunnell, James M., Jr.	–	29,987 R	59.1%	40.9%	59.1%	40.9%
1964	200,703	103,782	Williams, John J.	96,850	Carvel, Elbert N.	71	6,932 R	51.7%	48.3%	51.7%	48.3%
1960	194,964	98,874	Boggs, J. Caleb	96,090	Frear, J. Allen	–	2,784 R	50.7%	49.3%	50.7%	49.3%
1958	154,432	82,280	Williams, John J.	72,152	Carvel, Elbert N.	–	10,128 R	53.3%	46.7%	53.3%	46.7%
1954	144,900	62,389	Warburton, H. B.	82,511	Frear, J. Allen	–	20,122 D	43.1%	56.9%	43.1%	56.9%
1952	170,705	93,020	Williams, John J.	77,685	Bayard, A. I. duP.	–	15,335 R	54.5%	45.5%	54.5%	45.5%
1948	141,362	68,246	Buck, C. Douglas	71,888	Frear, J. Allen	1,228	3,642 D	48.3%	50.9%	48.7%	51.3%
1946	113,513	62,603	Williams, John J.	50,910	Tunnell, James M.	–	11,693 R	55.2%	44.8%	55.2%	44.8%

DELAWARE

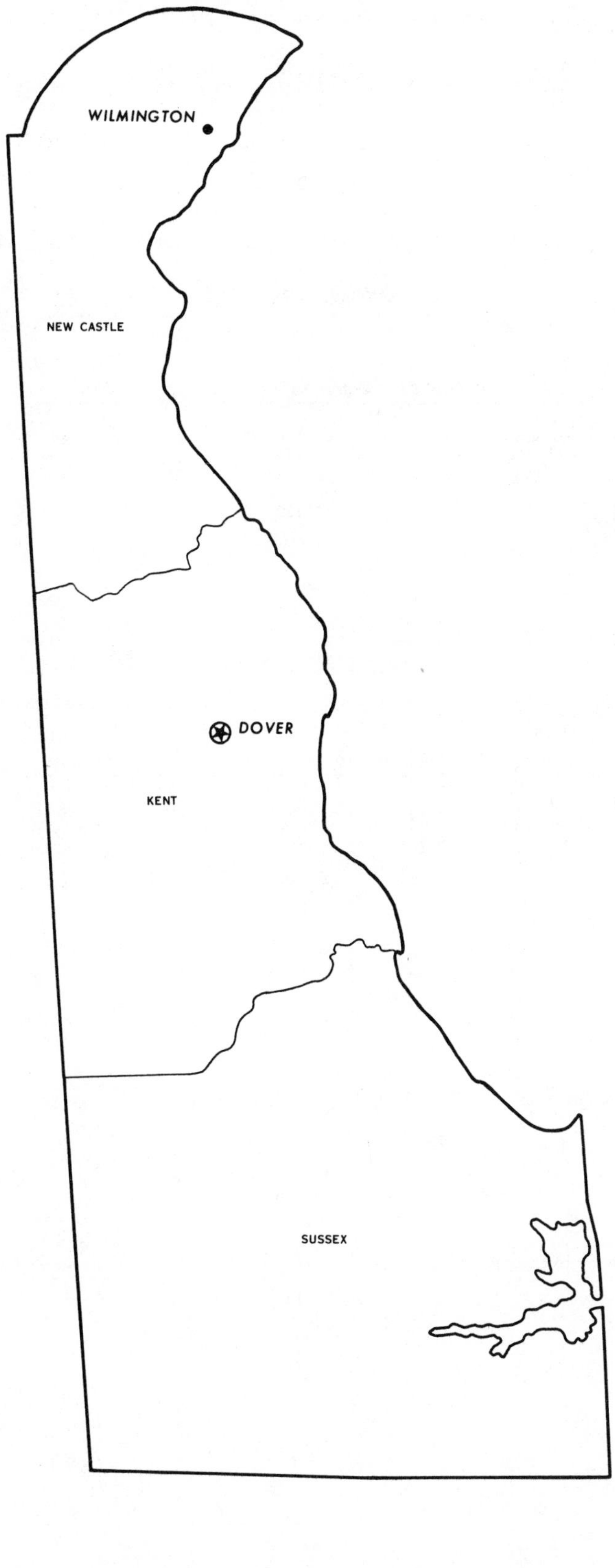

DELAWARE

PRESIDENT 1976

1970 Census Population	County	Total Vote	Republican	Democratic	Other	Rep.-Dem. Plurality	Percentage Total Vote Rep.	Total Vote Dem.	Major Vote Rep.	Major Vote Dem.
81,892	KENT	29,428	12,604	16,523	301	3,919 D	42.8%	56.1%	43.3%	56.7%
385,856	NEW CASTLE	170,338	80,074	87,521	2,743	7,447 D	47.0%	51.4%	47.8%	52.2%
80,356	SUSSEX	36,068	17,153	18,552	363	1,399 D	47.6%	51.4%	48.0%	52.0%
548,104	TOTAL	235,834	109,831	122,596	3,407	12,765 D	46.6%	52.0%	47.3%	52.7%

GOVERNOR 1976

1970 Census Population	County	Total Vote	Republican	Democratic	Other	Rep.-Dem. Plurality	Percentage Total Vote Rep.	Total Vote Dem.	Major Vote Rep.	Major Vote Dem.
81,892	KENT	28,802	11,849	16,540	413	4,691 D	41.1%	57.4%	41.7%	58.3%
385,856	NEW CASTLE	165,750	100,032	64,756	962	35,276 R	60.4%	39.1%	60.7%	39.3%
80,356	SUSSEX	35,011	18,650	16,184	177	2,466 R	53.3%	46.2%	53.5%	46.5%
548,104	TOTAL	229,563	130,531	97,480	1,552	33,051 R	56.9%	42.5%	57.2%	42.8%

SENATOR 1976

1970 Census Population	County	Total Vote	Republican	Democratic	Other	Rep.-Dem. Plurality	Percentage Total Vote Rep.	Total Vote Dem.	Major Vote Rep.	Major Vote Dem.
81,892	KENT	28,012	13,481	14,359	172	878 D	48.1%	51.3%	48.4%	51.6%
385,856	NEW CASTLE	162,828	93,267	68,610	951	24,657 R	57.3%	42.1%	57.6%	42.4%
80,356	SUSSEX	34,019	18,754	15,086	179	3,668 R	55.1%	44.3%	55.4%	44.6%
548,104	TOTAL	224,859	125,502	98,055	1,302	27,447 R	55.8%	43.6%	56.1%	43.9%

DELAWARE

CONGRESS

CD	Year	Total Vote	Republican Vote	Republican Candidate	Democratic Vote	Democratic Candidate	Other Vote	Rep.-Dem. Plurality	Percentage Total Vote Rep.	Percentage Total Vote Dem.	Percentage Major Vote Rep.	Percentage Major Vote Dem.
AL	1976	214,799	110,677	EVANS, THOMAS B.	102,431	SHIPLEY, SAMUEL L.	1,691	8,246 R	51.5%	47.7%	51.9%	48.1%
AL	1974	160,328	93,826	DUPONT, PIERRE	63,490	SOLES, JAMES	3,012	30,336 R	58.5%	39.6%	59.6%	40.4%
AL	1972	225,851	141,237	DUPONT, PIERRE	83,230	HANDLOFF, NORMA	1,384	58,007 R	62.5%	36.9%	62.9%	37.1%
AL	1970	160,313	86,125	DUPONT, PIERRE	71,429	DANIELLO, JOHN D.	2,759	14,696 R	53.7%	44.6%	54.7%	45.3%
AL	1968	200,820	117,827	ROTH, WILLIAM V.	82,993	MCDOWELL, HARRIS B.		34,834 R	58.7%	41.3%	58.7%	41.3%
AL	1966	163,103	90,961	ROTH, WILLIAM V.	72,142	MCDOWELL, HARRIS B.		18,819 R	55.8%	44.2%	55.8%	44.2%
AL	1964	198,691	86,254	SNOWDEN, JAMES H.	112,361	MCDOWELL, HARRIS B.	76	26,107 D	43.4%	56.6%	43.4%	56.6%
AL	1962	153,356	71,934	WILLIAMS, WILMER F.	81,166	MCDOWELL, HARRIS B.	256	9,232 D	46.9%	52.9%	47.0%	53.0%
AL	1960	194,564	96,337	MCKINSTRY, JAMES T.	98,227	MCDOWELL, HARRIS B.		1,890 D	49.5%	50.5%	49.5%	50.5%
AL	1958	152,896	76,099	HASKELL, HARRY G.	76,797	MCDOWELL, HARRIS B.		698 D	49.8%	50.2%	49.8%	50.2%
AL	1956	176,182	91,538	HASKELL, HARRY G.	84,644	MCDOWELL, HARRIS B.		6,894 R	52.0%	48.0%	52.0%	48.0%
AL	1954	144,236	65,035	MARTIN, LILLIAN	79,201	MCDOWELL, HARRIS B.		14,166 D	45.1%	54.9%	45.1%	54.9%
AL	1952	170,015	88,285	WARBURTON, H. B.	81,730	SCANNELL, JOSEPH S.		6,555 R	51.9%	48.1%	51.9%	48.1%
AL	1950	129,404	73,313	BOGGS, J. CALEB	56,091	WINCHESTER, H. M.		17,222 R	56.7%	43.3%	56.7%	43.3%
AL	1948	140,535	71,127	BOGGS, J. CALEB	68,909	MCGUIGAN, J. CARL	499	2,218 R	50.6%	49.0%	50.8%	49.2%
AL	1946	112,621	63,516	BOGGS, J. CALEB	49,105	TRAYNOR, PHILIP A.		14,411 R	56.4%	43.6%	56.4%	43.6%

DELAWARE

1976 GENERAL ELECTION

President — Other vote was 2,437 McCarthy (Non-Partisan); 645 Anderson (American); 136 LaRouche (U.S. Labor); 103 Bubar (Prohibition); 86 Levin (Socialist Labor). Original uncorrected canvass gave the vote in New Castle county as 80,023 Republican; 87,484 Democratic and 2,739 Other. The total state vote in the uncorrected canvass was 109,780 Republican; 122,559 Democratic; 3,403 Other.

Governor — Other vote was 1,255 Cripps (American); 297 Conner (Prohibition).

Senator — Other vote was 646 Gies (American); 440 McInerney (Non-Partisan); 216 Massimilla (Prohibition). Original uncorrected canvass gave the New Castle county vote as 93,219 Republican; 68,597 Democratic and 948 Other. The state-wide uncorrected totals were 125,454 Republican; 98,042 Democratic and 1,299 Other.

Congress — Other vote was 840 LoPresti (American); 347 Hollon (Socialist Labor); 346 Green (Prohibition); 158 Valenti (U.S. Labor). Original uncorrected canvass gave the vote at-large as 110,637 Republican; 102,411 Democratic; 1,690 Other.

1976 PRIMARIES

Party conventions nominate Delaware candidates, subject to a system of "challenge" primaries. Any candidate who receives at least 35 percent of the convention vote is entitled to challenge the endorsed candidate in a primary. No such primaries were held in 1976.

FLORIDA

GOVERNOR

Reubin Askew (D). Re-elected 1974 to a four-year term. Previously elected 1970.

SENATORS

Lawton Chiles (D). Re-elected 1976 to a six-year term. Previously elected 1970.

Richard Stone (D). Elected 1974 to a six-year term.

REPRESENTATIVES

1. Robert L. F. Sikes (D)
2. Don Fuqua (D)
3. Charles E. Bennett (D)
4. William V. Chappell (D)
5. Richard Kelly (R)
6. C. W. Young (R)
7. Sam M. Gibbons (D)
8. Andrew P. Ireland (D)
9. Louis Frey (R)
10. L. A. Bafalis (R)
11. Paul G. Rogers (D)
12. J. Herbert Burke (R)
13. William Lehman (D)
14. Claude Pepper (D)
15. Dante B. Fascell (D)

POSTWAR VOTE FOR GOVERNOR

	Total	Republican		Democratic		Other	Rep.-Dem.	Percentage			
								Total Vote		Major Vote	
Year	Vote	Vote	Candidate	Vote	Candidate	Vote	Plurality	Rep.	Dem.	Rep.	Dem.
1974	1,828,392	709,438	Thomas, Jerry	1,118,954	Askew, Reubin	–	409,516 D	38.8%	61.2%	38.8%	61.2%
1970	1,730,813	746,243	Kirk, Claude R.	984,305	Askew, Reubin	265	238,062 D	43.1%	56.9%	43.1%	56.9%
1966	1,489,661	821,190	Kirk, Claude R.	668,233	High, Robert King	238	152,957 R	55.1%	44.9%	55.1%	44.9%
1964s	1,663,481	686,297	Holley, Charles R.	933,554	Burns, Haydon	43,630	247,257 D	41.3%	56.1%	42.4%	57.6%
1960	1,419,343	569,936	Petersen, George C.	849,407	Bryant, Farris	–	279,471 D	40.2%	59.8%	40.2%	59.8%
1956	1,014,733	266,980	Washburne, W. A.	747,753	Collins, LeRoy	–	480,773 D	26.3%	73.7%	26.3%	73.7%
1954s	357,783	69,852	Watson, J. Tom	287,769	Collins, LeRoy	162	217,917 D	19.5%	80.4%	19.5%	80.5%
1952	834,518	210,009	Swan, Harry S.	624,463	McCarty, Dan	46	414,454 D	25.2%	74.8%	25.2%	74.8%
1948	457,638	76,153	Acker, Bert Lee	381,459	Warren, Fuller	26	305,306 D	16.6%	83.4%	16.6%	83.4%

The 1954 election was for a short term to fill a vacancy. The 1964 vote was for a two-year term to permit shifting the vote for Governor to non-Presidential years.

POSTWAR VOTE FOR SENATOR

	Total	Republican		Democratic		Other	Rep.-Dem.	Percentage			
								Total Vote		Major Vote	
Year	Vote	Vote	Candidate	Vote	Candidate	Vote	Plurality	Rep.	Dem.	Rep.	Dem.
1976	2,857,534	1,057,886	Grady, John	1,799,518	Chiles, Lawton	130	741,632 D	37.0%	63.0%	37.0%	63.0%
1974	1,800,539	736,674	Eckerd, Jack M.	781,031	Stone, Richard	282,834	44,357 D	40.9%	43.4%	48.5%	51.5%
1970	1,675,378	772,817	Cramer, William C.	902,438	Chiles, Lawton	123	129,621 D	46.1%	53.9%	46.1%	53.9%
1968	2,024,136	1,131,499	Gurney, Edward J.	892,637	Collins, LeRoy	–	238,862 R	55.9%	44.1%	55.9%	44.1%
1964	1,560,337	562,212	Kirk, Claude R.	997,585	Holland, Spessard L.	540	435,373 D	36.0%	63.9%	36.0%	64.0%
1962	939,207	281,381	Rupert, Emerson H.	657,633	Smathers, George A.	193	376,252 D	30.0%	70.0%	30.0%	70.0%
1958	542,069	155,956	Hyzer, Leland	386,113	Holland, Spessard L.	–	230,157 D	28.8%	71.2%	28.8%	71.2%
1956	655,418	–	–	655,418	Smathers, George A.	–	655,418 D	–	100.0%	–	100.0%
1952	617,800	–	–	616,665	Holland, Spessard L.	1,135	616,665 D	–	99.8%	–	100.0%
1950	313,487	74,228	Booth, John P.	238,987	Smathers, George A.	272	164,759 D	23.7%	76.2%	23.7%	76.3%
1946	198,640	42,408	Schad, J. Harry	156,232	Holland, Spessard L.	–	113,824 D	21.3%	78.7%	21.3%	78.7%

FLORIDA

Districts Established April 26, 1972

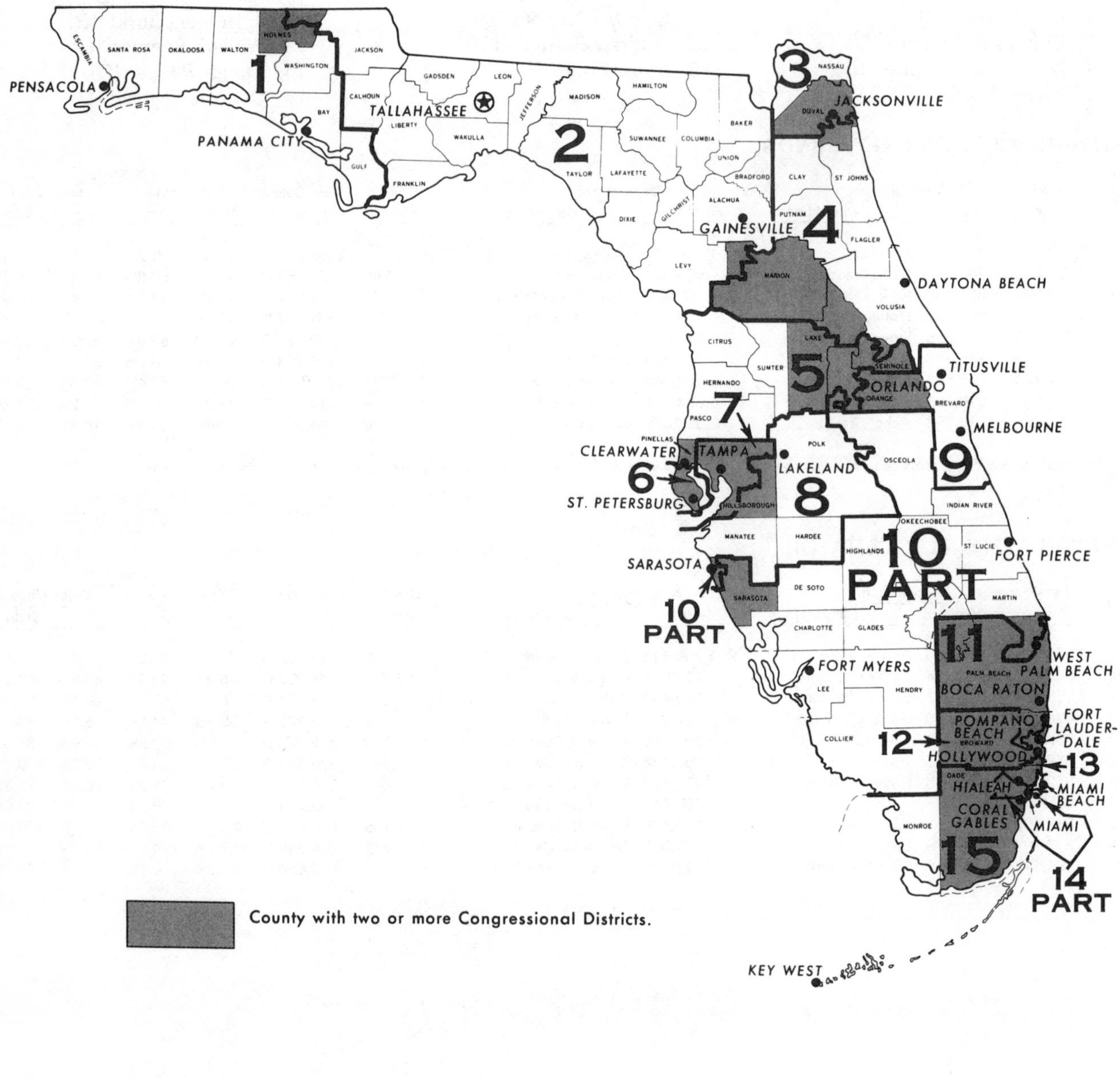

FLORIDA

PRESIDENT 1976

1970 Census Population	County	Total Vote	Republican	Democratic	Other	Rep.-Dem. Plurality	Percentage Total Vote Rep.	Percentage Total Vote Dem.	Percentage Major Vote Rep.	Percentage Major Vote Dem.
104,764	ALACHUA	44,578	15,546	27,895	1,137	12,349 D	34.9%	62.6%	35.8%	64.2%
9,242	BAKER	4,195	1,058	2,985	152	1,927 D	25.2%	71.2%	26.2%	73.8%
75,283	BAY	29,484	14,208	14,858	418	650 D	48.2%	50.4%	48.9%	51.1%
14,625	BRADFORD	5,617	1,680	3,868	69	2,188 D	29.9%	68.9%	30.3%	69.7%
230,006	BREVARD	92,364	44,470	46,421	1,473	1,951 D	48.1%	50.3%	48.9%	51.1%
620,100	BROWARD	342,343	161,411	176,491	4,441	15,080 D	47.1%	51.6%	47.8%	52.2%
7,624	CALHOUN	3,689	1,153	2,487	49	1,334 D	31.3%	67.4%	31.7%	68.3%
27,559	CHARLOTTE	23,333	12,703	10,300	330	2,403 R	54.4%	44.1%	55.2%	44.8%
19,196	CITRUS	17,707	7,973	9,438	296	1,465 D	45.0%	53.3%	45.8%	54.2%
32,059	CLAY	17,148	8,468	8,410	270	58 R	49.4%	49.0%	50.2%	49.8%
38,040	COLLIER	23,710	14,643	8,764	303	5,879 R	61.8%	37.0%	62.6%	37.4%
25,250	COLUMBIA	10,766	3,947	6,683	136	2,736 D	36.7%	62.1%	37.1%	62.9%
1,267,792	DADE	521,942	211,148	303,047	7,747	91,899 D	40.5%	58.1%	41.1%	58.9%
13,060	DE SOTO	4,822	2,000	2,715	107	715 D	41.5%	56.3%	42.4%	57.6%
5,480	DIXIE	2,752	558	2,169	25	1,611 D	20.3%	78.8%	20.5%	79.5%
528,865	DUVAL	182,561	74,997	105,912	1,652	30,915 D	41.1%	58.0%	41.5%	58.5%
205,334	ESCAMBIA	80,715	41,471	38,279	965	3,192 R	51.4%	47.4%	52.0%	48.0%
4,454	FLAGLER	3,373	1,262	2,086	25	824 D	37.4%	61.8%	37.7%	62.3%
7,065	FRANKLIN	2,973	1,054	1,859	60	805 D	35.5%	62.5%	36.2%	63.8%
39,184	GADSDEN	10,431	3,531	6,798	102	3,267 D	33.9%	65.2%	34.2%	65.8%
3,551	GILCHRIST	2,354	528	1,807	19	1,279 D	22.4%	76.8%	22.6%	77.4%
3,669	GLADES	1,965	624	1,311	30	687 D	31.8%	66.7%	32.2%	67.8%
10,096	GULF	4,281	1,584	2,641	56	1,057 D	37.0%	61.7%	37.5%	62.5%
7,787	HAMILTON	2,951	794	2,053	104	1,259 D	26.9%	69.6%	27.9%	72.1%
14,889	HARDEE	5,107	2,189	2,670	248	481 D	42.9%	52.3%	45.1%	54.9%
11,859	HENDRY	4,254	1,843	2,337	74	494 D	43.3%	54.9%	44.1%	55.9%
17,004	HERNANDO	13,732	5,793	7,717	222	1,924 D	42.2%	56.2%	42.9%	57.1%
29,507	HIGHLANDS	15,733	8,317	7,218	198	1,099 R	52.9%	45.9%	53.5%	46.5%
490,265	HILLSBOROUGH	175,145	78,504	94,589	2,052	16,085 D	44.8%	54.0%	45.4%	54.6%
10,720	HOLMES	5,180	1,850	3,256	74	1,406 D	35.7%	62.9%	36.2%	63.8%
35,992	INDIAN RIVER	18,654	9,818	8,512	324	1,306 R	52.6%	45.6%	53.6%	46.4%
34,434	JACKSON	12,652	4,795	7,687	170	2,892 D	37.9%	60.8%	38.4%	61.6%
8,778	JEFFERSON	3,749	1,361	2,310	78	949 D	36.3%	61.6%	37.1%	62.9%
2,892	LAFAYETTE	1,665	523	1,126	16	603 D	31.4%	67.6%	31.7%	68.3%
69,305	LAKE	34,787	19,976	14,369	442	5,607 R	57.4%	41.3%	58.2%	41.8%
105,216	LEE	69,789	38,038	30,567	1,184	7,471 R	54.5%	43.8%	55.4%	44.6%
103,047	LEON	53,443	23,739	28,729	975	4,990 D	44.4%	53.8%	45.2%	54.8%
12,756	LEVY	6,166	1,965	4,025	176	2,060 D	31.9%	65.3%	32.8%	67.2%
3,379	LIBERTY	1,776	620	1,137	19	517 D	34.9%	64.0%	35.3%	64.7%
13,481	MADISON	5,040	1,761	3,218	61	1,457 D	34.9%	63.8%	35.4%	64.6%
97,115	MANATEE	54,360	29,300	24,342	718	4,958 R	53.9%	44.8%	54.6%	45.4%
69,030	MARION	33,679	16,163	16,963	553	800 D	48.0%	50.4%	48.8%	51.2%
28,035	MARTIN	20,756	11,682	8,785	289	2,897 R	56.3%	42.3%	57.1%	42.9%
52,586	MONROE	19,757	8,232	11,079	446	2,847 D	41.7%	56.1%	42.6%	57.4%
20,626	NASSAU	9,140	3,136	5,896	108	2,760 D	34.3%	64.5%	34.7%	65.3%
88,187	OKALOOSA	33,295	18,598	14,210	487	4,388 R	55.9%	42.7%	56.7%	43.3%
11,233	OKEECHOBEE	4,825	1,598	3,184	43	1,586 D	33.1%	66.0%	33.4%	66.6%
344,311	ORANGE	130,437	70,451	58,442	1,544	12,009 R	54.0%	44.8%	54.7%	45.3%
25,267	OSCEOLA	14,175	7,062	6,893	220	169 R	49.8%	48.6%	50.6%	49.4%
348,753	PALM BEACH	198,657	98,236	96,705	3,716	1,531 R	49.5%	48.7%	50.4%	49.6%
75,955	PASCO	62,747	28,306	33,710	731	5,404 D	45.1%	53.7%	45.6%	54.4%
522,329	PINELLAS	295,569	150,003	141,879	3,687	8,124 R	50.8%	48.0%	51.4%	48.6%
227,222	POLK	92,706	44,238	47,286	1,182	3,048 D	47.7%	51.0%	48.3%	51.7%
36,290	PUTNAM	14,809	5,040	9,597	172	4,557 D	34.0%	64.8%	34.4%	65.6%
30,727	ST. JOHNS	14,371	6,660	7,412	299	752 D	46.3%	51.6%	47.3%	52.7%
50,836	ST. LUCIE	24,209	11,502	12,386	321	884 D	47.5%	51.2%	48.1%	51.9%
37,741	SANTA ROSA	17,412	9,122	8,020	270	1,102 R	52.4%	46.1%	53.2%	46.8%
120,413	SARASOTA	71,478	44,157	26,293	1,028	17,864 R	61.8%	36.8%	62.7%	37.3%
83,692	SEMINOLE	46,813	26,655	19,609	549	7,046 R	56.9%	41.9%	57.6%	42.4%
14,839	SUMTER	7,090	2,212	4,721	157	2,509 D	31.2%	66.6%	31.9%	68.1%
15,559	SUWANNEE	7,402	2,405	4,718	279	2,313 D	32.5%	63.7%	33.8%	66.2%
13,641	TAYLOR	5,406	1,983	3,370	53	1,387 D	36.7%	62.3%	37.0%	63.0%
8,112	UNION	2,040	544	1,480	16	936 D	26.7%	72.5%	26.9%	73.1%
169,487	VOLUSIA	88,225	37,523	49,161	1,541	11,638 D	42.5%	55.7%	43.3%	56.7%
6,308	WAKULLA	4,072	1,580	2,353	139	773 D	38.8%	57.8%	40.2%	59.8%
16,087	WALTON	8,279	2,927	5,196	156	2,269 D	35.4%	62.8%	36.0%	64.0%
11,453	WASHINGTON	5,996	2,313	3,566	117	1,253 D	38.6%	59.5%	39.3%	60.7%
6,789,443	TOTAL	3,150,631	1,469,531	1,636,000	45,100	166,469 D	46.6%	51.9%	47.3%	52.7%

FLORIDA

SENATOR 1976

1970 Census Population	County	Total Vote	Republican	Democratic	Other	Rep.-Dem. Plurality	Percentage Total Vote Rep.	Percentage Total Vote Dem.	Percentage Major Vote Rep.	Percentage Major Vote Dem.
104,764	ALACHUA	40,157	7,809	32,348		24,539 D	19.4%	80.6%	19.4%	80.6%
9,242	BAKER	3,572	1,000	2,572		1,572 D	28.0%	72.0%	28.0%	72.0%
75,283	BAY	26,831	10,371	16,460		6,089 D	38.7%	61.3%	38.7%	61.3%
14,625	BRADFORD	5,470	1,367	4,103		2,736 D	25.0%	75.0%	25.0%	75.0%
230,006	BREVARD	87,885	30,744	57,141		26,397 D	35.0%	65.0%	35.0%	65.0%
620,100	BROWARD	317,624	118,450	199,146	28	80,696 D	37.3%	62.7%	37.3%	62.7%
7,624	CALHOUN	3,222	890	2,332		1,442 D	27.6%	72.4%	27.6%	72.4%
27,559	CHARLOTTE	19,660	9,108	10,552		1,444 D	46.3%	53.7%	46.3%	53.7%
19,196	CITRUS	16,334	6,422	9,912		3,490 D	39.3%	60.7%	39.3%	60.7%
32,059	CLAY	15,845	6,345	9,500		3,155 D	40.0%	60.0%	40.0%	60.0%
38,040	COLLIER	21,863	11,308	10,554	1	754 R	51.7%	48.3%	51.7%	48.3%
25,250	COLUMBIA	9,649	2,830	6,819		3,989 D	29.3%	70.7%	29.3%	70.7%
1,267,792	DADE	444,324	139,501	304,770	53	165,269 D	31.4%	68.6%	31.4%	68.6%
13,060	DE SOTO	4,203	1,381	2,822		1,441 D	32.9%	67.1%	32.9%	67.1%
5,480	DIXIE	2,687	359	2,328		1,969 D	13.4%	86.6%	13.4%	86.6%
528,865	DUVAL	163,394	57,702	105,674	18	47,972 D	35.3%	64.7%	35.3%	64.7%
205,334	ESCAMBIA	74,045	25,369	48,676		23,307 D	34.3%	65.7%	34.3%	65.7%
4,454	FLAGLER	3,076	930	2,145	1	1,215 D	30.2%	69.7%	30.2%	69.8%
7,065	FRANKLIN	2,592	768	1,824		1,056 D	29.6%	70.4%	29.6%	70.4%
39,184	GADSDEN	9,029	2,589	6,440		3,851 D	28.7%	71.3%	28.7%	71.3%
3,551	GILCHRIST	2,315	333	1,982		1,649 D	14.4%	85.6%	14.4%	85.6%
3,669	GLADES	1,898	603	1,295		692 D	31.8%	68.2%	31.8%	68.2%
10,096	GULF	3,824	1,133	2,691		1,558 D	29.6%	70.4%	29.6%	70.4%
7,787	HAMILTON	2,486	673	1,813		1,140 D	27.1%	72.9%	27.1%	72.9%
14,889	HARDEE	4,761	1,919	2,842		923 D	40.3%	59.7%	40.3%	59.7%
11,859	HENDRY	3,976	1,878	2,098		220 D	47.2%	52.8%	47.2%	52.8%
17,004	HERNANDO	12,403	4,433	7,970		3,537 D	35.7%	64.3%	35.7%	64.3%
29,507	HIGHLANDS	14,453	6,688	7,764	1	1,076 D	46.3%	53.7%	46.3%	53.7%
490,265	HILLSBOROUGH	166,466	48,575	117,891		69,316 D	29.2%	70.8%	29.2%	70.8%
10,720	HOLMES	4,761	1,369	3,392		2,023 D	28.8%	71.2%	28.8%	71.2%
35,992	INDIAN RIVER	16,970	8,110	8,860		750 D	47.8%	52.2%	47.8%	52.2%
34,434	JACKSON	11,085	3,734	7,351		3,617 D	33.7%	66.3%	33.7%	66.3%
8,778	JEFFERSON	3,302	1,066	2,236		1,170 D	32.3%	67.7%	32.3%	67.7%
2,892	LAFAYETTE	1,296	408	888		480 D	31.5%	68.5%	31.5%	68.5%
69,305	LAKE	32,329	14,771	17,558		2,787 D	45.7%	54.3%	45.7%	54.3%
105,216	LEE	66,104	30,683	35,421		4,738 D	46.4%	53.6%	46.4%	53.6%
103,047	LEON	48,309	15,384	32,919	6	17,535 D	31.8%	68.1%	31.8%	68.2%
12,756	LEVY	5,483	1,309	4,173	1	2,864 D	23.9%	76.1%	23.9%	76.1%
3,379	LIBERTY	1,637	476	1,161		685 D	29.1%	70.9%	29.1%	70.9%
13,481	MADISON	3,608	1,287	2,321		1,034 D	35.7%	64.3%	35.7%	64.3%
97,115	MANATEE	50,598	22,546	28,052		5,506 D	44.6%	55.4%	44.6%	55.4%
69,030	MARION	30,879	13,570	17,309		3,739 D	43.9%	56.1%	43.9%	56.1%
28,035	MARTIN	18,660	9,320	9,340		20 D	49.9%	50.1%	49.9%	50.1%
52,586	MONROE	17,172	5,316	11,856		6,540 D	31.0%	69.0%	31.0%	69.0%
20,626	NASSAU	8,235	2,548	5,687		3,139 D	30.9%	69.1%	30.9%	69.1%
88,187	OKALOOSA	31,753	11,716	20,037		8,321 D	36.9%	63.1%	36.9%	63.1%
11,233	OKEECHOBEE	4,259	1,383	2,876		1,493 D	32.5%	67.5%	32.5%	67.5%
344,311	ORANGE	120,130	46,175	73,954	1	27,779 D	38.4%	61.6%	38.4%	61.6%
25,267	OSCEOLA	13,175	5,320	7,855		2,535 D	40.4%	59.6%	40.4%	59.6%
348,753	PALM BEACH	181,642	79,988	101,647	7	21,659 D	44.0%	56.0%	44.0%	56.0%
75,955	PASCO	56,073	22,037	34,036		11,999 D	39.3%	60.7%	39.3%	60.7%
522,329	PINELLAS	272,712	115,794	156,910	8	41,116 D	42.5%	57.5%	42.5%	57.5%
227,222	POLK	87,810	30,042	57,767	1	27,725 D	34.2%	65.8%	34.2%	65.8%
36,290	PUTNAM	13,699	4,390	9,309		4,919 D	32.0%	68.0%	32.0%	68.0%
30,727	ST. JOHNS	13,161	5,660	7,497	4	1,837 D	43.0%	57.0%	43.0%	57.0%
50,836	ST. LUCIE	21,292	9,730	11,562		1,832 D	45.7%	54.3%	45.7%	54.3%
37,741	SANTA ROSA	16,349	5,630	10,719		5,089 D	34.4%	65.6%	34.4%	65.6%
120,413	SARASOTA	64,159	30,092	34,067		3,975 D	46.9%	53.1%	46.9%	53.1%
83,692	SEMINOLE	40,821	17,043	23,778		6,735 D	41.8%	58.2%	41.8%	58.2%
14,839	SUMTER	6,045	1,703	4,342		2,639 D	28.2%	71.8%	28.2%	71.8%
15,559	SUWANNEE	6,634	2,251	4,383		2,132 D	33.9%	66.1%	33.9%	66.1%
13,641	TAYLOR	5,042	1,512	3,530		2,018 D	30.0%	70.0%	30.0%	70.0%
8,112	UNION	1,903	433	1,470		1,037 D	22.8%	77.2%	22.8%	77.2%
169,487	VOLUSIA	79,699	28,376	51,323		22,947 D	35.6%	64.4%	35.6%	64.4%
6,308	WAKULLA	3,564	1,438	2,126		688 D	40.3%	59.7%	40.3%	59.7%
16,087	WALTON	7,716	2,124	5,592		3,468 D	27.5%	72.5%	27.5%	72.5%
11,453	WASHINGTON	5,424	1,674	3,750		2,076 D	30.9%	69.1%	30.9%	69.1%
6,789,443	TOTAL	2,857,534	1,057,886	1,799,518	130	741,632 D	37.0%	63.0%	37.0%	63.0%

FLORIDA

CONGRESS

CD	Year	Total Vote	Republican Vote	Republican Candidate	Democratic Vote	Democratic Candidate	Other Vote	Rep.-Dem. Plurality	Percentage Total Vote Rep.	Total Vote Dem.	Major Vote Rep.	Major Vote Dem.
1	1976					SIKES, ROBERT L. F.						
1	1974					SIKES, ROBERT L. F.						
1	1972					SIKES, ROBERT L. F.						
2	1976					FUQUA, DON						
2	1974					FUQUA, DON						
2	1972					FUQUA, DON						
3	1976					BENNETT, CHARLES E.						
3	1974					BENNETT, CHARLES E.						
3	1972	123,660	22,219	BOWEN, JOHN F.	101,441	BENNETT, CHARLES E.		79,222 D	18.0%	82.0%	18.0%	82.0%
4	1976					CHAPPELL, WILLIAM V.						
4	1974	109,587	34,867	HAUSER, WARREN	74,720	CHAPPELL, WILLIAM V.		39,853 D	31.8%	68.2%	31.8%	68.2%
4	1972	165,501	72,960	FLEUCHAUS, P. T.	92,541	CHAPPELL, WILLIAM V.		19,581 D	44.1%	55.9%	44.1%	55.9%
5	1976	234,631	138,371	KELLY, RICHARD	96,260	SAUNDERS, JOANN		42,111 R	59.0%	41.0%	59.0%	41.0%
5	1974	142,088	74,954	KELLY, RICHARD	63,610	SAUNDERS, JOANN	3,524	11,344 R	52.8%	44.8%	54.1%	45.9%
5	1972	176,380	78,468	INSCO, JACK P.	97,902	GUNTER, WILLIAM D.	10	19,434 D	44.5%	55.5%	44.5%	55.5%
6	1976	232,218	151,371	YOUNG, C. W.	80,821	CAZARES, GABRIEL	26	70,550 R	65.2%	34.8%	65.2%	34.8%
6	1974	144,188	109,302	YOUNG, C. W.	34,886	MONROSE, MICKEY		74,416 R	75.8%	24.2%	75.8%	24.2%
6	1972	205,549	156,150	YOUNG, C. W.	49,399	PLUNKETT, MICHAEL O.		106,751 R	76.0%	24.0%	76.0%	24.0%
7	1976	156,338	53,599	OWENS, DUSTY	102,739	GIBBONS, SAM M.		49,140 D	34.3%	65.7%	34.3%	65.7%
7	1974					GIBBONS, SAM M.						
7	1972	135,274	43,343	CARTER, ROBERT A.	91,931	GIBBONS, SAM M.		48,588 D	32.0%	68.0%	32.0%	68.0%
8	1976	178,154	74,794	JOHNSON, ROBERT	103,360	IRELAND, ANDREW P.		28,566 D	42.0%	58.0%	42.0%	58.0%
8	1974	111,523	48,240	LOVINGOOD, JOE Z.	63,283	HALEY, JAMES A.		15,043 D	43.3%	56.7%	43.3%	56.7%
8	1972	153,988	64,920	THOMPSON, ROY	89,068	HALEY, JAMES A.		24,148 D	42.2%	57.8%	42.2%	57.8%
9	1976	167,139	130,509	FREY, LOUIS	36,630	ROSIER, JOSEPH A.		93,879 R	78.1%	21.9%	78.1%	21.9%
9	1974	112,481	86,226	FREY, LOUIS	26,255	ROWLAND, WILLIAM D.		59,971 R	76.7%	23.3%	76.7%	23.3%
9	1972			FREY, LOUIS								
10	1976	247,686	164,273	BAFALIS, L. A.	83,413	SIKES, BILL		80,860 R	66.3%	33.7%	66.3%	33.7%
10	1974	159,293	117,368	BAFALIS, L. A.	41,925	TUCKER, EVELYN		75,443 R	73.7%	26.3%	73.7%	26.3%
10	1972	182,963	113,461	BAFALIS, L. A.	69,502	SIKES, BILL		43,959 R	62.0%	38.0%	62.0%	38.0%
11	1976	218,437			199,031	ROGERS, PAUL G.	19,406	199,031 D		91.1%		100.0%
11	1974					ROGERS, PAUL G.						
11	1972	192,896	76,739	GUSTAFSON, JOEL KARL	116,157	ROGERS, PAUL G.		39,418 D	39.8%	60.2%	39.8%	60.2%
12	1976	199,076	107,268	BURKE, J. HERBERT	91,749	FRIEDMAN, CHARLES	59	15,519 R	53.9%	46.1%	53.9%	46.1%
12	1974	120,090	61,191	BURKE, J. HERBERT	58,899	FRIEDMAN, CHARLES		2,292 R	51.0%	49.0%	51.0%	49.0%
12	1972	176,276	110,750	BURKE, J. HERBERT	65,526	STEPHANIS, JAMES T.		45,224 R	62.8%	37.2%	62.8%	37.2%
13	1976	163,179	35,357	SPIEGELMAN, LEE A.	127,822	LEHMAN, WILLIAM		92,465 D	21.7%	78.3%	21.7%	78.3%
13	1974					LEHMAN, WILLIAM						
13	1972	149,676	57,418	BETHEL, PAUL D.	92,258	LEHMAN, WILLIAM		34,840 D	38.4%	61.6%	38.4%	61.6%
14	1976	113,439	30,774	ESTRELLA, EVELIO S.	82,665	PEPPER, CLAUDE		51,891 D	27.1%	72.9%	27.1%	72.9%
14	1974	65,862	20,383	CARRICARTE, MICHAEL A.	45,479	PEPPER, CLAUDE		25,096 D	30.9%	69.1%	30.9%	69.1%
14	1972	111,066	35,935	ESTRELLA, EVELIO S.	75,131	PEPPER, CLAUDE		39,196 D	32.4%	67.6%	32.4%	67.6%
15	1976	172,233	50,941	COBB, PAUL R.	121,292	FASCELL, DANTE B.		70,351 D	29.6%	70.4%	29.6%	70.4%
15	1974	96,508	28,444	CAPUA, S. PETER	68,064	FASCELL, DANTE B.		39,620 D	29.5%	70.5%	29.5%	70.5%
15	1972	158,281	68,320	RUBIN, ELLIS S.	89,961	FASCELL, DANTE B.		21,641 D	43.2%	56.8%	43.2%	56.8%

FLORIDA

1976 GENERAL ELECTION

President — Other vote was 23,643 McCarthy (Independent); 21,325 Anderson (American); 103 MacBride (write-in); 19 Levin (write-in); 8 Zeidler (write-in); 2 Miller (write-in).

Senator — Other vote was 123 Ice (write-in); 7 Adams (write-in).

Congress — Under present legislation, votes are not tallied in unopposed elections, so no total vote or candidate vote is available for unopposed Congressional elections. Other vote was scattered in CD's 6 and 12; Adams (American) in CD 11.

1976 PRIMARIES

SEPTEMBER 7 REPUBLICAN

Senator — 164,644 John Grady; 74,684 Walter Sims; 62,718 Helen S. Hansel.

Congress — Unopposed in eight CD's. No candidates in CD's 1, 2, 3, 4, and 11. Contested as follows:

CD 8 — 14,447 Robert Johnson; 11,399 Joe Z. Lovingood; 2,410 Lex Taylor; 2,065 David M. Molthrop.
CD 14 — 3,174 Evelio S. Estrella; 2,404 Herbert J. Hoodwin.

SEPTEMBER 7 DEMOCRATIC

Senator — Lawton Chiles, unopposed.

Congress — Unopposed in six CD's. Contested as follows:

CD 1 — 85,473 Robert L. F. Sikes; 31,441 John J. Benton.
CD 2 — 64,505 Don Fuqua; 41,398 Russell R. Bevis; 22,396 Jack Armstrong.
CD 4 — 55,511 William V. Chappell; 19,430 J. O. Townley; 8,035 Tommy Boney.
CD 5 — 34,982 JoAnn Saunders; 15,053 Miller Newton; 9,536 Sid Vihlen; 7,529 Don T. Reynolds; 3,094 James E. Sursely.
CD 8 — 36,048 Andrew P. Ireland; 14,876 Ray Mattox; 11,703 Jerome Pratt; 3,338 T. David Burns; 3,213 William A. Hartman; 1,251 William Willner.
CD 9 — 26,757 Joseph A. Rosier; 11,997 Frank J. Dama.
CD 10 — 38,244 Bill Sikes; 21,582 Robert F. Culpepper; 14,025 G. W. Bowers.
CD 12 — 12,452 Anne Kolb; 8,950 Charles Friedman; 5,172 Art Barker; 5,134 Andrew DeGraffenreidt; 5,125 John Lomelo; 4,523 Fred Lippman; 2,291 Joseph K. O'Brien; 1,765 Bill Brown.
CD 13 — 37,569 William Lehman; 7,866 Robert Renick; 5,798 E. C. Ackerman; 1,234 Dick Watson.

SEPTEMBER 28 REPUBLICAN RUN-OFF

Congress

CD 8 — 11,576 Robert Johnson; 7,776 Joe Z. Lovingood.

SEPTEMBER 28 DEMOCRATIC RUN-OFF

Congress

CD 5 — 30,534 JoAnn Saunders; 21,347 Miller Newton.
CD 12 — 16,032 Charles Friedman; 14,351 Anne Kolb.

GEORGIA

GOVERNOR

George Busbee (D). Elected 1974 to a four-year term.

SENATORS

Sam Nunn (D). Elected 1972 to a six-year term.

Herman Talmadge (D). Re-elected 1974 to a six-year term. Previously elected 1968, 1962, 1956.

REPRESENTATIVES

1. Ronald B. Ginn (D)
2. Dawson Mathis (D)
3. Jack Brinkley (D)
4. Elliott H. Levitas (D)
5. Andrew Young (D)
6. John J. Flynt (D)
7. Larry McDonald (D)
8. Billy Lee Evans (D)
9. Ed Jenkins (D)
10. Doug Barnard (D)

POSTWAR VOTE FOR GOVERNOR

	Total	Republican		Democratic		Other	Rep.-Dem.	Percentage			
								Total Vote		Major Vote	
Year	Vote	Vote	Candidate	Vote	Candidate	Vote	Plurality	Rep.	Dem.	Rep.	Dem.
1974	936,438	289,113	Thompson, Ronnie	646,777	Busbee, George	548	357,664 D	30.9%	69.1%	30.9%	69.1%
1970	1,046,663	424,983	Suit, Hal	620,419	Carter, Jimmy	1,261	195,436 D	40.6%	59.3%	40.7%	59.3%
1966	975,019	453,665	Callaway, Howard H.	450,626	Maddox, Lester	70,728	3,039 R	46.5%	46.2%	50.2%	49.8%
1962	311,691	–	–	311,524	Sanders, Carl E.	167	311,524 D	–	99.9%	–	100.0%
1958	168,497	–	–	168,414	Vandiver, Ernest	83	168,414 D	–	100.0%	–	100.0%
1954	331,966	–	–	331,899	Griffin, Marvin	67	331,899 D	–	100.0%	–	100.0%
1950	234,430	–	–	230,771	Talmadge, Herman	3,659	230,771 D	–	98.4%	–	100.0%
1948s	363,763	–	–	354,711	Talmadge, Herman	9,052	354,711 D	–	97.5%	–	100.0%
1946	145,403	–	–	143,279	Talmadge, Eugene	2,124	143,279 D	–	98.5%	–	100.0%

The 1948 election was for a short term to fill a vacancy. In 1966, in the absence of a majority for any candidate, the state legislature elected Lester Maddox to a four-year term.

POSTWAR VOTE FOR SENATOR

	Total	Republican		Democratic		Other	Rep.-Dem.	Percentage			
								Total Vote		Major Vote	
Year	Vote	Vote	Candidate	Vote	Candidate	Vote	Plurality	Rep.	Dem.	Rep.	Dem.
1974	874,555	246,866	Johnson, Jerry R.	627,376	Talmadge, Herman	313	380,510 D	28.2%	71.7%	28.2%	71.8%
1972	1,178,708	542,331	Thompson, Fletcher	635,970	Nunn, Sam	407	93,639 D	46.0%	54.0%	46.0%	54.0%
1968	1,141,889	256,796	Patton, E. Earl	885,093	Talmadge, Herman	–	628,297 D	22.5%	77.5%	22.5%	77.5%
1966	622,371	–	–	622,043	Russell, Richard B.	328	622,043 D	–	99.9%	–	100.0%
1962	306,250	–	–	306,250	Talmadge, Herman	–	306,250 D	–	100.0%	–	100.0%
1960	576,495	–	–	576,140	Russell, Richard B.	355	576,140 D	–	99.9%	–	100.0%
1956	541,267	–	–	541,094	Talmadge, Herman	173	541,094 D	–	100.0%	–	100.0%
1954	333,936	–	–	333,917	Russell, Richard B.	19	333,917 D	–	100.0%	–	100.0%
1950	261,293	–	–	261,290	George, Walter F.	3	261,290 D	–	100.0%	–	100.0%
1948	362,504	–	–	362,104	Russell, Richard B.	400	362,104 D	–	99.9%	–	100.0%

GEORGIA

Districts Established March 16, 1972

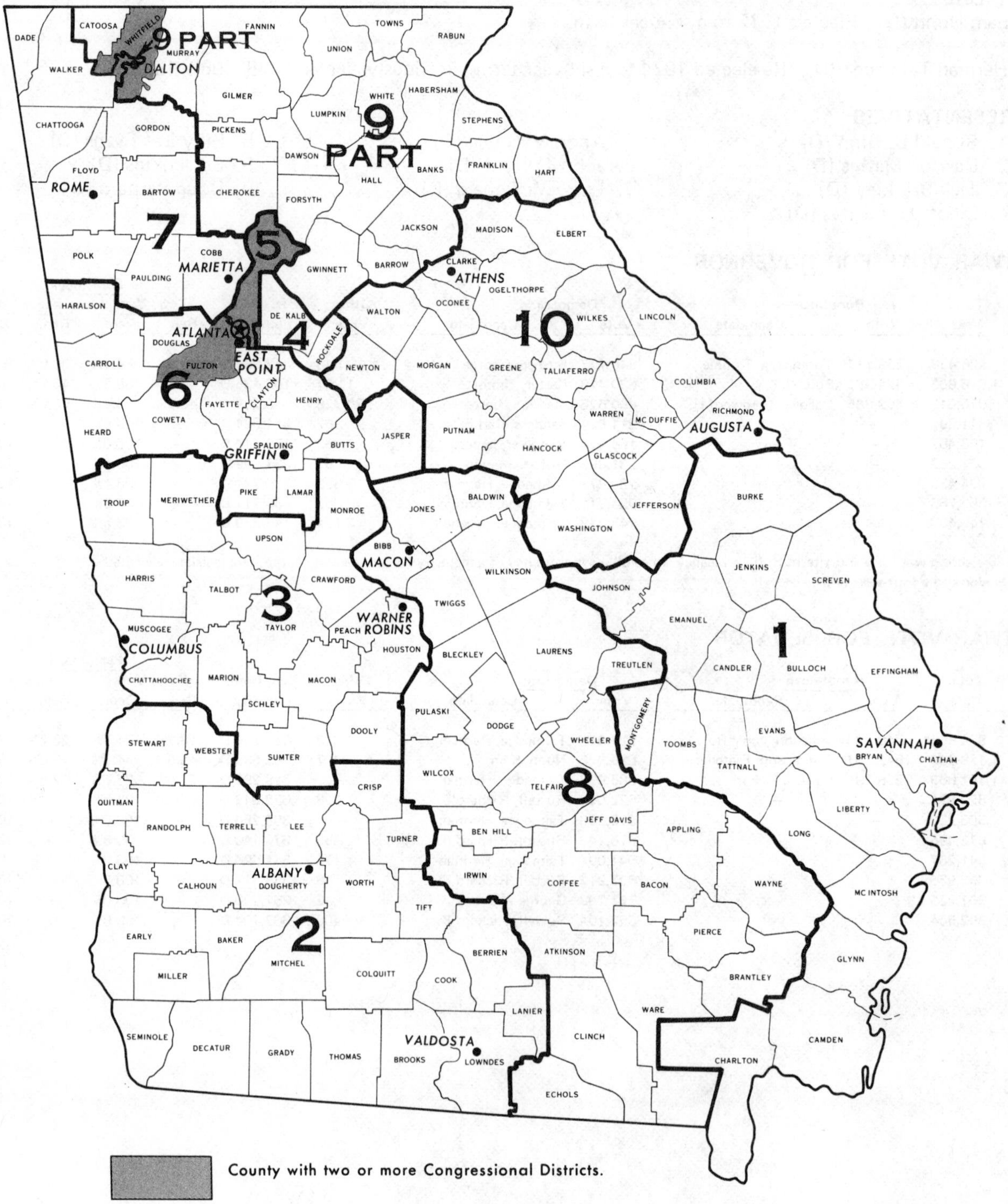

GEORGIA

PRESIDENT 1976

1970 Census Population	County	Total Vote	Republican	Democratic	Other	Rep.-Dem. Plurality	Percentage Total Vote Rep.	Total Vote Dem.	Major Vote Rep.	Major Vote Dem.
12,726	APPLING	4,546	961	3,585		2,624 D	21.1%	78.9%	21.1%	78.9%
5,879	ATKINSON	1,907	347	1,560		1,213 D	18.2%	81.8%	18.2%	81.8%
8,233	BACON	2,989	594	2,395		1,801 D	19.9%	80.1%	19.9%	80.1%
3,875	BAKER	1,467	305	1,162		857 D	20.8%	79.2%	20.8%	79.2%
34,240	BALDWIN	8,286	3,612	4,674		1,062 D	43.6%	56.4%	43.6%	56.4%
6,833	BANKS	2,717	330	2,387		2,057 D	12.1%	87.9%	12.1%	87.9%
16,859	BARROW	6,120	1,364	4,756		3,392 D	22.3%	77.7%	22.3%	77.7%
32,663	BARTOW	10,042	1,876	8,166		6,290 D	18.7%	81.3%	18.7%	81.3%
13,171	BEN HILL	3,263	814	2,449		1,635 D	24.9%	75.1%	24.9%	75.1%
11,556	BERRIEN	3,949	555	3,394		2,839 D	14.1%	85.9%	14.1%	85.9%
143,418	BIBB	44,721	12,819	31,902		19,083 D	28.7%	71.3%	28.7%	71.3%
10,291	BLECKLEY	3,577	972	2,605		1,633 D	27.2%	72.8%	27.2%	72.8%
5,940	BRANTLEY	2,652	358	2,294		1,936 D	13.5%	86.5%	13.5%	86.5%
13,739	BROOKS	3,755	1,102	2,653		1,551 D	29.3%	70.7%	29.3%	70.7%
6,539	BRYAN	2,806	761	2,045		1,284 D	27.1%	72.9%	27.1%	72.9%
31,585	BULLOCH	8,355	3,156	5,199		2,043 D	37.8%	62.2%	37.8%	62.2%
18,255	BURKE	4,579	1,565	3,014		1,449 D	34.2%	65.8%	34.2%	65.8%
10,560	BUTTS	3,717	819	2,898		2,079 D	22.0%	78.0%	22.0%	78.0%
6,606	CALHOUN	1,830	436	1,394		958 D	23.8%	76.2%	23.8%	76.2%
11,334	CAMDEN	3,957	995	2,962		1,967 D	25.1%	74.9%	25.1%	74.9%
6,412	CANDLER	2,034	646	1,388		742 D	31.8%	68.2%	31.8%	68.2%
45,404	CARROLL	13,690	3,640	10,050		6,410 D	26.6%	73.4%	26.6%	73.4%
28,271	CATOOSA	9,819	3,799	6,020		2,221 D	38.7%	61.3%	38.7%	61.3%
5,680	CHARLTON	2,202	452	1,750		1,298 D	20.5%	79.5%	20.5%	79.5%
187,767	CHATHAM	56,235	24,160	32,075		7,915 D	43.0%	57.0%	43.0%	57.0%
25,813	CHATTAHOOCHEE	684	178	506		328 D	26.0%	74.0%	26.0%	74.0%
20,541	CHATTOOGA	5,773	1,087	4,686		3,599 D	18.8%	81.2%	18.8%	81.2%
31,059	CHEROKEE	9,148	2,609	6,539		3,930 D	28.5%	71.5%	28.5%	71.5%
65,177	CLARKE	17,952	6,610	11,342		4,732 D	36.8%	63.2%	36.8%	63.2%
3,636	CLAY	1,242	295	947		652 D	23.8%	76.2%	23.8%	76.2%
98,043	CLAYTON	34,337	12,905	21,432		8,527 D	37.6%	62.4%	37.6%	62.4%
6,405	CLINCH	1,797	383	1,414		1,031 D	21.3%	78.7%	21.3%	78.7%
196,793	COBB	79,326	34,324	45,002		10,678 D	43.3%	56.7%	43.3%	56.7%
22,828	COFFEE	6,018	1,417	4,601		3,184 D	23.5%	76.5%	23.5%	76.5%
32,200	COLQUITT	9,109	2,181	6,928		4,747 D	23.9%	76.1%	23.9%	76.1%
22,327	COLUMBIA	8,097	3,423	4,674		1,251 D	42.3%	57.7%	42.3%	57.7%
12,129	COOK	3,552	670	2,882		2,212 D	18.9%	81.1%	18.9%	81.1%
32,310	COWETA	9,239	3,044	6,195		3,151 D	32.9%	67.1%	32.9%	67.1%
5,748	CRAWFORD	2,220	378	1,842		1,464 D	17.0%	83.0%	17.0%	83.0%
18,087	CRISP	5,075	1,328	3,747		2,419 D	26.2%	73.8%	26.2%	73.8%
9,910	DADE	3,651	1,388	2,263		875 D	38.0%	62.0%	38.0%	62.0%
3,639	DAWSON	1,754	370	1,384		1,014 D	21.1%	78.9%	21.1%	78.9%
22,310	DECATUR	6,236	2,500	3,736		1,236 D	40.1%	59.9%	40.1%	59.9%
415,387	DE KALB	154,032	67,160	86,872		19,712 D	43.6%	56.4%	43.6%	56.4%
15,658	DODGE	6,115	848	5,267		4,419 D	13.9%	86.1%	13.9%	86.1%
10,404	DOOLY	3,096	655	2,441		1,786 D	21.2%	78.8%	21.2%	78.8%
89,639	DOUGHERTY	20,798	9,337	11,461		2,124 D	44.9%	55.1%	44.9%	55.1%
28,659	DOUGLAS	11,764	3,959	7,805		3,846 D	33.7%	66.3%	33.7%	66.3%
12,682	EARLY	3,562	1,157	2,405		1,248 D	32.5%	67.5%	32.5%	67.5%
1,924	ECHOLS	696	111	585		474 D	15.9%	84.1%	15.9%	84.1%
13,632	EFFINGHAM	4,560	1,654	2,906		1,252 D	36.3%	63.7%	36.3%	63.7%
17,262	ELBERT	5,691	961	4,730		3,769 D	16.9%	83.1%	16.9%	83.1%
18,189	EMANUEL	6,096	1,493	4,603		3,110 D	24.5%	75.5%	24.5%	75.5%
7,290	EVANS	2,377	746	1,631		885 D	31.4%	68.6%	31.4%	68.6%
13,357	FANNIN	6,048	2,646	3,402		756 D	43.8%	56.3%	43.8%	56.3%
11,364	FAYETTE	6,555	2,837	3,718		881 D	43.3%	56.7%	43.3%	56.7%
73,742	FLOYD	22,864	7,713	15,151		7,438 D	33.7%	66.3%	33.7%	66.3%
16,928	FORSYTH	6,136	1,443	4,693		3,250 D	23.5%	76.5%	23.5%	76.5%
12,784	FRANKLIN	4,879	687	4,192		3,505 D	14.1%	85.9%	14.1%	85.9%
607,592	FULTON	191,401	61,552	129,849		68,297 D	32.2%	67.8%	32.2%	67.8%
8,956	GILMER	3,760	1,261	2,499		1,238 D	33.5%	66.5%	33.5%	66.5%
2,280	GLASCOCK	1,075	371	704		333 D	34.5%	65.5%	34.5%	65.5%
50,528	GLYNN	14,862	5,403	9,459		4,056 D	36.4%	63.6%	36.4%	63.6%
23,570	GORDON	7,750	1,698	6,052		4,354 D	21.9%	78.1%	21.9%	78.1%
17,826	GRADY	4,967	1,209	3,758		2,549 D	24.3%	75.7%	24.3%	75.7%

GEORGIA

PRESIDENT 1976

1970 Census Population	County	Total Vote	Republican	Democratic	Other	Rep.-Dem. Plurality	Percentage Total Vote Rep.	Total Vote Dem.	Major Vote Rep.	Major Vote Dem.
10,212	GREENE	3,186	652	2,534		1,882 D	20.5%	79.5%	20.5%	79.5%
72,349	GWINNETT	34,750	13,912	20,838		6,926 D	40.0%	60.0%	40.0%	60.0%
20,691	HABERSHAM	6,435	1,315	5,120		3,805 D	20.4%	79.6%	20.4%	79.6%
59,405	HALL	17,897	5,093	12,804		7,711 D	28.5%	71.5%	28.5%	71.5%
9,019	HANCOCK	2,768	651	2,117		1,466 D	23.5%	76.5%	23.5%	76.5%
15,927	HARALSON	5,851	1,301	4,550		3,249 D	22.2%	77.8%	22.2%	77.8%
11,520	HARRIS	4,405	1,544	2,861		1,317 D	35.1%	64.9%	35.1%	64.9%
15,814	HART	5,465	860	4,605		3,745 D	15.7%	84.3%	15.7%	84.3%
5,354	HEARD	2,026	433	1,593		1,160 D	21.4%	78.6%	21.4%	78.6%
23,724	HENRY	8,339	2,622	5,717		3,095 D	31.4%	68.6%	31.4%	68.6%
62,924	HOUSTON	18,568	5,404	13,164		7,760 D	29.1%	70.9%	29.1%	70.9%
8,036	IRWIN	2,573	561	2,012		1,451 D	21.8%	78.2%	21.8%	78.2%
21,093	JACKSON	7,170	1,239	5,931		4,692 D	17.3%	82.7%	17.3%	82.7%
5,760	JASPER	2,541	689	1,852		1,163 D	27.1%	72.9%	27.1%	72.9%
9,425	JEFF DAVIS	3,027	622	2,405		1,783 D	20.5%	79.5%	20.5%	79.5%
17,174	JEFFERSON	4,424	1,309	3,115		1,806 D	29.6%	70.4%	29.6%	70.4%
8,332	JENKINS	2,383	563	1,820		1,257 D	23.6%	76.4%	23.6%	76.4%
7,727	JOHNSON	2,908	698	2,210		1,512 D	24.0%	76.0%	24.0%	76.0%
12,218	JONES	4,788	1,317	3,471		2,154 D	27.5%	72.5%	27.5%	72.5%
10,688	LAMAR	3,632	847	2,785		1,938 D	23.3%	76.7%	23.3%	76.7%
5,031	LANIER	1,476	207	1,269		1,062 D	14.0%	86.0%	14.0%	86.0%
32,738	LAURENS	11,898	3,281	8,617		5,336 D	27.6%	72.4%	27.6%	72.4%
7,044	LEE	2,837	1,110	1,727		617 D	39.1%	60.9%	39.1%	60.9%
17,569	LIBERTY	4,307	979	3,328		2,349 D	22.7%	77.3%	22.7%	77.3%
5,895	LINCOLN	2,159	576	1,583		1,007 D	26.7%	73.3%	26.7%	73.3%
3,746	LONG	1,465	222	1,243		1,021 D	15.2%	84.8%	15.2%	84.8%
55,112	LOWNDES	13,342	4,512	8,830		4,318 D	33.8%	66.2%	33.8%	66.2%
8,728	LUMPKIN	2,848	547	2,301		1,754 D	19.2%	80.8%	19.2%	80.8%
15,276	MCDUFFIE	4,718	1,694	3,024		1,330 D	35.9%	64.1%	35.9%	64.1%
7,371	MCINTOSH	2,513	535	1,978		1,443 D	21.3%	78.7%	21.3%	78.7%
12,933	MACON	3,651	638	3,013		2,375 D	17.5%	82.5%	17.5%	82.5%
13,517	MADISON	4,482	1,115	3,367		2,252 D	24.9%	75.1%	24.9%	75.1%
5,099	MARION	1,605	291	1,314		1,023 D	18.1%	81.9%	18.1%	81.9%
19,461	MERIWETHER	6,280	1,450	4,830		3,380 D	23.1%	76.9%	23.1%	76.9%
6,397	MILLER	2,012	476	1,536		1,060 D	23.7%	76.3%	23.7%	76.3%
18,956	MITCHELL	6,067	1,572	4,495		2,923 D	25.9%	74.1%	25.9%	74.1%
10,991	MONROE	4,040	1,078	2,962		1,884 D	26.7%	73.3%	26.7%	73.3%
6,099	MONTGOMERY	2,236	626	1,610		984 D	28.0%	72.0%	28.0%	72.0%
9,904	MORGAN	3,178	904	2,274		1,370 D	28.4%	71.6%	28.4%	71.6%
12,986	MURRAY	4,400	889	3,511		2,622 D	20.2%	79.8%	20.2%	79.8%
167,377	MUSCOGEE	37,588	13,496	24,092		10,596 D	35.9%	64.1%	35.9%	64.1%
26,282	NEWTON	8,431	2,137	6,294		4,157 D	25.3%	74.7%	25.3%	74.7%
7,915	OCONEE	3,412	1,184	2,228		1,044 D	34.7%	65.3%	34.7%	65.3%
7,598	OGLETHORPE	2,665	811	1,854		1,043 D	30.4%	69.6%	30.4%	69.6%
17,520	PAULDING	6,852	1,432	5,420		3,988 D	20.9%	79.1%	20.9%	79.1%
15,990	PEACH	5,152	1,163	3,989		2,826 D	22.6%	77.4%	22.6%	77.4%
9,620	PICKENS	3,544	973	2,571		1,598 D	27.5%	72.5%	27.5%	72.5%
9,281	PIERCE	3,172	544	2,628		2,084 D	17.2%	82.8%	17.2%	82.8%
7,316	PIKE	2,679	776	1,903		1,127 D	29.0%	71.0%	29.0%	71.0%
29,656	POLK	8,059	1,944	6,115		4,171 D	24.1%	75.9%	24.1%	75.9%
8,066	PULASKI	2,803	485	2,318		1,833 D	17.3%	82.7%	17.3%	82.7%
8,394	PUTNAM	2,875	835	2,040		1,205 D	29.0%	71.0%	29.0%	71.0%
2,180	QUITMAN	990	313	677		364 D	31.6%	68.4%	31.6%	68.4%
8,327	RABUN	2,989	591	2,398		1,807 D	19.8%	80.2%	19.8%	80.2%
8,734	RANDOLPH	2,933	747	2,186		1,439 D	25.5%	74.5%	25.5%	74.5%
162,437	RICHMOND	41,935	17,893	24,042		6,149 D	42.7%	57.3%	42.7%	57.3%
18,152	ROCKDALE	7,614	2,974	4,640		1,666 D	39.1%	60.9%	39.1%	60.9%
3,097	SCHLEY	1,051	268	783		515 D	25.5%	74.5%	25.5%	74.5%
12,591	SCREVEN	3,344	1,176	2,168		992 D	35.2%	64.8%	35.2%	64.8%
7,059	SEMINOLE	2,755	681	2,074		1,393 D	24.7%	75.3%	24.7%	75.3%
39,514	SPALDING	11,332	3,739	7,593		3,854 D	33.0%	67.0%	33.0%	67.0%
20,331	STEPHENS	6,900	1,340	5,560		4,220 D	19.4%	80.6%	19.4%	80.6%
6,511	STEWART	2,065	433	1,632		1,199 D	21.0%	79.0%	21.0%	79.0%
26,931	SUMTER	7,381	2,053	5,328		3,275 D	27.8%	72.2%	27.8%	72.2%
6,625	TALBOT	2,093	459	1,634		1,175 D	21.9%	78.1%	21.9%	78.1%

GEORGIA

PRESIDENT 1976

1970 Census Population	County	Total Vote	Republican	Democratic	Other	Rep.-Dem. Plurality	Percentage Total Vote Rep.	Total Vote Dem.	Major Vote Rep.	Major Vote Dem.
2,423	TALIAFERRO	984	236	748		512 D	24.0%	76.0%	24.0%	76.0%
16,557	TATTNALL	4,882	1,326	3,556		2,230 D	27.2%	72.8%	27.2%	72.8%
7,865	TAYLOR	2,466	504	1,962		1,458 D	20.4%	79.6%	20.4%	79.6%
11,381	TELFAIR	4,171	637	3,534		2,897 D	15.3%	84.7%	15.3%	84.7%
11,416	TERRELL	3,516	1,168	2,348		1,180 D	33.2%	66.8%	33.2%	66.8%
34,515	THOMAS	9,410	3,263	6,147		2,884 D	34.7%	65.3%	34.7%	65.3%
27,288	TIFT	7,347	2,162	5,185		3,023 D	29.4%	70.6%	29.4%	70.6%
19,151	TOOMBS	6,173	2,126	4,047		1,921 D	34.4%	65.6%	34.4%	65.6%
4,565	TOWNS	2,961	1,175	1,786		611 D	39.7%	60.3%	39.7%	60.3%
5,647	TREUTLEN	2,032	465	1,567		1,102 D	22.9%	77.1%	22.9%	77.1%
44,466	TROUP	12,121	4,422	7,699		3,277 D	36.5%	63.5%	36.5%	63.5%
8,790	TURNER	2,681	416	2,265		1,849 D	15.5%	84.5%	15.5%	84.5%
8,222	TWIGGS	3,028	513	2,515		2,002 D	16.9%	83.1%	16.9%	83.1%
6,811	UNION	3,949	1,154	2,795		1,641 D	29.2%	70.8%	29.2%	70.8%
23,505	UPSON	7,116	2,897	4,219		1,322 D	40.7%	59.3%	40.7%	59.3%
50,691	WALKER	12,814	4,807	8,007		3,200 D	37.5%	62.5%	37.5%	62.5%
23,404	WALTON	7,089	1,687	5,402		3,715 D	23.8%	76.2%	23.8%	76.2%
33,525	WARE	10,380	2,661	7,719		5,058 D	25.6%	74.4%	25.6%	74.4%
6,669	WARREN	2,055	720	1,335		615 D	35.0%	65.0%	35.0%	65.0%
17,480	WASHINGTON	5,522	1,657	3,865		2,208 D	30.0%	70.0%	30.0%	70.0%
17,858	WAYNE	5,988	1,499	4,489		2,990 D	25.0%	75.0%	25.0%	75.0%
2,362	WEBSTER	787	165	622		457 D	21.0%	79.0%	21.0%	79.0%
4,596	WHEELER	1,722	344	1,378		1,034 D	20.0%	80.0%	20.0%	80.0%
7,742	WHITE	2,750	625	2,125		1,500 D	22.7%	77.3%	22.7%	77.3%
55,108	WHITFIELD	14,973	4,498	10,475		5,977 D	30.0%	70.0%	30.0%	70.0%
6,998	WILCOX	2,499	346	2,153		1,807 D	13.8%	86.2%	13.8%	86.2%
10,184	WILKES	3,528	1,067	2,461		1,394 D	30.2%	69.8%	30.2%	69.8%
9,393	WILKINSON	3,489	837	2,652		1,815 D	24.0%	76.0%	24.0%	76.0%
14,770	WORTH	3,946	1,156	2,790		1,634 D	29.3%	70.7%	29.3%	70.7%
4,589,575	TOTAL	1,467,458	483,743	979,409	4,306	495,666 D	33.0%	66.7%	33.1%	66.9%

GEORGIA

CONGRESS

CD	Year	Total Vote	Republican Vote	Republican Candidate	Democratic Vote	Democratic Candidate	Other Vote	Rep.-Dem. Plurality	Percentage Total Vote Rep.	Percentage Total Vote Dem.	Percentage Major Vote Rep.	Percentage Major Vote Dem.
1	1976	73,888			73,826	GINN, RONALD B.	62	73,826 D		99.9%		100.0%
1	1974	75,444	10,485	GOWAN, WILLIAM L.	64,958	GINN, RONALD B.	1	54,473 D	13.9%	86.1%	13.9%	86.1%
1	1972	55,267			55,256	GINN, RONALD B.	11	55,256 D		100.0%		100.0%
2	1976	96,026			95,807	MATHIS, DAWSON	219	95,807 D		99.8%		100.0%
2	1974	59,515			59,514	MATHIS, DAWSON	1	59,514 D		100.0%		100.0%
2	1972	65,999			65,997	MATHIS, DAWSON	2	65,997 D		100.0%		100.0%
3	1976	105,004	11,829	DUGAN, STEVE	93,174	BRINKLEY, JACK	1	81,345 D	11.3%	88.7%	11.3%	88.7%
3	1974	76,891	9,453	SAVAGE, CARL P.	67,438	BRINKLEY, JACK		57,985 D	12.3%	87.7%	12.3%	87.7%
3	1972	71,763			71,756	BRINKLEY, JACK	7	71,756 D		100.0%		100.0%
4	1976	161,412	51,140	WARREN, GEORGE	110,261	LEVITAS, ELLIOTT H.	11	59,121 D	31.7%	68.3%	31.7%	68.3%
4	1974	111,139	49,922	BLACKBURN, BEN B.	61,211	LEVITAS, ELLIOTT H.	6	11,289 D	44.9%	55.1%	44.9%	55.1%
4	1972	135,886	103,155	BLACKBURN, BEN B.	32,731	WELBORN, F. ODELL		70,424 R	75.9%	24.1%	75.9%	24.1%
5	1976	144,063	47,998	GADRIX, EDWARD W.	96,056	YOUNG, ANDREW	9	48,058 D	33.3%	66.7%	33.3%	66.7%
5	1974	96,667	27,397	LOWE, WYMAN C.	69,221	YOUNG, ANDREW	49	41,824 D	28.3%	71.6%	28.4%	71.6%
5	1972	136,810	64,495	COOK, RODNEY M.	72,289	YOUNG, ANDREW	26	7,794 D	47.1%	52.8%	47.2%	52.8%
6	1976	149,944	72,400	GINGRICH, NEWT	77,532	FLYNT, JOHN J.	12	5,132 D	48.3%	51.7%	48.3%	51.7%
6	1974	95,395	46,308	GINGRICH, NEWT	49,082	FLYNT, JOHN J.	5	2,774 D	48.5%	51.5%	48.5%	51.5%
6	1972	70,617			70,586	FLYNT, JOHN J.	31	70,586 D		100.0%		100.0%
7	1976	153,554	68,947	COLLINS, QUINCY	84,587	MCDONALD, LARRY	20	15,640 D	44.9%	55.1%	44.9%	55.1%
7	1974	95,477	47,450	COLLINS, QUINCY	47,993	MCDONALD, LARRY	34	543 D	49.7%	50.3%	49.7%	50.3%
7	1972	101,306	42,265	SHERRILL, CHARLES B.	59,031	DAVIS, JOHN W.	10	16,766 D	41.7%	58.3%	41.7%	58.3%
8	1976	130,978	39,623	ADAMS, BILLY	91,351	EVANS, BILLY LEE	4	51,728 D	30.3%	69.7%	30.3%	69.7%
8	1974	59,195			59,182	STUCKEY, W. S.	13	59,182 D		100.0%		100.0%
8	1972	114,272	42,986	THOMPSON, RONNIE	71,283	STUCKEY, W. S.	3	28,297 D	37.6%	62.4%	37.6%	62.4%
9	1976	143,357	29,954	WOFFORD, LOUISE	113,245	JENKINS, ED	158	83,291 D	20.9%	79.0%	20.9%	79.1%
9	1974	85,642	21,540	REEVES, RONALD D.	64,096	LANDRUM, PHIL M.	6	42,556 D	25.2%	74.8%	25.2%	74.8%
9	1972	71,809			71,801	LANDRUM, PHIL M.	8	71,801 D		100.0%		100.0%
10	1976	94,864			94,782	BARNARD, DOUG	82	94,782 D		99.9%		100.0%
10	1974	67,058	21,214	PLEGER, GARY	45,843	STEPHENS, ROBERT G.	1	24,629 D	31.6%	68.4%	31.6%	68.4%
10	1972	68,097			68,096	STEPHENS, ROBERT G.	1	68,096 D		100.0%		100.0%

GEORGIA

1976 GENERAL ELECTION

President — Other vote was all write-in for the following candidates: 1,168 Anderson; 1,071 Maddox; 991 McCarthy; 175 MacBride; 43 Camejo; 3 Hall; 3 Miller; 2 Levin; 2 Zeidler; 1 LaRouche; 847 scattered. Write-in votes are included in the state-wide total but are not available by county.

Congress — Other vote was scattered in CD's 3, 4, 5, 6, 7, 8 and 10; 53 Sevier (write-in) and 9 scattered in CD 1; 205 Goolsby (write-in) and 14 scattered in CD 2; 131 Ashworth (write-in) and 27 scattered in CD 9.

1976 PRIMARIES

AUGUST 10 REPUBLICAN

Congress — Unopposed in six CD's. No candidates in CD's 1, 2 and 10. Contested as follows:

CD 5 — 2,304 Edward W. Gadrix; 1,727 Marilyn Finley.

AUGUST 10 DEMOCRATIC

Congress — Unopposed in five CD's. Contested as follows:

CD 6 — 50,581 John J. Flynt; 26,745 Frank Bailey; 6,139 Bill Doll; 3,843 Gerald L. Churchill.
CD 7 — 47,168 Larry McDonald; 21,771 Ken Butterworth; 16,275 Ron Drake; 4,337 William O. Green.
CD 8 — 40,291 Wash Larsen; 30,475 Billy Lee Evans; 25,656 Joe Sports; 21,844 Harry Powell.
CD 9 — 33,491 Ed Jenkins; 25,792 J. Albert Minish; 22,392 Ray Gunnin; 15,416 Alton Bridges; 7,956 Bob Turner; 7,758 Joel B. Gunnells; 5,507 Jim Boyd; 1,885 Howard Richardson.
CD 10 — 25,945 Doug Barnard; 21,152 Mike Padgett; 16,309 Tom Harrold; 14,887 C. C. Moreland; 8,601 T. R. Ridgeway; 8,414 Betty Hemenway; 1,802 Wyman C. Lowe.

AUGUST 31 DEMOCRATIC RUN-OFF

Congress

CD 8 — 54,055 Billy Lee Evans; 50,582 Wash Larsen.
CD 9 — 58,905 Ed Jenkins; 47,963 J. Albert Minish.
CD 10 — 43,294 Doug Barnard; 40,495 Mike Padgett.

HAWAII

GOVERNOR
George R. Ariyoshi (D). Elected 1974 to a four-year term.

SENATORS
Daniel K. Inouye (D). Re-elected 1974 to a six-year term. Previously elected 1968, 1962.

Spark M. Matsunaga (D). Elected 1976 to a six-year term.

REPRESENTATIVES
1. Cecil Heftel (D)
2. Daniel K. Akaka (D)

POSTWAR VOTE FOR GOVERNOR

Year	Total Vote	Republican Vote	Republican Candidate	Democratic Vote	Democratic Candidate	Other Vote	Rep.-Dem. Plurality	Percentage Total Vote Rep.	Percentage Total Vote Dem.	Percentage Major Vote Rep.	Percentage Major Vote Dem.
1974	249,650	113,388	Crossley, Randolph	136,262	Ariyoshi, George R.	–	22,874 D	45.4%	54.6%	45.4%	54.6%
1970	239,061	101,249	King, Samuel P.	137,812	Burns, John A.	–	36,563 D	42.4%	57.6%	42.4%	57.6%
1966	213,164	104,324	Crossley, Randolph	108,840	Burns, John A.	–	4,516 D	48.9%	51.1%	48.9%	51.1%
1962	196,015	81,707	Quinn, William F.	114,308	Burns, John A.	–	32,601 D	41.7%	58.3%	41.7%	58.3%
1959	168,662	86,213	Quinn, William F.	82,074	Burns, John A.	375	4,139 R	51.1%	48.7%	51.2%	48.8%

POSTWAR VOTE FOR SENATOR

Year	Total Vote	Republican Vote	Republican Candidate	Democratic Vote	Democratic Candidate	Other Vote	Rep.-Dem. Plurality	Percentage Total Vote Rep.	Percentage Total Vote Dem.	Percentage Major Vote Rep.	Percentage Major Vote Dem.
1976	302,092	122,724	Quinn, William F.	162,305	Matsunaga, Spark M.	17,063	39,581 D	40.6%	53.7%	43.1%	56.9%
1974	250,221	–	–	207,454	Inouye, Daniel K.	42,767	207,454 D	–	82.9%	–	100.0%
1970	240,760	124,163	Fong, Hiram L.	116,597	Heftel, Cecil	–	7,566 R	51.6%	48.4%	51.6%	48.4%
1968	226,927	34,008	Thiessen, Wayne C.	189,248	Inouye, Daniel K.	3,671	155,240 D	15.0%	83.4%	15.2%	84.8%
1964	208,814	110,747	Fong, Hiram L.	96,789	Gill, Thomas P.	1,278	13,958 R	53.0%	46.4%	53.4%	46.6%
1962	196,361	60,067	Dillingham, Ben F.	136,294	Inouye, Daniel K.	–	76,227 D	30.6%	69.4%	30.6%	69.4%
1959	164,808	87,161	Fong, Hiram L.	77,647	Fasi, Frank F.	–	9,514 R	52.9%	47.1%	52.9%	47.1%
1959s	163,875	79,123	Tsukiyama, W. C.	83,700	Long, Oren E.	1,052	4,577 D	48.3%	51.1%	48.6%	51.4%

The two 1959 elections were held to indeterminate terms and the Senate later determined by lot that Senator Long would serve a short term, Senator Fong a full term.

HAWAII

Districts Established July 14, 1969

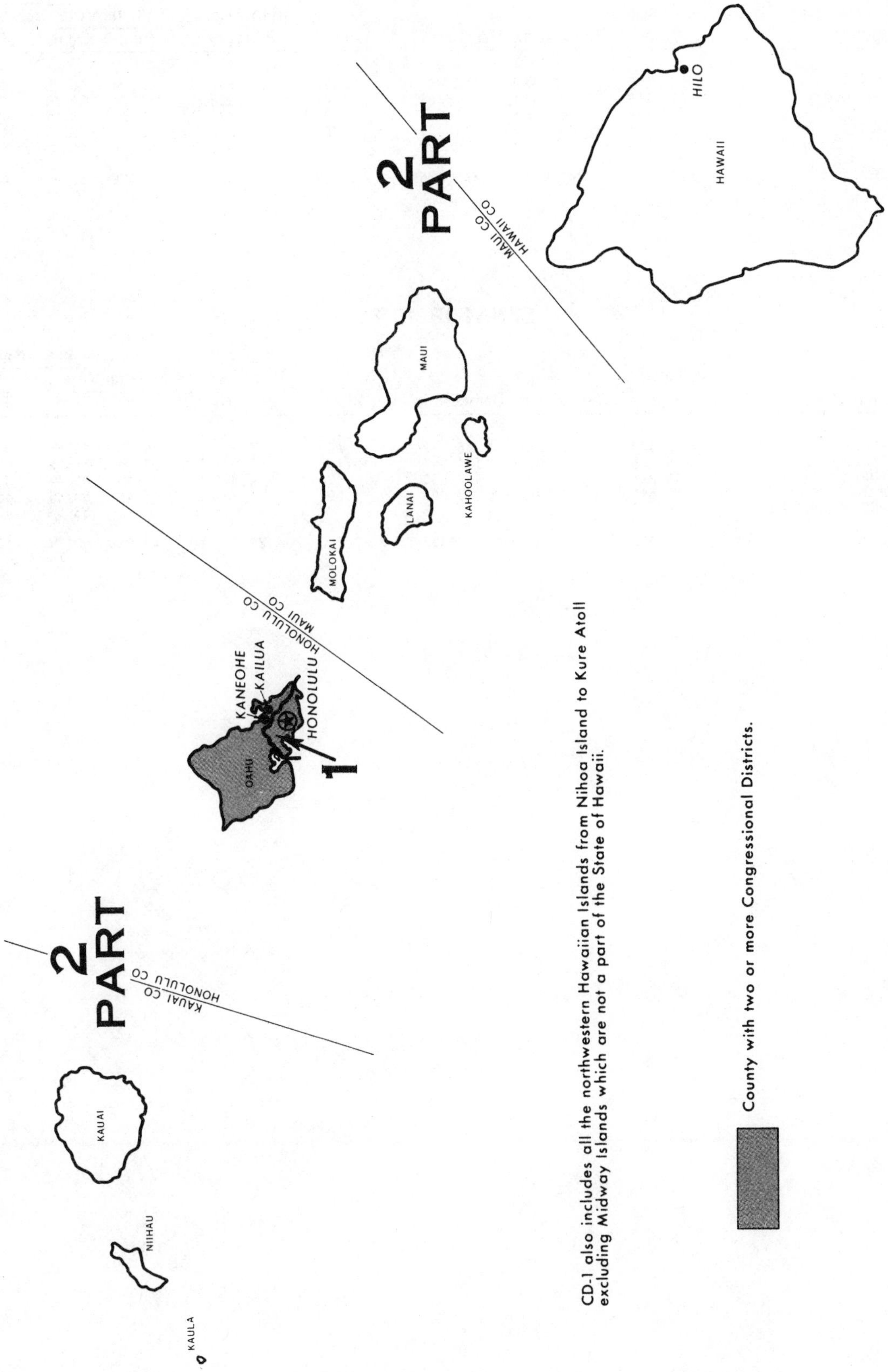

HAWAII

PRESIDENT 1976

1970 Census Population	County	Total Vote	Republican	Democratic	Other	Rep.-Dem. Plurality	Percentage Total Vote Rep.	Percentage Total Vote Dem.	Percentage Major Vote Rep.	Percentage Major Vote Dem.
63,468	HAWAII	31,765	15,366	15,960	439	594 D	48.4%	50.2%	49.1%	50.9%
630,528	HONOLULU	222,416	108,007	111,365	3,044	3,358 D	48.6%	50.1%	49.2%	50.8%
29,761	KAUAI	14,522	6,278	8,105	139	1,827 D	43.2%	55.8%	43.6%	56.4%
46,156	MAUI	22,538	10,318	11,921	299	1,603 D	45.8%	52.9%	46.4%	53.6%
	SPECIAL BALLOTS	60	34	24	2	10 R	56.7%	40.0%	58.6%	41.4%
769,913	TOTAL	291,301	140,003	147,375	3,923	7,372 D	48.1%	50.6%	48.7%	51.3%

SENATOR 1976

1970 Census Population	County	Total Vote	Republican	Democratic	Other	Rep.-Dem. Plurality	Percentage Total Vote Rep.	Percentage Total Vote Dem.	Percentage Major Vote Rep.	Percentage Major Vote Dem.
63,468	HAWAII	33,450	15,266	16,775	1,409	1,509 D	45.6%	50.1%	47.6%	52.4%
630,528	HONOLULU	229,776	92,002	124,009	13,765	32,007 D	40.0%	54.0%	42.6%	57.4%
29,761	KAUAI	15,221	5,197	9,500	524	4,303 D	34.1%	62.4%	35.4%	64.6%
46,156	MAUI	23,615	10,248	12,005	1,362	1,757 D	43.4%	50.8%	46.1%	53.9%
	SPECIAL BALLOTS	30	11	16	3	5 D	36.7%	53.3%	40.7%	59.3%
769,913	TOTAL	302,092	122,724	162,305	17,063	39,581 D	40.6%	53.7%	43.1%	56.9%

HAWAII

CONGRESS

CD	Year	Total Vote	Republican Vote	Republican Candidate	Democratic Vote	Democratic Candidate	Other Vote	Rep.-Dem. Plurality	Percentage Total Vote Rep.	Percentage Total Vote Dem.	Percentage Major Vote Rep.	Percentage Major Vote Dem.
1	1976	137,602	53,745	ROHLFING, FRED W.	60,050	HEFTEL, CECIL	23,807	6,305 D	39.1%	43.6%	47.2%	52.8%
1	1974	120,617	49,065	PAUL, WILLIAM B.	71,552	MATSUNAGA, SPARK M.		22,487 D	40.7%	59.3%	40.7%	59.3%
1	1972	134,964	61,138	ROHLFING, FRED W.	73,826	MATSUNAGA, SPARK M.		12,688 D	45.3%	54.7%	45.3%	54.7%
1	1970	117,175	31,764	COCKEY, RICHARD K.	85,411	MATSUNAGA, SPARK M.		53,647 D	27.1%	72.9%	27.1%	72.9%
2	1976	156,099	23,917	INOUYE, HANK	124,116	AKAKA, DANIEL K.	8,066	100,199 D	15.3%	79.5%	16.2%	83.8%
2	1974	138,810	51,894	CORAY, CARLA W.	86,916	MINK, PATSY		35,022 D	37.4%	62.6%	37.4%	62.6%
2	1972	139,899	60,043	HANSEN, DIANA	79,856	MINK, PATSY		19,813 D	42.9%	57.1%	42.9%	57.1%
2	1970	91,038			91,038	MINK, PATSY		91,038 D		100.0%		100.0%

HAWAII

1976 GENERAL ELECTION

President Other vote was MacBride (Libertarian). Special ballots include new resident and overseas votes.

Senator Other vote was 14,226 Hodges (People's); 1,433 Kimmel (Nonpartisan); 1,404 Johnson (Libertarian). Special ballots include new resident and overseas votes.

Congress Other vote was Hoshijo (Independents for Godly Government) in CD 1; in CD 2 as follows:

CD 2 3,461 Penaroza (Independents for Godly Government); 2,408 Cate (People's); 2,197 Smith (Libertarian).

1976 PRIMARIES

OCTOBER 2 REPUBLICAN

Senator 32,058 William F. Quinn; 2,170 Spencer J. Cabral.

Congress Unopposed in CD 1. Contested as follows:

CD 2 7,578 Hank Inouye; 6,872 Judy P. N. Stewart.

OCTOBER 2 DEMOCRATIC

Senator 105,731 Spark M. Matsunaga; 84,732 Patsy Mink; 6,369 Nathan N. Napoleon; 5,600 Floyd C. Loving; 4,728 Kamuela Price.

Congress Contested as follows:

CD 1 43,551 Cecil Heftel; 35,357 John P. Craven; 11,736 Hal Jones; 976 Christ P. Zivalich; 685 Warren A. Putzke.
CD 2 52,584 Daniel K. Akaka; 50,569 Joe Kuroda; 9,180 George B. Carter.

OCTOBER 2 INDEPENDENTS FOR GODLY GOVERNMENT

Senator None. No candidate.

Congress Unopposed in both CD's.

OCTOBER 2 LIBERTARIAN

Senator Rockne Johnson, unopposed.

Congress Unopposed in CD 2. No candidate in CD 1.

OCTOBER 2 NONPARTISAN

Senator James D. Kimmel, unopposed.

Congress No candidates in either CD.

OCTOBER 2 PEOPLE'S

Senator Anthony N. Hodges, unopposed.

Congress Unopposed in CD 2. No candidate in CD 1.

IDAHO

GOVERNOR

John V. Evans (D). Elected as Lieutenant-Governor in 1974 and succeeded upon the resignation of Governor Andrus in January 1977. Next election in 1978.

SENATORS

Frank Church (D). Re-elected 1974 to a six-year term. Previously elected 1968, 1962, 1956.

James A. McClure (R). Elected 1972 to a six-year term.

REPRESENTATIVES

1. Steven D. Symms (R)
2. George V. Hansen (R)

POSTWAR VOTE FOR GOVERNOR

								Percentage			
	Total	Republican		Democratic		Other	Rep.-Dem.	Total Vote		Major Vote	
Year	Vote	Vote	Candidate	Vote	Candidate	Vote	Plurality	Rep.	Dem.	Rep.	Dem.
1974	259,632	68,731	Murphy, Jack M.	184,142	Andrus, Cecil D.	6,759	115,411 D	26.5%	70.9%	27.2%	72.8%
1970	245,112	117,108	Samuelson, Don	128,004	Andrus, Cecil D.	–	10,896 D	47.8%	52.2%	47.8%	52.2%
1966	252,593	104,586	Samuelson, Don	93,744	Andrus, Cecil D.	54,263	10,842 R	41.4%	37.1%	52.7%	47.3%
1962	255,454	139,578	Smylie, Robert E.	115,876	Smith, Vernon K.	–	23,702 R	54.6%	45.4%	54.6%	45.4%
1958	239,046	121,810	Smylie, Robert E.	117,236	Derr, A. M.	–	4,574 R	51.0%	49.0%	51.0%	49.0%
1954	228,685	124,038	Smylie, Robert E.	104,647	Hamilton, Clark	–	19,391 R	54.2%	45.8%	54.2%	45.8%
1950	204,792	107,642	Jordan, Len B.	97,150	Wright, Calvin E.	–	10,492 R	52.6%	47.4%	52.6%	47.4%
1946	181,364	102,233	Robins, C. A.	79,131	Williams, Arnold	–	23,102 R	56.4%	43.6%	56.4%	43.6%

POSTWAR VOTE FOR SENATOR

								Percentage			
	Total	Republican		Democratic		Other	Rep.-Dem.	Total Vote		Major Vote	
Year	Vote	Vote	Candidate	Vote	Candidate	Vote	Plurality	Rep.	Dem.	Rep.	Dem.
1974	258,847	109,072	Smith, Robert L.	145,140	Church, Frank	4,635	36,068 D	42.1%	56.1%	42.9%	57.1%
1972	309,602	161,804	McClure, James A.	140,913	Davis, William E.	6,885	20,891 R	52.3%	45.5%	53.5%	46.5%
1968	287,876	114,394	Hansen, George V.	173,482	Church, Frank	–	59,088 D	39.7%	60.3%	39.7%	60.3%
1966	252,456	139,819	Jordan, Len B.	112,637	Harding, Ralph R.	–	27,182 R	55.4%	44.6%	55.4%	44.6%
1962	258,786	117,129	Hawley, Jack	141,657	Church, Frank	–	24,528 D	45.3%	54.7%	45.3%	54.7%
1962s	257,677	131,279	Jordan, Len B.	126,398	Pfost, Gracie	–	4,881 R	50.9%	49.1%	50.9%	49.1%
1960	292,096	152,648	Dworshak, Henry C.	139,448	McLaughlin, Bob	–	13,200 R	52.3%	47.7%	52.3%	47.7%
1956	265,292	102,781	Welker, Herman	149,096	Church, Frank	13,415	46,315 D	38.7%	56.2%	40.8%	59.2%
1954	226,408	142,269	Dworshak, Henry C.	84,139	Taylor, Glen H.	–	58,130 R	62.8%	37.2%	62.8%	37.2%
1950	201,417	124,237	Welker, Herman	77,180	Clark, D. Worth	–	47,057 R	61.7%	38.3%	61.7%	38.3%
1950s	201,970	104,068	Dworshak, Henry C.	97,902	Burtenshaw, Claude	–	6,166 R	51.5%	48.5%	51.5%	48.5%
1948	214,188	103,868	Dworshak, Henry C.	107,000	Miller, Bert H.	3,320	3,132 D	48.5%	50.0%	49.3%	50.7%
1946s	180,152	105,523	Dworshak, Henry C.	74,629	Donart, George E.	–	30,894 R	58.6%	41.4%	58.6%	41.4%

The 1946 election and one each of the 1962 and 1950 elections were for short terms to fill vacancies.

IDAHO

Districts Established April 13, 1971

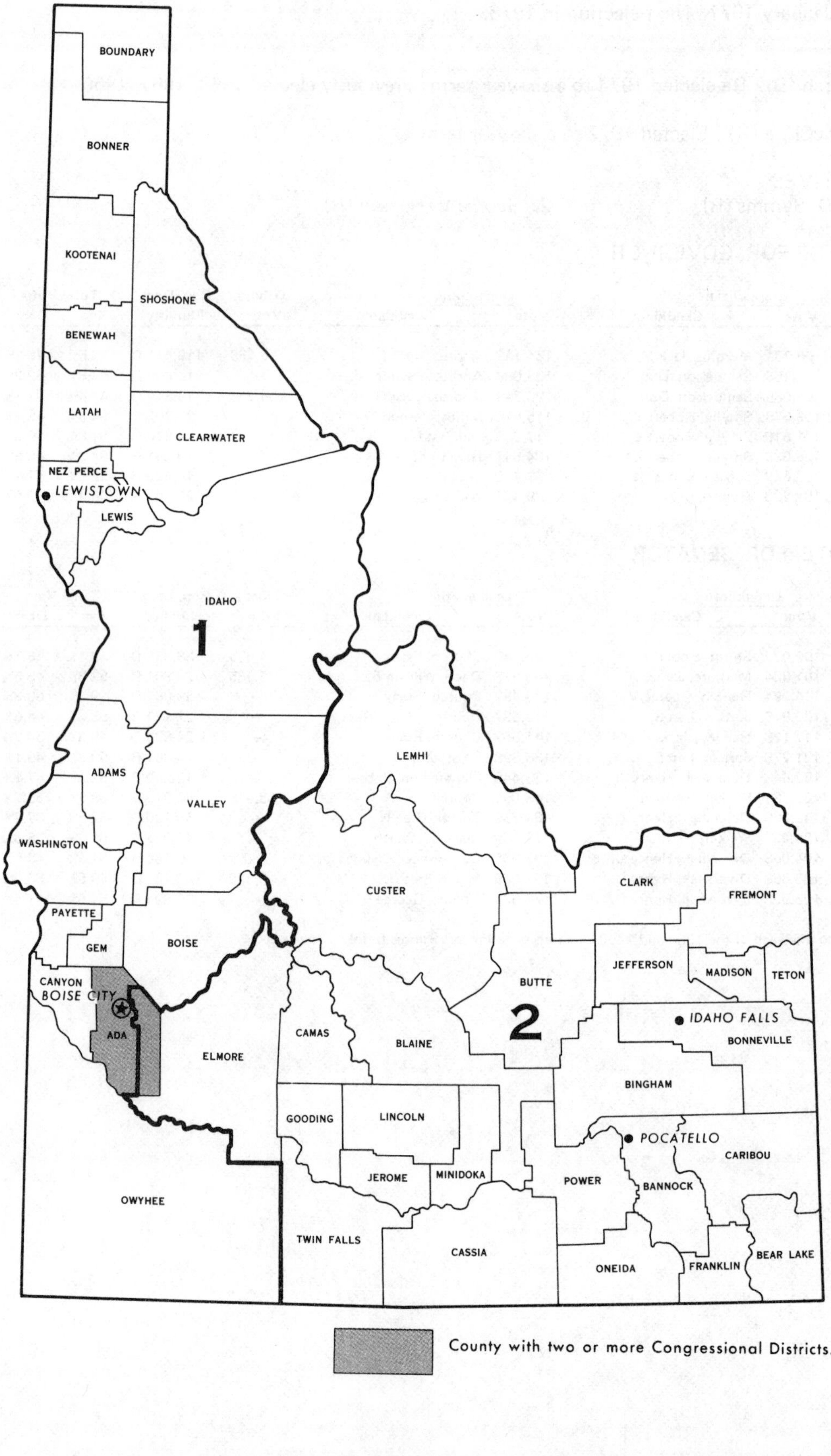
BOUNDARY
BONNER
KOOTENAI
SHOSHONE
BENEWAH
LATAH
CLEARWATER
NEZ PERCE
LEWISTOWN
LEWIS
IDAHO
1
LEMHI
ADAMS
VALLEY
WASHINGTON
CUSTER
CLARK
FREMONT
PAYETTE
GEM
BOISE
JEFFERSON
MADISON
TETON
CANYON
BOISE CITY
BUTTE
2
IDAHO FALLS
ADA
CAMAS
BLAINE
BONNEVILLE
ELMORE
BINGHAM
GOODING
LINCOLN
POCATELLO
CARIBOU
JEROME
MINIDOKA
POWER
BANNOCK
OWYHEE
TWIN FALLS
CASSIA
ONEIDA
FRANKLIN
BEAR LAKE
County with two or more Congressional Districts.

IDAHO

PRESIDENT 1976

1970 Census Population	County	Total Vote	Republican	Democratic	Other	Rep.-Dem. Plurality	Percentage Total Vote Rep.	Percentage Total Vote Dem.	Percentage Major Vote Rep.	Percentage Major Vote Dem.
112,230	ADA	64,530	41,135	21,125	2,270	20,010 R	63.7%	32.7%	66.1%	33.9%
2,877	ADAMS	1,492	809	639	44	170 R	54.2%	42.8%	55.9%	44.1%
52,200	BANNOCK	24,706	13,172	10,261	1,273	2,911 R	53.3%	41.5%	56.2%	43.8%
5,801	BEAR LAKE	3,154	2,094	960	100	1,134 R	66.4%	30.4%	68.6%	31.4%
6,230	BENEWAH	3,092	1,458	1,549	85	91 D	47.2%	50.1%	48.5%	51.5%
29,167	BINGHAM	12,121	7,327	4,347	447	2,980 R	60.4%	35.9%	62.8%	37.2%
5,749	BLAINE	3,966	2,176	1,604	186	572 R	54.9%	40.4%	57.6%	42.4%
1,763	BOISE	1,167	684	433	50	251 R	58.6%	37.1%	61.2%	38.8%
15,560	BONNER	8,897	4,549	4,065	283	484 R	51.1%	45.7%	52.8%	47.2%
52,457	BONNEVILLE	24,018	15,793	7,230	995	8,563 R	65.8%	30.1%	68.6%	31.4%
5,484	BOUNDARY	2,837	1,458	1,217	162	241 R	51.4%	42.9%	54.5%	45.5%
2,925	BUTTE	1,491	751	663	77	88 R	50.4%	44.5%	53.1%	46.9%
728	CAMAS	464	288	160	16	128 R	62.1%	34.5%	64.3%	35.7%
61,288	CANYON	27,813	17,263	9,460	1,090	7,803 R	62.1%	34.0%	64.6%	35.4%
6,534	CARIBOU	3,523	2,253	1,110	160	1,143 R	64.0%	31.5%	67.0%	33.0%
17,017	CASSIA	6,909	4,575	1,881	453	2,694 R	66.2%	27.2%	70.9%	29.1%
741	CLARK	524	334	169	21	165 R	63.7%	32.3%	66.4%	33.6%
10,871	CLEARWATER	3,342	1,469	1,752	121	283 D	44.0%	52.4%	45.6%	54.4%
2,967	CUSTER	1,421	850	516	55	334 R	59.8%	36.3%	62.2%	37.8%
17,479	ELMORE	5,122	2,808	2,164	150	644 R	54.8%	42.2%	56.5%	43.5%
7,373	FRANKLIN	4,080	2,720	1,157	203	1,563 R	66.7%	28.4%	70.2%	29.8%
8,710	FREMONT	4,232	2,581	1,445	206	1,136 R	61.0%	34.1%	64.1%	35.9%
9,387	GEM	4,605	2,401	1,978	226	423 R	52.1%	43.0%	54.8%	45.2%
8,645	GOODING	5,035	2,909	1,923	203	986 R	57.8%	38.2%	60.2%	39.8%
12,891	IDAHO	5,750	3,185	2,323	242	862 R	55.4%	40.4%	57.8%	42.2%
11,740	JEFFERSON	5,593	3,599	1,745	249	1,854 R	64.3%	31.2%	67.3%	32.7%
10,253	JEROME	5,192	3,188	1,800	204	1,388 R	61.4%	34.7%	63.9%	36.1%
35,332	KOOTENAI	18,317	10,493	7,225	599	3,268 R	57.3%	39.4%	59.2%	40.8%
24,891	LATAH	12,741	6,846	5,314	581	1,532 R	53.7%	41.7%	56.3%	43.7%
5,566	LEMHI	3,052	1,685	1,159	208	526 R	55.2%	38.0%	59.2%	40.8%
3,867	LEWIS	1,787	824	898	65	74 D	46.1%	50.3%	47.9%	52.1%
3,057	LINCOLN	1,593	909	615	69	294 R	57.1%	38.6%	59.6%	40.4%
13,452	MADISON	5,823	4,190	1,320	313	2,870 R	72.0%	22.7%	76.0%	24.0%
15,731	MINIDOKA	6,378	3,600	2,441	337	1,159 R	56.4%	38.3%	59.6%	40.4%
30,376	NEZ PERCE	12,819	6,151	6,324	344	173 D	48.0%	49.3%	49.3%	50.7%
2,864	ONEIDA	1,755	1,065	637	53	428 R	60.7%	36.3%	62.6%	37.4%
6,422	OWYHEE	2,649	1,519	1,054	76	465 R	57.3%	39.8%	59.0%	41.0%
12,401	PAYETTE	5,463	3,115	2,195	153	920 R	57.0%	40.2%	58.7%	41.3%
4,864	POWER	2,750	1,374	1,286	90	88 R	50.0%	46.8%	51.7%	48.3%
19,718	SHOSHONE	6,909	3,570	3,216	123	354 R	51.7%	46.5%	52.6%	47.4%
2,351	TETON	1,434	904	514	16	390 R	63.0%	35.8%	63.8%	36.2%
41,807	TWIN FALLS	19,298	12,659	6,085	554	6,574 R	65.6%	31.5%	67.5%	32.5%
3,609	VALLEY	2,366	1,374	897	95	477 R	58.1%	37.9%	60.5%	39.5%
7,633	WASHINGTON	3,861	2,044	1,693	124	351 R	52.9%	43.8%	54.7%	45.3%
713,008	TOTAL	344,071	204,151	126,549	13,371	77,602 R	59.3%	36.8%	61.7%	38.3%

IDAHO

CONGRESS

CD	Year	Total Vote	Republican Vote	Republican Candidate	Democratic Vote	Democratic Candidate	Other Vote	Rep.-Dem. Plurality	Percentage Total Vote Rep.	Percentage Total Vote Dem.	Percentage Major Vote Rep.	Percentage Major Vote Dem.
1	1976	175,495	95,833	SYMMS, STEVEN D.	79,662	PURSLEY, KEN		16,171 R	54.6%	45.4%	54.6%	45.4%
1	1974	129,405	75,404	SYMMS, STEVEN D.	54,001	COX, J. RAY		21,403 R	58.3%	41.7%	58.3%	41.7%
1	1972	153,376	85,270	SYMMS, STEVEN D.	68,106	WILLIAMS, ED		17,164 R	55.6%	44.4%	55.6%	44.4%
2	1976	166,412	84,175	HANSEN, GEORGE V.	82,237	KRESS, STAN		1,938 R	50.6%	49.4%	50.6%	49.4%
2	1974	120,873	67,274	HANSEN, GEORGE V.	53,599	HANSON, MAX		13,675 R	55.7%	44.3%	55.7%	44.3%
2	1972	148,178	102,537	HANSEN, ORVAL H.	40,081	LUDLOW, WILLIS	5,560	62,456 R	69.2%	27.0%	71.9%	28.1%

IDAHO

1976 GENERAL ELECTION

President — Other vote was 5,935 Maddox (American); 3,558 MacBridge (Libertarian); 1,194 McCarthy (write-in); 739 LaRouche (U.S. Labor); 493 Anderson (write-in); 14 Camejo (write-in); 5 Hall (write-in); 2 Zeidler (write-in); 1 Wright (write-in); 1,430 scattered. The vote for McCarthy in Bannock county was corrected from 82 to 74 which changed the state-wide total write-in votes from 3,147 to 3,139.

Congress

1976 PRIMARIES

AUGUST 3 REPUBLICAN

Congress — Unopposed in CD 1. Contested as follows:

CD 2 — 31,444 George V. Hansen; 12,177 Glen Wegner; 4,309 George Forschler.

AUGUST 3 DEMOCRATIC

Congress — Unopposed in CD 1. Contested as follows:

CD 2 — 13,623 Stan Kress; 10,846 Kelly Pearce.

ILLINOIS

GOVERNOR

James R. Thompson (R). Elected 1976 to a two-year term.

SENATORS

Charles H. Percy (R). Re-elected 1972 to a six-year term. Previously elected 1966.

Adlai E. Stevenson, III (D). Re-elected 1974 to a six-year term. Previously elected 1970 to fill out term vacated by the death of Senator Everett M. Dirksen.

REPRESENTATIVES

1. Ralph H. Metcalfe (D)
2. Morgan F. Murphy (D)
3. Martin A. Russo (D)
4. Edward J. Derwinski (R)
5. John G. Fary (D)
6. Henry J. Hyde (R)
7. Cardiss Collins (D)
8. Daniel Rostenkowski (D)
9. Sidney R. Yates (D)
10. Abner J. Mikva (D)
11. Frank Annunzio (D)
12. Philip M. Crane (R)
13. Robert McClory (R)
14. John N. Erlenborn (R)
15. Tom Corcoran (R)
16. John B. Anderson (R)
17. George M. O'Brien (R)
18. Robert H. Michel (R)
19. Tom Railsback (R)
20. Paul Findley (R)
21. Edward R. Madigan (R)
22. George E. Shipley (D)
23. Melvin Price (D)
24. Paul Simon (D)

POSTWAR VOTE FOR GOVERNOR

								Percentage			
	Total	Republican		Democratic		Other	Rep.-Dem.	Total Vote		Major Vote	
Year	Vote	Vote	Candidate	Vote	Candidate	Vote	Plurality	Rep.	Dem.	Rep.	Dem.
1976s	4,638,997	3,000,395	Thompson, James R.	1,610,258	Howlett, Michael J.	28,344	1,390,137 R	64.7%	34.7%	65.1%	34.9%
1972	4,678,804	2,293,809	Ogilvie, Richard B.	2,371,303	Walker, Daniel	13,692	77,494 D	49.0%	50.7%	49.2%	50.8%
1968	4,506,000	2,307,295	Ogilvie, Richard B.	2,179,501	Shapiro, Samuel H.	19,204	127,794 R	51.2%	48.4%	51.4%	48.6%
1964	4,657,500	2,239,095	Percy, Charles H.	2,418,394	Kerner, Otto	11	179,299 D	48.1%	51.9%	48.1%	51.9%
1960	4,674,187	2,070,479	Stratton, William G.	2,594,731	Kerner, Otto	8,977	524,252 D	44.3%	55.5%	44.4%	55.6%
1956	4,314,611	2,171,786	Stratton, William G.	2,134,909	Austin, Richard B.	7,916	36,877 R	50.3%	49.5%	50.4%	49.6%
1952	4,415,864	2,317,363	Stratton, William G.	2,089,721	Dixon, Sherwood	8,780	227,642 R	52.5%	47.3%	52.6%	47.4%
1948	3,940,257	1,678,007	Green, Dwight H.	2,250,074	Stevenson, Adlai E.	12,176	572,067 D	42.6%	57.1%	42.7%	57.3%

The 1976 vote was for a two-year term to permit shifting the vote for Governor to non-Presidential years.

POSTWAR VOTE FOR SENATOR

								Percentage			
	Total	Republican		Democratic		Other	Rep.-Dem.	Total Vote		Major Vote	
Year	Vote	Vote	Candidate	Vote	Candidate	Vote	Plurality	Rep.	Dem.	Rep.	Dem.
1974	2,914,666	1,084,884	Burditt, George M.	1,811,496	Stevenson, Adlai E., III	18,286	726,612 D	37.2%	62.2%	37.5%	62.5%
1972	4,608,380	2,867,078	Percy, Charles H.	1,721,031	Pucinski, Roman C.	20,271	1,146,047 R	62.2%	37.3%	62.5%	37.5%
1970s	3,599,272	1,519,718	Smith, Ralph T.	2,065,054	Stevenson, Adlai E., III	14,500	545,336 D	42.2%	57.4%	42.4%	57.6%
1968	4,449,757	2,358,947	Dirksen, Everett M.	2,073,242	Clark, William G.	17,568	285,705 R	53.0%	46.6%	53.2%	46.8%
1966	3,822,725	2,100,449	Percy, Charles H.	1,678,147	Douglas, Paul H.	44,129	422,302 R	54.9%	43.9%	55.6%	44.4%
1962	3,709,216	1,961,202	Dirksen, Everett M.	1,748,007	Yates, Sidney R.	7	213,195 R	52.9%	47.1%	52.9%	47.1%
1960	4,632,796	2,093,846	Witwer, Samuel W.	2,530,943	Douglas, Paul H.	8,007	437,097 D	45.2%	54.6%	45.3%	54.7%
1956	4,264,830	2,307,352	Dirksen, Everett M.	1,949,883	Stengel, Richard	7,595	357,469 R	54.1%	45.7%	54.2%	45.8%
1954	3,368,025	1,563,683	Meek, Joseph T.	1,804,338	Douglas, Paul H.	4	240,655 D	46.4%	53.6%	46.4%	53.6%
1950	3,622,673	1,951,984	Dirksen, Everett M.	1,657,630	Lucas, Scott W.	13,059	294,354 R	53.9%	45.8%	54.1%	45.9%
1948	3,900,285	1,740,026	Brooks, C. Wayland	2,147,754	Douglas, Paul H.	12,505	407,728 D	44.6%	55.1%	44.8%	55.2%

The 1970 election was for a short term to fill a vacancy.

ILLINOIS

Districts Established September 20,1971

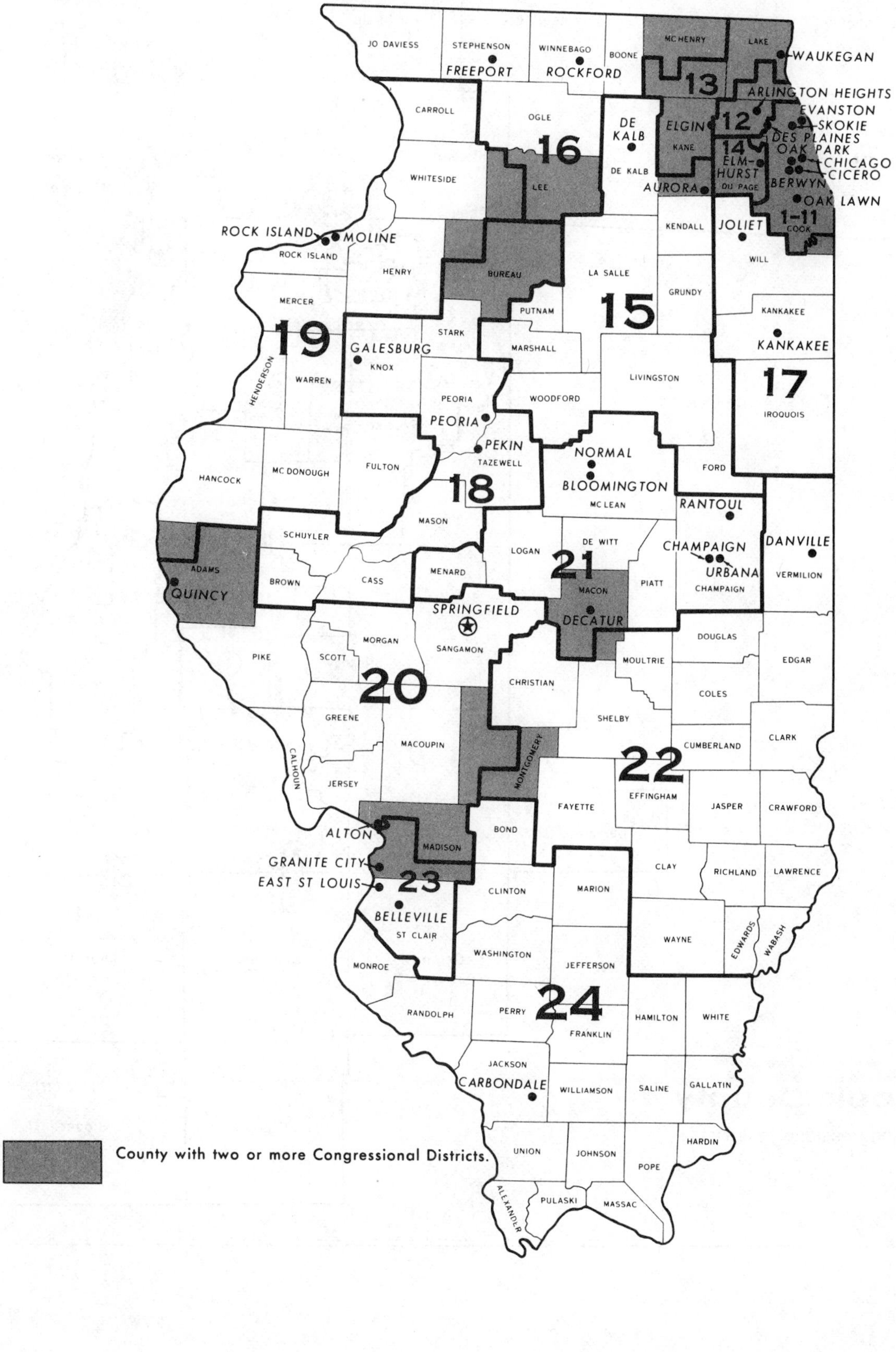

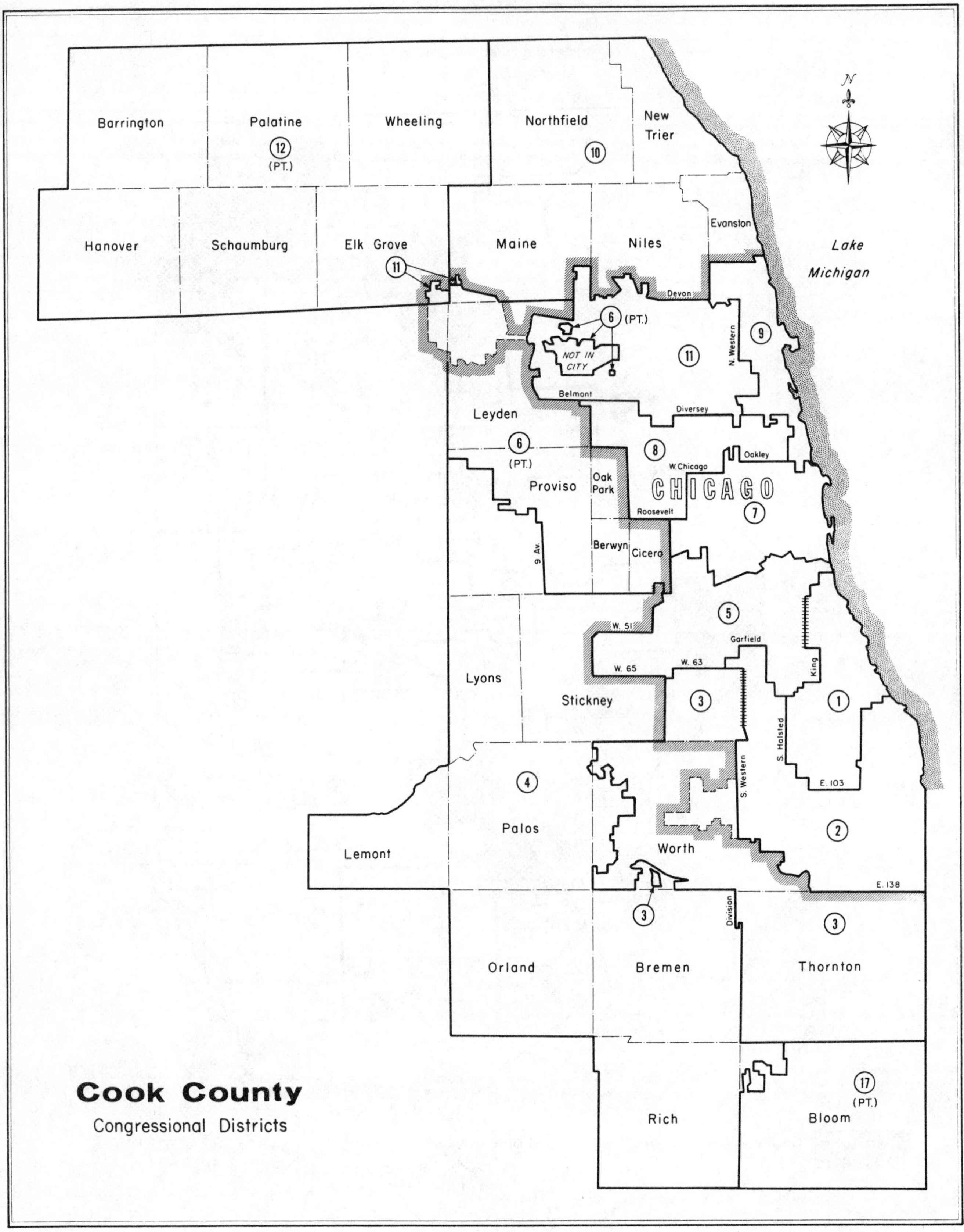

Cook County

Congressional Districts

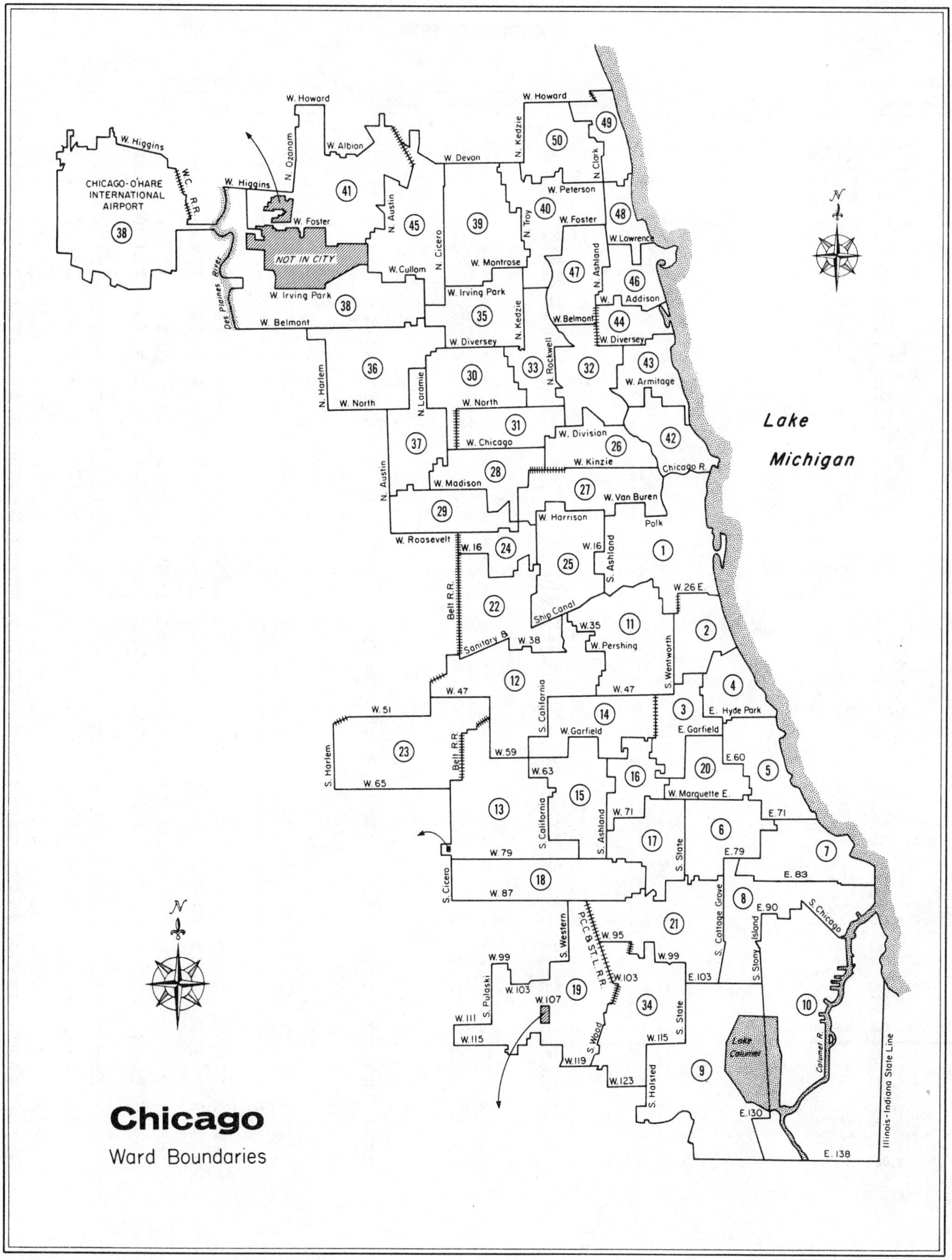

Chicago

Ward Boundaries

ILLINOIS

PRESIDENT 1976

1970 Census Population	County	Total Vote	Republican	Democratic	Other	Rep.-Dem. Plurality	Percentage Total Vote Rep.	Percentage Total Vote Dem.	Percentage Major Vote Rep.	Percentage Major Vote Dem.
70,861	ADAMS	30,485	18,189	11,926	370	6,263 R	59.7%	39.1%	60.4%	39.6%
12,015	ALEXANDER	5,658	2,349	3,246	63	897 D	41.5%	57.4%	42.0%	58.0%
14,012	BOND	7,478	3,716	3,682	80	34 R	49.7%	49.2%	50.2%	49.8%
25,440	BOONE	11,082	6,470	4,458	154	2,012 R	58.4%	40.2%	59.2%	40.8%
5,586	BROWN	3,103	1,519	1,533	51	14 D	49.0%	49.4%	49.8%	50.2%
38,541	BUREAU	18,648	10,854	7,566	228	3,288 R	58.2%	40.6%	58.9%	41.1%
5,675	CALHOUN	2,943	1,364	1,549	30	185 D	46.3%	52.6%	46.8%	53.2%
19,276	CARROLL	8,526	5,059	3,372	95	1,687 R	59.3%	39.5%	60.0%	40.0%
14,219	CASS	7,144	3,524	3,589	31	65 D	49.3%	50.2%	49.5%	50.5%
163,281	CHAMPAIGN	63,107	34,546	26,858	1,703	7,688 R	54.7%	42.6%	56.3%	43.7%
35,948	CHRISTIAN	16,960	7,445	9,306	209	1,861 D	43.9%	54.9%	44.4%	55.6%
16,216	CLARK	8,622	4,506	4,071	45	435 R	52.3%	47.2%	52.5%	47.5%
14,735	CLAY	7,729	3,860	3,837	32	23 R	49.9%	49.6%	50.1%	49.9%
28,315	CLINTON	13,671	7,245	6,275	151	970 R	53.0%	45.9%	53.6%	46.4%
47,815	COLES	20,162	11,021	8,639	502	2,382 R	54.7%	42.8%	56.1%	43.9%
5,492,369	COOK	2,209,581	987,498	1,180,814	41,269	193,316 D	44.7%	53.4%	45.5%	54.5%
19,824	CRAWFORD	10,622	5,522	5,007	93	515 R	52.0%	47.1%	52.4%	47.6%
9,772	CUMBERLAND	5,344	2,518	2,752	74	234 D	47.1%	51.5%	47.8%	52.2%
71,654	DE KALB	30,728	18,193	11,535	1,000	6,658 R	59.2%	37.5%	61.2%	38.8%
16,975	DE WITT	7,666	4,137	3,477	52	660 R	54.0%	45.4%	54.3%	45.7%
18,997	DOUGLAS	8,522	4,635	3,826	61	809 R	54.4%	44.9%	54.8%	45.2%
491,882	DU PAGE	254,547	175,055	72,137	7,355	102,918 R	68.8%	28.3%	70.8%	29.2%
21,591	EDGAR	11,021	5,842	5,058	121	784 R	53.0%	45.9%	53.6%	46.4%
7,090	EDWARDS	4,066	2,379	1,648	39	731 R	58.5%	40.5%	59.1%	40.9%
24,608	EFFINGHAM	13,391	7,194	5,952	245	1,242 R	53.7%	44.4%	54.7%	45.3%
20,752	FAYETTE	10,255	5,059	5,128	68	69 D	49.3%	50.0%	49.7%	50.3%
16,382	FORD	7,553	4,801	2,690	62	2,111 R	63.6%	35.6%	64.1%	35.9%
38,329	FRANKLIN	20,324	7,420	12,818	86	5,398 D	36.5%	63.1%	36.7%	63.3%
41,890	FULTON	19,090	9,588	9,314	188	274 R	50.2%	48.8%	50.7%	49.3%
7,418	GALLATIN	4,123	1,499	2,611	13	1,112 D	36.4%	63.3%	36.5%	63.5%
17,014	GREENE	7,827	3,706	4,057	64	351 D	47.3%	51.8%	47.7%	52.3%
26,535	GRUNDY	13,201	7,581	5,534	86	2,047 R	57.4%	41.9%	57.8%	42.2%
8,665	HAMILTON	5,498	2,433	3,036	29	603 D	44.3%	55.2%	44.5%	55.5%
23,645	HANCOCK	10,881	6,043	4,730	108	1,313 R	55.5%	43.5%	56.1%	43.9%
4,914	HARDIN	3,017	1,393	1,602	22	209 D	46.2%	53.1%	46.5%	53.5%
8,451	HENDERSON	4,407	2,210	2,152	45	58 R	50.1%	48.8%	50.7%	49.3%
53,217	HENRY	22,934	12,849	9,822	263	3,027 R	56.0%	42.8%	56.7%	43.3%
33,532	IROQUOIS	15,481	10,129	5,167	185	4,962 R	65.4%	33.4%	66.2%	33.8%
55,008	JACKSON	24,122	10,152	12,940	1,030	2,788 D	42.1%	53.6%	44.0%	56.0%
10,741	JASPER	5,650	2,794	2,772	84	22 R	49.5%	49.1%	50.2%	49.8%
31,446	JEFFERSON	16,520	7,422	8,989	109	1,567 D	44.9%	54.4%	45.2%	54.8%
18,492	JERSEY	8,983	4,273	4,625	85	352 D	47.6%	51.5%	48.0%	52.0%
21,766	JO DAVIESS	9,628	5,478	3,979	171	1,499 R	56.9%	41.3%	57.9%	42.1%
7,550	JOHNSON	4,628	2,417	2,182	29	235 R	52.2%	47.1%	52.6%	47.4%
251,005	KANE	95,374	59,275	34,057	2,042	25,218 R	62.2%	35.7%	63.5%	36.5%
97,250	KANKAKEE	42,108	23,003	18,394	711	4,609 R	54.6%	43.7%	55.6%	44.4%
26,374	KENDALL	13,349	9,011	4,202	136	4,809 R	67.5%	31.5%	68.2%	31.8%
61,280	KNOX	25,967	14,123	11,525	319	2,598 R	54.4%	44.4%	55.1%	44.9%
382,638	LAKE	153,204	92,231	57,741	3,232	34,490 R	60.2%	37.7%	61.5%	38.5%
111,409	LA SALLE	48,865	25,114	23,105	646	2,009 R	51.4%	47.3%	52.1%	47.9%
17,522	LAWRENCE	8,442	4,345	4,044	53	301 R	51.5%	47.9%	51.8%	48.2%
37,947	LEE	15,076	8,674	6,076	326	2,598 R	57.5%	40.3%	58.8%	41.2%
40,690	LIVINGSTON	15,640	10,097	5,174	369	4,923 R	64.6%	33.1%	66.1%	33.9%
33,538	LOGAN	14,386	8,623	5,686	77	2,937 R	59.9%	39.5%	60.3%	39.7%
36,653	MCDONOUGH	15,534	9,683	5,464	387	4,219 R	62.3%	35.2%	63.9%	36.1%
111,555	MCHENRY	54,989	37,115	16,799	1,075	20,316 R	67.5%	30.5%	68.8%	31.2%
104,389	MCLEAN	45,879	28,493	16,601	785	11,892 R	62.1%	36.2%	63.2%	36.8%
125,010	MACON	53,599	24,893	28,243	463	3,350 D	46.4%	52.7%	46.8%	53.2%
44,557	MACOUPIN	22,486	10,242	11,910	334	1,668 D	45.5%	53.0%	46.2%	53.8%
250,934	MADISON	101,998	44,183	56,457	1,358	12,274 D	43.3%	55.4%	43.9%	56.1%
38,986	MARION	18,720	8,729	9,834	157	1,105 D	46.6%	52.5%	47.0%	53.0%
13,302	MARSHALL	6,662	4,017	2,570	75	1,447 R	60.3%	38.6%	61.0%	39.0%
16,161	MASON	7,849	3,847	3,947	55	100 D	49.0%	50.3%	49.4%	50.6%
13,889	MASSAC	6,937	3,226	3,666	45	440 D	46.5%	52.8%	46.8%	53.2%
9,685	MENARD	5,479	3,137	2,301	41	836 R	57.3%	42.0%	57.7%	42.3%

ILLINOIS

PRESIDENT 1976

1970 Census Population	County	Total Vote	Republican	Democratic	Other	Rep.-Dem. Plurality	Percentage Total Vote Rep.	Total Vote Dem.	Major Vote Rep.	Major Vote Dem.
17,294	MERCER	8,982	4,816	4,090	76	726 R	53.6%	45.5%	54.1%	45.9%
18,831	MONROE	9,716	5,602	3,984	130	1,618 R	57.7%	41.0%	58.4%	41.6%
30,260	MONTGOMERY	15,848	7,379	8,322	147	943 D	46.6%	52.5%	47.0%	53.0%
36,174	MORGAN	16,489	8,885	7,403	201	1,482 R	53.9%	44.9%	54.5%	45.5%
13,263	MOULTRIE	6,169	2,803	3,332	34	529 D	45.4%	54.0%	45.7%	54.3%
42,867	OGLE	17,797	11,073	6,463	261	4,610 R	62.2%	36.3%	63.1%	36.9%
195,318	PEORIA	82,123	46,526	34,606	991	11,920 R	56.7%	42.1%	57.3%	42.7%
19,757	PERRY	11,395	5,286	5,976	133	690 D	46.4%	52.4%	46.9%	53.1%
15,509	PIATT	8,020	4,442	3,509	69	933 R	55.4%	43.8%	55.9%	44.1%
19,185	PIKE	10,110	4,975	5,006	129	31 D	49.2%	49.5%	49.8%	50.2%
3,857	POPE	2,275	1,187	1,070	18	117 R	52.2%	47.0%	52.6%	47.4%
8,741	PULASKI	4,345	1,836	2,489	20	653 D	42.3%	57.3%	42.5%	57.5%
5,007	PUTNAM	2,959	1,572	1,344	43	228 R	53.1%	45.4%	53.9%	46.1%
31,379	RANDOLPH	17,038	8,190	8,693	155	503 D	48.1%	51.0%	48.5%	51.5%
16,829	RICHLAND	8,057	4,434	3,485	138	949 R	55.0%	43.3%	56.0%	44.0%
166,734	ROCK ISLAND	71,261	34,007	35,994	1,260	1,987 D	47.7%	50.5%	48.6%	51.4%
285,176	ST. CLAIR	101,065	40,333	59,177	1,555	18,844 D	39.9%	58.6%	40.5%	59.5%
25,721	SALINE	13,493	5,970	7,472	51	1,502 D	44.2%	55.4%	44.4%	55.6%
161,335	SANGAMON	82,910	43,309	38,017	1,584	5,292 R	52.2%	45.9%	53.3%	46.7%
8,135	SCHUYLER	4,669	2,635	2,014	20	621 R	56.4%	43.1%	56.7%	43.3%
6,096	SCOTT	3,232	1,789	1,424	19	365 R	55.4%	44.1%	55.7%	44.3%
22,589	SHELBY	11,493	5,234	6,172	87	938 D	45.5%	53.7%	45.9%	54.1%
7,510	STARK	3,459	2,191	1,146	122	1,045 R	63.3%	33.1%	65.7%	34.3%
48,861	STEPHENSON	19,137	11,678	7,192	267	4,486 R	61.0%	37.6%	61.9%	38.1%
118,649	TAZEWELL	52,503	28,951	22,821	731	6,130 R	55.1%	43.5%	55.9%	44.1%
16,071	UNION	8,578	3,531	5,003	44	1,472 D	41.2%	58.3%	41.4%	58.6%
97,047	VERMILION	38,546	19,751	18,438	357	1,313 R	51.2%	47.8%	51.7%	48.3%
12,841	WABASH	6,227	3,388	2,781	58	607 R	54.4%	44.7%	54.9%	45.1%
21,595	WARREN	9,826	5,822	3,808	196	2,014 R	59.3%	38.8%	60.5%	39.5%
13,780	WASHINGTON	7,843	4,485	3,222	136	1,263 R	57.2%	41.1%	58.2%	41.8%
17,004	WAYNE	9,581	5,211	4,303	67	908 R	54.4%	44.9%	54.8%	45.2%
17,312	WHITE	9,933	4,600	5,306	27	706 D	46.3%	53.4%	46.4%	53.6%
62,877	WHITESIDE	25,854	14,308	11,255	291	3,053 R	55.3%	43.5%	56.0%	44.0%
249,498	WILL	114,695	61,784	51,103	1,808	10,681 R	53.9%	44.6%	54.7%	45.3%
49,021	WILLIAMSON	24,553	10,703	13,600	250	2,897 D	43.6%	55.4%	44.0%	56.0%
246,623	WINNEBAGO	97,360	52,736	42,399	2,225	10,337 R	54.2%	43.5%	55.4%	44.6%
28,012	WOODFORD	13,902	8,899	4,819	184	4,080 R	64.0%	34.7%	64.9%	35.1%
11,113,976	TOTAL	4,718,914	2,364,269	2,271,295	83,350	92,974 R	50.1%	48.1%	51.0%	49.0%

ILLINOIS

GOVERNOR 1976

1970 Census Population	County	Total Vote	Republican	Democratic	Other	Rep.-Dem. Plurality	Percentage Total Vote Rep.	Percentage Total Vote Dem.	Percentage Major Vote Rep.	Percentage Major Vote Dem.
70,861	ADAMS	30,101	22,726	7,301	74	15,425 R	75.5%	24.3%	75.7%	24.3%
12,015	ALEXANDER	5,465	2,557	2,880	28	323 D	46.8%	52.7%	47.0%	53.0%
14,012	BOND	7,316	4,644	2,659	13	1,985 R	63.5%	36.3%	63.6%	36.4%
25,440	BOONE	10,983	8,873	2,073	37	6,800 R	80.8%	18.9%	81.1%	18.9%
5,586	BROWN	3,041	2,043	966	32	1,077 R	67.2%	31.8%	67.9%	32.1%
38,541	BUREAU	18,372	13,182	5,144	46	8,038 R	71.8%	28.0%	71.9%	28.1%
5,675	CALHOUN	2,889	1,681	1,207	1	474 R	58.2%	41.8%	58.2%	41.8%
19,276	CARROLL	8,486	6,619	1,850	17	4,769 R	78.0%	21.8%	78.2%	21.8%
14,219	CASS	7,067	4,624	2,441	2	2,183 R	65.4%	34.5%	65.4%	34.6%
163,281	CHAMPAIGN	62,588	47,978	13,937	673	34,041 R	76.7%	22.3%	77.5%	22.5%
35,948	CHRISTIAN	16,873	10,945	5,880	48	5,065 R	64.9%	34.8%	65.1%	34.9%
16,216	CLARK	8,565	5,612	2,946	7	2,666 R	65.5%	34.4%	65.6%	34.4%
14,735	CLAY	7,645	4,947	2,693	5	2,254 R	64.7%	35.2%	64.8%	35.2%
28,315	CLINTON	13,488	8,658	4,815	15	3,843 R	64.2%	35.7%	64.3%	35.7%
47,815	COLES	19,554	14,343	5,128	83	9,215 R	73.4%	26.2%	73.7%	26.3%
5,492,369	COOK	2,166,567	1,240,751	910,409	15,407	330,342 R	57.3%	42.0%	57.7%	42.3%
19,824	CRAWFORD	10,525	7,035	3,479	11	3,556 R	66.8%	33.1%	66.9%	33.1%
9,772	CUMBERLAND	5,322	3,390	1,904	28	1,486 R	63.7%	35.8%	64.0%	36.0%
71,654	DE KALB	30,474	24,420	5,776	278	18,644 R	80.1%	19.0%	80.9%	19.1%
16,975	DE WITT	7,604	5,752	1,842	10	3,910 R	75.6%	24.2%	75.7%	24.3%
18,997	DOUGLAS	8,403	6,349	2,043	11	4,306 R	75.6%	24.3%	75.7%	24.3%
491,882	DU PAGE	252,616	205,873	43,715	3,028	162,158 R	81.5%	17.3%	82.5%	17.5%
21,591	EDGAR	10,952	6,982	3,935	35	3,047 R	63.8%	35.9%	64.0%	36.0%
7,090	EDWARDS	3,984	2,751	1,225	8	1,526 R	69.1%	30.7%	69.2%	30.8%
24,608	EFFINGHAM	13,293	8,622	4,599	72	4,023 R	64.9%	34.6%	65.2%	34.8%
20,752	FAYETTE	10,065	6,192	3,862	11	2,330 R	61.5%	38.4%	61.6%	38.4%
16,382	FORD	7,510	5,987	1,515	8	4,472 R	79.7%	20.2%	79.8%	20.2%
38,329	FRANKLIN	20,006	11,170	8,801	35	2,369 R	55.8%	44.0%	55.9%	44.1%
41,890	FULTON	18,987	12,647	6,278	62	6,369 R	66.6%	33.1%	66.8%	33.2%
7,418	GALLATIN	4,066	2,016	2,047	3	31 D	49.6%	50.3%	49.6%	50.4%
17,014	GREENE	7,722	5,000	2,712	10	2,288 R	64.8%	35.1%	64.8%	35.2%
26,535	GRUNDY	13,103	10,097	2,993	13	7,104 R	77.1%	22.8%	77.1%	22.9%
8,665	HAMILTON	5,396	3,318	2,073	5	1,245 R	61.5%	38.4%	61.5%	38.5%
23,645	HANCOCK	10,801	8,011	2,779	11	5,232 R	74.2%	25.7%	74.2%	25.8%
4,914	HARDIN	2,977	1,748	1,222	7	526 R	58.7%	41.0%	58.9%	41.1%
8,451	HENDERSON	4,374	2,880	1,490	4	1,390 R	65.8%	34.1%	65.9%	34.1%
53,217	HENRY	22,717	16,412	6,238	67	10,174 R	72.2%	27.5%	72.5%	27.5%
33,532	IROQUOIS	15,346	12,348	2,945	53	9,403 R	80.5%	19.2%	80.7%	19.3%
55,008	JACKSON	23,709	15,740	7,615	354	8,125 R	66.4%	32.1%	67.4%	32.6%
10,741	JASPER	5,617	3,552	2,060	5	1,492 R	63.2%	36.7%	63.3%	36.7%
31,446	JEFFERSON	16,294	10,252	6,019	23	4,233 R	62.9%	36.9%	63.0%	37.0%
18,492	JERSEY	8,897	5,593	3,296	8	2,297 R	62.9%	37.0%	62.9%	37.1%
21,766	JO DAVIESS	9,423	6,634	2,758	31	3,876 R	70.4%	29.3%	70.6%	29.4%
7,550	JOHNSON	4,546	3,073	1,467	6	1,606 R	67.6%	32.3%	67.7%	32.3%
251,005	KANE	92,944	72,760	19,707	477	53,053 R	78.3%	21.2%	78.7%	21.3%
97,250	KANKAKEE	41,537	28,303	13,013	221	15,290 R	68.1%	31.3%	68.5%	31.5%
26,374	KENDALL	13,399	11,556	1,821	22	9,735 R	86.2%	13.6%	86.4%	13.6%
61,280	KNOX	25,769	18,478	7,187	104	11,291 R	71.7%	27.9%	72.0%	28.0%
382,638	LAKE	149,680	118,839	30,056	785	88,783 R	79.4%	20.1%	79.8%	20.2%
111,409	LA SALLE	48,642	32,728	15,765	149	16,963 R	67.3%	32.4%	67.5%	32.5%
17,522	LAWRENCE	8,322	5,272	3,043	7	2,229 R	63.4%	36.6%	63.4%	36.6%
37,947	LEE	15,068	11,362	3,677	29	7,685 R	75.4%	24.4%	75.6%	24.4%
40,690	LIVINGSTON	15,083	11,514	3,517	52	7,997 R	76.3%	23.3%	76.6%	23.4%
33,538	LOGAN	14,294	10,735	3,549	10	7,186 R	75.1%	24.8%	75.2%	24.8%
36,653	MCDONOUGH	15,101	11,789	3,227	85	8,562 R	78.1%	21.4%	78.5%	21.5%
111,555	MCHENRY	54,844	45,280	9,341	223	35,939 R	82.6%	17.0%	82.9%	17.1%
104,389	MCLEAN	45,234	36,048	8,946	240	27,102 R	79.7%	19.8%	80.1%	19.9%
125,010	MACON	53,279	38,364	14,813	102	23,551 R	72.0%	27.8%	72.1%	27.9%
44,557	MACOUPIN	22,110	13,666	8,309	135	5,357 R	61.8%	37.6%	62.2%	37.8%
250,934	MADISON	100,127	59,451	40,412	264	19,039 R	59.4%	40.4%	59.5%	40.5%
38,986	MARION	18,489	10,687	7,753	49	2,934 R	57.8%	41.9%	58.0%	42.0%
13,302	MARSHALL	6,582	4,677	1,893	12	2,784 R	71.1%	28.8%	71.2%	28.8%
16,161	MASON	7,796	5,154	2,629	13	2,525 R	66.1%	33.7%	66.2%	33.8%
13,889	MASSAC	6,816	4,758	2,053	5	2,705 R	69.8%	30.1%	69.9%	30.1%
9,685	MENARD	5,410	3,944	1,461	5	2,483 R	72.9%	27.0%	73.0%	27.0%

ILLINOIS

GOVERNOR 1976

1970 Census Population	County	Total Vote	Republican	Democratic	Other	Rep.-Dem. Plurality	Percentage Total Vote Rep.	Total Vote Dem.	Major Vote Rep.	Major Vote Dem.
17,294	MERCER	8,885	6,527	2,350	8	4,177 R	73.5%	26.4%	73.5%	26.5%
18,831	MONROE	9,571	6,378	3,164	29	3,214 R	66.6%	33.1%	66.8%	33.2%
30,260	MONTGOMERY	15,645	9,842	5,793	10	4,049 R	62.9%	37.0%	62.9%	37.1%
36,174	MORGAN	16,182	11,117	5,021	44	6,096 R	68.7%	31.0%	68.9%	31.1%
13,263	MOULTRIE	6,019	4,359	1,656	4	2,703 R	72.4%	27.5%	72.5%	27.5%
42,867	OGLE	17,671	14,871	2,727	73	12,144 R	84.2%	15.4%	84.5%	15.5%
195,318	PEORIA	81,205	56,221	24,690	294	31,531 R	69.2%	30.4%	69.5%	30.5%
19,757	PERRY	11,170	6,720	4,412	38	2,308 R	60.2%	39.5%	60.4%	39.6%
15,509	PIATT	7,899	6,103	1,774	22	4,329 R	77.3%	22.5%	77.5%	22.5%
19,185	PIKE	9,918	6,562	3,265	91	3,297 R	66.2%	32.9%	66.8%	33.2%
3,857	POPE	2,243	1,517	723	3	794 R	67.6%	32.2%	67.7%	32.3%
8,741	PULASKI	4,161	2,256	1,898	7	358 R	54.2%	45.6%	54.3%	45.7%
5,007	PUTNAM	2,925	2,042	870	13	1,172 R	69.8%	29.7%	70.1%	29.9%
31,379	RANDOLPH	16,570	9,565	6,989	16	2,576 R	57.7%	42.2%	57.8%	42.2%
16,829	RICHLAND	7,977	5,423	2,500	54	2,923 R	68.0%	31.3%	68.4%	31.6%
166,734	ROCK ISLAND	69,356	45,970	22,846	540	23,124 R	66.3%	32.9%	66.8%	33.2%
285,176	ST. CLAIR	98,079	50,907	46,675	497	4,232 R	51.9%	47.6%	52.2%	47.8%
25,721	SALINE	13,313	7,783	5,517	13	2,266 R	58.5%	41.4%	58.5%	41.5%
161,335	SANGAMON	82,396	53,498	28,137	761	25,361 R	64.9%	34.1%	65.5%	34.5%
8,135	SCHUYLER	4,727	3,352	1,372	3	1,980 R	70.9%	29.0%	71.0%	29.0%
6,096	SCOTT	3,155	2,208	941	6	1,267 R	70.0%	29.8%	70.1%	29.9%
22,589	SHELBY	11,360	8,203	3,136	21	5,067 R	72.2%	27.6%	72.3%	27.7%
7,510	STARK	3,463	2,598	813	52	1,785 R	75.0%	23.5%	76.2%	23.8%
48,861	STEPHENSON	18,620	14,893	3,671	56	11,222 R	80.0%	19.7%	80.2%	19.8%
118,649	TAZEWELL	51,765	36,807	14,700	258	22,107 R	71.1%	28.4%	71.5%	28.5%
16,071	UNION	8,477	4,801	3,668	8	1,133 R	56.6%	43.3%	56.7%	43.3%
97,047	VERMILION	37,235	23,675	13,408	152	10,267 R	63.6%	36.0%	63.8%	36.2%
12,841	WABASH	6,066	3,623	2,427	16	1,196 R	59.7%	40.0%	59.9%	40.1%
21,595	WARREN	9,629	6,944	2,611	74	4,333 R	72.1%	27.1%	72.7%	27.3%
13,780	WASHINGTON	7,775	5,339	2,385	51	2,954 R	68.7%	30.7%	69.1%	30.9%
17,004	WAYNE	9,389	6,106	3,272	11	2,834 R	65.0%	34.8%	65.1%	34.9%
17,312	WHITE	9,631	5,608	4,013	10	1,595 R	58.2%	41.7%	58.3%	41.7%
62,877	WHITESIDE	25,561	19,051	6,437	73	12,614 R	74.5%	25.2%	74.7%	25.3%
249,498	WILL	114,144	81,497	32,226	421	49,271 R	71.4%	28.2%	71.7%	28.3%
49,021	WILLIAMSON	24,119	14,936	9,114	69	5,822 R	61.9%	37.8%	62.1%	37.9%
246,623	WINNEBAGO	94,778	73,114	20,839	825	52,275 R	77.1%	22.0%	77.8%	22.2%
28,012	WOODFORD	13,663	10,587	3,029	47	7,558 R	77.5%	22.2%	77.8%	22.2%
11,113,976	TOTAL	4,638,997	3,000,395	1,610,258	28,344	1,390,137 R	64.7%	34.7%	65.1%	34.9%

CHICAGO

PRESIDENT 1976

1970 Census Population	Ward	Total Vote	Republican	Democratic	Other	Rep.-Dem. Plurality	Percentage			
							Total Vote		Major Vote	
							Rep.	Dem.	Rep.	Dem.
68,950	WARD 1	17,059	3,498	13,338	223	9,840 D	20.5%	78.2%	20.8%	79.2%
75,533	WARD 2	18,550	1,740	16,509	301	14,769 D	9.4%	89.0%	9.5%	90.5%
68,992	WARD 3	15,403	884	14,329	190	13,445 D	5.7%	93.0%	5.8%	94.2%
68,549	WARD 4	19,628	2,235	16,991	402	14,756 D	11.4%	86.6%	11.6%	88.4%
66,918	WARD 5	23,763	4,144	18,809	810	14,665 D	17.4%	79.2%	18.1%	81.9%
67,715	WARD 6	24,295	2,137	21,907	251	19,770 D	8.8%	90.2%	8.9%	91.1%
	WARD 7	20,700	3,820	16,535	345	12,715 D	18.5%	79.9%	18.8%	81.2%
	WARD 8	26,921	1,836	24,795	290	22,959 D	6.8%	92.1%	6.9%	93.1%
66,932	WARD 9	19,962	1,961	17,783	218	15,822 D	9.8%	89.1%	9.9%	90.1%
67,074	WARD 10	28,461	8,975	19,084	402	10,109 D	31.5%	67.1%	32.0%	68.0%
66,549	WARD 11	29,254	7,097	21,807	350	14,710 D	24.3%	74.5%	24.6%	75.4%
66,389	WARD 12	28,573	12,704	15,399	470	2,695 D	44.5%	53.9%	45.2%	54.8%
56,766	WARD 13	36,120	18,149	17,383	588	766 R	50.2%	48.1%	51.1%	48.9%
66,638	WARD 14	23,904	7,727	15,792	385	8,065 D	32.3%	66.1%	32.9%	67.1%
67,502	WARD 15	24,464	6,867	17,239	358	10,372 D	28.1%	70.5%	28.5%	71.5%
65,890	WARD 16	17,566	822	16,557	187	15,735 D	4.7%	94.3%	4.7%	95.3%
68,514	WARD 17	18,638	907	17,547	184	16,640 D	4.9%	94.1%	4.9%	95.1%
67,720	WARD 18	30,258	10,804	19,023	431	8,219 D	35.7%	62.9%	36.2%	63.8%
66,876	WARD 19	35,157	18,857	15,587	713	3,270 R	53.6%	44.3%	54.7%	45.3%
69,504	WARD 20	19,228	1,465	17,549	214	16,084 D	7.6%	91.3%	7.7%	92.3%
67,181	WARD 21	27,911	1,771	25,863	277	24,092 D	6.3%	92.7%	6.4%	93.6%
68,276	WARD 22	17,959	4,398	13,258	303	8,860 D	24.5%	73.8%	24.9%	75.1%
66,437	WARD 23	32,792	16,224	15,966	602	258 R	49.5%	48.7%	50.4%	49.6%
67,369	WARD 24	14,636	508	13,989	139	13,481 D	3.5%	95.6%	3.5%	96.5%
66,131	WARD 25	15,210	2,719	12,308	183	9,589 D	17.9%	80.9%	18.1%	81.9%
68,562	WARD 26	18,287	4,757	13,239	291	8,482 D	26.0%	72.4%	26.4%	73.6%
67,816	WARD 27	14,706	901	13,617	188	12,716 D	6.1%	92.6%	6.2%	93.8%
69,293	WARD 28	14,602	601	13,839	162	13,238 D	4.1%	94.8%	4.2%	95.8%
67,023	WARD 29	15,095	866	14,070	159	13,204 D	5.7%	93.2%	5.8%	94.2%
65,760	WARD 30	23,838	9,980	13,370	488	3,390 D	41.9%	56.1%	42.7%	57.3%
66,866	WARD 31	19,680	3,851	15,544	285	11,693 D	19.6%	79.0%	19.9%	80.1%
67,704	WARD 32	19,107	5,316	13,404	387	8,088 D	27.8%	70.2%	28.4%	71.6%
68,514	WARD 33	20,496	7,165	12,908	423	5,743 D	35.0%	63.0%	35.7%	64.3%
67,953	WARD 34	25,351	1,510	23,641	200	22,131 D	6.0%	93.3%	6.0%	94.0%
65,434	WARD 35	27,184	13,496	13,112	576	384 R	49.6%	48.2%	50.7%	49.3%
68,089	WARD 36	33,636	16,547	16,475	614	72 R	49.2%	49.0%	50.1%	49.9%
66,974	WARD 37	22,273	4,867	17,057	349	12,190 D	21.9%	76.6%	22.2%	77.8%
64,071	WARD 38	33,706	17,995	15,095	616	2,900 R	53.4%	44.8%	54.4%	45.6%
68,755	WARD 39	27,464	12,965	13,929	570	964 D	47.2%	50.7%	48.2%	51.8%
65,533	WARD 40	27,668	11,998	15,051	619	3,053 D	43.4%	54.4%	44.4%	55.6%
66,932	WARD 41	40,579	23,713	16,109	757	7,604 R	58.4%	39.7%	59.5%	40.5%
69,355	WARD 42	29,341	12,937	15,662	742	2,725 D	44.1%	53.4%	45.2%	54.8%
69,173	WARD 43	33,574	15,788	16,342	1,444	554 D	47.0%	48.7%	49.1%	50.9%
66,575	WARD 44	24,444	9,743	13,776	925	4,033 D	39.9%	56.4%	41.4%	58.6%
67,071	WARD 45	35,110	19,091	15,320	699	3,771 R	54.4%	43.6%	55.5%	44.5%
65,242	WARD 46	21,308	7,887	12,791	630	4,904 D	37.0%	60.0%	38.1%	61.9%
68,280	WARD 47	26,811	11,965	14,266	580	2,301 D	44.6%	53.2%	45.6%	54.4%
67,982	WARD 48	24,031	10,031	13,323	677	3,292 D	41.7%	55.4%	43.0%	57.0%
68,548	WARD 49	27,922	10,614	16,028	1,280	5,414 D	38.0%	57.4%	39.8%	60.2%
67,000	WARD 50	34,822	12,498	21,442	882	8,944 D	35.9%	61.6%	36.8%	63.2%
3,366,957	TOTAL	1,227,447	389,331	814,757	23,359	425,426 D	31.7%	66.4%	32.3%	67.7%

CHICAGO

GOVERNOR 1976

1970 Census Population	Ward	Total Vote	Republican	Democratic	Other	Rep.-Dem. Plurality	Percentage Total Vote Rep.	Percentage Total Vote Dem.	Percentage Major Vote Rep.	Percentage Major Vote Dem.
68,950	WARD 1	16,638	4,586	11,920	132	7,334 D	27.6%	71.6%	27.8%	72.2%
75,533	WARD 2	17,494	4,758	12,520	216	7,762 D	27.2%	71.6%	27.5%	72.5%
68,992	WARD 3	14,551	2,316	12,054	181	9,738 D	15.9%	82.8%	16.1%	83.9%
68,549	WARD 4	18,502	5,450	12,775	277	7,325 D	29.5%	69.0%	29.9%	70.1%
66,918	WARD 5	22,777	12,050	10,179	548	1,871 R	52.9%	44.7%	54.2%	45.8%
67,715	WARD 6	22,947	6,648	16,028	271	9,380 D	29.0%	69.8%	29.3%	70.7%
	WARD 7	19,984	7,582	12,177	225	4,595 D	37.9%	60.9%	38.4%	61.6%
	WARD 8	25,989	8,417	17,360	212	8,943 D	32.4%	66.8%	32.7%	67.3%
66,932	WARD 9	19,380	5,602	13,625	153	8,023 D	28.9%	70.3%	29.1%	70.9%
67,074	WARD 10	27,684	11,818	15,669	197	3,851 D	42.7%	56.6%	43.0%	57.0%
66,549	WARD 11	28,558	6,740	21,664	154	14,924 D	23.6%	75.9%	23.7%	76.3%
66,389	WARD 12	27,738	13,870	13,666	202	204 R	50.0%	49.3%	50.4%	49.6%
56,766	WARD 13	35,384	17,852	17,345	187	507 R	50.5%	49.0%	50.7%	49.3%
66,638	WARD 14	23,386	8,440	14,755	191	6,315 D	36.1%	63.1%	36.4%	63.6%
67,502	WARD 15	23,809	8,255	15,369	185	7,114 D	34.7%	64.6%	34.9%	65.1%
65,890	WARD 16	16,871	2,737	13,958	176	11,221 D	16.2%	82.7%	16.4%	83.6%
68,514	WARD 17	17,880	4,017	13,632	231	9,615 D	22.5%	76.2%	22.8%	77.2%
67,720	WARD 18	29,578	12,679	16,715	184	4,036 D	42.9%	56.5%	43.1%	56.9%
66,876	WARD 19	34,914	17,183	17,536	195	353 D	49.2%	50.2%	49.5%	50.5%
69,504	WARD 20	18,236	3,755	14,294	187	10,539 D	20.6%	78.4%	20.8%	79.2%
67,181	WARD 21	26,675	8,537	17,830	308	9,293 D	32.0%	66.8%	32.4%	67.6%
68,276	WARD 22	17,402	5,907	11,326	169	5,419 D	33.9%	65.1%	34.3%	65.7%
66,437	WARD 23	32,176	17,141	14,832	203	2,309 R	53.3%	46.1%	53.6%	46.4%
67,369	WARD 24	13,967	1,588	12,245	134	10,657 D	11.4%	87.7%	11.5%	88.5%
66,131	WARD 25	15,080	3,589	11,380	111	7,791 D	23.8%	75.5%	24.0%	76.0%
68,562	WARD 26	17,515	5,560	11,792	163	6,232 D	31.7%	67.3%	32.0%	68.0%
67,816	WARD 27	14,307	1,583	12,547	177	10,964 D	11.1%	87.7%	11.2%	88.8%
69,293	WARD 28	14,010	1,985	11,850	175	9,865 D	14.2%	84.6%	14.3%	85.7%
67,023	WARD 29	14,544	2,470	11,907	167	9,437 D	17.0%	81.9%	17.2%	82.8%
65,760	WARD 30	23,199	12,345	10,572	282	1,773 R	53.2%	45.6%	53.9%	46.1%
66,866	WARD 31	19,096	4,829	14,092	175	9,263 D	25.3%	73.8%	25.5%	74.5%
67,704	WARD 32	18,494	6,721	11,566	207	4,845 D	36.3%	62.5%	36.8%	63.2%
68,514	WARD 33	19,849	9,147	10,502	200	1,355 D	46.1%	52.9%	46.6%	53.4%
67,953	WARD 34	24,552	5,869	18,442	241	12,573 D	23.9%	75.1%	24.1%	75.9%
65,434	WARD 35	26,535	16,678	9,641	216	7,037 R	62.9%	36.3%	63.4%	36.6%
68,089	WARD 36	32,884	18,190	14,408	286	3,782 R	55.3%	43.8%	55.8%	44.2%
66,974	WARD 37	21,643	7,006	14,453	184	7,447 D	32.4%	66.8%	32.6%	67.4%
64,071	WARD 38	32,915	20,123	12,546	246	7,577 R	61.1%	38.1%	61.6%	38.4%
68,755	WARD 39	27,009	15,533	11,304	172	4,229 R	57.5%	41.9%	57.9%	42.1%
65,533	WARD 40	27,150	15,359	11,550	241	3,809 R	56.6%	42.5%	57.1%	42.9%
66,932	WARD 41	39,823	24,356	15,243	224	9,113 R	61.2%	38.3%	61.5%	38.5%
69,355	WARD 42	28,635	15,446	12,925	264	2,521 R	53.9%	45.1%	54.4%	45.6%
69,173	WARD 43	32,684	22,002	10,254	428	11,748 R	67.3%	31.4%	68.2%	31.8%
66,575	WARD 44	23,816	13,619	9,873	324	3,746 R	57.2%	41.5%	58.0%	42.0%
67,071	WARD 45	34,555	20,859	13,453	243	7,406 R	60.4%	38.9%	60.8%	39.2%
65,242	WARD 46	20,923	10,860	9,800	263	1,060 R	51.9%	46.8%	52.6%	47.4%
68,280	WARD 47	26,392	13,926	12,268	198	1,658 R	52.8%	46.5%	53.2%	46.8%
67,982	WARD 48	23,271	12,954	10,045	272	2,909 R	55.7%	43.2%	56.3%	43.7%
68,548	WARD 49	27,426	14,294	12,743	389	1,551 R	52.1%	46.5%	52.9%	47.1%
67,000	WARD 50	34,062	18,170	15,627	265	2,543 R	53.3%	45.9%	53.8%	46.2%
3,366,957	TOTAL	1,192,889	511,401	670,257	11,231	158,856 D	42.9%	56.2%	43.3%	56.7%

ILLINOIS

CONGRESS

CD	Year	Total Vote	Republican Vote	Republican Candidate	Democratic Vote	Democratic Candidate	Other Vote	Rep.-Dem. Plurality	Percentage Total Vote Rep.	Percentage Total Vote Dem.	Percentage Major Vote Rep.	Percentage Major Vote Dem.
1	1976	137,193	10,147	RAYNER, A. A.	126,632	METCALFE, RALPH H.	414	116,485 D	7.4%	92.3%	7.4%	92.6%
1	1974	80,225	4,399	HAYNES, OSCAR H.	75,206	METCALFE, RALPH H.	620	70,807 D	5.5%	93.7%	5.5%	94.5%
1	1972	149,634	12,877	COGGS, LOUIS	136,755	METCALFE, RALPH H.	2	123,878 D	8.6%	91.4%	8.6%	91.4%
2	1976	150,335	23,037	LEAK, SPENCER	127,297	MURPHY, MORGAN F.	1	104,260 D	15.3%	84.7%	15.3%	84.7%
2	1974	75,198	9,386	GINDERSKE, JAMES J.	65,812	MURPHY, MORGAN F.		56,426 D	12.5%	87.5%	12.5%	87.5%
2	1972	153,698	38,391	DOYLE, JAMES E.	115,306	MURPHY, MORGAN F.	1	76,915 D	25.0%	75.0%	25.0%	75.0%
3	1976	196,365	79,434	BUIKEMA, RONALD	115,591	RUSSO, MARTIN A.	1,340	36,157 D	40.5%	58.9%	40.7%	59.3%
3	1974	124,227	58,891	HANRAHAN, ROBERT	65,336	RUSSO, MARTIN A.		6,445 D	47.4%	52.6%	47.4%	52.6%
3	1972	206,147	128,329	HANRAHAN, ROBERT	77,814	COMAN, DANIEL P.	4	50,515 R	62.3%	37.7%	62.3%	37.7%
4	1976	189,772	124,847	DERWINSKI, EDWARD J.	64,924	RODGER, RONALD A.	1	59,923 R	65.8%	34.2%	65.8%	34.2%
4	1974	115,524	68,428	DERWINSKI, EDWARD J.	47,096	RODGER, RONALD A.		21,332 R	59.2%	40.8%	59.2%	40.8%
4	1972	200,463	141,402	DERWINSKI, EDWARD J.	59,057	DORE, C. F.	4	82,345 R	70.5%	29.5%	70.5%	29.5%
5	1976	155,092	35,756	KROK, VINCENT S.	119,336	FARY, JOHN G.		83,580 D	23.1%	76.9%	23.1%	76.9%
5	1974	108,177	15,108	TOMS, WILLIAM	93,069	KLUCZYNSKI, JOHN C.		77,961 D	14.0%	86.0%	14.0%	86.0%
5	1972	166,544	45,264	JARZAB, LEONARD C.	121,278	KLUCZYNSKI, JOHN C.	2	76,014 D	27.2%	72.8%	27.2%	72.8%
6	1976	176,027	106,667	HYDE, HENRY J.	69,359	CLANCY, MARILYN D.	1	37,308 R	60.6%	39.4%	60.6%	39.4%
6	1974	123,681	66,027	HYDE, HENRY J.	57,654	HANRAHAN, EDWARD V.		8,373 R	53.4%	46.6%	53.4%	46.6%
6	1972	203,501	124,486	COLLIER, HAROLD R.	79,002	GALASSO, MICHAEL R.	13	45,484 R	61.2%	38.8%	61.2%	38.8%
7	1976	104,094	15,854	WARD, NEWELL	88,239	COLLINS, CARDISS	1	72,385 D	15.2%	84.8%	15.2%	84.8%
7	1974	72,762	8,800	METZGER, DONALD L.	63,962	COLLINS, CARDISS		55,162 D	12.1%	87.9%	12.1%	87.9%
7	1972	114,778	19,758	LENTO, THOMAS J.	95,018	COLLINS, GEORGE W.	2	75,260 D	17.2%	82.8%	17.2%	82.8%
8	1976	131,107	25,512	URBASZEWSKI, JOHN F.	105,595	ROSTENKOWSKI, DANIEL		80,083 D	19.5%	80.5%	19.5%	80.5%
8	1974	86,675	11,664	ODDO, SALVATORE E.	75,011	ROSTENKOWSKI, DANIEL		63,347 D	13.5%	86.5%	13.5%	86.5%
8	1972	149,219	38,758	STEPNOWSKI, EDWARD L.	110,457	ROSTENKOWSKI, DANIEL	4	71,699 D	26.0%	74.0%	26.0%	74.0%
9	1976	168,983	47,054	WAJERSKI, THOMAS J.	121,915	YATES, SIDNEY R.	14	74,861 D	27.8%	72.1%	27.8%	72.2%
9	1974	93,864			93,864	YATES, SIDNEY R.		93,864 D		100.0%		100.0%
9	1972	192,862	61,083	FETRIDGE, CLARK W.	131,777	YATES, SIDNEY R.	2	70,694 D	31.7%	68.3%	31.7%	68.3%
10	1976	213,414	106,603	YOUNG, SAMUEL H.	106,804	MIKVA, ABNER J.	7	201 D	50.0%	50.0%	50.0%	50.0%
10	1974	164,054	80,597	YOUNG, SAMUEL H.	83,457	MIKVA, ABNER J.		2,860 D	49.1%	50.9%	49.1%	50.9%
10	1972	233,929	120,681	YOUNG, SAMUEL H.	113,222	MIKVA, ABNER J.	26	7,459 R	51.6%	48.4%	51.6%	48.4%
11	1976	201,440	65,680	REBER, DANIEL C.	135,755	ANNUNZIO, FRANK	5	70,075 D	32.6%	67.4%	32.6%	67.4%
11	1974	141,723	39,182	ZADROZNY, MITCHELL G.	102,541	ANNUNZIO, FRANK		63,359 D	27.6%	72.4%	27.6%	72.4%
11	1972	222,415	103,773	HOELLEN, JOHN J.	118,637	ANNUNZIO, FRANK	5	14,864 D	46.7%	53.3%	46.7%	53.3%
12	1976	208,553	151,899	CRANE, PHILIP M.	56,644	FRANK, EDWIN L.	10	95,255 R	72.8%	27.2%	72.8%	27.2%
12	1974	115,780	70,731	CRANE, PHILIP M.	45,049	SPENCE, BETTY C.		25,682 R	61.1%	38.9%	61.1%	38.9%
12	1972	206,000	152,938	CRANE, PHILIP M.	53,055	FRANK, EDWIN L.	7	99,883 R	74.2%	25.8%	74.2%	25.8%
13	1976	164,266	109,726	MCCLORY, ROBERT	49,777	CUMMINGS, JAMES J.	4,763	59,949 R	66.8%	30.3%	68.8%	31.2%
13	1974	94,313	51,405	MCCLORY, ROBERT	42,903	BEETHAM, STANLEY W.	5	8,502 R	54.5%	45.5%	54.5%	45.5%
13	1972	159,738	98,201	MCCLORY, ROBERT	61,537	BEETHAM, STANLEY W.		36,664 R	61.5%	38.5%	61.5%	38.5%
14	1976	236,588	176,076	ERLENBORN, JOHN N.	60,505	FESE, MARIE A.	7	115,571 R	74.4%	25.6%	74.4%	25.6%
14	1974	116,699	77,718	ERLENBORN, JOHN N.	38,981	RENSHAW, ROBERT H.		38,737 R	66.6%	33.4%	66.6%	33.4%
14	1972	212,668	154,794	ERLENBORN, JOHN N.	57,874	WALL, JAMES M.		96,920 R	72.8%	27.2%	72.8%	27.2%
15	1976	190,231	102,555	CORCORAN, TOM	87,676	HALL, TIM L.		14,879 R	53.9%	46.1%	53.9%	46.1%
15	1974	119,007	54,278	CARLSON, CLIFFARD D.	61,912	HALL, TIM L.	2,817	7,634 D	45.6%	52.0%	46.7%	53.3%
15	1972	193,950	111,022	ARENDS, LESLIE C.	82,925	HALL, TIM L.	3	28,097 R	57.2%	42.8%	57.2%	42.8%
16	1976	168,328	114,324	ANDERSON, JOHN B.	54,002	EYTALIS, STEPHEN	2	60,322 R	67.9%	32.1%	67.9%	32.1%
16	1974	117,481	65,175	ANDERSON, JOHN B.	33,724	HUNGNESS, MARSHALL	18,582	31,451 R	55.5%	28.7%	65.9%	34.1%
16	1972	180,291	129,640	ANDERSON, JOHN B.	50,649	DEVINE, JOHN E.	2	78,991 R	71.9%	28.1%	71.9%	28.1%
17	1976	194,365	113,145	O BRIEN, GEORGE M.	81,220	KARLOCK, MERLIN		31,925 R	58.2%	41.8%	58.2%	41.8%
17	1974	116,525	59,984	O BRIEN, GEORGE M.	56,541	HOULIHAN, JOHN J.		3,443 R	51.5%	48.5%	51.5%	48.5%
17	1972	180,016	100,175	O BRIEN, GEORGE M.	79,840	HOULIHAN, JOHN J.	1	20,335 R	55.6%	44.4%	55.6%	44.4%
18	1976	187,130	108,028	MICHEL, ROBERT H.	79,102	RYAN, MATTHEW		28,926 R	57.7%	42.3%	57.7%	42.3%
18	1974	130,906	71,681	MICHEL, ROBERT H.	59,225	NORDVALL, STEPHEN L.		12,456 R	54.8%	45.2%	54.8%	45.2%
18	1972	191,921	124,407	MICHEL, ROBERT H.	67,514	NORDVALL, STEPHEN L.		56,893 R	64.8%	35.2%	64.8%	35.2%
19	1976	193,539	132,571	RAILSBACK, TOM	60,967	CRAVER, JOHN	1	71,604 R	68.5%	31.5%	68.5%	31.5%
19	1974	128,728	84,049	RAILSBACK, TOM	44,677	GENDE, JIM	2	39,372 R	65.3%	34.7%	65.3%	34.7%
19	1972	138,123	138,123	RAILSBACK, TOM				138,123 R	100.0%		100.0%	
20	1976	215,857	137,223	FINDLEY, PAUL	78,634	MACK, PETER F.		58,589 R	63.6%	36.4%	63.6%	36.4%
20	1974	153,987	84,426	FINDLEY, PAUL	69,551	MACK, PETER F.	10	14,875 R	54.8%	45.2%	54.8%	45.2%
20	1972	215,868	148,419	FINDLEY, PAUL	67,445	O SHEA, ROBERT S.	4	80,974 R	68.8%	31.2%	68.8%	31.2%
21	1976	184,035	137,037	MADIGAN, EDWARD R.	46,996	SCOTT, ANNA W.	2	90,041 R	74.5%	25.5%	74.5%	25.5%
21	1974	119,536	78,640	MADIGAN, EDWARD R.	40,896	SMALL, RICHARD N.		37,744 R	65.8%	34.2%	65.8%	34.2%
21	1972	182,496	99,966	MADIGAN, EDWARD R.	82,523	JOHNSON, LAWRENCE E.	7	17,443 R	54.8%	45.2%	54.8%	45.2%

ILLINOIS

CONGRESS

CD	Year	Total Vote	Republican Vote	Republican Candidate	Democratic Vote	Democratic Candidate	Other Vote	Rep.-Dem. Plurality	Percentage Total Vote Rep.	Percentage Total Vote Dem.	Percentage Major Vote Rep.	Percentage Major Vote Dem.
22	1976	210,289	81,102	MCGINNIS, RALPH Y.	129,187	SHIPLEY, GEORGE E.		48,085 D	38.6%	61.4%	38.6%	61.4%
22	1974	163,652	65,731	YOUNG, WILLIAM A.	97,921	SHIPLEY, GEORGE E.		32,190 D	40.2%	59.8%	40.2%	59.8%
22	1972	220,368	90,390	LAMKIN, ROBERT B.	124,589	SHIPLEY, GEORGE E.	5,389	34,199 D	41.0%	56.5%	42.0%	58.0%
23	1976	162,938	34,825	DRENOVAC, SAM P.	128,113	PRICE, MELVIN		93,288 D	21.4%	78.6%	21.4%	78.6%
23	1974	97,334	18,987	RANDOLPH, SCOTT R.	78,347	PRICE, MELVIN		59,360 D	19.5%	80.5%	19.5%	80.5%
23	1972	162,116	40,428	MAYS, ROBERT	121,682	PRICE, MELVIN	6	81,254 D	24.9%	75.1%	24.9%	75.1%
24	1976	226,110	73,766	PRINEAS, PETER G.	152,344	SIMON, PAUL		78,578 D	32.6%	67.4%	32.6%	67.4%
24	1974	182,051	73,634	OSHEL, VAL	108,417	SIMON, PAUL		34,783 D	40.4%	59.6%	40.4%	59.6%
24	1972	148,278			138,867	GRAY, KENNETH J.	9,411	138,867 D		93.7%		100.0%

ILLINOIS

1976 GENERAL ELECTION

President — Other vote was 55,939 McCarthy (Independent); 9,250 Hall (Communist); 8,057 MacBride (Libertarian); 3,615 Camejo (Socialist Workers); 2,422 Levin (Socialist Labor); 2,018 LaRouche (U.S. Labor); 387 Anderson (write-in); 1,662 scattered. In the final printed return – "The Official Vote" – the Schuyler county Republican vote was carried incorrectly as 22,635 and the Republican total vote incorrectly as 2,384,269.

Governor — The 1976 vote was for a two-year term to permit shifting the vote for Governor to non-Presidential years. Other vote was 10,091 Flory (Communist); 7,552 McCaffrey (Libertarian); 4,926 Haig (Socialist Workers); 3,147 LaForest (Socialist Labor); 2,302 Waffle (U.S. Labor); 326 scattered.

Congress — Other vote was DesLauiers (American Independent) in CD 13; 211 Simonsen (Workers), 198 Pulley (Socialist Workers) and 5 scattered in CD 1; 1,338 Collin (White Power) and 2 scattered in CD 3; and scattered in all other CD's.

CHICAGO

The boundary line between wards 7 and 8 was redrawn prior to the 1974 election and no population data is given for these wards.

President — Other vote was 13,671 McCarthy (Independent); 4,681 Hall (Communist); 1,758 MacBride (Libertarian); 1,520 Levin (Socialist Labor); 893 Camejo (Socialist Workers); 836 LaRouche (U.S. Labor). There were 714 write-in votes in Cook county, but these are not available by wards within the city of Chicago.

Governor — Other vote was 5,965 Flory (Communist); 1,618 LaForest (Socialist Labor); 1,565 McCaffrey (Libertarian); 1,192 Haig (Socialist Workers); 891 Waffle (U.S. Labor). There were 111 write-in votes in Cook county, but these are not available by wards within the city of Chicago.

1976 PRIMARIES

MARCH 16 REPUBLICAN

Governor — 625,457 James R. Thompson; 97,937 Richard H. Cooper; 170 scattered.

Congress — Unopposed in sixteen CD's. No candidate in CD 7; in that CD Newell Ward was named after the primary by the local party committee. Contested as follows:

- CD 3 — 14,692 Ronald Buikema; 4,218 Glen J. Allred; 3,005 Robert C. Gorman; 2,840 Carl L. Klein; 1 scattered.
- CD 8 — 2,640 John F. Urbaszewski; 774 Carl C. LoDico.
- CD 10 — 21,194 Samuel H. Young; 14,458 Daniel B. Hales; 6,683 John J. Nimrod.
- CD 11 — 5,911 Daniel C. Reber; 4,394 Mitchell G. Zadrosny; 3,050 Edward D. Kelley.
- CD 14 — 53,627 John N. Erlenborn; 10,528 William A. Broderick; 1 scattered.
- CD 15 — 18,798 Tom Corcoran; 15,705 James R. Washburn; 7,820 John A. Cunningham; 3,923 Walter B. Lunsford; 1,565 Clarence E. Batchelor.
- CD 20 — 36,139 Paul Findley; 4,017 Hank McCune.

ILLINOIS

MARCH 16 DEMOCRATIC

Governor	811,721 Michael J. Howlett; 696,380 Daniel Walker; 245 scattered.
Congress	Unopposed in seventeen CD's. Contested as follows:
CD 1	56,101 Ralph H. Metcalfe; 22,028 Erwin A. France.
CD 2	43,528 Morgan F. Murphy; 12,487 Andrew Tucker.
CD 6	23,105 Marilyn D. Clancy; 12,390 R. G. Patrick Logan.
CD 13	14,979 James J. Cummings; 12,148 F. James Lumber; 5 scattered.
CD 14	13,023 Marie A. Fese; 8,579 Winfield Green; 6,885 Nicholas F. Thomas; 3,573 Romaine Troost; 2 scattered.
CD 16	No candidates appeared on the ballot; there were 166 write-in votes for Stephen Eyatalis; 128 Margaret Brechon; 54 scattered.
CD 18	25,943 Matthew Ryan; 9,443 Virgil R. Grunkemeyer; 5,022 George W. Zaehringer; 7 scattered.

INDIANA

GOVERNOR

Otis R. Bowen (R). Re-elected 1976 to a four-year term. Previously elected 1972.

SENATORS

Birch Bayh (D). Re-elected 1974 to a six-year term. Previously elected 1968, 1962.

Richard G. Lugar (R). Elected 1976 to a six-year term.

REPRESENTATIVES

1. Adam Benjamin (D)
2. Floyd Fithian (D)
3. John Brademas (D)
4. J. Danforth Quayle (R)
5. Elwood H. Hillis (R)
6. David W. Evans (D)
7. John T. Myers (R)
8. David L. Cornwell (D)
9. Lee H. Hamilton (D)
10. Philip R. Sharp (D)
11. Andrew Jacobs, Jr. (D)

POSTWAR VOTE FOR GOVERNOR

		Republican		Democratic				Percentage			
	Total					Other	Rep.-Dem.	Total Vote		Major Vote	
Year	Vote	Vote	Candidate	Vote	Candidate	Vote	Plurality	Rep.	Dem.	Rep.	Dem.
1976	2,175,324	1,236,555	Bowen, Otis R.	927,243	Conrad, Larry A.	11,526	309,312 R	56.8%	42.6%	57.1%	42.9%
1972	2,120,847	1,203,903	Bowen, Otis R.	900,489	Welsh, Matthew E.	16,455	303,414 R	56.8%	42.5%	57.2%	42.8%
1968	2,049,072	1,080,271	Whitcomb, Edgar D.	965,816	Rock, Robert L.	2,985	114,455 R	52.7%	47.1%	52.8%	47.2%
1964	2,072,915	901,342	Ristine, Richard O.	1,164,620	Branigin, Roger D.	6,953	263,278 D	43.5%	56.2%	43.6%	56.4%
1960	2,128,965	1,049,540	Parker, Crawford F.	1,072,717	Welsh, Matthew E.	6,708	23,177 D	49.3%	50.4%	49.5%	50.5%
1956	1,954,290	1,086,868	Handley, Harold W.	859,393	Tucker, Ralph	8,029	227,475 R	55.6%	44.0%	55.8%	44.2%
1952	1,931,869	1,075,685	Craig, George N.	841,984	Watkins, John A.	14,200	233,701 R	55.7%	43.6%	56.1%	43.9%
1948	1,652,321	745,892	Creighton, Hobart	884,995	Schricker, Henry F.	21,434	139,103 D	45.1%	53.6%	45.7%	54.3%

POSTWAR VOTE FOR SENATOR

		Republican		Democratic				Percentage			
	Total					Other	Rep.-Dem.	Total Vote		Major Vote	
Year	Vote	Vote	Candidate	Vote	Candidate	Vote	Plurality	Rep.	Dem.	Rep.	Dem.
1976	2,171,187	1,275,833	Lugar, Richard G.	878,522	Hartke, R. Vance	16,832	397,311 R	58.8%	40.5%	59.2%	40.8%
1974	1,752,978	814,117	Lugar, Richard G.	889,269	Bayh, Birch	49,592	75,152 D	46.4%	50.7%	47.8%	52.2%
1970	1,737,697	866,707	Roudebush, Richard	870,990	Hartke, R. Vance	–	4,283 D	49.9%	50.1%	49.9%	50.1%
1968	2,053,118	988,571	Ruckelshaus, William	1,060,456	Bayh, Birch	4,091	71,885 D	48.1%	51.7%	48.2%	51.8%
1964	2,076,963	941,519	Bontrager, D. Russell	1,128,505	Hartke, R. Vance	6,939	186,986 D	45.3%	54.3%	45.5%	54.5%
1962	1,800,038	894,547	Capehart, Homer E.	905,491	Bayh, Birch	–	10,944 D	49.7%	50.3%	49.7%	50.3%
1958	1,724,598	731,635	Handley, Harold W.	973,636	Hartke, R. Vance	19,327	242,001 D	42.4%	56.5%	42.9%	57.1%
1956	1,963,986	1,084,262	Capehart, Homer E.	871,781	Wickard, Claude	7,943	212,481 R	55.2%	44.4%	55.4%	44.6%
1952	1,946,118	1,020,605	Jenner, William E.	911,169	Schricker, Henry F.	14,344	109,436 R	52.4%	46.8%	52.8%	47.2%
1950	1,598,724	844,303	Capehart, Homer E.	741,025	Campbell, Alex M.	13,396	103,278 R	52.8%	46.4%	53.3%	46.7%
1946	1,347,434	739,809	Jenner, William E.	584,288	Townsend, M. Clifford	23,337	155,521 R	54.9%	43.4%	55.9%	44.1%

INDIANA

Districts Established February 16, 1972

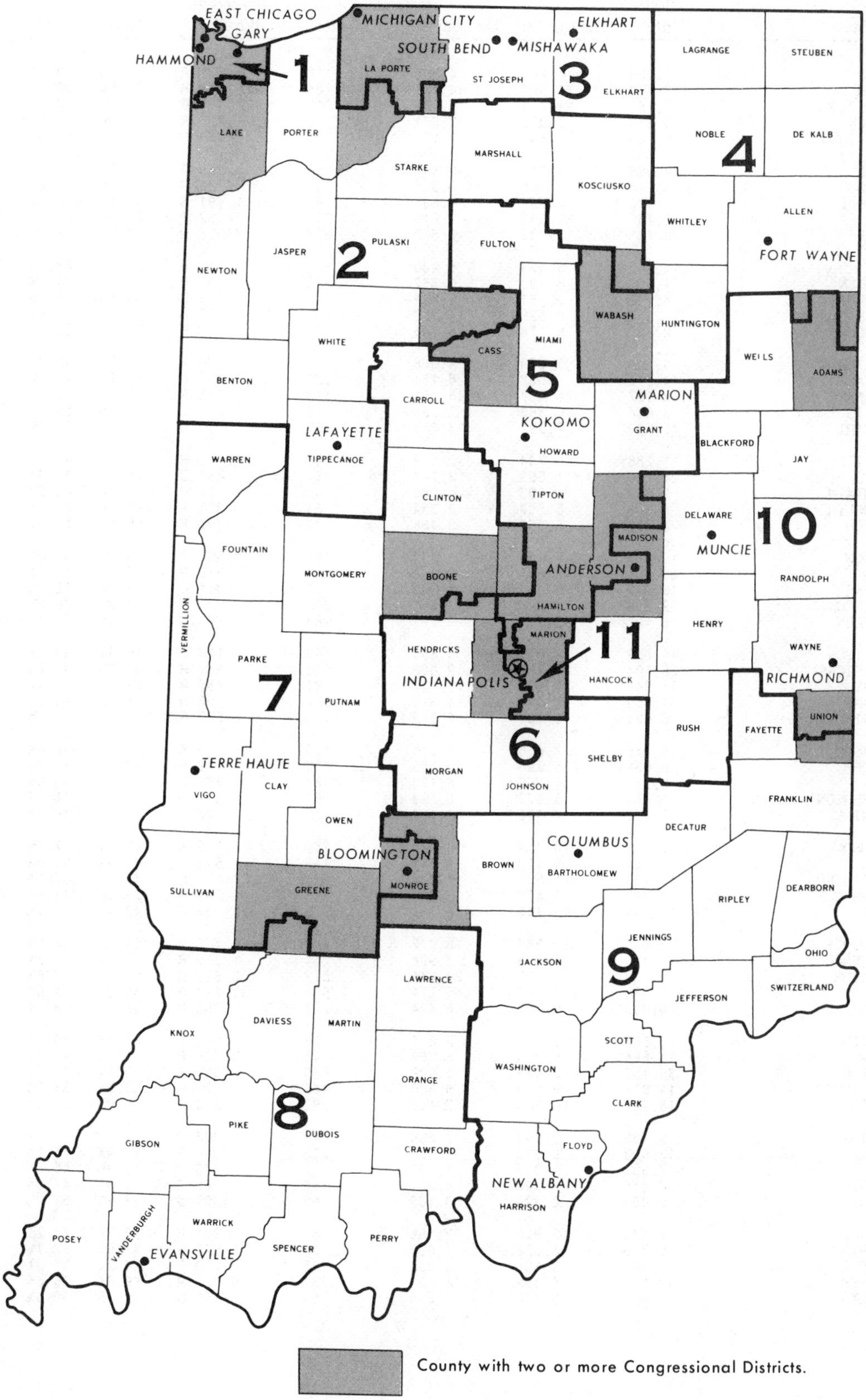

County with two or more Congressional Districts.

INDIANA

PRESIDENT 1976

1970 Census Population	County	Total Vote	Republican	Democratic	Other	Rep.-Dem. Plurality	Percentage Total Vote Rep.	Percentage Total Vote Dem.	Percentage Major Vote Rep.	Percentage Major Vote Dem.
26,871	ADAMS	11,306	6,280	4,908	118	1,372 R	55.5%	43.4%	56.1%	43.9%
280,455	ALLEN	117,769	71,321	44,744	1,704	26,577 R	60.6%	38.0%	61.4%	38.6%
57,022	BARTHOLOMEW	26,187	14,771	11,203	213	3,568 R	56.4%	42.8%	56.9%	43.1%
11,262	BENTON	5,234	3,093	2,071	70	1,022 R	59.1%	39.6%	59.9%	40.1%
15,888	BLACKFORD	6,120	2,886	3,174	60	288 D	47.2%	51.9%	47.6%	52.4%
30,870	BOONE	14,986	9,214	5,686	86	3,528 R	61.5%	37.9%	61.8%	38.2%
9,057	BROWN	4,904	2,466	2,381	57	85 R	50.3%	48.6%	50.9%	49.1%
17,734	CARROLL	8,493	4,797	3,606	90	1,191 R	56.5%	42.5%	57.1%	42.9%
40,456	CASS	18,231	10,342	7,610	279	2,732 R	56.7%	41.7%	57.6%	42.4%
75,876	CLARK	29,731	12,732	16,670	329	3,938 D	42.8%	56.1%	43.3%	56.7%
23,933	CLAY	11,265	5,674	5,433	158	241 R	50.4%	48.2%	51.1%	48.9%
30,547	CLINTON	14,963	8,199	6,662	102	1,537 R	54.8%	44.5%	55.2%	44.8%
8,033	CRAWFORD	4,948	2,181	2,721	46	540 D	44.1%	55.0%	44.5%	55.5%
26,602	DAVIESS	11,838	6,829	4,952	57	1,877 R	57.7%	41.8%	58.0%	42.0%
29,430	DEARBORN	12,595	6,176	6,348	71	172 D	49.0%	50.4%	49.3%	50.7%
22,738	DECATUR	9,985	5,555	4,365	65	1,190 R	55.6%	43.7%	56.0%	44.0%
30,837	DE KALB	14,246	7,860	6,151	235	1,709 R	55.2%	43.2%	56.1%	43.9%
129,219	DELAWARE	52,087	26,417	25,151	519	1,266 R	50.7%	48.3%	51.2%	48.8%
30,934	DUBOIS	13,884	6,383	7,385	116	1,002 D	46.0%	53.2%	46.4%	53.6%
126,529	ELKHART	45,429	27,291	17,581	557	9,710 R	60.1%	38.7%	60.8%	39.2%
26,216	FAYETTE	11,288	5,704	5,519	65	185 R	50.5%	48.9%	50.8%	49.2%
55,622	FLOYD	24,255	11,259	12,744	252	1,485 D	46.4%	52.5%	46.9%	53.1%
18,257	FOUNTAIN	9,052	4,903	4,089	60	814 R	54.2%	45.2%	54.5%	45.5%
16,943	FRANKLIN	6,845	3,557	3,234	54	323 R	52.0%	47.2%	52.4%	47.6%
16,984	FULTON	8,703	5,083	3,488	132	1,595 R	58.4%	40.1%	59.3%	40.7%
30,444	GIBSON	15,599	7,105	8,430	64	1,325 D	45.5%	54.0%	45.7%	54.3%
83,955	GRANT	30,554	16,847	13,468	239	3,379 R	55.1%	44.1%	55.6%	44.4%
26,894	GREENE	13,843	6,442	7,263	138	821 D	46.5%	52.5%	47.0%	53.0%
54,532	HAMILTON	29,958	21,828	7,857	273	13,971 R	72.9%	26.2%	73.5%	26.5%
35,096	HANCOCK	16,427	10,072	6,191	164	3,881 R	61.3%	37.7%	61.9%	38.1%
20,423	HARRISON	10,699	4,911	5,685	103	774 D	45.9%	53.1%	46.3%	53.7%
53,974	HENDRICKS	26,104	16,725	9,066	313	7,659 R	64.1%	34.7%	64.8%	35.2%
52,603	HENRY	21,848	11,620	10,137	91	1,483 R	53.2%	46.4%	53.4%	46.6%
83,198	HOWARD	34,653	19,571	14,815	267	4,756 R	56.5%	42.8%	56.9%	43.1%
34,970	HUNTINGTON	15,890	9,182	6,515	193	2,667 R	57.8%	41.0%	58.5%	41.5%
33,187	JACKSON	15,358	7,615	7,610	133	5 R	49.6%	49.6%	50.0%	50.0%
20,429	JASPER	8,884	5,398	3,286	200	2,112 R	60.8%	37.0%	62.2%	37.8%
23,575	JAY	8,817	4,606	4,124	87	482 R	52.2%	46.8%	52.8%	47.2%
27,006	JEFFERSON	11,873	5,573	6,139	161	566 D	46.9%	51.7%	47.6%	52.4%
19,454	JENNINGS	9,012	4,505	4,430	77	75 R	50.0%	49.2%	50.4%	49.6%
61,138	JOHNSON	26,749	16,414	10,075	260	6,339 R	61.4%	37.7%	62.0%	38.0%
41,546	KNOX	18,860	9,100	9,612	148	512 D	48.3%	51.0%	48.6%	51.4%
48,127	KOSCIUSKO	22,124	14,505	7,328	291	7,177 R	65.6%	33.1%	66.4%	33.6%
20,890	LA GRANGE	6,772	3,876	2,835	61	1,041 R	57.2%	41.9%	57.8%	42.2%
546,253	LAKE	212,741	90,119	120,700	1,922	30,581 D	42.4%	56.7%	42.7%	57.3%
105,342	LA PORTE	40,655	21,989	18,217	449	3,772 R	54.1%	44.8%	54.7%	45.3%
38,038	LAWRENCE	17,440	9,278	7,908	254	1,370 R	53.2%	45.3%	54.0%	46.0%
138,451	MADISON	62,820	32,437	29,811	572	2,626 R	51.6%	47.5%	52.1%	47.9%
792,299	MARION	325,576	177,767	145,274	2,535	32,493 R	54.6%	44.6%	55.0%	45.0%
34,986	MARSHALL	16,408	9,707	6,424	277	3,283 R	59.2%	39.2%	60.2%	39.8%
10,969	MARTIN	5,565	2,702	2,827	36	125 D	48.6%	50.8%	48.9%	51.1%
39,246	MIAMI	14,665	8,263	6,257	145	2,006 R	56.3%	42.7%	56.9%	43.1%
84,849	MONROE	36,182	18,938	16,609	635	2,329 R	52.3%	45.9%	53.3%	46.7%
33,930	MONTGOMERY	14,977	9,509	5,320	148	4,189 R	63.5%	35.5%	64.1%	35.9%
44,176	MORGAN	18,427	10,983	7,181	263	3,802 R	59.6%	39.0%	60.5%	39.5%
11,606	NEWTON	5,483	3,204	2,236	43	968 R	58.4%	40.8%	58.9%	41.1%
31,382	NOBLE	13,013	6,885	5,875	253	1,010 R	52.9%	45.1%	54.0%	46.0%
4,289	OHIO	2,337	1,027	1,300	10	273 D	43.9%	55.6%	44.1%	55.9%
16,968	ORANGE	8,476	4,399	4,031	46	368 R	51.9%	47.6%	52.2%	47.8%
12,163	OWEN	6,055	2,896	3,103	56	207 D	47.8%	51.2%	48.3%	51.7%
14,600	PARKE	7,144	3,929	3,158	57	771 R	55.0%	44.2%	55.4%	44.6%
19,075	PERRY	9,746	4,088	5,620	38	1,532 D	41.9%	57.7%	42.1%	57.9%
12,281	PIKE	7,101	3,138	3,938	25	800 D	44.2%	55.5%	44.3%	55.7%
87,114	PORTER	42,658	25,489	16,468	701	9,021 R	59.8%	38.6%	60.8%	39.2%
21,740	POSEY	10,488	5,136	5,298	54	162 D	49.0%	50.5%	49.2%	50.8%

INDIANA

PRESIDENT 1976

1970 Census Population	County	Total Vote	Republican	Democratic	Other	Rep.-Dem. Plurality	Percentage Total Vote Rep.	Percentage Total Vote Dem.	Percentage Major Vote Rep.	Percentage Major Vote Dem.
12,534	PULASKI	6,615	3,586	2,813	216	773 R	54.2%	42.5%	56.0%	44.0%
26,932	PUTNAM	11,297	6,063	5,116	118	947 R	53.7%	45.3%	54.2%	45.8%
28,915	RANDOLPH	12,320	6,891	5,330	99	1,561 R	55.9%	43.3%	56.4%	43.6%
21,138	RIPLEY	10,157	5,293	4,792	72	501 R	52.1%	47.2%	52.5%	47.5%
20,352	RUSH	7,830	4,723	3,052	55	1,671 R	60.3%	39.0%	60.7%	39.3%
245,045	ST. JOSEPH	100,324	50,358	49,156	810	1,202 R	50.2%	49.0%	50.6%	49.4%
17,144	SCOTT	6,966	2,657	4,229	80	1,572 D	38.1%	60.7%	38.6%	61.4%
37,797	SHELBY	16,150	8,918	7,098	134	1,820 R	55.2%	44.0%	55.7%	44.3%
17,134	SPENCER	8,990	4,166	4,796	28	630 D	46.3%	53.3%	46.5%	53.5%
19,280	STARKE	9,241	4,354	4,753	134	399 D	47.1%	51.4%	47.8%	52.2%
20,159	STEUBEN	8,575	5,079	3,323	173	1,756 R	59.2%	38.8%	60.4%	39.6%
19,889	SULLIVAN	9,006	3,747	5,198	61	1,451 D	41.6%	57.7%	41.9%	58.1%
6,306	SWITZERLAND	3,491	1,329	2,150	12	821 D	38.1%	61.6%	38.2%	61.8%
109,378	TIPPECANOE	47,587	29,186	17,850	551	11,336 R	61.3%	37.5%	62.1%	37.9%
16,650	TIPTON	8,328	4,776	3,428	124	1,348 R	57.3%	41.2%	58.2%	41.8%
6,582	UNION	2,800	1,631	1,160	9	471 R	58.3%	41.4%	58.4%	41.6%
168,772	VANDERBURGH	73,211	37,975	34,911	325	3,064 R	51.9%	47.7%	52.1%	47.9%
16,793	VERMILLION	8,538	3,674	4,791	73	1,117 D	43.0%	56.1%	43.4%	56.6%
114,528	VIGO	48,610	23,555	24,684	371	1,129 D	48.5%	50.8%	48.8%	51.2%
35,553	WABASH	14,340	8,534	5,704	102	2,830 R	59.5%	39.8%	59.9%	40.1%
8,705	WARREN	4,312	2,377	1,906	29	471 R	55.1%	44.2%	55.5%	44.5%
27,972	WARRICK	15,096	7,200	7,804	92	604 D	47.7%	51.7%	48.0%	52.0%
19,278	WASHINGTON	8,318	3,794	4,409	115	615 D	45.6%	53.0%	46.3%	53.7%
79,109	WAYNE	29,191	16,697	12,306	188	4,391 R	57.2%	42.2%	57.6%	42.4%
23,821	WELLS	9,934	5,596	4,250	88	1,346 R	56.3%	42.8%	56.8%	43.2%
20,995	WHITE	10,369	6,287	3,963	119	2,324 R	60.6%	38.2%	61.3%	38.7%
23,395	WHITLEY	12,441	6,761	5,445	235	1,316 R	54.3%	43.8%	55.4%	44.6%
5,193,669	TOTAL	2,220,362	1,183,958	1,014,714	21,690	169,244 R	53.3%	45.7%	53.8%	46.2%

INDIANA

GOVERNOR 1976

1970 Census Population	County	Total Vote	Republican	Democratic	Other	Rep.-Dem. Plurality	Percentage Total Vote Rep.	Percentage Total Vote Dem.	Percentage Major Vote Rep.	Percentage Major Vote Dem.
26,871	ADAMS	11,102	6,025	5,008	69	1,017 R	54.3%	45.1%	54.6%	45.4%
280,455	ALLEN	114,856	71,985	41,859	1,012	30,126 R	62.7%	36.4%	63.2%	36.8%
57,022	BARTHOLOMEW	25,935	15,340	10,507	88	4,833 R	59.1%	40.5%	59.3%	40.7%
11,262	BENTON	5,094	3,295	1,776	23	1,519 R	64.7%	34.9%	65.0%	35.0%
15,888	BLACKFORD	6,030	3,212	2,794	24	418 R	53.3%	46.3%	53.5%	46.5%
30,870	BOONE	14,907	9,540	5,311	56	4,229 R	64.0%	35.6%	64.2%	35.8%
9,057	BROWN	4,807	2,637	2,145	25	492 R	54.9%	44.6%	55.1%	44.9%
17,734	CARROLL	8,271	5,249	2,994	28	2,255 R	63.5%	36.2%	63.7%	36.3%
40,456	CASS	17,934	11,112	6,688	134	4,424 R	62.0%	37.3%	62.4%	37.6%
75,876	CLARK	28,031	13,764	14,150	117	386 D	49.1%	50.5%	49.3%	50.7%
23,933	CLAY	11,108	6,161	4,865	82	1,296 R	55.5%	43.8%	55.9%	44.1%
30,547	CLINTON	14,829	8,706	6,082	41	2,624 R	58.7%	41.0%	58.9%	41.1%
8,033	CRAWFORD	4,847	2,341	2,501	5	160 D	48.3%	51.6%	48.3%	51.7%
26,602	DAVIESS	11,554	6,886	4,648	20	2,238 R	59.6%	40.2%	59.7%	40.3%
29,430	DEARBORN	12,303	5,970	6,306	27	336 D	48.5%	51.3%	48.6%	51.4%
22,738	DECATUR	9,831	5,611	4,206	14	1,405 R	57.1%	42.8%	57.2%	42.8%
30,837	DE KALB	13,987	7,930	5,894	163	2,036 R	56.7%	42.1%	57.4%	42.6%
129,219	DELAWARE	51,674	27,144	24,111	419	3,033 R	52.5%	46.7%	53.0%	47.0%
30,934	DUBOIS	13,509	6,438	7,049	22	611 D	47.7%	52.2%	47.7%	52.3%
126,529	ELKHART	44,610	30,832	13,548	230	17,284 R	69.1%	30.4%	69.5%	30.5%
26,216	FAYETTE	11,092	5,631	5,437	24	194 R	50.8%	49.0%	50.9%	49.1%
55,622	FLOYD	23,569	11,807	11,703	59	104 R	50.1%	49.7%	50.2%	49.8%
18,257	FOUNTAIN	8,858	5,273	3,556	29	1,717 R	59.5%	40.1%	59.7%	40.3%
16,943	FRANKLIN	6,524	3,257	3,237	30	20 R	49.9%	49.6%	50.2%	49.8%
16,984	FULTON	8,604	5,727	2,804	73	2,923 R	66.6%	32.6%	67.1%	32.9%
30,444	GIBSON	15,205	7,316	7,861	28	545 D	48.1%	51.7%	48.2%	51.8%
83,955	GRANT	30,396	17,494	12,764	138	4,730 R	57.6%	42.0%	57.8%	42.2%
26,894	GREENE	13,586	7,175	6,380	31	795 R	52.8%	47.0%	52.9%	47.1%
54,532	HAMILTON	28,998	21,751	7,102	145	14,649 R	75.0%	24.5%	75.4%	24.6%
35,096	HANCOCK	16,136	10,197	5,849	90	4,348 R	63.2%	36.2%	63.5%	36.5%
20,423	HARRISON	10,312	5,069	5,224	19	155 D	49.2%	50.7%	49.2%	50.8%
53,974	HENDRICKS	25,922	17,345	8,427	150	8,918 R	66.9%	32.5%	67.3%	32.7%
52,603	HENRY	21,726	12,232	9,373	121	2,859 R	56.3%	43.1%	56.6%	43.4%
83,198	HOWARD	34,482	20,653	13,734	95	6,919 R	59.9%	39.8%	60.1%	39.9%
34,970	HUNTINGTON	15,556	9,648	5,804	104	3,844 R	62.0%	37.3%	62.4%	37.6%
33,187	JACKSON	15,115	8,007	7,071	37	936 R	53.0%	46.8%	53.1%	46.9%
20,429	JASPER	8,547	5,745	2,697	105	3,048 R	67.2%	31.6%	68.1%	31.9%
23,575	JAY	8,710	4,788	3,869	53	919 R	55.0%	44.4%	55.3%	44.7%
27,006	JEFFERSON	11,443	5,704	5,704	35	R	49.8%	49.8%	50.0%	50.0%
19,454	JENNINGS	8,880	4,532	4,310	38	222 R	51.0%	48.5%	51.3%	48.7%
61,138	JOHNSON	26,098	16,752	9,181	165	7,571 R	64.2%	35.2%	64.6%	35.4%
41,546	KNOX	18,572	9,658	8,884	30	774 R	52.0%	47.8%	52.1%	47.9%
48,127	KOSCIUSKO	21,873	15,435	6,192	246	9,243 R	70.6%	28.3%	71.4%	28.6%
20,890	LA GRANGE	6,550	4,132	2,374	44	1,758 R	63.1%	36.2%	63.5%	36.5%
546,253	LAKE	203,270	86,971	115,485	814	28,514 D	42.8%	56.8%	43.0%	57.0%
105,342	LA PORTE	39,889	22,919	16,686	284	6,233 R	57.5%	41.8%	57.9%	42.1%
38,038	LAWRENCE	17,124	9,513	7,537	74	1,976 R	55.6%	44.0%	55.8%	44.2%
138,451	MADISON	62,567	33,238	28,956	373	4,282 R	53.1%	46.3%	53.4%	46.6%
792,299	MARION	323,510	180,472	141,410	1,628	39,062 R	55.8%	43.7%	56.1%	43.9%
34,986	MARSHALL	16,317	11,514	4,601	202	6,913 R	70.6%	28.2%	71.4%	28.6%
10,969	MARTIN	5,436	2,671	2,753	12	82 D	49.1%	50.6%	49.2%	50.8%
39,246	MIAMI	14,509	8,787	5,673	49	3,114 R	60.6%	39.1%	60.8%	39.2%
84,849	MONROE	35,104	21,795	13,163	146	8,632 R	62.1%	37.5%	62.3%	37.7%
33,930	MONTGOMERY	14,908	10,008	4,844	56	5,164 R	67.1%	32.5%	67.4%	32.6%
44,176	MORGAN	18,256	11,598	6,535	123	5,063 R	63.5%	35.8%	64.0%	36.0%
11,606	NEWTON	5,345	3,215	2,085	45	1,130 R	60.1%	39.0%	60.7%	39.3%
31,382	NOBLE	12,807	7,211	5,449	147	1,762 R	56.3%	42.5%	57.0%	43.0%
4,289	OHIO	2,261	1,100	1,151	10	51 D	48.7%	50.9%	48.9%	51.1%
16,968	ORANGE	8,219	4,434	3,762	23	672 R	53.9%	45.8%	54.1%	45.9%
12,163	OWEN	5,955	3,180	2,736	39	444 R	53.4%	45.9%	53.8%	46.2%
14,600	PARKE	6,899	4,118	2,755	26	1,363 R	59.7%	39.9%	59.9%	40.1%
19,075	PERRY	9,565	4,204	5,339	22	1,135 D	44.0%	55.8%	44.1%	55.9%
12,281	PIKE	6,848	3,266	3,551	31	285 D	47.7%	51.9%	47.9%	52.1%
87,114	PORTER	41,214	25,917	14,903	394	11,014 R	62.9%	36.2%	63.5%	36.5%
21,740	POSEY	10,167	5,219	4,913	35	306 R	51.3%	48.3%	51.5%	48.5%

INDIANA

GOVERNOR 1976

1970 Census Population	County	Total Vote	Republican	Democratic	Other	Rep.-Dem. Plurality	Percentage Total Vote Rep.	Percentage Total Vote Dem.	Percentage Major Vote Rep.	Percentage Major Vote Dem.
12,534	PULASKI	6,447	3,979	2,269	199	1,710 R	61.7%	35.2%	63.7%	36.3%
26,932	PUTNAM	10,987	6,645	4,255	87	2,390 R	60.5%	38.7%	61.0%	39.0%
28,915	RANDOLPH	12,221	7,379	4,754	88	2,625 R	60.4%	38.9%	60.8%	39.2%
21,138	RIPLEY	9,773	5,263	4,470	40	793 R	53.9%	45.7%	54.1%	45.9%
20,352	RUSH	7,791	5,016	2,762	13	2,254 R	64.4%	35.5%	64.5%	35.5%
245,045	ST. JOSEPH	98,513	62,836	35,347	330	27,489 R	63.8%	35.9%	64.0%	36.0%
17,144	SCOTT	6,687	2,843	3,790	54	947 D	42.5%	56.7%	42.9%	57.1%
37,797	SHELBY	15,897	9,398	6,456	43	2,942 R	59.1%	40.6%	59.3%	40.7%
17,134	SPENCER	8,993	4,262	4,718	13	456 D	47.4%	52.5%	47.5%	52.5%
19,280	STARKE	8,948	4,980	3,873	95	1,107 R	55.7%	43.3%	56.3%	43.7%
20,159	STEUBEN	8,413	5,287	2,998	128	2,289 R	62.8%	35.6%	63.8%	36.2%
19,889	SULLIVAN	8,571	4,099	4,443	29	344 D	47.8%	51.8%	48.0%	52.0%
6,306	SWITZERLAND	3,231	1,291	1,935	5	644 D	40.0%	59.9%	40.0%	60.0%
109,378	TIPPECANOE	46,832	31,143	15,425	264	15,718 R	66.5%	32.9%	66.9%	33.1%
16,650	TIPTON	8,229	5,029	3,155	45	1,874 R	61.1%	38.3%	61.4%	38.6%
6,582	UNION	2,729	1,645	1,076	8	569 R	60.3%	39.4%	60.5%	39.5%
168,772	VANDERBURGH	71,489	39,703	31,443	343	8,260 R	55.5%	44.0%	55.8%	44.2%
16,793	VERMILLION	8,204	3,971	4,193	40	222 D	48.4%	51.1%	48.6%	51.4%
114,528	VIGO	47,656	24,651	22,865	140	1,786 R	51.7%	48.0%	51.9%	48.1%
35,553	WABASH	14,033	9,165	4,837	31	4,328 R	65.3%	34.5%	65.5%	34.5%
8,705	WARREN	4,234	2,514	1,704	16	810 R	59.4%	40.2%	59.6%	40.4%
27,972	WARRICK	14,778	7,616	7,106	56	510 R	51.5%	48.1%	51.7%	48.3%
19,278	WASHINGTON	8,023	4,019	3,962	42	57 R	50.1%	49.4%	50.4%	49.6%
79,109	WAYNE	28,374	17,069	11,175	130	5,894 R	60.2%	39.4%	60.4%	39.6%
23,821	WELLS	9,741	5,989	3,707	45	2,282 R	61.5%	38.1%	61.8%	38.2%
20,995	WHITE	10,134	6,927	3,142	65	3,785 R	68.4%	31.0%	68.8%	31.2%
23,395	WHITLEY	12,253	6,980	5,117	156	1,863 R	57.0%	41.8%	57.7%	42.3%
5,193,669	TOTAL	2,175,324	1,236,555	927,243	11,526	309,312 R	56.8%	42.6%	57.1%	42.9%

INDIANA

SENATOR 1976

1970 Census Population	County	Total Vote	Republican	Democratic	Other	Rep.-Dem. Plurality	Percentage Total Vote Rep.	Percentage Total Vote Dem.	Percentage Major Vote Rep.	Percentage Major Vote Dem.
26,871	ADAMS	11,056	6,612	4,234	210	2,378 R	59.8%	38.3%	61.0%	39.0%
280,455	ALLEN	114,618	75,424	37,904	1,290	37,520 R	65.8%	33.1%	66.6%	33.4%
57,022	BARTHOLOMEW	25,892	16,628	9,112	152	7,516 R	64.2%	35.2%	64.6%	35.4%
11,262	BENTON	5,116	3,279	1,805	32	1,474 R	64.1%	35.3%	64.5%	35.5%
15,888	BLACKFORD	6,025	3,420	2,560	45	860 R	56.8%	42.5%	57.2%	42.8%
30,870	BOONE	14,867	9,701	5,055	111	4,646 R	65.3%	34.0%	65.7%	34.3%
9,057	BROWN	4,816	2,735	2,042	39	693 R	56.8%	42.4%	57.3%	42.7%
17,734	CARROLL	8,374	5,254	3,079	41	2,175 R	62.7%	36.8%	63.1%	36.9%
40,456	CASS	17,992	11,372	6,420	200	4,952 R	63.2%	35.7%	63.9%	36.1%
75,876	CLARK	28,523	14,774	13,581	168	1,193 R	51.8%	47.6%	52.1%	47.9%
23,933	CLAY	11,173	6,260	4,793	120	1,467 R	56.0%	42.9%	56.6%	43.4%
30,547	CLINTON	14,839	8,621	6,142	76	2,479 R	58.1%	41.4%	58.4%	41.6%
8,033	CRAWFORD	4,899	2,377	2,512	10	135 D	48.5%	51.3%	48.6%	51.4%
26,602	DAVIESS	11,677	7,090	4,557	30	2,533 R	60.7%	39.0%	60.9%	39.1%
29,430	DEARBORN	12,169	6,001	6,125	43	124 D	49.3%	50.3%	49.5%	50.5%
22,738	DECATUR	9,851	5,852	3,963	36	1,889 R	59.4%	40.2%	59.6%	40.4%
30,837	DE KALB	13,938	8,492	5,236	210	3,256 R	60.9%	37.6%	61.9%	38.1%
129,219	DELAWARE	51,286	30,962	19,708	616	11,254 R	60.4%	38.4%	61.1%	38.9%
30,934	DUBOIS	13,585	7,076	6,469	40	607 R	52.1%	47.6%	52.2%	47.8%
126,529	ELKHART	44,105	29,264	14,557	284	14,707 R	66.4%	33.0%	66.8%	33.2%
26,216	FAYETTE	11,022	5,848	5,134	40	714 R	53.1%	46.6%	53.3%	46.7%
55,622	FLOYD	23,583	12,838	10,669	76	2,169 R	54.4%	45.2%	54.6%	45.4%
18,257	FOUNTAIN	8,925	5,222	3,665	38	1,557 R	58.5%	41.1%	58.8%	41.2%
16,943	FRANKLIN	6,590	3,364	3,188	38	176 R	51.0%	48.4%	51.3%	48.7%
16,984	FULTON	8,586	5,701	2,734	151	2,967 R	66.4%	31.8%	67.6%	32.4%
30,444	GIBSON	15,382	8,203	7,137	42	1,066 R	53.3%	46.4%	53.5%	46.5%
83,955	GRANT	30,313	18,501	11,568	244	6,933 R	61.0%	38.2%	61.5%	38.5%
26,894	GREENE	13,525	7,168	6,316	41	852 R	53.0%	46.7%	53.2%	46.8%
54,532	HAMILTON	29,047	22,627	6,185	235	16,442 R	77.9%	21.3%	78.5%	21.5%
35,096	HANCOCK	16,184	10,566	5,471	147	5,095 R	65.3%	33.8%	65.9%	34.1%
20,423	HARRISON	10,354	5,547	4,776	31	771 R	53.6%	46.1%	53.7%	46.3%
53,974	HENDRICKS	25,866	17,793	7,773	300	10,020 R	68.8%	30.1%	69.6%	30.4%
52,603	HENRY	21,712	12,418	9,148	146	3,270 R	57.2%	42.1%	57.6%	42.4%
83,198	HOWARD	33,969	21,679	12,146	144	9,533 R	63.8%	35.8%	64.1%	35.9%
34,970	HUNTINGTON	15,475	9,901	5,442	132	4,459 R	64.0%	35.2%	64.5%	35.5%
33,187	JACKSON	15,053	8,402	6,605	46	1,797 R	55.8%	43.9%	56.0%	44.0%
20,429	JASPER	8,553	5,519	2,882	152	2,637 R	64.5%	33.7%	65.7%	34.3%
23,575	JAY	8,712	5,071	3,544	97	1,527 R	58.2%	40.7%	58.9%	41.1%
27,006	JEFFERSON	11,536	6,026	5,474	36	552 R	52.2%	47.5%	52.4%	47.6%
19,454	JENNINGS	8,823	4,772	4,012	39	760 R	54.1%	45.5%	54.3%	45.7%
61,138	JOHNSON	26,209	17,326	8,338	545	8,988 R	66.1%	31.8%	67.5%	32.5%
41,546	KNOX	18,566	10,620	7,901	45	2,719 R	57.2%	42.6%	57.3%	42.7%
48,127	KOSCIUSKO	21,862	15,565	5,929	368	9,636 R	71.2%	27.1%	72.4%	27.6%
20,890	LA GRANGE	6,592	4,161	2,369	62	1,792 R	63.1%	35.9%	63.7%	36.3%
546,253	LAKE	203,669	89,203	113,584	882	24,381 D	43.8%	55.8%	44.0%	56.0%
105,342	LA PORTE	39,874	23,362	16,161	351	7,201 R	58.6%	40.5%	59.1%	40.9%
38,038	LAWRENCE	17,074	10,512	6,460	102	4,052 R	61.6%	37.8%	61.9%	38.1%
138,451	MADISON	62,330	35,345	26,492	493	8,853 R	56.7%	42.5%	57.2%	42.8%
792,299	MARION	322,642	186,760	133,490	2,392	53,270 R	57.9%	41.4%	58.3%	41.7%
34,986	MARSHALL	16,088	10,739	5,158	191	5,581 R	66.8%	32.1%	67.6%	32.4%
10,969	MARTIN	5,520	2,829	2,678	13	151 R	51.3%	48.5%	51.4%	48.6%
39,246	MIAMI	14,461	9,149	5,244	68	3,905 R	63.3%	36.3%	63.6%	36.4%
84,849	MONROE	34,820	23,242	11,384	194	11,858 R	66.7%	32.7%	67.1%	32.9%
33,930	MONTGOMERY	14,859	10,224	4,535	100	5,689 R	68.8%	30.5%	69.3%	30.7%
44,176	MORGAN	18,102	11,602	6,290	210	5,312 R	64.1%	34.7%	64.8%	35.2%
11,606	NEWTON	5,342	3,135	2,135	72	1,000 R	58.7%	40.0%	59.5%	40.5%
31,382	NOBLE	12,811	7,690	4,905	216	2,785 R	60.0%	38.3%	61.1%	38.9%
4,289	OHIO	2,245	1,056	1,170	19	114 D	47.0%	52.1%	47.4%	52.6%
16,968	ORANGE	8,311	4,656	3,600	55	1,056 R	56.0%	43.3%	56.4%	43.6%
12,163	OWEN	5,986	3,161	2,756	69	405 R	52.8%	46.0%	53.4%	46.6%
14,600	PARKE	6,989	4,183	2,745	61	1,438 R	59.9%	39.3%	60.4%	39.6%
19,075	PERRY	9,661	4,747	4,885	29	138 D	49.1%	50.6%	49.3%	50.7%
12,281	PIKE	7,018	3,433	3,544	41	111 D	48.9%	50.5%	49.2%	50.8%
87,114	PORTER	41,210	26,401	14,336	473	12,065 R	64.1%	34.8%	64.8%	35.2%
21,740	POSEY	10,196	6,115	4,005	76	2,110 R	60.0%	39.3%	60.4%	39.6%

INDIANA

SENATOR 1976

1970 Census Population	County	Total Vote	Republican	Democratic	Other	Rep.-Dem. Plurality	Percentage Total Vote Rep.	Total Vote Dem.	Major Vote Rep.	Major Vote Dem.
12,534	PULASKI	6,433	3,837	2,348	248	1,489 R	59.6%	36.5%	62.0%	38.0%
26,932	PUTNAM	11,018	6,632	4,192	194	2,440 R	60.2%	38.0%	61.3%	38.7%
28,915	RANDOLPH	12,277	7,271	4,864	142	2,407 R	59.2%	39.6%	59.9%	40.1%
21,138	RIPLEY	9,625	5,271	4,292	62	979 R	54.8%	44.6%	55.1%	44.9%
20,352	RUSH	7,775	5,015	2,728	32	2,287 R	64.5%	35.1%	64.8%	35.2%
245,045	ST. JOSEPH	97,834	58,518	38,878	438	19,640 R	59.8%	39.7%	60.1%	39.9%
17,144	SCOTT	6,622	2,977	3,579	66	602 D	45.0%	54.0%	45.4%	54.6%
37,797	SHELBY	15,963	9,453	6,425	85	3,028 R	59.2%	40.2%	59.5%	40.5%
17,134	SPENCER	8,980	4,535	4,429	16	106 R	50.5%	49.3%	50.6%	49.4%
19,280	STARKE	8,905	4,745	4,047	113	698 R	53.3%	45.4%	54.0%	46.0%
20,159	STEUBEN	8,192	5,390	2,634	168	2,756 R	65.8%	32.2%	67.2%	32.8%
19,889	SULLIVAN	8,679	4,126	4,515	38	389 D	47.5%	52.0%	47.7%	52.3%
6,306	SWITZERLAND	3,197	1,261	1,923	13	662 D	39.4%	60.2%	39.6%	60.4%
109,378	TIPPECANOE	46,837	32,646	13,871	320	18,775 R	69.7%	29.6%	70.2%	29.8%
16,650	TIPTON	8,178	5,180	2,915	83	2,265 R	63.3%	35.6%	64.0%	36.0%
6,582	UNION	2,764	1,682	1,070	12	612 R	60.9%	38.7%	61.1%	38.9%
168,772	VANDERBURGH	69,951	42,666	26,758	527	15,908 R	61.0%	38.3%	61.5%	38.5%
16,793	VERMILLION	8,383	4,015	4,307	61	292 D	47.9%	51.4%	48.2%	51.8%
114,528	VIGO	47,623	25,543	21,936	144	3,607 R	53.6%	46.1%	53.8%	46.2%
35,553	WABASH	13,937	9,013	4,864	60	4,149 R	64.7%	34.9%	64.9%	35.1%
8,705	WARREN	4,261	2,537	1,701	23	836 R	59.5%	39.9%	59.9%	40.1%
27,972	WARRICK	14,450	8,555	5,769	126	2,786 R	59.2%	39.9%	59.7%	40.3%
19,278	WASHINGTON	7,996	4,203	3,744	49	459 R	52.6%	46.8%	52.9%	47.1%
79,109	WAYNE	28,603	17,130	11,202	271	5,928 R	59.9%	39.2%	60.5%	39.5%
23,821	WELLS	9,669	6,099	3,434	136	2,665 R	63.1%	35.5%	64.0%	36.0%
20,995	WHITE	10,248	6,674	3,456	118	3,218 R	65.1%	33.7%	65.9%	34.1%
23,395	WHITLEY	12,339	7,283	4,824	232	2,459 R	59.0%	39.1%	60.2%	39.8%
5,193,669	TOTAL	2,171,187	1,275,833	878,522	16,832	397,311 R	58.8%	40.5%	59.2%	40.8%

INDIANA

CONGRESS

			Republican		Democratic				Percentage			
		Total					Other	Rep.-Dem.	Total Vote		Major Vote	
CD	Year	Vote	Vote	Candidate	Vote	Candidate	Vote	Plurality	Rep.	Dem.	Rep.	Dem.
1	1976	169,911	48,756	BILLINGS, ROBERT J.	121,155	BENJAMIN, ADAM		72,399 D	28.7%	71.3%	28.7%	71.3%
1	1974	104,552	32,793	HARKIN, JOSEPH D.	71,759	MADDEN, RAY J.		38,966 D	31.4%	68.6%	31.4%	68.6%
1	1972	168,535	72,662	HALLER, BRUCE R.	95,873	MADDEN, RAY J.		23,211 D	43.1%	56.9%	43.1%	56.9%
2	1976	214,795	95,505	ERWIN, WILLIAM W.	117,617	FITHIAN, FLOYD	1,673	22,112 D	44.5%	54.8%	44.8%	55.2%
2	1974	166,806	64,950	LANDGREBE, EARL F.	101,856	FITHIAN, FLOYD		36,906 D	38.9%	61.1%	38.9%	61.1%
2	1972	201,939	110,406	LANDGREBE, EARL F.	91,533	FITHIAN, FLOYD		18,873 R	54.7%	45.3%	54.7%	45.3%
3	1976	178,871	77,094	THORSON, THOMAS L.	101,777	BRADEMAS, JOHN		24,683 D	43.1%	56.9%	43.1%	56.9%
3	1974	139,422	50,116	BLACK, VIRGINIA R.	89,306	BRADEMAS, JOHN		39,190 D	35.9%	64.1%	35.9%	64.1%
3	1972	188,202	81,369	NEWMAN, DON M.	103,949	BRADEMAS, JOHN	2,884	22,580 D	43.2%	55.2%	43.9%	56.1%
4	1976	198,183	107,762	QUAYLE, J. DANFORTH	88,361	ROUSH, J. EDWARD	2,060	19,401 R	54.4%	44.6%	54.9%	45.1%
4	1974	161,219	75,031	HELMKE, WALTER P.	83,604	ROUSH, J. EDWARD	2,584	8,573 D	46.5%	51.9%	47.3%	52.7%
4	1972	194,819	94,492	BLOOM, ALLAN	100,327	ROUSH, J. EDWARD		5,835 D	48.5%	51.5%	48.5%	51.5%
5	1976	206,001	127,194	HILLIS, ELWOOD H.	78,807	STOUT, WILLIAM C.		48,387 R	61.7%	38.3%	61.7%	38.3%
5	1974	168,570	95,331	HILLIS, ELWOOD H.	73,239	SEBREE, WILLIAM T.		22,092 R	56.6%	43.4%	56.6%	43.4%
5	1972	194,438	124,692	HILLIS, ELWOOD H.	69,746	WILLIAMS, KATHLEEN Z.		54,946 R	64.1%	35.9%	64.1%	35.9%
6	1976	192,627	86,854	CRANE, DAVID G.	105,773	EVANS, DAVID W.		18,919 D	45.1%	54.9%	45.1%	54.9%
6	1974	149,548	71,134	BRAY, WILLIAM G.	78,414	EVANS, DAVID W.		7,280 D	47.6%	52.4%	47.6%	52.4%
6	1972	173,595	112,525	BRAY, WILLIAM G.	61,070	EVANS, DAVID W.		51,455 R	64.8%	35.2%	64.8%	35.2%
7	1976	207,360	130,005	MYERS, JOHN T.	77,355	TIPTON, JOHN E.		52,650 R	62.7%	37.3%	62.7%	37.3%
7	1974	175,351	100,128	MYERS, JOHN T.	73,802	TIPTON, ELDEN C.	1,421	26,326 R	57.1%	42.1%	57.6%	42.4%
7	1972	208,833	128,688	MYERS, JOHN T.	80,145	HENEGAR, WARREN		48,543 R	61.6%	38.4%	61.6%	38.4%
8	1976	216,026	107,013	BELL, BELDEN	109,013	CORNWELL, DAVID L.		2,000 D	49.5%	50.5%	49.5%	50.5%
8	1974	187,417	87,296	ZION, ROGER H.	100,121	HAYES, PHILIP H.		12,825 D	46.6%	53.4%	46.6%	53.4%
8	1972	211,221	133,850	ZION, ROGER H.	77,371	DEEN, RICHARD L.		56,479 R	63.4%	36.6%	63.4%	36.6%
9	1976	136,056			136,056	HAMILTON, LEE H.		136,056 D		100.0%		100.0%
9	1974	165,529	47,881	COX, DELSON	117,648	HAMILTON, LEE H.		69,767 D	28.9%	71.1%	28.9%	71.1%
9	1972	195,023	72,325	JOHNSON, WILLIAM A.	122,698	HAMILTON, LEE H.		50,373 D	37.1%	62.9%	37.1%	62.9%
10	1976	191,449	76,890	FRAZIER, WILLIAM G.	114,559	SHARP, PHILIP R.		37,669 D	40.2%	59.8%	40.2%	59.8%
10	1974	157,119	71,701	DENNIS, DAVID W.	85,418	SHARP, PHILIP R.		13,717 D	45.6%	54.4%	45.6%	54.4%
10	1972	186,554	106,798	DENNIS, DAVID W.	79,756	SHARP, PHILIP R.		27,042 R	57.2%	42.8%	57.2%	42.8%
11	1976	191,859	74,829	BUELL, LAWRENCE L.	115,895	JACOBS, ANDREW, JR.	1,135	41,066 D	39.0%	60.4%	39.2%	60.8%
11	1974	155,301	73,793	HUDNUT, WILLIAM H.	81,508	JACOBS, ANDREW, JR.		7,715 D	47.5%	52.5%	47.5%	52.5%
11	1972	187,077	95,839	HUDNUT, WILLIAM H.	91,238	JACOBS, ANDREW, JR.		4,601 R	51.2%	48.8%	51.2%	48.8%

INDIANA

1976 GENERAL ELECTION

President Other vote was 14,048 Anderson (American); 5,695 Camejo (Socialist Workers); 1,947 LaRouche (U.S. Labor). Early uncorrected canvass gave the Republican total state vote as 1,185,958.

Governor Other vote was 9,850 Talbot (American); 1,676 Washington (U.S. Labor).

Senator Other vote was 14,321 Lee (American); 2,511 Hoagland (U.S. Labor). Early uncorrected canvass gave the Democratic total state vote as 868,522.

Congress Other vote was Logan (American) in CD 2; Gran (American) in CD 4; and Eineman (American) in CD 11.

1976 PRIMARIES

MAY 4 REPUBLICAN

Governor Otis R. Bowen, unopposed.

Senator 393,064 Richard G. Lugar; 179,203 Edgar D. Whitcomb; 28,329 William Costas.

Congress Unopposed in two CD's. Gary L. Cook, the unopposed candidate in CD 9, withdrew after the primary and no substitution was made. Contested as follows:

CD 1 10,639 Robert J. Billings; 3,783 Thaddeus Romanowski.
CD 2 36,191 William W. Erwin; 19,035 Glenn H. Sullivan; 9,443 J. Philip Oppenheim; 1,406 Robert L. Van Gorp; 1,227 Milan D. Tesanovich.
CD 3 21,089 Thomas L. Thorson; 14,411 Jack A. Donis.
CD 4 36,634 J. Danforth Quayle; 21,199 Dennis L. Wright.
CD 6 30,520 David G. Crane; 17,466 Robert H. Bales; 5,890 James D. Bowyer; 1,981 Chester Coomer.
CD 7 53,057 John T. Myers; 6,879 Ernest R. Boykin.
CD 8 25,029 Belden Bell; 18,565 Alton Davis; 6,757 Barbara J. Marting.
CD 10 25,884 William G. Frazier; 23,833 Roger F. Marsh; 5,722 Robert J. Luellen.
CD 11 32,883 Lawrence L. Buell; 7,477 Eugene R. Barnett; 3,211 Remus L. Sanders; 1,921 Logan D. Murley.

MAY 4 DEMOCRATIC

Governor 358,421 Larry A. Conrad; 105,965 Jack L. New; 91,606 Robert J. Fair.

Senator 304,076 R. Vance Hartke; 268,790 Philip H. Hayes.

Congress Unopposed in two CD's. Contested as follows:

CD 1 53,267 Adam Benjamin; 32,584 Ray J. Madden; 4,428 Raymond J. Bell; 1,932 Michael P. Rogan; 1,840 Mirko Acamovic; 1,059 William M. Hebert.
CD 3 40,648 John Brademas; 7,549 Lawrence D. Vandewalle; 4,671 Edward J. Malo.
CD 4 32,638 J. Edward Roush; 5,046 Stephen G. Hope.
CD 5 16,672 William C. Stout; 15,203 Ernest L. Bradley; 6,875 John C. Salomone.
CD 6 30,073 David W. Evans; 3,201 James H. Logan.
CD 7 30,567 John E. Tipton; 18,653 Jon Pekel; 14,744 James M. Mason.
CD 8 30,559 David L. Cornwell; 9,467 Clark Field; 8,410 John H. Blair; 8,206 Donald E. Buttram; 5,049 Richard L. Deen; 1,030 Franklin D. R. Enochs.
CD 10 40,263 Philip R. Sharp; 2,643 Robert L. Murphy; 2,495 Randall S. Harmon.
CD 11 32,933 Andrew Jacobs, Jr.; 1,883 Paul D. Hibner; 1,733 Steven D. Snyder.

IOWA

GOVERNOR

Robert Ray (R). Re-elected 1974 to a four-year term. Previously elected 1972, 1970, 1968.

SENATORS

Richard Clark (D). Elected 1972 to a six-year term.

John C. Culver (D). Elected 1974 to a six-year term.

REPRESENTATIVES

1. James Leach (R)
2. Michael Blouin (D)
3. Charles E. Grassley (R)
4. Neal Smith (D)
5. Tom Harkin (D)
6. Berkley Bedell (D)

POSTWAR VOTE FOR GOVERNOR

								Percentage			
	Total	Republican		Democratic		Other	Rep.-Dem.	Total Vote		Major Vote	
Year	Vote	Vote	Candidate	Vote	Candidate	Vote	Plurality	Rep.	Dem.	Rep.	Dem.
1974	920,458	534,518	Ray, Robert	377,553	Schaben, James F.	8,387	156,965 R	58.1%	41.0%	58.6%	41.4%
1972	1,210,222	707,177	Ray, Robert	487,282	Franzenburg, Paul	15,763	219,895 R	58.4%	40.3%	59.2%	40.8%
1970	791,241	403,394	Ray, Robert	368,911	Fulton, Robert	18,936	34,483 R	51.0%	46.6%	52.2%	47.8%
1968	1,136,489	614,328	Ray, Robert	521,216	Franzenburg, Paul	945	93,112 R	54.1%	45.9%	54.1%	45.9%
1966	893,175	394,518	Murray, William G.	494,259	Hughes, Harold E.	4,398	99,741 D	44.2%	55.3%	44.4%	55.6%
1964	1,167,734	365,131	Hultman, Evan	794,610	Hughes, Harold E.	7,993	429,479 D	31.3%	68.0%	31.5%	68.5%
1962	819,854	388,955	Erbe, Norman A.	430,899	Hughes, Harold E.	–	41,944 D	47.4%	52.6%	47.4%	52.6%
1960	1,237,089	645,026	Erbe, Norman A.	592,063	McManus, E. J.	–	52,963 R	52.1%	47.9%	52.1%	47.9%
1958	859,095	394,071	Murray, William G.	465,024	Loveless, Herschel C.	–	70,953 D	45.9%	54.1%	45.9%	54.1%
1956	1,204,235	587,383	Hoegh, Leo A.	616,852	Loveless, Herschel C.	–	29,469 D	48.8%	51.2%	48.8%	51.2%
1954	848,592	435,944	Hoegh, Leo A.	410,255	Herring, Clyde E.	2,393	25,689 R	51.4%	48.3%	51.5%	48.5%
1952	1,230,045	638,388	Beardsley, William	587,671	Loveless, Herschel C.	3,986	50,717 R	51.9%	47.8%	52.1%	47.9%
1950	857,213	506,642	Beardsley, William	347,176	Gillette, Lester S.	3,395	159,466 R	59.1%	40.5%	59.3%	40.7%
1948	994,833	553,900	Beardsley, William	434,432	Switzer, Carroll O.	6,501	119,468 R	55.7%	43.7%	56.0%	44.0%
1946	631,681	362,592	Blue, Robert D.	266,190	Miles, Frank	2,899	96,402 R	57.4%	42.1%	57.7%	42.3%

The term of office of Iowa's Governor was increased from two to four years effective with the 1974 election.

POSTWAR VOTE FOR SENATOR

								Percentage			
	Total	Republican		Democratic		Other	Rep.-Dem.	Total Vote		Major Vote	
Year	Vote	Vote	Candidate	Vote	Candidate	Vote	Plurality	Rep.	Dem.	Rep.	Dem.
1974	889,561	420,546	Stanley, David M.	462,947	Culver, John C.	6,068	42,401 D	47.3%	52.0%	47.6%	52.4%
1972	1,203,333	530,525	Miller, Jack	662,637	Clark, Richard	10,171	132,112 D	44.1%	55.1%	44.5%	55.5%
1968	1,144,086	568,469	Stanley, David M.	574,884	Hughes, Harold E.	733	6,415 D	49.7%	50.2%	49.7%	50.3%
1966	857,496	522,339	Miller, Jack	324,114	Smith, E. B.	11,043	198,225 R	60.9%	37.8%	61.7%	38.3%
1962	807,972	431,364	Hickenlooper, Bourke B.	376,602	Smith, E. B.	6	54,762 R	53.4%	46.6%	53.4%	46.6%
1960	1,237,582	642,463	Miller, Jack	595,119	Loveless, Herschel C.	–	47,344 R	51.9%	48.1%	51.9%	48.1%
1956	1,178,655	635,499	Hickenlooper, Bourke B.	543,156	Evans, R. M.	–	92,343 R	53.9%	46.1%	53.9%	46.1%
1954	847,355	442,409	Martin, Thomas E.	402,712	Gillette, Guy	2,234	39,697 R	52.2%	47.5%	52.3%	47.7%
1950	858,523	470,613	Hickenlooper, Bourke B.	383,766	Loveland, A. J.	4,144	86,847 R	54.8%	44.7%	55.1%	44.9%
1948	1,000,412	415,778	Wilson, George A.	578,226	Gillette, Guy	6,408	162,448 D	41.6%	57.8%	41.8%	58.2%

IOWA

Districts Established March 6, 1971

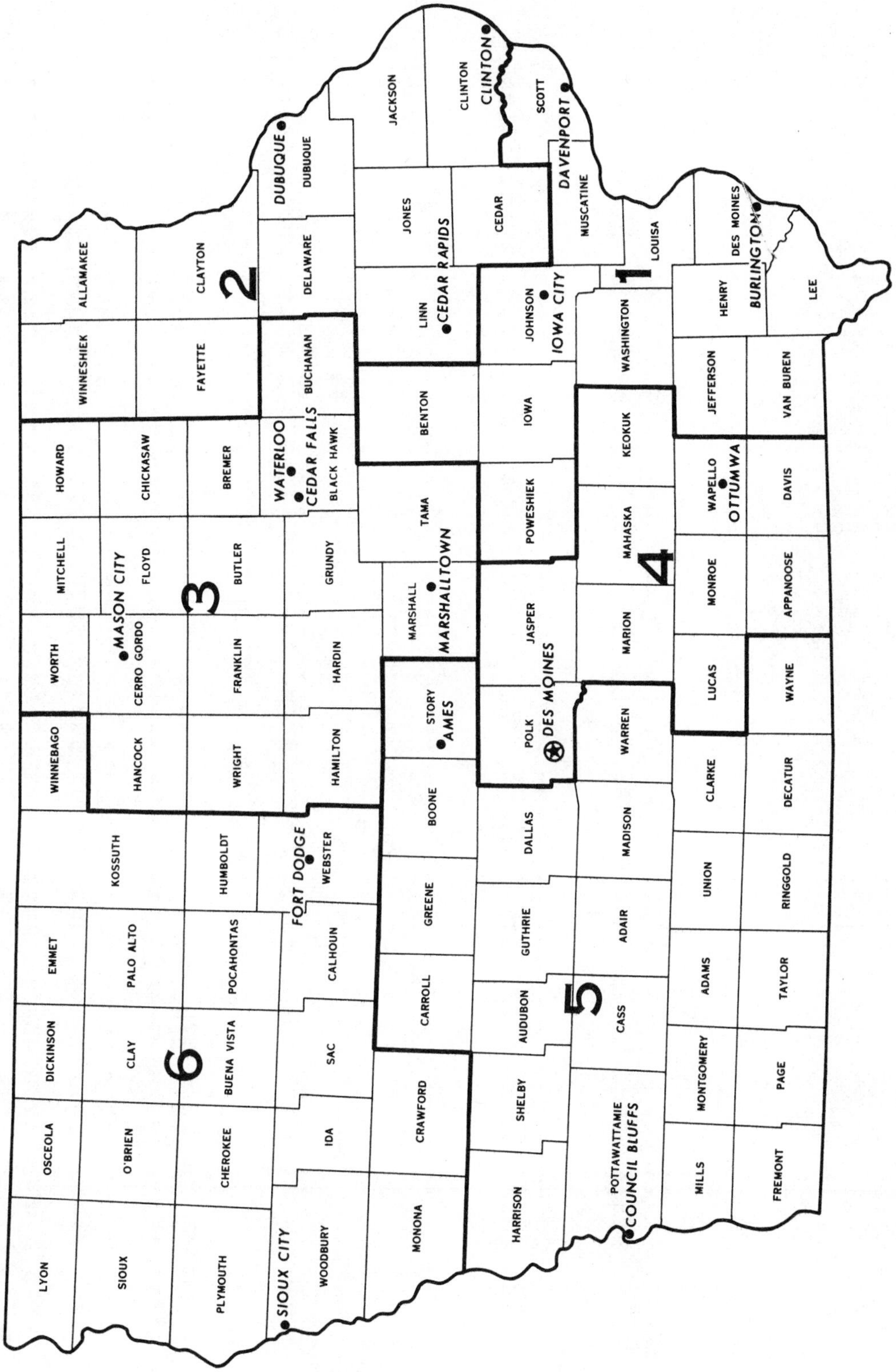

IOWA

PRESIDENT 1976

1970 Census Population	County	Total Vote	Republican	Democratic	Other	Rep.-Dem. Plurality	Percentage Total Vote Rep.	Percentage Total Vote Dem.	Percentage Major Vote Rep.	Percentage Major Vote Dem.
9,487	ADAIR	4,722	2,326	2,294	102	32 R	49.3%	48.6%	50.3%	49.7%
6,322	ADAMS	2,937	1,388	1,507	42	119 D	47.3%	51.3%	47.9%	52.1%
14,968	ALLAMAKEE	6,303	3,648	2,568	87	1,080 R	57.9%	40.7%	58.7%	41.3%
15,007	APPANOOSE	6,558	3,036	3,424	98	388 D	46.3%	52.2%	47.0%	53.0%
9,595	AUDUBON	4,133	1,978	2,104	51	126 D	47.9%	50.9%	48.5%	51.5%
22,885	BENTON	10,703	5,014	5,514	175	500 D	46.8%	51.5%	47.6%	52.4%
132,916	BLACK HAWK	61,715	30,994	29,508	1,213	1,486 R	50.2%	47.8%	51.2%	48.8%
26,470	BOONE	12,263	5,413	6,595	255	1,182 D	44.1%	53.8%	45.1%	54.9%
22,737	BREMER	10,685	6,252	4,203	230	2,049 R	58.5%	39.3%	59.8%	40.2%
21,746	BUCHANAN	9,223	4,794	4,258	171	536 R	52.0%	46.2%	53.0%	47.0%
20,693	BUENA VISTA	9,567	5,126	4,227	214	899 R	53.6%	44.2%	54.8%	45.2%
16,953	BUTLER	6,808	4,207	2,503	98	1,704 R	61.8%	36.8%	62.7%	37.3%
14,287	CALHOUN	6,300	3,215	3,001	84	214 R	51.0%	47.6%	51.7%	48.3%
22,912	CARROLL	9,608	4,094	5,333	181	1,239 D	42.6%	55.5%	43.4%	56.6%
17,007	CASS	7,549	4,589	2,866	94	1,723 R	60.8%	38.0%	61.6%	38.4%
17,655	CEDAR	7,822	4,308	3,354	160	954 R	55.1%	42.9%	56.2%	43.8%
49,335	CERRO GORDO	22,196	10,604	11,189	403	585 D	47.8%	50.4%	48.7%	51.3%
17,269	CHEROKEE	7,478	3,993	3,358	127	635 R	53.4%	44.9%	54.3%	45.7%
14,969	CHICKASAW	6,988	3,432	3,503	53	71 D	49.1%	50.1%	49.5%	50.5%
7,581	CLARKE	4,149	1,737	2,333	79	596 D	41.9%	56.2%	42.7%	57.3%
18,464	CLAY	8,500	4,548	3,776	176	772 R	53.5%	44.4%	54.6%	45.4%
20,606	CLAYTON	8,807	4,826	3,804	177	1,022 R	54.8%	43.2%	55.9%	44.1%
56,749	CLINTON	24,534	12,401	11,746	387	655 R	50.5%	47.9%	51.4%	48.6%
19,116	CRAWFORD	7,948	3,879	3,903	166	24 D	48.8%	49.1%	49.8%	50.2%
26,085	DALLAS	12,247	5,308	6,722	217	1,414 D	43.3%	54.9%	44.1%	55.9%
8,207	DAVIS	4,129	1,631	2,426	72	795 D	39.5%	58.8%	40.2%	59.8%
9,737	DECATUR	4,707	1,932	2,698	77	766 D	41.0%	57.3%	41.7%	58.3%
18,770	DELAWARE	7,481	4,161	3,168	152	993 R	55.6%	42.3%	56.8%	43.2%
46,982	DES MOINES	20,536	9,023	11,268	245	2,245 D	43.9%	54.9%	44.5%	55.5%
12,565	DICKINSON	7,010	3,795	3,074	141	721 R	54.1%	43.9%	55.2%	44.8%
90,609	DUBUQUE	39,049	17,459	20,548	1,042	3,089 D	44.7%	52.6%	45.9%	54.1%
14,009	EMMET	5,687	2,872	2,720	95	152 R	50.5%	47.8%	51.4%	48.6%
26,898	FAYETTE	12,102	6,618	5,220	264	1,398 R	54.7%	43.1%	55.9%	44.1%
19,860	FLOYD	9,178	4,361	4,646	171	285 D	47.5%	50.6%	48.4%	51.6%
13,255	FRANKLIN	5,843	3,056	2,682	105	374 R	52.3%	45.9%	53.3%	46.7%
9,282	FREMONT	4,176	2,163	1,964	49	199 R	51.8%	47.0%	52.4%	47.6%
12,716	GREENE	5,989	2,811	3,094	84	283 D	46.9%	51.7%	47.6%	52.4%
14,119	GRUNDY	6,660	4,173	2,410	77	1,763 R	62.7%	36.2%	63.4%	36.6%
12,243	GUTHRIE	5,641	2,644	2,873	124	229 D	46.9%	50.9%	47.9%	52.1%
18,383	HAMILTON	8,025	3,932	3,953	140	21 D	49.0%	49.3%	49.9%	50.1%
13,330	HANCOCK	6,187	3,127	2,975	85	152 R	50.5%	48.1%	51.2%	48.8%
22,248	HARDIN	9,328	4,682	4,479	167	203 R	50.2%	48.0%	51.1%	48.9%
16,240	HARRISON	6,790	3,489	3,228	73	261 R	51.4%	47.5%	51.9%	48.1%
18,114	HENRY	7,887	3,848	3,882	157	34 D	48.8%	49.2%	49.8%	50.2%
11,442	HOWARD	5,616	2,618	2,917	81	299 D	46.6%	51.9%	47.3%	52.7%
12,519	HUMBOLDT	5,841	3,075	2,677	89	398 R	52.6%	45.8%	53.5%	46.5%
9,190	IDA	4,555	2,590	1,868	97	722 R	56.9%	41.0%	58.1%	41.9%
15,419	IOWA	7,411	3,926	3,367	118	559 R	53.0%	45.4%	53.8%	46.2%
20,839	JACKSON	8,886	4,221	4,467	198	246 D	47.5%	50.3%	48.6%	51.4%
35,425	JASPER	16,786	7,728	8,783	275	1,055 D	46.0%	52.3%	46.8%	53.2%
15,774	JEFFERSON	7,244	3,746	3,377	121	369 R	51.7%	46.6%	52.6%	47.4%
72,127	JOHNSON	38,710	16,090	20,208	2,412	4,118 D	41.6%	52.2%	44.3%	55.7%
19,868	JONES	8,831	4,463	4,245	123	218 R	50.5%	48.1%	51.3%	48.7%
13,943	KEOKUK	6,504	2,920	3,482	102	562 D	44.9%	53.5%	45.6%	54.4%
22,937	KOSSUTH	10,046	4,653	5,190	203	537 D	46.3%	51.7%	47.3%	52.7%
42,996	LEE	17,465	8,195	9,017	253	822 D	46.9%	51.6%	47.6%	52.4%
163,213	LINN	76,397	36,513	38,252	1,632	1,739 D	47.8%	50.1%	48.8%	51.2%
10,682	LOUISA	4,441	2,284	2,089	68	195 R	51.4%	47.0%	52.2%	47.8%
10,163	LUCAS	4,894	2,071	2,733	90	662 D	42.3%	55.8%	43.1%	56.9%
13,340	LYON	5,554	3,558	1,870	126	1,688 R	64.1%	33.7%	65.5%	34.5%
11,558	MADISON	5,910	2,681	3,109	120	428 D	45.4%	52.6%	46.3%	53.7%
22,177	MAHASKA	10,251	5,267	4,838	146	429 R	51.4%	47.2%	52.1%	47.9%
26,352	MARION	11,857	5,429	6,226	202	797 D	45.8%	52.5%	46.6%	53.4%
41,076	MARSHALL	18,630	9,562	8,695	373	867 R	51.3%	46.7%	52.4%	47.6%
11,832	MILLS	4,710	2,722	1,908	80	814 R	57.8%	40.5%	58.8%	41.2%

IOWA

PRESIDENT 1976

1970 Census Population	County	Total Vote	Republican	Democratic	Other	Rep.-Dem. Plurality	Percentage Total Vote Rep.	Percentage Total Vote Dem.	Percentage Major Vote Rep.	Percentage Major Vote Dem.
13,108	MITCHELL	5,892	2,887	2,906	99	19 D	49.0%	49.3%	49.8%	50.2%
12,069	MONONA	5,370	2,636	2,661	73	25 D	49.1%	49.6%	49.8%	50.2%
9,357	MONROE	3,996	1,581	2,360	55	779 D	39.6%	59.1%	40.1%	59.9%
12,781	MONTGOMERY	5,974	3,673	2,229	72	1,444 R	61.5%	37.3%	62.2%	37.8%
37,181	MUSCATINE	14,496	7,697	6,567	232	1,130 R	53.1%	45.3%	54.0%	46.0%
17,522	O BRIEN	7,506	4,643	2,732	131	1,911 R	61.9%	36.4%	63.0%	37.0%
8,555	OSCEOLA	3,341	1,955	1,309	77	646 R	58.5%	39.2%	59.9%	40.1%
18,507	PAGE	8,335	5,343	2,865	127	2,478 R	64.1%	34.4%	65.1%	34.9%
13,289	PALO ALTO	5,904	2,623	3,182	99	559 D	44.4%	53.9%	45.2%	54.8%
24,312	PLYMOUTH	10,016	5,590	4,284	142	1,306 R	55.8%	42.8%	56.6%	43.4%
12,729	POCAHONTAS	5,889	2,700	3,055	134	355 D	45.8%	51.9%	46.9%	53.1%
286,101	POLK	137,763	62,316	71,917	3,530	9,601 D	45.2%	52.2%	46.4%	53.6%
86,991	POTTAWATTAMIE	32,519	17,264	14,754	501	2,510 R	53.1%	45.4%	53.9%	46.1%
18,803	POWESHIEK	8,735	4,194	4,360	181	166 D	48.0%	49.9%	49.0%	51.0%
6,373	RINGGOLD	3,336	1,543	1,739	54	196 D	46.3%	52.1%	47.0%	53.0%
15,573	SAC	6,493	3,347	2,996	150	351 R	51.5%	46.1%	52.8%	47.2%
142,687	SCOTT	65,940	35,021	29,771	1,148	5,250 R	53.1%	45.1%	54.1%	45.9%
15,528	SHELBY	6,261	3,301	2,851	109	450 R	52.7%	45.5%	53.7%	46.3%
27,996	SIOUX	12,935	9,448	3,322	165	6,126 R	73.0%	25.7%	74.0%	26.0%
62,783	STORY	35,476	18,394	15,717	1,365	2,677 R	51.8%	44.3%	53.9%	46.1%
20,147	TAMA	9,107	4,379	4,580	148	201 D	48.1%	50.3%	48.9%	51.1%
8,790	TAYLOR	4,054	2,059	1,947	48	112 R	50.8%	48.0%	51.4%	48.6%
13,557	UNION	5,948	2,873	2,955	120	82 D	48.3%	49.7%	49.3%	50.7%
8,643	VAN BUREN	3,671	1,804	1,807	60	3 D	49.1%	49.2%	50.0%	50.0%
42,149	WAPELLO	17,268	6,786	10,249	233	3,463 D	39.3%	59.4%	39.8%	60.2%
27,432	WARREN	14,108	6,099	7,653	356	1,554 D	43.2%	54.2%	44.3%	55.7%
18,967	WASHINGTON	7,807	4,218	3,448	141	770 R	54.0%	44.2%	55.0%	45.0%
8,405	WAYNE	3,995	1,781	2,145	69	364 D	44.6%	53.7%	45.4%	54.6%
48,391	WEBSTER	19,995	9,068	10,543	384	1,475 D	45.4%	52.7%	46.2%	53.8%
12,990	WINNEBAGO	6,346	3,315	2,950	81	365 R	52.2%	46.5%	52.9%	47.1%
21,758	WINNESHIEK	9,149	4,765	4,158	226	607 R	52.1%	45.4%	53.4%	46.6%
103,052	WOODBURY	43,287	22,853	19,664	770	3,189 R	52.8%	45.4%	53.8%	46.2%
8,968	WORTH	4,425	1,964	2,399	62	435 D	44.4%	54.2%	45.0%	55.0%
17,294	WRIGHT	7,282	3,544	3,637	101	93 D	48.7%	49.9%	49.4%	50.6%
2,825,041	TOTAL	1,279,306	632,863	619,931	26,512	12,932 R	49.5%	48.5%	50.5%	49.5%

IOWA

CONGRESS

CD	Year	Total Vote	Republican Vote	Republican Candidate	Democratic Vote	Democratic Candidate	Other Vote	Rep.-Dem. Plurality	Percentage Total Vote Rep.	Percentage Total Vote Dem.	Percentage Major Vote Rep.	Percentage Major Vote Dem.
1	1976	211,204	109,694	LEACH, JAMES A.	101,024	MEZVINSKY, EDWARD	486	8,670 R	51.9%	47.8%	52.1%	47.9%
1	1974	139,240	63,540	LEACH, JAMES A.	75,687	MEZVINSKY, EDWARD	13	12,147 D	45.6%	54.4%	45.6%	54.4%
1	1972	200,633	91,609	SCHWENGEL, FRED	107,099	MEZVINSKY, EDWARD	1,925	15,490 D	45.7%	53.4%	46.1%	53.9%
2	1976	204,556	100,344	RILEY, TOM	102,980	BLOUIN, MICHAEL	1,232	2,636 D	49.1%	50.3%	49.4%	50.6%
2	1974	143,628	69,088	RILEY, TOM	73,416	BLOUIN, MICHAEL	1,124	4,328 D	48.1%	51.1%	48.5%	51.5%
2	1972	195,156	79,667	ELLSWORTH, THEODORE R.	115,489	CULVER, JOHN C.		35,822 D	40.8%	59.2%	40.8%	59.2%
3	1976	208,943	117,957	GRASSLEY, CHARLES E.	90,981	RAPP, STEPHEN J.	5	26,976 R	56.5%	43.5%	56.5%	43.5%
3	1974	152,371	77,468	GRASSLEY, CHARLES E.	74,895	RAPP, STEPHEN J.	8	2,573 R	50.8%	49.2%	50.8%	49.2%
3	1972	195,965	109,113	GROSS, H. R.	86,848	TAYLOR, LYLE D.	4	22,265 R	55.7%	44.3%	55.7%	44.3%
4	1976	210,364	65,013	MINOR, CHARLES E.	145,343	SMITH, NEAL	8	80,330 D	30.9%	69.1%	30.9%	69.1%
4	1974	151,429	53,756	DICK, CHUCK	96,755	SMITH, NEAL	918	42,999 D	35.5%	63.9%	35.7%	64.3%
4	1972	210,588	85,156	KYL, JOHN	125,431	SMITH, NEAL	1	40,275 D	40.4%	59.6%	40.4%	59.6%
5	1976	209,062	71,377	FULK, KENNETH R.	135,600	HARKIN, TOM	2,085	64,223 D	34.1%	64.9%	34.5%	65.5%
5	1974	158,835	77,683	SCHERLE, WILLIAM J.	81,146	HARKIN, TOM	6	3,463 D	48.9%	51.1%	48.9%	51.1%
5	1972	196,536	108,596	SCHERLE, WILLIAM J.	87,937	HARKIN, TOM	3	20,659 R	55.3%	44.7%	55.3%	44.7%
6	1976	198,012	62,292	SOPER, JOANNE D.	133,507	BEDELL, BERKLEY	2,213	71,215 D	31.5%	67.4%	31.8%	68.2%
6	1974	158,012	71,695	MAYNE, WILEY	86,315	BEDELL, BERKLEY	2	14,620 D	45.4%	54.6%	45.4%	54.6%
6	1972	196,858	103,284	MAYNE, WILEY	93,574	BEDELL, BERKLEY		9,710 R	52.5%	47.5%	52.5%	47.5%

IOWA

1976 GENERAL ELECTION

President — Other vote was 20,051 McCarthy (Independent); 3,040 Anderson (American); 1,452 MacBride (Libertarian); 554 Hall (Communist); 267 Camejo (Socialist Workers); 241 LaRouche (U.S. Labor); 234 Zeidler (Socialist); 167 Levin (Socialist Labor); 506 scattered.

Congress — Other vote was scattered in CD's 3 and 4; Smith (American) in CD 1; 741 Robertson (Independent), 485 Oxley (American) and 6 scattered in CD 2; 2,075 Hayes (American) and 10 scattered in CD 5; 2,203 Mincer (American) and 10 scattered in CD 6.

1976 PRIMARIES

JUNE 8 REPUBLICAN

Congress — Unopposed in five CD's. Contested as follows:

CD 5 — 18,259 Kenneth R. Fulk; 14,050 John S. Murray.

JUNE 8 DEMOCRATIC

Congress — Unopposed in five CD's. Contested as follows:

CD 2 — 20,831 Michael Blouin; 3,256 James D. Roberson.

KANSAS

GOVERNOR

Robert F. Bennett (R). Elected 1974 to a four-year term.

SENATORS

Robert Dole (R). Re-elected 1974 to a six-year term. Previously elected 1968.

James B. Pearson (R). Re-elected 1972 to a six-year term. Previously elected 1966 and in 1962 to fill out term vacated by the death of Senator Andrew F. Schoeppel; had been appointed January 1962 to fill this same vacancy.

REPRESENTATIVES

1. Keith Sebelius (R)
2. Martha Keys (D)
3. Larry Winn (R)
4. Dan Glickman (D)
5. Joe Skubitz (R)

POSTWAR VOTE FOR GOVERNOR

	Total	Republican		Democratic		Other	Rep.-Dem.	Percentage			
								Total Vote		Major Vote	
Year	Vote	Vote	Candidate	Vote	Candidate	Vote	Plurality	Rep.	Dem.	Rep.	Dem.
1974	783,875	387,792	Bennett, Robert F.	384,115	Miller, Vern	11,968	3,677 R	49.5%	49.0%	50.2%	49.8%
1972	921,552	341,440	Kay, Morris	571,256	Docking, Robert	8,856	229,816 D	37.1%	62.0%	37.4%	62.6%
1970	745,196	333,227	Frizzell, Kent	404,611	Docking, Robert	7,358	71,384 D	44.7%	54.3%	45.2%	54.8%
1968	862,473	410,673	Harman, Rick	447,269	Docking, Robert	4,531	36,596 D	47.6%	51.9%	47.9%	52.1%
1966	692,955	304,325	Avery, William H.	380,030	Docking, Robert	8,600	75,705 D	43.9%	54.8%	44.5%	55.5%
1964	850,414	432,667	Avery, William H.	400,264	Wiles, Harry G.	17,483	32,403 R	50.9%	47.1%	51.9%	48.1%
1962	638,798	341,257	Anderson, John	291,285	Saffels, Dale E.	6,256	49,972 R	53.4%	45.6%	54.0%	46.0%
1960	922,522	511,534	Anderson, John	402,261	Docking, George	8,727	109,273 R	55.4%	43.6%	56.0%	44.0%
1958	735,939	313,036	Reed, Clyde M.	415,506	Docking, George	7,397	102,470 D	42.5%	56.5%	43.0%	57.0%
1956	864,935	364,340	Shaw, Warren W.	479,701	Docking, George	20,894	115,361 D	42.1%	55.5%	43.2%	56.8%
1954	622,633	329,868	Hall, Fred	286,218	Docking, George	6,547	43,650 R	53.0%	46.0%	53.5%	46.5%
1952	872,139	491,338	Arn, Edward F.	363,482	Rooney, Charles	17,319	127,856 R	56.3%	41.7%	57.5%	42.5%
1950	619,310	333,001	Arn, Edward F.	275,494	Anderson, Kenneth	10,815	57,507 R	53.8%	44.5%	54.7%	45.3%
1948	760,407	433,396	Carlson, Frank	307,485	Carpenter, Randolph	19,526	125,911 R	57.0%	40.4%	58.5%	41.5%
1946	577,694	309,064	Carlson, Frank	254,283	Woodring, Harry H.	14,347	54,781 R	53.5%	44.0%	54.9%	45.1%

The term of office of Kansas' Governor was increased from two to four years effective with the 1974 election.

POSTWAR VOTE FOR SENATOR

	Total	Republican		Democratic		Other	Rep.-Dem.	Percentage			
								Total Vote		Major Vote	
Year	Vote	Vote	Candidate	Vote	Candidate	Vote	Plurality	Rep.	Dem.	Rep.	Dem.
1974	794,437	403,983	Dole, Robert	390,451	Roy, William R.	3	13,532 R	50.9%	49.1%	50.9%	49.1%
1972	871,722	622,591	Pearson, James B.	200,764	Tetzlaff, Arch O.	48,367	421,827 R	71.4%	23.0%	75.6%	24.4%
1968	817,096	490,911	Dole, Robert	315,911	Robinson, William I.	10,274	175,000 R	60.1%	38.7%	60.8%	39.2%
1966	671,345	350,077	Pearson, James B.	303,223	Breeding, J. Floyd	18,045	46,854 R	52.1%	45.2%	53.6%	46.4%
1962	622,232	388,500	Carlson, Frank	223,630	Smith, K. L.	10,102	164,870 R	62.4%	35.9%	63.5%	36.5%
1962s	613,250	344,689	Pearson, James B.	260,756	Aylward, Paul L.	7,805	83,933 R	56.2%	42.5%	56.9%	43.1%
1960	888,592	485,499	Schoeppel, Andrew F.	388,895	Theis, Frank	14,198	96,604 R	54.6%	43.8%	55.5%	44.5%
1956	825,280	477,822	Carlson, Frank	333,939	Hart, George	13,519	143,883 R	57.9%	40.5%	58.9%	41.1%
1954	618,063	348,144	Schoeppel, Andrew F.	258,575	McGill, George	11,344	89,569 R	56.3%	41.8%	57.4%	42.6%
1950	619,104	335,880	Carlson, Frank	271,365	Aiken, Paul	11,859	64,515 R	54.3%	43.8%	55.3%	44.7%
1948	716,342	393,412	Schoeppel, Andrew F.	305,987	McGill, George	16,943	87,425 R	54.9%	42.7%	56.3%	43.7%

One of the 1962 elections was for a short term to fill a vacancy.

KANSAS

Districts Established March 30, 1971

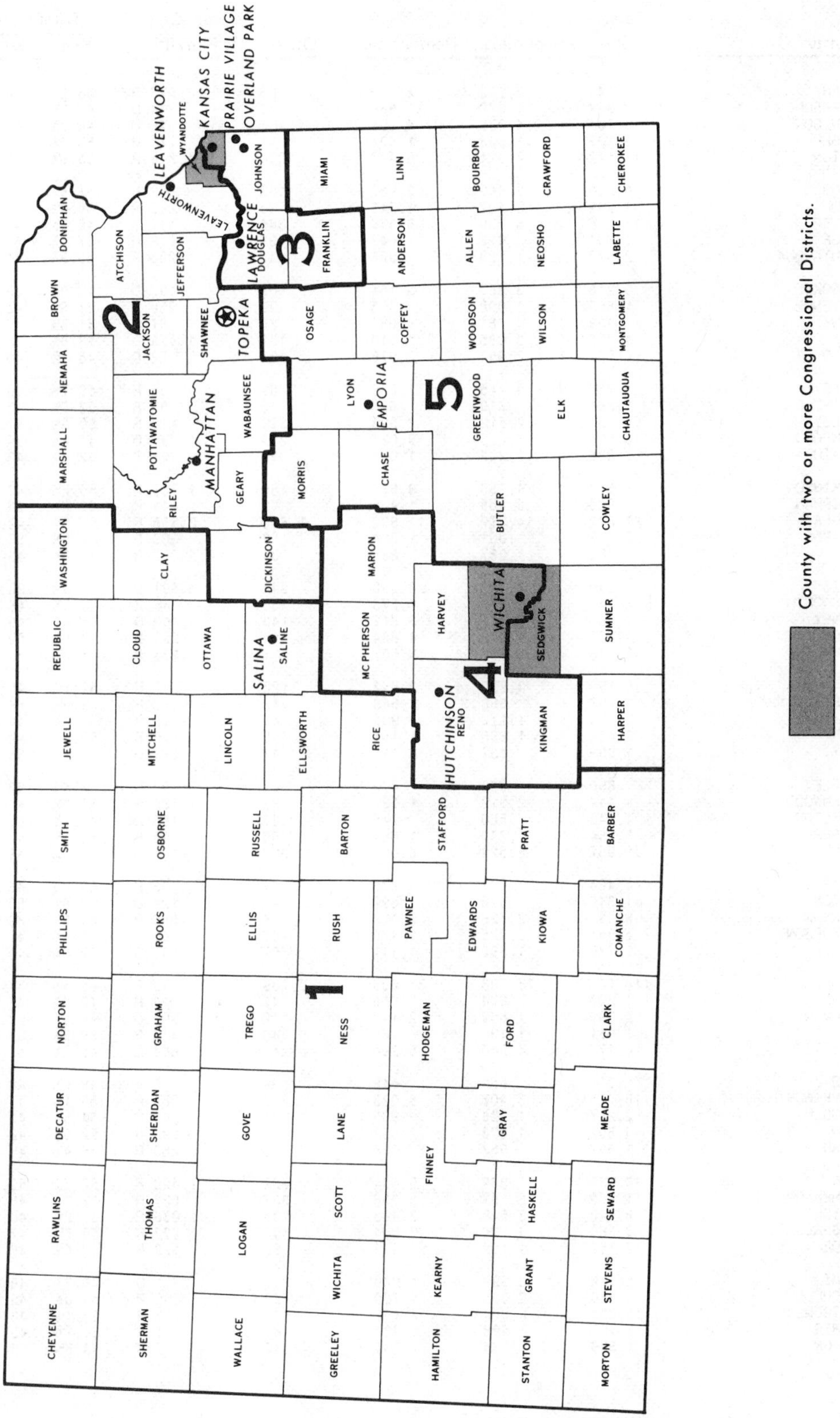

KANSAS

PRESIDENT 1976

1970 Census Population	County	Total Vote	Republican	Democratic	Other	Rep.-Dem. Plurality	Percentage Total Vote Rep.	Percentage Total Vote Dem.	Percentage Major Vote Rep.	Percentage Major Vote Dem.
15,043	ALLEN	6,141	3,269	2,746	126	523 R	53.2%	44.7%	54.3%	45.7%
8,501	ANDERSON	3,844	1,872	1,886	86	14 D	48.7%	49.1%	49.8%	50.2%
19,165	ATCHISON	8,344	4,030	4,108	206	78 D	48.3%	49.2%	49.5%	50.5%
7,016	BARBER	3,109	1,568	1,494	47	74 R	50.4%	48.1%	51.2%	48.8%
30,663	BARTON	13,142	7,311	5,497	334	1,814 R	55.6%	41.8%	57.1%	42.9%
15,215	BOURBON	6,929	3,589	3,237	103	352 R	51.8%	46.7%	52.6%	47.4%
11,685	BROWN	5,245	3,407	1,745	93	1,662 R	65.0%	33.3%	66.1%	33.9%
38,658	BUTLER	17,316	8,390	8,540	386	150 D	48.5%	49.3%	49.6%	50.4%
3,408	CHASE	1,601	922	643	36	279 R	57.6%	40.2%	58.9%	41.1%
4,642	CHAUTAUQUA	2,078	1,159	866	53	293 R	55.8%	41.7%	57.2%	42.8%
21,549	CHEROKEE	9,218	3,957	5,154	107	1,197 D	42.9%	55.9%	43.4%	56.6%
4,256	CHEYENNE	1,805	1,008	758	39	250 R	55.8%	42.0%	57.1%	42.9%
2,896	CLARK	1,469	761	680	28	81 R	51.8%	46.3%	52.8%	47.2%
9,890	CLAY	4,832	3,085	1,610	137	1,475 R	63.8%	33.3%	65.7%	34.3%
13,466	CLOUD	6,061	2,954	2,976	131	22 D	48.7%	49.1%	49.8%	50.2%
7,397	COFFEY	3,783	2,145	1,549	89	596 R	56.7%	40.9%	58.1%	41.9%
2,702	COMANCHE	1,364	719	630	15	89 R	52.7%	46.2%	53.3%	46.7%
35,012	COWLEY	14,931	7,513	7,095	323	418 R	50.3%	47.5%	51.4%	48.6%
37,850	CRAWFORD	16,504	7,225	9,021	258	1,796 D	43.8%	54.7%	44.5%	55.5%
4,988	DECATUR	2,336	1,232	1,011	93	221 R	52.7%	43.3%	54.9%	45.1%
19,993	DICKINSON	8,617	4,759	3,672	186	1,087 R	55.2%	42.6%	56.4%	43.6%
9,107	DONIPHAN	3,969	2,469	1,428	72	1,041 R	62.2%	36.0%	63.4%	36.6%
57,932	DOUGLAS	27,842	14,277	11,922	1,643	2,355 R	51.3%	42.8%	54.5%	45.5%
4,581	EDWARDS	2,357	1,001	1,304	52	303 D	42.5%	55.3%	43.4%	56.6%
3,858	ELK	1,982	1,087	865	30	222 R	54.8%	43.6%	55.7%	44.3%
24,730	ELLIS	11,240	4,719	6,280	241	1,561 D	42.0%	55.9%	42.9%	57.1%
6,146	ELLSWORTH	3,246	1,618	1,573	55	45 R	49.8%	48.5%	50.7%	49.3%
19,029	FINNEY	7,667	3,711	3,813	143	102 D	48.4%	49.7%	49.3%	50.7%
22,587	FORD	9,827	4,679	4,934	214	255 D	47.6%	50.2%	48.7%	51.3%
20,007	FRANKLIN	8,578	4,760	3,607	211	1,153 R	55.5%	42.0%	56.9%	43.1%
28,111	GEARY	6,196	3,230	2,843	123	387 R	52.1%	45.9%	53.2%	46.8%
3,940	GOVE	1,757	860	848	49	12 R	48.9%	48.3%	50.4%	49.6%
4,751	GRAHAM	2,088	1,112	936	40	176 R	53.3%	44.8%	54.3%	45.7%
5,961	GRANT	2,422	1,226	1,151	45	75 R	50.6%	47.5%	51.6%	48.4%
4,516	GRAY	1,989	837	1,111	41	274 D	42.1%	55.9%	43.0%	57.0%
1,819	GREELEY	896	389	479	28	90 D	43.4%	53.5%	44.8%	55.2%
9,141	GREENWOOD	4,144	2,319	1,737	88	582 R	56.0%	41.9%	57.2%	42.8%
2,747	HAMILTON	1,343	560	746	37	186 D	41.7%	55.5%	42.9%	57.1%
7,871	HARPER	3,554	1,777	1,681	96	96 R	50.0%	47.3%	51.4%	48.6%
27,236	HARVEY	12,987	6,624	6,003	360	621 R	51.0%	46.2%	52.5%	47.5%
3,672	HASKELL	1,464	761	676	27	85 R	52.0%	46.2%	53.0%	47.0%
2,662	HODGEMAN	1,315	576	697	42	121 D	43.8%	53.0%	45.2%	54.8%
10,342	JACKSON	4,968	2,725	2,129	114	596 R	54.9%	42.9%	56.1%	43.9%
11,945	JEFFERSON	5,851	3,225	2,470	156	755 R	55.1%	42.2%	56.6%	43.4%
6,099	JEWELL	2,770	1,592	1,111	67	481 R	57.5%	40.1%	58.9%	41.1%
220,073	JOHNSON	114,142	75,798	35,605	2,739	40,193 R	66.4%	31.2%	68.0%	32.0%
3,047	KEARNY	1,377	674	658	45	16 R	48.9%	47.8%	50.6%	49.4%
8,886	KINGMAN	4,093	1,839	2,142	112	303 D	44.9%	52.3%	46.2%	53.8%
4,088	KIOWA	1,984	1,180	764	40	416 R	59.5%	38.5%	60.7%	39.3%
25,775	LABETTE	10,177	4,640	5,294	243	654 D	45.6%	52.0%	46.7%	53.3%
2,707	LANE	1,331	651	646	34	5 R	48.9%	48.5%	50.2%	49.8%
53,340	LEAVENWORTH	16,778	8,407	8,022	349	385 R	50.1%	47.8%	51.2%	48.8%
4,582	LINCOLN	2,247	1,225	985	37	240 R	54.5%	43.8%	55.4%	44.6%
7,770	LINN	3,602	1,873	1,681	48	192 R	52.0%	46.7%	52.7%	47.3%
3,814	LOGAN	1,697	957	694	46	263 R	56.4%	40.9%	58.0%	42.0%
32,071	LYON	13,428	7,062	5,634	732	1,428 R	52.6%	42.0%	55.6%	44.4%
24,778	MCPHERSON	11,860	6,187	5,366	307	821 R	52.2%	45.2%	53.6%	46.4%
13,935	MARION	6,140	3,519	2,483	138	1,036 R	57.3%	40.4%	58.6%	41.4%
13,139	MARSHALL	6,360	3,226	3,004	130	222 R	50.7%	47.2%	51.8%	48.2%
4,912	MEADE	2,152	1,109	983	60	126 R	51.5%	45.7%	53.0%	47.0%
19,254	MIAMI	8,216	3,999	4,000	217	1 D	48.7%	48.7%	50.0%	50.0%
8,010	MITCHELL	3,880	2,095	1,700	85	395 R	54.0%	43.8%	55.2%	44.8%
39,949	MONTGOMERY	16,391	8,864	7,157	370	1,707 R	54.1%	43.7%	55.3%	44.7%
6,432	MORRIS	3,102	1,698	1,337	67	361 R	54.7%	43.1%	55.9%	44.1%
3,576	MORTON	1,509	738	735	36	3 R	48.9%	48.7%	50.1%	49.9%

KANSAS

PRESIDENT 1976

1970 Census Population	County	Total Vote	Republican	Democratic	Other	Rep.-Dem. Plurality	Percentage Total Vote Rep.	Total Vote Dem.	Major Vote Rep.	Major Vote Dem.
11,825	NEMAHA	5,441	2,759	2,586	96	173 R	50.7%	47.5%	51.6%	48.4%
18,812	NEOSHO	8,024	4,038	3,842	144	196 R	50.3%	47.9%	51.2%	48.8%
4,791	NESS	2,184	1,016	1,106	62	90 D	46.5%	50.6%	47.9%	52.1%
7,279	NORTON	3,635	2,201	1,337	97	864 R	60.6%	36.8%	62.2%	37.8%
13,352	OSAGE	5,828	2,945	2,755	128	190 R	50.5%	47.3%	51.7%	48.3%
6,416	OSBORNE	2,840	1,574	1,190	76	384 R	55.4%	41.9%	56.9%	43.1%
6,183	OTTAWA	3,082	1,629	1,393	60	236 R	52.9%	45.2%	53.9%	46.1%
8,484	PAWNEE	3,751	1,692	1,959	100	267 D	45.1%	52.2%	46.3%	53.7%
7,888	PHILLIPS	3,675	2,317	1,264	94	1,053 R	63.0%	34.4%	64.7%	35.3%
11,755	POTTAWATOMIE	5,897	3,483	2,316	98	1,167 R	59.1%	39.3%	60.1%	39.9%
10,056	PRATT	4,850	2,427	2,307	116	120 R	50.0%	47.6%	51.3%	48.7%
4,393	RAWLINS	2,131	1,148	903	80	245 R	53.9%	42.4%	56.0%	44.0%
60,765	RENO	26,512	11,212	14,620	680	3,408 D	42.3%	55.1%	43.4%	56.6%
8,498	REPUBLIC	3,994	2,294	1,617	83	677 R	57.4%	40.5%	58.7%	41.3%
12,320	RICE	5,765	2,584	3,056	125	472 D	44.8%	53.0%	45.8%	54.2%
56,788	RILEY	16,568	9,518	6,540	510	2,978 R	57.4%	39.5%	59.3%	40.7%
7,628	ROOKS	3,137	1,664	1,412	61	252 R	53.0%	45.0%	54.1%	45.9%
5,117	RUSH	2,581	1,170	1,359	52	189 D	45.3%	52.7%	46.3%	53.7%
9,428	RUSSELL	4,669	3,165	1,453	51	1,712 R	67.8%	31.1%	68.5%	31.5%
46,592	SALINE	20,107	11,218	8,476	413	2,742 R	55.8%	42.2%	57.0%	43.0%
5,606	SCOTT	2,183	1,195	919	69	276 R	54.7%	42.1%	56.5%	43.5%
350,694	SEDGWICK	137,629	69,828	63,989	3,812	5,839 R	50.7%	46.5%	52.2%	47.8%
15,744	SEWARD	5,615	3,604	1,907	104	1,697 R	64.2%	34.0%	65.4%	34.6%
155,322	SHAWNEE	67,370	37,101	28,578	1,691	8,523 R	55.1%	42.4%	56.5%	43.5%
3,859	SHERIDAN	1,705	838	793	74	45 R	49.1%	46.5%	51.4%	48.6%
7,792	SHERMAN	3,332	1,671	1,573	88	98 R	50.2%	47.2%	51.5%	48.5%
6,757	SMITH	3,436	2,009	1,333	94	676 R	58.5%	38.8%	60.1%	39.9%
5,943	STAFFORD	3,162	1,430	1,659	73	229 D	45.2%	52.5%	46.3%	53.7%
2,287	STANTON	1,040	510	489	41	21 R	49.0%	47.0%	51.1%	48.9%
4,198	STEVENS	2,205	1,262	901	42	361 R	57.2%	40.9%	58.3%	41.7%
23,553	SUMNER	10,340	4,645	5,385	310	740 D	44.9%	52.1%	46.3%	53.7%
7,501	THOMAS	4,164	2,246	1,802	116	444 R	53.9%	43.3%	55.5%	44.5%
4,436	TREGO	2,068	1,025	1,003	40	22 R	49.6%	48.5%	50.5%	49.5%
6,397	WABAUNSEE	3,336	1,921	1,354	61	567 R	57.6%	40.6%	58.7%	41.3%
2,215	WALLACE	1,137	600	486	51	114 R	52.8%	42.7%	55.2%	44.8%
9,249	WASHINGTON	4,213	2,543	1,564	106	979 R	60.4%	37.1%	61.9%	38.1%
3,274	WICHITA	1,238	593	614	31	21 D	47.9%	49.6%	49.1%	50.9%
11,317	WILSON	4,818	2,682	2,047	89	635 R	55.7%	42.5%	56.7%	43.3%
4,789	WOODSON	2,041	1,104	904	33	200 R	54.1%	44.3%	55.0%	45.0%
186,845	WYANDOTTE	62,555	23,141	37,478	1,936	14,337 D	37.0%	59.9%	38.2%	61.8%
2,249,071	TOTAL	957,845	502,752	430,421	24,672	72,331 R	52.5%	44.9%	53.9%	46.1%

KANSAS

CONGRESS

		Total	Republican		Democratic		Other	Rep.-Dem.	Percentage			
									Total Vote		Major Vote	
CD	Year	Vote	Vote	Candidate	Vote	Candidate	Vote	Plurality	Rep.	Dem.	Rep.	Dem.
1	1976	194,772	142,311	SEBELIUS, KEITH	52,459	YOWELL, RANDY	2	89,852 R	73.1%	26.9%	73.1%	26.9%
1	1974	173,868	101,565	SEBELIUS, KEITH	57,326	SMITH, DONALD C.	14,977	44,239 R	58.4%	33.0%	63.9%	36.1%
1	1972	188,658	145,712	SEBELIUS, KEITH	40,678	COOVER, MORRIS	2,268	105,034 R	77.2%	21.6%	78.2%	21.8%
2	1976	174,861	82,946	FREEMAN, ROSS R.	88,645	KEYS, MARTHA	3,270	5,699 D	47.4%	50.7%	48.3%	51.7%
2	1974	154,239	67,650	PETERSON, JOHN C.	84,864	KEYS, MARTHA	1,725	17,214 D	43.9%	55.0%	44.4%	55.6%
2	1972	175,345	65,071	MCATEE, CHARLES D.	106,276	ROY, WILLIAM R.	3,998	41,205 D	37.1%	60.6%	38.0%	62.0%
3	1976	179,865	123,578	WINN, LARRY	52,110	RHOADS, PHILIP S.	4,177	71,468 R	68.7%	29.0%	70.3%	29.7%
3	1974	142,650	89,694	WINN, LARRY	49,976	WELLS, SAMUEL J.	2,980	39,718 R	62.9%	35.0%	64.2%	35.8%
3	1972	172,406	122,358	WINN, LARRY	43,777	BARSOTTI, CHARLES	6,271	78,581 R	71.0%	25.4%	73.6%	26.4%
4	1976	179,168	86,832	SHRIVER, GARNER E.	90,067	GLICKMAN, DAN	2,269	3,235 D	48.5%	50.3%	49.1%	50.9%
4	1974	144,131	70,401	SHRIVER, GARNER E.	61,210	CHANEY, BERT	12,520	9,191 R	48.8%	42.5%	53.5%	46.5%
4	1972	164,127	120,120	SHRIVER, GARNER E.	40,753	STEVENS, JOHN S.	3,254	79,367 R	73.2%	24.8%	74.7%	25.3%
5	1976	180,625	109,573	SKUBITZ, JOE	65,340	OLSON, VIRGIL L.	5,712	44,233 R	60.7%	36.2%	62.6%	37.4%
5	1974	160,670	88,646	SKUBITZ, JOE	72,024	GAINES, FRANK		16,622 R	55.2%	44.8%	55.2%	44.8%
5	1972	177,829	128,639	SKUBITZ, JOE	49,169	KITCH, LLOYD L.	21	79,470 R	72.3%	27.6%	72.3%	27.7%

KANSAS

1976 GENERAL ELECTION

President Other vote was 13,185 McCarthy (Independent); 4,724 Anderson (American); 3,242 MacBride (Independent); 2,118 Maddox (Conservative); 1,403 Bubar (Prohibition).

Congress Other vote was scattered in CD 1; 1,933 Ijams (American) and 1,337 Scoggin (Prohibition) in CD 2; 4,162 Hyatt (American) and 15 scattered in CD 3; Cowdrey (American) in CD 4; Rutherford (American) in CD 5.

1976 PRIMARIES

AUGUST 3 REPUBLICAN

Congress Unopposed in three CD's. Contested as follows:

CD 2 19,621 Ross R. Freeman; 8,456 Ken E. Johnson; 5,929 Nina Strahm; 4,029 Lawrence E. Beckwith; 2,697 Richard W. Fatherley; 1,487 Charles Ijams; 1,171 C. D. Rose.

CD 5 33,843 Joe Skubitz; 8,770 William F. Tyler.

AUGUST 3 DEMOCRATIC

Congress Unopposed in two CD's. Contested as follows:

CD 1 16,342 Randy Yowell; 9,777 Bill Addington.

CD 4 19,713 Dan Glickman; 8,075 Jack Williams; 2,137 Aron R. Russell; 1,746 Bill Linker.

CD 5 10,035 Virgil L. Olson; 9,738 Kay Camin; 9,137 John A. Barnes.

KENTUCKY

GOVERNOR

Julian Carroll (D). Elected 1975 to a four-year term. Had been elected as Lieutenant-Governor in 1971 and succeeded upon Governor Ford's election to the Senate in November, 1974.

SENATORS

Wendell H. Ford (D). Elected 1974 to a six-year term.

Walter Huddleston (D). Elected 1972 to a six-year term.

REPRESENTATIVES

1. Carroll Hubbard (D)
2. William H. Natcher (D)
3. Romano L. Mazzoli (D)
4. M. G. Snyder (R)
5. Tim Lee Carter (R)
6. John Breckinridge (D)
7. Carl D. Perkins (D)

POSTWAR VOTE FOR GOVERNOR

Year	Total Vote	Republican Vote	Republican Candidate	Democratic Vote	Democratic Candidate	Other Vote	Rep.-Dem. Plurality	Percentage Total Vote Rep.	Percentage Total Vote Dem.	Percentage Major Vote Rep.	Percentage Major Vote Dem.
1975	748,157	277,998	Gable, Robert E.	470,159	Carroll, Julian	–	192,161 D	37.2%	62.8%	37.2%	62.8%
1971	930,790	412,653	Emberton, Thomas	470,720	Ford, Wendell H.	47,417	58,067 D	44.3%	50.6%	46.7%	53.3%
1967	886,946	454,123	Nunn, Louie B.	425,674	Ward, Henry	7,149	28,449 R	51.2%	48.0%	51.6%	48.4%
1963	886,047	436,496	Nunn, Louie B.	449,551	Breathitt, Edward T.	–	13,055 D	49.3%	50.7%	49.3%	50.7%
1959	853,005	336,456	Robsion, John M.	516,549	Combs, Bert T.	–	180,093 D	39.4%	60.6%	39.4%	60.6%
1955	778,488	322,671	Denney, Edwin R.	451,647	Chandler, Albert B.	4,170	128,976 D	41.4%	58.0%	41.7%	58.3%
1951	634,359	288,014	Siler, Eugene	346,345	Wetherby, Lawrence	–	58,331 D	45.4%	54.6%	45.4%	54.6%
1947	672,372	287,130	Dummit, Eldon S.	385,242	Clements, Earle C.	–	98,112 D	42.7%	57.3%	42.7%	57.3%

POSTWAR VOTE FOR SENATOR

Year	Total Vote	Republican Vote	Republican Candidate	Democratic Vote	Democratic Candidate	Other Vote	Rep.-Dem. Plurality	Percentage Total Vote Rep.	Percentage Total Vote Dem.	Percentage Major Vote Rep.	Percentage Major Vote Dem.
1974	745,994	328,982	Cook, Marlow W.	399,406	Ford, Wendell H.	17,606	70,424 D	44.1%	53.5%	45.2%	54.8%
1972	1,037,861	494,337	Nunn, Louie B.	528,550	Huddleston, Walter	14,974	34,213 D	47.6%	50.9%	48.3%	51.7%
1968	942,865	484,260	Cook, Marlow W.	448,960	Peden, Katherine	9,645	35,300 R	51.4%	47.6%	51.9%	48.1%
1966	749,884	483,805	Cooper, John Sherman	266,079	Brown, J. Y.	–	217,726 R	64.5%	35.5%	64.5%	35.5%
1962	820,088	432,648	Morton, Thruston B.	387,440	Wyatt, Wilson W.	–	45,208 R	52.8%	47.2%	52.8%	47.2%
1960	1,088,377	644,087	Cooper, John Sherman	444,290	Johnson, Keen	–	199,797 R	59.2%	40.8%	59.2%	40.8%
1956	1,006,825	506,903	Morton, Thruston B.	499,922	Clements, Earle C.	–	6,981 R	50.3%	49.7%	50.3%	49.7%
1956s	1,011,645	538,505	Cooper, John Sherman	473,140	Wetherby, Lawrence	–	65,365 R	53.2%	46.8%	53.2%	46.8%
1954	797,057	362,948	Cooper, John Sherman	434,109	Barkley, Alben W.	–	71,161 D	45.5%	54.5%	45.5%	54.5%
1952s	960,228	494,576	Cooper, John Sherman	465,652	Underwood, Thomas R.	–	28,924 R	51.5%	48.5%	51.5%	48.5%
1950	617,121	278,368	Dawson, Charles L.	334,249	Clements, Earle C.	4,504	55,881 D	45.1%	54.2%	45.4%	54.6%
1948	794,469	383,776	Cooper, John Sherman	408,256	Chapman, Virgil	2,437	24,480 D	48.3%	51.4%	48.5%	51.5%
1946s	615,119	327,652	Cooper, John Sherman	285,829	Brown, J. Y.	1,638	41,823 R	53.3%	46.5%	53.4%	46.6%

One of the elections in 1956 and those in 1952 and 1946 were for short terms to fill vacancies.

KENTUCKY

Districts Established June 27, 1972

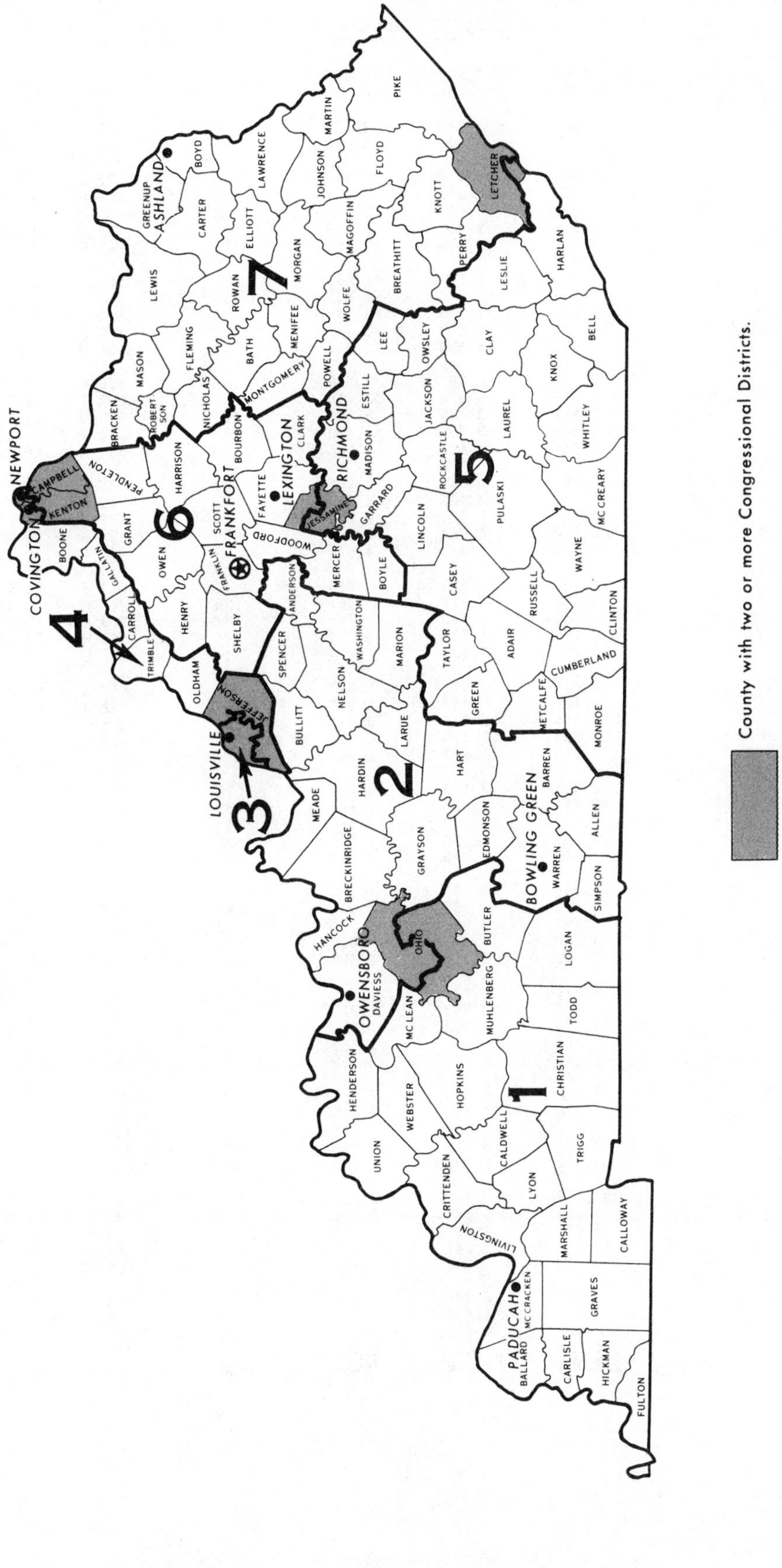

KENTUCKY

PRESIDENT 1976

1970 Census Population	County	Total Vote	Republican	Democratic	Other	Rep.-Dem. Plurality	Percentage Total Vote Rep.	Percentage Total Vote Dem.	Percentage Major Vote Rep.	Percentage Major Vote Dem.
13,037	ADAIR	5,634	3,201	2,366	67	835 R	56.8%	42.0%	57.5%	42.5%
12,598	ALLEN	4,778	2,508	2,231	39	277 R	52.5%	46.7%	52.9%	47.1%
9,358	ANDERSON	4,132	1,682	2,388	62	706 D	40.7%	57.8%	41.3%	58.7%
8,276	BALLARD	3,693	649	2,794	250	2,145 D	17.6%	75.7%	18.8%	81.2%
28,677	BARREN	9,771	3,797	5,878	96	2,081 D	38.9%	60.2%	39.2%	60.8%
9,235	BATH	3,071	938	2,113	20	1,175 D	30.5%	68.8%	30.7%	69.3%
31,087	BELL	10,483	5,035	5,284	164	249 D	48.0%	50.4%	48.8%	51.2%
32,812	BOONE	11,385	5,602	5,602	181	R	49.2%	49.2%	50.0%	50.0%
18,476	BOURBON	5,904	2,260	3,504	140	1,244 D	38.3%	59.3%	39.2%	60.8%
52,376	BOYD	20,459	9,106	11,150	203	2,044 D	44.5%	54.5%	45.0%	55.0%
21,090	BOYLE	7,703	3,511	4,095	97	584 D	45.6%	53.2%	46.2%	53.8%
7,227	BRACKEN	2,495	879	1,577	39	698 D	35.2%	63.2%	35.8%	64.2%
14,221	BREATHITT	4,576	1,014	3,544	18	2,530 D	22.2%	77.4%	22.2%	77.8%
14,789	BRECKINRIDGE	6,111	2,698	3,347	66	649 D	44.1%	54.8%	44.6%	55.4%
26,090	BULLITT	9,477	3,639	5,623	215	1,984 D	38.4%	59.3%	39.3%	60.7%
9,723	BUTLER	3,981	2,363	1,588	30	775 R	59.4%	39.9%	59.8%	40.2%
13,179	CALDWELL	4,899	1,808	3,016	75	1,208 D	36.9%	61.6%	37.5%	62.5%
27,692	CALLOWAY	11,507	3,171	8,141	195	4,970 D	27.6%	70.7%	28.0%	72.0%
88,561	CAMPBELL	28,821	15,798	12,423	600	3,375 R	54.8%	43.1%	56.0%	44.0%
5,354	CARLISLE	2,456	435	1,985	36	1,550 D	17.7%	80.8%	18.0%	82.0%
8,523	CARROLL	3,099	815	2,251	33	1,436 D	26.3%	72.6%	26.6%	73.4%
19,850	CARTER	7,133	3,185	3,915	33	730 D	44.7%	54.9%	44.9%	55.1%
12,930	CASEY	5,032	3,379	1,602	51	1,777 R	67.2%	31.8%	67.8%	32.2%
56,224	CHRISTIAN	12,914	4,964	7,845	105	2,881 D	38.4%	60.7%	38.8%	61.2%
24,090	CLARK	7,768	3,114	4,575	79	1,461 D	40.1%	58.9%	40.5%	59.5%
18,481	CLAY	5,336	3,652	1,674	10	1,978 R	68.4%	31.4%	68.6%	31.4%
8,174	CLINTON	3,389	2,354	987	48	1,367 R	69.5%	29.1%	70.5%	29.5%
8,493	CRITTENDEN	3,352	1,596	1,715	41	119 D	47.6%	51.2%	48.2%	51.8%
6,850	CUMBERLAND	2,527	1,653	853	21	800 R	65.4%	33.8%	66.0%	34.0%
79,486	DAVIESS	27,454	12,826	14,114	514	1,288 D	46.7%	51.4%	47.6%	52.4%
8,751	EDMONSON	3,411	1,976	1,418	17	558 R	57.9%	41.6%	58.2%	41.8%
5,933	ELLIOTT	2,461	455	1,987	19	1,532 D	18.5%	80.7%	18.6%	81.4%
12,752	ESTILL	4,314	2,250	2,034	30	216 R	52.2%	47.1%	52.5%	47.5%
174,323	FAYETTE	64,989	35,170	28,012	1,807	7,158 R	54.1%	43.1%	55.7%	44.3%
11,366	FLEMING	3,983	1,647	2,317	19	670 D	41.4%	58.2%	41.5%	58.5%
35,889	FLOYD	13,333	3,108	10,151	74	7,043 D	23.3%	76.1%	23.4%	76.6%
34,481	FRANKLIN	16,441	5,536	10,475	430	4,939 D	33.7%	63.7%	34.6%	65.4%
10,183	FULTON	3,470	1,060	2,370	40	1,310 D	30.5%	68.3%	30.9%	69.1%
4,134	GALLATIN	1,623	436	1,164	23	728 D	26.9%	71.7%	27.3%	72.8%
9,457	GARRARD	3,988	2,045	1,887	56	158 R	51.3%	47.3%	52.0%	48.0%
9,999	GRANT	3,634	1,212	2,336	86	1,124 D	33.4%	64.3%	34.2%	65.8%
30,939	GRAVES	12,420	3,195	8,982	243	5,787 D	25.7%	72.3%	26.2%	73.8%
16,445	GRAYSON	6,790	3,658	3,064	68	594 R	53.9%	45.1%	54.4%	45.6%
10,350	GREEN	4,519	2,397	2,085	37	312 R	53.0%	46.1%	53.5%	46.5%
33,192	GREENUP	12,013	5,062	6,880	71	1,818 D	42.1%	57.3%	42.4%	57.6%
7,080	HANCOCK	2,747	1,124	1,562	61	438 D	40.9%	56.9%	41.8%	58.2%
78,421	HARDIN	15,185	6,965	7,977	243	1,012 D	45.9%	52.5%	46.6%	53.4%
37,370	HARLAN	12,006	4,624	7,300	82	2,676 D	38.5%	60.8%	38.8%	61.2%
14,158	HARRISON	5,551	1,911	3,582	58	1,671 D	34.4%	64.5%	34.8%	65.2%
13,980	HART	5,244	2,013	3,189	42	1,176 D	38.4%	60.8%	38.7%	61.3%
36,031	HENDERSON	12,118	4,053	7,916	149	3,863 D	33.4%	65.3%	33.9%	66.1%
10,910	HENRY	4,220	1,192	2,985	43	1,793 D	28.2%	70.7%	28.5%	71.5%
6,264	HICKMAN	2,716	585	2,035	96	1,450 D	21.5%	74.9%	22.3%	77.7%
38,167	HOPKINS	12,990	5,115	7,749	126	2,634 D	39.4%	59.7%	39.8%	60.2%
10,005	JACKSON	3,466	2,766	680	20	2,086 R	79.8%	19.6%	80.3%	19.7%
695,055	JEFFERSON	259,445	130,262	122,731	6,452	7,531 R	50.2%	47.3%	51.5%	48.5%
17,430	JESSAMINE	6,004	3,081	2,795	128	286 R	51.3%	46.6%	52.4%	47.6%
17,539	JOHNSON	8,635	4,891	3,683	61	1,208 R	56.6%	42.7%	57.0%	43.0%
129,440	KENTON	41,680	22,087	18,833	760	3,254 R	53.0%	45.2%	54.0%	46.0%
14,698	KNOTT	5,779	962	4,762	55	3,800 D	16.6%	82.4%	16.8%	83.2%
23,689	KNOX	8,661	4,931	3,642	88	1,289 R	56.9%	42.1%	57.5%	42.5%
10,672	LARUE	3,655	1,409	2,207	39	798 D	38.5%	60.4%	39.0%	61.0%
27,386	LAUREL	10,073	6,186	3,813	74	2,373 R	61.4%	37.9%	61.9%	38.1%
10,726	LAWRENCE	4,283	1,838	2,402	43	564 D	42.9%	56.1%	43.3%	56.7%
6,587	LEE	2,563	1,449	1,091	23	358 R	56.5%	42.6%	57.0%	43.0%

KENTUCKY

PRESIDENT 1976

1970 Census Population	County	Total Vote	Republican	Democratic	Other	Rep.-Dem. Plurality	Percentage Total Vote Rep.	Percentage Total Vote Dem.	Percentage Major Vote Rep.	Percentage Major Vote Dem.
11,623	LESLIE	5,271	3,770	1,478	23	2,292 R	71.5%	28.0%	71.8%	28.2%
23,165	LETCHER	7,748	3,122	4,590	36	1,468 D	40.3%	59.2%	40.5%	59.5%
12,355	LEWIS	4,332	2,383	1,929	20	454 R	55.0%	44.5%	55.3%	44.7%
16,663	LINCOLN	5,925	2,694	3,198	33	504 D	45.5%	54.0%	45.7%	54.3%
7,596	LIVINGSTON	3,415	878	2,497	40	1,619 D	25.7%	73.1%	26.0%	74.0%
21,793	LOGAN	7,389	2,430	4,850	109	2,420 D	32.9%	65.6%	33.4%	66.6%
5,562	LYON	2,221	585	1,606	30	1,021 D	26.3%	72.3%	26.7%	73.3%
58,281	MCCRACKEN	22,687	6,997	14,956	734	7,959 D	30.8%	65.9%	31.9%	68.1%
12,548	MCCREARY	5,142	3,272	1,827	43	1,445 R	63.6%	35.5%	64.2%	35.8%
9,062	MCLEAN	3,593	1,212	2,346	35	1,134 D	33.7%	65.3%	34.1%	65.9%
42,730	MADISON	14,114	6,581	7,299	234	718 D	46.6%	51.7%	47.4%	52.6%
10,443	MAGOFFIN	4,263	1,793	2,451	19	658 D	42.1%	57.5%	42.2%	57.8%
16,714	MARION	5,322	1,723	3,520	79	1,797 D	32.4%	66.1%	32.9%	67.1%
20,381	MARSHALL	9,614	2,578	6,906	130	4,328 D	26.8%	71.8%	27.2%	72.8%
9,377	MARTIN	3,413	2,120	1,267	26	853 R	62.1%	37.1%	62.6%	37.4%
17,273	MASON	6,004	2,529	3,397	78	868 D	42.1%	56.6%	42.7%	57.3%
18,796	MEADE	4,868	1,755	3,030	83	1,275 D	36.1%	62.2%	36.7%	63.3%
4,050	MENIFEE	1,356	304	1,041	11	737 D	22.4%	76.8%	22.6%	77.4%
15,960	MERCER	5,991	2,451	3,411	129	960 D	40.9%	56.9%	41.8%	58.2%
8,177	METCALFE	3,266	1,356	1,877	33	521 D	41.5%	57.5%	41.9%	58.1%
11,642	MONROE	4,795	3,352	1,412	31	1,940 R	69.9%	29.4%	70.4%	29.6%
15,364	MONTGOMERY	5,234	2,032	3,141	61	1,109 D	38.8%	60.0%	39.3%	60.7%
10,019	MORGAN	3,897	973	2,897	27	1,924 D	25.0%	74.3%	25.1%	74.9%
27,537	MUHLENBERG	11,449	4,292	7,058	99	2,766 D	37.5%	61.6%	37.8%	62.2%
23,477	NELSON	7,504	2,804	4,454	246	1,650 D	37.4%	59.4%	38.6%	61.4%
6,508	NICHOLAS	2,378	738	1,582	58	844 D	31.0%	66.5%	31.8%	68.2%
18,790	OHIO	7,337	3,764	3,508	65	256 R	51.3%	47.8%	51.8%	48.2%
14,687	OLDHAM	6,631	3,695	2,819	117	876 R	55.7%	42.5%	56.7%	43.3%
7,470	OWEN	3,051	676	2,332	43	1,656 D	22.2%	76.4%	22.5%	77.5%
5,023	OWSLEY	1,367	1,053	305	9	748 R	77.0%	22.3%	77.5%	22.5%
9,949	PENDLETON	3,427	1,230	2,147	50	917 D	35.9%	62.6%	36.4%	63.6%
26,259	PERRY	10,116	4,434	5,633	49	1,199 D	43.8%	55.7%	44.0%	56.0%
61,059	PIKE	23,691	9,178	14,320	193	5,142 D	38.7%	60.4%	39.1%	60.9%
7,704	POWELL	3,029	1,148	1,859	22	711 D	37.9%	61.4%	38.2%	61.8%
35,234	PULASKI	15,083	9,226	5,752	105	3,474 R	61.2%	38.1%	61.6%	38.4%
2,163	ROBERTSON	828	275	546	7	271 D	33.2%	65.9%	33.5%	66.5%
12,305	ROCKCASTLE	4,013	2,583	1,408	22	1,175 R	64.4%	35.1%	64.7%	35.3%
17,010	ROWAN	5,868	2,244	3,541	83	1,297 D	38.2%	60.3%	38.8%	61.2%
10,542	RUSSELL	4,732	2,882	1,803	47	1,079 R	60.9%	38.1%	61.5%	38.5%
17,948	SCOTT	5,638	2,408	3,118	112	710 D	42.7%	55.3%	43.6%	56.4%
18,999	SHELBY	6,847	2,916	3,841	90	925 D	42.6%	56.1%	43.2%	56.8%
13,054	SIMPSON	4,299	1,481	2,782	36	1,301 D	34.4%	64.7%	34.7%	65.3%
5,488	SPENCER	1,983	742	1,209	32	467 D	37.4%	61.0%	38.0%	62.0%
17,138	TAYLOR	6,866	3,337	3,456	73	119 D	48.6%	50.3%	49.1%	50.9%
10,823	TODD	3,597	1,095	2,436	66	1,341 D	30.4%	67.7%	31.0%	69.0%
8,620	TRIGG	3,745	991	2,727	27	1,736 D	26.5%	72.8%	26.7%	73.3%
5,349	TRIMBLE	2,113	517	1,568	28	1,051 D	24.5%	74.2%	24.8%	75.2%
15,882	UNION	5,312	1,716	3,540	56	1,824 D	32.3%	66.6%	32.6%	67.4%
57,432	WARREN	19,291	9,439	9,657	195	218 D	48.9%	50.1%	49.4%	50.6%
10,728	WASHINGTON	4,235	1,765	2,376	94	611 D	41.7%	56.1%	42.6%	57.4%
14,268	WAYNE	5,817	3,243	2,537	37	706 R	55.8%	43.6%	56.1%	43.9%
13,282	WEBSTER	4,970	1,402	3,523	45	2,121 D	28.2%	70.9%	28.5%	71.5%
24,145	WHITLEY	10,392	6,100	4,212	80	1,888 R	58.7%	40.5%	59.2%	40.8%
5,669	WOLFE	2,458	659	1,777	22	1,118 D	26.8%	72.3%	27.1%	72.9%
14,434	WOODFORD	5,465	2,646	2,689	130	43 D	48.4%	49.2%	49.6%	50.4%
3,219,311	TOTAL	1,167,142	531,852	615,717	19,573	83,865 D	45.6%	52.8%	46.3%	53.7%

KENTUCKY

GOVERNOR 1975

1970 Census Population	County	Total Vote	Republican	Democratic	Other	Rep.-Dem. Plurality	Percentage Total Vote Rep.	Percentage Total Vote Dem.	Percentage Major Vote Rep.	Percentage Major Vote Dem.
13,037	ADAIR	4,337	2,266	2,071		195 R	52.2%	47.8%	52.2%	47.8%
12,598	ALLEN	3,251	1,312	1,939		627 D	40.4%	59.6%	40.4%	59.6%
9,358	ANDERSON	2,721	713	2,008		1,295 D	26.2%	73.8%	26.2%	73.8%
8,276	BALLARD	2,114	136	1,978		1,842 D	6.4%	93.6%	6.4%	93.6%
28,677	BARREN	6,487	2,009	4,478		2,469 D	31.0%	69.0%	31.0%	69.0%
9,235	BATH	2,166	462	1,704		1,242 D	21.3%	78.7%	21.3%	78.7%
31,087	BELL	7,355	3,349	4,006		657 D	45.5%	54.5%	45.5%	54.5%
32,812	BOONE	6,446	2,083	4,363		2,280 D	32.3%	67.7%	32.3%	67.7%
18,476	BOURBON	4,220	1,088	3,132		2,044 D	25.8%	74.2%	25.8%	74.2%
52,376	BOYD	16,459	5,898	10,561		4,663 D	35.8%	64.2%	35.8%	64.2%
21,090	BOYLE	4,451	1,270	3,181		1,911 D	28.5%	71.5%	28.5%	71.5%
7,227	BRACKEN	1,481	344	1,137		793 D	23.2%	76.8%	23.2%	76.8%
14,221	BREATHITT	3,179	361	2,818		2,457 D	11.4%	88.6%	11.4%	88.6%
14,789	BRECKINRIDGE	4,726	1,936	2,790		854 D	41.0%	59.0%	41.0%	59.0%
26,090	BULLITT	6,212	2,430	3,782		1,352 D	39.1%	60.9%	39.1%	60.9%
9,723	BUTLER	2,886	1,684	1,202		482 R	58.4%	41.6%	58.4%	41.6%
13,179	CALDWELL	3,067	615	2,452		1,837 D	20.1%	79.9%	20.1%	79.9%
27,692	CALLOWAY	5,033	685	4,348		3,663 D	13.6%	86.4%	13.6%	86.4%
88,561	CAMPBELL	18,937	6,351	12,586		6,235 D	33.5%	66.5%	33.5%	66.5%
5,354	CARLISLE	1,526	130	1,396		1,266 D	8.5%	91.5%	8.5%	91.5%
8,523	CARROLL	2,067	429	1,638		1,209 D	20.8%	79.2%	20.8%	79.2%
19,850	CARTER	4,849	1,997	2,852		855 D	41.2%	58.8%	41.2%	58.8%
12,930	CASEY	3,385	1,982	1,403		579 R	58.6%	41.4%	58.6%	41.4%
56,224	CHRISTIAN	5,844	1,237	4,607		3,370 D	21.2%	78.8%	21.2%	78.8%
24,090	CLARK	4,086	1,232	2,854		1,622 D	30.2%	69.8%	30.2%	69.8%
18,481	CLAY	4,844	2,178	2,666		488 D	45.0%	55.0%	45.0%	55.0%
8,174	CLINTON	1,978	1,143	835		308 R	57.8%	42.2%	57.8%	42.2%
8,493	CRITTENDEN	2,451	1,012	1,439		427 D	41.3%	58.7%	41.3%	58.7%
6,850	CUMBERLAND	2,208	1,191	1,017		174 R	53.9%	46.1%	53.9%	46.1%
79,486	DAVIESS	19,108	5,189	13,919		8,730 D	27.2%	72.8%	27.2%	72.8%
8,751	EDMONSON	2,244	1,335	909		426 R	59.5%	40.5%	59.5%	40.5%
5,933	ELLIOTT	1,257	172	1,085		913 D	13.7%	86.3%	13.7%	86.3%
12,752	ESTILL	3,776	1,962	1,814		148 R	52.0%	48.0%	52.0%	48.0%
174,323	FAYETTE	35,171	13,442	21,729		8,287 D	38.2%	61.8%	38.2%	61.8%
11,366	FLEMING	2,762	946	1,816		870 D	34.3%	65.7%	34.3%	65.7%
35,889	FLOYD	6,949	1,367	5,582		4,215 D	19.7%	80.3%	19.7%	80.3%
34,481	FRANKLIN	12,770	2,270	10,500		8,230 D	17.8%	82.2%	17.8%	82.2%
10,183	FULTON	2,027	237	1,790		1,553 D	11.7%	88.3%	11.7%	88.3%
4,134	GALLATIN	1,138	232	906		674 D	20.4%	79.6%	20.4%	79.6%
9,457	GARRARD	2,804	1,442	1,362		80 R	51.4%	48.6%	51.4%	48.6%
9,999	GRANT	1,955	390	1,565		1,175 D	19.9%	80.1%	19.9%	80.1%
30,939	GRAVES	6,691	812	5,879		5,067 D	12.1%	87.9%	12.1%	87.9%
16,445	GRAYSON	5,590	2,850	2,740		110 R	51.0%	49.0%	51.0%	49.0%
10,350	GREEN	3,963	1,996	1,967		29 R	50.4%	49.6%	50.4%	49.6%
33,192	GREENUP	7,404	2,592	4,812		2,220 D	35.0%	65.0%	35.0%	65.0%
7,080	HANCOCK	1,600	459	1,141		682 D	28.7%	71.3%	28.7%	71.3%
78,421	HARDIN	9,529	3,439	6,090		2,651 D	36.1%	63.9%	36.1%	63.9%
37,370	HARLAN	8,073	2,470	5,603		3,133 D	30.6%	69.4%	30.6%	69.4%
14,158	HARRISON	2,568	541	2,027		1,486 D	21.1%	78.9%	21.1%	78.9%
13,980	HART	4,192	1,292	2,900		1,608 D	30.8%	69.2%	30.8%	69.2%
36,031	HENDERSON	5,957	908	5,049		4,141 D	15.2%	84.8%	15.2%	84.8%
10,910	HENRY	2,987	637	2,350		1,713 D	21.3%	78.7%	21.3%	78.7%
6,264	HICKMAN	1,838	211	1,627		1,416 D	11.5%	88.5%	11.5%	88.5%
38,167	HOPKINS	6,339	1,106	5,233		4,127 D	17.4%	82.6%	17.4%	82.6%
10,005	JACKSON	1,901	1,187	714		473 R	62.4%	37.6%	62.4%	37.6%
695,055	JEFFERSON	184,607	91,946	92,661		715 D	49.8%	50.2%	49.8%	50.2%
17,430	JESSAMINE	2,815	1,017	1,798		781 D	36.1%	63.9%	36.1%	63.9%
17,539	JOHNSON	3,930	2,004	1,926		78 R	51.0%	49.0%	51.0%	49.0%
129,440	KENTON	26,320	8,496	17,824		9,328 D	32.3%	67.7%	32.3%	67.7%
14,698	KNOTT	3,970	656	3,314		2,658 D	16.5%	83.5%	16.5%	83.5%
23,689	KNOX	4,604	2,084	2,520		436 D	45.3%	54.7%	45.3%	54.7%
10,672	LARUE	2,520	851	1,669		818 D	33.8%	66.2%	33.8%	66.2%
27,386	LAUREL	5,474	2,920	2,554		366 R	53.3%	46.7%	53.3%	46.7%
10,726	LAWRENCE	2,939	1,266	1,673		407 D	43.1%	56.9%	43.1%	56.9%
6,587	LEE	1,860	894	966		72 D	48.1%	51.9%	48.1%	51.9%

KENTUCKY

GOVERNOR 1975

1970 Census Population	County	Total Vote	Republican	Democratic	Other	Rep.-Dem. Plurality	Percentage Total Vote Rep.	Percentage Total Vote Dem.	Percentage Major Vote Rep.	Percentage Major Vote Dem.
11,623	LESLIE	2,180	1,047	1,133		86 D	48.0%	52.0%	48.0%	52.0%
23,165	LETCHER	5,163	1,595	3,568		1,973 D	30.9%	69.1%	30.9%	69.1%
12,355	LEWIS	3,111	1,747	1,364		383 R	56.2%	43.8%	56.2%	43.8%
16,663	LINCOLN	4,377	1,916	2,461		545 D	43.8%	56.2%	43.8%	56.2%
7,596	LIVINGSTON	1,943	294	1,649		1,355 D	15.1%	84.9%	15.1%	84.9%
21,793	LOGAN	4,579	855	3,724		2,869 D	18.7%	81.3%	18.7%	81.3%
5,562	LYON	1,425	193	1,232		1,039 D	13.5%	86.5%	13.5%	86.5%
58,281	MCCRACKEN	15,320	1,143	14,177		13,034 D	7.5%	92.5%	7.5%	92.5%
12,548	MCCREARY	3,635	2,609	1,026		1,583 R	71.8%	28.2%	71.8%	28.2%
9,062	MCLEAN	2,074	434	1,640		1,206 D	20.9%	79.1%	20.9%	79.1%
42,730	MADISON	8,575	2,914	5,661		2,747 D	34.0%	66.0%	34.0%	66.0%
10,443	MAGOFFIN	4,073	1,611	2,462		851 D	39.6%	60.4%	39.6%	60.4%
16,714	MARION	3,506	739	2,767		2,028 D	21.1%	78.9%	21.1%	78.9%
20,381	MARSHALL	4,989	630	4,359		3,729 D	12.6%	87.4%	12.6%	87.4%
9,377	MARTIN	1,217	793	424		369 R	65.2%	34.8%	65.2%	34.8%
17,273	MASON	3,516	965	2,551		1,586 D	27.4%	72.6%	27.4%	72.6%
18,796	MEADE	3,253	972	2,281		1,309 D	29.9%	70.1%	29.9%	70.1%
4,050	MENIFEE	765	147	618		471 D	19.2%	80.8%	19.2%	80.8%
15,960	MERCER	3,822	1,375	2,447		1,072 D	36.0%	64.0%	36.0%	64.0%
8,177	METCALFE	2,830	1,033	1,797		764 D	36.5%	63.5%	36.5%	63.5%
11,642	MONROE	3,061	1,501	1,560		59 D	49.0%	51.0%	49.0%	51.0%
15,364	MONTGOMERY	2,448	706	1,742		1,036 D	28.8%	71.2%	28.8%	71.2%
10,019	MORGAN	1,925	283	1,642		1,359 D	14.7%	85.3%	14.7%	85.3%
27,537	MUHLENBERG	7,269	2,012	5,257		3,245 D	27.7%	72.3%	27.7%	72.3%
23,477	NELSON	5,003	1,437	3,566		2,129 D	28.7%	71.3%	28.7%	71.3%
6,508	NICHOLAS	1,212	264	948		684 D	21.8%	78.2%	21.8%	78.2%
18,790	OHIO	4,339	2,048	2,291		243 D	47.2%	52.8%	47.2%	52.8%
14,687	OLDHAM	3,845	1,694	2,151		457 D	44.1%	55.9%	44.1%	55.9%
7,470	OWEN	1,937	292	1,645		1,353 D	15.1%	84.9%	15.1%	84.9%
5,023	OWSLEY	1,126	560	566		6 D	49.7%	50.3%	49.7%	50.3%
9,949	PENDLETON	1,761	402	1,359		957 D	22.8%	77.2%	22.8%	77.2%
26,259	PERRY	6,980	2,372	4,608		2,236 D	34.0%	66.0%	34.0%	66.0%
61,059	PIKE	10,510	3,134	7,376		4,242 D	29.8%	70.2%	29.8%	70.2%
7,704	POWELL	1,855	815	1,040		225 D	43.9%	56.1%	43.9%	56.1%
35,234	PULASKI	10,553	5,878	4,675		1,203 R	55.7%	44.3%	55.7%	44.3%
2,163	ROBERTSON	476	113	363		250 D	23.7%	76.3%	23.7%	76.3%
12,305	ROCKCASTLE	2,877	1,751	1,126		625 R	60.9%	39.1%	60.9%	39.1%
17,010	ROWAN	3,882	1,137	2,745		1,608 D	29.3%	70.7%	29.3%	70.7%
10,542	RUSSELL	3,267	1,763	1,504		259 R	54.0%	46.0%	54.0%	46.0%
17,948	SCOTT	2,938	700	2,238		1,538 D	23.8%	76.2%	23.8%	76.2%
18,999	SHELBY	3,948	1,143	2,805		1,662 D	29.0%	71.0%	29.0%	71.0%
13,054	SIMPSON	2,635	480	2,155		1,675 D	18.2%	81.8%	18.2%	81.8%
5,488	SPENCER	1,350	402	948		546 D	29.8%	70.2%	29.8%	70.2%
17,138	TAYLOR	4,712	1,891	2,821		930 D	40.1%	59.9%	40.1%	59.9%
10,823	TODD	1,638	259	1,379		1,120 D	15.8%	84.2%	15.8%	84.2%
8,620	TRIGG	2,455	344	2,111		1,767 D	14.0%	86.0%	14.0%	86.0%
5,349	TRIMBLE	1,433	307	1,126		819 D	21.4%	78.6%	21.4%	78.6%
15,882	UNION	2,445	415	2,030		1,615 D	17.0%	83.0%	17.0%	83.0%
57,432	WARREN	11,728	3,845	7,883		4,038 D	32.8%	67.2%	32.8%	67.2%
10,728	WASHINGTON	2,827	911	1,916		1,005 D	32.2%	67.8%	32.2%	67.8%
14,268	WAYNE	4,192	2,334	1,858		476 R	55.7%	44.3%	55.7%	44.3%
13,282	WEBSTER	2,795	395	2,400		2,005 D	14.1%	85.9%	14.1%	85.9%
24,145	WHITLEY	5,571	2,988	2,583		405 R	53.6%	46.4%	53.6%	46.4%
5,669	WOLFE	1,095	213	882		669 D	19.5%	80.5%	19.5%	80.5%
14,434	WOODFORD	3,318	1,056	2,262		1,206 D	31.8%	68.2%	31.8%	68.2%
3,219,311	TOTAL	748,157	277,998	470,159		192,161 D	37.2%	62.8%	37.2%	62.8%

KENTUCKY

CONGRESS

CD	Year	Total Vote	Republican Vote	Republican Candidate	Democratic Vote	Democratic Candidate	Other Vote	Rep.-Dem. Plurality	Percentage Total Vote Rep.	Percentage Total Vote Dem.	Percentage Major Vote Rep.	Percentage Major Vote Dem.
1	1976	144,985	26,089	BERSKY, BOB	118,886	HUBBARD, CARROLL	10	92,797 D	18.0%	82.0%	18.0%	82.0%
1	1974	90,465	16,937	BANKEN, CHARLES T.	70,723	HUBBARD, CARROLL	2,805	53,786 D	18.7%	78.2%	19.3%	80.7%
1	1972	125,662	42,286	BANKEN, CHARLES T.	81,456	STUBBLEFIELD, FRANK	1,920	39,170 D	33.7%	64.8%	34.2%	65.8%
2	1976	130,920	51,900	BAKER, WALTER A.	79,016	NATCHER, WILLIAM H.	4	27,116 D	39.6%	60.4%	39.6%	60.4%
2	1974	77,400	18,312	EDDLEMAN, ART	56,502	NATCHER, WILLIAM H.	2,586	38,190 D	23.7%	73.0%	24.5%	75.5%
2	1972	123,307	47,436	CARTER, J. C.	75,871	NATCHER, WILLIAM H.		28,435 D	38.5%	61.5%	38.5%	61.5%
3	1976	140,744	58,019	RAMSEY, DENZIL J.	80,496	MAZZOLI, ROMANO L.	2,229	22,477 D	41.2%	57.2%	41.9%	58.1%
3	1974	108,475	28,813	BARCLAY, VINCENT N.	75,571	MAZZOLI, ROMANO L.	4,091	46,758 D	26.6%	69.7%	27.6%	72.4%
3	1972	139,671	51,634	KAELIN, PHIL	86,810	MAZZOLI, ROMANO L.	1,227	35,176 D	37.0%	62.2%	37.3%	62.7%
4	1976	174,502	97,493	SNYDER, M. G.	77,009	WINTERBERG, EDWARD J.		20,484 R	55.9%	44.1%	55.9%	44.1%
4	1974	123,384	63,845	SNYDER, M. G.	59,539	HUBBARD, KYLE T.		4,306 R	51.7%	48.3%	51.7%	48.3%
4	1972	150,234	110,902	SNYDER, M. G.	39,332	ROGERS, JAMES W.		71,570 R	73.8%	26.2%	73.8%	26.2%
5	1976	150,473	100,204	CARTER, TIM LEE	49,128	SMITH, CHARLES C.	1,141	51,076 R	66.6%	32.6%	67.1%	32.9%
5	1974	97,882	66,709	CARTER, TIM LEE	28,706	WILLIS, LYLE LEONARD	2,467	38,003 R	68.2%	29.3%	69.9%	30.1%
5	1972	148,565	109,264	CARTER, TIM LEE	39,301	WILLIS, LYLE LEONARD		69,963 R	73.5%	26.5%	73.5%	26.5%
6	1976	96,493			90,695	BRECKINRIDGE, JOHN	5,798	90,695 D		94.0%		100.0%
6	1974	87,416	21,039	ROGERS, THOMAS F.	63,010	BRECKINRIDGE, JOHN	3,367	41,971 D	24.1%	72.1%	25.0%	75.0%
6	1972	145,412	68,012	JACKSON, LABAN P.	76,185	BRECKINRIDGE, JOHN	1,215	8,173 D	46.8%	52.4%	47.2%	52.8%
7	1976	150,831	40,381	THOMAS, GRANVILLE	110,450	PERKINS, CARL D.		70,069 D	26.8%	73.2%	26.8%	73.2%
7	1974	94,203	22,982	THOMAS, GRANVILLE	71,221	PERKINS, CARL D.		48,239 D	24.4%	75.6%	24.4%	75.6%
7	1972	153,126	58,286	HOLCOMB, ROBERT	94,840	PERKINS, CARL D.		36,554 D	38.1%	61.9%	38.1%	61.9%

KENTUCKY

1975 GENERAL ELECTION

Governor

1975 PRIMARIES

MAY 27 REPUBLICAN

Governor 38,113 Robert E. Gable; 16,855 Elmer Begley; 10,844 T. William Klein; 8,426 Granville Thomas.

MAY 27 DEMOCRATIC

Governor 263,965 Julian Carroll; 113,285 Todd Hollenbach; 14,901 Mary Louise Foust; 5,838 Robert McC. Johnson.

1976 GENERAL ELECTION

President Other vote was 8,308 Anderson (American); 6,837 McCarthy (Independent); 2,328 Maddox (American Independent); 814 MacBride (Libertarian); 510 LaRouche (U.S. Labor); 426 Hall (Communist); 350 Camejo (Socialist Workers).

Congress Other vote was scattered in CD's 1 and 2; Chambers (American) in CD 3; 1,125 Cullum (American) and 16 scattered in CD 5; 5,795 McCord (American) and 3 scattered in CD 6.

1976 PRIMARIES

MAY 25 REPUBLICAN

Congress Unopposed in three CD's. No candidate in CD 6. Contested as follows:

CD 1 2,111 Bob Bersky; 1,425 Arthur L. McLaughlin.
CD 3 8,734 Denzil J. Ramsey; 4,811 Shirley Murray.
CD 5 28,502 Tim Lee Carter; 2,368 Elmer Begley; 1,108 Thurman J. Hamlin.

MAY 25 DEMOCRATIC

Congress Unopposed in two CD's. Contested as follows:

CD 3 23,906 Romano L. Mazzoli; 18,081 James E. Lawrence; 641 Philip V. Baker.
CD 4 17,158 Edward J. Winterberg; 14,878 George C. Martin.
CD 5 7,106 Charles C. Smith; 2,642 Jesse M. Ramey; 2,401 Lyle Leonard Willis; 2,172 Hubert L. Marcum; 1,083 Nick Augusta.
CD 6 36,887 John Breckinridge; 4,942 Victor E. Privett.
CD 7 34,097 Carl D. Perkins; 3,952 Ray Adkins.

LOUISIANA

GOVERNOR

Edwin W. Edwards (D). Re-elected December 1975 to a four-year term. Previously elected February 1972.

SENATORS

J. Bennett Johnston (D). Elected 1972 to a six-year term.

Russell B. Long (D). Re-elected 1974 to a six-year term. Previously elected 1968, 1962, 1956, 1950, and in 1948 to fill out term vacated by the death of Senator John H. Overton.

REPRESENTATIVES

1. Richard A. Tonry (D)
2. Lindy Boggs (D)
3. David C. Treen (R)
4. Joe D. Waggonner (D)
5. Jerry Huckaby (D)
6. W. Henson Moore (R)
7. John B. Breaux (D)
8. Gillis W. Long (D)

POSTWAR VOTE FOR GOVERNOR

Year	Total Vote	Republican Vote	Republican Candidate	Democratic Vote	Democratic Candidate	Other Vote	Rep.-Dem. Plurality	Percentage Total Vote Rep.	Percentage Total Vote Dem.	Percentage Major Vote Rep.	Percentage Major Vote Dem.
1975	430,095	–	–	430,095	Edwards, Edwin W.	–	430,095 D	–	100.0%	–	100.0%
1972	1,121,570	480,424	Treen, David C.	641,146	Edwards, Edwin W.	–	160,722 D	42.8%	57.2%	42.8%	57.2%
1968	372,762	–	–	372,762	McKeithen, John J.	–	372,762 D	–	100.0%	–	100.0%
1964	773,390	297,753	Lyons, C. H.	469,589	McKeithen, John J.	6,048	171,836 D	38.5%	60.7%	38.8%	61.2%
1960	506,562	86,135	Grevemberg, F. C.	407,907	Davis, Jimmie H.	12,520	321,772 D	17.0%	80.5%	17.4%	82.6%
1956	172,291	–	–	172,291	Long, Earl K.	–	172,291 D	–	100.0%	–	100.0%
1952	123,681	4,958	Bagwell, Harrison G.	118,723	Kennon, Robert F.	–	113,765 D	4.0%	96.0%	4.0%	96.0%
1948	76,566	–	–	76,566	Long, Earl K.	–	76,566 D	–	100.0%	–	100.0%

POSTWAR VOTE FOR SENATOR

Year	Total Vote	Republican Vote	Republican Candidate	Democratic Vote	Democratic Candidate	Other Vote	Rep.-Dem. Plurality	Percentage Total Vote Rep.	Percentage Total Vote Dem.	Percentage Major Vote Rep.	Percentage Major Vote Dem.
1974	434,643	–	–	434,643	Long, Russell B.	–	434,643 D	–	100.0%	–	100.0%
1972	1,084,904	206,846	Toledano, Ben C.	598,987	Johnston, J. Bennett	279,071	392,141 D	19.1%	55.2%	25.7%	74.3%
1968	518,586	–	–	518,586	Long, Russell B.	–	518,586 D	–	100.0%	–	100.0%
1966	437,695	–	–	437,695	Ellender, Allen J.	–	437,695 D	–	100.0%	–	100.0%
1962	421,904	103,066	O'Hearn, Taylor W.	318,838	Long, Russell B.	–	215,772 D	24.4%	75.6%	24.4%	75.6%
1960	541,928	109,698	Reese, George W.	432,228	Ellender, Allen J.	2	322,530 D	20.2%	79.8%	20.2%	79.8%
1956	335,564	–	–	335,564	Long, Russell B.	–	335,564 D	–	100.0%	–	100.0%
1954	207,115	–	–	207,115	Ellender, Allen J.	–	207,115 D	–	100.0%	–	100.0%
1950	251,838	30,931	Gerth, Charles S.	220,907	Long, Russell B.	–	189,976 D	12.3%	87.7%	12.3%	87.7%
1948	330,124	–	–	330,115	Ellender, Allen J.	9	330,115 D	–	100.0%	–	100.0%
1948s	408,667	102,331	Clarke, Clem S.	306,336	Long Russell B.	–	204,005 D	25.0%	75.0%	25.0%	75.0%

One of the 1948 elections was for a short term to fill a vacancy.

LOUISIANA

Districts Established June 1, 1972

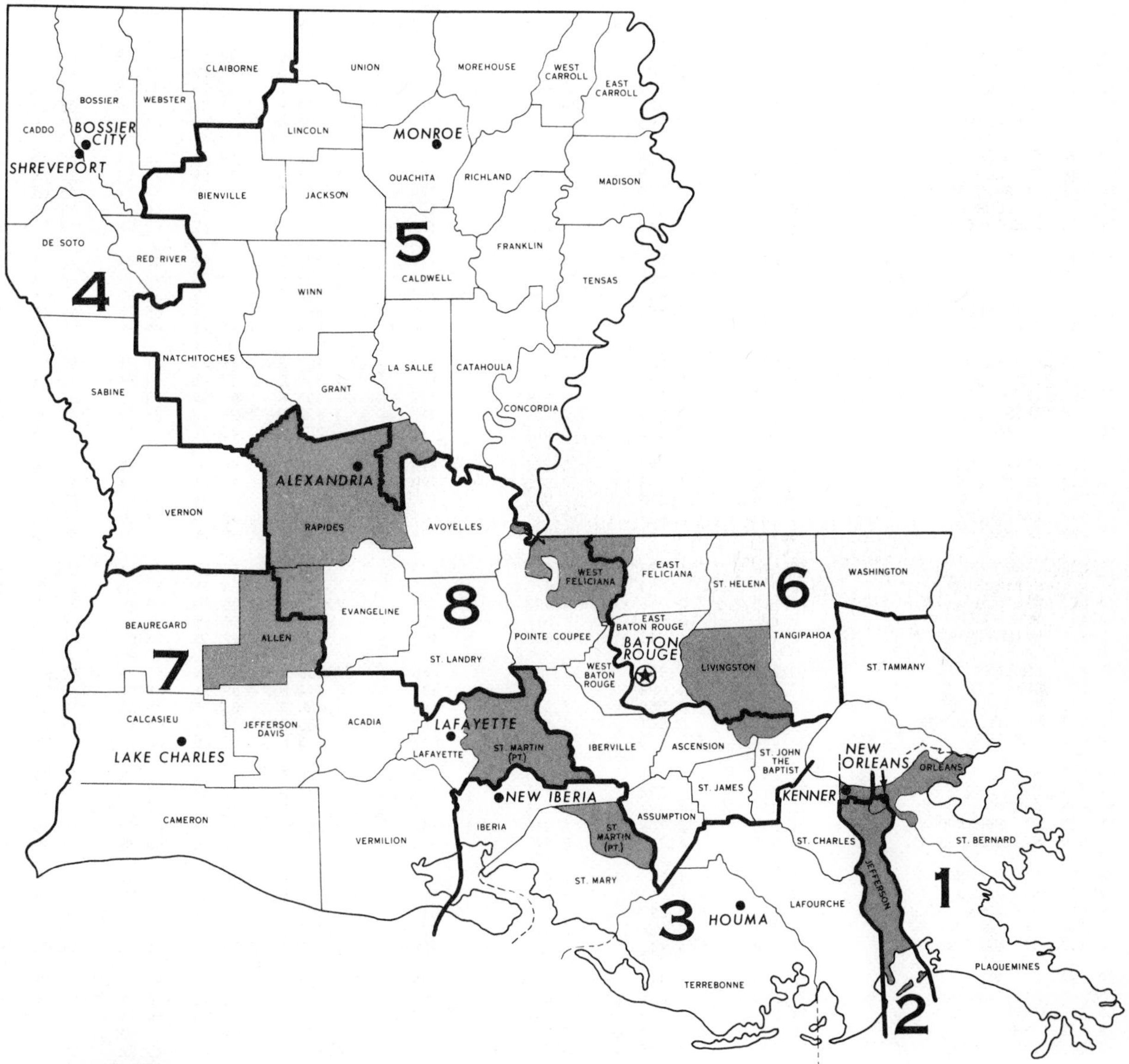

Parish with two or more Congressional Districts.

LOUISIANA

PRESIDENT 1976

1970 Census Population	Parish	Total Vote	Republican	Democratic	Other	Rep.-Dem. Plurality	Percentage Total Vote Rep.	Percentage Total Vote Dem.	Percentage Major Vote Rep.	Percentage Major Vote Dem.
52,109	ACADIA	17,648	6,296	10,814	538	4,518 D	35.7%	61.3%	36.8%	63.2%
20,794	ALLEN	7,673	2,080	5,373	220	3,293 D	27.1%	70.0%	27.9%	72.1%
37,086	ASCENSION	13,978	4,435	9,100	443	4,665 D	31.7%	65.1%	32.8%	67.2%
19,654	ASSUMPTION	7,711	3,117	4,401	193	1,284 D	40.4%	57.1%	41.5%	58.5%
37,751	AVOYELLES	13,315	4,574	8,104	637	3,530 D	34.4%	60.9%	36.1%	63.9%
22,888	BEAUREGARD	8,786	3,196	5,322	268	2,126 D	36.4%	60.6%	37.5%	62.5%
16,024	BIENVILLE	6,011	2,499	3,402	110	903 D	41.6%	56.6%	42.3%	57.7%
63,703	BOSSIER	20,487	12,132	8,062	293	4,070 R	59.2%	39.4%	60.1%	39.9%
230,184	CADDO	74,340	42,627	30,593	1,120	12,034 R	57.3%	41.2%	58.2%	41.8%
145,415	CALCASIEU	52,595	17,485	33,980	1,130	16,495 D	33.2%	64.6%	34.0%	66.0%
9,354	CALDWELL	3,806	1,890	1,830	86	60 R	49.7%	48.1%	50.8%	49.2%
8,194	CAMERON	3,338	819	2,432	87	1,613 D	24.5%	72.9%	25.2%	74.8%
11,769	CATAHOULA	4,767	2,086	2,547	134	461 D	43.8%	53.4%	45.0%	55.0%
17,024	CLAIBORNE	6,207	3,216	2,891	100	325 R	51.8%	46.6%	52.7%	47.3%
22,578	CONCORDIA	7,912	3,849	3,892	171	43 D	48.6%	49.2%	49.7%	50.3%
22,764	DE SOTO	8,348	3,601	4,630	117	1,029 D	43.1%	55.5%	43.7%	56.3%
285,167	EAST BATON ROUGE	103,807	51,655	49,956	2,196	1,699 R	49.8%	48.1%	50.8%	49.2%
12,884	EAST CARROLL	4,158	1,681	2,367	110	686 D	40.4%	56.9%	41.5%	58.5%
17,657	EAST FELICIANA	5,323	1,668	3,485	170	1,817 D	31.3%	65.5%	32.4%	67.6%
31,932	EVANGELINE	11,558	3,715	7,578	265	3,863 D	32.1%	65.6%	32.9%	67.1%
23,946	FRANKLIN	7,991	3,947	3,824	220	123 R	49.4%	47.9%	50.8%	49.2%
13,671	GRANT	6,136	2,280	3,670	186	1,390 D	37.2%	59.8%	38.3%	61.7%
57,397	IBERIA	20,753	10,392	9,984	377	408 R	50.1%	48.1%	51.0%	49.0%
30,746	IBERVILLE	11,389	3,822	7,254	313	3,432 D	33.6%	63.7%	34.5%	65.5%
15,963	JACKSON	7,060	3,310	3,605	145	295 D	46.9%	51.1%	47.9%	52.1%
338,229	JEFFERSON	127,560	71,787	53,257	2,516	18,530 R	56.3%	41.8%	57.4%	42.6%
29,554	JEFFERSON DAVIS	10,278	3,603	6,376	299	2,773 D	35.1%	62.0%	36.1%	63.9%
111,745	LAFAYETTE	43,699	22,805	19,918	976	2,887 R	52.2%	45.6%	53.4%	46.6%
68,941	LAFOURCHE	26,266	11,434	14,131	701	2,697 D	43.5%	53.8%	44.7%	55.3%
13,295	LA SALLE	6,310	3,161	2,961	188	200 R	50.1%	46.9%	51.6%	48.4%
33,800	LINCOLN	11,969	6,828	4,971	170	1,857 R	57.0%	41.5%	57.9%	42.1%
36,511	LIVINGSTON	15,895	5,555	9,875	465	4,320 D	34.9%	62.1%	36.0%	64.0%
15,065	MADISON	7,128	2,096	4,933	99	2,837 D	29.4%	69.2%	29.8%	70.2%
32,463	MOREHOUSE	9,692	5,418	4,017	257	1,401 R	55.9%	41.4%	57.4%	42.6%
35,219	NATCHITOCHES	12,417	5,248	6,692	477	1,444 D	42.3%	53.9%	44.0%	56.0%
593,471	ORLEANS	168,304	70,925	93,130	4,249	22,205 D	42.1%	55.3%	43.2%	56.8%
115,387	OUACHITA	40,451	24,082	15,738	631	8,344 R	59.5%	38.9%	60.5%	39.5%
25,225	PLAQUEMINES	8,855	6,052	2,614	189	3,438 R	68.3%	29.5%	69.8%	30.2%
22,002	POINTE COUPEE	7,876	2,567	5,147	162	2,580 D	32.6%	65.4%	33.3%	66.7%
118,078	RAPIDES	39,264	17,766	20,851	647	3,085 D	45.2%	53.1%	46.0%	54.0%
9,226	RED RIVER	3,707	1,728	1,906	73	178 D	46.6%	51.4%	47.6%	52.4%
21,774	RICHLAND	7,270	3,630	3,495	145	135 R	49.9%	48.1%	50.9%	49.1%
18,638	SABINE	8,351	3,531	4,555	265	1,024 D	42.3%	54.5%	43.7%	56.3%
51,185	ST. BERNARD	26,508	12,707	12,969	832	262 D	47.9%	48.9%	49.5%	50.5%
29,550	ST. CHARLES	11,505	4,270	6,872	363	2,602 D	37.1%	59.7%	38.3%	61.7%
9,937	ST. HELENA	3,788	1,046	2,622	120	1,576 D	27.6%	69.2%	28.5%	71.5%
19,733	ST. JAMES	7,466	2,751	4,531	184	1,780 D	36.8%	60.7%	37.8%	62.2%
23,813	ST. JOHN THE BAPTIST	9,609	3,597	5,700	312	2,103 D	37.4%	59.3%	38.7%	61.3%
80,364	ST. LANDRY	26,243	9,956	15,613	674	5,657 D	37.9%	59.5%	38.9%	61.1%
32,453	ST. MARTIN	12,433	4,112	7,992	329	3,880 D	33.1%	64.3%	34.0%	66.0%
60,752	ST. MARY	18,708	8,919	9,401	388	482 D	47.7%	50.3%	48.7%	51.3%
63,585	ST. TAMMANY	31,399	15,822	14,691	886	1,131 R	50.4%	46.8%	51.9%	48.1%
65,875	TANGIPAHOA	24,311	9,242	14,432	637	5,190 D	38.0%	59.4%	39.0%	61.0%
9,732	TENSAS	3,677	1,553	2,081	43	528 D	42.2%	56.6%	42.7%	57.3%
76,049	TERREBONNE	24,282	12,895	10,627	760	2,268 R	53.1%	43.8%	54.8%	45.2%
18,447	UNION	7,905	4,139	3,600	166	539 R	52.4%	45.5%	53.5%	46.5%
43,071	VERMILION	17,850	6,133	11,246	471	5,113 D	34.4%	63.0%	35.3%	64.7%
53,794	VERNON	10,465	3,970	6,202	293	2,232 D	37.9%	59.3%	39.0%	61.0%
41,987	WASHINGTON	16,073	5,677	10,000	396	4,323 D	35.3%	62.2%	36.2%	63.8%
39,939	WEBSTER	15,017	7,550	7,286	181	264 R	50.3%	48.5%	50.9%	49.1%
16,864	WEST BATON ROUGE	5,884	1,913	3,809	162	1,896 D	32.5%	64.7%	33.4%	66.6%
13,028	WEST CARROLL	5,112	2,407	2,595	110	188 D	47.1%	50.8%	48.1%	51.9%
11,376	WEST FELICIANA	2,926	990	1,890	46	900 D	33.8%	64.6%	34.4%	65.6%
16,369	WINN	6,889	3,209	3,543	137	334 D	46.6%	51.4%	47.5%	52.5%
3,643,180	TOTAL	1,278,439	587,446	661,365	29,628	73,919 D	46.0%	51.7%	47.0%	53.0%

LOUISIANA
GOVERNOR 1975
Primary Election

1970 Census Population	Parish	Total Vote	Jones	Edwards	Other	Jones-Edwards Plurality	Percentage: Total Vote		Percentage: Major Vote	
							Jones	Edwards	Jones	Edwards
52,109	ACADIA	22,020	2,561	18,217	1,242	15,656 E	11.6%	82.7%	12.3%	87.7%
20,794	ALLEN	9,505	2,511	5,374	1,620	2,863 E	26.4%	56.5%	31.8%	68.2%
37,086	ASCENSION	16,028	3,176	9,856	2,996	6,680 E	19.8%	61.5%	24.4%	75.6%
19,654	ASSUMPTION	8,185	1,900	5,423	862	3,523 E	23.2%	66.3%	25.9%	74.1%
37,751	AVOYELLES	14,831	3,166	9,163	2,502	5,997 E	21.3%	61.8%	25.7%	74.3%
22,888	BEAUREGARD	9,771	3,814	4,759	1,198	945 E	39.0%	48.7%	44.5%	55.5%
16,024	BIENVILLE	6,960	1,881	4,437	642	2,556 E	27.0%	63.8%	29.8%	70.2%
63,703	BOSSIER	15,250	5,353	9,081	816	3,728 E	35.1%	59.5%	37.1%	62.9%
230,184	CADDO	53,653	20,112	30,737	2,804	10,625 E	37.5%	57.3%	39.6%	60.4%
145,415	CALCASIEU	50,666	19,074	27,992	3,600	8,918 E	37.6%	55.2%	40.5%	59.5%
9,354	CALDWELL	4,176	1,487	1,413	1,276	74 J	35.6%	33.8%	51.3%	48.7%
8,194	CAMERON	4,049	1,097	2,568	384	1,471 E	27.1%	63.4%	29.9%	70.1%
11,769	CATAHOULA	5,604	1,726	2,606	1,272	880 E	30.8%	46.5%	39.8%	60.2%
17,024	CLAIBORNE	6,190	1,666	3,963	561	2,297 E	26.9%	64.0%	29.6%	70.4%
22,578	CONCORDIA	9,082	2,923	4,618	1,541	1,695 E	32.2%	50.8%	38.8%	61.2%
22,764	DE SOTO	8,273	2,089	5,587	597	3,498 E	25.3%	67.5%	27.2%	72.8%
285,167	EAST BATON ROUGE	85,292	22,538	44,265	18,489	21,727 E	26.4%	51.9%	33.7%	66.3%
12,884	EAST CARROLL	4,840	987	3,178	675	2,191 E	20.4%	65.7%	23.7%	76.3%
17,657	EAST FELICIANA	5,517	1,141	2,754	1,622	1,613 E	20.7%	49.9%	29.3%	70.7%
31,932	EVANGELINE	14,346	3,044	9,482	1,820	6,438 E	21.2%	66.1%	24.3%	75.7%
23,946	FRANKLIN	8,799	3,262	3,359	2,178	97 E	37.1%	38.2%	49.3%	50.7%
13,671	GRANT	7,079	2,851	2,751	1,477	100 J	40.3%	38.9%	50.9%	49.1%
57,397	IBERIA	21,847	3,933	14,783	3,131	10,850 E	18.0%	67.7%	21.0%	79.0%
30,746	IBERVILLE	13,155	1,974	8,608	2,573	6,634 E	15.0%	65.4%	18.7%	81.3%
15,963	JACKSON	7,263	2,079	4,041	1,143	1,962 E	28.6%	55.6%	34.0%	66.0%
338,229	JEFFERSON	103,505	20,051	73,337	10,117	53,286 E	19.4%	70.9%	21.5%	78.5%
29,554	JEFFERSON DAVIS	11,263	3,359	7,126	778	3,767 E	29.8%	63.3%	32.0%	68.0%
111,745	LAFAYETTE	38,021	6,825	26,534	4,662	19,709 E	18.0%	69.8%	20.5%	79.5%
68,941	LAFOURCHE	27,455	4,249	19,894	3,312	15,645 E	15.5%	72.5%	17.6%	82.4%
13,295	LA SALLE	7,373	2,810	2,874	1,689	64 E	38.1%	39.0%	49.4%	50.6%
33,800	LINCOLN	11,089	4,140	5,385	1,564	1,245 E	37.3%	48.6%	43.5%	56.5%
36,511	LIVINGSTON	18,558	4,714	8,324	5,520	3,610 E	25.4%	44.9%	36.2%	63.8%
15,065	MADISON	5,942	1,135	4,057	750	2,922 E	19.1%	68.3%	21.9%	78.1%
32,463	MOREHOUSE	10,781	3,887	5,519	1,375	1,632 E	36.1%	51.2%	41.3%	58.7%
35,219	NATCHITOCHES	12,723	3,701	7,370	1,652	3,669 E	29.1%	57.9%	33.4%	66.6%
593,471	ORLEANS	135,893	23,913	98,550	13,430	74,637 E	17.6%	72.5%	19.5%	80.5%
115,387	OUACHITA	32,932	9,893	17,575	5,464	7,682 E	30.0%	53.4%	36.0%	64.0%
25,225	PLAQUEMINES	7,307	708	6,301	298	5,593 E	9.7%	86.2%	10.1%	89.9%
22,002	POINTE COUPEE	9,081	1,252	6,360	1,469	5,108 E	13.8%	70.0%	16.4%	83.6%
118,078	RAPIDES	35,904	12,252	17,811	5,841	5,559 E	34.1%	49.6%	40.8%	59.2%
9,226	RED RIVER	4,522	1,216	2,908	398	1,692 E	26.9%	64.3%	29.5%	70.5%
21,774	RICHLAND	7,924	2,718	3,628	1,578	910 E	34.3%	45.8%	42.8%	57.2%
18,638	SABINE	8,912	2,343	5,595	974	3,252 E	26.3%	62.8%	29.5%	70.5%
51,185	ST. BERNARD	25,332	4,305	19,025	2,002	14,720 E	17.0%	75.1%	18.5%	81.5%
29,550	ST. CHARLES	12,430	2,405	8,626	1,399	6,221 E	19.3%	69.4%	21.8%	78.2%
9,937	ST. HELENA	4,771	1,192	2,607	972	1,415 E	25.0%	54.6%	31.4%	68.6%
19,733	ST. JAMES	8,119	1,343	5,797	979	4,454 E	16.5%	71.4%	18.8%	81.2%
23,813	ST. JOHN THE BAPTIST	10,772	1,770	7,877	1,125	6,107 E	16.4%	73.1%	18.3%	81.7%
80,364	ST. LANDRY	32,235	4,971	22,513	4,751	17,542 E	15.4%	69.8%	18.1%	81.9%
32,453	ST. MARTIN	14,052	1,280	8,575	4,197	7,295 E	9.1%	61.0%	13.0%	87.0%
60,752	ST. MARY	18,548	3,565	12,996	1,987	9,431 E	19.2%	70.1%	21.5%	78.5%
63,585	ST. TAMMANY	25,055	6,823	14,489	3,743	7,666 E	27.2%	57.8%	32.0%	68.0%
65,875	TANGIPAHOA	27,009	7,997	15,244	3,768	7,247 E	29.6%	56.4%	34.4%	65.6%
9,732	TENSAS	3,937	800	2,527	610	1,727 E	20.3%	64.2%	24.0%	76.0%
76,049	TERREBONNE	24,097	4,469	16,384	3,244	11,915 E	18.5%	68.0%	21.4%	78.6%
18,447	UNION	8,097	2,698	3,782	1,617	1,084 E	33.3%	46.7%	41.6%	58.4%
43,071	VERMILION	19,950	3,049	14,845	2,056	11,796 E	15.3%	74.4%	17.0%	83.0%
53,794	VERNON	11,831	3,752	6,068	2,011	2,316 E	31.7%	51.3%	38.2%	61.8%
41,987	WASHINGTON	18,211	5,509	10,041	2,661	4,532 E	30.3%	55.1%	35.4%	64.6%
39,939	WEBSTER	14,587	4,791	8,720	1,076	3,929 E	32.8%	59.8%	35.5%	64.5%
16,864	WEST BATON ROUGE	6,070	910	4,067	1,093	3,157 E	15.0%	67.0%	18.3%	81.7%
13,028	WEST CARROLL	5,626	1,586	2,718	1,322	1,132 E	28.2%	48.3%	36.8%	63.2%
11,376	WEST FELICIANA	3,162	633	1,930	599	1,297 E	20.0%	61.0%	24.7%	75.3%
16,369	WINN	7,547	2,861	3,113	1,573	252 E	37.9%	41.2%	47.9%	52.1%
3,643,180	TOTAL	1,203,004	292,220	750,107	160,677	457,887 E	24.3%	62.4%	28.0%	72.0%

LOUISIANA

GOVERNOR 1975

1970 Census Population	Parish	Total Vote	Republican	Democratic	Other	Rep.-Dem. Plurality	Percentage Total Vote Rep.	Percentage Total Vote Dem.	Percentage Major Vote Rep.	Percentage Major Vote Dem.
52,109	ACADIA	4,408		4,408		4,408 D		100.0%		100.0%
20,794	ALLEN	4,262		4,262		4,262 D		100.0%		100.0%
37,086	ASCENSION	5,099		5,099		5,099 D		100.0%		100.0%
19,654	ASSUMPTION	3,120		3,120		3,120 D		100.0%		100.0%
37,751	AVOYELLES	1,908		1,908		1,908 D		100.0%		100.0%
22,888	BEAUREGARD	2,672		2,672		2,672 D		100.0%		100.0%
16,024	BIENVILLE	2,453		2,453		2,453 D		100.0%		100.0%
63,703	BOSSIER	6,227		6,227		6,227 D		100.0%		100.0%
230,184	CADDO	19,285		19,285		19,285 D		100.0%		100.0%
145,415	CALCASIEU	17,226		17,226		17,226 D		100.0%		100.0%
9,354	CALDWELL	764		764		764 D		100.0%		100.0%
8,194	CAMERON	945		945		945 D		100.0%		100.0%
11,769	CATAHOULA	2,082		2,082		2,082 D		100.0%		100.0%
17,024	CLAIBORNE	2,528		2,528		2,528 D		100.0%		100.0%
22,578	CONCORDIA	2,351		2,351		2,351 D		100.0%		100.0%
22,764	DE SOTO	2,387		2,387		2,387 D		100.0%		100.0%
285,167	EAST BATON ROUGE	44,668		44,668		44,668 D		100.0%		100.0%
12,884	EAST CARROLL	1,306		1,306		1,306 D		100.0%		100.0%
17,657	EAST FELICIANA	2,372		2,372		2,372 D		100.0%		100.0%
31,932	EVANGELINE	3,152		3,152		3,152 D		100.0%		100.0%
23,946	FRANKLIN	2,490		2,490		2,490 D		100.0%		100.0%
13,671	GRANT	2,802		2,802		2,802 D		100.0%		100.0%
57,397	IBERIA	3,730		3,730		3,730 D		100.0%		100.0%
30,746	IBERVILLE	5,787		5,787		5,787 D		100.0%		100.0%
15,963	JACKSON	3,228		3,228		3,228 D		100.0%		100.0%
338,229	JEFFERSON	41,465		41,465		41,465 D		100.0%		100.0%
29,554	JEFFERSON DAVIS	3,592		3,592		3,592 D		100.0%		100.0%
111,745	LAFAYETTE	14,925		14,925		14,925 D		100.0%		100.0%
68,941	LAFOURCHE	14,092		14,092		14,092 D		100.0%		100.0%
13,295	LA SALLE	3,104		3,104		3,104 D		100.0%		100.0%
33,800	LINCOLN	5,357		5,357		5,357 D		100.0%		100.0%
36,511	LIVINGSTON	5,251		5,251		5,251 D		100.0%		100.0%
15,065	MADISON	1,062		1,062		1,062 D		100.0%		100.0%
32,463	MOREHOUSE	4,729		4,729		4,729 D		100.0%		100.0%
35,219	NATCHITOCHES	5,043		5,043		5,043 D		100.0%		100.0%
593,471	ORLEANS	54,091		54,091		54,091 D		100.0%		100.0%
115,387	OUACHITA	11,874		11,874		11,874 D		100.0%		100.0%
25,225	PLAQUEMINES	958		958		958 D		100.0%		100.0%
22,002	POINTE COUPEE	2,373		2,373		2,373 D		100.0%		100.0%
118,078	RAPIDES	10,719		10,719		10,719 D		100.0%		100.0%
9,226	RED RIVER	823		823		823 D		100.0%		100.0%
21,774	RICHLAND	2,810		2,810		2,810 D		100.0%		100.0%
18,638	SABINE	2,214		2,214		2,214 D		100.0%		100.0%
51,185	ST. BERNARD	4,814		4,814		4,814 D		100.0%		100.0%
29,550	ST. CHARLES	6,711		6,711		6,711 D		100.0%		100.0%
9,937	ST. HELENA	1,277		1,277		1,277 D		100.0%		100.0%
19,733	ST. JAMES	1,868		1,868		1,868 D		100.0%		100.0%
23,813	ST. JOHN THE BAPTIST	3,322		3,322		3,322 D		100.0%		100.0%
80,364	ST. LANDRY	5,296		5,296		5,296 D		100.0%		100.0%
32,453	ST. MARTIN	3,463		3,463		3,463 D		100.0%		100.0%
60,752	ST. MARY	4,231		4,231		4,231 D		100.0%		100.0%
63,585	ST. TAMMANY	9,684		9,684		9,684 D		100.0%		100.0%
65,875	TANGIPAHOA	12,071		12,071		12,071 D		100.0%		100.0%
9,732	TENSAS	406		406		406 D		100.0%		100.0%
76,049	TERREBONNE	13,046		13,046		13,046 D		100.0%		100.0%
18,447	UNION	3,292		3,292		3,292 D		100.0%		100.0%
43,071	VERMILION	4,930		4,930		4,930 D		100.0%		100.0%
53,794	VERNON	3,953		3,953		3,953 D		100.0%		100.0%
41,987	WASHINGTON	6,463		6,463		6,463 D		100.0%		100.0%
39,939	WEBSTER	3,443		3,443		3,443 D		100.0%		100.0%
16,864	WEST BATON ROUGE	3,257		3,257		3,257 D		100.0%		100.0%
13,028	WEST CARROLL	2,817		2,817		2,817 D		100.0%		100.0%
11,376	WEST FELICIANA	824		824		824 D		100.0%		100.0%
16,369	WINN	3,193		3,193		3,193 D		100.0%		100.0%
3,643,180	TOTAL	430,095		430,095		430,095 D		100.0%		100.0%

LOUISIANA

CONGRESS

CD	Year	Total Vote	Republican Vote	Republican Candidate	Democratic Vote	Democratic Candidate	Other Vote	Rep.-Dem. Plurality	Percentage Total Vote Rep.	Percentage Total Vote Dem.	Percentage Major Vote Rep.	Percentage Major Vote Dem.
1	1976	130,558	56,679	LIVINGSTON, BOB	61,652	TONRY, RICHARD A.	12,227	4,973 D	43.4%	47.2%	47.9%	52.1%
1	1974	48,452			48,452	HEBERT, F. EDWARD		48,452 D		100.0%		100.0%
1	1972	78,156			78,156	HEBERT, F. EDWARD		78,156 D		100.0%		100.0%
2	1976	92,827			85,923	BOGGS, LINDY	6,904	85,923 D		92.6%		100.0%
2	1974	65,756	9,632	MORPHOS, DIANE	53,802	BOGGS, LINDY	2,322	44,170 D	14.6%	81.8%	15.2%	84.8%
2	1972	68,093			68,093	BOGGS, HALE		68,093 D		100.0%		100.0%
3	1976	148,863	109,135	TREEN, DAVID C.	39,728	SCHEUERMANN, DAVID H.		69,407 R	73.3%	26.7%	73.3%	26.7%
3	1974	94,986	55,574	TREEN, DAVID C.	39,412	GRISBAUM, CHARLES		16,162 R	58.5%	41.5%	58.5%	41.5%
3	1972	131,611	71,090	TREEN, DAVID C.	60,521	WATKINS, J. LOUIS		10,569 R	54.0%	46.0%	54.0%	46.0%
4	1976	76,406			76,406	WAGGONNER, JOE D.		76,406 D		100.0%		100.0%
4	1974	47,371			47,371	WAGGONNER, JOE D.		47,371 D		100.0%		100.0%
4	1972	74,397			74,397	WAGGONNER, JOE D.		74,397 D		100.0%		100.0%
5	1976	159,270	75,574	SPOONER, FRANK	83,696	HUCKABY, JERRY		8,122 D	47.5%	52.5%	47.5%	52.5%
5	1974	43,068			43,068	PASSMAN, OTTO E.		43,068 D		100.0%		100.0%
5	1972	64,027			64,027	PASSMAN, OTTO E.		64,027 D		100.0%		100.0%
6	1976	152,992	99,780	MOORE, W. HENSON	53,212	DE BLIEUX, J. D.		46,568 R	65.2%	34.8%	65.2%	34.8%
6	1975	138,168	74,802	MOORE, W. HENSON	63,366	LACAZE, JEFF		11,436 R	54.1%	45.9%	54.1%	45.9%
6	1972	84,275			84,275	RARICK, JOHN R.		84,275 D		100.0%		100.0%
7	1976	140,610	23,414	HUFF, CHARLES F.	117,196	BREAUX, JOHN B.		93,782 D	16.7%	83.3%	16.7%	83.3%
7	1974	66,537			59,406	BREAUX, JOHN B.	7,131	59,406 D		89.3%		100.0%
7	1972	71,901			71,901	BREAUX, JOHN B.		71,901 D		100.0%		100.0%
8	1976	112,811			106,285	LONG, GILLIS W.	6,526	106,285 D		94.2%		100.0%
8	1974	41,704			41,704	LONG, GILLIS W.		41,704 D		100.0%		100.0%
8	1972	105,968	15,517	STRICKLAND, ROY C.	72,607	LONG, GILLIS W.	17,844	57,090 D	14.6%	68.5%	17.6%	82.4%

LOUISIANA

1975 GENERAL ELECTION

Governor There was no run-off election for Governor in 1975 under the new non-party election law; therefore the vote in the first election of November 1st is carried here in addition to the December 13th vote. In the November contest there were six candidates on the ballot, all Democrats. The vote was as follows: 750,107 Edwin W. Edwards; 292,220 Robert C. Jones, 146,368 Wade O. Martin; 5,307 Ken Lewis; 4,664 A. Roswell Thompson; 4,338 Cecilia M. Pizzo. The first Gubernatorial table in the data section gives the details of the vote for Edwards and Jones with the votes for Martin, Lewis, Thompson and Pizzo grouped in the "other" column. Users should note that Martin ran second in six parishes. The second table in the data section gives the detail of the vote on December 13th in which Governor Edwards received 430,095 votes as the only name on the ballot.

1975 PRIMARIES

NOVEMBER 1

Governor As of 1975 the Louisiana state legislature eliminated the partisan primary. There is now an open primary election with candidates from all parties running on the same ballot. Any candidate who receives a majority is elected; if no candidate receives 50 percent, there is a run-off between the top two finishers. In 1975 there were six candidates on the ballot, all Democrats. Edwin W. Edwards received 62.4% of the total vote and no run-off was required. See note in the general election section for details of the voting.

1976 GENERAL ELECTION

President Other vote was 10,058 Maddox (American); 7,417 Hall (Communist); 6,588 McCarthy (Independent); 3,325 MacBride (Libertarian); 2,240 Camejo (Socialist Workers).

Congress Other vote was Rarick (Independent) in CD 1; Hillery (Independent) in CD 2; Courtney (Independent) in CD 8.

1976 PRIMARIES

AUGUST 14 REPUBLICAN

Congress Unopposed in six CD's. No candidates in CD's 4 and 8. Thomas F. Jordan, the unopposed candidate in CD 2, withdrew after the primary and no substitution was made.

AUGUST 14 DEMOCRATIC

Congress Unopposed in two CD's. Contested as follows:

CD 1 38,429 James A. Moreau; 18,837 Richard A. Tonry; 12,659 David F. Dixon; 10,343 Salvadore E. Gutierrez; 6,335 William T. Bergeron; 682 Albert L. Dart; 475 Sanford Krasnoff.
CD 2 48,312 Lindy Boggs; 6,896 Matt P. Miller; 2,874 Travis J. Chiasson.
CD 3 35,869 David H. Scheuermann; 18,044 Warren J. Moity.
CD 4 36,997 Joe D. Waggonner; 7,779 T. A. Wilson.
CD 5 45,700 Jerry Huckaby; 40,697 Otto E. Passman.
CD 6 59,253 J. D. DeBlieux; 23,087 Bobby G. Pailette.

OCTOBER 2 DEMOCRATIC RUN-OFF

Congress

CD 1 48,798 Richard A. Tonry; 48,446 James A. Moreau.

MAINE

GOVERNOR

James B. Longley (I). Elected 1974 to a four-year term.

SENATORS

William D. Hathaway (D). Elected 1972 to a six-year term.

Edmund S. Muskie (D). Re-elected 1976 to a six-year term. Previously elected 1970, 1964, September 1958.

REPRESENTATIVES

1. David F. Emery (R)
2. William S. Cohen (R)

POSTWAR VOTE FOR GOVERNOR

								Percentage			
	Total	Republican		Democratic		Other	Rep.-Dem.	Total Vote		Major Vote	
Year	Vote	Vote	Candidate	Vote	Candidate	Vote	Plurality	Rep.	Dem.	Rep.	Dem.
1974	363,945	84,176	Erwin, James S.	132,219	Mitchell, George J.	147,550	48,043 D	23.1%	36.3%	38.9%	61.1%
1970	325,386	162,248	Erwin, James S.	163,138	Curtis, Kenneth M.	–	890 D	49.9%	50.1%	49.9%	50.1%
1966	323,838	151,802	Reed, John H.	172,036	Curtis, Kenneth M.	–	20,234 D	46.9%	53.1%	46.9%	53.1%
1962	292,725	146,604	Reed, John H.	146,121	Dolloff, Maynard C.	–	483 R	50.1%	49.9%	50.1%	49.9%
1960s	417,315	219,768	Reed, John H.	197,547	Coffin, Frank M.	–	22,221 R	52.7%	47.3%	52.7%	47.3%
1958	280,295	134,572	Hildreth, Horace A.	145,723	Clauson, Clinton A.	–	11,151 D	48.0%	52.0%	48.0%	52.0%
1956	304,649	124,395	Trafton, Willis A.	180,254	Muskie, Edmund S.	–	55,859 D	40.8%	59.2%	40.8%	59.2%
1954	248,971	113,298	Cross, Burton M.	135,673	Muskie, Edmund S.	–	22,375 D	45.5%	54.5%	45.5%	54.5%
1952	248,441	128,532	Cross, Burton M.	82,538	Oliver, James C.	37,371	45,994 R	51.7%	33.2%	60.9%	39.1%
1950	241,177	145,823	Payne, Frederick G.	94,304	Grant, Earl S.	1,050	51,519 R	60.5%	39.1%	60.7%	39.3%
1948	222,500	145,956	Payne, Frederick G.	76,544	Lausier, Louis B.	–	69,412 R	65.6%	34.4%	65.6%	34.4%
1946	179,951	110,327	Hildreth, Horace A.	69,624	Clark, F. Davis	–	40,703 R	61.3%	38.7%	61.3%	38.7%

The term of office of Maine's Governor was increased from two to four years effective with the 1958 election. The election in 1960 was for a short term to fill a vacancy. In 1974 James B. Longley, an Independent candidate, polled 142,464 votes (39.1% of the total vote) and won the election with a 10,245 plurality.

POSTWAR VOTE FOR SENATOR

								Percentage			
	Total	Republican		Democratic		Other	Rep.-Dem.	Total Vote		Major Vote	
Year	Vote	Vote	Candidate	Vote	Candidate	Vote	Plurality	Rep.	Dem.	Rep.	Dem.
1976	486,254	193,489	Monks, Robert A. G.	292,704	Muskie, Edmund S.	61	99,215 D	39.8%	60.2%	39.8%	60.2%
1972	421,310	197,040	Smith, Margaret Chase	224,270	Hathaway, William D.	–	27,230 D	46.8%	53.2%	46.8%	53.2%
1970	323,860	123,906	Bishop, Neil S.	199,954	Muskie, Edmund S.	–	76,048 D	38.3%	61.7%	38.3%	61.7%
1966	319,535	188,291	Smith, Margaret Chase	131,136	Violette, Elmer H.	108	57,155 R	58.9%	41.0%	58.9%	41.1%
1964	380,551	127,040	McIntire, Clifford	253,511	Muskie, Edmund S.	–	126,471 D	33.4%	66.6%	33.4%	66.6%
1960	416,699	256,890	Smith, Margaret Chase	159,809	Cormier, Lucia M.	–	97,081 R	61.6%	38.4%	61.6%	38.4%
1958	284,226	111,522	Payne, Frederick G.	172,704	Muskie, Edmund S.	–	61,182 D	39.2%	60.8%	39.2%	60.8%
1954	246,605	144,530	Smith, Margaret Chase	102,075	Fullam, Paul A.	–	42,455 R	58.6%	41.4%	58.6%	41.4%
1952	237,164	139,205	Payne, Frederick G.	82,665	Dube, Roger P.	15,294	56,540 R	58.7%	34.9%	62.7%	37.3%
1948	223,256	159,182	Smith, Margaret Chase	64,074	Scolten, Adrian H.	–	95,108 R	71.3%	28.7%	71.3%	28.7%
1946	175,014	111,215	Brewster, Owen	63,799	MacDonald, Peter	–	47,416 R	63.5%	36.5%	63.5%	36.5%

MAINE

Districts Established June 21, 1971

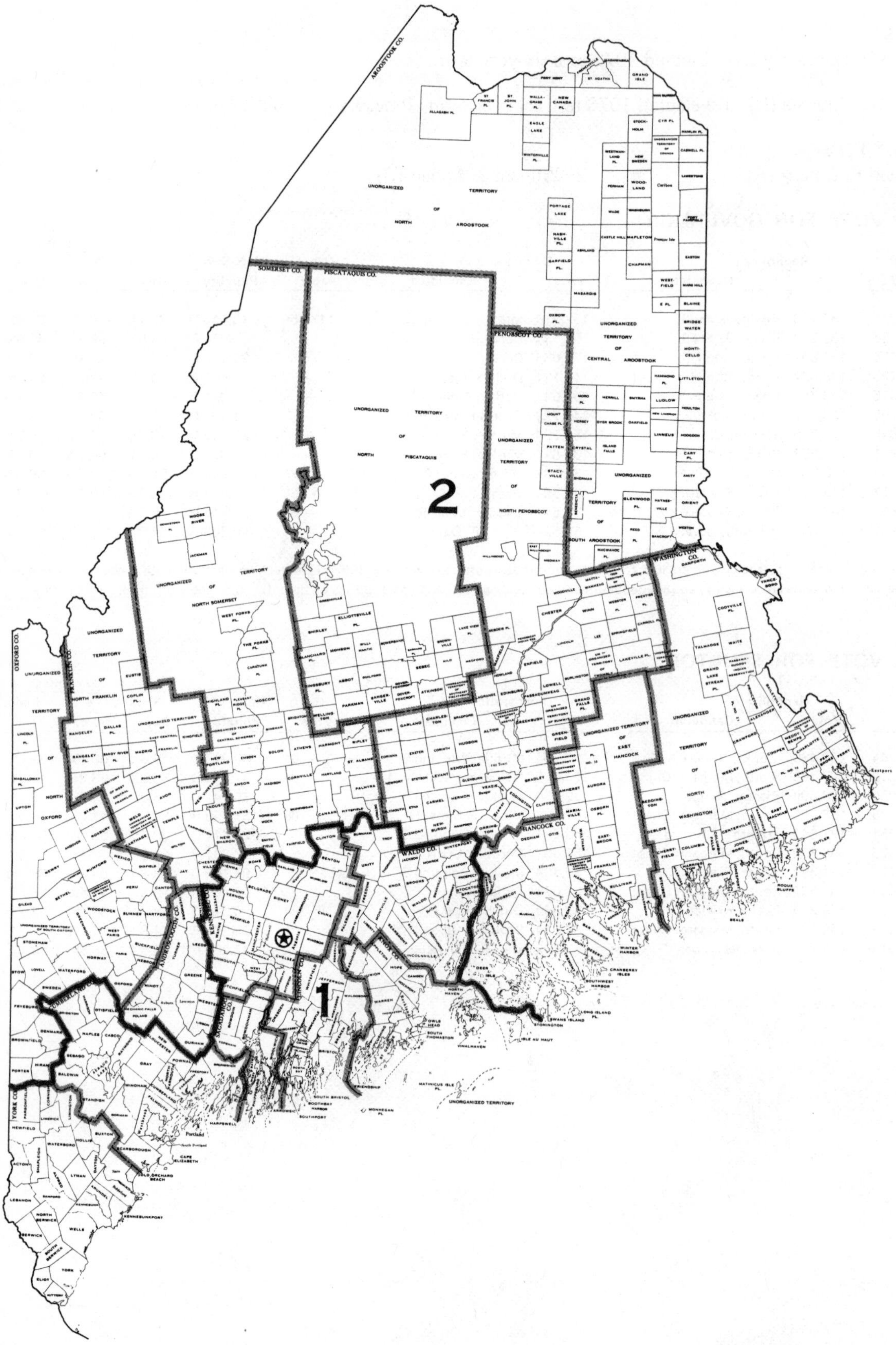

MAINE

PRESIDENT 1976

1970 Census Population	County	Total Vote	Republican	Democratic	Other	Rep.-Dem. Plurality	Percentage Total Vote Rep.	Percentage Total Vote Dem.	Percentage Major Vote Rep.	Percentage Major Vote Dem.
91,279	ANDROSCOGGIN	43,665	16,330	26,484	851	10,154 D	37.4%	60.7%	38.1%	61.9%
94,078	AROOSTOOK	32,051	15,550	15,484	1,017	66 R	48.5%	48.3%	50.1%	49.9%
192,528	CUMBERLAND	98,626	48,959	47,007	2,660	1,952 R	49.6%	47.7%	51.0%	49.0%
22,444	FRANKLIN	11,384	5,799	5,140	445	659 R	50.9%	45.2%	53.0%	47.0%
34,590	HANCOCK	19,647	12,064	6,725	858	5,339 R	61.4%	34.2%	64.2%	35.8%
95,247	KENNEBEC	47,412	22,534	23,473	1,405	939 D	47.5%	49.5%	49.0%	51.0%
29,013	KNOX	14,786	8,315	5,922	549	2,393 R	56.2%	40.1%	58.4%	41.6%
20,537	LINCOLN	12,797	7,554	4,818	425	2,736 R	59.0%	37.6%	61.1%	38.9%
43,457	OXFORD	21,516	10,551	10,340	625	211 R	49.0%	48.1%	50.5%	49.5%
125,393	PENOBSCOT	55,613	29,016	24,672	1,925	4,344 R	52.2%	44.4%	54.0%	46.0%
16,285	PISCATAQUIS	8,090	4,084	3,727	279	357 R	50.5%	46.1%	52.3%	47.7%
23,452	SAGADAHOC	11,876	5,988	5,529	359	459 R	50.4%	46.6%	52.0%	48.0%
40,597	SOMERSET	18,966	8,868	9,465	633	597 D	46.8%	49.9%	48.4%	51.6%
23,328	WALDO	11,633	6,289	4,853	491	1,436 R	54.1%	41.7%	56.4%	43.6%
29,859	WASHINGTON	14,235	7,039	6,644	552	395 R	49.4%	46.7%	51.4%	48.6%
111,576	YORK	60,919	27,380	31,996	1,543	4,616 D	44.9%	52.5%	46.1%	53.9%
993,663	TOTAL	483,216	236,320	232,279	14,617	4,041 R	48.9%	48.1%	50.4%	49.6%

SENATOR 1976

1970 Census Population	County	Total Vote	Republican	Democratic	Other	Rep.-Dem. Plurality	Percentage Total Vote Rep.	Percentage Total Vote Dem.	Percentage Major Vote Rep.	Percentage Major Vote Dem.
91,279	ANDROSCOGGIN	43,777	13,658	30,119		16,461 D	31.2%	68.8%	31.2%	68.8%
94,078	AROOSTOOK	32,197	13,351	18,846		5,495 D	41.5%	58.5%	41.5%	58.5%
192,528	CUMBERLAND	99,587	36,195	63,392		27,197 D	36.3%	63.7%	36.3%	63.7%
22,444	FRANKLIN	11,348	4,625	6,723		2,098 D	40.8%	59.2%	40.8%	59.2%
34,590	HANCOCK	19,844	10,455	9,389		1,066 R	52.7%	47.3%	52.7%	47.3%
95,247	KENNEBEC	47,617	18,408	29,209		10,801 D	38.7%	61.3%	38.7%	61.3%
29,013	KNOX	14,980	6,772	8,208		1,436 D	45.2%	54.8%	45.2%	54.8%
20,537	LINCOLN	12,967	6,255	6,712		457 D	48.2%	51.8%	48.2%	51.8%
43,457	OXFORD	21,745	8,635	13,110		4,475 D	39.7%	60.3%	39.7%	60.3%
125,393	PENOBSCOT	55,796	23,360	32,436		9,076 D	41.9%	58.1%	41.9%	58.1%
16,285	PISCATAQUIS	8,149	3,681	4,468		787 D	45.2%	54.8%	45.2%	54.8%
23,452	SAGADAHOC	12,019	4,327	7,692		3,365 D	36.0%	64.0%	36.0%	64.0%
40,597	SOMERSET	19,114	8,624	10,490		1,866 D	45.1%	54.9%	45.1%	54.9%
23,328	WALDO	11,674	5,799	5,875		76 D	49.7%	50.3%	49.7%	50.3%
29,859	WASHINGTON	14,298	6,294	8,004		1,710 D	44.0%	56.0%	44.0%	56.0%
111,576	YORK	61,081	23,050	38,031		14,981 D	37.7%	62.3%	37.7%	62.3%
993,663	TOTAL	486,254	193,489	292,704	61	99,215 D	39.8%	60.2%	39.8%	60.2%

MAINE

PRESIDENT 1976

1970 Census Population	City/Town	Total Vote	Republican	Democratic	Other	Rep.-Dem. Plurality	Percentage Total Vote Rep.	Percentage Total Vote Dem.	Percentage Major Vote Rep.	Percentage Major Vote Dem.
24,151	AUBURN	10,940	4,959	5,782	199	823 D	45.3%	52.9%	46.2%	53.8%
21,945	AUGUSTA	9,824	4,593	4,961	270	368 D	46.8%	50.5%	48.1%	51.9%
33,168	BANGOR	12,521	6,725	5,385	411	1,340 R	53.7%	43.0%	55.5%	44.5%
9,679	BATH	4,511	2,414	1,977	120	437 R	53.5%	43.8%	55.0%	45.0%
5,957	BELFAST	2,638	1,528	1,009	101	519 R	57.9%	38.2%	60.2%	39.8%
19,983	BIDDEFORD	9,483	1,966	7,335	182	5,369 D	20.7%	77.3%	21.1%	78.9%
9,300	BREWER	4,416	2,639	1,694	83	945 R	59.8%	38.4%	60.9%	39.1%
16,195	BRUNSWICK	6,562	2,915	3,418	229	503 D	44.4%	52.1%	46.0%	54.0%
7,873	CAPE ELIZABETH	5,202	3,448	1,639	115	1,809 R	66.3%	31.5%	67.8%	32.2%
10,419	CARIBOU	3,483	1,924	1,468	91	456 R	55.2%	42.1%	56.7%	43.3%
5,684	FAIRFIELD	2,469	1,091	1,310	68	219 D	44.2%	53.1%	45.4%	54.6%
6,291	FALMOUTH	3,974	2,512	1,383	79	1,129 R	63.2%	34.8%	64.5%	35.5%
5,657	FARMINGTON	2,921	1,603	1,140	178	463 R	54.9%	39.0%	58.4%	41.6%
6,685	GARDINER	3,094	1,505	1,507	82	2 D	48.6%	48.7%	50.0%	50.0%
7,839	GORHAM	4,556	2,350	2,087	119	263 R	51.6%	45.8%	53.0%	47.0%
8,111	HOULTON	2,856	1,906	844	106	1,062 R	66.7%	29.6%	69.3%	30.7%
5,646	KENNEBUNK	3,476	2,127	1,270	79	857 R	61.2%	36.5%	62.6%	37.4%
11,028	KITTERY	3,817	2,069	1,660	88	409 R	54.2%	43.5%	55.5%	44.5%
41,779	LEWISTON	19,609	5,369	13,899	341	8,530 D	27.4%	70.9%	27.9%	72.1%
8,745	LIMESTONE	957	466	473	18	7 D	48.7%	49.4%	49.6%	50.4%
6,544	LISBON	3,136	1,372	1,700	64	328 D	43.8%	54.2%	44.7%	55.3%
5,585	MADAWASKA	1,873	441	1,398	34	957 D	23.5%	74.6%	24.0%	76.0%
7,742	MILLINOCKET	3,569	1,686	1,770	113	84 D	47.2%	49.6%	48.8%	51.2%
5,404	OLD ORCHARD BEACH	3,030	1,196	1,748	86	552 D	39.5%	57.7%	40.6%	59.4%
9,057	OLD TOWN	4,136	1,660	2,307	169	647 D	40.1%	55.8%	41.8%	58.2%
9,989	ORONO	4,137	2,115	1,807	215	308 R	51.1%	43.7%	53.9%	46.1%
65,116	PORTLAND	27,126	11,598	14,708	820	3,110 D	42.8%	54.2%	44.1%	55.9%
11,452	PRESQUE ISLE	4,091	2,377	1,602	112	775 R	58.1%	39.2%	59.7%	40.3%
8,505	ROCKLAND	3,127	1,735	1,292	100	443 R	55.5%	41.3%	57.3%	42.7%
9,363	RUMFORD	4,076	1,509	2,465	102	956 D	37.0%	60.5%	38.0%	62.0%
11,678	SACO	6,180	2,398	3,650	132	1,252 D	38.8%	59.1%	39.6%	60.4%
15,812	SANFORD	7,750	3,087	4,485	178	1,398 D	39.8%	57.9%	40.8%	59.2%
7,845	SCARBOROUGH	4,788	2,526	2,160	102	366 R	52.8%	45.1%	53.9%	46.1%
7,601	SKOWHEGAN	3,584	1,676	1,814	94	138 D	46.8%	50.6%	48.0%	52.0%
23,267	SOUTH PORTLAND	10,817	5,080	5,470	267	390 D	47.0%	50.6%	48.2%	51.8%
5,022	TOPSHAM	2,320	1,007	1,260	53	253 D	43.4%	54.3%	44.4%	55.6%
18,192	WATERVILLE	8,234	3,319	4,660	255	1,341 D	40.3%	56.6%	41.6%	58.4%
14,444	WESTBROOK	7,251	3,209	3,900	142	691 D	44.3%	53.8%	45.1%	54.9%
6,593	WINDHAM	4,215	2,095	2,031	89	64 R	49.7%	48.2%	50.8%	49.2%
7,299	WINSLOW	3,838	1,383	2,367	88	984 D	36.0%	61.7%	36.9%	63.1%
5,690	YORK TOWN	3,975	2,403	1,453	119	950 R	60.5%	36.6%	62.3%	37.7%

MAINE

SENATOR 1976

1970 Census Population	City/Town	Total Vote	Republican	Democratic	Other	Rep.-Dem. Plurality	Percentage Total Vote Rep.	Total Vote Dem.	Major Vote Rep.	Major Vote Dem.
24,151	AUBURN	10,989	4,171	6,818		2,647 D	38.0%	62.0%	38.0%	62.0%
21,945	AUGUSTA	9,814	3,665	6,149		2,484 D	37.3%	62.7%	37.3%	62.7%
33,168	BANGOR	12,455	4,930	7,525		2,595 D	39.6%	60.4%	39.6%	60.4%
9,679	BATH	4,532	1,467	3,065		1,598 D	32.4%	67.6%	32.4%	67.6%
5,957	BELFAST	2,640	1,318	1,322		4 D	49.9%	50.1%	49.9%	50.1%
19,983	BIDDEFORD	9,555	1,991	7,564		5,573 D	20.8%	79.2%	20.8%	79.2%
9,300	BREWER	4,380	2,064	2,316		252 D	47.1%	52.9%	47.1%	52.9%
16,195	BRUNSWICK	6,663	2,375	4,288		1,913 D	35.6%	64.4%	35.6%	64.4%
7,873	CAPE ELIZABETH	5,235	2,612	2,623		11 D	49.9%	50.1%	49.9%	50.1%
10,419	CARIBOU	3,441	1,551	1,890		339 D	45.1%	54.9%	45.1%	54.9%
5,684	FAIRFIELD	2,497	977	1,520		543 D	39.1%	60.9%	39.1%	60.9%
6,291	FALMOUTH	3,948	1,849	2,099		250 D	46.8%	53.2%	46.8%	53.2%
5,657	FARMINGTON	2,859	1,221	1,638		417 D	42.7%	57.3%	42.7%	57.3%
6,685	GARDINER	3,114	1,253	1,861		608 D	40.2%	59.8%	40.2%	59.8%
7,839	GORHAM	4,671	1,783	2,888		1,105 D	38.2%	61.8%	38.2%	61.8%
8,111	HOULTON	2,859	1,377	1,482		105 D	48.2%	51.8%	48.2%	51.8%
5,646	KENNEBUNK	3,506	1,504	2,002		498 D	42.9%	57.1%	42.9%	57.1%
11,028	KITTERY	3,818	1,599	2,219		620 D	41.9%	58.1%	41.9%	58.1%
41,779	LEWISTON	19,522	4,329	15,193		10,864 D	22.2%	77.8%	22.2%	77.8%
8,745	LIMESTONE	971	431	540		109 D	44.4%	55.6%	44.4%	55.6%
6,544	LISBON	3,197	1,095	2,102		1,007 D	34.3%	65.7%	34.3%	65.7%
5,585	MADAWASKA	1,911	455	1,456		1,001 D	23.8%	76.2%	23.8%	76.2%
7,742	MILLINOCKET	3,609	1,293	2,316		1,023 D	35.8%	64.2%	35.8%	64.2%
5,404	OLD ORCHARD BEACH	3,060	1,041	2,019		978 D	34.0%	66.0%	34.0%	66.0%
9,057	OLD TOWN	4,162	1,303	2,859		1,556 D	31.3%	68.7%	31.3%	68.7%
9,989	ORONO	4,122	1,335	2,787		1,452 D	32.4%	67.6%	32.4%	67.6%
65,116	PORTLAND	27,352	8,055	19,297		11,242 D	29.4%	70.6%	29.4%	70.6%
11,452	PRESQUE ISLE	4,008	1,878	2,130		252 D	46.9%	53.1%	46.9%	53.1%
8,505	ROCKLAND	3,118	1,364	1,754		390 D	43.7%	56.3%	43.7%	56.3%
9,363	RUMFORD	4,159	1,189	2,970		1,781 D	28.6%	71.4%	28.6%	71.4%
11,678	SACO	6,187	1,933	4,254		2,321 D	31.2%	68.8%	31.2%	68.8%
15,812	SANFORD	7,801	2,589	5,212		2,623 D	33.2%	66.8%	33.2%	66.8%
7,845	SCARBOROUGH	4,806	1,849	2,957		1,108 D	38.5%	61.5%	38.5%	61.5%
7,601	SKOWHEGAN	3,623	1,558	2,065		507 D	43.0%	57.0%	43.0%	57.0%
23,267	SOUTH PORTLAND	10,854	3,594	7,260		3,666 D	33.1%	66.9%	33.1%	66.9%
5,022	TOPSHAM	2,337	782	1,555		773 D	33.5%	66.5%	33.5%	66.5%
18,192	WATERVILLE	8,184	2,394	5,790		3,396 D	29.3%	70.7%	29.3%	70.7%
14,444	WESTBROOK	7,367	2,375	4,992		2,617 D	32.2%	67.8%	32.2%	67.8%
6,593	WINDHAM	4,246	1,633	2,613		980 D	38.5%	61.5%	38.5%	61.5%
7,299	WINSLOW	3,900	1,065	2,835		1,770 D	27.3%	72.7%	27.3%	72.7%
5,690	YORK TOWN	3,980	2,022	1,958		64 R	50.8%	49.2%	50.8%	49.2%

MAINE

CONGRESS

CD	Year	Total Vote	Republican Vote	Republican Candidate	Democratic Vote	Democratic Candidate	Other Vote	Rep.-Dem. Plurality	Percentage Total Vote Rep.	Percentage Total Vote Dem.	Percentage Major Vote Rep.	Percentage Major Vote Dem.
1	1976	253,643	145,523	EMERY, DAVID F.	108,105	BARTON, FREDERICK D.	15	37,418 R	57.4%	42.6%	57.4%	42.6%
1	1974	187,727	94,203	EMERY, DAVID F.	93,524	KYROS, PETER N.		679 R	50.2%	49.8%	50.2%	49.8%
1	1972	217,996	88,588	PORTEOUS, L. ROBERT	129,408	KYROS, PETER N.		40,820 D	40.6%	59.4%	40.6%	59.4%
1	1970	168,154	68,671	SPEERS, RONALD T.	99,483	KYROS, PETER N.		30,812 D	40.8%	59.2%	40.8%	59.2%
1	1968	200,450	86,949	HILDRETH, HORACE, JR.	113,501	KYROS, PETER N.		26,552 D	43.4%	56.6%	43.4%	56.6%
1	1966	161,384	72,984	GARLAND, PETER A.	81,302	KYROS, PETER N.	7,098	8,318 D	45.2%	50.4%	47.3%	52.7%
1	1964	190,593	95,398	TUPPER, STANLEY R.	95,195	CURTIS, KENNETH M.		203 R	50.1%	49.9%	50.1%	49.9%
1	1962	143,993	85,864	TUPPER, STANLEY R.	58,129	KELLAM, RONALD L.		27,735 R	59.6%	40.4%	59.6%	40.4%
2	1976	219,570	169,292	COHEN, WILLIAM S.	43,150	COONEY, LEIGHTON	7,128	126,142 R	77.1%	19.7%	79.7%	20.3%
2	1974	165,553	118,154	COHEN, WILLIAM S.	47,399	GARTLEY, MARKHAM L.		70,755 R	71.4%	28.6%	71.4%	28.6%
2	1972	195,415	106,280	COHEN, WILLIAM S.	89,135	VIOLETTE, ELMER H.		17,145 R	54.4%	45.6%	54.4%	45.6%
2	1970	149,877	53,642	CONNERS, MAYNARD G.	96,235	HATHAWAY, WILLIAM D.		42,593 D	35.8%	64.2%	35.8%	64.2%
2	1968	183,767	81,398	SHUTE, ELDEN H.	102,369	HATHAWAY, WILLIAM D.		20,971 D	44.3%	55.7%	44.3%	55.7%
2	1966	151,432	65,476	FOLEY, HOWARD M.	85,956	HATHAWAY, WILLIAM D.		20,480 D	43.2%	56.8%	43.2%	56.8%
2	1964	178,909	67,978	MACLEOD, KENNETH P.	110,931	HATHAWAY, WILLIAM D.		42,953 D	38.0%	62.0%	38.0%	62.0%
2	1962	141,508	72,349	MCINTIRE, CLIFFORD	69,159	HATHAWAY, WILLIAM D.		3,190 R	51.1%	48.9%	51.1%	48.9%

MAINE

1976 GENERAL ELECTION

In addition to the county-by-county figures, 1976 data are presented for selected Maine communities. Since not all jurisdictions of the state are listed in this special tabulation, state-wide totals are shown only with the county-by-county statistics.

President	Other vote was 10,874 McCarthy (Independent); 3,495 Bubar (Prohibition); 28 Anderson (write-in); 14 Hall (write-in); 11 MacBride (write-in); 8 Maddox (write-in); 1 Camejo (write-in); 1 Levin (write-in); 185 scattered.
Senator	State-wide other vote total includes 61 scattered votes not available by county or city/town.
Congress	Other vote was scattered in CD 1; 7,105 Kaye (Independent) and 23 scattered in CD 2.

1976 PRIMARIES

JUNE 8 REPUBLICAN

Senator	65,224 Robert A. G. Monks; 12,552 Plato Truman.
Congress	Unopposed in both CD's.

JUNE 8 DEMOCRATIC

Senator	Edmund S. Muskie, unopposed.
Congress	Unopposed in CD 2. Contested as follows:
CD 1	9,906 Frederick D. Barton; 8,204 James E. Mitchell; 7,568 Neil Rolde; 5,127 David W. Bustin; 5,099 Bruce M. Reeves; 3,570 Gilbert R. Boucher; 1,994 Donald G. Lowry.

MARYLAND

GOVERNOR

Marvin Mandel (D). Re-elected 1974 to a four-year term. Previously elected 1970 and in January 1969 by the State Legislature on the resignation of Governor Spiro T. Agnew.

SENATORS

Charles Mathias (R). Re-elected 1974 to a six-year term. Previously elected 1968.

Paul S. Sarbanes (D). Elected 1976 to a six-year term.

REPRESENTATIVES

1. Robert E. Bauman (R)
2. Clarence D. Long (D)
3. Barbara A. Mikulski (D)
4. Marjorie S. Holt (R)
5. Gladys N. Spellman (D)
6. Goodloe E. Byron (D)
7. Parren J. Mitchell (D)
8. Newton I. Steers (R)

POSTWAR VOTE FOR GOVERNOR

								Percentage			
	Total	Republican		Democratic		Other	Rep.-Dem.	Total Vote		Major Vote	
Year	Vote	Vote	Candidate	Vote	Candidate	Vote	Plurality	Rep.	Dem.	Rep.	Dem.
1974	949,097	346,449	Gore, Louise	602,648	Mandel, Marvin	–	256,199 D	36.5%	63.5%	36.5%	63.5%
1970	973,099	314,336	Blair, C. Stanley	639,579	Mandel, Marvin	19,184	325,243 D	32.3%	65.7%	33.0%	67.0%
1966	918,761	455,318	Agnew, Spiro T.	373,543	Mahoney, George P.	89,900	81,775 R	49.6%	40.7%	54.9%	45.1%
1962	775,101	343,051	Small, Frank	432,045	Tawes, J. Millard	5	88,994 D	44.3%	55.7%	44.3%	55.7%
1958	763,234	278,173	Devereux, James	485,061	Tawes, J. Millard	–	206,888 D	36.4%	63.6%	36.4%	63.6%
1954	700,484	381,451	McKeldin, Theodore	319,033	Byrd, Harry C.	–	62,418 R	54.5%	45.5%	54.5%	45.5%
1950	645,631	369,807	McKeldin, Theodore	275,824	Lane, William P.	–	93,983 R	57.3%	42.7%	57.3%	42.7%
1946	489,836	221,752	McKeldin, Theodore	268,084	Lane, William P.	–	46,332 D	45.3%	54.7%	45.3%	54.7%

POSTWAR VOTE FOR SENATOR

								Percentage			
	Total	Republican		Democratic		Other	Rep.-Dem.	Total Vote		Major Vote	
Year	Vote	Vote	Candidate	Vote	Candidate	Vote	Plurality	Rep.	Dem.	Rep.	Dem.
1976	1,365,568	530,439	Beall, J. Glenn, Jr.	772,101	Sarbanes, Paul S.	63,028	241,662 D	38.8%	56.5%	40.7%	59.3%
1974	877,786	503,223	Mathias, Charles	374,563	Mikulski, Barbara A.	–	128,660 R	57.3%	42.7%	57.3%	42.7%
1970	956,370	484,960	Beall, J. Glenn, Jr.	460,422	Tydings, Joseph D.	10,988	24,538 R	50.7%	48.1%	51.3%	48.7%
1968	1,133,727	541,893	Mathias, Charles	443,367	Brewster, Daniel B.	148,467	98,526 R	47.8%	39.1%	55.0%	45.0%
1964	1,081,049	402,393	Beall, J. Glenn	678,649	Tydings, Joseph D.	7	276,256 D	37.2%	62.8%	37.2%	62.8%
1962	714,248	270,312	Miller, Edward T.	443,935	Brewster, Daniel B.	1	173,623 D	37.8%	62.2%	37.8%	62.2%
1958	749,291	382,021	Beall, J. Glenn	367,270	D'Alesandro, Thomas	–	14,751 R	51.0%	49.0%	51.0%	49.0%
1956	892,167	473,059	Butler, John Marshall	419,108	Mahoney, George P.	–	53,951 R	53.0%	47.0%	53.0%	47.0%
1952	856,193	449,823	Beall, J. Glenn	406,370	Mahoney, George P.	–	43,453 R	52.5%	47.5%	52.5%	47.5%
1950	615,614	326,291	Butler, John Marshall	283,180	Tydings, Millard E.	6,143	43,111 R	53.0%	46.0%	53.5%	46.5%
1946	472,232	235,000	Markey, David John	237,232	O'Conor, Herbert R.	–	2,232 D	49.8%	50.2%	49.8%	50.2%

MARYLAND

Districts Established March 21, 1972

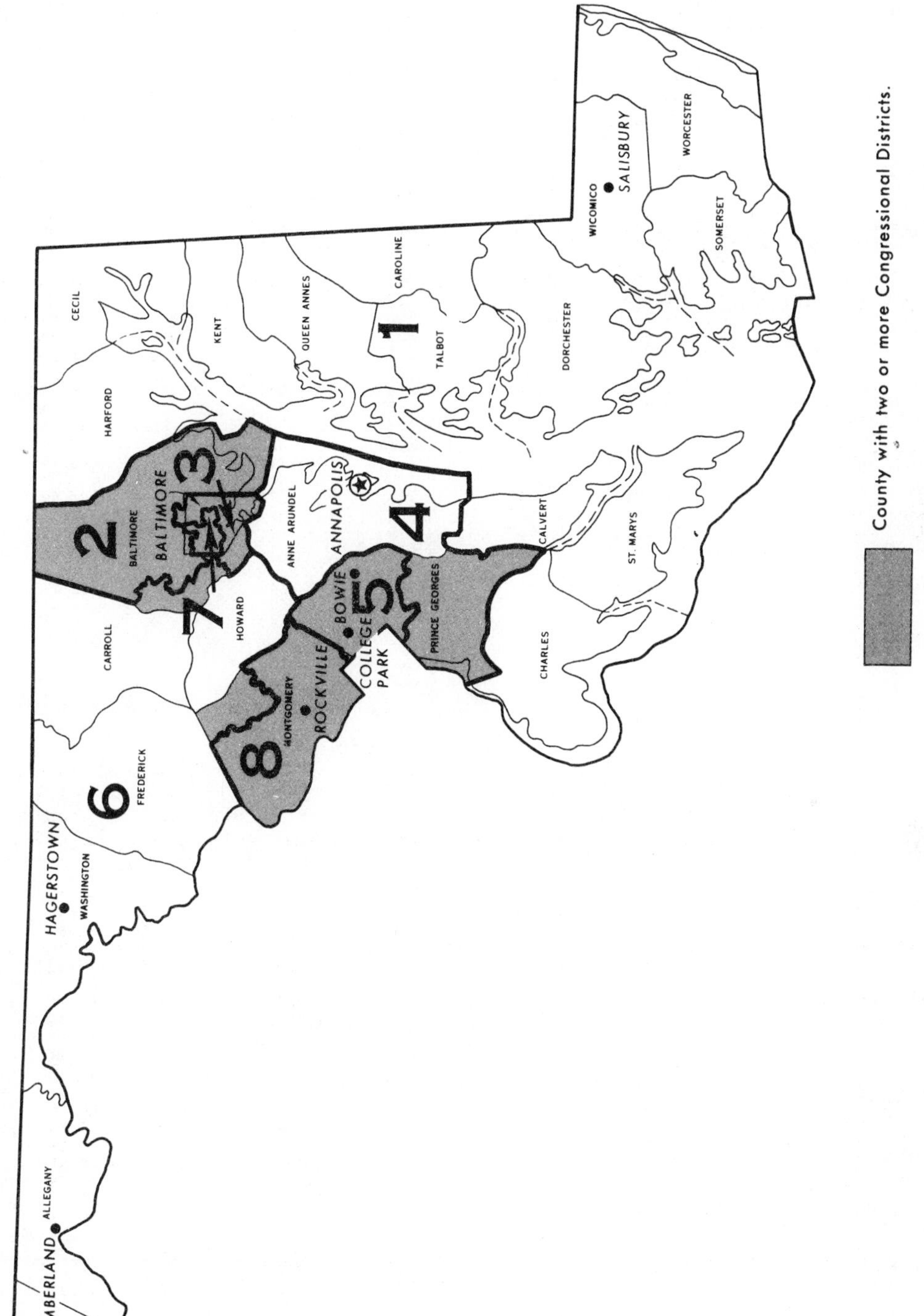

MARYLAND

PRESIDENT 1976

1970 Census Population	County	Total Vote	Republican	Democratic	Other	Rep.-Dem. Plurality	Percentage Total Vote Rep.	Total Vote Dem.	Major Vote Rep.	Major Vote Dem.
84,044	ALLEGANY	31,496	15,435	15,967	94	532 D	49.0%	50.7%	49.2%	50.8%
297,539	ANNE ARUNDEL	116,100	61,353	54,351	396	7,002 R	52.8%	46.8%	53.0%	47.0%
905,759	BALTIMORE CITY	261,832	81,762	178,593	1,477	96,831 D	31.2%	68.2%	31.4%	68.6%
621,077	BALTIMORE COUNTY	262,866	143,293	118,505	1,068	24,788 R	54.5%	45.1%	54.7%	45.3%
20,682	CALVERT	8,074	3,439	4,626	9	1,187 D	42.6%	57.3%	42.6%	57.4%
19,781	CAROLINE	6,140	3,114	3,017	9	97 R	50.7%	49.1%	50.8%	49.2%
69,006	CARROLL	25,684	15,661	9,940	83	5,721 R	61.0%	38.7%	61.2%	38.8%
53,291	CECIL	16,811	7,833	8,950	28	1,117 D	46.6%	53.2%	46.7%	53.3%
47,678	CHARLES	17,343	7,792	9,525	26	1,733 D	44.9%	54.9%	45.0%	55.0%
29,405	DORCHESTER	9,301	4,768	4,528	5	240 R	51.3%	48.7%	51.3%	48.7%
84,927	FREDERICK	32,704	17,941	14,542	221	3,399 R	54.9%	44.5%	55.2%	44.8%
21,476	GARRETT	8,000	4,640	3,332	28	1,308 R	58.0%	41.7%	58.2%	41.8%
115,378	HARFORD	44,227	24,309	19,890	28	4,419 R	55.0%	45.0%	55.0%	45.0%
61,911	HOWARD	42,007	21,200	20,533	274	667 R	50.5%	48.9%	50.8%	49.2%
16,146	KENT	6,041	2,821	3,211	9	390 D	46.7%	53.2%	46.8%	53.2%
522,809	MONTGOMERY	256,177	122,674	131,098	2,405	8,424 D	47.9%	51.2%	48.3%	51.7%
660,567	PRINCE GEORGES	193,966	81,027	111,743	1,196	30,716 D	41.8%	57.6%	42.0%	58.0%
18,422	QUEEN ANNES	6,966	3,479	3,457	30	22 R	49.9%	49.6%	50.2%	49.8%
47,388	ST. MARYS	12,905	5,640	7,227	38	1,587 D	43.7%	56.0%	43.8%	56.2%
18,924	SOMERSET	6,727	3,254	3,472	1	218 D	48.4%	51.6%	48.4%	51.6%
23,682	TALBOT	9,590	5,848	3,715	27	2,133 R	61.0%	38.7%	61.2%	38.8%
103,829	WASHINGTON	36,233	20,194	15,902	137	4,292 R	55.7%	43.9%	55.9%	44.1%
54,236	WICOMICO	19,977	10,537	9,412	28	1,125 R	52.7%	47.1%	52.8%	47.2%
24,442	WORCESTER	8,730	4,647	4,076	7	571 R	53.2%	46.7%	53.3%	46.7%
3,922,399	TOTAL	1,439,897	672,661	759,612	7,624	86,951 D	46.7%	52.8%	47.0%	53.0%

SENATOR 1976

1970 Census Population	County	Total Vote	Republican	Democratic	Other	Rep.-Dem. Plurality	Percentage Total Vote Rep.	Total Vote Dem.	Major Vote Rep.	Major Vote Dem.
84,044	ALLEGANY	29,912	14,680	13,802	1,430	878 R	49.1%	46.1%	51.5%	48.5%
297,539	ANNE ARUNDEL	109,503	49,655	54,435	5,413	4,780 D	45.3%	49.7%	47.7%	52.3%
905,759	BALTIMORE CITY	249,020	51,375	191,916	5,729	140,541 D	20.6%	77.1%	21.1%	78.9%
621,077	BALTIMORE COUNTY	252,580	102,011	140,163	10,406	38,152 D	40.4%	55.5%	42.1%	57.9%
20,682	CALVERT	7,118	2,943	3,785	390	842 D	41.3%	53.2%	43.7%	56.3%
19,781	CAROLINE	5,546	2,835	2,488	223	347 R	51.1%	44.9%	53.3%	46.7%
69,006	CARROLL	24,408	13,884	9,233	1,291	4,651 R	56.9%	37.8%	60.1%	39.9%
53,291	CECIL	15,362	6,815	8,016	531	1,201 D	44.4%	52.2%	46.0%	54.0%
47,678	CHARLES	15,792	7,067	8,100	625	1,033 D	44.8%	51.3%	46.6%	53.4%
29,405	DORCHESTER	8,155	3,811	3,968	376	157 D	46.7%	48.7%	49.0%	51.0%
84,927	FREDERICK	31,053	17,510	11,551	1,992	5,959 R	56.4%	37.2%	60.3%	39.7%
21,476	GARRETT	7,135	4,674	2,212	249	2,462 R	65.5%	31.0%	67.9%	32.1%
115,378	HARFORD	41,900	18,277	21,359	2,264	3,082 D	43.6%	51.0%	46.1%	53.9%
61,911	HOWARD	40,220	16,346	21,168	2,706	4,822 D	40.6%	52.6%	43.6%	56.4%
16,146	KENT	5,514	2,575	2,742	197	167 D	46.7%	49.7%	48.4%	51.6%
522,809	MONTGOMERY	246,735	98,974	130,981	16,780	32,007 D	40.1%	53.1%	43.0%	57.0%
660,567	PRINCE GEORGES	181,964	67,331	105,736	8,897	38,405 D	37.0%	58.1%	38.9%	61.1%
18,422	QUEEN ANNES	6,407	3,029	3,115	263	86 D	47.3%	48.6%	49.3%	50.7%
47,388	ST. MARYS	11,647	4,652	6,429	566	1,777 D	39.9%	55.2%	42.0%	58.0%
18,924	SOMERSET	5,918	2,832	2,950	136	118 D	47.9%	49.8%	49.0%	51.0%
23,682	TALBOT	8,827	4,884	3,420	523	1,464 R	55.3%	38.7%	58.8%	41.2%
103,829	WASHINGTON	34,069	21,497	11,347	1,225	10,150 R	63.1%	33.3%	65.5%	34.5%
54,236	WICOMICO	19,022	8,709	9,767	546	1,058 D	45.8%	51.3%	47.1%	52.9%
24,442	WORCESTER	7,761	4,073	3,418	270	655 R	52.5%	44.0%	54.4%	45.6%
3,922,399	TOTAL	1,365,568	530,439	772,101	63,028	241,662 D	38.8%	56.5%	40.7%	59.3%

MARYLAND

CONGRESS

CD	Year	Total Vote	Republican Vote	Republican Candidate	Democratic Vote	Democratic Candidate	Other Vote	Rep.-Dem. Plurality	Percentage Total Vote Rep.	Percentage Total Vote Dem.	Percentage Major Vote Rep.	Percentage Major Vote Dem.
1	1976	158,912	85,919	BAUMAN, ROBERT E.	72,993	DYSON, ROY		12,926 R	54.1%	45.9%	54.1%	45.9%
1	1974	112,423	59,570	BAUMAN, ROBERT E.	52,853	HATEM, THOMAS J.		6,717 R	53.0%	47.0%	53.0%	47.0%
1	1972	122,465	86,326	MILLS, WILLIAM O.	36,139	HARGREAVES, JOHN R.		50,187 R	70.5%	29.5%	70.5%	29.5%
2	1976	196,303	35,258	SENEY, JOHN M.	139,196	LONG, CLARENCE D.	21,849	103,938 D	18.0%	70.9%	20.2%	79.8%
2	1974	133,861	30,639	SENEY, JOHN M.	103,222	LONG, CLARENCE D.		72,583 D	22.9%	77.1%	22.9%	77.1%
2	1972	187,465	64,119	BISHOP, JOHN J.	123,346	LONG, CLARENCE D.		59,227 D	34.2%	65.8%	34.2%	65.8%
3	1976	143,461	36,447	CULOTTA, SAMUEL A.	107,014	MIKULSKI, BARBARA A.		70,567 D	25.4%	74.6%	25.4%	74.6%
3	1974	111,185	17,967	MATHEWS, WILLIAM H.	93,218	SARBANES, PAUL S.		75,251 D	16.2%	83.8%	16.2%	83.8%
3	1972	133,535	40,442	MORROW, ROBERT D.	93,093	SARBANES, PAUL S.		52,651 D	30.3%	69.7%	30.3%	69.7%
4	1976	165,013	95,158	HOLT, MARJORIE S.	69,855	FORNOS, WERNER H.		25,303 R	57.7%	42.3%	57.7%	42.3%
4	1974	105,267	61,208	HOLT, MARJORIE S.	44,059	WINELAND, FRED L.		17,149 R	58.1%	41.9%	58.1%	41.9%
4	1972	147,411	87,534	HOLT, MARJORIE S.	59,877	FORNOS, WERNER H.		27,657 R	59.4%	40.6%	59.4%	40.6%
5	1976	134,893	57,057	BURCHAM, JOHN B.	77,836	SPELLMAN, GLADYS N.		20,779 D	42.3%	57.7%	42.3%	57.7%
5	1974	86,016	40,805	BURCHAM, JOHN B.	45,211	SPELLMAN, GLADYS N.		4,406 D	47.4%	52.6%	47.4%	52.6%
5	1972	143,065	90,016	HOGAN, LAWRENCE J.	53,049	CONROY, EDWARD T.		36,967 R	62.9%	37.1%	62.9%	37.1%
6	1976	179,004	52,203	BOND, ARTHUR T.	126,801	BYRON, GOODLOE E.		74,598 D	29.2%	70.8%	29.2%	70.8%
6	1974	123,298	32,416	WAMPLER, ELTON R.	90,882	BYRON, GOODLOE E.		58,466 D	26.3%	73.7%	26.3%	73.7%
6	1972	165,542	58,259	MASON, EDWARD J.	107,283	BYRON, GOODLOE E.		49,024 D	35.2%	64.8%	35.2%	64.8%
7	1976	100,633			94,991	MITCHELL, PARREN J.	5,642	94,991 D		94.4%		100.0%
7	1974	43,252			43,252	MITCHELL, PARREN J.		43,252 D		100.0%		100.0%
7	1972	104,625	20,876	ADAIR, VERDELL	83,749	MITCHELL, PARREN J.		62,873 D	20.0%	80.0%	20.0%	80.0%
8	1976	237,652	111,274	STEERS, NEWTON I.	100,343	DAVIS, LANNY	26,035	10,931 R	46.8%	42.2%	52.6%	47.4%
8	1974	158,787	104,675	GUDE, GILBERT	54,112	KRAMER, SIDNEY		50,563 R	65.9%	34.1%	65.9%	34.1%
8	1972	214,838	137,287	GUDE, GILBERT	77,551	ANASTASI, JOSEPH G.		59,736 R	63.9%	36.1%	63.9%	36.1%

MARYLAND

1976 GENERAL ELECTION

President — Other vote was 4,541 McCarthy (Independent); 321 Anderson (American); 261 Camejo (Socialist Workers); 255 MacBride (Libertarian); 171 Maddox (American Independent); 68 Hall (Communist); 21 LaRouche (U.S. Labor); 16 Zeidler (Socialist); 8 Miller (Restoration); 8 Wright (People's); 7 Levin (Socialist Labor); 2 Bubar (Prohibition); 1,945 scattered.

Senator — Other vote was 62,750 Bradley (Independent); 278 scattered.

Congress — Other vote was Meroney (Independent) in CD 2; Salisbury (Independent) in CD 7; Ficker (Independent) in CD 8.

1976 PRIMARIES

MAY 18 REPUBLICAN

Senator — J. Glenn Beall, Jr., unopposed.

Congress — Unopposed in three CD's. No candidate in CD 7. Contested as follows:

CD 2 — 7,502 John M. Seney; 4,066 Walter S. Kenton; 3,580 John L. Koenig.
CD 3 — 3,146 Samuel A. Culotta; 2,708 Richard L. Andrews; 2,645 Jeffrey W. Boyd.
CD 5 — 8,884 John B. Burcham; 1,569 Leo L. Emery; 1,178 Jonathan J. Stanley; 921 Frederick C. Taylor.
CD 8 — 14,681 Newton I. Steers; 8,402 Austin B. Rohrbaugh; 2,021 Albert N. Nunn; 1,960 Thomas S. Fess; 1,739 Peter Larsen; 1,517 Wallace Barlow; 1,302 Howard D. Greyber; 1,117 Peter James; 902 Frederick L. Garwood; 776 Abraham H. Kalish.

MAY 18 DEMOCRATIC

Senator — 302,983 Paul S. Sarbanes; 191,875 Joseph D. Tydings; 12,606 David E. Shaw; 11,892 Howard L. Gates; 11,256 Roy L. Chambers; 9,256 William A. Albaugh; 5,904 Walter G. Finch; 1,982 Monroe Cornish.

Congress — Unopposed in two CD's. Contested as follows:

CD 1 — 23,387 Roy Dyson; 7,984 Sally M. Johnson; 5,887 Edward G. Post.
CD 3 — 37,188 Barbara A. Mikulski; 14,994 J. Joseph Curran; 10,753 R. Charles Avara; 10,647 John C. Byrnes; 7,147 John A. Pica; 931 DeHaven L. Smith; 735 Morgan L. Amaimo; 622 J. Robert Rutkowski; 426 Gerard A. Gloss; 412 Thomas W. Smith; 251 Jacquelyn Vincent.
CD 4 — 14,918 Werner H. Fornos; 11,097 Charles S. Blumenthal; 8,221 Cecelia A. Fabula; 7,880 Charles G. McIntosh; 6,932 Casey Hughes; 1,382 Marvin O. Morris.
CD 5 — 31,478 Gladys N. Spellman; 8,275 Thomas J. Mooney; 3,550 Richard E. Lee.
CD 6 — 33,003 Goodloe E. Byron; 26,540 Dan Rupli.
CD 8 — 24,429 Lanny Davis; 19,897 Frank Mankiewicz; 16,690 Idamae T. Garrott; 14,247 Charles A. Docter; 11,677 Lucille Maurer; 1,481 John H. MacArthur; 870 John J. Seiden; 786 Robert R. Fustero; 531 George W. Benns; 440 Robert J. Roosevelt; 379 David Dunnell.

MASSACHUSETTS

GOVERNOR

Michael S. Dukakis (D). Elected 1974 to a four-year term.

SENATORS

Edward W. Brooke (R). Re-elected 1972 to a six-year term. Previously elected 1966.

Edward M. Kennedy (D). Re-elected 1976 to a six-year term. Previously elected 1970, 1964, and in 1962 to fill out term vacated by the resignation of Senator John F. Kennedy.

REPRESENTATIVES

1. Silvio O. Conte (R)
2. Edward P. Boland (D)
3. Joseph D. Early (D)
4. Robert F. Drinan (D)
5. Paul E. Tsongas (D)
6. Michael J. Harrington (D)
7. Edward J. Markey (D)
8. Thomas P. O'Neill (D)
9. John J. Moakley (D)
10. Margaret M. Heckler (R)
11. James A. Burke (D)
12. Gerry E. Studds (D)

POSTWAR VOTE FOR GOVERNOR

								Percentage			
	Total	Republican		Democratic		Other	Rep.-Dem.	Total Vote		Major Vote	
Year	Vote	Vote	Candidate	Vote	Candidate	Vote	Plurality	Rep.	Dem.	Rep.	Dem.
1974	1,854,798	784,353	Sargent, Francis W.	992,284	Dukakis, Michael S.	78,161	207,931 D	42.3%	53.5%	44.1%	55.9%
1970	1,867,906	1,058,623	Sargent, Francis W.	799,269	White, Kevin H.	10,014	259,354 R	56.7%	42.8%	57.0%	43.0%
1966	2,041,177	1,277,358	Volpe, John A.	752,720	McCormack, Edward J.	11,099	524,638 R	62.6%	36.9%	62.9%	37.1%
1964	2,340,130	1,176,462	Volpe, John A.	1,153,416	Bellotti, Francis X.	10,252	23,046 R	50.3%	49.3%	50.5%	49.5%
1962	2,109,089	1,047,891	Volpe, John A.	1,053,322	Peabody, Endicott	7,876	5,431 D	49.7%	49.9%	49.9%	50.1%
1960	2,417,133	1,269,295	Volpe, John A.	1,130,810	Ward, Joseph D.	17,028	138,485 R	52.5%	46.8%	52.9%	47.1%
1958	1,899,117	818,463	Gibbons, Charles	1,067,020	Furcolo, Foster	13,634	248,557 D	43.1%	56.2%	43.4%	56.6%
1956	2,339,884	1,096,759	Whittier, Sumner G.	1,234,618	Furcolo, Foster	8,507	137,859 D	46.9%	52.8%	47.0%	53.0%
1954	1,903,774	985,339	Herter, Christian A.	910,087	Murphy, Robert F.	8,348	75,252 R	51.8%	47.8%	52.0%	48.0%
1952	2,356,298	1,175,955	Herter, Christian A.	1,161,499	Dever, Paul A.	18,844	14,456 R	49.9%	49.3%	50.3%	49.7%
1950	1,910,180	824,069	Coolidge, Arthur W.	1,074,570	Dever, Paul A.	11,541	250,501 D	43.1%	56.3%	43.4%	56.6%
1948	2,099,250	849,895	Bradford, Robert F.	1,239,247	Dever, Paul A.	10,108	389,352 D	40.5%	59.0%	40.7%	59.3%
1946	1,683,452	911,152	Bradford, Robert F.	762,743	Tobin, Maurice	9,557	148,409 R	54.1%	45.3%	54.4%	45.6%

The term of office of Massachusetts' Governor was increased from two to four years effective with the 1966 election.

POSTWAR VOTE FOR SENATOR

								Percentage			
	Total	Republican		Democratic		Other	Rep.-Dem.	Total Vote		Major Vote	
Year	Vote	Vote	Candidate	Vote	Candidate	Vote	Plurality	Rep.	Dem.	Rep.	Dem.
1976	2,491,255	722,641	Robertson, Michael	1,726,657	Kennedy, Edward M.	41,957	1,004,016 D	29.0%	69.3%	29.5%	70.5%
1972	2,370,676	1,505,932	Brooke, Edward W.	823,278	Droney, John J.	41,466	682,654 R	63.5%	34.7%	64.7%	35.3%
1970	1,935,607	715,978	Spaulding, Josiah A.	1,202,856	Kennedy, Edward M.	16,773	486,878 D	37.0%	62.1%	37.3%	62.7%
1966	1,999,949	1,213,473	Brooke, Edward W.	774,761	Peabody, Endicott	11,715	438,712 R	60.7%	38.7%	61.0%	39.0%
1964	2,312,028	587,663	Whitmore, Howard	1,716,907	Kennedy, Edward M.	7,458	1,129,244 D	25.4%	74.3%	25.5%	74.5%
1962s	2,097,085	877,669	Lodge, George C.	1,162,611	Kennedy, Edward M.	56,805	284,942 D	41.9%	55.4%	43.0%	57.0%
1960	2,417,813	1,358,556	Saltonstall, Leverett	1,050,725	O'Connor, Thomas J.	8,532	307,831 R	56.2%	43.5%	56.4%	43.6%
1958	1,862,041	488,318	Celeste, Vincent J.	1,362,926	Kennedy, John F.	10,797	874,608 D	26.2%	73.2%	26.4%	73.6%
1954	1,892,710	956,605	Saltonstall, Leverett	927,899	Furcolo, Foster	8,206	28,706 R	50.5%	49.0%	50.8%	49.2%
1952	2,360,425	1,141,247	Lodge, Henry Cabot	1,211,984	Kennedy, John F.	7,194	70,737 D	48.3%	51.3%	48.5%	51.5%
1948	2,055,798	1,088,475	Saltonstall, Leverett	954,398	Fitzgerald, John I.	12,925	134,077 R	52.9%	46.4%	53.3%	46.7%
1946	1,662,063	989,736	Lodge, Henry Cabot	660,200	Walsh, David I.	12,127	329,536 R	59.5%	39.7%	60.0%	40.0%

The 1962 election was for a short term to fill a vacancy.

MASSACHUSETTS

Districts Established November 12, 1971

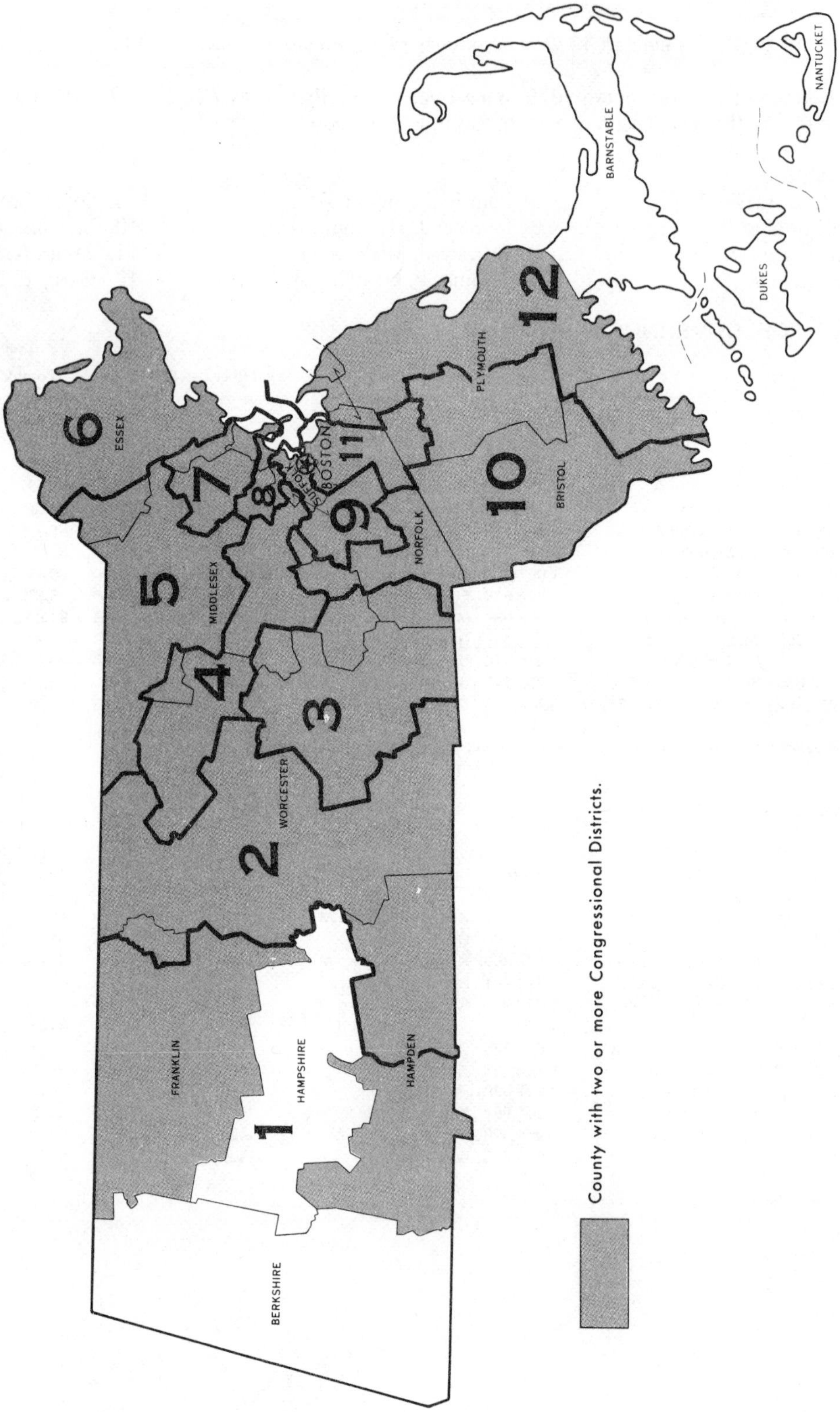

MASSACHUSETTS

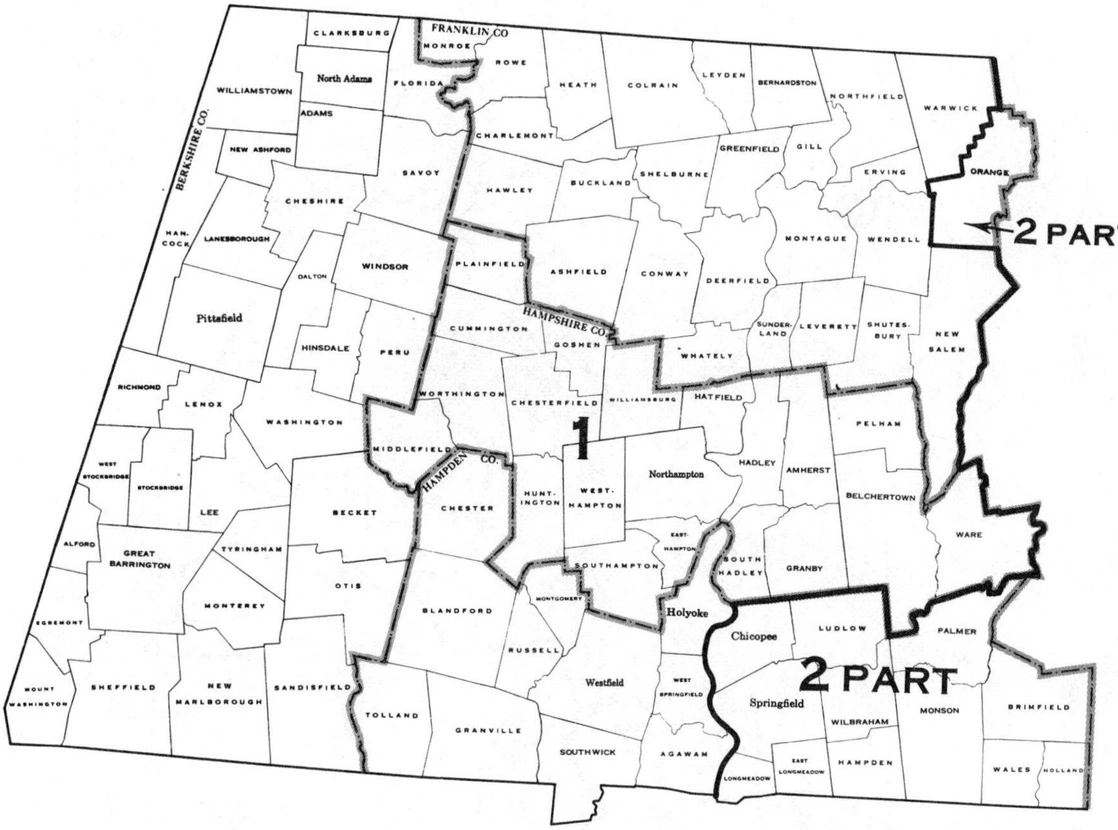

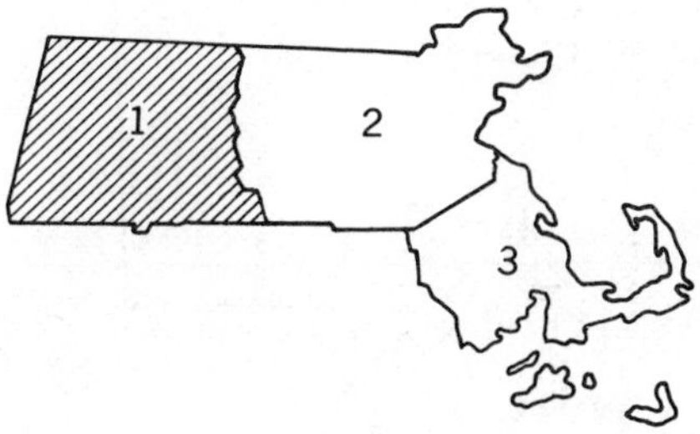

MASSACHUSETTS

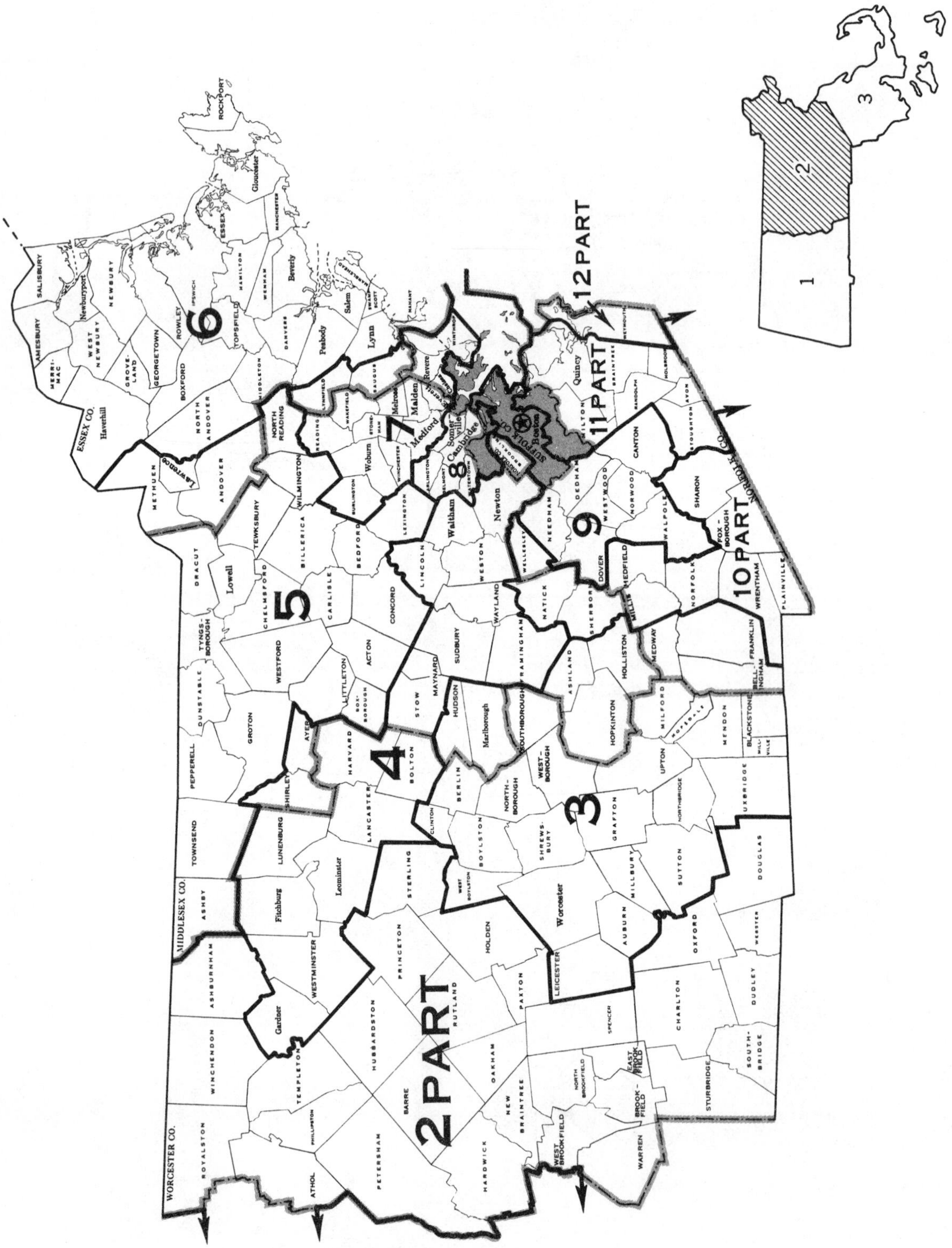

MASSACHUSETTS

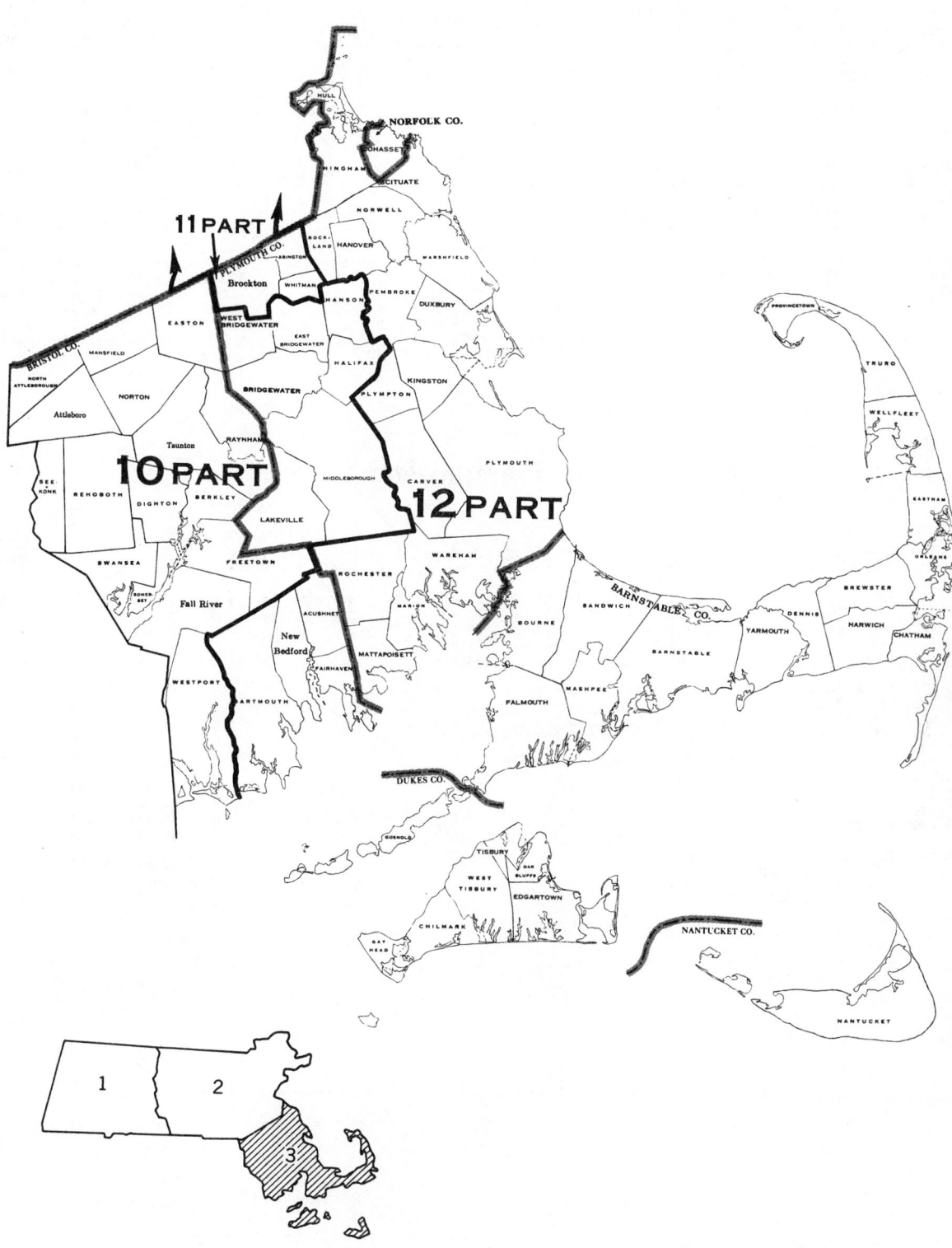

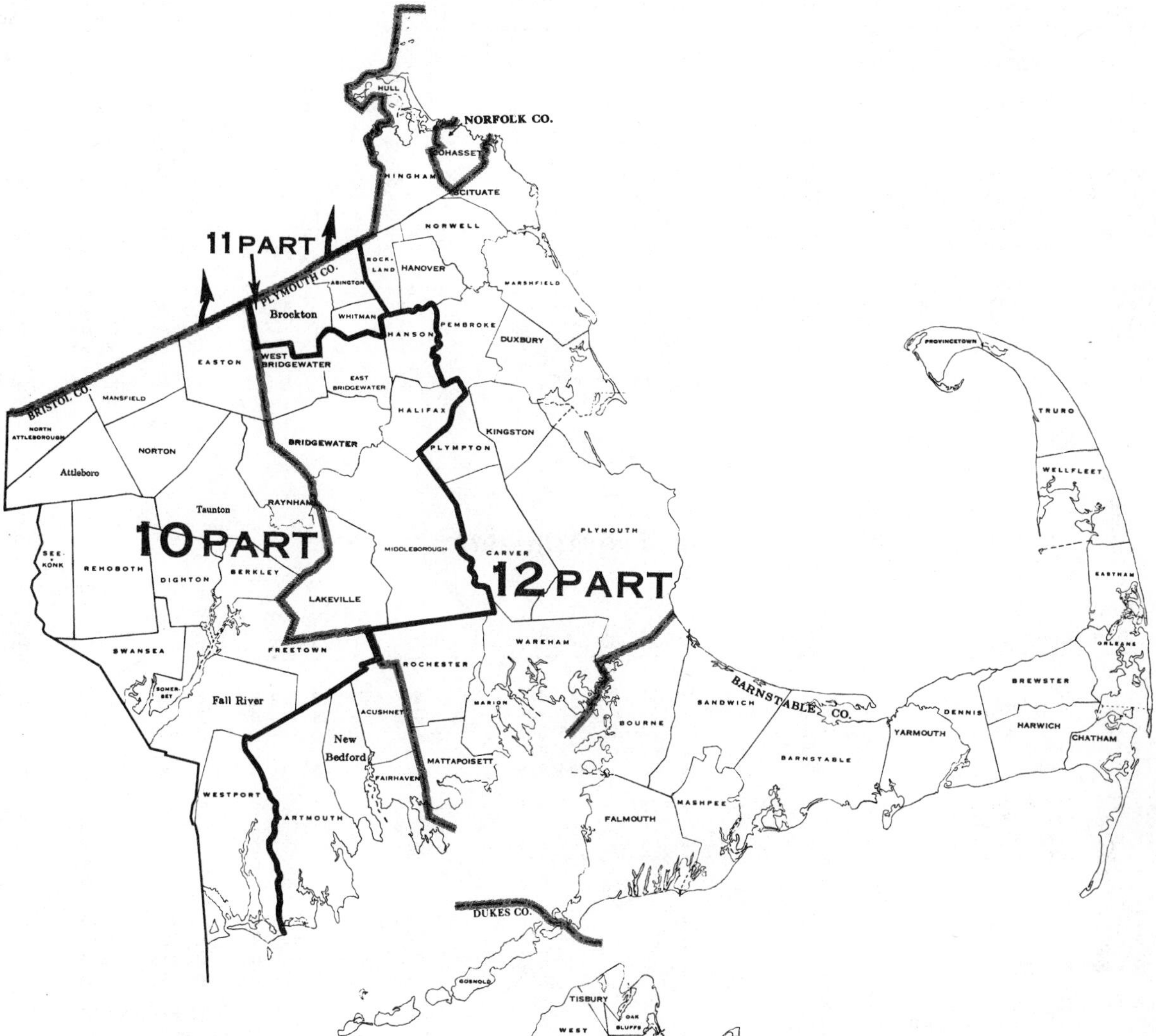

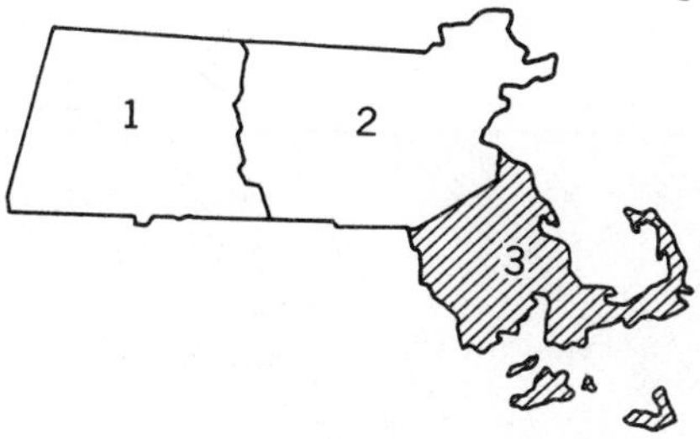

MASSACHUSETTS

PRESIDENT 1976

1970 Census Population	County	Total Vote	Republican	Democratic	Other	Rep.-Dem. Plurality	Percentage: Total Vote Rep.	Total Vote Dem.	Major Vote Rep.	Major Vote Dem.
96,656	BARNSTABLE	73,117	39,295	31,268	2,554	8,027 R	53.7%	42.8%	55.7%	44.3%
149,402	BERKSHIRE	68,871	27,462	39,337	2,072	11,875 D	39.9%	57.1%	41.1%	58.9%
444,301	BRISTOL	191,771	69,957	116,318	5,496	46,361 D	36.5%	60.7%	37.6%	62.4%
6,117	DUKES	5,135	2,365	2,513	257	148 D	46.1%	48.9%	48.5%	51.5%
637,887	ESSEX	301,444	125,538	165,710	10,196	40,172 D	41.6%	55.0%	43.1%	56.9%
59,210	FRANKLIN	31,181	14,837	14,985	1,359	148 D	47.6%	48.1%	49.8%	50.2%
459,050	HAMPDEN	185,290	70,008	110,028	5,254	40,020 D	37.8%	59.4%	38.9%	61.1%
123,981	HAMPSHIRE	60,075	22,219	34,947	2,909	12,728 D	37.0%	58.2%	38.9%	61.1%
1,397,268	MIDDLESEX	643,382	260,044	359,919	23,419	99,875 D	40.4%	55.9%	41.9%	58.1%
3,774	NANTUCKET	2,626	1,399	1,115	112	284 R	53.3%	42.5%	55.6%	44.4%
605,051	NORFOLK	302,616	136,628	155,342	10,646	18,714 D	45.1%	51.3%	46.8%	53.2%
333,314	PLYMOUTH	164,433	74,684	83,663	6,086	8,979 D	45.4%	50.9%	47.2%	52.8%
735,190	SUFFOLK	232,372	80,623	142,010	9,739	61,387 D	34.7%	61.1%	36.2%	63.8%
637,969	WORCESTER	285,245	105,217	172,320	7,708	67,103 D	36.9%	60.4%	37.9%	62.1%
5,689,170	TOTAL	2,547,558	1,030,276	1,429,475	87,807	399,199 D	40.4%	56.1%	41.9%	58.1%

SENATOR 1976

1970 Census Population	County	Total Vote	Republican	Democratic	Other	Rep.-Dem. Plurality	Percentage: Total Vote Rep.	Total Vote Dem.	Major Vote Rep.	Major Vote Dem.
96,656	BARNSTABLE	71,804	29,064	41,833	907	12,769 D	40.5%	58.3%	41.0%	59.0%
149,402	BERKSHIRE	67,222	18,361	47,806	1,055	29,445 D	27.3%	71.1%	27.7%	72.3%
444,301	BRISTOL	188,293	49,774	136,040	2,479	86,266 D	26.4%	72.2%	26.8%	73.2%
6,117	DUKES	5,028	1,567	3,320	141	1,753 D	31.2%	66.0%	32.1%	67.9%
637,887	ESSEX	295,311	84,255	206,996	4,060	122,741 D	28.5%	70.1%	28.9%	71.1%
59,210	FRANKLIN	30,719	9,625	20,385	709	10,760 D	31.3%	66.4%	32.1%	67.9%
459,050	HAMPDEN	180,452	53,122	124,231	3,099	71,109 D	29.4%	68.8%	30.0%	70.0%
123,981	HAMPSHIRE	59,003	16,195	41,226	1,582	25,031 D	27.4%	69.9%	28.2%	71.8%
1,397,268	MIDDLESEX	632,765	172,859	448,237	11,669	275,378 D	27.3%	70.8%	27.8%	72.2%
3,774	NANTUCKET	2,573	891	1,623	59	732 D	34.6%	63.1%	35.4%	64.6%
605,051	NORFOLK	295,872	98,847	192,432	4,593	93,585 D	33.4%	65.0%	33.9%	66.1%
333,314	PLYMOUTH	160,803	55,049	103,549	2,205	48,500 D	34.2%	64.4%	34.7%	65.3%
735,190	SUFFOLK	219,476	58,394	155,204	5,878	96,810 D	26.6%	70.7%	27.3%	72.7%
637,969	WORCESTER	281,934	74,638	203,775	3,521	129,137 D	26.5%	72.3%	26.8%	73.2%
5,689,170	TOTAL	2,491,255	722,641	1,726,657	41,957	1,004,016 D	29.0%	69.3%	29.5%	70.5%

MASSACHUSETTS

PRESIDENT 1976

1970 Census Population	City/Town	Total Vote	Republican	Democratic	Other	Rep.-Dem. Plurality	Percentage Total Vote Rep.	Percentage Total Vote Dem.	Percentage Major Vote Rep.	Percentage Major Vote Dem.
21,717	AGAWAM	10,400	4,032	6,090	278	2,058 D	38.8%	58.6%	39.8%	60.2%
26,331	AMHERST	11,091	3,254	6,848	989	3,594 D	29.3%	61.7%	32.2%	67.8%
23,695	ANDOVER	13,095	7,214	5,464	417	1,750 R	55.1%	41.7%	56.9%	43.1%
53,524	ARLINGTON	27,849	11,353	15,530	966	4,177 D	40.8%	55.8%	42.2%	57.8%
32,907	ATTLEBORO	12,381	5,903	6,073	405	170 D	47.7%	49.1%	49.3%	50.7%
28,285	BELMONT	16,158	7,750	7,854	554	104 D	48.0%	48.6%	49.7%	50.3%
38,348	BEVERLY	19,053	9,027	9,399	627	372 D	47.4%	49.3%	49.0%	51.0%
31,648	BILLERICA	13,593	5,199	7,964	430	2,765 D	38.2%	58.6%	39.5%	60.5%
641,071	BOSTON	191,648	67,604	115,802	8,242	48,198 D	35.3%	60.4%	36.9%	63.1%
35,050	BRAINTREE	18,555	8,242	9,695	618	1,453 D	44.4%	52.3%	45.9%	54.1%
89,040	BROCKTON	33,413	12,661	19,421	1,331	6,760 D	37.9%	58.1%	39.5%	60.5%
58,886	BROOKLINE	28,579	11,407	15,874	1,298	4,467 D	39.9%	55.5%	41.8%	58.2%
21,980	BURLINGTON	10,511	4,259	5,919	333	1,660 D	40.5%	56.3%	41.8%	58.2%
100,361	CAMBRIDGE	42,308	10,424	29,052	2,832	18,628 D	24.6%	68.7%	26.4%	73.6%
31,432	CHELMSFORD	15,468	7,610	7,408	450	202 R	49.2%	47.9%	50.7%	49.3%
30,625	CHELSEA	10,937	2,824	7,724	389	4,900 D	25.8%	70.6%	26.8%	73.2%
66,676	CHICOPEE	26,114	7,496	17,874	744	10,378 D	28.7%	68.4%	29.5%	70.5%
26,151	DANVERS	11,801	5,553	5,786	462	233 D	47.1%	49.0%	49.0%	51.0%
26,938	DEDHAM	13,473	6,137	6,853	483	716 D	45.6%	50.9%	47.2%	52.8%
42,485	EVERETT	17,872	5,649	11,599	624	5,950 D	31.6%	64.9%	32.8%	67.2%
96,898	FALL RIVER	37,077	10,065	26,126	886	16,061 D	27.1%	70.5%	27.8%	72.2%
43,343	FITCHBURG	16,848	4,582	11,891	375	7,309 D	27.2%	70.6%	27.8%	72.2%
64,048	FRAMINGHAM	30,050	13,903	15,387	760	1,484 D	46.3%	51.2%	47.5%	52.5%
27,941	GLOUCESTER	12,820	5,582	6,795	443	1,213 D	43.5%	53.0%	45.1%	54.9%
46,120	HAVERHILL	20,091	7,347	12,227	517	4,880 D	36.6%	60.9%	37.5%	62.5%
50,112	HOLYOKE	19,231	6,653	11,955	623	5,302 D	34.6%	62.2%	35.8%	64.2%
66,915	LAWRENCE	25,996	5,996	19,245	755	13,249 D	23.1%	74.0%	23.8%	76.2%
32,939	LEOMINSTER	14,609	4,833	9,399	377	4,566 D	33.1%	64.3%	34.0%	66.0%
31,886	LEXINGTON	16,925	7,814	8,494	617	680 D	46.2%	50.2%	47.9%	52.1%
94,239	LOWELL	36,880	11,328	24,609	943	13,281 D	30.7%	66.7%	31.5%	68.5%
90,294	LYNN	34,432	11,580	21,430	1,422	9,850 D	33.6%	62.2%	35.1%	64.9%
56,127	MALDEN	25,134	8,503	15,346	1,285	6,843 D	33.8%	61.1%	35.7%	64.3%
21,295	MARBLEHEAD	12,749	7,311	5,014	424	2,297 R	57.3%	39.3%	59.3%	40.7%
27,936	MARLBOROUGH	13,309	5,189	7,700	420	2,511 D	39.0%	57.9%	40.3%	59.7%
64,397	MEDFORD	29,096	9,918	18,236	942	8,318 D	34.1%	62.7%	35.2%	64.8%
33,180	MELROSE	15,835	7,916	7,440	479	476 R	50.0%	47.0%	51.5%	48.5%
35,456	METHUEN	17,663	5,767	11,476	420	5,709 D	32.7%	65.0%	33.4%	66.6%
27,190	MILTON	15,402	7,526	7,400	476	126 R	48.9%	48.0%	50.4%	49.6%
31,057	NATICK	14,776	6,973	7,281	522	308 D	47.2%	49.3%	48.9%	51.1%
29,748	NEEDHAM	16,612	9,381	6,695	536	2,686 R	56.5%	40.3%	58.4%	41.6%
101,777	NEW BEDFORD	37,741	11,122	25,543	1,076	14,421 D	29.5%	67.7%	30.3%	69.7%
91,066	NEWTON	45,266	18,372	25,116	1,778	6,744 D	40.6%	55.5%	42.2%	57.8%
29,664	NORTHAMPTON	13,466	4,944	7,848	674	2,904 D	36.7%	58.3%	38.6%	61.4%
30,815	NORWOOD	14,986	6,297	8,213	476	1,916 D	42.0%	54.8%	43.4%	56.6%
48,080	PEABODY	22,177	7,774	13,610	793	5,836 D	35.1%	61.4%	36.4%	63.6%
57,020	PITTSFIELD	25,238	9,575	14,907	756	5,332 D	37.9%	59.1%	39.1%	60.9%
87,966	QUINCY	43,263	17,622	24,082	1,559	6,460 D	40.7%	55.7%	42.3%	57.7%
27,035	RANDOLPH	13,647	4,781	8,352	514	3,571 D	35.0%	61.2%	36.4%	63.6%
22,539	READING	11,905	6,401	5,077	427	1,324 R	53.8%	42.6%	55.8%	44.2%
43,159	REVERE	19,954	6,093	13,105	756	7,012 D	30.5%	65.7%	31.7%	68.3%
40,556	SALEM	18,405	6,072	11,474	859	5,402 D	33.0%	62.3%	34.6%	65.4%
25,110	SAUGUS	12,343	4,800	7,172	371	2,372 D	38.9%	58.1%	40.1%	59.9%
88,779	SOMERVILLE	31,199	8,444	21,312	1,443	12,868 D	27.1%	68.3%	28.4%	71.6%
163,905	SPRINGFIELD	53,043	17,959	33,533	1,551	15,574 D	33.9%	63.2%	34.9%	65.1%
20,725	STONEHAM	10,380	4,512	5,461	407	949 D	43.5%	52.6%	45.2%	54.8%
23,459	STOUGHTON	10,998	4,323	6,327	348	2,004 D	39.3%	57.5%	40.6%	59.4%
43,756	TAUNTON	17,966	6,049	11,329	588	5,280 D	33.7%	63.1%	34.8%	65.2%
22,755	TEWKSBURY	10,145	3,932	5,923	290	1,991 D	38.8%	58.4%	39.9%	60.1%
25,402	WAKEFIELD	12,983	5,761	6,726	496	965 D	44.4%	51.8%	46.1%	53.9%
61,582	WALTHAM	23,679	9,439	13,552	688	4,113 D	39.9%	57.2%	41.1%	58.9%
39,307	WATERTOWN	17,689	6,177	10,753	759	4,576 D	34.9%	60.8%	36.5%	63.5%
28,051	WELLESLEY	14,783	8,878	5,422	483	3,456 R	60.1%	36.7%	62.1%	37.9%
28,461	WEST SPRINGFIELD	12,343	5,380	6,628	335	1,248 D	43.6%	53.7%	44.8%	55.2%
31,433	WESTFIELD	15,009	5,998	8,587	424	2,589 D	40.0%	57.2%	41.1%	58.9%
54,610	WEYMOUTH	25,395	10,682	13,582	1,131	2,900 D	42.1%	53.5%	44.0%	56.0%
22,269	WINCHESTER	11,260	6,006	4,868	386	1,138 R	53.3%	43.2%	55.2%	44.8%
20,335	WINTHROP	9,833	4,102	5,379	352	1,277 D	41.7%	54.7%	43.3%	56.7%
37,406	WOBURN	16,959	5,901	10,493	565	4,592 D	34.8%	61.9%	36.0%	64.0%
176,572	WORCESTER CITY	68,669	21,992	44,723	1,954	22,731 D	32.0%	65.1%	33.0%	67.0%

MASSACHUSETTS

SENATOR 1976

1970 Census Population	City/Town	Total Vote	Republican	Democratic	Other	Rep.-Dem. Plurality	Percentage Total Vote Rep.	Total Vote Dem.	Major Vote Rep.	Major Vote Dem.
21,717	AGAWAM	10,013	2,868	6,968	177	4,100 D	28.6%	69.6%	29.2%	70.8%
26,331	AMHERST	10,599	2,128	7,822	649	5,694 D	20.1%	73.8%	21.4%	78.6%
23,695	ANDOVER	12,708	5,168	7,389	151	2,221 D	40.7%	58.1%	41.2%	58.8%
53,524	ARLINGTON	27,608	7,621	19,535	452	11,914 D	27.6%	70.8%	28.1%	71.9%
32,907	ATTLEBORO	11,827	3,988	7,654	185	3,666 D	33.7%	64.7%	34.3%	65.7%
28,285	BELMONT	16,022	5,240	10,522	260	5,282 D	32.7%	65.7%	33.2%	66.8%
38,348	BEVERLY	18,878	5,761	12,907	210	7,146 D	30.5%	68.4%	30.9%	69.1%
31,648	BILLERICA	12,983	3,539	9,204	240	5,665 D	27.3%	70.9%	27.8%	72.2%
641,071	BOSTON	180,571	50,609	124,899	5,063	74,290 D	28.0%	69.2%	28.8%	71.2%
35,050	BRAINTREE	18,404	6,681	11,431	292	4,750 D	36.3%	62.1%	36.9%	63.1%
89,040	BROCKTON	31,927	9,037	22,370	520	13,333 D	28.3%	70.1%	28.8%	71.2%
58,886	BROOKLINE	27,939	6,550	20,818	571	14,268 D	23.4%	74.5%	23.9%	76.1%
21,980	BURLINGTON	10,316	2,751	7,377	188	4,626 D	26.7%	71.5%	27.2%	72.8%
100,361	CAMBRIDGE	41,724	6,048	33,699	1,977	27,651 D	14.5%	80.8%	15.2%	84.8%
31,432	CHELMSFORD	15,342	5,357	9,784	201	4,427 D	34.9%	63.8%	35.4%	64.6%
30,625	CHELSEA	10,741	1,636	8,860	245	7,224 D	15.2%	82.5%	15.6%	84.4%
66,676	CHICOPEE	25,879	6,176	19,188	515	13,012 D	23.9%	74.1%	24.3%	75.7%
26,151	DANVERS	11,246	3,741	7,358	147	3,617 D	33.3%	65.4%	33.7%	66.3%
26,938	DEDHAM	12,920	4,728	7,932	260	3,204 D	36.6%	61.4%	37.3%	62.7%
42,485	EVERETT	17,270	3,625	13,212	433	9,587 D	21.0%	76.5%	21.5%	78.5%
96,898	FALL RIVER	36,416	5,338	30,629	449	25,291 D	14.7%	84.1%	14.8%	85.2%
43,343	FITCHBURG	16,599	3,287	13,155	157	9,868 D	19.8%	79.3%	20.0%	80.0%
64,048	FRAMINGHAM	29,933	9,039	20,637	257	11,598 D	30.2%	68.9%	30.5%	69.5%
27,941	GLOUCESTER	12,659	3,356	9,144	159	5,788 D	26.5%	72.2%	26.8%	73.2%
46,120	HAVERHILL	19,907	4,536	15,137	234	10,601 D	22.8%	76.0%	23.1%	76.9%
50,112	HOLYOKE	18,346	4,737	13,209	400	8,472 D	25.8%	72.0%	26.4%	73.6%
66,915	LAWRENCE	25,730	4,031	21,205	494	17,174 D	15.7%	82.4%	16.0%	84.0%
32,939	LEOMINSTER	13,761	3,274	10,376	111	7,102 D	23.8%	75.4%	24.0%	76.0%
31,886	LEXINGTON	16,576	5,442	10,864	270	5,422 D	32.8%	65.5%	33.4%	66.6%
94,239	LOWELL	36,458	7,083	28,898	477	21,815 D	19.4%	79.3%	19.7%	80.3%
90,294	LYNN	32,776	7,780	24,451	545	16,671 D	23.7%	74.6%	24.1%	75.9%
56,127	MALDEN	24,556	5,024	19,117	415	14,093 D	20.5%	77.9%	20.8%	79.2%
21,295	MARBLEHEAD	12,635	4,990	7,523	122	2,533 D	39.5%	59.5%	39.9%	60.1%
27,936	MARLBOROUGH	13,246	3,267	9,809	170	6,542 D	24.7%	74.1%	25.0%	75.0%
64,397	MEDFORD	28,744	6,525	21,652	567	15,127 D	22.7%	75.3%	23.2%	76.8%
33,180	MELROSE	15,534	5,571	9,733	230	4,162 D	35.9%	62.7%	36.4%	63.6%
35,456	METHUEN	17,524	4,132	13,138	254	9,006 D	23.6%	75.0%	23.9%	76.1%
27,190	MILTON	15,184	5,569	9,449	166	3,880 D	36.7%	62.2%	37.1%	62.9%
31,057	NATICK	14,535	4,712	9,611	212	4,899 D	32.4%	66.1%	32.9%	67.1%
29,748	NEEDHAM	15,895	6,868	8,815	212	1,947 D	43.2%	55.5%	43.8%	56.2%
101,777	NEW BEDFORD	37,278	7,963	28,709	606	20,746 D	21.4%	77.0%	21.7%	78.3%
91,066	NEWTON	44,366	10,790	32,877	699	22,087 D	24.3%	74.1%	24.7%	75.3%
29,664	NORTHAMPTON	13,296	3,329	9,647	320	6,318 D	25.0%	72.6%	25.7%	74.3%
30,815	NORWOOD	14,885	4,433	10,247	205	5,814 D	29.8%	68.8%	30.2%	69.8%
48,080	PEABODY	21,963	4,900	16,765	298	11,865 D	22.3%	76.3%	22.6%	77.4%
57,020	PITTSFIELD	24,492	6,463	17,620	409	11,157 D	26.4%	71.9%	26.8%	73.2%
87,966	QUINCY	42,756	13,675	28,297	784	14,622 D	32.0%	66.2%	32.6%	67.4%
27,035	RANDOLPH	13,006	3,124	9,671	211	6,547 D	24.0%	74.4%	24.4%	75.6%
22,539	READING	11,397	4,533	6,695	169	2,162 D	39.8%	58.7%	40.4%	59.6%
43,159	REVERE	18,588	3,608	14,568	412	10,960 D	19.4%	78.4%	19.9%	80.1%
40,556	SALEM	17,415	3,532	13,636	247	10,104 D	20.3%	78.3%	20.6%	79.4%
25,110	SAUGUS	12,279	3,539	8,557	183	5,018 D	28.8%	69.7%	29.3%	70.7%
88,779	SOMERVILLE	30,861	5,484	24,325	1,052	18,841 D	17.8%	78.8%	18.4%	81.6%
163,905	SPRINGFIELD	50,879	12,887	36,992	1,000	24,105 D	25.3%	72.7%	25.8%	74.2%
20,725	STONEHAM	9,924	2,988	6,778	158	3,790 D	30.1%	68.3%	30.6%	69.4%
23,459	STOUGHTON	10,622	2,948	7,451	223	4,503 D	27.8%	70.1%	28.3%	71.7%
43,756	TAUNTON	17,871	5,795	11,937	139	6,142 D	32.4%	66.8%	32.7%	67.3%
22,755	TEWKSBURY	10,066	2,672	7,254	140	4,582 D	26.5%	72.1%	26.9%	73.1%
25,402	WAKEFIELD	12,410	3,884	8,353	173	4,469 D	31.3%	67.3%	31.7%	68.3%
61,582	WALTHAM	23,004	5,508	17,075	421	11,567 D	23.9%	74.2%	24.4%	75.6%
39,307	WATERTOWN	17,365	3,845	13,155	365	9,310 D	22.1%	75.8%	22.6%	77.4%
28,051	WELLESLEY	14,204	6,619	7,430	155	811 D	46.6%	52.3%	47.1%	52.9%
28,461	WEST SPRINGFIELD	11,975	4,233	7,574	168	3,341 D	35.3%	63.2%	35.9%	64.1%
31,433	WESTFIELD	14,845	4,524	10,109	212	5,585 D	30.5%	68.1%	30.9%	69.1%
54,610	WEYMOUTH	24,033	8,062	15,501	470	7,439 D	33.5%	64.5%	34.2%	65.8%
22,269	WINCHESTER	11,056	4,155	6,739	162	2,584 D	37.6%	61.0%	38.1%	61.9%
20,335	WINTHROP	9,576	2,541	6,877	158	4,336 D	26.5%	71.8%	27.0%	73.0%
37,406	WOBURN	16,788	3,869	12,587	332	8,718 D	23.0%	75.0%	23.5%	76.5%
176,572	WORCESTER CITY	68,161	15,343	51,853	965	36,510 D	22.5%	76.1%	22.8%	77.2%

MASSACHUSETTS

CONGRESS

CD	Year	Total Vote	Republican Vote	Republican Candidate	Democratic Vote	Democratic Candidate	Other Vote	Rep.-Dem. Plurality	Percentage Total Vote Rep.	Percentage Total Vote Dem.	Percentage Major Vote Rep.	Percentage Major Vote Dem.
1	1976	215,870	137,652	CONTE, SILVIO O.	78,181	MCCOLGAN, EDWARD A.	37	59,471 R	63.8%	36.2%	63.8%	36.2%
1	1974	150,816	107,285	CONTE, SILVIO O.	43,524	MANNING, THOMAS R.	7	63,761 R	71.1%	28.9%	71.1%	28.9%
1	1972	159,429	159,282	CONTE, SILVIO O.			147	159,282 R	99.9%		100.0%	
2	1976	185,755	41,563	SWANK, THOMAS P.	134,408	BOLAND, EDWARD P.	9,784	92,845 D	22.4%	72.4%	23.6%	76.4%
2	1974	105,793			105,763	BOLAND, EDWARD P.	30	105,763 D		100.0%		100.0%
2	1972	137,625			137,616	BOLAND, EDWARD P.	9	137,616 D		100.0%		100.0%
3	1976	168,568			168,520	EARLY, JOSEPH D.	48	168,520 D		100.0%		100.0%
3	1974	158,120	60,717	LIONETT, DAVID J.	78,244	EARLY, JOSEPH D.	19,159	17,527 D	38.4%	49.5%	43.7%	56.3%
3	1972	156,839			156,703	DONOHUE, HAROLD D.	136	156,703 D		99.9%		100.0%
4	1976	209,835	100,562	MASON, ARTHUR D.	109,268	DRINAN, ROBERT F.	5	8,706 D	47.9%	52.1%	47.9%	52.1%
4	1974	151,996	21,922	MANDELL, ALVIN	77,286	DRINAN, ROBERT F.	52,788	55,364 D	14.4%	50.8%	22.1%	77.9%
4	1972	205,047	93,927	LINSKY, MARTIN A.	99,977	DRINAN, ROBERT F.	11,143	6,050 D	45.8%	48.8%	48.4%	51.6%
5	1976	214,263	70,036	DURKIN, ROGER P.	144,217	TSONGAS, PAUL E.	10	74,181 D	32.7%	67.3%	32.7%	67.3%
5	1974	164,117	64,596	CRONIN, PAUL W.	99,518	TSONGAS, PAUL E.	3	34,922 D	39.4%	60.6%	39.4%	60.6%
5	1972	207,623	110,970	CRONIN, PAUL W.	92,847	KERRY, JOHN F.	3,806	18,123 R	53.4%	44.7%	54.4%	45.6%
6	1976	221,813	91,655	BRONSON, WILLIAM E.	121,562	HARRINGTON, MICHAEL J.	8,596	29,907 D	41.3%	54.8%	43.0%	57.0%
6	1974	119,301			119,278	HARRINGTON, MICHAEL J.	23	119,278 D		100.0%		100.0%
6	1972	218,078	78,381	MOSELEY, JAMES B.	139,697	HARRINGTON, MICHAEL J.		61,316 D	35.9%	64.1%	35.9%	64.1%
7	1976	210,809	37,063	DALY, RICHARD W.	162,126	MARKEY, EDWARD J.	11,620	125,063 D	17.6%	76.9%	18.6%	81.4%
7	1974	153,127			122,165	MACDONALD, TORBERT	30,962	122,165 D		79.8%		100.0%
7	1972	199,562	64,357	ALIBERTI, JOAN M.	135,193	MACDONALD, TORBERT	12	70,836 D	32.2%	67.7%	32.3%	67.7%
8	1976	178,850	33,437	BARNSTEAD, WILLIAM A.	133,131	O NEILL, THOMAS P.	12,282	99,694 D	18.7%	74.4%	20.1%	79.9%
8	1974	121,845			107,042	O NEILL, THOMAS P.	14,803	107,042 D		87.9%		100.0%
8	1972	160,687			142,470	O NEILL, THOMAS P.	18,217	142,470 D		88.7%		100.0%
9	1976	149,371	34,547	CUNNINGHAM, ROBERT G.	103,901	MOAKLEY, JOHN J.	10,923	69,354 D	23.1%	69.6%	25.0%	75.0%
9	1974	106,158			94,804	MOAKLEY, JOHN J.	11,354	94,804 D		89.3%		100.0%
9	1972	163,288	23,177	MILLER, HOWARD M.	67,143	HICKS, LOUISE DAY	72,968	43,966 D	14.2%	41.1%	25.7%	74.3%
10	1976	176,691	176,604	HECKLER, MARGARET M.			87	176,604 R	100.0%		100.0%	
10	1974	155,868	99,993	HECKLER, MARGARET M.	55,871	MONAHAN, BARRY F.	4	44,122 R	64.2%	35.8%	64.2%	35.8%
10	1972	161,765	161,708	HECKLER, MARGARET M.			57	161,708 R	100.0%		100.0%	
11	1976	191,055			131,789	BURKE, JAMES A.	59,266	131,789 D		69.0%		100.0%
11	1974	125,991			125,978	BURKE, JAMES A.	13	125,978 D		100.0%		100.0%
11	1972	154,453			154,397	BURKE, JAMES A.	56	154,397 D		100.0%		100.0%
12	1976	222,504			222,418	STUDDS, GERRY E.	86	222,418 D		100.0%		100.0%
12	1974	185,569	46,787	MACKAY, J. ALAN	138,779	STUDDS, GERRY E.	3	91,992 D	25.2%	74.8%	25.2%	74.8%
12	1972	234,305	116,592	WEEKS, WILLIAM D.	117,710	STUDDS, GERRY E.	3	1,118 D	49.8%	50.2%	49.8%	50.2%

MASSACHUSETTS

1976 GENERAL ELECTION

In addition to the county-by-county figures, 1976 data are presented for selected Massachusetts communities. Since not all jurisdictions of the state are listed in this special tabulation, state-wide totals are shown only with the county-by-county statistics.

President	Other vote was 65,637 McCarthy (Independent); 8,138 Camejo (Socialist Workers); 7,555 Anderson (American); 4,922 LaRouche (U.S. Labor); 135 MacBride (write-in); 33 Wright (write-in); 19 Levin (write-in); 14 Bubar (write-in); 1,354 scattered.
Senator	Other vote was 26,283 Evans (Socialist Workers); 15,517 Lowry (U.S. Labor); 157 scattered.
Congress	John J. Moakley, the Democratic candidate in CD 9, was previously elected as an Independent in that district in 1972. Other vote was scattered in CD's 1, 3, 4, 5, 10 and 12; 9,776 McCarthy (U.S. Labor) and 8 scattered in CD 2; 8,589 McGowan (Independent) and 7 scattered in CD 6; 59,240 DeBenedictis (Independent) and 26 scattered in CD 11; in other CD's as follows:
CD 7	6,851 Murphy (Independent); 4,748 Chickles (Independent); 21 scattered.
CD 8	8,233 DiDonato (Independent); 4,022 Kahian (American) and 27 scattered.
CD 9	7,862 O'Loughlin (Independent); 3,058 MacWarren (Socialist Workers); 3 scattered.

1976 PRIMARIES

SEPTEMBER 14 REPUBLICAN

Senator	Michael Robertson, unopposed.
Congress	Unopposed in seven CD's. No candidates in CD's 3, 11 and 12. Contested as follows:
CD 6	7,479 William E. Bronson; 4,965 George C. Vlahos; 2 scattered.
CD 7	No candidates appeared on the ballot; there were 2,015 write-in votes for Richard W. Daly and 33 scattered.

SEPTEMBER 14 DEMOCRATIC

Senator	534,725 Edward M. Kennedy; 117,496 Robert E. Dinsmore; 59,315 Frederick C. Langone; 12,399 Bernard Shannon; 53 scattered.
Congress	Unopposed in five CD's. No candidate in CD 10. Contested as follows:
CD 1	19,694 Edward A. McColgan; 19,681 Edward M. O'Brien; 23 scattered.
CD 7	22,137 Edward J. Markey; 16,298 Joseph E. Croken; 13,797 Vincent LoPresti; 13,757 Stephen McGrail; 12,838 George R. McCarthy; 5,989 William G. Reinstein; 5,143 William F. Hogan; 5,083 Robert F. Donovan; 4,266 Jack Leff; 1,759 Robert S. Leo; 852 Rose Marie Turino; 756 Bartholomew J. Conte; 1 scattered.
CD 8	51,406 Thomas P. O'Neill; 22,298 Edward F. Galotti; 4 scattered.
CD 9	39,291 John J. Moakley; 19,125 Robert O. Flynn; 2 scattered.
CD 11	39,872 James A. Burke; 29,722 Patrick H. McCarthy; 5 scattered.
CD 12	49,919 Gerry E. Studds; 9,133 Edmund Dinis; 6 scattered.

MICHIGAN

GOVERNOR

William G. Milliken (R). Re-elected 1974 to a four-year term. Previously elected 1970; as Lieutenant Governor became Governor January 1969 on the resignation of Governor George W. Romney.

SENATORS

Robert P. Griffin (R). Re-elected 1972 to a six-year term. Previously elected 1966; had been appointed May 1966 to fill out term vacated by the death of Senator Patrick V. McNamara.

Donald W. Riegle (D). Elected 1976 to a six-year term.

REPRESENTATIVES

1. John Conyers (D)
2. Carl D. Pursell (R)
3. Garry Brown (R)
4. Dave Stockman (R)
5. Harold S. Sawyer (R)
6. M. Robert Carr (D)
7. Dale E. Kildee (D)
8. J. Robert Traxler (D)
9. Guy Vander Jagt (R)
10. Elford A. Cederberg (R)
11. Philip E. Ruppe (R)
12. David E. Bonior (D)
13. Charles C. Diggs (D)
14. Lucien N. Nedzi (D)
15. William D. Ford (D)
16. John D. Dingell, Jr. (D)
17. William M. Brodhead (D)
18. James J. Blanchard (D)
19. William S. Broomfield (R)

POSTWAR VOTE FOR GOVERNOR

								Percentage			
	Total	Republican		Democratic		Other	Rep.-Dem.	Total Vote		Major Vote	
Year	Vote	Vote	Candidate	Vote	Candidate	Vote	Plurality	Rep.	Dem.	Rep.	Dem.
1974	2,657,017	1,356,865	Milliken, William G.	1,242,247	Levin, Sander	57,905	114,618 R	51.1%	46.8%	52.2%	47.8%
1970	2,656,162	1,339,047	Milliken, William G.	1,294,638	Levin, Sander	22,477	44,409 R	50.4%	48.7%	50.8%	49.2%
1966	2,461,909	1,490,430	Romney, George W.	963,383	Ferency, Zoltan A.	8,096	527,047 R	60.5%	39.1%	60.7%	39.3%
1964	3,158,102	1,764,355	Romney, George W.	1,381,442	Staebler, Neil	12,305	382,913 R	55.9%	43.7%	56.1%	43.9%
1962	2,764,839	1,420,086	Romney, George W.	1,339,513	Swainson, John B.	5,240	80,573 R	51.4%	48.4%	51.5%	48.5%
1960	3,255,991	1,602,022	Bagwell, Paul D.	1,643,634	Swainson, John B.	10,335	41,612 D	49.2%	50.5%	49.4%	50.6%
1958	2,312,184	1,078,089	Bagwell, Paul D.	1,225,533	Williams, G. Mennen	8,562	147,444 D	46.6%	53.0%	46.8%	53.2%
1956	3,049,651	1,376,376	Cobo, Albert E.	1,666,689	Williams, G. Mennen	6,586	290,313 D	45.1%	54.7%	45.2%	54.8%
1954	2,187,027	963,300	Leonard, Donald S.	1,216,308	Williams, G. Mennen	7,419	253,008 D	44.0%	55.6%	44.2%	55.8%
1952	2,865,980	1,423,275	Alger, Fred M.	1,431,893	Williams, G. Mennen	10,812	8,618 D	49.7%	50.0%	49.8%	50.2%
1950	1,879,382	933,998	Kelly, Harry F.	935,152	Williams, G. Mennen	10,232	1,154 D	49.7%	49.8%	50.0%	50.0%
1948	2,113,122	964,810	Sigler, Kim	1,128,664	Williams, G. Mennen	19,648	163,854 D	45.7%	53.4%	46.1%	53.9%
1946	1,665,475	1,003,878	Sigler, Kim	644,540	Van Wagoner, Murray	17,057	359,338 R	60.3%	38.7%	60.9%	39.1%

The term of office of Michigan's Governor was increased from two to four years effective with the 1966 election.

POSTWAR VOTE FOR SENATOR

								Percentage			
	Total	Republican		Democratic		Other	Rep.-Dem.	Total Vote		Major Vote	
Year	Vote	Vote	Candidate	Vote	Candidate	Vote	Plurality	Rep.	Dem.	Rep.	Dem.
1976	3,490,664	1,635,087	Esch, Marvin L.	1,831,031	Riegle, Donald W.	24,546	195,944 D	46.8%	52.5%	47.2%	52.8%
1972	3,406,906	1,781,065	Griffin, Robert P.	1,577,178	Kelley, Frank J.	48,663	203,887 R	52.3%	46.3%	53.0%	47.0%
1970	2,610,839	858,470	Romney, Lenore	1,744,716	Hart, Philip A.	7,653	886,246 D	32.9%	66.8%	33.0%	67.0%
1966	2,439,365	1,363,530	Griffin, Robert P.	1,069,484	Williams, G. Mennen	6,351	294,046 R	55.9%	43.8%	56.0%	44.0%
1964	3,101,667	1,096,272	Peterson, Elly M.	1,996,912	Hart, Philip A.	8,483	900,640 D	35.3%	64.4%	35.4%	64.6%
1960	3,226,647	1,548,873	Bentley, Alvin M.	1,669,179	McNamara, Patrick V.	8,595	120,306 D	48.0%	51.7%	48.1%	51.9%
1958	2,271,644	1,046,963	Potter, Charles E.	1,216,966	Hart, Philip A.	7,715	170,003 D	46.1%	53.6%	46.2%	53.8%
1954	2,144,840	1,049,420	Ferguson, Homer	1,088,550	McNamara, Patrick V.	6,870	39,130 D	48.9%	50.8%	49.1%	50.9%
1952	2,821,133	1,428,352	Potter, Charles E.	1,383,416	Moody, Blair	9,365	44,936 R	50.6%	49.0%	50.8%	49.2%
1948	2,062,097	1,045,156	Ferguson, Homer	1,000,329	Hook, Frank E.	16,612	44,827 R	50.7%	48.5%	51.1%	48.9%
1946	1,618,720	1,085,570	Vandenberg, Arthur	517,923	Lee, James H.	15,227	567,647 R	67.1%	32.0%	67.7%	32.3%

MICHIGAN

Districts Established May 15, 1972

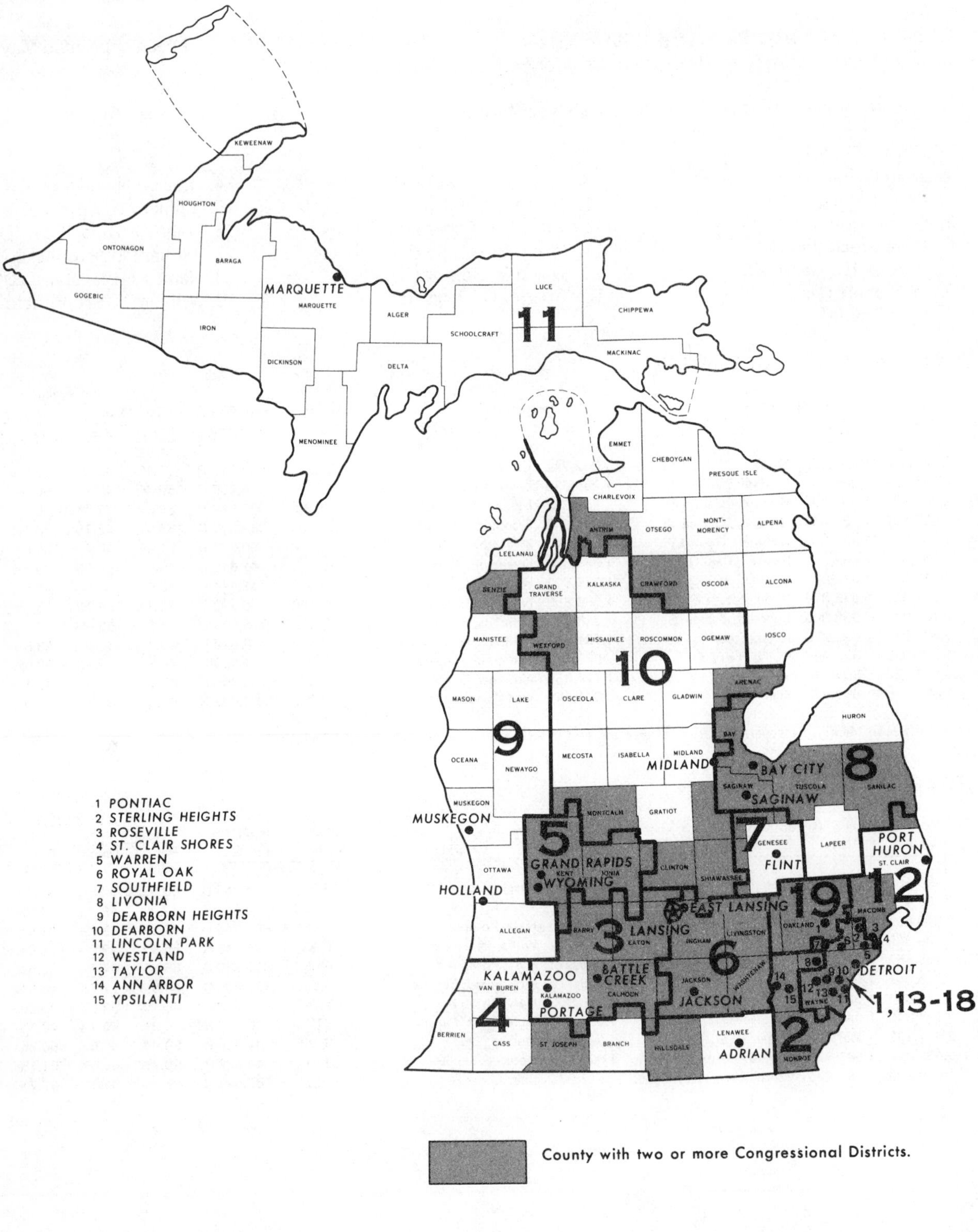

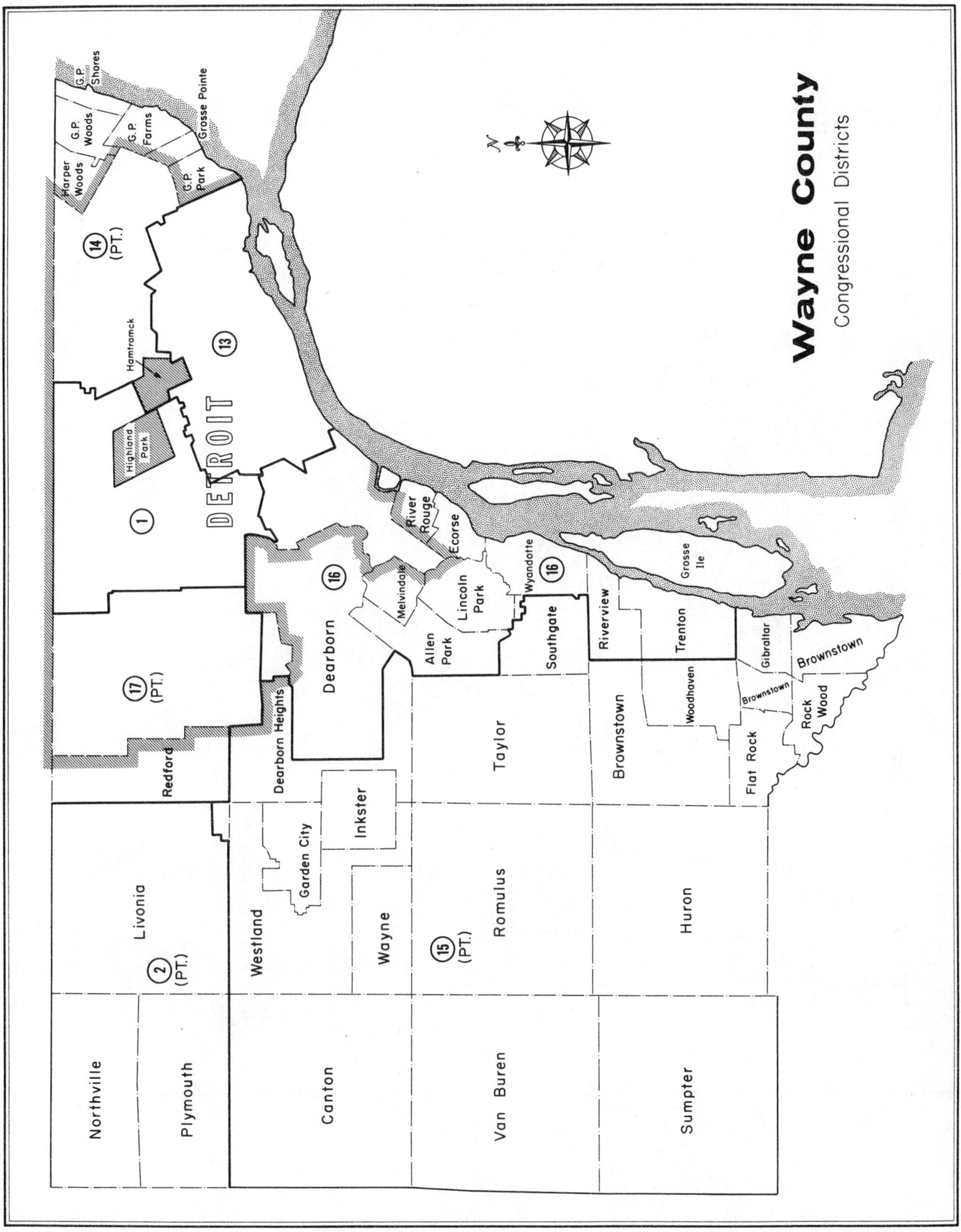
Wayne County
Congressional Districts
N
DETROIT
1
13
14 (PT.)
16
17 (PT.)
2 (PT.)
15 (PT.)
Harper Woods
G.P. Woods
G.P. Shores
G.P. Farms
Grosse Pointe
G.P. Park
Hamtramck
Highland Park
River Rouge
Ecorse
Wyandotte
Melvindale
Lincoln Park
Allen Park
Dearborn
Dearborn Heights
Redford
Southgate
Riverview
Trenton
Grosse Ile
Gibraltar
Brownstown
Woodhaven
Rock Wood
Flat Rock
Taylor
Inkster
Garden City
Westland
Wayne
Romulus
Huron
Livonia
Northville
Plymouth
Canton
Van Buren
Sumpter

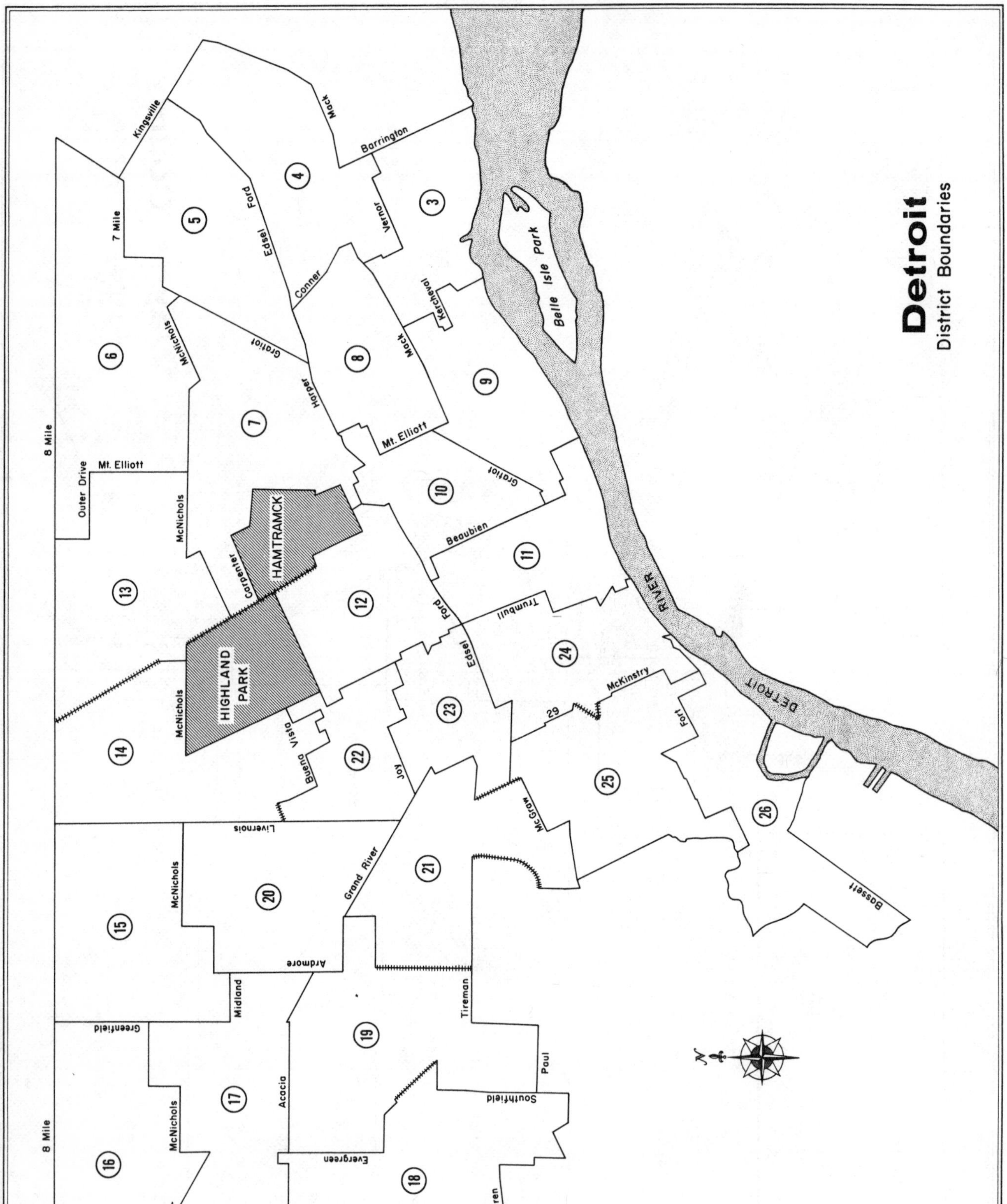
Detroit
District Boundaries
Belle Isle Park
DETROIT RIVER
HIGHLAND PARK
HAMTRAMCK
8 Mile
7 Mile
Kingsville
Mack
Barrington
Edsel Ford
Vernor
Conner
Kercheval
Gratiot
McNichols
Harper
Mt. Elliott
Outer Drive
Beaubien
Carpenter
Ford
Trumbull
Edsel
McKinstry
29
Fort
Buena Vista
Joy
McGraw
Livernois
Grand River
Ardmore
Midland
Greenfield
Tireman
Acacia
Paul
Southfield
Evergreen
Warren
Hazelton
Fenkell
Dale
Five Points
Bassett

MICHIGAN

PRESIDENT 1976

1970 Census Population	County	Total Vote	Republican	Democratic	Other	Rep.-Dem. Plurality	Percentage Total Vote Rep.	Percentage Total Vote Dem.	Percentage Major Vote Rep.	Percentage Major Vote Dem.
7,113	ALCONA	4,403	2,328	2,038	37	290 R	52.9%	46.3%	53.3%	46.7%
8,568	ALGER	4,161	1,722	2,379	60	657 D	41.4%	57.2%	42.0%	58.0%
66,575	ALLEGAN	29,471	19,330	9,794	347	9,536 R	65.6%	33.2%	66.4%	33.6%
30,708	ALPENA	12,866	6,380	6,310	176	70 R	49.6%	49.0%	50.3%	49.7%
12,612	ANTRIM	7,518	4,369	3,032	117	1,337 R	58.1%	40.3%	59.0%	41.0%
11,149	ARENAC	5,423	2,687	2,695	41	8 D	49.5%	49.7%	49.9%	50.1%
7,789	BARAGA	3,614	1,788	1,778	48	10 R	49.5%	49.2%	50.1%	49.9%
38,166	BARRY	18,388	11,178	6,967	243	4,211 R	60.8%	37.9%	61.6%	38.4%
117,339	BAY	49,689	23,174	25,958	557	2,784 D	46.6%	52.2%	47.2%	52.8%
8,593	BENZIE	5,038	3,085	1,891	62	1,194 R	61.2%	37.5%	62.0%	38.0%
163,875	BERRIEN	66,798	40,835	25,163	800	15,672 R	61.1%	37.7%	61.9%	38.1%
37,906	BRANCH	14,802	8,251	6,301	250	1,950 R	55.7%	42.6%	56.7%	43.3%
141,963	CALHOUN	56,520	30,390	25,229	901	5,161 R	53.8%	44.6%	54.6%	45.4%
43,312	CASS	17,939	9,893	7,843	203	2,050 R	55.1%	43.7%	55.8%	44.2%
16,541	CHARLEVOIX	9,258	5,145	3,953	160	1,192 R	55.6%	42.7%	56.6%	43.4%
16,573	CHEBOYGAN	8,878	4,894	3,880	104	1,014 R	55.1%	43.7%	55.8%	44.2%
32,412	CHIPPEWA	13,175	7,025	6,022	128	1,003 R	53.3%	45.7%	53.8%	46.2%
16,695	CLARE	9,126	4,879	4,153	94	726 R	53.5%	45.5%	54.0%	46.0%
48,492	CLINTON	21,353	13,475	7,549	329	5,926 R	63.1%	35.4%	64.1%	35.9%
6,482	CRAWFORD	4,303	2,359	1,889	55	470 R	54.8%	43.9%	55.5%	44.5%
35,924	DELTA	17,033	7,809	9,027	197	1,218 D	45.8%	53.0%	46.4%	53.6%
23,753	DICKINSON	12,177	5,922	6,134	121	212 D	48.6%	50.4%	49.1%	50.9%
68,892	EATON	34,750	22,120	12,083	547	10,037 R	63.7%	34.8%	64.7%	35.3%
18,331	EMMET	10,104	5,910	4,013	181	1,897 R	58.5%	39.7%	59.6%	40.4%
444,341	GENESEE	171,438	80,004	88,967	2,467	8,963 D	46.7%	51.9%	47.3%	52.7%
13,471	GLADWIN	7,567	3,794	3,719	54	75 R	50.1%	49.1%	50.5%	49.5%
20,676	GOGEBIC	10,392	3,953	6,341	98	2,388 D	38.0%	61.0%	38.4%	61.6%
39,175	GRAND TRAVERSE	21,150	13,505	7,263	382	6,242 R	63.9%	34.3%	65.0%	35.0%
39,246	GRATIOT	15,118	9,526	5,429	163	4,097 R	63.0%	35.9%	63.7%	36.3%
37,171	HILLSDALE	14,955	9,307	5,427	221	3,880 R	62.2%	36.3%	63.2%	36.8%
34,652	HOUGHTON	15,600	8,049	7,352	199	697 R	51.6%	47.1%	52.3%	47.7%
34,083	HURON	15,176	9,297	5,721	158	3,576 R	61.3%	37.7%	61.9%	38.1%
261,039	INGHAM	119,327	66,729	47,890	4,708	18,839 R	55.9%	40.1%	58.2%	41.8%
45,848	IONIA	18,791	11,737	6,820	234	4,917 R	62.5%	36.3%	63.2%	36.8%
24,905	IOSCO	10,498	5,500	4,875	123	625 R	52.4%	46.4%	53.0%	47.0%
13,813	IRON	7,718	3,224	4,401	93	1,177 D	41.8%	57.0%	42.3%	57.7%
44,594	ISABELLA	18,345	10,577	7,281	487	3,296 R	57.7%	39.7%	59.2%	40.8%
143,274	JACKSON	58,457	32,873	24,726	858	8,147 R	56.2%	42.3%	57.1%	42.9%
201,550	KALAMAZOO	87,085	51,462	33,411	2,212	18,051 R	59.1%	38.4%	60.6%	39.4%
5,272	KALKASKA	4,291	2,280	1,957	54	323 R	53.1%	45.6%	53.8%	46.2%
411,044	KENT	188,633	126,805	59,000	2,828	67,805 R	67.2%	31.3%	68.2%	31.8%
2,264	KEWEENAW	1,271	606	658	7	52 D	47.7%	51.8%	47.9%	52.1%
5,661	LAKE	3,808	1,598	2,179	31	581 D	42.0%	57.2%	42.3%	57.7%
52,317	LAPEER	22,215	12,349	9,503	363	2,846 R	55.6%	42.8%	56.5%	43.5%
10,872	LEELANAU	6,803	4,240	2,437	126	1,803 R	62.3%	35.8%	63.5%	36.5%
81,609	LENAWEE	33,435	18,397	14,610	428	3,787 R	55.0%	43.7%	55.7%	44.3%
58,967	LIVINGSTON	32,486	19,437	12,415	634	7,022 R	59.8%	38.2%	61.0%	39.0%
6,789	LUCE	2,495	1,379	1,099	17	280 R	55.3%	44.0%	55.6%	44.4%
9,660	MACKINAC	5,627	3,107	2,452	68	655 R	55.2%	43.6%	55.9%	44.1%
625,309	MACOMB	258,603	132,499	121,176	4,928	11,323 R	51.2%	46.9%	52.2%	47.8%
20,094	MANISTEE	10,134	5,532	4,479	123	1,053 R	54.6%	44.2%	55.3%	44.7%
64,686	MARQUETTE	26,315	12,984	12,837	494	147 R	49.3%	48.8%	50.3%	49.7%
22,612	MASON	11,516	6,812	4,541	163	2,271 R	59.2%	39.4%	60.0%	40.0%
27,992	MECOSTA	12,221	7,287	4,725	209	2,562 R	59.6%	38.7%	60.7%	39.3%
24,587	MENOMINEE	11,357	5,633	5,596	128	37 R	49.6%	49.3%	50.2%	49.8%
63,769	MIDLAND	30,101	17,631	11,959	511	5,672 R	58.6%	39.7%	59.6%	40.4%
7,126	MISSAUKEE	4,681	2,943	1,688	50	1,255 R	62.9%	36.1%	63.5%	36.5%
118,479	MONROE	44,597	20,676	23,290	631	2,614 D	46.4%	52.2%	47.0%	53.0%
39,660	MONTCALM	17,294	10,439	6,684	171	3,755 R	60.4%	38.6%	61.0%	39.0%
5,247	MONTMORENCY	3,617	1,882	1,684	51	198 R	52.0%	46.6%	52.8%	47.2%
157,426	MUSKEGON	63,407	35,548	27,013	846	8,535 R	56.1%	42.6%	56.8%	43.2%
27,992	NEWAYGO	14,050	8,258	5,622	170	2,636 R	58.8%	40.0%	59.5%	40.5%
907,871	OAKLAND	416,205	244,271	164,266	7,668	80,005 R	58.7%	39.5%	59.8%	40.2%
17,984	OCEANA	8,798	5,236	3,427	135	1,809 R	59.5%	39.0%	60.4%	39.6%
11,903	OGEMAW	6,824	3,212	3,545	67	333 D	47.1%	51.9%	47.5%	52.5%

MICHIGAN

PRESIDENT 1976

1970 Census Population	County	Total Vote	Republican	Democratic	Other	Rep.-Dem. Plurality	Percentage Total Vote Rep.	Total Vote Dem.	Major Vote Rep.	Major Vote Dem.
10,548	ONTONAGON	5,607	2,462	3,104	41	642 D	43.9%	55.4%	44.2%	55.8%
14,838	OSCEOLA	7,178	4,467	2,603	108	1,864 R	62.2%	36.3%	63.2%	36.8%
4,726	OSCODA	2,677	1,541	1,108	28	433 R	57.6%	41.4%	58.2%	41.8%
10,422	OTSEGO	5,952	3,155	2,724	73	431 R	53.0%	45.8%	53.7%	46.3%
128,181	OTTAWA	66,370	49,196	16,381	793	32,815 R	74.1%	24.7%	75.0%	25.0%
12,836	PRESQUE ISLE	6,948	3,545	3,334	69	211 R	51.0%	48.0%	51.5%	48.5%
9,892	ROSCOMMON	8,401	4,608	3,691	102	917 R	54.9%	43.9%	55.5%	44.5%
219,743	SAGINAW	84,071	46,765	36,280	1,026	10,485 R	55.6%	43.2%	56.3%	43.7%
120,175	ST. CLAIR	49,889	26,311	22,734	844	3,577 R	52.7%	45.6%	53.6%	46.4%
47,392	ST. JOSEPH	19,295	11,784	7,306	205	4,478 R	61.1%	37.9%	61.7%	38.3%
34,889	SANILAC	16,856	10,597	6,042	217	4,555 R	62.9%	35.8%	63.7%	36.3%
8,226	SCHOOLCRAFT	4,154	1,933	2,158	63	225 D	46.5%	51.9%	47.3%	52.7%
63,075	SHIAWASSEE	27,721	15,113	12,202	406	2,911 R	54.5%	44.0%	55.3%	44.7%
48,603	TUSCOLA	20,144	12,059	7,932	153	4,127 R	59.9%	39.4%	60.3%	39.7%
56,173	VAN BUREN	24,302	13,615	10,366	321	3,249 R	56.0%	42.7%	56.8%	43.2%
234,103	WASHTENAW	111,689	56,807	50,917	3,965	5,890 R	50.9%	45.6%	52.7%	47.3%
2,666,751	WAYNE	912,990	348,588	548,767	15,635	200,179 D	38.2%	60.1%	38.8%	61.2%
19,717	WEXFORD	10,317	5,670	4,519	128	1,151 R	55.0%	43.8%	55.6%	44.4%
8,875,083	TOTAL	3,653,749	1,893,742	1,696,714	63,293	197,028 R	51.8%	46.4%	52.7%	47.3%

MICHIGAN

SENATOR 1976

1970 Census Population	County	Total Vote	Republican	Democratic	Other	Rep.-Dem. Plurality	Percentage Total Vote Rep.	Percentage Total Vote Dem.	Percentage Major Vote Rep.	Percentage Major Vote Dem.
7,113	ALCONA	4,074	2,058	2,000	16	58 R	50.5%	49.1%	50.7%	49.3%
8,568	ALGER	3,710	1,334	2,363	13	1,029 D	36.0%	63.7%	36.1%	63.9%
66,575	ALLEGAN	28,178	17,691	10,357	130	7,334 R	62.8%	36.8%	63.1%	36.9%
30,708	ALPENA	12,058	5,027	6,974	57	1,947 D	41.7%	57.8%	41.9%	58.1%
12,612	ANTRIM	7,008	4,238	2,744	26	1,494 R	60.5%	39.2%	60.7%	39.3%
11,149	ARENAC	5,124	2,358	2,758	8	400 D	46.0%	53.8%	46.1%	53.9%
7,789	BARAGA	3,330	1,408	1,895	27	487 D	42.3%	56.9%	42.6%	57.4%
38,166	BARRY	17,402	9,869	7,475	58	2,394 R	56.7%	43.0%	56.9%	43.1%
117,339	BAY	47,315	18,485	28,653	177	10,168 D	39.1%	60.6%	39.2%	60.8%
8,593	BENZIE	4,771	2,987	1,763	21	1,224 R	62.6%	37.0%	62.9%	37.1%
163,875	BERRIEN	62,481	37,653	24,497	331	13,156 R	60.3%	39.2%	60.6%	39.4%
37,906	BRANCH	14,099	7,458	6,565	76	893 R	52.9%	46.6%	53.2%	46.8%
141,963	CALHOUN	54,161	26,139	27,803	219	1,664 D	48.3%	51.3%	48.5%	51.5%
43,312	CASS	16,649	8,954	7,588	107	1,366 R	53.8%	45.6%	54.1%	45.9%
16,541	CHARLEVOIX	8,726	4,802	3,874	50	928 R	55.0%	44.4%	55.3%	44.7%
16,573	CHEBOYGAN	8,030	4,143	3,861	26	282 R	51.6%	48.1%	51.8%	48.2%
32,412	CHIPPEWA	12,118	6,220	5,843	55	377 R	51.3%	48.2%	51.6%	48.4%
16,695	CLARE	8,584	4,347	4,207	30	140 R	50.6%	49.0%	50.8%	49.2%
48,492	CLINTON	20,546	12,218	8,198	130	4,020 R	59.5%	39.9%	59.8%	40.2%
6,482	CRAWFORD	3,887	2,153	1,717	17	436 R	55.4%	44.2%	55.6%	44.4%
35,924	DELTA	15,798	5,951	9,732	115	3,781 D	37.7%	61.6%	37.9%	62.1%
23,753	DICKINSON	10,897	4,581	6,242	74	1,661 D	42.0%	57.3%	42.3%	57.7%
68,892	EATON	33,177	19,284	13,651	242	5,633 R	58.1%	41.1%	58.6%	41.4%
18,331	EMMET	9,488	5,563	3,865	60	1,698 R	58.6%	40.7%	59.0%	41.0%
444,341	GENESEE	165,521	61,550	103,036	935	41,486 D	37.2%	62.2%	37.4%	62.6%
13,471	GLADWIN	7,051	3,289	3,736	26	447 D	46.6%	53.0%	46.8%	53.2%
20,676	GOGEBIC	9,523	3,168	6,301	54	3,133 D	33.3%	66.2%	33.5%	66.5%
39,175	GRAND TRAVERSE	20,365	12,607	7,621	137	4,986 R	61.9%	37.4%	62.3%	37.7%
39,246	GRATIOT	14,495	8,575	5,845	75	2,730 R	59.2%	40.3%	59.5%	40.5%
37,171	HILLSDALE	13,841	8,533	5,219	89	3,314 R	61.7%	37.7%	62.0%	38.0%
34,652	HOUGHTON	14,480	6,516	7,882	82	1,366 D	45.0%	54.4%	45.3%	54.7%
34,083	HURON	13,962	8,060	5,835	67	2,225 R	57.7%	41.8%	58.0%	42.0%
261,039	INGHAM	115,299	54,826	57,954	2,519	3,128 D	47.6%	50.3%	48.6%	51.4%
45,848	IONIA	17,409	9,858	7,466	85	2,392 R	56.6%	42.9%	56.9%	43.1%
24,905	IOSCO	10,072	4,919	5,126	27	207 D	48.8%	50.9%	49.0%	51.0%
13,813	IRON	7,083	2,712	4,344	27	1,632 D	38.3%	61.3%	38.4%	61.6%
44,594	ISABELLA	17,511	8,628	8,683	200	55 D	49.3%	49.6%	49.8%	50.2%
143,274	JACKSON	55,836	28,649	26,780	407	1,869 R	51.3%	48.0%	51.7%	48.3%
201,550	KALAMAZOO	82,635	43,588	38,563	484	5,025 R	52.7%	46.7%	53.1%	46.9%
5,272	KALKASKA	3,972	2,089	1,859	24	230 R	52.6%	46.8%	52.9%	47.1%
411,044	KENT	182,211	110,584	70,578	1,049	40,006 R	60.7%	38.7%	61.0%	39.0%
2,264	KEWEENAW	1,133	489	641	3	152 D	43.2%	56.6%	43.3%	56.7%
5,661	LAKE	3,530	1,554	1,965	11	411 D	44.0%	55.7%	44.2%	55.8%
52,317	LAPEER	21,641	10,117	11,371	153	1,254 D	46.7%	52.5%	47.1%	52.9%
10,872	LEELANAU	6,551	4,097	2,403	51	1,694 R	62.5%	36.7%	63.0%	37.0%
81,609	LENAWEE	31,709	17,680	13,883	146	3,797 R	55.8%	43.8%	56.0%	44.0%
58,967	LIVINGSTON	31,500	17,948	13,355	197	4,593 R	57.0%	42.4%	57.3%	42.7%
6,789	LUCE	2,286	1,230	1,049	7	181 R	53.8%	45.9%	54.0%	46.0%
9,660	MACKINAC	5,126	2,684	2,419	23	265 R	52.4%	47.2%	52.6%	47.4%
625,309	MACOMB	246,484	107,827	136,888	1,769	29,061 D	43.7%	55.5%	44.1%	55.9%
20,094	MANISTEE	9,528	5,143	4,339	46	804 R	54.0%	45.5%	54.2%	45.8%
64,686	MARQUETTE	24,598	9,702	14,770	126	5,068 D	39.4%	60.0%	39.6%	60.4%
22,612	MASON	11,200	6,083	5,042	75	1,041 R	54.3%	45.0%	54.7%	45.3%
27,992	MECOSTA	11,647	6,736	4,847	64	1,889 R	57.8%	41.6%	58.2%	41.8%
24,587	MENOMINEE	10,084	4,689	5,347	48	658 D	46.5%	53.0%	46.7%	53.3%
63,769	MIDLAND	29,524	15,911	13,379	234	2,532 R	53.9%	45.3%	54.3%	45.7%
7,126	MISSAUKEE	4,414	2,845	1,552	17	1,293 R	64.5%	35.2%	64.7%	35.3%
118,479	MONROE	42,861	21,592	21,103	166	489 R	50.4%	49.2%	50.6%	49.4%
39,660	MONTCALM	16,362	9,260	7,043	59	2,217 R	56.6%	43.0%	56.8%	43.2%
5,247	MONTMORENCY	3,221	1,796	1,407	18	389 R	55.8%	43.7%	56.1%	43.9%
157,426	MUSKEGON	61,141	31,915	28,957	269	2,958 R	52.2%	47.4%	52.4%	47.6%
27,992	NEWAYGO	13,472	7,754	5,671	47	2,083 R	57.6%	42.1%	57.8%	42.2%
907,871	OAKLAND	401,135	209,225	189,209	2,701	20,016 R	52.2%	47.2%	52.5%	47.5%
17,984	OCEANA	8,353	4,711	3,606	36	1,105 R	56.4%	43.2%	56.6%	43.4%
11,903	OGEMAW	6,416	2,903	3,495	18	592 D	45.2%	54.5%	45.4%	54.6%

MICHIGAN

SENATOR 1976

1970 Census Population	County	Total Vote	Republican	Democratic	Other	Rep.-Dem. Plurality	Percentage Total Vote Rep.	Percentage Total Vote Dem.	Percentage Major Vote Rep.	Percentage Major Vote Dem.
10,548	ONTONAGON	4,929	1,880	3,036	13	1,156 D	38.1%	61.6%	38.2%	61.8%
14,838	OSCEOLA	6,863	4,252	2,583	28	1,669 R	62.0%	37.6%	62.2%	37.8%
4,726	OSCODA	2,517	1,442	1,069	6	373 R	57.3%	42.5%	57.4%	42.6%
10,422	OTSEGO	5,461	2,929	2,506	26	423 R	53.6%	45.9%	53.9%	46.1%
128,181	OTTAWA	64,389	45,931	18,230	228	27,701 R	71.3%	28.3%	71.6%	28.4%
12,836	PRESQUE ISLE	6,394	2,954	3,423	17	469 D	46.2%	53.5%	46.3%	53.7%
9,892	ROSCOMMON	7,958	4,314	3,616	28	698 R	54.2%	45.4%	54.4%	45.6%
219,743	SAGINAW	81,957	40,686	40,598	673	88 R	49.6%	49.5%	50.1%	49.9%
120,175	ST. CLAIR	47,978	22,746	24,932	300	2,186 D	47.4%	52.0%	47.7%	52.3%
47,392	ST. JOSEPH	18,029	10,680	7,287	62	3,393 R	59.2%	40.4%	59.4%	40.6%
34,889	SANILAC	15,735	9,634	6,053	48	3,581 R	61.2%	38.5%	61.4%	38.6%
8,226	SCHOOLCRAFT	3,730	1,521	2,187	22	666 D	40.8%	58.6%	41.0%	59.0%
63,075	SHIAWASSEE	26,661	13,166	13,337	158	171 D	49.4%	50.0%	49.7%	50.3%
48,603	TUSCOLA	18,818	10,292	8,456	70	1,836 R	54.7%	44.9%	54.9%	45.1%
56,173	VAN BUREN	22,883	12,261	10,527	95	1,734 R	53.6%	46.0%	53.8%	46.2%
234,103	WASHTENAW	108,434	55,179	52,165	1,090	3,014 R	50.9%	48.1%	51.4%	48.6%
2,666,751	WAYNE	871,403	293,096	571,298	7,009	278,202 D	33.6%	65.6%	33.9%	66.1%
19,717	WEXFORD	9,732	5,161	4,534	37	627 R	53.0%	46.6%	53.2%	46.8%
8,875,083	TOTAL	3,490,664	1,635,087	1,831,031	24,546	195,944 D	46.8%	52.5%	47.2%	52.8%

Detroit

PRESIDENT 1976

1970 Census Population	District	Total Vote	Republican	Democratic	Other	Rep.-Dem. Plurality	Percentage Total Vote Rep.	Percentage Total Vote Dem.	Percentage Major Vote Rep.	Percentage Major Vote Dem.
	DISTRICT 3	11,256	1,288	9,844	124	8,556 D	11.4%	87.5%	11.6%	88.4%
	DISTRICT 4	18,576	7,974	10,244	358	2,270 D	42.9%	55.1%	43.8%	56.2%
	DISTRICT 5	21,435	10,557	10,450	428	107 R	49.3%	48.8%	50.3%	49.7%
	DISTRICT 6	23,530	10,555	12,587	388	2,032 D	44.9%	53.5%	45.6%	54.4%
	DISTRICT 7	15,343	3,816	11,296	231	7,480 D	24.9%	73.6%	25.3%	74.7%
	DISTRICT 8	16,276	804	15,375	97	14,571 D	4.9%	94.5%	5.0%	95.0%
	DISTRICT 9	13,315	2,288	10,786	241	8,498 D	17.2%	81.0%	17.5%	82.5%
	DISTRICT 10	9,021	1,083	7,820	118	6,737 D	12.0%	86.7%	12.2%	87.8%
	DISTRICT 11	8,285	1,548	6,540	197	4,992 D	18.7%	78.9%	19.1%	80.9%
	DISTRICT 12	13,786	993	12,608	185	11,615 D	7.2%	91.5%	7.3%	92.7%
	DISTRICT 13	20,340	2,977	17,139	224	14,162 D	14.6%	84.3%	14.8%	85.2%
	DISTRICT 14	20,036	3,119	16,549	368	13,430 D	15.6%	82.6%	15.9%	84.1%
	DISTRICT 15	27,226	1,896	25,081	249	23,185 D	7.0%	92.1%	7.0%	93.0%
	DISTRICT 16	21,523	8,076	13,013	434	4,937 D	37.5%	60.5%	38.3%	61.7%
	DISTRICT 17	22,377	8,734	13,090	553	4,356 D	39.0%	58.5%	40.0%	60.0%
	DISTRICT 18	20,491	9,041	11,053	397	2,012 D	44.1%	53.9%	45.0%	55.0%
	DISTRICT 19	18,839	5,074	13,474	291	8,400 D	26.9%	71.5%	27.4%	72.6%
	DISTRICT 20	19,903	989	18,737	177	17,748 D	5.0%	94.1%	5.0%	95.0%
	DISTRICT 21	19,459	2,133	17,139	187	15,006 D	11.0%	88.1%	11.1%	88.9%
	DISTRICT 22	17,177	710	16,360	107	15,650 D	4.1%	95.2%	4.2%	95.8%
	DISTRICT 23	14,925	626	14,212	87	13,586 D	4.2%	95.2%	4.2%	95.8%
	DISTRICT 24	8,513	1,063	7,327	123	6,264 D	12.5%	86.1%	12.7%	87.3%
	DISTRICT 25	14,206	4,500	9,454	252	4,954 D	31.7%	66.5%	32.2%	67.8%
	DISTRICT 26	8,760	1,190	7,500	70	6,310 D	13.6%	85.6%	13.7%	86.3%
	ABSENTEE	40,931	16,925	23,368	638	6,443 D	41.4%	57.1%	42.0%	58.0%
1,511,482	TOTAL	445,529	107,959	331,046	6,524	223,087 D	24.2%	74.3%	24.6%	75.4%

SENATOR 1976

1970 Census Population	District	Total Vote	Republican	Democratic	Other	Rep.-Dem. Plurality	Percentage Total Vote Rep.	Percentage Total Vote Dem.	Percentage Major Vote Rep.	Percentage Major Vote Dem.
	DISTRICT 3	10,508	1,098	9,305	105	8,207 D	10.4%	88.6%	10.6%	89.4%
	DISTRICT 4	17,638	6,674	10,778	186	4,104 D	37.8%	61.1%	38.2%	61.8%
	DISTRICT 5	20,565	8,683	11,734	148	3,051 D	42.2%	57.1%	42.5%	57.5%
	DISTRICT 6	22,518	8,396	13,993	129	5,597 D	37.3%	62.1%	37.5%	62.5%
	DISTRICT 7	14,436	2,921	11,403	112	8,482 D	20.2%	79.0%	20.4%	79.6%
	DISTRICT 8	15,240	528	14,603	109	14,075 D	3.5%	95.8%	3.5%	96.5%
	DISTRICT 9	12,095	1,894	10,053	148	8,159 D	15.7%	83.1%	15.9%	84.1%
	DISTRICT 10	8,225	747	7,376	102	6,629 D	9.1%	89.7%	9.2%	90.8%
	DISTRICT 11	7,628	1,242	6,254	132	5,012 D	16.3%	82.0%	16.6%	83.4%
	DISTRICT 12	13,005	797	11,987	221	11,190 D	6.1%	92.2%	6.2%	93.8%
	DISTRICT 13	18,933	2,274	16,509	150	14,235 D	12.0%	87.2%	12.1%	87.9%
	DISTRICT 14	18,945	2,554	16,190	201	13,636 D	13.5%	85.5%	13.6%	86.4%
	DISTRICT 15	25,620	1,478	23,968	174	22,490 D	5.8%	93.6%	5.8%	94.2%
	DISTRICT 16	20,858	6,699	13,997	162	7,298 D	32.1%	67.1%	32.4%	67.6%
	DISTRICT 17	21,504	7,493	13,794	217	6,301 D	34.8%	64.1%	35.2%	64.8%
	DISTRICT 18	19,783	7,229	12,414	140	5,185 D	36.5%	62.8%	36.8%	63.2%
	DISTRICT 19	18,014	4,020	13,860	134	9,840 D	22.3%	76.9%	22.5%	77.5%
	DISTRICT 20	18,609	921	17,570	118	16,649 D	4.9%	94.4%	5.0%	95.0%
	DISTRICT 21	18,304	1,611	16,560	133	14,949 D	8.8%	90.5%	8.9%	91.1%
	DISTRICT 22	15,958	556	15,311	91	14,755 D	3.5%	95.9%	3.5%	96.5%
	DISTRICT 23	13,761	470	13,196	95	12,726 D	3.4%	95.9%	3.4%	96.6%
	DISTRICT 24	7,944	840	7,003	101	6,163 D	10.6%	88.2%	10.7%	89.3%
	DISTRICT 25	13,434	3,404	9,895	135	6,491 D	25.3%	73.7%	25.6%	74.4%
	DISTRICT 26	8,218	898	7,282	38	6,384 D	10.9%	88.6%	11.0%	89.0%
	ABSENTEE	40,431	14,847	25,229	355	10,382 D	36.7%	62.4%	37.0%	63.0%
1,511,482	TOTAL	422,174	88,274	330,264	3,636	241,990 D	20.9%	78.2%	21.1%	78.9%

MICHIGAN

CONGRESS

			Republican		Democratic				Percentage			
		Total					Other	Rep.-Dem.	Total Vote		Major Vote	
CD	Year	Vote	Vote	Candidate	Vote	Candidate	Vote	Plurality	Rep.	Dem.	Rep.	Dem.
1	1976	136,585	8,927	HOOD, ISAAC	126,161	CONYERS, JOHN	1,497	117,234 D	6.5%	92.4%	6.6%	93.4%
1	1974	107,573	9,358	GIRARDOT, WALTER F.	97,620	CONYERS, JOHN	595	88,262 D	8.7%	90.7%	8.7%	91.3%
1	1972	148,603	16,096	GIRARDOT, WALTER F.	131,353	CONYERS, JOHN	1,154	115,257 D	10.8%	88.4%	10.9%	89.1%
2	1976	191,746	95,397	PURSELL, CARL D.	95,053	PIERCE, EDWARD C.	1,296	344 R	49.8%	49.6%	50.1%	49.9%
2	1974	138,160	72,245	ESCH, MARVIN L.	62,755	REUTHER, JOHN S.	3,160	9,490 R	52.3%	45.4%	53.5%	46.5%
2	1972	184,396	103,321	ESCH, MARVIN L.	79,762	STEMPIEN, MARVIN R.	1,313	23,559 R	56.0%	43.3%	56.4%	43.6%
3	1976	196,163	99,231	BROWN, GARRY	95,261	WOLPE, HOWARD	1,671	3,970 R	50.6%	48.6%	51.0%	49.0%
3	1974	137,139	70,157	BROWN, GARRY	65,212	TODD, PAUL H.	1,770	4,945 R	51.2%	47.6%	51.8%	48.2%
3	1972	185,937	110,082	BROWN, GARRY	74,114	BRIGNALL, JAMES T.	1,741	35,968 R	59.2%	39.9%	59.8%	40.2%
4	1976	179,746	107,881	STOCKMAN, DAVE	69,655	DAUGHERTY, RICHARD E.	2,210	38,226 R	60.0%	38.8%	60.8%	39.2%
4	1974	121,925	64,731	HUTCHINSON, EDWARD	55,469	DAUGHERTY, RICHARD E.	1,725	9,262 R	53.1%	45.5%	53.9%	46.1%
4	1972	165,326	111,185	HUTCHINSON, EDWARD	54,141	JAMESON, CHARLES W.		57,044 R	67.3%	32.7%	67.3%	32.7%
5	1976	205,452	109,589	SAWYER, HAROLD S.	94,973	VANDER VEEN, RICHARD F.	890	14,616 R	53.3%	46.2%	53.6%	46.4%
5	1974	153,475	66,659	GOEBEL, PAUL G.	80,778	VANDER VEEN, RICHARD F.	6,038	14,119 D	43.4%	52.6%	45.2%	54.8%
5	1972	193,229	118,027	FORD, GERALD R.	72,782	MCKEE, JEAN	2,420	45,245 R	61.1%	37.7%	61.9%	38.1%
6	1976	206,514	96,008	TAYLOR, CLIFFORD W.	108,909	CARR, M. ROBERT	1,597	12,901 D	46.5%	52.7%	46.9%	53.1%
6	1974	149,986	73,309	TAYLOR, CLIFFORD W.	73,956	CARR, M. ROBERT	2,721	647 D	48.9%	49.3%	49.8%	50.2%
6	1972	192,875	97,666	CHAMBERLAIN, C. E.	95,209	CARR, M. ROBERT		2,457 R	50.6%	49.4%	50.6%	49.4%
7	1976	177,582	50,301	WIDGERY, ROBIN	124,260	KILDEE, DALE E.	3,021	73,959 D	28.3%	70.0%	28.8%	71.2%
7	1974	125,129	41,603	EASTMAN, ROBERT E.	81,014	RIEGLE, DONALD W.	2,512	39,411 D	33.2%	64.7%	33.9%	66.1%
7	1972	163,539	114,656	RIEGLE, DONALD W.	48,883	MATTISON, EUGENE L.		65,773 R	70.1%	29.9%	70.1%	29.9%
8	1976	186,632	75,323	DENTON, E. BRADY	110,127	TRAXLER, J. ROBERT	1,182	34,804 D	40.4%	59.0%	40.6%	59.4%
8	1974	141,854	61,578	SPARLING, JAMES M.	77,795	TRAXLER, J. ROBERT	2,481	16,217 D	43.4%	54.8%	44.2%	55.8%
8	1972	169,750	100,597	HARVEY, JAMES	66,873	HART, JEROME	2,280	33,724 R	59.3%	39.4%	60.1%	39.9%
9	1976	209,704	146,712	VANDER JAGT, GUY	61,641	FAWLEY, STEPHEN E.	1,351	85,071 R	70.0%	29.4%	70.4%	29.6%
9	1974	154,811	87,551	VANDER JAGT, GUY	65,235	HALBOWER, NORM	2,025	22,316 R	56.6%	42.1%	57.3%	42.7%
9	1972	190,614	132,268	VANDER JAGT, GUY	56,236	OLSON, LARRY H.	2,110	76,032 R	69.4%	29.5%	70.2%	29.8%
10	1976	210,191	118,726	CEDERBERG, ELFORD A.	89,980	ALBOSTA, DONALD J.	1,485	28,746 R	56.5%	42.8%	56.9%	43.1%
10	1974	146,937	78,897	CEDERBERG, ELFORD A.	67,467	MARBLE, SAMUEL D.	573	11,430 R	53.7%	45.9%	53.9%	46.1%
10	1972	181,886	121,368	CEDERBERG, ELFORD A.	56,149	GRAVES, BENNIE D.	4,369	65,219 R	66.7%	30.9%	68.4%	31.6%
11	1976	217,117	118,871	RUPPE, PHILIP E.	97,325	BROUILLETTE, FRANCIS D.	921	21,546 R	54.7%	44.8%	55.0%	45.0%
11	1974	163,536	83,293	RUPPE, PHILIP E.	79,793	BROUILLETTE, FRANCIS D.	450	3,500 R	50.9%	48.8%	51.1%	48.9%
11	1972	195,609	135,786	RUPPE, PHILIP E.	58,334	MCNAMARA, JAMES E.	1,489	77,452 R	69.4%	29.8%	69.9%	30.1%
12	1976	180,877	85,326	SEROTKIN, DAVID M.	94,815	BONIOR, DAVID E.	736	9,489 D	47.2%	52.4%	47.4%	52.6%
12	1974	124,415	34,293	TYZA, EUGENE J.	89,822	O HARA, JAMES G.	300	55,529 D	27.6%	72.2%	27.6%	72.4%
12	1972	164,018	80,667	SEROTKIN, DAVID M.	83,351	O HARA, JAMES G.		2,684 D	49.2%	50.8%	49.2%	50.8%
13	1976	93,690	9,002	GOLDEN, RICHARD A.	83,387	DIGGS, CHARLES C.	1,301	74,385 D	9.6%	89.0%	9.7%	90.3%
13	1974	72,403	8,036	MCCALL, GEORGE E.	63,246	DIGGS, CHARLES C.	1,121	55,210 D	11.1%	87.4%	11.3%	88.7%
13	1972	113,928	15,180	EDWARDS, LEONARD T.	97,562	DIGGS, CHARLES C.	1,186	82,382 D	13.3%	85.6%	13.5%	86.5%
14	1976	161,668	52,995	GETZ, JOHN E.	107,503	NEDZI, LUCIEN N.	1,170	54,508 D	32.8%	66.5%	33.0%	67.0%
14	1974	131,925	35,723	STEIGER, HERBERT O.	93,973	NEDZI, LUCIEN N.	2,229	58,250 D	27.1%	71.2%	27.5%	72.5%
14	1972	171,196	77,273	MCGRATH, ROBERT V.	93,923	NEDZI, LUCIEN N.		16,650 D	45.1%	54.9%	45.1%	54.9%
15	1976	158,553	39,177	WALASKAY, JAMES D.	117,313	FORD, WILLIAM D.	2,063	78,136 D	24.7%	74.0%	25.0%	75.0%
15	1974	110,910	23,028	UNDERWOOD, JACK A.	86,601	FORD, WILLIAM D.	1,281	63,573 D	20.8%	78.1%	21.0%	79.0%
15	1972	147,530	48,504	FACKLER, ERNEST C.	97,054	FORD, WILLIAM D.	1,972	48,550 D	32.9%	65.8%	33.3%	66.7%
16	1976	160,351	36,378	ROSTRON, WILLIAM E.	121,682	DINGELL, JOHN D., JR.	2,291	85,304 D	22.7%	75.9%	23.0%	77.0%
16	1974	123,284	25,248	ENGLISH, WALLACE D.	95,834	DINGELL, JOHN D., JR.	2,202	70,586 D	20.5%	77.7%	20.9%	79.1%
16	1972	162,683	48,414	ROSTRON, WILLIAM E.	110,715	DINGELL, JOHN D., JR.	3,554	62,301 D	29.8%	68.1%	30.4%	69.6%
17	1976	175,474	60,476	BURDICK, JAMES W.	112,746	BRODHEAD, WILLIAM M.	2,252	52,270 D	34.5%	64.3%	34.9%	65.1%
17	1974	135,674	39,856	GALLAGHER, KENNETH C.	94,242	BRODHEAD, WILLIAM M.	1,576	54,386 D	29.4%	69.5%	29.7%	70.3%
17	1972	185,633	60,337	JUDD, RALPH E.	123,331	GRIFFITHS, MARTHA W.	1,965	62,994 D	32.5%	66.4%	32.9%	67.1%
18	1976	186,196	60,995	OLSEN, JOHN E.	123,113	BLANCHARD, JAMES J.	2,088	62,118 D	32.8%	66.1%	33.1%	66.9%
18	1974	142,232	57,133	HUBER, ROBERT J.	83,523	BLANCHARD, JAMES J.	1,576	26,390 D	40.2%	58.7%	40.6%	59.4%
18	1972	180,633	95,053	HUBER, ROBERT J.	85,580	COOPER, DANIEL S.		9,473 R	52.6%	47.4%	52.6%	47.4%
19	1976	197,649	131,799	BROOMFIELD, WILLIAM S.	64,337	BECKER, DOROTHEA	1,513	67,462 R	66.7%	32.6%	67.2%	32.8%
19	1974	138,052	86,846	BROOMFIELD, WILLIAM S.	50,924	MONTGOMERY, GEORGE F.	282	35,922 R	62.9%	36.9%	63.0%	37.0%
19	1972	175,789	123,697	BROOMFIELD, WILLIAM S.	50,355	MONTGOMERY, GEORGE F.	1,737	73,342 R	70.4%	28.6%	71.1%	28.9%

MICHIGAN

1976 GENERAL ELECTION

President — Other vote was 47,905 McCarthy (Independent); 5,406 MacBride (Libertarian); 3,504 Wright (Human Rights); 1,804 Camejo (Socialist Workers); 1,366 LaRouche (U.S. Labor); 1,148 Levin (Socialist Labor); 2,160 scattered.

Senator — Other vote was 8,842 Erwin (Libertarian); 7,281 Albert (Human Rights); 3,399 Reimers (Socialist Workers); 2,554 Girard (Socialist Labor); 2,218 Signorelli (U.S. Labor); 252 scattered.

Congress — Other vote was as follows:

CD 1 — 727 McGregor (American Independent); 306 Washington (Socialist Workers); 245 Jones (Libertarian); 216 Nelson (U.S. Labor); 3 scattered.
CD 2 — 598 Carroll (Human Rights); 403 McKenna (Libertarian); 287 Ziegler (U.S. Labor); 8 scattered.
CD 3 — 1,208 Walter (American Independent); 334 Todd (Libertarian); 124 Stevens (U.S. Labor); 5 scattered.
CD 4 — 1,789 Friske (American Independent); 288 Severance (Libertarian); 124 Hilty (U.S. Labor); 9 scattered.
CD 5 — 477 Berman (Libertarian); 399 Powell (U.S. Labor); 14 scattered.
CD 6 — 1,398 McClure (Human Rights); 189 Rothstein (U.S. Labor); 10 scattered.
CD 7 — 1,451 Sabin (American Independent); 835 Max Dean (U.S. Labor); 735 Hoffman (Libertarian).
CD 8 — 973 Johns (American Independent); 209 Thill (U.S. Labor).
CD 9 — 1,021 Hesselink (American Independent); 204 Powell (U.S. Labor); 123 Friesser (Socialist Labor); 3 scattered.
CD 10 — 1,256 Lawrence Dean (American Independent); 222 D'Urso (U.S. Labor); 7 scattered.
CD 11 — 537 Pape (American Independent); 231 Aho (Human Rights); 151 Hoffman (U.S. Labor); 2 scattered.
CD 12 — 441 Clark (Libertarian); 285 Kronberg (U.S. Labor); 10 scattered.
CD 13 — 449 Houle (American Independent); 366 Hawkins (Socialist Workers); 285 Brown (U.S. Labor); 198 DeWaters (Libertarian); 3 scattered.
CD 14 — 473 Geary (Human Rights); 303 Moser (Libertarian); 198 Hilty (U.S. Labor); 194 Severs (Socialist Workers); 2 scattered.
CD 15 — 776 Fuhrmann (American Independent); 746 Augustin (Libertarian); 306 Sarkisian (Socialist Labor); 232 Douglas (U.S. Labor); 3 scattered.
CD 16 — 1,009 Miller (American Independent); 484 Hancock (Libertarian); 463 Dalto (U.S. Labor); 328 Bechler (Socialist Workers); 7 scattered.
CD 17 — 1,382 Bakken (American Independent); 390 Wallace (Socialist Workers); 285 Novess (Libertarian); 194 Elliott (U.S. Labor); 1 scattered.
CD 18 — 1,143 Drexler (American Independent); 396 Rising (Libertarian); 289 Keller (U.S. Labor); 259 Horvath (Socialist Labor); 1 scattered.
CD 19 — 751 Muotka (American Independent); 496 Barbone (Libertarian); 262 Simpson (U.S. Labor); 4 scattered.

DETROIT

Population data not available by districts in Detroit.

President — Other vote was 4,609 McCarthy (Independent); 505 Wright (Human Rights); 493 Camejo (Socialist Workers); 416 MacBride (Libertarian); 260 LaRouche (U.S. Labor); 241 Levin (Socialist Labor). There were 419 write-in votes in Wayne county, but these are not available by wards within the city of Detroit.

Senator — Other vote was 1,003 Albert (Human Rights); 918 Erwin (Libertarian); 843 Reimers (Socialist Workers); 485 Girard (Socialist Labor); 387 Signorelli (U.S. Labor). There were 65 write-in votes in Wayne county, but these are not available by wards within the city of Detroit.

MICHIGAN

1976 PRIMARIES

AUGUST 3 REPUBLICAN

Senator 209,250 Marvin L. Esch; 129,917 Thomas E. Brennan; 82,092 Robert J. Huber; 51,852 Deane Baker.

Congress Unopposed in nine CD's. Contested as follows:

CD 1	622 Isaac Hood; 591 Reba W. Hawkins.
CD 2	14,229 Carl D. Pursell; 10,648 Ron Trowbridge.
CD 3	24,229 Garry Brown; 13,509 John J. H. Schwarz.
CD 4	28,871 Dave Stockman; 13,564 Lee Boothby; 2,809 David S. Frazer; 2,243 Helen R. Take.
CD 5	27,729 Harold S. Sawyer; 11,213 Charles M. Wiersma; 6,561 Walter J. Russell.
CD 8	20,380 E. Brady Denton; 11,048 Mark Nelson; 2,141 Carl B. Flynn; 1,599 Gary R. Kitts.
CD 11	36,588 Philip E. Ruppe; 7,886 Malcolm W. Dale.
CD 12	10,074 David M. Serotkin; 5,709 Lawrence P. Zatkoff; 2,460 Larry Lick; 1,391 William A. Froberg; 525 Eugene J. Tyza.
CD 13	844 Richard A. Golden; 283 Lanell Buffington.
CD 18	7,028 John E. Olsen; 5,112 Al Zaparackas.

AUGUST 3 DEMOCRATIC

Senator 325,705 Donald W. Riegle; 208,310 Richard H. Austin; 170,473 James G. O'Hara; 30,655 James L. Elsman.

Congress Unopposed in eight CD's. Contested as follows:

CD 1	35,700 John Conyers; 3,054 Russell S. Brown; 2,781 Lawrence E. Elliott.
CD 2	19,053 Edward C. Pierce; 9,435 Marvin R. Stempien; 3,984 Delbert J. Hoffman; 2,523 Mary F. Robek; 1,461 John M. Spillson.
CD 3	11,863 Howard Wolpe; 7,719 Brian Hampton.
CD 5	16,976 Richard F. Vander Veen; 6,155 John E. Leach.
CD 7	39,704 Dale E. Kildee; 12,227 Dave Benjamin.
CD 10	14,437 Donald J. Albosta; 8,117 Samuel D. Marble; 6,609 Patrick Casey.
CD 12	18,283 David E. Bonior; 15,677 John T. Bowman; 6,172 Kim Moran; 5,659 James A. Scandirito; 3,251 Charlotte M. Boyd.
CD 14	36,998 Lucien N. Nedzi; 6,033 Theodore C. Spiro.
CD 16	36,477 John D. Dingell, Jr.; 7,951 Charles J. Nemeth.
CD 17	36,785 William M. Brodhead; 3,803 Harry V. Teachout.
CD 19	9,638 Dorothea Becker; 8,781 Betty F. Collier.

MINNESOTA

GOVERNOR

Rudy Perpich (D). Elected as Lieutenant-Governor in 1974 and succeeded upon the resignation of Governor Anderson in December 1976. Next election in 1978.

SENATORS

Wendell R. Anderson (D). Appointed December 1976 to fill out term vacated by the resignation of Senator Walter F. Mondale to become Vice-President. Next election in 1978.

Hubert H. Humphrey (D). Re-elected 1976 to a six-year term. Previously elected 1970, 1960, 1954, 1948.

REPRESENTATIVES

1. Albert H. Quie (R)
2. Tom Hagedorn (R)
3. Bill Frenzel (R)
4. Bruce F. Vento (D)
5. Donald M. Fraser (D)
6. Richard M. Nolan (D)
7. Bob Bergland (D)
8. James L. Oberstar (D)

POSTWAR VOTE FOR GOVERNOR

		Republican		Democratic				Percentage			
								Total Vote		Major Vote	
Year	Total Vote	Vote	Candidate	Vote	Candidate	Other Vote	Rep.-Dem. Plurality	Rep.	Dem.	Rep.	Dem.
1974	1,252,898	367,722	Johnson, John W.	786,787	Anderson, Wendell R.	98,389	419,065 D	29.3%	62.8%	31.9%	68.1%
1970	1,365,443	621,780	Head, Douglas M.	737,921	Anderson, Wendell R.	5,742	116,141 D	45.5%	54.0%	45.7%	54.3%
1966	1,295,058	680,593	LeVander, Harold	607,943	Rolvaag, Karl F.	6,522	72,650 R	52.6%	46.9%	52.8%	47.2%
1962	1,246,904	619,751	Andersen, Elmer L.	619,842	Rolvaag, Karl F.	7,311	91 D	49.7%	49.7%	50.0%	50.0%
1960	1,550,265	783,813	Andersen, Elmer L.	760,934	Freeman, Orville L.	5,518	22,879 R	50.6%	49.1%	50.7%	49.3%
1958	1,159,915	490,731	MacKinnon, George	658,326	Freeman, Orville L.	10,858	167,595 D	42.3%	56.8%	42.7%	57.3%
1956	1,422,161	685,196	Nelsen, Ancher	731,180	Freeman, Orville L.	5,785	45,984 D	48.2%	51.4%	48.4%	51.6%
1954	1,151,417	538,865	Anderson, C. Elmer	607,099	Freeman, Orville L.	5,453	68,234 D	46.8%	52.7%	47.0%	53.0%
1952	1,418,869	785,125	Anderson, C. Elmer	624,480	Freeman, Orville L.	9,264	160,645 R	55.3%	44.0%	55.7%	44.3%
1950	1,046,632	635,800	Youngdahl, Luther	400,637	Peterson, Harry H.	10,195	235,163 R	60.7%	38.3%	61.3%	38.7%
1948	1,210,894	643,572	Youngdahl, Luther	545,766	Halsted, Charles L.	21,556	97,806 R	53.1%	45.1%	54.1%	45.9%
1946	880,348	519,067	Youngdahl, Luther	349,565	Barker, Harold H.	11,716	169,502 R	59.0%	39.7%	59.8%	40.2%

The term of office of Minnesota's Governor was increased from two to four years effective with the 1962 election.

POSTWAR VOTE FOR SENATOR

		Republican		Democratic				Percentage			
								Total Vote		Major Vote	
Year	Total Vote	Vote	Candidate	Vote	Candidate	Other Vote	Rep.-Dem. Plurality	Rep.	Dem.	Rep.	Dem.
1976	1,912,068	478,611	Brekke, Gerald W.	1,290,736	Humphrey, Hubert H.	142,721	812,125 D	25.0%	67.5%	27.1%	72.9%
1972	1,731,653	742,121	Hansen, Philip	981,340	Mondale, Walter F.	8,192	239,219 D	42.9%	56.7%	43.1%	56.9%
1970	1,364,887	568,025	MacGregor, Clark	788,256	Humphrey, Hubert H.	8,606	220,231 D	41.6%	57.8%	41.9%	58.1%
1966	1,271,426	574,868	Forsythe, Robert A.	685,840	Mondale, Walter F.	10,718	110,972 D	45.2%	53.9%	45.6%	54.4%
1964	1,543,590	605,933	Whitney, Wheelock	931,353	McCarthy, Eugene J.	6,304	325,420 D	39.3%	60.3%	39.4%	60.6%
1960	1,536,839	648,586	Peterson, P. K.	884,168	Humphrey, Hubert H.	4,085	235,582 D	42.2%	57.5%	42.3%	57.7%
1958	1,150,883	536,629	Thye, Edward J.	608,847	McCarthy, Eugene J.	5,407	72,218 D	46.6%	52.9%	46.8%	53.2%
1954	1,138,952	479,619	Bjornson, Val	642,193	Humphrey, Hubert H.	17,140	162,574 D	42.1%	56.4%	42.8%	57.2%
1952	1,387,419	785,649	Thye, Edward J.	590,011	Carlson, William E.	11,759	195,638 R	56.6%	42.5%	57.1%	42.9%
1948	1,220,250	485,801	Ball, Joseph H.	729,494	Humphrey, Hubert H.	4,955	243,693 D	39.8%	59.8%	40.0%	60.0%
1946	878,731	517,775	Thye, Edward J.	349,520	Jorgenson, Theodore	11,436	168,255 R	58.9%	39.8%	59.7%	40.3%

MINNESOTA

Districts Established June 7, 1971

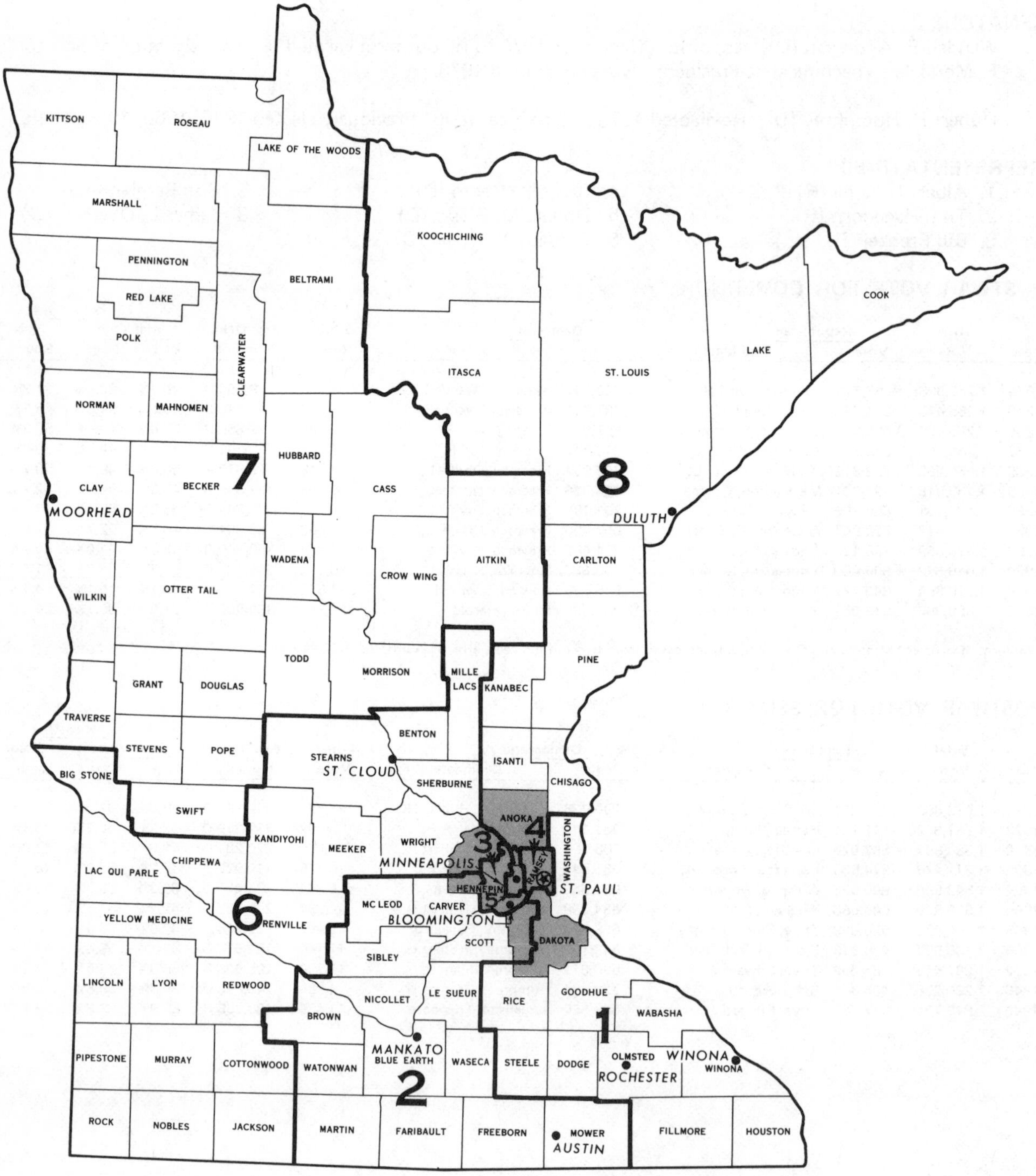

MINNESOTA

PRESIDENT 1976

1970 Census Population	County	Total Vote	Republican	Democratic	Other	Rep.-Dem. Plurality	Percentage Total Vote Rep.	Total Vote Dem.	Major Vote Rep.	Major Vote Dem.
11,403	AITKIN	6,949	2,476	4,308	165	1,832 D	35.6%	62.0%	36.5%	63.5%
154,556	ANOKA	78,315	27,863	48,173	2,279	20,310 D	35.6%	61.5%	36.6%	63.4%
24,372	BECKER	12,575	5,611	6,597	367	986 D	44.6%	52.5%	46.0%	54.0%
26,373	BELTRAMI	13,285	5,214	7,540	531	2,326 D	39.2%	56.8%	40.9%	59.1%
20,841	BENTON	10,965	4,099	6,235	631	2,136 D	37.4%	56.9%	39.7%	60.3%
7,941	BIG STONE	4,011	1,332	2,581	98	1,249 D	33.2%	64.3%	34.0%	66.0%
52,322	BLUE EARTH	25,688	11,998	12,930	760	932 D	46.7%	50.3%	48.1%	51.9%
28,887	BROWN	14,039	7,479	5,792	768	1,687 R	53.3%	41.3%	56.4%	43.6%
28,072	CARLTON	13,952	4,371	9,247	334	4,876 D	31.3%	66.3%	32.1%	67.9%
28,310	CARVER	16,363	8,199	7,574	590	625 R	50.1%	46.3%	52.0%	48.0%
17,323	CASS	10,234	4,443	5,424	367	981 D	43.4%	53.0%	45.0%	55.0%
15,109	CHIPPEWA	8,051	3,254	4,648	149	1,394 D	40.4%	57.7%	41.2%	58.8%
17,492	CHISAGO	10,867	3,874	6,625	368	2,751 D	35.6%	61.0%	36.9%	63.1%
46,585	CLAY	21,711	10,317	10,876	518	559 D	47.5%	50.1%	48.7%	51.3%
8,013	CLEARWATER	4,016	1,374	2,437	205	1,063 D	34.2%	60.7%	36.1%	63.9%
3,423	COOK	2,130	1,034	1,018	78	16 R	48.5%	47.8%	50.4%	49.6%
14,887	COTTONWOOD	7,859	3,906	3,813	140	93 R	49.7%	48.5%	50.6%	49.4%
34,826	CROW WING	19,608	8,072	10,653	883	2,581 D	41.2%	54.3%	43.1%	56.9%
139,808	DAKOTA	84,080	37,542	44,253	2,285	6,711 D	44.7%	52.6%	45.9%	54.1%
13,037	DODGE	6,598	3,446	3,009	143	437 R	52.2%	45.6%	53.4%	46.6%
22,892	DOUGLAS	13,321	5,910	7,097	314	1,187 D	44.4%	53.3%	45.4%	54.6%
20,896	FARIBAULT	10,848	5,577	5,049	222	528 R	51.4%	46.5%	52.5%	47.5%
21,916	FILLMORE	10,957	5,984	4,758	215	1,226 R	54.6%	43.4%	55.7%	44.3%
38,064	FREEBORN	18,018	8,220	9,470	328	1,250 D	45.6%	52.6%	46.5%	53.5%
34,763	GOODHUE	19,352	9,967	8,926	459	1,041 R	51.5%	46.1%	52.8%	47.2%
7,462	GRANT	4,338	1,635	2,624	79	989 D	37.7%	60.5%	38.4%	61.6%
960,080	HENNEPIN	483,378	211,892	257,380	14,106	45,488 D	43.8%	53.2%	45.2%	54.8%
17,556	HOUSTON	8,926	4,853	3,861	212	992 R	54.4%	43.3%	55.7%	44.3%
10,583	HUBBARD	6,502	2,985	3,196	321	211 D	45.9%	49.2%	48.3%	51.7%
16,560	ISANTI	9,428	3,159	6,013	256	2,854 D	33.5%	63.8%	34.4%	65.6%
35,530	ITASCA	20,281	6,646	12,979	656	6,333 D	32.8%	64.0%	33.9%	66.1%
14,352	JACKSON	7,298	2,870	4,311	117	1,441 D	39.3%	59.1%	40.0%	60.0%
9,775	KANABEC	5,311	1,943	3,188	180	1,245 D	36.6%	60.0%	37.9%	62.1%
30,548	KANDIYOHI	17,145	6,664	9,992	489	3,328 D	38.9%	58.3%	40.0%	60.0%
6,853	KITTSON	3,629	1,555	2,008	66	453 D	42.8%	55.3%	43.6%	56.4%
17,131	KOOCHICHING	8,010	2,893	4,846	271	1,953 D	36.1%	60.5%	37.4%	62.6%
11,164	LAC QUI PARLE	6,065	2,292	3,647	126	1,355 D	37.8%	60.1%	38.6%	61.4%
13,351	LAKE	6,619	2,313	3,973	333	1,660 D	34.9%	60.0%	36.8%	63.2%
3,987	LAKE OF THE WOODS	1,968	757	1,105	106	348 D	38.5%	56.1%	40.7%	59.3%
21,332	LE SUEUR	11,396	4,565	6,556	275	1,991 D	40.1%	57.5%	41.0%	59.0%
8,143	LINCOLN	4,272	1,599	2,594	79	995 D	37.4%	60.7%	38.1%	61.9%
24,273	LYON	12,470	5,036	7,122	312	2,086 D	40.4%	57.1%	41.4%	58.6%
27,662	MCLEOD	13,245	6,519	6,249	477	270 R	49.2%	47.2%	51.1%	48.9%
5,638	MAHNOMEN	2,621	905	1,590	126	685 D	34.5%	60.7%	36.3%	63.7%
13,060	MARSHALL	6,490	2,605	3,744	141	1,139 D	40.1%	57.7%	41.0%	59.0%
24,316	MARTIN	12,488	6,484	5,672	332	812 R	51.9%	45.4%	53.3%	46.7%
18,810	MEEKER	9,765	4,097	5,295	373	1,198 D	42.0%	54.2%	43.6%	56.4%
15,703	MILLE LACS	8,670	3,212	5,172	286	1,960 D	37.0%	59.7%	38.3%	61.7%
26,949	MORRISON	13,294	4,590	8,176	528	3,586 D	34.5%	61.5%	36.0%	64.0%
43,783	MOWER	21,487	8,163	12,837	487	4,674 D	38.0%	59.7%	38.9%	61.1%
12,508	MURRAY	6,399	2,605	3,685	109	1,080 D	40.7%	57.6%	41.4%	58.6%
24,518	NICOLLET	12,245	6,071	5,777	397	294 R	49.6%	47.2%	51.2%	48.8%
23,208	NOBLES	10,735	4,503	6,034	198	1,531 D	41.9%	56.2%	42.7%	57.3%
10,008	NORMAN	5,012	1,983	2,946	83	963 D	39.6%	58.8%	40.2%	59.8%
84,104	OLMSTED	39,617	24,030	14,676	911	9,354 R	60.7%	37.0%	62.1%	37.9%
46,097	OTTER TAIL	24,510	12,113	11,881	516	232 R	49.4%	48.5%	50.5%	49.5%
13,266	PENNINGTON	6,948	3,023	3,787	138	764 D	43.5%	54.5%	44.4%	55.6%
16,821	PINE	8,887	3,057	5,442	388	2,385 D	34.4%	61.2%	36.0%	64.0%
12,791	PIPESTONE	6,402	3,018	3,272	112	254 D	47.1%	51.1%	48.0%	52.0%
34,435	POLK	16,052	6,552	9,078	422	2,526 D	40.8%	56.6%	41.9%	58.1%
11,107	POPE	6,127	2,251	3,746	130	1,495 D	36.7%	61.1%	37.5%	62.5%
476,255	RAMSEY	228,067	86,480	133,682	7,905	47,202 D	37.9%	58.6%	39.3%	60.7%
5,388	RED LAKE	2,613	737	1,748	128	1,011 D	28.2%	66.9%	29.7%	70.3%
20,024	REDWOOD	9,822	4,926	4,525	371	401 R	50.2%	46.1%	52.1%	47.9%
21,139	RENVILLE	10,545	4,482	5,762	301	1,280 D	42.5%	54.6%	43.8%	56.2%

MINNESOTA

PRESIDENT 1976

1970 Census Population	County	Total Vote	Republican	Democratic	Other	Rep.-Dem. Plurality	Percentage Total Vote Rep.	Percentage Total Vote Dem.	Percentage Major Vote Rep.	Percentage Major Vote Dem.
41,582	RICE	19,607	8,311	10,590	706	2,279 D	42.4%	54.0%	44.0%	56.0%
11,346	ROCK	5,739	2,892	2,769	78	123 R	50.4%	48.2%	51.1%	48.9%
11,569	ROSEAU	5,755	2,382	3,215	158	833 D	41.4%	55.9%	42.6%	57.4%
220,693	ST. LOUIS	114,075	35,331	75,040	3,704	39,709 D	31.0%	65.8%	32.0%	68.0%
32,423	SCOTT	17,622	7,154	9,912	556	2,758 D	40.6%	56.2%	41.9%	58.1%
18,344	SHERBURNE	11,442	4,361	6,678	403	2,317 D	38.1%	58.4%	39.5%	60.5%
15,845	SIBLEY	7,860	3,871	3,752	237	119 R	49.2%	47.7%	50.8%	49.2%
95,400	STEARNS	47,821	19,574	25,027	3,220	5,453 D	40.9%	52.3%	43.9%	56.1%
26,931	STEELE	13,648	7,053	6,263	332	790 R	51.7%	45.9%	53.0%	47.0%
11,218	STEVENS	5,793	2,484	3,171	138	687 D	42.9%	54.7%	43.9%	56.1%
13,177	SWIFT	6,762	2,190	4,428	144	2,238 D	32.4%	65.5%	33.1%	66.9%
22,114	TODD	11,248	4,278	6,530	440	2,252 D	38.0%	58.1%	39.6%	60.4%
6,254	TRAVERSE	3,207	1,130	2,020	57	890 D	35.2%	63.0%	35.9%	64.1%
17,224	WABASHA	9,049	4,484	4,286	279	198 R	49.6%	47.4%	51.1%	48.9%
12,412	WADENA	6,424	3,048	3,164	212	116 D	47.4%	49.3%	49.1%	50.9%
16,663	WASECA	8,805	4,582	4,002	221	580 R	52.0%	45.5%	53.4%	46.6%
82,948	WASHINGTON	48,583	20,716	26,454	1,413	5,738 D	42.6%	54.5%	43.9%	56.1%
13,298	WATONWAN	6,662	3,351	3,177	134	174 R	50.3%	47.7%	51.3%	48.7%
9,389	WILKIN	4,112	1,882	2,103	127	221 D	45.8%	51.1%	47.2%	52.8%
44,409	WINONA	21,914	10,436	10,939	539	503 D	47.6%	49.9%	48.8%	51.2%
38,933	WRIGHT	23,464	9,314	13,379	771	4,065 D	39.7%	57.0%	41.0%	59.0%
14,516	YELLOW MEDICINE	7,470	2,946	4,337	187	1,391 D	39.4%	58.1%	40.5%	59.5%
3,805,069	TOTAL	1,949,931	819,395	1,070,440	60,096	251,045 D	42.0%	54.9%	43.4%	56.6%

MINNESOTA

SENATOR 1976

1970 Census Population	County	Total Vote	Republican	Democratic	Other	Rep.-Dem. Plurality	Percentage Total Vote Rep.	Percentage Total Vote Dem.	Percentage Major Vote Rep.	Percentage Major Vote Dem.
11,403	AITKIN	6,935	1,808	4,693	434	2,885 D	26.1%	67.7%	27.8%	72.2%
154,556	ANOKA	78,509	13,657	57,571	7,281	43,914 D	17.4%	73.3%	19.2%	80.8%
24,372	BECKER	12,658	3,900	8,295	463	4,395 D	30.8%	65.5%	32.0%	68.0%
26,373	BELTRAMI	13,265	3,392	9,031	842	5,639 D	25.6%	68.1%	27.3%	72.7%
20,841	BENTON	10,754	2,294	6,667	1,793	4,373 D	21.3%	62.0%	25.6%	74.4%
7,941	BIG STONE	3,975	868	2,882	225	2,014 D	21.8%	72.5%	23.1%	76.9%
52,322	BLUE EARTH	25,698	7,421	16,738	1,539	9,317 D	28.9%	65.1%	30.7%	69.3%
28,887	BROWN	13,920	4,285	7,179	2,456	2,894 D	30.8%	51.6%	37.4%	62.6%
28,072	CARLTON	13,925	2,370	11,265	290	8,895 D	17.0%	80.9%	17.4%	82.6%
28,310	CARVER	16,262	4,724	9,297	2,241	4,573 D	29.0%	57.2%	33.7%	66.3%
17,323	CASS	10,194	2,900	6,092	1,202	3,192 D	28.4%	59.8%	32.3%	67.7%
15,109	CHIPPEWA	7,991	2,180	5,361	450	3,181 D	27.3%	67.1%	28.9%	71.1%
17,492	CHISAGO	10,713	2,066	7,204	1,443	5,138 D	19.3%	67.2%	22.3%	77.7%
46,585	CLAY	21,068	6,064	14,619	385	8,555 D	28.8%	69.4%	29.3%	70.7%
8,013	CLEARWATER	4,039	923	2,804	312	1,881 D	22.9%	69.4%	24.8%	75.2%
3,423	COOK	2,095	697	1,326	72	629 D	33.3%	63.3%	34.5%	65.5%
14,887	COTTONWOOD	7,766	2,586	4,705	475	2,119 D	33.3%	60.6%	35.5%	64.5%
34,826	CROW WING	19,400	4,751	11,641	3,008	6,890 D	24.5%	60.0%	29.0%	71.0%
139,808	DAKOTA	82,353	20,418	55,377	6,558	34,959 D	24.8%	67.2%	26.9%	73.1%
13,037	DODGE	6,541	2,212	3,911	418	1,699 D	33.8%	59.8%	36.1%	63.9%
22,892	DOUGLAS	13,449	3,712	8,471	1,266	4,759 D	27.6%	63.0%	30.5%	69.5%
20,896	FARIBAULT	10,410	3,570	6,288	552	2,718 D	34.3%	60.4%	36.2%	63.8%
21,916	FILLMORE	10,819	3,951	6,411	457	2,460 D	36.5%	59.3%	38.1%	61.9%
38,064	FREEBORN	17,518	5,251	11,925	342	6,674 D	30.0%	68.1%	30.6%	69.4%
34,763	GOODHUE	19,201	6,380	11,144	1,677	4,764 D	33.2%	58.0%	36.4%	63.6%
7,462	GRANT	4,368	1,126	3,088	154	1,962 D	25.8%	70.7%	26.7%	73.3%
960,080	HENNEPIN	467,528	119,121	316,130	32,277	197,009 D	25.5%	67.6%	27.4%	72.6%
17,556	HOUSTON	8,811	3,004	5,534	273	2,530 D	34.1%	62.8%	35.2%	64.8%
10,583	HUBBARD	6,533	2,004	3,914	615	1,910 D	30.7%	59.9%	33.9%	66.1%
16,560	ISANTI	9,422	1,907	6,424	1,091	4,517 D	20.2%	68.2%	22.9%	77.1%
35,530	ITASCA	20,171	4,220	15,002	949	10,782 D	20.9%	74.4%	22.0%	78.0%
14,352	JACKSON	7,262	1,926	5,034	302	3,108 D	26.5%	69.3%	27.7%	72.3%
9,775	KANABEC	5,320	1,198	3,378	744	2,180 D	22.5%	63.5%	26.2%	73.8%
30,548	KANDIYOHI	16,824	3,563	11,405	1,856	7,842 D	21.2%	67.8%	23.8%	76.2%
6,853	KITTSON	3,646	1,053	2,517	76	1,464 D	28.9%	69.0%	29.5%	70.5%
17,131	KOOCHICHING	7,998	1,710	5,999	289	4,289 D	21.4%	75.0%	22.2%	77.8%
11,164	LAC QUI PARLE	6,022	1,567	4,152	303	2,585 D	26.0%	68.9%	27.4%	72.6%
13,351	LAKE	6,618	1,465	4,627	526	3,162 D	22.1%	69.9%	24.0%	76.0%
3,987	LAKE OF THE WOODS	1,969	406	1,278	285	872 D	20.6%	64.9%	24.1%	75.9%
21,332	LE SUEUR	11,361	2,887	7,467	1,007	4,580 D	25.4%	65.7%	27.9%	72.1%
8,143	LINCOLN	4,264	1,032	3,169	63	2,137 D	24.2%	74.3%	24.6%	75.4%
24,273	LYON	12,392	3,206	8,676	510	5,470 D	25.9%	70.0%	27.0%	73.0%
27,662	MCLEOD	12,750	3,947	7,165	1,638	3,218 D	31.0%	56.2%	35.5%	64.5%
5,638	MAHNOMEN	2,660	725	1,824	111	1,099 D	27.3%	68.6%	28.4%	71.6%
13,060	MARSHALL	6,544	1,671	4,697	176	3,026 D	25.5%	71.8%	26.2%	73.8%
24,316	MARTIN	12,378	4,577	6,443	1,358	1,866 D	37.0%	52.1%	41.5%	58.5%
18,810	MEEKER	9,759	2,723	5,983	1,053	3,260 D	27.9%	61.3%	31.3%	68.7%
15,703	MILLE LACS	8,634	1,847	5,634	1,153	3,787 D	21.4%	65.3%	24.7%	75.3%
26,949	MORRISON	13,351	2,951	8,801	1,599	5,850 D	22.1%	65.9%	25.1%	74.9%
43,783	MOWER	20,615	4,644	15,351	620	10,707 D	22.5%	74.5%	23.2%	76.8%
12,508	MURRAY	5,802	1,617	4,060	125	2,443 D	27.9%	70.0%	28.5%	71.5%
24,518	NICOLLET	12,261	4,087	7,265	909	3,178 D	33.3%	59.3%	36.0%	64.0%
23,208	NOBLES	10,641	2,725	7,765	151	5,040 D	25.6%	73.0%	26.0%	74.0%
10,008	NORMAN	5,112	1,346	3,697	69	2,351 D	26.3%	72.3%	26.7%	73.3%
84,104	OLMSTED	37,801	12,996	22,614	2,191	9,618 D	34.4%	59.8%	36.5%	63.5%
46,097	OTTER TAIL	23,966	8,443	14,434	1,089	5,991 D	35.2%	60.2%	36.9%	63.1%
13,266	PENNINGTON	7,002	1,835	4,884	283	3,049 D	26.2%	69.8%	27.3%	72.7%
16,821	PINE	9,065	1,810	6,145	1,110	4,335 D	20.0%	67.8%	22.8%	77.2%
12,791	PIPESTONE	6,305	1,916	4,327	62	2,411 D	30.4%	68.6%	30.7%	69.3%
34,435	POLK	16,670	4,288	11,779	603	7,491 D	25.7%	70.7%	26.7%	73.3%
11,107	POPE	6,077	1,460	4,197	420	2,737 D	24.0%	69.1%	25.8%	74.2%
476,255	RAMSEY	220,541	48,330	155,307	16,904	106,977 D	21.9%	70.4%	23.7%	76.3%
5,388	RED LAKE	2,656	478	2,038	140	1,560 D	18.0%	76.7%	19.0%	81.0%
20,024	REDWOOD	9,165	3,182	5,346	637	2,164 D	34.7%	58.3%	37.3%	62.7%
21,139	RENVILLE	10,558	2,724	6,630	1,204	3,906 D	25.8%	62.8%	29.1%	70.9%

MINNESOTA

SENATOR 1976

1970 Census Population	County	Total Vote	Republican	Democratic	Other	Rep.-Dem. Plurality	Percentage Total Vote Rep.	Percentage Total Vote Dem.	Percentage Major Vote Rep.	Percentage Major Vote Dem.
41,582	RICE	19,228	5,120	12,597	1,511	7,477 D	26.6%	65.5%	28.9%	71.1%
11,346	ROCK	5,632	1,937	3,633	62	1,696 D	34.4%	64.5%	34.8%	65.2%
11,569	ROSEAU	5,816	1,600	3,862	354	2,262 D	27.5%	66.4%	29.3%	70.7%
220,693	ST. LOUIS	112,083	19,725	89,724	2,634	69,999 D	17.6%	80.1%	18.0%	82.0%
32,423	SCOTT	17,299	3,747	11,506	2,046	7,759 D	21.7%	66.5%	24.6%	75.4%
18,344	SHERBURNE	11,439	2,451	7,524	1,464	5,073 D	21.4%	65.8%	24.6%	75.4%
15,845	SIBLEY	7,806	2,610	4,330	866	1,720 D	33.4%	55.5%	37.6%	62.4%
95,400	STEARNS	46,910	10,076	27,793	9,041	17,717 D	21.5%	59.2%	26.6%	73.4%
26,931	STEELE	13,119	4,487	7,909	723	3,422 D	34.2%	60.3%	36.2%	63.8%
11,218	STEVENS	5,826	1,495	3,955	376	2,460 D	25.7%	67.9%	27.4%	72.6%
13,177	SWIFT	6,809	1,259	5,118	432	3,859 D	18.5%	75.2%	19.7%	80.3%
22,114	TODD	11,243	2,670	7,201	1,372	4,531 D	23.7%	64.0%	27.0%	73.0%
6,254	TRAVERSE	3,216	716	2,385	115	1,669 D	22.3%	74.2%	23.1%	76.9%
17,224	WABASHA	9,000	2,737	5,417	846	2,680 D	30.4%	60.2%	33.6%	66.4%
12,412	WADENA	6,472	2,028	3,751	693	1,723 D	31.3%	58.0%	35.1%	64.9%
16,663	WASECA	8,733	3,291	4,980	462	1,689 D	37.7%	57.0%	39.8%	60.2%
82,948	WASHINGTON	48,042	11,931	32,059	4,052	20,128 D	24.8%	66.7%	27.1%	72.9%
13,298	WATONWAN	6,628	2,346	3,824	458	1,478 D	35.4%	57.7%	38.0%	62.0%
9,389	WILKIN	4,183	1,332	2,764	87	1,432 D	31.8%	66.1%	32.5%	67.5%
44,409	WINONA	21,461	5,848	14,825	788	8,977 D	27.2%	69.1%	28.3%	71.7%
38,933	WRIGHT	23,381	5,174	15,459	2,748	10,285 D	22.1%	66.1%	25.1%	74.9%
14,516	YELLOW MEDICINE	7,462	1,934	5,043	485	3,109 D	25.9%	67.6%	27.7%	72.3%
3,805,069	TOTAL	1,912,068	478,611	1,290,736	142,721	812,125 D	25.0%	67.5%	27.1%	72.9%

MINNESOTA

CONGRESS

CD	Year	Total Vote	Republican Vote	Republican Candidate	Democratic Vote	Democratic Candidate	Other Vote	Rep.-Dem. Plurality	Percentage Total Vote Rep.	Percentage Total Vote Dem.	Percentage Major Vote Rep.	Percentage Major Vote Dem.
1	1976	231,780	158,177	QUIE, ALBERT H.	70,630	OLSON, ROBERT C.	2,973	87,547 R	68.2%	30.5%	69.1%	30.9%
1	1974	152,011	95,138	QUIE, ALBERT H.	56,868	SCOTT, ULRIC	5	38,270 R	62.6%	37.4%	62.6%	37.4%
1	1972	201,804	142,698	QUIE, ALBERT H.	59,106	THOMPSON, CHARLES S.		83,592 R	70.7%	29.3%	70.7%	29.3%
2	1976	245,816	148,322	HAGEDORN, TOM	97,488	GRIFFIN, GLORIA	6	50,834 R	60.3%	39.7%	60.3%	39.7%
2	1974	165,920	88,071	HAGEDORN, TOM	77,780	BABCOCK, STEVE	69	10,291 R	53.1%	46.9%	53.1%	46.9%
2	1972	217,783	124,350	NELSEN, ANCHER	93,433	TURNBULL, CHARLES V.		30,917 R	57.1%	42.9%	57.1%	42.9%
3	1976	225,459	149,013	FRENZEL, BILL	72,044	COUGHLIN, JEROME W.	4,402	76,969 R	66.1%	32.0%	67.4%	32.6%
3	1974	137,955	83,325	FRENZEL, BILL	54,630	RIGGS, ROBERT		28,695 R	60.4%	39.6%	60.4%	39.6%
3	1972	210,942	132,638	FRENZEL, BILL	66,070	BELL, JIM	12,234	66,568 R	62.9%	31.3%	66.8%	33.2%
4	1976	200,635	59,767	ENGEBRETSON, ANDREW	133,282	VENTO, BRUCE F.	7,586	73,515 D	29.8%	66.4%	31.0%	69.0%
4	1974	125,529	30,083	RHEINBERGER, JOSEPH A.	95,437	KARTH, JOSEPH E.	9	65,354 D	24.0%	76.0%	24.0%	76.0%
4	1972	191,078	52,786	THOMPSON, STEVE	138,292	KARTH, JOSEPH E.		85,506 D	27.6%	72.4%	27.6%	72.4%
5	1976	195,596	50,764	ERDALL, RICHARD M.	138,213	FRASER, DONALD M.	6,619	87,449 D	26.0%	70.7%	26.9%	73.1%
5	1974	122,045	30,146	RATTE, PHIL	90,012	FRASER, DONALD M.	1,887	59,866 D	24.7%	73.8%	25.1%	74.9%
5	1972	205,200	50,014	DAVISSON, ALLAN	135,108	FRASER, DONALD M.	20,078	85,094 D	24.4%	65.8%	27.0%	73.0%
6	1976	246,710	99,201	ANDERSON, JAMES	147,507	NOLAN, RICHARD M.	2	48,306 D	40.2%	59.8%	40.2%	59.8%
6	1974	174,263	77,797	GRUNSETH, JON	96,465	NOLAN, RICHARD M.	1	18,668 D	44.6%	55.4%	44.6%	55.4%
6	1972	224,492	114,537	ZWACH, JOHN M.	109,955	NOLAN, RICHARD M.		4,582 R	51.0%	49.0%	51.0%	49.0%
7	1976	241,664	64,333	LEISETH, BOB	174,080	BERGLAND, BOB	3,251	109,747 D	26.6%	72.0%	27.0%	73.0%
7	1974	172,266	43,054	REBER, DAN	129,207	BERGLAND, BOB	5	86,153 D	25.0%	75.0%	25.0%	75.0%
7	1972	225,350	92,283	HAAVEN, JON O.	133,067	BERGLAND, BOB		40,784 D	41.0%	59.0%	41.0%	59.0%
8	1976	206,844			206,755	OBERSTAR, JAMES L.	89	206,755 D		100.0%		100.0%
8	1974	169,013	44,298	ARNOLD, JEROME	104,740	OBERSTAR, JAMES L.	19,975	60,442 D	26.2%	62.0%	29.7%	70.3%
8	1972	213,137	51,314	JOHNSON, EDWARD	161,823	BLATNIK, JOHN A.		110,509 D	24.1%	75.9%	24.1%	75.9%

MINNESOTA

1976 GENERAL ELECTION

In Minnesota the Democratic party is known as the Democratic-Farmer-Labor party and the Republican party as Independent-Republican; candidates appear on the ballot with these designations. Socialist Labor candidates appear on the ballot with the designation Industrial Government.

1976 GENERAL ELECTION

President — Other vote was 35,490 McCarthy (McCarthy '76 Principle); 13,592 Anderson (American); 4,149 Camejo (Socialist Workers); 3,529 MacBride (Libertarian); 1,092 Hall (Communist); 635 Wright (People's); 543 LaRouche (International Development Bank); 370 Levin (Industrial Government); 354 Zeidler (Socialist); 342 scattered.

Senator — Original uncorrected canvass gave the Republican total vote as 478,602. Other vote was 125,612 Helm (American); 9,380 Peterson (Socialist Workers); 5,476 Miller (Libertarian); 2,214 Savola (Communist); 39 scattered.

Congress — Other vote was scattered in CD's 2, 6 and 8; Mathias (American) in CD 3; 2,966 Duwe (American) and 7 scattered in CD 1; 3,214 Carlson (Libertarian) and 37 scattered in CD 7; in other CD's as follows:

CD 4 — 3,040 Uhl (Independent); 2,720 Piotrowski (Libertarian); 1,790 Schwartz (Socialist Workers); 36 scattered.

CD 5 — 3,189 Kirkham (American); 1,824 Frank (Socialist Workers); 1,070 Haws (Libertarian); 536 Brust (Workers).

1976 PRIMARIES

SEPTEMBER 14 REPUBLICAN

Senator — 76,183 Gerald W. Brekke; 32,115 Richard Franson; 13,014 John H. Glover; 9,307 Roland Riemers; 9,150 Bea Mooney.

Congress — Unopposed in six CD's. No candidate in CD 8. Contested as follows:

CD 4 — 9,354 Andrew Engebretson; 7,388 Dean Fenner.

SEPTEMBER 14 DEMOCRATIC

Senator — 317,632 Hubert H. Humphrey; 30,262 Dick Bullock.

Congress — Unopposed in four CD's. Contested as follows:

CD 1 — 15,460 Robert C. Olson; 9,263 Lynn W. Carlson; 3,382 Marion M. Doxtater.

CD 3 — 10,674 Jerome W. Coughlin; 6,446 Joel A. Saliterman.

CD 4 — 35,025 Bruce F. Vento; 15,669 John S. Connolly; 14,921 Robert W. Mattson; 787 Terry Brown; 537 Howard J. Parker.

CD 5 — 38,155 Donald M. Fraser; 3,563 Phil Ratte.

MISSISSIPPI

GOVERNOR

Cliff Finch (D). Elected 1975 to a four-year term.

SENATORS

James O. Eastland (D). Re-elected 1972 to a six-year term. Previously elected 1966, 1960, 1954, 1948, 1942. Also served in the Senate from June to September, 1941.

John Stennis (D). Re-elected 1976 to a six-year term. Previously elected 1970, 1964, 1958, 1952, and in 1947 to fill out term vacated by the death of Senator Theodore Bilbo.

REPRESENTATIVES

1. Jamie L. Whitten (D)
2. David R. Bowen (D)
3. G. V. Montgomery (D)
4. Thad Cochran (R)
5. Trent Lott (R)

POSTWAR VOTE FOR GOVERNOR

		Republican		Democratic				Percentage			
	Total					Other	Rep.-Dem.	Total Vote		Major Vote	
Year	Vote	Vote	Candidate	Vote	Candidate	Vote	Plurality	Rep.	Dem.	Rep.	Dem.
1975	708,033	319,632	Carmichael, Gil	369,568	Finch, Cliff	18,833	49,936 D	45.1%	52.2%	46.4%	53.6%
1971	780,537	–	–	601,122	Waller, William L.	179,415	601,122 D	–	77.0%	–	100.0%
1967	448,697	133,379	Phillips, Rubel L.	315,318	Williams, John Bell	–	181,939 D	29.7%	70.3%	29.7%	70.3%
1963	363,971	138,515	Phillips, Rubel L.	225,456	Johnson, Paul B.	–	86,941 D	38.1%	61.9%	38.1%	61.9%
1959	57,671	–	–	57,671	Barnett, Ross R.	–	57,671 D	–	100.0%	–	100.0%
1955	40,707	–	–	40,707	Coleman, James P.	–	40,707 D	–	100.0%	–	100.0%
1951	43,422	–	–	43,422	White, Hugh	–	43,422 D	–	100.0%	–	100.0%
1947	166,095	–	–	161,993	Wright, Fielding L.	4,102	161,993 D	–	97.5%	–	100.0%

POSTWAR VOTE FOR SENATOR

		Republican		Democratic				Percentage			
	Total					Other	Rep.-Dem.	Total Vote		Major Vote	
Year	Vote	Vote	Candidate	Vote	Candidate	Vote	Plurality	Rep.	Dem.	Rep.	Dem.
1976	554,433	–	–	554,433	Stennis, John	–	554,433 D	–	100.0%	–	100.0%
1972	645,746	249,779	Carmichael, Gil	375,102	Eastland, James O.	20,865	125,323 D	38.7%	58.1%	40.0%	60.0%
1970	324,215	–	–	286,622	Stennis, John	37,593	286,622 D	–	88.4%	–	100.0%
1966	393,900	105,150	Walker, Prentiss	258,248	Eastland, James O.	30,502	153,098 D	26.7%	65.6%	28.9%	71.1%
1964	343,364	–	–	343,364	Stennis, John	–	343,364 D	–	100.0%	–	100.0%
1960	266,148	21,807	Moore, Joe A.	244,341	Eastland, James O.	–	222,534 D	8.2%	91.8%	8.2%	91.8%
1958	61,039	–	–	61,039	Stennis, John	–	61,039 D	–	100.0%	–	100.0%
1954	105,526	4,678	White, James A.	100,848	Eastland, James O.	–	96,170 D	4.4%	95.6%	4.4%	95.6%
1952	233,919	–	–	233,919	Stennis, John	–	233,919 D	–	100.0%	–	100.0%
1948	151,478	–	–	151,478	Eastland, James O.	–	151,478 D	–	100.0%	–	100.0%
1947s	193,709		(See note below)								
1946	46,747	–	–	46,747	Bilbo, Theodore	–	46,747 D	–	100.0%	–	100.0%

The 1947 election was for a short term to fill a vacancy and was held without party designation or nomination; John Stennis polled 52,068 votes (26.9% of the total vote) and won the election with a 6,343 plurality.

MISSISSIPPI

Districts Established March 1, 1972

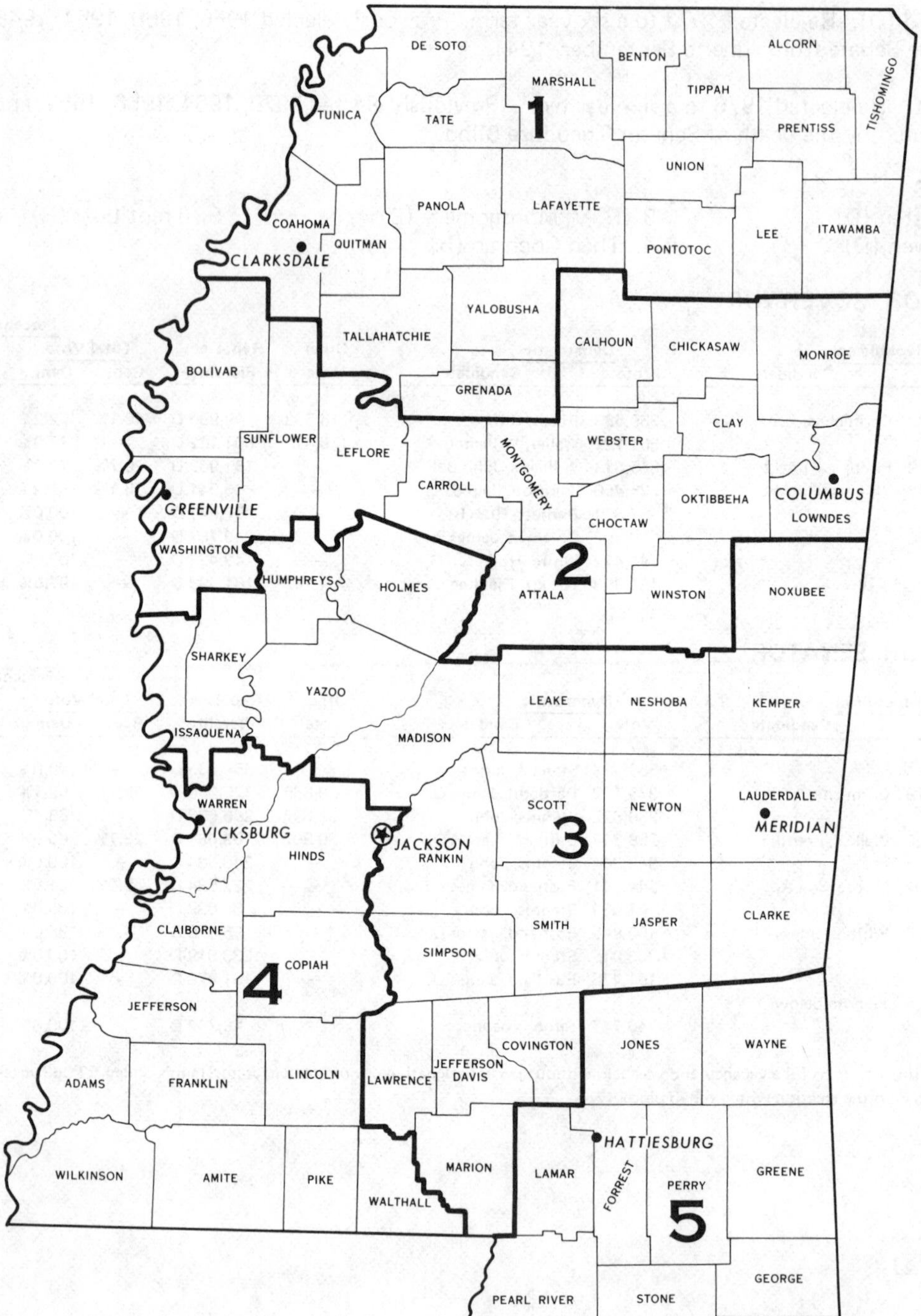

MISSISSIPPI

PRESIDENT 1976

1970 Census Population	County	Total Vote	Republican	Democratic	Other	Rep.-Dem. Plurality	Percentage Total Vote Rep.	Total Vote Dem.	Major Vote Rep.	Major Vote Dem.
37,293	ADAMS	13,861	6,431	6,619	811	188 D	46.4%	47.8%	49.3%	50.7%
27,179	ALCORN	10,770	3,430	6,995	345	3,565 D	31.8%	64.9%	32.9%	67.1%
13,763	AMITE	4,999	2,256	2,574	169	318 D	45.1%	51.5%	46.7%	53.3%
19,570	ATTALA	7,423	3,146	4,068	209	922 D	42.4%	54.8%	43.6%	56.4%
7,505	BENTON	3,209	790	2,375	44	1,585 D	24.6%	74.0%	25.0%	75.0%
49,409	BOLIVAR	12,875	5,136	7,561	178	2,425 D	39.9%	58.7%	40.5%	59.5%
14,623	CALHOUN	4,788	1,892	2,724	172	832 D	39.5%	56.9%	41.0%	59.0%
9,397	CARROLL	3,167	1,561	1,566	40	5 D	49.3%	49.4%	49.9%	50.1%
16,805	CHICKASAW	5,723	2,581	2,891	251	310 D	45.1%	50.5%	47.2%	52.8%
8,440	CHOCTAW	3,172	1,562	1,520	90	42 R	49.2%	47.9%	50.7%	49.3%
10,086	CLAIBORNE	3,852	1,078	2,657	117	1,579 D	28.0%	69.0%	28.9%	71.1%
15,049	CLARKE	5,995	2,935	2,816	244	119 R	49.0%	47.0%	51.0%	49.0%
18,840	CLAY	6,837	3,017	3,514	306	497 D	44.1%	51.4%	46.2%	53.8%
40,447	COAHOMA	11,113	4,269	6,412	432	2,143 D	38.4%	57.7%	40.0%	60.0%
24,749	COPIAH	8,646	4,108	4,267	271	159 D	47.5%	49.4%	49.1%	50.9%
14,002	COVINGTON	5,568	2,591	2,862	115	271 D	46.5%	51.4%	47.5%	52.5%
35,885	DE SOTO	14,312	6,240	7,756	316	1,516 D	43.6%	54.2%	44.6%	55.4%
57,849	FORREST	19,120	10,770	7,914	436	2,856 R	56.3%	41.4%	57.6%	42.4%
8,011	FRANKLIN	3,395	1,719	1,578	98	141 R	50.6%	46.5%	52.1%	47.9%
12,459	GEORGE	5,229	1,957	3,072	200	1,115 D	37.4%	58.7%	38.9%	61.1%
8,545	GREENE	3,770	1,538	2,127	105	589 D	40.8%	56.4%	42.0%	58.0%
19,854	GRENADA	7,020	3,569	3,263	188	306 R	50.8%	46.5%	52.2%	47.8%
17,387	HANCOCK	7,842	3,765	3,855	222	90 D	48.0%	49.2%	49.4%	50.6%
134,582	HARRISON	37,139	19,207	16,569	1,363	2,638 R	51.7%	44.6%	53.7%	46.3%
214,973	HINDS	75,756	45,803	28,748	1,205	17,055 R	60.5%	37.9%	61.4%	38.6%
23,120	HOLMES	7,203	2,438	4,616	149	2,178 D	33.8%	64.1%	34.6%	65.4%
14,601	HUMPHREYS	3,774	1,445	2,172	157	727 D	38.3%	57.6%	40.0%	60.0%
2,737	ISSAQUENA	954	325	567	62	242 D	34.1%	59.4%	36.4%	63.6%
16,847	ITAWAMBA	6,705	2,153	4,480	72	2,327 D	32.1%	66.8%	32.5%	67.5%
87,975	JACKSON	31,082	17,177	12,533	1,372	4,644 R	55.3%	40.3%	57.8%	42.2%
15,994	JASPER	5,513	2,356	3,109	48	753 D	42.7%	56.4%	43.1%	56.9%
9,295	JEFFERSON	3,426	782	2,562	82	1,780 D	22.8%	74.8%	23.4%	76.6%
12,936	JEFFERSON DAVIS	4,698	1,868	2,747	83	879 D	39.8%	58.5%	40.5%	59.5%
56,357	JONES	21,552	11,098	10,139	315	959 R	51.5%	47.0%	52.3%	47.7%
10,233	KEMPER	4,160	1,680	2,436	44	756 D	40.4%	58.6%	40.8%	59.2%
24,181	LAFAYETTE	8,351	3,735	4,375	241	640 D	44.7%	52.4%	46.1%	53.9%
15,209	LAMAR	7,414	4,056	3,109	249	947 R	54.7%	41.9%	56.6%	43.4%
67,087	LAUDERDALE	24,446	14,273	9,813	360	4,460 R	58.4%	40.1%	59.3%	40.7%
11,137	LAWRENCE	4,436	2,109	2,242	85	133 D	47.5%	50.5%	48.5%	51.5%
17,085	LEAKE	6,508	2,952	3,415	141	463 D	45.4%	52.5%	46.4%	53.6%
46,148	LEE	16,333	7,366	8,504	463	1,138 D	45.1%	52.1%	46.4%	53.6%
42,111	LEFLORE	12,589	5,872	6,135	582	263 D	46.6%	48.7%	48.9%	51.1%
26,198	LINCOLN	10,392	6,084	4,043	265	2,041 R	58.5%	38.9%	60.1%	39.9%
49,700	LOWNDES	14,700	8,003	6,181	516	1,822 R	54.4%	42.0%	56.4%	43.6%
29,737	MADISON	11,316	4,838	6,240	238	1,402 D	42.8%	55.1%	43.7%	56.3%
22,871	MARION	10,737	5,300	5,283	154	17 R	49.4%	49.2%	50.1%	49.9%
24,027	MARSHALL	9,226	2,242	6,769	215	4,527 D	24.3%	73.4%	24.9%	75.1%
34,043	MONROE	11,234	4,737	6,097	400	1,360 D	42.2%	54.3%	43.7%	56.3%
12,918	MONTGOMERY	4,827	2,278	2,410	139	132 D	47.2%	49.9%	48.6%	51.4%
20,802	NESHOBA	7,819	3,859	3,891	69	32 D	49.4%	49.8%	49.8%	50.2%
18,983	NEWTON	6,690	3,813	2,741	136	1,072 R	57.0%	41.0%	58.2%	41.8%
14,288	NOXUBEE	4,136	1,860	2,121	155	261 D	45.0%	51.3%	46.7%	53.3%
28,752	OKTIBBEHA	9,725	5,194	4,339	192	855 R	53.4%	44.6%	54.5%	45.5%
26,829	PANOLA	9,067	3,341	5,517	209	2,176 D	36.8%	60.8%	37.7%	62.3%
27,802	PEARL RIVER	9,665	4,332	5,024	309	692 D	44.8%	52.0%	46.3%	53.7%
9,065	PERRY	3,725	1,527	1,965	233	438 D	41.0%	52.8%	43.7%	56.3%
31,756	PIKE	11,751	5,659	5,749	343	90 D	48.2%	48.9%	49.6%	50.4%
17,363	PONTOTOC	6,491	2,245	4,066	180	1,821 D	34.6%	62.6%	35.6%	64.4%
20,133	PRENTISS	6,977	2,362	4,431	184	2,069 D	33.9%	63.5%	34.8%	65.2%
15,888	QUITMAN	4,045	1,287	2,621	137	1,334 D	31.8%	64.8%	32.9%	67.1%
43,933	RANKIN	18,878	11,507	6,937	434	4,570 R	61.0%	36.7%	62.4%	37.6%
21,369	SCOTT	7,468	3,649	3,643	176	6 R	48.9%	48.8%	50.0%	50.0%
8,937	SHARKEY	2,449	1,024	1,283	142	259 D	41.8%	52.4%	44.4%	55.6%
19,947	SIMPSON	7,960	4,291	3,600	69	691 R	53.9%	45.2%	54.4%	45.6%
13,561	SMITH	5,748	3,147	2,434	167	713 R	54.7%	42.3%	56.4%	43.6%

MISSISSIPPI

PRESIDENT 1976

1970 Census Population	County	Total Vote	Republican	Democratic	Other	Rep.-Dem. Plurality	Percentage Total Vote Rep.	Total Vote Dem.	Major Vote Rep.	Major Vote Dem.
8,101	STONE	3,278	1,575	1,648	55	73 D	48.0%	50.3%	48.9%	51.1%
37,047	SUNFLOWER	8,024	3,456	4,322	246	866 D	43.1%	53.9%	44.4%	55.6%
19,338	TALLAHATCHIE	5,252	2,146	2,991	115	845 D	40.9%	56.9%	41.8%	58.2%
18,544	TATE	6,436	2,497	3,747	192	1,250 D	38.8%	58.2%	40.0%	60.0%
15,852	TIPPAH	6,274	1,887	4,260	127	2,373 D	30.1%	67.9%	30.7%	69.3%
14,940	TISHOMINGO	5,839	1,969	3,734	136	1,765 D	33.7%	63.9%	34.5%	65.5%
11,854	TUNICA	2,756	951	1,695	110	744 D	34.5%	61.5%	35.9%	64.1%
19,096	UNION	7,659	2,507	5,021	131	2,514 D	32.7%	65.6%	33.3%	66.7%
12,500	WALTHALL	4,927	2,110	2,650	167	540 D	42.8%	53.8%	44.3%	55.7%
44,981	WARREN	15,705	8,699	6,299	707	2,400 R	55.4%	40.1%	58.0%	42.0%
70,581	WASHINGTON	18,146	7,474	9,650	1,022	2,176 D	41.2%	53.2%	43.6%	56.4%
16,650	WAYNE	6,422	3,022	3,306	94	284 D	47.1%	51.5%	47.8%	52.2%
10,047	WEBSTER	4,281	1,943	2,218	120	275 D	45.4%	51.8%	46.7%	53.3%
11,099	WILKINSON	3,845	1,273	2,514	58	1,241 D	33.1%	65.4%	33.6%	66.4%
18,406	WINSTON	7,792	3,659	3,956	177	297 D	47.0%	50.8%	48.0%	52.0%
11,915	YALOBUSHA	4,503	1,808	2,603	92	795 D	40.2%	57.8%	41.0%	59.0%
27,304	YAZOO	8,471	4,255	4,053	163	202 R	50.2%	47.8%	51.2%	48.8%
2,216,912	TOTAL	769,361	366,846	381,309	21,206	14,463 D	47.7%	49.6%	49.0%	51.0%

MISSISSIPPI

GOVERNOR 1975

1970 Census Population	County	Total Vote	Republican	Democratic	Other	Rep.-Dem. Plurality	Percentage Total Vote Rep.	Percentage Total Vote Dem.	Percentage Major Vote Rep.	Percentage Major Vote Dem.
37,293	ADAMS	12,151	6,431	5,286	434	1,145 R	52.9%	43.5%	54.9%	45.1%
27,179	ALCORN	11,590	3,789	7,721	80	3,932 D	32.7%	66.6%	32.9%	67.1%
13,763	AMITE	4,961	1,669	3,243	49	1,574 D	33.6%	65.4%	34.0%	66.0%
19,570	ATTALA	7,203	2,686	4,252	265	1,566 D	37.3%	59.0%	38.7%	61.3%
7,505	BENTON	2,745	642	2,067	36	1,425 D	23.4%	75.3%	23.7%	76.3%
49,409	BOLIVAR	10,173	4,177	5,089	907	912 D	41.1%	50.0%	45.1%	54.9%
14,623	CALHOUN	5,380	1,722	3,482	176	1,760 D	32.0%	64.7%	33.1%	66.9%
9,397	CARROLL	3,350	1,089	2,192	69	1,103 D	32.5%	65.4%	33.2%	66.8%
16,805	CHICKASAW	6,101	2,441	3,511	149	1,070 D	40.0%	57.5%	41.0%	59.0%
8,440	CHOCTAW	3,109	900	2,186	23	1,286 D	28.9%	70.3%	29.2%	70.8%
10,086	CLAIBORNE	4,311	1,239	2,249	823	1,010 D	28.7%	52.2%	35.5%	64.5%
15,049	CLARKE	6,347	2,908	3,387	52	479 D	45.8%	53.4%	46.2%	53.8%
18,840	CLAY	6,300	2,915	3,165	220	250 D	46.3%	50.2%	47.9%	52.1%
40,447	COAHOMA	8,405	3,759	4,270	376	511 D	44.7%	50.8%	46.8%	53.2%
24,749	COPIAH	8,438	3,446	4,843	149	1,397 D	40.8%	57.4%	41.6%	58.4%
14,002	COVINGTON	5,646	2,046	3,501	99	1,455 D	36.2%	62.0%	36.9%	63.1%
35,885	DE SOTO	11,128	2,671	8,336	121	5,665 D	24.0%	74.9%	24.3%	75.7%
57,849	FORREST	17,161	9,746	7,245	170	2,501 R	56.8%	42.2%	57.4%	42.6%
8,011	FRANKLIN	3,835	1,223	2,538	74	1,315 D	31.9%	66.2%	32.5%	67.5%
12,459	GEORGE	5,144	1,548	3,570	26	2,022 D	30.1%	69.4%	30.2%	69.8%
8,545	GREENE	4,284	1,226	3,028	30	1,802 D	28.6%	70.7%	28.8%	71.2%
19,854	GRENADA	6,633	3,163	3,308	162	145 D	47.7%	49.9%	48.9%	51.1%
17,387	HANCOCK	6,913	2,894	3,951	68	1,057 D	41.9%	57.2%	42.3%	57.7%
134,582	HARRISON	30,185	17,463	12,284	438	5,179 R	57.9%	40.7%	58.7%	41.3%
214,973	HINDS	65,817	41,894	20,392	3,531	21,502 R	63.7%	31.0%	67.3%	32.7%
23,120	HOLMES	7,397	2,947	4,068	382	1,121 D	39.8%	55.0%	42.0%	58.0%
14,601	HUMPHREYS	4,356	1,587	2,445	324	858 D	36.4%	56.1%	39.4%	60.6%
2,737	ISSAQUENA	874	253	556	65	303 D	28.9%	63.6%	31.3%	68.7%
16,847	ITAWAMBA	6,563	1,942	4,583	38	2,641 D	29.6%	69.8%	29.8%	70.2%
87,975	JACKSON	24,209	13,524	10,352	333	3,172 R	55.9%	42.8%	56.6%	43.4%
15,994	JASPER	5,420	2,246	3,038	136	792 D	41.4%	56.1%	42.5%	57.5%
9,295	JEFFERSON	3,247	824	2,344	79	1,520 D	25.4%	72.2%	26.0%	74.0%
12,936	JEFFERSON DAVIS	4,575	1,526	2,925	124	1,399 D	33.4%	63.9%	34.3%	65.7%
56,357	JONES	21,611	10,665	10,660	286	5 R	49.3%	49.3%	50.0%	50.0%
10,233	KEMPER	3,955	1,576	2,312	67	736 D	39.8%	58.5%	40.5%	59.5%
24,181	LAFAYETTE	6,700	3,326	3,300	74	26 R	49.6%	49.3%	50.2%	49.8%
15,209	LAMAR	6,591	2,844	3,717	30	873 D	43.1%	56.4%	43.3%	56.7%
67,087	LAUDERDALE	22,135	12,411	9,251	473	3,160 R	56.1%	41.8%	57.3%	42.7%
11,137	LAWRENCE	4,648	1,871	2,682	95	811 D	40.3%	57.7%	41.1%	58.9%
17,085	LEAKE	6,799	2,370	4,288	141	1,918 D	34.9%	63.1%	35.6%	64.4%
46,148	LEE	14,987	7,493	7,211	283	282 R	50.0%	48.1%	51.0%	49.0%
42,111	LEFLORE	11,524	6,069	4,905	550	1,164 R	52.7%	42.6%	55.3%	44.7%
26,198	LINCOLN	10,160	4,532	5,468	160	936 D	44.6%	53.8%	45.3%	54.7%
49,700	LOWNDES	11,934	6,906	4,899	129	2,007 R	57.9%	41.1%	58.5%	41.5%
29,737	MADISON	10,367	4,698	4,884	785	186 D	45.3%	47.1%	49.0%	51.0%
22,871	MARION	9,336	4,868	4,303	165	565 R	52.1%	46.1%	53.1%	46.9%
24,027	MARSHALL	9,163	2,438	6,470	255	4,032 D	26.6%	70.6%	27.4%	72.6%
34,043	MONROE	9,866	4,425	5,278	163	853 D	44.9%	53.5%	45.6%	54.4%
12,918	MONTGOMERY	4,872	1,675	3,010	187	1,335 D	34.4%	61.8%	35.8%	64.2%
20,802	NESHOBA	8,798	3,708	4,963	127	1,255 D	42.1%	56.4%	42.8%	57.2%
18,983	NEWTON	7,570	3,411	4,074	85	663 D	45.1%	53.8%	45.6%	54.4%
14,288	NOXUBEE	4,016	1,757	2,146	113	389 D	43.8%	53.4%	45.0%	55.0%
28,752	OKTIBBEHA	7,779	5,219	2,449	111	2,770 R	67.1%	31.5%	68.1%	31.9%
26,829	PANOLA	9,255	1,421	7,658	176	6,237 D	15.4%	82.7%	15.7%	84.3%
27,802	PEARL RIVER	9,618	3,614	5,918	86	2,304 D	37.6%	61.5%	37.9%	62.1%
9,065	PERRY	4,021	1,356	2,628	37	1,272 D	33.7%	65.4%	34.0%	66.0%
31,756	PIKE	10,782	4,669	5,301	812	632 D	43.3%	49.2%	46.8%	53.2%
17,363	PONTOTOC	7,023	2,336	4,640	47	2,304 D	33.3%	66.1%	33.5%	66.5%
20,133	PRENTISS	6,966	2,236	4,678	52	2,442 D	32.1%	67.2%	32.3%	67.7%
15,888	QUITMAN	4,286	1,273	2,946	67	1,673 D	29.7%	68.7%	30.2%	69.8%
43,933	RANKIN	17,277	9,335	7,674	268	1,661 R	54.0%	44.4%	54.9%	45.1%
21,369	SCOTT	8,193	3,437	4,498	258	1,061 D	42.0%	54.9%	43.3%	56.7%
8,937	SHARKEY	2,538	1,003	1,397	138	394 D	39.5%	55.0%	41.8%	58.2%
19,947	SIMPSON	8,229	3,453	4,573	203	1,120 D	42.0%	55.6%	43.0%	57.0%
13,561	SMITH	6,160	2,355	3,734	71	1,379 D	38.2%	60.6%	38.7%	61.3%

MISSISSIPPI

GOVERNOR 1975

1970 Census Population	County	Total Vote	Republican	Democratic	Other	Rep.-Dem. Plurality	Percentage Total Vote Rep.	Percentage Total Vote Dem.	Percentage Major Vote Rep.	Percentage Major Vote Dem.
8,101	STONE	3,624	1,658	1,916	50	258 D	45.8%	52.9%	46.4%	53.6%
37,047	SUNFLOWER	6,993	2,943	3,835	215	892 D	42.1%	54.8%	43.4%	56.6%
19,338	TALLAHATCHIE	4,939	1,121	3,783	35	2,662 D	22.7%	76.6%	22.9%	77.1%
18,544	TATE	5,180	1,293	3,801	86	2,508 D	25.0%	73.4%	25.4%	74.6%
15,852	TIPPAH	5,670	1,796	3,811	63	2,015 D	31.7%	67.2%	32.0%	68.0%
14,940	TISHOMINGO	5,286	1,404	3,861	21	2,457 D	26.6%	73.0%	26.7%	73.3%
11,854	TUNICA	2,176	545	1,608	23	1,063 D	25.0%	73.9%	25.3%	74.7%
19,096	UNION	6,677	2,554	4,063	60	1,509 D	38.3%	60.9%	38.6%	61.4%
12,500	WALTHALL	5,030	1,845	2,957	228	1,112 D	36.7%	58.8%	38.4%	61.6%
44,981	WARREN	12,254	7,221	4,708	325	2,513 R	58.9%	38.4%	60.5%	39.5%
70,581	WASHINGTON	14,351	7,370	6,325	656	1,045 R	51.4%	44.1%	53.8%	46.2%
16,650	WAYNE	6,315	2,321	3,930	64	1,609 D	36.8%	62.2%	37.1%	62.9%
10,047	WEBSTER	4,290	1,333	2,930	27	1,597 D	31.1%	68.3%	31.3%	68.7%
11,099	WILKINSON	4,249	1,469	2,713	67	1,244 D	34.6%	63.9%	35.1%	64.9%
18,406	WINSTON	7,262	3,044	4,092	126	1,048 D	41.9%	56.3%	42.7%	57.3%
11,915	YALOBUSHA	4,433	954	3,421	58	2,467 D	21.5%	77.2%	21.8%	78.2%
27,304	YAZOO	8,194	3,475	4,492	227	1,017 D	42.4%	54.8%	43.6%	56.4%
2,216,912	TOTAL	708,033	319,632	369,568	18,833	49,936 D	45.1%	52.2%	46.4%	53.6%

MISSISSIPPI

SENATOR 1976

1970 Census Population	County	Total Vote	Republican	Democratic	Other	Rep.-Dem. Plurality	Percentage Total Vote Rep.	Percentage Total Vote Dem.	Percentage Major Vote Rep.	Percentage Major Vote Dem.
37,293	ADAMS	5,969		5,969		5,969 D		100.0%		100.0%
27,179	ALCORN	6,923		6,923		6,923 D		100.0%		100.0%
13,763	AMITE	4,099		4,099		4,099 D		100.0%		100.0%
19,570	ATTALA	5,855		5,855		5,855 D		100.0%		100.0%
7,505	BENTON	1,958		1,958		1,958 D		100.0%		100.0%
49,409	BOLIVAR	6,169		6,169		6,169 D		100.0%		100.0%
14,623	CALHOUN	3,940		3,940		3,940 D		100.0%		100.0%
9,397	CARROLL	2,109		2,109		2,109 D		100.0%		100.0%
16,805	CHICKASAW	3,880		3,880		3,880 D		100.0%		100.0%
8,440	CHOCTAW	2,511		2,511		2,511 D		100.0%		100.0%
10,086	CLAIBORNE	1,897		1,897		1,897 D		100.0%		100.0%
15,049	CLARKE	5,113		5,113		5,113 D		100.0%		100.0%
18,840	CLAY	5,548		5,548		5,548 D		100.0%		100.0%
40,447	COAHOMA	4,779		4,779		4,779 D		100.0%		100.0%
24,749	COPIAH	5,843		5,843		5,843 D		100.0%		100.0%
14,002	COVINGTON	4,104		4,104		4,104 D		100.0%		100.0%
35,885	DE SOTO	10,531		10,531		10,531 D		100.0%		100.0%
57,849	FORREST	16,535		16,535		16,535 D		100.0%		100.0%
8,011	FRANKLIN	2,040		2,040		2,040 D		100.0%		100.0%
12,459	GEORGE	4,446		4,446		4,446 D		100.0%		100.0%
8,545	GREENE	2,808		2,808		2,808 D		100.0%		100.0%
19,854	GRENADA	5,315		5,315		5,315 D		100.0%		100.0%
17,387	HANCOCK	6,682		6,682		6,682 D		100.0%		100.0%
134,582	HARRISON	31,114		31,114		31,114 D		100.0%		100.0%
214,973	HINDS	61,256		61,256		61,256 D		100.0%		100.0%
23,120	HOLMES	4,807		4,807		4,807 D		100.0%		100.0%
14,601	HUMPHREYS	2,642		2,642		2,642 D		100.0%		100.0%
2,737	ISSAQUENA	388		388		388 D		100.0%		100.0%
16,847	ITAWAMBA	4,499		4,499		4,499 D		100.0%		100.0%
87,975	JACKSON	25,657		25,657		25,657 D		100.0%		100.0%
15,994	JASPER	4,511		4,511		4,511 D		100.0%		100.0%
9,295	JEFFERSON	2,068		2,068		2,068 D		100.0%		100.0%
12,936	JEFFERSON DAVIS	1,882		1,882		1,882 D		100.0%		100.0%
56,357	JONES	15,740		15,740		15,740 D		100.0%		100.0%
10,233	KEMPER	3,406		3,406		3,406 D		100.0%		100.0%
24,181	LAFAYETTE	6,457		6,457		6,457 D		100.0%		100.0%
15,209	LAMAR	5,205		5,205		5,205 D		100.0%		100.0%
67,087	LAUDERDALE	18,885		18,885		18,885 D		100.0%		100.0%
11,137	LAWRENCE	3,106		3,106		3,106 D		100.0%		100.0%
17,085	LEAKE	5,499		5,499		5,499 D		100.0%		100.0%
46,148	LEE	9,477		9,477		9,477 D		100.0%		100.0%
42,111	LEFLORE	8,562		8,562		8,562 D		100.0%		100.0%
26,198	LINCOLN	8,240		8,240		8,240 D		100.0%		100.0%
49,700	LOWNDES	11,905		11,905		11,905 D		100.0%		100.0%
29,737	MADISON	6,068		6,068		6,068 D		100.0%		100.0%
22,871	MARION	7,630		7,630		7,630 D		100.0%		100.0%
24,027	MARSHALL	5,246		5,246		5,246 D		100.0%		100.0%
34,043	MONROE	8,398		8,398		8,398 D		100.0%		100.0%
12,918	MONTGOMERY	3,095		3,095		3,095 D		100.0%		100.0%
20,802	NESHOBA	7,043		7,043		7,043 D		100.0%		100.0%
18,983	NEWTON	6,068		6,068		6,068 D		100.0%		100.0%
14,288	NOXUBEE	2,376		2,376		2,376 D		100.0%		100.0%
28,752	OKTIBBEHA	7,641		7,641		7,641 D		100.0%		100.0%
26,829	PANOLA	5,183		5,183		5,183 D		100.0%		100.0%
27,802	PEARL RIVER	7,909		7,909		7,909 D		100.0%		100.0%
9,065	PERRY	3,184		3,184		3,184 D		100.0%		100.0%
31,756	PIKE	8,755		8,755		8,755 D		100.0%		100.0%
17,363	PONTOTOC	4,595		4,595		4,595 D		100.0%		100.0%
20,133	PRENTISS	4,440		4,440		4,440 D		100.0%		100.0%
15,888	QUITMAN	2,177		2,177		2,177 D		100.0%		100.0%
43,933	RANKIN	15,797		15,797		15,797 D		100.0%		100.0%
21,369	SCOTT	5,219		5,219		5,219 D		100.0%		100.0%
8,937	SHARKEY	1,119		1,119		1,119 D		100.0%		100.0%
19,947	SIMPSON	6,734		6,734		6,734 D		100.0%		100.0%
13,561	SMITH	4,386		4,386		4,386 D		100.0%		100.0%

MISSISSIPPI

SENATOR 1976

1970 Census Population	County	Total Vote	Republican	Democratic	Other	Rep.-Dem. Plurality	Percentage Total Vote Rep.	Percentage Total Vote Dem.	Percentage Major Vote Rep.	Percentage Major Vote Dem.
8,101	STONE	2,655		2,655		2,655 D		100.0%		100.0%
37,047	SUNFLOWER	6,224		6,224		6,224 D		100.0%		100.0%
19,338	TALLAHATCHIE	2,573		2,573		2,573 D		100.0%		100.0%
18,544	TATE	4,809		4,809		4,809 D		100.0%		100.0%
15,852	TIPPAH	3,489		3,489		3,489 D		100.0%		100.0%
14,940	TISHOMINGO	3,911		3,911		3,911 D		100.0%		100.0%
11,854	TUNICA	1,268		1,268		1,268 D		100.0%		100.0%
19,096	UNION	5,689		5,689		5,689 D		100.0%		100.0%
12,500	WALTHALL	3,219		3,219		3,219 D		100.0%		100.0%
44,981	WARREN	7,828		7,828		7,828 D		100.0%		100.0%
70,581	WASHINGTON	9,268		9,268		9,268 D		100.0%		100.0%
16,650	WAYNE	5,217		5,217		5,217 D		100.0%		100.0%
10,047	WEBSTER	3,380		3,380		3,380 D		100.0%		100.0%
11,099	WILKINSON	2,019		2,019		2,019 D		100.0%		100.0%
18,406	WINSTON	6,438		6,438		6,438 D		100.0%		100.0%
11,915	YALOBUSHA	3,649		3,649		3,649 D		100.0%		100.0%
27,304	YAZOO	5,374		5,374		5,374 D		100.0%		100.0%
2,216,912	TOTAL	554,433		554,433		554,433 D		100.0%		100.0%

MISSISSIPPI

CONGRESS

CD	Year	Total Vote	Republican Vote	Republican Candidate	Democratic Vote	Democratic Candidate	Other Vote	Rep.-Dem. Plurality	Percentage Total Vote Rep.	Percentage Total Vote Dem.	Percentage Major Vote Rep.	Percentage Major Vote Dem.
1	1976	93,687			93,687	WHITTEN, JAMIE L.		93,687 D		100.0%		100.0%
1	1974	44,408			39,158	WHITTEN, JAMIE L.	5,250	39,158 D		88.2%		100.0%
1	1972	87,526			87,526	WHITTEN, JAMIE L.		87,526 D		100.0%		100.0%
2	1970	59,781			51,689	WHITTEN, JAMIE L.	8,092	51,689 D		86.5%		100.0%
2	1968	71,260			71,260	WHITTEN, JAMIE L.		71,260 D		100.0%		100.0%
2	1966	64,242	10,622	WISE, S. B.	53,620	WHITTEN, JAMIE L.		42,998 D	16.5%	83.5%	16.5%	83.5%
2	1976	119,173	42,601	BYRD, ROLAND	75,092	BOWEN, DAVID R.	1,480	32,491 D	35.7%	63.0%	36.2%	63.8%
2	1974	57,358	15,876	HILBUN, BEN F.	37,909	BOWEN, DAVID R.	3,573	22,033 D	27.7%	66.1%	29.5%	70.5%
2	1972	112,837	39,117	BUTLER, CARL	69,892	BOWEN, DAVID R.	3,828	30,775 D	34.7%	61.9%	35.9%	64.1%
3	1976	137,409	8,321	CLEVELAND, DOROTHY C.	129,088	MONTGOMERY, G. V.		120,767 D	6.1%	93.9%	6.1%	93.9%
3	1974	43,020			43,020	MONTGOMERY, G. V.		43,020 D		100.0%		100.0%
3	1972	105,722			105,722	MONTGOMERY, G. V.		105,722 D		100.0%		100.0%
4	1976	132,991	101,132	COCHRAN, THAD	28,737	DAVIS, STERLING P.	3,122	72,395 R	76.0%	21.6%	77.9%	22.1%
4	1974	89,201	62,634	COCHRAN, THAD	25,699	DEAN, KENNETH L.	868	36,935 R	70.2%	28.8%	70.9%	29.1%
4	1972	141,374	67,655	COCHRAN, THAD	62,148	BODRON, ELLIS B.	11,571	5,507 R	47.9%	44.0%	52.1%	47.9%
3	1970	79,374	28,847	LEE, RAY	50,527	GRIFFIN, CHARLES H.		21,680 D	36.3%	63.7%	36.3%	63.7%
3	1968	82,896			82,896	GRIFFIN, CHARLES H.		82,896 D		100.0%		100.0%
3	1966	86,595			71,377	WILLIAMS, JOHN BELL	15,218	71,377 D		82.4%		100.0%
5	1976	153,278	104,554	LOTT, TRENT	48,724	BLESSEY, GERALD		55,830 R	68.2%	31.8%	68.2%	31.8%
5	1974	71,922	52,489	LOTT, TRENT	10,333	MURPHEY, WALTER W.	9,100	42,156 R	73.0%	14.4%	83.6%	16.4%
5	1972	140,614	77,826	LOTT, TRENT	62,101	STONE, BEN	687	15,725 R	55.3%	44.2%	55.6%	44.4%

MISSISSIPPI

1975 GENERAL ELECTION

Governor Original uncorrected canvass gave the Republican total vote as 319,932. Other vote was Kirksey (Independent).

1975 PRIMARIES

AUGUST 5 REPUBLICAN

Governor Gil Carmichael, unopposed.

AUGUST 5 DEMOCRATIC

Governor 286,652 William Winter; 253,829 Cliff Finch; 179,472 Maurice Dantin; 50,606 John A. Eaves; 11,966 Leman Gandy; 7,369 David L. Perkins.

AUGUST 26 DEMOCRATIC RUN-OFF

Governor 442,864 Cliff Finch; 324,749 William Winter.

1976 GENERAL ELECTION

President Original uncorrected canvass gave the Republican total vote as 381,329; the MacBride Independent vote as 2,787; the Republican vote in Jefferson Davis county as 1,808; the Democratic vote in Noxubee county as 3,121. Other vote was 6,678 Anderson (American); 4,861 Maddox (Independent); 4,074 McCarthy (Independent); 2,805 Camejo (Independent); 2,788 MacBride (Independent).

Congress Other vote was Wells (American) in CD 2; 1,862 Norman (American) and 1,260 Latham (Independent) in CD 4.

1976 PRIMARIES

JUNE 1 REPUBLICAN

Senator None. No candidate.

Congress No candidate in CD 1. All other CD's unopposed.

JUNE 1 DEMOCRATIC

Senator 157,943 John Stennis; 27,016 E. Michael Marks.

Congress Unopposed in all CD's.

MISSOURI

GOVERNOR

Joseph P. Teasdale (D). Elected 1976 to a four-year term.

SENATORS

John C. Danforth (R). Elected 1976 to a six-year term.

Thomas F. Eagleton (D). Re-elected 1974 to a six-year term. Previously elected 1968.

REPRESENTATIVES

1. William Clay (D)
2. Robert A. Young (D)
3. Richard A. Gephardt (D)
4. Ike Skelton (D)
5. Richard Bolling (D)
6. E. Thomas Coleman (R)
7. Gene Taylor (R)
8. Richard Ichord (D)
9. Harold Volkmer (D)
10. Bill D. Burlison (D)

POSTWAR VOTE FOR GOVERNOR

								Percentage			
	Total	Republican		Democratic		Other	Rep.-Dem.	Total Vote		Major Vote	
Year	Vote	Vote	Candidate	Vote	Candidate	Vote	Plurality	Rep.	Dem.	Rep.	Dem.
1976	1,933,575	958,110	Bond, Christopher	971,184	Teasdale, Joseph P.	4,281	13,074 D	49.6%	50.2%	49.7%	50.3%
1972	1,865,683	1,029,451	Bond, Christopher	832,751	Dowd, Edward L.	3,481	196,700 R	55.2%	44.6%	55.3%	44.7%
1968	1,764,602	691,797	Roos, Lawrence K.	1,072,805	Hearnes, Warren E.	–	381,008 D	39.2%	60.8%	39.2%	60.8%
1964	1,789,600	678,949	Shepley, Ethan	1,110,651	Hearnes, Warren E.	–	431,702 D	37.9%	62.1%	37.9%	62.1%
1960	1,887,331	792,131	Farmer, Edward G.	1,095,200	Dalton, John M.	–	303,069 D	42.0%	58.0%	42.0%	58.0%
1956	1,808,338	866,810	Hocker, Lon	941,528	Blair, James T.	–	74,718 D	47.9%	52.1%	47.9%	52.1%
1952	1,871,095	886,370	Elliott, Howard	983,166	Donnelly, Phil M.	1,559	96,796 D	47.4%	52.5%	47.4%	52.6%
1948	1,567,338	670,064	Thompson, Murray	893,092	Smith, Forrest	4,182	223,028 D	42.8%	57.0%	42.9%	57.1%

POSTWAR VOTE FOR SENATOR

								Percentage			
	Total	Republican		Democratic		Other	Rep.-Dem.	Total Vote		Major Vote	
Year	Vote	Vote	Candidate	Vote	Candidate	Vote	Plurality	Rep.	Dem.	Rep.	Dem.
1976	1,914,777	1,090,067	Danforth, John C.	813,571	Hearnes, Warren E.	11,139	276,496 R	56.9%	42.5%	57.3%	42.7%
1974	1,224,303	480,900	Curtis, Thomas B.	735,433	Eagleton, Thomas F.	7,970	254,533 D	39.3%	60.1%	39.5%	60.5%
1970	1,283,912	617,903	Danforth, John C.	655,431	Symington, Stuart	10,578	37,528 D	48.1%	51.0%	48.5%	51.5%
1968	1,737,958	850,544	Curtis, Thomas B.	887,414	Eagleton, Thomas F.	–	36,870 D	48.9%	51.1%	48.9%	51.1%
1964	1,783,043	596,377	Bradshaw, Jean P.	1,186,666	Symington, Stuart	–	590,289 D	33.4%	66.6%	33.4%	66.6%
1962	1,222,259	555,330	Kemper, Crosby	666,929	Long, Edward V.	–	111,599 D	45.4%	54.6%	45.4%	54.6%
1960s	1,880,232	880,576	Hocker, Lon	999,656	Long, Edward V.	–	119,080 D	46.8%	53.2%	46.8%	53.2%
1958	1,173,903	393,847	Palmer, Hazel	780,056	Symington, Stuart	–	386,209 D	33.6%	66.4%	33.6%	66.4%
1956	1,800,984	785,048	Douglas, Herbert	1,015,936	Hennings, Thomas C.	–	230,888 D	43.6%	56.4%	43.6%	56.4%
1952	1,868,083	858,170	Kem, James P.	1,008,523	Symington, Stuart	1,390	150,353 D	45.9%	54.0%	46.0%	54.0%
1950	1,279,414	592,922	Donnell, Forrest C.	685,732	Hennings, Thomas C.	760	92,810 D	46.3%	53.6%	46.4%	53.6%
1946	1,084,100	572,556	Kem, James P.	511,544	Briggs, Frank P.	–	61,012 R	52.8%	47.2%	52.8%	47.2%

The 1960 election was for a short term to fill a vacancy.

MISSOURI

Districts Established February 22, 1972

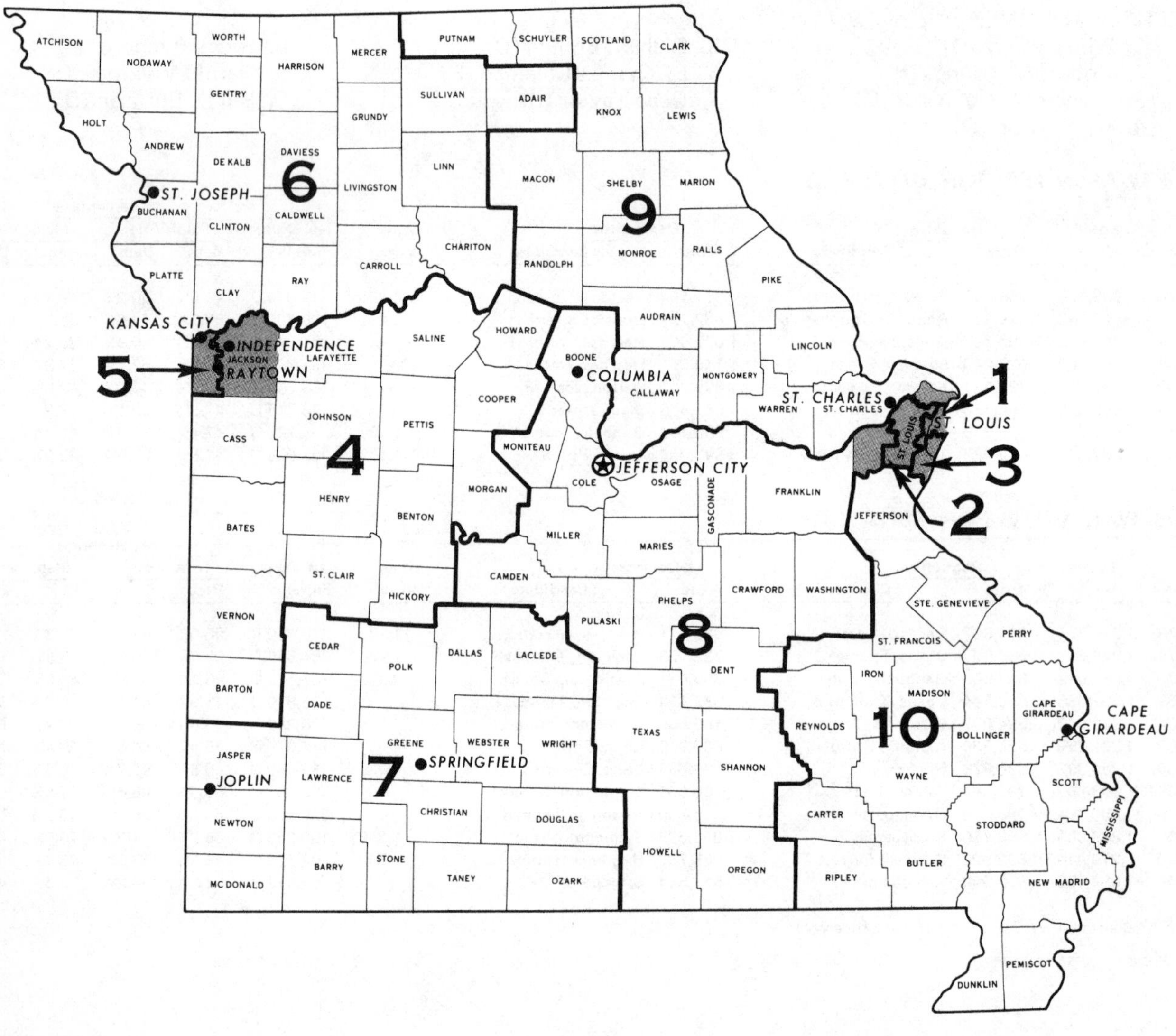

County with two or more Congressional Districts.

MISSOURI

PRESIDENT 1976

1970 Census Population	County	Total Vote	Republican	Democratic	Other	Rep.-Dem. Plurality	Percentage Total Vote Rep.	Percentage Total Vote Dem.	Percentage Major Vote Rep.	Percentage Major Vote Dem.
22,472	ADAIR	9,133	5,249	3,684	200	1,565 R	57.5%	40.3%	58.8%	41.2%
11,913	ANDREW	6,213	3,130	3,042	41	88 R	50.4%	49.0%	50.7%	49.3%
9,240	ATCHISON	3,930	1,960	1,926	44	34 R	49.9%	49.0%	50.4%	49.6%
25,362	AUDRAIN	11,032	5,378	5,600	54	222 D	48.7%	50.8%	49.0%	51.0%
19,597	BARRY	10,148	5,053	5,046	49	7 R	49.8%	49.7%	50.0%	50.0%
10,431	BARTON	5,077	2,708	2,326	43	382 R	53.3%	45.8%	53.8%	46.2%
15,468	BATES	7,684	3,350	4,288	46	938 D	43.6%	55.8%	43.9%	56.1%
9,695	BENTON	5,587	2,875	2,684	28	191 R	51.5%	48.0%	51.7%	48.3%
8,820	BOLLINGER	4,862	2,113	2,740	9	627 D	43.5%	56.4%	43.5%	56.5%
80,911	BOONE	34,893	16,373	17,674	846	1,301 D	46.9%	50.7%	48.1%	51.9%
86,915	BUCHANAN	34,124	16,446	17,427	251	981 D	48.2%	51.1%	48.6%	51.4%
33,529	BUTLER	12,485	5,669	6,759	57	1,090 D	45.4%	54.1%	45.6%	54.4%
8,351	CALDWELL	4,233	2,094	2,113	26	19 D	49.5%	49.9%	49.8%	50.2%
25,950	CALLAWAY	10,059	5,115	4,843	101	272 R	50.8%	48.1%	51.4%	48.6%
13,315	CAMDEN	8,510	4,469	3,975	66	494 R	52.5%	46.7%	52.9%	47.1%
49,350	CAPE GIRARDEAU	23,164	12,607	10,440	117	2,167 R	54.4%	45.1%	54.7%	45.3%
12,565	CARROLL	6,077	2,936	3,114	27	178 D	48.3%	51.2%	48.5%	51.5%
3,878	CARTER	2,007	842	1,154	11	312 D	42.0%	57.5%	42.2%	57.8%
39,448	CASS	16,330	7,182	9,008	140	1,826 D	44.0%	55.2%	44.4%	55.6%
9,424	CEDAR	4,965	2,752	2,192	21	560 R	55.4%	44.1%	55.7%	44.3%
11,084	CHARITON	5,204	2,128	3,055	21	927 D	40.9%	58.7%	41.1%	58.9%
15,124	CHRISTIAN	8,442	4,553	3,830	59	723 R	53.9%	45.4%	54.3%	45.7%
8,260	CLARK	3,274	1,582	1,679	13	97 D	48.3%	51.3%	48.5%	51.5%
123,644	CLAY	52,315	24,962	26,609	744	1,647 D	47.7%	50.9%	48.4%	51.6%
12,462	CLINTON	6,272	2,807	3,424	41	617 D	44.8%	54.6%	45.0%	55.0%
46,228	COLE	22,503	14,370	7,949	184	6,421 R	63.9%	35.3%	64.4%	35.6%
14,732	COOPER	6,809	3,694	3,087	28	607 R	54.3%	45.3%	54.5%	45.5%
14,828	CRAWFORD	6,833	3,224	3,565	44	341 D	47.2%	52.2%	47.5%	52.5%
6,850	DADE	3,710	2,015	1,681	14	334 R	54.3%	45.3%	54.5%	45.5%
10,054	DALLAS	4,910	2,430	2,453	27	23 D	49.5%	50.0%	49.8%	50.2%
8,420	DAVIESS	4,191	1,919	2,250	22	331 D	45.8%	53.7%	46.0%	54.0%
7,305	DE KALB	3,779	1,739	2,023	17	284 D	46.0%	53.5%	46.2%	53.8%
11,457	DENT	5,401	2,433	2,931	37	498 D	45.0%	54.3%	45.4%	54.6%
9,268	DOUGLAS	4,667	2,652	1,981	34	671 R	56.8%	42.4%	57.2%	42.8%
33,742	DUNKLIN	10,443	3,314	7,107	22	3,793 D	31.7%	68.1%	31.8%	68.2%
55,116	FRANKLIN	24,342	12,242	11,695	405	547 R	50.3%	48.0%	51.1%	48.9%
11,878	GASCONADE	5,682	3,925	1,702	55	2,223 R	69.1%	30.0%	69.8%	30.2%
8,060	GENTRY	4,035	1,772	2,249	14	477 D	43.9%	55.7%	44.1%	55.9%
152,929	GREENE	72,205	37,691	33,824	690	3,867 R	52.2%	46.8%	52.7%	47.3%
11,819	GRUNDY	5,273	2,646	2,597	30	49 R	50.2%	49.3%	50.5%	49.5%
10,257	HARRISON	4,813	2,478	2,304	31	174 R	51.5%	47.9%	51.8%	48.2%
18,451	HENRY	9,497	4,168	5,282	47	1,114 D	43.9%	55.6%	44.1%	55.9%
4,481	HICKORY	2,822	1,403	1,398	21	5 R	49.7%	49.5%	50.1%	49.9%
6,654	HOLT	3,318	1,777	1,529	12	248 R	53.6%	46.1%	53.8%	46.2%
10,561	HOWARD	4,494	1,690	2,769	35	1,079 D	37.6%	61.6%	37.9%	62.1%
23,521	HOWELL	10,035	4,692	5,265	78	573 D	46.8%	52.5%	47.1%	52.9%
9,529	IRON	4,434	1,765	2,646	23	881 D	39.8%	59.7%	40.0%	60.0%
654,558	JACKSON	235,441	101,401	130,120	3,920	28,719 D	43.1%	55.3%	43.8%	56.2%
79,852	JASPER	32,149	17,086	14,910	153	2,176 R	53.1%	46.4%	53.4%	46.6%
105,248	JEFFERSON	43,915	18,261	25,159	495	6,898 D	41.6%	57.3%	42.1%	57.9%
34,172	JOHNSON	11,220	5,513	5,551	156	38 D	49.1%	49.5%	49.8%	50.2%
5,692	KNOX	2,556	1,216	1,319	21	103 D	47.6%	51.6%	48.0%	52.0%
19,944	LACLEDE	8,475	4,067	4,381	27	314 D	48.0%	51.7%	48.1%	51.9%
26,626	LAFAYETTE	13,305	6,823	6,410	72	413 R	51.3%	48.2%	51.6%	48.4%
24,585	LAWRENCE	11,137	5,784	5,315	38	469 R	51.9%	47.7%	52.1%	47.9%
10,993	LEWIS	4,497	1,983	2,486	28	503 D	44.1%	55.3%	44.4%	55.6%
18,041	LINCOLN	8,140	3,581	4,473	86	892 D	44.0%	55.0%	44.5%	55.5%
15,125	LINN	7,236	3,114	4,092	30	978 D	43.0%	56.6%	43.2%	56.8%
15,368	LIVINGSTON	6,857	3,010	3,819	28	809 D	43.9%	55.7%	44.1%	55.9%
12,357	MCDONALD	6,108	2,949	3,111	48	162 D	48.3%	50.9%	48.7%	51.3%
15,432	MACON	7,688	3,360	4,296	32	936 D	43.7%	55.9%	43.9%	56.1%
8,641	MADISON	3,989	1,739	2,229	21	490 D	43.6%	55.9%	43.8%	56.2%
6,851	MARIES	3,294	1,485	1,796	13	311 D	45.1%	54.5%	45.3%	54.7%
28,121	MARION	11,663	5,501	6,124	38	623 D	47.2%	52.5%	47.3%	52.7%
4,910	MERCER	2,207	1,025	1,177	5	152 D	46.4%	53.3%	46.5%	53.5%

MISSOURI

PRESIDENT 1976

1970 Census Population	County	Total Vote	Republican	Democratic	Other	Rep.-Dem. Plurality	Percentage Total Vote Rep.	Percentage Total Vote Dem.	Percentage Major Vote Rep.	Percentage Major Vote Dem.
15,026	MILLER	6,866	4,095	2,739	32	1,356 R	59.6%	39.9%	59.9%	40.1%
16,647	MISSISSIPPI	5,116	1,733	3,366	17	1,633 D	33.9%	65.8%	34.0%	66.0%
10,742	MONITEAU	5,555	3,077	2,462	16	615 R	55.4%	44.3%	55.6%	44.4%
9,542	MONROE	4,650	1,585	3,039	26	1,454 D	34.1%	65.4%	34.3%	65.7%
11,000	MONTGOMERY	5,243	2,665	2,535	43	130 R	50.8%	48.4%	51.3%	48.8%
10,068	MORGAN	5,595	2,831	2,738	26	93 R	50.6%	48.9%	50.8%	49.2%
23,420	NEW MADRID	8,136	2,798	5,319	19	2,521 D	34.4%	65.4%	34.5%	65.5%
32,901	NEWTON	14,301	7,142	7,045	114	97 R	49.9%	49.3%	50.3%	49.7%
22,467	NODAWAY	9,534	4,558	4,875	101	317 D	47.8%	51.1%	48.3%	51.7%
9,180	OREGON	3,712	1,122	2,564	26	1,442 D	30.2%	69.1%	30.4%	69.6%
10,994	OSAGE	5,269	3,224	2,015	30	1,209 R	61.2%	38.2%	61.5%	38.5%
6,226	OZARK	3,105	1,754	1,341	10	413 R	56.5%	43.2%	56.7%	43.3%
26,373	PEMISCOT	7,236	2,541	4,681	14	2,140 D	35.1%	64.7%	35.2%	64.8%
14,393	PERRY	6,918	4,086	2,801	31	1,285 R	59.1%	40.5%	59.3%	40.7%
34,137	PETTIS	15,296	7,344	7,887	65	543 D	48.0%	51.6%	48.2%	51.8%
29,567	PHELPS	12,512	6,153	6,261	98	108 D	49.2%	50.0%	49.6%	50.4%
16,928	PIKE	7,162	3,355	3,770	37	415 D	46.8%	52.6%	47.1%	52.9%
32,081	PLATTE	17,054	8,103	8,651	300	548 D	47.5%	50.7%	48.4%	51.6%
15,415	POLK	7,590	3,893	3,663	34	230 R	51.3%	48.3%	51.5%	48.5%
53,967	PULASKI	7,267	2,865	4,370	32	1,505 D	39.4%	60.1%	39.6%	60.4%
5,916	PUTNAM	2,550	1,444	1,097	9	347 R	56.6%	43.0%	56.8%	43.2%
7,764	RALLS	3,682	1,334	2,318	30	984 D	36.2%	63.0%	36.5%	63.5%
22,434	RANDOLPH	9,481	3,594	5,839	48	2,245 D	37.9%	61.6%	38.1%	61.9%
17,599	RAY	8,461	2,853	5,535	73	2,682 D	33.7%	65.4%	34.0%	66.0%
6,106	REYNOLDS	3,030	879	2,143	8	1,264 D	29.0%	70.7%	29.1%	70.9%
9,803	RIPLEY	4,245	1,640	2,577	28	937 D	38.6%	60.7%	38.9%	61.1%
92,954	ST. CHARLES	48,704	26,105	22,063	536	4,042 R	53.6%	45.3%	54.2%	45.8%
7,667	ST. CLAIR	4,103	1,808	2,271	24	463 D	44.1%	55.3%	44.3%	55.7%
36,818	ST. FRANCOIS	15,911	7,002	8,852	57	1,850 D	44.0%	55.6%	44.2%	55.8%
622,236	ST. LOUIS CITY	179,784	58,367	118,703	2,714	60,336 D	32.5%	66.0%	33.0%	67.0%
951,353	ST. LOUIS COUNTY	452,626	246,988	196,915	8,723	50,073 R	54.6%	43.5%	55.6%	44.4%
12,867	STE. GENEVIEVE	5,372	2,241	3,091	40	850 D	41.7%	57.5%	42.0%	58.0%
24,837	SALINE	10,845	4,883	5,890	72	1,007 D	45.0%	54.3%	45.3%	54.7%
4,665	SCHUYLER	2,620	1,193	1,417	10	224 D	45.5%	54.1%	45.7%	54.3%
5,499	SCOTLAND	2,752	1,286	1,449	17	163 D	46.7%	52.7%	47.0%	53.0%
33,250	SCOTT	13,576	5,473	8,075	28	2,602 D	40.3%	59.5%	40.4%	59.6%
7,196	SHANNON	2,971	989	1,960	22	971 D	33.3%	66.0%	33.5%	66.5%
7,906	SHELBY	3,702	1,453	2,227	22	774 D	39.2%	60.2%	39.5%	60.5%
25,771	STODDARD	10,111	3,989	6,097	25	2,108 D	39.5%	60.3%	39.5%	60.5%
9,921	STONE	5,842	3,457	2,358	27	1,099 R	59.2%	40.4%	59.4%	40.6%
7,572	SULLIVAN	4,484	2,141	2,313	30	172 D	47.7%	51.6%	48.1%	51.9%
13,023	TANEY	8,344	4,696	3,626	22	1,070 R	56.3%	43.5%	56.4%	43.6%
18,320	TEXAS	8,018	3,338	4,638	42	1,300 D	41.6%	57.8%	41.9%	58.1%
19,065	VERNON	8,684	3,715	4,921	48	1,206 D	42.8%	56.7%	43.0%	57.0%
9,699	WARREN	5,430	3,214	2,164	52	1,050 R	59.2%	39.9%	59.8%	40.2%
15,086	WASHINGTON	6,108	2,526	3,543	39	1,017 D	41.4%	58.0%	41.6%	58.4%
8,546	WAYNE	4,958	1,963	2,987	8	1,024 D	39.6%	60.2%	39.7%	60.3%
15,562	WEBSTER	7,315	3,510	3,759	46	249 D	48.0%	51.4%	48.3%	51.7%
3,359	WORTH	1,749	771	969	9	198 D	44.1%	55.4%	44.3%	55.7%
13,667	WRIGHT	6,191	3,397	2,781	13	616 R	54.9%	44.9%	55.0%	45.0%
4,677,399	TOTAL	1,953,600	927,443	998,387	27,770	70,944 D	47.5%	51.1%	48.2%	51.8%

MISSOURI

GOVERNOR 1976

1970 Census Population	County	Total Vote	Republican	Democratic	Other	Rep.-Dem. Plurality	Percentage Total Vote Rep.	Percentage Total Vote Dem.	Percentage Major Vote Rep.	Percentage Major Vote Dem.
22,472	ADAIR	8,991	5,635	3,350	6	2,285 R	62.7%	37.3%	62.7%	37.3%
11,913	ANDREW	6,178	3,510	2,662	6	848 R	56.8%	43.1%	56.9%	43.1%
9,240	ATCHISON	3,877	2,245	1,630	2	615 R	57.9%	42.0%	57.9%	42.1%
25,362	AUDRAIN	11,091	5,598	5,485	8	113 R	50.5%	49.5%	50.5%	49.5%
19,597	BARRY	10,136	5,713	4,416	7	1,297 R	56.4%	43.6%	56.4%	43.6%
10,431	BARTON	4,899	3,088	1,808	3	1,280 R	63.0%	36.9%	63.1%	36.9%
15,468	BATES	7,632	3,568	4,059	5	491 D	46.8%	53.2%	46.8%	53.2%
9,695	BENTON	5,550	2,950	2,597	3	353 R	53.2%	46.8%	53.2%	46.8%
8,820	BOLLINGER	4,803	2,338	2,465		127 D	48.7%	51.3%	48.7%	51.3%
80,911	BOONE	35,356	18,017	17,179	160	838 R	51.0%	48.6%	51.2%	48.8%
86,915	BUCHANAN	34,222	17,054	17,120	48	66 D	49.8%	50.0%	49.9%	50.1%
33,529	BUTLER	12,264	6,489	5,742	33	747 R	52.9%	46.8%	53.1%	46.9%
8,351	CALDWELL	4,211	2,313	1,892	6	421 R	54.9%	44.9%	55.0%	45.0%
25,950	CALLAWAY	10,061	5,226	4,801	34	425 R	51.9%	47.7%	52.1%	47.9%
13,315	CAMDEN	8,541	4,873	3,655	13	1,218 R	57.1%	42.8%	57.1%	42.9%
49,350	CAPE GIRARDEAU	23,099	13,079	10,013	7	3,066 R	56.6%	43.3%	56.6%	43.4%
12,565	CARROLL	6,054	3,335	2,703	16	632 R	55.1%	44.6%	55.2%	44.8%
3,878	CARTER	1,967	985	980	2	5 R	50.1%	49.8%	50.1%	49.9%
39,448	CASS	16,199	7,113	9,057	29	1,944 D	43.9%	55.9%	44.0%	56.0%
9,424	CEDAR	4,945	3,003	1,933	9	1,070 R	60.7%	39.1%	60.8%	39.2%
11,084	CHARITON	5,179	2,302	2,872	5	570 D	44.4%	55.5%	44.5%	55.5%
15,124	CHRISTIAN	8,398	4,984	3,397	17	1,587 R	59.3%	40.5%	59.5%	40.5%
8,260	CLARK	3,259	1,930	1,326	3	604 R	59.2%	40.7%	59.3%	40.7%
123,644	CLAY	51,776	24,836	26,710	230	1,874 D	48.0%	51.6%	48.2%	51.8%
12,462	CLINTON	6,210	2,966	3,235	9	269 D	47.8%	52.1%	47.8%	52.2%
46,228	COLE	22,517	12,904	9,602	11	3,302 R	57.3%	42.6%	57.3%	42.7%
14,732	COOPER	6,696	3,757	2,939		818 R	56.1%	43.9%	56.1%	43.9%
14,828	CRAWFORD	6,820	3,376	3,439	5	63 D	49.5%	50.4%	49.5%	50.5%
6,850	DADE	3,714	2,295	1,416	3	879 R	61.8%	38.1%	61.8%	38.2%
10,054	DALLAS	4,881	2,717	2,154	10	563 R	55.7%	44.1%	55.8%	44.2%
8,420	DAVIESS	4,180	2,226	1,950	4	276 R	53.3%	46.7%	53.3%	46.7%
7,305	DE KALB	3,755	1,967	1,785	3	182 R	52.4%	47.5%	52.4%	47.6%
11,457	DENT	5,396	2,597	2,796	3	199 D	48.1%	51.8%	48.2%	51.8%
9,268	DOUGLAS	4,604	2,924	1,667	13	1,257 R	63.5%	36.2%	63.7%	36.3%
33,742	DUNKLIN	10,111	4,131	5,974	6	1,843 D	40.9%	59.1%	40.9%	59.1%
55,116	FRANKLIN	24,240	11,913	12,221	106	308 D	49.1%	50.4%	49.4%	50.6%
11,878	GASCONADE	5,656	3,910	1,743	3	2,167 R	69.1%	30.8%	69.2%	30.8%
8,060	GENTRY	4,015	2,049	1,960	6	89 R	51.0%	48.8%	51.1%	48.9%
152,929	GREENE	71,157	41,212	29,691	254	11,521 R	57.9%	41.7%	58.1%	41.9%
11,819	GRUNDY	5,252	3,039	2,207	6	832 R	57.9%	42.0%	57.9%	42.1%
10,257	HARRISON	4,766	2,946	1,813	7	1,133 R	61.8%	38.0%	61.9%	38.1%
18,451	HENRY	9,439	4,217	5,213	9	996 D	44.7%	55.2%	44.7%	55.3%
4,481	HICKORY	2,821	1,527	1,283	11	244 R	54.1%	45.5%	54.3%	45.7%
6,654	HOLT	3,308	1,936	1,368	4	568 R	58.5%	41.4%	58.6%	41.4%
10,561	HOWARD	4,452	1,834	2,617	1	783 D	41.2%	58.8%	41.2%	58.8%
23,521	HOWELL	9,940	5,673	4,251	16	1,422 R	57.1%	42.8%	57.2%	42.8%
9,529	IRON	4,369	2,043	2,315	11	272 D	46.8%	53.0%	46.9%	53.1%
654,558	JACKSON	233,958	97,030	135,746	1,182	38,716 D	41.5%	58.0%	41.7%	58.3%
79,852	JASPER	32,060	20,731	11,305	24	9,426 R	64.7%	35.3%	64.7%	35.3%
105,248	JEFFERSON	43,837	19,858	23,904	75	4,046 D	45.3%	54.5%	45.4%	54.6%
34,172	JOHNSON	10,986	5,584	5,332	70	252 R	50.8%	48.5%	51.2%	48.8%
5,692	KNOX	2,556	1,355	1,198	3	157 R	53.0%	46.9%	53.1%	46.9%
19,944	LACLEDE	8,459	4,846	3,599	14	1,247 R	57.3%	42.5%	57.4%	42.6%
26,626	LAFAYETTE	13,243	7,064	6,161	18	903 R	53.3%	46.5%	53.4%	46.6%
24,585	LAWRENCE	11,154	6,633	4,513	8	2,120 R	59.5%	40.5%	59.5%	40.5%
10,993	LEWIS	4,448	2,379	2,067	2	312 R	53.5%	46.5%	53.5%	46.5%
18,041	LINCOLN	8,101	3,670	4,421	10	751 D	45.3%	54.6%	45.4%	54.6%
15,125	LINN	7,237	3,487	3,743	7	256 D	48.2%	51.7%	48.2%	51.8%
15,368	LIVINGSTON	6,793	3,309	3,474	10	165 D	48.7%	51.1%	48.8%	51.2%
12,357	MCDONALD	6,073	3,711	2,362		1,349 R	61.1%	38.9%	61.1%	38.9%
15,432	MACON	7,652	3,807	3,836	9	29 D	49.8%	50.1%	49.8%	50.2%
8,641	MADISON	3,961	1,994	1,966	1	28 R	50.3%	49.6%	50.4%	49.6%
6,851	MARIES	3,307	1,507	1,799	1	292 D	45.6%	54.4%	45.6%	54.4%
28,121	MARION	11,662	6,298	5,359	5	939 R	54.0%	46.0%	54.0%	46.0%
4,910	MERCER	2,184	1,366	815	3	551 R	62.5%	37.3%	62.6%	37.4%

MISSOURI

GOVERNOR 1976

1970 Census Population	County	Total Vote	Republican	Democratic	Other	Rep.-Dem. Plurality	Percentage Total Vote Rep.	Percentage Total Vote Dem.	Percentage Major Vote Rep.	Percentage Major Vote Dem.
15,026	MILLER	6,858	4,130	2,722	6	1,408 R	60.2%	39.7%	60.3%	39.7%
16,647	MISSISSIPPI	4,937	1,617	3,316	4	1,699 D	32.8%	67.2%	32.8%	67.2%
10,742	MONITEAU	5,547	3,084	2,462	1	622 R	55.6%	44.4%	55.6%	44.4%
9,542	MONROE	4,632	1,724	2,903	5	1,179 D	37.2%	62.7%	37.3%	62.7%
11,000	MONTGOMERY	5,241	2,764	2,474	3	290 R	52.7%	47.2%	52.8%	47.2%
10,068	MORGAN	5,572	3,066	2,504	2	562 R	55.0%	44.9%	55.0%	45.0%
23,420	NEW MADRID	7,818	2,951	4,863	4	1,912 D	37.7%	62.2%	37.8%	62.2%
32,901	NEWTON	14,220	8,721	5,393	106	3,328 R	61.3%	37.9%	61.8%	38.2%
22,467	NODAWAY	9,446	4,817	4,629		188 R	51.0%	49.0%	51.0%	49.0%
9,180	OREGON	3,630	1,350	2,277	3	927 D	37.2%	62.7%	37.2%	62.8%
10,994	OSAGE	5,290	2,893	2,395	2	498 R	54.7%	45.3%	54.7%	45.3%
6,226	OZARK	3,054	1,886	1,167	1	719 R	61.8%	38.2%	61.8%	38.2%
26,373	PEMISCOT	6,692	2,743	3,939	10	1,196 D	41.0%	58.9%	41.1%	58.9%
14,393	PERRY	6,851	4,416	2,428	7	1,988 R	64.5%	35.4%	64.5%	35.5%
34,137	PETTIS	15,211	7,119	8,082	10	963 D	46.8%	53.1%	46.8%	53.2%
29,567	PHELPS	12,448	6,307	6,131	10	176 R	50.7%	49.3%	50.7%	49.3%
16,928	PIKE	7,093	3,549	3,540	4	9 R	50.0%	49.9%	50.1%	49.9%
32,081	PLATTE	17,045	8,386	8,603	56	217 D	49.2%	50.5%	49.4%	50.6%
15,415	POLK	7,567	4,245	3,310	12	935 R	56.1%	43.7%	56.2%	43.8%
53,967	PULASKI	7,184	3,262	3,917	5	655 D	45.4%	54.5%	45.4%	54.6%
5,916	PUTNAM	2,510	1,704	804	2	900 R	67.9%	32.0%	67.9%	32.1%
7,764	RALLS	3,661	1,550	2,110	1	560 D	42.3%	57.6%	42.3%	57.7%
22,434	RANDOLPH	9,466	3,823	5,638	5	1,815 D	40.4%	59.6%	40.4%	59.6%
17,599	RAY	8,395	3,203	5,167	25	1,964 D	38.2%	61.5%	38.3%	61.7%
6,106	REYNOLDS	2,959	1,175	1,781	3	606 D	39.7%	60.2%	39.7%	60.3%
9,803	RIPLEY	4,169	1,972	2,190	7	218 D	47.3%	52.5%	47.4%	52.6%
92,954	ST. CHARLES	48,599	25,646	22,916	37	2,730 R	52.8%	47.2%	52.8%	47.2%
7,667	ST. CLAIR	4,089	2,052	2,030	7	22 R	50.2%	49.6%	50.3%	49.7%
36,818	ST. FRANCOIS	15,827	7,569	8,251	7	682 D	47.8%	52.1%	47.8%	52.2%
622,236	ST. LOUIS CITY	174,764	57,177	117,304	283	60,127 D	32.7%	67.1%	32.8%	67.2%
951,353	ST. LOUIS COUNTY	449,938	243,804	205,250	884	38,554 R	54.2%	45.6%	54.3%	45.7%
12,867	STE. GENEVIEVE	5,354	2,260	3,089	5	829 D	42.2%	57.7%	42.3%	57.7%
24,837	SALINE	10,777	5,299	5,461	17	162 D	49.2%	50.7%	49.2%	50.8%
4,665	SCHUYLER	2,617	1,383	1,232	2	151 R	52.8%	47.1%	52.9%	47.1%
5,499	SCOTLAND	2,746	1,559	1,187		372 R	56.8%	43.2%	56.8%	43.2%
33,250	SCOTT	13,352	5,558	7,793	1	2,235 D	41.6%	58.4%	41.6%	58.4%
7,196	SHANNON	2,913	1,187	1,722	4	535 D	40.7%	59.1%	40.8%	59.2%
7,906	SHELBY	3,689	1,590	2,096	3	506 D	43.1%	56.8%	43.1%	56.9%
25,771	STODDARD	9,934	4,617	5,315	2	698 D	46.5%	53.5%	46.5%	53.5%
9,921	STONE	5,784	3,815	1,960	9	1,855 R	66.0%	33.9%	66.1%	33.9%
7,572	SULLIVAN	4,418	2,379	2,039		340 R	53.8%	46.2%	53.8%	46.2%
13,023	TANEY	8,300	5,265	3,025	10	2,240 R	63.4%	36.4%	63.5%	36.5%
18,320	TEXAS	7,974	3,804	4,163	7	359 D	47.7%	52.2%	47.7%	52.3%
19,065	VERNON	8,668	4,618	4,029	21	589 R	53.3%	46.5%	53.4%	46.6%
9,699	WARREN	5,444	3,296	2,146	2	1,150 R	60.5%	39.4%	60.6%	39.4%
15,086	WASHINGTON	6,075	2,855	3,210	10	355 D	47.0%	52.8%	47.1%	52.9%
8,546	WAYNE	4,918	2,428	2,489	1	61 D	49.4%	50.6%	49.4%	50.6%
15,562	WEBSTER	7,308	3,842	3,455	11	387 R	52.6%	47.3%	52.7%	47.3%
3,359	WORTH	1,737	898	839		59 R	51.7%	48.3%	51.7%	48.3%
13,667	WRIGHT	6,130	3,780	2,347	3	1,433 R	61.7%	38.3%	61.7%	38.3%
4,677,399	TOTAL	1,933,575	958,110	971,184	4,281	13,074 D	49.6%	50.2%	49.7%	50.3%

MISSOURI

SENATOR 1976

1970 Census Population	County	Total Vote	Republican	Democratic	Other	Rep.-Dem. Plurality	Percentage Total Vote Rep.	Percentage Total Vote Dem.	Percentage Major Vote Rep.	Percentage Major Vote Dem.
22,472	ADAIR	9,030	6,312	2,686	32	3,626 R	69.9%	29.7%	70.1%	29.9%
11,913	ANDREW	6,150	3,827	2,264	59	1,563 R	62.2%	36.8%	62.8%	37.2%
9,240	ATCHISON	3,879	2,132	1,741	6	391 R	55.0%	44.9%	55.0%	45.0%
25,362	AUDRAIN	10,934	6,753	4,163	18	2,590 R	61.8%	38.1%	61.9%	38.1%
19,597	BARRY	10,047	6,247	3,772	28	2,475 R	62.2%	37.5%	62.4%	37.6%
10,431	BARTON	4,879	3,251	1,620	8	1,631 R	66.6%	33.2%	66.7%	33.3%
15,468	BATES	7,603	3,996	3,582	25	414 R	52.6%	47.1%	52.7%	47.3%
9,695	BENTON	5,516	3,402	2,086	28	1,316 R	61.7%	37.8%	62.0%	38.0%
8,820	BOLLINGER	4,787	2,352	2,435		83 D	49.1%	50.9%	49.1%	50.9%
80,911	BOONE	34,929	24,856	9,559	514	15,297 R	71.2%	27.4%	72.2%	27.8%
86,915	BUCHANAN	33,791	18,326	15,325	140	3,001 R	54.2%	45.4%	54.5%	45.5%
33,529	BUTLER	12,302	7,028	5,212	62	1,816 R	57.1%	42.4%	57.4%	42.6%
8,351	CALDWELL	4,201	2,585	1,584	32	1,001 R	61.5%	37.7%	62.0%	38.0%
25,950	CALLAWAY	9,978	6,222	3,712	44	2,510 R	62.4%	37.2%	62.6%	37.4%
13,315	CAMDEN	8,480	5,488	2,954	38	2,534 R	64.7%	34.8%	65.0%	35.0%
49,350	CAPE GIRARDEAU	23,033	13,259	9,743	31	3,516 R	57.6%	42.3%	57.6%	42.4%
12,565	CARROLL	5,974	3,740	2,190	44	1,550 R	62.6%	36.7%	63.1%	36.9%
3,878	CARTER	1,959	1,033	922	4	111 R	52.7%	47.1%	52.8%	47.2%
39,448	CASS	16,065	8,446	7,533	86	913 R	52.6%	46.9%	52.9%	47.1%
9,424	CEDAR	4,919	3,286	1,609	24	1,677 R	66.8%	32.7%	67.1%	32.9%
11,084	CHARITON	5,144	3,021	2,107	16	914 R	58.7%	41.0%	58.9%	41.1%
15,124	CHRISTIAN	8,363	5,770	2,535	58	3,235 R	69.0%	30.3%	69.5%	30.5%
8,260	CLARK	3,240	1,938	1,298	4	640 R	59.8%	40.1%	59.9%	40.1%
123,644	CLAY	50,807	29,499	20,838	470	8,661 R	58.1%	41.0%	58.6%	41.4%
12,462	CLINTON	6,192	3,361	2,799	32	562 R	54.3%	45.2%	54.6%	45.4%
46,228	COLE	22,414	14,148	8,212	54	5,936 R	63.1%	36.6%	63.3%	36.7%
14,732	COOPER	6,664	4,346	2,301	17	2,045 R	65.2%	34.5%	65.4%	34.6%
14,828	CRAWFORD	6,783	3,585	3,177	21	408 R	52.9%	46.8%	53.0%	47.0%
6,850	DADE	3,681	2,570	1,103	8	1,467 R	69.8%	30.0%	70.0%	30.0%
10,054	DALLAS	4,808	3,054	1,726	28	1,328 R	63.5%	35.9%	63.9%	36.1%
8,420	DAVIESS	4,146	2,423	1,691	32	732 R	58.4%	40.8%	58.9%	41.1%
7,305	DE KALB	3,743	2,148	1,577	18	571 R	57.4%	42.1%	57.7%	42.3%
11,457	DENT	5,377	2,914	2,433	30	481 R	54.2%	45.2%	54.5%	45.5%
9,268	DOUGLAS	4,523	3,152	1,330	41	1,822 R	69.7%	29.4%	70.3%	29.7%
33,742	DUNKLIN	10,069	3,482	6,577	10	3,095 D	34.6%	65.3%	34.6%	65.4%
55,116	FRANKLIN	24,018	12,035	11,814	169	221 R	50.1%	49.2%	50.5%	49.5%
11,878	GASCONADE	5,596	4,107	1,483	6	2,624 R	73.4%	26.5%	73.5%	26.5%
8,060	GENTRY	4,008	2,166	1,819	23	347 R	54.0%	45.4%	54.4%	45.6%
152,929	GREENE	70,503	48,377	21,436	690	26,941 R	68.6%	30.4%	69.3%	30.7%
11,819	GRUNDY	5,177	3,522	1,633	22	1,889 R	68.0%	31.5%	68.3%	31.7%
10,257	HARRISON	4,725	2,958	1,740	27	1,218 R	62.6%	36.8%	63.0%	37.0%
18,451	HENRY	9,385	5,132	4,217	36	915 R	54.7%	44.9%	54.9%	45.1%
4,481	HICKORY	2,796	1,769	1,012	15	757 R	63.3%	36.2%	63.6%	36.4%
6,654	HOLT	3,287	2,061	1,213	13	848 R	62.7%	36.9%	63.0%	37.0%
10,561	HOWARD	4,410	2,423	1,983	4	440 R	54.9%	45.0%	55.0%	45.0%
23,521	HOWELL	9,797	6,345	3,385	67	2,960 R	64.8%	34.6%	65.2%	34.8%
9,529	IRON	4,354	1,998	2,333	23	335 D	45.9%	53.6%	46.1%	53.9%
654,558	JACKSON	231,443	119,423	109,714	2,306	9,709 R	51.6%	47.4%	52.1%	47.9%
79,852	JASPER	31,905	18,858	13,004	43	5,854 R	59.1%	40.8%	59.2%	40.8%
105,248	JEFFERSON	43,557	21,847	21,522	188	325 R	50.2%	49.4%	50.4%	49.6%
34,172	JOHNSON	10,990	6,609	4,259	122	2,350 R	60.1%	38.8%	60.8%	39.2%
5,692	KNOX	2,541	1,563	972	6	591 R	61.5%	38.3%	61.7%	38.3%
19,944	LACLEDE	8,407	5,512	2,862	33	2,650 R	65.6%	34.0%	65.8%	34.2%
26,626	LAFAYETTE	13,169	7,687	5,427	55	2,260 R	58.4%	41.2%	58.6%	41.4%
24,585	LAWRENCE	11,079	7,392	3,667	20	3,725 R	66.7%	33.1%	66.8%	33.2%
10,993	LEWIS	4,383	2,496	1,876	11	620 R	56.9%	42.8%	57.1%	42.9%
18,041	LINCOLN	8,099	4,337	3,729	33	608 R	53.5%	46.0%	53.8%	46.2%
15,125	LINN	7,209	4,019	3,173	17	846 R	55.7%	44.0%	55.9%	44.1%
15,368	LIVINGSTON	6,768	4,172	2,565	31	1,607 R	61.6%	37.9%	61.9%	38.1%
12,357	MCDONALD	5,984	3,552	2,432		1,120 R	59.4%	40.6%	59.4%	40.6%
15,432	MACON	7,602	4,661	2,917	24	1,744 R	61.3%	38.4%	61.5%	38.5%
8,641	MADISON	3,946	2,025	1,913	8	112 R	51.3%	48.5%	51.4%	48.6%
6,851	MARIES	3,276	1,791	1,479	6	312 R	54.7%	45.1%	54.8%	45.2%
28,121	MARION	11,523	6,220	5,286	17	934 R	54.0%	45.9%	54.1%	45.9%
4,910	MERCER	2,162	1,429	730	3	699 R	66.1%	33.8%	66.2%	33.8%

MISSOURI

SENATOR 1976

1970 Census Population	County	Total Vote	Republican	Democratic	Other	Rep.-Dem. Plurality	Percentage Total Vote Rep.	Total Vote Dem.	Major Vote Rep.	Major Vote Dem.
15,026	MILLER	6,830	4,560	2,260	10	2,300 R	66.8%	33.1%	66.9%	33.1%
16,647	MISSISSIPPI	4,998	1,273	3,721	4	2,448 D	25.5%	74.4%	25.5%	74.5%
10,742	MONITEAU	5,508	3,407	2,098	3	1,309 R	61.9%	38.1%	61.9%	38.1%
9,542	MONROE	4,591	2,319	2,253	19	66 R	50.5%	49.1%	50.7%	49.3%
11,000	MONTGOMERY	5,209	3,149	2,055	5	1,094 R	60.5%	39.5%	60.5%	39.5%
10,068	MORGAN	5,519	3,374	2,139	6	1,235 R	61.1%	38.8%	61.2%	38.8%
23,420	NEW MADRID	7,875	2,591	5,283	1	2,692 D	32.9%	67.1%	32.9%	67.1%
32,901	NEWTON	13,982	8,347	5,439	196	2,908 R	59.7%	38.9%	60.5%	39.5%
22,467	NODAWAY	9,383	6,047	3,336		2,711 R	64.4%	35.6%	64.4%	35.6%
9,180	OREGON	3,579	1,558	1,997	24	439 D	43.5%	55.8%	43.8%	56.2%
10,994	OSAGE	5,382	3,510	1,868	4	1,642 R	65.2%	34.7%	65.3%	34.7%
6,226	OZARK	3,020	2,035	980	5	1,055 R	67.4%	32.5%	67.5%	32.5%
26,373	PEMISCOT	6,822	1,922	4,890	10	2,968 D	28.2%	71.7%	28.2%	71.8%
14,393	PERRY	6,810	4,341	2,460	9	1,881 R	63.7%	36.1%	63.8%	36.2%
34,137	PETTIS	15,144	8,911	6,217	16	2,694 R	58.8%	41.1%	58.9%	41.1%
29,567	PHELPS	12,398	7,392	4,981	25	2,411 R	59.6%	40.2%	59.7%	40.3%
16,928	PIKE	7,009	4,399	2,595	15	1,804 R	62.8%	37.0%	62.9%	37.1%
32,081	PLATTE	15,502	9,128	6,152	222	2,976 R	58.9%	39.7%	59.7%	40.3%
15,415	POLK	7,549	4,837	2,681	31	2,156 R	64.1%	35.5%	64.3%	35.7%
53,967	PULASKI	7,140	3,612	3,502	26	110 R	50.6%	49.0%	50.8%	49.2%
5,916	PUTNAM	2,505	1,707	795	3	912 R	68.1%	31.7%	68.2%	31.8%
7,764	RALLS	3,615	1,763	1,846	6	83 D	48.8%	51.1%	48.9%	51.1%
22,434	RANDOLPH	9,277	5,124	4,144	9	980 R	55.2%	44.7%	55.3%	44.7%
17,599	RAY	8,374	3,978	4,329	67	351 D	47.5%	51.7%	47.9%	52.1%
6,106	REYNOLDS	2,949	1,227	1,713	9	486 D	41.6%	58.1%	41.7%	58.3%
9,803	RIPLEY	4,148	1,898	2,246	4	348 D	45.8%	54.1%	45.8%	54.2%
92,954	ST. CHARLES	48,424	29,001	19,244	179	9,757 R	59.9%	39.7%	60.1%	39.9%
7,667	ST. CLAIR	4,067	2,356	1,688	23	668 R	57.9%	41.5%	58.3%	41.7%
36,818	ST. FRANCOIS	15,791	8,267	7,503	21	764 R	52.4%	47.5%	52.4%	47.6%
622,236	ST. LOUIS CITY	172,451	68,287	103,526	638	35,239 D	39.6%	60.0%	39.7%	60.3%
951,353	ST. LOUIS COUNTY	445,016	280,154	162,056	2,806	118,098 R	63.0%	36.4%	63.4%	36.6%
12,867	STE. GENEVIEVE	5,327	2,691	2,625	11	66 R	50.5%	49.3%	50.6%	49.4%
24,837	SALINE	10,673	6,291	4,347	35	1,944 R	58.9%	40.7%	59.1%	40.9%
4,665	SCHUYLER	2,573	1,583	978	12	605 R	61.5%	38.0%	61.8%	38.2%
5,499	SCOTLAND	2,722	1,630	1,092		538 R	59.9%	40.1%	59.9%	40.1%
33,250	SCOTT	13,251	5,249	7,992	10	2,743 D	39.6%	60.3%	39.6%	60.4%
7,196	SHANNON	2,884	1,409	1,453	22	44 D	48.9%	50.4%	49.2%	50.8%
7,906	SHELBY	3,669	1,911	1,751	7	160 R	52.1%	47.7%	52.2%	47.8%
25,771	STODDARD	9,911	4,267	5,635	9	1,368 D	43.1%	56.9%	43.1%	56.9%
9,921	STONE	5,729	4,110	1,576	43	2,534 R	71.7%	27.5%	72.3%	27.7%
7,572	SULLIVAN	4,381	2,650	1,729	2	921 R	60.5%	39.5%	60.5%	39.5%
13,023	TANEY	8,175	5,813	2,340	22	3,473 R	71.1%	28.6%	71.3%	28.7%
18,320	TEXAS	7,894	4,389	3,468	37	921 R	55.6%	43.9%	55.9%	44.1%
19,065	VERNON	8,540	4,943	3,570	27	1,373 R	57.9%	41.8%	58.1%	41.9%
9,699	WARREN	5,410	3,414	1,980	16	1,434 R	63.1%	36.6%	63.3%	36.7%
15,086	WASHINGTON	6,034	2,832	3,183	19	351 D	46.9%	52.8%	47.1%	52.9%
8,546	WAYNE	4,872	2,355	2,514	3	159 D	48.3%	51.6%	48.4%	51.6%
15,562	WEBSTER	7,253	4,407	2,798	48	1,609 R	60.8%	38.6%	61.2%	38.8%
3,359	WORTH	1,715	1,065	646	4	419 R	62.1%	37.7%	62.2%	37.8%
13,667	WRIGHT	6,071	4,146	1,906	19	2,240 R	68.3%	31.4%	68.5%	31.5%
4,677,399	TOTAL	1,914,777	1,090,067	813,571	11,139	276,496 R	56.9%	42.5%	57.3%	42.7%

MISSOURI

CONGRESS

CD	Year	Total Vote	Republican Vote	Republican Candidate	Democratic Vote	Democratic Candidate	Other Vote	Rep.-Dem. Plurality	Percentage Total Vote Rep.	Percentage Total Vote Dem.	Percentage Major Vote Rep.	Percentage Major Vote Dem.
1	1976	133,226	45,874	WITHERSPOON, ROBERT L.	87,310	CLAY, WILLIAM	42	41,436 D	34.4%	65.5%	34.4%	65.6%
1	1974	90,640	28,707	MARTIN, ARTHUR O.	61,933	CLAY, WILLIAM		33,226 D	31.7%	68.3%	31.7%	68.3%
1	1972	148,694	53,596	FUNSCH, RICHARD O.	95,098	CLAY, WILLIAM		41,502 D	36.0%	64.0%	36.0%	64.0%
2	1976	218,461	106,811	SNYDER, ROBERT O.	111,568	YOUNG, ROBERT A.	82	4,757 D	48.9%	51.1%	48.9%	51.1%
2	1974	141,003	55,026	OHLENDORF, HOWARD C.	85,977	SYMINGTON, JAMES W.		30,951 D	39.0%	61.0%	39.0%	61.0%
2	1972	211,524	77,192	COOPER, JOHN W.	134,332	SYMINGTON, JAMES W.		57,140 D	36.5%	63.5%	36.5%	63.5%
3	1976	180,743	65,623	BADARACCO, JOSEPH L.	115,109	GEPHARDT, RICHARD A.	11	49,486 D	36.3%	63.7%	36.3%	63.7%
3	1974	129,541	31,489	RAISCH, JOANN P.	96,201	SULLIVAN, LEONOR K.	1,851	64,712 D	24.3%	74.3%	24.7%	75.3%
3	1972	179,353	54,523	HOLST, ALBERT	124,365	SULLIVAN, LEONOR K.	465	69,842 D	30.4%	69.3%	30.5%	69.5%
4	1976	207,562	91,605	KING, RICHARD A.	115,955	SKELTON, IKE	2	24,350 D	44.1%	55.9%	44.1%	55.9%
4	1974	121,502	39,055	PATTERSON, CLAUDE	82,447	RANDALL, WILLIAM J.		43,392 D	32.1%	67.9%	32.1%	67.9%
4	1972	188,359	80,228	BARROWS, RAYMOND E.	108,131	RANDALL, WILLIAM J.		27,903 D	42.6%	57.4%	42.6%	57.4%
5	1976	148,302	41,681	COLLINS, JOANNE	100,876	BOLLING, RICHARD	5,745	59,195 D	28.1%	68.0%	29.2%	70.8%
5	1974	82,605	24,669	MCDONOUGH, JOHN J.	57,081	BOLLING, RICHARD	855	32,412 D	29.9%	69.1%	30.2%	69.8%
5	1972	149,450	53,257	RICE, VERNON E.	93,812	BOLLING, RICHARD	2,381	40,555 D	35.6%	62.8%	36.2%	63.8%
6	1976	206,707	120,969	COLEMAN, E. THOMAS	83,755	MAXFIELD, MORGAN	1,983	37,214 R	58.5%	40.5%	59.1%	40.9%
6	1974	128,756	27,147	SPEERS, GROVER H.	101,609	LITTON, JERRY		74,462 D	21.1%	78.9%	21.1%	78.9%
6	1972	201,657	91,610	SLOAN, RUSSELL	110,047	LITTON, JERRY		18,437 D	45.4%	54.6%	45.4%	54.6%
7	1976	215,515	133,656	TAYLOR, GENE	81,848	HAWKINS, DOLAN G.	11	51,808 R	62.0%	38.0%	62.0%	38.0%
7	1974	152,440	79,787	TAYLOR, GENE	72,653	FRANKS, RICHARD L.		7,134 R	52.3%	47.7%	52.3%	47.7%
7	1972	208,393	132,780	TAYLOR, GENE	75,613	THOMAS, WILLIAM		57,167 R	63.7%	36.3%	63.7%	36.3%
8	1976	196,650	60,179	LEICK, CHARLES R.	132,386	ICHORD, RICHARD	4,085	72,207 D	30.6%	67.3%	31.3%	68.7%
8	1974	123,964	37,369	NOLAND, JAMES A.	86,595	ICHORD, RICHARD		49,226 D	30.1%	69.9%	30.1%	69.9%
8	1972	181,136	68,580	COUNTIE, DAVID R.	112,556	ICHORD, RICHARD		43,976 D	37.9%	62.1%	37.9%	62.1%
9	1976	215,144	94,816	FRAPPIER, J. H.	120,325	VOLKMER, HAROLD	3	25,509 D	44.1%	55.9%	44.1%	55.9%
9	1974	131,864	44,318	BISCHOF, MILTON	87,546	HUNGATE, WILLIAM L.		43,228 D	33.6%	66.4%	33.6%	66.4%
9	1972	198,678	66,528	PRANGE, ROBERT L.	132,150	HUNGATE, WILLIAM L.		65,622 D	33.5%	66.5%	33.5%	66.5%
10	1976	182,706	51,024	CARRON, JOE	131,675	BURLISON, BILL D.	7	80,651 D	27.9%	72.1%	27.9%	72.1%
10	1974	106,727	29,050	FARROW, TRUMAN	77,677	BURLISON, BILL D.		48,627 D	27.2%	72.8%	27.2%	72.8%
10	1972	165,384	59,083	SVENDROWSKI, FRANK	106,301	BURLISON, BILL D.		47,218 D	35.7%	64.3%	35.7%	64.3%

MISSOURI

1976 GENERAL ELECTION

President Original uncorrected canvass gave the Republican total vote as 928,808; the Democratic total vote as 999,163 and the McCarthy Independent total vote as 24,329. Other vote was 24,029 McCarthy (Independent); 3,741 scattered. State-wide other vote total includes the 3,741 scattered votes not available by county.

Governor Other vote was 4,215 Striler (Non-partisan); 66 scattered. State-wide other vote total includes the 66 scattered votes not available by county.

Senator Other vote was 10,822 Petty (Non-partisan); 317 scattered. State-wide other vote total includes the 317 scattered votes not available by county.

Congress Other vote was scattered in CD's 1, 2, 3, 4, 7, 9 and 10; Moore (Independent) in CD 5; 1,937 Thompson (Independent) and 46 scattered in CD 6; 4,082 Leiderman (Independent) and 3 scattered in CD 8.

1976 PRIMARIES

AUGUST 3 REPUBLICAN

Governor 286,377 Christopher Bond; 24,975 Harvey Euge.

Senator 284,025 John C. Danforth; 19,796 Gregory Hansman.

Congress Unopposed in three CD's. Contested as follows:

CD 1 4,615 Robert L. Witherspoon; 2,804 Percy Gray; 2,007 Authur O. Martin.
CD 2 13,906 Robert O. Snyder; 13,572 Bob Chase; 3,039 Jack Cooper; 1,747 Leo Eickhoff; 1,669 John R. Stoeffler; 1,244 Robert H. Blanke; 980 Hugh V. Murray.
CD 3 16,845 Joseph L. Badaracco; 8,330 Paul A. Koch.
CD 4 14,310 Richard A. King; 12,033 Robert T. Johnson.
CD 5 6,415 Joanne Collins; 6,242 John McDonough.
CD 9 16,136 J. H. Frappier; 8,562 David Doctorian.
CD 10 13,692 Joe Carron; 4,463 M. Francis Svendrowski.

AUGUST 3 DEMOCRATIC

Governor 419,656 Joseph P. Teasdale; 340,208 William Cason; 18,180 Byron Sparks; 12,539 Milton Morris; 11,568 Roy Bean; 10,746 George D. Weber; 9,735 Charles Baker; 5,779 Douglas V. White; 4,842 Roy Smith.

Senator 401,822 Jerry Litton; 233,544 Warren E. Hearnes; 222,681 James W. Symington; 10,894 Charles B. Wheeler; 4,865 William McK. Thomas; 4,784 Lee C. Sutton; 2,030 Jim C. Tyler; 1,923 Norman L. Tucker; 1,425 Terry Richards; 1,207 Horace Kingery. Mr. Litton died primary day and Warren E. Hearnes was substituted by the state central committee.

Congress Unopposed in two CD's. Contested as follows:

CD 1 38,735 William Clay; 7,614 Dan E. McGovern; 5,178 James P. Troupe; 5,164 Takuri Tei; 3,169 Felix J. Panlasigui; 2,535 Elsa D. Hill; 1,400 Arnold L. Totter.
CD 2 42,621 Robert A. Young; 41,561 Jack J. Schramm; 2,942 Fred E. Bradley; 1,470 Edward P. Roche.
CD 3 48,874 Richard A. Gephardt; 32,791 Donald J. Gralike; 2,960 Victoria Schmidt; 2,680 Marie S. Nowak.
CD 4 37,201 Ike Skelton; 26,853 Jack Gant; 14,446 Don Manford; 3,574 Adelaide Miller; 3,565 Art Lamb; 3,386 Ross Edwards; 1,612 Forest Nave; 1,095 Lane Leard; 665 William M. Biggs.
CD 5 48,510 Richard Bolling; 19,113 John Shockey.
CD 6 50,047 Morgan Maxfield; 26,715 Pat Danner; 22,757 Charles Broomfield; 9,121 Vern King; 2,152 H. N. Sutherland; 1,942 Bill Davis; 907 Sandra Finley.

MISSOURI

CD 9 36,168 Harold Volkmer; 18,291 Joseph Afshari; 14,439 Jerry Welch; 12,271 Tom Walsh; 8,695 Jean Berg; 6,001 Ken Maurer; 3,274 Gene Weathers; 3,045 Connie Cook; 875 R. E. Laramie; 584 John W. Williamson; 319 Thomas Willsie.

CD 10 71,213 Bill D. Burlison; 15,470 Richard Flotran; 15,164 W. F. McKee.

AUGUST 3 INDEPENDENT (NON-PARTISAN)

Under Missouri law, if more than one independent candidate files for a given office, a primary is held to determine the Non-Partisan ballot designation in November. In 1976 there was one such contest:

Congress

CD 5 296 William F. Moore; 203 Jimie Kelso.

MONTANA

GOVERNOR

Thomas L. Judge (D). Re-elected 1976 to a four-year term. Previously elected 1972.

SENATORS

John Melcher (D). Elected 1976 to a six-year term.

Lee Metcalf (D). Re-elected 1972 to a six-year term. Previously elected 1966, 1960.

REPRESENTATIVES

1. Max S. Baucus (D)
2. Ron Marlenee (R)

POSTWAR VOTE FOR GOVERNOR

Year	Total Vote	Republican Vote	Republican Candidate	Democratic Vote	Democratic Candidate	Other Vote	Rep.-Dem. Plurality	Percentage Total Vote Rep.	Percentage Total Vote Dem.	Percentage Major Vote Rep.	Percentage Major Vote Dem.
1976	316,720	115,848	Woodahl, Robert	195,420	Judge, Thomas L.	5,452	79,572 D	36.6%	61.7%	37.2%	62.8%
1972	318,754	146,231	Smith, Ed	172,523	Judge, Thomas L.	–	26,292 D	45.9%	54.1%	45.9%	54.1%
1968	278,112	116,432	Babcock, Tim M.	150,481	Anderson, Forrest H.	11,199	34,049 D	41.9%	54.1%	43.6%	56.4%
1964	280,975	144,113	Babcock, Tim M.	136,862	Renne, Roland	–	7,251 R	51.3%	48.7%	51.3%	48.7%
1960	279,881	154,230	Nutter, Donald G.	125,651	Cannon, Paul	–	28,579 R	55.1%	44.9%	55.1%	44.9%
1956	270,366	138,878	Aronson, J. Hugo	131,488	Olsen, Arnold H.	–	7,390 R	51.4%	48.6%	51.4%	48.6%
1952	263,792	134,423	Aronson, J. Hugo	129,369	Bonner, John W.	–	5,054 R	51.0%	49.0%	51.0%	49.0%
1948	222,964	97,792	Ford, Sam C.	124,267	Bonner, John W.	905	26,475 D	43.9%	55.7%	44.0%	56.0%

POSTWAR VOTE FOR SENATOR

Year	Total Vote	Republican Vote	Republican Candidate	Democratic Vote	Democratic Candidate	Other Vote	Rep.-Dem. Plurality	Percentage Total Vote Rep.	Percentage Total Vote Dem.	Percentage Major Vote Rep.	Percentage Major Vote Dem.
1976	321,445	115,213	Burger, Stanley C.	206,232	Melcher, John	–	91,019 D	35.8%	64.2%	35.8%	64.2%
1972	314,925	151,316	Hibbard, Henry S.	163,609	Metcalf, Lee	–	12,293 D	48.0%	52.0%	48.0%	52.0%
1970	247,869	97,809	Wallace, Harold E.	150,060	Mansfield, Mike	–	52,251 D	39.5%	60.5%	39.5%	60.5%
1966	259,863	121,697	Babcock, Tim M.	138,166	Metcalf, Lee	–	16,469 D	46.8%	53.2%	46.8%	53.2%
1964	280,010	99,367	Blewett, Alex	180,643	Mansfield, Mike	–	81,276 D	35.5%	64.5%	35.5%	64.5%
1960	276,612	136,281	Fjare, Orvin B.	140,331	Metcalf, Lee	–	4,050 D	49.3%	50.7%	49.3%	50.7%
1958	229,483	54,573	Welch, Lou W.	174,910	Mansfield, Mike	–	120,337 D	23.8%	76.2%	23.8%	76.2%
1954	227,454	112,863	D'Ewart, Wesley A.	114,591	Murray, James E.	–	1,728 D	49.6%	50.4%	49.6%	50.4%
1952	262,297	127,360	Ecton, Zales N.	133,109	Mansfield, Mike	1,828	5,749 D	48.6%	50.7%	48.9%	51.1%
1948	221,003	94,458	David, Tom J.	125,193	Murray, James E.	1,352	30,735 D	42.7%	56.6%	43.0%	57.0%
1946	190,566	101,901	Ecton, Zales N.	86,476	Erickson, Leif	2,189	15,425 R	53.5%	45.4%	54.1%	45.9%

MONTANA

Districts Established March 3, 1971

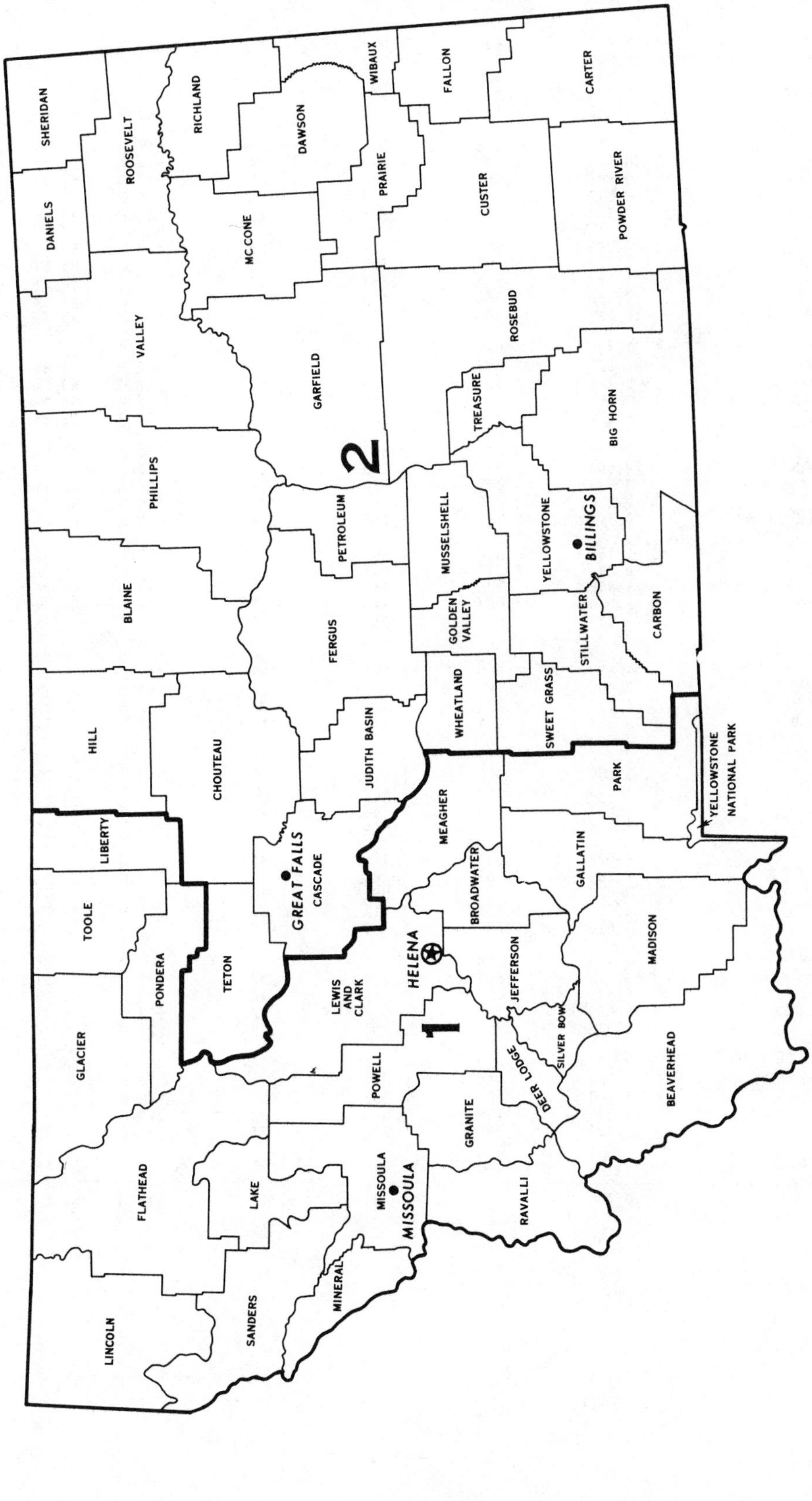

MONTANA

PRESIDENT 1976

1970 Census Population	County	Total Vote	Republican	Democratic	Other	Rep.-Dem. Plurality	Percentage Total Vote Rep.	Percentage Total Vote Dem.	Percentage Major Vote Rep.	Percentage Major Vote Dem.
8,187	BEAVERHEAD	3,543	2,461	1,013	69	1,448 R	69.5%	28.6%	70.8%	29.2%
10,057	BIG HORN	3,630	1,615	1,962	53	347 D	44.5%	54.0%	45.1%	54.9%
6,727	BLAINE	2,739	1,349	1,356	34	7 D	49.3%	49.5%	49.9%	50.1%
2,526	BROADWATER	1,389	820	557	12	263 R	59.0%	40.1%	59.5%	40.5%
7,080	CARBON	4,045	2,121	1,853	71	268 R	52.4%	45.8%	53.4%	46.6%
1,956	CARTER	972	558	344	70	214 R	57.4%	35.4%	61.9%	38.1%
81,804	CASCADE	30,511	15,289	14,678	544	611 R	50.1%	48.1%	51.0%	49.0%
6,473	CHOUTEAU	3,465	1,814	1,568	83	246 R	52.4%	45.3%	53.6%	46.4%
12,174	CUSTER	5,647	3,120	2,425	102	695 R	55.3%	42.9%	56.3%	43.7%
3,083	DANIELS	1,639	816	797	26	19 R	49.8%	48.6%	50.6%	49.4%
11,269	DAWSON	4,960	2,639	2,201	120	438 R	53.2%	44.4%	54.5%	45.5%
15,652	DEER LODGE	6,176	2,197	3,859	120	1,662 D	35.6%	62.5%	36.3%	63.7%
4,050	FALLON	1,797	934	847	16	87 R	52.0%	47.1%	52.4%	47.6%
12,611	FERGUS	6,160	3,556	2,470	134	1,086 R	57.7%	40.1%	59.0%	41.0%
39,460	FLATHEAD	18,845	10,494	7,827	524	2,667 R	55.7%	41.5%	57.3%	42.7%
32,505	GALLATIN	17,460	11,062	6,215	183	4,847 R	63.4%	35.6%	64.0%	36.0%
1,796	GARFIELD	922	625	273	24	352 R	67.8%	29.6%	69.6%	30.4%
10,783	GLACIER	3,724	1,892	1,755	77	137 R	50.8%	47.1%	51.9%	48.1%
931	GOLDEN VALLEY	569	302	255	12	47 R	53.1%	44.8%	54.2%	45.8%
2,737	GRANITE	1,272	746	509	17	237 R	58.6%	40.0%	59.4%	40.6%
17,358	HILL	7,260	3,274	3,878	108	604 D	45.1%	53.4%	45.8%	54.2%
5,238	JEFFERSON	2,654	1,387	1,210	57	177 R	52.3%	45.6%	53.4%	46.6%
2,667	JUDITH BASIN	1,614	809	772	33	37 R	50.1%	47.8%	51.2%	48.8%
14,445	LAKE	7,210	3,809	3,253	148	556 R	52.8%	45.1%	53.9%	46.1%
33,281	LEWIS AND CLARK	18,517	10,155	8,118	244	2,037 R	54.8%	43.8%	55.6%	44.4%
2,359	LIBERTY	1,163	638	506	19	132 R	54.9%	43.5%	55.8%	44.2%
18,063	LINCOLN	6,283	3,017	3,146	120	129 D	48.0%	50.1%	49.0%	51.0%
2,875	MCCONE	1,499	730	749	20	19 D	48.7%	50.0%	49.4%	50.6%
5,014	MADISON	2,610	1,688	870	52	818 R	64.7%	33.3%	66.0%	34.0%
2,122	MEAGHER	939	565	364	10	201 R	60.2%	38.8%	60.8%	39.2%
2,958	MINERAL	1,514	679	819	16	140 D	44.8%	54.1%	45.3%	54.7%
58,263	MISSOULA	31,837	16,350	15,099	388	1,251 R	51.4%	47.4%	52.0%	48.0%
3,734	MUSSELSHELL	2,065	1,117	922	26	195 R	54.1%	44.6%	54.8%	45.2%
11,197	PARK	5,740	3,281	2,364	95	917 R	57.2%	41.2%	58.1%	41.9%
675	PETROLEUM	331	211	110	10	101 R	63.7%	33.2%	65.7%	34.3%
5,386	PHILLIPS	2,486	1,347	1,117	22	230 R	54.2%	44.9%	54.7%	45.3%
6,611	PONDERA	3,150	1,666	1,413	71	253 R	52.9%	44.9%	54.1%	45.9%
2,862	POWDER RIVER	1,235	683	429	123	254 R	55.3%	34.7%	61.4%	38.6%
6,660	POWELL	2,951	1,610	1,302	39	308 R	54.6%	44.1%	55.3%	44.7%
1,752	PRAIRIE	1,019	597	415	7	182 R	58.6%	40.7%	59.0%	41.0%
14,409	RAVALLI	8,694	4,894	3,504	296	1,390 R	56.3%	40.3%	58.3%	41.7%
9,837	RICHLAND	4,263	2,189	1,961	113	228 R	51.3%	46.0%	52.7%	47.3%
10,365	ROOSEVELT	3,928	1,822	2,061	45	239 D	46.4%	52.5%	46.9%	53.1%
6,032	ROSEBUD	3,006	1,538	1,413	55	125 R	51.2%	47.0%	52.1%	47.9%
7,093	SANDERS	3,576	1,738	1,725	113	13 R	48.6%	48.2%	50.2%	49.8%
5,779	SHERIDAN	2,714	1,114	1,560	40	446 D	41.0%	57.5%	41.7%	58.3%
41,981	SILVER BOW	19,110	7,506	11,377	227	3,871 D	39.3%	59.5%	39.8%	60.2%
4,632	STILLWATER	2,635	1,446	1,143	46	303 R	54.9%	43.4%	55.9%	44.1%
2,980	SWEET GRASS	1,659	1,135	502	22	633 R	68.4%	30.3%	69.3%	30.7%
6,116	TETON	3,345	1,730	1,506	109	224 R	51.7%	45.0%	53.5%	46.5%
5,839	TOOLE	2,603	1,469	1,080	54	389 R	56.4%	41.5%	57.6%	42.4%
1,069	TREASURE	564	315	239	10	76 R	55.9%	42.4%	56.9%	43.1%
11,471	VALLEY	4,959	2,520	2,352	87	168 R	50.8%	47.4%	51.7%	48.3%
2,529	WHEATLAND	1,320	755	535	30	220 R	57.2%	40.5%	58.5%	41.5%
1,465	WIBAUX	691	308	352	31	44 D	44.6%	50.9%	46.7%	53.3%
87,367	YELLOWSTONE	44,125	25,201	18,329	595	6,872 R	57.1%	41.5%	57.9%	42.1%
694,409	TOTAL	328,734	173,703	149,259	5,772	24,444 R	52.8%	45.4%	53.8%	46.2%

MONTANA

GOVERNOR 1976

1970 Census Population	County	Total Vote	Republican	Democratic	Other	Rep.-Dem. Plurality	Percentage Total Vote Rep.	Percentage Total Vote Dem.	Percentage Major Vote Rep.	Percentage Major Vote Dem.
8,187	BEAVERHEAD	3,367	1,682	1,685		3 D	50.0%	50.0%	50.0%	50.0%
10,057	BIG HORN	3,527	1,171	2,327	29	1,156 D	33.2%	66.0%	33.5%	66.5%
6,727	BLAINE	2,730	914	1,679	137	765 D	33.5%	61.5%	35.2%	64.8%
2,526	BROADWATER	1,353	565	677	111	112 D	41.8%	50.0%	45.5%	54.5%
7,080	CARBON	3,936	1,500	2,436		936 D	38.1%	61.9%	38.1%	61.9%
1,956	CARTER	957	466	472	19	6 D	48.7%	49.3%	49.7%	50.3%
81,804	CASCADE	28,867	8,596	19,944	327	11,348 D	29.8%	69.1%	30.1%	69.9%
6,473	CHOUTEAU	3,416	1,097	1,853	466	756 D	32.1%	54.2%	37.2%	62.8%
12,174	CUSTER	5,478	1,734	3,396	348	1,662 D	31.7%	62.0%	33.8%	66.2%
3,083	DANIELS	1,609	686	917	6	231 D	42.6%	57.0%	42.8%	57.2%
11,269	DAWSON	4,919	1,704	3,107	108	1,403 D	34.6%	63.2%	35.4%	64.6%
15,652	DEER LODGE	5,967	1,922	4,045		2,123 D	32.2%	67.8%	32.2%	67.8%
4,050	FALLON	1,781	765	999	17	234 D	43.0%	56.1%	43.4%	56.6%
12,611	FERGUS	6,173	2,316	3,626	231	1,310 D	37.5%	58.7%	39.0%	61.0%
39,460	FLATHEAD	18,442	7,209	11,233		4,024 D	39.1%	60.9%	39.1%	60.9%
32,505	GALLATIN	15,997	6,809	9,188		2,379 D	42.6%	57.4%	42.6%	57.4%
1,796	GARFIELD	873	147	244	482	97 D	16.8%	27.9%	37.6%	62.4%
10,783	GLACIER	3,589	1,127	2,299	163	1,172 D	31.4%	64.1%	32.9%	67.1%
931	GOLDEN VALLEY	567	218	331	18	113 D	38.4%	58.4%	39.7%	60.3%
2,737	GRANITE	1,252	581	671		90 D	46.4%	53.6%	46.4%	53.6%
17,358	HILL	7,414	2,343	4,919	152	2,576 D	31.6%	66.3%	32.3%	67.7%
5,238	JEFFERSON	2,507	936	1,571		635 D	37.3%	62.7%	37.3%	62.7%
2,667	JUDITH BASIN	1,563	515	940	108	425 D	32.9%	60.1%	35.4%	64.6%
14,445	LAKE	7,177	3,392	3,629	156	237 D	47.3%	50.6%	48.3%	51.7%
33,281	LEWIS AND CLARK	17,845	5,871	11,381	593	5,510 D	32.9%	63.8%	34.0%	66.0%
2,359	LIBERTY	1,134	368	617	149	249 D	32.5%	54.4%	37.4%	62.6%
18,063	LINCOLN	6,064	1,968	4,096		2,128 D	32.5%	67.5%	32.5%	67.5%
2,875	MCCONE	1,483	543	848	92	305 D	36.6%	57.2%	39.0%	61.0%
5,014	MADISON	2,561	1,431	1,100	30	331 R	55.9%	43.0%	56.5%	43.5%
2,122	MEAGHER	873	363	510		147 D	41.6%	58.4%	41.6%	58.4%
2,958	MINERAL	1,497	465	1,032		567 D	31.1%	68.9%	31.1%	68.9%
58,263	MISSOULA	30,580	11,334	18,723	523	7,389 D	37.1%	61.2%	37.7%	62.3%
3,734	MUSSELSHELL	2,061	692	1,308	61	616 D	33.6%	63.5%	34.6%	65.4%
11,197	PARK	5,599	2,100	3,499		1,399 D	37.5%	62.5%	37.5%	62.5%
675	PETROLEUM	324	112	171	41	59 D	34.6%	52.8%	39.6%	60.4%
5,386	PHILLIPS	2,440	929	1,460	51	531 D	38.1%	59.8%	38.9%	61.1%
6,611	PONDERA	2,922	960	1,962		1,002 D	32.9%	67.1%	32.9%	67.1%
2,862	POWDER RIVER	1,215	585	567	63	18 R	48.1%	46.7%	50.8%	49.2%
6,660	POWELL	2,855	1,201	1,568	86	367 D	42.1%	54.9%	43.4%	56.6%
1,752	PRAIRIE	999	429	555	15	126 D	42.9%	55.6%	43.6%	56.4%
14,409	RAVALLI	8,354	3,597	4,757		1,160 D	43.1%	56.9%	43.1%	56.9%
9,837	RICHLAND	4,144	1,630	2,514		884 D	39.3%	60.7%	39.3%	60.7%
10,365	ROOSEVELT	3,897	1,280	2,580	37	1,300 D	32.8%	66.2%	33.2%	66.8%
6,032	ROSEBUD	2,866	1,016	1,850		834 D	35.5%	64.5%	35.5%	64.5%
7,093	SANDERS	3,472	1,550	1,880	42	330 D	44.6%	54.1%	45.2%	54.8%
5,779	SHERIDAN	2,629	1,057	1,552	20	495 D	40.2%	59.0%	40.5%	59.5%
41,981	SILVER BOW	18,409	6,084	12,252	73	6,168 D	33.0%	66.6%	33.2%	66.8%
4,632	STILLWATER	2,536	1,022	1,514		492 D	40.3%	59.7%	40.3%	59.7%
2,980	SWEET GRASS	1,563	702	644	217	58 R	44.9%	41.2%	52.2%	47.8%
6,116	TETON	3,294	1,375	1,753	166	378 D	41.7%	53.2%	44.0%	56.0%
5,839	TOOLE	2,391	907	1,484		577 D	37.9%	62.1%	37.9%	62.1%
1,069	TREASURE	557	197	331	29	134 D	35.4%	59.4%	37.3%	62.7%
11,471	VALLEY	4,788	1,851	2,842	95	991 D	38.7%	59.4%	39.4%	60.6%
2,529	WHEATLAND	1,233	464	769		305 D	37.6%	62.4%	37.6%	62.4%
1,465	WIBAUX	675	264	411		147 D	39.1%	60.9%	39.1%	60.9%
87,367	YELLOWSTONE	41,999	15,106	26,702	191	11,596 D	36.0%	63.6%	36.1%	63.9%
694,409	TOTAL	316,720	115,848	195,420	5,452	79,572 D	36.6%	61.7%	37.2%	62.8%

MONTANA

SENATOR 1976

1970 Census Population	County	Total Vote	Republican	Democratic	Other	Rep.-Dem. Plurality	Percentage Total Vote Rep.	Total Vote Dem.	Major Vote Rep.	Major Vote Dem.
8,187	BEAVERHEAD	3,553	1,990	1,563		427 R	56.0%	44.0%	56.0%	44.0%
10,057	BIG HORN	3,601	1,203	2,398		1,195 D	33.4%	66.6%	33.4%	66.6%
6,727	BLAINE	2,783	912	1,871		959 D	32.8%	67.2%	32.8%	67.2%
2,526	BROADWATER	1,403	673	730		57 D	48.0%	52.0%	48.0%	52.0%
7,080	CARBON	4,092	1,402	2,690		1,288 D	34.3%	65.7%	34.3%	65.7%
1,956	CARTER	983	425	558		133 D	43.2%	56.8%	43.2%	56.8%
81,804	CASCADE	29,378	8,856	20,522		11,666 D	30.1%	69.9%	30.1%	69.9%
6,473	CHOUTEAU	3,539	1,335	2,204		869 D	37.7%	62.3%	37.7%	62.3%
12,174	CUSTER	5,704	1,982	3,722		1,740 D	34.7%	65.3%	34.7%	65.3%
3,083	DANIELS	1,657	539	1,118		579 D	32.5%	67.5%	32.5%	67.5%
11,269	DAWSON	5,017	1,835	3,182		1,347 D	36.6%	63.4%	36.6%	63.4%
15,652	DEER LODGE	5,593	1,261	4,332		3,071 D	22.5%	77.5%	22.5%	77.5%
4,050	FALLON	1,806	746	1,060		314 D	41.3%	58.7%	41.3%	58.7%
12,611	FERGUS	6,312	2,713	3,599		886 D	43.0%	57.0%	43.0%	57.0%
39,460	FLATHEAD	18,746	7,728	11,018		3,290 D	41.2%	58.8%	41.2%	58.8%
32,505	GALLATIN	15,742	7,596	8,146		550 D	48.3%	51.7%	48.3%	51.7%
1,796	GARFIELD	930	382	548		166 D	41.1%	58.9%	41.1%	58.9%
10,783	GLACIER	3,717	1,429	2,288		859 D	38.4%	61.6%	38.4%	61.6%
931	GOLDEN VALLEY	576	221	355		134 D	38.4%	61.6%	38.4%	61.6%
2,737	GRANITE	1,312	595	717		122 D	45.4%	54.6%	45.4%	54.6%
17,358	HILL	7,305	2,023	5,282		3,259 D	27.7%	72.3%	27.7%	72.3%
5,238	JEFFERSON	2,697	1,019	1,678		659 D	37.8%	62.2%	37.8%	62.2%
2,667	JUDITH BASIN	1,638	596	1,042		446 D	36.4%	63.6%	36.4%	63.6%
14,445	LAKE	7,294	3,323	3,971		648 D	45.6%	54.4%	45.6%	54.4%
33,281	LEWIS AND CLARK	16,723	6,435	10,288		3,853 D	38.5%	61.5%	38.5%	61.5%
2,359	LIBERTY	1,183	542	641		99 D	45.8%	54.2%	45.8%	54.2%
18,063	LINCOLN	6,172	1,841	4,331		2,490 D	29.8%	70.2%	29.8%	70.2%
2,875	MCCONE	1,523	559	964		405 D	36.7%	63.3%	36.7%	63.3%
5,014	MADISON	2,663	1,493	1,170		323 R	56.1%	43.9%	56.1%	43.9%
2,122	MEAGHER	950	441	509		68 D	46.4%	53.6%	46.4%	53.6%
2,958	MINERAL	1,521	413	1,108		695 D	27.2%	72.8%	27.2%	72.8%
58,263	MISSOULA	31,950	10,196	21,754		11,558 D	31.9%	68.1%	31.9%	68.1%
3,734	MUSSELSHELL	2,095	603	1,492		889 D	28.8%	71.2%	28.8%	71.2%
11,197	PARK	5,808	2,300	3,508		1,208 D	39.6%	60.4%	39.6%	60.4%
675	PETROLEUM	337	149	188		39 D	44.2%	55.8%	44.2%	55.8%
5,386	PHILLIPS	2,501	904	1,597		693 D	36.1%	63.9%	36.1%	63.9%
6,611	PONDERA	3,169	1,277	1,892		615 D	40.3%	59.7%	40.3%	59.7%
2,862	POWDER RIVER	1,270	600	670		70 D	47.2%	52.8%	47.2%	52.8%
6,660	POWELL	2,718	1,009	1,709		700 D	37.1%	62.9%	37.1%	62.9%
1,752	PRAIRIE	1,025	423	602		179 D	41.3%	58.7%	41.3%	58.7%
14,409	RAVALLI	8,782	4,150	4,632		482 D	47.3%	52.7%	47.3%	52.7%
9,837	RICHLAND	4,310	1,707	2,603		896 D	39.6%	60.4%	39.6%	60.4%
10,365	ROOSEVELT	3,970	1,423	2,547		1,124 D	35.8%	64.2%	35.8%	64.2%
6,032	ROSEBUD	3,039	602	2,437		1,835 D	19.8%	80.2%	19.8%	80.2%
7,093	SANDERS	3,568	1,268	2,300		1,032 D	35.5%	64.5%	35.5%	64.5%
5,779	SHERIDAN	2,726	836	1,890		1,054 D	30.7%	69.3%	30.7%	69.3%
41,981	SILVER BOW	17,246	4,052	13,194		9,142 D	23.5%	76.5%	23.5%	76.5%
4,632	STILLWATER	2,677	948	1,729		781 D	35.4%	64.6%	35.4%	64.6%
2,980	SWEET GRASS	1,659	845	814		31 R	50.9%	49.1%	50.9%	49.1%
6,116	TETON	3,376	1,389	1,987		598 D	41.1%	58.9%	41.1%	58.9%
5,839	TOOLE	2,647	1,153	1,494		341 D	43.6%	56.4%	43.6%	56.4%
1,069	TREASURE	573	142	431		289 D	24.8%	75.2%	24.8%	75.2%
11,471	VALLEY	4,845	1,746	3,099		1,353 D	36.0%	64.0%	36.0%	64.0%
2,529	WHEATLAND	1,338	496	842		346 D	37.1%	62.9%	37.1%	62.9%
1,465	WIBAUX	712	225	487		262 D	31.6%	68.4%	31.6%	68.4%
87,367	YELLOWSTONE	42,991	14,262	28,729		14,467 D	33.2%	66.8%	33.2%	66.8%
694,409	TOTAL	321,445	115,213	206,232		91,019 D	35.8%	64.2%	35.8%	64.2%

MONTANA

CONGRESS

CD	Year	Total Vote	Republican Vote	Republican Candidate	Democratic Vote	Democratic Candidate	Other Vote	Rep.-Dem. Plurality	Percentage Total Vote Rep.	Percentage Total Vote Dem.	Percentage Major Vote Rep.	Percentage Major Vote Dem.
1	1976	167,784	56,297	DIEHL, W. D.	111,487	BAUCUS, MAX S.		55,190 D	33.6%	66.4%	33.6%	66.4%
1	1974	135,613	61,309	SHOUP, RICHARD G.	74,304	BAUCUS, MAX S.		12,995 D	45.2%	54.8%	45.2%	54.8%
1	1972	164,446	88,373	SHOUP, RICHARD G.	76,073	OLSEN, ARNOLD H.		12,300 R	53.7%	46.3%	53.7%	46.3%
2	1976	153,121	84,149	MARLENEE, RON	68,972	TOWE, THOMAS E.		15,177 R	55.0%	45.0%	55.0%	45.0%
2	1974	118,533	43,853	MCDONALD, JOHN K.	74,680	MELCHER, JOHN		30,827 D	37.0%	63.0%	37.0%	63.0%
2	1972	150,587	36,063	FORESTER, RICHARD L.	114,524	MELCHER, JOHN		78,461 D	23.9%	76.1%	23.9%	76.1%

MONTANA

Population total includes 64 persons living in Yellowstone National Park and not under any county jurisdiction.

1976 GENERAL ELECTION

President Other vote was Anderson (Americanist for President).

Governor Other vote was Mahoney (write-in).

Senator

Congress

1976 PRIMARIES

JUNE 1 REPUBLICAN

Governor 47,629 Robert Woodahl; 36,420 John K. McDonald.

Senator 32,313 Stanley C. Burger; 27,257 Dave Drum; 15,129 John F. Tierney; 5,258 Larry L. Gilbert.

Congress Unopposed in CD 1. Contested as follows:

CD 2 15,742 Ron Marlenee; 11,724 John Cavan; 5,763 Math J. Dasinger; 4,518 Sam Kitzenberg; 1,073 Ben C. Worm.

JUNE 1 DEMOCRATIC

Governor Thomas L. Judge, unopposed.

Senator 89,413 John Melcher; 11,593 Ray E. Gulick.

Congress Unopposed in CD 1. Contested as follows:

CD 2 15,198 Thomas E. Towe; 13,661 Pat McKittrick; 7,056 Thomas G. Monahan; 5,880 Clyde Jarvis; 4,952 Jerry J. Cate.

NEBRASKA

GOVERNOR

J. J. Exon (D). Re-elected 1974 to a four-year term. Previously elected 1970.

SENATORS

Carl T. Curtis (R). Re-elected 1972 to a six-year term. Previously elected 1966, 1960, 1954.

Edward Zorinsky (D). Elected 1976 to a six-year term.

REPRESENTATIVES

1. Charles Thone (R)
2. John J. Cavanaugh (D)
3. Virginia Smith (R)

POSTWAR VOTE FOR GOVERNOR

		Republican		Democratic				Percentage			
	Total					Other	Rep.-Dem.	Total Vote		Major Vote	
Year	Vote	Vote	Candidate	Vote	Candidate	Vote	Plurality	Rep.	Dem.	Rep.	Dem.
1974	451,306	159,780	Marvel, Richard D.	267,012	Exon, J. J.	24,514	107,232 D	35.4%	59.2%	37.4%	62.6%
1970	461,619	201,994	Tiemann, Norbert T.	248,552	Exon, J. J.	11,073	46,558 D	43.8%	53.8%	44.8%	55.2%
1966	486,396	299,245	Tiemann, Norbert T.	186,985	Sorensen, Philip C.	166	112,260 R	61.5%	38.4%	61.5%	38.5%
1964	578,090	231,029	Burney, Dwight W.	347,026	Morrison, Frank B.	35	115,997 D	40.0%	60.0%	40.0%	60.0%
1962	464,585	221,885	Seaton, Fred A.	242,669	Morrison, Frank B.	31	20,784 D	47.8%	52.2%	47.8%	52.2%
1960	598,971	287,302	Cooper, John R.	311,344	Morrison, Frank B.	325	24,042 D	48.0%	52.0%	48.0%	52.0%
1958	421,067	209,705	Anderson, Victor E.	211,345	Brooks, Ralph G.	17	1,640 D	49.8%	50.2%	49.8%	50.2%
1956	567,933	308,293	Anderson, Victor E.	228,048	Sorrell, Frank	31,592	80,245 R	54.3%	40.2%	57.5%	42.5%
1954	414,841	250,080	Anderson, Victor E.	164,753	Ritchie, William	8	85,327 R	60.3%	39.7%	60.3%	39.7%
1952	595,714	366,009	Crosby, Robert B.	229,700	Raecke, Walter R.	5	136,309 R	61.4%	38.6%	61.4%	38.6%
1950	449,720	247,081	Peterson, Val	202,638	Raecke, Walter R.	1	44,443 R	54.9%	45.1%	54.9%	45.1%
1948	476,352	286,119	Peterson, Val	190,214	Sorrell, Frank	19	95,905 R	60.1%	39.9%	60.1%	39.9%
1946	380,835	249,468	Peterson, Val	131,367	Sorrell, Frank	–	118,101 R	65.5%	34.5%	65.5%	34.5%

The term of office of Nebraska's Governor was increased from two to four years effective with the 1966 election.

POSTWAR VOTE FOR SENATOR

		Republican		Democratic				Percentage			
	Total					Other	Rep.-Dem.	Total Vote		Major Vote	
Year	Vote	Vote	Candidate	Vote	Candidate	Vote	Plurality	Rep.	Dem.	Rep.	Dem.
1976	598,314	284,284	McCollister, John Y.	313,809	Zorinsky, Edward	221	29,525 D	47.5%	52.4%	47.5%	52.5%
1972	568,580	301,841	Curtis, Carl T.	265,922	Carpenter, Terry	817	35,919 R	53.1%	46.8%	53.2%	46.8%
1970	458,966	240,894	Hruska, Roman L.	217,681	Morrison, Frank B.	391	23,213 R	52.5%	47.4%	52.5%	47.5%
1966	485,101	296,116	Curtis, Carl T.	187,950	Morrison, Frank B.	1,035	108,166 R	61.0%	38.7%	61.2%	38.8%
1964	563,401	345,772	Hruska, Roman L.	217,605	Arndt, Raymond W.	24	128,167 R	61.4%	38.6%	61.4%	38.6%
1960	598,743	352,748	Curtis, Carl T.	245,837	Conrad, Robert	158	106,911 R	58.9%	41.1%	58.9%	41.1%
1958	417,385	232,227	Hruska, Roman L.	185,152	Morrison, Frank B.	6	47,075 R	55.6%	44.4%	55.6%	44.4%
1954	418,691	255,695	Curtis, Carl T.	162,990	Neville, Keith	6	92,705 R	61.1%	38.9%	61.1%	38.9%
1954s	411,225	250,341	Hruska, Roman L.	160,881	Green, James F.	3	89,460 R	60.9%	39.1%	60.9%	39.1%
1952	591,749	408,971	Butler, Hugh	164,660	Long, Stanley D.	18,118	244,311 R	69.1%	27.8%	71.3%	28.7%
1952s	581,750	369,841	Griswold, Dwight	211,898	Ritchie, William	11	157,943 R	63.6%	36.4%	63.6%	36.4%
1948	471,895	267,575	Wherry, Kenneth S.	204,320	Carpenter, Terry	–	63,255 R	56.7%	43.3%	56.7%	43.3%
1946	382,958	271,208	Butler, Hugh	111,750	Mekota, John E.	–	159,458 R	70.8%	29.2%	70.8%	29.2%

One each of the 1954 and 1952 elections was for a short term to fill a vacancy.

NEBRASKA

Districts Established January 11, 1968

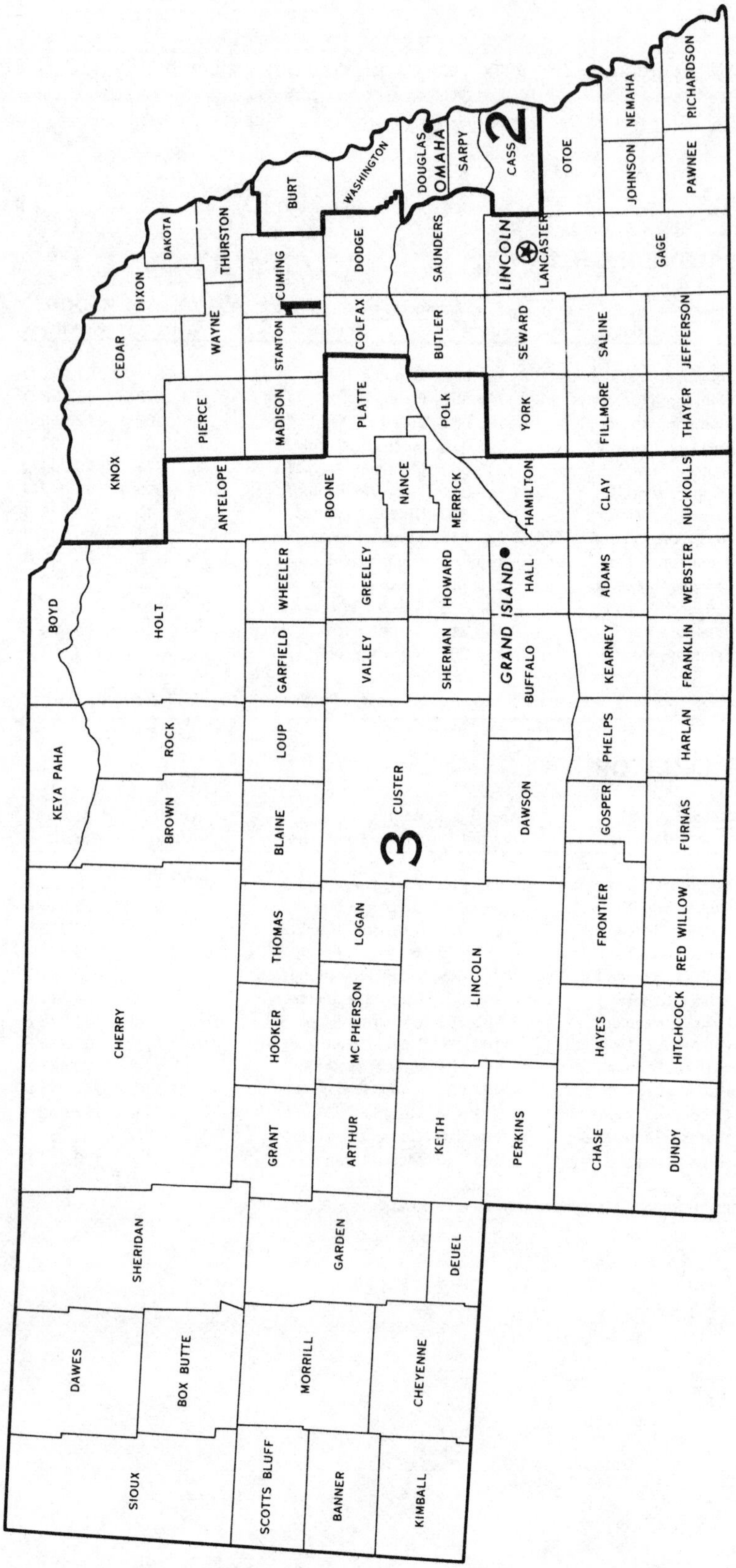

NEBRASKA

PRESIDENT 1976

1970 Census Population	County	Total Vote	Republican	Democratic	Other	Rep.-Dem. Plurality	Percentage Total Vote Rep.	Total Vote Dem.	Major Vote Rep.	Major Vote Dem.
30,553	ADAMS	12,839	7,623	4,959	257	2,664 R	59.4%	38.6%	60.6%	39.4%
9,047	ANTELOPE	3,887	2,488	1,325	74	1,163 R	64.0%	34.1%	65.3%	34.7%
606	ARTHUR	262	193	64	5	129 R	73.7%	24.4%	75.1%	24.9%
1,034	BANNER	513	281	210	22	71 R	54.8%	40.9%	57.2%	42.8%
847	BLAINE	422	281	133	8	148 R	66.6%	31.5%	67.9%	32.1%
8,190	BOONE	3,437	2,035	1,329	73	706 R	59.2%	38.7%	60.5%	39.5%
10,094	BOX BUTTE	4,579	2,956	1,516	107	1,440 R	64.6%	33.1%	66.1%	33.9%
3,752	BOYD	1,821	1,004	792	25	212 R	55.1%	43.5%	55.9%	44.1%
4,021	BROWN	1,836	1,241	557	38	684 R	67.6%	30.3%	69.0%	31.0%
31,222	BUFFALO	12,777	8,095	4,308	374	3,787 R	63.4%	33.7%	65.3%	34.7%
9,247	BURT	3,967	2,510	1,375	82	1,135 R	63.3%	34.7%	64.6%	35.4%
9,461	BUTLER	4,271	1,809	2,337	125	528 D	42.4%	54.7%	43.6%	56.4%
18,076	CASS	7,141	3,807	3,205	129	602 R	53.3%	44.9%	54.3%	45.7%
12,192	CEDAR	4,760	2,415	2,225	120	190 R	50.7%	46.7%	52.0%	48.0%
4,129	CHASE	1,937	1,146	725	66	421 R	59.2%	37.4%	61.3%	38.7%
6,846	CHERRY	3,192	2,197	906	89	1,291 R	68.8%	28.4%	70.8%	29.2%
10,778	CHEYENNE	4,052	2,285	1,665	102	620 R	56.4%	41.1%	57.8%	42.2%
8,266	CLAY	3,703	2,254	1,369	80	885 R	60.9%	37.0%	62.2%	37.8%
9,498	COLFAX	4,123	2,364	1,666	93	698 R	57.3%	40.4%	58.7%	41.3%
12,034	CUMING	4,774	3,303	1,374	97	1,929 R	69.2%	28.8%	70.6%	29.4%
14,092	CUSTER	6,175	3,935	1,985	255	1,950 R	63.7%	32.1%	66.5%	33.5%
13,137	DAKOTA	4,995	2,631	2,292	72	339 R	52.7%	45.9%	53.4%	46.6%
9,761	DAWES	3,910	2,446	1,286	178	1,160 R	62.6%	32.9%	65.5%	34.5%
19,467	DAWSON	7,985	5,413	2,395	177	3,018 R	67.8%	30.0%	69.3%	30.7%
2,717	DEUEL	1,191	776	398	17	378 R	65.2%	33.4%	66.1%	33.9%
7,453	DIXON	3,338	1,981	1,286	71	695 R	59.3%	38.5%	60.6%	39.4%
34,782	DODGE	14,481	8,982	5,283	216	3,699 R	62.0%	36.5%	63.0%	37.0%
389,455	DOUGLAS	158,707	93,204	61,877	3,626	31,327 R	58.7%	39.0%	60.1%	39.9%
2,926	DUNDY	1,263	774	457	32	317 R	61.3%	36.2%	62.9%	37.1%
8,137	FILLMORE	3,671	2,098	1,489	84	609 R	57.2%	40.6%	58.5%	41.5%
4,566	FRANKLIN	2,163	1,170	941	52	229 R	54.1%	43.5%	55.4%	44.6%
3,982	FRONTIER	1,635	994	588	53	406 R	60.8%	36.0%	62.8%	37.2%
6,897	FURNAS	3,061	1,844	1,126	91	718 R	60.2%	36.8%	62.1%	37.9%
25,719	GAGE	9,908	5,206	4,512	190	694 R	52.5%	45.5%	53.6%	46.4%
2,929	GARDEN	1,442	928	445	69	483 R	64.4%	30.9%	67.6%	32.4%
2,411	GARFIELD	1,121	726	343	52	383 R	64.8%	30.6%	67.9%	32.1%
2,178	GOSPER	1,009	654	332	23	322 R	64.8%	32.9%	66.3%	33.7%
1,019	GRANT	446	314	116	16	198 R	70.4%	26.0%	73.0%	27.0%
4,000	GREELEY	1,709	787	877	45	90 D	46.1%	51.3%	47.3%	52.7%
42,851	HALL	17,386	10,935	6,079	372	4,856 R	62.9%	35.0%	64.3%	35.7%
8,867	HAMILTON	4,181	2,737	1,337	107	1,400 R	65.5%	32.0%	67.2%	32.8%
4,357	HARLAN	2,255	1,325	879	51	446 R	58.8%	39.0%	60.1%	39.9%
1,530	HAYES	695	411	267	17	144 R	59.1%	38.4%	60.6%	39.4%
4,051	HITCHCOCK	1,732	898	786	48	112 R	51.8%	45.4%	53.3%	46.7%
12,933	HOLT	5,278	3,389	1,751	138	1,638 R	64.2%	33.2%	65.9%	34.1%
939	HOOKER	427	326	98	3	228 R	76.3%	23.0%	76.9%	23.1%
6,807	HOWARD	2,736	1,362	1,316	58	46 R	49.8%	48.1%	50.9%	49.1%
10,436	JEFFERSON	4,789	2,628	2,068	93	560 R	54.9%	43.2%	56.0%	44.0%
5,743	JOHNSON	2,455	1,298	1,115	42	183 R	52.9%	45.4%	53.8%	46.2%
6,707	KEARNEY	3,124	1,830	1,219	75	611 R	58.6%	39.0%	60.0%	40.0%
8,487	KEITH	3,760	2,485	1,139	136	1,346 R	66.1%	30.3%	68.6%	31.4%
1,340	KEYA PAHA	667	405	245	17	160 R	60.7%	36.7%	62.3%	37.7%
6,009	KIMBALL	2,001	1,257	696	48	561 R	62.8%	34.8%	64.4%	35.6%
11,723	KNOX	4,654	2,610	1,922	122	688 R	56.1%	41.3%	57.6%	42.4%
167,972	LANCASTER	69,131	39,041	28,301	1,789	10,740 R	56.5%	40.9%	58.0%	42.0%
29,538	LINCOLN	12,739	7,076	5,355	308	1,721 R	55.5%	42.0%	56.9%	43.1%
991	LOGAN	494	283	196	15	87 R	57.3%	39.7%	59.1%	40.9%
854	LOUP	456	299	140	17	159 R	65.6%	30.7%	68.1%	31.9%
623	MCPHERSON	333	221	104	8	117 R	66.4%	31.2%	68.0%	32.0%
27,402	MADISON	11,455	7,846	3,433	176	4,413 R	68.5%	30.0%	69.6%	30.4%
8,751	MERRICK	3,702	2,229	1,360	113	869 R	60.2%	36.7%	62.1%	37.9%
5,813	MORRILL	2,379	1,351	971	57	380 R	56.8%	40.8%	58.2%	41.8%
5,142	NANCE	2,113	1,121	936	56	185 R	53.1%	44.3%	54.5%	45.5%
8,976	NEMAHA	3,544	2,093	1,406	45	687 R	59.1%	39.7%	59.8%	40.2%
7,404	NUCKOLLS	3,224	1,753	1,424	47	329 R	54.4%	44.2%	55.2%	44.8%

NEBRASKA

PRESIDENT 1976

1970 Census Population	County	Total Vote	Republican	Democratic	Other	Rep.-Dem. Plurality	Percentage Total Vote Rep.	Percentage Total Vote Dem.	Percentage Major Vote Rep.	Percentage Major Vote Dem.
15,576	OTOE	6,237	3,715	2,436	86	1,279 R	59.6%	39.1%	60.4%	39.6%
4,473	PAWNEE	1,873	990	845	38	145 R	52.9%	45.1%	54.0%	46.0%
3,423	PERKINS	1,649	981	622	46	359 R	59.5%	37.7%	61.2%	38.8%
9,553	PHELPS	4,509	3,210	1,168	131	2,042 R	71.2%	25.9%	73.3%	26.7%
8,493	PIERCE	3,244	2,172	1,004	68	1,168 R	67.0%	30.9%	68.4%	31.6%
26,508	PLATTE	11,179	7,217	3,693	269	3,524 R	64.6%	33.0%	66.2%	33.8%
6,468	POLK	3,053	1,797	1,190	66	607 R	58.9%	39.0%	60.2%	39.8%
12,191	RED WILLOW	4,810	2,978	1,722	110	1,256 R	61.9%	35.8%	63.4%	36.6%
12,277	RICHARDSON	5,627	3,119	2,416	92	703 R	55.4%	42.9%	56.4%	43.6%
2,231	ROCK	1,009	732	255	22	477 R	72.5%	25.3%	74.2%	25.8%
12,809	SALINE	5,662	2,330	3,205	127	875 D	41.2%	56.6%	42.1%	57.9%
65,007	SARPY	19,716	11,917	7,385	414	4,532 R	60.4%	37.5%	61.7%	38.3%
17,018	SAUNDERS	7,502	3,844	3,507	151	337 R	51.2%	46.7%	52.3%	47.7%
36,432	SCOTTS BLUFF	11,468	6,887	4,298	283	2,589 R	60.1%	37.5%	61.6%	38.4%
14,460	SEWARD	5,950	3,220	2,610	120	610 R	54.1%	43.9%	55.2%	44.8%
7,285	SHERIDAN	2,953	2,003	810	140	1,193 R	67.8%	27.4%	71.2%	28.8%
4,725	SHERMAN	2,093	935	1,078	80	143 D	44.7%	51.5%	46.4%	53.6%
2,034	SIOUX	883	532	329	22	203 R	60.2%	37.3%	61.8%	38.2%
5,758	STANTON	2,286	1,469	764	53	705 R	64.3%	33.4%	65.8%	34.2%
7,779	THAYER	3,360	1,994	1,315	51	679 R	59.3%	39.1%	60.3%	39.7%
954	THOMAS	468	343	103	22	240 R	73.3%	22.0%	76.9%	23.1%
6,942	THURSTON	2,393	1,290	1,021	82	269 R	53.9%	42.7%	55.8%	44.2%
5,783	VALLEY	2,769	1,587	1,042	140	545 R	57.3%	37.6%	60.4%	39.6%
13,310	WASHINGTON	6,111	3,799	2,233	79	1,566 R	62.2%	36.5%	63.0%	37.0%
10,400	WAYNE	3,708	2,521	1,089	98	1,432 R	68.0%	29.4%	69.8%	30.2%
5,396	WEBSTER	2,441	1,267	1,130	44	137 R	51.9%	46.3%	52.9%	47.1%
1,054	WHEELER	436	274	146	16	128 R	62.8%	33.5%	65.2%	34.8%
13,685	YORK	6,066	4,223	1,665	178	2,558 R	69.6%	27.4%	71.7%	28.3%
1,483,791	TOTAL	607,668	359,705	233,692	14,271	126,013 R	59.2%	38.5%	60.6%	39.4%

NEBRASKA

SENATOR 1976

1970 Census Population	County	Total Vote	Republican	Democratic	Other	Rep.-Dem. Plurality	Percentage: Total Vote Rep.	Total Vote Dem.	Major Vote Rep.	Major Vote Dem.
30,553	ADAMS	13,067	7,038	6,027	2	1,011 R	53.9%	46.1%	53.9%	46.1%
9,047	ANTELOPE	3,959	2,401	1,558		843 R	60.6%	39.4%	60.6%	39.4%
606	ARTHUR	252	184	68		116 R	73.0%	27.0%	73.0%	27.0%
1,034	BANNER	518	334	184		150 R	64.5%	35.5%	64.5%	35.5%
847	BLAINE	415	291	124		167 R	70.1%	29.9%	70.1%	29.9%
8,190	BOONE	3,434	1,847	1,587		260 R	53.8%	46.2%	53.8%	46.2%
10,094	BOX BUTTE	4,585	2,845	1,740		1,105 R	62.1%	37.9%	62.1%	37.9%
3,752	BOYD	1,620	909	711		198 R	56.1%	43.9%	56.1%	43.9%
4,021	BROWN	1,848	1,300	548		752 R	70.3%	29.7%	70.3%	29.7%
31,222	BUFFALO	12,708	6,879	5,827	2	1,052 R	54.1%	45.9%	54.1%	45.9%
9,247	BURT	4,037	2,147	1,890		257 R	53.2%	46.8%	53.2%	46.8%
9,461	BUTLER	3,992	1,422	2,570		1,148 D	35.6%	64.4%	35.6%	64.4%
18,076	CASS	7,155	3,074	4,081		1,007 D	43.0%	57.0%	43.0%	57.0%
12,192	CEDAR	4,541	2,484	2,057		427 R	54.7%	45.3%	54.7%	45.3%
4,129	CHASE	1,916	1,189	727		462 R	62.1%	37.9%	62.1%	37.9%
6,846	CHERRY	3,132	2,182	950		1,232 R	69.7%	30.3%	69.7%	30.3%
10,778	CHEYENNE	3,707	2,118	1,589		529 R	57.1%	42.9%	57.1%	42.9%
8,266	CLAY	3,708	2,110	1,598		512 R	56.9%	43.1%	56.9%	43.1%
9,498	COLFAX	4,187	1,813	2,374		561 D	43.3%	56.7%	43.3%	56.7%
12,034	CUMING	4,823	2,537	2,286		251 R	52.6%	47.4%	52.6%	47.4%
14,092	CUSTER	6,148	3,661	2,487		1,174 R	59.5%	40.5%	59.5%	40.5%
13,137	DAKOTA	4,901	2,276	2,625		349 D	46.4%	53.6%	46.4%	53.6%
9,761	DAWES	3,853	2,461	1,392		1,069 R	63.9%	36.1%	63.9%	36.1%
19,467	DAWSON	7,700	4,794	2,906		1,888 R	62.3%	37.7%	62.3%	37.7%
2,717	DEUEL	1,195	800	395		405 R	66.9%	33.1%	66.9%	33.1%
7,453	DIXON	3,262	2,037	1,225		812 R	62.4%	37.6%	62.4%	37.6%
34,782	DODGE	14,466	5,887	8,577	2	2,690 D	40.7%	59.3%	40.7%	59.3%
389,455	DOUGLAS	153,343	56,054	97,126	163	41,072 D	36.6%	63.3%	36.6%	63.4%
2,926	DUNDY	1,195	782	412	1	370 R	65.4%	34.5%	65.5%	34.5%
8,137	FILLMORE	3,655	2,007	1,647	1	360 R	54.9%	45.1%	54.9%	45.1%
4,566	FRANKLIN	2,074	1,135	939		196 R	54.7%	45.3%	54.7%	45.3%
3,982	FRONTIER	1,640	981	659		322 R	59.8%	40.2%	59.8%	40.2%
6,897	FURNAS	2,902	1,787	1,115		672 R	61.6%	38.4%	61.6%	38.4%
25,719	GAGE	9,913	4,762	5,146	5	384 D	48.0%	51.9%	48.1%	51.9%
2,929	GARDEN	1,411	909	502		407 R	64.4%	35.6%	64.4%	35.6%
2,411	GARFIELD	1,105	698	407		291 R	63.2%	36.8%	63.2%	36.8%
2,178	GOSPER	1,003	637	366		271 R	63.5%	36.5%	63.5%	36.5%
1,019	GRANT	441	295	146		149 R	66.9%	33.1%	66.9%	33.1%
4,000	GREELEY	1,679	753	926		173 D	44.8%	55.2%	44.8%	55.2%
42,851	HALL	16,144	8,137	8,007		130 R	50.4%	49.6%	50.4%	49.6%
8,867	HAMILTON	4,072	2,480	1,592		888 R	60.9%	39.1%	60.9%	39.1%
4,357	HARLAN	2,237	1,275	962		313 R	57.0%	43.0%	57.0%	43.0%
1,530	HAYES	675	459	216		243 R	68.0%	32.0%	68.0%	32.0%
4,051	HITCHCOCK	1,731	968	763		205 R	55.9%	44.1%	55.9%	44.1%
12,933	HOLT	5,099	3,154	1,945		1,209 R	61.9%	38.1%	61.9%	38.1%
939	HOOKER	427	304	123		181 R	71.2%	28.8%	71.2%	28.8%
6,807	HOWARD	2,792	1,213	1,579		366 D	43.4%	56.6%	43.4%	56.6%
10,436	JEFFERSON	4,822	2,664	2,158		506 R	55.2%	44.8%	55.2%	44.8%
5,743	JOHNSON	2,390	1,131	1,255	4	124 D	47.3%	52.5%	47.4%	52.6%
6,707	KEARNEY	3,006	1,506	1,500		6 R	50.1%	49.9%	50.1%	49.9%
8,487	KEITH	3,729	2,220	1,509		711 R	59.5%	40.5%	59.5%	40.5%
1,340	KEYA PAHA	633	477	156		321 R	75.4%	24.6%	75.4%	24.6%
6,009	KIMBALL	2,020	1,293	727		566 R	64.0%	36.0%	64.0%	36.0%
11,723	KNOX	4,587	2,664	1,923		741 R	58.1%	41.9%	58.1%	41.9%
167,972	LANCASTER	68,053	30,462	37,584	7	7,122 D	44.8%	55.2%	44.8%	55.2%
29,538	LINCOLN	12,837	5,880	6,957		1,077 D	45.8%	54.2%	45.8%	54.2%
991	LOGAN	481	282	199		83 R	58.6%	41.4%	58.6%	41.4%
854	LOUP	452	272	180		92 R	60.2%	39.8%	60.2%	39.8%
623	MCPHERSON	324	223	101		122 R	68.8%	31.2%	68.8%	31.2%
27,402	MADISON	11,515	6,736	4,777	2	1,959 R	58.5%	41.5%	58.5%	41.5%
8,751	MERRICK	3,701	2,022	1,679		343 R	54.6%	45.4%	54.6%	45.4%
5,813	MORRILL	2,404	1,421	983		438 R	59.1%	40.9%	59.1%	40.9%
5,142	NANCE	2,086	961	1,125		164 D	46.1%	53.9%	46.1%	53.9%
8,976	NEMAHA	3,576	1,670	1,906		236 D	46.7%	53.3%	46.7%	53.3%
7,404	NUCKOLLS	3,212	1,576	1,636		60 D	49.1%	50.9%	49.1%	50.9%

NEBRASKA

SENATOR 1976

1970 Census Population	County	Total Vote	Republican	Democratic	Other	Rep.-Dem. Plurality	Percentage Total Vote Rep.	Total Vote Dem.	Major Vote Rep.	Major Vote Dem.
15,576	OTOE	6,367	2,929	3,433	5	504 D	46.0%	53.9%	46.0%	54.0%
4,473	PAWNEE	1,876	947	929		18 R	50.5%	49.5%	50.5%	49.5%
3,423	PERKINS	1,634	973	661		312 R	59.5%	40.5%	59.5%	40.5%
9,553	PHELPS	4,469	2,962	1,505	2	1,457 R	66.3%	33.7%	66.3%	33.7%
8,493	PIERCE	3,199	2,113	1,085	1	1,028 R	66.1%	33.9%	66.1%	33.9%
26,508	PLATTE	11,166	5,554	5,608	4	54 D	49.7%	50.2%	49.8%	50.2%
6,468	POLK	3,030	1,481	1,549		68 D	48.9%	51.1%	48.9%	51.1%
12,191	RED WILLOW	4,832	2,962	1,870		1,092 R	61.3%	38.7%	61.3%	38.7%
12,277	RICHARDSON	5,483	2,691	2,791	1	100 D	49.1%	50.9%	49.1%	50.9%
2,231	ROCK	996	689	307		382 R	69.2%	30.8%	69.2%	30.8%
12,809	SALINE	5,612	2,057	3,555		1,498 D	36.7%	63.3%	36.7%	63.3%
65,007	SARPY	19,744	7,798	11,934	12	4,136 D	39.5%	60.4%	39.5%	60.5%
17,018	SAUNDERS	7,571	2,955	4,613	3	1,658 D	39.0%	60.9%	39.0%	61.0%
36,432	SCOTTS BLUFF	12,148	6,946	5,202		1,744 R	57.2%	42.8%	57.2%	42.8%
14,460	SEWARD	5,813	2,781	3,032		251 D	47.8%	52.2%	47.8%	52.2%
7,285	SHERIDAN	2,922	2,059	863		1,196 R	70.5%	29.5%	70.5%	29.5%
4,725	SHERMAN	2,089	889	1,200		311 D	42.6%	57.4%	42.6%	57.4%
2,034	SIOUX	886	577	309		268 R	65.1%	34.9%	65.1%	34.9%
5,758	STANTON	2,292	1,204	1,088		116 R	52.5%	47.5%	52.5%	47.5%
7,779	THAYER	3,375	1,932	1,443		489 R	57.2%	42.8%	57.2%	42.8%
954	THOMAS	469	338	131		207 R	72.1%	27.9%	72.1%	27.9%
6,942	THURSTON	2,340	1,205	1,131	4	74 R	51.5%	48.3%	51.6%	48.4%
5,783	VALLEY	2,777	1,520	1,257		263 R	54.7%	45.3%	54.7%	45.3%
13,310	WASHINGTON	6,171	1,773	4,398		2,625 D	28.7%	71.3%	28.7%	71.3%
10,400	WAYNE	3,647	2,256	1,391		865 R	61.9%	38.1%	61.9%	38.1%
5,396	WEBSTER	2,462	1,355	1,107		248 R	55.0%	45.0%	55.0%	45.0%
1,054	WHEELER	428	259	169		90 R	60.5%	39.5%	60.5%	39.5%
13,685	YORK	6,021	3,809	2,212		1,597 R	63.3%	36.7%	63.3%	36.7%
1,483,791	TOTAL	598,314	284,284	313,809	221	29,525 D	47.5%	52.4%	47.5%	52.5%

NEBRASKA

CONGRESS

CD	Year	Total Vote	Republican Vote	Republican Candidate	Democratic Vote	Democratic Candidate	Other Vote	Rep.-Dem. Plurality	Percentage Total Vote Rep.	Percentage Total Vote Dem.	Percentage Major Vote Rep.	Percentage Major Vote Dem.
1	1976	200,272	146,558	THONE, CHARLES	53,703	ANDERSON, PAULINE F.	11	92,855 R	73.2%	26.8%	73.2%	26.8%
1	1974	154,454	82,353	THONE, CHARLES	72,099	DYAS, HESS	2	10,254 R	53.3%	46.7%	53.3%	46.7%
1	1972	197,436	126,789	THONE, CHARLES	70,570	BERG, DARREL E.	77	56,219 R	64.2%	35.7%	64.2%	35.8%
1	1970	156,305	79,131	THONE, CHARLES	36,240	BURROWS, GEORGE	40,934	42,891 R	50.6%	23.2%	68.6%	31.4%
1	1968	180,622	97,697	DENNEY, ROBERT V.	78,374	CALLAN, CLAIR A.	4,551	19,323 R	54.1%	43.4%	55.5%	44.5%
2	1976	194,775	88,352	TERRY, LEE	106,296	CAVANAUGH, JOHN J.	127	17,944 D	45.4%	54.6%	45.4%	54.6%
2	1974	131,925	72,731	MCCOLLISTER, JOHN Y.	59,142	LYNCH, DANIEL C.	52	13,589 R	55.1%	44.8%	55.2%	44.8%
2	1972	179,387	114,669	MCCOLLISTER, JOHN Y.	64,696	COONEY, PATRICK L.	22	49,973 R	63.9%	36.1%	63.9%	36.1%
2	1970	134,387	69,671	MCCOLLISTER, JOHN Y.	64,620	HLAVACEK, JOHN	96	5,051 R	51.8%	48.1%	51.9%	48.1%
2	1968	158,977	87,683	CUNNINGHAM, GLENN	71,254	MORRISON, MRS. FRANK	40	16,429 R	55.2%	44.8%	55.2%	44.8%
3	1976	206,765	150,720	SMITH, VIRGINIA	51,012	HANSEN, JAMES T.	5,033	99,708 R	72.9%	24.7%	74.7%	25.3%
3	1974	161,312	80,992	SMITH, VIRGINIA	80,255	ZIEBARTH, WAYNE W.	65	737 R	50.2%	49.8%	50.2%	49.8%
3	1972	192,023	133,607	MARTIN, DAVE	58,378	FITZGERALD, WARREN	38	75,229 R	69.6%	30.4%	69.6%	30.4%
3	1970	157,407	93,705	MARTIN, DAVE	63,698	SEARCY, DONALD	4	30,007 R	59.5%	40.5%	59.5%	40.5%
3	1968	182,572	123,838	MARTIN, DAVE	58,728	DEAN, J. B.	6	65,110 R	67.8%	32.2%	67.8%	32.2%

NEBRASKA

1976 GENERAL ELECTION

President — There was a minor confusion in the presentation of the election data from the state. The special ballots for President were carried in a separate table. These new resident votes are included in the figures presented here. In the "Official Report" a printers error of 233,287 appeared as the Democratic total vote for President. Other vote was 9,409 McCarthy (Independent); 3,380 Maddox (American); 1,482 MacBride (Libertarian).

Senator — Original uncorrected canvass gave the Republican vote in Platte county as 554 and the Republican total vote as 279,284. The data here includes the four special ballots cast for the Democratic candidate. Other vote was 58 Etchison (write-in) and 163 scattered.

Congress — In CD 1 the data includes the four special ballots cast for the Democratic candidate. Other vote was scattered in CD's 1 and 2; 5,025 Steen (American) and 8 scattered in CD 3.

1976 PRIMARIES

MAY 11 REPUBLICAN

Senator — 150,732 John Y. McCollister; 41,519 Richard F. Proud; 122 scattered.

Congress — Unopposed in CD 1. Contested as follows:

CD 2 — 24,846 Lee Terry; 13,150 P. J. Morgan; 12,949 Monte Taylor; 2,327 Joe B. Moss.
CD 3 — 60,615 Virginia Smith; 21,235 John W. DeCamp.

MAY 11 DEMOCRATIC

Senator — 79,988 Edward Zorinsky; 77,384 Hess Dyas; 7,194 Lenore R. Etchison; 107 scattered.

Congress — Unopposed in two CD's. Contested as follows:

CD 3 — 24,093 James T. Hansen; 18,697 William H. Hodge.

NEVADA

GOVERNOR

Mike O'Callaghan (D). Re-elected 1974 to a four-year term. Previously elected 1970.

SENATORS

Howard W. Cannon (D). Re-elected 1976 to a six-year term. Previously elected 1970, 1964, 1958.

Paul Laxalt (R). Elected 1974 to a six-year term.

REPRESENTATIVE

At-Large. James Santini (D)

POSTWAR VOTE FOR GOVERNOR

		Republican		Democratic				Percentage			
	Total					Other	Rep.-Dem.	Total Vote		Major Vote	
Year	Vote	Vote	Candidate	Vote	Candidate	Vote	Plurality	Rep.	Dem.	Rep.	Dem.
1974	169,358	28,959	Crumpler, Shirley	114,114	O'Callaghan, Mike	26,285	85,155 D	17.1%	67.4%	20.2%	79.8%
1970	146,991	64,400	Fike, Ed	70,697	O'Callaghan, Mike	11,894	6,297 D	43.8%	48.1%	47.7%	52.3%
1966	137,677	71,807	Laxalt, Paul	65,870	Sawyer, Grant	–	5,937 R	52.2%	47.8%	52.2%	47.8%
1962	96,929	32,145	Gragson, Oran K.	64,784	Sawyer, Grant	–	32,639 D	33.2%	66.8%	33.2%	66.8%
1958	84,889	34,025	Russell, Charles H.	50,864	Sawyer, Grant	–	16,839 D	40.1%	59.9%	40.1%	59.9%
1954	78,462	41,665	Russell, Charles H.	36,797	Pittman, Vail	–	4,868 R	53.1%	46.9%	53.1%	46.9%
1950	61,773	35,609	Russell, Charles H.	26,164	Pittman, Vail	–	9,445 R	57.6%	42.4%	57.6%	42.4%
1946	49,902	21,247	Jepson, Melvin E.	28,655	Pittman, Vail	–	7,408 D	42.6%	57.4%	42.6%	57.4%

POSTWAR VOTE FOR SENATOR

		Republican		Democratic				Percentage			
	Total					Other	Rep.-Dem.	Total Vote		Major Vote	
Year	Vote	Vote	Candidate	Vote	Candidate	Vote	Plurality	Rep.	Dem.	Rep.	Dem.
1976	201,980	63,471	Towell, David	127,295	Cannon, Howard W.	11,214	63,824 D	31.4%	63.0%	33.3%	66.7%
1974	169,473	79,605	Laxalt, Paul	78,981	Reid, Harry	10,887	624 R	47.0%	46.6%	50.2%	49.8%
1970	147,768	60,838	Raggio, William J.	85,187	Cannon, Howard W.	1,743	24,349 D	41.2%	57.6%	41.7%	58.3%
1968	152,690	69,068	Fike, Ed	83,622	Bible, Alan	–	14,554 D	45.2%	54.8%	45.2%	54.8%
1964	134,624	67,288	Laxalt, Paul	67,336	Cannon, Howard W.	–	48 D	50.0%	50.0%	50.0%	50.0%
1962	97,192	33,749	Wright, William B.	63,443	Bible, Alan	–	29,694 D	34.7%	65.3%	34.7%	65.3%
1958	84,492	35,760	Malone, George W.	48,732	Cannon, Howard W.	–	12,972 D	42.3%	57.7%	42.3%	57.7%
1956	96,389	45,712	Young, Clifton	50,677	Bible, Alan	–	4,965 D	47.4%	52.6%	47.4%	52.6%
1954s	77,513	32,470	Brown, Ernest S.	45,043	Bible, Alan	–	12,573 D	41.9%	58.1%	41.9%	58.1%
1952	81,090	41,906	Malone, George W.	39,184	Mechling, Thomas B.	–	2,722 R	51.7%	48.3%	51.7%	48.3%
1950	61,762	25,933	Marshall, George E.	35,829	McCarran, Pat	–	9,896 D	42.0%	58.0%	42.0%	58.0%
1946	50,354	27,801	Malone, George W.	22,553	Bunker, Berkeley	–	5,248 R	55.2%	44.8%	55.2%	44.8%

The 1954 election was for a short term to fill a vacancy.

NEVADA

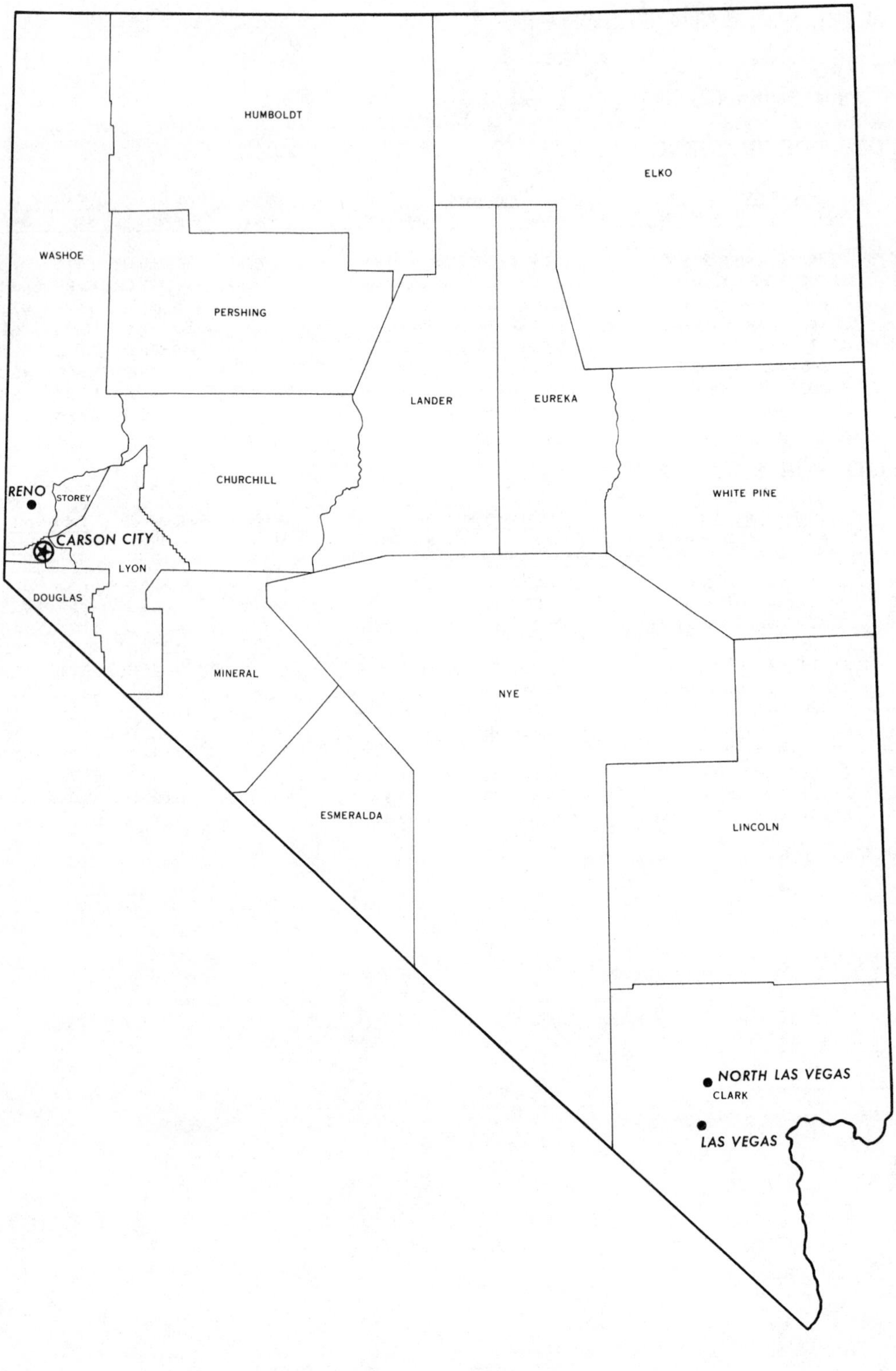
HUMBOLDT
ELKO
WASHOE
PERSHING
LANDER
EUREKA
RENO
STOREY
CHURCHILL
WHITE PINE
CARSON CITY
LYON
DOUGLAS
MINERAL
NYE
ESMERALDA
LINCOLN
NORTH LAS VEGAS
CLARK
LAS VEGAS

NEVADA

PRESIDENT 1976

1970 Census Population	County	Total Vote	Republican	Democratic	Other	Rep.-Dem. Plurality	Percentage Total Vote Rep.	Percentage Total Vote Dem.	Percentage Major Vote Rep.	Percentage Major Vote Dem.
15,468	CARSON CITY	9,761	5,282	3,874	605	1,408 R	54.1%	39.7%	57.7%	42.3%
10,513	CHURCHILL	4,446	2,358	1,800	288	558 R	53.0%	40.5%	56.7%	43.3%
273,288	CLARK	102,812	48,236	51,178	3,398	2,942 D	46.9%	49.8%	48.5%	51.5%
6,882	DOUGLAS	5,282	3,095	1,934	253	1,161 R	58.6%	36.6%	61.5%	38.5%
13,958	ELKO	5,459	3,293	1,955	211	1,338 R	60.3%	35.8%	62.7%	37.3%
629	ESMERALDA	416	181	214	21	33 D	43.5%	51.4%	45.8%	54.2%
948	EUREKA	467	272	163	32	109 R	58.2%	34.9%	62.5%	37.5%
6,375	HUMBOLDT	2,585	1,380	1,074	131	306 R	53.4%	41.5%	56.2%	43.8%
2,666	LANDER	1,123	561	518	44	43 R	50.0%	46.1%	52.0%	48.0%
2,557	LINCOLN	1,399	700	642	57	58 R	50.0%	45.9%	52.2%	47.8%
8,221	LYON	4,162	2,068	1,866	228	202 R	49.7%	44.8%	52.6%	47.4%
7,051	MINERAL	2,594	1,104	1,361	129	257 D	42.6%	52.5%	44.8%	55.2%
5,599	NYE	2,415	1,027	1,261	127	234 D	42.5%	52.2%	44.9%	55.1%
2,670	PERSHING	1,353	635	633	85	2 R	46.9%	46.8%	50.1%	49.9%
695	STOREY	636	274	310	52	36 D	43.1%	48.7%	46.9%	53.1%
121,068	WASHOE	53,227	29,264	21,687	2,276	7,577 R	55.0%	40.7%	57.4%	42.6%
10,150	WHITE PINE	3,739	1,543	2,009	187	466 D	41.3%	53.7%	43.4%	56.6%
488,738	TOTAL	201,876	101,273	92,479	8,124	8,794 R	50.2%	45.8%	52.3%	47.7%

SENATOR 1976

1970 Census Population	County	Total Vote	Republican	Democratic	Other	Rep.-Dem. Plurality	Percentage Total Vote Rep.	Percentage Total Vote Dem.	Percentage Major Vote Rep.	Percentage Major Vote Dem.
15,468	CARSON CITY	9,732	4,257	4,726	749	469 D	43.7%	48.6%	47.4%	52.6%
10,513	CHURCHILL	4,424	2,019	2,202	203	183 D	45.6%	49.8%	47.8%	52.2%
273,288	CLARK	102,637	22,328	76,099	4,210	53,771 D	21.8%	74.1%	22.7%	77.3%
6,882	DOUGLAS	5,322	2,272	2,638	412	366 D	42.7%	49.6%	46.3%	53.7%
13,958	ELKO	5,543	2,493	2,844	206	351 D	45.0%	51.3%	46.7%	53.3%
629	ESMERALDA	419	140	248	31	108 D	33.4%	59.2%	36.1%	63.9%
948	EUREKA	506	251	240	15	11 R	49.6%	47.4%	51.1%	48.9%
6,375	HUMBOLDT	2,641	1,224	1,301	116	77 D	46.3%	49.3%	48.5%	51.5%
2,666	LANDER	1,145	463	612	70	149 D	40.4%	53.4%	43.1%	56.9%
2,557	LINCOLN	1,412	475	890	47	415 D	33.6%	63.0%	34.8%	65.2%
8,221	LYON	4,212	1,878	2,060	274	182 D	44.6%	48.9%	47.7%	52.3%
7,051	MINERAL	2,672	621	1,957	94	1,336 D	23.2%	73.2%	24.1%	75.9%
5,599	NYE	2,441	610	1,724	107	1,114 D	25.0%	70.6%	26.1%	73.9%
2,670	PERSHING	1,360	563	750	47	187 D	41.4%	55.1%	42.9%	57.1%
695	STOREY	629	242	336	51	94 D	38.5%	53.4%	41.9%	58.1%
121,068	WASHOE	53,126	22,251	26,462	4,413	4,211 D	41.9%	49.8%	45.7%	54.3%
10,150	WHITE PINE	3,759	1,384	2,206	169	822 D	36.8%	58.7%	38.6%	61.4%
488,738	TOTAL	201,980	63,471	127,295	11,214	63,824 D	31.4%	63.0%	33.3%	66.7%

NEVADA

CONGRESS

CD	Year	Total Vote	Republican Vote	Republican Candidate	Democratic Vote	Democratic Candidate	Other Vote	Rep.-Dem. Plurality	Percentage Total Vote Rep.	Percentage Total Vote Dem.	Percentage Major Vote Rep.	Percentage Major Vote Dem.
AL	1976	199,863	24,124	EARHART, WALDEN C.	153,996	SANTINI, JAMES	21,743	129,872 D	12.1%	77.1%	13.5%	86.5%
AL	1974	167,966	61,182	TOWELL, DAVID	93,665	SANTINI, JAMES	13,119	32,483 D	36.4%	55.8%	39.5%	60.5%
AL	1972	180,462	94,113	TOWELL, DAVID	86,349	BILBRAY, JAMES H.		7,764 R	52.2%	47.8%	52.2%	47.8%
AL	1970	137,643	24,147	CHARLES, J. ROBERT	113,496	BARING, WALTER S.		89,349 D	17.5%	82.5%	17.5%	82.5%
AL	1968	144,345	40,209	SLATTERY, JAMES M.	104,136	BARING, WALTER S.		63,927 D	27.9%	72.1%	27.9%	72.1%
AL	1966	127,850	41,383	KRAEMER, RALPH L.	86,467	BARING, WALTER S.		45,084 D	32.4%	67.6%	32.4%	67.6%
AL	1964	130,737	47,989	VON TOBEL, GEORGE	82,748	BARING, WALTER S.		34,759 D	36.7%	63.3%	36.7%	63.3%
AL	1962	93,324	26,458	ADAIR, J. CARLTON	66,866	BARING, WALTER S.		40,408 D	28.4%	71.6%	28.4%	71.6%
AL	1960	103,602	43,986	MALONE, GEORGE W.	59,616	BARING, WALTER S.		15,630 D	42.5%	57.5%	42.5%	57.5%
AL	1958	82,328	27,275	HORTON, ROBERT C.	55,053	BARING, WALTER S.		27,778 D	33.1%	66.9%	33.1%	66.9%
AL	1956	94,254	43,154	HORTON, RICHARD W.	51,100	BARING, WALTER S.		7,946 D	45.8%	54.2%	45.8%	54.2%
AL	1954	77,639	42,321	YOUNG, CLIFTON	35,318	BARING, WALTER S.		7,003 R	54.5%	45.5%	54.5%	45.5%
AL	1952	80,595	40,683	YOUNG, CLIFTON	39,912	BARING, WALTER S.		771 R	50.5%	49.5%	50.5%	49.5%
AL	1950	60,328	28,485	MACKENZIE, A. E.	31,843	BARING, WALTER S.		3,358 D	47.2%	52.8%	47.2%	52.8%
AL	1948	58,705	28,972	RUSSELL, CHARLES H.	29,733	BARING, WALTER S.		761 D	49.4%	50.6%	49.4%	50.6%
AL	1946	49,046	28,859	RUSSELL, CHARLES H.	20,187	MCEACHIN, MALCOLM		8,672 R	58.8%	41.2%	58.8%	41.2%

NEVADA

1976 GENERAL ELECTION

President Other vote was 1,519 MacBride (Libertarian); 1,497 Maddox (Independent American); 5,108 "None of these Candidates".

Senator Other vote was 3,619 Young (Independent American); 2,307 Becan (Libertarian); 5,288 "None of these Candidates".

Congress Other vote at-large was 12,038 Hansen (Independent American); 2,825 Burns (Libertarian); 6,880 "None of these Candidates".

1976 PRIMARIES

SEPTEMBER 14 REPUBLICAN

Senator 25,960 David Towell; 5,964 S. M. Cavnar; 1,439 Robert Charles; 5,164 "None of these candidates".

Congress Contested as follows:

AL 9,831 Walden C. Earhart; 8,097 Anthony Dart; 16,097 "None of these candidates".

SEPTEMBER 14 DEMOCRATIC

Senator 61,407 Howard W. Cannon; 2,761 C. Harrison Cundiff; 2,563 Rowena M. Von Wolff; 4,817 "None of these candidates".

Congress Unopposed at-large.

NEW HAMPSHIRE

GOVERNOR

Meldrim Thomson (R). Re-elected 1976 to a two-year term. Previously elected 1974, 1972.

SENATORS

John A. Durkin (D). Elected September 1975 to the remaining years of the six-year term to which the 1974 election was held. That election was voided when the Senate declared the seat vacant in July 1975. Next election in 1980.

Thomas J. McIntyre (D). Re-elected 1972 to a six-year term. Previously elected 1966, and in 1962 to fill out term vacated by the death of Senator Styles Bridges.

REPRESENTATIVES

1. Norman E. D'Amours (D)
2. James C. Cleveland (R)

POSTWAR VOTE FOR GOVERNOR

								Percentage			
	Total	Republican		Democratic		Other	Rep.-Dem.	Total Vote		Major Vote	
Year	Vote	Vote	Candidate	Vote	Candidate	Vote	Plurality	Rep.	Dem.	Rep.	Dem.
1976	342,669	197,589	Thomson, Meldrim	145,015	Spanos, Harry V.	65	52,574 R	57.7%	42.3%	57.7%	42.3%
1974	226,665	115,933	Thomson, Meldrim	110,591	Leonard, Richard W.	141	5,342 R	51.1%	48.8%	51.2%	48.8%
1972	323,102	133,702	Thomson, Meldrim	126,107	Crowley, Roger J.	63,293	7,595 R	41.4%	39.0%	51.5%	48.5%
1970	222,441	102,298	Peterson, Walter R.	98,098	Crowley, Roger J.	22,045	4,200 R	46.0%	44.1%	51.0%	49.0%
1968	285,342	149,902	Peterson, Walter R.	135,378	Bussiere, Emile R.	62	14,524 R	52.5%	47.4%	52.5%	47.5%
1966	233,642	107,259	Gregg, Hugh	125,882	King, John W.	501	18,623 D	45.9%	53.9%	46.0%	54.0%
1964	285,863	94,824	Pillsbury, John	190,863	King, John W.	176	96,039 D	33.2%	66.8%	33.2%	66.8%
1962	230,048	94,567	Pillsbury, John	135,481	King, John W.	–	40,914 D	41.1%	58.9%	41.1%	58.9%
1960	290,527	161,123	Powell, Wesley	129,404	Boutin, Bernard L.	–	31,719 R	55.5%	44.5%	55.5%	44.5%
1958	206,745	106,790	Powell, Wesley	99,955	Boutin, Bernard L.	–	6,835 R	51.7%	48.3%	51.7%	48.3%
1956	258,695	141,578	Dwinell, Lane	117,117	Shaw, John	–	24,461 R	54.7%	45.3%	54.7%	45.3%
1954	194,631	107,287	Dwinell, Lane	87,344	Shaw, John	–	19,943 R	55.1%	44.9%	55.1%	44.9%
1952	265,715	167,791	Gregg, Hugh	97,924	Craig, William H.	–	69,867 R	63.1%	36.9%	63.1%	36.9%
1950	191,239	108,907	Adams, Sherman	82,258	Bingham, Robert P.	74	26,649 R	56.9%	43.0%	57.0%	43.0%
1948	222,571	116,212	Adams, Sherman	105,207	Hill, Herbert W.	1,152	11,005 R	52.2%	47.3%	52.5%	47.5%
1946	163,451	103,204	Dale, Charles M.	60,247	Keefe, F. Clyde	–	42,957 R	63.1%	36.9%	63.1%	36.9%

POSTWAR VOTE FOR SENATOR

								Percentage			
	Total	Republican		Democratic		Other	Rep.-Dem.	Total Vote		Major Vote	
Year	Vote	Vote	Candidate	Vote	Candidate	Vote	Plurality	Rep.	Dem.	Rep.	Dem.
1975s	262,682	113,007	Wyman, Louis C.	140,778	Durkin, John A.	8,897	27,771 D	43.0%	53.6%	44.5%	55.5%
1974	223,363	110,926	Wyman, Louis C.	110,924	Durkin, John A.	1,513	2 R	49.7%	49.7%	50.0%	50.0%
1972	324,354	139,852	Powell, Wesley	184,495	McIntyre, Thomas J.	7	44,643 D	43.1%	56.9%	43.1%	56.9%
1968	286,989	170,163	Cotton, Norris	116,816	King, John W.	10	53,347 R	59.3%	40.7%	59.3%	40.7%
1966	229,305	105,241	Thyng, Harrison R.	123,888	McIntyre, Thomas J.	176	18,647 D	45.9%	54.0%	45.9%	54.1%
1962	224,479	134,035	Cotton, Norris	90,444	Catalfo, Alfred	–	43,591 R	59.7%	40.3%	59.7%	40.3%
1962s	224,811	107,199	Bass, Perkins	117,612	McIntyre, Thomas J.	–	10,413 D	47.7%	52.3%	47.7%	52.3%
1960	287,545	173,521	Bridges, Styles	114,024	Hill, Herbert W.	–	59,497 R	60.3%	39.7%	60.3%	39.7%
1956	251,943	161,424	Cotton, Norris	90,519	Pickett, Laurence M.	–	70,905 R	64.1%	35.9%	64.1%	35.9%
1954	194,536	117,150	Bridges, Styles	77,386	Morin, Gerard L.	–	39,764 R	60.2%	39.8%	60.2%	39.8%
1954s	189,558	114,068	Cotton, Norris	75,490	Betley, Stanley J.	–	38,578 R	60.2%	39.8%	60.2%	39.8%
1950	190,573	106,142	Tobey, Charles W.	72,473	Kelley, Emmet J.	11,958	33,669 R	55.7%	38.0%	59.4%	40.6%
1948	222,898	129,600	Bridges, Styles	91,760	Fortin, Alfred E.	1,538	37,840 R	58.1%	41.2%	58.5%	41.5%

The 1975 election and one each of the 1962 and 1954 elections were for short terms to fill vacancies.

NEW HAMPSHIRE

Districts Established March 1, 1972

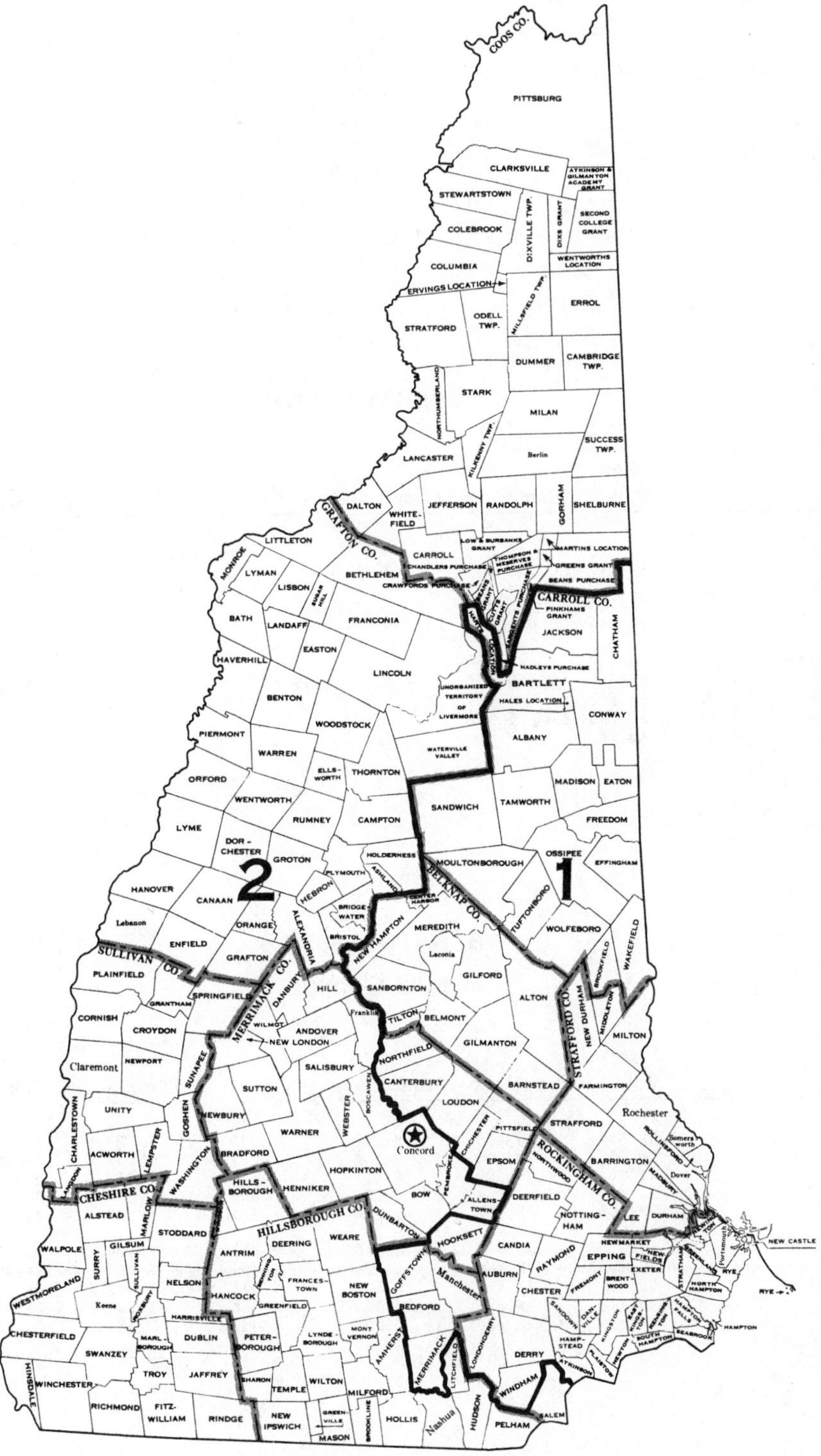

NEW HAMPSHIRE

PRESIDENT 1976

1970 Census Population	County	Total Vote	Republican	Democratic	Other	Rep.-Dem. Plurality	Percentage Total Vote Rep.	Total Vote Dem.	Major Vote Rep.	Major Vote Dem.
32,367	BELKNAP	16,249	9,876	6,143	230	3,733 R	60.8%	37.8%	61.7%	38.3%
18,548	CARROLL	12,198	8,561	3,374	263	5,187 R	70.2%	27.7%	71.7%	28.3%
52,364	CHESHIRE	23,305	12,554	10,388	363	2,166 R	53.9%	44.6%	54.7%	45.3%
34,291	COOS	14,638	7,094	7,385	159	291 D	48.5%	50.5%	49.0%	51.0%
54,914	GRAFTON	23,914	14,430	8,996	488	5,434 R	60.3%	37.6%	61.6%	38.4%
223,941	HILLSBOROUGH	100,880	53,581	45,544	1,755	8,037 R	53.1%	45.1%	54.1%	45.9%
80,925	MERRIMACK	37,282	21,853	14,865	564	6,988 R	58.6%	39.9%	59.5%	40.5%
138,951	ROCKINGHAM	68,130	36,738	30,051	1,341	6,687 R	53.9%	44.1%	55.0%	45.0%
70,431	STRAFFORD	29,815	14,569	14,566	680	3 R	48.9%	48.9%	50.0%	50.0%
30,949	SULLIVAN	13,207	6,679	6,323	205	356 R	50.6%	47.9%	51.4%	48.6%
737,681	TOTAL	339,618	185,935	147,635	6,048	38,300 R	54.7%	43.5%	55.7%	44.3%

GOVERNOR 1976

1970 Census Population	County	Total Vote	Republican	Democratic	Other	Rep.-Dem. Plurality	Percentage Total Vote Rep.	Total Vote Dem.	Major Vote Rep.	Major Vote Dem.
32,367	BELKNAP	16,720	10,310	6,406	4	3,904 R	61.7%	38.3%	61.7%	38.3%
18,548	CARROLL	12,572	9,391	3,181		6,210 R	74.7%	25.3%	74.7%	25.3%
52,364	CHESHIRE	23,626	11,055	12,566	5	1,511 D	46.8%	53.2%	46.8%	53.2%
34,291	COOS	14,783	9,437	5,346		4,091 R	63.8%	36.2%	63.8%	36.2%
54,914	GRAFTON	24,391	14,600	9,781	10	4,819 R	59.9%	40.1%	59.9%	40.1%
223,941	HILLSBOROUGH	99,620	60,008	39,590	22	20,418 R	60.2%	39.7%	60.3%	39.7%
80,925	MERRIMACK	38,674	18,950	19,716	8	766 D	49.0%	51.0%	49.0%	51.0%
138,951	ROCKINGHAM	68,763	41,728	27,026	9	14,702 R	60.7%	39.3%	60.7%	39.3%
70,431	STRAFFORD	29,740	15,568	14,168	4	1,400 R	52.3%	47.6%	52.4%	47.6%
30,949	SULLIVAN	13,780	6,542	7,235	3	693 D	47.5%	52.5%	47.5%	52.5%
737,681	TOTAL	342,669	197,589	145,015	65	52,574 R	57.7%	42.3%	57.7%	42.3%

SENATOR 1975
Special Election

1970 Census Population	County	Total Vote	Republican	Democratic	Other	Rep.-Dem. Plurality	Percentage Total Vote Rep.	Total Vote Dem.	Major Vote Rep.	Major Vote Dem.
32,367	BELKNAP	13,117	6,219	6,356	542	137 D	47.4%	48.5%	49.5%	50.5%
18,548	CARROLL	9,047	5,866	2,834	347	3,032 R	64.8%	31.3%	67.4%	32.6%
52,364	CHESHIRE	17,161	6,503	9,987	671	3,484 D	37.9%	58.2%	39.4%	60.6%
34,291	COOS	11,464	4,164	6,891	409	2,727 D	36.3%	60.1%	37.7%	62.3%
54,914	GRAFTON	17,506	8,387	8,254	865	133 R	47.9%	47.1%	50.4%	49.6%
223,941	HILLSBOROUGH	80,110	34,751	42,550	2,809	7,799 D	43.4%	53.1%	45.0%	55.0%
80,925	MERRIMACK	30,751	12,884	16,696	1,171	3,812 D	41.9%	54.3%	43.6%	56.4%
138,951	ROCKINGHAM	50,101	22,217	26,806	1,078	4,589 D	44.3%	53.5%	45.3%	54.7%
70,431	STRAFFORD	23,109	8,296	14,145	668	5,849 D	35.9%	61.2%	37.0%	63.0%
30,949	SULLIVAN	10,316	3,720	6,259	337	2,539 D	36.1%	60.7%	37.3%	62.7%
737,681	TOTAL	262,682	113,007	140,778	8,897	27,771 D	43.0%	53.6%	44.5%	55.5%

NEW HAMPSHIRE

PRESIDENT 1976

1970 Census Population	City/Town	Total Vote	Republican	Democratic	Other	Rep.-Dem. Plurality	Percentage Total Vote Rep.	Percentage Total Vote Dem.	Percentage Major Vote Rep.	Percentage Major Vote Dem.
5,859	BEDFORD	3,337	2,240	1,059	38	1,181 R	67.1%	31.7%	67.9%	32.1%
15,256	BERLIN	6,533	2,338	4,142	53	1,804 D	35.8%	63.4%	36.1%	63.9%
14,221	CLAREMONT	4,996	2,152	2,792	52	640 D	43.1%	55.9%	43.5%	56.5%
30,022	CONCORD	12,051	6,627	5,256	168	1,371 R	55.0%	43.6%	55.8%	44.2%
11,712	DERRY	5,554	3,144	2,272	138	872 R	56.6%	40.9%	58.1%	41.9%
20,850	DOVER	8,855	4,204	4,386	265	182 D	47.5%	49.5%	48.9%	51.1%
8,869	DURHAM	3,034	1,484	1,390	160	94 R	48.9%	45.8%	51.6%	48.4%
8,892	EXETER	4,407	2,506	1,816	85	690 R	56.9%	41.2%	58.0%	42.0%
7,292	FRANKLIN	2,815	1,479	1,310	26	169 R	52.5%	46.5%	53.0%	47.0%
9,284	GOFFSTOWN	3,940	2,311	1,575	54	736 R	58.7%	40.0%	59.5%	40.5%
8,011	HAMPTON	4,588	2,676	1,890	22	786 R	58.3%	41.2%	58.6%	41.4%
8,494	HANOVER	3,212	1,483	1,614	115	131 D	46.2%	50.2%	47.9%	52.1%
5,564	HOOKSETT	2,658	1,613	985	60	628 R	60.7%	37.1%	62.1%	37.9%
10,638	HUDSON	4,837	2,249	2,508	80	259 D	46.5%	51.9%	47.3%	52.7%
20,467	KEENE	8,262	4,499	3,667	96	832 R	54.5%	44.4%	55.1%	44.9%
14,888	LACONIA	5,981	3,311	2,640	30	671 R	55.4%	44.1%	55.6%	44.4%
9,725	LEBANON	3,864	2,029	1,779	56	250 R	52.5%	46.0%	53.3%	46.7%
5,290	LITTLETON	2,314	1,520	748	46	772 R	65.7%	32.3%	67.0%	33.0%
5,346	LONDONDERRY	3,423	1,991	1,334	98	657 R	58.2%	39.0%	59.9%	40.1%
87,754	MANCHESTER	34,197	17,506	16,243	448	1,263 R	51.2%	47.5%	51.9%	48.1%
8,595	MERRIMACK TOWN	5,064	2,859	2,126	79	733 R	56.5%	42.0%	57.4%	42.6%
6,622	MILFORD	3,218	1,974	1,142	102	832 R	61.3%	35.5%	63.4%	36.6%
55,820	NASHUA	24,594	11,103	13,014	477	1,911 D	45.1%	52.9%	46.0%	54.0%
5,899	NEWPORT	2,324	1,234	1,061	29	173 R	53.1%	45.7%	53.8%	46.2%
5,408	PELHAM	2,927	1,296	1,562	69	266 D	44.3%	53.4%	45.3%	54.7%
25,717	PORTSMOUTH	8,625	4,169	4,303	153	134 D	48.3%	49.9%	49.2%	50.8%
17,938	ROCHESTER	7,516	3,801	3,641	74	160 R	50.6%	48.4%	51.1%	48.9%
20,142	SALEM	9,210	3,994	4,983	233	989 D	43.4%	54.1%	44.5%	55.5%
9,026	SOMERSWORTH	3,709	1,361	2,297	51	936 D	36.7%	61.9%	37.2%	62.8%

NEW HAMPSHIRE

GOVERNOR 1976

1970 Census Population	City/Town	Total Vote	Republican	Democratic	Other	Rep.-Dem. Plurality	Percentage Total Vote Rep.	Total Vote Dem.	Major Vote Rep.	Major Vote Dem.
5,859	BEDFORD	3,488	2,539	949		1,590 R	72.8%	27.2%	72.8%	27.2%
15,256	BERLIN	6,568	3,605	2,963		642 R	54.9%	45.1%	54.9%	45.1%
14,221	CLAREMONT	5,180	2,136	3,044		908 D	41.2%	58.8%	41.2%	58.8%
30,022	CONCORD	12,460	4,537	7,923		3,386 D	36.4%	63.6%	36.4%	63.6%
11,712	DERRY	5,558	3,956	1,597	5	2,359 R	71.2%	28.7%	71.2%	28.8%
20,850	DOVER	8,885	4,396	4,487	2	91 D	49.5%	50.5%	49.5%	50.5%
8,869	DURHAM	3,018	811	2,207		1,396 D	26.9%	73.1%	26.9%	73.1%
8,892	EXETER	4,296	2,171	2,125		46 R	50.5%	49.5%	50.5%	49.5%
7,292	FRANKLIN	2,949	1,486	1,463		23 R	50.4%	49.6%	50.4%	49.6%
9,284	GOFFSTOWN	4,168	2,793	1,375		1,418 R	67.0%	33.0%	67.0%	33.0%
8,011	HAMPTON	4,565	2,452	2,113		339 R	53.7%	46.3%	53.7%	46.3%
8,494	HANOVER	3,201	872	2,327	2	1,455 D	27.2%	72.7%	27.3%	72.7%
5,564	HOOKSETT	2,743	1,879	864		1,015 R	68.5%	31.5%	68.5%	31.5%
10,638	HUDSON	4,864	2,699	2,162	3	537 R	55.5%	44.4%	55.5%	44.5%
20,467	KEENE	8,402	3,235	5,164	3	1,929 D	38.5%	61.5%	38.5%	61.5%
14,888	LACONIA	6,121	3,358	2,763		595 R	54.9%	45.1%	54.9%	45.1%
9,725	LEBANON	3,879	1,759	2,120		361 D	45.3%	54.7%	45.3%	54.7%
5,290	LITTLETON	2,353	1,666	683	4	983 R	70.8%	29.0%	70.9%	29.1%
5,346	LONDONDERRY	3,450	2,485	965		1,520 R	72.0%	28.0%	72.0%	28.0%
87,754	MANCHESTER	33,314	20,410	12,901	3	7,509 R	61.3%	38.7%	61.3%	38.7%
8,595	MERRIMACK TOWN	5,060	3,383	1,669	8	1,714 R	66.9%	33.0%	67.0%	33.0%
6,622	MILFORD	3,253	2,135	1,116	2	1,019 R	65.6%	34.3%	65.7%	34.3%
55,820	NASHUA	23,666	11,769	11,895	2	126 D	49.7%	50.3%	49.7%	50.3%
5,899	NEWPORT	2,486	1,091	1,395		304 D	43.9%	56.1%	43.9%	56.1%
5,408	PELHAM	2,895	1,835	1,059	1	776 R	63.4%	36.6%	63.4%	36.6%
25,717	PORTSMOUTH	8,466	3,267	5,198	1	1,931 D	38.6%	61.4%	38.6%	61.4%
17,938	ROCHESTER	7,314	4,451	2,861	2	1,590 R	60.9%	39.1%	60.9%	39.1%
20,142	SALEM	9,484	6,005	3,479		2,526 R	63.3%	36.7%	63.3%	36.7%
9,026	SOMERSWORTH	3,674	1,769	1,905		136 D	48.1%	51.9%	48.1%	51.9%

NEW HAMPSHIRE

SENATOR 1975
Special Election

1970 Census Population	City/Town	Total Vote	Republican	Democratic	Other	Rep.-Dem. Plurality	Percentage Total Vote Rep.	Percentage Total Vote Dem.	Percentage Major Vote Rep.	Percentage Major Vote Dem.
5,859	BEDFORD	2,860	1,729	1,023	108	706 R	60.5%	35.8%	62.8%	37.2%
15,256	BERLIN	5,314	1,150	4,022	142	2,872 D	21.6%	75.7%	22.2%	77.8%
14,221	CLAREMONT	4,239	1,228	2,912	99	1,684 D	29.0%	68.7%	29.7%	70.3%
30,022	CONCORD	10,218	3,829	6,128	261	2,299 D	37.5%	60.0%	38.5%	61.5%
11,712	DERRY	3,679	1,921	1,650	108	271 R	52.2%	44.8%	53.8%	46.2%
20,850	DOVER	7,123	2,356	4,625	142	2,269 D	33.1%	64.9%	33.7%	66.3%
8,869	DURHAM	2,275	701	1,533	41	832 D	30.8%	67.4%	31.4%	68.6%
8,892	EXETER	3,717	1,777	1,867	73	90 D	47.8%	50.2%	48.8%	51.2%
7,292	FRANKLIN	2,364	756	1,433	175	677 D	32.0%	60.6%	34.5%	65.5%
9,284	GOFFSTOWN	3,395	1,746	1,507	142	239 R	51.4%	44.4%	53.7%	46.3%
8,011	HAMPTON	3,384	1,373	1,977	34	604 D	40.6%	58.4%	41.0%	59.0%
8,494	HANOVER	2,312	742	1,542	28	800 D	32.1%	66.7%	32.5%	67.5%
5,564	HOOKSETT	2,212	1,115	996	101	119 R	50.4%	45.0%	52.8%	47.2%
10,638	HUDSON	3,318	1,061	2,158	99	1,097 D	32.0%	65.0%	33.0%	67.0%
20,467	KEENE	6,400	2,200	4,001	199	1,801 D	34.4%	62.5%	35.5%	64.5%
14,888	LACONIA	5,095	2,038	2,912	145	874 D	40.0%	57.2%	41.2%	58.8%
9,725	LEBANON	2,623	842	1,743	38	901 D	32.1%	66.5%	32.6%	67.4%
5,290	LITTLETON	1,887	974	814	99	160 R	51.6%	43.1%	54.5%	45.5%
5,346	LONDONDERRY	2,018	1,034	900	84	134 R	51.2%	44.6%	53.5%	46.5%
87,754	MANCHESTER	32,052	14,462	16,639	951	2,177 D	45.1%	51.9%	46.5%	53.5%
8,595	MERRIMACK TOWN	3,379	1,417	1,826	136	409 D	41.9%	54.0%	43.7%	56.3%
6,622	MILFORD	2,487	1,261	1,108	118	153 R	50.7%	44.6%	53.2%	46.8%
55,820	NASHUA	17,093	4,854	11,694	545	6,840 D	28.4%	68.4%	29.3%	70.7%
5,899	NEWPORT	1,816	684	1,054	78	370 D	37.7%	58.0%	39.4%	60.6%
5,408	PELHAM	1,912	677	1,216	19	539 D	35.4%	63.6%	35.8%	64.2%
25,717	PORTSMOUTH	6,609	2,085	4,440	84	2,355 D	31.5%	67.2%	32.0%	68.0%
17,938	ROCHESTER	6,051	2,360	3,463	228	1,103 D	39.0%	57.2%	40.5%	59.5%
20,142	SALEM	6,581	2,242	4,269	70	2,027 D	34.1%	64.9%	34.4%	65.6%
9,026	SOMERSWORTH	2,821	768	1,987	66	1,219 D	27.2%	70.4%	27.9%	72.1%

NEW HAMPSHIRE

CONGRESS

			Republican		Democratic				Percentage			
		Total					Other	Rep.-Dem.	Total Vote		Major Vote	
CD	Year	Vote	Vote	Candidate	Vote	Candidate	Vote	Plurality	Rep.	Dem.	Rep.	Dem.
1	1976	158,465	48,087	ADAMS, JOHN	107,806	D AMOURS, NORMAN E.	2,572	59,719 D	30.3%	68.0%	30.8%	69.2%
1	1974	112,004	53,610	BANKS, DAVID A.	58,388	D AMOURS, NORMAN E.	6	4,778 D	47.9%	52.1%	47.9%	52.1%
1	1972	158,749	115,732	WYMAN, LOUIS C.	42,996	MERROW, CHESTER E.	21	72,736 R	72.9%	27.1%	72.9%	27.1%
2	1976	166,709	100,911	CLEVELAND, JAMES C.	65,792	GRANDMAISON, J. JOSEPH	6	35,119 R	60.5%	39.5%	60.5%	39.5%
2	1974	107,538	69,068	CLEVELAND, JAMES C.	38,463	BLISS, HELEN L.	7	30,605 R	64.2%	35.8%	64.2%	35.8%
2	1972	158,285	107,021	CLEVELAND, JAMES C.	51,259	OFFICER, CHARLES B.	5	55,762 R	67.6%	32.4%	67.6%	32.4%

NEW HAMPSHIRE

In addition to the county-by-county figures, 1975 and 1976 data are presented for selected New Hampshire communities. Since not all jurisdictions of the state are listed in this special tabulation, state-wide totals are shown only with the county-by-county statistics.

1975 SPECIAL ELECTION

Senator — The election of November 1974 was contested in the Senate due to the closeness of the vote, and no member was seated. The Senate declared the seat vacant and a special election was called for September 16, 1975. Other vote was 8,787 Chimento (American); 110 scattered.

1976 GENERAL ELECTION

President — Original uncorrected canvass gave the Democratic vote in Hillsborough county as 45,554; the other vote in Hillsborough county as 1,754; the Democratic total state-wide vote as 147,645; the other total state-wide vote as 6,047. Other vote was 4,095 McCarthy (McCarthy '76); 936 MacBride (Libertarian); 186 LaRouche (U.S. Labor); 161 Camejo (Socialist Workers); 66 Levin (Socialist Labor); 604 scattered.

Governor — Original uncorrected canvass gave the Democratic vote in Hillsborough county as 39,230; the Democratic total state vote as 144,655. Other vote was scattered.

Congress — Other vote was 2,349 O'Brien (Libertarian), 193 Wyman (write-in), 30 scattered in CD 1; scattered in CD 2.

1976 PRIMARIES

SEPTEMBER 14 REPUBLICAN

Governor — 52,968 Meldrim Thomson; 26,728 Gerald J. Zeiller; 2,257 Ralph Brewster.

Congress — Unopposed in CD 2. Contested as follows:

CD 1 — 12,195 John Adams; 7,944 Edward E. Hewson; 5,670 Calvin Warburton; 5,202 Richard I. Ellis.

SEPTEMBER 15 DEMOCRATIC

Governor — 21,589 Harry V. Spanos; 15,758 James A. Connor; 13,629 Hugh J. Gallen; 1,242 Carmen C. Chimento.

Congress — Unopposed in CD 1. Contested as follows:

CD 2 — 17,570 J. Joseph Grandmaison; 4,692 Richard H. Diotte.

NEW JERSEY

GOVERNOR

Brendan T. Byrne (D). Elected 1973 to a four-year term.

SENATORS

Clifford P. Case (R). Re-elected 1972 to a six-year term. Previously elected 1966, 1960, 1954.

Harrison Williams (D). Re-elected 1976 to a six-year term. Previously elected 1970, 1964, 1958.

REPRESENTATIVES

1. James J. Florio (D)
2. William J. Hughes (D)
3. James J. Howard (D)
4. Frank Thompson (D)
5. Millicent Fenwick (R)
6. Edwin B. Forsythe (R)
7. Andrew Maguire (D)
8. Robert A. Roe (D)
9. Harold C. Hollenbeck (R)
10. Peter W. Rodino (D)
11. Joseph G. Minish (D)
12. Matthew J. Rinaldo (R)
13. Helen S. Meyner (D)
14. Joseph A. LeFante (D)
15. Edward J. Patten (D)

POSTWAR VOTE FOR GOVERNOR

								Percentage			
	Total	Republican		Democratic		Other	Rep.-Dem.	Total Vote		Major Vote	
Year	Vote	Vote	Candidate	Vote	Candidate	Vote	Plurality	Rep.	Dem.	Rep.	Dem.
1973	2,122,009	676,235	Sandman, Charles W.	1,414,613	Byrne, Brendan T.	31,161	738,378 D	31.9%	66.7%	32.3%	67.7%
1969	2,366,606	1,411,905	Cahill, William T.	911,003	Meyner, Robert B.	43,698	500,902 R	59.7%	38.5%	60.8%	39.2%
1965	2,229,583	915,996	Dumont, Wayne	1,279,568	Hughes, Richard J.	34,019	363,572 D	41.1%	57.4%	41.7%	58.3%
1961	2,152,662	1,049,274	Mitchell, James P.	1,084,194	Hughes, Richard J.	19,194	34,920 D	48.7%	50.4%	49.2%	50.8%
1957	2,018,488	897,321	Forbes, Malcolm S.	1,101,130	Meyner, Robert B.	20,037	203,809 D	44.5%	54.6%	44.9%	55.1%
1953	1,810,812	809,068	Troast, Paul L.	962,710	Meyner, Robert B.	39,034	153,642 D	44.7%	53.2%	45.7%	54.3%
1949	1,718,788	885,882	Driscoll, Alfred	810,022	Wene, Elmer H.	22,884	75,860 R	51.5%	47.1%	52.2%	47.8%
1946	1,414,527	807,378	Driscoll, Alfred	585,960	Hansen, Lewis G.	21,189	221,418 R	57.1%	41.4%	57.9%	42.1%

The term of office of New Jersey's Governor was increased from three to four years effective with the 1949 election.

POSTWAR VOTE FOR SENATOR

								Percentage			
	Total	Republican		Democratic		Other	Rep.-Dem.	Total Vote		Major Vote	
Year	Vote	Vote	Candidate	Vote	Candidate	Vote	Plurality	Rep.	Dem.	Rep.	Dem.
1976	2,771,390	1,054,508	Norcross, David F.	1,681,140	Williams, Harrison	35,742	626,632 D	38.0%	60.7%	38.5%	61.5%
1972	2,791,907	1,743,854	Case, Clifford P.	963,573	Krebs, Paul J.	84,480	780,281 R	62.5%	34.5%	64.4%	35.6%
1970	2,142,105	903,026	Gross, Nelson G.	1,157,074	Williams, Harrison	82,005	254,048 D	42.2%	54.0%	43.8%	56.2%
1966	2,131,188	1,279,343	Case, Clifford P.	788,021	Wilentz, Warren W.	63,824	491,322 R	60.0%	37.0%	61.9%	38.1%
1964	2,710,441	1,011,610	Shanley, Bernard M.	1,678,051	Williams, Harrison	20,780	666,441 D	37.3%	61.9%	37.6%	62.4%
1960	2,664,556	1,483,832	Case, Clifford P.	1,151,385	Lord, Thorn	29,339	332,447 R	55.7%	43.2%	56.3%	43.7%
1958	1,881,329	882,287	Kean, Robert W.	966,832	Williams, Harrison	32,210	84,545 D	46.9%	51.4%	47.7%	52.3%
1954	1,770,557	861,528	Case, Clifford P.	858,158	Howell, Charles R.	50,871	3,370 R	48.7%	48.5%	50.1%	49.9%
1952	2,318,232	1,286,782	Smith, H. Alexander	1,011,187	Alexander, Archibald	20,263	275,595 R	55.5%	43.6%	56.0%	44.0%
1948	1,869,882	934,720	Hendrickson, Robert	884,414	Alexander, Archibald	50,748	50,306 R	50.0%	47.3%	51.4%	48.6%
1946	1,367,155	799,808	Smith, H. Alexander	548,458	Brunner, George E.	18,889	251,350 R	58.5%	40.1%	59.3%	40.7%

NEW JERSEY

Districts Established April 12, 1972

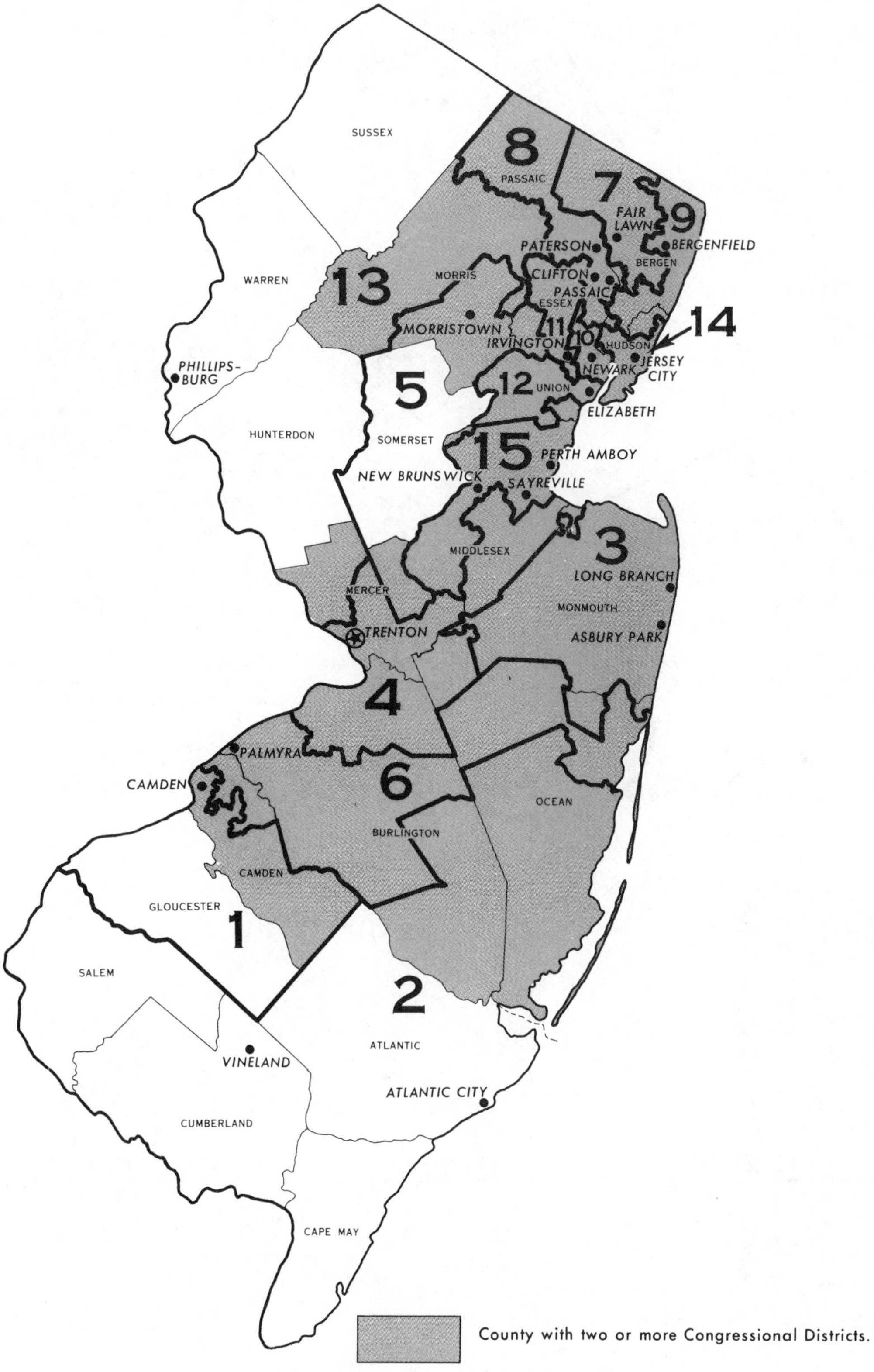

NEW JERSEY

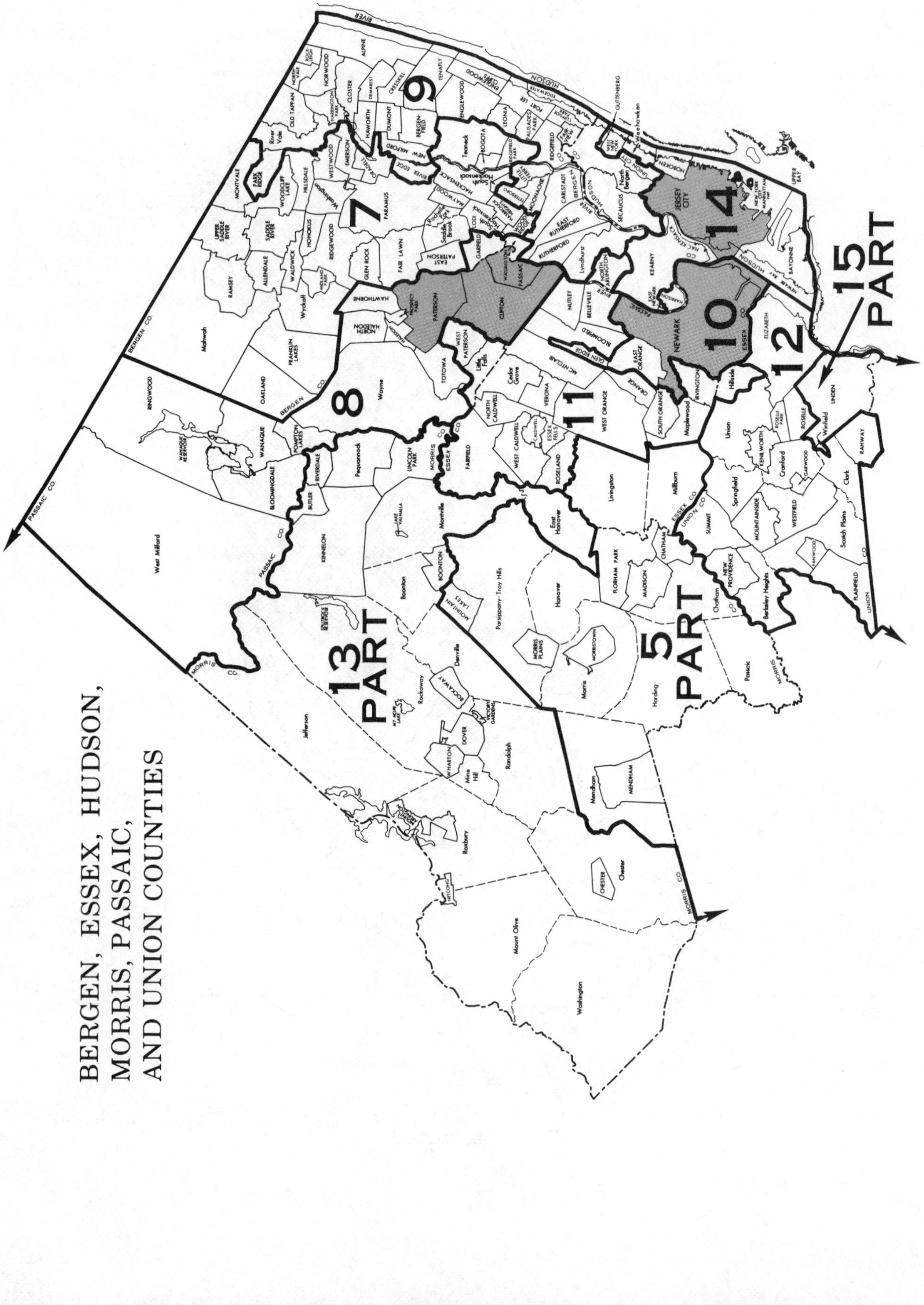

BERGEN, ESSEX, HUDSON, MORRIS, PASSAIC, AND UNION COUNTIES

NEW JERSEY

PRESIDENT 1976

1970 Census Population	County	Total Vote	Republican	Democratic	Other	Rep.-Dem. Plurality	Percentage Total Vote Rep.	Percentage Total Vote Dem.	Percentage Major Vote Rep.	Percentage Major Vote Dem.
175,043	ATLANTIC	80,630	36,733	41,965	1,932	5,232 D	45.6%	52.0%	46.7%	53.3%
898,012	BERGEN	424,853	237,331	180,738	6,784	56,593 R	55.9%	42.5%	56.8%	43.2%
323,132	BURLINGTON	126,820	60,960	63,309	2,551	2,349 D	48.1%	49.9%	49.1%	50.9%
456,291	CAMDEN	195,611	82,801	108,854	3,956	26,053 D	42.3%	55.6%	43.2%	56.8%
59,554	CAPE MAY	36,667	19,498	16,489	680	3,009 R	53.2%	45.0%	54.2%	45.8%
121,374	CUMBERLAND	50,287	20,535	29,165	587	8,630 D	40.8%	58.0%	41.3%	58.7%
929,986	ESSEX	315,812	133,911	174,434	7,467	40,523 D	42.4%	55.2%	43.4%	56.6%
172,681	GLOUCESTER	75,302	34,888	38,726	1,688	3,838 D	46.3%	51.4%	47.4%	52.6%
609,266	HUDSON	212,730	92,636	116,241	3,853	23,605 D	43.5%	54.6%	44.3%	55.7%
69,718	HUNTERDON	32,966	19,616	12,592	758	7,024 R	59.5%	38.2%	60.9%	39.1%
303,968	MERCER	130,856	58,453	69,621	2,782	11,168 D	44.7%	53.2%	45.6%	54.4%
583,813	MIDDLESEX	240,864	113,539	122,859	4,466	9,320 D	47.1%	51.0%	48.0%	52.0%
459,379	MONMOUTH	202,790	110,104	88,956	3,730	21,148 R	54.3%	43.9%	55.3%	44.7%
383,454	MORRIS	172,373	105,921	63,749	2,703	42,172 R	61.4%	37.0%	62.4%	37.6%
208,470	OCEAN	136,781	77,875	56,413	2,493	21,462 R	56.9%	41.2%	58.0%	42.0%
460,782	PASSAIC	166,226	85,102	76,194	4,930	8,908 R	51.2%	45.8%	52.8%	47.2%
60,346	SALEM	24,977	11,639	12,826	512	1,187 D	46.6%	51.4%	47.6%	52.4%
198,372	SOMERSET	89,691	51,260	36,258	2,173	15,002 R	57.2%	40.4%	58.6%	41.4%
77,528	SUSSEX	39,229	23,613	14,759	857	8,854 R	60.2%	37.6%	61.5%	38.5%
543,116	UNION	228,902	118,019	106,267	4,616	11,752 R	51.6%	46.4%	52.6%	47.4%
73,879	WARREN	30,105	15,254	14,238	613	1,016 R	50.7%	47.3%	51.7%	48.3%
7,168,164	TOTAL	3,014,472	1,509,688	1,444,653	60,131	65,035 R	50.1%	47.9%	51.1%	48.9%

SENATOR 1976

1970 Census Population	County	Total Vote	Republican	Democratic	Other	Rep.-Dem. Plurality	Percentage Total Vote Rep.	Percentage Total Vote Dem.	Percentage Major Vote Rep.	Percentage Major Vote Dem.
175,043	ATLANTIC	70,421	25,500	43,769	1,152	18,269 D	36.2%	62.2%	36.8%	63.2%
898,012	BERGEN	396,090	163,830	226,964	5,296	63,134 D	41.4%	57.3%	41.9%	58.1%
323,132	BURLINGTON	117,614	49,573	67,404	637	17,831 D	42.1%	57.3%	42.4%	57.6%
456,291	CAMDEN	175,511	62,876	110,639	1,996	47,763 D	35.8%	63.0%	36.2%	63.8%
59,554	CAPE MAY	31,670	13,839	17,641	190	3,802 D	43.7%	55.7%	44.0%	56.0%
121,374	CUMBERLAND	46,521	15,761	30,578	182	14,817 D	33.9%	65.7%	34.0%	66.0%
929,986	ESSEX	286,972	87,771	194,533	4,668	106,762 D	30.6%	67.8%	31.1%	68.9%
172,681	GLOUCESTER	73,067	26,533	45,772	762	19,239 D	36.3%	62.6%	36.7%	63.3%
609,266	HUDSON	196,464	61,135	132,508	2,821	71,373 D	31.1%	67.4%	31.6%	68.4%
69,718	HUNTERDON	30,504	14,782	15,520	202	738 D	48.5%	50.9%	48.8%	51.2%
303,968	MERCER	120,062	40,883	77,959	1,220	37,076 D	34.1%	64.9%	34.4%	65.6%
583,813	MIDDLESEX	221,202	74,841	143,452	2,909	68,611 D	33.8%	64.9%	34.3%	65.7%
459,379	MONMOUTH	188,612	73,979	112,687	1,946	38,708 D	39.2%	59.7%	39.6%	60.4%
383,454	MORRIS	157,326	76,127	79,546	1,653	3,419 D	48.4%	50.6%	48.9%	51.1%
208,470	OCEAN	126,493	58,525	66,317	1,651	7,792 D	46.3%	52.4%	46.9%	53.1%
460,782	PASSAIC	147,709	56,409	88,218	3,082	31,809 D	38.2%	59.7%	39.0%	61.0%
60,346	SALEM	23,906	8,847	14,853	206	6,006 D	37.0%	62.1%	37.3%	62.7%
198,372	SOMERSET	82,797	36,740	44,665	1,392	7,925 D	44.4%	53.9%	45.1%	54.9%
77,528	SUSSEX	38,066	18,032	19,546	488	1,514 D	47.4%	51.3%	48.0%	52.0%
543,116	UNION	211,408	77,404	131,033	2,971	53,629 D	36.6%	62.0%	37.1%	62.9%
73,879	WARREN	28,972	11,118	17,536	318	6,418 D	38.4%	60.5%	38.8%	61.2%
7,168,164	TOTAL	2,771,390	1,054,508	1,681,140	35,742	626,632 D	38.0%	60.7%	38.5%	61.5%

NEW JERSEY

CONGRESS

			Republican		Democratic				Percentage			
									Total Vote		Major Vote	
CD	Year	Total Vote	Vote	Candidate	Vote	Candidate	Other Vote	Rep.-Dem. Plurality	Rep.	Dem.	Rep.	Dem.
1	1976	194,898	56,363	MCCULLOUGH, JOSEPH I.	136,624	FLORIO, JAMES J.	1,911	80,261 D	28.9%	70.1%	29.2%	70.8%
1	1974	140,468	54,069	HUNT, JOHN E.	80,768	FLORIO, JAMES J.	5,631	26,699 D	38.5%	57.5%	40.1%	59.9%
1	1972	186,026	97,650	HUNT, JOHN E.	87,492	FLORIO, JAMES J.	884	10,158 R	52.5%	47.0%	52.7%	47.3%
2	1976	229,668	87,915	HURLEY, JAMES R.	141,753	HUGHES, WILLIAM J.		53,838 D	38.3%	61.7%	38.3%	61.7%
2	1974	191,520	79,064	SANDMAN, CHARLES W.	109,763	HUGHES, WILLIAM J.	2,693	30,699 D	41.3%	57.3%	41.9%	58.1%
2	1972	202,470	133,096	SANDMAN, CHARLES W.	69,374	ROSE, JOHN D.		63,722 R	65.7%	34.3%	65.7%	34.3%
3	1976	204,739	75,934	SICILIANO, RALPH A.	127,164	HOWARD, JAMES J.	1,641	51,230 D	37.1%	62.1%	37.4%	62.6%
3	1974	153,906	45,932	CLARK, KENNETH W.	105,979	HOWARD, JAMES J.	1,995	60,047 D	29.8%	68.9%	30.2%	69.8%
3	1972	196,178	92,285	DOWD, WILLIAM F.	103,893	HOWARD, JAMES J.		11,608 D	47.0%	53.0%	47.0%	53.0%
4	1976	170,868	54,789	INDYK, JOSEPH S.	113,281	THOMPSON, FRANK	2,798	58,492 D	32.1%	66.3%	32.6%	67.4%
4	1974	122,992	40,797	KELLER, HENRY J.	82,195	THOMPSON, FRANK		41,398 D	33.2%	66.8%	33.2%	66.8%
4	1972	169,236	71,030	GARIBALDI, PETER P.	98,206	THOMPSON, FRANK		27,176 D	42.0%	58.0%	42.0%	58.0%
5	1976	206,106	137,803	FENWICK, MILLICENT	64,598	NERO, F. R.	3,705	73,205 R	66.9%	31.3%	68.1%	31.9%
5	1974	152,758	81,498	FENWICK, MILLICENT	66,380	BOHEN, FREDERICK M.	4,880	15,118 R	53.4%	43.5%	55.1%	44.9%
5	1972	205,386	127,310	FRELINGHUYSEN, PETER	78,076	BOHEN, FREDERICK M.		49,234 R	62.0%	38.0%	62.0%	38.0%
6	1976	214,304	125,920	FORSYTHE, EDWIN B.	85,053	COSTA, CATHERINE A.	3,331	40,867 R	58.8%	39.7%	59.7%	40.3%
6	1974	154,712	81,190	FORSYTHE, EDWIN B.	70,353	YATES, CHARLES B.	3,169	10,837 R	52.5%	45.5%	53.6%	46.4%
6	1972	196,821	123,610	FORSYTHE, EDWIN B.	71,113	BRENNAN, FRANCIS P.	2,098	52,497 R	62.8%	36.1%	63.5%	36.5%
7	1976	213,150	92,624	SHEEHAN, JAMES J.	120,526	MAGUIRE, ANDREW		27,902 D	43.5%	56.5%	43.5%	56.5%
7	1974	160,705	71,377	WIDNALL, WILLIAM B.	79,808	MAGUIRE, ANDREW	9,520	8,431 D	44.4%	49.7%	47.2%	52.8%
7	1972	214,634	124,365	WIDNALL, WILLIAM B.	85,712	LESEMANN, ARTHUR J.	4,557	38,653 R	57.9%	39.9%	59.2%	40.8%
8	1976	154,196	44,775	DOTY, BESSIE	108,841	ROE, ROBERT A.	580	64,066 D	29.0%	70.6%	29.1%	70.9%
8	1974	113,327	27,839	SCHMIDT, HERMAN	83,724	ROE, ROBERT A.	1,764	55,885 D	24.6%	73.9%	25.0%	75.0%
8	1972	165,454	61,073	JOHNSON, WALTER E.	104,381	ROE, ROBERT A.		43,308 D	36.9%	63.1%	36.9%	63.1%
9	1976	202,344	107,454	HOLLENBECK, HAROLD C.	89,723	HELSTOSKI, HENRY	5,167	17,731 R	53.1%	44.3%	54.5%	45.5%
9	1974	154,362	50,859	PARETI, HAROLD A.	99,592	HELSTOSKI, HENRY	3,911	48,733 D	32.9%	64.5%	33.8%	66.2%
9	1972	214,290	94,747	SCHIAFFO, ALFRED D.	119,543	HELSTOSKI, HENRY		24,796 D	44.2%	55.8%	44.2%	55.8%
10	1976	106,775	17,129	GRANDISON, TONY	88,245	RODINO, PETER W.	1,401	71,116 D	16.0%	82.6%	16.3%	83.7%
10	1974	65,538	9,936	TALIAFERRO, JOHN R.	53,094	RODINO, PETER W.	2,508	43,158 D	15.2%	81.0%	15.8%	84.2%
10	1972	118,257	23,949	MILLER, KENNETH C.	94,308	RODINO, PETER W.		70,359 D	20.3%	79.7%	20.3%	79.7%
11	1976	190,808	59,397	POEKEL, CHARLES A.	129,026	MINISH, JOSEPH G.	2,385	69,629 D	31.1%	67.6%	31.5%	68.5%
11	1974	142,915	42,036	GRANT, WILLIAM B.	98,957	MINISH, JOSEPH G.	1,922	56,921 D	29.4%	69.2%	29.8%	70.2%
11	1972	209,102	82,957	WALDOR, MILTON A.	120,277	MINISH, JOSEPH G.	5,868	37,320 D	39.7%	57.5%	40.8%	59.2%
12	1976	187,282	136,973	RINALDO, MATTHEW J.	49,189	BUGGELLI, RICHARD A.	1,120	87,784 R	73.1%	26.3%	73.6%	26.4%
12	1974	142,843	92,829	RINALDO, MATTHEW J.	46,246	LEVIN, ADAM K.	3,768	46,583 R	65.0%	32.4%	66.7%	33.3%
12	1972	201,179	127,690	RINALDO, MATTHEW J.	72,758	ENGLISH, JERRY F.	731	54,932 R	63.5%	36.2%	63.7%	36.3%
13	1976	209,051	100,050	SCHLUTER, WILLIAM E.	105,291	MEYNER, HELEN S.	3,710	5,241 D	47.9%	50.4%	48.7%	51.3%
13	1974	150,209	64,166	MARAZITI, JOSEPH J.	86,043	MEYNER, HELEN S.		21,877 D	42.7%	57.3%	42.7%	57.3%
13	1972	196,958	109,640	MARAZITI, JOSEPH J.	84,492	MEYNER, HELEN S.	2,826	25,148 R	55.7%	42.9%	56.5%	43.5%
14	1976	146,768	66,319	CAMPENNI, ANTHONY L.	73,174	LEFANTE, JOSEPH A.	7,275	6,855 D	45.2%	49.9%	47.5%	52.5%
14	1974	106,935	17,231	SHERIDAN, CLAIRE J.	85,438	DANIELS, DOMINICK V.	4,266	68,207 D	16.1%	79.9%	16.8%	83.2%
14	1972	168,363	57,683	BOZZONE, RICHARD T.	103,089	DANIELS, DOMINICK V.	7,591	45,406 D	34.3%	61.2%	35.9%	64.1%
15	1976	179,836	54,487	WILEY, CHARLES W.	106,170	PATTEN, EDWARD J.	19,179	51,683 D	30.3%	59.0%	33.9%	66.1%
15	1974	130,367	35,875	HAMMESFAHR, ERNEST J.	92,593	PATTEN, EDWARD J.	1,899	56,718 D	27.5%	71.0%	27.9%	72.1%
15	1972	187,555	89,400	BROOKS, FULLER H.	98,155	PATTEN, EDWARD J.		8,755 D	47.7%	52.3%	47.7%	52.3%

NEW JERSEY

1976 GENERAL ELECTION

President — Other vote was 32,717 McCarthy (Independent); 9,449 MacBride (Libertarian); 7,716 Maddox (American); 3,686 Levin (Socialist Labor); 1,662 Hall (Communist); 1,650 LaRouche (Labor); 1,184 Camejo (Socialist Workers); 1,044 Wright (People's); 554 Bubar (Prohibition); 469 Zeidler (Socialist).

Senator — Other vote was 19,907 Cundari (Libertarian); 9,185 Doganiero (Socialist Labor); 6,650 Johnson (Labor). There is a small discrepancy between the official Republican total vote and the addition of the various county totals.

Congress — Other vote was Swirsky (Libertarian) in CD 3; Doll (Libertarian) in CD 8; in other CD's as follows:

CD 1 — 800 Smith (Libertarian); 784 Sloan (Independent); 327 Bowen (Labor).
CD 4 — 1,431 Mahalchik (Independent); 946 Moyers (Libertarian); 421 Greenspan (Labor).
CD 5 — 1,723 Rehmke (Libertarian); 1,483 Giammarco (Independent); 499 Viola (Independent).
CD 6 — 1,154 Amber (American); 1,016 Brown (Libertarian); 933 Byrne (Independent); 228 Silverstein (Independent).
CD 9 — 1,814 Shaw (Independent); 1,759 Primich (Libertarian); 1,594 Terlizzi (Independent).
CD 10 — 862 McAdam (Libertarian); 330 Stewart (Socialist Workers); 209 Mack (Labor).
CD 11 — 1,749 Kupchik (Libertarian); 636 Rogers (Independent).
CD 12 — 642 Geyer (American); 478 Miskell (Labor).
CD 13 — 2,160 DeMott (Independent); 1,550 Mayer (Independent).
CD 14 — 3,979 McCarthy (Independent); 1,969 Jones (Independent); 452 Bronn (Labor); 446 Ryley (Libertarian); 429 Bergonzi (Independent).
CD 15 — 14,543 Adams (Independent); 3,916 Klein (Independent); 720 Todd (Labor).

1976 PRIMARIES

JUNE 8 REPUBLICAN

Senator — 196,457 David F. Norcross; 45,472 Martin E. Wendelken; 27,672 James E. Parker; 17,892 N. Leonard Smith.

Congress — Unopposed in eleven CD's. Contested as follows:

CD 2 — 32,948 James R. Hurley; 5,255 Robert F. Dufala.
CD 3 — 18,691 Ralph A. Siciliano; 5,504 Joseph L. Heimbold.
CD 7 — 14,603 James J. Sheehan; 11,293 James A. Quaremba; 4,258 Gerald L. Williams.
CD 13 — 19,686 William E. Schluter; 8,558 Jay R. Rosner.

JUNE 8 DEMOCRATIC

Senator — 378,553 Harrison Williams; 66,178 Stephen J. Foley.

Congress — Unopposed in ten CD's. In CD 9 the Democratic primary was declared void due to problems in handling the absentee ballots and a new primary was held on September 21. Robert L. Mauro, the third candidate in the original primary, withdrew from the special primary. The vote in CD 9 below is for the September 21 special primary. Contested as follows:

CD 2 — 23,230 William J. Hughes; 2,723 Solveig I. Henschen.
CD 8 — 15,149 Robert A. Roe; 2,101 Frances Aires.
CD 9 — 20,286 Henry Helstoski; 17,180 Byron M. Baer.
CD 12 — 16,277 Richard A. Buggelli; 8,114 Adrian H. Freund.
CD 13 — 21,784 Helen S. Meyner; 3,605 Edward J. Gaffney; 1,541 Ray Rollinson.

NEW MEXICO

GOVERNOR

Jerry Apodaca (D). Elected 1974 to a four-year term.

SENATORS

Peter V. Domenici (R). Elected 1972 to a six-year term.

Harrison Schmitt (R). Elected 1976 to a six-year term.

REPRESENTATIVES

1. Manuel Lujan, Jr. (R)
2. Harold L. Runnels (D)

POSTWAR VOTE FOR GOVERNOR

Year	Total Vote	Republican Vote	Republican Candidate	Democratic Vote	Democratic Candidate	Other Vote	Rep.-Dem. Plurality	Percentage Total Vote Rep.	Percentage Total Vote Dem.	Percentage Major Vote Rep.	Percentage Major Vote Dem.
1974	328,742	160,430	Skeen, Joseph R.	164,172	Apodaca, Jerry	4,140	3,742 D	48.8%	49.9%	49.4%	50.6%
1970	290,375	134,640	Domenici, Peter V.	148,835	King, Bruce	6,900	14,195 D	46.4%	51.3%	47.5%	52.5%
1968	318,975	160,140	Cargo, David F.	157,230	Chavez, Fabian	1,605	2,910 R	50.2%	49.3%	50.5%	49.5%
1966	260,232	134,625	Cargo, David F.	125,587	Lusk, Thomas E.	20	9,038 R	51.7%	48.3%	51.7%	48.3%
1964	318,042	126,540	Tucker, Merle H.	191,497	Campbell, Jack M.	5	64,957 D	39.8%	60.2%	39.8%	60.2%
1962	247,135	116,184	Mechem, Edwin L.	130,933	Campbell, Jack M.	18	14,749 D	47.0%	53.0%	47.0%	53.0%
1960	305,542	153,765	Mechem, Edwin L.	151,777	Burroughs, John	–	1,988 R	50.3%	49.7%	50.3%	49.7%
1958	205,048	101,567	Mechem, Edwin L.	103,481	Burroughs, John	–	1,914 D	49.5%	50.5%	49.5%	50.5%
1956	251,751	131,488	Mechem, Edwin L.	120,263	Simms, John F.	–	11,225 R	52.2%	47.8%	52.2%	47.8%
1954	193,956	83,373	Stockton, Alvin	110,583	Simms, John F.	–	27,210 D	43.0%	57.0%	43.0%	57.0%
1952	240,150	129,116	Mechem, Edwin L.	111,034	Grantham, Everett	–	18,082 R	53.8%	46.2%	53.8%	46.2%
1950	180,205	96,846	Mechem, Edwin L.	83,359	Miles, John E.	–	13,487 R	53.7%	46.3%	53.7%	46.3%
1948	189,992	86,023	Lujan, Manuel	103,969	Mabry, Thomas J.	–	17,946 D	45.3%	54.7%	45.3%	54.7%
1946	132,930	62,875	Safford, Edward L.	70,055	Mabry, Thomas J.	–	7,180 D	47.3%	52.7%	47.3%	52.7%

The term of office for New Mexico's Governor was increased from two to four years effective with the 1970 election.

POSTWAR VOTE FOR SENATOR

Year	Total Vote	Republican Vote	Republican Candidate	Democratic Vote	Democratic Candidate	Other Vote	Rep.-Dem. Plurality	Percentage Total Vote Rep.	Percentage Total Vote Dem.	Percentage Major Vote Rep.	Percentage Major Vote Dem.
1976	413,141	234,681	Schmitt, Harrison	176,382	Montoya, Joseph M.	2,078	58,299 R	56.8%	42.7%	57.1%	42.9%
1972	378,330	204,253	Domenici, Peter V.	173,815	Daniels, Jack	262	30,438 R	54.0%	45.9%	54.0%	46.0%
1970	289,906	135,004	Carter, Anderson	151,486	Montoya, Joseph M.	3,416	16,482 D	46.6%	52.3%	47.1%	52.9%
1966	258,203	120,988	Carter, Anderson	137,205	Anderson, Clinton P.	10	16,217 D	46.9%	53.1%	46.9%	53.1%
1964	325,774	147,562	Mechem, Edwin L.	178,209	Montoya, Joseph M.	3	30,647 D	45.3%	54.7%	45.3%	54.7%
1960	300,551	109,897	Colwes, William F.	190,654	Anderson, Clinton P.	–	80,757 D	36.6%	63.4%	36.6%	63.4%
1958	203,323	75,827	Atchley, Forrest S.	127,496	Chavez, Dennis	–	51,669 D	37.3%	62.7%	37.3%	62.7%
1954	194,422	83,071	Mechem, Edwin L.	111,351	Anderson, Clinton P.	–	28,280 D	42.7%	57.3%	42.7%	57.3%
1952	239,711	117,168	Hurley, Patrick J.	122,543	Chavez, Dennis	–	5,375 D	48.9%	51.1%	48.9%	51.1%
1948	188,495	80,226	Hurley, Patrick J.	108,269	Anderson, Clinton P.	–	28,043 D	42.6%	57.4%	42.6%	57.4%
1946	133,282	64,632	Hurley, Patrick J.	68,650	Chavez, Dennis	–	4,018 D	48.5%	51.5%	48.5%	51.5%

NEW MEXICO

Districts Established May 15, 1968

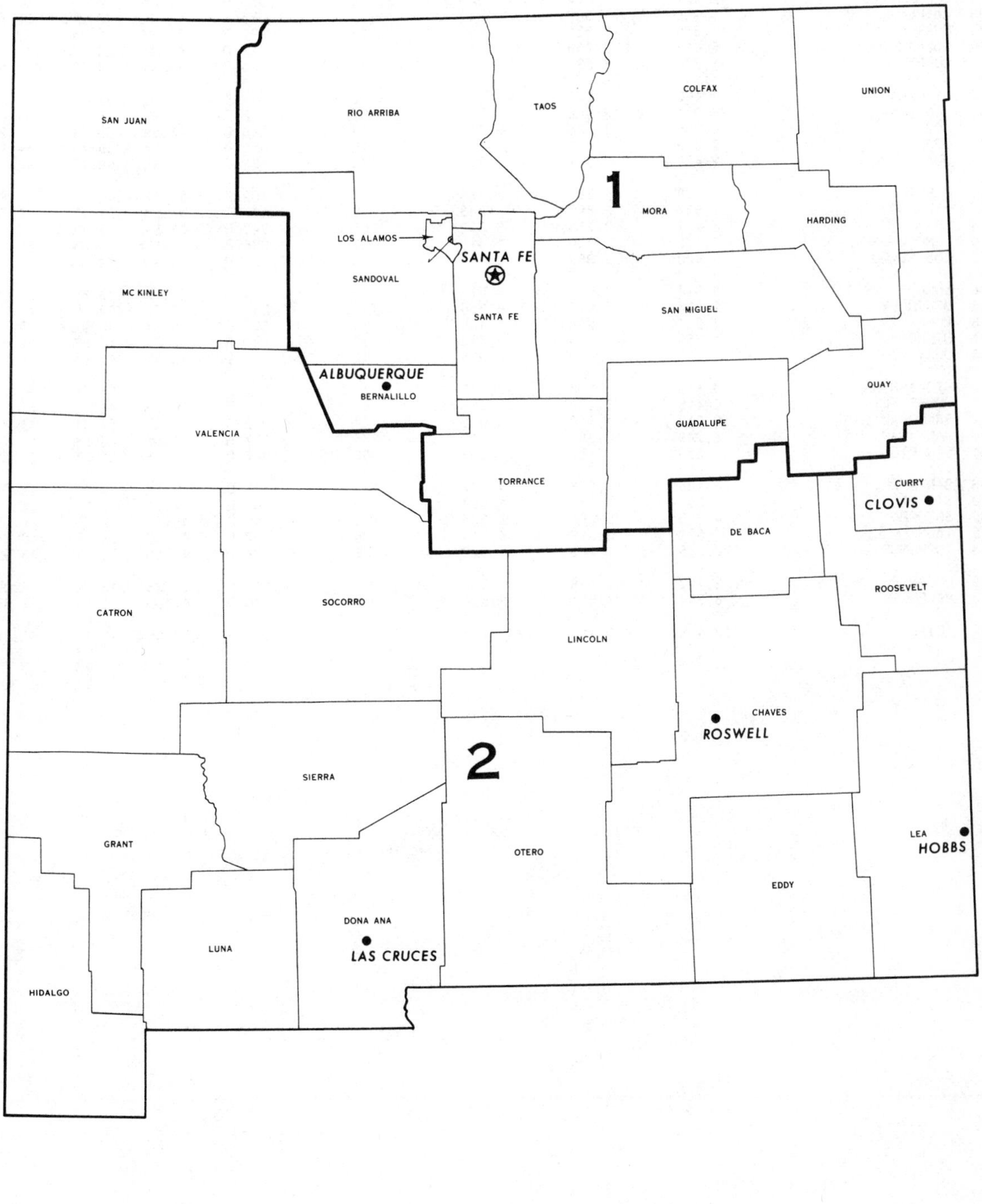

NEW MEXICO

PRESIDENT 1976

1970 Census Population	County	Total Vote	Republican	Democratic	Other	Rep.-Dem. Plurality	Percentage Total Vote Rep.	Percentage Total Vote Dem.	Percentage Major Vote Rep.	Percentage Major Vote Dem.
315,774	BERNALILLO	142,921	76,614	63,949	2,358	12,665 R	53.6%	44.7%	54.5%	45.5%
2,198	CATRON	1,135	602	517	16	85 R	53.0%	45.6%	53.8%	46.2%
43,335	CHAVES	17,985	10,631	7,139	215	3,492 R	59.1%	39.7%	59.8%	40.2%
12,170	COLFAX	5,018	2,259	2,718	41	459 D	45.0%	54.2%	45.4%	54.6%
39,517	CURRY	11,374	6,232	5,004	138	1,228 R	54.8%	44.0%	55.5%	44.5%
2,547	DE BACA	1,160	556	597	7	41 D	47.9%	51.5%	48.2%	51.8%
69,773	DONA ANA	26,261	13,888	12,036	337	1,852 R	52.9%	45.8%	53.6%	46.4%
41,119	EDDY	16,905	7,698	9,073	134	1,375 D	45.5%	53.7%	45.9%	54.1%
22,030	GRANT	9,349	4,095	5,176	78	1,081 D	43.8%	55.4%	44.2%	55.8%
4,969	GUADALUPE	2,456	1,047	1,379	30	332 D	42.6%	56.1%	43.2%	56.8%
1,348	HARDING	678	387	285	6	102 R	57.1%	42.0%	57.6%	42.4%
4,734	HIDALGO	1,837	891	938	8	47 D	48.5%	51.1%	48.7%	51.3%
49,554	LEA	15,457	8,773	6,533	151	2,240 R	56.8%	42.3%	57.3%	42.7%
7,560	LINCOLN	3,772	2,320	1,415	37	905 R	61.5%	37.5%	62.1%	37.9%
15,198	LOS ALAMOS	8,429	5,383	2,890	156	2,493 R	63.9%	34.3%	65.1%	34.9%
11,706	LUNA	5,914	2,966	2,872	76	94 R	50.2%	48.6%	50.8%	49.2%
43,208	MCKINLEY	11,624	4,617	6,856	151	2,239 D	39.7%	59.0%	40.2%	59.8%
4,673	MORA	2,361	904	1,438	19	534 D	38.3%	60.9%	38.6%	61.4%
41,097	OTERO	11,380	5,914	5,333	133	581 R	52.0%	46.9%	52.6%	47.4%
10,903	QUAY	4,197	2,059	2,095	43	36 D	49.1%	49.9%	49.6%	50.4%
25,170	RIO ARRIBA	10,455	3,213	7,125	117	3,912 D	30.7%	68.1%	31.1%	68.9%
16,479	ROOSEVELT	6,445	3,269	3,111	65	158 R	50.7%	48.3%	51.2%	48.8%
17,492	SANDOVAL	9,319	4,110	5,072	137	962 D	44.1%	54.4%	44.8%	55.2%
52,517	SAN JUAN	19,742	10,852	8,615	275	2,237 R	55.0%	43.6%	55.7%	44.3%
21,951	SAN MIGUEL	8,523	3,162	5,204	157	2,042 D	37.1%	61.1%	37.8%	62.2%
53,756	SANTA FE	26,165	11,576	14,127	462	2,551 D	44.2%	54.0%	45.0%	55.0%
7,189	SIERRA	3,264	1,665	1,564	35	101 R	51.0%	47.9%	51.6%	48.4%
9,763	SOCORRO	4,980	2,265	2,606	109	341 D	45.5%	52.3%	46.5%	53.5%
17,516	TAOS	7,532	3,012	4,414	106	1,402 D	40.0%	58.6%	40.6%	59.4%
5,290	TORRANCE	3,015	1,462	1,526	27	64 D	48.5%	50.6%	48.9%	51.1%
4,925	UNION	2,152	1,146	975	31	171 R	53.3%	45.3%	54.0%	46.0%
40,539	VALENCIA	16,604	7,851	8,566	187	715 D	47.3%	51.6%	47.8%	52.2%
1,016,000	TOTAL	418,409	211,419	201,148	5,842	10,271 R	50.5%	48.1%	51.2%	48.8%

NEW MEXICO

SENATOR 1976

1970 Census Population	County	Total Vote	Republican	Democratic	Other	Rep.-Dem. Plurality	Percentage Total Vote Rep.	Percentage Total Vote Dem.	Percentage Major Vote Rep.	Percentage Major Vote Dem.
315,774	BERNALILLO	141,786	88,976	51,876	934	37,100 R	62.8%	36.6%	63.2%	36.8%
2,198	CATRON	1,119	664	449	6	215 R	59.3%	40.1%	59.7%	40.3%
43,335	CHAVES	17,799	12,269	5,502	28	6,767 R	68.9%	30.9%	69.0%	31.0%
12,170	COLFAX	4,948	2,740	2,201	7	539 R	55.4%	44.5%	55.5%	44.5%
39,517	CURRY	10,708	6,402	4,285	21	2,117 R	59.8%	40.0%	59.9%	40.1%
2,547	DE BACA	1,111	620	489	2	131 R	55.8%	44.0%	55.9%	44.1%
69,773	DONA ANA	25,927	14,885	10,960	82	3,925 R	57.4%	42.3%	57.6%	42.4%
41,119	EDDY	16,797	9,178	7,589	30	1,589 R	54.6%	45.2%	54.7%	45.3%
22,030	GRANT	9,410	5,159	4,225	26	934 R	54.8%	44.9%	55.0%	45.0%
4,969	GUADALUPE	2,431	799	1,626	6	827 D	32.9%	66.9%	32.9%	67.1%
1,348	HARDING	678	406	271	1	135 R	59.9%	40.0%	60.0%	40.0%
4,734	HIDALGO	1,814	1,001	808	5	193 R	55.2%	44.5%	55.3%	44.7%
49,554	LEA	15,087	8,719	6,336	32	2,383 R	57.8%	42.0%	57.9%	42.1%
7,560	LINCOLN	3,720	2,450	1,258	12	1,192 R	65.9%	33.8%	66.1%	33.9%
15,198	LOS ALAMOS	8,385	4,406	3,959	20	447 R	52.5%	47.2%	52.7%	47.3%
11,706	LUNA	5,838	3,295	2,526	17	769 R	56.4%	43.3%	56.6%	43.4%
43,208	MCKINLEY	11,269	4,794	6,434	41	1,640 D	42.5%	57.1%	42.7%	57.3%
4,673	MORA	2,330	845	1,482	3	637 D	36.3%	63.6%	36.3%	63.7%
41,097	OTERO	11,269	6,436	4,774	59	1,662 R	57.1%	42.4%	57.4%	42.6%
10,903	QUAY	4,112	2,376	1,732	4	644 R	57.8%	42.1%	57.8%	42.2%
25,170	RIO ARRIBA	10,335	3,233	6,946	156	3,713 D	31.3%	67.2%	31.8%	68.2%
16,479	ROOSEVELT	6,310	4,157	2,138	15	2,019 R	65.9%	33.9%	66.0%	34.0%
17,492	SANDOVAL	9,248	4,378	4,820	50	442 D	47.3%	52.1%	47.6%	52.4%
52,517	SAN JUAN	19,500	12,391	7,030	79	5,361 R	63.5%	36.1%	63.8%	36.2%
21,951	SAN MIGUEL	8,256	3,091	5,108	57	2,017 D	37.4%	61.9%	37.7%	62.3%
53,756	SANTA FE	25,893	12,490	13,193	210	703 D	48.2%	51.0%	48.6%	51.4%
7,189	SIERRA	3,219	1,887	1,322	10	565 R	58.6%	41.1%	58.8%	41.2%
9,763	SOCORRO	4,944	2,415	2,495	34	80 D	48.8%	50.5%	49.2%	50.8%
17,516	TAOS	7,436	2,899	4,472	65	1,573 D	39.0%	60.1%	39.3%	60.7%
5,290	TORRANCE	2,977	1,674	1,291	12	383 R	56.2%	43.4%	56.5%	43.5%
4,925	UNION	2,088	1,322	757	9	565 R	63.3%	36.3%	63.6%	36.4%
40,539	VALENCIA	16,397	8,324	8,028	45	296 R	50.8%	49.0%	50.9%	49.1%
1,016,000	TOTAL	413,141	234,681	176,382	2,078	58,299 R	56.8%	42.7%	57.1%	42.9%

NEW MEXICO

CONGRESS

			Republican		Democratic				Percentage			
		Total					Other	Rep.-Dem.	Total Vote		Major Vote	
CD	Year	Vote	Vote	Candidate	Vote	Candidate	Vote	Plurality	Rep.	Dem.	Rep.	Dem.
1	1976	225,592	162,587	LUJAN, MANUEL, JR.	61,800	GARCIA, RAYMOND	1,205	100,787 R	72.1%	27.4%	72.5%	27.5%
1	1974	181,334	106,268	LUJAN, MANUEL, JR.	71,968	MONDRAGON, ROBERT A.	3,098	34,300 R	58.6%	39.7%	59.6%	40.4%
1	1972	212,672	118,403	LUJAN, MANUEL, JR.	94,239	GALLEGOS, EUGENE	30	24,164 R	55.7%	44.3%	55.7%	44.3%
1	1970	158,368	91,187	LUJAN, MANUEL, JR.	64,598	CHAVEZ, FABIAN	2,583	26,589 R	57.6%	40.8%	58.5%	41.5%
1	1968	167,488	88,517	LUJAN, MANUEL, JR.	78,117	MORRIS, THOMAS G.	854	10,400 R	52.8%	46.6%	53.1%	46.9%
2	1976	175,713	52,131	TRUBEY, DONALD W.	123,563	RUNNELS, HAROLD L.	19	71,432 D	29.7%	70.3%	29.7%	70.3%
2	1974	135,038	43,045	TRUBEY, DONALD W.	90,127	RUNNELS, HAROLD L.	1,866	47,082 D	31.9%	66.7%	32.3%	67.7%
2	1972	160,981	44,784	PRESSON, GEORGE E.	116,152	RUNNELS, HAROLD L.	45	71,368 D	27.8%	72.2%	27.8%	72.2%
2	1970	126,990	61,074	FOREMAN, ED	64,518	RUNNELS, HAROLD L.	1,398	3,444 D	48.1%	50.8%	48.6%	51.4%
2	1968	142,364	71,857	FOREMAN, ED	69,858	WALKER, E. S. JOHNNY	649	1,999 R	50.5%	49.1%	50.7%	49.3%

NEW MEXICO

1976 GENERAL ELECTION

President — Other vote was 2,462 Camejo (Socialist Workers); 1,161 McCarthy (write-in); 1,110 MacBride (Libertarian); 240 Zeidler (Socialist); 211 Bubar (Prohibition); 106 Anderson (write-in); 31 Maddox (write-in); 19 Hall (write-in); 1 LaRouche (write-in); 501 scattered.

Senator — Other vote was 1,087 Borunda (Raza Unida); 906 Dillon (American Independent); 85 scattered.

Congress — Other vote was 1,159 Aragon (Raza Unida) and 46 scattered in CD 1; scattered in CD 2.

1976 PRIMARIES

JUNE 1 REPUBLICAN

Senator — 34,074 Harrison Schmitt; 10,965 Eugene W. Peirce; 2,481 Arthur A. Lavine.

Congress — Unopposed in both CD's.

JUNE 1 DEMOCRATIC

Senator — 96,063 Joseph M. Montoya; 48,824 Robert R. Sims; 11 scattered.

Congress — Unopposed in CD 2. Contested as follows:

CD 1 — 42,188 Raymond Garcia; 19,882 Quinn D. Mizer.

NEW YORK

GOVERNOR

Hugh L. Carey (D). Elected 1974 to a four-year term.

SENATORS

Jacob K. Javits (R). Re-elected 1974 to a six-year term. Previously elected 1968, 1962, 1956.

Daniel P. Moynihan (D). Elected 1976 to a six-year term.

REPRESENTATIVES

1. Otis G. Pike (D)
2. Thomas J. Downey (D)
3. Jerome A. Ambro (D)
4. Norman F. Lent (R)
5. John W. Wydler (R)
6. Lester L. Wolff (D)
7. Joseph P. Addabbo (D)
8. Benjamin Rosenthal (D)
9. James J. Delaney (D)
10. Mario Biaggi (D)
11. James H. Scheuer (D)
12. Shirley Chisholm (D)
13. Stephen J. Solarz (D)
14. Frederick W. Richmond (D)
15. Leo C. Zeferetti (D)
16. Elizabeth Holtzman (D)
17. John M. Murphy (D)
18. Edward I. Koch (D)
19. Charles B. Rangel (D)
20. Theodore S. Weiss (D)
21. Herman Badillo (D)
22. Jonathan Bingham (D)
23. Bruce F. Caputo (R)
24. Richard L. Ottinger (D)
25. Hamilton Fish (R)
26. Benjamin A. Gilman (R)
27. Matthew F. McHugh (D)
28. Samuel S. Stratton (D)
29. Edward W. Pattison (D)
30. Robert C. McEwen (R)
31. Donald J. Mitchell (R)
32. James M. Hanley (D)
33. William F. Walsh (R)
34. Frank J. Horton (R)
35. Barber B. Conable (R)
36. John J. LaFalce (D)
37. Henry J. Nowak (D)
38. Jack F. Kemp (R)
39. Stanley N. Lundine (D)

POSTWAR VOTE FOR GOVERNOR

								Percentage			
	Total	Republican		Democratic		Other	Rep.-Dem.	Total Vote		Major Vote	
Year	Vote	Vote	Candidate	Vote	Candidate	Vote	Plurality	Rep.	Dem.	Rep.	Dem.
1974	5,293,176	2,219,667	Wilson, Malcolm	3,028,503	Carey, Hugh L.	45,006	808,836 D	41.9%	57.2%	42.3%	57.7%
1970	6,013,064	3,151,432	Rockefeller, Nelson A.	2,421,426	Goldberg, Arthur	440,206	730,006 R	52.4%	40.3%	56.5%	43.5%
1966	6,031,585	2,690,626	Rockefeller, Nelson A.	2,298,363	O'Connor, Frank D.	1,042,596	392,263 R	44.6%	38.1%	53.9%	46.1%
1962	5,805,631	3,081,587	Rockefeller, Nelson A.	2,552,418	Morgenthau, Robert M.	171,626	529,169 R	53.1%	44.0%	54.7%	45.3%
1958	5,712,665	3,126,929	Rockefeller, Nelson A.	2,553,895	Harriman, Averell	31,841	573,034 R	54.7%	44.7%	55.0%	45.0%
1954	5,161,942	2,549,613	Ives, Irving M.	2,560,738	Harriman, Averell	51,591	11,125 D	49.4%	49.6%	49.9%	50.1%
1950	5,308,889	2,819,523	Dewey, Thomas E.	2,246,855	Lynch, Walter A.	242,511	572,668 R	53.1%	42.3%	55.7%	44.3%
1946	4,964,552	2,825,633	Dewey, Thomas E.	2,138,482	Mead, James M.	437	687,151 R	56.9%	43.1%	56.9%	43.1%

POSTWAR VOTE FOR SENATOR

								Percentage			
	Total	Republican		Democratic		Other	Rep.-Dem.	Total Vote		Major Vote	
Year	Vote	Vote	Candidate	Vote	Candidate	Vote	Plurality	Rep.	Dem.	Rep.	Dem.
1976	6,319,755	2,836,633	Buckley, James L.	3,422,594	Moynihan, Daniel P.	60,528	585,961 D	44.9%	54.2%	45.3%	54.7%
1974	5,163,600	2,340,188	Javits, Jacob K.	1,973,781	Clark, Ramsey	849,631	366,407 R	45.3%	38.2%	54.2%	45.8%
1970	5,904,782	1,434,472	Goodell, Charles	2,171,232	Ottinger, Richard L.	2,299,078	736,760 D	24.3%	36.8%	39.8%	60.2%
1968	6,581,587	3,269,772	Javits, Jacob K.	2,150,695	O'Dwyer, Paul	1,161,120	1,119,077 R	49.7%	32.7%	60.3%	39.7%
1964	7,151,686	3,104,056	Keating, Kenneth B.	3,823,749	Kennedy, Robert F.	223,881	719,693 D	43.4%	53.5%	44.8%	55.2%
1962	5,700,186	3,269,417	Javits, Jacob K.	2,289,341	Donovan, James B.	141,428	980,076 R	57.4%	40.2%	58.8%	41.2%
1958	5,602,088	2,842,942	Keating, Kenneth B.	2,709,950	Hogan, Frank S.	49,196	132,992 R	50.7%	48.4%	51.2%	48.8%
1956	6,991,136	3,723,933	Javits, Jacob K.	3,265,159	Wagner, Robert F.	2,044	458,774 R	53.3%	46.7%	53.3%	46.7%
1952	6,980,259	3,853,934	Ives, Irving M.	2,521,736	Cashmore, John	604,589	1,332,198 R	55.2%	36.1%	60.4%	39.6%
1950	5,228,403	2,367,353	Hanley, Joe R.	2,632,313	Lehman, Herbert H.	228,737	264,960 D	45.3%	50.3%	47.4%	52.6%
1949s	4,966,878	2,384,381	Dulles, John Foster	2,582,438	Lehman, Herbert H.	59	198,057 D	48.0%	52.0%	48.0%	52.0%
1946	4,867,564	2,559,365	Ives, Irving M.	2,308,112	Lehman, Herbert H.	87	251,253 R	52.6%	47.4%	52.6%	47.4%

The 1949 election was for a short term to fill a vacancy. In 1970 James L. Buckley, the Conservative candidate, polled 2,288,190 votes (38.8% of the total vote) and won the election with a 116,958 plurality.

NEW YORK

Districts Established March 28, 1972

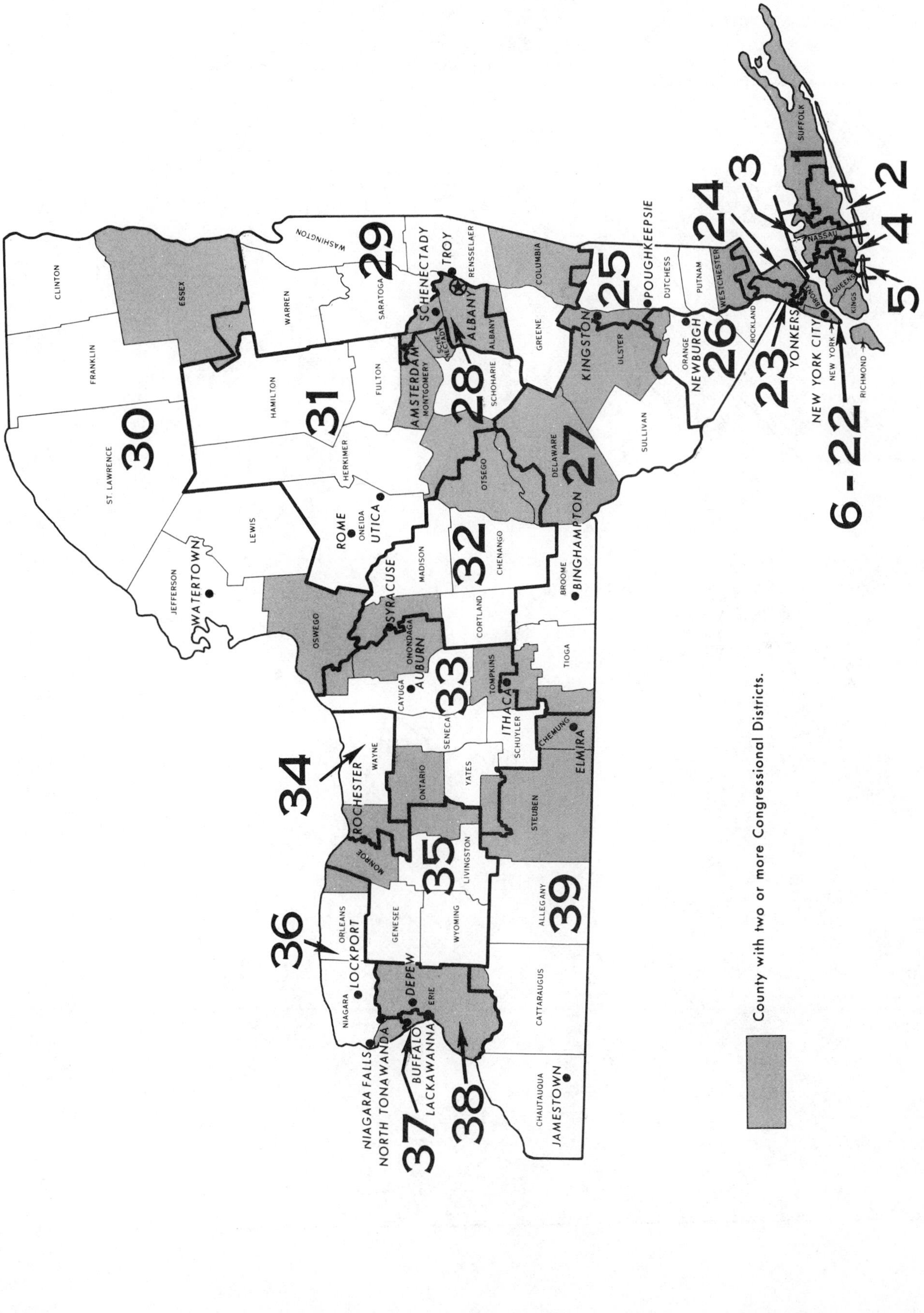

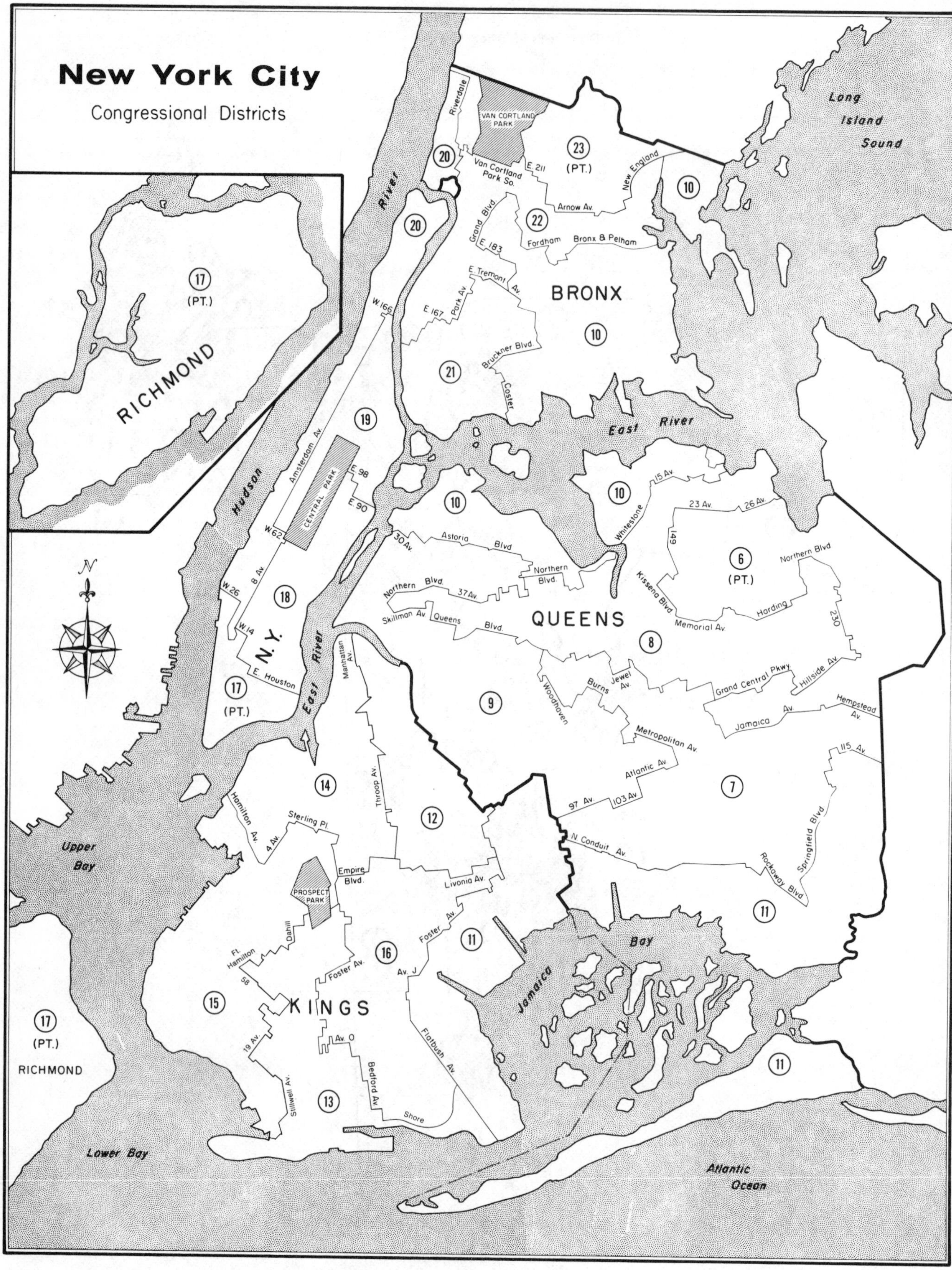
New York City
Congressional Districts
RICHMOND
17
(PT.)
Hudson
River
Riverdale
VAN CORTLAND PARK
Van Cortland Park So.
E. 211
23
(PT.)
Arnow Av.
New England
Long Island Sound
20
22
Grand Blvd.
E. 183
Fordham
Bronx & Pelham
E. Tremont Av.
Park Av.
E. 167
W. 166
BRONX
10
21
Bruckner Blvd.
Coster
19
East River
Amsterdam Av.
CENTRAL PARK
E. 98
E. 90
W. 62
15 Av.
Whitestone
23 Av.
26 Av.
149
6
(PT.)
Northern Blvd.
30 Av.
Astoria Blvd
Northern Blvd.
37 Av.
Kissena Blvd
Harding
Memorial Av.
230
QUEENS
8
Skillman Av
Queens Blvd.
8 Av.
W. 26
W. 14
18
N.Y.
E. Houston
Manhattan Av.
Woodhaven
Burns
Jewel Av.
Grand Central Pkwy.
Hillside Av.
Hempstead Av.
Jamaica Av.
9
Metropolitan Av.
Atlantic Av.
115 Av.
7
14
Throop Av.
12
97 Av.
103 Av.
Hamilton Av.
4 Av.
Sterling Pl
Upper Bay
N. Conduit Av.
Springfield Blvd.
Rockaway Blvd.
Empire Blvd.
Livonia Av.
PROSPECT PARK
11
Dahill
Ft. Hamilton
58
Foster Av.
16
Av. J
Bay
Jamaica
KINGS
15
19 Av.
Av. O
Bedford Av.
Flatbush Av.
Stillwell Av.
13
Shore
RICHMOND
Lower Bay
Atlantic Ocean

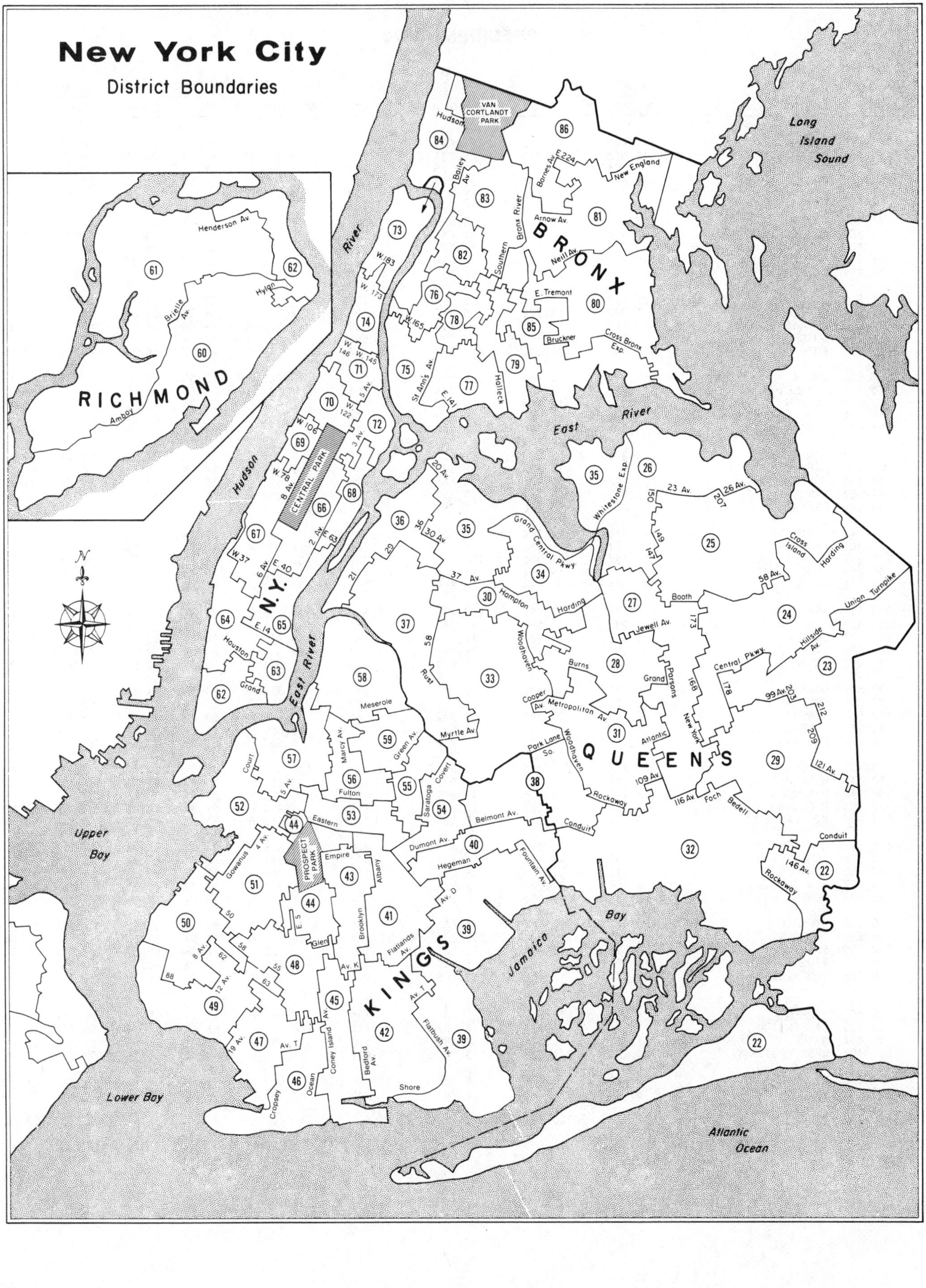
New York City
District Boundaries
RICHMOND
BRONX
N.Y.
QUEENS
KINGS
Long Island Sound
Hudson River
East River
Upper Bay
Lower Bay
Jamaica Bay
Atlantic Ocean
VAN CORTLANDT PARK
CENTRAL PARK
PROSPECT PARK
Henderson Av.
Hylan
Brielle Av.
Amboy
Hudson
Bailey Av
Southern
Bronx River
Barnes Av.
E. 224
New England
Arnow Av.
Neill Av.
E. Tremont
Bruckner
Cross Bronx Exp.
Halleck
St Ann's Av.
E. 141
W. 183
W. 173
W. 165
W. 146
W. 145
5 Av.
W. 122
W. 106
3 Av.
W. 78
8 Av.
2 Av.
E. 63
W. 37
6 Av.
E. 40
E. 14
Houston
Grand
20 Av.
36
30 Av.
29
21
37 Av.
Whitestone Exp.
23 Av.
26 Av.
150
207
149
147
Grand Central Pkwy
Hampton
Harding
Booth
58 Av.
Cross Island
Union Turnpike
Jewell Av.
173
58
Rust
Woodhaven
Burns
Grand
Parsons
168
Central Pkwy.
Hillside Av.
178
99 Av.
203
212
209
121 Av.
Cooper Av.
Metropolitan Av.
Myrtle Av.
Park Lane So.
Atlantic
New York
109 Av.
116 Av.
Foch
Bedell
Rockaway
Conduit
146 Av.
Meserole
Marcy Av.
Green Av.
Court
5 Av.
Fulton
Saratoga
Covert
Eastern
Belmont Av.
Dumont Av.
Hegeman
Fountain Av.
Empire
Albany
4 Av.
Gowanus
E. 5
Brooklyn
Av. D
Glen
Flatlands Av.
50
58
8 Av.
62
55
63
88
12 Av.
Av. K
19 Av.
Av. T
Coney Island Av.
Bedford Av.
Flatbush Av.
Ocean
Cropsey
Shore
22
23
24
25
26
27
28
29
30
31
32
33
34
35
36
37
38
39
40
41
42
43
44
45
46
47
48
49
50
51
52
53
54
55
56
57
58
59
60
61
62
63
64
65
66
67
68
69
70
71
72
73
74
75
76
77
78
79
80
81
82
83
84
85
86

NEW YORK

PRESIDENT 1976

1970 Census Population	County	Total Vote	Republican	Democratic	Other	Rep.-Dem. Plurality	Percentage Total Vote Rep.	Total Vote Dem.	Major Vote Rep.	Major Vote Dem.
285,618	ALBANY	142,409	69,592	71,616	1,201	2,024 D	48.9%	50.3%	49.3%	50.7%
46,458	ALLEGANY	18,010	11,769	6,134	107	5,635 R	65.3%	34.1%	65.7%	34.3%
1,472,216	BRONX	337,391	96,842	238,786	1,763	141,944 D	28.7%	70.8%	28.9%	71.1%
221,815	BROOME	90,658	50,340	39,827	491	10,513 R	55.5%	43.9%	55.8%	44.2%
81,666	CATTARAUGUS	33,422	19,469	13,768	185	5,701 R	58.3%	41.2%	58.6%	41.4%
77,439	CAYUGA	33,343	19,775	13,348	220	6,427 R	59.3%	40.0%	59.7%	40.3%
147,305	CHAUTAUQUA	61,436	33,730	27,447	259	6,283 R	54.9%	44.7%	55.1%	44.9%
101,537	CHEMUNG	38,026	20,640	17,207	179	3,433 R	54.3%	45.3%	54.5%	45.5%
46,368	CHENANGO	19,837	12,384	7,356	97	5,028 R	62.4%	37.1%	62.7%	37.3%
72,934	CLINTON	27,103	15,433	11,555	115	3,878 R	56.9%	42.6%	57.2%	42.8%
51,519	COLUMBIA	26,574	15,871	10,514	189	5,357 R	59.7%	39.6%	60.2%	39.8%
45,894	CORTLAND	18,300	11,222	6,947	131	4,275 R	61.3%	38.0%	61.8%	38.2%
44,718	DELAWARE	19,827	12,443	7,254	130	5,189 R	62.8%	36.6%	63.2%	36.8%
222,295	DUTCHESS	89,505	51,312	37,531	662	13,781 R	57.3%	41.9%	57.8%	42.2%
1,113,491	ERIE	452,843	220,310	229,397	3,136	9,087 D	48.7%	50.7%	49.0%	51.0%
34,631	ESSEX	16,824	10,194	6,556	74	3,638 R	60.6%	39.0%	60.9%	39.1%
43,931	FRANKLIN	16,152	8,846	7,248	58	1,598 R	54.8%	44.9%	55.0%	45.0%
52,637	FULTON	21,629	12,161	9,323	145	2,838 R	56.2%	43.1%	56.6%	43.4%
58,722	GENESEE	25,536	14,567	10,803	166	3,764 R	57.0%	42.3%	57.4%	42.6%
33,136	GREENE	19,264	11,370	7,740	154	3,630 R	59.0%	40.2%	59.5%	40.5%
4,714	HAMILTON	3,370	2,306	1,052	12	1,254 R	68.4%	31.2%	68.7%	31.3%
67,440	HERKIMER	28,377	15,362	12,875	140	2,487 R	54.1%	45.4%	54.4%	45.6%
88,508	JEFFERSON	34,028	20,401	13,503	124	6,898 R	60.0%	39.7%	60.2%	39.8%
2,601,852	KINGS	613,643	190,728	419,382	3,533	228,654 D	31.1%	68.3%	31.3%	68.7%
23,644	LEWIS	9,633	5,840	3,764	29	2,076 R	60.6%	39.1%	60.8%	39.2%
54,041	LIVINGSTON	23,819	14,044	9,629	146	4,415 R	59.0%	40.4%	59.3%	40.7%
62,864	MADISON	24,591	15,674	8,822	95	6,852 R	63.7%	35.9%	64.0%	36.0%
711,917	MONROE	303,434	167,303	134,739	1,392	32,564 R	55.1%	44.4%	55.4%	44.6%
55,883	MONTGOMERY	24,730	13,281	11,271	178	2,010 R	53.7%	45.6%	54.1%	45.9%
1,422,905	NASSAU	637,438	329,176	302,869	5,393	26,307 R	51.6%	47.5%	52.1%	47.9%
1,524,541	NEW YORK	460,838	117,702	337,438	5,698	219,736 D	25.5%	73.2%	25.9%	74.1%
235,720	NIAGARA	90,239	46,101	43,667	471	2,434 R	51.1%	48.4%	51.4%	48.6%
273,037	ONEIDA	105,988	57,655	47,779	554	9,876 R	54.4%	45.1%	54.7%	45.3%
472,185	ONONDAGA	192,578	115,474	76,097	1,007	39,377 R	60.0%	39.5%	60.3%	39.7%
78,849	ONTARIO	35,441	21,118	14,044	279	7,074 R	59.6%	39.6%	60.1%	39.9%
220,558	ORANGE	90,677	49,685	40,362	630	9,323 R	54.8%	44.5%	55.2%	44.8%
37,305	ORLEANS	15,023	8,994	5,927	102	3,067 R	59.9%	39.5%	60.3%	39.7%
100,897	OSWEGO	40,463	23,949	16,332	182	7,617 R	59.2%	40.4%	59.5%	40.5%
56,181	OTSEGO	24,754	14,796	9,787	171	5,009 R	59.8%	39.5%	60.2%	39.8%
56,696	PUTNAM	30,711	18,523	11,963	225	6,560 R	60.3%	39.0%	60.8%	39.2%
1,973,708	QUEENS	627,352	244,396	379,907	3,049	135,511 D	39.0%	60.6%	39.1%	60.9%
152,510	RENSSELAER	69,653	40,229	28,979	445	11,250 R	57.8%	41.6%	58.1%	41.9%
295,443	RICHMOND	105,477	56,995	47,867	615	9,128 R	54.0%	45.4%	54.4%	45.6%
229,903	ROCKLAND	101,489	52,087	48,673	729	3,414 R	51.3%	48.0%	51.7%	48.3%
111,991	ST. LAWRENCE	39,934	22,249	17,503	182	4,746 R	55.7%	43.8%	56.0%	44.0%
121,679	SARATOGA	62,486	38,296	23,768	422	14,528 R	61.3%	38.0%	61.7%	38.3%
160,979	SCHENECTADY	73,450	40,789	31,838	823	8,951 R	55.5%	43.3%	56.2%	43.8%
24,750	SCHOHARIE	12,515	7,154	5,250	111	1,904 R	57.2%	41.9%	57.7%	42.3%
16,737	SCHUYLER	7,189	4,267	2,885	37	1,382 R	59.4%	40.1%	59.7%	40.3%
35,083	SENECA	13,508	7,659	5,745	104	1,914 R	56.7%	42.5%	57.1%	42.9%
99,546	STEUBEN	38,015	23,164	14,685	166	8,479 R	60.9%	38.6%	61.2%	38.8%
1,116,672	SUFFOLK	460,048	248,908	208,263	2,877	40,645 R	54.1%	45.3%	54.4%	45.6%
52,580	SULLIVAN	28,096	13,709	14,189	198	480 D	48.8%	50.5%	49.1%	50.9%
46,513	TIOGA	18,893	11,824	6,969	100	4,855 R	62.6%	36.9%	62.9%	37.1%
76,879	TOMPKINS	28,671	15,463	12,808	400	2,655 R	53.9%	44.7%	54.7%	45.3%
141,241	ULSTER	66,155	35,353	30,190	612	5,163 R	53.4%	45.6%	53.9%	46.1%
49,402	WARREN	21,912	14,548	7,264	100	7,284 R	66.4%	33.2%	66.7%	33.3%
52,725	WASHINGTON	21,324	13,946	7,262	116	6,684 R	65.4%	34.1%	65.8%	34.2%
79,404	WAYNE	31,562	19,324	12,061	177	7,263 R	61.2%	38.2%	61.6%	38.4%
891,409	WESTCHESTER	384,296	208,527	173,153	2,616	35,374 R	54.3%	45.1%	54.6%	45.4%
37,688	WYOMING	15,539	9,726	5,737	76	3,989 R	62.6%	36.9%	62.9%	37.1%
19,831	YATES	8,742	5,796	2,903	43	2,893 R	66.3%	33.2%	66.6%	33.4%
18,190,740	TOTAL	6,534,170	3,100,791	3,389,558	43,821	288,767 D	47.5%	51.9%	47.8%	52.2%

NEW YORK

SENATOR 1976

1970 Census Population	County	Total Vote	Republican	Democratic	Other	Rep.-Dem. Plurality	Percentage Total Vote Rep.	Percentage Total Vote Dem.	Percentage Major Vote Rep.	Percentage Major Vote Dem.
285,618	ALBANY	140,883	58,984	80,852	1,047	21,868 D	41.9%	57.4%	42.2%	57.8%
46,458	ALLEGANY	17,469	11,217	6,182	70	5,035 R	64.2%	35.4%	64.5%	35.5%
1,472,216	BRONX	317,203	86,554	227,044	3,605	140,490 D	27.3%	71.6%	27.6%	72.4%
221,815	BROOME	87,112	47,444	39,120	548	8,324 R	54.5%	44.9%	54.8%	45.2%
81,666	CATTARAUGUS	31,953	18,075	13,686	192	4,389 R	56.6%	42.8%	56.9%	43.1%
77,439	CAYUGA	32,621	20,384	12,055	182	8,329 R	62.5%	37.0%	62.8%	37.2%
147,305	CHAUTAUQUA	59,517	30,767	28,485	265	2,282 R	51.7%	47.9%	51.9%	48.1%
101,537	CHEMUNG	36,755	21,505	15,094	156	6,411 R	58.5%	41.1%	58.8%	41.2%
46,368	CHENANGO	19,445	13,257	6,103	85	7,154 R	68.2%	31.4%	68.5%	31.5%
72,934	CLINTON	25,982	14,743	11,045	194	3,698 R	56.7%	42.5%	57.2%	42.8%
51,519	COLUMBIA	25,755	15,305	10,272	178	5,033 R	59.4%	39.9%	59.8%	40.2%
45,894	CORTLAND	17,731	11,644	5,975	112	5,669 R	65.7%	33.7%	66.1%	33.9%
44,718	DELAWARE	19,175	11,971	7,072	132	4,899 R	62.4%	36.9%	62.9%	37.1%
222,295	DUTCHESS	87,701	51,226	35,760	715	15,466 R	58.4%	40.8%	58.9%	41.1%
1,113,491	ERIE	428,757	195,045	230,714	2,998	35,669 D	45.5%	53.8%	45.8%	54.2%
34,631	ESSEX	16,037	9,873	6,062	102	3,811 R	61.6%	37.8%	62.0%	38.0%
43,931	FRANKLIN	15,337	9,101	6,165	71	2,936 R	59.3%	40.2%	59.6%	40.4%
52,637	FULTON	20,831	11,880	8,803	148	3,077 R	57.0%	42.3%	57.4%	42.6%
58,722	GENESEE	24,786	14,365	10,312	109	4,053 R	58.0%	41.6%	58.2%	41.8%
33,136	GREENE	19,140	11,442	7,538	160	3,904 R	59.8%	39.4%	60.3%	39.7%
4,714	HAMILTON	3,182	2,263	901	18	1,362 R	71.1%	28.3%	71.5%	28.5%
67,440	HERKIMER	27,111	15,980	10,969	162	5,011 R	58.9%	40.5%	59.3%	40.7%
88,508	JEFFERSON	32,253	19,643	12,435	175	7,208 R	60.9%	38.6%	61.2%	38.8%
2,601,852	KINGS	587,023	158,271	421,661	7,091	263,390 D	27.0%	71.8%	27.3%	72.7%
23,644	LEWIS	9,322	6,307	2,975	40	3,332 R	67.7%	31.9%	67.9%	32.1%
54,041	LIVINGSTON	23,257	13,589	9,534	134	4,055 R	58.4%	41.0%	58.8%	41.2%
62,864	MADISON	23,812	16,074	7,590	148	8,484 R	67.5%	31.9%	67.9%	32.1%
711,917	MONROE	295,905	142,379	151,423	2,103	9,044 D	48.1%	51.2%	48.5%	51.5%
55,883	MONTGOMERY	23,799	12,634	11,002	163	1,632 R	53.1%	46.2%	53.5%	46.5%
1,422,905	NASSAU	625,247	296,841	324,170	4,236	27,329 D	47.5%	51.8%	47.8%	52.2%
1,524,541	NEW YORK	437,458	93,953	329,759	13,746	235,806 D	21.5%	75.4%	22.2%	77.8%
235,720	NIAGARA	86,513	42,243	43,905	365	1,662 D	48.8%	50.7%	49.0%	51.0%
273,037	ONEIDA	103,179	59,581	43,181	417	16,400 R	57.7%	41.9%	58.0%	42.0%
472,185	ONONDAGA	188,015	119,175	67,748	1,092	51,427 R	63.4%	36.0%	63.8%	36.2%
78,849	ONTARIO	34,690	20,728	13,764	198	6,964 R	59.8%	39.7%	60.1%	39.9%
220,558	ORANGE	88,785	50,334	37,945	506	12,389 R	56.7%	42.7%	57.0%	43.0%
37,305	ORLEANS	14,447	8,481	5,896	70	2,585 R	58.7%	40.8%	59.0%	41.0%
100,897	OSWEGO	38,717	24,946	13,522	249	11,424 R	64.4%	34.9%	64.8%	35.2%
56,181	OTSEGO	24,134	14,478	9,485	171	4,993 R	60.0%	39.3%	60.4%	39.6%
56,696	PUTNAM	30,196	17,132	12,835	229	4,297 R	56.7%	42.5%	57.2%	42.8%
1,973,708	QUEENS	611,309	210,732	395,040	5,537	184,308 D	34.5%	64.6%	34.8%	65.2%
152,510	RENSSELAER	66,575	35,305	30,880	390	4,425 R	53.0%	46.4%	53.3%	46.7%
295,443	RICHMOND	103,483	48,900	53,930	653	5,030 D	47.3%	52.1%	47.6%	52.4%
229,903	ROCKLAND	99,483	45,024	53,541	918	8,517 D	45.3%	53.8%	45.7%	54.3%
111,991	ST. LAWRENCE	38,182	23,164	14,706	312	8,458 R	60.7%	38.5%	61.2%	38.8%
121,679	SARATOGA	60,114	35,356	24,324	434	11,032 R	58.8%	40.5%	59.2%	40.8%
160,979	SCHENECTADY	70,912	37,354	32,796	762	4,558 R	52.7%	46.2%	53.2%	46.8%
24,750	SCHOHARIE	12,235	7,367	4,768	100	2,599 R	60.2%	39.0%	60.7%	39.3%
16,737	SCHUYLER	6,967	4,593	2,330	44	2,263 R	65.9%	33.4%	66.3%	33.7%
35,083	SENECA	13,173	8,197	4,897	79	3,300 R	62.2%	37.2%	62.6%	37.4%
99,546	STEUBEN	37,000	23,138	13,687	175	9,451 R	62.5%	37.0%	62.8%	37.2%
1,116,672	SUFFOLK	449,691	238,543	208,126	3,022	30,417 R	53.0%	46.3%	53.4%	46.6%
52,580	SULLIVAN	27,366	13,289	13,873	204	584 D	48.6%	50.7%	48.9%	51.1%
46,513	TIOGA	18,314	11,696	6,530	88	5,166 R	63.9%	35.7%	64.2%	35.8%
76,879	TOMPKINS	27,866	14,986	12,401	479	2,585 R	53.8%	44.5%	54.7%	45.3%
141,241	ULSTER	64,409	35,810	27,813	786	7,997 R	55.6%	43.2%	56.3%	43.7%
49,402	WARREN	20,867	13,867	6,897	103	6,970 R	66.5%	33.1%	66.8%	33.2%
52,725	WASHINGTON	20,543	13,784	6,656	103	7,128 R	67.1%	32.4%	67.4%	32.6%
79,404	WAYNE	30,623	18,724	11,750	149	6,974 R	61.1%	38.4%	61.4%	38.6%
891,409	WESTCHESTER	375,724	181,552	190,497	3,675	8,945 D	48.3%	50.7%	48.8%	51.2%
37,688	WYOMING	15,125	9,448	5,596	81	3,852 R	62.5%	37.0%	62.8%	37.2%
19,831	YATES	8,559	5,990	2,517	52	3,473 R	70.0%	29.4%	70.4%	29.6%
18,190,740	TOTAL	6,319,755	2,836,633	3,422,594	60,528	585,961 D	44.9%	54.2%	45.3%	54.7%

New York City
Bronx County
PRESIDENT 1976

1970 Census Population	Assembly District	Total Vote	Republican	Democratic	Other	Rep.-Dem. Plurality	Percentage Total Vote Rep.	Percentage Total Vote Dem.	Percentage Major Vote Rep.	Percentage Major Vote Dem.
122,641	DISTRICT 75	17,189	2,048	15,055	86	13,007 D	11.9%	87.6%	12.0%	88.0%
122,637	DISTRICT 76	17,668	2,058	15,523	87	13,465 D	11.6%	87.9%	11.7%	88.3%
122,643	DISTRICT 77	12,195	1,043	11,110	42	10,067 D	8.6%	91.1%	8.6%	91.4%
122,641	DISTRICT 78	12,221	727	11,447	47	10,720 D	5.9%	93.7%	6.0%	94.0%
122,649	DISTRICT 79	10,606	895	9,670	41	8,775 D	8.4%	91.2%	8.5%	91.5%
122,641	DISTRICT 80	38,502	21,910	16,428	164	5,482 R	56.9%	42.7%	57.1%	42.9%
122,642	DISTRICT 81	58,771	12,527	45,827	417	33,300 D	21.3%	78.0%	21.5%	78.5%
122,641	DISTRICT 82	20,833	5,697	15,017	119	9,320 D	27.3%	72.1%	27.5%	72.5%
122,640	DISTRICT 83	39,886	14,662	24,970	254	10,308 D	36.8%	62.6%	37.0%	63.0%
122,644	DISTRICT 84	37,288	9,429	27,660	199	18,231 D	25.3%	74.2%	25.4%	74.6%
122,641	DISTRICT 85	36,085	11,408	24,549	128	13,141 D	31.6%	68.0%	31.7%	68.3%
122,641	DISTRICT 86	36,147	14,438	21,530	179	7,092 D	39.9%	59.6%	40.1%	59.9%
1,472,216	TOTAL	337,391	96,842	238,786	1,763	141,944 D	28.7%	70.8%	28.9%	71.1%

New York City
Kings County
PRESIDENT 1976

1970 Census Population	Assembly District	Total Vote	Republican	Democratic	Other	Rep.-Dem. Plurality	Percentage Total Vote Rep.	Percentage Total Vote Dem.	Percentage Major Vote Rep.	Percentage Major Vote Dem.
65,884	DISTRICT 38	10,839	5,027	5,771	41	744 D	46.4%	53.2%	46.6%	53.4%
120,767	DISTRICT 39	42,332	10,309	31,862	161	21,553 D	24.4%	75.3%	24.4%	75.6%
120,769	DISTRICT 40	14,825	1,230	13,540	55	12,310 D	8.3%	91.3%	8.3%	91.7%
120,767	DISTRICT 41	30,719	8,653	21,936	130	13,283 D	28.2%	71.4%	28.3%	71.7%
120,767	DISTRICT 42	46,777	18,737	27,820	220	9,083 D	40.1%	59.5%	40.2%	59.8%
120,767	DISTRICT 43	24,264	5,891	18,175	198	12,284 D	24.3%	74.9%	24.5%	75.5%
120,768	DISTRICT 44	35,018	9,720	24,944	354	15,224 D	27.8%	71.2%	28.0%	72.0%
120,769	DISTRICT 45	48,444	11,914	36,249	281	24,335 D	24.6%	74.8%	24.7%	75.3%
120,769	DISTRICT 46	39,326	8,752	30,296	278	21,544 D	22.3%	77.0%	22.4%	77.6%
120,768	DISTRICT 47	36,620	13,599	22,862	159	9,263 D	37.1%	62.4%	37.3%	62.7%
120,768	DISTRICT 48	38,758	12,690	25,886	182	13,196 D	32.7%	66.8%	32.9%	67.1%
120,768	DISTRICT 49	37,260	22,314	14,821	125	7,493 R	59.9%	39.8%	60.1%	39.9%
120,768	DISTRICT 50	33,388	18,967	14,274	147	4,693 R	56.8%	42.8%	57.1%	42.9%
120,768	DISTRICT 51	29,104	13,188	15,722	194	2,534 D	45.3%	54.0%	45.6%	54.4%
120,768	DISTRICT 52	27,867	8,890	18,649	328	9,759 D	31.9%	66.9%	32.3%	67.7%
120,768	DISTRICT 53	16,960	1,403	15,440	117	14,037 D	8.3%	91.0%	8.3%	91.7%
120,769	DISTRICT 54	12,782	756	11,991	35	11,235 D	5.9%	93.8%	5.9%	94.1%
120,768	DISTRICT 55	12,764	1,311	11,401	52	10,090 D	10.3%	89.3%	10.3%	89.7%
120,768	DISTRICT 56	17,123	2,076	14,985	62	12,909 D	12.1%	87.5%	12.2%	87.8%
120,768	DISTRICT 57	22,358	4,165	17,968	225	13,803 D	18.6%	80.4%	18.8%	81.2%
120,768	DISTRICT 58	21,542	8,809	12,613	120	3,804 D	40.9%	58.6%	41.1%	58.9%
120,768	DISTRICT 59	14,573	2,327	12,177	69	9,850 D	16.0%	83.6%	16.0%	84.0%
2,601,852	TOTAL	613,643	190,728	419,382	3,533	228,654 D	31.1%	68.3%	31.3%	68.7%

New York City
New York County
PRESIDENT 1976

1970 Census Population	Assembly District	Total Vote	Republican	Democratic	Other	Rep.-Dem. Plurality	Percentage Total Vote Rep.	Percentage Total Vote Dem.	Percentage Major Vote Rep.	Percentage Major Vote Dem.
71,490	DISTRICT 62	15,555	4,531	10,868	156	6,337 D	29.1%	69.9%	29.4%	70.6%
122,312	DISTRICT 63	23,722	4,367	18,880	475	14,513 D	18.4%	79.6%	18.8%	81.2%
122,312	DISTRICT 64	47,815	11,300	35,335	1,180	24,035 D	23.6%	73.9%	24.2%	75.8%
122,312	DISTRICT 65	54,731	20,401	33,773	557	13,372 D	37.3%	61.7%	37.7%	62.3%
122,312	DISTRICT 66	51,381	22,446	28,612	323	6,166 D	43.7%	55.7%	44.0%	56.0%
122,312	DISTRICT 67	43,709	10,927	32,234	548	21,307 D	25.0%	73.7%	25.3%	74.7%
122,312	DISTRICT 68	43,341	15,014	27,930	397	12,916 D	34.6%	64.4%	35.0%	65.0%
122,312	DISTRICT 69	44,553	7,269	36,400	884	29,131 D	16.3%	81.7%	16.6%	83.4%
122,312	DISTRICT 70	26,287	3,262	22,676	349	19,414 D	12.4%	86.3%	12.6%	87.4%
122,312	DISTRICT 71	27,027	2,113	24,784	130	22,671 D	7.8%	91.7%	7.9%	92.1%
122,312	DISTRICT 72	21,262	2,547	18,633	82	16,086 D	12.0%	87.6%	12.0%	88.0%
122,311	DISTRICT 73	34,003	10,209	23,369	425	13,160 D	30.0%	68.7%	30.4%	69.6%
122,312	DISTRICT 74	27,452	3,316	23,944	192	20,628 D	12.1%	87.2%	12.2%	87.8%
1,524,541	TOTAL	460,838	117,702	337,438	5,698	219,736 D	25.5%	73.2%	25.9%	74.1%

New York City
Queens County
PRESIDENT 1976

1970 Census Population	Assembly District	Total Vote	Republican	Democratic	Other	Rep.-Dem. Plurality	Percentage Total Vote Rep.	Percentage Total Vote Dem.	Percentage Major Vote Rep.	Percentage Major Vote Dem.
120,768	DISTRICT 22	38,633	12,512	25,971	150	13,459 D	32.4%	67.2%	32.5%	67.5%
120,768	DISTRICT 23	39,972	18,519	21,280	173	2,761 D	46.3%	53.2%	46.5%	53.5%
120,768	DISTRICT 24	48,730	13,714	34,755	261	21,041 D	28.1%	71.3%	28.3%	71.7%
120,768	DISTRICT 25	46,759	24,394	22,137	228	2,257 R	52.2%	47.3%	52.4%	47.6%
120,768	DISTRICT 26	45,272	15,085	29,955	232	14,870 D	33.3%	66.2%	33.5%	66.5%
120,768	DISTRICT 27	39,064	10,403	28,442	219	18,039 D	26.6%	72.8%	26.8%	73.2%
120,769	DISTRICT 28	47,080	13,332	33,525	223	20,193 D	28.3%	71.2%	28.5%	71.5%
120,768	DISTRICT 29	31,894	3,507	28,288	99	24,781 D	11.0%	88.7%	11.0%	89.0%
120,769	DISTRICT 30	35,098	13,679	21,231	188	7,552 D	39.0%	60.5%	39.2%	60.8%
120,768	DISTRICT 31	37,888	20,387	17,333	168	3,054 R	53.8%	45.7%	54.0%	46.0%
120,768	DISTRICT 32	33,596	8,217	25,221	158	17,004 D	24.5%	75.1%	24.6%	75.4%
120,768	DISTRICT 33	40,063	24,756	15,150	157	9,606 R	61.8%	37.8%	62.0%	38.0%
120,768	DISTRICT 34	29,172	9,608	19,413	151	9,805 D	32.9%	66.5%	33.1%	66.9%
120,768	DISTRICT 35	36,369	18,401	17,783	185	618 R	50.6%	48.9%	50.9%	49.1%
120,768	DISTRICT 36	30,032	11,257	18,562	213	7,305 D	37.5%	61.8%	37.8%	62.2%
120,768	DISTRICT 37	31,079	16,730	14,182	167	2,548 R	53.8%	45.6%	54.1%	45.9%
54,884	DISTRICT 38	16,651	9,895	6,679	77	3,216 R	59.4%	40.1%	59.7%	40.3%
1,973,708	TOTAL	627,352	244,396	379,907	3,049	135,511 D	39.0%	60.6%	39.1%	60.9%

New York City
Richmond County
PRESIDENT 1976

1970 Census Population	Assembly District	Total Vote	Republican	Democratic	Other	Rep.-Dem. Plurality	Percentage Total Vote Rep.	Percentage Total Vote Dem.	Percentage Major Vote Rep.	Percentage Major Vote Dem.
122,311	DISTRICT 60	46,768	27,478	19,053	237	8,425 R	58.8%	40.7%	59.1%	40.9%
122,311	DISTRICT 61	45,123	23,446	21,428	249	2,018 R	52.0%	47.5%	52.2%	47.8%
50,821	DISTRICT 62	13,586	6,071	7,386	129	1,315 D	44.7%	54.4%	45.1%	54.9%
295,443	TOTAL	105,477	56,995	47,867	615	9,128 R	54.0%	45.4%	54.4%	45.6%

New York City
PRESIDENT 1976

1970 Census Population	County	Total Vote	Republican	Democratic	Other	Rep.-Dem. Plurality	Percentage Total Vote Rep.	Percentage Total Vote Dem.	Percentage Major Vote Rep.	Percentage Major Vote Dem.
1,472,216	BRONX	337,391	96,842	238,786	1,763	141,944 D	28.7%	70.8%	28.9%	71.1%
2,601,852	KINGS	613,643	190,728	419,382	3,533	228,654 D	31.1%	68.3%	31.3%	68.7%
1,524,541	NEW YORK	460,838	117,702	337,438	5,698	219,736 D	25.5%	73.2%	25.9%	74.1%
1,973,708	QUEENS	627,352	244,396	379,907	3,049	135,511 D	39.0%	60.6%	39.1%	60.9%
295,443	RICHMOND	105,477	56,995	47,867	615	9,128 R	54.0%	45.4%	54.4%	45.6%
7,867,760	TOTAL	2,144,701	706,663	1,423,380	14,658	716,717 D	32.9%	66.4%	33.2%	66.8%

New York City
Bronx County
SENATOR 1976

1970 Census Population	Assembly District	Total Vote	Republican	Democratic	Other	Rep.-Dem. Plurality	Percentage Total Vote Rep.	Percentage Total Vote Dem.	Percentage Major Vote Rep.	Percentage Major Vote Dem.
122,641	DISTRICT 75	14,397	2,463	11,748	186	9,285 D	17.1%	81.6%	17.3%	82.7%
122,637	DISTRICT 76	15,800	2,618	12,959	223	10,341 D	16.6%	82.0%	16.8%	83.2%
122,643	DISTRICT 77	9,996	1,264	8,624	108	7,360 D	12.6%	86.3%	12.8%	87.2%
122,641	DISTRICT 78	10,561	1,429	8,988	144	7,559 D	13.5%	85.1%	13.7%	86.3%
122,649	DISTRICT 79	9,211	1,390	7,720	101	6,330 D	15.1%	83.8%	15.3%	84.7%
122,641	DISTRICT 80	36,895	18,796	17,876	223	920 R	50.9%	48.5%	51.3%	48.7%
122,642	DISTRICT 81	57,110	10,505	45,797	808	35,292 D	18.4%	80.2%	18.7%	81.3%
122,641	DISTRICT 82	19,545	5,156	14,197	192	9,041 D	26.4%	72.6%	26.6%	73.4%
122,640	DISTRICT 83	38,972	11,809	26,730	433	14,921 D	30.3%	68.6%	30.6%	69.4%
122,644	DISTRICT 84	36,179	7,615	28,070	494	20,455 D	21.0%	77.6%	21.3%	78.7%
122,641	DISTRICT 85	33,917	10,654	22,948	315	12,294 D	31.4%	67.7%	31.7%	68.3%
122,641	DISTRICT 86	34,620	12,855	21,387	378	8,532 D	37.1%	61.8%	37.5%	62.5%
1,472,216	TOTAL	317,203	86,554	227,044	3,605	140,490 D	27.3%	71.6%	27.6%	72.4%

New York City
Kings County
SENATOR 1976

1970 Census Population	Assembly District	Total Vote	Republican	Democratic	Other	Rep.-Dem. Plurality	Percentage Total Vote Rep.	Percentage Total Vote Dem.	Percentage Major Vote Rep.	Percentage Major Vote Dem.
65,884	DISTRICT 38	10,688	4,695	5,902	91	1,207 D	43.9%	55.2%	44.3%	55.7%
120,767	DISTRICT 39	41,479	7,654	33,591	234	25,937 D	18.5%	81.0%	18.6%	81.4%
120,769	DISTRICT 40	13,364	2,105	11,085	174	8,980 D	15.8%	82.9%	16.0%	84.0%
120,767	DISTRICT 41	29,911	7,141	22,505	265	15,364 D	23.9%	75.2%	24.1%	75.9%
120,767	DISTRICT 42	46,162	14,759	31,127	276	16,368 D	32.0%	67.4%	32.2%	67.8%
120,767	DISTRICT 43	23,241	5,545	17,252	444	11,707 D	23.9%	74.2%	24.3%	75.7%
120,768	DISTRICT 44	34,106	7,744	25,573	789	17,829 D	22.7%	75.0%	23.2%	76.8%
120,769	DISTRICT 45	47,804	7,419	39,920	465	32,501 D	15.5%	83.5%	15.7%	84.3%
120,769	DISTRICT 46	38,309	6,333	31,513	463	25,180 D	16.5%	82.3%	16.7%	83.3%
120,768	DISTRICT 47	35,501	10,464	24,786	251	14,322 D	29.5%	69.8%	29.7%	70.3%
120,768	DISTRICT 48	38,310	7,762	30,288	260	22,526 D	20.3%	79.1%	20.4%	79.6%
120,768	DISTRICT 49	35,978	18,653	17,126	199	1,527 R	51.8%	47.6%	52.1%	47.9%
120,768	DISTRICT 50	32,378	16,014	16,161	203	147 D	49.5%	49.9%	49.8%	50.2%
120,768	DISTRICT 51	27,872	10,526	16,985	361	6,459 D	37.8%	60.9%	38.3%	61.7%
120,768	DISTRICT 52	26,775	7,608	18,270	897	10,662 D	28.4%	68.2%	29.4%	70.6%
120,768	DISTRICT 53	15,328	2,485	12,498	345	10,013 D	16.2%	81.5%	16.6%	83.4%
120,769	DISTRICT 54	10,727	1,684	8,903	140	7,219 D	15.7%	83.0%	15.9%	84.1%
120,768	DISTRICT 55	11,505	2,121	9,263	121	7,142 D	18.4%	80.5%	18.6%	81.4%
120,768	DISTRICT 56	14,950	2,754	11,995	201	9,241 D	18.4%	80.2%	18.7%	81.3%
120,768	DISTRICT 57	20,452	4,580	15,260	612	10,680 D	22.4%	74.6%	23.1%	76.9%
120,768	DISTRICT 58	19,594	7,582	11,854	158	4,272 D	38.7%	60.5%	39.0%	61.0%
120,768	DISTRICT 59	12,589	2,643	9,804	142	7,161 D	21.0%	77.9%	21.2%	78.8%
2,601,852	TOTAL	587,023	158,271	421,661	7,091	263,390 D	27.0%	71.8%	27.3%	72.7%

New York City
New York County
SENATOR 1976

1970 Census Population	Assembly District	Total Vote	Republican	Democratic	Other	Rep.-Dem. Plurality	Percentage Total Vote Rep.	Percentage Total Vote Dem.	Percentage Major Vote Rep.	Percentage Major Vote Dem.
71,490	DISTRICT 62	14,694	3,571	10,566	557	6,995 D	24.3%	71.9%	25.3%	74.7%
122,312	DISTRICT 63	22,007	3,527	17,537	943	14,010 D	16.0%	79.7%	16.7%	83.3%
122,312	DISTRICT 64	46,172	9,298	33,950	2,924	24,652 D	20.1%	73.5%	21.5%	78.5%
122,312	DISTRICT 65	53,557	15,255	37,309	993	22,054 D	28.5%	69.7%	29.0%	71.0%
122,312	DISTRICT 66	50,372	15,342	34,445	585	19,103 D	30.5%	68.4%	30.8%	69.2%
122,312	DISTRICT 67	42,094	7,971	32,739	1,384	24,768 D	18.9%	77.8%	19.6%	80.4%
122,312	DISTRICT 68	41,579	10,999	29,838	742	18,839 D	26.5%	71.8%	26.9%	73.1%
122,312	DISTRICT 69	42,388	5,791	33,900	2,697	28,109 D	13.7%	80.0%	14.6%	85.4%
122,312	DISTRICT 70	24,165	3,891	19,171	1,103	15,280 D	16.1%	79.3%	16.9%	83.1%
122,312	DISTRICT 71	24,196	3,583	20,201	412	16,618 D	14.8%	83.5%	15.1%	84.9%
122,312	DISTRICT 72	18,986	3,093	15,652	241	12,559 D	16.3%	82.4%	16.5%	83.5%
122,311	DISTRICT 73	32,789	7,552	24,583	654	17,031 D	23.0%	75.0%	23.5%	76.5%
122,312	DISTRICT 74	24,459	4,080	19,868	511	15,788 D	16.7%	81.2%	17.0%	83.0%
1,524,541	TOTAL	437,458	93,953	329,759	13,746	235,806 D	21.5%	75.4%	22.2%	77.8%

New York City
Queens County
SENATOR 1976

1970 Census Population	Assembly District	Total Vote	Republican	Democratic	Other	Rep.-Dem. Plurality	Percentage Total Vote Rep.	Percentage Total Vote Dem.	Percentage Major Vote Rep.	Percentage Major Vote Dem.
120,768	DISTRICT 22	37,933	9,823	27,851	259	18,028 D	25.9%	73.4%	26.1%	73.9%
120,768	DISTRICT 23	38,999	17,031	21,662	306	4,631 D	43.7%	55.5%	44.0%	56.0%
120,768	DISTRICT 24	48,119	10,270	37,372	477	27,102 D	21.3%	77.7%	21.6%	78.4%
120,768	DISTRICT 25	46,270	20,998	24,903	369	3,905 D	45.4%	53.8%	45.7%	54.3%
120,768	DISTRICT 26	44,523	12,177	31,926	420	19,749 D	27.3%	71.7%	27.6%	72.4%
120,768	DISTRICT 27	37,964	9,084	28,502	378	19,418 D	23.9%	75.1%	24.2%	75.8%
120,769	DISTRICT 28	46,788	8,432	37,984	372	29,552 D	18.0%	81.2%	18.2%	81.8%
120,768	DISTRICT 29	29,863	6,456	22,940	467	16,484 D	21.6%	76.8%	22.0%	78.0%
120,769	DISTRICT 30	34,452	11,013	23,085	354	12,072 D	32.0%	67.0%	32.3%	67.7%
120,768	DISTRICT 31	37,057	17,847	18,948	262	1,101 D	48.2%	51.1%	48.5%	51.5%
120,768	DISTRICT 32	32,135	8,764	22,950	421	14,186 D	27.3%	71.4%	27.6%	72.4%
120,768	DISTRICT 33	39,052	21,682	17,153	217	4,529 R	55.5%	43.9%	55.8%	44.2%
120,768	DISTRICT 34	27,782	8,521	18,960	301	10,439 D	30.7%	68.2%	31.0%	69.0%
120,768	DISTRICT 35	35,301	15,782	19,255	264	3,473 D	44.7%	54.5%	45.0%	55.0%
120,768	DISTRICT 36	28,657	10,028	18,289	340	8,261 D	35.0%	63.8%	35.4%	64.6%
120,768	DISTRICT 37	30,181	14,141	15,797	243	1,656 D	46.9%	52.3%	47.2%	52.8%
54,884	DISTRICT 38	16,233	8,683	7,463	87	1,220 R	53.5%	46.0%	53.8%	46.2%
1,973,708	TOTAL	611,309	210,732	395,040	5,537	184,308 D	34.5%	64.6%	34.8%	65.2%

New York City
Richmond County
SENATOR 1976

1970 Census Population	Assembly District	Total Vote	Republican	Democratic	Other	Rep.-Dem. Plurality	Percentage Total Vote Rep.	Total Vote Dem.	Major Vote Rep.	Major Vote Dem.
122,311	DISTRICT 60	46,226	23,328	22,653	245	675 R	50.5%	49.0%	50.7%	49.3%
122,311	DISTRICT 61	44,110	20,149	23,720	241	3,571 D	45.7%	53.8%	45.9%	54.1%
50,821	DISTRICT 62	13,147	5,423	7,557	167	2,134 D	41.2%	57.5%	41.8%	58.2%
295,443	TOTAL	103,483	48,900	53,930	653	5,030 D	47.3%	52.1%	47.6%	52.4%

New York City

SENATOR 1976

1970 Census Population	County	Total Vote	Republican	Democratic	Other	Rep.-Dem. Plurality	Percentage Total Vote Rep.	Total Vote Dem.	Major Vote Rep.	Major Vote Dem.
1,472,216	BRONX	317,203	86,554	227,044	3,605	140,490 D	27.3%	71.6%	27.6%	72.4%
2,601,852	KINGS	587,023	158,271	421,661	7,091	263,390 D	27.0%	71.8%	27.3%	72.7%
1,524,541	NEW YORK	437,458	93,953	329,759	13,746	235,806 D	21.5%	75.4%	22.2%	77.8%
1,973,708	QUEENS	611,309	210,732	395,040	5,537	184,308 D	34.5%	64.6%	34.8%	65.2%
295,443	RICHMOND	103,483	48,900	53,930	653	5,030 D	47.3%	52.1%	47.6%	52.4%
7,867,760	TOTAL	2,056,476	598,410	1,427,434	30,632	829,024 D	29.1%	69.4%	29.5%	70.5%

NEW YORK

CONGRESS

CD	Year	Total Vote	Republican Vote	Republican Candidate	Democratic Vote	Democratic Candidate	Other Vote	Rep.-Dem. Plurality	Percentage Total Vote Rep.	Percentage Total Vote Dem.	Percentage Major Vote Rep.	Percentage Major Vote Dem.
1	1976	207,468	61,671	NICOSIA, SALVATORE C.	135,528	*PIKE, OTIS G.	10,269	73,857 D	29.7%	65.3%	31.3%	68.7%
1	1974	155,681	44,513	SALLAH, DONALD R.	101,130	PIKE, OTIS G.	10,038	56,617 D	28.6%	65.0%	30.6%	69.4%
1	1972	195,444	72,133	BOYD, JOSEPH H.	102,628	PIKE, OTIS G.	20,683	30,495 D	36.9%	52.5%	41.3%	58.7%
2	1976	159,902	67,755	*COHALAN, PETER F.	91,241	*DOWNEY, THOMAS J.	906	23,486 D	42.4%	57.1%	42.6%	57.4%
2	1974	119,451	53,344	GROVER, JAMES R.	58,289	DOWNEY, THOMAS J.	7,818	4,945 D	44.7%	48.8%	47.8%	52.2%
2	1972	151,015	99,348	GROVER, JAMES R.	49,454	DENNISON, FERN C.	2,213	49,894 R	65.8%	32.7%	66.8%	33.2%
3	1976	181,439	84,824	*HOGAN, HOWARD T.	94,265	AMBRO, JEROME A.	2,350	9,441 D	46.8%	52.0%	47.4%	52.6%
3	1974	147,560	67,986	*RONCALLO, ANGELO D.	76,383	AMBRO, JEROME A.	3,191	8,397 D	46.1%	51.8%	47.1%	52.9%
3	1972	195,160	103,620	RONCALLO, ANGELO D.	73,429	BALES, CARTER F.	18,111	30,191 R	53.1%	37.6%	58.5%	41.5%
4	1976	190,029	106,058	*LENT, NORMAN F.	83,971	*HALPERN, GERALD P.		22,087 R	55.8%	44.2%	55.8%	44.2%
4	1974	159,204	85,382	*LENT, NORMAN F.	73,822	*ORENSTEIN, FRANKLIN H.		11,560 R	53.6%	46.4%	53.6%	46.4%
4	1972	201,034	125,422	LENT, NORMAN F.	72,280	HOROWITZ, ELAINE B.	3,332	53,142 R	62.4%	36.0%	63.4%	36.6%
5	1976	198,234	110,366	*WYDLER, JOHN W.	87,868	*LOWENSTEIN, ALLARD K.		22,498 R	55.7%	44.3%	55.7%	44.3%
5	1974	169,033	91,677	*WYDLER, JOHN W.	77,356	*LOWENSTEIN, ALLARD K.		14,321 R	54.2%	45.8%	54.2%	45.8%
5	1972	213,542	133,332	WYDLER, JOHN W.	67,709	STECKLER, FERNE M.	12,501	65,623 R	62.4%	31.7%	66.3%	33.7%
6	1976	181,947	60,567	BALLETTA, VINCENT	112,422	*WOLFF, LESTER L.	8,958	51,855 D	33.3%	61.8%	35.0%	65.0%
6	1974	151,765	50,528	*LAYNE, EDYTHE	101,237	*WOLFF, LESTER L.		50,709 D	33.3%	66.7%	33.3%	66.7%
6	1972	212,658	103,038	*GALLAGHER, JOHN T.	109,620	*WOLFF, LESTER L.		6,582 D	48.5%	51.5%	48.5%	51.5%
7	1976	113,373			107,312	*ADDABBO, JOSEPH P.	6,061	107,312 D		94.7%		100.0%
7	1974	83,972			83,972	*ADDABBO, JOSEPH P.		83,972 D		100.0%		100.0%
7	1972	137,459	28,296	HALL, JOHN E.	103,110	*ADDABBO, JOSEPH P.	6,053	74,814 D	20.6%	75.0%	21.5%	78.5%
8	1976	137,861	30,191	*LEMISHOW, ALBERT	107,295	*ROSENTHAL, BENJAMIN	375	77,104 D	21.9%	77.8%	22.0%	78.0%
8	1974	114,180	23,980	*LEMISHOW, ALBERT	90,200	*ROSENTHAL, BENJAMIN		66,220 D	21.0%	79.0%	21.0%	79.0%
8	1972	170,459	60,166	*LA PINA, FRANK	110,293	*ROSENTHAL, BENJAMIN		50,127 D	35.3%	64.7%	35.3%	64.7%
9	1976	115,195			109,552	*DELANEY, JAMES J.	5,643	109,552 D		95.1%		100.0%
9	1974	99,155			92,231	*DELANEY, JAMES J.	6,924	92,231 D		93.0%		100.0%
9	1972	151,288			141,323	*DELANEY, JAMES J.	9,965	141,323 D		93.4%		100.0%
10	1976	115,962			106,222	*BIAGGI, MARIO	9,740	106,222 D		91.6%		100.0%
10	1974	91,422			75,375	*BIAGGI, MARIO	16,047	75,375 D		82.4%		100.0%
10	1972	138,597			130,200	*BIAGGI, MARIO	8,397	130,200 D		93.9%		100.0%
11	1976	114,458	19,203	CUCCIA, ARTHUR	84,770	SCHEUER, JAMES H.	10,485	65,567 D	16.8%	74.1%	18.5%	81.5%
11	1974	86,351	12,297	DESBOROUGH, EDWARD G.	62,388	SCHEUER, JAMES H.	11,666	50,091 D	14.2%	72.2%	16.5%	83.5%
11	1972	137,546	43,105	*SOLOMON, MELVIN	87,869	BRASCO, FRANK J.	6,572	44,764 D	31.3%	63.9%	32.9%	67.1%
12	1976	49,632	5,336	MORANCIE, HORACE L.	43,203	*CHISHOLM, SHIRLEY	1,093	37,867 D	10.8%	87.0%	11.0%	89.0%
12	1974	32,979	4,577	VOYTICKY, FRANCIS J.	26,446	*CHISHOLM, SHIRLEY	1,956	21,869 D	13.9%	80.2%	14.8%	85.2%
13	1976	132,224	21,600	*DOBOSH, JACK N.	110,624	*SOLARZ, STEPHEN J.		89,024 D	16.3%	83.7%	16.3%	83.7%
13	1974	111,237	20,229	*DOBOSH, JACK N.	91,008	*SOLARZ, STEPHEN J.		70,779 D	18.2%	81.8%	18.2%	81.8%
14	1976	65,591	8,977	*GARGIULO, FRANK X.	55,723	*RICHMOND, FREDERICK W.	891	46,746 D	13.7%	85.0%	13.9%	86.1%
14	1974	46,551	5,360	CARBAJAL, MICHAEL	33,195	RICHMOND, FREDERICK W.	7,996	27,835 D	11.5%	71.3%	13.9%	86.1%
15	1976	109,487	33,641	D ANGELO, RONALD J.	69,242	*ZEFERETTI, LEO C.	6,604	35,601 D	30.7%	63.2%	32.7%	67.3%
15	1974	91,922	34,814	CANADE, AUSTEN D.	53,733	*ZEFERETTI, LEO C.	3,375	18,919 D	37.9%	58.5%	39.3%	60.7%
16	1976	113,418	19,423	*PEMBERTON, GLADYS	93,995	*HOLTZMAN, ELIZABETH		74,572 D	17.1%	82.9%	17.1%	82.9%
16	1974	93,816	19,806	*GENTILI, JOSEPH L.	74,010	*HOLTZMAN, ELIZABETH		54,204 D	21.1%	78.9%	21.1%	78.9%
16	1972	147,892	33,828	MACCHIO, NICHOLAS R.	96,984	HOLTZMAN, ELIZABETH	17,080	63,156 D	22.9%	65.6%	25.9%	74.1%
17	1976	135,915	27,734	GROSSBERGER, KENNETH	89,126	MURPHY, JOHN M.	19,055	61,392 D	20.4%	65.6%	23.7%	76.3%
17	1974	110,504	28,269	BIONDOLILLO, FRANK J.	63,805	MURPHY, JOHN M.	18,430	35,536 D	25.6%	57.7%	30.7%	69.3%
17	1972	153,064	60,812	*BELARDINO, MARIO D.	92,252	MURPHY, JOHN M.		31,440 D	39.7%	60.3%	39.7%	60.3%
18	1976	149,422	29,728	LANDAU, SONIA	112,187	*KOCH, EDWARD I.	7,507	82,459 D	19.9%	75.1%	20.9%	79.1%
18	1974	119,903	22,560	BOOGAERTS, JOHN	91,985	*KOCH, EDWARD I.	5,358	69,425 D	18.8%	76.7%	19.7%	80.3%
18	1972	178,894	52,379	*LANGLEY, JANE P.	125,117	*KOCH, EDWARD I.	1,398	72,738 D	29.3%	69.9%	29.5%	70.5%
19	1976	94,481			91,672	*RANGEL, CHARLES B.	2,809	91,672 D		97.0%		100.0%
19	1974	65,185			63,146	*RANGEL, CHARLES B.	2,039	63,146 D		96.9%		100.0%
19	1972	108,769			104,427	*RANGEL, CHARLES B.	4,342	104,427 D		96.0%		100.0%
20	1976	110,490	14,114	WEISEMAN, DENISE T.	91,977	*WEISS, THEODORE S.	4,399	77,863 D	12.8%	83.2%	13.3%	86.7%
20	1974	96,638	15,053	POSNER, STEPHEN	76,074	*ABZUG, BELLA S.	5,511	61,021 D	15.6%	78.7%	16.5%	83.5%
20	1972	153,492	18,024	LEVY, ANNETTE F.	85,558	ABZUG, BELLA S.	49,910	67,534 D	11.7%	55.7%	17.4%	82.6%
21	1976	41,883			41,285	*BADILLO, HERMAN	598	41,285 D		98.6%		100.0%
21	1974	28,984			28,025	*BADILLO, HERMAN	959	28,025 D		96.7%		100.0%
21	1972	55,744	6,366	RAMOS, MANUEL A.	48,441	*BADILLO, HERMAN	937	42,075 D	11.4%	86.9%	11.6%	88.4%
22	1976	106,592	11,130	SLOTKIN, PAUL	92,044	*BINGHAM, JONATHAN	3,418	80,914 D	10.4%	86.4%	10.8%	89.2%
22	1974	90,632	8,142	BLACK, ROBERT	77,157	*BINGHAM, JONATHAN	5,333	69,015 D	9.0%	85.1%	9.5%	90.5%
22	1972	140,493	33,045	*AVARELLO, CHARLES A.	107,448	*BINGHAM, JONATHAN		74,403 D	23.5%	76.5%	23.5%	76.5%

NEW YORK

CONGRESS

CD	Year	Total Vote	Republican Vote	Republican Candidate	Democratic Vote	Democratic Candidate	Other Vote	Rep.-Dem. Plurality	Percentage Total Vote Rep.	Percentage Total Vote Dem.	Percentage Major Vote Rep.	Percentage Major Vote Dem.
23	1976	173,430	93,006	*CAPUTO, BRUCE F.	80,424	*MEYER, J. EDWARD		12,582 R	53.6%	46.4%	53.6%	46.4%
23	1974	139,469	80,361	*PEYSER, PETER A.	59,108	*GREENAWALT, WILLIAM S.		21,253 R	57.6%	42.4%	57.6%	42.4%
23	1972	198,072	99,737	*PEYSER, PETER A.	98,335	*OTTINGER, RICHARD L.		1,402 R	50.4%	49.6%	50.4%	49.6%
24	1976	183,012	81,111	*HICKS, DAVID V.	99,761	OTTINGER, RICHARD L.	2,140	18,650 D	44.3%	54.5%	44.8%	55.2%
24	1974	142,722	60,180	*STEPHENS, CHARLES J.	82,542	OTTINGER, RICHARD L.		22,362 D	42.2%	57.8%	42.2%	57.8%
24	1972	206,797	98,818	*VERGARI, CARL A.	107,979	*REID, OGDEN R.		9,161 D	47.8%	52.2%	47.8%	52.2%
25	1976	197,650	139,434	*FISH, HAMILTON	58,216	PEYSER, MINNA P.		81,218 R	70.5%	29.5%	70.5%	29.5%
25	1974	159,037	103,799	*FISH, HAMILTON	53,357	ANGELL, NICHOLAS B.	1,881	50,442 R	65.3%	33.6%	66.0%	34.0%
25	1972	201,536	144,386	*FISH, HAMILTON	54,271	BURNS, JOHN M.	2,879	90,115 R	71.6%	26.9%	72.7%	27.3%
26	1976	183,981	120,049	GILMAN, BENJAMIN A.	60,511	MALONEY, JOHN R.	3,421	59,538 R	65.3%	32.9%	66.5%	33.5%
26	1974	151,068	81,562	GILMAN, BENJAMIN A.	58,161	*DOW, JOHN G.	11,345	23,401 R	54.0%	38.5%	58.4%	41.6%
26	1972	190,424	90,922	GILMAN, BENJAMIN A.	74,906	DOW, JOHN G.	24,596	16,016 R	47.7%	39.3%	54.8%	45.2%
27	1976	190,674	63,626	*HARTER, WILLIAM H.	127,048	*MCHUGH, MATTHEW F.		63,422 D	33.4%	66.6%	33.4%	66.6%
27	1974	158,361	68,273	LIBOUS, ALFRED J.	83,562	*MCHUGH, MATTHEW F.	6,526	15,289 D	43.1%	52.8%	45.0%	55.0%
27	1972	184,828	114,902	ROBISON, HOWARD W.	55,076	BLAZER, DAVID H.	14,850	59,826 R	62.2%	29.8%	67.6%	32.4%
28	1976	215,162	44,053	*BRADT, MARY	170,034	STRATTON, SAMUEL S.	1,075	125,981 D	20.5%	79.0%	20.6%	79.4%
28	1974	193,982	33,493	WAGNER, WAYNE E.	156,439	STRATTON, SAMUEL S.	4,050	122,946 D	17.3%	80.6%	17.6%	82.4%
28	1972	228,018	45,623	*RYAN, JOHN F.	182,395	STRATTON, SAMUEL S.		136,772 D	20.0%	80.0%	20.0%	80.0%
29	1976	214,222	96,476	MARTINO, JOSEPH A.	100,663	*PATTISON, EDWARD W.	17,083	4,187 D	45.0%	47.0%	48.9%	51.1%
29	1974	184,092	83,768	*KING, CARLETON	100,324	*PATTISON, EDWARD W.		16,556 D	45.5%	54.5%	45.5%	54.5%
29	1972	212,090	148,170	*KING, CARLETON	63,920	*GORDON, HAROLD B.		84,250 R	69.9%	30.1%	69.9%	30.1%
30	1976	171,515	95,564	*MCEWEN, ROBERT C.	75,951	BARTLE, NORMA A.		19,613 R	55.7%	44.3%	55.7%	44.3%
30	1974	142,010	78,117	*MCEWEN, ROBERT C.	63,893	*TUBBY, ROGER W.		14,224 R	55.0%	45.0%	55.0%	45.0%
30	1972	172,981	114,193	*MCEWEN, ROBERT C.	58,788	*LABAFF, ERNEST J.		55,405 R	66.0%	34.0%	66.0%	34.0%
31	1976	185,175	123,143	*MITCHELL, DONALD J.	62,032	MAXWELL, ANITA		61,111 R	66.5%	33.5%	66.5%	33.5%
31	1974	158,239	94,319	*MITCHELL, DONALD J.	59,639	REILE, DONALD J.	4,281	34,680 R	59.6%	37.7%	61.3%	38.7%
31	1972	193,221	98,454	*MITCHELL, DONALD J.	75,513	CASTLE, ROBERT	19,254	22,941 R	51.0%	39.1%	56.6%	43.4%
32	1976	185,140	81,597	*WORTLEY, GEORGE C.	101,419	HANLEY, JAMES M.	2,124	19,822 D	44.1%	54.8%	44.6%	55.4%
32	1974	150,039	61,379	*BUSH, WILLIAM E.	88,660	HANLEY, JAMES M.		27,281 D	40.9%	59.1%	40.9%	59.1%
32	1972	194,932	83,451	*KOLDIN, LEONARD C.	111,481	HANLEY, JAMES M.		28,030 D	42.8%	57.2%	42.8%	57.2%
33	1976	182,755	125,163	WALSH, WILLIAM F.	48,855	WELCH, CHARLES R.	8,737	76,308 R	68.5%	26.7%	71.9%	28.1%
33	1974	149,091	97,380	WALSH, WILLIAM F.	45,043	BOCKMAN, ROBERT H.	6,668	52,337 R	65.3%	30.2%	68.4%	31.6%
33	1972	185,178	132,139	*WALSH, WILLIAM F.	53,039	KADYS, CLARENCE		79,100 R	71.4%	28.6%	71.4%	28.6%
34	1976	192,196	126,566	HORTON, FRANK J.	58,247	LARSEN, WILLIAM C.	7,383	68,319 R	65.9%	30.3%	68.5%	31.5%
34	1974	156,365	105,585	HORTON, FRANK J.	45,408	GOSSIN, IRENE	5,372	60,177 R	67.5%	29.0%	69.9%	30.1%
34	1972	198,003	142,803	HORTON, FRANK J.	46,509	RUBENS, JACK	8,691	96,294 R	72.1%	23.5%	75.4%	24.6%
35	1976	187,915	120,738	CONABLE, BARBER B.	67,177	*MACALUSO, MICHAEL		53,561 R	64.3%	35.7%	64.3%	35.7%
35	1974	159,058	90,269	CONABLE, BARBER B.	63,012	COSTANZA, MARGARET	5,777	27,257 R	56.8%	39.6%	58.9%	41.1%
35	1972	187,580	127,298	CONABLE, BARBER B.	53,321	SPENCER, TERENCE J.	6,961	73,977 R	67.9%	28.4%	70.5%	29.5%
36	1976	184,947	61,701	*ARGEN, RALPH J.	123,246	*LAFALCE, JOHN J.		61,545 D	33.4%	66.6%	33.4%	66.6%
36	1974	151,940	61,442	*ROURKE, RUSSELL A.	90,498	*LAFALCE, JOHN J.		29,056 D	40.4%	59.6%	40.4%	59.6%
36	1972	192,333	110,238	*SMITH, HENRY P.	82,095	*MCCARTHY, MAX		28,143 R	57.3%	42.7%	57.3%	42.7%
37	1976	127,951	23,660	KIMBOROUGH, CALVIN	100,042	*NOWAK, HENRY J.	4,249	76,382 D	18.5%	78.2%	19.1%	80.9%
37	1974	112,116	27,531	*BALA, JOSEPH R.	84,064	*NOWAK, HENRY J.	521	56,533 D	24.6%	75.0%	24.7%	75.3%
37	1972	158,708	44,103	*MCLAUGHLIN, WILLIAM F.	114,605	*DULSKI, THADDEUS J.		70,502 D	27.8%	72.2%	27.8%	72.2%
38	1976	212,009	165,702	*KEMP, JACK F.	46,307	*GERACI, PETER J.		119,395 R	78.2%	21.8%	78.2%	21.8%
38	1974	175,616	126,687	*KEMP, JACK F.	48,929	*WICKS, BARBARA C.		77,758 R	72.1%	27.9%	72.1%	27.9%
38	1972	214,552	156,967	*KEMP, JACK F.	57,585	*LORUSSO, ANTHONY P.		99,382 R	73.2%	26.8%	73.2%	26.8%
39	1976	178,004	68,018	*SNOWDEN, RICHARD A.	109,986	LUNDINE, STANLEY N.		41,968 D	38.2%	61.8%	38.2%	61.8%
39	1974	145,019	87,321	HASTINGS, JAMES F.	53,866	*PARMENT, WILLIAM L.	3,832	33,455 R	60.2%	37.1%	61.8%	38.2%
39	1972	175,400	126,147	*HASTINGS, JAMES F.	49,253	WHITE, WILBUR		76,894 R	71.9%	28.1%	71.9%	28.1%

NEW YORK

1976 GENERAL ELECTION

President — The Republican candidate was also the Conservative nominee and 274,878 of his votes were received as the Conservative candidate. The Democratic candidate was also the Liberal nominee and 145,393 of his votes were received as the Liberal candidate. Other vote was 12,197 MacBride (Free Libertarian); 10,270 Hall (Communist); 6,996 Camejo (Socialist Workers); 5,413 LaRouche (Labor); 4,303 McCarthy (write-in); 451 Anderson (write-in); 97 Maddox (write-in); 28 Levin (write-in); 14 Zeidler (write-in); 4,052 scattered. Original uncorrected canvass gave the total write-in vote as 8,975.

Senator — The Republican candidate was also the Conservative nominee and 311,494 of his votes were received as the Conservative candidate. The Democratic candidate was also the Liberal nominee and 184,083 of his votes were received as the Liberal candidate. Other vote was 25,141 Aptheker (Communist); 16,350 Gallo (Socialist Workers); 10,943 Nixon (Free Libertarian); 6,716 Boyd (Labor); 1,378 scattered.

Congress — Original uncorrected canvass gave the Republican vote in CD 25 as 122,958. The boundary lines of CD's 12, 13, 14 and 15 were redrawn prior to the 1974 election. Other vote was Morgan (Conservative) in CD 1; Davidson (Liberal) in CD 2; York (Liberal) in CD 3; Gammans (Conservative) in CD 6; Jones (Socialist Workers) in CD 7; Brown (Socialist Workers) in CD 8; Kluger (Liberal) in CD 9; Shepherd (Conservative) in CD 12; Paone (Liberal) in CD 15; Lindsley (Conservative) in CD 21; Bonner (Conservative) in CD 22; Assante (Liberal) in CD 24; Victor (Liberal) in CD 26; Lewis (Labor) in CD 28; Colvin (Liberal) in CD 32; Cook (Conservative) in CD 34; Grimm (Conservative) in CD 37; in other CD's as follows:

CD 10	5,868 Fuchs (Conservative); 3,872 Hagan (Liberal).
CD 11	6,316 Levinson (Conservative); 4,169 Rothenberg (Liberal).
CD 14	678 Wright (Socialist Workers); 213 Flateau (Workers).
CD 17	10,399 Peters (Conservative); 8,656 Schneir (Liberal).
CD 18	6,319 McConnell (Conservative); 1,188 Garza (Socialist Workers).
CD 19	2,169 Cole (Conservative); 640 Halyard (Workers).
CD 20	3,323 Dinsmore (Conservative); 1,076 Steinberg (Workers).
CD 29	15,337 DeYoung (Conservative); 1,314 Brooks (Mayflower); 432 Ferran (Co-Equal Citizens).
CD 33	5,980 Elkins (Conservative); 2,757 Reiner (Liberal).

NEW YORK CITY

The city is composed of five counties, each of which for municipal government purposes is known as a borough. Names of the counties and boroughs are the same save in the case of New York county (Manhattan borough) and Kings county (Brooklyn borough). The boundaries of the 38th and 62nd Assembly Districts cross county lines. The 38th District is part in Kings and part in Queens; the 62nd District is part in Richmond, part in New York.

President — The Republican vote includes 78,921 votes cast for Ford as the Conservative candidate, and the Democratic vote includes 84,425 votes cast for Carter as the Liberal candidate. Other vote was 5,332 Hall (Communist); 3,660 Camejo (Socialist Workers); 2,202 MacBride (Free Libertarian); 2,117 LaRouche (Labor); 795 McCarthy (write-in); 552 scattered.

Senator — The Republican vote includes 91,742 votes cast for Buckley as the Conservative candidate, and the Democratic vote includes 97,548 votes cast for Moynihan as the Liberal candidate. Other vote was 16,154 Aptheker (Communist); 7,130 Gallo (Socialist Workers); 4,929 Nixon (Free Libertarian); 2,168 Boyd (Labor); 251 scattered.

NEW YORK

1976 PRIMARIES

SEPTEMBER 14 REPUBLICAN

Senator 242,527 James L. Buckley; 101,629 Peter A. Peyser.

Congress Unopposed in twenty-nine CD's. Democratic candidates were endorsed in CD's 7, 9, 10, 19, and 21. Bernard L. Ploscowe, the unopposed candidate in CD 20, died after the primary and Denise T. Weiseman was substituted by the local party committee. Contested as follows:

CD 9 3,488 James J. Delaney; 1,807 James E. Eagan.
CD 25 12,745 Hamilton Fish; 1,298 Sanford P. Cohen.
CD 27 18,832 William H. Harter; 5,418 Imogene Calogero.
CD 28 No candidates appeared on the ballot; write-in votes were 83 Samuel S. Stratton and 33 Mary Bradt. Mr. Stratton declined the endorsement and Mary Bradt the Conservative candidate became the endorsed candidate.
CD 29 16,091 Joseph A. Martino; 9,089 James E. DeYoung; 3,920 Thomas J. Myles.

SEPTEMBER 14 DEMOCRATIC

Senator 333,697 Daniel P. Moynihan; 323,705 Bella S. Abzug; 94,191 Ramsey Clark; 82,689 Paul O'Dwyer; 82,331 Abraham J. Hirschfeld.

Congress Unopposed in twenty-eight CD's. Contested as follows:

CD 2 8,066 Thomas J. Downey; 1,108 John R. Mawn.
CD 11 24,366 James H. Scheuer; 9,727 Bryan Levinson.
CD 12 10,602 Shirley Chisholm; 7,364 Samuel D. Wright; 1,915 Luz P. Vega.
CD 14 14,977 Frederick W. Richmond; 3,822 Irving Gross.
CD 15 11,800 Leo C. Zeferetti; 8,066 Arthur J. Paone; 4,357 Robert Chira; 867 Daniel J. Kisha.
CD 17 17,383 John M. Murphy; 7,295 Ned Schneier; 3,774 Peter J. Murray.
CD 21 13,622 Herman Badillo; 4,721 Ramon S. Velez.
CD 22 28,251 Jonathan Bingham; 4,614 Richard J. Waksman.
CD 23 11,898 J. Edward Meyer; 4,089 Robert N. Rickles; 2,803 Jeffrey M. Bernbach; 2,784 Robert J. Conlan; 2,575 Dominick Iannacone.
CD 26 5,472 John R. Maloney; 5,264 Frederick F. Johnson; 4,131 Eugene R. Victor.
CD 37 19,065 Henry J. Nowak; 5,944 Charles Poth.

SEPTEMBER 14 CONSERVATIVE

Senator James L. Buckley, unopposed.

Congress Major party candidates endorsed or nominees unopposed in all CD's in which a candidate was named except CD's 6, 25 and 27. In those CD's contested as follows:

CD 6 317 Nelson J. Gammans; 264 Vincent Balletta.
CD 25 427 Hamilton Fish; 366 Donald Badgley.
CD 27 289 William H. Harter; 228 Imogene Calogero.

SEPTEMBER 14 LIBERAL

Senator Henry J. Stern, unopposed. Mr. Stern withdrew after the primary and Daniel P. Moynihan was substituted by the state committee.

Congress Major party candidates endorsed or nominees unopposed in all CD's in which a candidate was named.

NORTH CAROLINA

GOVERNOR

James B. Hunt (D). Elected 1976 to a four-year term.

SENATORS

Jesse Helms (R). Elected 1972 to a six-year term.

Robert Morgan (D). Elected 1974 to a six-year term.

REPRESENTATIVES

1. Walter B. Jones (D)
2. L. H. Fountain (D)
3. Charles Whitley (D)
4. Ike F. Andrews (D)
5. Stephen L. Neal (D)
6. L. Richardson Preyer (D)
7. Charles G. Rose (D)
8. W. G. Hefner (D)
9. James G. Martin (R)
10. James T. Broyhill (R)
11. Lamar Gudger (D)

POSTWAR VOTE FOR GOVERNOR

								Percentage			
	Total	Republican		Democratic		Other	Rep.-Dem.	Total Vote		Major Vote	
Year	Vote	Vote	Candidate	Vote	Candidate	Vote	Plurality	Rep.	Dem.	Rep.	Dem.
1976	1,663,824	564,102	Flaherty, David T.	1,081,293	Hunt, James B.	18,429	517,191 D	33.9%	65.0%	34.3%	65.7%
1972	1,504,785	767,470	Holshouser, James E.	729,104	Bowles, Hargrove	8,211	38,366 R	51.0%	48.5%	51.3%	48.7%
1968	1,558,308	737,075	Gardner, James C.	821,233	Scott, Robert W.	–	84,158 D	47.3%	52.7%	47.3%	52.7%
1964	1,396,508	606,165	Gavin, Robert L.	790,343	Moore, Dan K.	–	184,178 D	43.4%	56.6%	43.4%	56.6%
1960	1,350,360	613,975	Gavin, Robert L.	735,248	Sanford, Terry	1,137	121,273 D	45.5%	54.4%	45.5%	54.5%
1956	1,135,859	375,379	Hayes, Kyle	760,480	Hodges, Luther H.	–	385,101 D	33.0%	67.0%	33.0%	67.0%
1952	1,179,635	383,329	Seawell, H. F.	796,306	Umstead, William B.	–	412,977 D	32.5%	67.5%	32.5%	67.5%
1948	780,525	206,166	Pritchard, George	570,995	Scott, William Kerr	3,364	364,829 D	26.4%	73.2%	26.5%	73.5%

POSTWAR VOTE FOR SENATOR

								Percentage			
	Total	Republican		Democratic		Other	Rep.-Dem.	Total Vote		Major Vote	
Year	Vote	Vote	Candidate	Vote	Candidate	Vote	Plurality	Rep.	Dem.	Rep.	Dem.
1974	1,020,367	377,618	Stevens, William E.	633,775	Morgan, Robert	8,974	256,157 D	37.0%	62.1%	37.3%	62.7%
1972	1,472,541	795,248	Helms, Jesse	677,293	Galifianakis, Nick	–	117,955 R	54.0%	46.0%	54.0%	46.0%
1968	1,437,340	566,934	Somers, Robert V.	870,406	Ervin, Sam J.	–	303,472 D	39.4%	60.6%	39.4%	60.6%
1966	901,978	400,502	Shallcross, John S.	501,440	Jordan, B. Everett	36	100,938 D	44.4%	55.6%	44.4%	55.6%
1962	813,155	321,635	Greene, Claude L.	491,520	Ervin, Sam J.	–	169,885 D	39.6%	60.4%	39.6%	60.4%
1960	1,291,485	497,964	Hayes, Kyle	793,521	Jordan, B. Everett	–	295,557 D	38.6%	61.4%	38.6%	61.4%
1958s	616,469	184,977	Clarke, Richard C.	431,492	Jordan, B. Everett	–	246,515 D	30.0%	70.0%	30.0%	70.0%
1956	1,098,828	367,475	Johnson, Joel A.	731,353	Ervin, Sam J.	–	363,878 D	33.4%	66.6%	33.4%	66.6%
1954	619,634	211,322	West, Paul C.	408,312	Scott, William Kerr	–	196,990 D	34.1%	65.9%	34.1%	65.9%
1954s	410,574	–	–	410,574	Ervin, Sam J.	–	410,574 D	–	100.0%	–	100.0%
1950	548,276	171,804	Leavitt, Halsey B.	376,472	Hoey, Clyde R.	–	204,668 D	31.3%	68.7%	31.3%	68.7%
1950s	544,924	177,753	Gavin, E. L.	364,912	Smith, Willis	2,259	187,159 D	32.6%	67.0%	32.8%	67.2%
1948	764,559	220,307	Wilkinson, John A.	540,762	Broughton, J. M.	3,490	320,455 D	28.8%	70.7%	28.9%	71.1%

The election in 1958, and one each in 1954 and 1950 were for short terms to fill vacancies.

NORTH CAROLINA

Districts Established April 29, 1971

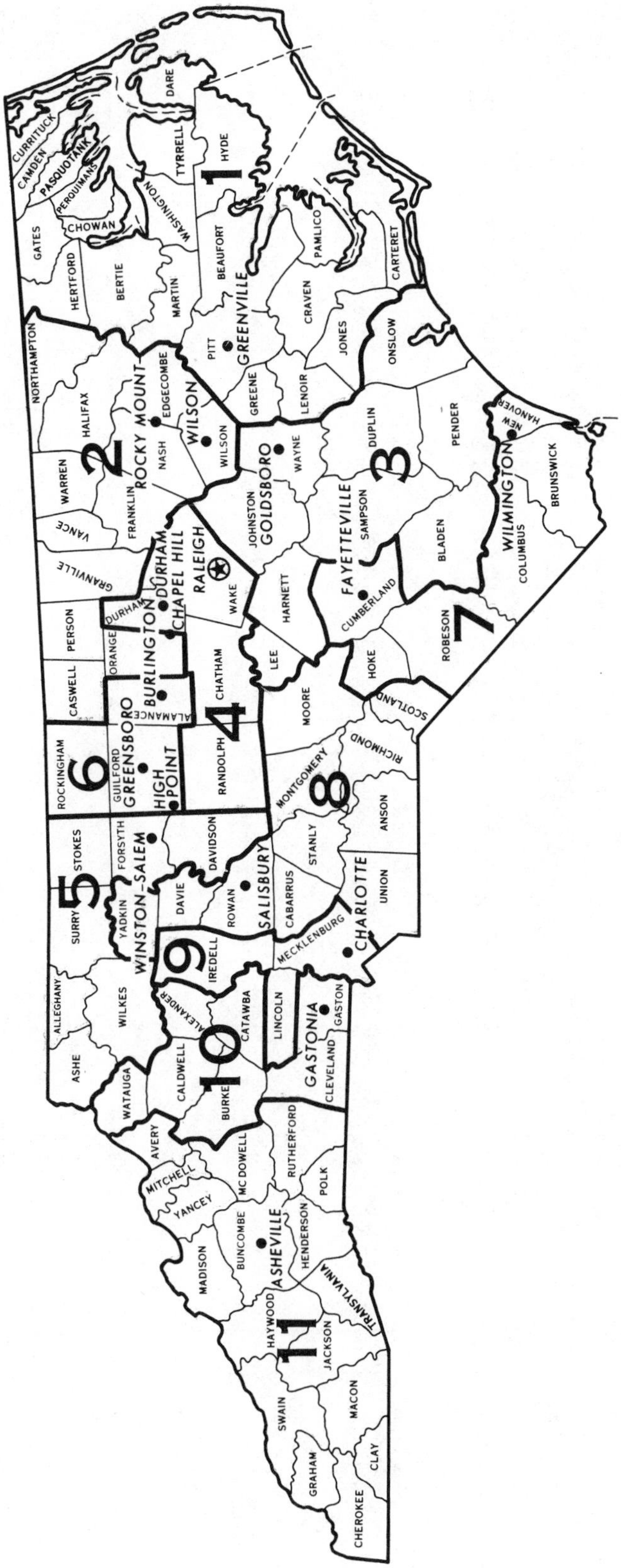

NORTH CAROLINA

PRESIDENT 1976

1970 Census Population	County	Total Vote	Republican	Democratic	Other	Rep.-Dem. Plurality	Percentage Total Vote Rep.	Percentage Total Vote Dem.	Percentage Major Vote Rep.	Percentage Major Vote Dem.
96,362	ALAMANCE	30,247	12,680	17,371	196	4,691 D	41.9%	57.4%	42.2%	57.8%
19,466	ALEXANDER	9,975	4,661	5,287	27	626 D	46.7%	53.0%	46.9%	53.1%
8,134	ALLEGHANY	4,099	1,532	2,550	17	1,018 D	37.4%	62.2%	37.5%	62.5%
23,488	ANSON	6,425	1,608	4,796	21	3,188 D	25.0%	74.6%	25.1%	74.9%
19,571	ASHE	10,155	4,937	5,193	25	256 D	48.6%	51.1%	48.7%	51.3%
12,655	AVERY	4,995	3,085	1,869	41	1,216 R	61.8%	37.4%	62.3%	37.7%
35,980	BEAUFORT	10,467	4,677	5,728	62	1,051 D	44.7%	54.7%	44.9%	55.1%
20,528	BERTIE	5,470	1,332	4,117	21	2,785 D	24.4%	75.3%	24.4%	75.6%
26,477	BLADEN	7,589	1,546	6,009	34	4,463 D	20.4%	79.2%	20.5%	79.5%
24,223	BRUNSWICK	11,066	3,636	7,377	53	3,741 D	32.9%	66.7%	33.0%	67.0%
145,056	BUNCOMBE	49,426	22,461	26,633	332	4,172 D	45.4%	53.9%	45.8%	54.2%
60,364	BURKE	24,440	10,070	14,254	116	4,184 D	41.2%	58.3%	41.4%	58.6%
74,629	CABARRUS	24,644	12,455	12,049	140	406 R	50.5%	48.9%	50.8%	49.2%
56,699	CALDWELL	21,875	9,872	11,894	109	2,022 D	45.1%	54.4%	45.4%	54.6%
5,453	CAMDEN	1,809	562	1,231	16	669 D	31.1%	68.0%	31.3%	68.7%
31,603	CARTERET	12,939	5,786	7,080	73	1,294 D	44.7%	54.7%	45.0%	55.0%
19,055	CASWELL	5,489	1,761	3,707	21	1,946 D	32.1%	67.5%	32.2%	67.8%
90,873	CATAWBA	35,718	18,696	16,862	160	1,834 R	52.3%	47.2%	52.6%	47.4%
29,554	CHATHAM	10,730	4,279	6,397	54	2,118 D	39.9%	59.6%	40.1%	59.9%
16,330	CHEROKEE	6,849	3,210	3,571	68	361 D	46.9%	52.1%	47.3%	52.7%
10,764	CHOWAN	2,890	1,019	1,862	9	843 D	35.3%	64.4%	35.4%	64.6%
5,180	CLAY	3,012	1,428	1,569	15	141 D	47.4%	52.1%	47.6%	52.4%
72,556	CLEVELAND	22,605	8,106	14,406	93	6,300 D	35.9%	63.7%	36.0%	64.0%
46,937	COLUMBUS	14,401	3,184	11,148	69	7,964 D	22.1%	77.4%	22.2%	77.8%
62,554	CRAVEN	13,549	5,881	7,553	115	1,672 D	43.4%	55.7%	43.8%	56.2%
212,042	CUMBERLAND	38,694	14,226	24,297	171	10,071 D	36.8%	62.8%	36.9%	63.1%
6,976	CURRITUCK	2,972	954	1,999	19	1,045 D	32.1%	67.3%	32.3%	67.7%
6,995	DARE	3,891	1,680	2,191	20	511 D	43.2%	56.3%	43.4%	56.6%
95,627	DAVIDSON	36,863	18,813	17,859	191	954 R	51.0%	48.4%	51.3%	48.7%
18,855	DAVIE	8,463	4,772	3,635	56	1,137 R	56.4%	43.0%	56.8%	43.2%
38,015	DUPLIN	11,694	3,912	7,696	86	3,784 D	33.5%	65.8%	33.7%	66.3%
132,681	DURHAM	41,575	18,945	22,425	205	3,480 D	45.6%	53.9%	45.8%	54.2%
52,341	EDGECOMBE	12,970	4,850	8,001	119	3,151 D	37.4%	61.7%	37.7%	62.3%
214,348	FORSYTH	78,934	38,886	39,561	487	675 D	49.3%	50.1%	49.6%	50.4%
26,820	FRANKLIN	8,097	2,630	5,405	62	2,775 D	32.5%	66.8%	32.7%	67.3%
148,415	GASTON	42,776	19,727	22,878	171	3,151 D	46.1%	53.5%	46.3%	53.7%
8,524	GATES	3,028	722	2,291	15	1,569 D	23.8%	75.7%	24.0%	76.0%
6,562	GRAHAM	3,424	1,621	1,791	12	170 D	47.3%	52.3%	47.5%	52.5%
32,762	GRANVILLE	8,251	2,955	5,244	52	2,289 D	35.8%	63.6%	36.0%	64.0%
14,967	GREENE	4,126	1,356	2,740	30	1,384 D	32.9%	66.4%	33.1%	66.9%
288,590	GUILFORD	92,740	45,441	46,826	473	1,385 D	49.0%	50.5%	49.2%	50.8%
53,884	HALIFAX	13,254	5,257	7,892	105	2,635 D	39.7%	59.5%	40.0%	60.0%
49,667	HARNETT	14,988	5,935	8,992	61	3,057 D	39.6%	60.0%	39.8%	60.2%
41,710	HAYWOOD	16,655	5,885	10,692	78	4,807 D	35.3%	64.2%	35.5%	64.5%
42,804	HENDERSON	19,156	10,830	8,155	171	2,675 R	56.5%	42.6%	57.0%	43.0%
23,529	HERTFORD	5,511	1,517	3,986	8	2,469 D	27.5%	72.3%	27.6%	72.4%
16,436	HOKE	4,123	920	3,186	17	2,266 D	22.3%	77.3%	22.4%	77.6%
5,571	HYDE	1,718	623	1,084	11	461 D	36.3%	63.1%	36.5%	63.5%
72,197	IREDELL	25,142	11,573	13,295	274	1,722 D	46.0%	52.9%	46.5%	53.5%
21,593	JACKSON	8,798	3,536	5,223	39	1,687 D	40.2%	59.4%	40.4%	59.6%
61,737	JOHNSTON	18,881	8,511	10,301	69	1,790 D	45.1%	54.6%	45.2%	54.8%
9,779	JONES	3,011	948	2,016	47	1,068 D	31.5%	67.0%	32.0%	68.0%
30,467	LEE	8,834	3,691	5,104	39	1,413 D	41.8%	57.8%	42.0%	58.0%
55,204	LENOIR	15,484	7,715	7,650	119	65 R	49.8%	49.4%	50.2%	49.8%
32,682	LINCOLN	16,214	6,682	9,462	70	2,780 D	41.2%	58.4%	41.4%	58.6%
30,648	MCDOWELL	10,750	4,450	6,246	54	1,796 D	41.4%	58.1%	41.6%	58.4%
15,788	MACON	8,123	3,673	4,406	44	733 D	45.2%	54.2%	45.5%	54.5%
16,003	MADISON	5,896	2,446	3,433	17	987 D	41.5%	58.2%	41.6%	58.4%
24,730	MARTIN	6,478	1,931	4,518	29	2,587 D	29.8%	69.7%	29.9%	70.1%
354,656	MECKLENBURG	125,549	61,715	63,198	636	1,483 D	49.2%	50.3%	49.4%	50.6%
13,447	MITCHELL	5,781	3,728	2,031	22	1,697 R	64.5%	35.1%	64.7%	35.3%
19,267	MONTGOMERY	7,214	2,872	4,308	34	1,436 D	39.8%	59.7%	40.0%	60.0%
39,048	MOORE	15,030	7,577	7,373	80	204 R	50.4%	49.1%	50.7%	49.3%
59,122	NASH	17,617	8,477	8,937	203	460 D	48.1%	50.7%	48.7%	51.3%
82,996	NEW HANOVER	28,502	13,687	14,504	311	817 D	48.0%	50.9%	48.6%	51.4%

NORTH CAROLINA

PRESIDENT 1976

1970 Census Population	County	Total Vote	Republican	Democratic	Other	Rep.-Dem. Plurality	Percentage Total Vote Rep.	Percentage Total Vote Dem.	Percentage Major Vote Rep.	Percentage Major Vote Dem.
24,009	NORTHAMPTON	6,380	1,238	5,118	24	3,880 D	19.4%	80.2%	19.5%	80.5%
103,126	ONSLOW	13,978	5,953	7,954	71	2,001 D	42.6%	56.9%	42.8%	57.2%
57,707	ORANGE	25,297	9,302	15,755	240	6,453 D	36.8%	62.3%	37.1%	62.9%
9,467	PAMLICO	3,209	1,068	2,113	28	1,045 D	33.3%	65.8%	33.6%	66.4%
26,824	PASQUOTANK	6,996	2,651	4,302	43	1,651 D	37.9%	61.5%	38.1%	61.9%
18,149	PENDER	6,538	2,063	4,422	53	2,359 D	31.6%	67.6%	31.8%	68.2%
8,351	PERQUIMANS	2,581	909	1,666	6	757 D	35.2%	64.5%	35.3%	64.7%
25,914	PERSON	7,038	3,038	3,977	23	939 D	43.2%	56.5%	43.3%	56.7%
73,900	PITT	21,309	9,532	11,636	141	2,104 D	44.7%	54.6%	45.0%	55.0%
11,735	POLK	5,812	2,605	3,155	52	550 D	44.8%	54.3%	45.2%	54.8%
76,358	RANDOLPH	27,212	14,337	12,714	161	1,623 R	52.7%	46.7%	53.0%	47.0%
39,889	RICHMOND	11,665	2,848	8,793	24	5,945 D	24.4%	75.4%	24.5%	75.5%
84,842	ROBESON	25,699	4,907	20,695	97	15,788 D	19.1%	80.5%	19.2%	80.8%
72,402	ROCKINGHAM	22,872	9,362	13,413	97	4,051 D	40.9%	58.6%	41.1%	58.9%
90,035	ROWAN	30,248	14,644	15,363	241	719 D	48.4%	50.8%	48.8%	51.2%
47,337	RUTHERFORD	17,124	6,718	10,361	45	3,643 D	39.2%	60.5%	39.3%	60.7%
44,954	SAMPSON	15,902	6,968	8,869	65	1,901 D	43.8%	55.8%	44.0%	56.0%
26,929	SCOTLAND	6,391	1,932	4,430	29	2,498 D	30.2%	69.3%	30.4%	69.6%
42,822	STANLY	18,190	8,845	9,262	83	417 D	48.6%	50.9%	48.8%	51.2%
23,782	STOKES	12,711	6,029	6,647	35	618 D	47.4%	52.3%	47.6%	52.4%
51,415	SURRY	17,490	7,403	10,024	63	2,621 D	42.3%	57.3%	42.5%	57.5%
7,861	SWAIN	3,771	1,608	2,151	12	543 D	42.6%	57.0%	42.8%	57.2%
19,713	TRANSYLVANIA	8,795	4,089	4,636	70	547 D	46.5%	52.7%	46.9%	53.1%
3,806	TYRRELL	1,305	403	900	2	497 D	30.9%	69.0%	30.9%	69.1%
54,714	UNION	16,847	6,184	10,578	85	4,394 D	36.7%	62.8%	36.9%	63.1%
32,691	VANCE	9,461	3,813	5,620	28	1,807 D	40.3%	59.4%	40.4%	59.6%
228,453	WAKE	88,947	44,291	44,005	651	286 R	49.8%	49.5%	50.2%	49.8%
15,810	WARREN	4,635	1,427	3,185	23	1,758 D	30.8%	68.7%	30.9%	69.1%
14,038	WASHINGTON	4,364	1,486	2,840	38	1,354 D	34.1%	65.1%	34.4%	65.6%
23,404	WATAUGA	10,834	5,400	5,358	76	42 R	49.8%	49.5%	50.2%	49.8%
85,408	WAYNE	19,002	9,607	9,265	130	342 R	50.6%	48.8%	50.9%	49.1%
49,524	WILKES	22,032	11,768	10,176	88	1,592 R	53.4%	46.2%	53.6%	46.4%
57,486	WILSON	15,087	6,795	8,209	83	1,414 D	45.0%	54.4%	45.3%	54.7%
24,599	YADKIN	10,471	5,916	4,497	58	1,419 R	56.5%	42.9%	56.8%	43.2%
12,629	YANCEY	6,650	2,688	3,932	30	1,244 D	40.4%	59.1%	40.6%	59.4%
5,082,059	TOTAL	1,678,914	741,960	927,365	9,589	185,405 D	44.2%	55.2%	44.4%	55.6%

NORTH CAROLINA

GOVERNOR 1976

1970 Census Population	County	Total Vote	Republican	Democratic	Other	Rep.-Dem. Plurality	Percentage Total Vote Rep.	Total Vote Dem.	Major Vote Rep.	Major Vote Dem.
96,362	ALAMANCE	30,573	10,147	19,918	508	9,771 D	33.2%	65.1%	33.8%	66.2%
19,466	ALEXANDER	9,854	4,178	5,650	26	1,472 D	42.4%	57.3%	42.5%	57.5%
8,134	ALLEGHANY	4,124	1,373	2,739	12	1,366 D	33.3%	66.4%	33.4%	66.6%
23,488	ANSON	6,357	967	5,375	15	4,408 D	15.2%	84.6%	15.2%	84.8%
19,571	ASHE	10,051	4,623	5,398	30	775 D	46.0%	53.7%	46.1%	53.9%
12,655	AVERY	4,869	2,821	2,014	34	807 R	57.9%	41.4%	58.3%	41.7%
35,980	BEAUFORT	10,299	2,959	7,282	58	4,323 D	28.7%	70.7%	28.9%	71.1%
20,528	BERTIE	5,004	595	4,377	32	3,782 D	11.9%	87.5%	12.0%	88.0%
26,477	BLADEN	7,363	861	6,432	70	5,571 D	11.7%	87.4%	11.8%	88.2%
24,223	BRUNSWICK	11,042	2,898	8,055	89	5,157 D	26.2%	72.9%	26.5%	73.5%
145,056	BUNCOMBE	50,619	18,670	31,557	392	12,887 D	36.9%	62.3%	37.2%	62.8%
60,364	BURKE	24,124	9,349	14,708	67	5,359 D	38.8%	61.0%	38.9%	61.1%
74,629	CABARRUS	24,380	9,684	14,542	154	4,858 D	39.7%	59.6%	40.0%	60.0%
56,699	CALDWELL	21,642	9,346	12,220	76	2,874 D	43.2%	56.5%	43.3%	56.7%
5,453	CAMDEN	1,754	259	1,489	6	1,230 D	14.8%	84.9%	14.8%	85.2%
31,603	CARTERET	12,827	4,437	8,292	98	3,855 D	34.6%	64.6%	34.9%	65.1%
19,055	CASWELL	5,323	886	4,377	60	3,491 D	16.6%	82.2%	16.8%	83.2%
90,873	CATAWBA	35,241	16,119	19,017	105	2,898 D	45.7%	54.0%	45.9%	54.1%
29,554	CHATHAM	10,636	3,491	6,915	230	3,424 D	32.8%	65.0%	33.5%	66.5%
16,330	CHEROKEE	6,951	3,001	3,886	64	885 D	43.2%	55.9%	43.6%	56.4%
10,764	CHOWAN	2,999	450	2,529	20	2,079 D	15.0%	84.3%	15.1%	84.9%
5,180	CLAY	2,963	1,355	1,599	9	244 D	45.7%	54.0%	45.9%	54.1%
72,556	CLEVELAND	22,131	5,530	16,526	75	10,996 D	25.0%	74.7%	25.1%	74.9%
46,937	COLUMBUS	14,216	2,152	11,994	70	9,842 D	15.1%	84.4%	15.2%	84.8%
62,554	CRAVEN	13,713	3,556	10,012	145	6,456 D	25.9%	73.0%	26.2%	73.8%
212,042	CUMBERLAND	39,020	9,654	28,646	720	18,992 D	24.7%	73.4%	25.2%	74.8%
6,976	CURRITUCK	2,833	442	2,381	10	1,939 D	15.6%	84.0%	15.7%	84.3%
6,995	DARE	3,898	1,062	2,811	25	1,749 D	27.2%	72.1%	27.4%	72.6%
95,627	DAVIDSON	36,406	15,660	20,493	253	4,833 D	43.0%	56.3%	43.3%	56.7%
18,855	DAVIE	8,300	4,161	4,076	63	85 R	50.1%	49.1%	50.5%	49.5%
38,015	DUPLIN	11,370	2,470	8,787	113	6,317 D	21.7%	77.3%	21.9%	78.1%
132,681	DURHAM	41,011	14,134	26,091	786	11,957 D	34.5%	63.6%	35.1%	64.9%
52,341	EDGECOMBE	12,791	3,051	9,567	173	6,516 D	23.9%	74.8%	24.2%	75.8%
214,348	FORSYTH	76,414	29,334	46,085	995	16,751 D	38.4%	60.3%	38.9%	61.1%
26,820	FRANKLIN	7,807	1,511	6,129	167	4,618 D	19.4%	78.5%	19.8%	80.2%
148,415	GASTON	41,158	14,039	26,980	139	12,941 D	34.1%	65.6%	34.2%	65.8%
8,524	GATES	2,794	255	2,524	15	2,269 D	9.1%	90.3%	9.2%	90.8%
6,562	GRAHAM	3,343	1,425	1,914	4	489 D	42.6%	57.3%	42.7%	57.3%
32,762	GRANVILLE	8,049	1,457	6,453	139	4,996 D	18.1%	80.2%	18.4%	81.6%
14,967	GREENE	4,105	798	3,260	47	2,462 D	19.4%	79.4%	19.7%	80.3%
288,590	GUILFORD	92,223	33,146	57,345	1,732	24,199 D	35.9%	62.2%	36.6%	63.4%
53,884	HALIFAX	13,116	2,994	9,900	222	6,906 D	22.8%	75.5%	23.2%	76.8%
49,667	HARNETT	14,860	4,454	10,186	220	5,732 D	30.0%	68.5%	30.4%	69.6%
41,710	HAYWOOD	16,474	4,817	11,601	56	6,784 D	29.2%	70.4%	29.3%	70.7%
42,804	HENDERSON	19,438	9,477	9,823	138	346 D	48.8%	50.5%	49.1%	50.9%
23,529	HERTFORD	5,219	576	4,613	30	4,037 D	11.0%	88.4%	11.1%	88.9%
16,436	HOKE	4,075	566	3,472	37	2,906 D	13.9%	85.2%	14.0%	86.0%
5,571	HYDE	1,712	345	1,353	14	1,008 D	20.2%	79.0%	20.3%	79.7%
72,197	IREDELL	24,932	9,109	15,567	256	6,458 D	36.5%	62.4%	36.9%	63.1%
21,593	JACKSON	9,345	3,459	5,838	48	2,379 D	37.0%	62.5%	37.2%	62.8%
61,737	JOHNSTON	18,716	5,981	12,447	288	6,466 D	32.0%	66.5%	32.5%	67.5%
9,779	JONES	2,956	462	2,454	40	1,992 D	15.6%	83.0%	15.8%	84.2%
30,467	LEE	9,229	3,001	6,063	165	3,062 D	32.5%	65.7%	33.1%	66.9%
55,204	LENOIR	15,264	4,206	10,874	184	6,668 D	27.6%	71.2%	27.9%	72.1%
32,682	LINCOLN	16,025	6,032	9,960	33	3,928 D	37.6%	62.2%	37.7%	62.3%
30,648	MCDOWELL	10,615	3,571	7,011	33	3,440 D	33.6%	66.0%	33.7%	66.3%
15,788	MACON	8,072	3,212	4,830	30	1,618 D	39.8%	59.8%	39.9%	60.1%
16,003	MADISON	6,010	2,258	3,730	22	1,472 D	37.6%	62.1%	37.7%	62.3%
24,730	MARTIN	6,510	1,070	5,387	53	4,317 D	16.4%	82.7%	16.6%	83.4%
354,656	MECKLENBURG	123,371	47,363	74,833	1,175	27,470 D	38.4%	60.7%	38.8%	61.2%
13,447	MITCHELL	5,618	3,457	2,145	16	1,312 R	61.5%	38.2%	61.7%	38.3%
19,267	MONTGOMERY	7,161	2,454	4,633	74	2,179 D	34.3%	64.7%	34.6%	65.4%
39,048	MOORE	14,806	6,291	8,168	347	1,877 D	42.5%	55.2%	43.5%	56.5%
59,122	NASH	17,429	5,484	11,548	397	6,064 D	31.5%	66.3%	32.2%	67.8%
82,996	NEW HANOVER	27,696	8,493	18,815	388	10,322 D	30.7%	67.9%	31.1%	68.9%

NORTH CAROLINA

GOVERNOR 1976

1970 Census Population	County	Total Vote	Republican	Democratic	Other	Rep.-Dem. Plurality	Percentage Total Vote Rep.	Total Vote Dem.	Major Vote Rep.	Major Vote Dem.
24,009	NORTHAMPTON	6,371	557	5,733	81	5,176 D	8.7%	90.0%	8.9%	91.1%
103,126	ONSLOW	13,744	3,233	10,421	90	7,188 D	23.5%	75.8%	23.7%	76.3%
57,707	ORANGE	24,428	7,338	16,515	575	9,177 D	30.0%	67.6%	30.8%	69.2%
9,467	PAMLICO	3,098	696	2,377	25	1,681 D	22.5%	76.7%	22.6%	77.4%
26,824	PASQUOTANK	6,806	1,267	5,486	53	4,219 D	18.6%	80.6%	18.8%	81.2%
18,149	PENDER	6,242	1,441	4,747	54	3,306 D	23.1%	76.0%	23.3%	76.7%
8,351	PERQUIMANS	2,529	351	2,169	9	1,818 D	13.9%	85.8%	13.9%	86.1%
25,914	PERSON	6,865	1,937	4,733	195	2,796 D	28.2%	68.9%	29.0%	71.0%
73,900	PITT	20,847	5,256	15,421	170	10,165 D	25.2%	74.0%	25.4%	74.6%
11,735	POLK	5,854	2,342	3,464	48	1,122 D	40.0%	59.2%	40.3%	59.7%
76,358	RANDOLPH	27,860	13,050	14,426	384	1,376 D	46.8%	51.8%	47.5%	52.5%
39,889	RICHMOND	11,124	2,113	8,889	122	6,776 D	19.0%	79.9%	19.2%	80.8%
84,842	ROBESON	24,909	2,539	22,212	158	19,673 D	10.2%	89.2%	10.3%	89.7%
72,402	ROCKINGHAM	22,607	6,698	15,614	295	8,916 D	29.6%	69.1%	30.0%	70.0%
90,035	ROWAN	29,857	11,641	17,970	246	6,329 D	39.0%	60.2%	39.3%	60.7%
47,337	RUTHERFORD	16,922	5,413	11,430	79	6,017 D	32.0%	67.5%	32.1%	67.9%
44,954	SAMPSON	15,810	5,980	9,718	112	3,738 D	37.8%	61.5%	38.1%	61.9%
26,929	SCOTLAND	6,162	1,213	4,907	42	3,694 D	19.7%	79.6%	19.8%	80.2%
42,822	STANLY	18,066	7,764	10,249	53	2,485 D	43.0%	56.7%	43.1%	56.9%
23,782	STOKES	12,662	5,431	7,174	57	1,743 D	42.9%	56.7%	43.1%	56.9%
51,415	SURRY	18,761	7,002	11,639	120	4,637 D	37.3%	62.0%	37.6%	62.4%
7,861	SWAIN	4,031	1,483	2,530	18	1,047 D	36.8%	62.8%	37.0%	63.0%
19,713	TRANSYLVANIA	8,932	3,454	5,396	82	1,942 D	38.7%	60.4%	39.0%	61.0%
3,806	TYRRELL	1,257	215	1,039	3	824 D	17.1%	82.7%	17.1%	82.9%
54,714	UNION	16,484	4,563	11,839	82	7,276 D	27.7%	71.8%	27.8%	72.2%
32,691	VANCE	9,341	2,166	7,028	147	4,862 D	23.2%	75.2%	23.6%	76.4%
228,453	WAKE	89,947	32,165	55,599	2,183	23,434 D	35.8%	61.8%	36.6%	63.4%
15,810	WARREN	4,377	793	3,482	102	2,689 D	18.1%	79.6%	18.5%	81.5%
14,038	WASHINGTON	4,471	904	3,535	32	2,631 D	20.2%	79.1%	20.4%	79.6%
23,404	WATAUGA	10,632	4,695	5,884	53	1,189 D	44.2%	55.3%	44.4%	55.6%
85,408	WAYNE	19,153	6,778	12,067	308	5,289 D	35.4%	63.0%	36.0%	64.0%
49,524	WILKES	22,254	11,027	11,143	84	116 D	49.6%	50.1%	49.7%	50.3%
57,486	WILSON	15,333	3,332	11,796	205	8,464 D	21.7%	76.9%	22.0%	78.0%
24,599	YADKIN	10,185	5,332	4,795	58	537 R	52.4%	47.1%	52.7%	47.3%
12,629	YANCEY	6,677	2,495	4,170	12	1,675 D	37.4%	62.5%	37.4%	62.6%
5,082,059	TOTAL	1,663,824	564,102	1,081,293	18,429	517,191 D	33.9%	65.0%	34.3%	65.7%

NORTH CAROLINA

CONGRESS

CD	Year	Total Vote	Republican Vote	Republican Candidate	Democratic Vote	Democratic Candidate	Other Vote	Rep.-Dem. Plurality	Percentage Total Vote Rep.	Percentage Total Vote Dem.	Percentage Major Vote Rep.	Percentage Major Vote Dem.
1	1976	129,964	29,295	WARD, JOSEPH M.	98,611	JONES, WALTER B.	2,058	69,316 D	22.5%	75.9%	22.9%	77.1%
1	1974	71,420	16,097	MCMULLAN, HARRY	55,323	JONES, WALTER B.		39,226 D	22.5%	77.5%	22.5%	77.5%
1	1972	112,501	35,063	BONNER, J. JORDAN	77,438	JONES, WALTER B.		42,375 D	31.2%	68.8%	31.2%	68.8%
2	1976	113,561			113,368	FOUNTAIN, L. H.	193	113,368 D		99.8%		100.0%
2	1974	52,786			52,786	FOUNTAIN, L. H.		52,786 D		100.0%		100.0%
2	1972	123,991	35,193	LITTLE, ERICK P.	88,798	FOUNTAIN, L. H.		53,605 D	28.4%	71.6%	28.4%	71.6%
3	1976	112,286	35,089	BLANCHARD, WILLARD J.	77,193	WHITLEY, CHARLES	4	42,104 D	31.2%	68.7%	31.3%	68.7%
3	1974	50,931			50,931	HENDERSON, DAVID N.		50,931 D		100.0%		100.0%
3	1972	56,968			56,968	HENDERSON, DAVID N.		56,968 D		100.0%		100.0%
4	1976	152,100	59,917	GALLEMORE, JOHNNIE L.	92,165	ANDREWS, IKE F.	18	32,248 D	39.4%	60.6%	39.4%	60.6%
4	1974	96,791	33,521	PURRINGTON, WARD	62,600	ANDREWS, IKE F.	670	29,079 D	34.6%	64.7%	34.9%	65.1%
4	1972	145,044	71,972	HAWKE, JACK	73,072	ANDREWS, IKE F.		1,100 D	49.6%	50.4%	49.6%	50.4%
5	1976	182,166	83,129	MIZELL, WILMER D.	98,789	NEAL, STEPHEN L.	248	15,660 D	45.6%	54.2%	45.7%	54.3%
5	1974	124,241	59,182	MIZELL, WILMER D.	64,634	NEAL, STEPHEN L.	425	5,452 D	47.6%	52.0%	47.8%	52.2%
5	1972	156,361	101,375	MIZELL, WILMER D.	54,986	HAYS, BROOKS		46,389 R	64.8%	35.2%	64.8%	35.2%
6	1976	107,812			103,851	PREYER, L. RICHARDSON	3,961	103,851 D		96.3%		100.0%
6	1974	88,764	31,906	RITCHIE, R. S.	56,507	PREYER, L. RICHARDSON	351	24,601 D	35.9%	63.7%	36.1%	63.9%
6	1972	87,489			82,158	PREYER, L. RICHARDSON	5,331	82,158 D		93.9%		100.0%
7	1976	117,419	21,955	VAUGHAN, M. H.	95,463	ROSE, CHARLES G.	1	73,508 D	18.7%	81.3%	18.7%	81.3%
7	1974	49,780			49,780	ROSE, CHARLES G.		49,780 D		100.0%		100.0%
7	1972	94,937	36,726	SCOTT, JERRY C.	57,348	ROSE, CHARLES G.	863	20,622 D	38.7%	60.4%	39.0%	61.0%
8	1976	151,081	49,094	EAGLE, CARL	99,296	HEFNER, W. G.	2,691	50,202 D	32.5%	65.7%	33.1%	66.9%
8	1974	108,091	46,500	RUTH, EARL B.	61,591	HEFNER, W. G.		15,091 D	43.0%	57.0%	43.0%	57.0%
8	1972	136,258	82,060	RUTH, EARL B.	54,198	CLARK, RICHARD		27,862 R	60.2%	39.8%	60.2%	39.8%
9	1976	153,796	82,297	MARTIN, JAMES G.	70,847	GOODMAN, ARTHUR	652	11,450 R	53.5%	46.1%	53.7%	46.3%
9	1974	93,877	51,032	MARTIN, JAMES G.	41,387	SHORT, MILTON	1,458	9,645 R	54.4%	44.1%	55.2%	44.8%
9	1972	136,527	80,356	MARTIN, JAMES G.	56,171	BEATTY, JAMES		24,185 R	58.9%	41.1%	58.9%	41.1%
10	1976	167,072	99,882	BROYHILL, JAMES T.	67,190	HUNT, JOHN J.		32,692 R	59.8%	40.2%	59.8%	40.2%
10	1974	116,513	63,382	BROYHILL, JAMES T.	53,131	RHYNE, JACK L.		10,251 R	54.4%	45.6%	54.4%	45.6%
10	1972	142,144	103,119	BROYHILL, JAMES T.	39,025	BECK, PAUL L.		64,094 R	72.5%	27.5%	72.5%	27.5%
11	1976	184,421	88,752	BRIGGS, BRUCE	93,857	GUDGER, LAMAR	1,812	5,105 D	48.1%	50.9%	48.6%	51.4%
11	1974	135,146	45,983	GILMAN, ALBERT F.	89,163	TAYLOR, ROY A.		43,180 D	34.0%	66.0%	34.0%	66.0%
11	1972	158,527	64,062	LEDBETTER, JESSE I.	94,465	TAYLOR, ROY A.		30,403 D	40.4%	59.6%	40.4%	59.6%

NORTH CAROLINA

1976 GENERAL ELECTION

President — Other vote was 5,607 Anderson (American); 2,219 MacBride (Libertarian); 755 LaRouche (Labor); 780 McCarthy (write-in); 228 scattered.

Governor — Other vote was 13,604 Seawell (American); 4,764 Andrews (Libertarian); 61 scattered.

Congress — Other vote was scattered in CD's 2, 3, 4 and 7; 2,050 Parker (American) and 8 scattered in CD 1; 246 Hooks (U.S. Labor) and 2 scattered in CD 5; 2,156 Ligon (American) and 535 Bell (U.S. Labor) in CD 8; 644 Schlanger (U.S. Labor) and 8 scattered in CD 9; 1,796 Underwood (American) and 16 scattered in CD 11; in CD 6 as follows:

CD 6 — 2,137 Wagle (Libertarian); 1,823 Porter (U.S. Labor); 1 scattered.

1976 PRIMARIES

AUGUST 17 REPUBLICAN

Governor — 57,663 David T. Flaherty; 37,573 Coy C. Privette; 16,149 J. F. Alexander; 4,467 Wallace E. McCall.

Congress — Unopposed in five CD's. No candidates in CD's 2 and 6. Contested as follows:

CD 1 — 2,771 Joseph M. Ward; 2,438 Harold Stroud.
CD 4 — 6,424 Johnnie L. Gallemore; 3,048 Lenzie G. Barnes.
CD 8 — 7,663 Carl Eagle; 6,299 Gilbert L. Boger.
CD 11 — 11,117 Bruce Briggs; 4,461 Ralph Ledford; 3,057 Walter Sheppard.

AUGUST 17 DEMOCRATIC

Governor — 362,102 James B. Hunt; 157,815 Edward M. O'Herron; 121,673 George Wood; 31,338 Thomas E. Strickland; 5,003 Jetter Barker.

Congress — Unopposed in four CD's. Contested as follows:

CD 1 — 47,616 Walter B. Jones; 23,704 James J. Bonner.
CD 2 — 38,530 L. H. Fountain; 25,080 J. Russell Kirby; 6,825 Elbert Rudasill; 4,945 Henry B. Thorpe.
CD 3 — 28,749 Jimmy L. Love; 25,342 Charles Whitley; 4,695 Jimmy Hatcher; 2,000 Joseph R. Overby.
CD 5 — 40,597 Stephen L. Neal; 5,368 Marion C. Wardlow.
CD 9 — 31,910 Arthur Goodman; 9,913 Robert H. Sieburg.
CD 10 — 32,079 John J. Hunt; 19,025 E. Eugene Poston.
CD 11 — 20,489 Lamar Gudger; 18,318 Glenn Brown; 17,399 R. P. Thomas; 5,015 Michael E. Vaughn; 898 Roy P. Gibbens.

SEPTEMBER 14 REPUBLICAN RUN-OFF

Governor — 45,661 David T. Flaherty; 29,810 Coy C. Privette.

SEPTEMBER 14 DEMOCRATIC RUN-OFF

Congress

CD 3 — 29,974 Charles Whitley; 26,037 Jimmy L. Love.
CD 11 — 22,767 Lamar Gudger; 21,995 Glenn Brown.

NORTH DAKOTA

GOVERNOR

Arthur A. Link (D). Re-elected 1976 to a four-year term. Previously elected 1972.

SENATORS

Quentin N. Burdick (D). Re-elected 1976 to a six-year term. Previously elected 1970, 1964, and in June 1960 to fill out term vacated by the death of Senator William Langer.

Milton R. Young (R). Re-elected 1974 to a six-year term. Previously elected 1968, 1962, 1956, 1950, and in June 1946 to fill out term vacated by the death of Senator John Moses; had been appointed March 1945 to fill this same vacancy.

REPRESENTATIVE

At-Large. Mark Andrews (R)

POSTWAR VOTE FOR GOVERNOR

								Percentage			
	Total	Republican		Democratic		Other	Rep.-Dem.	Total Vote		Major Vote	
Year	Vote	Vote	Candidate	Vote	Candidate	Vote	Plurality	Rep.	Dem.	Rep.	Dem.
1976	297,249	138,321	Elkin, Richard	153,309	Link, Arthur A.	5,619	14,988 D	46.5%	51.6%	47.4%	52.6%
1972	281,931	138,032	Larsen, Richard	143,899	Link, Arthur A.	–	5,867 D	49.0%	51.0%	49.0%	51.0%
1968	248,000	108,382	McCarney, Robert P.	135,955	Guy, William L.	3,663	27,573 D	43.7%	54.8%	44.4%	55.6%
1964	262,661	116,247	Halcrow, Donald M.	146,414	Guy, William L.	–	30,167 D	44.3%	55.7%	44.3%	55.7%
1962	228,509	113,251	Andrews, Mark	115,258	Guy, William L.	–	2,007 D	49.6%	50.4%	49.6%	50.4%
1960	275,375	122,486	Dahl, C. P.	136,148	Guy, William L.	16,741	13,662 D	44.5%	49.4%	47.4%	52.6%
1958	210,599	111,836	Davis, John E.	98,763	Lord, John F.	–	13,073 R	53.1%	46.9%	53.1%	46.9%
1956	252,435	147,566	Davis, John E.	104,869	Warner, Wallace E.	–	42,697 R	58.5%	41.5%	58.5%	41.5%
1954	193,501	124,253	Brunsdale, C. Norman	69,248	Bymers, Cornelius	–	55,005 R	64.2%	35.8%	64.2%	35.8%
1952	253,934	199,944	Brunsdale, C. Norman	53,990	Johnson, Ole C.	–	145,954 R	78.7%	21.3%	78.7%	21.3%
1950	183,772	121,822	Brunsdale, C. Norman	61,950	Byerly, Clyde G.	–	59,872 R	66.3%	33.7%	66.3%	33.7%
1948	214,858	131,764	Aandahl, Fred G.	80,555	Henry, Howard	2,539	51,209 R	61.3%	37.5%	62.1%	37.9%
1946	169,391	116,672	Aandahl, Fred G.	52,719	Burdick, Quentin N.	–	63,953 R	68.9%	31.1%	68.9%	31.1%

The term of office of North Dakota's Governor was increased from two to four years effective with the 1964 election.

POSTWAR VOTE FOR SENATOR

								Percentage			
	Total	Republican		Democratic		Other	Rep.-Dem.	Total Vote		Major Vote	
Year	Vote	Vote	Candidate	Vote	Candidate	Vote	Plurality	Rep.	Dem.	Rep.	Dem.
1976	283,062	103,466	Stroup, Richard	175,772	Burdick, Quentin N.	3,824	72,306 D	36.6%	62.1%	37.1%	62.9%
1974	235,661	114,117	Young, Milton R.	113,931	Guy, William L.	7,613	186 R	48.4%	48.3%	50.0%	50.0%
1970	219,560	82,996	Kleppe, Tom	134,519	Burdick, Quentin N.	2,045	51,523 D	37.8%	61.3%	38.2%	61.8%
1968	239,776	154,968	Young, Milton R.	80,815	Lashkowitz, Herschel	3,993	74,153 R	64.6%	33.7%	65.7%	34.3%
1964	258,945	109,681	Kleppe, Tom	149,264	Burdick, Quentin N.	–	39,583 D	42.4%	57.6%	42.4%	57.6%
1962	223,737	135,705	Young, Milton R.	88,032	Lanier, William	–	47,673 R	60.7%	39.3%	60.7%	39.3%
1960s	210,349	103,475	Davis, John E.	104,593	Burdick, Quentin N.	2,281	1,118 D	49.2%	49.7%	49.7%	50.3%
1958	204,635	117,070	Langer, William	84,892	Vendsel, Raymond	2,673	32,178 R	57.2%	41.5%	58.0%	42.0%
1956	244,161	155,305	Young, Milton R.	87,919	Burdick, Quentin N.	937	67,386 R	63.6%	36.0%	63.9%	36.1%
1952	237,995	157,907	Langer, William	55,347	Morrison, Harold A.	24,741	102,560 R	66.3%	23.3%	74.0%	26.0%
1950	186,716	126,209	Young, Milton R.	60,507	O'Brien, Harry	–	65,702 R	67.6%	32.4%	67.6%	32.4%
1946	165,382	88,210	Langer, William	38,368	Larson, Abner B.	38,804	49,842 R	53.3%	23.2%	69.7%	30.3%
1946s	136,852	75,998	Young, Milton R.	37,507	Lanier, William	23,347	38,491 R	55.5%	27.4%	67.0%	33.0%

The 1960 and 1946 special elections were held in June for short terms to fill vacancies.

NORTH DAKOTA

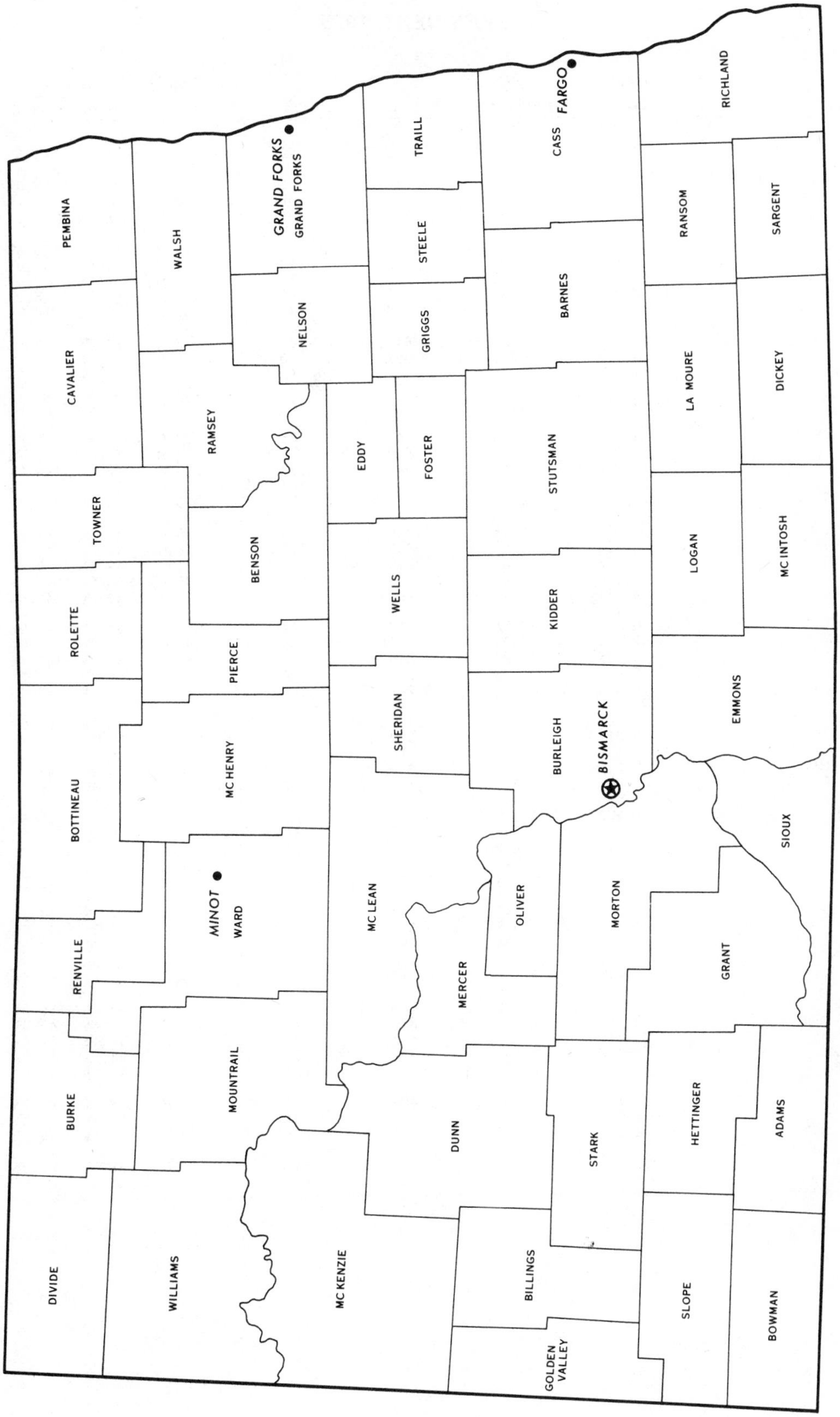

NORTH DAKOTA

PRESIDENT 1976

1970 Census Population	County	Total Vote	Republican	Democratic	Other	Rep.-Dem. Plurality	Percentage Total Vote Rep.	Percentage Total Vote Dem.	Percentage Major Vote Rep.	Percentage Major Vote Dem.
3,832	ADAMS	1,937	940	959	38	19 D	48.5%	49.5%	49.5%	50.5%
14,669	BARNES	7,462	4,011	3,321	130	690 R	53.8%	44.5%	54.7%	45.3%
8,245	BENSON	3,725	1,689	1,973	63	284 D	45.3%	53.0%	46.1%	53.9%
1,198	BILLINGS	684	351	285	48	66 R	51.3%	41.7%	55.2%	44.8%
9,496	BOTTINEAU	4,700	2,638	1,987	75	651 R	56.1%	42.3%	57.0%	43.0%
3,901	BOWMAN	1,998	1,033	911	54	122 R	51.7%	45.6%	53.1%	46.9%
4,739	BURKE	2,089	1,087	899	103	188 R	52.0%	43.0%	54.7%	45.3%
40,714	BURLEIGH	23,549	13,680	9,188	681	4,492 R	58.1%	39.0%	59.8%	40.2%
73,653	CASS	41,411	22,583	17,879	949	4,704 R	54.5%	43.2%	55.8%	44.2%
8,213	CAVALIER	4,300	2,046	2,178	76	132 D	47.6%	50.7%	48.4%	51.6%
6,976	DICKEY	3,709	2,027	1,612	70	415 R	54.7%	43.5%	55.7%	44.3%
4,564	DIVIDE	1,978	881	1,057	40	176 D	44.5%	53.4%	45.5%	54.5%
4,895	DUNN	2,157	1,041	1,051	65	10 D	48.3%	48.7%	49.8%	50.2%
4,103	EDDY	2,054	890	1,123	41	233 D	43.3%	54.7%	44.2%	55.8%
7,200	EMMONS	2,984	1,370	1,459	155	89 D	45.9%	48.9%	48.4%	51.6%
4,832	FOSTER	2,305	1,120	1,147	38	27 D	48.6%	49.8%	49.4%	50.6%
2,611	GOLDEN VALLEY	1,208	633	479	96	154 R	52.4%	39.7%	56.9%	43.1%
61,102	GRAND FORKS	26,218	13,820	11,545	853	2,275 R	52.7%	44.0%	54.5%	45.5%
5,009	GRANT	2,258	1,205	952	101	253 R	53.4%	42.2%	55.9%	44.1%
4,184	GRIGGS	2,262	1,086	1,122	54	36 D	48.0%	49.6%	49.2%	50.8%
5,075	HETTINGER	2,302	1,135	1,095	72	40 R	49.3%	47.6%	50.9%	49.1%
4,362	KIDDER	2,023	954	936	133	18 R	47.2%	46.3%	50.5%	49.5%
7,117	LA MOURE	3,538	1,735	1,718	85	17 R	49.0%	48.6%	50.2%	49.8%
4,245	LOGAN	1,876	944	809	123	135 R	50.3%	43.1%	53.9%	46.1%
8,977	MCHENRY	4,111	2,043	1,994	74	49 R	49.7%	48.5%	50.6%	49.4%
5,545	MCINTOSH	2,776	1,785	912	79	873 R	64.3%	32.9%	66.2%	33.8%
6,127	MCKENZIE	2,978	1,595	1,335	48	260 R	53.6%	44.8%	54.4%	45.6%
11,251	MCLEAN	5,665	2,729	2,815	121	86 D	48.2%	49.7%	49.2%	50.8%
6,175	MERCER	3,414	1,982	1,298	134	684 R	58.1%	38.0%	60.4%	39.6%
20,310	MORTON	10,462	4,921	5,241	300	320 D	47.0%	50.1%	48.4%	51.6%
8,437	MOUNTRAIL	3,708	1,430	2,189	89	759 D	38.6%	59.0%	39.5%	60.5%
5,776	NELSON	3,015	1,336	1,610	69	274 D	44.3%	53.4%	45.3%	54.7%
2,322	OLIVER	1,140	575	529	36	46 R	50.4%	46.4%	52.1%	47.9%
10,728	PEMBINA	5,209	2,810	2,274	125	536 R	53.9%	43.7%	55.3%	44.7%
6,323	PIERCE	2,887	1,396	1,434	57	38 D	48.4%	49.7%	49.3%	50.7%
12,915	RAMSEY	6,502	3,293	3,096	113	197 R	50.6%	47.6%	51.5%	48.5%
7,102	RANSOM	3,456	1,696	1,715	45	19 D	49.1%	49.6%	49.7%	50.3%
3,828	RENVILLE	1,846	812	1,008	26	196 D	44.0%	54.6%	44.6%	55.4%
18,089	RICHLAND	9,785	4,991	4,592	202	399 R	51.0%	46.9%	52.1%	47.9%
11,549	ROLETTE	3,693	1,094	2,531	68	1,437 D	29.6%	68.5%	30.2%	69.8%
5,937	SARGENT	3,031	1,344	1,644	43	300 D	44.3%	54.2%	45.0%	55.0%
3,232	SHERIDAN	1,536	935	569	32	366 R	60.9%	37.0%	62.2%	37.8%
3,632	SIOUX	1,081	354	697	30	343 D	32.7%	64.5%	33.7%	66.3%
1,484	SLOPE	726	355	347	24	8 R	48.9%	47.8%	50.6%	49.4%
19,613	STARK	8,760	4,374	4,076	310	298 R	49.9%	46.5%	51.8%	48.2%
3,749	STEELE	1,926	835	1,066	25	231 D	43.4%	55.3%	43.9%	56.1%
23,550	STUTSMAN	10,780	5,653	4,883	244	770 R	52.4%	45.3%	53.7%	46.3%
4,645	TOWNER	2,234	993	1,216	25	223 D	44.4%	54.4%	45.0%	55.0%
9,571	TRAILL	5,251	2,800	2,352	99	448 R	53.3%	44.8%	54.3%	45.7%
16,251	WALSH	7,309	3,518	3,555	236	37 D	48.1%	48.6%	49.7%	50.3%
58,560	WARD	22,721	12,751	9,484	486	3,267 R	56.1%	41.7%	57.3%	42.7%
7,847	WELLS	3,767	1,941	1,742	84	199 R	51.5%	46.2%	52.7%	47.3%
19,301	WILLIAMS	8,692	4,230	4,189	273	41 R	48.7%	48.2%	50.2%	49.8%
617,761	TOTAL	297,188	153,470	136,078	7,640	17,392 R	51.6%	45.8%	53.0%	47.0%

NORTH DAKOTA

GOVERNOR 1976

1970 Census Population	County	Total Vote	Republican	Democratic	Other	Rep.-Dem. Plurality	Percentage Total Vote Rep.	Percentage Total Vote Dem.	Percentage Major Vote Rep.	Percentage Major Vote Dem.
3,832	ADAMS	1,969	1,035	890	44	145 R	52.6%	45.2%	53.8%	46.2%
14,669	BARNES	7,529	3,562	3,896	71	334 D	47.3%	51.7%	47.8%	52.2%
8,245	BENSON	3,736	1,415	2,288	33	873 D	37.9%	61.2%	38.2%	61.8%
1,198	BILLINGS	685	347	311	27	36 R	50.7%	45.4%	52.7%	47.3%
9,496	BOTTINEAU	4,896	2,487	2,363	46	124 R	50.8%	48.3%	51.3%	48.7%
3,901	BOWMAN	2,013	1,026	978	9	48 R	51.0%	48.6%	51.2%	48.8%
4,739	BURKE	2,109	935	1,066	108	131 D	44.3%	50.5%	46.7%	53.3%
40,714	BURLEIGH	23,748	12,734	10,371	643	2,363 R	53.6%	43.7%	55.1%	44.9%
73,653	CASS	40,664	19,988	20,296	380	308 D	49.2%	49.9%	49.6%	50.4%
8,213	CAVALIER	4,287	1,850	2,375	62	525 D	43.2%	55.4%	43.8%	56.2%
6,976	DICKEY	3,600	1,875	1,702	23	173 R	52.1%	47.3%	52.4%	47.6%
4,564	DIVIDE	2,026	788	1,196	42	408 D	38.9%	59.0%	39.7%	60.3%
4,895	DUNN	2,188	920	1,222	46	302 D	42.0%	55.9%	43.0%	57.0%
4,103	EDDY	2,089	844	1,220	25	376 D	40.4%	58.4%	40.9%	59.1%
7,200	EMMONS	3,085	1,614	1,273	198	341 R	52.3%	41.3%	55.9%	44.1%
4,832	FOSTER	2,360	1,076	1,270	14	194 D	45.6%	53.8%	45.9%	54.1%
2,611	GOLDEN VALLEY	1,222	628	526	68	102 R	51.4%	43.0%	54.4%	45.6%
61,102	GRAND FORKS	25,489	11,781	13,204	504	1,423 D	46.2%	51.8%	47.2%	52.8%
5,009	GRANT	2,298	1,205	852	241	353 R	52.4%	37.1%	58.6%	41.4%
4,184	GRIGGS	2,334	1,017	1,290	27	273 D	43.6%	55.3%	44.1%	55.9%
5,075	HETTINGER	2,336	1,143	1,107	86	36 R	48.9%	47.4%	50.8%	49.2%
4,362	KIDDER	2,077	930	991	156	61 D	44.8%	47.7%	48.4%	51.6%
7,117	LA MOURE	3,551	1,705	1,803	43	98 D	48.0%	50.8%	48.6%	51.4%
4,245	LOGAN	1,870	991	758	121	233 R	53.0%	40.5%	56.7%	43.3%
8,977	MCHENRY	4,268	1,919	2,289	60	370 D	45.0%	53.6%	45.6%	54.4%
5,545	MCINTOSH	2,818	1,817	932	69	885 R	64.5%	33.1%	66.1%	33.9%
6,127	MCKENZIE	3,091	1,385	1,668	38	283 D	44.8%	54.0%	45.4%	54.6%
11,251	MCLEAN	5,866	2,677	3,083	106	406 D	45.6%	52.6%	46.5%	53.5%
6,175	MERCER	3,545	1,797	1,641	107	156 R	50.7%	46.3%	52.3%	47.7%
20,310	MORTON	10,599	4,755	5,524	320	769 D	44.9%	52.1%	46.3%	53.7%
8,437	MOUNTRAIL	3,717	1,319	2,352	46	1,033 D	35.5%	63.3%	35.9%	64.1%
5,776	NELSON	3,036	1,106	1,876	54	770 D	36.4%	61.8%	37.1%	62.9%
2,322	OLIVER	1,208	561	598	49	37 D	46.4%	49.5%	48.4%	51.6%
10,728	PEMBINA	5,159	2,394	2,695	70	301 D	46.4%	52.2%	47.0%	53.0%
6,323	PIERCE	3,005	1,440	1,528	37	88 D	47.9%	50.8%	48.5%	51.5%
12,915	RAMSEY	6,612	3,031	3,539	42	508 D	45.8%	53.5%	46.1%	53.9%
7,102	RANSOM	3,434	1,531	1,879	24	348 D	44.6%	54.7%	44.9%	55.1%
3,828	RENVILLE	1,853	732	1,090	31	358 D	39.5%	58.8%	40.2%	59.8%
18,089	RICHLAND	9,757	4,310	5,333	114	1,023 D	44.2%	54.7%	44.7%	55.3%
11,549	ROLETTE	3,748	1,142	2,576	30	1,434 D	30.5%	68.7%	30.7%	69.3%
5,937	SARGENT	3,064	1,167	1,876	21	709 D	38.1%	61.2%	38.4%	61.6%
3,232	SHERIDAN	1,596	940	610	46	330 R	58.9%	38.2%	60.6%	39.4%
3,632	SIOUX	1,101	359	722	20	363 D	32.6%	65.6%	33.2%	66.8%
1,484	SLOPE	739	357	369	13	12 D	48.3%	49.9%	49.2%	50.8%
19,613	STARK	8,570	3,949	4,320	301	371 D	46.1%	50.4%	47.8%	52.2%
3,749	STEELE	1,935	748	1,176	11	428 D	38.7%	60.8%	38.9%	61.1%
23,550	STUTSMAN	10,649	5,438	5,057	154	381 R	51.1%	47.5%	51.8%	48.2%
4,645	TOWNER	2,238	916	1,291	31	375 D	40.9%	57.7%	41.5%	58.5%
9,571	TRAILL	5,357	2,550	2,771	36	221 D	47.6%	51.7%	47.9%	52.1%
16,251	WALSH	7,317	2,893	4,286	138	1,393 D	39.5%	58.6%	40.3%	59.7%
58,560	WARD	22,495	10,037	12,018	440	1,981 D	44.6%	53.4%	45.5%	54.5%
7,847	WELLS	3,811	1,858	1,885	68	27 D	48.8%	49.5%	49.6%	50.4%
19,301	WILLIAMS	8,500	3,297	5,077	126	1,780 D	38.8%	59.7%	39.4%	60.6%
617,761	TOTAL	297,249	138,321	153,309	5,619	14,988 D	46.5%	51.6%	47.4%	52.6%

NORTH DAKOTA

SENATOR 1976

1970 Census Population	County	Total Vote	Republican	Democratic	Other	Rep.-Dem. Plurality	Percentage Total Vote Rep.	Percentage Total Vote Dem.	Percentage Major Vote Rep.	Percentage Major Vote Dem.
3,832	ADAMS	1,850	760	1,080	10	320 D	41.1%	58.4%	41.3%	58.7%
14,669	BARNES	7,245	2,742	4,450	53	1,708 D	37.8%	61.4%	38.1%	61.9%
8,245	BENSON	3,616	1,103	2,488	25	1,385 D	30.5%	68.8%	30.7%	69.3%
1,198	BILLINGS	634	286	329	19	43 D	45.1%	51.9%	46.5%	53.5%
9,496	BOTTINEAU	4,679	1,900	2,759	20	859 D	40.6%	59.0%	40.8%	59.2%
3,901	BOWMAN	1,888	734	1,147	7	413 D	38.9%	60.8%	39.0%	61.0%
4,739	BURKE	1,989	709	1,207	73	498 D	35.6%	60.7%	37.0%	63.0%
40,714	BURLEIGH	22,606	9,800	12,355	451	2,555 D	43.4%	54.7%	44.2%	55.8%
73,653	CASS	39,405	14,104	24,970	331	10,866 D	35.8%	63.4%	36.1%	63.9%
8,213	CAVALIER	4,134	1,234	2,867	33	1,633 D	29.9%	69.4%	30.1%	69.9%
6,976	DICKEY	3,487	1,523	1,928	36	405 D	43.7%	55.3%	44.1%	55.9%
4,564	DIVIDE	1,910	527	1,365	18	838 D	27.6%	71.5%	27.9%	72.1%
4,895	DUNN	2,116	832	1,244	40	412 D	39.3%	58.8%	40.1%	59.9%
4,103	EDDY	2,024	630	1,380	14	750 D	31.1%	68.2%	31.3%	68.7%
7,200	EMMONS	2,912	1,142	1,627	143	485 D	39.2%	55.9%	41.2%	58.8%
4,832	FOSTER	2,259	777	1,465	17	688 D	34.4%	64.9%	34.7%	65.3%
2,611	GOLDEN VALLEY	1,106	459	597	50	138 D	41.5%	54.0%	43.5%	56.5%
61,102	GRAND FORKS	24,395	8,267	15,728	400	7,461 D	33.9%	64.5%	34.5%	65.5%
5,009	GRANT	2,102	948	1,082	72	134 D	45.1%	51.5%	46.7%	53.3%
4,184	GRIGGS	2,278	745	1,511	22	766 D	32.7%	66.3%	33.0%	67.0%
5,075	HETTINGER	2,213	872	1,303	38	431 D	39.4%	58.9%	40.1%	59.9%
4,362	KIDDER	1,894	703	1,079	112	376 D	37.1%	57.0%	39.5%	60.5%
7,117	LA MOURE	3,455	1,402	2,017	36	615 D	40.6%	58.4%	41.0%	59.0%
4,245	LOGAN	1,813	779	929	105	150 D	43.0%	51.2%	45.6%	54.4%
8,977	MCHENRY	3,964	1,458	2,493	13	1,035 D	36.8%	62.9%	36.9%	63.1%
5,545	MCINTOSH	2,666	1,464	1,138	64	326 R	54.9%	42.7%	56.3%	43.7%
6,127	MCKENZIE	2,916	1,211	1,673	32	462 D	41.5%	57.4%	42.0%	58.0%
11,251	MCLEAN	5,650	2,476	3,116	58	640 D	43.8%	55.2%	44.3%	55.7%
6,175	MERCER	3,480	1,888	1,514	78	374 R	54.3%	43.5%	55.5%	44.5%
20,310	MORTON	10,223	3,639	6,423	161	2,784 D	35.6%	62.8%	36.2%	63.8%
8,437	MOUNTRAIL	3,489	1,247	2,213	29	966 D	35.7%	63.4%	36.0%	64.0%
5,776	NELSON	2,946	831	2,082	33	1,251 D	28.2%	70.7%	28.5%	71.5%
2,322	OLIVER	1,173	526	622	25	96 D	44.8%	53.0%	45.8%	54.2%
10,728	PEMBINA	4,935	1,608	3,274	53	1,666 D	32.6%	66.3%	32.9%	67.1%
6,323	PIERCE	2,749	1,012	1,719	18	707 D	36.8%	62.5%	37.1%	62.9%
12,915	RAMSEY	6,160	2,093	4,032	35	1,939 D	34.0%	65.5%	34.2%	65.8%
7,102	RANSOM	3,194	1,110	2,067	17	957 D	34.8%	64.7%	34.9%	65.1%
3,828	RENVILLE	1,794	584	1,197	13	613 D	32.6%	66.7%	32.8%	67.2%
18,089	RICHLAND	8,837	2,890	5,859	88	2,969 D	32.7%	66.3%	33.0%	67.0%
11,549	ROLETTE	3,593	794	2,778	21	1,984 D	22.1%	77.3%	22.2%	77.8%
5,937	SARGENT	2,932	904	2,007	21	1,103 D	30.8%	68.5%	31.1%	68.9%
3,232	SHERIDAN	1,432	765	646	21	119 R	53.4%	45.1%	54.2%	45.8%
3,632	SIOUX	1,066	271	777	18	506 D	25.4%	72.9%	25.9%	74.1%
1,484	SLOPE	680	250	414	16	164 D	36.8%	60.9%	37.7%	62.3%
19,613	STARK	7,873	2,692	4,988	193	2,296 D	34.2%	63.4%	35.1%	64.9%
3,749	STEELE	1,875	575	1,295	5	720 D	30.7%	69.1%	30.7%	69.3%
23,550	STUTSMAN	10,227	4,092	6,018	117	1,926 D	40.0%	58.8%	40.5%	59.5%
4,645	TOWNER	2,155	668	1,478	9	810 D	31.0%	68.6%	31.1%	68.9%
9,571	TRAILL	5,195	1,882	3,290	23	1,408 D	36.2%	63.3%	36.4%	63.6%
16,251	WALSH	7,045	2,057	4,885	103	2,828 D	29.2%	69.3%	29.6%	70.4%
58,560	WARD	21,123	7,565	13,250	308	5,685 D	35.8%	62.7%	36.3%	63.7%
7,847	WELLS	3,634	1,452	2,149	33	697 D	40.0%	59.1%	40.3%	59.7%
19,301	WILLIAMS	8,046	2,484	5,468	94	2,984 D	30.9%	68.0%	31.2%	68.8%
617,761	TOTAL	283,062	103,466	175,772	3,824	72,306 D	36.6%	62.1%	37.1%	62.9%

NORTH DAKOTA

CONGRESS

CD	Year	Total Vote	Republican Vote	Republican Candidate	Democratic Vote	Democratic Candidate	Other Vote	Rep.-Dem. Plurality	Percentage Total Vote Rep.	Percentage Total Vote Dem.	Percentage Major Vote Rep.	Percentage Major Vote Dem.
AL	1976	289,881	181,018	ANDREWS, MARK	104,263	OMDAHL, LLOYD B.	4,600	76,755 R	62.4%	36.0%	63.5%	36.5%
AL	1974	233,688	130,184	ANDREWS, MARK	103,504	DORGAN, BYRON L.		26,680 R	55.7%	44.3%	55.7%	44.3%
AL	1972	268,721	195,360	ANDREWS, MARK	72,850	ISTA, RICHARD	511	122,510 R	72.7%	27.1%	72.8%	27.2%

NORTH DAKOTA

1976 GENERAL ELECTION

President Other vote was 3,796 Anderson (American); 2,952 McCarthy (Independent); 269 Maddox (American Independent); 253 MacBride (Libertarian); 142 LaRouche (U.S. Labor); 84 Hall (Communist); 63 Bubar (Prohibition); 43 Camejo (Socialist Workers); 38 Zeidler (Socialist). Original uncorrected canvass gave the Hall vote as 85, the MacBride vote as 256, and the Anderson vote as 3,698 (98 votes had been omitted in Mercer county).

Governor Other vote was Vaaler (American).

Senator Other vote was Haggard (American).

Congress Other vote at-large was Kleppe (American).

1976 PRIMARIES

SEPTEMBER 7 REPUBLICAN

Governor 54,427 Richard Elkin; 12,013 Herb Geving.

Senator Richard Stroup, unopposed.

Congress Unopposed at-large.

SEPTEMBER 7 DEMOCRATIC

Governor Arthur A. Link, unopposed.

Senator Quentin N. Burdick, unopposed.

Congress Contested as follows:

AL 46,382 Lloyd B. Omdahl; 7,281 Tarfin Teigen.

SEPTEMBER 7 AMERICAN

Governor Martin Vaaler, unopposed.

Senator Clarence Haggard, unopposed.

Congress Unopposed at-large.

OHIO

GOVERNOR

James A. Rhodes (R). Elected 1974 to a four-year term. Previously elected 1966, 1962.

SENATORS

John H. Glenn (D). Elected 1974 to a six-year term.

Howard Metzenbaum (D). Elected 1976 to a six-year term.

REPRESENTATIVES

1. Willis D. Gradison (R)
2. Thomas A. Luken (D)
3. Charles W. Whalen (R)
4. Tennyson Guyer (R)
5. Delbert L. Latta (R)
6. William H. Harsha (R)
7. Clarence Brown, Jr. (R)
8. Thomas N. Kindness (R)
9. Thomas L. Ashley (D)
10. Clarence E. Miller (R)
11. J. William Stanton (R)
12. Samuel L. Devine (R)
13. Donald J. Pease (D)
14. John F. Seiberling (D)
15. Chalmers P. Wylie (R)
16. Ralph S. Regula (R)
17. John M. Ashbrook (R)
18. Douglas Applegate (D)
19. Charles J. Carney (D)
20. Mary Rose Oakar (D)
21. Louis Stokes (D)
22. Charles A. Vanik (D)
23. Ronald M. Mottl (D)

POSTWAR VOTE FOR GOVERNOR

Year	Total Vote	Republican Vote	Republican Candidate	Democratic Vote	Democratic Candidate	Other Vote	Rep.-Dem. Plurality	Percentage Total Vote Rep.	Percentage Total Vote Dem.	Percentage Major Vote Rep.	Percentage Major Vote Dem.
1974	3,072,010	1,493,679	Rhodes James A.	1,482,191	Gilligan, John J.	96,140	11,488 R	48.6%	48.2%	50.2%	49.8%
1970	3,184,133	1,382,659	Cloud, Roger	1,725,560	Gilligan, John J.	75,914	342,901 D	43.4%	54.2%	44.5%	55.5%
1966	2,887,331	1,795,277	Rhodes, James A.	1,092,054	Reams, Frazier, Jr.	–	703,223 R	62.2%	37.8%	62.2%	37.8%
1962	3,116,711	1,836,190	Rhodes, James A.	1,280,521	DiSalle, Michael V.	–	555,669 R	58.9%	41.1%	58.9%	41.1%
1958	3,284,134	1,414,874	O'Neill, C. William	1,869,260	DiSalle, Michael V.	–	454,386 D	43.1%	56.9%	43.1%	56.9%
1956	3,542,091	1,984,988	O'Neill, C. William	1,557,103	DiSalle, Michael V.	–	427,885 R	56.0%	44.0%	56.0%	44.0%
1954	2,597,790	1,192,528	Rhodes, James A.	1,405,262	Lausche, Frank J.	–	212,734 D	45.9%	54.1%	45.9%	54.1%
1952	3,605,168	1,590,058	Taft, Charles P.	2,015,110	Lausche, Frank J.	–	425,052 D	44.1%	55.9%	44.1%	55.9%
1950	2,892,819	1,370,570	Ebright, Don H.	1,522,249	Lausche, Frank J.	–	151,679 D	47.4%	52.6%	47.4%	52.6%
1948	3,018,289	1,398,514	Herbert, Thomas J.	1,619,775	Lausche, Frank J.	–	221,261 D	46.3%	53.7%	46.3%	53.7%
1946	2,303,750	1,166,550	Herbert, Thomas J.	1,125,997	Lausche, Frank J.	11,203	40,553 R	50.6%	48.9%	50.9%	49.1%

The term of office of Ohio's Governor was increased from two to four years effective with the 1958 election.

POSTWAR VOTE FOR SENATOR

Year	Total Vote	Republican Vote	Republican Candidate	Democratic Vote	Democratic Candidate	Other Vote	Rep.-Dem. Plurality	Percentage Total Vote Rep.	Percentage Total Vote Dem.	Percentage Major Vote Rep.	Percentage Major Vote Dem.
1976	3,920,613	1,823,774	Taft, Robert A., Jr.	1,941,113	Metzenbaum, Howard	155,726	117,339 D	46.5%	49.5%	48.4%	51.6%
1974	2,987,951	918,133	Perk, Ralph J.	1,930,670	Glenn, John H.	139,148	1,012,537 D	30.7%	64.6%	32.2%	67.8%
1970	3,151,274	1,565,682	Taft, Robert A., Jr.	1,495,262	Metzenbaum, Howard	90,330	70,420 R	49.7%	47.4%	51.2%	48.8%
1968	3,743,121	1,928,964	Saxbe, William B.	1,814,152	Gilligan, John J.	5	114,812 R	51.5%	48.5%	51.5%	48.5%
1964	3,830,389	1,906,781	Taft, Robert A., Jr.	1,923,608	Young, Stephen M.	–	16,827 D	49.8%	50.2%	49.8%	50.2%
1962	2,994,986	1,151,173	Briley, John M.	1,843,813	Lausche, Frank J.	–	692,640 D	38.4%	61.6%	38.4%	61.6%
1958	3,149,410	1,497,199	Bricker, John W.	1,652,211	Young, Stephen M.	–	155,012 D	47.5%	52.5%	47.5%	52.5%
1956	3,525,499	1,660,910	Bender, George H.	1,864,589	Lausche, Frank J.	–	203,679 D	47.1%	52.9%	47.1%	52.9%
1954s	2,512,778	1,257,874	Bender, George H.	1,254,904	Burke, Thomas A.	–	2,970 R	50.1%	49.9%	50.1%	49.9%
1952	3,442,291	1,878,961	Bricker, John W.	1,563,330	DiSalle, Michael V.	–	315,631 R	54.6%	45.4%	54.6%	45.4%
1950	2,860,102	1,645,643	Taft, Robert A.	1,214,459	Ferguson, Joseph T.	–	431,184 R	57.5%	42.5%	57.5%	42.5%
1946	2,237,269	1,275,774	Bricker, John W.	947,610	Huffman, James W.	13,885	328,164 R	57.0%	42.4%	57.4%	42.6%

The 1954 election was for a short term to fill a vacancy.

OHIO

Districts Established January 20, 1972

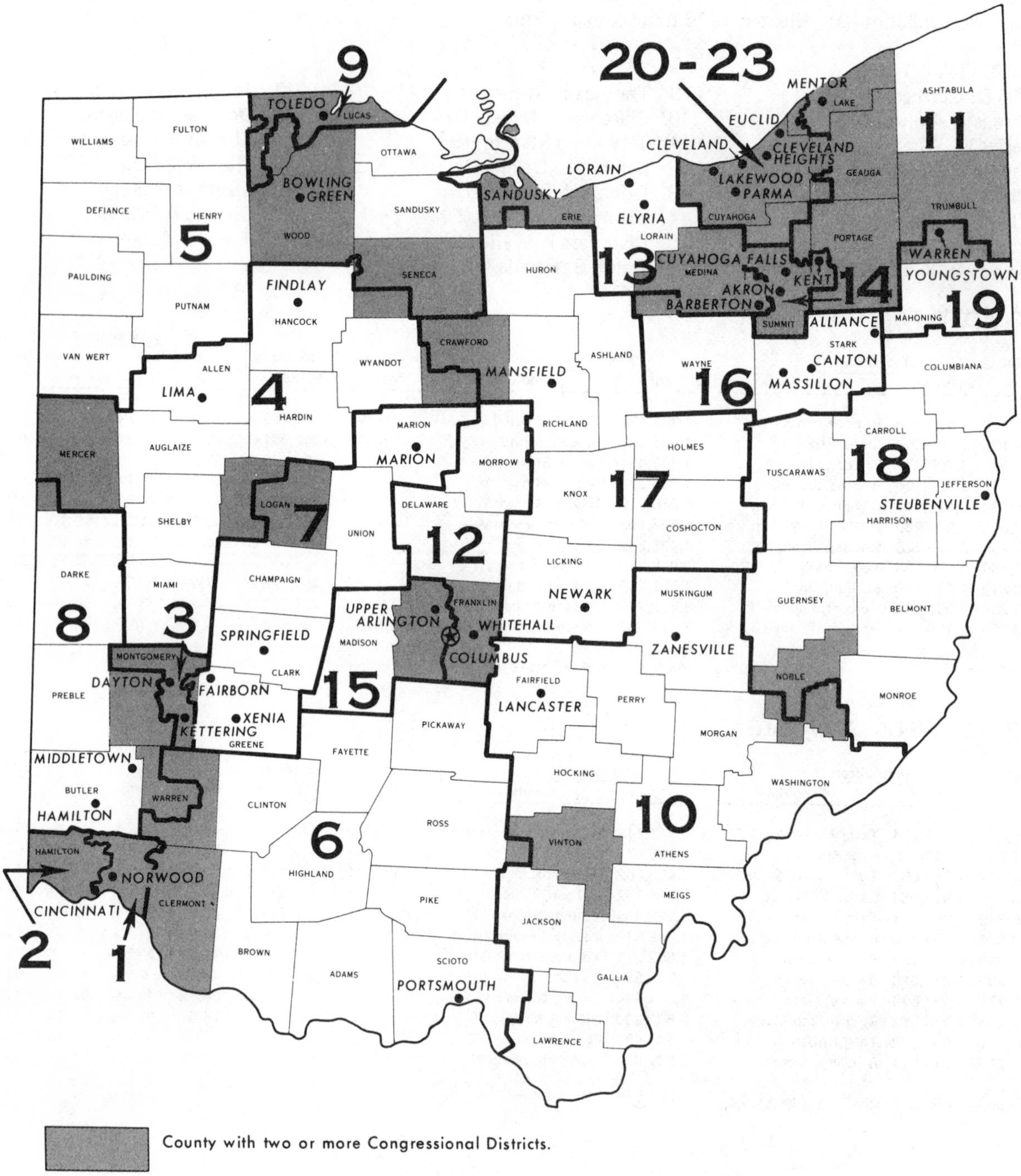

OHIO

PRESIDENT 1976

1970 Census Population	County	Total Vote	Republican	Democratic	Other	Rep.-Dem. Plurality	Percentage Total Vote Rep.	Percentage Total Vote Dem.	Percentage Major Vote Rep.	Percentage Major Vote Dem.
18,957	ADAMS	8,780	4,197	4,450	133	253 D	47.8%	50.7%	48.5%	51.5%
111,144	ALLEN	39,167	23,721	14,627	819	9,094 R	60.6%	37.3%	61.9%	38.1%
43,303	ASHLAND	17,354	9,761	7,205	388	2,556 R	56.2%	41.5%	57.5%	42.5%
98,237	ASHTABULA	38,625	16,885	20,883	857	3,998 D	43.7%	54.1%	44.7%	55.3%
54,889	ATHENS	19,016	8,387	9,896	733	1,509 D	44.1%	52.0%	45.9%	54.1%
38,602	AUGLAIZE	15,965	9,772	5,840	353	3,932 R	61.2%	36.6%	62.6%	37.4%
80,917	BELMONT	35,219	13,550	21,162	507	7,612 D	38.5%	60.1%	39.0%	61.0%
26,635	BROWN	10,126	4,549	5,432	145	883 D	44.9%	53.6%	45.6%	54.4%
226,207	BUTLER	86,217	49,625	35,123	1,469	14,502 R	57.6%	40.7%	58.6%	41.4%
21,579	CARROLL	10,325	5,091	5,006	228	85 R	49.3%	48.5%	50.4%	49.6%
30,491	CHAMPAIGN	11,502	6,526	4,748	228	1,778 R	56.7%	41.3%	57.9%	42.1%
157,115	CLARK	54,660	26,745	26,135	1,780	610 R	48.9%	47.8%	50.6%	49.4%
95,725	CLERMONT	35,037	19,616	14,850	571	4,766 R	56.0%	42.4%	56.9%	43.1%
31,464	CLINTON	11,737	6,597	4,959	181	1,638 R	56.2%	42.3%	57.1%	42.9%
108,310	COLUMBIANA	46,367	22,318	23,096	953	778 D	48.1%	49.8%	49.1%	50.9%
33,486	COSHOCTON	12,496	6,361	5,827	308	534 R	50.9%	46.6%	52.2%	47.8%
50,364	CRAWFORD	18,870	10,801	7,553	516	3,248 R	57.2%	40.0%	58.8%	41.2%
1,721,300	CUYAHOGA	623,222	255,594	349,186	18,442	93,592 D	41.0%	56.0%	42.3%	57.7%
49,141	DARKE	21,953	11,580	9,901	472	1,679 R	52.7%	45.1%	53.9%	46.1%
36,949	DEFIANCE	13,679	7,526	5,850	303	1,676 R	55.0%	42.8%	56.3%	43.7%
42,908	DELAWARE	19,853	12,285	7,058	510	5,227 R	61.9%	35.6%	63.5%	36.5%
75,909	ERIE	29,478	14,742	13,843	893	899 R	50.0%	47.0%	51.6%	48.4%
73,301	FAIRFIELD	33,079	19,098	13,361	620	5,737 R	57.7%	40.4%	58.8%	41.2%
25,461	FAYETTE	10,364	5,719	4,477	168	1,242 R	55.2%	43.2%	56.1%	43.9%
833,249	FRANKLIN	340,712	189,645	141,624	9,443	48,021 R	55.7%	41.6%	57.2%	42.8%
33,071	FULTON	12,949	7,891	4,850	208	3,041 R	60.9%	37.5%	61.9%	38.1%
25,239	GALLIA	10,317	5,198	4,971	148	227 R	50.4%	48.2%	51.1%	48.9%
62,977	GEAUGA	26,269	15,004	10,449	816	4,555 R	57.1%	39.8%	58.9%	41.1%
125,057	GREENE	44,077	22,598	20,245	1,234	2,353 R	51.3%	45.9%	52.7%	47.3%
37,665	GUERNSEY	15,524	7,746	7,573	205	173 R	49.9%	48.8%	50.6%	49.4%
924,018	HAMILTON	353,079	211,267	135,605	6,207	75,662 R	59.8%	38.4%	60.9%	39.1%
61,217	HANCOCK	25,333	15,983	8,548	802	7,435 R	63.1%	33.7%	65.2%	34.8%
30,813	HARDIN	11,075	6,076	4,650	349	1,426 R	54.9%	42.0%	56.6%	43.4%
17,013	HARRISON	7,681	3,509	4,070	102	561 D	45.7%	53.0%	46.3%	53.7%
27,058	HENRY	12,470	7,656	4,592	222	3,064 R	61.4%	36.8%	62.5%	37.5%
28,996	HIGHLAND	13,331	6,853	6,327	151	526 R	51.4%	47.5%	52.0%	48.0%
20,322	HOCKING	9,396	4,114	5,126	156	1,012 D	43.8%	54.6%	44.5%	55.5%
23,024	HOLMES	5,299	2,870	2,242	187	628 R	54.2%	42.3%	56.1%	43.9%
49,587	HURON	18,066	9,386	7,742	938	1,644 R	52.0%	42.9%	54.8%	45.2%
27,174	JACKSON	12,822	5,987	6,699	136	712 D	46.7%	52.2%	47.2%	52.8%
96,193	JEFFERSON	37,825	14,839	22,318	668	7,479 D	39.2%	59.0%	39.9%	60.1%
41,795	KNOX	17,081	9,290	7,361	430	1,929 R	54.4%	43.1%	55.8%	44.2%
197,200	LAKE	79,408	36,390	40,734	2,284	4,344 D	45.8%	51.3%	47.2%	52.8%
56,868	LAWRENCE	22,995	10,668	12,072	255	1,404 D	46.4%	52.5%	46.9%	53.1%
107,799	LICKING	43,733	23,518	19,247	968	4,271 R	53.8%	44.0%	55.0%	45.0%
35,072	LOGAN	15,402	9,092	5,949	361	3,143 R	59.0%	38.6%	60.4%	39.6%
256,843	LORAIN	94,711	39,459	52,387	2,865	12,928 D	41.7%	55.3%	43.0%	57.0%
484,370	LUCAS	183,907	76,069	103,658	4,180	27,589 D	41.4%	56.4%	42.3%	57.7%
28,318	MADISON	12,161	7,074	4,885	202	2,189 R	58.2%	40.2%	59.2%	40.8%
303,424	MAHONING	125,294	46,314	75,837	3,143	29,523 D	37.0%	60.5%	37.9%	62.1%
64,724	MARION	24,620	13,141	10,962	517	2,179 R	53.4%	44.5%	54.5%	45.5%
82,717	MEDINA	36,249	19,066	16,251	932	2,815 R	52.6%	44.8%	54.0%	46.0%
19,799	MEIGS	10,348	4,942	5,262	144	320 D	47.8%	50.9%	48.4%	51.6%
35,265	MERCER	14,849	7,678	6,724	447	954 R	51.7%	45.3%	53.3%	46.7%
84,342	MIAMI	32,413	18,686	13,074	653	5,612 R	57.6%	40.3%	58.8%	41.2%
15,739	MONROE	7,132	2,728	4,296	108	1,568 D	38.3%	60.2%	38.8%	61.2%
606,148	MONTGOMERY	211,436	100,223	106,468	4,745	6,245 D	47.4%	50.4%	48.5%	51.5%
12,375	MORGAN	5,809	2,971	2,727	111	244 R	51.1%	46.9%	52.1%	47.9%
21,348	MORROW	10,912	5,814	4,870	228	944 R	53.3%	44.6%	54.4%	45.6%
77,826	MUSKINGUM	30,070	15,358	14,178	534	1,180 R	51.1%	47.1%	52.0%	48.0%
10,428	NOBLE	5,730	3,007	2,612	111	395 R	52.5%	45.6%	53.5%	46.5%
37,099	OTTAWA	18,299	8,241	9,646	412	1,405 D	45.0%	52.7%	46.1%	53.9%
19,329	PAULDING	6,987	3,593	3,229	165	364 R	51.4%	46.2%	52.7%	47.3%
27,434	PERRY	12,138	5,637	6,268	233	631 D	46.4%	51.6%	47.3%	52.7%
40,071	PICKAWAY	14,045	7,695	5,907	443	1,788 R	54.8%	42.1%	56.6%	43.4%

OHIO

PRESIDENT 1976

1970 Census Population	County	Total Vote	Republican	Democratic	Other	Rep.-Dem. Plurality	Percentage Total Vote Rep.	Percentage Total Vote Dem.	Percentage Major Vote Rep.	Percentage Major Vote Dem.
19,114	PIKE	9,574	3,729	5,734	111	2,005 D	38.9%	59.9%	39.4%	60.6%
125,868	PORTAGE	43,824	17,927	24,417	1,480	6,490 D	40.9%	55.7%	42.3%	57.7%
34,719	PREBLE	12,747	6,654	5,850	243	804 R	52.2%	45.9%	53.2%	46.8%
31,134	PUTNAM	12,710	7,332	5,035	343	2,297 R	57.7%	39.6%	59.3%	40.7%
129,997	RICHLAND	49,251	24,310	23,065	1,876	1,245 R	49.4%	46.8%	51.3%	48.7%
61,211	ROSS	22,751	11,477	10,743	531	734 R	50.4%	47.2%	51.7%	48.3%
60,983	SANDUSKY	24,867	13,074	11,202	591	1,872 R	52.6%	45.0%	53.9%	46.1%
76,951	SCIOTO	31,488	13,021	18,019	448	4,998 D	41.4%	57.2%	41.9%	58.1%
60,696	SENECA	22,516	11,730	10,074	712	1,656 R	52.1%	44.7%	53.8%	46.2%
37,748	SHELBY	14,859	8,011	6,414	434	1,597 R	53.9%	43.2%	55.5%	44.5%
372,210	STARK	145,709	72,607	70,012	3,090	2,595 R	49.8%	48.0%	50.9%	49.1%
553,371	SUMMIT	209,350	80,415	123,711	5,224	43,296 D	38.4%	59.1%	39.4%	60.6%
232,579	TRUMBULL	92,544	36,469	53,828	2,247	17,359 D	39.4%	58.2%	40.4%	59.6%
77,211	TUSCARAWAS	31,841	14,279	16,880	682	2,601 D	44.8%	53.0%	45.8%	54.2%
23,786	UNION	12,043	7,464	4,377	202	3,087 R	62.0%	36.3%	63.0%	37.0%
29,194	VAN WERT	14,284	8,344	5,689	251	2,655 R	58.4%	39.8%	59.5%	40.5%
9,420	VINTON	4,846	2,148	2,629	69	481 D	44.3%	54.3%	45.0%	55.0%
84,925	WARREN	29,935	16,115	13,349	471	2,766 R	53.8%	44.6%	54.7%	45.3%
57,160	WASHINGTON	21,096	11,513	8,914	669	2,599 R	54.6%	42.3%	56.4%	43.6%
87,123	WAYNE	30,754	16,976	13,087	691	3,889 R	55.2%	42.6%	56.5%	43.5%
33,669	WILLIAMS	12,762	7,596	4,920	246	2,676 R	59.5%	38.6%	60.7%	39.3%
89,722	WOOD	37,131	19,331	16,926	874	2,405 R	52.1%	45.6%	53.3%	46.7%
21,826	WYANDOT	9,946	5,661	4,043	242	1,618 R	56.9%	40.6%	58.3%	41.7%
10,652,017	TOTAL	4,111,873	2,000,505	2,011,621	99,747	11,116 D	48.7%	48.9%	49.9%	50.1%

OHIO

SENATOR 1976

1970 Census Population	County	Total Vote	Republican	Democratic	Other	Rep.-Dem. Plurality	Percentage Total Vote Rep.	Total Vote Dem.	Major Vote Rep.	Major Vote Dem.
18,957	ADAMS	8,448	4,143	4,060	245	83 R	49.0%	48.1%	50.5%	49.5%
111,144	ALLEN	39,229	21,920	15,774	1,535	6,146 R	55.9%	40.2%	58.2%	41.8%
43,303	ASHLAND	16,865	9,879	6,514	472	3,365 R	58.6%	38.6%	60.3%	39.7%
98,237	ASHTABULA	38,011	17,032	19,910	1,069	2,878 D	44.8%	52.4%	46.1%	53.9%
54,889	ATHENS	18,464	7,822	10,097	545	2,275 D	42.4%	54.7%	43.7%	56.3%
38,602	AUGLAIZE	15,604	8,916	6,040	648	2,876 R	57.1%	38.7%	59.6%	40.4%
80,917	BELMONT	33,934	12,669	20,051	1,214	7,382 D	37.3%	59.1%	38.7%	61.3%
26,635	BROWN	9,651	4,176	5,181	294	1,005 D	43.3%	53.7%	44.6%	55.4%
226,207	BUTLER	85,380	45,482	37,589	2,309	7,893 R	53.3%	44.0%	54.8%	45.2%
21,579	CARROLL	9,993	5,264	4,384	345	880 R	52.7%	43.9%	54.6%	45.4%
30,491	CHAMPAIGN	11,503	6,454	4,761	288	1,693 R	56.1%	41.4%	57.5%	42.5%
157,115	CLARK	51,995	22,882	25,439	3,674	2,557 D	44.0%	48.9%	47.4%	52.6%
95,725	CLERMONT	34,806	17,436	16,241	1,129	1,195 R	50.1%	46.7%	51.8%	48.2%
31,464	CLINTON	11,628	6,504	4,853	271	1,651 R	55.9%	41.7%	57.3%	42.7%
108,310	COLUMBIANA	45,318	21,008	22,719	1,591	1,711 D	46.4%	50.1%	48.0%	52.0%
33,486	COSHOCTON	11,337	5,697	4,356	1,284	1,341 R	50.3%	38.4%	56.7%	43.3%
50,364	CRAWFORD	18,444	10,571	7,191	682	3,380 R	57.3%	39.0%	59.5%	40.5%
1,721,300	CUYAHOGA	551,574	195,920	320,873	34,781	124,953 D	35.5%	58.2%	37.9%	62.1%
49,141	DARKE	21,735	11,317	9,706	712	1,611 R	52.1%	44.7%	53.8%	46.2%
36,949	DEFIANCE	13,481	7,664	5,299	518	2,365 R	56.9%	39.3%	59.1%	40.9%
42,908	DELAWARE	19,611	11,470	7,576	565	3,894 R	58.5%	38.6%	60.2%	39.8%
75,909	ERIE	27,544	12,694	13,014	1,836	320 D	46.1%	47.2%	49.4%	50.6%
73,301	FAIRFIELD	33,039	18,137	13,996	906	4,141 R	54.9%	42.4%	56.4%	43.6%
25,461	FAYETTE	9,961	5,579	4,128	254	1,451 R	56.0%	41.4%	57.5%	42.5%
833,249	FRANKLIN	325,663	165,042	147,745	12,876	17,297 R	50.7%	45.4%	52.8%	47.2%
33,071	FULTON	12,661	8,010	4,343	308	3,667 R	63.3%	34.3%	64.8%	35.2%
25,239	GALLIA	9,807	5,251	4,216	340	1,035 R	53.5%	43.0%	55.5%	44.5%
62,977	GEAUGA	25,392	12,684	11,496	1,212	1,188 R	50.0%	45.3%	52.5%	47.5%
125,057	GREENE	43,876	20,702	21,840	1,334	1,138 D	47.2%	49.8%	48.7%	51.3%
37,665	GUERNSEY	14,964	8,012	6,597	355	1,415 R	53.5%	44.1%	54.8%	45.2%
924,018	HAMILTON	346,090	186,437	151,187	8,466	35,250 R	53.9%	43.7%	55.2%	44.8%
61,217	HANCOCK	23,688	14,167	6,562	2,959	7,605 R	59.8%	27.7%	68.3%	31.7%
30,813	HARDIN	10,479	5,383	3,610	1,486	1,773 R	51.4%	34.4%	59.9%	40.1%
17,013	HARRISON	7,351	3,548	3,601	202	53 D	48.3%	49.0%	49.6%	50.4%
27,058	HENRY	12,096	7,797	3,918	381	3,879 R	64.5%	32.4%	66.6%	33.4%
28,996	HIGHLAND	13,103	6,862	5,959	282	903 R	52.4%	45.5%	53.5%	46.5%
20,322	HOCKING	9,117	4,029	4,859	229	830 D	44.2%	53.3%	45.3%	54.7%
23,024	HOLMES	5,208	3,075	1,853	280	1,222 R	59.0%	35.6%	62.4%	37.6%
49,587	HURON	17,026	9,072	6,764	1,190	2,308 R	53.3%	39.7%	57.3%	42.7%
27,174	JACKSON	11,973	5,958	5,689	326	269 R	49.8%	47.5%	51.2%	48.8%
96,193	JEFFERSON	36,729	13,625	21,932	1,172	8,307 D	37.1%	59.7%	38.3%	61.7%
41,795	KNOX	16,296	8,271	7,042	983	1,229 R	50.8%	43.2%	54.0%	46.0%
197,200	LAKE	69,798	29,694	35,397	4,707	5,703 D	42.5%	50.7%	45.6%	54.4%
56,868	LAWRENCE	21,701	10,785	10,178	738	607 R	49.7%	46.9%	51.4%	48.6%
107,799	LICKING	42,980	21,653	19,992	1,335	1,661 R	50.4%	46.5%	52.0%	48.0%
35,072	LOGAN	15,247	8,837	5,918	492	2,919 R	58.0%	38.8%	59.9%	40.1%
256,843	LORAIN	91,600	38,457	50,397	2,746	11,940 D	42.0%	55.0%	43.3%	56.7%
484,370	LUCAS	172,611	78,903	87,672	6,036	8,769 D	45.7%	50.8%	47.4%	52.6%
28,318	MADISON	11,678	6,487	4,908	283	1,579 R	55.5%	42.0%	56.9%	43.1%
303,424	MAHONING	110,044	39,310	67,174	3,560	27,864 D	35.7%	61.0%	36.9%	63.1%
64,724	MARION	24,483	12,712	11,104	667	1,608 R	51.9%	45.4%	53.4%	46.6%
82,717	MEDINA	36,140	18,330	16,995	815	1,335 R	50.7%	47.0%	51.9%	48.1%
19,799	MEIGS	9,660	4,868	4,507	285	361 R	50.4%	46.7%	51.9%	48.1%
35,265	MERCER	14,536	7,025	6,560	951	465 R	48.3%	45.1%	51.7%	48.3%
84,342	MIAMI	32,405	17,869	13,712	824	4,157 R	55.1%	42.3%	56.6%	43.4%
15,739	MONROE	6,717	2,690	3,842	185	1,152 D	40.0%	57.2%	41.2%	58.8%
606,148	MONTGOMERY	203,135	89,109	106,616	7,410	17,507 D	43.9%	52.5%	45.5%	54.5%
12,375	MORGAN	5,743	3,075	2,509	159	566 R	53.5%	43.7%	55.1%	44.9%
21,348	MORROW	10,720	5,815	4,565	340	1,250 R	54.2%	42.6%	56.0%	44.0%
77,826	MUSKINGUM	29,555	14,329	14,437	789	108 D	48.5%	48.8%	49.8%	50.2%
10,428	NOBLE	5,512	2,990	2,351	171	639 R	54.2%	42.7%	56.0%	44.0%
37,099	OTTAWA	17,799	8,674	8,611	514	63 R	48.7%	48.4%	50.2%	49.8%
19,329	PAULDING	6,685	3,599	2,710	376	889 R	53.8%	40.5%	57.0%	43.0%
27,434	PERRY	11,982	5,416	6,244	322	828 D	45.2%	52.1%	46.4%	53.6%
40,071	PICKAWAY	12,890	6,308	4,773	1,809	1,535 R	48.9%	37.0%	56.9%	43.1%

OHIO

SENATOR 1976

1970 Census Population	County	Total Vote	Republican	Democratic	Other	Rep.-Dem. Plurality	Percentage Total Vote Rep.	Percentage Total Vote Dem.	Percentage Major Vote Rep.	Percentage Major Vote Dem.
19,114	PIKE	9,276	3,807	5,327	142	1,520 D	41.0%	57.4%	41.7%	58.3%
125,868	PORTAGE	43,773	17,849	24,773	1,151	6,924 D	40.8%	56.6%	41.9%	58.1%
34,719	PREBLE	12,722	6,554	5,821	347	733 R	51.5%	45.8%	53.0%	47.0%
31,134	PUTNAM	12,367	6,861	5,002	504	1,859 R	55.5%	40.4%	57.8%	42.2%
129,997	RICHLAND	46,069	22,317	20,630	3,122	1,687 R	48.4%	44.8%	52.0%	48.0%
61,211	ROSS	20,674	10,320	8,495	1,859	1,825 R	49.9%	41.1%	54.8%	45.2%
60,983	SANDUSKY	24,483	13,383	10,237	863	3,146 R	54.7%	41.8%	56.7%	43.3%
76,951	SCIOTO	30,821	12,940	17,201	680	4,261 D	42.0%	55.8%	42.9%	57.1%
60,696	SENECA	22,276	12,133	9,247	896	2,886 R	54.5%	41.5%	56.7%	43.3%
37,748	SHELBY	14,420	7,084	6,468	868	616 R	49.1%	44.9%	52.3%	47.7%
372,210	STARK	145,380	71,430	69,983	3,967	1,447 R	49.1%	48.1%	50.5%	49.5%
553,371	SUMMIT	208,785	82,163	121,598	5,024	39,435 D	39.4%	58.2%	40.3%	59.7%
232,579	TRUMBULL	87,226	33,052	51,357	2,817	18,305 D	37.9%	58.9%	39.2%	60.8%
77,211	TUSCARAWAS	31,247	14,821	15,492	934	671 D	47.4%	49.6%	48.9%	51.1%
23,786	UNION	11,787	7,096	4,323	368	2,773 R	60.2%	36.7%	62.1%	37.9%
29,194	VAN WERT	13,676	7,607	5,401	668	2,206 R	55.6%	39.5%	58.5%	41.5%
9,420	VINTON	4,527	2,087	2,286	154	199 D	46.1%	50.5%	47.7%	52.3%
84,925	WARREN	29,697	15,224	13,759	714	1,465 R	51.3%	46.3%	52.5%	47.5%
57,160	WASHINGTON	19,614	10,820	8,010	784	2,810 R	55.2%	40.8%	57.5%	42.5%
87,123	WAYNE	30,567	17,689	12,140	738	5,549 R	57.9%	39.7%	59.3%	40.7%
33,669	WILLIAMS	12,462	7,693	4,366	403	3,327 R	61.7%	35.0%	63.8%	36.2%
89,722	WOOD	36,440	19,598	15,498	1,344	4,100 R	53.8%	42.5%	55.8%	44.2%
21,826	WYANDOT	9,629	5,750	3,562	317	2,188 R	59.7%	37.0%	61.7%	38.3%
10,652,017	TOTAL	3,920,613	1,823,774	1,941,113	155,726	117,339 D	46.5%	49.5%	48.4%	51.6%

OHIO

CONGRESS

CD	Year	Total Vote	Republican Vote	Republican Candidate	Democratic Vote	Democratic Candidate	Other Vote	Rep.-Dem. Plurality	Percentage Total Vote Rep.	Percentage Total Vote Dem.	Percentage Major Vote Rep.	Percentage Major Vote Dem.
1	1976	169,516	109,789	GRADISON, WILLIS D.	56,995	BOWEN, WILLIAM F.	2,732	52,794 R	64.8%	33.6%	65.8%	34.2%
1	1974	137,991	70,284	GRADISON, WILLIS D.	67,685	LUKEN, THOMAS A.	22	2,599 R	50.9%	49.1%	50.9%	49.1%
1	1972	170,044	119,469	KEATING, WILLIAM J.	50,575	HEISER, KARL F.		68,894 R	70.3%	29.7%	70.3%	29.7%
2	1976	171,637	83,459	CLANCY, DONALD D.	88,178	LUKEN, THOMAS A.		4,719 D	48.6%	51.4%	48.6%	51.4%
2	1974	134,042	71,512	CLANCY, DONALD D.	62,530	WOLTERMAN, E. W.		8,982 R	53.4%	46.6%	53.4%	46.6%
2	1972	175,198	109,961	CLANCY, DONALD D.	65,237	MANES, PENNY		44,724 R	62.8%	37.2%	62.8%	37.2%
3	1976	145,374	100,871	WHALEN, CHARLES W.	33,873	STUBBS, LEONARD	10,630	66,998 R	69.4%	23.3%	74.9%	25.1%
3	1974	82,159	82,159	WHALEN, CHARLES W.				82,159 R	100.0%		100.0%	
3	1972	146,072	111,253	WHALEN, CHARLES W.	34,819	LELAK, JOHN W.		76,434 R	76.2%	23.8%	76.2%	23.8%
4	1976	172,957	121,173	GUYER, TENNYSON	51,784	DORSEY, CLINTON G.		69,389 R	70.1%	29.9%	70.1%	29.9%
4	1974	132,739	81,674	GUYER, TENNYSON	51,065	GEHRLICH, JAMES L.		30,609 R	61.5%	38.5%	61.5%	38.5%
4	1972	174,828	109,612	GUYER, TENNYSON	65,216	NICHOLAS, DIMITRI		44,396 R	62.7%	37.3%	62.7%	37.3%
5	1976	185,214	124,910	LATTA, DELBERT L.	60,304	EDWARDS, BRUCE		64,606 R	67.4%	32.6%	67.4%	32.6%
5	1974	142,552	89,161	LATTA, DELBERT L.	53,391	EDWARDS, BRUCE		35,770 R	62.5%	37.5%	62.5%	37.5%
5	1972	181,497	132,032	LATTA, DELBERT L.	49,465	EDWARDS, BRUCE		82,567 R	72.7%	27.3%	72.7%	27.3%
6	1976	174,131	107,064	HARSHA, WILLIAM H.	67,067	STRICKLAND, TED		39,997 R	61.5%	38.5%	61.5%	38.5%
6	1974	135,716	93,400	HARSHA, WILLIAM H.	42,316	WOOD, LLOYD A.		51,084 R	68.8%	31.2%	68.8%	31.2%
6	1972	128,394	128,394	HARSHA, WILLIAM H.				128,394 R	100.0%		100.0%	
7	1976	155,782	101,027	BROWN, CLARENCE, JR.	54,755	FRANKE, DOROTHY		46,272 R	64.9%	35.1%	64.9%	35.1%
7	1974	121,419	73,503	BROWN, CLARENCE, JR.	34,828	NELSON, PATRICK L.	13,088	38,675 R	60.5%	28.7%	67.9%	32.1%
7	1972	153,295	112,350	BROWN, CLARENCE, JR.			40,945	112,350 R	73.3%		100.0%	
8	1976	161,357	110,775	KINDNESS, THOMAS N.	46,424	GRIFFIN, JOHN W.	4,158	64,351 R	68.7%	28.8%	70.5%	29.5%
8	1974	120,415	51,097	KINDNESS, THOMAS N.	45,701	STRINKO, T. EDWARD	23,617	5,396 R	42.4%	38.0%	52.8%	47.2%
8	1972	153,394	80,050	POWELL, WALTER E.	73,344	RUPPERT, JAMES D.		6,706 R	52.2%	47.8%	52.2%	47.8%
9	1976	167,969	73,919	FINKBEINER, C. S.	91,040	ASHLEY, THOMAS L.	3,010	17,121 D	44.0%	54.2%	44.8%	55.2%
9	1974	122,775	57,892	FINKBEINER, C. S.	64,831	ASHLEY, THOMAS L.	52	6,939 D	47.2%	52.8%	47.2%	52.8%
9	1972	159,838	49,388	RICHARDS, JOSEPH C.	110,450	ASHLEY, THOMAS L.		61,062 D	30.9%	69.1%	30.9%	69.1%
10	1976	184,904	127,147	MILLER, CLARENCE E.	57,757	PLUMMER, JAMES A.		69,390 R	68.8%	31.2%	68.8%	31.2%
10	1974	142,854	100,521	MILLER, CLARENCE E.	42,333	BUMPASS, H. KENT		58,188 R	70.4%	29.6%	70.4%	29.6%
10	1972	177,139	129,683	MILLER, CLARENCE E.	47,456	WHEALEY, ROBERT H.		82,227 R	73.2%	26.8%	73.2%	26.8%
11	1976	168,264	120,716	STANTON, J. WILLIAM	47,548	WEST, THOMAS R.		73,168 R	71.7%	28.3%	71.7%	28.3%
11	1974	131,857	79,756	STANTON, J. WILLIAM	52,017	COFFEY, MICHAEL D.	84	27,739 R	60.5%	39.4%	60.5%	39.5%
11	1972	156,732	106,841	STANTON, J. WILLIAM	49,891	CALLAHAN, DENNIS M.		56,950 R	68.2%	31.8%	68.2%	31.8%
12	1976	195,840	90,987	DEVINE, SAMUEL L.	89,424	RYAN, FRAN	15,429	1,563 R	46.5%	45.7%	50.4%	49.6%
12	1974	144,121	73,303	DEVINE, SAMUEL L.	70,818	RYAN, FRAN		2,485 R	50.9%	49.1%	50.9%	49.1%
12	1972	184,729	103,655	DEVINE, SAMUEL L.	81,074	GOODRICH, JAMES W.		22,581 R	56.1%	43.9%	56.1%	43.9%
13	1976	163,683	49,828	MATHNA, WOODROW W.	108,061	PEASE, DONALD J.	5,794	58,233 D	30.4%	66.0%	31.6%	68.4%
13	1974	126,647	72,881	MOSHER, CHARLES A.	53,766	RITENAUER, FRED M.		19,115 R	57.5%	42.5%	57.5%	42.5%
13	1972	163,233	111,242	MOSHER, CHARLES A.	51,991	RYAN, JOHN M.		59,251 R	68.1%	31.9%	68.1%	31.9%
14	1976	164,188	39,917	HOUSTON, JAMES E.	121,652	SEIBERLING, JOHN F.	2,619	81,735 D	24.3%	74.1%	24.7%	75.3%
14	1974	124,534	30,603	FIGETAKIS, MARK	93,931	SEIBERLING, JOHN F.		63,328 D	24.6%	75.4%	24.6%	75.4%
14	1972	181,558	46,490	HOLT, NORMAN W.	135,068	SEIBERLING, JOHN F.		88,578 D	25.6%	74.4%	25.6%	74.4%
15	1976	167,371	109,630	WYLIE, CHALMERS P.	57,741	MCGEE, MANLEY L.		51,889 R	65.5%	34.5%	65.5%	34.5%
15	1974	129,059	79,376	WYLIE, CHALMERS P.	49,683	MCGEE, MANLEY L.		29,693 R	61.5%	38.5%	61.5%	38.5%
15	1972	175,913	115,779	WYLIE, CHALMERS P.	55,314	MCGEE, MANLEY L.	4,820	60,465 R	65.8%	31.4%	67.7%	32.3%
16	1976	174,091	116,374	REGULA, RALPH S.	55,671	FREEDOM, JOHN G.	2,046	60,703 R	66.8%	32.0%	67.6%	32.4%
16	1974	141,740	92,986	REGULA, RALPH S.	48,754	FREEDOM, JOHN G.		44,232 R	65.6%	34.4%	65.6%	34.4%
16	1972	177,942	102,013	REGULA, RALPH S.	75,929	MUSSER, VIRGIL L.		26,084 R	57.3%	42.7%	57.3%	42.7%
17	1976	167,042	94,874	ASHBROOK, JOHN M.	72,168	MCDONALD, JOHN C.		22,706 R	56.8%	43.2%	56.8%	43.2%
17	1974	134,053	70,708	ASHBROOK, JOHN M.	63,342	NOBLE, DAVID D.	3	7,366 R	52.7%	47.3%	52.7%	47.3%
17	1972	161,554	92,666	ASHBROOK, JOHN M.	62,512	BECK, RAYMOND C.	6,376	30,154 R	57.4%	38.7%	59.7%	40.3%
18	1976	185,834	45,735	MCCOY, RALPH R.	116,901	APPLEGATE, DOUGLAS	23,198	71,166 D	24.6%	62.9%	28.1%	71.9%
18	1974	137,832	47,385	ROMIG, RALPH H.	90,447	HAYS, WAYNE L.		43,062 D	34.4%	65.6%	34.4%	65.6%
18	1972	183,235	54,572	STEWART, ROBERT	128,663	HAYS, WAYNE L.		74,091 D	29.8%	70.2%	29.8%	70.2%
19	1976	179,895	86,162	HUNTER, JACK C.	90,386	CARNEY, CHARLES J.	3,347	4,224 D	47.9%	50.2%	48.8%	51.2%
19	1974	134,358	36,649	RIPPLE, JAMES L.	97,709	CARNEY, CHARLES J.		61,060 D	27.3%	72.7%	27.3%	72.7%
19	1972	171,913	61,934	PARR, NORMAN M.	109,979	CARNEY, CHARLES J.		48,045 D	36.0%	64.0%	36.0%	64.0%
20	1976	121,976			98,785	OAKAR, MARY ROSE	23,191	98,785 D		81.0%		100.0%
20	1974	99,396	12,991	FRANTZ, ROBERT A.	86,405	STANTON, JAMES V.		73,414 D	13.1%	86.9%	13.1%	86.9%
20	1972	139,219	16,624	VILT, THOMAS E.	117,302	STANTON, JAMES V.	5,293	100,678 D	11.9%	84.3%	12.4%	87.6%
21	1976	109,626	12,434	SPARKS, BARBARA	91,903	STOKES, LOUIS	5,289	79,469 D	11.3%	83.8%	11.9%	88.1%
21	1974	71,955	12,986	MACK, BILL	58,969	STOKES, LOUIS		45,983 D	18.0%	82.0%	18.0%	82.0%
21	1972	122,339	13,861	JOHNSON, JAMES D.	99,190	STOKES, LOUIS	9,288	85,329 D	11.3%	81.1%	12.3%	87.7%

OHIO

CONGRESS

CD	Year	Total Vote	Republican Vote	Republican Candidate	Democratic Vote	Democratic Candidate	Other Vote	Rep.-Dem. Plurality	Percentage Total Vote Rep.	Percentage Total Vote Dem.	Percentage Major Vote Rep.	Percentage Major Vote Dem.
22	1976	176,723	42,727	HANNA, HARRY A.	128,535	VANIK, CHARLES A.	5,461	85,808 D	24.2%	72.7%	24.9%	75.1%
22	1974	143,256	30,585	FRANZ, WILLIAM J.	112,671	VANIK, CHARLES A.		82,086 D	21.3%	78.7%	21.3%	78.7%
22	1972	197,844	64,577	GROPP, DONALD W.	126,462	VANIK, CHARLES A.	6,805	61,885 D	32.6%	63.9%	33.8%	66.2%
23	1976	178,380	47,804	SCANLON, MICHAEL T.	130,576	MOTTL, RONALD M.		82,772 D	26.8%	73.2%	26.8%	73.2%
23	1974	153,455	46,810	MASTICS, GEORGE E.	53,338	MOTTL, RONALD M.	53,307	6,528 D	30.5%	34.8%	46.7%	53.3%
23	1972	199,631	98,594	MINSHALL, WILLIAM E.	94,366	KUCINICH, DENNIS J.	6,671	4,228 R	49.4%	47.3%	51.1%	48.9%

OHIO

1976 GENERAL ELECTION

President — Other vote was 58,258 McCarthy (Independent); 15,529 Maddox (American); 8,961 MacBride (Independent); 7,817 Hall (Independent); 4,717 Camejo (Independent); 4,335 LaRouche (Independent); 68 Levin (write-in); 62 Bubar (write-in). Vote detailed here is for the recount.

Senator — Other vote was 53,657 O'Neill (Independent); 36,979 Babcock (American); 33,285 Fundaburk (Independent); 31,805 Singler (Independent).

Congress — Other vote was Martinson (Independent) in CD 1; 5,758 Hurst (Independent) and 4,872 Austin (Independent) in CD 3; Payton (Independent) in CD 8; 1,533 Emery (Independent) and 1,477 Galonsky (Independent) in CD 9; Moss (Independent) in CD 12; Cortez (Independent) in CD 13; Meyer (Independent) in CD 14; 1,969 Festerly (American) and 77 scattered in CD 16; 21,537 Crabbe (Independent) and 1,661 Bashline (write-in) in CD 18; 2,258 Zurbrugg (Independent) and 1,089 Untch (Independent) in CD 19; Held (Independent) in CD 20; Curry (Independent) in CD 21; Lippitt (American) in CD 22.

1976 PRIMARIES

JUNE 8 REPUBLICAN

Senator — Robert A. Taft, Jr., unopposed.

Congress — Unopposed in fourteen CD's. Contested as follows:

CD 1	33,167 Willis D. Gradison; 10,544 William E. Flax.
CD 3	18,899 Charles W. Whalen; 14,534 Billy R. Shepherd; 2,525 H. Quinn Licklider.
CD 8	34,046 Thomas N. Kindness; 5,855 John R. Brown.
CD 13	14,567 Woodrow W. Mathna; 11,511 Peter A. Walderzak.
CD 17	35,836 John M. Ashbrook; 7,326 Donald C. Wickham.
CD 19	25,702 Jack C. Hunter; 1,909 Joseph J. Rohan.
CD 20	No candidates appeared on the ballot; there were 191 write-in votes for Thomas L. McSweeney. Mr. McSweeney withdrew and no substitution was made.
CD 22	12,156 Harry A. Hanna; 10,281 Kent R. Minshall; 5,780 William J. Franz.
CD 23	22,554 Michael T. Scanlon; 6,644 John D. DuRoss.

JUNE 8 DEMOCRATIC

Senator — 576,124 Howard Metzenbaum; 400,552 James V. Stanton; 62,979 James D. Nolan; 35,522 Richard B. Kay.

Congress — Unopposed in seven CD's. Contested as follows:

CD 2	16,949 Thomas A. Luken; 9,760 W. Emerson Rhodes; 2,051 John T. Conboy.
CD 6	14,891 Ted Strickland; 10,626 Paul H. McCarthy; 8,966 Barbara E. Taylor.
CD 9	31,519 Thomas L. Ashley; 13,182 Corey Garber.
CD 10	26,150 James A. Plummer; 8,601 J. Kermit Gatten.
CD 11	13,704 Thomas R. West; 11,916 Robert P. Woodman; 6,185 Gary A. Tisor.
CD 12	37,183 Fran Ryan; 9,463 Jack Ruzicho.
CD 13	27,389 Donald J. Pease; 10,278 John M. Ryan; 5,316 Robert C. Salkowitz.
CD 14	57,179 John F. Seiberling; 6,315 Raymond A. Sullivan; 2,732 Robert Marmaduke.
CD 15	16,641 Manley L. McGee; 16,048 David C. Sweet.
CD 16	37,575 John G. Freedom; 14,116 Owen S. Hand.
CD 18	42,716 Wayne L. Hays; 26,971 Nick B. Karnick. Mr. Hays withdrew after the primary and Douglas Applegate was substituted by the local party committee.
CD 19	44,909 Charles J. Carney; 19,536 George Beelen; 4,642 Gary J. Thompson; 4,480 S. Michael Kirwan; 2,216 Edith Tomich; 1,124 James E. Simones.

OHIO

CD 20	14,408 Mary Rose Oakar; 11,037 Anthony J. Celebrezze, Jr.; 10,761 Michael L. Climaco; 9,885 Basil M. Russo; 5,044 Raymond A. Stachewicz; 2,987 James P. Celebrezze; 1,569 Ronald J. Novak; 1,289 Donald T. Gallagher; 1,010 John T. Flanigan; 833 Norbert G. Dennerll; 650 Michael G. Kelly; 539 Edward A. Ginley.
CD 21	35,061 Louis Stokes; 9,210 Owen L. Heggs.
CD 22	55,813 Charles A. Vanik; 4,075 William J. Kennick.
CD 23	45,308 Ronald M. Mottl; 3,460 Arthur M. Shinn.

OKLAHOMA

GOVERNOR

David L. Boren (D). Elected 1974 to a four-year term.

SENATORS

Dewey F. Bartlett (R). Elected 1972 to a six-year term.

Henry Bellmon (R). Re-elected 1974 to a six-year term. Previously elected 1968.

REPRESENTATIVES

1. James R. Jones (D)
2. Ted M. Risenhoover (D)
3. Wes Watkins (D)
4. Tom Steed (D)
5. M. H. Edwards (R)
6. Glenn English (D)

POSTWAR VOTE FOR GOVERNOR

		Republican		Democratic				Percentage			
	Total					Other	Rep.-Dem.	Total Vote		Major Vote	
Year	Vote	Vote	Candidate	Vote	Candidate	Vote	Plurality	Rep.	Dem.	Rep.	Dem.
1974	804,848	290,459	Inhofe, James M.	514,389	Boren, David L.	–	223,930 D	36.1%	63.9%	36.1%	63.9%
1970	698,790	336,157	Bartlett, Dewey F.	338,338	Hall, David	24,295	2,181 D	48.1%	48.4%	49.8%	50.2%
1966	677,258	377,078	Bartlett, Dewey F.	296,328	Moore, Preston J.	3,852	80,750 R	55.7%	43.8%	56.0%	44.0%
1962	709,763	392,316	Bellmon, Henry	315,357	Atkinson, W. P.	2,090	76,959 R	55.3%	44.4%	55.4%	44.6%
1958	538,839	107,495	Ferguson, Phil	399,504	Edmondson, J. Howard	31,840	292,009 D	19.9%	74.1%	21.2%	78.8%
1954	609,194	251,808	Sparks, Reuben K.	357,386	Gary, Raymond	–	105,578 D	41.3%	58.7%	41.3%	58.7%
1950	644,276	313,205	Ferguson, Jo O.	329,308	Murray, Johnston	1,763	16,103 D	48.6%	51.1%	48.7%	51.3%
1946	494,599	227,426	Flynn, Olney F.	259,491	Turner, Roy J.	7,682	32,065 D	46.0%	52.5%	46.7%	53.3%

POSTWAR VOTE FOR SENATOR

		Republican		Democratic				Percentage			
	Total					Other	Rep.-Dem.	Total Vote		Major Vote	
Year	Vote	Vote	Candidate	Vote	Candidate	Vote	Plurality	Rep.	Dem.	Rep.	Dem.
1974	791,809	390,997	Bellmon, Henry	387,162	Edmondson, Ed	13,650	3,835 R	49.4%	48.9%	50.2%	49.8%
1972	1,005,148	516,934	Bartlett, Dewey F.	478,212	Edmondson, Ed	10,002	38,722 R	51.4%	47.6%	51.9%	48.1%
1968	909,119	470,120	Bellmon, Henry	419,658	Monroney, A. S. Mike	19,341	50,462 R	51.7%	46.2%	52.8%	47.2%
1966	638,742	295,585	Patterson, Pat J.	343,157	Harris, Fred R.	–	47,572 D	46.3%	53.7%	46.3%	53.7%
1964s	912,174	445,392	Wilkinson, Bud	466,782	Harris, Fred R.	–	21,390 D	48.8%	51.2%	48.8%	51.2%
1962	664,712	307,966	Crawford, B. Hayden	353,890	Monroney, A. S. Mike	2,856	45,924 D	46.3%	53.2%	46.5%	53.5%
1960	864,475	385,646	Crawford, B. Hayden	474,116	Kerr, Robert S.	4,713	88,470 D	44.6%	54.8%	44.9%	55.1%
1956	831,142	371,146	McKeever, Douglas	459,996	Monroney, A. S. Mike	–	88,850 D	44.7%	55.3%	44.7%	55.3%
1954	600,120	262,013	Mock, Fred M.	335,127	Kerr, Robert S.	2,980	73,114 D	43.7%	55.8%	43.9%	56.1%
1950	631,177	285,224	Alexander, W. H.	345,953	Monroney, A. S. Mike	–	60,729 D	45.2%	54.8%	45.2%	54.8%
1948	708,931	265,169	Rizley, Ross	441,654	Kerr, Robert S.	2,108	176,485 D	37.4%	62.3%	37.5%	62.5%

The 1964 election was for a short term to fill a vacancy.

OKLAHOMA

Districts Established April 3, 1972

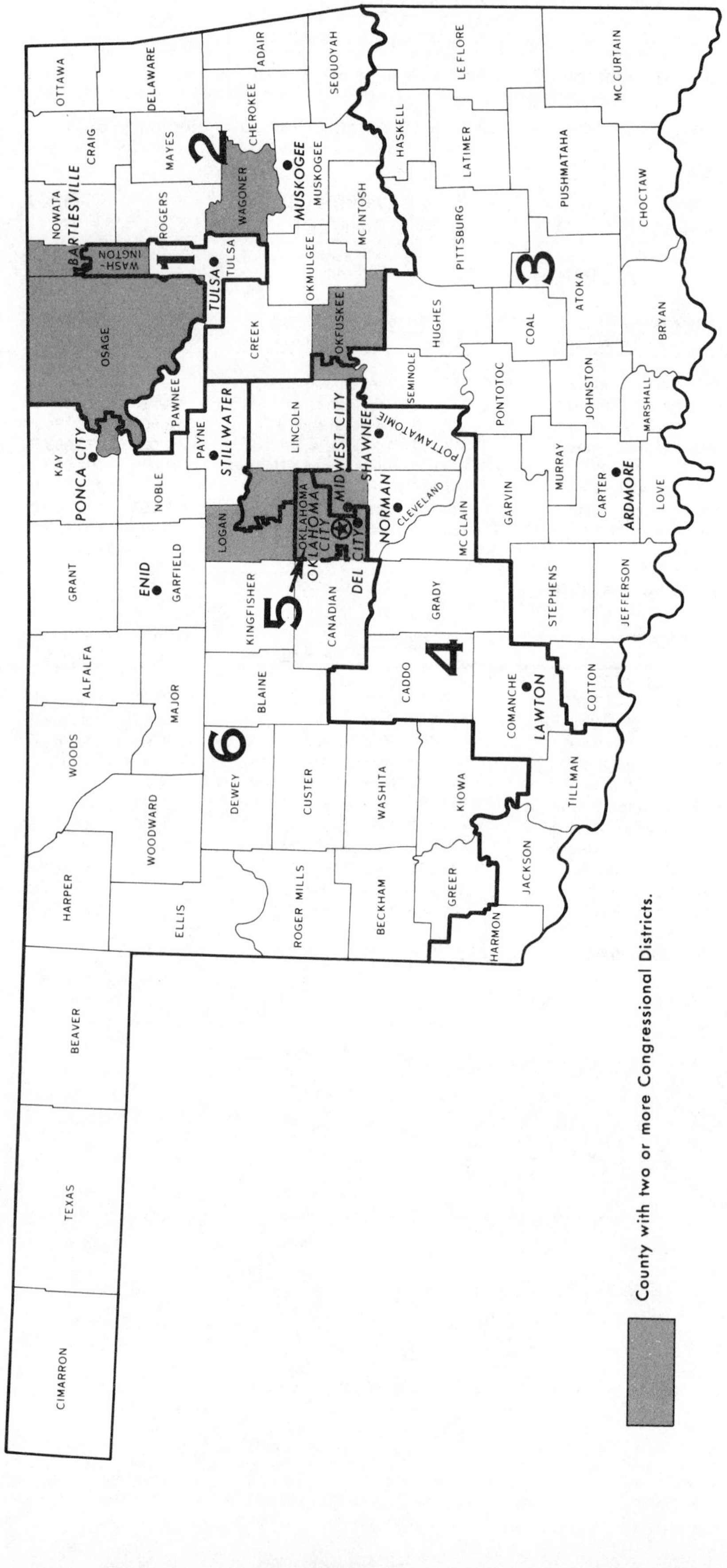

OKLAHOMA

PRESIDENT 1976

1970 Census Population	County	Total Vote	Republican	Democratic	Other	Rep.-Dem. Plurality	Percentage Total Vote Rep.	Percentage Total Vote Dem.	Percentage Major Vote Rep.	Percentage Major Vote Dem.
15,141	ADAIR	6,259	3,013	3,183	63	170 D	48.1%	50.9%	48.6%	51.4%
7,224	ALFALFA	3,897	2,113	1,725	59	388 R	54.2%	44.3%	55.1%	44.9%
10,972	ATOKA	4,402	1,098	3,276	28	2,178 D	24.9%	74.4%	25.1%	74.9%
6,282	BEAVER	3,061	1,801	1,213	47	588 R	58.8%	39.6%	59.8%	40.2%
15,754	BECKHAM	6,935	2,351	4,530	54	2,179 D	33.9%	65.3%	34.2%	65.8%
11,794	BLAINE	5,056	2,682	2,297	77	385 R	53.0%	45.4%	53.9%	46.1%
25,552	BRYAN	10,293	2,848	7,410	35	4,562 D	27.7%	72.0%	27.8%	72.2%
28,931	CADDO	11,327	3,854	7,382	91	3,528 D	34.0%	65.2%	34.3%	65.7%
32,245	CANADIAN	17,339	9,766	7,288	285	2,478 R	56.3%	42.0%	57.3%	42.7%
37,349	CARTER	15,070	6,668	8,319	83	1,651 D	44.2%	55.2%	44.5%	55.5%
23,174	CHEROKEE	10,564	4,443	6,006	115	1,563 D	42.1%	56.9%	42.5%	57.5%
15,141	CHOCTAW	6,140	1,821	4,269	50	2,448 D	29.7%	69.5%	29.9%	70.1%
4,145	CIMARRON	1,879	872	962	45	90 D	46.4%	51.2%	47.5%	52.5%
81,839	CLEVELAND	43,281	22,098	20,054	1,129	2,044 R	51.1%	46.3%	52.4%	47.6%
5,525	COAL	2,566	769	1,774	23	1,005 D	30.0%	69.1%	30.2%	69.8%
108,144	COMANCHE	26,303	13,163	12,910	230	253 R	50.0%	49.1%	50.5%	49.5%
6,832	COTTON	3,064	1,127	1,911	26	784 D	36.8%	62.4%	37.1%	62.9%
14,722	CRAIG	6,178	2,540	3,577	61	1,037 D	41.1%	57.9%	41.5%	58.5%
45,532	CREEK	17,591	8,458	8,964	169	506 D	48.1%	51.0%	48.5%	51.5%
22,665	CUSTER	9,546	4,847	4,597	102	250 R	50.8%	48.2%	51.3%	48.7%
17,767	DELAWARE	8,657	3,642	4,924	91	1,282 D	42.1%	56.9%	42.5%	57.5%
5,656	DEWEY	2,825	1,230	1,540	55	310 D	43.5%	54.5%	44.4%	55.6%
5,129	ELLIS	2,746	1,429	1,256	61	173 R	52.0%	45.7%	53.2%	46.8%
56,343	GARFIELD	23,474	14,202	8,969	303	5,233 R	60.5%	38.2%	61.3%	38.7%
24,874	GARVIN	10,785	3,905	6,797	83	2,892 D	36.2%	63.0%	36.5%	63.5%
29,354	GRADY	11,955	4,686	7,155	114	2,469 D	39.2%	59.8%	39.6%	60.4%
7,117	GRANT	3,588	1,685	1,853	50	168 D	47.0%	51.6%	47.6%	52.4%
7,979	GREER	3,308	1,164	2,113	31	949 D	35.2%	63.9%	35.5%	64.5%
5,136	HARMON	2,045	666	1,371	8	705 D	32.6%	67.0%	32.7%	67.3%
5,151	HARPER	2,320	1,303	978	39	325 R	56.2%	42.2%	57.1%	42.9%
9,578	HASKELL	4,818	1,401	3,388	29	1,987 D	29.1%	70.3%	29.3%	70.7%
13,228	HUGHES	5,956	1,715	4,185	56	2,470 D	28.8%	70.3%	29.1%	70.9%
30,902	JACKSON	8,163	3,189	4,914	60	1,725 D	39.1%	60.2%	39.4%	60.6%
7,125	JEFFERSON	3,285	956	2,303	26	1,347 D	29.1%	70.1%	29.3%	70.7%
7,870	JOHNSTON	3,934	1,127	2,765	42	1,638 D	28.6%	70.3%	29.0%	71.0%
48,791	KAY	22,086	12,441	9,371	274	3,070 R	56.3%	42.4%	57.0%	43.0%
12,857	KINGFISHER	5,897	3,443	2,372	82	1,071 R	58.4%	40.2%	59.2%	40.8%
12,532	KIOWA	5,420	1,971	3,403	46	1,432 D	36.4%	62.8%	36.7%	63.3%
8,601	LATIMER	4,028	1,312	2,661	55	1,349 D	32.6%	66.1%	33.0%	67.0%
32,137	LE FLORE	13,085	4,907	8,033	145	3,126 D	37.5%	61.4%	37.9%	62.1%
19,482	LINCOLN	9,550	4,429	4,988	133	559 D	46.4%	52.2%	47.0%	53.0%
19,645	LOGAN	9,136	4,382	4,594	160	212 D	48.0%	50.3%	48.8%	51.2%
5,637	LOVE	2,778	846	1,923	9	1,077 D	30.5%	69.2%	30.6%	69.4%
14,157	MCCLAIN	6,572	2,444	4,048	80	1,604 D	37.2%	61.6%	37.6%	62.4%
28,642	MCCURTAIN	11,080	3,423	7,560	97	4,137 D	30.9%	68.2%	31.2%	68.8%
12,472	MCINTOSH	6,015	1,822	4,145	48	2,323 D	30.3%	68.9%	30.5%	69.5%
7,529	MAJOR	3,697	2,282	1,357	58	925 R	61.7%	36.7%	62.7%	37.3%
7,682	MARSHALL	4,324	1,358	2,939	27	1,581 D	31.4%	68.0%	31.6%	68.4%
23,302	MAYES	11,419	5,040	6,298	81	1,258 D	44.1%	55.2%	44.5%	55.5%
10,669	MURRAY	4,536	1,563	2,932	41	1,369 D	34.5%	64.6%	34.8%	65.2%
59,542	MUSKOGEE	25,155	10,287	14,678	190	4,391 D	40.9%	58.4%	41.2%	58.8%
10,043	NOBLE	4,965	2,634	2,278	53	356 R	53.1%	45.9%	53.6%	46.4%
9,773	NOWATA	4,311	2,077	2,195	39	118 D	48.2%	50.9%	48.6%	51.4%
10,683	OKFUSKEE	4,325	1,630	2,663	32	1,033 D	37.7%	61.6%	38.0%	62.0%
526,805	OKLAHOMA	210,113	119,120	87,185	3,808	31,935 R	56.7%	41.5%	57.7%	42.3%
35,358	OKMULGEE	13,963	5,333	8,499	131	3,166 D	38.2%	60.9%	38.6%	61.4%
29,750	OSAGE	13,348	6,398	6,832	118	434 D	47.9%	51.2%	48.4%	51.6%
29,800	OTTAWA	12,515	4,985	7,446	84	2,461 D	39.8%	59.5%	40.1%	59.9%
11,338	PAWNEE	6,201	3,111	3,031	59	80 R	50.2%	48.9%	50.7%	49.3%
50,654	PAYNE	23,888	13,481	9,987	420	3,494 R	56.4%	41.8%	57.4%	42.6%
37,521	PITTSBURG	15,692	4,807	10,743	142	5,936 D	30.6%	68.5%	30.9%	69.1%
27,867	PONTOTOC	12,486	4,895	7,466	125	2,571 D	39.2%	59.8%	39.6%	60.4%
43,134	POTTAWATOMIE	20,571	9,090	11,255	226	2,165 D	44.2%	54.7%	44.7%	55.3%
9,385	PUSHMATAHA	4,376	1,360	2,987	29	1,627 D	31.1%	68.3%	31.3%	68.7%
4,452	ROGER MILLS	2,243	873	1,346	24	473 D	38.9%	60.0%	39.3%	60.7%

OKLAHOMA

PRESIDENT 1976

1970 Census Population	County	Total Vote	Republican	Democratic	Other	Rep.-Dem. Plurality	Percentage Total Vote Rep.	Total Vote Dem.	Major Vote Rep.	Major Vote Dem.
28,425	ROGERS	14,815	7,318	7,368	129	50 D	49.4%	49.7%	49.8%	50.2%
25,144	SEMINOLE	10,202	4,237	5,874	91	1,637 D	41.5%	57.6%	41.9%	58.1%
23,370	SEQUOYAH	9,884	3,938	5,873	73	1,935 D	39.8%	59.4%	40.1%	59.9%
35,902	STEPHENS	17,020	7,099	9,795	126	2,696 D	41.7%	57.5%	42.0%	58.0%
16,352	TEXAS	6,580	3,919	2,591	70	1,328 R	59.6%	39.4%	60.2%	39.8%
12,901	TILLMAN	4,695	1,802	2,852	41	1,050 D	38.4%	60.7%	38.7%	61.3%
400,709	TULSA	176,300	108,653	65,298	2,349	43,355 R	61.6%	37.0%	62.5%	37.5%
22,163	WAGONER	11,057	5,071	5,879	107	808 D	45.9%	53.2%	46.3%	53.7%
42,277	WASHINGTON	21,670	14,560	6,898	212	7,662 R	67.2%	31.8%	67.9%	32.1%
12,141	WASHITA	5,531	2,165	3,304	62	1,139 D	39.1%	59.7%	39.6%	60.4%
11,920	WOODS	5,421	2,788	2,530	103	258 R	51.4%	46.7%	52.4%	47.6%
15,537	WOODWARD	6,691	3,782	2,807	102	975 R	56.5%	42.0%	57.4%	42.6%
2,559,253	TOTAL	1,092,251	545,708	532,442	14,101	13,266 R	50.0%	48.7%	50.6%	49.4%

OKLAHOMA

CONGRESS

CD	Year	Total Vote	Republican Vote	Republican Candidate	Democratic Vote	Democratic Candidate	Other Vote	Rep.-Dem. Plurality	Percentage Total Vote Rep.	Percentage Total Vote Dem.	Percentage Major Vote Rep.	Percentage Major Vote Dem.
1	1976	187,044	84,374	INHOFE, JAMES M.	100,945	JONES, JAMES R.	1,725	16,571 D	45.1%	54.0%	45.5%	54.5%
1	1974	129,856	41,697	MIZER, GEORGE A.	88,159	JONES, JAMES R.		46,462 D	32.1%	67.9%	32.1%	67.9%
1	1972	168,652	73,786	HEWGLEY, J. M.	91,864	JONES, JAMES R.	3,002	18,078 D	43.8%	54.5%	44.5%	55.5%
2	1976	189,743	87,341	STEWART, E. L.	102,402	RISENHOOVER, TED M.		15,061 D	46.0%	54.0%	46.0%	54.0%
2	1974	132,156	54,110	KEEN, RALPH F.	78,046	RISENHOOVER, TED M.		23,936 D	40.9%	59.1%	40.9%	59.1%
2	1972	147,742	42,632	TOLIVER, EMERY H.	105,110	MCSPADDEN, CLEM R.		62,478 D	28.9%	71.1%	28.9%	71.1%
3	1976	184,565	31,732	BEASLEY, GERALD	151,271	WATKINS, WES	1,562	119,539 D	17.2%	82.0%	17.3%	82.7%
3	1974					ALBERT, CARL						
3	1972	108,974			101,732	ALBERT, CARL	7,242	101,732 D		93.4%		100.0%
4	1976	155,357	34,170	STANLEY, M. C.	116,425	STEED, TOM	4,762	82,255 D	22.0%	74.9%	22.7%	77.3%
4	1974					STEED, TOM						
4	1972	120,062	34,484	CROZIER, WILLIAM E.	85,578	STEED, TOM		51,094 D	28.7%	71.3%	28.7%	71.3%
5	1976	157,764	78,651	EDWARDS, M. H.	74,752	DUNLAP, TOM	4,361	3,899 R	49.9%	47.4%	51.3%	48.7%
5	1974	100,812	48,705	EDWARDS, M. H.	52,107	JARMAN, JOHN		3,402 D	48.3%	51.7%	48.3%	51.7%
5	1972	115,421	45,711	KELLER, LLEWELLYN L.	69,710	JARMAN, JOHN		23,999 D	39.6%	60.4%	39.6%	60.4%
6	1976	193,451	55,953	MCCURLEY, CAROL	137,498	ENGLISH, GLENN		81,545 D	28.9%	71.1%	28.9%	71.1%
6	1974	143,488	63,731	CAMP, JOHN N.	76,392	ENGLISH, GLENN	3,365	12,661 D	44.4%	53.2%	45.5%	54.5%
6	1972	156,230	113,567	CAMP, JOHN N.	42,663	SCHMITT, WILLIAM P.		70,904 R	72.7%	27.3%	72.7%	27.3%

OKLAHOMA

1976 GENERAL ELECTION

President — Other vote was McCarthy (Independent).

Congress — Other vote was Mackintoch (Independent) in CD 1; Finley (Independent) in CD 3; Trent (Independent) in CD 4; in CD 5 as follows:

CD 5 — 1,353 Wofley (Independent); 1,348 Parker (Independent); 886 Smith (Independent); 774 Buchanan (Independent).

1976 PRIMARIES

AUGUST 24 REPUBLICAN

Congress — Contested as follows:

CD 1 — 17,707 James M. Inhofe; 6,751 Frank Keating; 2,057 Mary Warner.
CD 2 — 7,956 E. L. Stewart; 6,126 John R. Drummond.
CD 3 — 2,516 Gerald Beasley; 2,493 Tom Pate.
CD 4 — 2,778 M. C. Stanley; 2,635 Stacy Autry.
CD 5 — 10,960 M. H. Edwards; 9,873 G. T. Blankenship; 1,014 George V. McClintic.
CD 6 — 8,906 Stephen Jones; 7,367 Carol McCurley; 4,231 John Duck.

AUGUST 24 DEMOCRATIC

Congress — Unopposed in two CD's. Contested as follows:

CD 1 — 31,912 James R. Jones; 8,113 Dick E. Richardson.
CD 2 — 49,590 Ted M. Risenhoover; 37,348 W. A. Drew Edmondson; 9,486 Richard E. Hancock.
CD 3 — 46,550 Wes Watkins; 36,509 Charles Ward; 21,673 Hamp Baker; 17,681 Gary E. Payne; 989 Marvin D. Andrews; 391 Eugene V. Poling.
CD 5 — 21,846 Tom Dunlap; 16,313 Tony Zahn; 12,578 Jerry Gilbert.

SEPTEMBER 21 REPUBLICAN RUN-OFF

Congress

CD 6 — 7,442 Carol McCurley; 5,403 Stephen Jones.

SEPTEMBER 21 DEMOCRATIC RUN-OFF

Congress

CD 3 — 71,428 Wes Watkins; 41,345 Charles Ward.
CD 5 — 23,717 Tom Dunlap; 21,259 Tony Zahn.

OREGON

GOVERNOR

Robert W. Straub (D). Elected 1974 to a four-year term.

SENATORS

Mark Hatfield (R). Re-elected 1972 to a six-year term. Previously elected 1966.

Robert W. Packwood (R). Re-elected 1974 to a six-year term. Previously elected 1968.

REPRESENTATIVES

1. Les AuCoin (D)
2. Albert C. Ullman (D)
3. Robert B. Duncan (D)
4. James Weaver (D)

POSTWAR VOTE FOR GOVERNOR

								Percentage			
	Total	Republican		Democratic		Other	Rep.-Dem.	Total Vote		Major Vote	
Year	Vote	Vote	Candidate	Vote	Candidate	Vote	Plurality	Rep.	Dem.	Rep.	Dem.
1974	770,574	324,751	Atiyeh, Victor	444,812	Straub, Robert W.	1,011	120,061 D	42.1%	57.7%	42.2%	57.8%
1970	666,394	369,964	McCall, Tom	293,892	Straub, Robert W.	2,538	76,072 R	55.5%	44.1%	55.7%	44.3%
1966	682,862	377,346	McCall, Tom	305,008	Straub, Robert W.	508	72,338 R	55.3%	44.7%	55.3%	44.7%
1962	637,407	345,497	Hatfield, Mark	265,359	Thornton, Robert Y.	26,551	80,138 R	54.2%	41.6%	56.6%	43.4%
1958	599,994	331,900	Hatfield, Mark	267,934	Holmes, Robert D.	160	63,966 R	55.3%	44.7%	55.3%	44.7%
1956s	731,279	361,840	Smith, Elmo E.	369,439	Holmes, Robert D.	–	7,599 D	49.5%	50.5%	49.5%	50.5%
1954	566,701	322,522	Patterson, Paul	244,179	Carson, Joseph K.	–	78,343 R	56.9%	43.1%	56.9%	43.1%
1950	505,910	334,160	McKay, Douglas	171,750	Flegel, Austin F.	–	162,410 R	66.1%	33.9%	66.1%	33.9%
1948s	509,633	271,295	McKay, Douglas	226,958	Wallace, Lew	11,380	44,337 R	53.2%	44.5%	54.4%	45.6%
1946	344,155	237,681	Snell, Earl	106,474	Donaugh, Carl C.	–	131,207 R	69.1%	30.9%	69.1%	30.9%

The elections in 1956 and 1948 were for short terms to fill vacancies.

POSTWAR VOTE FOR SENATOR

								Percentage			
	Total	Republican		Democratic		Other	Rep.-Dem.	Total Vote		Major Vote	
Year	Vote	Vote	Candidate	Vote	Candidate	Vote	Plurality	Rep.	Dem.	Rep.	Dem.
1974	766,414	420,984	Packwood, Robert W.	338,591	Roberts, Betty	6,839	82,393 R	54.9%	44.2%	55.4%	44.6%
1972	920,833	494,671	Hatfield, Mark	425,036	Morse, Wayne L.	1,126	69,635 R	53.7%	46.2%	53.8%	46.2%
1968	814,176	408,646	Packwood, Robert W.	405,353	Morse, Wayne L.	177	3,293 R	50.2%	49.8%	50.2%	49.8%
1966	685,067	354,391	Hatfield, Mark	330,374	Duncan, Robert B.	302	24,017 R	51.7%	48.2%	51.8%	48.2%
1962	636,558	291,587	Unander, Sig	344,716	Morse, Wayne L.	255	53,129 D	45.8%	54.2%	45.8%	54.2%
1960	755,875	343,009	Smith, Elmo E.	412,757	Neuberger, Maurine	109	69,748 D	45.4%	54.6%	45.4%	54.6%
1956	732,254	335,405	McKay, Douglas	396,849	Morse, Wayne L.	–	61,444 D	45.8%	54.2%	45.8%	54.2%
1954	569,088	283,313	Cordon, Guy	285,775	Neuberger, Richard L.	–	2,462 D	49.8%	50.2%	49.8%	50.2%
1950	503,455	376,510	Morse, Wayne L.	116,780	Latourette, Howard	10,165	259,730 R	74.8%	23.2%	76.3%	23.7%
1948	498,570	299,295	Cordon, Guy	199,275	Wilson, Manley J.	–	100,020 R	60.0%	40.0%	60.0%	40.0%

OREGON

Districts Established July 2, 1971

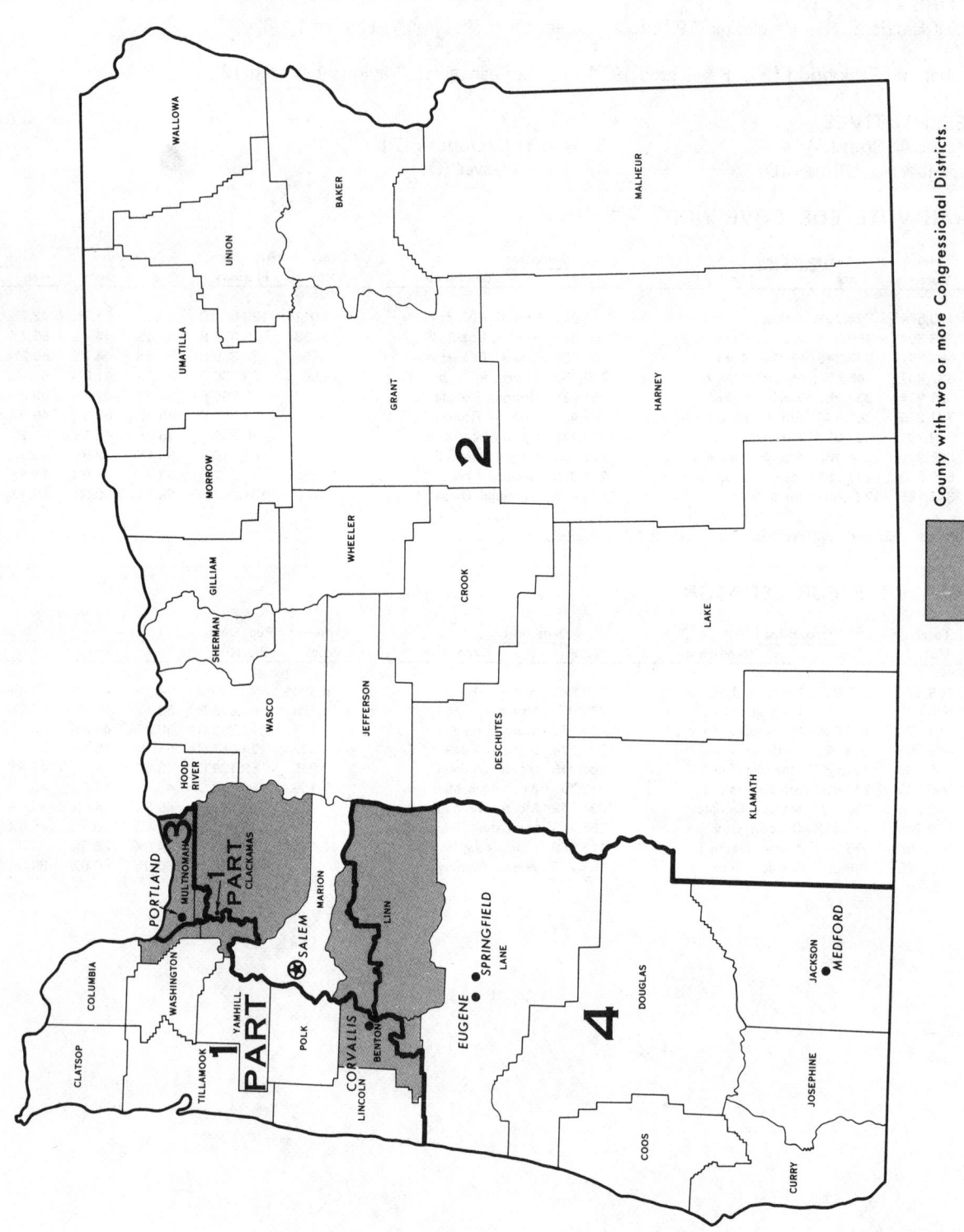

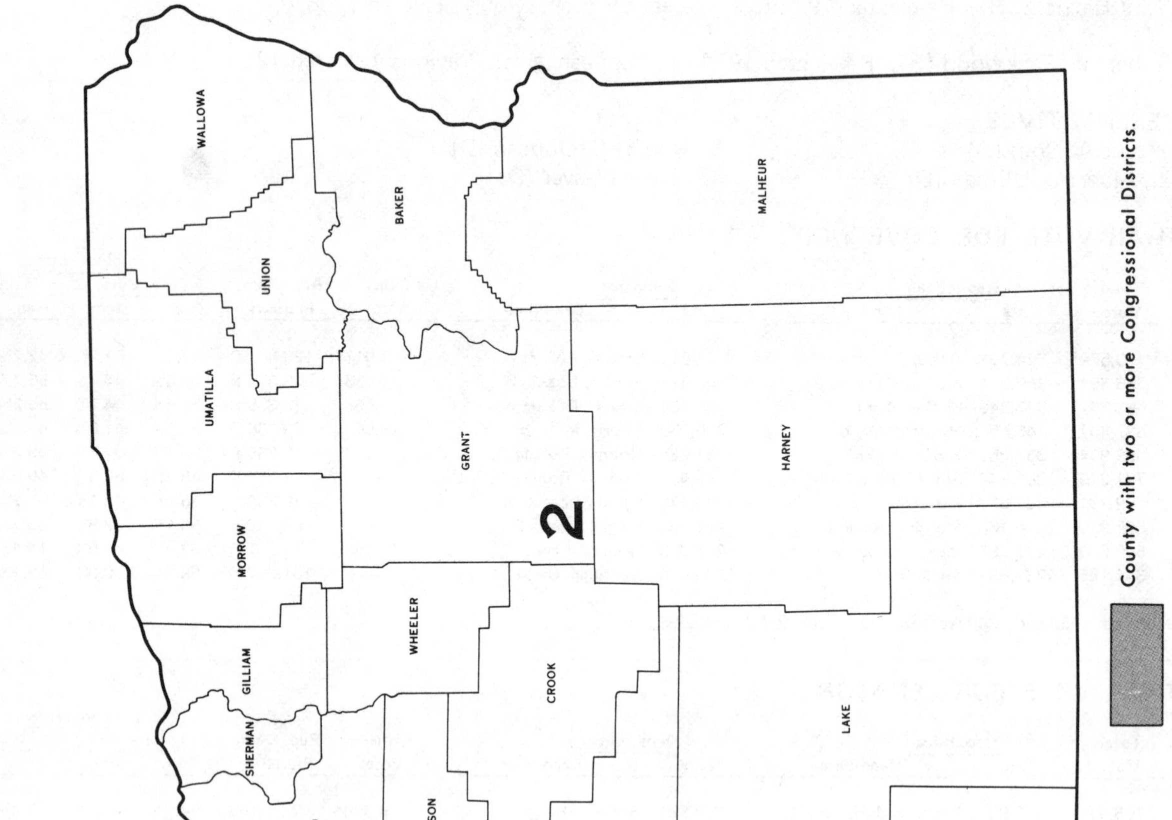

OREGON

PRESIDENT 1976

1970 Census Population	County	Total Vote	Republican	Democratic	Other	Rep.-Dem. Plurality	Percentage Total Vote Rep.	Percentage Total Vote Dem.	Percentage Major Vote Rep.	Percentage Major Vote Dem.
14,919	BAKER	6,919	3,340	3,306	273	34 R	48.3%	47.8%	50.3%	49.7%
53,776	BENTON	29,307	15,555	11,887	1,865	3,668 R	53.1%	40.6%	56.7%	43.3%
166,088	CLACKAMAS	93,959	47,671	42,504	3,784	5,167 R	50.7%	45.2%	52.9%	47.1%
28,473	CLATSOP	13,616	6,178	6,690	748	512 D	45.4%	49.1%	48.0%	52.0%
28,790	COLUMBIA	13,859	5,226	8,005	628	2,779 D	37.7%	57.8%	39.5%	60.5%
56,515	COOS	24,725	9,481	14,168	1,076	4,687 D	38.3%	57.3%	40.1%	59.9%
9,985	CROOK	4,777	2,093	2,536	148	443 D	43.8%	53.1%	45.2%	54.8%
13,006	CURRY	6,507	2,962	3,227	318	265 D	45.5%	49.6%	47.9%	52.1%
30,442	DESCHUTES	19,382	9,054	9,480	848	426 D	46.7%	48.9%	48.9%	51.1%
71,743	DOUGLAS	32,973	16,500	14,965	1,508	1,535 R	50.0%	45.4%	52.4%	47.6%
2,342	GILLIAM	1,166	612	508	46	104 R	52.5%	43.6%	54.6%	45.4%
6,996	GRANT	3,206	1,640	1,393	173	247 R	51.2%	43.4%	54.1%	45.9%
7,215	HARNEY	3,407	1,652	1,567	188	85 R	48.5%	46.0%	51.3%	48.7%
13,187	HOOD RIVER	6,636	3,210	3,114	312	96 R	48.4%	46.9%	50.8%	49.2%
94,533	JACKSON	50,236	24,237	23,384	2,615	853 R	48.2%	46.5%	50.9%	49.1%
8,548	JEFFERSON	3,777	1,810	1,769	198	41 R	47.9%	46.8%	50.6%	49.4%
35,746	JOSEPHINE	21,110	10,726	9,061	1,323	1,665 R	50.8%	42.9%	54.2%	45.8%
50,021	KLAMATH	22,187	11,649	9,659	879	1,990 R	52.5%	43.5%	54.7%	45.3%
6,343	LAKE	3,088	1,575	1,381	132	194 R	51.0%	44.7%	53.3%	46.7%
213,358	LANE	108,367	46,245	56,479	5,643	10,234 D	42.7%	52.1%	45.0%	55.0%
25,755	LINCOLN	13,199	5,755	6,685	759	930 D	43.6%	50.6%	46.3%	53.7%
71,914	LINN	31,241	14,128	15,776	1,337	1,648 D	45.2%	50.5%	47.2%	52.8%
23,169	MALHEUR	9,610	5,682	3,507	421	2,175 R	59.1%	36.5%	61.8%	38.2%
151,309	MARION	72,331	35,497	33,781	3,053	1,716 R	49.1%	46.7%	51.2%	48.8%
4,465	MORROW	2,367	1,091	1,162	114	71 D	46.1%	49.1%	48.4%	51.6%
556,667	MULTNOMAH	253,159	112,400	129,060	11,699	16,660 D	44.4%	51.0%	46.6%	53.4%
35,349	POLK	17,530	8,528	8,141	861	387 R	48.6%	46.4%	51.2%	48.8%
2,139	SHERMAN	1,109	567	491	51	76 R	51.1%	44.3%	53.6%	46.4%
17,930	TILLAMOOK	8,867	4,033	4,456	378	423 D	45.5%	50.3%	47.5%	52.5%
44,923	UMATILLA	18,031	9,345	7,985	701	1,360 R	51.8%	44.3%	53.9%	46.1%
19,377	UNION	9,829	5,111	4,280	438	831 R	52.0%	43.5%	54.4%	45.6%
6,247	WALLOWA	3,149	1,693	1,310	146	383 R	53.8%	41.6%	56.4%	43.6%
20,133	WASCO	9,240	4,258	4,560	422	302 D	46.1%	49.4%	48.3%	51.7%
157,920	WASHINGTON	90,611	52,376	34,847	3,388	17,529 R	57.8%	38.5%	60.0%	40.0%
1,849	WHEELER	779	355	402	22	47 D	45.6%	51.6%	46.9%	53.1%
40,213	YAMHILL	19,620	9,885	8,881	854	1,004 R	50.4%	45.3%	52.7%	47.3%
2,091,385	TOTAL	1,029,876	492,120	490,407	47,349	1,713 R	47.8%	47.6%	50.1%	49.9%

OREGON

CONGRESS

CD	Year	Total Vote	Republican Vote	Republican Candidate	Democratic Vote	Democratic Candidate	Other Vote	Rep.-Dem. Plurality	Percentage Total Vote Rep.	Percentage Total Vote Dem.	Percentage Major Vote Rep.	Percentage Major Vote Dem.
1	1976	264,000	109,140	BLADINE, PHIL	154,844	AUCOIN, LES	16	45,704 D	41.3%	58.7%	41.3%	58.7%
1	1974	204,592	89,848	O SCANNLAIN, DIARMUID	114,629	AUCOIN, LES	115	24,781 D	43.9%	56.0%	43.9%	56.1%
1	1972	242,798	166,476	WYATT, WENDELL	76,307	BUNCH, RALPH E.	15	90,169 R	68.6%	31.4%	68.6%	31.4%
2	1976	240,761	67,431	MERCER, THOMAS H.	173,313	ULLMAN, ALBERT C.	17	105,882 D	28.0%	72.0%	28.0%	72.0%
2	1974	180,449	39,441	BROWN, KENNETH A.	140,963	ULLMAN, ALBERT C.	45	101,522 D	21.9%	78.1%	21.9%	78.1%
2	1972	178,728			178,537	ULLMAN, ALBERT C.	191	178,537 D		99.9%		100.0%
3	1976	177,051			148,503	DUNCAN, ROBERT B.	28,548	148,503 D		83.9%		100.0%
3	1974	183,537	54,080	PIACENTINI, JOHN	129,290	DUNCAN, ROBERT B.	167	75,210 D	29.5%	70.4%	29.5%	70.5%
3	1972	226,030	84,697	WALSH, MIKE	141,046	GREEN, EDITH	287	56,349 D	37.5%	62.4%	37.5%	62.5%
4	1976	244,852	85,943	LAUSMANN, JERRY	122,475	WEAVER, JAMES	36,434	36,532 D	35.1%	50.0%	41.2%	58.8%
4	1974	184,617	86,950	DELLENBACK, JOHN R.	97,580	WEAVER, JAMES	87	10,630 D	47.1%	52.9%	47.1%	52.9%
4	1972	222,174	138,965	DELLENBACK, JOHN R.	83,134	PORTER, CHARLES O.	75	55,831 R	62.5%	37.4%	62.6%	37.4%

OREGON

1976 GENERAL ELECTION

President — Vote detailed here is for the recount. Original uncorrected canvass gave the McCarthy vote as 40,192. Other vote was 40,207 McCarthy (Independent); 1,035 Anderson (write-in); 6,107 scattered.

Congress — Other vote was scattered in CD's 1 and 2; 28,245 Simon (Independent) and 303 scattered in CD 3; in CD 4 as follows:

CD 4 — 22,104 Howard (Independent); 14,307 Nathan (Independent); 23 scattered.

1976 PRIMARIES

MAY 25 REPUBLICAN

Congress — Unopposed in CD 1. Contested as follows:

CD 2 — 26,437 Thomas H. Mercer; 19,329 Cecil R. Kariker; 14,750 Terry L. Hicks; 599 scattered.
CD 3 — No candidates appeared on the ballot; there were 662 write-in votes for Robert B. Duncan and 354 scattered. Mr. Duncan was the unopposed Democratic candidate in CD 3.
CD 4 — 43,158 Jerry Lausmann; 12,862 Donald E. Turner; 4,842 Donald G. Lavin; 275 scattered.

MAY 25 DEMOCRATIC

Congress — Unopposed in three CD's. Contested as follows:

CD 4 — 65,302 James Weaver; 15,954 Charles O. Porter; 14,672 Jerry Running Foxe; 237 scattered.

PENNSYLVANIA

GOVERNOR

Milton Shapp (D). Re-elected 1974 to a four-year term. Previously elected 1970.

SENATORS

H. John Heinz (R). Elected 1976 to a six-year term.

Richard S. Schweiker (R). Re-elected 1974 to a six-year term. Previously elected 1968.

REPRESENTATIVES

1. Michael Myers (D)
2. Robert N. C. Nix (D)
3. Raymond F. Lederer (D)
4. Joshua Eilberg (D)
5. Richard T. Schulze (R)
6. Gus Yatron (D)
7. Robert W. Edgar (D)
8. Peter H. Kostmayer (D)
9. E. G. Shuster (R)
10. Joseph M. McDade (R)
11. Daniel J. Flood (D)
12. John P. Murtha (D)
13. R. Lawrence Coughlin (R)
14. William S. Moorhead (D)
15. Fred B. Rooney (D)
16. Robert S. Walker (R)
17. Allen E. Ertel (D)
18. Douglas Walgren (D)
19. William F. Goodling (R)
20. Joseph M. Gaydos (D)
21. John H. Dent (D)
22. Austin J. Murphy (D)
23. Joseph S. Ammerman (D)
24. Marc L. Marks (R)
25. Gary A. Myers (R)

POSTWAR VOTE FOR GOVERNOR

Year	Total Vote	Republican Vote	Republican Candidate	Democratic Vote	Democratic Candidate	Other Vote	Rep.-Dem. Plurality	Percentage Total Vote Rep.	Total Vote Dem.	Major Vote Rep.	Major Vote Dem.
1974	3,491,234	1,578,917	Lewis, Andrew L.	1,878,252	Shapp, Milton	34,065	299,335 D	45.2%	53.8%	45.7%	54.3%
1970	3,700,060	1,542,854	Broderick, Raymond	2,043,029	Shapp, Milton	114,177	500,175 D	41.7%	55.2%	43.0%	57.0%
1966	4,050,668	2,110,349	Shafer, Raymond P.	1,868,719	Shapp, Milton	71,600	241,630 R	52.1%	46.1%	53.0%	47.0%
1962	4,378,042	2,424,918	Scranton, William W.	1,938,627	Dilworth, Richardson	14,497	486,291 R	55.4%	44.3%	55.6%	44.4%
1958	3,986,918	1,948,769	McGonigle, A. T.	2,024,852	Lawrence, David	13,297	76,083 D	48.9%	50.8%	49.0%	51.0%
1954	3,720,457	1,717,070	Wood, Lloyd H.	1,996,266	Leader, George M.	7,121	279,196 D	46.2%	53.7%	46.2%	53.8%
1950	3,540,059	1,796,119	Fine, John S.	1,710,355	Dilworth, Richardson	33,585	85,764 R	50.7%	48.3%	51.2%	48.8%
1946	3,123,994	1,828,462	Duff, James H.	1,270,947	Rice, John S.	24,585	557,515 R	58.5%	40.7%	59.0%	41.0%

POSTWAR VOTE FOR SENATOR

Year	Total Vote	Republican Vote	Republican Candidate	Democratic Vote	Democratic Candidate	Other Vote	Rep.-Dem. Plurality	Percentage Total Vote Rep.	Total Vote Dem.	Major Vote Rep.	Major Vote Dem.
1976	4,546,353	2,381,891	Heinz, H. John	2,126,977	Green, William J., III	37,485	254,914 R	52.4%	46.8%	52.8%	47.2%
1974	3,477,812	1,843,317	Schweiker, Richard S.	1,596,121	Flaherty, Peter	38,374	247,196 R	53.0%	45.9%	53.6%	46.4%
1970	3,644,305	1,874,106	Scott, Hugh	1,653,774	Sesler, William G.	116,425	220,332 R	51.4%	45.4%	53.1%	46.9%
1968	4,624,218	2,399,762	Schweiker, Richard S.	2,117,662	Clark, Joseph S.	106,794	282,100 R	51.9%	45.8%	53.1%	46.9%
1964	4,803,835	2,429,858	Scott, Hugh	2,359,223	Blatt, Genevieve	14,754	70,635 R	50.6%	49.1%	50.7%	49.3%
1962	4,383,475	2,134,649	Van Zandt, James E.	2,238,383	Clark, Joseph S.	10,443	103,734 D	48.7%	51.1%	48.8%	51.2%
1958	3,988,622	2,042,586	Scott, Hugh	1,929,821	Leader, George M.	16,215	112,765 R	51.2%	48.4%	51.4%	48.6%
1956	4,529,874	2,250,671	Duff, James H.	2,268,641	Clark, Joseph S.	10,562	17,970 D	49.7%	50.1%	49.8%	50.2%
1952	4,519,761	2,331,034	Martin, Edward	2,168,546	Bard, Guy Kurtz	20,181	162,488 R	51.6%	48.0%	51.8%	48.2%
1950	3,548,703	1,820,400	Duff, James H.	1,694,076	Myers, Francis J.	34,227	126,324 R	51.3%	47.7%	51.8%	48.2%
1946	3,127,860	1,853,458	Martin, Edward	1,245,338	Guffey, Joseph F.	29,064	608,120 R	59.3%	39.8%	59.8%	40.2%

PENNSYLVANIA

Districts Established January 25, 1972

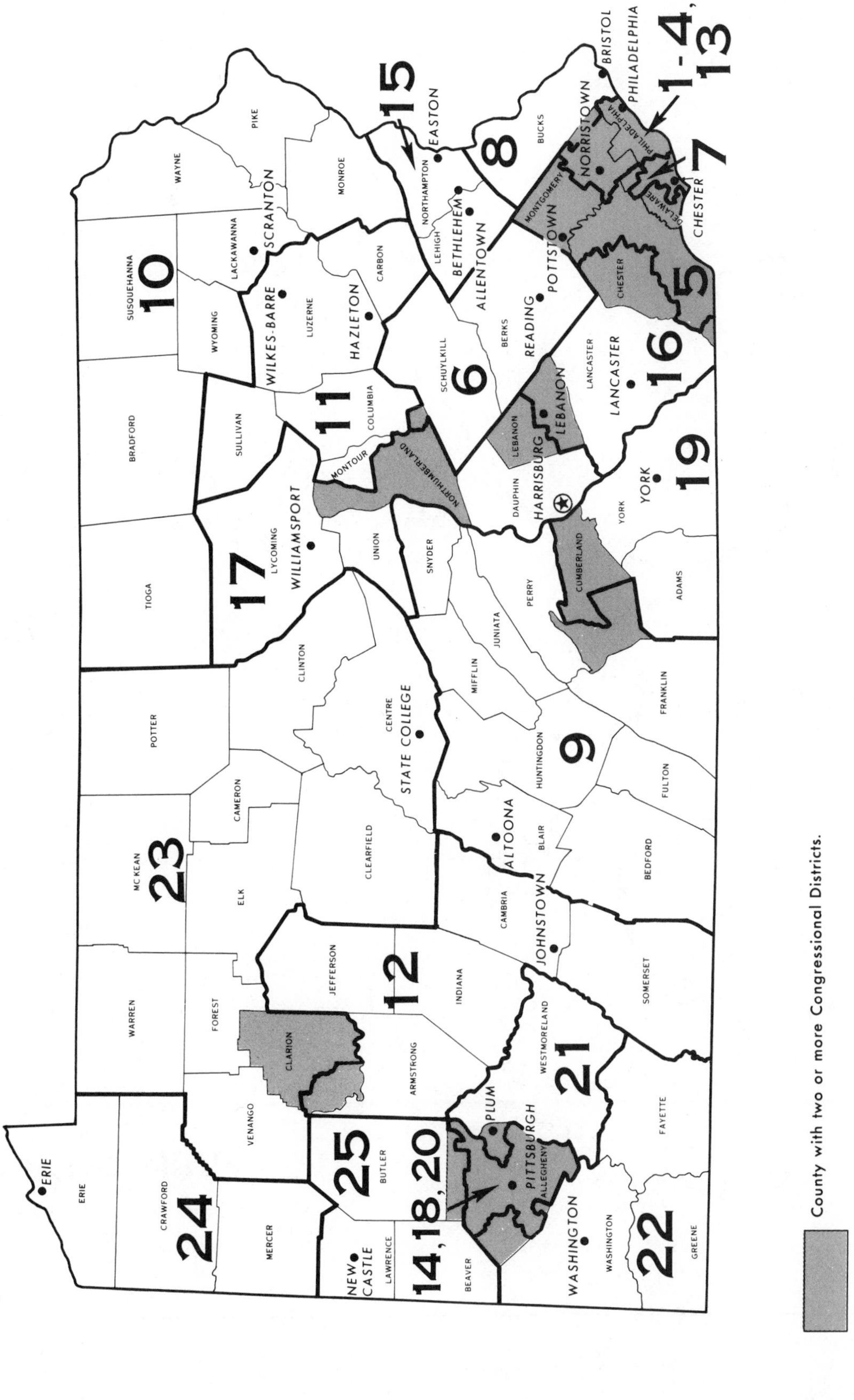

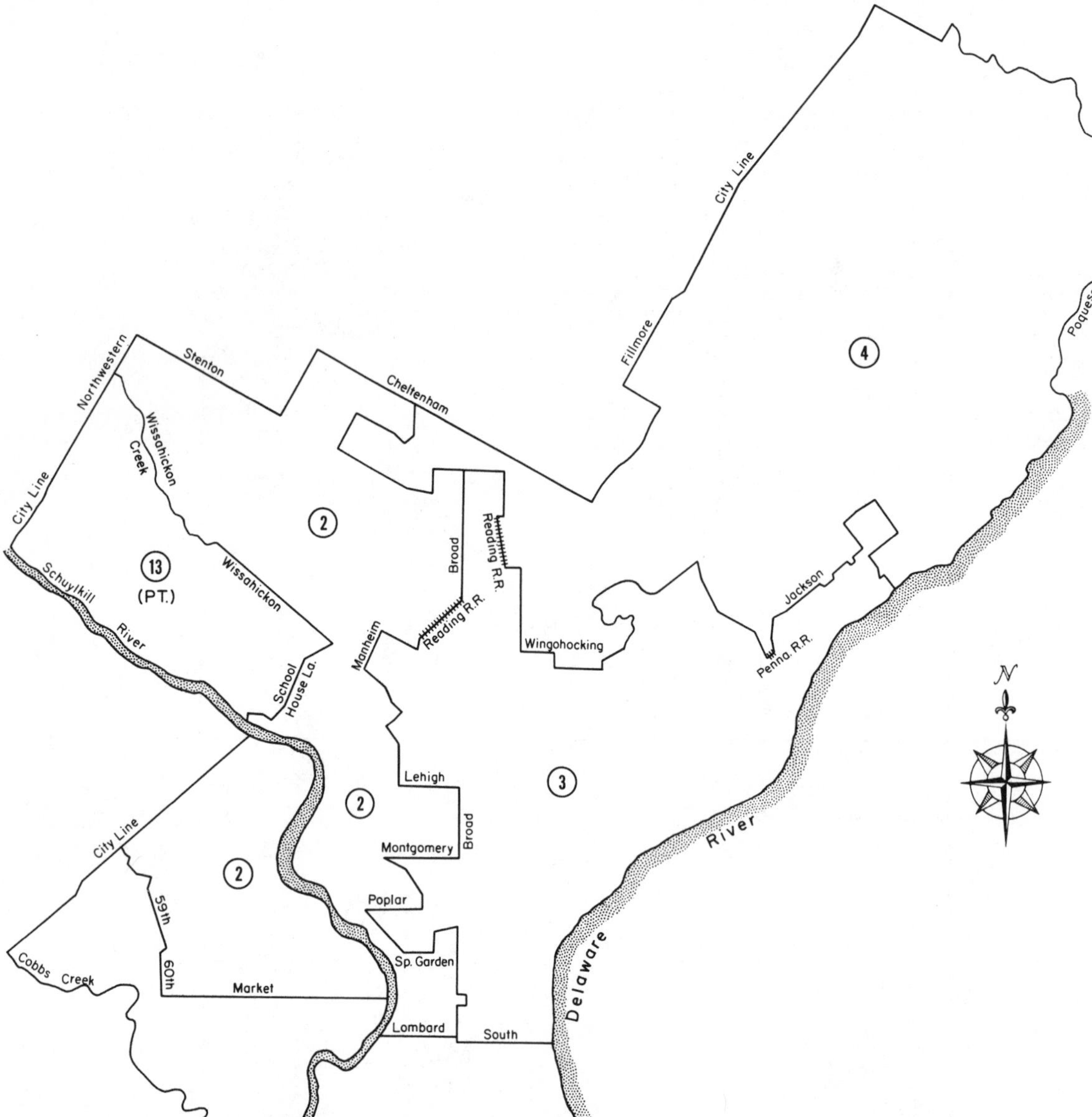

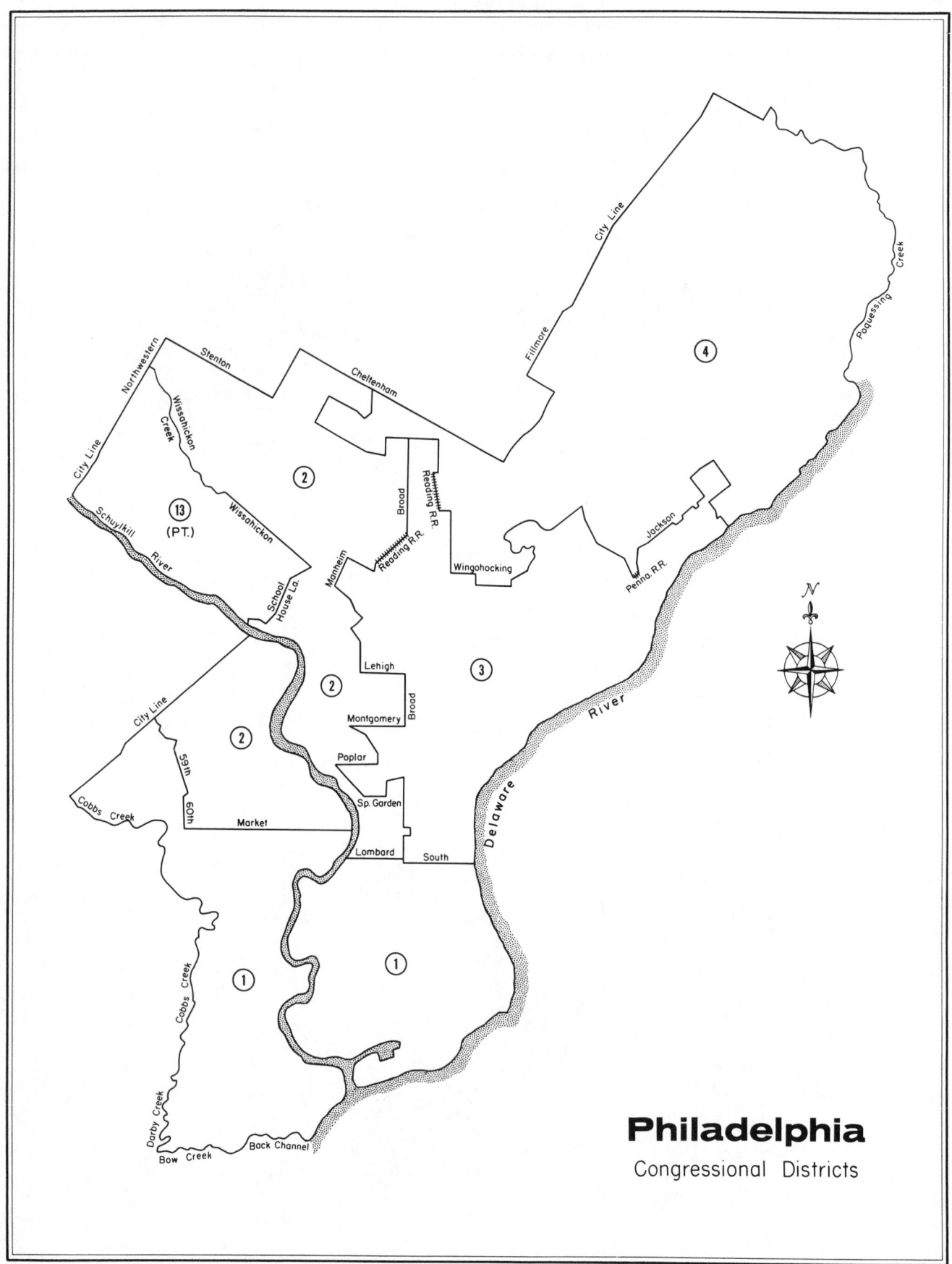

Philadelphia

Congressional Districts

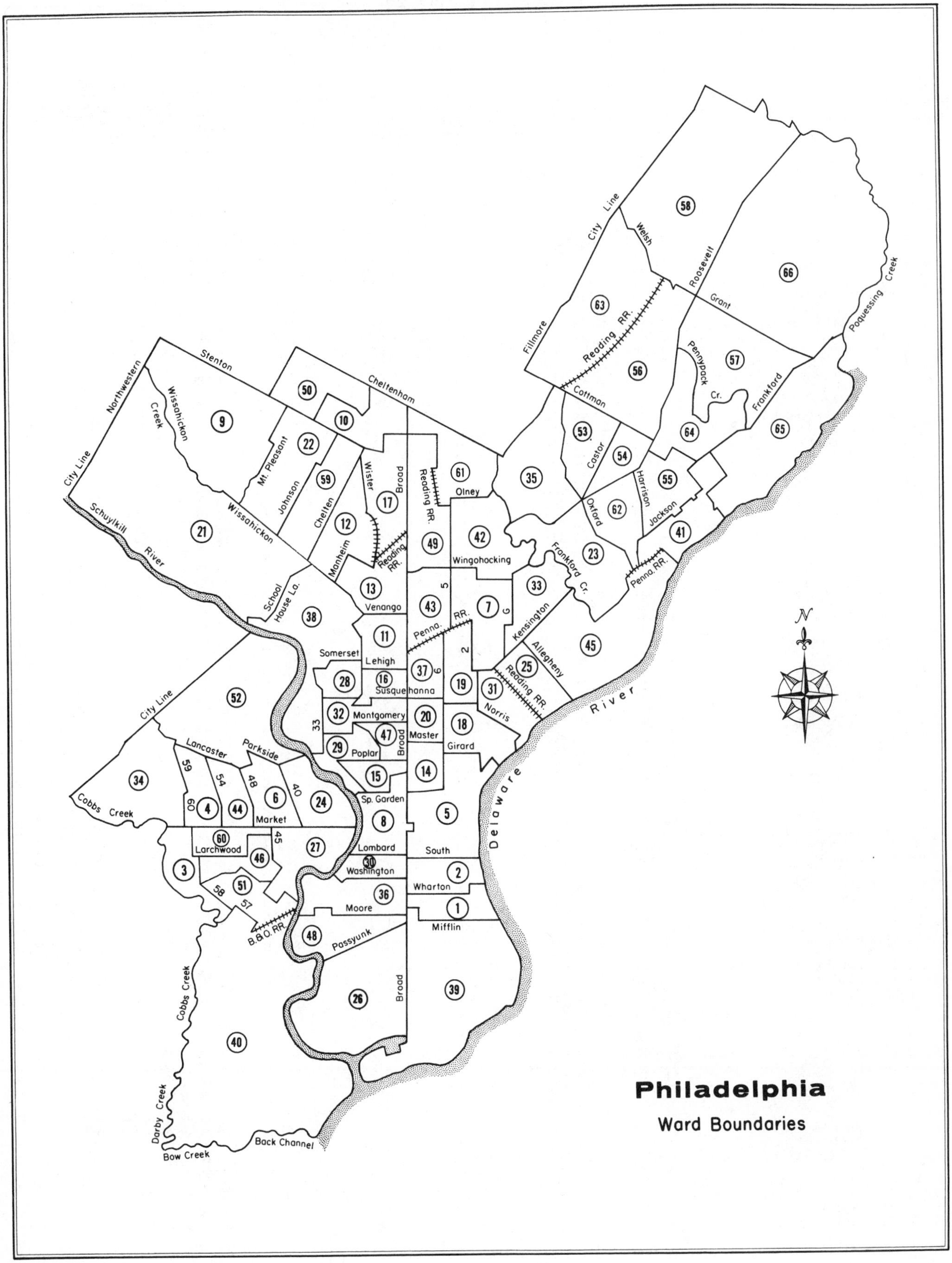
Philadelphia
Ward Boundaries
City Line
Welsh
Roosevelt
Grant
Poquessing Creek
Fillmore
Reading RR.
Pennypack Cr.
Frankford
Cottman
Castor
Oxford
Harrison
Jackson
Frankford Cr.
Penna. RR.
Stenton
Northwestern
Wissahickon Creek
Cheltenham
Mt. Pleasant
Johnson
Chelten
Wister
Broad
Reading RR.
Olney
Wingohocking
Manheim
Schuylkill River
Wissahickon
School House La.
Venango
Somerset
Lehigh
Penna. RR.
Kensington
Allegheny
Susquehanna
Montgomery
Master
Girard
Norris
Reading RR.
Poplar
Lancaster
Parkside
Sp. Garden
Cobbs Creek
Market
Larchwood
Lombard
South
Washington
Wharton
Moore
Mifflin
B.&O. RR.
Passyunk
Delaware River
Cobbs Creek
Darby Creek
Bow Creek
Back Channel
N
1
2
3
4
5
6
7
8
9
10
11
12
13
14
15
16
17
18
19
20
21
22
23
24
25
26
27
28
29
30
31
32
33
34
35
36
37
38
39
40
41
42
43
44
45
46
47
48
49
50
51
52
53
54
55
56
57
58
59
60
61
62
63
64
65
66

PENNSYLVANIA

PRESIDENT 1976

1970 Census Population	County	Total Vote	Republican	Democratic	Other	Rep.-Dem. Plurality	Percentage Total Vote Rep.	Total Vote Dem.	Major Vote Rep.	Major Vote Dem.
56,937	ADAMS	21,322	12,133	8,771	418	3,362 R	56.9%	41.1%	58.0%	42.0%
1,605,016	ALLEGHENY	647,857	303,127	328,343	16,387	25,216 D	46.8%	50.7%	48.0%	52.0%
75,590	ARMSTRONG	29,050	13,378	15,179	493	1,801 D	46.1%	52.3%	46.8%	53.2%
208,418	BEAVER	81,150	33,593	46,117	1,440	12,524 D	41.4%	56.8%	42.1%	57.9%
42,353	BEDFORD	16,138	9,355	6,652	131	2,703 R	58.0%	41.2%	58.4%	41.6%
296,382	BERKS	107,553	54,452	50,994	2,107	3,458 R	50.6%	47.4%	51.6%	48.4%
135,356	BLAIR	47,366	28,290	18,397	679	9,893 R	59.7%	38.8%	60.6%	39.4%
57,962	BRADFORD	21,034	12,851	7,913	270	4,938 R	61.1%	37.6%	61.9%	38.1%
415,056	BUCKS	168,923	85,628	79,838	3,457	5,790 R	50.7%	47.3%	51.7%	48.3%
127,941	BUTLER	50,198	26,366	22,611	1,221	3,755 R	52.5%	45.0%	53.8%	46.2%
186,785	CAMBRIA	72,128	32,469	38,797	862	6,328 D	45.0%	53.8%	45.6%	54.4%
7,096	CAMERON	2,977	1,616	1,319	42	297 R	54.3%	44.3%	55.1%	44.9%
50,573	CARBON	19,973	8,883	10,791	299	1,908 D	44.5%	54.0%	45.2%	54.8%
99,267	CENTRE	40,437	21,177	17,867	1,393	3,310 R	52.4%	44.2%	54.2%	45.8%
278,311	CHESTER	112,026	67,686	42,712	1,628	24,974 R	60.4%	38.1%	61.3%	38.7%
38,414	CLARION	15,210	8,360	6,585	265	1,775 R	55.0%	43.3%	55.9%	44.1%
74,619	CLEARFIELD	27,685	13,626	13,714	345	88 D	49.2%	49.5%	49.8%	50.2%
37,721	CLINTON	12,564	5,858	6,532	174	674 D	46.6%	52.0%	47.3%	52.7%
55,114	COLUMBIA	23,925	11,508	12,051	366	543 D	48.1%	50.4%	48.8%	51.2%
81,342	CRAWFORD	30,610	15,301	14,712	597	589 R	50.0%	48.1%	51.0%	49.0%
158,177	CUMBERLAND	64,270	39,950	23,008	1,312	16,942 R	62.2%	35.8%	63.5%	36.5%
223,834	DAUPHIN	83,122	46,819	34,342	1,961	12,477 R	56.3%	41.3%	57.7%	42.3%
600,035	DELAWARE	270,894	148,679	117,252	4,963	31,427 R	54.9%	43.3%	55.9%	44.1%
37,770	ELK	13,109	6,159	6,713	237	554 D	47.0%	51.2%	47.8%	52.2%
263,654	ERIE	107,439	49,641	55,385	2,413	5,744 D	46.2%	51.6%	47.3%	52.7%
154,667	FAYETTE	53,244	20,021	32,232	991	12,211 D	37.6%	60.5%	38.3%	61.7%
4,926	FOREST	2,187	1,135	1,017	35	118 R	51.9%	46.5%	52.7%	47.3%
100,833	FRANKLIN	35,389	20,009	14,643	737	5,366 R	56.5%	41.4%	57.7%	42.3%
10,776	FULTON	4,052	2,219	1,737	96	482 R	54.8%	42.9%	56.1%	43.9%
36,090	GREENE	14,219	5,293	8,769	157	3,476 D	37.2%	61.7%	37.6%	62.4%
39,108	HUNTINGDON	13,462	7,843	5,410	209	2,433 R	58.3%	40.2%	59.2%	40.8%
79,451	INDIANA	30,949	15,786	14,650	513	1,136 R	51.0%	47.3%	51.9%	48.1%
43,695	JEFFERSON	17,130	9,437	7,456	237	1,981 R	55.1%	43.5%	55.9%	44.1%
16,712	JUNIATA	7,206	3,991	3,105	110	886 R	55.4%	43.1%	56.2%	43.8%
234,107	LACKAWANNA	102,797	43,354	57,685	1,758	14,331 D	42.2%	56.1%	42.9%	57.1%
319,693	LANCASTER	109,676	72,106	35,533	2,037	36,573 R	65.7%	32.4%	67.0%	33.0%
107,374	LAWRENCE	42,640	18,546	23,337	757	4,791 D	43.5%	54.7%	44.3%	55.7%
99,665	LEBANON	33,330	20,880	11,785	665	9,095 R	62.6%	35.4%	63.9%	36.1%
255,304	LEHIGH	95,308	46,895	46,620	1,793	275 R	49.2%	48.9%	50.1%	49.9%
342,301	LUZERNE	136,009	60,058	74,655	1,296	14,597 D	44.2%	54.9%	44.6%	55.4%
113,296	LYCOMING	42,082	22,648	18,635	799	4,013 R	53.8%	44.3%	54.9%	45.1%
51,915	MCKEAN	16,926	10,305	6,424	197	3,881 R	60.9%	38.0%	61.6%	38.4%
127,175	MERCER	48,235	22,469	25,041	725	2,572 D	46.6%	51.9%	47.3%	52.7%
45,268	MIFFLIN	14,109	7,698	6,210	201	1,488 R	54.6%	44.0%	55.3%	44.7%
45,422	MONROE	20,165	10,228	9,544	393	684 R	50.7%	47.3%	51.7%	48.3%
623,799	MONTGOMERY	273,169	155,480	112,644	5,045	42,836 R	56.9%	41.2%	58.0%	42.0%
16,508	MONTOUR	6,075	3,259	2,727	89	532 R	53.6%	44.9%	54.4%	45.6%
214,368	NORTHAMPTON	76,961	32,926	42,514	1,521	9,588 D	42.8%	55.2%	43.6%	56.4%
99,190	NORTHUMBERLAND	38,876	19,283	18,939	654	344 R	49.6%	48.7%	50.5%	49.5%
28,615	PERRY	12,320	7,454	4,605	261	2,849 R	60.5%	37.4%	61.8%	38.2%
1,948,609	PHILADELPHIA	746,197	239,000	494,579	12,618	255,579 D	32.0%	66.3%	32.6%	67.4%
11,818	PIKE	7,146	4,241	2,775	130	1,466 R	59.3%	38.8%	60.4%	39.6%
16,395	POTTER	6,891	3,828	2,983	80	845 R	55.6%	43.3%	56.2%	43.8%
160,089	SCHUYLKILL	66,948	31,944	33,905	1,099	1,961 D	47.7%	50.6%	48.5%	51.5%
29,269	SNYDER	9,929	6,557	3,097	275	3,460 R	66.0%	31.2%	67.9%	32.1%
76,037	SOMERSET	29,685	15,960	13,452	273	2,508 R	53.8%	45.3%	54.3%	45.7%
5,961	SULLIVAN	2,951	1,584	1,347	20	237 R	53.7%	45.6%	54.0%	46.0%
34,344	SUSQUEHANNA	14,682	8,331	6,075	276	2,256 R	56.7%	41.4%	57.8%	42.2%
39,691	TIOGA	14,405	8,417	5,795	193	2,622 R	58.4%	40.2%	59.2%	40.8%
28,603	UNION	9,902	6,309	3,405	188	2,904 R	63.7%	34.4%	64.9%	35.1%
62,353	VENANGO	21,311	12,270	8,653	388	3,617 R	57.6%	40.6%	58.6%	41.4%
47,682	WARREN	16,170	8,508	7,412	250	1,096 R	52.6%	45.8%	53.4%	46.6%
210,876	WASHINGTON	83,251	32,827	49,317	1,107	16,490 D	39.4%	59.2%	40.0%	60.0%
29,581	WAYNE	12,310	7,811	4,244	255	3,567 R	63.5%	34.5%	64.8%	35.2%
376,935	WESTMORELAND	136,134	59,172	74,217	2,745	15,045 D	43.5%	54.5%	44.4%	55.6%
19,082	WYOMING	9,455	5,705	3,628	122	2,077 R	60.3%	38.4%	61.1%	38.9%
272,603	YORK	99,944	56,912	41,281	1,751	15,631 R	56.9%	41.3%	58.0%	42.0%
11,793,909	TOTAL	4,620,787	2,205,604	2,328,677	86,506	123,073 D	47.7%	50.4%	48.6%	51.4%

PENNSYLVANIA

SENATOR 1976

1970 Census Population	County	Total Vote	Republican	Democratic	Other	Rep.-Dem. Plurality	Percentage: Total Vote Rep.	Percentage: Total Vote Dem.	Percentage: Major Vote Rep.	Percentage: Major Vote Dem.
56,937	ADAMS	21,125	12,098	8,871	156	3,227 R	57.3%	42.0%	57.7%	42.3%
1,605,016	ALLEGHENY	637,960	420,816	209,061	8,083	211,755 R	66.0%	32.8%	66.8%	33.2%
75,590	ARMSTRONG	28,917	18,393	10,413	111	7,980 R	63.6%	36.0%	63.9%	36.1%
208,418	BEAVER	81,049	45,514	35,105	430	10,409 R	56.2%	43.3%	56.5%	43.5%
42,353	BEDFORD	16,167	9,737	6,386	44	3,351 R	60.2%	39.5%	60.4%	39.6%
296,382	BERKS	105,200	54,266	49,938	996	4,328 R	51.6%	47.5%	52.1%	47.9%
135,356	BLAIR	47,228	28,542	18,482	204	10,060 R	60.4%	39.1%	60.7%	39.3%
57,962	BRADFORD	20,294	12,569	7,543	182	5,026 R	61.9%	37.2%	62.5%	37.5%
415,056	BUCKS	167,559	84,748	81,325	1,486	3,423 R	50.6%	48.5%	51.0%	49.0%
127,941	BUTLER	49,609	32,255	16,881	473	15,374 R	65.0%	34.0%	65.6%	34.4%
186,785	CAMBRIA	72,250	41,098	30,907	245	10,191 R	56.9%	42.8%	57.1%	42.9%
7,096	CAMERON	2,954	1,728	1,212	14	516 R	58.5%	41.0%	58.8%	41.2%
50,573	CARBON	19,528	9,215	10,164	149	949 D	47.2%	52.0%	47.6%	52.4%
99,267	CENTRE	40,058	21,093	18,698	267	2,395 R	52.7%	46.7%	53.0%	47.0%
278,311	CHESTER	111,183	68,579	41,992	612	26,587 R	61.7%	37.8%	62.0%	38.0%
38,414	CLARION	15,154	9,241	5,806	107	3,435 R	61.0%	38.3%	61.4%	38.6%
74,619	CLEARFIELD	27,044	14,051	12,866	127	1,185 R	52.0%	47.6%	52.2%	47.8%
37,721	CLINTON	12,419	5,874	6,450	95	576 D	47.3%	51.9%	47.7%	52.3%
55,114	COLUMBIA	23,727	10,965	12,598	164	1,633 D	46.2%	53.1%	46.5%	53.5%
81,342	CRAWFORD	29,838	16,647	12,800	391	3,847 R	55.8%	42.9%	56.5%	43.5%
158,177	CUMBERLAND	63,045	40,603	21,811	631	18,792 R	64.4%	34.6%	65.1%	34.9%
223,834	DAUPHIN	80,881	48,916	31,028	937	17,888 R	60.5%	38.4%	61.2%	38.8%
600,035	DELAWARE	267,362	141,651	124,088	1,623	17,563 R	53.0%	46.4%	53.3%	46.7%
37,770	ELK	13,052	6,896	6,108	48	788 R	52.8%	46.8%	53.0%	47.0%
263,654	ERIE	103,913	54,770	47,851	1,292	6,919 R	52.7%	46.0%	53.4%	46.6%
154,667	FAYETTE	52,291	25,337	26,262	692	925 D	48.5%	50.2%	49.1%	50.9%
4,926	FOREST	2,181	1,285	886	10	399 R	58.9%	40.6%	59.2%	40.8%
100,833	FRANKLIN	34,873	19,037	15,276	560	3,761 R	54.6%	43.8%	55.5%	44.5%
10,776	FULTON	3,935	2,064	1,835	36	229 R	52.5%	46.6%	52.9%	47.1%
36,090	GREENE	14,185	6,836	7,290	59	454 D	48.2%	51.4%	48.4%	51.6%
39,108	HUNTINGDON	13,440	7,937	5,394	109	2,543 R	59.1%	40.1%	59.5%	40.5%
79,451	INDIANA	30,896	19,116	11,631	149	7,485 R	61.9%	37.6%	62.2%	37.8%
43,695	JEFFERSON	17,144	10,473	6,599	72	3,874 R	61.1%	38.5%	61.3%	38.7%
16,712	JUNIATA	7,203	4,053	3,097	53	956 R	56.3%	43.0%	56.7%	43.3%
234,107	LACKAWANNA	99,437	43,247	55,327	863	12,080 D	43.5%	55.6%	43.9%	56.1%
319,693	LANCASTER	108,167	72,617	34,266	1,284	38,351 R	67.1%	31.7%	67.9%	32.1%
107,374	LAWRENCE	42,279	20,848	21,125	306	277 D	49.3%	50.0%	49.7%	50.3%
99,665	LEBANON	32,733	20,835	11,571	327	9,264 R	63.7%	35.3%	64.3%	35.7%
255,304	LEHIGH	93,530	48,105	44,699	726	3,406 R	51.4%	47.8%	51.8%	48.2%
342,301	LUZERNE	132,122	59,826	71,834	462	12,008 D	45.3%	54.4%	45.4%	54.6%
113,296	LYCOMING	41,326	22,470	18,413	443	4,057 R	54.4%	44.6%	55.0%	45.0%
51,915	MCKEAN	16,197	9,715	6,290	192	3,425 R	60.0%	38.8%	60.7%	39.3%
127,175	MERCER	45,967	24,841	20,720	406	4,121 R	54.0%	45.1%	54.5%	45.5%
45,268	MIFFLIN	13,935	8,093	5,740	102	2,353 R	58.1%	41.2%	58.5%	41.5%
45,422	MONROE	19,748	10,105	9,461	182	644 R	51.2%	47.9%	51.6%	48.4%
623,799	MONTGOMERY	269,996	148,800	119,593	1,603	29,207 R	55.1%	44.3%	55.4%	44.6%
16,508	MONTOUR	6,047	3,217	2,783	47	434 R	53.2%	46.0%	53.6%	46.4%
214,368	NORTHAMPTON	75,277	34,059	40,407	811	6,348 D	45.2%	53.7%	45.7%	54.3%
99,190	NORTHUMBERLAND	37,972	19,477	18,041	454	1,436 R	51.3%	47.5%	51.9%	48.1%
28,615	PERRY	12,230	7,639	4,482	109	3,157 R	62.5%	36.6%	63.0%	37.0%
1,948,609	PHILADELPHIA	730,941	210,445	516,294	4,202	305,849 D	28.8%	70.6%	29.0%	71.0%
11,818	PIKE	6,853	4,033	2,754	66	1,279 R	58.9%	40.2%	59.4%	40.6%
16,395	POTTER	6,698	3,617	3,039	42	578 R	54.0%	45.4%	54.3%	45.7%
160,089	SCHUYLKILL	67,031	33,156	33,214	661	58 D	49.5%	49.6%	50.0%	50.0%
29,269	SNYDER	9,811	6,699	3,002	110	3,697 R	68.3%	30.6%	69.1%	30.9%
76,037	SOMERSET	29,650	18,458	11,080	112	7,378 R	62.3%	37.4%	62.5%	37.5%
5,961	SULLIVAN	2,925	1,547	1,371	7	176 R	52.9%	46.9%	53.0%	47.0%
34,344	SUSQUEHANNA	14,381	8,395	5,837	149	2,558 R	58.4%	40.6%	59.0%	41.0%
39,691	TIOGA	14,218	8,852	5,246	120	3,606 R	62.3%	36.9%	62.8%	37.2%
28,603	UNION	9,843	6,412	3,346	85	3,066 R	65.1%	34.0%	65.7%	34.3%
62,353	VENANGO	21,167	13,675	7,389	103	6,286 R	64.6%	34.9%	64.9%	35.1%
47,682	WARREN	15,752	8,987	6,615	150	2,372 R	57.1%	42.0%	57.6%	42.4%
210,876	WASHINGTON	83,039	47,196	35,433	410	11,763 R	56.8%	42.7%	57.1%	42.9%
29,581	WAYNE	11,770	7,303	4,275	192	3,028 R	62.0%	36.3%	63.1%	36.9%
376,935	WESTMORELAND	134,068	78,802	54,028	1,238	24,774 R	58.8%	40.3%	59.3%	40.7%
19,082	WYOMING	9,401	5,760	3,576	65	2,184 R	61.3%	38.0%	61.7%	38.3%
272,603	YORK	98,178	58,257	39,072	849	19,185 R	59.3%	39.8%	59.9%	40.1%
11,793,909	TOTAL	4,546,353	2,381,891	2,126,977	37,485	254,914 R	52.4%	46.8%	52.8%	47.2%

Philadelphia

PRESIDENT 1976

1970 Census Population	Ward	Total Vote	Republican	Democratic	Other	Rep.-Dem. Plurality	Percentage Total Vote Rep.	Percentage Total Vote Dem.	Percentage Major Vote Rep.	Percentage Major Vote Dem.
25,046	WARD 1	11,154	4,421	6,595	138	2,174 D	39.6%	59.1%	40.1%	59.9%
29,249	WARD 2	10,125	3,841	6,119	165	2,278 D	37.9%	60.4%	38.6%	61.4%
27,991	WARD 3	9,924	719	9,141	64	8,422 D	7.2%	92.1%	7.3%	92.7%
27,226	WARD 4	9,342	873	8,390	79	7,517 D	9.3%	89.8%	9.4%	90.6%
22,917	WARD 5	9,607	3,740	5,568	299	1,828 D	38.9%	58.0%	40.2%	59.8%
25,203	WARD 6	6,406	467	5,888	51	5,421 D	7.3%	91.9%	7.3%	92.7%
26,992	WARD 7	9,204	3,144	5,913	147	2,769 D	34.2%	64.2%	34.7%	65.3%
30,425	WARD 8	14,573	5,544	8,619	410	3,075 D	38.0%	59.1%	39.1%	60.9%
18,594	WARD 9	9,495	4,735	4,529	231	206 R	49.9%	47.7%	51.1%	48.9%
29,858	WARD 10	10,433	1,254	9,060	119	7,806 D	12.0%	86.8%	12.2%	87.8%
26,385	WARD 11	6,501	669	5,773	59	5,104 D	10.3%	88.8%	10.4%	89.6%
30,054	WARD 12	8,958	1,832	6,870	256	5,038 D	20.5%	76.7%	21.1%	78.9%
26,982	WARD 13	8,307	1,290	6,875	142	5,585 D	15.5%	82.8%	15.8%	84.2%
15,099	WARD 14	3,016	383	2,585	48	2,202 D	12.7%	85.7%	12.9%	87.1%
23,167	WARD 15	7,700	2,813	4,703	184	1,890 D	36.5%	61.1%	37.4%	62.6%
24,584	WARD 16	6,921	537	6,295	89	5,758 D	7.8%	91.0%	7.9%	92.1%
30,299	WARD 17	10,549	1,279	9,147	123	7,868 D	12.1%	86.7%	12.3%	87.7%
23,765	WARD 18	6,335	2,132	4,084	119	1,952 D	33.7%	64.5%	34.3%	65.7%
25,818	WARD 19	5,136	848	4,226	62	3,378 D	16.5%	82.3%	16.7%	83.3%
15,128	WARD 20	2,902	293	2,576	33	2,283 D	10.1%	88.8%	10.2%	89.8%
53,291	WARD 21	23,481	12,187	10,882	412	1,305 R	51.9%	46.3%	52.8%	47.2%
29,912	WARD 22	12,582	2,367	9,977	238	7,610 D	18.8%	79.3%	19.2%	80.8%
27,436	WARD 23	10,929	4,647	6,064	218	1,417 D	42.5%	55.5%	43.4%	56.6%
22,191	WARD 24	5,119	489	4,520	110	4,031 D	9.6%	88.3%	9.8%	90.2%
27,498	WARD 25	10,228	3,912	6,131	185	2,219 D	38.2%	59.9%	39.0%	61.0%
28,881	WARD 26	11,767	5,551	6,064	152	513 D	47.2%	51.5%	47.8%	52.2%
24,903	WARD 27	8,791	2,349	6,138	304	3,789 D	26.7%	69.8%	27.7%	72.3%
24,128	WARD 28	6,833	408	6,366	59	5,958 D	6.0%	93.2%	6.0%	94.0%
22,180	WARD 29	6,172	639	5,463	70	4,824 D	10.4%	88.5%	10.5%	89.5%
19,734	WARD 30	5,392	893	4,405	94	3,512 D	16.6%	81.7%	16.9%	83.1%
22,225	WARD 31	8,093	3,339	4,601	153	1,262 D	41.3%	56.9%	42.1%	57.9%
42,606	WARD 32	10,135	791	9,163	181	8,372 D	7.8%	90.4%	7.9%	92.1%
26,875	WARD 33	11,687	4,742	6,728	217	1,986 D	40.6%	57.6%	41.3%	58.7%
48,267	WARD 34	19,967	5,790	13,936	241	8,146 D	29.0%	69.8%	29.4%	70.6%
36,679	WARD 35	16,766	8,265	8,162	339	103 R	49.3%	48.7%	50.3%	49.7%
47,404	WARD 36	16,781	2,837	13,712	232	10,875 D	16.9%	81.7%	17.1%	82.9%
29,158	WARD 37	5,703	482	5,155	66	4,673 D	8.5%	90.4%	8.6%	91.4%
28,451	WARD 38	8,295	2,425	5,751	119	3,326 D	29.2%	69.3%	29.7%	70.3%
55,790	WARD 39	23,028	9,705	13,048	275	3,343 D	42.1%	56.7%	42.7%	57.3%
54,572	WARD 40	20,738	7,665	12,708	365	5,043 D	37.0%	61.3%	37.6%	62.4%
26,185	WARD 41	11,447	5,053	6,128	266	1,075 D	44.1%	53.5%	45.2%	54.8%
32,134	WARD 42	13,123	5,476	7,409	238	1,933 D	41.7%	56.5%	42.5%	57.5%
27,757	WARD 43	7,990	1,791	6,083	116	4,292 D	22.4%	76.1%	22.7%	77.3%
20,484	WARD 44	7,818	1,471	6,274	73	4,803 D	18.8%	80.3%	19.0%	81.0%
28,708	WARD 45	12,516	4,871	7,385	260	2,514 D	38.9%	59.0%	39.7%	60.3%
28,684	WARD 46	10,037	1,244	8,485	308	7,241 D	12.4%	84.5%	12.8%	87.2%
17,714	WARD 47	4,488	414	4,027	47	3,613 D	9.2%	89.7%	9.3%	90.7%
27,873	WARD 48	10,817	4,403	6,262	152	1,859 D	40.7%	57.9%	41.3%	58.7%
32,278	WARD 49	10,532	2,908	7,392	232	4,484 D	27.6%	70.2%	28.2%	71.8%
32,953	WARD 50	13,065	2,075	10,822	168	8,747 D	15.9%	82.8%	16.1%	83.9%
33,191	WARD 51	8,166	852	7,236	78	6,384 D	10.4%	88.6%	10.5%	89.5%
32,573	WARD 52	15,803	3,380	12,246	177	8,866 D	21.4%	77.5%	21.6%	78.4%
25,084	WARD 53	13,798	4,997	8,563	238	3,566 D	36.2%	62.1%	36.9%	63.1%
23,403	WARD 54	13,809	4,117	9,459	233	5,342 D	29.8%	68.5%	30.3%	69.7%
32,726	WARD 55	16,348	7,672	8,358	318	686 D	46.9%	51.1%	47.9%	52.1%
35,007	WARD 56	20,761	7,793	12,656	312	4,863 D	37.5%	61.0%	38.1%	61.9%
31,957	WARD 57	15,069	6,364	8,450	255	2,086 D	42.2%	56.1%	43.0%	57.0%
43,125	WARD 58	22,881	10,292	12,280	309	1,988 D	45.0%	53.7%	45.6%	54.4%
28,540	WARD 59	10,779	1,952	8,601	226	6,649 D	18.1%	79.8%	18.5%	81.5%
26,725	WARD 60	9,580	653	8,846	81	8,193 D	6.8%	92.3%	6.9%	93.1%
29,591	WARD 61	14,971	7,005	7,646	320	641 D	46.8%	51.1%	47.8%	52.2%
30,632	WARD 62	14,476	6,350	7,835	291	1,485 D	43.9%	54.1%	44.8%	55.2%
27,287	WARD 63	13,505	6,561	6,696	248	135 D	48.6%	49.6%	49.5%	50.5%
18,570	WARD 64	9,802	4,595	5,042	165	447 D	46.9%	51.4%	47.7%	52.3%
26,457	WARD 65	11,035	4,536	6,289	210	1,753 D	41.1%	57.0%	41.9%	58.1%
52,008	WARD 66	23,678	11,543	11,734	401	191 D	48.7%	49.6%	49.6%	50.4%
	SPECIAL BALLOTS	828	335	445	48	110 D	40.5%	53.7%	42.9%	57.1%
1,948,609	TOTAL	746,197	239,000	494,579	12,618	255,579 D	32.0%	66.3%	32.6%	67.4%

Philadelphia

SENATOR 1976

1970 Census Population	Ward	Total Vote	Republican	Democratic	Other	Rep.-Dem. Plurality	Percentage Total Vote Rep.	Percentage Total Vote Dem.	Percentage Major Vote Rep.	Percentage Major Vote Dem.
25,046	WARD 1	10,878	3,950	6,881	47	2,931 D	36.3%	63.3%	36.5%	63.5%
29,249	WARD 2	9,863	3,510	6,252	101	2,742 D	35.6%	63.4%	36.0%	64.0%
27,991	WARD 3	9,663	1,030	8,595	38	7,565 D	10.7%	88.9%	10.7%	89.3%
27,226	WARD 4	9,126	1,106	7,980	40	6,874 D	12.1%	87.4%	12.2%	87.8%
22,917	WARD 5	8,677	2,913	5,679	85	2,766 D	33.6%	65.4%	33.9%	66.1%
25,203	WARD 6	6,208	640	5,541	27	4,901 D	10.3%	89.3%	10.4%	89.6%
26,992	WARD 7	9,127	2,556	6,525	46	3,969 D	28.0%	71.5%	28.1%	71.9%
30,425	WARD 8	14,268	5,140	9,035	93	3,895 D	36.0%	63.3%	36.3%	63.7%
18,594	WARD 9	9,488	4,320	5,125	43	805 D	45.5%	54.0%	45.7%	54.3%
29,858	WARD 10	10,264	1,531	8,680	53	7,149 D	14.9%	84.6%	15.0%	85.0%
26,385	WARD 11	6,339	686	5,623	30	4,937 D	10.8%	88.7%	10.9%	89.1%
30,054	WARD 12	8,746	1,855	6,770	121	4,915 D	21.2%	77.4%	21.5%	78.5%
26,982	WARD 13	8,115	1,335	6,721	59	5,386 D	16.5%	82.8%	16.6%	83.4%
15,099	WARD 14	2,959	480	2,454	25	1,974 D	16.2%	82.9%	16.4%	83.6%
23,167	WARD 15	7,557	2,384	5,119	54	2,735 D	31.5%	67.7%	31.8%	68.2%
24,584	WARD 16	6,746	651	6,014	81	5,363 D	9.7%	89.1%	9.8%	90.2%
30,299	WARD 17	10,435	1,410	8,975	50	7,565 D	13.5%	86.0%	13.6%	86.4%
23,765	WARD 18	6,223	1,653	4,527	43	2,874 D	26.6%	72.7%	26.7%	73.3%
25,818	WARD 19	4,948	761	4,148	39	3,387 D	15.4%	83.8%	15.5%	84.5%
15,128	WARD 20	2,834	351	2,457	26	2,106 D	12.4%	86.7%	12.5%	87.5%
53,291	WARD 21	22,931	10,426	12,421	84	1,995 D	45.5%	54.2%	45.6%	54.4%
29,912	WARD 22	12,574	2,640	9,847	87	7,207 D	21.0%	78.3%	21.1%	78.9%
27,436	WARD 23	10,827	3,889	6,874	64	2,985 D	35.9%	63.5%	36.1%	63.9%
22,191	WARD 24	4,951	650	4,255	46	3,605 D	13.1%	85.9%	13.3%	86.7%
27,498	WARD 25	10,181	3,230	6,899	52	3,669 D	31.7%	67.8%	31.9%	68.1%
28,881	WARD 26	11,467	4,939	6,454	74	1,515 D	43.1%	56.3%	43.4%	56.6%
24,903	WARD 27	8,500	2,217	6,187	96	3,970 D	26.1%	72.8%	26.4%	73.6%
24,128	WARD 28	6,591	565	5,986	40	5,421 D	8.6%	90.8%	8.6%	91.4%
22,180	WARD 29	5,971	711	5,228	32	4,517 D	11.9%	87.6%	12.0%	88.0%
19,734	WARD 30	5,534	1,120	4,352	62	3,232 D	20.2%	78.6%	20.5%	79.5%
22,225	WARD 31	8,017	2,775	5,197	45	2,422 D	34.6%	64.8%	34.8%	65.2%
42,606	WARD 32	9,651	972	8,569	110	7,597 D	10.1%	88.8%	10.2%	89.8%
26,875	WARD 33	11,637	3,514	8,087	36	4,573 D	30.2%	69.5%	30.3%	69.7%
48,267	WARD 34	19,545	5,248	14,200	97	8,952 D	26.9%	72.7%	27.0%	73.0%
36,679	WARD 35	16,633	7,013	9,537	83	2,524 D	42.2%	57.3%	42.4%	57.6%
47,404	WARD 36	16,461	2,692	13,648	121	10,956 D	16.4%	82.9%	16.5%	83.5%
29,158	WARD 37	5,461	510	4,925	26	4,415 D	9.3%	90.2%	9.4%	90.6%
28,451	WARD 38	7,988	2,254	5,706	28	3,452 D	28.2%	71.4%	28.3%	71.7%
55,790	WARD 39	22,211	8,434	13,662	115	5,228 D	38.0%	61.5%	38.2%	61.8%
54,572	WARD 40	20,429	6,840	13,511	78	6,671 D	33.5%	66.1%	33.6%	66.4%
26,185	WARD 41	11,347	4,168	7,101	78	2,933 D	36.7%	62.6%	37.0%	63.0%
32,134	WARD 42	12,966	4,741	8,158	67	3,417 D	36.6%	62.9%	36.8%	63.2%
27,757	WARD 43	7,889	1,558	6,286	45	4,728 D	19.7%	79.7%	19.9%	80.1%
20,484	WARD 44	6,793	856	5,889	48	5,033 D	12.6%	86.7%	12.7%	87.3%
28,708	WARD 45	12,311	3,742	8,477	92	4,735 D	30.4%	68.9%	30.6%	69.4%
28,684	WARD 46	9,813	1,502	8,159	152	6,657 D	15.3%	83.1%	15.5%	84.5%
17,714	WARD 47	4,440	433	3,975	32	3,542 D	9.8%	89.5%	9.8%	90.2%
27,873	WARD 48	10,573	4,079	6,443	51	2,364 D	38.6%	60.9%	38.8%	61.2%
32,278	WARD 49	10,384	2,685	7,633	66	4,948 D	25.9%	73.5%	26.0%	74.0%
32,953	WARD 50	12,773	2,318	10,401	54	8,083 D	18.1%	81.4%	18.2%	81.8%
33,191	WARD 51	8,015	1,090	6,881	44	5,791 D	13.6%	85.9%	13.7%	86.3%
32,573	WARD 52	15,514	2,999	12,444	71	9,445 D	19.3%	80.2%	19.4%	80.6%
25,084	WARD 53	13,545	4,137	9,344	64	5,207 D	30.5%	69.0%	30.7%	69.3%
23,403	WARD 54	13,641	3,358	10,227	56	6,869 D	24.6%	75.0%	24.7%	75.3%
32,726	WARD 55	16,142	6,257	9,819	66	3,562 D	38.8%	60.8%	38.9%	61.1%
35,007	WARD 56	20,443	6,613	13,745	85	7,132 D	32.3%	67.2%	32.5%	67.5%
31,957	WARD 57	14,901	5,383	9,460	58	4,077 D	36.1%	63.5%	36.3%	63.7%
43,125	WARD 58	22,535	8,677	13,784	74	5,107 D	38.5%	61.2%	38.6%	61.4%
28,540	WARD 59	10,526	2,101	8,344	81	6,243 D	20.0%	79.3%	20.1%	79.9%
26,725	WARD 60	9,751	883	8,821	47	7,938 D	9.1%	90.5%	9.1%	90.9%
29,591	WARD 61	14,783	5,982	8,725	76	2,743 D	40.5%	59.0%	40.7%	59.3%
30,632	WARD 62	14,341	5,242	9,029	70	3,787 D	36.6%	63.0%	36.7%	63.3%
27,287	WARD 63	13,358	5,458	7,856	44	2,398 D	40.9%	58.8%	41.0%	59.0%
18,570	WARD 64	9,653	3,865	5,742	46	1,877 D	40.0%	59.5%	40.2%	59.8%
26,457	WARD 65	10,905	3,764	7,092	49	3,328 D	34.5%	65.0%	34.7%	65.3%
52,008	WARD 66	23,575	9,653	13,813	109	4,160 D	40.9%	58.6%	41.1%	58.9%
1,948,609	TOTAL	730,941	210,445	516,294	4,202	305,849 D	28.8%	70.6%	29.0%	71.0%

PENNSYLVANIA

CONGRESS

CD	Year	Total Vote	Republican Vote	Republican Candidate	Democratic Vote	Democratic Candidate	Other Vote	Rep.-Dem. Plurality	Percentage Total Vote Rep.	Percentage Total Vote Dem.	Percentage Major Vote Rep.	Percentage Major Vote Dem.
1	1976	159,205	40,191	FANELLI, SAMUEL N.	117,087	MYERS, MICHAEL	1,927	76,896 D	25.2%	73.5%	25.6%	74.4%
1	1974	127,901	29,772	NIGRO, RUSSELL M.	96,988	BARRETT, WILLIAM A.	1,141	67,216 D	23.3%	75.8%	23.5%	76.5%
1	1972	179,932	59,807	PEDICONE, GUS A.	118,953	BARRETT, WILLIAM A.	1,172	59,146 D	33.2%	66.1%	33.5%	66.5%
2	1976	149,369	37,907	WOODS, JESSE W.	109,855	NIX, ROBERT N. C.	1,607	71,948 D	25.4%	73.5%	25.7%	74.3%
2	1974	101,386	26,353	WOODS, JESSE W.	75,033	NIX, ROBERT N. C.		48,680 D	26.0%	74.0%	26.0%	74.0%
2	1972	153,262	45,753	BRYANT, FREDERICK D.	107,509	NIX, ROBERT N. C.		61,756 D	29.9%	70.1%	29.9%	70.1%
3	1976	134,818	35,491	SHADE, TERRENCE J.	98,627	LEDERER, RAYMOND F.	700	63,136 D	26.3%	73.2%	26.5%	73.5%
3	1974	112,367	27,692	COLBERT, RICHARD P.	84,675	GREEN, WILLIAM J., III		56,983 D	24.6%	75.4%	24.6%	75.4%
3	1972	159,704	57,787	MARROLETTI, ALFRED	101,144	GREEN, WILLIAM J., III	773	43,357 D	36.2%	63.3%	36.4%	63.6%
4	1976	214,590	69,700	MUGFORD, JAMES E.	144,890	EILBERG, JOSHUA		75,190 D	32.5%	67.5%	32.5%	67.5%
4	1974	174,640	50,688	EINHORN, ISADORE	123,952	EILBERG, JOSHUA		73,264 D	29.0%	71.0%	29.0%	71.0%
4	1972	231,118	102,013	PFENDER, WILLIAM	129,105	EILBERG, JOSHUA		27,092 D	44.1%	55.9%	44.1%	55.9%
5	1976	200,981	119,682	SCHULZE, RICHARD T.	81,299	CAMPOLO, ANTHONY		38,383 R	59.5%	40.5%	59.5%	40.5%
5	1974	140,152	83,526	SCHULZE, RICHARD T.	56,626	MCDERMOTT, LEO D.		26,900 R	59.6%	40.4%	59.6%	40.4%
5	1972	187,675	121,346	WARE, JOHN H.	66,329	YERGER, BROWER B.		55,017 R	64.7%	35.3%	64.7%	35.3%
6	1976	180,998	46,103	POSTUPACK, STEPHEN	133,624	YATRON, GUS	1,271	87,521 D	25.5%	73.8%	25.7%	74.3%
6	1974	148,952	35,805	POSTUPACK, STEPHEN	111,127	YATRON, GUS	2,020	75,322 D	24.0%	74.6%	24.4%	75.6%
6	1972	185,408	64,076	HUBLER, EUGENE W.	119,557	YATRON, GUS	1,775	55,481 D	34.6%	64.5%	34.9%	65.1%
7	1976	202,351	92,788	KENNEY, JOHN M.	109,436	EDGAR, ROBERT W.	127	16,648 D	45.9%	54.1%	45.9%	54.1%
7	1974	162,295	70,894	MCEWEN, STEPHEN J.	89,680	EDGAR, ROBERT W.	1,721	18,786 D	43.7%	55.3%	44.2%	55.8%
7	1972	202,200	122,622	WILLIAMS, LAWRENCE	79,578	BOWIE, STUART S.		43,044 R	60.6%	39.4%	60.6%	39.4%
8	1976	189,623	92,543	RENNINGER, JOHN S.	93,855	KOSTMAYER, PETER H.	3,225	1,312 D	48.8%	49.5%	49.6%	50.4%
8	1974	133,891	75,313	BIESTER, EDWARD G.	54,815	MOYER, WILLIAM B.	3,763	20,498 R	56.2%	40.9%	57.9%	42.1%
8	1972	179,881	115,799	BIESTER, EDWARD G.	64,069	WILLIAMS, ALAN	13	51,730 R	64.4%	35.6%	64.4%	35.6%
9	1976	154,359	154,359	*SHUSTER, E. G.				154,359 R	100.0%		100.0%	
9	1974	130,725	73,881	SHUSTER, E. G.	56,844	FORD, ROBERT D.		17,037 R	56.5%	43.5%	56.5%	43.5%
9	1972	155,341	95,913	SHUSTER, E. G.	59,386	COLLINS, EARL P.	42	36,527 R	61.7%	38.2%	61.8%	38.2%
10	1976	200,143	125,218	MCDADE, JOSEPH M.	74,925	MITCHELL, EDWARD		50,293 R	62.6%	37.4%	62.6%	37.4%
10	1974	155,194	100,793	MCDADE, JOSEPH M.	54,401	HANLON, THOMAS J.		46,392 R	64.9%	35.1%	64.9%	35.1%
10	1972	195,221	143,670	MCDADE, JOSEPH M.	51,550	COVELESKIE, STANLEY R.	1	92,120 R	73.6%	26.4%	73.6%	26.4%
11	1976	183,796	53,621	WILLIAMS, HOWARD G.	130,175	FLOOD, DANIEL J.		76,554 D	29.2%	70.8%	29.2%	70.8%
11	1974	149,678	38,106	MUZYKA, RICHARD A.	111,572	FLOOD, DANIEL J.		73,466 D	25.5%	74.5%	25.5%	74.5%
11	1972	182,146	57,809	AYERS, DONALD B.	124,336	FLOOD, DANIEL J.	1	66,527 D	31.7%	68.3%	31.7%	68.3%
12	1976	180,993	58,489	HUMES, TED	122,504	MURTHA, JOHN P.		64,015 D	32.3%	67.7%	32.3%	67.7%
12	1974	153,619	64,416	FOX, HARRY M.	89,193	MURTHA, JOHN P.	10	24,777 D	41.9%	58.1%	41.9%	58.1%
12	1972	179,947	122,628	SAYLOR, JOHN P.	57,314	MURPHY, JOSEPH	5	65,314 R	68.1%	31.9%	68.1%	31.9%
13	1976	206,140	130,705	COUGHLIN, R. LAWRENCE	75,435	STRICK, GERTRUDE		55,270 R	63.4%	36.6%	63.4%	36.6%
13	1974	158,418	98,985	COUGHLIN, R. LAWRENCE	59,433	CURRY, LAWRENCE H.		39,552 R	62.5%	37.5%	62.5%	37.5%
13	1972	208,818	139,085	COUGHLIN, R. LAWRENCE	69,728	CAMP, KATHERINE L.	5	69,357 R	66.6%	33.4%	66.6%	33.4%
14	1976	159,644	43,308	BRADLEY, JOHN F.	114,472	MOORHEAD, WILLIAM S.	1,864	71,164 D	27.1%	71.7%	27.4%	72.6%
14	1974	120,332	27,116	DAVIS, ZACHARY T.	93,169	MOORHEAD, WILLIAM S.	47	66,053 D	22.5%	77.4%	22.5%	77.5%
14	1972	178,907	72,275	CATARINELLA, ROLAND S.	106,158	MOORHEAD, WILLIAM S.	474	33,883 D	40.4%	59.3%	40.5%	59.5%
15	1976	166,890	57,616	SIVULICH, ALICE B.	108,844	ROONEY, FRED B.	430	51,228 D	34.5%	65.2%	34.6%	65.4%
15	1974	85,905			85,905	ROONEY, FRED B.		85,905 D		100.0%		100.0%
15	1972	164,500	64,560	STEIGERWALT, WARDELL F.	99,937	ROONEY, FRED B.	3	35,377 D	39.2%	60.8%	39.2%	60.8%
16	1976	156,455	97,527	WALKER, ROBERT S.	57,836	MINNEY, MICHAEL J.	1,092	39,691 R	62.3%	37.0%	62.8%	37.2%
16	1974	115,168	73,130	ESHLEMAN, EDWIN D.	40,273	MINNEY, MICHAEL J.	1,765	32,857 R	63.5%	35.0%	64.5%	35.5%
16	1972	152,827	112,292	ESHLEMAN, EDWIN D.	40,534	GARRETT, SHIRLEY S.	1	71,758 R	73.5%	26.5%	73.5%	26.5%
17	1976	169,864	82,370	HEPFORD, H. JOSEPH	86,158	ERTEL, ALLEN E.	1,336	3,788 D	48.5%	50.7%	48.9%	51.1%
17	1974	134,850	70,274	SCHNEEBELI, HERMAN	64,576	WAMBACH, PETER C.		5,698 R	52.1%	47.9%	52.1%	47.9%
17	1972	166,494	120,214	SCHNEEBELI, HERMAN	44,202	RIPPON, DONALD J.	2,078	76,012 R	72.2%	26.5%	73.1%	26.9%
18	1976	191,381	77,594	CASEY, ROBERT J.	113,787	WALGREN, DOUGLAS		36,193 D	40.5%	59.5%	40.5%	59.5%
18	1974	149,471	107,723	HEINZ, H. JOHN	41,706	MCARDLE, FRANCIS J.	42	66,017 R	72.1%	27.9%	72.1%	27.9%
18	1972	198,472	144,521	HEINZ, H. JOHN	53,929	WALGREN, DOUGLAS	22	90,592 R	72.8%	27.2%	72.8%	27.2%
19	1976	175,784	124,098	GOODLING, WILLIAM F.	51,686	NOLL, RICHARD P.		72,412 R	70.6%	29.4%	70.6%	29.4%
19	1974	129,158	66,417	GOODLING, WILLIAM F.	61,414	BERGER, ARTHUR L.	1,327	5,003 R	51.4%	47.5%	52.0%	48.0%
19	1972	162,587	93,536	GOODLING, GEORGE A.	67,018	NOLL, RICHARD P.	2,033	26,518 R	57.5%	41.2%	58.3%	41.7%
20	1976	180,055	44,432	KOSTELAC, JOHN P.	134,961	GAYDOS, JOSEPH M.	662	90,529 D	24.7%	75.0%	24.8%	75.2%
20	1974	137,393	25,129	ANDERKO, JOSEPH J.	112,237	GAYDOS, JOSEPH M.	27	87,108 D	18.3%	81.7%	18.3%	81.7%
20	1972	191,764	73,817	HUNT, WILLIAM R.	117,933	GAYDOS, JOSEPH M.	14	44,116 D	38.5%	61.5%	38.5%	61.5%
21	1976	166,923	67,763	MILLER, ROBERT H.	99,160	DENT, JOHN H.		31,397 D	40.6%	59.4%	40.6%	59.4%
21	1974	126,822	38,111	SCONING, CHARLES L.	88,701	DENT, JOHN H.	10	50,590 D	30.1%	69.9%	30.1%	69.9%
21	1972	168,032	63,812	YOUNG, THOMAS H.	104,203	DENT, JOHN H.	17	40,391 D	38.0%	62.0%	38.0%	62.0%

PENNSYLVANIA

CONGRESS

CD	Year	Total Vote	Republican Vote	Republican Candidate	Democratic Vote	Democratic Candidate	Other Vote	Rep.-Dem. Plurality	Percentage Total Vote Rep.	Percentage Total Vote Dem.	Percentage Major Vote Rep.	Percentage Major Vote Dem.
22	1976	175,416	77,030	FISCHER, ROGER	97,036	MURPHY, AUSTIN J.	1,350	20,006 D	43.9%	55.3%	44.3%	55.7%
22	1974	131,628	41,706	MONTGOMERY, JAMES R.	83,654	MORGAN, THOMAS E.	6,268	41,948 D	31.7%	63.6%	33.3%	66.7%
22	1972	165,934	65,005	MONTGOMERY, JAMES R.	100,918	MORGAN, THOMAS E.	11	35,913 D	39.2%	60.8%	39.2%	60.8%
23	1976	169,462	73,641	JOHNSON, ALBERT W.	95,821	AMMERMAN, JOSEPH S.		22,180 D	43.5%	56.5%	43.5%	56.5%
23	1974	127,403	67,192	JOHNSON, ALBERT W.	60,211	MAST, YATES		6,981 R	52.7%	47.3%	52.7%	47.3%
23	1972	160,428	90,615	JOHNSON, ALBERT W.	69,813	KASSAB, ERNEST A.		20,802 R	56.5%	43.5%	56.5%	43.5%
24	1976	182,526	101,048	MARKS, MARC L.	79,937	VIGORITO, JOSEPH P.	1,541	21,111 R	55.4%	43.8%	55.8%	44.2%
24	1974	131,197	54,277	SCALZITTI, CLEMENT R.	76,920	VIGORITO, JOSEPH P.		22,643 D	41.4%	58.6%	41.4%	58.6%
24	1972	177,498	55,406	LEVENHAGEN, ALVIN W.	122,092	VIGORITO, JOSEPH P.		66,686 D	31.2%	68.8%	31.2%	68.8%
24	1970	140,848	44,395	MERRICK, WAYNE R.	94,029	VIGORITO, JOSEPH P.	2,424	49,634 D	31.5%	66.8%	32.1%	67.9%
24	1968	174,958	66,429	EDWARDS, JOHN V.	106,869	VIGORITO, JOSEPH P.	1,660	40,440 D	38.0%	61.1%	38.3%	61.7%
24	1966	154,148	68,955	WEAVER, JAMES D.	85,193	VIGORITO, JOSEPH P.		16,238 D	44.7%	55.3%	44.7%	55.3%
24	1964	182,440	89,828	WEAVER, JAMES D.	92,612	VIGORITO, JOSEPH P.		2,784 D	49.2%	50.8%	49.2%	50.8%
24	1962	159,962	82,213	WEAVER, JAMES D.	77,749	JOYCE, PETER J.		4,464 R	51.4%	48.6%	51.4%	48.6%
24	1960	186,647	95,149	KEARNS, CARROLL D.	91,498	HAMPTON, CHESTER C.		3,651 R	51.0%	49.0%	51.0%	49.0%
24	1958	142,807	76,870	KEARNS, CARROLL D.	65,937	O BRIEN, JAMES P.		10,933 R	53.8%	46.2%	53.8%	46.2%
24	1956	162,449	93,824	KEARNS, CARROLL D.	68,625	THOMAS, WILLIAM D.		25,199 R	57.8%	42.2%	57.8%	42.2%
24	1954	126,847	66,005	KEARNS, CARROLL D.	60,842	ROGERS, EDMUND T.		5,163 R	52.0%	48.0%	52.0%	48.0%
24	1952	158,066	90,276	KEARNS, CARROLL D.	67,790	BEBELL, CLINTON J.		22,486 R	57.1%	42.9%	57.1%	42.9%
28	1950	118,664	67,604	KEARNS, CARROLL D.	51,060	FILIPKOWSKI, STEVE		16,544 R	57.0%	43.0%	57.0%	43.0%
28	1948	119,678	65,276	KEARNS, CARROLL D.	54,402	KENNEDY, JAMES A.		10,874 R	54.5%	45.5%	54.5%	45.5%
28	1946	89,001	56,835	KEARNS, CARROLL D.	32,166	WEBB, CHARLES W.		24,669 R	63.9%	36.1%	63.9%	36.1%
25	1976	182,489	103,632	MYERS, GARY A.	78,857	ATKINSON, EUGENE V.		24,775 R	56.8%	43.2%	56.8%	43.2%
25	1974	138,732	74,645	MYERS, GARY A.	64,049	CLARK, FRANK M.	38	10,596 R	53.8%	46.2%	53.8%	46.2%
25	1972	174,693	77,123	MYERS, GARY A.	97,549	CLARK, FRANK M.	21	20,426 D	44.1%	55.8%	44.2%	55.8%

PENNSYLVANIA

1976 GENERAL ELECTION

President Other vote was 50,584 McCarthy (McCarthy '76); 25,344 Maddox (Constitutional); 3,009 Camejo (Socialist Workers); 2,744 LaRouche (Labor); 1,891 Hall (Communist); 2,934 scattered.

Senator Other vote was 26,028 Watson (Constitutional); 5,484 Stanton (Socialist Workers); 3,637 Salera (Labor); 2,097 Kinces (Communist); 239 scattered.

Congress In CD 9 E. G. Shuster, the Democratic candidate, also had the Republican endorsement. Other vote was 1,341 Fraenzl (Socialist Workers) and 586 Moss (Labor) in CD 1; 1,106 Austin (Socialist Workers), 287 Thomas (Independent Conservative), and 214 Grant (Revolutionary Workers) in CD 2; Douglas (Labor) in CD 3; Fisher (Constitutional) in CD 6; Cinger (Labor) in CD 7; Graham (Constitutional) in CD 8; 1,370 Hoag (Socialist Workers) and 494 Brady (Labor) in CD 14; Coates (Labor) in CD 15; 743 Haas (Independent) and 349 Ross (Labor) in CD 16; Dublin (Constitutional) in CD 17; Billington (Labor) in CD 20; Wilson (American) in CD 22; Hereford (American) in CD 24.

PHILADELPHIA

Philadelphia city and county are coterminous.

President In a few wards, there are minor discrepancies between the Republican ward totals as published by the Voter Registration Division in their annual report and ward totals as furnished this office by the Election Department. Special ballots were short Presidential ballots cast by new residents. Other vote was 7,864 McCarthy (McCarthy '76); 2,178 Maddox (Constitutional); 927 LaRouche (Labor); 914 Camejo (Socialist Workers); 735 Hall (Communist).

Senator Other vote was 1,522 Watson (Constitutional); 1,127 Stanton (Socialist Workers); 930 Salera (Labor); 623 Kinces (Communist).

1976 PRIMARIES

APRIL 27 REPUBLICAN

Senator 358,715 H. John Heinz; 332,513 Arlen Specter; 160,379 George R. Packard; 46,828 C. Homer Brown; 29,160 Mary E. Foltz; 20,421 Francis Worley; 2,665 scattered.

Congress Unopposed in fifteen CD's. Douglas C. Flynn, the unopposed candidate in CD 15, withdrew after the primary and Alice B. Sivulich was substituted by the local party committee. Contested as follows:

CD 1 6,236 Samuel N. Fanelli; 4,772 George Kelly.
CD 6 15,681 Stephen Postupack; 8,990 Norman W. Bertasavage.
CD 7 36,874 John M. Kenney; 11,249 John J. Golden.
CD 8 13,552 John S. Renninger; 12,862 James L. Wright; 6,228 James S. Kiel; 6,073 William A. Duff; 1,109 Duncan E. Beaton.
CD 16 11,669 Robert S. Walker; 9,138 Marvin E. Miller; 8,894 Al Lewis; 8,045 Darvin E. Boyd; 7,329 William A. Drury; 4,756 Richard M. Scott; 4,434 Herbert C. Mearig; 3,475 Norman O. Aamodt; 1,066 Alonzo B. Baxter; 888 Richard L. Mohler; 287 Donald F. Krank.
CD 17 25,558 H. Joseph Hepford; 16,246 W. Crawford Murdoch; 8,150 David J. Lu.
CD 18 11,266 Robert J. Casey; 9,977 Ted Jacob; 8,207 Keith Swenson; 8,154 Jim Kelly; 5,932 Dennis Unkovic; 343 Joseph Imburgia.
CD 22 No candidates names appeared on the ballot; Roger Fischer received 3,042 write-in votes and became the nominee.
CD 23 26,690 Albert W. Johnson; 22,143 Charles M. Seeger; 2,239 Gregory M. Leshock.
CD 24 23,206 Marc L. Marks; 17,825 Neil McLaughlin.

PENNSYLVANIA

APRIL 27 DEMOCRATIC

Senator 762,733 William J. Green, III; 345,264 Jeanette Reibman; 2,058 scattered.

Congress Unopposed in eight CD's. No candidate in CD 9. Contested as follows:

CD 1	39,783 William A. Barrett; 13,381 Robert G. Allman. Mr. Barrett died shortly before the primary and Michael Myers was substituted after the primary by the local party committee.
CD 2	27,700 Robert N. C. Nix; 27,361 William H. Gray; 2,887 William H. Blake.
CD 3	24,468 Raymond F. Lederer; 6,477 Richard M. Moszczynski; 4,991 Bette Henderson; 3,179 Kenneth N. Clemente; 2,105 Joe Mikuliak; 1,900 Joseph S. Henderson.
CD 5	14,440 Anthony Campolo; 8,079 Nicholas S. Smola.
CD 8	12,842 Peter H. Kostmayer; 9,449 Joseph H. Pavlak; 5,511 Wynne James; 4,146 Stephen R. Lahoda; 3,296 Edward W. Kelley.
CD 9	No candidates names appeared on the ballot; E. G. Shuster, the unopposed Republican candidate, received 11,044 write-in votes and became the nominee.
CD 10	28,462 Edward Mitchell; 7,134 Michael Petsko; 4,046 Gene Basalyga.
CD 13	18,470 Gertrude Strick; 9,292 Edward H. Johnson.
CD 17	15,057 Allen E. Ertel; 11,927 Harold Swenson; 8,260 Anthony Petrucci; 2,357 Donald J. Rippon.
CD 18	28,955 Douglas Walgren; 14,333 Neal V. Musmanno; 5,877 Peter Block; 4,507 Vincent J. Dipasquale; 3,439 Frank J. Mahr; 3,427 George F. Cepek; 2,956 Mike Della Vecchia; 1,545 Jerry D. Freeble.
CD 19	21,248 Richard P. Noll; 8,982 Rajeshwar Kumar.
CD 20	64,953 Joseph M. Gaydos; 15,688 John E. Pribanic.
CD 21	40,362 John H. Dent; 24,071 John A. Cicco.
CD 22	26,358 Austin J. Murphy; 24,122 Fred L. Lebder; 18,723 John Hook; 12,249 Steven A. Stepanian; 3,452 Emmett Nepa; 2,521 Jim Dugan; 1,235 Robert M. Luzier; 947 David A. Bertovich; 924 Frederick H. Sivavec; 864 John Tomikel; 580 Michael J. Defino; 471 Donald J. Skillin.
CD 23	28,203 Joseph S. Ammerman; 13,027 Peter Atigan.
CD 24	33,483 Joseph P. Vigorito; 20,867 Louis J. Tullio; 6,448 Vincent N. DeLuca; 4,045 Robert T. O'Hara.
CD 25	28,898 Eugene V. Atkinson; 16,832 Frank M. Clark; 14,763 Thomas A. Shumaker; 4,023 Eugene D. Pace.

APRIL 27 CONSTITUTIONAL

Senator Andrew J. Watson, unopposed.

Congress Unopposed in the three CD's in which candidates were entered. C. George Mitchell, the unopposed candidate in CD 8, withdrew after the primary and Robert B. Graham was substituted by the local party committee.

RHODE ISLAND

GOVERNOR

J. Joseph Garrahy (D). Elected 1976 to a two-year term.

SENATORS

John H. Chafee (R). Elected 1976 to a six-year term.

Claiborne Pell (D). Re-elected 1972 to a six-year term. Previously elected 1966, 1960.

REPRESENTATIVES

1. Fernand St. Germain (D)
2. Edward P. Beard (D)

POSTWAR VOTE FOR GOVERNOR

		Republican		Democratic				Percentage			
								Total Vote		Major Vote	
Year	Total Vote	Vote	Candidate	Vote	Candidate	Other Vote	Rep.-Dem. Plurality	Rep.	Dem.	Rep.	Dem.
1976	398,683	178,254	Taft, James L.	218,561	Garrahy, J. Joseph	1,868	40,307 D	44.7%	54.8%	44.9%	55.1%
1974	321,660	69,224	Nugent, James W.	252,436	Noel, Philip W.	–	183,212 D	21.5%	78.5%	21.5%	78.5%
1972	412,866	194,315	DeSimone, Herbert F.	216,953	Noel, Philip W.	1,598	22,638 D	47.1%	52.5%	47.2%	52.8%
1970	346,342	171,549	DeSimone, Herbert F.	173,420	Licht, Frank	1,373	1,871 D	49.5%	50.1%	49.7%	50.3%
1968	383,725	187,958	Chafee, John H.	195,766	Licht, Frank	1	7,808 D	49.0%	51.0%	49.0%	51.0%
1966	332,064	210,202	Chafee, John H.	121,862	Hobbs, Horace E.	–	88,340 R	63.3%	36.7%	63.3%	36.7%
1964	391,668	239,501	Chafee, John H.	152,165	Gallogly, Edward P.	2	87,336 R	61.1%	38.9%	61.1%	38.9%
1962	327,506	163,952	Chafee, John H.	163,554	Notte, John A.	–	398 R	50.1%	49.9%	50.1%	49.9%
1960	401,362	174,044	Del Sesto, Christopher	227,318	Notte, John A.	–	53,274 D	43.4%	56.6%	43.4%	56.6%
1958	346,780	176,505	Del Sesto, Christopher	170,275	Roberts, Dennis J.	–	6,230 R	50.9%	49.1%	50.9%	49.1%
1956	383,919	191,604	Del Sesto, Christopher	192,315	Roberts, Dennis J.	–	711 D	49.9%	50.1%	49.9%	50.1%
1954	328,670	137,131	Lewis, Dean J.	189,595	Roberts, Dennis J.	1,944	52,464 D	41.7%	57.7%	42.0%	58.0%
1952	409,689	194,102	Archambault, Raoul	215,587	Roberts, Dennis J.	–	21,485 D	47.4%	52.6%	47.4%	52.6%
1950	296,809	120,684	Lachapelle, E. T.	176,125	Roberts, Dennis J.	–	55,441 D	40.7%	59.3%	40.7%	59.3%
1948	323,863	124,441	Ruerat, Albert P.	198,056	Pastore, John O.	1,366	73,615 D	38.4%	61.2%	38.6%	61.4%
1946	275,341	126,456	Murphy, John G.	148,885	Pastore, John O.	–	22,429 D	45.9%	54.1%	45.9%	54.1%

POSTWAR VOTE FOR SENATOR

		Republican		Democratic				Percentage			
								Total Vote		Major Vote	
Year	Total Vote	Vote	Candidate	Vote	Candidate	Other Vote	Rep.-Dem. Plurality	Rep.	Dem.	Rep.	Dem.
1976	398,906	230,329	Chafee, John H.	167,665	Lorber, Richard P.	912	62,664 R	57.7%	42.0%	57.9%	42.1%
1972	413,432	188,990	Chafee, John H.	221,942	Pell, Claiborne	2,500	32,952 D	45.7%	53.7%	46.0%	54.0%
1970	341,222	107,351	McLaughlin, John	230,469	Pastore, John O.	3,402	123,118 D	31.5%	67.5%	31.8%	68.2%
1966	324,173	104,838	Briggs, Ruth M.	219,331	Pell, Claiborne	4	114,493 D	32.3%	67.7%	32.3%	67.7%
1964	386,322	66,715	Lagueux, Ronald R.	319,607	Pastore, John O.	–	252,892 D	17.3%	82.7%	17.3%	82.7%
1960	399,983	124,408	Archambault, Raoul	275,575	Pell, Claiborne	–	151,167 D	31.1%	68.9%	31.1%	68.9%
1958	344,519	122,353	Ewing, Bayard	222,166	Pastore, John O.	–	99,813 D	35.5%	64.5%	35.5%	64.5%
1954	326,624	132,970	Sundlun, Walter I.	193,654	Green, Theodore F.	–	60,684 D	40.7%	59.3%	40.7%	59.3%
1952	410,978	185,850	Ewing, Bayard	225,128	Pastore, John O.	–	39,278 D	45.2%	54.8%	45.2%	54.8%
1950s	297,909	114,184	Levy, Austin T.	183,725	Pastore, John O.	–	69,541 D	48.3%	61.7%	38.3%	61.7%
1948	320,420	130,262	Hazard, Thomas P.	190,158	Green, Theodore F.	–	59,896 D	40.7%	59.3%	40.7%	59.3%
1946	273,528	122,780	Dyer, W. Gurnee	150,748	McGrath, J. Howard	–	27,968 D	44.9%	55.1%	44.9%	55.1%

The election in 1950 was for a short term to fill a vacancy.

RHODE ISLAND

Districts Established January 31, 1972

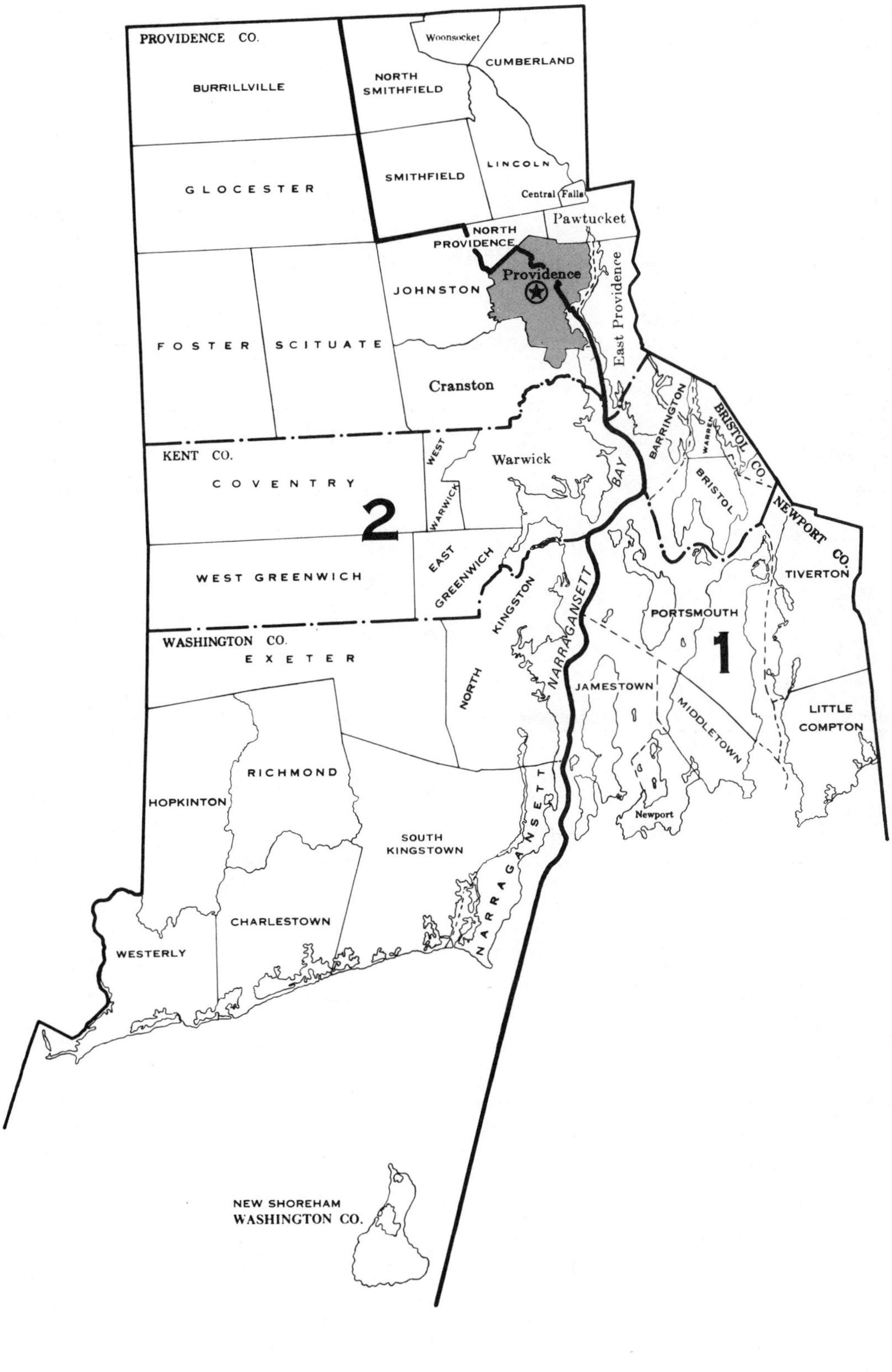
PROVIDENCE CO.
BURRILLVILLE
Woonsocket
CUMBERLAND
NORTH SMITHFIELD
GLOCESTER
SMITHFIELD
LINCOLN
Central Falls
Pawtucket
NORTH PROVIDENCE
Providence
JOHNSTON
East Providence
FOSTER
SCITUATE
Cranston
BARRINGTON
WARREN
BRISTOL CO.
KENT CO.
WEST WARWICK
Warwick
BRISTOL
BAY
COVENTRY
2
NEWPORT CO.
WEST GREENWICH
EAST GREENWICH
NORTH KINGSTON
NARRAGANSETT
TIVERTON
PORTSMOUTH
1
WASHINGTON CO.
EXETER
JAMESTOWN
MIDDLETOWN
LITTLE COMPTON
RICHMOND
HOPKINTON
Newport
SOUTH KINGSTOWN
NARRAGANSETT
CHARLESTOWN
WESTERLY
NEW SHOREHAM
WASHINGTON CO.

RHODE ISLAND

PRESIDENT 1976

1970 Census Population	County	Total Vote	Republican	Democratic	Other	Rep.-Dem. Plurality	Percentage Total Vote Rep.	Total Vote Dem.	Major Vote Rep.	Major Vote Dem.
45,937	BRISTOL	21,425	10,131	11,228	66	1,097 D	47.3%	52.4%	47.4%	52.6%
142,382	KENT	70,213	34,131	35,855	227	1,724 D	48.6%	51.1%	48.8%	51.2%
94,228	NEWPORT	33,107	15,155	17,768	184	2,613 D	45.8%	53.7%	46.0%	54.0%
581,470	PROVIDENCE	249,817	103,976	144,805	1,036	40,829 D	41.6%	58.0%	41.8%	58.2%
85,706	WASHINGTON	36,022	17,856	17,980	186	124 D	49.6%	49.9%	49.8%	50.2%
949,723	TOTAL	411,170	181,249	227,636	2,285	46,387 D	44.1%	55.4%	44.3%	55.7%

GOVERNOR 1976

1970 Census Population	County	Total Vote	Republican	Democratic	Other	Rep.-Dem. Plurality	Percentage Total Vote Rep.	Total Vote Dem.	Major Vote Rep.	Major Vote Dem.
45,937	BRISTOL	20,861	10,233	10,532	96	299 D	49.1%	50.5%	49.3%	50.7%
142,382	KENT	69,114	35,556	33,250	308	2,306 R	51.4%	48.1%	51.7%	48.3%
94,228	NEWPORT	31,190	14,193	16,802	195	2,609 D	45.5%	53.9%	45.8%	54.2%
581,470	PROVIDENCE	242,639	99,522	142,024	1,093	42,502 D	41.0%	58.5%	41.2%	58.8%
85,706	WASHINGTON	34,879	18,750	15,953	176	2,797 R	53.8%	45.7%	54.0%	46.0%
949,723	TOTAL	398,683	178,254	218,561	1,868	40,307 D	44.7%	54.8%	44.9%	55.1%

SENATOR 1976

1970 Census Population	County	Total Vote	Republican	Democratic	Other	Rep.-Dem. Plurality	Percentage Total Vote Rep.	Total Vote Dem.	Major Vote Rep.	Major Vote Dem.
45,937	BRISTOL	21,028	13,333	7,652	43	5,681 R	63.4%	36.4%	63.5%	36.5%
142,382	KENT	69,108	43,676	25,323	109	18,353 R	63.2%	36.6%	63.3%	36.7%
94,228	NEWPORT	31,491	17,321	14,112	58	3,209 R	55.0%	44.8%	55.1%	44.9%
581,470	PROVIDENCE	242,355	133,937	107,837	581	26,100 R	55.3%	44.5%	55.4%	44.6%
85,706	WASHINGTON	34,924	22,062	12,741	121	9,321 R	63.2%	36.5%	63.4%	36.6%
949,723	TOTAL	398,906	230,329	167,665	912	62,664 R	57.7%	42.0%	57.9%	42.1%

RHODE ISLAND

PRESIDENT 1976

1970 Census Population	City/Town	Total Vote	Republican	Democratic	Other	Rep.-Dem. Plurality	Percentage Total Vote Rep.	Percentage Total Vote Dem.	Percentage Major Vote Rep.	Percentage Major Vote Dem.
17,554	BARRINGTON	9,005	5,225	3,757	23	1,468 R	58.0%	41.7%	58.2%	41.8%
17,860	BRISTOL TOWN	7,786	3,082	4,681	23	1,599 D	39.6%	60.1%	39.7%	60.3%
10,087	BURRILLVILLE	4,517	1,838	2,659	20	821 D	40.7%	58.9%	40.9%	59.1%
18,716	CENTRAL FALLS	6,640	2,278	4,337	25	2,059 D	34.3%	65.3%	34.4%	65.6%
2,863	CHARLESTOWN	1,903	1,030	865	8	165 R	54.1%	45.5%	54.4%	45.6%
22,947	COVENTRY	10,975	5,244	5,695	36	451 D	47.8%	51.9%	47.9%	52.1%
74,287	CRANSTON	37,066	17,769	19,150	147	1,381 D	47.9%	51.7%	48.1%	51.9%
26,605	CUMBERLAND	12,627	5,805	6,784	38	979 D	46.0%	53.7%	46.1%	53.9%
9,577	EAST GREENWICH	4,827	3,052	1,763	12	1,289 R	63.2%	36.5%	63.4%	36.6%
48,207	EAST PROVIDENCE	21,783	9,770	11,940	73	2,170 D	44.9%	54.8%	45.0%	55.0%
3,245	EXETER	1,335	694	632	9	62 R	52.0%	47.3%	52.3%	47.7%
2,626	FOSTER	1,431	763	660	8	103 R	53.3%	46.1%	53.6%	46.4%
5,160	GLOCESTER	2,869	1,446	1,411	12	35 R	50.4%	49.2%	50.6%	49.4%
5,392	HOPKINTON	2,139	1,119	1,016	4	103 R	52.3%	47.5%	52.4%	47.6%
2,911	JAMESTOWN	2,086	1,015	1,053	18	38 D	48.7%	50.5%	49.1%	50.9%
22,037	JOHNSTON	11,300	4,345	6,916	39	2,571 D	38.5%	61.2%	38.6%	61.4%
16,182	LINCOLN	8,775	4,429	4,323	23	106 R	50.5%	49.3%	50.6%	49.4%
2,385	LITTLE COMPTON	1,512	844	658	10	186 R	55.8%	43.5%	56.2%	43.8%
29,290	MIDDLETOWN	6,335	3,168	3,120	47	48 R	50.0%	49.3%	50.4%	49.6%
7,138	NARRAGANSETT	4,807	2,307	2,470	30	163 D	48.0%	51.4%	48.3%	51.7%
34,562	NEWPORT CITY	11,239	4,952	6,216	71	1,264 D	44.1%	55.3%	44.3%	55.7%
489	NEW SHOREHAM	678	331	342	5	11 D	48.8%	50.4%	49.2%	50.8%
29,793	NORTH KINGSTOWN	8,683	4,861	3,768	54	1,093 R	56.0%	43.4%	56.3%	43.7%
24,337	NORTH PROVIDENCE	14,664	5,955	8,673	36	2,718 D	40.6%	59.1%	40.7%	59.3%
9,349	NORTH SMITHFIELD	4,731	2,139	2,581	11	442 D	45.2%	54.6%	45.3%	54.7%
76,984	PAWTUCKET	28,735	11,741	16,858	136	5,117 D	40.9%	58.7%	41.1%	58.9%
12,521	PORTSMOUTH	6,034	2,800	3,209	25	409 D	46.4%	53.2%	46.6%	53.4%
179,116	PROVIDENCE CITY	64,483	24,100	39,996	387	15,896 D	37.4%	62.0%	37.6%	62.4%
2,625	RICHMOND	1,321	622	693	6	71 D	47.1%	52.5%	47.3%	52.7%
7,489	SCITUATE	4,204	2,479	1,708	17	771 R	59.0%	40.6%	59.2%	40.8%
13,468	SMITHFIELD	6,598	3,146	3,437	15	291 D	47.7%	52.1%	47.8%	52.2%
16,913	SOUTH KINGSTOWN	6,784	3,395	3,341	48	54 R	50.0%	49.2%	50.4%	49.6%
12,559	TIVERTON	5,901	2,376	3,512	13	1,136 D	40.3%	59.5%	40.4%	59.6%
10,523	WARREN	4,634	1,824	2,790	20	966 D	39.4%	60.2%	39.5%	60.5%
83,694	WARWICK	42,202	20,642	21,414	146	772 D	48.9%	50.7%	49.1%	50.9%
17,248	WESTERLY	8,372	3,497	4,853	22	1,356 D	41.8%	58.0%	41.9%	58.1%
1,841	WEST GREENWICH	1,132	563	564	5	1 D	49.7%	49.8%	50.0%	50.0%
24,323	WEST WARWICK	11,077	4,630	6,419	28	1,789 D	41.8%	57.9%	41.9%	58.1%
46,820	WOONSOCKET	19,394	5,973	13,372	49	7,399 D	30.8%	68.9%	30.9%	69.1%
949,723	TOTAL	411,170	181,249	227,636	2,285	46,387 D	44.1%	55.4%	44.3%	55.7%

RHODE ISLAND

GOVERNOR 1976

1970 Census Population	City/Town	Total Vote	Republican	Democratic	Other	Rep.-Dem. Plurality	Percentage Total Vote Rep.	Percentage Total Vote Dem.	Percentage Major Vote Rep.	Percentage Major Vote Dem.
17,554	BARRINGTON	8,826	5,302	3,478	46	1,824 R	60.1%	39.4%	60.4%	39.6%
17,860	BRISTOL TOWN	7,537	2,977	4,523	37	1,546 D	39.5%	60.0%	39.7%	60.3%
10,087	BURRILLVILLE	4,414	1,863	2,531	20	668 D	42.2%	57.3%	42.4%	57.6%
18,716	CENTRAL FALLS	6,365	2,066	4,275	24	2,209 D	32.5%	67.2%	32.6%	67.4%
2,863	CHARLESTOWN	1,870	1,146	710	14	436 R	61.3%	38.0%	61.7%	38.3%
22,947	COVENTRY	10,815	5,727	5,050	38	677 R	53.0%	46.7%	53.1%	46.9%
74,287	CRANSTON	37,056	20,878	16,052	126	4,826 R	56.3%	43.3%	56.5%	43.5%
26,605	CUMBERLAND	12,304	5,353	6,917	34	1,564 D	43.5%	56.2%	43.6%	56.4%
9,577	EAST GREENWICH	4,717	3,091	1,606	20	1,485 R	65.5%	34.0%	65.8%	34.2%
48,207	EAST PROVIDENCE	21,229	9,284	11,852	93	2,568 D	43.7%	55.8%	43.9%	56.1%
3,245	EXETER	1,314	773	532	9	241 R	58.8%	40.5%	59.2%	40.8%
2,626	FOSTER	1,393	844	540	9	304 R	60.6%	38.8%	61.0%	39.0%
5,160	GLOCESTER	2,834	1,635	1,189	10	446 R	57.7%	42.0%	57.9%	42.1%
5,392	HOPKINTON	2,082	1,178	903	1	275 R	56.6%	43.4%	56.6%	43.4%
2,911	JAMESTOWN	2,022	1,100	909	13	191 R	54.4%	45.0%	54.8%	45.2%
22,037	JOHNSTON	11,020	3,946	7,029	45	3,083 D	35.8%	63.8%	36.0%	64.0%
16,182	LINCOLN	8,580	4,183	4,368	29	185 D	48.8%	50.9%	48.9%	51.1%
2,385	LITTLE COMPTON	1,432	904	513	15	391 R	63.1%	35.8%	63.8%	36.2%
29,290	MIDDLETOWN	6,050	2,833	3,178	39	345 D	46.8%	52.5%	47.1%	52.9%
7,138	NARRAGANSETT	4,646	2,361	2,252	33	109 R	50.8%	48.5%	51.2%	48.8%
34,562	NEWPORT CITY	10,546	4,188	6,279	79	2,091 D	39.7%	59.5%	40.0%	60.0%
489	NEW SHOREHAM	661	302	357	2	55 D	45.7%	54.0%	45.8%	54.2%
29,793	NORTH KINGSTOWN	8,482	5,199	3,232	51	1,967 R	61.3%	38.1%	61.7%	38.3%
24,337	NORTH PROVIDENCE	14,405	4,926	9,438	41	4,512 D	34.2%	65.5%	34.3%	65.7%
9,349	NORTH SMITHFIELD	4,551	2,125	2,405	21	280 D	46.7%	52.8%	46.9%	53.1%
76,984	PAWTUCKET	27,673	10,495	17,061	117	6,566 D	37.9%	61.7%	38.1%	61.9%
12,521	PORTSMOUTH	5,777	2,845	2,912	20	67 D	49.2%	50.4%	49.4%	50.6%
179,116	PROVIDENCE CITY	61,623	20,537	40,697	389	20,160 D	33.3%	66.0%	33.5%	66.5%
2,625	RICHMOND	1,295	660	629	6	31 R	51.0%	48.6%	51.2%	48.8%
7,489	SCITUATE	4,181	2,666	1,490	25	1,176 R	63.8%	35.6%	64.1%	35.9%
13,468	SMITHFIELD	6,458	3,018	3,420	20	402 D	46.7%	53.0%	46.9%	53.1%
16,913	SOUTH KINGSTOWN	6,564	3,741	2,770	53	971 R	57.0%	42.2%	57.5%	42.5%
12,559	TIVERTON	5,363	2,323	3,011	29	688 D	43.3%	56.1%	43.6%	56.4%
10,523	WARREN	4,498	1,954	2,531	13	577 D	43.4%	56.3%	43.6%	56.4%
83,694	WARWICK	41,682	21,469	20,003	210	1,466 R	51.5%	48.0%	51.8%	48.2%
17,248	WESTERLY	7,965	3,390	4,568	7	1,178 D	42.6%	57.4%	42.6%	57.4%
1,841	WEST GREENWICH	1,110	550	552	8	2 D	49.5%	49.7%	49.9%	50.1%
24,323	WEST WARWICK	10,790	4,719	6,039	32	1,320 D	43.7%	56.0%	43.9%	56.1%
46,820	WOONSOCKET	18,553	5,703	12,760	90	7,057 D	30.7%	68.8%	30.9%	69.1%
949,723	TOTAL	398,683	178,254	218,561	1,868	40,307 D	44.7%	54.8%	44.9%	55.1%

RHODE ISLAND

SENATOR 1976

1970 Census Population	City/Town	Total Vote	Republican	Democratic	Other	Rep.-Dem. Plurality	Percentage Total Vote Rep.	Percentage Total Vote Dem.	Percentage Major Vote Rep.	Percentage Major Vote Dem.
17,554	BARRINGTON	8,824	6,522	2,286	16	4,236 R	73.9%	25.9%	74.0%	26.0%
17,860	BRISTOL TOWN	7,668	4,215	3,433	20	782 R	55.0%	44.8%	55.1%	44.9%
10,087	BURRILLVILLE	4,461	2,404	2,049	8	355 R	53.9%	45.9%	54.0%	46.0%
18,716	CENTRAL FALLS	6,429	3,286	3,135	8	151 R	51.1%	48.8%	51.2%	48.8%
2,863	CHARLESTOWN	1,866	1,215	644	7	571 R	65.1%	34.5%	65.4%	34.6%
22,947	COVENTRY	10,832	6,782	4,033	17	2,749 R	62.6%	37.2%	62.7%	37.3%
74,287	CRANSTON	36,517	21,854	14,600	63	7,254 R	59.8%	40.0%	59.9%	40.1%
26,605	CUMBERLAND	12,400	7,692	4,695	13	2,997 R	62.0%	37.9%	62.1%	37.9%
9,577	EAST GREENWICH	4,740	3,591	1,145	4	2,446 R	75.8%	24.2%	75.8%	24.2%
48,207	EAST PROVIDENCE	21,428	12,462	8,934	32	3,528 R	58.2%	41.7%	58.2%	41.8%
3,245	EXETER	1,319	839	473	7	366 R	63.6%	35.9%	63.9%	36.1%
2,626	FOSTER	1,414	908	505	1	403 R	64.2%	35.7%	64.3%	35.7%
5,160	GLOCESTER	2,848	1,862	985	1	877 R	65.4%	34.6%	65.4%	34.6%
5,392	HOPKINTON	2,095	1,293	801	1	492 R	61.7%	38.2%	61.7%	38.3%
2,911	JAMESTOWN	2,049	1,256	779	14	477 R	61.3%	38.0%	61.7%	38.3%
22,037	JOHNSTON	11,020	5,624	5,384	12	240 R	51.0%	48.9%	51.1%	48.9%
16,182	LINCOLN	8,610	5,656	2,951	3	2,705 R	65.7%	34.3%	65.7%	34.3%
2,385	LITTLE COMPTON	1,451	1,020	426	5	594 R	70.3%	29.4%	70.5%	29.5%
29,290	MIDDLETOWN	6,081	3,445	2,636		809 R	56.7%	43.3%	56.7%	43.3%
7,138	NARRAGANSETT	4,617	3,001	1,601	15	1,400 R	65.0%	34.7%	65.2%	34.8%
34,562	NEWPORT CITY	10,576	5,459	5,100	17	359 R	51.6%	48.2%	51.7%	48.3%
489	NEW SHOREHAM	673	458	213	2	245 R	68.1%	31.6%	68.3%	31.7%
29,793	NORTH KINGSTOWN	8,492	5,874	2,583	35	3,291 R	69.2%	30.4%	69.5%	30.5%
24,337	NORTH PROVIDENCE	14,411	7,602	6,790	19	812 R	52.8%	47.1%	52.8%	47.2%
9,349	NORTH SMITHFIELD	4,599	2,726	1,870	3	856 R	59.3%	40.7%	59.3%	40.7%
76,984	PAWTUCKET	27,641	15,390	12,199	52	3,191 R	55.7%	44.1%	55.8%	44.2%
12,521	PORTSMOUTH	5,833	3,326	2,499	8	827 R	57.0%	42.8%	57.1%	42.9%
179,116	PROVIDENCE CITY	61,247	30,686	30,235	326	451 R	50.1%	49.4%	50.4%	49.6%
2,625	RICHMOND	1,288	780	504	4	276 R	60.6%	39.1%	60.7%	39.3%
7,489	SCITUATE	4,182	3,039	1,132	11	1,907 R	72.7%	27.1%	72.9%	27.1%
13,468	SMITHFIELD	6,472	4,035	2,425	12	1,610 R	62.3%	37.5%	62.5%	37.5%
16,913	SOUTH KINGSTOWN	6,566	4,499	2,025	42	2,474 R	68.5%	30.8%	69.0%	31.0%
12,559	TIVERTON	5,501	2,815	2,672	14	143 R	51.2%	48.6%	51.3%	48.7%
10,523	WARREN	4,536	2,596	1,933	7	663 R	57.2%	42.6%	57.3%	42.7%
83,694	WARWICK	41,578	26,500	15,003	75	11,497 R	63.7%	36.1%	63.9%	36.1%
17,248	WESTERLY	8,008	4,103	3,897	8	206 R	51.2%	48.7%	51.3%	48.7%
1,841	WEST GREENWICH	1,120	669	449	2	220 R	59.7%	40.1%	59.8%	40.2%
24,323	WEST WARWICK	10,838	6,134	4,693	11	1,441 R	56.6%	43.3%	56.7%	43.3%
46,820	WOONSOCKET	18,676	8,711	9,948	17	1,237 D	46.6%	53.3%	46.7%	53.3%
949,723	TOTAL	398,906	230,329	167,665	912	62,664 R	57.7%	42.0%	57.9%	42.1%

RHODE ISLAND

CONGRESS

CD	Year	Total Vote	Republican Vote	Republican Candidate	Democratic Vote	Democratic Candidate	Other Vote	Rep.-Dem. Plurality	Percentage Total Vote Rep.	Percentage Total Vote Dem.	Percentage Major Vote Rep.	Percentage Major Vote Dem.
1	1976	187,002	68,080	SLOCUM, JOHN J.	116,674	ST. GERMAIN, FERNAND	2,248	48,594 D	36.4%	62.4%	36.8%	63.2%
1	1974	144,384	39,096	BARONE, ERNEST	105,288	ST. GERMAIN, FERNAND		66,192 D	27.1%	72.9%	27.1%	72.9%
1	1972	193,592	67,125	FEELEY, JOHN M.	120,705	ST. GERMAIN, FERNAND	5,762	53,580 D	34.7%	62.4%	35.7%	64.3%
2	1976	201,912	45,438	IANNITTI, THOMAS V.	154,453	BEARD, EDWARD P.	2,021	109,015 D	22.5%	76.5%	22.7%	77.3%
2	1974	159,487	34,728	ROTONDO, VINCENT J.	124,759	BEARD, EDWARD P.		90,031 D	21.8%	78.2%	21.8%	78.2%
2	1972	194,400	71,661	RYAN, DONALD P.	122,739	TIERNAN, ROBERT O.		51,078 D	36.9%	63.1%	36.9%	63.1%

RHODE ISLAND

1976 GENERAL ELECTION

In addition to the county-by-county figures, 1976 data are presented by cities and towns.

President — Other vote was 715 MacBride (Libertarian); 479 McCarthy (write-in); 462 Camejo (Socialist Workers); 334 Hall (Communist); 188 Levin (Socialist Labor); 24 Anderson (write-in); 1 Maddox (write-in); 82 scattered. State-wide other vote total includes 586 write-in votes not available by county or city/town.

Governor — Other vote was 1,267 Swift (Independent); 601 Engel (Libertarian).

Senator — Other vote was Cann (Communist).

Congress — Other vote was Morrissey (Independent) in CD 1; Pacia (Independent) in CD 2.

1976 PRIMARIES

SEPTEMBER 14 REPUBLICAN

Governor — James L. Taft, unopposed.

Senator — John H. Chafee, unopposed.

Congress — Unopposed in both CD's.

SEPTEMBER 14 DEMOCRATIC

Governor — 113,625 J. Joseph Garrahy; 24,314 Giovanni Folcarelli.

Senator — 60,118 Richard P. Lorber; 60,018 Philip W. Noel; 25,456 John P. Hawkins; 5,500 Paul E. Goulding; 4,481 Ralph J. Perrotta; 2,160 John E. Caddick; 962 Earl F. Pasbach; 447 Arthur E. Marley.

Congress — Contested as follows:

CD 1 — 51,122 Fernand St. Germain; 11,689 Norman J. Jacques.
CD 2 — 59,106 Edward P. Beard; 13,419 Eugene J. McCaffrey; 6,471 Louis H. Pastore; 5,858 Martin T. Byrne.

SOUTH CAROLINA

GOVERNOR

James B. Edwards (R). Elected 1974 to a four-year term.

SENATORS

Ernest F. Hollings (D). Re-elected 1974 to a six-year term. Previously elected 1968, and in 1966 to fill out term vacated by the death of Senator Olin D. Johnston.

Strom Thurmond (R). Re-elected 1972 to a six-year term. Previously elected 1966, 1960 and in 1956 to fill out term vacated by his own resignation in April 1956; had been elected to this term in 1954 as an Independent Democrat. Also served in the Senate from December 1954 to January 1955. Changed party affiliation from Democrat to Republican in September 1964.

REPRESENTATIVES

1. Mendel J. Davis (D)
2. Floyd Spence (R)
3. Butler Derrick (D)
4. James R. Mann (D)
5. Kenneth L. Holland (D)
6. John W. Jenrette (D)

POSTWAR VOTE FOR GOVERNOR

		Republican		Democratic				Percentage			
								Total Vote		Major Vote	
Year	Total Vote	Vote	Candidate	Vote	Candidate	Other Vote	Rep.-Dem. Plurality	Rep.	Dem.	Rep.	Dem.
1974	523,199	266,109	Edwards, James B.	248,938	Dorn, W. J. Bryan	8,152	17,171 R	50.9%	47.6%	51.7%	48.3%
1970	484,857	221,233	Watson, Albert W.	250,551	West, John C.	13,073	29,318 D	45.6%	51.7%	46.9%	53.1%
1966	439,942	184,088	Rogers, Joseph O.	255,854	McNair, Robert E.	–	71,766 D	41.8%	58.2%	41.8%	58.2%
1962	253,721	–	–	253,704	Russell, Donald S.	17	253,704 D	–	100.0%	–	100.0%
1958	77,740	–	–	77,714	Hollings, Ernest F.	26	77,714 D	–	100.0%	–	100.0%
1954	214,212	–	–	214,204	Timmerman, George B.	8	214,204 D	–	100.0%	–	100.0%
1950	50,642	–	–	50,633	Byrnes, James F.	9	50,633 D	–	100.0%	–	100.0%
1946	26,520	–	–	26,520	Thurmond, Strom	–	26,520 D	–	100.0%	–	100.0%

POSTWAR VOTE FOR SENATOR

		Republican		Democratic				Percentage			
								Total Vote		Major Vote	
Year	Total Vote	Vote	Candidate	Vote	Candidate	Other Vote	Rep.-Dem. Plurality	Rep.	Dem.	Rep.	Dem.
1974	512,397	146,645	Bush, Gwenyfred	356,126	Hollings, Ernest F.	9,626	209,481 D	28.6%	69.5%	29.2%	70.8%
1972	672,246	426,601	Thurmond, Strom	245,457	Zeigler, Eugene N.	188	181,144 R	63.5%	36.5%	63.5%	36.5%
1968	652,855	248,780	Parker, Marshall	404,060	Hollings, Ernest F.	15	155,280 D	38.1%	61.9%	38.1%	61.9%
1966	436,252	271,297	Thurmond, Strom	164,955	Morrah, Bradley	–	106,342 R	62.2%	37.8%	62.2%	37.8%
1966s	435,822	212,032	Parker, Marshall	223,790	Hollings, Ernest F.	–	11,758 D	48.7%	51.3%	48.7%	51.3%
1962	312,647	133,930	Workman, W. D.	178,712	Johnston, Olin D.	5	44,782 D	42.8%	57.2%	42.8%	57.2%
1960	330,266	–	–	330,164	Thurmond, Strom	102	330,164 D	–	100.0%	–	100.0%
1956	279,845	49,695	Crawford, Leon P.	230,150	Johnston, Olin D.	–	180,455 D	17.8%	82.2%	17.8%	82.2%
1956s	251,907	–	–	251,907	Thurmond, Strom	–	251,907 D	–	100.0%	–	100.0%
1954	227,232	–	–	83,525	Brown, Edgar A.	143,707	83,525 D	–	36.8%	–	100.0%
1950	50,277	–	–	50,240	Johnston, Olin D.	37	50,240 D	–	99.9%	–	100.0%
1948	141,006	5,008	Gerald, J. Bates	135,998	Maybank, Burnet R.	–	130,990 D	3.6%	96.4%	3.6%	96.4%

One each of the 1966 and 1956 elections was for a short term to fill a vacancy. In 1954, Strom Thurmond polled 143,444 votes as an Independent Democratic write-in candidate (63.1% of the total vote) and won the election with a 59,919 plurality.

SOUTH CAROLINA

Districts Established November 11, 1971

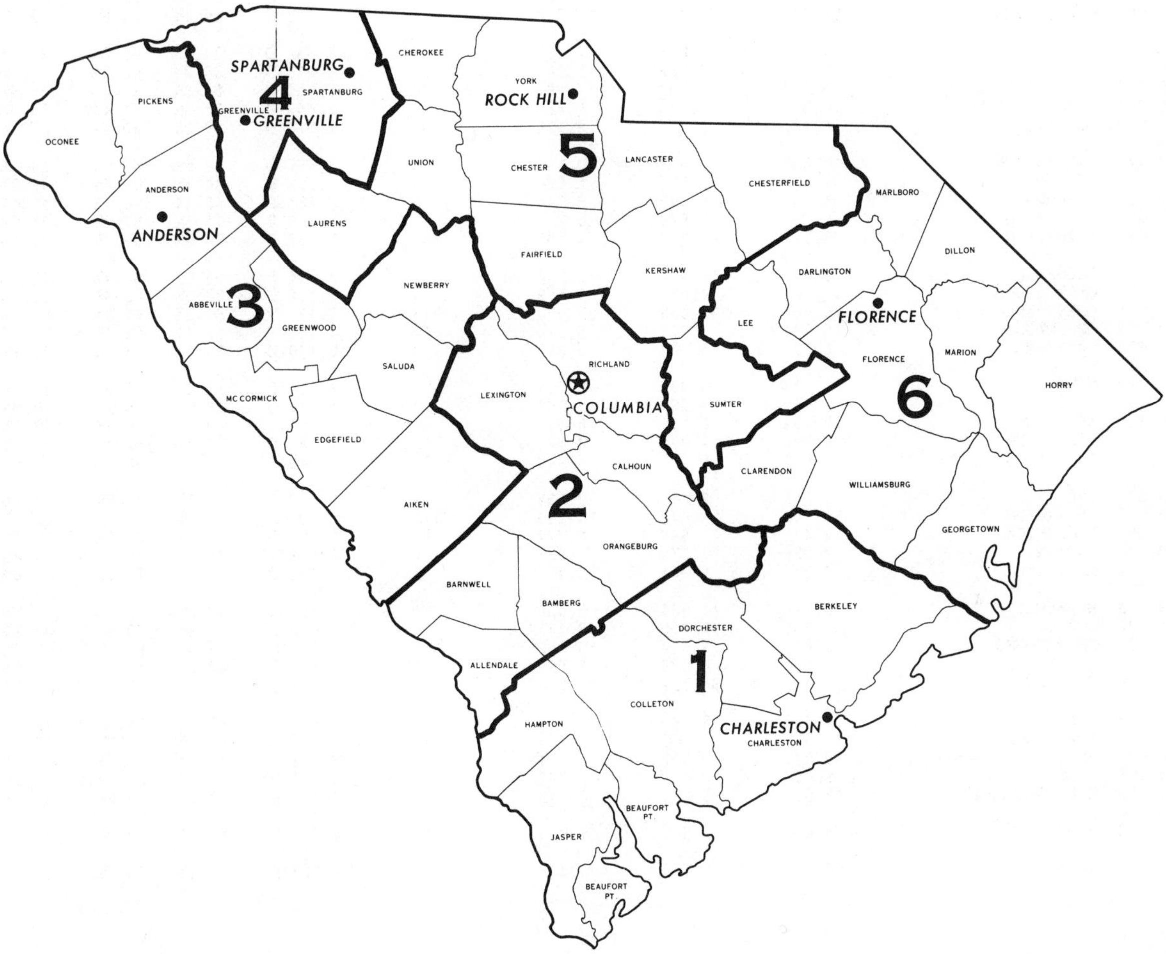

SOUTH CAROLINA

PRESIDENT 1976

1970 Census Population	County	Total Vote	Republican	Democratic	Other	Rep.-Dem. Plurality	Percentage Total Vote Rep.	Percentage Total Vote Dem.	Percentage Major Vote Rep.	Percentage Major Vote Dem.
21,112	ABBEVILLE	6,527	1,791	4,700	36	2,909 D	27.4%	72.0%	27.6%	72.4%
91,023	AIKEN	31,173	16,011	14,927	235	1,084 R	51.4%	47.9%	51.8%	48.2%
9,692	ALLENDALE	3,709	1,064	2,634	11	1,570 D	28.7%	71.0%	28.8%	71.2%
105,474	ANDERSON	28,654	9,496	19,002	156	9,506 D	33.1%	66.3%	33.3%	66.7%
15,950	BAMBERG	5,218	1,849	3,330	39	1,481 D	35.4%	63.8%	35.7%	64.3%
17,176	BARNWELL	6,652	2,569	4,083		1,514 D	38.6%	61.4%	38.6%	61.4%
51,136	BEAUFORT	12,052	5,935	6,049	68	114 D	49.2%	50.2%	49.5%	50.5%
56,199	BERKELEY	16,795	6,981	9,741	73	2,760 D	41.6%	58.0%	41.7%	58.3%
10,780	CALHOUN	3,468	1,382	2,055	31	673 D	39.9%	59.3%	40.2%	59.8%
247,650	CHARLESTON	69,265	34,010	34,328	927	318 D	49.1%	49.6%	49.8%	50.2%
36,791	CHEROKEE	11,732	3,931	7,765	36	3,834 D	33.5%	66.2%	33.6%	66.4%
29,811	CHESTER	8,212	2,982	5,200	30	2,218 D	36.3%	63.3%	36.4%	63.6%
33,667	CHESTERFIELD	10,250	2,537	7,687	26	5,150 D	24.8%	75.0%	24.8%	75.2%
25,604	CLARENDON	8,561	3,040	5,489	32	2,449 D	35.5%	64.1%	35.6%	64.4%
27,622	COLLETON	8,522	3,324	5,134	64	1,810 D	39.0%	60.2%	39.3%	60.7%
53,442	DARLINGTON	16,899	6,678	10,165	56	3,487 D	39.5%	60.2%	39.6%	60.4%
28,838	DILLON	7,639	2,527	5,089	23	2,562 D	33.1%	66.6%	33.2%	66.8%
32,421	DORCHESTER	14,779	6,695	8,046	38	1,351 D	45.3%	54.4%	45.4%	54.6%
15,692	EDGEFIELD	5,144	1,878	3,216	50	1,338 D	36.5%	62.5%	36.9%	63.1%
19,999	FAIRFIELD	5,990	1,817	4,155	18	2,338 D	30.3%	69.4%	30.4%	69.6%
89,636	FLORENCE	29,938	13,539	16,294	105	2,755 D	45.2%	54.4%	45.4%	54.6%
33,500	GEORGETOWN	11,293	4,068	7,169	56	3,101 D	36.0%	63.5%	36.2%	63.8%
240,546	GREENVILLE	75,961	39,099	35,923	939	3,176 R	51.5%	47.3%	52.1%	47.9%
49,686	GREENWOOD	15,991	5,974	9,976	41	4,002 D	37.4%	62.4%	37.5%	62.5%
15,878	HAMPTON	5,725	1,773	3,923	29	2,150 D	31.0%	68.5%	31.1%	68.9%
69,992	HORRY	25,117	9,339	15,720	58	6,381 D	37.2%	62.6%	37.3%	62.7%
11,885	JASPER	4,140	1,221	2,903	16	1,682 D	29.5%	70.1%	29.6%	70.4%
34,727	KERSHAW	12,402	6,126	6,211	65	85 D	49.4%	50.1%	49.7%	50.3%
43,328	LANCASTER	13,394	4,997	8,324	73	3,327 D	37.3%	62.1%	37.5%	62.5%
49,713	LAURENS	12,831	5,300	7,440	91	2,140 D	41.3%	58.0%	41.6%	58.4%
18,323	LEE	6,257	2,357	3,869	31	1,512 D	37.7%	61.8%	37.9%	62.1%
89,012	LEXINGTON	36,143	21,442	14,339	362	7,103 R	59.3%	39.7%	59.9%	40.1%
7,955	MCCORMICK	2,431	640	1,774	17	1,134 D	26.3%	73.0%	26.5%	73.5%
30,270	MARION	9,024	3,076	5,927	21	2,851 D	34.1%	65.7%	34.2%	65.8%
27,151	MARLBORO	7,377	1,961	5,409	7	3,448 D	26.6%	73.3%	26.6%	73.4%
29,273	NEWBERRY	10,024	4,931	5,034	59	103 D	49.2%	50.2%	49.5%	50.5%
40,728	OCONEE	12,333	3,805	8,447	81	4,642 D	30.9%	68.5%	31.1%	68.9%
69,789	ORANGEBURG	22,604	8,794	13,652	158	4,858 D	38.9%	60.4%	39.2%	60.8%
58,956	PICKENS	16,655	8,029	8,505	121	476 D	48.2%	51.1%	48.6%	51.4%
233,868	RICHLAND	70,153	32,727	36,855	571	4,128 D	46.7%	52.5%	47.0%	53.0%
14,528	SALUDA	4,853	2,085	2,715	53	630 D	43.0%	55.9%	43.4%	56.6%
173,631	SPARTANBURG	48,820	20,456	27,925	439	7,469 D	41.9%	57.2%	42.3%	57.7%
78,885	SUMTER	19,949	9,332	10,471	146	1,139 D	46.8%	52.5%	47.1%	52.9%
29,133	UNION	9,867	3,463	6,363	41	2,900 D	35.1%	64.5%	35.2%	64.8%
34,203	WILLIAMSBURG	14,055	5,275	8,745	35	3,470 D	37.5%	62.2%	37.6%	62.4%
85,216	YORK	24,005	9,843	14,099	63	4,256 D	41.0%	58.7%	41.1%	58.9%
2,589,891	TOTAL	802,583	346,149	450,807	5,627	104,658 D	43.1%	56.2%	43.4%	56.6%

SOUTH CAROLINA

CONGRESS

CD	Year	Total Vote	Republican Vote	Republican Candidate	Democratic Vote	Democratic Candidate	Other Vote	Rep.-Dem. Plurality	Percentage Total Vote Rep.	Percentage Total Vote Dem.	Percentage Major Vote Rep.	Percentage Major Vote Dem.
1	1976	130,503	40,598	ROWELL, LONNIE	89,891	DAVIS, MENDEL J.	14	49,293 D	31.1%	68.9%	31.1%	68.9%
1	1974	86,777	22,450	RAST, GEORGE B.	63,111	DAVIS, MENDEL J.	1,216	40,661 D	25.9%	72.7%	26.2%	73.8%
1	1972	113,094	51,469	LIMEHOUSE, J. SIDI	61,625	DAVIS, MENDEL J.		10,156 D	45.5%	54.5%	45.5%	54.5%
2	1976	144,995	83,426	SPENCE, FLOYD	60,602	LIVINGSTON, CLYDE B.	967	22,824 R	57.5%	41.8%	57.9%	42.1%
2	1974	105,091	58,936	SPENCE, FLOYD	45,205	PERRY, MATTHEW J.	950	13,731 R	56.1%	43.0%	56.6%	43.4%
2	1972	83,590	83,543	SPENCE, FLOYD			47	83,543 R	99.9%		100.0%	
3	1976	117,855			117,740	DERRICK, BUTLER	115	117,740 D		99.9%		100.0%
3	1974	89,166	34,046	PARKER, MARSHALL	55,120	DERRICK, BUTLER		21,074 D	38.2%	61.8%	38.2%	61.8%
3	1972	109,757	27,173	ETHRIDGE, ROY	82,579	DORN, W. J. BRYAN	5	55,406 D	24.8%	75.2%	24.8%	75.2%
3	1970	80,689	19,981	BALLARD, H. GRADY	60,708	DORN, W. J. BRYAN		40,727 D	24.8%	75.2%	24.8%	75.2%
3	1968	112,057	35,463	GRISSO, JOHN	74,104	DORN, W. J. BRYAN	2,490	38,641 D	31.6%	66.1%	32.4%	67.6%
3	1966	74,205	31,331	GRISSO, JOHN	42,874	DORN, W. J. BRYAN		11,543 D	42.2%	57.8%	42.2%	57.8%
4	1976	124,765	32,983	WATKINS, ROBERT L.	91,721	MANN, JAMES R.	61	58,738 D	26.4%	73.5%	26.4%	73.6%
4	1974	71,255	26,185	WATKINS, ROBERT L.	45,070	MANN, JAMES R.		18,885 D	36.7%	63.3%	36.7%	63.3%
4	1972	98,389	33,363	WHATLEY, WAYNE N.	64,989	MANN, JAMES R.	37	31,626 D	33.9%	66.1%	33.9%	66.1%
5	1976	128,510	62,095	RICHARDSON, BOBBY	66,073	HOLLAND, KENNETH L.	342	3,978 D	48.3%	51.4%	48.4%	51.6%
5	1974	77,545	29,294	PHILLIPS, B. LEONARD	47,614	HOLLAND, KENNETH L.	637	18,320 D	37.8%	61.4%	38.1%	61.9%
5	1972	108,968	42,620	PHILLIPS, B. LEONARD	66,343	GETTYS, TOM S.	5	23,723 D	39.1%	60.9%	39.1%	60.9%
6	1976	136,896	60,288	YOUNG, EDWARD L.	75,916	JENRETTE, JOHN W.	692	15,628 D	44.0%	55.5%	44.3%	55.7%
6	1974	87,378	41,982	YOUNG, EDWARD L.	45,396	JENRETTE, JOHN W.		3,414 D	48.0%	52.0%	48.0%	52.0%
6	1972	116,859	63,527	YOUNG, EDWARD L.	53,324	JENRETTE, JOHN W.	8	10,203 R	54.4%	45.6%	54.4%	45.6%

SOUTH CAROLINA

1976 GENERAL ELECTION

President — Other vote was 2,996 Anderson (American); 1,950 Maddox (Independent); 289 McCarthy (write-in); 53 MacBride (write-in); 8 Camejo (write-in); 2 LaRouche (write-in); 1 Hall (write-in); 328 scattered.

Congress — Other vote was scattered in CD's 1, 3 and 4; 950 O'Neal (Independent) and 17 scattered in CD 2; 298 Hough (Independent) and 44 scattered in CD 5; 687 Dillingham (Independent) and 5 scattered in CD 6.

1976 PRIMARIES

JUNE 8 REPUBLICAN

Congress — Unopposed in four CD's. No candidate in CD 3. George D. Grice, the unopposed candidate in CD 1, withdrew after the primary and Lonnie Rowell was substituted by the local party committee. Contested as follows:

CD 4 — 4,857 Robert L. Watkins; 2,677 Charles W. Harte.

JUNE 8 DEMOCRATIC

Congress — Unopposed in four CD's. Contested as follows:

CD 1 — 37,811 Mendel J. Davis; 6,926 Milton J. Dukes.
CD 6 — 51,128 John W. Jenrette; 22,054 Cooper Tedder; 10,252 Bill R. Craig; 4,119 Richard N. Bennett; 1,390 Goldie Gause.

SOUTH DAKOTA

GOVERNOR

Richard F. Kneip (D). Re-elected 1974 to a four-year term. Previously elected 1972, 1970.

SENATORS

James Abourezk (D). Elected 1972 to a six-year term.

George S. McGovern (D). Re-elected 1974 to a six-year term. Previously elected 1968, 1962.

REPRESENTATIVES

1. Larry Pressler (R)
2. James Abdnor (R)

POSTWAR VOTE FOR GOVERNOR

		Republican		Democratic				Percentage			
								Total Vote		Major Vote	
Year	Total Vote	Vote	Candidate	Vote	Candidate	Other Vote	Rep.-Dem. Plurality	Rep.	Dem.	Rep.	Dem.
1974	278,228	129,077	Olson, John E.	149,151	Kneip, Richard F.	–	20,074 D	46.4%	53.6%	46.4%	53.6%
1972	308,177	123,165	Thompson, Carveth	185,012	Kneip, Richard F.	–	61,847 D	40.0%	60.0%	40.0%	60.0%
1970	239,963	108,347	Farrar, Frank	131,616	Kneip, Richard F.	–	23,269 D	45.2%	54.8%	45.2%	54.8%
1968	276,906	159,646	Farrar, Frank	117,260	Chamberlin, Robert	–	42,386 R	57.7%	42.3%	57.7%	42.3%
1966	228,214	131,710	Boe, Nils A.	96,504	Chamberlin, Robert	–	35,206 R	57.7%	42.3%	57.7%	42.3%
1964	290,570	150,151	Boe, Nils A.	140,419	Lindley, John F.	–	9,732 R	51.7%	48.3%	51.7%	48.3%
1962	256,120	143,682	Gubbrud, Archie M.	112,438	Herseth, Ralph	–	31,244 R	56.1%	43.9%	56.1%	43.9%
1960	304,625	154,530	Gubbrud, Archie M.	150,095	Herseth, Ralph	–	4,435 R	50.7%	49.3%	50.7%	49.3%
1958	258,281	125,520	Saunders, Phil	132,761	Herseth, Ralph	–	7,241 D	48.6%	51.4%	48.6%	51.4%
1956	292,017	158,819	Foss, Joe J.	133,198	Herseth, Ralph	–	25,621 R	54.4%	45.6%	54.4%	45.6%
1954	236,255	133,878	Foss, Joe J.	102,377	Martin, Ed. C.	–	31,501 R	56.7%	43.3%	56.7%	43.3%
1952	289,515	203,102	Anderson, Sigurd	86,413	Iverson, Sherman A.	–	116,689 R	70.2%	29.8%	70.2%	29.8%
1950	253,316	154,254	Anderson, Sigurd	99,062	Robbie, Joseph	–	55,192 R	60.9%	39.1%	60.9%	39.1%
1948	245,372	149,883	Mickelson, George	95,489	Volz, Harold J.	–	54,394 R	61.1%	38.9%	61.1%	38.9%
1946	162,292	108,998	Mickelson, George	53,294	Haeder, Richard	–	55,704 R	67.2%	32.8%	67.2%	32.8%

The term of office of South Dakota's Governor was increased from two to four years effective with the 1974 election.

POSTWAR VOTE FOR SENATOR

		Republican		Democratic				Percentage			
								Total Vote		Major Vote	
Year	Total Vote	Vote	Candidate	Vote	Candidate	Other Vote	Rep.-Dem. Plurality	Rep.	Dem.	Rep.	Dem.
1974	278,884	130,955	Thorsness, Leo K.	147,929	McGovern, George S.	–	16,974 D	47.0%	53.0%	47.0%	53.0%
1972	306,386	131,613	Hirsch, Robert W.	174,773	Abourezk, James	–	43,160 D	43.0%	57.0%	43.0%	57.0%
1968	279,912	120,951	Gubbrud, Archie M.	158,961	McGovern, George S.	–	38,010 D	43.2%	56.8%	43.2%	56.8%
1966	227,080	150,517	Mundt, Karl E.	76,563	Wright, Donn H.	–	73,954 R	66.3%	33.7%	66.3%	33.7%
1962	254,319	126,861	Bottum, Joe H.	127,458	McGovern, George S.	–	597 D	49.9%	50.1%	49.9%	50.1%
1960	305,442	160,181	Mundt, Karl E.	145,261	McGovern, George S.	–	14,920 R	52.4%	47.6%	52.4%	47.6%
1956	290,622	147,621	Case, Francis	143,001	Holum, Kenneth	–	4,620 R	50.8%	49.2%	50.8%	49.2%
1954	235,745	135,071	Mundt, Karl E.	100,674	Holum, Kenneth	–	34,397 R	57.3%	42.7%	57.3%	42.7%
1950	251,362	160,670	Case, Francis	90,692	Engel, John A.	–	69,978 R	63.9%	36.1%	63.9%	36.1%
1948	242,833	144,084	Mundt, Karl E.	98,749	Engel, John A.	–	45,335 R	59.3%	40.7%	59.3%	40.7%

SOUTH DAKOTA

Districts Established March 25, 1971

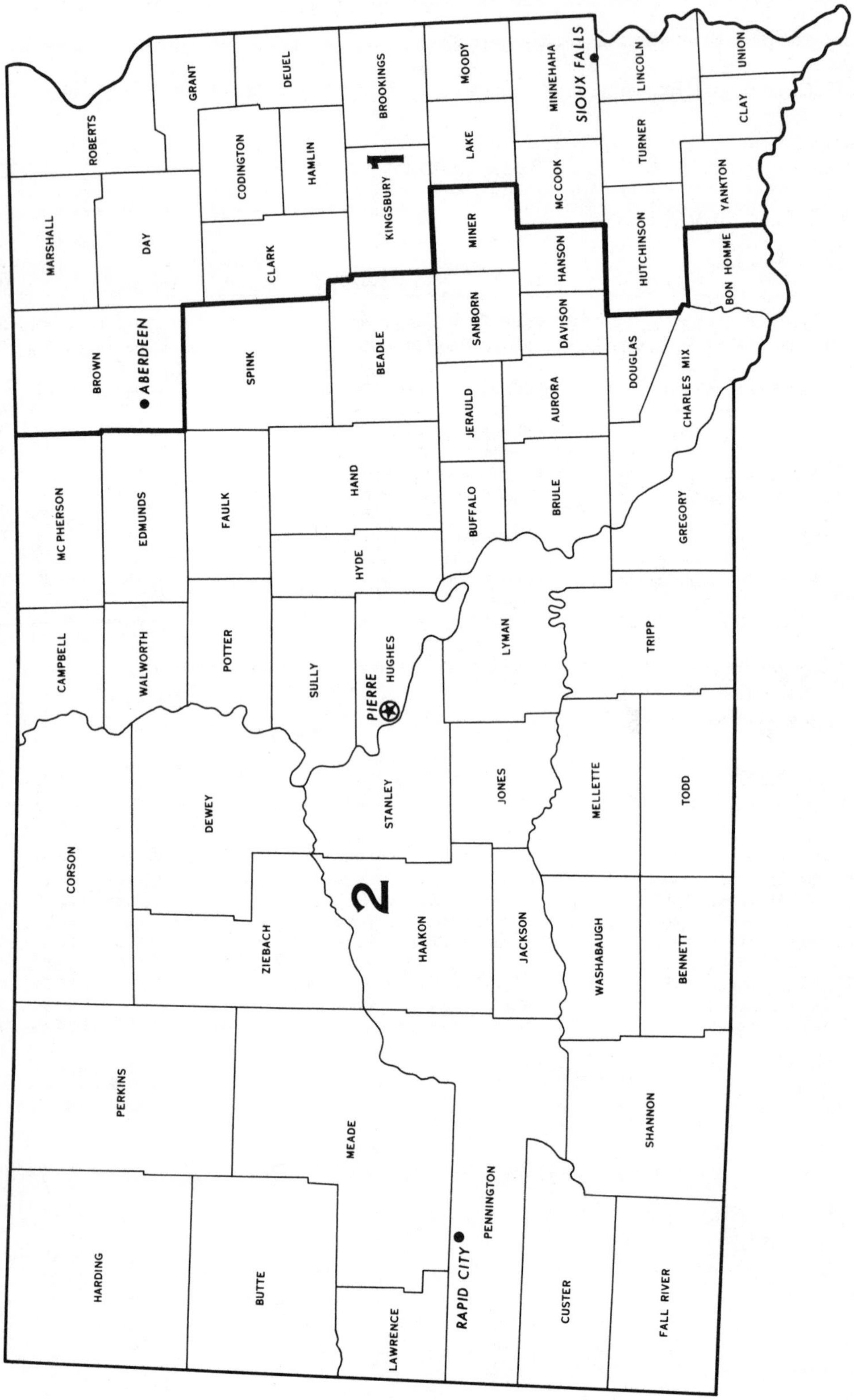

SOUTH DAKOTA

PRESIDENT 1976

1970 Census Population	County	Total Vote	Republican	Democratic	Other	Rep.-Dem. Plurality	Percentage Total Vote Rep.	Percentage Total Vote Dem.	Percentage Major Vote Rep.	Percentage Major Vote Dem.
4,183	AURORA	2,109	831	1,269	9	438 D	39.4%	60.2%	39.6%	60.4%
20,877	BEADLE	9,666	4,758	4,846	62	88 D	49.2%	50.1%	49.5%	50.5%
3,088	BENNETT	1,111	610	481	20	129 R	54.9%	43.3%	55.9%	44.1%
8,577	BON HOMME	4,073	1,897	2,154	22	257 D	46.6%	52.9%	46.8%	53.2%
22,158	BROOKINGS	10,026	5,278	4,685	63	593 R	52.6%	46.7%	53.0%	47.0%
36,920	BROWN	16,633	7,609	8,888	136	1,279 D	45.7%	53.4%	46.1%	53.9%
5,870	BRULE	2,723	1,175	1,534	14	359 D	43.2%	56.3%	43.4%	56.6%
1,739	BUFFALO	434	194	240		46 D	44.7%	55.3%	44.7%	55.3%
7,825	BUTTE	3,472	2,055	1,366	51	689 R	59.2%	39.3%	60.1%	39.9%
2,866	CAMPBELL	1,391	897	489	5	408 R	64.5%	35.2%	64.7%	35.3%
9,994	CHARLES MIX	4,394	1,779	2,593	22	814 D	40.5%	59.0%	40.7%	59.3%
5,515	CLARK	2,838	1,449	1,376	13	73 R	51.1%	48.5%	51.3%	48.7%
12,923	CLAY	5,301	2,647	2,593	61	54 R	49.9%	48.9%	50.5%	49.5%
19,140	CODINGTON	9,213	4,504	4,680	29	176 D	48.9%	50.8%	49.0%	51.0%
4,994	CORSON	1,823	846	967	10	121 D	46.4%	53.0%	46.7%	53.3%
4,698	CUSTER	2,405	1,373	995	37	378 R	57.1%	41.4%	58.0%	42.0%
17,319	DAVISON	8,248	3,688	4,510	50	822 D	44.7%	54.7%	45.0%	55.0%
8,713	DAY	4,257	1,617	2,610	30	993 D	38.0%	61.3%	38.3%	61.7%
5,686	DEUEL	2,652	1,177	1,465	10	288 D	44.4%	55.2%	44.5%	55.5%
5,170	DEWEY	1,534	820	706	8	114 R	53.5%	46.0%	53.7%	46.3%
4,569	DOUGLAS	2,295	1,315	975	5	340 R	57.3%	42.5%	57.4%	42.6%
5,548	EDMUNDS	2,932	1,294	1,629	9	335 D	44.1%	55.6%	44.3%	55.7%
7,505	FALL RIVER	3,615	2,046	1,537	32	509 R	56.6%	42.5%	57.1%	42.9%
3,893	FAULK	1,937	868	1,063	6	195 D	44.8%	54.9%	45.0%	55.0%
9,005	GRANT	4,464	2,051	2,398	15	347 D	45.9%	53.7%	46.1%	53.9%
6,710	GREGORY	3,145	1,475	1,658	12	183 D	46.9%	52.7%	47.1%	52.9%
2,802	HAAKON	1,312	812	477	23	335 R	61.9%	36.4%	63.0%	37.0%
5,520	HAMLIN	2,866	1,452	1,402	12	50 R	50.7%	48.9%	50.9%	49.1%
5,883	HAND	2,994	1,510	1,477	7	33 R	50.4%	49.3%	50.6%	49.4%
3,781	HANSON	1,707	693	1,005	9	312 D	40.6%	58.9%	40.8%	59.2%
1,855	HARDING	945	470	459	16	11 R	49.7%	48.6%	50.6%	49.4%
11,632	HUGHES	6,536	3,997	2,506	33	1,491 R	61.2%	38.3%	61.5%	38.5%
10,379	HUTCHINSON	4,906	2,822	2,062	22	760 R	57.5%	42.0%	57.8%	42.2%
2,515	HYDE	1,263	687	572	4	115 R	54.4%	45.3%	54.6%	45.4%
1,531	JACKSON	865	532	313	20	219 R	61.5%	36.2%	63.0%	37.0%
3,310	JERAULD	1,669	821	845	3	24 D	49.2%	50.6%	49.3%	50.7%
1,882	JONES	890	515	374	1	141 R	57.9%	42.0%	57.9%	42.1%
7,657	KINGSBURY	3,617	1,844	1,762	11	82 R	51.0%	48.7%	51.1%	48.9%
11,456	LAKE	5,476	2,530	2,930	16	400 D	46.2%	53.5%	46.3%	53.7%
17,453	LAWRENCE	7,449	4,206	3,102	141	1,104 R	56.5%	41.6%	57.6%	42.4%
11,761	LINCOLN	6,084	3,105	2,957	22	148 R	51.0%	48.6%	51.2%	48.8%
4,060	LYMAN	1,739	892	831	16	61 R	51.3%	47.8%	51.8%	48.2%
7,246	MCCOOK	3,578	1,744	1,822	12	78 D	48.7%	50.9%	48.9%	51.1%
5,022	MCPHERSON	2,367	1,662	693	12	969 R	70.2%	29.3%	70.6%	29.4%
5,965	MARSHALL	2,967	1,233	1,721	13	488 D	41.6%	58.0%	41.7%	58.3%
17,020	MEADE	5,690	3,096	2,478	116	618 R	54.4%	43.6%	55.5%	44.5%
2,420	MELLETTE	949	508	429	12	79 R	53.5%	45.2%	54.2%	45.8%
4,454	MINER	2,140	839	1,289	12	450 D	39.2%	60.2%	39.4%	60.6%
95,209	MINNEHAHA	45,556	23,286	22,068	202	1,218 R	51.1%	48.4%	51.3%	48.7%
7,622	MOODY	3,428	1,475	1,942	11	467 D	43.0%	56.7%	43.2%	56.8%
59,349	PENNINGTON	23,699	13,352	10,058	289	3,294 R	56.3%	42.4%	57.0%	43.0%
4,769	PERKINS	2,592	1,298	1,262	32	36 R	50.1%	48.7%	50.7%	49.3%
4,449	POTTER	2,052	1,136	908	8	228 R	55.4%	44.2%	55.6%	44.4%
11,678	ROBERTS	4,820	1,915	2,890	15	975 D	39.7%	60.0%	39.9%	60.1%
3,697	SANBORN	1,912	881	1,025	6	144 D	46.1%	53.6%	46.2%	53.8%
8,198	SHANNON	1,081	301	756	24	455 D	27.8%	69.9%	28.5%	71.5%
10,595	SPINK	4,679	2,003	2,650	26	647 D	42.8%	56.6%	43.0%	57.0%
2,457	STANLEY	1,189	637	548	4	89 R	53.6%	46.1%	53.8%	46.2%
2,362	SULLY	1,139	630	505	4	125 R	55.3%	44.3%	55.5%	44.5%
6,606	TODD	1,434	583	826	25	243 D	40.7%	57.6%	41.4%	58.6%
8,171	TRIPP	3,817	1,980	1,822	15	158 R	51.9%	47.7%	52.1%	47.9%
9,872	TURNER	4,618	2,694	1,906	18	788 R	58.3%	41.3%	58.6%	41.4%
9,643	UNION	4,860	2,297	2,540	23	243 D	47.3%	52.3%	47.5%	52.5%
7,842	WALWORTH	3,728	2,187	1,516	25	671 R	58.7%	40.7%	59.1%	40.9%
1,389	WASHABAUGH	526	229	276	21	47 D	43.5%	52.5%	45.3%	54.7%
19,039	YANKTON	8,087	4,029	3,987	71	42 R	49.8%	49.3%	50.3%	49.7%
2,221	ZIEBACH	761	369	370	22	1 D	48.5%	48.6%	49.9%	50.1%
666,257	TOTAL	300,678	151,505	147,068	2,105	4,437 R	50.4%	48.9%	50.7%	49.3%

SOUTH DAKOTA

CONGRESS

CD	Year	Total Vote	Republican Vote	Republican Candidate	Democratic Vote	Democratic Candidate	Other Vote	Rep.-Dem. Plurality	Percentage Total Vote Rep.	Percentage Total Vote Dem.	Percentage Major Vote Rep.	Percentage Major Vote Dem.
1	1976	152,402	121,587	PRESSLER, LARRY	29,533	GUFFEY, JAMES V.	1,282	92,054 R	79.8%	19.4%	80.5%	19.5%
1	1974	141,605	78,266	PRESSLER, LARRY	63,339	DENHOLM, FRANK E.		14,927 R	55.3%	44.7%	55.3%	44.7%
1	1972	156,031	61,589	VICKERMAN, JOHN	94,442	DENHOLM, FRANK E.		32,853 D	39.5%	60.5%	39.5%	60.5%
2	1976	142,569	99,601	ABDNOR, JAMES	42,968	MICKELSON, GRACE		56,633 R	69.9%	30.1%	69.9%	30.1%
2	1974	130,865	88,746	ABDNOR, JAMES	42,119	WEILAND, JACK		46,627 R	67.8%	32.2%	67.8%	32.2%
2	1972	144,961	79,546	ABDNOR, JAMES	65,415	MCKEEVER, PATRICK		14,131 R	54.9%	45.1%	54.9%	45.1%

TENNESSEE

PRESIDENT 1976

1970 Census Population	County	Total Vote	Republican	Democratic	Other	Rep.-Dem. Plurality	Percentage Total Vote Rep.	Percentage Total Vote Dem.	Percentage Major Vote Rep.	Percentage Major Vote Dem.
29,936	OBION	10,320	2,986	7,204	130	4,218 D	28.9%	69.8%	29.3%	70.7%
14,866	OVERTON	5,047	1,115	3,897	35	2,782 D	22.1%	77.2%	22.2%	77.8%
5,238	PERRY	2,201	520	1,660	21	1,140 D	23.6%	75.4%	23.9%	76.1%
3,774	PICKETT	1,944	986	948	10	38 R	50.7%	48.8%	51.0%	49.0%
11,669	POLK	5,155	1,835	3,284	36	1,449 D	35.6%	63.7%	35.8%	64.2%
35,487	PUTNAM	12,708	4,079	8,485	144	4,406 D	32.1%	66.8%	32.5%	67.5%
17,202	RHEA	7,241	3,449	3,735	57	286 D	47.6%	51.6%	48.0%	52.0%
38,881	ROANE	16,491	7,121	9,216	154	2,095 D	43.2%	55.9%	43.6%	56.4%
29,102	ROBERTSON	10,114	2,505	7,547	62	5,042 D	24.8%	74.6%	24.9%	75.1%
59,428	RUTHERFORD	23,082	7,921	14,854	307	6,933 D	34.3%	64.4%	34.8%	65.2%
14,762	SCOTT	4,730	2,432	2,260	38	172 R	51.4%	47.8%	51.8%	48.2%
6,331	SEQUATCHIE	2,842	1,065	1,733	44	668 D	37.5%	61.0%	38.1%	61.9%
28,241	SEVIER	11,814	7,608	3,993	213	3,615 R	64.4%	33.8%	65.6%	34.4%
722,014	SHELBY	279,601	128,646	147,893	3,062	19,247 D	46.0%	52.9%	46.5%	53.5%
12,509	SMITH	5,136	1,332	3,753	51	2,421 D	25.9%	73.1%	26.2%	73.8%
7,319	STEWART	2,972	510	2,442	20	1,932 D	17.2%	82.2%	17.3%	82.7%
127,329	SULLIVAN	46,762	22,087	23,353	1,322	1,266 D	47.2%	49.9%	48.6%	51.4%
56,106	SUMNER	22,007	7,946	13,848	213	5,902 D	36.1%	62.9%	36.5%	63.5%
28,001	TIPTON	9,072	3,329	5,667	76	2,338 D	36.7%	62.5%	37.0%	63.0%
5,155	TROUSDALE	1,726	332	1,385	9	1,053 D	19.2%	80.2%	19.3%	80.7%
15,254	UNICOI	5,782	3,211	2,526	45	685 R	55.5%	43.7%	56.0%	44.0%
9,072	UNION	3,457	1,801	1,631	25	170 R	52.1%	47.2%	52.5%	47.5%
3,758	VAN BUREN	1,442	346	1,085	11	739 D	24.0%	75.2%	24.2%	75.8%
26,972	WARREN	9,115	2,364	6,666	85	4,302 D	25.9%	73.1%	26.2%	73.8%
73,924	WASHINGTON	29,032	14,770	13,951	311	819 R	50.9%	48.1%	51.4%	48.6%
12,365	WAYNE	4,511	2,597	1,891	23	706 R	57.6%	41.9%	57.9%	42.1%
28,827	WEAKLEY	9,696	2,875	6,605	216	3,730 D	29.7%	68.1%	30.3%	69.7%
16,355	WHITE	5,314	1,382	3,874	58	2,492 D	26.0%	72.9%	26.3%	73.7%
34,330	WILLIAMSON	16,266	7,880	8,183	203	303 D	48.4%	50.3%	49.1%	50.9%
36,999	WILSON	15,362	4,696	10,537	129	5,841 D	30.6%	68.6%	30.8%	69.2%
3,924,164	TOTAL	1,476,345	633,969	825,879	16,497	191,910 D	42.9%	55.9%	43.4%	56.6%

TENNESSEE

SENATOR 1976

1970 Census Population	County	Total Vote	Republican	Democratic	Other	Rep.-Dem. Plurality	Percentage Total Vote Rep.	Percentage Total Vote Dem.	Percentage Major Vote Rep.	Percentage Major Vote Dem.
60,300	ANDERSON	23,527	11,130	12,266	131	1,136 D	47.3%	52.1%	47.6%	52.4%
25,039	BEDFORD	10,170	3,278	6,843	49	3,565 D	32.2%	67.3%	32.4%	67.6%
12,126	BENTON	5,648	1,807	3,833	8	2,026 D	32.0%	67.9%	32.0%	68.0%
7,643	BLEDSOE	3,453	1,900	1,551	2	349 R	55.0%	44.9%	55.1%	44.9%
63,744	BLOUNT	25,187	14,707	10,387	93	4,320 R	58.4%	41.2%	58.6%	41.4%
50,686	BRADLEY	17,990	10,399	7,535	56	2,864 R	57.8%	41.9%	58.0%	42.0%
26,045	CAMPBELL	9,157	4,457	4,665	35	208 D	48.7%	50.9%	48.9%	51.1%
8,467	CANNON	3,337	962	2,367	8	1,405 D	28.8%	70.9%	28.9%	71.1%
25,741	CARROLL	9,494	4,344	5,125	25	781 D	45.8%	54.0%	45.9%	54.1%
43,259	CARTER	15,292	8,248	6,977	67	1,271 R	53.9%	45.6%	54.2%	45.8%
13,199	CHEATHAM	5,577	1,596	3,949	32	2,353 D	28.6%	70.8%	28.8%	71.2%
9,927	CHESTER	4,404	2,072	2,320	12	248 D	47.0%	52.7%	47.2%	52.8%
19,420	CLAIBORNE	6,349	3,337	2,998	14	339 R	52.6%	47.2%	52.7%	47.3%
6,624	CLAY	2,624	1,018	1,595	11	577 D	38.8%	60.8%	39.0%	61.0%
25,283	COCKE	7,902	5,134	2,743	25	2,391 R	65.0%	34.7%	65.2%	34.8%
32,572	COFFEE	11,763	4,496	7,225	42	2,729 D	38.2%	61.4%	38.4%	61.6%
14,402	CROCKETT	4,557	2,127	2,417	13	290 D	46.7%	53.0%	46.8%	53.2%
20,733	CUMBERLAND	8,576	4,436	4,109	31	327 R	51.7%	47.9%	51.9%	48.1%
447,877	DAVIDSON	159,152	65,993	91,864	1,295	25,871 D	41.5%	57.7%	41.8%	58.2%
9,457	DECATUR	4,005	1,817	2,179	9	362 D	45.4%	54.4%	45.5%	54.5%
11,151	DE KALB	4,604	1,467	3,124	13	1,657 D	31.9%	67.9%	32.0%	68.0%
21,977	DICKSON	8,780	2,589	6,158	33	3,569 D	29.5%	70.1%	29.6%	70.4%
30,427	DYER	10,108	4,424	5,622	62	1,198 D	43.8%	55.6%	44.0%	56.0%
22,692	FAYETTE	5,868	2,278	3,482	108	1,204 D	38.8%	59.3%	39.5%	60.5%
12,593	FENTRESS	3,596	1,801	1,790	5	11 R	50.1%	49.8%	50.2%	49.8%
27,244	FRANKLIN	10,395	3,256	7,092	47	3,836 D	31.3%	68.2%	31.5%	68.5%
47,871	GIBSON	15,303	6,086	9,184	33	3,098 D	39.8%	60.0%	39.9%	60.1%
22,138	GILES	7,004	2,122	4,856	26	2,734 D	30.3%	69.3%	30.4%	69.6%
13,948	GRAINGER	4,759	2,874	1,871	14	1,003 R	60.4%	39.3%	60.6%	39.4%
47,630	GREENE	15,492	8,659	6,787	46	1,872 R	55.9%	43.8%	56.1%	43.9%
10,631	GRUNDY	3,629	1,275	2,349	5	1,074 D	35.1%	64.7%	35.2%	64.8%
38,696	HAMBLEN	14,237	7,223	6,969	45	254 R	50.7%	48.9%	50.9%	49.1%
254,236	HAMILTON	94,427	56,894	37,099	434	19,795 R	60.3%	39.3%	60.5%	39.5%
6,719	HANCOCK	2,009	1,266	734	9	532 R	63.0%	36.5%	63.3%	36.7%
22,435	HARDEMAN	6,055	2,419	3,605	31	1,186 D	40.0%	59.5%	40.2%	59.8%
18,212	HARDIN	6,513	3,265	3,232	16	33 R	50.1%	49.6%	50.3%	49.7%
33,726	HAWKINS	11,971	6,486	5,456	29	1,030 R	54.2%	45.6%	54.3%	45.7%
19,596	HAYWOOD	5,577	2,128	3,428	21	1,300 D	38.2%	61.5%	38.3%	61.7%
17,291	HENDERSON	7,294	4,261	3,018	15	1,243 R	58.4%	41.4%	58.5%	41.5%
23,749	HENRY	9,550	2,988	6,538	24	3,550 D	31.3%	68.5%	31.4%	68.6%
12,096	HICKMAN	4,695	1,232	3,457	6	2,225 D	26.2%	73.6%	26.3%	73.7%
5,845	HOUSTON	2,348	519	1,820	9	1,301 D	22.1%	77.5%	22.2%	77.8%
13,560	HUMPHREYS	5,276	1,518	3,745	13	2,227 D	28.8%	71.0%	28.8%	71.2%
8,141	JACKSON	3,509	630	2,878	1	2,248 D	18.0%	82.0%	18.0%	82.0%
24,940	JEFFERSON	9,302	5,742	3,532	28	2,210 R	61.7%	38.0%	61.9%	38.1%
11,569	JOHNSON	4,144	2,737	1,396	11	1,341 R	66.0%	33.7%	66.2%	33.8%
276,293	KNOX	105,844	61,500	43,550	794	17,950 R	58.1%	41.1%	58.5%	41.5%
7,896	LAKE	2,297	571	1,706	20	1,135 D	24.9%	74.3%	25.1%	74.9%
20,271	LAUDERDALE	6,800	2,235	4,524	41	2,289 D	32.9%	66.5%	33.1%	66.9%
29,097	LAWRENCE	11,917	5,271	6,616	30	1,345 D	44.2%	55.5%	44.3%	55.7%
6,761	LEWIS	2,923	683	2,235	5	1,552 D	23.4%	76.5%	23.4%	76.6%
24,318	LINCOLN	7,207	2,005	5,178	24	3,173 D	27.8%	71.8%	27.9%	72.1%
24,266	LOUDON	8,986	4,800	4,143	43	657 R	53.4%	46.1%	53.7%	46.3%
35,462	MCMINN	13,668	7,405	6,229	34	1,176 R	54.2%	45.6%	54.3%	45.7%
18,369	MCNAIRY	7,513	3,467	4,024	22	557 D	46.1%	53.6%	46.3%	53.7%
12,315	MACON	3,951	2,067	1,875	9	192 R	52.3%	47.5%	52.4%	47.6%
65,727	MADISON	23,695	12,060	11,490	145	570 R	50.9%	48.5%	51.2%	48.8%
20,577	MARION	7,526	3,863	3,641	22	222 R	51.3%	48.4%	51.5%	48.5%
17,319	MARSHALL	6,131	2,009	4,100	22	2,091 D	32.8%	66.9%	32.9%	67.1%
44,028	MAURY	13,885	6,285	7,547	53	1,262 D	45.3%	54.4%	45.4%	54.6%
5,219	MEIGS	2,216	1,141	1,071	4	70 R	51.5%	48.3%	51.6%	48.4%
23,475	MONROE	10,646	5,688	4,922	36	766 R	53.4%	46.2%	53.6%	46.4%
62,721	MONTGOMERY	17,903	6,471	11,340	92	4,869 D	36.1%	63.3%	36.3%	63.7%
3,568	MOORE	1,397	380	1,014	3	634 D	27.2%	72.6%	27.3%	72.7%
13,619	MORGAN	4,785	1,932	2,838	15	906 D	40.4%	59.3%	40.5%	59.5%

TENNESSEE

SENATOR 1976

1970 Census Population	County	Total Vote	Republican	Democratic	Other	Rep.-Dem. Plurality	Percentage Total Vote Rep.	Percentage Total Vote Dem.	Percentage Major Vote Rep.	Percentage Major Vote Dem.
29,936	OBION	9,635	2,851	6,752	32	3,901 D	29.6%	70.1%	29.7%	70.3%
14,866	OVERTON	4,899	1,258	3,631	10	2,373 D	25.7%	74.1%	25.7%	74.3%
5,238	PERRY	2,149	587	1,555	7	968 D	27.3%	72.4%	27.4%	72.6%
3,774	PICKETT	1,897	1,004	891	2	113 R	52.9%	47.0%	53.0%	47.0%
11,669	POLK	5,148	2,119	3,010	19	891 D	41.2%	58.5%	41.3%	58.7%
35,487	PUTNAM	12,350	4,498	7,810	42	3,312 D	36.4%	63.2%	36.5%	63.5%
17,202	RHEA	7,175	3,919	3,241	15	678 R	54.6%	45.2%	54.7%	45.3%
38,881	ROANE	16,186	7,363	8,772	51	1,409 D	45.5%	54.2%	45.6%	54.4%
29,102	ROBERTSON	9,945	2,866	7,049	30	4,183 D	28.8%	70.9%	28.9%	71.1%
59,428	RUTHERFORD	22,452	9,113	13,159	180	4,046 D	40.6%	58.6%	40.9%	59.1%
14,762	SCOTT	4,447	2,587	1,846	14	741 R	58.2%	41.5%	58.4%	41.6%
6,331	SEQUATCHIE	2,802	1,389	1,411	2	22 D	49.6%	50.4%	49.6%	50.4%
28,241	SEVIER	11,215	7,589	3,589	37	4,000 R	67.7%	32.0%	67.9%	32.1%
722,014	SHELBY	265,139	127,439	136,312	1,388	8,873 D	48.1%	51.4%	48.3%	51.7%
12,509	SMITH	5,006	1,401	3,595	10	2,194 D	28.0%	71.8%	28.0%	72.0%
7,319	STEWART	2,881	662	2,216	3	1,554 D	23.0%	76.9%	23.0%	77.0%
127,329	SULLIVAN	44,270	21,035	22,554	681	1,519 D	47.5%	50.9%	48.3%	51.7%
56,106	SUMNER	21,674	8,761	12,781	132	4,020 D	40.4%	59.0%	40.7%	59.3%
28,001	TIPTON	9,104	3,345	5,722	37	2,377 D	36.7%	62.9%	36.9%	63.1%
5,155	TROUSDALE	1,702	440	1,255	7	815 D	25.9%	73.7%	26.0%	74.0%
15,254	UNICOI	5,540	3,064	2,462	14	602 R	55.3%	44.4%	55.4%	44.6%
9,072	UNION	3,296	1,824	1,457	15	367 R	55.3%	44.2%	55.6%	44.4%
3,758	VAN BUREN	1,408	482	926		444 D	34.2%	65.8%	34.2%	65.8%
26,972	WARREN	8,956	2,573	6,354	29	3,781 D	28.7%	70.9%	28.8%	71.2%
73,924	WASHINGTON	27,160	14,478	12,537	145	1,941 R	53.3%	46.2%	53.6%	46.4%
12,365	WAYNE	4,335	2,528	1,804	3	724 R	58.3%	41.6%	58.4%	41.6%
28,827	WEAKLEY	11,265	3,256	7,951	58	4,695 D	28.9%	70.6%	29.1%	70.9%
16,355	WHITE	5,303	1,666	3,607	30	1,941 D	31.4%	68.0%	31.6%	68.4%
34,330	WILLIAMSON	15,808	8,445	7,253	110	1,192 R	53.4%	45.9%	53.8%	46.2%
36,999	WILSON	15,000	5,459	9,465	76	4,006 D	36.4%	63.1%	36.6%	63.4%
3,924,164	TOTAL	1,432,046	673,231	751,180	7,635	77,949 D	47.0%	52.5%	47.3%	52.7%

TENNESSEE

CONGRESS

CD	Year	Total Vote	Republican		Democratic		Other Vote	Rep.-Dem. Plurality	Percentage			
									Total Vote		Major Vote	
			Vote	Candidate	Vote	Candidate			Rep.	Dem.	Rep.	Dem.
1	1976	168,734	97,781	QUILLEN, JAMES H.	69,507	BLEVINS, LLOYD	1,446	28,274 R	57.9%	41.2%	58.5%	41.5%
1	1974	118,917	76,394	QUILLEN, JAMES H.	42,523	BLEVINS, LLOYD		33,871 R	64.2%	35.8%	64.2%	35.8%
1	1972	139,608	110,868	QUILLEN, JAMES H.	28,736	CANTOR, BERNARD	4	82,132 R	79.4%	20.6%	79.4%	20.6%
2	1976	186,707	117,256	DUNCAN, JOHN J.	69,449	ROWLAND, MIKE	2	47,807 R	62.8%	37.2%	62.8%	37.2%
2	1974	123,339	87,419	DUNCAN, JOHN J.	35,920	BROWN, JESSE B.		51,499 R	70.9%	29.1%	70.9%	29.1%
2	1972	109,925	109,925	DUNCAN, JOHN J.				109,925 R	100.0%		100.0%	
3	1976	183,569	57,116	BAKER, LAMAR	123,872	LLOYD, MARILYN	2,581	66,756 D	31.1%	67.5%	31.6%	68.4%
3	1974	121,198	55,580	BAKER, LAMAR	61,926	LLOYD, MARILYN	3,692	6,346 D	45.9%	51.1%	47.3%	52.7%
3	1972	149,443	82,561	BAKER, LAMAR	62,536	SOMPAYRAC, HOWARD	4,346	20,025 R	55.2%	41.8%	56.9%	43.1%
4	1976	122,723			115,392	GORE, ALBERT, JR.	7,331	115,392 D		94.0%		100.0%
4	1974	94,918			94,847	EVINS, JOE L.	71	94,847 D		99.9%		100.0%
4	1972	114,731	21,689	FINNEY, BILLY JO	93,042	EVINS, JOE L.		71,353 D	18.9%	81.1%	18.9%	81.1%
5	1976	136,151			125,830	ALLEN, CLIFFORD	10,321	125,830 D		92.4%		100.0%
5	1974	88,350			88,206	FULTON, RICHARD	144	88,206 D		99.8%		100.0%
5	1972	149,464	55,067	ADAMS, ALFRED	93,555	FULTON, RICHARD	842	38,488 D	36.8%	62.6%	37.1%	62.9%
6	1976	181,375	116,905	BEARD, ROBIN L.	64,462	BASS, ROSS	8	52,443 R	64.5%	35.5%	64.5%	35.5%
7	1976	105,847			105,832	JONES, ED	15	105,832 D		100.0%		100.0%
8	1976	165,954	63,819	ALISSANDRATOS, A. D.	100,683	FORD, HAROLD E.	1,452	36,864 D	38.5%	60.7%	38.8%	61.2%

TENNESSEE

1976 GENERAL ELECTION

President — Original uncorrected canvass gave the scattered vote total as 230. Other vote was 5,769 Anderson (Independent); 5,004 McCarthy (Independent); 2,303 Maddox (Independent); 1,375 MacBride (Independent); 547 Hall (Independent); 512 LaRouche (Independent); 442 Bubar (Independent); 316 Miller (Independent); 229 scattered.

Senator — Original uncorrected canvass gave the other vote total in Hawkins county as 22. Other vote was 5,137 Bates (Independent); 1,406 Jacox (Independent); 1,061 Zandi (Independent); 31 scattered.

Congress — A minor adjustment was made in the Congressional District boundaries of CD's 6, 7 and 8 by court order in March 1976. The change involved only seven precincts in the Memphis area. Other vote was scattered in CD's 2, 6 and 7; 967 Bobic (Independent), 476 Joyner (Independent) and 3 scattered in CD 1; 2,340 Dover (Independent) and 241 Hill (Independent) in CD 3; 10,292 Bissell (Independent) and 29 scattered in CD 5; 1,450 Flanagan (Independent) and 2 scattered in CD 8.

1976 PRIMARIES

AUGUST 5 REPUBLICAN

Senator — William E. Brock, unopposed.

Congress — Unopposed in CD 6. No candidates in CD's 4 and 7. Contested as follows:

CD 1 — 45,361 James H. Quillen; 5,422 John Curtis.
CD 2 — 45,877 John J. Duncan; 1,704 Hubert D. Patty.
CD 3 — 26,191 LaMar Baker; 2,750 Kent Feary.
CD 5 — 2,819 Roy Skinner; 1,743 Jesse D. McDonald; 4 scattered. Mr. Skinner withdrew after the primary and no substitution was made.
CD 8 — 15,286 A. D. Alissandratos; 1,628 Joe Cooper.

AUGUST 5 DEMOCRATIC

Senator — 244,930 James R. Sasser; 171,716 John J. Hooker; 54,125 Harry Sadler; 44,056 David Bolin; 29,864 Lester Kefauver; 4,695 Edward Brown; 4,461 William T. Hardison; 2 scattered.

Congress — Unopposed in three CD's. Contested as follows:

CD 2 — 25,358 Mike Rowland; 8,151 Oliver Smith; 3,899 Margaret Francis.
CD 4 — 37,680 Albert Gore, Jr.; 34,121 Stanley Rogers; 19,856 T. Tommy Cutrer; 13,917 Ben H. McFarlin; 5,359 Larry S. Irby; 3,667 Sarah King; 1,456 William H. Long; 875 Robert Paulk; 795 William J. Kelton.
CD 5 — 59,241 Clifford Allen; 4,607 Porter Freeman; 3,402 Joe McEwen; 1 scattered.
CD 6 — 31,740 Ross Bass; 13,524 Henry Ragan; 8,311 Pat Sutton; 3,181 James Williams.
CD 7 — 56,058 Ed Jones; 37,121 Larry Bates; 1,126 Willie Burns.

TEXAS

GOVERNOR

Dolph Briscoe (D). Re-elected 1974 to a four-year term. Previously elected 1972.

SENATORS

Lloyd Bentsen (D). Re-elected 1976 to a six-year term. Previously elected 1970.

John G. Tower (R). Re-elected 1972 to a six-year term. Previously elected 1966, and in May 1961 to fill out term vacated by the resignation of Senator Lyndon B. Johnson.

REPRESENTATIVES

1. Sam B. Hall (D)
2. Charles Wilson (D)
3. James M. Collins (R)
4. Ray Roberts (D)
5. Jim Mattox (D)
6. Olin E. Teague (D)
7. W. R. Archer (R)
8. Bob Eckhardt (D)
9. Jack B. Brooks (D)
10. Jake Pickle (D)
11. W. R. Poage (D)
12. James C. Wright (D)
13. John Hightower (D)
14. John Young (D)
15. Eligio de la Garza (D)
16. Richard C. White (D)
17. Omar Burleson (D)
18. Barbara Jordan (D)
19. George H. Mahon (D)
20. Henry B. Gonzalez (D)
21. Robert Krueger (D)
22. Bob Gammage (D)
23. Abraham Kazen (D)
24. Dale Milford (D)

POSTWAR VOTE FOR GOVERNOR

		Republican		Democratic				Percentage			
	Total					Other	Rep.-Dem.	Total Vote		Major Vote	
Year	Vote	Vote	Candidate	Vote	Candidate	Vote	Plurality	Rep.	Dem.	Rep.	Dem.
1974	1,654,984	514,725	Granberry, Jim	1,016,334	Briscoe, Dolph	123,925	501,609 D	31.1%	61.4%	33.6%	66.4%
1972	3,410,128	1,534,060	Grover, Henry C.	1,633,970	Briscoe, Dolph	242,098	99,910 D	45.0%	47.9%	48.4%	51.6%
1970	2,235,847	1,037,723	Eggers, Paul W.	1,197,726	Smith, Preston	398	160,003 D	46.4%	53.6%	46.4%	53.6%
1968	2,916,509	1,254,333	Eggers, Paul W.	1,662,019	Smith, Preston	157	407,686 D	43.0%	57.0%	43.0%	57.0%
1966	1,425,861	368,025	Kennerly, T. E.	1,037,517	Connally, John B.	20,319	669,492 D	25.8%	72.8%	26.2%	73.8%
1964	2,544,753	661,675	Crichton, Jack	1,877,793	Connally, John B.	5,285	1,216,118 D	26.0%	73.8%	26.1%	73.9%
1962	1,569,181	715,025	Cox, Jack	847,036	Connally, John B.	7,120	132,011 D	45.6%	54.0%	45.8%	54.2%
1960	2,250,718	612,963	Steger, William M.	1,637,755	Daniel, Price	–	1,024,792 D	27.2%	72.8%	27.2%	72.8%
1958	789,133	94,098	Mayer, Edwin S.	695,035	Daniel, Price	–	600,937 D	11.9%	88.1%	11.9%	88.1%
1956	1,828,161	271,088	Bryant, William R.	1,433,051	Daniel, Price	124,022	1,161,963 D	14.8%	78.4%	15.9%	84.1%
1954	636,892	66,154	Adams, Tod R.	569,533	Shivers, Allan	1,205	503,379 D	10.4%	89.4%	10.4%	89.6%
1952	1,881,202	–	–	1,844,530	Shivers, Allan	36,672	1,844,530 D	–	98.1%	–	100.0%
1950	394,747	39,737	Currie, Ralph W.	355,010	Shivers, Allan	–	315,273 D	10.1%	89.9%	10.1%	89.9%
1948	1,208,860	177,399	Lane, Alvin H.	1,024,160	Jester, Beauford	7,301	846,761 D	14.7%	84.7%	14.8%	85.2%
1946	378,744	33,231	Nolte, Eugene	345,513	Jester, Beauford	–	312,282 D	8.8%	91.2%	8.8%	91.2%

The term of office of Texas' Governor was increased from two to four years effective with the 1974 election.

POSTWAR VOTE FOR SENATOR

		Republican		Democratic				Percentage			
	Total					Other	Rep.-Dem.	Total Vote		Major Vote	
Year	Vote	Vote	Candidate	Vote	Candidate	Vote	Plurality	Rep.	Dem.	Rep.	Dem.
1976	3,874,516	1,636,370	Steelman, Alan	2,199,956	Bentsen, Lloyd	38,190	563,586 D	42.2%	56.8%	42.7%	57.3%
1972	3,413,903	1,822,877	Tower, John G.	1,511,985	Sanders, Barefoot	79,041	310,892 R	53.4%	44.3%	54.7%	45.3%
1970	2,231,671	1,035,794	Bush, George	1,194,069	Bentsen, Lloyd	1,808	158,275 D	46.4%	53.5%	46.5%	53.5%
1966	1,493,182	842,501	Tower, John G.	643,855	Carr, Waggoner	6,826	198,646 R	56.4%	43.1%	56.7%	43.3%
1964	2,603,856	1,134,337	Bush, George	1,463,958	Yarborough, Ralph	5,561	329,621 D	43.6%	56.2%	43.7%	56.3%
1961s	886,091	448,217	Tower, John G.	437,874	Blakley, William A.	–	10,343 R	50.6%	49.4%	50.6%	49.4%
1960	2,253,784	926,653	Tower, John G.	1,306,625	Johnson, Lyndon B.	20,506	379,972 D	41.1%	58.0%	41.5%	58.5%
1958	787,128	185,926	Whittenburg, Roy	587,030	Yarborough, Ralph	14,172	401,104 D	23.6%	74.6%	24.1%	75.9%
1957s	957,298		(See note below)								
1954	636,475	94,131	Watson, Carlos G.	539,319	Johnson, Lyndon B.	3,025	445,188 D	14.8%	84.7%	14.9%	85.1%
1952	1,895,192	–	–	1,895,192	Daniel, Price	–	1,895,192 D	–	100.0%	–	100.0%
1948	1,061,563	349,665	Porter, Jack	702,985	Johnson, Lyndon B.	8,913	353,320 D	32.9%	66.2%	33.2%	66.8%
1946	380,681	43,750	Sells, Murray C.	336,931	Connally, Tom	–	293,181 D	11.5%	88.5%	11.5%	88.5%

The 1961 election (May) and the 1957 election (April) were for short terms to fill vacancies. Though neither vote was held with official party designations, the 1961 vote above was a run-off contest between unofficial party candidates. In 1957 there was a single ballot without run-off and Ralph Yarborough polled 364,605 votes (38.1% of the total vote) and won the election with a 73,802 plurality.

TEXAS

Districts Established October 17, 1973

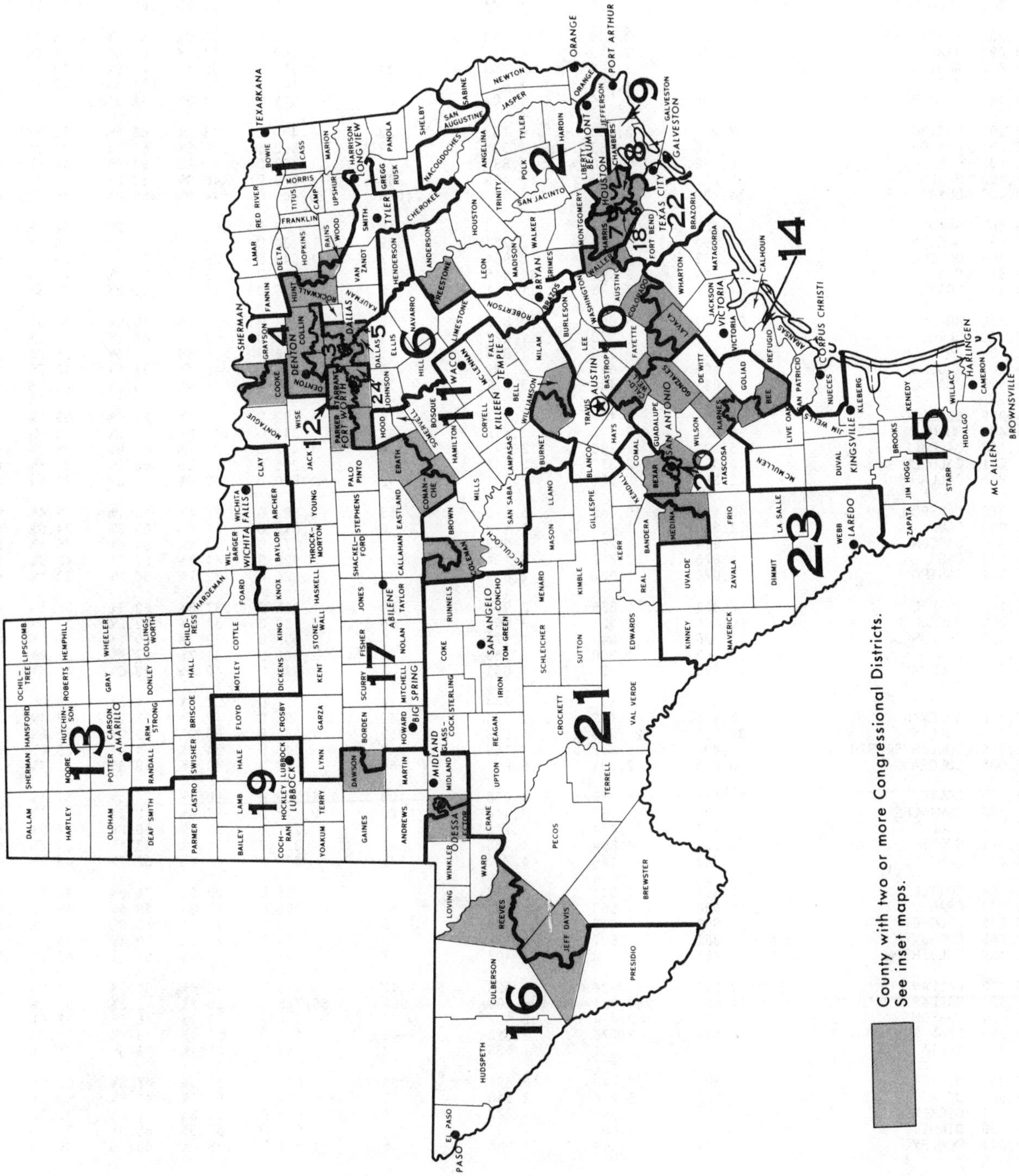

TEXAS

PRESIDENT 1976

1970 Census Population	County	Total Vote	Republican	Democratic	Other	Rep.-Dem. Plurality	Percentage Total Vote Rep.	Percentage Total Vote Dem.	Percentage Major Vote Rep.	Percentage Major Vote Dem.
27,789	ANDERSON	9,715	4,172	5,499	44	1,327 D	42.9%	56.6%	43.1%	56.9%
10,372	ANDREWS	3,937	2,127	1,777	33	350 R	54.0%	45.1%	54.5%	45.5%
49,349	ANGELINA	17,112	7,223	9,750	139	2,527 D	42.2%	57.0%	42.6%	57.4%
8,902	ARANSAS	4,181	1,985	2,136	60	151 D	47.5%	51.1%	48.2%	51.8%
5,759	ARCHER	2,561	966	1,577	18	611 D	37.7%	61.6%	38.0%	62.0%
1,895	ARMSTRONG	1,027	506	513	8	7 D	49.3%	50.0%	49.7%	50.3%
18,696	ATASCOSA	7,072	2,415	4,565	92	2,150 D	34.1%	64.6%	34.6%	65.4%
13,831	AUSTIN	5,033	2,686	2,313	34	373 R	53.4%	46.0%	53.7%	46.3%
8,487	BAILEY	2,627	1,255	1,356	16	101 D	47.8%	51.6%	48.1%	51.9%
4,747	BANDERA	2,766	1,554	1,183	29	371 R	56.2%	42.8%	56.8%	43.2%
17,297	BASTROP	7,204	2,383	4,788	33	2,405 D	33.1%	66.5%	33.2%	66.8%
5,221	BAYLOR	2,130	783	1,335	12	552 D	36.8%	62.7%	37.0%	63.0%
22,737	BEE	6,722	2,953	3,690	79	737 D	43.9%	54.9%	44.5%	55.5%
124,483	BELL	32,912	15,126	17,499	287	2,373 D	46.0%	53.2%	46.4%	53.6%
830,460	BEXAR	271,430	121,176	146,581	3,673	25,405 D	44.6%	54.0%	45.3%	54.7%
3,567	BLANCO	1,956	1,015	923	18	92 R	51.9%	47.2%	52.4%	47.6%
888	BORDEN	390	150	234	6	84 D	38.5%	60.0%	39.1%	60.9%
10,966	BOSQUE	4,883	1,912	2,954	17	1,042 D	39.2%	60.5%	39.3%	60.7%
67,813	BOWIE	22,214	9,590	12,445	179	2,855 D	43.2%	56.0%	43.5%	56.5%
108,312	BRAZORIA	41,744	19,475	21,711	558	2,236 D	46.7%	52.0%	47.3%	52.7%
57,978	BRAZOS	26,700	15,685	10,628	387	5,057 R	58.7%	39.8%	59.6%	40.4%
7,780	BREWSTER	2,624	1,368	1,227	29	141 R	52.1%	46.8%	52.7%	47.3%
2,794	BRISCOE	1,119	285	823	11	538 D	25.5%	73.5%	25.7%	74.3%
8,005	BROOKS	3,429	641	2,782	6	2,141 D	18.7%	81.1%	18.7%	81.3%
25,877	BROWN	10,095	4,483	5,577	35	1,094 D	44.4%	55.2%	44.6%	55.4%
9,999	BURLESON	4,081	1,142	2,924	15	1,782 D	28.0%	71.6%	28.1%	71.9%
11,420	BURNET	6,636	2,777	3,818	41	1,041 D	41.8%	57.5%	42.1%	57.9%
21,178	CALDWELL	5,921	2,235	3,647	39	1,412 D	37.7%	61.6%	38.0%	62.0%
17,831	CALHOUN	6,061	2,377	3,642	42	1,265 D	39.2%	60.1%	39.5%	60.5%
8,205	CALLAHAN	3,864	1,581	2,241	42	660 D	40.9%	58.0%	41.4%	58.6%
140,368	CAMERON	42,111	16,448	25,310	353	8,862 D	39.1%	60.1%	39.4%	60.6%
8,005	CAMP	3,285	1,133	2,146	6	1,013 D	34.5%	65.3%	34.6%	65.4%
6,358	CARSON	2,824	1,269	1,542	13	273 D	44.9%	54.6%	45.1%	54.9%
24,133	CASS	8,875	3,712	5,134	29	1,422 D	41.8%	57.8%	42.0%	58.0%
10,394	CASTRO	3,076	1,007	2,033	36	1,026 D	32.7%	66.1%	33.1%	66.9%
12,187	CHAMBERS	4,852	1,835	2,927	90	1,092 D	37.8%	60.3%	38.5%	61.5%
32,008	CHEROKEE	10,465	3,921	6,509	35	2,588 D	37.5%	62.2%	37.6%	62.4%
6,605	CHILDRESS	2,626	1,043	1,578	5	535 D	39.7%	60.1%	39.8%	60.2%
8,079	CLAY	3,783	1,200	2,568	15	1,368 D	31.7%	67.9%	31.8%	68.2%
5,326	COCHRAN	1,739	701	1,031	7	330 D	40.3%	59.3%	40.5%	59.5%
3,087	COKE	1,377	517	844	16	327 D	37.5%	61.3%	38.0%	62.0%
10,288	COLEMAN	3,955	1,669	2,264	22	595 D	42.2%	57.2%	42.4%	57.6%
66,920	COLLIN	36,000	21,608	14,039	353	7,569 R	60.0%	39.0%	60.6%	39.4%
4,755	COLLINGSWORTH	1,804	629	1,169	6	540 D	34.9%	64.8%	35.0%	65.0%
17,638	COLORADO	6,075	2,991	3,028	56	37 D	49.2%	49.8%	49.7%	50.3%
24,165	COMAL	10,554	6,377	4,068	109	2,309 R	60.4%	38.5%	61.1%	38.9%
11,898	COMANCHE	4,731	1,297	3,414	20	2,117 D	27.4%	72.2%	27.5%	72.5%
2,937	CONCHO	1,195	474	715	6	241 D	39.7%	59.8%	39.9%	60.1%
23,471	COOKE	9,329	4,804	4,483	42	321 R	51.5%	48.1%	51.7%	48.3%
35,311	CORYELL	8,929	4,140	4,710	79	570 D	46.4%	52.7%	46.8%	53.2%
3,204	COTTLE	1,361	311	1,047	3	736 D	22.9%	76.9%	22.9%	77.1%
4,172	CRANE	1,680	963	664	53	299 R	57.3%	39.5%	59.2%	40.8%
3,885	CROCKETT	1,608	802	804	2	2 D	49.9%	50.0%	49.9%	50.1%
9,085	CROSBY	3,092	897	2,176	19	1,279 D	29.0%	70.4%	29.2%	70.8%
3,429	CULBERSON	787	373	407	7	34 D	47.4%	51.7%	47.8%	52.2%
6,012	DALLAM	2,007	936	1,029	42	93 D	46.6%	51.3%	47.6%	52.4%
1,327,321	DALLAS	464,385	263,081	196,303	5,001	66,778 R	56.7%	42.3%	57.3%	42.7%
16,604	DAWSON	4,653	2,474	2,162	17	312 R	53.2%	46.5%	53.4%	46.6%
18,999	DEAF SMITH	5,435	2,776	2,613	46	163 R	51.1%	48.1%	51.5%	48.5%
4,927	DELTA	1,991	421	1,563	7	1,142 D	21.1%	78.5%	21.2%	78.8%
75,633	DENTON	39,692	20,440	18,887	365	1,553 R	51.5%	47.6%	52.0%	48.0%
18,660	DE WITT	5,327	2,754	2,540	33	214 R	51.7%	47.7%	52.0%	48.0%
3,737	DICKENS	1,571	343	1,222	6	879 D	21.8%	77.8%	21.9%	78.1%
9,039	DIMMIT	2,624	890	1,721	13	831 D	33.9%	65.6%	34.1%	65.9%
3,641	DONLEY	1,804	704	1,095	5	391 D	39.0%	60.7%	39.1%	60.9%

TEXAS

PRESIDENT 1976

1970 Census Population	County	Total Vote	Republican	Democratic	Other	Rep.-Dem. Plurality	Percentage: Total Vote Rep.	Total Vote Dem.	Major Vote Rep.	Major Vote Dem.
11,722	DUVAL	4,941	661	4,267	13	3,606 D	13.4%	86.4%	13.4%	86.6%
18,092	EASTLAND	6,695	2,340	4,320	35	1,980 D	35.0%	64.5%	35.1%	64.9%
91,805	ECTOR	30,328	18,973	10,802	553	8,171 R	62.6%	35.6%	63.7%	36.3%
2,107	EDWARDS	672	412	258	2	154 R	61.3%	38.4%	61.5%	38.5%
46,638	ELLIS	17,055	6,996	9,991	68	2,995 D	41.0%	58.6%	41.2%	58.8%
359,291	EL PASO	89,465	42,697	45,477	1,291	2,780 D	47.7%	50.8%	48.4%	51.6%
18,141	ERATH	7,790	2,925	4,821	44	1,896 D	37.5%	61.9%	37.8%	62.2%
17,300	FALLS	6,567	2,261	4,277	29	2,016 D	34.4%	65.1%	34.6%	65.4%
22,705	FANNIN	7,985	2,102	5,845	38	3,743 D	26.3%	73.2%	26.5%	73.5%
17,650	FAYETTE	6,493	3,030	3,428	35	398 D	46.7%	52.8%	46.9%	53.1%
6,344	FISHER	2,576	573	1,993	10	1,420 D	22.2%	77.4%	22.3%	77.7%
11,044	FLOYD	3,414	1,402	1,991	21	589 D	41.1%	58.3%	41.3%	58.7%
2,211	FOARD	950	240	706	4	466 D	25.3%	74.3%	25.4%	74.6%
52,314	FORT BEND	28,787	17,354	11,264	169	6,090 R	60.3%	39.1%	60.6%	39.4%
5,291	FRANKLIN	2,404	758	1,636	10	878 D	31.5%	68.1%	31.7%	68.3%
11,116	FREESTONE	4,361	1,674	2,679	8	1,005 D	38.4%	61.4%	38.5%	61.5%
11,159	FRIO	3,908	1,280	2,598	30	1,318 D	32.8%	66.5%	33.0%	67.0%
11,593	GAINES	3,544	1,643	1,880	21	237 D	46.4%	53.0%	46.6%	53.4%
169,812	GALVESTON	63,735	25,251	37,873	611	12,622 D	39.6%	59.4%	40.0%	60.0%
5,289	GARZA	1,725	755	957	13	202 D	43.8%	55.5%	44.1%	55.9%
10,553	GILLESPIE	4,885	3,541	1,260	84	2,281 R	72.5%	25.8%	73.8%	26.2%
1,155	GLASSCOCK	413	218	190	5	28 R	52.8%	46.0%	53.4%	46.6%
4,869	GOLIAD	1,731	846	875	10	29 D	48.9%	50.5%	49.2%	50.8%
16,375	GONZALES	5,026	1,789	3,219	18	1,430 D	35.6%	64.0%	35.7%	64.3%
26,949	GRAY	9,962	6,010	3,872	80	2,138 R	60.3%	38.9%	60.8%	39.2%
83,225	GRAYSON	29,095	11,981	17,015	99	5,034 D	41.2%	58.5%	41.3%	58.7%
75,929	GREGG	27,612	17,582	9,827	203	7,755 R	63.7%	35.6%	64.1%	35.9%
11,855	GRIMES	4,148	1,473	2,656	19	1,183 D	35.5%	64.0%	35.7%	64.3%
33,554	GUADALUPE	12,935	6,766	6,054	115	712 R	52.3%	46.8%	52.8%	47.2%
34,137	HALE	11,007	5,390	5,580	37	190 D	49.0%	50.7%	49.1%	50.9%
6,015	HALL	2,314	671	1,633	10	962 D	29.0%	70.6%	29.1%	70.9%
7,198	HAMILTON	3,189	1,176	1,981	32	805 D	36.9%	62.1%	37.3%	62.7%
6,351	HANSFORD	2,406	1,401	983	22	418 R	58.2%	40.9%	58.8%	41.2%
6,795	HARDEMAN	2,225	805	1,403	17	598 D	36.2%	63.1%	36.5%	63.5%
29,996	HARDIN	10,688	4,046	6,558	84	2,512 D	37.9%	61.4%	38.2%	61.8%
1,741,912	HARRIS	685,264	357,536	321,897	5,831	35,639 R	52.2%	47.0%	52.6%	47.4%
44,841	HARRISON	15,639	7,787	7,796	56	9 D	49.8%	49.8%	50.0%	50.0%
2,782	HARTLEY	1,597	811	774	12	37 R	50.8%	48.5%	51.2%	48.8%
8,512	HASKELL	3,359	838	2,512	9	1,674 D	24.9%	74.8%	25.0%	75.0%
27,642	HAYS	12,875	5,714	7,005	156	1,291 D	44.4%	54.4%	44.9%	55.1%
3,084	HEMPHILL	1,578	858	707	13	151 R	54.4%	44.8%	54.8%	45.2%
26,466	HENDERSON	12,937	4,658	8,245	34	3,587 D	36.0%	63.7%	36.1%	63.9%
181,535	HIDALGO	54,593	19,199	35,021	373	15,822 D	35.2%	64.1%	35.4%	64.6%
22,596	HILL	8,032	2,680	5,327	25	2,647 D	33.4%	66.3%	33.5%	66.5%
20,396	HOCKLEY	7,130	3,137	3,949	44	812 D	44.0%	55.4%	44.3%	55.7%
6,368	HOOD	5,061	1,857	3,181	23	1,324 D	36.7%	62.9%	36.9%	63.1%
20,710	HOPKINS	7,592	2,556	4,992	44	2,436 D	33.7%	65.8%	33.9%	66.1%
17,855	HOUSTON	5,421	2,229	3,179	13	950 D	41.1%	58.6%	41.2%	58.8%
37,796	HOWARD	11,972	4,899	6,984	89	2,085 D	40.9%	58.3%	41.2%	58.8%
2,392	HUDSPETH	881	395	479	7	84 D	44.8%	54.4%	45.2%	54.8%
47,948	HUNT	15,314	6,676	8,543	95	1,867 D	43.6%	55.8%	43.9%	56.1%
24,443	HUTCHINSON	9,933	6,137	3,691	105	2,446 R	61.8%	37.2%	62.4%	37.6%
1,070	IRION	604	302	297	5	5 R	50.0%	49.2%	50.4%	49.6%
6,711	JACK	2,871	1,049	1,814	8	765 D	36.5%	63.2%	36.6%	63.4%
12,975	JACKSON	4,433	1,884	2,524	25	640 D	42.5%	56.9%	42.7%	57.3%
24,692	JASPER	8,607	3,167	5,422	18	2,255 D	36.8%	63.0%	36.9%	63.1%
1,527	JEFF DAVIS	607	288	309	10	21 D	47.4%	50.9%	48.2%	51.8%
244,773	JEFFERSON	80,546	32,451	47,581	514	15,130 D	40.3%	59.1%	40.5%	59.5%
4,654	JIM HOGG	2,074	429	1,645		1,216 D	20.7%	79.3%	20.7%	79.3%
33,032	JIM WELLS	11,550	3,547	7,961	42	4,414 D	30.7%	68.9%	30.8%	69.2%
45,769	JOHNSON	18,127	7,194	10,864	69	3,670 D	39.7%	59.9%	39.8%	60.2%
16,106	JONES	5,416	2,072	3,318	26	1,246 D	38.3%	61.3%	38.4%	61.6%
13,462	KARNES	4,718	1,675	2,996	47	1,321 D	35.5%	63.5%	35.9%	64.1%
32,392	KAUFMAN	10,204	3,867	6,302	35	2,435 D	37.9%	61.8%	38.0%	62.0%
6,964	KENDALL	3,793	2,543	1,190	60	1,353 R	67.0%	31.4%	68.1%	31.9%

TEXAS

PRESIDENT 1976

1970 Census Population	County	Total Vote	Republican	Democratic	Other	Rep.-Dem. Plurality	Percentage Total Vote Rep.	Total Vote Dem.	Major Vote Rep.	Major Vote Dem.
678	KENEDY	205	65	139	1	74 D	31.7%	67.8%	31.9%	68.1%
1,434	KENT	647	171	474	2	303 D	26.4%	73.3%	26.5%	73.5%
19,454	KERR	9,978	6,021	3,767	190	2,254 R	60.3%	37.8%	61.5%	38.5%
3,904	KIMBLE	1,632	846	759	27	87 R	51.8%	46.5%	52.7%	47.3%
464	KING	197	96	100	1	4 D	48.7%	50.8%	49.0%	51.0%
2,006	KINNEY	843	318	516	9	198 D	37.7%	61.2%	38.1%	61.9%
33,166	KLEBERG	9,647	3,771	5,803	73	2,032 D	39.1%	60.2%	39.4%	60.6%
5,972	KNOX	2,060	551	1,498	11	947 D	26.7%	72.7%	26.9%	73.1%
36,062	LAMAR	13,076	4,443	8,601	32	4,158 D	34.0%	65.8%	34.1%	65.9%
17,770	LAMB	5,815	2,413	3,374	28	961 D	41.5%	58.0%	41.7%	58.3%
9,323	LAMPASAS	3,982	1,563	2,376	43	813 D	39.3%	59.7%	39.7%	60.3%
5,014	LA SALLE	1,983	677	1,294	12	617 D	34.1%	65.3%	34.3%	65.7%
17,903	LAVACA	5,964	2,466	3,458	40	992 D	41.3%	58.0%	41.6%	58.4%
8,048	LEE	3,303	1,348	1,937	18	589 D	40.8%	58.6%	41.0%	59.0%
8,738	LEON	3,261	1,161	2,085	15	924 D	35.6%	63.9%	35.8%	64.2%
33,014	LIBERTY	11,704	4,552	7,086	66	2,534 D	38.9%	60.5%	39.1%	60.9%
18,100	LIMESTONE	5,900	2,045	3,825	30	1,780 D	34.7%	64.8%	34.8%	65.2%
3,486	LIPSCOMB	1,569	911	644	14	267 R	58.1%	41.0%	58.6%	41.4%
6,697	LIVE OAK	2,961	1,287	1,656	18	369 D	43.5%	55.9%	43.7%	56.3%
6,979	LLANO	4,324	1,947	2,361	16	414 D	45.0%	54.6%	45.2%	54.8%
164	LOVING	86	47	35	4	12 R	54.7%	40.7%	57.3%	42.7%
179,295	LUBBOCK	63,707	38,478	24,797	432	13,681 R	60.4%	38.9%	60.8%	39.2%
9,107	LYNN	2,757	1,166	1,575	16	409 D	42.3%	57.1%	42.5%	57.5%
8,571	MCCULLOCH	3,207	1,300	1,888	19	588 D	40.5%	58.9%	40.8%	59.2%
147,553	MCLENNAN	55,970	25,370	30,091	509	4,721 D	45.3%	53.8%	45.7%	54.3%
1,095	MCMULLEN	411	217	194		23 R	52.8%	47.2%	52.8%	47.2%
7,693	MADISON	2,961	1,062	1,885	14	823 D	35.9%	63.7%	36.0%	64.0%
8,517	MARION	3,167	1,291	1,860	16	569 D	40.8%	58.7%	41.0%	59.0%
4,774	MARTIN	1,618	698	907	13	209 D	43.1%	56.1%	43.5%	56.5%
3,356	MASON	1,640	805	814	21	9 D	49.1%	49.6%	49.7%	50.3%
27,913	MATAGORDA	8,731	3,679	4,971	81	1,292 D	42.1%	56.9%	42.5%	57.5%
18,093	MAVERICK	3,802	924	2,840	38	1,916 D	24.3%	74.7%	24.5%	75.5%
20,249	MEDINA	6,988	3,252	3,681	55	429 D	46.5%	52.7%	46.9%	53.1%
2,646	MENARD	1,000	441	543	16	102 D	44.1%	54.3%	44.8%	55.2%
65,433	MIDLAND	27,195	19,178	7,725	292	11,453 R	70.5%	28.4%	71.3%	28.7%
20,028	MILAM	7,315	2,404	4,871	40	2,467 D	32.9%	66.6%	33.0%	67.0%
4,212	MILLS	1,710	684	1,012	14	328 D	40.0%	59.2%	40.3%	59.7%
9,073	MITCHELL	2,804	1,058	1,730	16	672 D	37.7%	61.7%	37.9%	62.1%
15,326	MONTAGUE	6,294	2,182	4,087	25	1,905 D	34.7%	64.9%	34.8%	65.2%
49,479	MONTGOMERY	29,659	15,739	13,718	202	2,021 R	53.1%	46.3%	53.4%	46.6%
14,060	MOORE	5,575	2,759	2,767	49	8 D	49.5%	49.6%	49.9%	50.1%
12,310	MORRIS	4,931	1,843	3,071	17	1,228 D	37.4%	62.3%	37.5%	62.5%
2,178	MOTLEY	961	428	522	11	94 D	44.5%	54.3%	45.1%	54.9%
36,362	NACOGDOCHES	14,141	7,315	6,697	129	618 R	51.7%	47.4%	52.2%	47.8%
31,150	NAVARRO	11,068	4,012	6,995	61	2,983 D	36.2%	63.2%	36.4%	63.6%
11,657	NEWTON	4,502	1,011	3,468	23	2,457 D	22.5%	77.0%	22.6%	77.4%
16,220	NOLAN	5,545	2,431	3,094	20	663 D	43.8%	55.8%	44.0%	56.0%
237,544	NUECES	86,325	32,797	52,755	773	19,958 D	38.0%	61.1%	38.3%	61.7%
9,704	OCHILTREE	3,587	2,471	1,084	32	1,387 R	68.9%	30.2%	69.5%	30.5%
2,258	OLDHAM	911	354	554	3	200 D	38.9%	60.8%	39.0%	61.0%
71,170	ORANGE	24,484	9,147	15,177	160	6,030 D	37.4%	62.0%	37.6%	62.4%
28,962	PALO PINTO	7,905	2,684	5,170	51	2,486 D	34.0%	65.4%	34.2%	65.8%
15,894	PANOLA	6,977	3,218	3,731	28	513 D	46.1%	53.5%	46.3%	53.7%
33,888	PARKER	12,969	4,692	8,186	91	3,494 D	36.2%	63.1%	36.4%	63.6%
10,509	PARMER	3,417	1,487	1,914	16	427 D	43.5%	56.0%	43.7%	56.3%
13,748	PECOS	4,233	2,234	1,971	28	263 R	52.8%	46.6%	53.1%	46.9%
14,457	POLK	6,967	2,529	4,384	54	1,855 D	36.3%	62.9%	36.6%	63.4%
90,511	POTTER	26,036	13,819	11,917	300	1,902 R	53.1%	45.8%	53.7%	46.3%
4,842	PRESIDIO	1,936	687	1,232	17	545 D	35.5%	63.6%	35.8%	64.2%
3,752	RAINS	1,855	510	1,339	6	829 D	27.5%	72.2%	27.6%	72.4%
53,885	RANDALL	26,524	17,115	9,074	335	8,041 R	64.5%	34.2%	65.4%	34.6%
3,239	REAGAN	1,234	666	563	5	103 R	54.0%	45.6%	54.2%	45.8%
2,013	REAL	969	448	510	11	62 D	46.2%	52.6%	46.8%	53.2%
14,298	RED RIVER	5,533	1,852	3,670	11	1,818 D	33.5%	66.3%	33.5%	66.5%
16,526	REEVES	4,342	1,711	2,613	18	902 D	39.4%	60.2%	39.6%	60.4%

TEXAS

PRESIDENT 1976

1970 Census Population	County	Total Vote	Republican	Democratic	Other	Rep.-Dem. Plurality	Percentage Total Vote Rep.	Percentage Total Vote Dem.	Percentage Major Vote Rep.	Percentage Major Vote Dem.
9,494	REFUGIO	3,765	1,537	2,218	10	681 D	40.8%	58.9%	40.9%	59.1%
967	ROBERTS	562	350	202	10	148 R	62.3%	35.9%	63.4%	36.6%
14,389	ROBERTSON	4,996	1,244	3,741	11	2,497 D	24.9%	74.9%	25.0%	75.0%
7,046	ROCKWALL	3,936	2,087	1,828	21	259 R	53.0%	46.4%	53.3%	46.7%
12,108	RUNNELS	4,282	2,203	2,068	11	135 R	51.4%	48.3%	51.6%	48.4%
34,102	RUSK	12,915	6,800	6,063	52	737 R	52.7%	46.9%	52.9%	47.1%
7,187	SABINE	3,296	904	2,391	1	1,487 D	27.4%	72.5%	27.4%	72.6%
7,858	SAN AUGUSTINE	2,870	1,047	1,817	6	770 D	36.5%	63.3%	36.6%	63.4%
6,702	SAN JACINTO	3,529	1,094	2,406	29	1,312 D	31.0%	68.2%	31.3%	68.7%
47,288	SAN PATRICIO	15,395	5,853	9,469	73	3,616 D	38.0%	61.5%	38.2%	61.8%
5,540	SAN SABA	2,005	582	1,408	15	826 D	29.0%	70.2%	29.2%	70.8%
2,277	SCHLEICHER	993	516	468	9	48 R	52.0%	47.1%	52.4%	47.6%
15,760	SCURRY	5,459	2,797	2,639	23	158 R	51.2%	48.3%	51.5%	48.5%
3,323	SHACKELFORD	1,518	748	764	6	16 D	49.3%	50.3%	49.5%	50.5%
19,672	SHELBY	7,387	2,695	4,680	12	1,985 D	36.5%	63.4%	36.5%	63.5%
3,657	SHERMAN	1,416	679	718	19	39 D	48.0%	50.7%	48.6%	51.4%
97,096	SMITH	39,275	22,238	16,856	181	5,382 R	56.6%	42.9%	56.9%	43.1%
2,793	SOMERVELL	1,391	332	1,054	5	722 D	23.9%	75.8%	24.0%	76.0%
17,707	STARR	5,325	664	4,646	15	3,982 D	12.5%	87.2%	12.5%	87.5%
8,414	STEPHENS	3,429	1,621	1,796	12	175 D	47.3%	52.4%	47.4%	52.6%
1,056	STERLING	381	202	174	5	28 R	53.0%	45.7%	53.7%	46.3%
2,397	STONEWALL	1,070	252	812	6	560 D	23.6%	75.9%	23.7%	76.3%
3,175	SUTTON	1,609	831	768	10	63 R	51.6%	47.7%	52.0%	48.0%
10,373	SWISHER	3,577	753	2,811	13	2,058 D	21.1%	78.6%	21.1%	78.9%
716,317	TARRANT	248,631	124,433	122,287	1,911	2,146 R	50.0%	49.2%	50.4%	49.6%
97,853	TAYLOR	34,543	19,822	14,453	268	5,369 R	57.4%	41.8%	57.8%	42.2%
1,940	TERRELL	642	317	321	4	4 D	49.4%	50.0%	49.7%	50.3%
14,118	TERRY	5,001	2,113	2,859	29	746 D	42.3%	57.2%	42.5%	57.5%
2,205	THROCKMORTON	1,016	356	658	2	302 D	35.0%	64.8%	35.1%	64.9%
16,702	TITUS	6,822	2,603	4,205	14	1,602 D	38.2%	61.6%	38.2%	61.8%
71,047	TOM GREEN	23,554	12,316	11,064	174	1,252 R	52.3%	47.0%	52.7%	47.3%
295,516	TRAVIS	152,213	71,031	78,585	2,597	7,554 D	46.7%	51.6%	47.5%	52.5%
7,628	TRINITY	3,154	1,042	2,100	12	1,058 D	33.0%	66.6%	33.2%	66.8%
12,417	TYLER	5,318	1,965	3,322	31	1,357 D	36.9%	62.5%	37.2%	62.8%
20,976	UPSHUR	8,211	3,272	4,902	37	1,630 D	39.8%	59.7%	40.0%	60.0%
4,697	UPTON	1,561	869	686	6	183 R	55.7%	43.9%	55.9%	44.1%
17,348	UVALDE	5,449	3,103	2,299	47	804 R	56.9%	42.2%	57.4%	42.6%
27,471	VAL VERDE	8,152	3,476	4,603	73	1,127 D	42.6%	56.5%	43.0%	57.0%
22,155	VAN ZANDT	9,898	3,385	6,449	64	3,064 D	34.2%	65.2%	34.4%	65.6%
53,766	VICTORIA	17,028	9,594	7,326	108	2,268 R	56.3%	43.0%	56.7%	43.3%
27,680	WALKER	10,171	4,974	5,105	92	131 D	48.9%	50.2%	49.4%	50.6%
14,285	WALLER	4,862	1,992	2,828	42	836 D	41.0%	58.2%	41.3%	58.7%
13,019	WARD	4,218	2,123	2,046	49	77 R	50.3%	48.5%	50.9%	49.1%
18,842	WASHINGTON	6,500	3,820	2,635	45	1,185 R	58.8%	40.5%	59.2%	40.8%
72,859	WEBB	14,698	4,222	10,362	114	6,140 D	28.7%	70.5%	28.9%	71.1%
36,729	WHARTON	10,644	4,682	5,914	48	1,232 D	44.0%	55.6%	44.2%	55.8%
6,434	WHEELER	2,888	1,273	1,598	17	325 D	44.1%	55.3%	44.3%	55.7%
121,862	WICHITA	41,266	19,024	22,017	225	2,993 D	46.1%	53.4%	46.4%	53.6%
15,355	WILBARGER	5,476	2,145	3,280	51	1,135 D	39.2%	59.9%	39.5%	60.5%
15,570	WILLACY	4,557	1,542	2,984	31	1,442 D	33.8%	65.5%	34.1%	65.9%
37,305	WILLIAMSON	17,010	7,481	9,355	174	1,874 D	44.0%	55.0%	44.4%	55.6%
13,041	WILSON	5,902	1,926	3,973	3	2,047 D	32.6%	67.3%	32.6%	67.4%
9,640	WINKLER	3,266	1,842	1,382	42	460 R	56.4%	42.3%	57.1%	42.9%
19,687	WISE	8,013	2,856	5,133	24	2,277 D	35.6%	64.1%	35.7%	64.3%
18,589	WOOD	7,226	3,076	4,107	43	1,031 D	42.6%	56.8%	42.8%	57.2%
7,344	YOAKUM	2,680	1,477	1,181	22	296 R	55.1%	44.1%	55.6%	44.4%
15,400	YOUNG	6,166	2,652	3,473	41	821 D	43.0%	56.3%	43.3%	56.7%
4,352	ZAPATA	1,682	462	1,216	4	754 D	27.5%	72.3%	27.5%	72.5%
11,370	ZAVALA	2,578	735	1,822	21	1,087 D	28.5%	70.7%	28.7%	71.3%
11,196,730	TOTAL	4,071,884	1,953,300	2,082,319	36,265	129,019 D	48.0%	51.1%	48.4%	51.6%

TEXAS

SENATOR 1976

1970 Census Population	County	Total Vote	Republican	Democratic	Other	Rep.-Dem. Plurality	Percentage Total Vote Rep.	Percentage Total Vote Dem.	Percentage Major Vote Rep.	Percentage Major Vote Dem.
27,789	ANDERSON	9,166	3,099	6,050	17	2,951 D	33.8%	66.0%	33.9%	66.1%
10,372	ANDREWS	3,695	1,882	1,796	17	86 R	50.9%	48.6%	51.2%	48.8%
49,349	ANGELINA	16,496	4,770	11,619	107	6,849 D	28.9%	70.4%	29.1%	70.9%
8,902	ARANSAS	4,081	1,676	2,357	48	681 D	41.1%	57.8%	41.6%	58.4%
5,759	ARCHER	2,443	558	1,883	2	1,325 D	22.8%	77.1%	22.9%	77.1%
1,895	ARMSTRONG	967	327	637	3	310 D	33.8%	65.9%	33.9%	66.1%
18,696	ATASCOSA	6,363	1,556	4,759	48	3,203 D	24.5%	74.8%	24.6%	75.4%
13,831	AUSTIN	4,876	2,082	2,780	14	698 D	42.7%	57.0%	42.8%	57.2%
8,487	BAILEY	2,492	957	1,532	3	575 D	38.4%	61.5%	38.4%	61.6%
4,747	BANDERA	2,577	1,124	1,439	14	315 D	43.6%	55.8%	43.9%	56.1%
17,297	BASTROP	6,679	1,821	4,827	31	3,006 D	27.3%	72.3%	27.4%	72.6%
5,221	BAYLOR	2,039	499	1,538	2	1,039 D	24.5%	75.4%	24.5%	75.5%
22,737	BEE	6,410	2,073	4,246	91	2,173 D	32.3%	66.2%	32.8%	67.2%
124,483	BELL	30,782	12,292	18,323	167	6,031 D	39.9%	59.5%	40.2%	59.8%
830,460	BEXAR	259,893	99,364	156,097	4,432	56,733 D	38.2%	60.1%	38.9%	61.1%
3,567	BLANCO	1,809	706	1,094	9	388 D	39.0%	60.5%	39.2%	60.8%
888	BORDEN	378	104	274		170 D	27.5%	72.5%	27.5%	72.5%
10,966	BOSQUE	4,674	1,769	2,898	7	1,129 D	37.8%	62.0%	37.9%	62.1%
67,813	BOWIE	21,595	6,657	14,798	140	8,141 D	30.8%	68.5%	31.0%	69.0%
108,312	BRAZORIA	40,997	15,096	25,342	559	10,246 D	36.8%	61.8%	37.3%	62.7%
57,978	BRAZOS	26,144	14,302	11,441	401	2,861 R	54.7%	43.8%	55.6%	44.4%
7,780	BREWSTER	2,545	894	1,610	41	716 D	35.1%	63.3%	35.7%	64.3%
2,794	BRISCOE	1,066	175	888	3	713 D	16.4%	83.3%	16.5%	83.5%
8,005	BROOKS	3,176	411	2,729	36	2,318 D	12.9%	85.9%	13.1%	86.9%
25,877	BROWN	9,726	4,301	5,401	24	1,100 D	44.2%	55.5%	44.3%	55.7%
9,999	BURLESON	3,856	889	2,955	12	2,066 D	23.1%	76.6%	23.1%	76.9%
11,420	BURNET	6,418	2,523	3,883	12	1,360 D	39.3%	60.5%	39.4%	60.6%
21,178	CALDWELL	5,568	1,748	3,769	51	2,021 D	31.4%	67.7%	31.7%	68.3%
17,831	CALHOUN	5,679	1,838	3,792	49	1,954 D	32.4%	66.8%	32.6%	67.4%
8,205	CALLAHAN	3,736	1,221	2,499	16	1,278 D	32.7%	66.9%	32.8%	67.2%
140,368	CAMERON	39,051	13,545	25,168	338	11,623 D	34.7%	64.4%	35.0%	65.0%
8,005	CAMP	3,102	897	2,203	2	1,306 D	28.9%	71.0%	28.9%	71.1%
6,358	CARSON	2,730	963	1,763	4	800 D	35.3%	64.6%	35.3%	64.7%
24,133	CASS	8,151	2,613	5,529	9	2,916 D	32.1%	67.8%	32.1%	67.9%
10,394	CASTRO	2,978	929	2,021	28	1,092 D	31.2%	67.9%	31.5%	68.5%
12,187	CHAMBERS	4,771	1,358	3,341	72	1,983 D	28.5%	70.0%	28.9%	71.1%
32,008	CHEROKEE	10,066	3,074	6,978	14	3,904 D	30.5%	69.3%	30.6%	69.4%
6,605	CHILDRESS	2,454	726	1,727	1	1,001 D	29.6%	70.4%	29.6%	70.4%
8,079	CLAY	3,500	834	2,664	2	1,830 D	23.8%	76.1%	23.8%	76.2%
5,326	COCHRAN	1,610	404	1,198	8	794 D	25.1%	74.4%	25.2%	74.8%
3,087	COKE	1,351	364	980	7	616 D	26.9%	72.5%	27.1%	72.9%
10,288	COLEMAN	3,814	1,259	2,546	9	1,287 D	33.0%	66.8%	33.1%	66.9%
66,920	COLLIN	35,160	19,393	15,473	294	3,920 R	55.2%	44.0%	55.6%	44.4%
4,755	COLLINGSWORTH	1,690	421	1,268	1	847 D	24.9%	75.0%	24.9%	75.1%
17,638	COLORADO	5,772	2,107	3,630	35	1,523 D	36.5%	62.9%	36.7%	63.3%
24,165	COMAL	10,164	4,974	5,128	62	154 D	48.9%	50.5%	49.2%	50.8%
11,898	COMANCHE	4,546	1,174	3,369	3	2,195 D	25.8%	74.1%	25.8%	74.2%
2,937	CONCHO	1,174	209	963	2	754 D	17.8%	82.0%	17.8%	82.2%
23,471	COOKE	9,128	4,800	4,315	13	485 R	52.6%	47.3%	52.7%	47.3%
35,311	CORYELL	8,495	4,367	4,104	24	263 R	51.4%	48.3%	51.6%	48.4%
3,204	COTTLE	1,290	192	1,091	7	899 D	14.9%	84.6%	15.0%	85.0%
4,172	CRANE	1,577	513	847	217	334 D	32.5%	53.7%	37.7%	62.3%
3,885	CROCKETT	1,468	393	1,041	34	648 D	26.8%	70.9%	27.4%	72.6%
9,085	CROSBY	2,920	559	2,328	33	1,769 D	19.1%	79.7%	19.4%	80.6%
3,429	CULBERSON	682	214	449	19	235 D	31.4%	65.8%	32.3%	67.7%
6,012	DALLAM	1,861	724	1,129	8	405 D	38.9%	60.7%	39.1%	60.9%
1,327,321	DALLAS	445,039	262,947	178,931	3,161	84,016 R	59.1%	40.2%	59.5%	40.5%
16,604	DAWSON	4,385	1,624	2,746	15	1,122 D	37.0%	62.6%	37.2%	62.8%
18,999	DEAF SMITH	5,183	2,146	2,994	43	848 D	41.4%	57.8%	41.8%	58.2%
4,927	DELTA	1,953	478	1,474	1	996 D	24.5%	75.5%	24.5%	75.5%
75,633	DENTON	38,428	20,852	17,307	269	3,545 R	54.3%	45.0%	54.6%	45.4%
18,660	DE WITT	5,129	2,249	2,868	12	619 D	43.8%	55.9%	44.0%	56.0%
3,737	DICKENS	1,457	258	1,194	5	936 D	17.7%	81.9%	17.8%	82.2%
9,039	DIMMIT	2,464	533	1,895	36	1,362 D	21.6%	76.9%	22.0%	78.0%
3,641	DONLEY	1,689	507	1,178	4	671 D	30.0%	69.7%	30.1%	69.9%

TEXAS

SENATOR 1976

1970 Census Population	County	Total Vote	Republican	Democratic	Other	Rep.-Dem. Plurality	Percentage Total Vote Rep.	Percentage Total Vote Dem.	Percentage Major Vote Rep.	Percentage Major Vote Dem.
11,722	DUVAL	4,784	532	4,236	16	3,704 D	11.1%	88.5%	11.2%	88.8%
18,092	EASTLAND	6,460	1,955	4,489	16	2,534 D	30.3%	69.5%	30.3%	69.7%
91,805	ECTOR	29,767	14,637	14,572	558	65 R	49.2%	49.0%	50.1%	49.9%
2,107	EDWARDS	616	231	385		154 D	37.5%	62.5%	37.5%	62.5%
46,638	ELLIS	16,477	6,286	10,132	59	3,846 D	38.2%	61.5%	38.3%	61.7%
359,291	EL PASO	90,884	28,596	57,759	4,529	29,163 D	31.5%	63.6%	33.1%	66.9%
18,141	ERATH	7,598	2,533	5,045	20	2,512 D	33.3%	66.4%	33.4%	66.6%
17,300	FALLS	6,050	1,790	4,240	20	2,450 D	29.6%	70.1%	29.7%	70.3%
22,705	FANNIN	7,769	1,777	5,986	6	4,209 D	22.9%	77.0%	22.9%	77.1%
17,650	FAYETTE	6,132	2,014	4,102	16	2,088 D	32.8%	66.9%	32.9%	67.1%
6,344	FISHER	2,187	436	1,742	9	1,306 D	19.9%	79.7%	20.0%	80.0%
11,044	FLOYD	3,233	990	2,229	14	1,239 D	30.6%	68.9%	30.8%	69.2%
2,211	FOARD	907	148	758	1	610 D	16.3%	83.6%	16.3%	83.7%
52,314	FORT BEND	27,355	13,350	13,879	126	529 D	48.8%	50.7%	49.0%	51.0%
5,291	FRANKLIN	2,287	567	1,718	2	1,151 D	24.8%	75.1%	24.8%	75.2%
11,116	FREESTONE	3,420	1,154	2,262	4	1,108 D	33.7%	66.1%	33.8%	66.2%
11,159	FRIO	3,450	891	2,516	43	1,625 D	25.8%	72.9%	26.2%	73.8%
11,593	GAINES	3,380	1,271	2,098	11	827 D	37.6%	62.1%	37.7%	62.3%
169,812	GALVESTON	59,991	19,985	39,327	679	19,342 D	33.3%	65.6%	33.7%	66.3%
5,289	GARZA	1,526	472	1,050	4	578 D	30.9%	68.8%	31.0%	69.0%
10,553	GILLESPIE	4,739	2,670	2,044	25	626 R	56.3%	43.1%	56.6%	43.4%
1,155	GLASSCOCK	404	159	244	1	85 D	39.4%	60.4%	39.5%	60.5%
4,869	GOLIAD	1,600	580	1,017	3	437 D	36.3%	63.6%	36.3%	63.7%
16,375	GONZALES	4,472	1,237	3,218	17	1,981 D	27.7%	72.0%	27.8%	72.2%
26,949	GRAY	9,477	4,649	4,810	18	161 D	49.1%	50.8%	49.1%	50.9%
83,225	GRAYSON	27,684	10,668	16,945	71	6,277 D	38.5%	61.2%	38.6%	61.4%
75,929	GREGG	25,792	14,936	10,743	113	4,193 R	57.9%	41.7%	58.2%	41.8%
11,855	GRIMES	3,914	1,113	2,782	19	1,669 D	28.4%	71.1%	28.6%	71.4%
33,554	GUADALUPE	12,275	5,717	6,501	57	784 D	46.6%	53.0%	46.8%	53.2%
34,137	HALE	10,473	4,267	6,161	45	1,894 D	40.7%	58.8%	40.9%	59.1%
6,015	HALL	2,207	465	1,739	3	1,274 D	21.1%	78.8%	21.1%	78.9%
7,198	HAMILTON	3,037	1,251	1,781	5	530 D	41.2%	58.6%	41.3%	58.7%
6,351	HANSFORD	2,374	1,119	1,255		136 D	47.1%	52.9%	47.1%	52.9%
6,795	HARDEMAN	2,104	572	1,530	2	958 D	27.2%	72.7%	27.2%	72.8%
29,996	HARDIN	10,150	3,012	7,094	44	4,082 D	29.7%	69.9%	29.8%	70.2%
1,741,912	HARRIS	638,676	295,074	337,970	5,632	42,896 D	46.2%	52.9%	46.6%	53.4%
44,841	HARRISON	13,703	5,100	8,542	61	3,442 D	37.2%	62.3%	37.4%	62.6%
2,782	HARTLEY	1,516	563	950	3	387 D	37.1%	62.7%	37.2%	62.8%
8,512	HASKELL	3,256	605	2,644	7	2,039 D	18.6%	81.2%	18.6%	81.4%
27,642	HAYS	11,943	4,646	7,179	118	2,533 D	38.9%	60.1%	39.3%	60.7%
3,084	HEMPHILL	1,454	570	882	2	312 D	39.2%	60.7%	39.3%	60.7%
26,466	HENDERSON	12,384	4,298	8,067	19	3,769 D	34.7%	65.1%	34.8%	65.2%
181,535	HIDALGO	50,311	15,460	34,389	462	18,929 D	30.7%	68.4%	31.0%	69.0%
22,596	HILL	7,679	2,391	5,276	12	2,885 D	31.1%	68.7%	31.2%	68.8%
20,396	HOCKLEY	6,769	2,117	4,629	23	2,512 D	31.3%	68.4%	31.4%	68.6%
6,368	HOOD	4,786	1,712	3,059	15	1,347 D	35.8%	63.9%	35.9%	64.1%
20,710	HOPKINS	7,288	2,205	5,070	13	2,865 D	30.3%	69.6%	30.3%	69.7%
17,855	HOUSTON	4,911	1,249	3,648	14	2,399 D	25.4%	74.3%	25.5%	74.5%
37,796	HOWARD	11,727	4,197	7,438	92	3,241 D	35.8%	63.4%	36.1%	63.9%
2,392	HUDSPETH	767	162	604	1	442 D	21.1%	78.7%	21.1%	78.9%
47,948	HUNT	14,521	6,149	8,319	53	2,170 D	42.3%	57.3%	42.5%	57.5%
24,443	HUTCHINSON	9,536	4,901	4,604	31	297 R	51.4%	48.3%	51.6%	48.4%
1,070	IRION	546	158	380	8	222 D	28.9%	69.6%	29.4%	70.6%
6,711	JACK	2,699	685	2,010	4	1,325 D	25.4%	74.5%	25.4%	74.6%
12,975	JACKSON	4,202	1,546	2,635	21	1,089 D	36.8%	62.7%	37.0%	63.0%
24,692	JASPER	8,209	2,457	5,736	16	3,279 D	29.9%	69.9%	30.0%	70.0%
1,527	JEFF DAVIS	556	177	356	23	179 D	31.8%	64.0%	33.2%	66.8%
244,773	JEFFERSON	79,583	25,597	53,405	581	27,808 D	32.2%	67.1%	32.4%	67.6%
4,654	JIM HOGG	1,895	239	1,656		1,417 D	12.6%	87.4%	12.6%	87.4%
33,032	JIM WELLS	11,081	2,571	8,459	51	5,888 D	23.2%	76.3%	23.3%	76.7%
45,769	JOHNSON	17,015	6,287	10,687	41	4,400 D	36.9%	62.8%	37.0%	63.0%
16,106	JONES	5,176	1,602	3,561	13	1,959 D	31.0%	68.8%	31.0%	69.0%
13,462	KARNES	4,472	1,178	3,264	30	2,086 D	26.3%	73.0%	26.5%	73.5%
32,392	KAUFMAN	9,853	3,456	6,388	9	2,932 D	35.1%	64.8%	35.1%	64.9%
6,964	KENDALL	3,567	1,901	1,638	28	263 R	53.3%	45.9%	53.7%	46.3%

TEXAS

SENATOR 1976

1970 Census Population	County	Total Vote	Republican	Democratic	Other	Rep.-Dem. Plurality	Percentage Total Vote Rep.	Percentage Total Vote Dem.	Percentage Major Vote Rep.	Percentage Major Vote Dem.
678	KENEDY	195	50	145		95 D	25.6%	74.4%	25.6%	74.4%
1,434	KENT	612	121	491		370 D	19.8%	80.2%	19.8%	80.2%
19,454	KERR	9,527	4,967	4,445	115	522 R	52.1%	46.7%	52.8%	47.2%
3,904	KIMBLE	1,398	385	1,002	11	617 D	27.5%	71.7%	27.8%	72.2%
464	KING	180	52	128		76 D	28.9%	71.1%	28.9%	71.1%
2,006	KINNEY	785	190	590	5	400 D	24.2%	75.2%	24.4%	75.6%
33,166	KLEBERG	9,260	3,195	5,985	80	2,790 D	34.5%	64.6%	34.8%	65.2%
5,972	KNOX	1,952	311	1,641		1,330 D	15.9%	84.1%	15.9%	84.1%
36,062	LAMAR	12,349	4,330	8,003	16	3,673 D	35.1%	64.8%	35.1%	64.9%
17,770	LAMB	5,460	1,703	3,734	23	2,031 D	31.2%	68.4%	31.3%	68.7%
9,323	LAMPASAS	3,736	1,466	2,256	14	790 D	39.2%	60.4%	39.4%	60.6%
5,014	LA SALLE	1,494	391	1,074	29	683 D	26.2%	71.9%	26.7%	73.3%
17,903	LAVACA	5,677	1,786	3,879	12	2,093 D	31.5%	68.3%	31.5%	68.5%
8,048	LEE	2,962	804	2,153	5	1,349 D	27.1%	72.7%	27.2%	72.8%
8,738	LEON	2,901	811	2,084	6	1,273 D	28.0%	71.8%	28.0%	72.0%
33,014	LIBERTY	11,057	3,451	7,568	38	4,117 D	31.2%	68.4%	31.3%	68.7%
18,100	LIMESTONE	5,669	1,818	3,839	12	2,021 D	32.1%	67.7%	32.1%	67.9%
3,486	LIPSCOMB	1,444	596	848		252 D	41.3%	58.7%	41.3%	58.7%
6,697	LIVE OAK	2,816	941	1,862	13	921 D	33.4%	66.1%	33.6%	66.4%
6,979	LLANO	4,173	1,695	2,471	7	776 D	40.6%	59.2%	40.7%	59.3%
164	LOVING	65	25	40		15 D	38.5%	61.5%	38.5%	61.5%
179,295	LUBBOCK	60,760	27,617	32,723	420	5,106 D	45.5%	53.9%	45.8%	54.2%
9,107	LYNN	2,645	665	1,973	7	1,308 D	25.1%	74.6%	25.2%	74.8%
8,571	MCCULLOCH	2,924	784	2,125	15	1,341 D	26.8%	72.7%	27.0%	73.0%
147,553	MCLENNAN	54,557	23,741	30,595	221	6,854 D	43.5%	56.1%	43.7%	56.3%
1,095	MCMULLEN	392	154	237	1	83 D	39.3%	60.5%	39.4%	60.6%
7,693	MADISON	2,738	748	1,982	8	1,234 D	27.3%	72.4%	27.4%	72.6%
8,517	MARION	2,836	813	2,020	3	1,207 D	28.7%	71.2%	28.7%	71.3%
4,774	MARTIN	1,475	440	1,030	5	590 D	29.8%	69.8%	29.9%	70.1%
3,356	MASON	1,551	577	964	10	387 D	37.2%	62.2%	37.4%	62.6%
27,913	MATAGORDA	8,367	2,874	5,429	64	2,555 D	34.3%	64.9%	34.6%	65.4%
18,093	MAVERICK	3,524	560	2,930	34	2,370 D	15.9%	83.1%	16.0%	84.0%
20,249	MEDINA	6,632	2,270	4,324	38	2,054 D	34.2%	65.2%	34.4%	65.6%
2,646	MENARD	951	261	680	10	419 D	27.4%	71.5%	27.7%	72.3%
65,433	MIDLAND	25,563	15,281	10,033	249	5,248 R	59.8%	39.2%	60.4%	39.6%
20,028	MILAM	7,042	1,904	5,126	12	3,222 D	27.0%	72.8%	27.1%	72.9%
4,212	MILLS	1,627	669	957	1	288 D	41.1%	58.8%	41.1%	58.9%
9,073	MITCHELL	2,707	877	1,823	7	946 D	32.4%	67.3%	32.5%	67.5%
15,326	MONTAGUE	5,667	1,743	3,917	7	2,174 D	30.8%	69.1%	30.8%	69.2%
49,479	MONTGOMERY	28,152	12,649	15,328	175	2,679 D	44.9%	54.4%	45.2%	54.8%
14,060	MOORE	5,308	1,940	3,357	11	1,417 D	36.5%	63.2%	36.6%	63.4%
12,310	MORRIS	4,589	1,366	3,219	4	1,853 D	29.8%	70.1%	29.8%	70.2%
2,178	MOTLEY	899	272	621	6	349 D	30.3%	69.1%	30.5%	69.5%
36,362	NACOGDOCHES	13,423	6,095	7,255	73	1,160 D	45.4%	54.0%	45.7%	54.3%
31,150	NAVARRO	10,496	3,264	7,212	20	3,948 D	31.1%	68.7%	31.2%	68.8%
11,657	NEWTON	4,097	717	3,372	8	2,655 D	17.5%	82.3%	17.5%	82.5%
16,220	NOLAN	5,377	1,949	3,423	5	1,474 D	36.2%	63.7%	36.3%	63.7%
237,544	NUECES	82,990	27,339	54,940	711	27,601 D	32.9%	66.2%	33.2%	66.8%
9,704	OCHILTREE	3,378	1,645	1,727	6	82 D	48.7%	51.1%	48.8%	51.2%
2,258	OLDHAM	794	266	519	9	253 D	33.5%	65.4%	33.9%	66.1%
71,170	ORANGE	23,638	7,338	16,202	98	8,864 D	31.0%	68.5%	31.2%	68.8%
28,962	PALO PINTO	7,719	2,367	5,320	32	2,953 D	30.7%	68.9%	30.8%	69.2%
15,894	PANOLA	6,465	2,103	4,354	8	2,251 D	32.5%	67.3%	32.6%	67.4%
33,888	PARKER	12,611	4,275	8,281	55	4,006 D	33.9%	65.7%	34.0%	66.0%
10,509	PARMER	3,283	1,147	2,133	3	986 D	34.9%	65.0%	35.0%	65.0%
13,748	PECOS	4,004	1,505	2,421	78	916 D	37.6%	60.5%	38.3%	61.7%
14,457	POLK	6,295	1,803	4,458	34	2,655 D	28.6%	70.8%	28.8%	71.2%
90,511	POTTER	25,362	10,337	14,692	333	4,355 D	40.8%	57.9%	41.3%	58.7%
4,842	PRESIDIO	1,591	371	1,191	29	820 D	23.3%	74.9%	23.8%	76.2%
3,752	RAINS	1,730	466	1,262	2	796 D	26.9%	72.9%	27.0%	73.0%
53,885	RANDALL	26,009	12,766	13,012	231	246 D	49.1%	50.0%	49.5%	50.5%
3,239	REAGAN	1,187	402	783	2	381 D	33.9%	66.0%	33.9%	66.1%
2,013	REAL	871	244	616	11	372 D	28.0%	70.7%	28.4%	71.6%
14,298	RED RIVER	4,933	1,153	3,779	1	2,626 D	23.4%	76.6%	23.4%	76.6%
16,526	REEVES	3,773	1,258	2,416	99	1,158 D	33.3%	64.0%	34.2%	65.8%

TEXAS

SENATOR 1976

1970 Census Population	County	Total Vote	Republican	Democratic	Other	Rep.-Dem. Plurality	Percentage Total Vote Rep.	Total Vote Dem.	Major Vote Rep.	Major Vote Dem.
9,494	REFUGIO	3,469	1,011	2,441	17	1,430 D	29.1%	70.4%	29.3%	70.7%
967	ROBERTS	532	252	278	2	26 D	47.4%	52.3%	47.5%	52.5%
14,389	ROBERTSON	4,715	1,011	3,691	13	2,680 D	21.4%	78.3%	21.5%	78.5%
7,046	ROCKWALL	3,827	1,995	1,827	5	168 R	52.1%	47.7%	52.2%	47.8%
12,108	RUNNELS	3,926	1,198	2,727	1	1,529 D	30.5%	69.5%	30.5%	69.5%
34,102	RUSK	11,149	5,016	6,086	47	1,070 D	45.0%	54.6%	45.2%	54.8%
7,187	SABINE	3,075	608	2,464	3	1,856 D	19.8%	80.1%	19.8%	80.2%
7,858	SAN AUGUSTINE	2,667	651	2,012	4	1,361 D	24.4%	75.4%	24.4%	75.6%
6,702	SAN JACINTO	3,227	821	2,386	20	1,565 D	25.4%	73.9%	25.6%	74.4%
47,288	SAN PATRICIO	14,841	5,003	9,753	85	4,750 D	33.7%	65.7%	33.9%	66.1%
5,540	SAN SABA	1,945	514	1,426	5	912 D	26.4%	73.3%	26.5%	73.5%
2,277	SCHLEICHER	956	305	638	13	333 D	31.9%	66.7%	32.3%	67.7%
15,760	SCURRY	5,242	2,123	3,106	13	983 D	40.5%	59.3%	40.6%	59.4%
3,323	SHACKELFORD	1,382	524	850	8	326 D	37.9%	61.5%	38.1%	61.9%
19,672	SHELBY	6,950	1,473	5,472	5	3,999 D	21.2%	78.7%	21.2%	78.8%
3,657	SHERMAN	1,350	500	844	6	344 D	37.0%	62.5%	37.2%	62.8%
97,096	SMITH	37,092	19,977	17,042	73	2,935 R	53.9%	45.9%	54.0%	46.0%
2,793	SOMERVELL	1,366	361	1,002	3	641 D	26.4%	73.4%	26.5%	73.5%
17,707	STARR	5,115	474	4,630	11	4,156 D	9.3%	90.5%	9.3%	90.7%
8,414	STEPHENS	3,176	1,361	1,810	5	449 D	42.9%	57.0%	42.9%	57.1%
1,056	STERLING	368	121	247		126 D	32.9%	67.1%	32.9%	67.1%
2,397	STONEWALL	1,046	182	862	2	680 D	17.4%	82.4%	17.4%	82.6%
3,175	SUTTON	1,494	449	1,013	32	564 D	30.1%	67.8%	30.7%	69.3%
10,373	SWISHER	3,461	590	2,867	4	2,277 D	17.0%	82.8%	17.1%	82.9%
716,317	TARRANT	237,148	109,663	125,385	2,100	15,722 D	46.2%	52.9%	46.7%	53.3%
97,853	TAYLOR	32,333	15,708	16,506	119	798 D	48.6%	51.1%	48.8%	51.2%
1,940	TERRELL	596	185	406	5	221 D	31.0%	68.1%	31.3%	68.7%
14,118	TERRY	4,720	1,468	3,235	17	1,767 D	31.1%	68.5%	31.2%	68.8%
2,205	THROCKMORTON	975	227	746	2	519 D	23.3%	76.5%	23.3%	76.7%
16,702	TITUS	6,293	2,021	4,267	5	2,246 D	32.1%	67.8%	32.1%	67.9%
71,047	TOM GREEN	23,176	9,130	13,788	258	4,658 D	39.4%	59.5%	39.8%	60.2%
295,516	TRAVIS	148,809	66,422	76,818	5,569	10,396 D	44.6%	51.6%	46.4%	53.6%
7,628	TRINITY	2,890	566	2,311	13	1,745 D	19.6%	80.0%	19.7%	80.3%
12,417	TYLER	4,849	1,418	3,416	15	1,998 D	29.2%	70.4%	29.3%	70.7%
20,976	UPSHUR	7,565	2,664	4,884	17	2,220 D	35.2%	64.6%	35.3%	64.7%
4,697	UPTON	1,490	571	900	19	329 D	38.3%	60.4%	38.8%	61.2%
17,348	UVALDE	5,166	2,028	3,090	48	1,062 D	39.3%	59.8%	39.6%	60.4%
27,471	VAL VERDE	7,821	2,252	5,494	75	3,242 D	28.8%	70.2%	29.1%	70.9%
22,155	VAN ZANDT	9,608	3,180	6,410	18	3,230 D	33.1%	66.7%	33.2%	66.8%
53,766	VICTORIA	16,507	8,406	7,952	149	454 R	50.9%	48.2%	51.4%	48.6%
27,680	WALKER	9,545	3,902	5,560	83	1,658 D	40.9%	58.3%	41.2%	58.8%
14,285	WALLER	4,597	1,469	3,106	22	1,637 D	32.0%	67.6%	32.1%	67.9%
13,019	WARD	3,996	1,814	2,159	23	345 D	45.4%	54.0%	45.7%	54.3%
18,842	WASHINGTON	6,219	2,377	3,826	16	1,449 D	38.2%	61.5%	38.3%	61.7%
72,859	WEBB	12,984	2,453	10,359	172	7,906 D	18.9%	79.8%	19.1%	80.9%
36,729	WHARTON	10,247	3,737	6,464	46	2,727 D	36.5%	63.1%	36.6%	63.4%
6,434	WHEELER	2,675	1,015	1,655	5	640 D	37.9%	61.9%	38.0%	62.0%
121,862	WICHITA	40,078	14,321	25,647	110	11,326 D	35.7%	64.0%	35.8%	64.2%
15,355	WILBARGER	5,121	1,213	3,886	22	2,673 D	23.7%	75.9%	23.8%	76.2%
15,570	WILLACY	4,295	1,096	3,178	21	2,082 D	25.5%	74.0%	25.6%	74.4%
37,305	WILLIAMSON	15,988	6,219	9,690	79	3,471 D	38.9%	60.6%	39.1%	60.9%
13,041	WILSON	5,383	1,432	3,934	17	2,502 D	26.6%	73.1%	26.7%	73.3%
9,640	WINKLER	3,087	1,220	1,846	21	626 D	39.5%	59.8%	39.8%	60.2%
19,687	WISE	7,749	2,387	5,351	11	2,964 D	30.8%	69.1%	30.8%	69.2%
18,589	WOOD	6,992	2,815	4,147	30	1,332 D	40.3%	59.3%	40.4%	59.6%
7,344	YOAKUM	2,547	1,048	1,486	13	438 D	41.1%	58.3%	41.4%	58.6%
15,400	YOUNG	5,925	1,988	3,924	13	1,936 D	33.6%	66.2%	33.6%	66.4%
4,352	ZAPATA	1,575	306	1,260	9	954 D	19.4%	80.0%	19.5%	80.5%
11,370	ZAVALA	1,938	429	1,467	42	1,038 D	22.1%	75.7%	22.6%	77.4%
11,196,730	TOTAL	3,874,516	1,636,370	2,199,956	38,190	563,586 D	42.2%	56.8%	42.7%	57.3%

TEXAS

CONGRESS

CD	Year	Total Vote	Republican Vote	Republican Candidate	Democratic Vote	Democratic Candidate	Other Vote	Rep.-Dem. Plurality	Percentage Total Vote Rep.	Percentage Total Vote Dem.	Percentage Major Vote Rep.	Percentage Major Vote Dem.
1	1976	161,745	26,334	HOGAN, JAMES	135,384	HALL, SAM B.	27	109,050 D	16.3%	83.7%	16.3%	83.7%
1	1974	72,050	22,619	FARRIS, JAMES W.	49,426	PATMAN, WRIGHT	5	26,807 D	31.4%	68.6%	31.4%	68.6%
2	1976	140,971			133,910	WILSON, CHARLES	7,061	133,910 D		95.0%		100.0%
2	1974	57,132			57,096	WILSON, CHARLES	36	57,096 D		99.9%		100.0%
3	1976	231,430	171,343	COLLINS, JAMES M.	60,070	SHACKELFORD, LES E.	17	111,273 R	74.0%	26.0%	74.0%	26.0%
3	1974	98,130	63,489	COLLINS, JAMES M.	34,623	COLLUM, HAROLD	18	28,866 R	64.7%	35.3%	64.7%	35.3%
4	1976	168,038	62,641	GLENN, FRANK S.	105,394	ROBERTS, RAY	3	42,753 D	37.3%	62.7%	37.3%	62.7%
4	1974	64,329	16,113	LETOURNEAU, DICK	48,209	ROBERTS, RAY	7	32,096 D	25.0%	74.9%	25.1%	74.9%
5	1976	125,778	56,056	JUDY, NANCY	67,871	MATTOX, JIM	1,851	11,815 D	44.6%	54.0%	45.2%	54.8%
5	1974	54,637	28,446	STEELMAN, ALAN	26,190	MCKOOL, MIKE	1	2,256 R	52.1%	47.9%	52.1%	47.9%
6	1976	180,549	60,316	MOWERY, WES	119,025	TEAGUE, OLIN E.	1,208	58,709 D	33.4%	65.9%	33.6%	66.4%
6	1974	64,256	10,908	NIGLIAZZO, CARL	53,345	TEAGUE, OLIN E.	3	42,437 D	17.0%	83.0%	17.0%	83.0%
7	1976	193,127	193,127	ARCHER, W. R.				193,127 R	100.0%		100.0%	
7	1974	88,887	70,363	ARCHER, W. R.	18,524	BRADY, JIM		51,839 R	79.2%	20.8%	79.2%	20.8%
8	1976	139,163	54,566	GEARHART, NICK	84,404	ECKHARDT, BOB	193	29,838 D	39.2%	60.7%	39.3%	60.7%
8	1974	41,763	11,605	WHITEFIELD, DONALD D.	30,158	ECKHARDT, BOB		18,553 D	27.8%	72.2%	27.8%	72.2%
9	1976	113,016			112,945	BROOKS, JACK B.	71	112,945 D		99.9%		100.0%
9	1974	60,210	22,935	FERGUSON, COLEMAN R.	37,275	BROOKS, JACK B.		14,340 D	38.1%	61.9%	38.1%	61.9%
10	1976	209,172	48,482	MCCLURE, PAUL	160,683	PICKLE, JAKE	7	112,201 D	23.2%	76.8%	23.2%	76.8%
10	1974	94,814	18,560	WEISS, PAUL A.	76,240	PICKLE, JAKE	14	57,680 D	19.6%	80.4%	19.6%	80.4%
11	1976	160,563	68,373	BURGESS, JACK	92,142	POAGE, W. R.	48	23,769 D	42.6%	57.4%	42.6%	57.4%
11	1974	57,411	9,883	CLEMENTS, DON	46,828	POAGE, W. R.	700	36,945 D	17.2%	81.6%	17.4%	82.6%
12	1976	134,259	31,941	DURHAM, W. R.	101,814	WRIGHT, JAMES C.	504	69,873 D	23.8%	75.8%	23.9%	76.1%
12	1974	54,175	11,543	GARVEY, JAMES S.	42,632	WRIGHT, JAMES C.		31,089 D	21.3%	78.7%	21.3%	78.7%
13	1976	171,682	69,328	PRICE, ROBERT	101,798	HIGHTOWER, JOHN	556	32,470 D	40.4%	59.3%	40.5%	59.5%
13	1974	92,182	39,087	PRICE, ROBERT	53,094	HIGHTOWER, JOHN	1	14,007 D	42.4%	57.6%	42.4%	57.6%
14	1976	152,416	58,788	HOLFORD, L. DEAN	93,589	YOUNG, JOHN	39	34,801 D	38.6%	61.4%	38.6%	61.4%
14	1974	41,076			41,066	YOUNG, JOHN	10	41,066 D		100.0%		100.0%
15	1976	138,285	35,446	MCDONALD, R. L.	102,837	DE LA GARZA, ELIGIO	2	67,391 D	25.6%	74.4%	25.6%	74.4%
15	1974	42,568			42,567	DE LA GARZA, ELIGIO	1	42,567 D		100.0%		100.0%
16	1976	124,448	52,499	SHACKELFORD, VIC	71,876	WHITE, RICHARD C.	73	19,377 D	42.2%	57.8%	42.2%	57.8%
16	1974	42,897			42,880	WHITE, RICHARD C.	17	42,880 D		100.0%		100.0%
17	1976	127,683			127,613	BURLESON, OMAR	70	127,613 D		99.9%		100.0%
17	1974	64,969			64,959	BURLESON, OMAR	10	64,959 D		100.0%		100.0%
18	1976	109,876	15,381	WRIGHT, SAM H.	93,953	JORDAN, BARBARA	542	78,572 D	14.0%	85.5%	14.1%	85.9%
18	1974	43,168	6,053	MITCHELL, ROBBINS	36,597	JORDAN, BARBARA	518	30,544 D	14.0%	84.8%	14.2%	85.8%
19	1976	160,901	72,991	REESE, JIM	87,908	MAHON, GEORGE H.	2	14,917 D	45.4%	54.6%	45.4%	54.6%
19	1974	49,634			49,619	MAHON, GEORGE H.	15	49,619 D		100.0%		100.0%
20	1976	90,181			90,173	GONZALEZ, HENRY B.	8	90,173 D		100.0%		100.0%
20	1974	39,358			39,358	GONZALEZ, HENRY B.		39,358 D		100.0%		100.0%
21	1976	210,315	56,211	LOCKE, BOBBY A.	149,395	KRUEGER, ROBERT	4,709	93,184 D	26.7%	71.0%	27.3%	72.7%
21	1974	101,761	45,959	HARLAN, DOUG	53,543	KRUEGER, ROBERT	2,259	7,584 D	45.2%	52.6%	46.2%	53.8%
22	1976	192,802	96,267	PAUL, RON	96,535	GAMMAGE, BOB		268 D	49.9%	50.1%	49.9%	50.1%
22	1974	68,718	19,483	PAUL, RON	47,783	CASEY, ROBERT R.	1,452	28,300 D	28.4%	69.5%	29.0%	71.0%
23	1976	96,524			96,481	KAZEN, ABRAHAM	43	96,481 D		100.0%		100.0%
23	1974	47,257			47,249	KAZEN, ABRAHAM	8	47,249 D		100.0%		100.0%
24	1976	130,531	47,075	BERMAN, LEO	82,743	MILFORD, DALE	713	35,668 D	36.1%	63.4%	36.3%	63.7%
24	1974	47,437	9,698	BEAMAN, JOSEPH	36,085	MILFORD, DALE	1,654	26,387 D	20.4%	76.1%	21.2%	78.8%

TEXAS

1976 GENERAL ELECTION

President — Original uncorrected canvass gave the Republican vote in Lamar county as 4,437 and the total Republican vote as 1,953,294. Other vote was 20,118 McCarthy (Independent); 11,442 Anderson (American); 1,723 Camejo (Socialist Workers); 189 MacBride (write-in); 41 Maddox (write-in); 2,752 scattered.

Senator — Other vote was 20,549 Vasquez (Socialist Workers); 17,355 Gallion (American); 286 scattered.

Congress — The data for CD 2 in the Congressional table is for the recount; original vote was 96,433 Gammage (Democrat); 96,197 Paul (Republican) and 2 scattered. Other vote was Lantz (Socialist Workers) in CD 8; Kutchinski (American) in CD 12; Zapata (Socialist Workers) in CD 18; 6,992 Doyle (American) and 69 scattered in CD 2; 1,841 McDonnell (American) and 10 scattered in CD 5; 1,193 Pinon (American) and 15 scattered in CD 6; 547 Hathcock (American) and 9 scattered in CD 13; 2,515 Carrillo (Raza Unida), 2,179 Gallion (American) and 15 scattered in CD 21; 704 Armstrong (American) and 9 scattered in CD 24; scattered in all other CD's.

1976 PRIMARIES

MAY 1 REPUBLICAN

Senator — 251,252 Alan Steelman; 64,404 Hugh Sweeney; 40,651 Louis Leman.

Congress — Unopposed in twelve CD's. No candidates in CD's 2, 9, 17, 20 and 23. Contested as follows:

CD 1 — 3,868 James Hogan; 1,758 Jessalyn Davis.
CD 3 — 42,126 James M. Collins; 15,006 Roger Chafin.
CD 6 — 11,816 Wes Mowery; 1,897 Carl Nigliazzo.
CD 10 — 7,152 Paul McClure; 5,487 Billy Murray.
CD 21 — 14,056 Bobby A. Locke; 12,199 C. J. Calnan.
CD 22 — 19,119 Ron Paul; 1,341 Joe W. Jones.
CD 24 — 7,536 Leo Berman; 5,569 Lowry Davison.

MAY 1 DEMOCRATIC

Senator — 970,983 Lloyd Bentsen; 427,597 Phil Gramm; 109,715 Hugh Wilson; 19,870 Leon Dugi; 1,003 scattered.

Congress — Unopposed in nine CD's. No candidate in CD 7. Contested as follows:

CD 1 — 27,787 Sam B. Hall; 24,929 Glen Jones; 23,126 Thelby Parish; 18,448 Fred Hudson; 16,182 George L. Preston; 6,768 James Allison; 3,294 Jess Nickerson; 2,758 John E. Wade; 1,472 Sam Taylor; 999 Kenneth V. Burkhalter.
CD 2 — 89,349 Charles Wilson; 27,327 Richard Brown.
CD 3 — 19,458 Les E. Shackelford; 7,432 Clarence M. Lambright.
CD 4 — 52,232 Ray Roberts; 20,950 David H. Brown; 7,309 Ben H. Zollner.
CD 5 — 19,289 Jim Mattox; 10,757 Wes Wise; 1,628 B. D. Howard.
CD 6 — 40,181 Olin E. Teague; 33,884 Ron Godbey.
CD 8 — 18,690 Bob Eckhardt; 4,279 Perry Roach.
CD 10 — 88,949 Jake Pickle; 18,528 E. H. Meadows.
CD 11 — 59,481 W. R. Poage; 21,947 Steve S. Alexander.
CD 15 — 69,987 Eligio de la Garza; 20,740 Angel N. Gonzales.
CD 16 — 38,468 Richard C. White; 23,583 George A. McAlmon; 4,867 Edgar Griggs; 923 Jack Gregory.
CD 21 — 64,478 Robert Krueger; 10,323 Joe Sullivan.
CD 22 — 32,276 Bob Gammage; 11,062 John S. Brunson; 4,634 J. Charles Whitfield.
CD 24 — 18,232 Dale Milford; 7,900 James Ross.

JUNE 5 DEMOCRATIC RUN-OFF

Congress

CD 1 — 50,082 Sam B. Hall; 45,836 Glen Jones.

UTAH

GOVERNOR

Scott M. Matheson (D). Elected 1976 to a four-year term.

SENATORS

E. J. Garn (R). Elected 1974 to a six-year term.

Orrin G. Hatch (R). Elected 1976 to a six-year term.

REPRESENTATIVES

1. K. Gunn McKay (D)
2. Dan Marriott (R)

POSTWAR VOTE FOR GOVERNOR

Year	Total Vote	Republican Vote	Republican Candidate	Democratic Vote	Democratic Candidate	Other Vote	Rep.-Dem. Plurality	Percentage Total Vote Rep.	Percentage Total Vote Dem.	Percentage Major Vote Rep.	Percentage Major Vote Dem.
1976	539,649	248,027	Romney, Vernon B.	280,706	Matheson, Scott M.	10,916	32,679 D	46.0%	52.0%	46.9%	53.1%
1972	476,447	144,449	Strike, Nicholas L.	331,998	Rampton, Calvin L.	–	187,549 D	30.3%	69.7%	30.3%	69.7%
1968	421,012	131,729	Buehner, Carl W.	289,283	Rampton, Calvin L.	–	157,554 D	31.3%	68.7%	31.3%	68.7%
1964	398,256	171,300	Melich, Mitchell	226,956	Rampton, Calvin L.	–	55,656 D	43.0%	57.0%	43.0%	57.0%
1960	371,489	195,634	Clyde, George D.	175,855	Barlocker, W. A.	–	19,779 R	52.7%	47.3%	52.7%	47.3%
1956	332,889	127,164	Clyde, George D.	111,297	Romney, L. C.	94,428	15,867 R	38.2%	33.4%	53.3%	46.7%
1952	327,704	180,516	Lee, J. Bracken	147,188	Glade, Earl J.	–	33,328 R	55.1%	44.9%	55.1%	44.9%
1948	275,067	151,253	Lee, J. Bracken	123,814	Maw, Herbert B.	–	27,439 R	55.0%	45.0%	55.0%	45.0%

POSTWAR VOTE FOR SENATOR

Year	Total Vote	Republican Vote	Republican Candidate	Democratic Vote	Democratic Candidate	Other Vote	Rep.-Dem. Plurality	Percentage Total Vote Rep.	Percentage Total Vote Dem.	Percentage Major Vote Rep.	Percentage Major Vote Dem.
1976	540,108	290,221	Hatch, Orrin G.	241,948	Moss, Frank E.	7,939	48,273 R	53.7%	44.8%	54.5%	45.5%
1974	420,642	210,299	Garn, E. J.	185,377	Owens, Wayne	24,966	24,922 R	50.0%	44.1%	53.1%	46.9%
1970	374,303	159,004	Burton, Laurence J.	210,207	Moss, Frank E.	5,092	51,203 D	42.5%	56.2%	43.1%	56.9%
1968	419,262	225,075	Bennett, Wallace F.	192,168	Weilenmann, Milton	2,019	32,907 R	53.7%	45.8%	53.9%	46.1%
1964	397,384	169,562	Wilkinson, Ernest L.	227,822	Moss, Frank E.	–	58,260 D	42.7%	57.3%	42.7%	57.3%
1962	318,411	166,755	Bennett, Wallace F.	151,656	King, David S.	–	15,099 R	52.4%	47.6%	52.4%	47.6%
1958	291,311	101,471	Watkins, Arthur V.	112,827	Moss, Frank E.	77,013	11,356 D	34.8%	38.7%	47.4%	52.6%
1956	330,381	178,261	Bennett, Wallace F.	152,120	Hopkin, Alonzo F.	–	26,141 R	54.0%	46.0%	54.0%	46.0%
1952	327,033	177,435	Watkins, Arthur V.	149,598	Granger, Walter K.	–	27,837 R	54.3%	45.7%	54.3%	45.7%
1950	264,440	142,427	Bennett, Wallace F.	121,198	Thomas, Elbert D.	815	21,229 R	53.9%	45.8%	54.0%	46.0%
1946	197,399	101,142	Watkins, Arthur V.	96,257	Murdock, Abe	–	4,885 R	51.2%	48.8%	51.2%	48.8%

UTAH

Districts Established February 6,1971

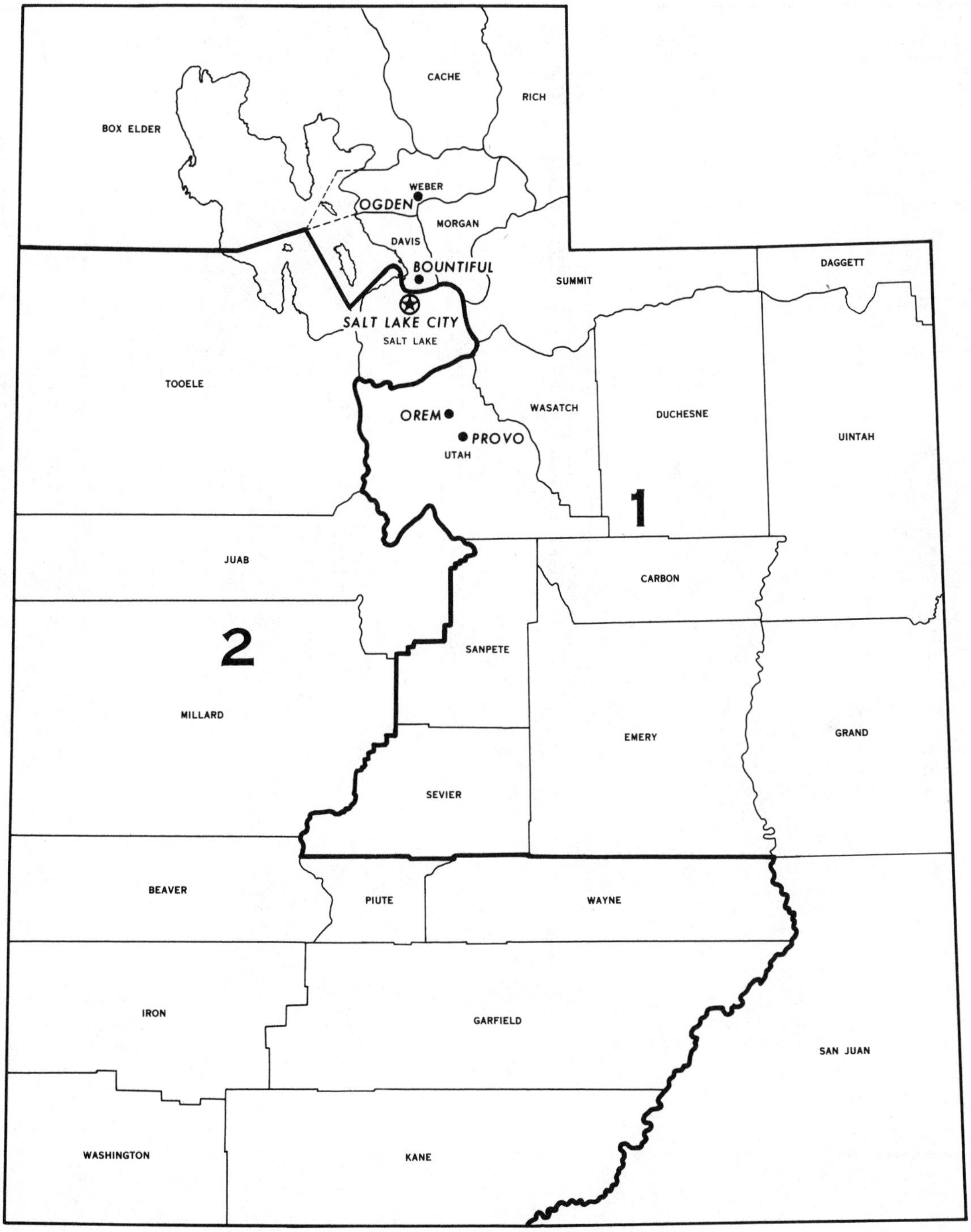

UTAH

PRESIDENT 1976

1970 Census Population	County	Total Vote	Republican	Democratic	Other	Rep.-Dem. Plurality	Percentage Total Vote Rep.	Total Vote Dem.	Major Vote Rep.	Major Vote Dem.
3,800	BEAVER	2,076	1,088	963	25	125 R	52.4%	46.4%	53.0%	47.0%
28,129	BOX ELDER	13,501	9,319	3,353	829	5,966 R	69.0%	24.8%	73.5%	26.5%
42,331	CACHE	23,194	16,636	5,430	1,128	11,206 R	71.7%	23.4%	75.4%	24.6%
15,647	CARBON	8,683	3,360	5,157	166	1,797 D	38.7%	59.4%	39.5%	60.5%
666	DAGGETT	365	217	131	17	86 R	59.5%	35.9%	62.4%	37.6%
99,028	DAVIS	47,097	31,216	14,084	1,797	17,132 R	66.3%	29.9%	68.9%	31.1%
7,299	DUCHESNE	3,982	2,619	1,110	253	1,509 R	65.8%	27.9%	70.2%	29.8%
5,137	EMERY	3,643	1,717	1,771	155	54 D	47.1%	48.6%	49.2%	50.8%
3,157	GARFIELD	1,776	1,163	539	74	624 R	65.5%	30.3%	68.3%	31.7%
6,688	GRAND	2,855	1,781	931	143	850 R	62.4%	32.6%	65.7%	34.3%
12,177	IRON	6,833	4,757	1,700	376	3,057 R	69.6%	24.9%	73.7%	26.3%
4,574	JUAB	2,501	1,290	1,091	120	199 R	51.6%	43.6%	54.2%	45.8%
2,421	KANE	1,509	1,094	330	85	764 R	72.5%	21.9%	76.8%	23.2%
6,988	MILLARD	3,963	2,484	1,224	255	1,260 R	62.7%	30.9%	67.0%	33.0%
3,983	MORGAN	2,154	1,356	701	97	655 R	63.0%	32.5%	65.9%	34.1%
1,164	PIUTE	675	377	265	33	112 R	55.9%	39.3%	58.7%	41.3%
1,615	RICH	806	541	248	17	293 R	67.1%	30.8%	68.6%	31.4%
458,607	SALT LAKE	238,777	144,100	86,659	8,018	57,441 R	60.3%	36.3%	62.4%	37.6%
9,606	SAN JUAN	3,222	1,856	1,182	184	674 R	57.6%	36.7%	61.1%	38.9%
10,976	SANPETE	5,935	3,683	1,925	327	1,758 R	62.1%	32.4%	65.7%	34.3%
10,103	SEVIER	5,650	3,686	1,564	400	2,122 R	65.2%	27.7%	70.2%	29.8%
5,879	SUMMIT	3,763	2,316	1,282	165	1,034 R	61.5%	34.1%	64.4%	35.6%
21,545	TOOELE	9,251	4,657	4,371	223	286 R	50.3%	47.2%	51.6%	48.4%
12,684	UINTAH	5,807	4,017	1,342	448	2,675 R	69.2%	23.1%	75.0%	25.0%
137,776	UTAH	70,993	49,328	18,327	3,338	31,001 R	69.5%	25.8%	72.9%	27.1%
5,863	WASATCH	3,150	1,940	1,092	118	848 R	61.6%	34.7%	64.0%	36.0%
13,669	WASHINGTON	8,414	5,944	1,893	577	4,051 R	70.6%	22.5%	75.8%	24.2%
1,483	WAYNE	939	555	334	50	221 R	59.1%	35.6%	62.4%	37.6%
126,278	WEBER	59,684	34,811	23,111	1,762	11,700 R	58.3%	38.7%	60.1%	39.9%
1,059,273	TOTAL	541,198	337,908	182,110	21,180	155,798 R	62.4%	33.6%	65.0%	35.0%

UTAH

GOVERNOR 1976

1970 Census Population	County	Total Vote	Republican	Democratic	Other	Rep.-Dem. Plurality	Percentage Total Vote Rep.	Percentage Total Vote Dem.	Percentage Major Vote Rep.	Percentage Major Vote Dem.
3,800	BEAVER	2,054	760	1,270	24	510 D	37.0%	61.8%	37.4%	62.6%
28,129	BOX ELDER	13,465	7,241	5,681	543	1,560 R	53.8%	42.2%	56.0%	44.0%
42,331	CACHE	23,074	12,713	9,528	833	3,185 R	55.1%	41.3%	57.2%	42.8%
15,647	CARBON	8,639	1,971	6,601	67	4,630 D	22.8%	76.4%	23.0%	77.0%
666	DAGGETT	357	164	185	8	21 D	45.9%	51.8%	47.0%	53.0%
99,028	DAVIS	47,124	23,618	22,420	1,086	1,198 R	50.1%	47.6%	51.3%	48.7%
7,299	DUCHESNE	3,964	1,941	1,874	149	67 R	49.0%	47.3%	50.9%	49.1%
5,137	EMERY	3,618	1,348	2,180	90	832 D	37.3%	60.3%	38.2%	61.8%
3,157	GARFIELD	1,761	920	774	67	146 R	52.2%	44.0%	54.3%	45.7%
6,688	GRAND	2,801	1,100	1,653	48	553 D	39.3%	59.0%	40.0%	60.0%
12,177	IRON	6,810	2,787	3,878	145	1,091 D	40.9%	56.9%	41.8%	58.2%
4,574	JUAB	2,506	1,172	1,285	49	113 D	46.8%	51.3%	47.7%	52.3%
2,421	KANE	1,499	789	663	47	126 R	52.6%	44.2%	54.3%	45.7%
6,988	MILLARD	3,944	2,046	1,746	152	300 R	51.9%	44.3%	54.0%	46.0%
3,983	MORGAN	2,172	1,065	1,049	58	16 R	49.0%	48.3%	50.4%	49.6%
1,164	PIUTE	661	344	284	33	60 R	52.0%	43.0%	54.8%	45.2%
1,615	RICH	808	407	392	9	15 R	50.4%	48.5%	50.9%	49.1%
458,607	SALT LAKE	238,035	100,346	134,442	3,247	34,096 D	42.2%	56.5%	42.7%	57.3%
9,606	SAN JUAN	3,101	1,592	1,434	75	158 R	51.3%	46.2%	52.6%	47.4%
10,976	SANPETE	5,914	3,070	2,650	194	420 R	51.9%	44.8%	53.7%	46.3%
10,103	SEVIER	5,626	2,773	2,307	546	466 R	49.3%	41.0%	54.6%	45.4%
5,879	SUMMIT	3,711	1,638	1,997	76	359 D	44.1%	53.8%	45.1%	54.9%
21,545	TOOELE	9,160	3,432	5,596	132	2,164 D	37.5%	61.1%	38.0%	62.0%
12,684	UINTAH	5,799	3,334	2,204	261	1,130 R	57.5%	38.0%	60.2%	39.8%
137,776	UTAH	70,798	39,422	29,693	1,683	9,729 R	55.7%	41.9%	57.0%	43.0%
5,863	WASATCH	3,132	1,582	1,507	43	75 R	50.5%	48.1%	51.2%	48.8%
13,669	WASHINGTON	8,598	4,972	3,335	291	1,637 R	57.8%	38.8%	59.9%	40.1%
1,483	WAYNE	932	430	392	110	38 R	46.1%	42.1%	52.3%	47.7%
126,278	WEBER	59,586	25,050	33,686	850	8,636 D	42.0%	56.5%	42.6%	57.4%
1,059,273	TOTAL	539,649	248,027	280,706	10,916	32,679 D	46.0%	52.0%	46.9%	53.1%

UTAH

SENATOR 1976

1970 Census Population	County	Total Vote	Republican	Democratic	Other	Rep.-Dem. Plurality	Percentage Total Vote Rep.	Percentage Total Vote Dem.	Percentage Major Vote Rep.	Percentage Major Vote Dem.
3,800	BEAVER	2,057	984	1,063	10	79 D	47.8%	51.7%	48.1%	51.9%
28,129	BOX ELDER	13,493	7,544	5,546	403	1,998 R	55.9%	41.1%	57.6%	42.4%
42,331	CACHE	23,204	14,809	7,903	492	6,906 R	63.8%	34.1%	65.2%	34.8%
15,647	CARBON	8,683	2,791	5,848	44	3,057 D	32.1%	67.3%	32.3%	67.7%
666	DAGGETT	354	187	164	3	23 R	52.8%	46.3%	53.3%	46.7%
99,028	DAVIS	47,333	26,264	20,371	698	5,893 R	55.5%	43.0%	56.3%	43.7%
7,299	DUCHESNE	4,001	2,622	1,305	74	1,317 R	65.5%	32.6%	66.8%	33.2%
5,137	EMERY	3,626	1,564	2,005	57	441 D	43.1%	55.3%	43.8%	56.2%
3,157	GARFIELD	1,767	1,170	570	27	600 R	66.2%	32.3%	67.2%	32.8%
6,688	GRAND	2,753	1,750	966	37	784 R	63.6%	35.1%	64.4%	35.6%
12,177	IRON	6,754	4,279	2,356	119	1,923 R	63.4%	34.9%	64.5%	35.5%
4,574	JUAB	2,511	1,241	1,230	40	11 R	49.4%	49.0%	50.2%	49.8%
2,421	KANE	1,501	1,069	406	26	663 R	71.2%	27.0%	72.5%	27.5%
6,988	MILLARD	3,962	2,545	1,345	72	1,200 R	64.2%	33.9%	65.4%	34.6%
3,983	MORGAN	2,168	1,153	983	32	170 R	53.2%	45.3%	54.0%	46.0%
1,164	PIUTE	669	395	263	11	132 R	59.0%	39.3%	60.0%	40.0%
1,615	RICH	814	522	290	2	232 R	64.1%	35.6%	64.3%	35.7%
458,607	SALT LAKE	238,032	119,610	115,127	3,295	4,483 R	50.2%	48.4%	51.0%	49.0%
9,606	SAN JUAN	3,123	1,955	1,118	50	837 R	62.6%	35.8%	63.6%	36.4%
10,976	SANPETE	5,927	3,546	2,275	106	1,271 R	59.8%	38.4%	60.9%	39.1%
10,103	SEVIER	5,616	3,558	1,832	226	1,726 R	63.4%	32.6%	66.0%	34.0%
5,879	SUMMIT	3,733	2,017	1,645	71	372 R	54.0%	44.1%	55.1%	44.9%
21,545	TOOELE	9,250	3,693	5,472	85	1,779 D	39.9%	59.2%	40.3%	59.7%
12,684	UINTAH	5,799	4,157	1,499	143	2,658 R	71.7%	25.8%	73.5%	26.5%
137,776	UTAH	70,929	45,733	24,223	973	21,510 R	64.5%	34.2%	65.4%	34.6%
5,863	WASATCH	3,152	1,760	1,362	30	398 R	55.8%	43.2%	56.4%	43.6%
13,669	WASHINGTON	8,356	5,982	2,222	152	3,760 R	71.6%	26.6%	72.9%	27.1%
1,483	WAYNE	947	626	306	15	320 R	66.1%	32.3%	67.2%	32.8%
126,278	WEBER	59,594	26,695	32,253	646	5,558 D	44.8%	54.1%	45.3%	54.7%
1,059,273	TOTAL	540,108	290,221	241,948	7,939	48,273 R	53.7%	44.8%	54.5%	45.5%

UTAH

CONGRESS

CD	Year	Total Vote	Republican Vote	Republican Candidate	Democratic Vote	Democratic Candidate	Other Vote	Rep.-Dem. Plurality	Percentage Total Vote Rep.	Percentage Total Vote Dem.	Percentage Major Vote Rep.	Percentage Major Vote Dem.
1	1976	267,531	106,542	FERGUSON, JOE H.	155,631	MCKAY, K. GUNN	5,358	49,089 D	39.8%	58.2%	40.6%	59.4%
1	1974	199,264	62,807	INKLEY, RON W.	124,793	MCKAY, K. GUNN	11,664	61,986 D	31.5%	62.6%	33.5%	66.5%
1	1972	229,366	96,296	WOLTHUIS, ROBERT K.	127,027	MCKAY, K. GUNN	6,043	30,731 D	42.0%	55.4%	43.1%	56.9%
2	1976	276,300	144,861	MARRIOTT, DAN	110,931	HOWE, ALLAN T.	20,508	33,930 R	52.4%	40.1%	56.6%	43.4%
2	1974	213,698	100,259	HARMSEN, STEPHEN M.	105,739	HOWE, ALLAN T.	7,700	5,480 D	46.9%	49.5%	48.7%	51.3%
2	1972	243,702	107,185	LLOYD, SHERMAN P.	132,832	OWENS, WAYNE	3,685	25,647 D	44.0%	54.5%	44.7%	55.3%

UTAH

1976 GENERAL ELECTION

President	Original uncorrected canvass gave the Anderson (American) total vote as 13,304. Other vote was 13,284 Anderson (American); 3,907 McCarthy (Independent); 2,438 MacBride (Libertarian); 1,162 Maddox (Concerned Citizens); 268 Camejo (Independent); 121 Hall (Independent).
Governor	Original uncorrected canvass gave the Democratic total vote as 280,606. Other vote was 7,201 Brown (American); 3,715 Bates (Concerned Citizens).
Senator	Original uncorrected canvass gave the Democratic total vote as 223,948. Other vote was 4,913 Batchelor (American); 3,026 Trotter (Libertarian).
Congress	Other vote was Gerlach (American) in CD 1; McCarthy (write-in) in CD 2. Original canvass omitted the McCarthy write-in vote in CD 2.

1976 PRIMARIES

SEPTEMBER 14 REPUBLICAN

Governor	87,251 Vernon B. Romney; 76,139 Dixie L. Leavitt.
Senator	104,490 Orrin G. Hatch; 57,249 Jack Carlson.
Congress	Contested as follows:
CD 1	39,456 Joe H. Ferguson; 35,334 Calvin Black.
CD 2	56,071 Dan Marriott; 25,524 J. Preston Hughes.

SEPTEMBER 14 DEMOCRATIC

Governor	50,505 Scott M. Matheson; 35,154 John P. Creer.
Senator	Frank E. Moss, unopposed.
Congress	Unopposed in both CD's.

VERMONT

GOVERNOR

Richard A. Snelling (R). Elected 1976 to a two-year term.

SENATORS

Patrick J. Leahy (D). Elected 1974 to a six-year term.

Robert T. Stafford (R). Re-elected 1976 to a six-year term. Previously elected January 1972 to fill out term vacated by the death of Senator Winston L. Prouty; had been appointed September 1971 to fill this same vacancy.

REPRESENTATIVE

At-Large. James M. Jeffords (R)

POSTWAR VOTE FOR GOVERNOR

								Percentage			
	Total	Republican		Democratic		Other	Rep.-Dem.	Total Vote		Major Vote	
Year	Vote	Vote	Candidate	Vote	Candidate	Vote	Plurality	Rep.	Dem.	Rep.	Dem.
1976	185,929	99,268	Snelling, Richard A.	75,262	Hackel, Stella B.	11,399	24,006 R	53.4%	40.5%	56.9%	43.1%
1974	141,156	53,672	Kennedy, Walter L.	79,842	Salmon, Thomas P.	7,642	26,170 D	38.0%	56.6%	40.2%	59.8%
1972	189,237	82,491	Hackett, Luther F.	104,533	Salmon, Thomas P.	2,213	22,042 D	43.6%	55.2%	44.1%	55.9%
1970	153,528	87,458	Davis, Deane C.	66,028	O'Brien, Leo	42	21,430 R	57.0%	43.0%	57.0%	43.0%
1968	161,089	89,387	Davis, Deane C.	71,656	Daley, John J.	46	17,731 R	55.5%	44.5%	55.5%	44.5%
1966	136,262	57,577	Snelling, Richard A.	78,669	Hoff, Philip H.	16	21,092 D	42.3%	57.7%	42.3%	57.7%
1964	164,199	57,576	Foote, Ralph A.	106,611	Hoff, Philip H.	12	49,035 D	35.1%	64.9%	35.1%	64.9%
1962	121,422	60,035	Keyser, F. Ray	61,383	Hoff, Philip H.	4	1,348 D	49.4%	50.6%	49.4%	50.6%
1960	164,632	92,861	Keyser, F. Ray	71,755	Niquette, Russell F.	16	21,106 R	56.4%	43.6%	56.4%	43.6%
1958	123,728	62,222	Stafford, Robert T.	61,503	Leddy, Bernard J.	3	719 R	50.3%	49.7%	50.3%	49.7%
1956	153,809	88,379	Johnson, Joseph B.	65,420	Branon, E. Frank	10	22,959 R	57.5%	42.5%	57.5%	42.5%
1954	114,360	59,778	Johnson, Joseph B.	54,554	Branon, E. Frank	28	5,224 R	52.3%	47.7%	52.3%	47.7%
1952	150,862	78,338	Emerson, Lee E.	60,051	Larrow, Robert W.	12,473	18,287 R	51.9%	39.8%	56.6%	43.4%
1950	87,155	64,915	Emerson, Lee E.	22,227	Moran, J. Edward	13	42,688 R	74.5%	25.5%	74.5%	25.5%
1948	120,183	86,394	Gibson, Ernest W., Jr.	33,588	Ryan, Charles F.	201	52,806 R	71.9%	27.9%	72.0%	28.0%
1946	72,044	57,849	Gibson, Ernest W., Jr.	14,096	Coburn, Berthold	99	43,753 R	80.3%	19.6%	80.4%	19.6%

POSTWAR VOTE FOR SENATOR

								Percentage			
	Total	Republican		Democratic		Other	Rep.-Dem.	Total Vote		Major Vote	
Year	Vote	Vote	Candidate	Vote	Candidate	Vote	Plurality	Rep.	Dem.	Rep.	Dem.
1976	189,060	94,481	Stafford, Robert T.	85,682	Salmon, Thomas P.	8,897	8,799 R	50.0%	45.3%	52.4%	47.6%
1974	142,772	66,223	Mallary, Richard W.	70,629	Leahy, Patrick J.	5,920	4,406 D	46.4%	49.5%	48.4%	51.6%
1972s	71,348	45,888	Stafford, Robert T.	23,842	Major, Randolph T.	1,618	22,046 R	64.3%	33.4%	65.8%	34.2%
1970	154,899	91,198	Prouty, Winston L.	62,271	Hoff, Philip H.	1,430	28,927 R	58.9%	40.2%	59.4%	40.6%
1968	157,375	157,154	Aiken, George D.	–	–	221	157,154 R	99.9%	–	100.0%	–
1964	164,350	87,879	Prouty, Winston L.	76,457	Fayette, Frederick J.	14	11,422 R	53.5%	46.5%	53.5%	46.5%
1962	121,571	81,241	Aiken, George D.	40,134	Johnson, W. Robert	196	41,107 R	66.8%	33.0%	66.9%	33.1%
1958	124,442	64,900	Prouty, Winston L.	59,536	Fayette, Frederick J.	6	5,364 R	52.2%	47.8%	52.2%	47.8%
1956	155,289	103,101	Aiken, George D.	52,184	O'Shea, Bernard G.	4	50,917 R	66.4%	33.6%	66.4%	33.6%
1952	154,052	111,406	Flanders, Ralph E.	42,630	Johnston, Allan R.	16	68,776 R	72.3%	27.7%	72.3%	27.7%
1950	89,171	69,543	Aiken, George D.	19,608	Bigelow, James E.	20	49,935 R	78.0%	22.0%	78.0%	22.0%
1946	73,340	54,729	Flanders, Ralph E.	18,594	McDevitt, Charles P.	17	36,135 R	74.6%	25.4%	74.6%	25.4%

In 1968 the Republican candidate won both major party nominations. The 1972 election was held in January for a short term to fill a vacancy.

VERMONT

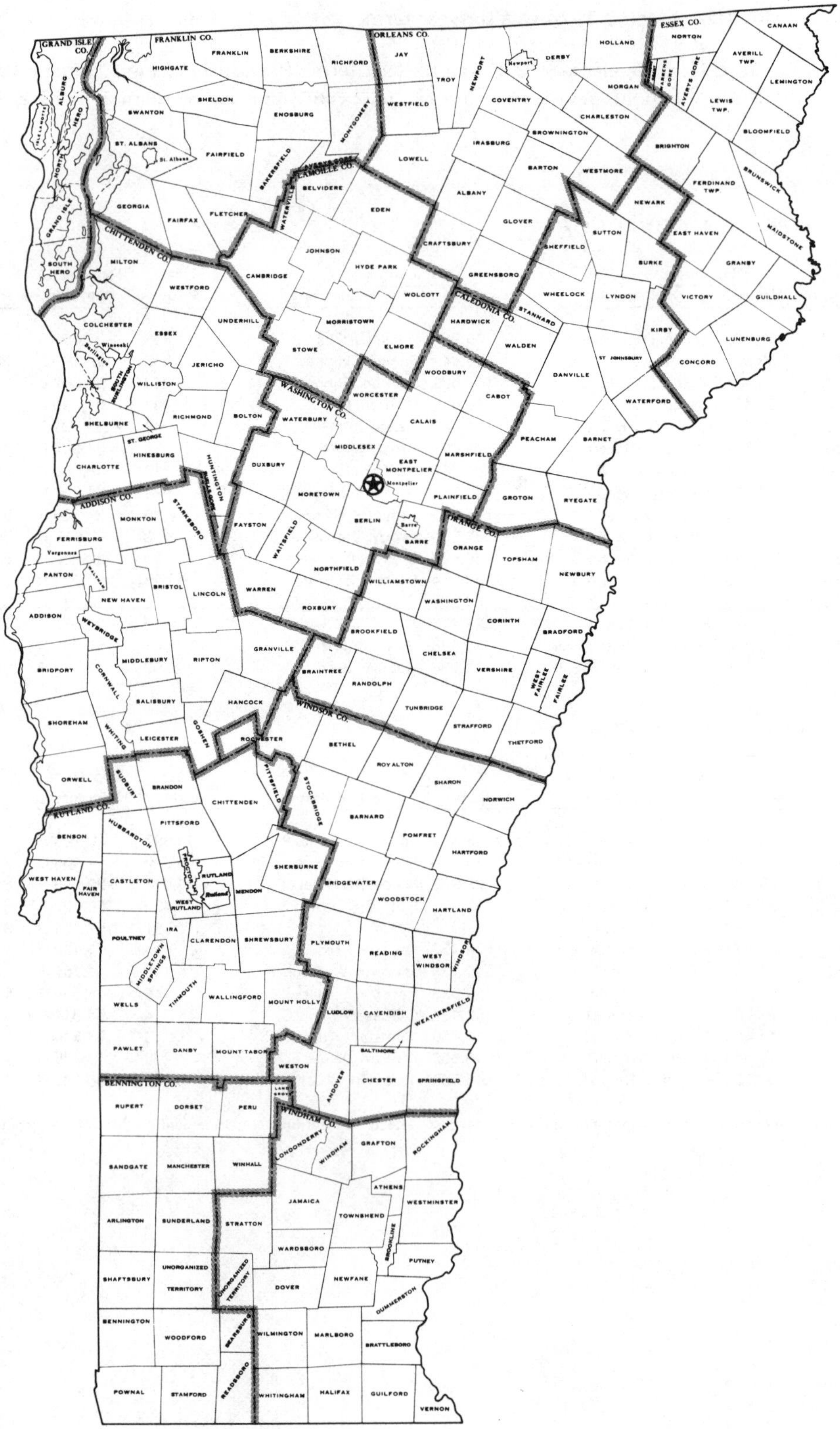
GRAND ISLE CO.
FRANKLIN CO.
ORLEANS CO.
ESSEX CO.
LAMOILLE CO.
CHITTENDEN CO.
CALEDONIA CO.
WASHINGTON CO.
ADDISON CO.
ORANGE CO.
WINDSOR CO.
RUTLAND CO.
BENNINGTON CO.
WINDHAM CO.
ALBURG
NORTH HERO
GRAND ISLE
SOUTH HERO
FRANKLIN
BERKSHIRE
RICHFORD
HIGHGATE
SHELDON
SWANTON
ENOSBURG
MONTGOMERY
ST. ALBANS
St. Albans
FAIRFIELD
BAKERSFIELD
GEORGIA
FAIRFAX
FLETCHER
JAY
TROY
NEWPORT
Newport
DERBY
HOLLAND
NORTON
CANAAN
AVERILL TWP
LEMINGTON
WESTFIELD
COVENTRY
MORGAN
CHARLESTON
LEWIS TWP.
BLOOMFIELD
IRASBURG
BROWNINGTON
LOWELL
BARTON
WESTMORE
BRIGHTON
BRUNSWICK
FERDINAND TWP.
ALBANY
NEWARK
MAIDSTONE
BELVIDERE
WATERVILLE
EDEN
GLOVER
SUTTON
EAST HAVEN
JOHNSON
HYDE PARK
CRAFTSBURY
SHEFFIELD
BURKE
GRANBY
CAMBRIDGE
GREENSBORO
WHEELOCK
LYNDON
VICTORY
GUILDHALL
MILTON
WESTFORD
WOLCOTT
STANNARD
UNDERHILL
MORRISTOWN
HARDWICK
KIRBY
LUNENBURG
COLCHESTER
Winooski
ESSEX
STOWE
ELMORE
WALDEN
ST. JOHNSBURY
CONCORD
JERICHO
WOODBURY
DANVILLE
WILLISTON
SOUTH BURLINGTON
WORCESTER
CABOT
RICHMOND
BOLTON
WATERFORD
WATERBURY
CALAIS
SHELBURNE
ST. GEORGE
PEACHAM
BARNET
HINESBURG
MIDDLESEX
CHARLOTTE
HUNTINGTON
DUXBURY
EAST MONTPELIER
MARSHFIELD
Montpelier
MORETOWN
PLAINFIELD
GROTON
RYEGATE
MONKTON
STARKSBORO
FAYSTON
BERLIN
Barre
FERRISBURG
Vergennes
WAITSFIELD
BARRE
ORANGE
TOPSHAM
PANTON
NORTHFIELD
NEWBURY
BRISTOL
WILLIAMSTOWN
NEW HAVEN
LINCOLN
WARREN
WASHINGTON
ADDISON
WEYBRIDGE
ROXBURY
CORINTH
BROOKFIELD
BRADFORD
MIDDLEBURY
RIPTON
GRANVILLE
CHELSEA
BRIDPORT
CORNWALL
BRAINTREE
VERSHIRE
RANDOLPH
WEST FAIRLEE
FAIRLEE
SALISBURY
HANCOCK
TUNBRIDGE
SHOREHAM
WHITING
LEICESTER
GOSHEN
ROCHESTER
STRAFFORD
THETFORD
BETHEL
ORWELL
SUDBURY
BRANDON
ROYALTON
PITTSFIELD
SHARON
CHITTENDEN
STOCKBRIDGE
NORWICH
BENSON
HUBBARDTON
PITTSFORD
BARNARD
POMFRET
HARTFORD
PROCTOR
RUTLAND
SHERBURNE
WEST HAVEN
CASTLETON
MENDON
BRIDGEWATER
FAIR HAVEN
Rutland
WEST RUTLAND
WOODSTOCK
HARTLAND
POULTNEY
IRA
CLARENDON
SHREWSBURY
PLYMOUTH
READING
WEST WINDSOR
WINDSOR
MIDDLETOWN SPRINGS
TINMOUTH
WALLINGFORD
MOUNT HOLLY
LUDLOW
CAVENDISH
WEATHERSFIELD
WELLS
PAWLET
DANBY
MOUNT TABOR
BALTIMORE
WESTON
ANDOVER
CHESTER
SPRINGFIELD
RUPERT
DORSET
PERU
LANDGROVE
LONDONDERRY
WINDHAM
GRAFTON
ROCKINGHAM
SANDGATE
MANCHESTER
WINHALL
ATHENS
JAMAICA
WESTMINSTER
TOWNSHEND
ARLINGTON
SUNDERLAND
STRATTON
BROOKLINE
WARDSBORO
PUTNEY
SHAFTSBURY
UNORGANIZED TERRITORY
DOVER
NEWFANE
DUMMERSTON
BENNINGTON
WOODFORD
SEARSBURG
WILMINGTON
MARLBORO
BRATTLEBORO
POWNAL
STAMFORD
READSBORO
WHITINGHAM
HALIFAX
GUILFORD
VERNON

VERMONT

PRESIDENT 1976

1970 Census Population	County	Total Vote	Republican	Democratic	Other	Rep.-Dem. Plurality	Percentage Total Vote Rep.	Percentage Total Vote Dem.	Percentage Major Vote Rep.	Percentage Major Vote Dem.
24,266	ADDISON	10,129	5,726	4,164	239	1,562 R	56.5%	41.1%	57.9%	42.1%
29,282	BENNINGTON	12,387	6,712	5,443	232	1,269 R	54.2%	43.9%	55.2%	44.8%
22,789	CALEDONIA	9,193	5,488	3,511	194	1,977 R	59.7%	38.2%	61.0%	39.0%
99,131	CHITTENDEN	41,348	22,013	17,992	1,343	4,021 R	53.2%	43.5%	55.0%	45.0%
5,416	ESSEX	2,188	1,161	1,002	25	159 R	53.1%	45.8%	53.7%	46.3%
31,282	FRANKLIN	11,977	6,190	5,610	177	580 R	51.7%	46.8%	52.5%	47.5%
3,574	GRAND ISLE	1,908	1,004	866	38	138 R	52.6%	45.4%	53.7%	46.3%
13,309	LAMOILLE	5,740	3,535	2,016	189	1,519 R	61.6%	35.1%	63.7%	36.3%
17,676	ORANGE	8,132	4,768	3,171	193	1,597 R	58.6%	39.0%	60.1%	39.9%
20,153	ORLEANS	7,772	4,075	3,561	136	514 R	52.4%	45.8%	53.4%	46.6%
52,637	RUTLAND	21,724	11,565	9,778	381	1,787 R	53.2%	45.0%	54.2%	45.8%
47,659	WASHINGTON	20,254	10,919	8,764	571	2,155 R	53.9%	43.3%	55.5%	44.5%
33,476	WINDHAM	15,223	7,928	6,794	501	1,134 R	52.1%	44.6%	53.9%	46.1%
44,082	WINDSOR	19,691	11,001	8,282	408	2,719 R	55.9%	42.1%	57.1%	42.9%
444,732	TOTAL	187,765	102,085	80,954	4,726	21,131 R	54.4%	43.1%	55.8%	44.2%

GOVERNOR 1976

1970 Census Population	County	Total Vote	Republican	Democratic	Other	Rep.-Dem. Plurality	Percentage Total Vote Rep.	Percentage Total Vote Dem.	Percentage Major Vote Rep.	Percentage Major Vote Dem.
24,266	ADDISON	10,108	5,268	4,118	722	1,150 R	52.1%	40.7%	56.1%	43.9%
29,282	BENNINGTON	11,910	7,659	3,826	425	3,833 R	64.3%	32.1%	66.7%	33.3%
22,789	CALEDONIA	9,203	5,478	3,406	319	2,072 R	59.5%	37.0%	61.7%	38.3%
99,131	CHITTENDEN	41,126	18,787	18,844	3,495	57 D	45.7%	45.8%	49.9%	50.1%
5,416	ESSEX	2,126	1,066	1,004	56	62 R	50.1%	47.2%	51.5%	48.5%
31,282	FRANKLIN	12,042	4,513	7,221	308	2,708 D	37.5%	60.0%	38.5%	61.5%
3,574	GRAND ISLE	1,912	778	1,053	81	275 D	40.7%	55.1%	42.5%	57.5%
13,309	LAMOILLE	5,694	3,164	2,066	464	1,098 R	55.6%	36.3%	60.5%	39.5%
17,676	ORANGE	8,088	4,956	2,654	478	2,302 R	61.3%	32.8%	65.1%	34.9%
20,153	ORLEANS	7,728	3,561	3,900	267	339 D	46.1%	50.5%	47.7%	52.3%
52,637	RUTLAND	21,820	12,093	8,553	1,174	3,540 R	55.4%	39.2%	58.6%	41.4%
47,659	WASHINGTON	20,254	11,405	7,162	1,687	4,243 R	56.3%	35.4%	61.4%	38.6%
33,476	WINDHAM	14,459	8,734	4,826	899	3,908 R	60.4%	33.4%	64.4%	35.6%
44,082	WINDSOR	19,377	11,806	6,629	942	5,177 R	60.9%	34.2%	64.0%	36.0%
444,732	TOTAL	185,929	99,268	75,262	11,399	24,006 R	53.4%	40.5%	56.9%	43.1%

SENATOR 1976

1970 Census Population	County	Total Vote	Republican	Democratic	Other	Rep.-Dem. Plurality	Percentage Total Vote Rep.	Percentage Total Vote Dem.	Percentage Major Vote Rep.	Percentage Major Vote Dem.
24,266	ADDISON	10,220	5,668	3,956	596	1,712 R	55.5%	38.7%	58.9%	41.1%
29,282	BENNINGTON	12,261	5,406	6,538	317	1,132 D	44.1%	53.3%	45.3%	54.7%
22,789	CALEDONIA	9,213	5,084	3,791	338	1,293 R	55.2%	41.1%	57.3%	42.7%
99,131	CHITTENDEN	40,922	19,419	19,255	2,248	164 R	47.5%	47.1%	50.2%	49.8%
5,416	ESSEX	2,189	1,134	980	75	154 R	51.8%	44.8%	53.6%	46.4%
31,282	FRANKLIN	12,265	6,373	5,528	364	845 R	52.0%	45.1%	53.6%	46.4%
3,574	GRAND ISLE	1,950	956	923	71	33 R	49.0%	47.3%	50.9%	49.1%
13,309	LAMOILLE	5,803	3,238	2,220	345	1,018 R	55.8%	38.3%	59.3%	40.7%
17,676	ORANGE	8,268	4,638	3,221	409	1,417 R	56.1%	39.0%	59.0%	41.0%
20,153	ORLEANS	7,892	3,569	4,023	300	454 D	45.2%	51.0%	47.0%	53.0%
52,637	RUTLAND	22,228	11,687	9,625	916	2,062 R	52.6%	43.3%	54.8%	45.2%
47,659	WASHINGTON	20,471	10,103	8,953	1,415	1,150 R	49.4%	43.7%	53.0%	47.0%
33,476	WINDHAM	15,225	6,758	7,855	612	1,097 D	44.4%	51.6%	46.2%	53.8%
44,082	WINDSOR	20,057	10,448	8,814	795	1,634 R	52.1%	43.9%	54.2%	45.8%
444,732	TOTAL	189,060	94,481	85,682	8,897	8,799 R	50.0%	45.3%	52.4%	47.6%

VERMONT

PRESIDENT 1976

1970 Census Population	City/Town	Total Vote	Republican	Democratic	Other	Rep.-Dem. Plurality	Percentage Total Vote Rep.	Total Vote Dem.	Major Vote Rep.	Major Vote Dem.
10,209	BARRE CITY	3,819	1,895	1,858	66	37 R	49.6%	48.7%	50.5%	49.5%
6,509	BARRE TOWN	2,783	1,492	1,261	30	231 R	53.6%	45.3%	54.2%	45.8%
14,586	BENNINGTON TOWN	4,851	2,241	2,525	85	284 D	46.2%	52.1%	47.0%	53.0%
12,239	BRATTLEBORO	4,710	2,397	2,190	123	207 R	50.9%	46.5%	52.3%	47.7%
38,633	BURLINGTON	14,094	6,566	6,889	639	323 D	46.6%	48.9%	48.8%	51.2%
8,776	COLCHESTER	3,893	2,118	1,668	107	450 R	54.4%	42.8%	55.9%	44.1%
10,951	ESSEX TOWN	5,099	3,148	1,853	98	1,295 R	61.7%	36.3%	62.9%	37.1%
6,477	HARTFORD	2,444	1,400	1,009	35	391 R	57.3%	41.3%	58.1%	41.9%
6,532	MIDDLEBURY	2,590	1,394	1,108	88	286 R	53.8%	42.8%	55.7%	44.3%
8,609	MONTPELIER	3,717	2,267	1,363	87	904 R	61.0%	36.7%	62.5%	37.5%
5,501	ROCKINGHAM	2,223	1,051	1,118	54	67 D	47.3%	50.3%	48.5%	51.5%
19,293	RUTLAND CITY	7,254	3,470	3,650	134	180 D	47.8%	50.3%	48.7%	51.3%
8,082	ST. ALBANS CITY	3,109	1,719	1,359	31	360 R	55.3%	43.7%	55.8%	44.2%
8,409	ST. JOHNSBURY	3,019	1,753	1,219	47	534 R	58.1%	40.4%	59.0%	41.0%
10,032	SOUTH BURLINGTON	4,409	2,581	1,700	128	881 R	58.5%	38.6%	60.3%	39.7%
10,063	SPRINGFIELD	4,232	2,247	1,913	72	334 R	53.1%	45.2%	54.0%	46.0%
7,309	WINOOSKI	2,070	730	1,295	45	565 D	35.3%	62.6%	36.0%	64.0%

GOVERNOR 1976

1970 Census Population	City/Town	Total Vote	Republican	Democratic	Other	Rep.-Dem. Plurality	Percentage Total Vote Rep.	Total Vote Dem.	Major Vote Rep.	Major Vote Dem.
10,209	BARRE CITY	3,792	2,028	1,586	178	442 R	53.5%	41.8%	56.1%	43.9%
6,509	BARRE TOWN	2,788	1,546	1,118	124	428 R	55.5%	40.1%	58.0%	42.0%
14,586	BENNINGTON TOWN	4,589	2,773	1,630	186	1,143 R	60.4%	35.5%	63.0%	37.0%
12,239	BRATTLEBORO	4,404	2,685	1,474	245	1,211 R	61.0%	33.5%	64.6%	35.4%
38,633	BURLINGTON	13,797	5,868	6,276	1,653	408 D	42.5%	45.5%	48.3%	51.7%
8,776	COLCHESTER	3,900	1,799	1,861	240	62 D	46.1%	47.7%	49.2%	50.8%
10,951	ESSEX TOWN	5,054	2,502	2,257	295	245 R	49.5%	44.7%	52.6%	47.4%
6,477	HARTFORD	2,387	1,535	772	80	763 R	64.3%	32.3%	66.5%	33.5%
6,532	MIDDLEBURY	2,525	1,338	917	270	421 R	53.0%	36.3%	59.3%	40.7%
8,609	MONTPELIER	3,782	2,367	1,176	239	1,191 R	62.6%	31.1%	66.8%	33.2%
5,501	ROCKINGHAM	2,147	1,124	947	76	177 R	52.4%	44.1%	54.3%	45.7%
19,293	RUTLAND CITY	7,222	3,669	3,135	418	534 R	50.8%	43.4%	53.9%	46.1%
8,082	ST. ALBANS CITY	3,201	1,180	1,974	47	794 D	36.9%	61.7%	37.4%	62.6%
8,409	ST. JOHNSBURY	3,008	1,803	1,128	77	675 R	59.9%	37.5%	61.5%	38.5%
10,032	SOUTH BURLINGTON	4,503	2,157	2,023	323	134 R	47.9%	44.9%	51.6%	48.4%
10,063	SPRINGFIELD	4,023	2,322	1,517	184	805 R	57.7%	37.7%	60.5%	39.5%
7,309	WINOOSKI	2,002	467	1,430	105	963 D	23.3%	71.4%	24.6%	75.4%

SENATOR 1976

1970 Census Population	City/Town	Total Vote	Republican	Democratic	Other	Rep.-Dem. Plurality	Percentage Total Vote Rep.	Total Vote Dem.	Major Vote Rep.	Major Vote Dem.
10,209	BARRE CITY	3,909	1,657	2,076	176	419 D	42.4%	53.1%	44.4%	55.6%
6,509	BARRE TOWN	2,819	1,374	1,341	104	33 R	48.7%	47.6%	50.6%	49.4%
14,586	BENNINGTON TOWN	4,638	1,819	2,702	117	883 D	39.2%	58.3%	40.2%	59.8%
12,239	BRATTLEBORO	4,609	2,039	2,414	156	375 D	44.2%	52.4%	45.8%	54.2%
38,633	BURLINGTON	13,594	5,775	6,862	957	1,087 D	42.5%	50.5%	45.7%	54.3%
8,776	COLCHESTER	3,960	1,753	2,039	168	286 D	44.3%	51.5%	46.2%	53.8%
10,951	ESSEX TOWN	4,947	2,664	2,114	169	550 R	53.9%	42.7%	55.8%	44.2%
6,477	HARTFORD	2,466	1,311	1,082	73	229 R	53.2%	43.9%	54.8%	45.2%
6,532	MIDDLEBURY	2,564	1,375	1,022	167	353 R	53.6%	39.9%	57.4%	42.6%
8,609	MONTPELIER	3,668	1,986	1,514	168	472 R	54.1%	41.3%	56.7%	43.3%
5,501	ROCKINGHAM	2,294	716	1,516	62	800 D	31.2%	66.1%	32.1%	67.9%
19,293	RUTLAND CITY	7,275	3,480	3,507	288	27 D	47.8%	48.2%	49.8%	50.2%
8,082	ST. ALBANS CITY	3,172	1,747	1,364	61	383 R	55.1%	43.0%	56.2%	43.8%
8,409	ST. JOHNSBURY	3,068	1,567	1,411	90	156 R	51.1%	46.0%	52.6%	47.4%
10,032	SOUTH BURLINGTON	4,485	2,334	1,980	171	354 R	52.0%	44.1%	54.1%	45.9%
10,063	SPRINGFIELD	4,246	2,087	1,988	171	99 R	49.2%	46.8%	51.2%	48.8%
7,309	WINOOSKI	1,947	613	1,257	77	644 D	31.5%	64.6%	32.8%	67.2%

VERMONT

CONGRESS

			Republican		Democratic				Percentage			
		Total					Other	Rep.-Dem.	Total Vote		Major Vote	
CD	Year	Vote	Vote	Candidate	Vote	Candidate	Vote	Plurality	Rep.	Dem.	Rep.	Dem.
AL	1976	184,783	124,458	JEFFORDS, JAMES M.	60,202	*BURGESS, JOHN A.	123	64,256 R	67.4%	32.6%	67.4%	32.6%
AL	1974	140,899	74,561	JEFFORDS, JAMES M.	56,342	*CAIN, FRANCIS J.	9,996	18,219 R	52.9%	40.0%	57.0%	43.0%
AL	1972	186,028	120,924	MALLARY, RICHARD W.	65,062	MEYER, WILLIAM H.	42	55,862 R	65.0%	35.0%	65.0%	35.0%
AL	1970	152,557	103,806	STAFFORD, ROBERT T.	44,415	O SHEA, BERNARD G.	4,336	59,391 R	68.0%	29.1%	70.0%	30.0%
AL	1968	157,133	156,956	*STAFFORD, ROBERT T.			177	156,956 R	99.9%		100.0%	
AL	1966	135,748	89,097	STAFFORD, ROBERT T.	46,643	RYAN, WILLIAM J.	8	42,454 R	65.6%	34.4%	65.6%	34.4%
AL	1964	163,452	92,252	STAFFORD, ROBERT T.	71,193	O SHEA, BERNARD G.	7	21,059 R	56.4%	43.6%	56.4%	43.6%
AL	1962	121,381	68,822	STAFFORD, ROBERT T.	52,535	RAYNOLDS, HAROLD	24	16,287 R	56.7%	43.3%	56.7%	43.3%
AL	1960	166,035	94,905	STAFFORD, ROBERT T.	71,111	MEYER, WILLIAM H.	19	23,794 R	57.2%	42.8%	57.2%	42.8%
AL	1958	122,702	59,536	ARTHUR, HAROLD J.	63,131	MEYER, WILLIAM H.	35	3,595 D	48.5%	51.5%	48.5%	51.5%
AL	1956	154,536	103,736	PROUTY, WINSTON L.	50,797	ST. AMOUR, CAMILLE	3	52,939 R	67.1%	32.9%	67.1%	32.9%
AL	1954	114,289	70,143	PROUTY, WINSTON L.	44,141	BOYLAN, JOHN J.	5	26,002 R	61.4%	38.6%	61.4%	38.6%
AL	1952	153,060	109,871	PROUTY, WINSTON L.	43,187	COMINGS, HERBERT B.	2	66,684 R	71.8%	28.2%	71.8%	28.2%
AL	1950	88,851	65,248	PROUTY, WINSTON L.	22,709	COMINGS, HERBERT B.	894	42,539 R	73.4%	25.6%	74.2%	25.8%
AL	1948	121,968	74,076	PLUMLEY, CHARLES A.	47,767	READY, ROBERT W.	125	26,309 R	60.7%	39.2%	60.8%	39.2%
AL	1946	73,066	46,985	PLUMLEY, CHARLES A.	26,056	CALDBECK, MATTHEW J.	25	20,929 R	64.3%	35.7%	64.3%	35.7%

VERMONT

1976 GENERAL ELECTION

In addition to the county-by-county figures, 1976 data are presented for selected Vermont communities. Since not all jurisdictions of the state are listed in this tabulation, state-wide totals are shown only with the county-by-county statistics.

President — The Democratic candidate was also the Independent Vermonters nominee and 991 of his votes were received as the IV candidate. The Rutland county vote includes corrected figures from Rutland City; original vote from Rutland City was 1,772 Ford (Republican) and 1,395 Carter (Democratic and Independent Vermonters). State-wide other vote total includes 99 scattered votes not available by county or city/town. Other vote was 4,001 McCarthy (McCarthy '76); 430 Camejo (Socialist Workers); 196 LaRouche (U.S. Labor); 99 scattered.

Governor — The Democratic candidate was also the Independent Vermonters nominee and 2,501 of his votes were received as the IV candidate. The Republican candidate was also the Bipartisan Vermonters nominee and 1,062 of his votes were received as the BV candidate. State-wide other vote total includes 82 scattered votes not available by county or city/town. Other vote was 11,317 Sanders (Liberty Union); 82 scattered.

Senator — The Democratic candidate was also the Independent Vermonters nominee and 3,508 of his votes were received as the IV candidate. State-wide other vote total includes 96 scattered votes not available by county or city/town. Other vote was 8,801 Kaufman (Liberty Union); 96 scattered.

Congress — The Democratic at-large candidate was also the Independent Vermonters nominee and 3,149 of his votes were received as the IV candidate. Other vote at-large was scattered.

1976 PRIMARIES

SEPTEMBER 14 REPUBLICAN

Governor — 24,279 Richard A. Snelling; 9,429 William G. Craig; 579 scattered.

Senator — 24,338 Robert T. Stafford; 10,911 John J. Welch; 178 scattered.

Congress — Unopposed at-large.

SEPTEMBER 14 DEMOCRATIC

Governor — 18,522 Stella B. Hackel; 14,725 Brian D. Burns; 8,809 Robert O'Brien; 71 scattered.

Senator — 21,674 Thomas P. Salmon; 19,238 Scott Skinner; 178 scattered.

Congress — Contested as follows:

AL — 26,654 John A. Burgess; 4,637 Robert W. Santway; 3,065 John T. Schnebly; 260 scattered.

SEPTEMBER 14 LIBERTY UNION

Governor — Bernard Sanders, unopposed.

Senator — 362 Nancy Kaufman; 146 John Medeiros; 12 scattered.

Congress — None. No candidate.

VIRGINIA

GOVERNOR

Mills E. Godwin (R). Elected 1973 to a four-year term. Previously elected 1965 as a Democrat.

SENATORS

Harry Flood Byrd, Jr. (I). Re-elected 1976 to a six-year term. Previously elected 1970 as an Independent and 1966 as a Democrat to fill out term vacated by the resignation of Senator Harry Flood Byrd; had been appointed November 1965 to fill this same vacancy.

William L. Scott (R). Elected 1972 to a six-year term.

REPRESENTATIVES

1. Paul Trible (R)
2. G. W. Whitehurst (R)
3. David Satterfield (D)
4. Robert W. Daniel (R)
5. W. C. Daniel (D)
6. M. Caldwell Butler (R)
7. J. Kenneth Robinson (R)
8. Herbert E. Harris (D)
9. William C. Wampler (R)
10. Joseph L. Fisher (D)

POSTWAR VOTE FOR GOVERNOR

	Total	Republican		Democratic		Other	Rep.-Dem.	Percentage			
								Total Vote		Major Vote	
Year	Vote	Vote	Candidate	Vote	Candidate	Vote	Plurality	Rep.	Dem.	Rep.	Dem.
1973	1,035,495	525,075	Godwin, Mills E.	–	–	510,420	525,075 R	50.7%	–	100.0%	–
1969	915,764	480,869	Holton, Linwood	415,695	Battle, William C.	19,200	65,174 R	52.5%	45.4%	53.6%	46.4%
1965	562,789	212,207	Holton, Linwood	269,526	Godwin, Mills E.	81,056	57,319 D	37.7%	47.9%	44.1%	55.9%
1961	394,490	142,567	Pearson, H. Clyde	251,861	Harrison, Albertis	62	109,294 D	36.1%	63.8%	36.1%	63.9%
1957	517,655	188,628	Dalton, Ted	326,921	Almond, J. Lindsay	2,106	138,293 D	36.4%	63.2%	36.6%	63.4%
1953	414,025	183,328	Dalton, Ted	226,998	Stanley, Thomas B.	3,699	43,670 D	44.3%	54.8%	44.7%	55.3%
1949	262,350	71,991	Johnson, Walter	184,772	Battle, John S.	5,587	112,781 D	27.4%	70.4%	28.0%	72.0%
1945	168,783	52,386	Landreth, S. Floyd	112,355	Tuck, William M.	4,042	59,969 D	31.0%	66.6%	31.8%	68.2%

POSTWAR VOTE FOR SENATOR

	Total	Republican		Democratic		Other	Rep.-Dem.	Percentage			
								Total Vote		Major Vote	
Year	Vote	Vote	Candidate	Vote	Candidate	Vote	Plurality	Rep.	Dem.	Rep.	Dem.
1976	1,557,500	–	–	596,009	Zumwalt, Elmo R.	961,491	596,009 D	–	38.3%	–	100.0%
1972	1,396,268	718,337	Scott, William L.	643,963	Spong, William B.	33,968	74,374 R	51.4%	46.1%	52.7%	47.3%
1970	946,751	145,031	Garland, Ray	295,057	Rawlings, George C.	506,663	150,026 D	15.3%	31.2%	33.0%	67.0%
1966	733,879	245,681	Ould, James P.	429,855	Spong, William B.	58,343	184,174 D	33.5%	58.6%	36.4%	63.6%
1966s	729,839	272,804	Traylor, Lawrence M.	389,028	Byrd, Harry Flood, Jr.	68,007	116,224 D	37.4%	53.3%	41.2%	58.8%
1964	928,363	176,624	May, Richard A.	592,260	Byrd, Harry Flood	159,479	415,636 D	19.0%	63.8%	23.0%	77.0%
1960	622,820	–	–	506,169	Robertson, A. Willis	116,651	506,169 D	–	81.3%	–	100.0%
1958	457,640	–	–	317,221	Byrd, Harry Flood	140,419	317,221 D	–	69.3%	–	100.0%
1954	306,510	–	–	244,844	Robertson, A. Willis	61,666	244,844 D	–	79.9%	–	100.0%
1952	543,516	–	–	398,677	Byrd, Harry Flood	144,839	398,677 D	–	73.4%	–	100.0%
1948	386,178	118,546	Woods, Robert	253,865	Robertson, A. Willis	13,767	135,319 D	30.7%	65.7%	31.8%	68.2%
1946	252,863	77,005	Parsons, Lester S.	163,960	Byrd, Harry Flood	11,898	86,955 D	30.5%	64.8%	32.0%	68.0%
1946s	248,962	72,253	Woods, Robert	169,680	Robertson, A. Willis	7,029	97,427 D	29.0%	68.2%	29.9%	70.1%

One each of the 1966 and 1946 elections was for a short term to fill a vacancy. In 1970 Harry Flood Byrd, Jr., the Independent candidate, polled 506,633 votes (53.5% of the total vote) and won the election with a 211,576 plurality. In 1976 Harry Flood Byrd, Jr., polled 890,778 votes as an Independent candidate (57.2% of the total vote) and won the election with a 294,769 plurality.

VIRGINIA

Districts Established March 11, 1972

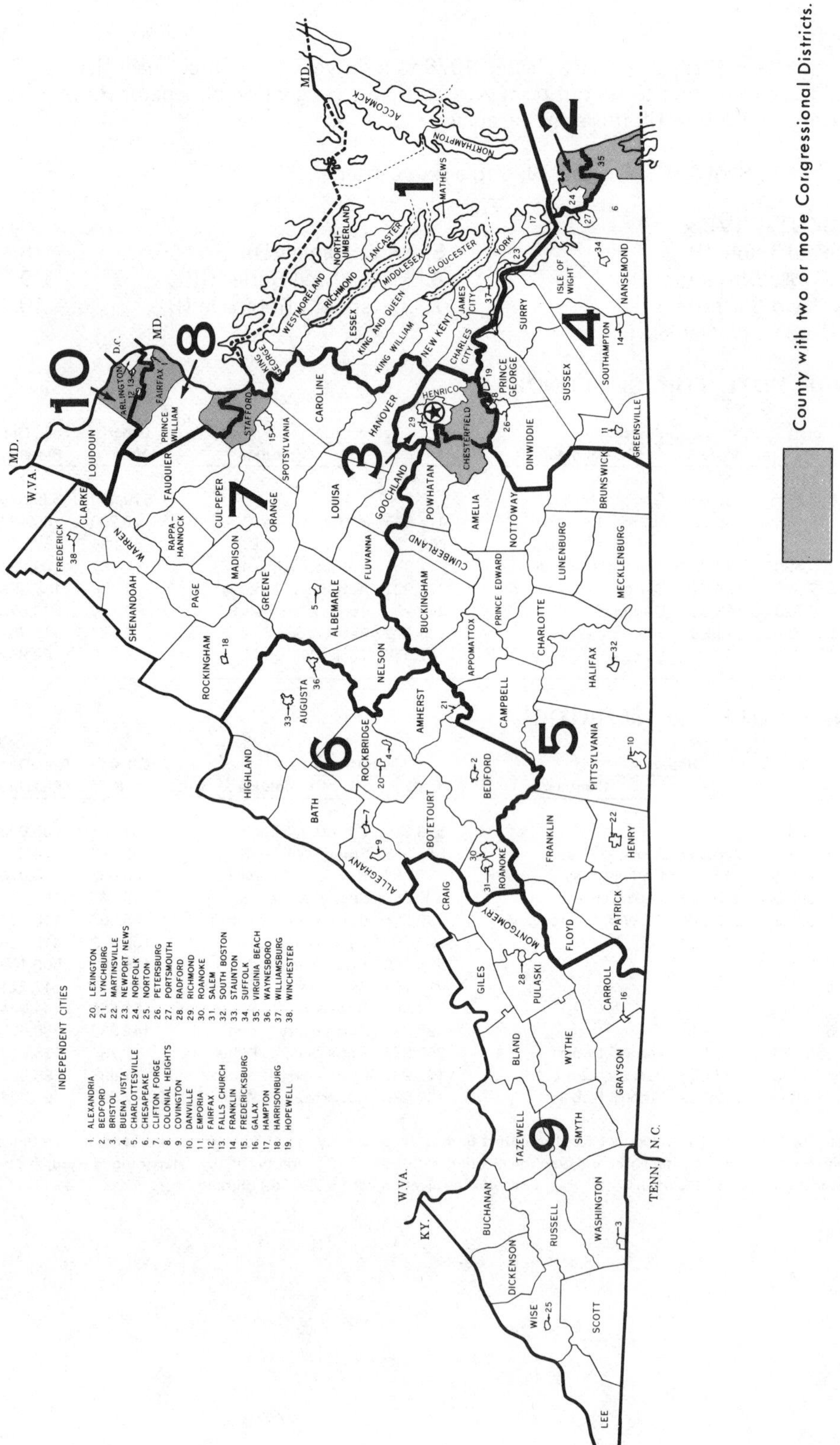

VIRGINIA

PRESIDENT 1976

1970 Census Population	County	Total Vote	Republican	Democratic	Other	Rep.-Dem. Plurality	Percentage Total Vote Rep.	Percentage Total Vote Dem.	Percentage Major Vote Rep.	Percentage Major Vote Dem.
29,004	ACCOMACK	9,536	4,494	4,807	235	313 D	47.1%	50.4%	48.3%	51.7%
37,780	ALBEMARLE	16,632	9,084	7,310	238	1,774 R	54.6%	44.0%	55.4%	44.6%
12,461	ALLEGHANY	4,265	1,756	2,462	47	706 D	41.2%	57.7%	41.6%	58.4%
7,592	AMELIA	3,458	1,634	1,715	109	81 D	47.3%	49.6%	48.8%	51.2%
26,072	AMHERST	7,776	3,956	3,675	145	281 R	50.9%	47.3%	51.8%	48.2%
9,784	APPOMATTOX	3,863	1,964	1,702	197	262 R	50.8%	44.1%	53.6%	46.4%
174,284	ARLINGTON	64,599	30,972	32,536	1,091	1,564 D	47.9%	50.4%	48.8%	51.2%
44,220	AUGUSTA	14,692	8,452	5,626	614	2,826 R	57.5%	38.3%	60.0%	40.0%
5,192	BATH	1,932	888	1,029	15	141 D	46.0%	53.3%	46.3%	53.7%
26,728	BEDFORD	9,246	4,189	4,766	291	577 D	45.3%	51.5%	46.8%	53.2%
5,423	BLAND	2,017	1,047	961	9	86 R	51.9%	47.6%	52.1%	47.9%
18,193	BOTETOURT	7,573	3,343	4,021	209	678 D	44.1%	53.1%	45.4%	54.6%
16,172	BRUNSWICK	5,668	2,387	3,071	210	684 D	42.1%	54.2%	43.7%	56.3%
32,071	BUCHANAN	10,728	3,850	5,791	1,087	1,941 D	35.9%	54.0%	39.9%	60.1%
10,597	BUCKINGHAM	3,758	1,487	2,179	92	692 D	39.6%	58.0%	40.6%	59.4%
43,319	CAMPBELL	12,245	7,442	4,354	449	3,088 R	60.8%	35.6%	63.1%	36.9%
13,925	CAROLINE	4,796	1,648	3,064	84	1,416 D	34.4%	63.9%	35.0%	65.0%
23,092	CARROLL	8,968	4,820	4,010	138	810 R	53.7%	44.7%	54.6%	45.4%
6,158	CHARLES CITY	1,951	439	1,455	57	1,016 D	22.5%	74.6%	23.2%	76.8%
11,551	CHARLOTTE	4,394	2,023	2,312	59	289 D	46.0%	52.6%	46.7%	53.3%
76,855	CHESTERFIELD	42,436	27,812	14,126	498	13,686 R	65.5%	33.3%	66.3%	33.7%
8,102	CLARKE	2,794	1,440	1,276	78	164 R	51.5%	45.7%	53.0%	47.0%
3,524	CRAIG	1,667	546	1,103	18	557 D	32.8%	66.2%	33.1%	66.9%
18,218	CULPEPER	6,696	3,659	2,892	145	767 R	54.6%	43.2%	55.9%	44.1%
6,179	CUMBERLAND	2,757	1,284	1,302	171	18 D	46.6%	47.2%	49.7%	50.3%
16,077	DICKENSON	8,209	3,471	4,583	155	1,112 D	42.3%	55.8%	43.1%	56.9%
25,046	DINWIDDIE	6,473	2,413	3,873	187	1,460 D	37.3%	59.8%	38.4%	61.6%
7,099	ESSEX	2,730	1,380	1,306	44	74 R	50.5%	47.8%	51.4%	48.6%
455,021	FAIRFAX COUNTY	205,957	110,424	92,037	3,496	18,387 R	53.6%	44.7%	54.5%	45.5%
26,375	FAUQUIER	9,111	4,715	4,002	394	713 R	51.8%	43.9%	54.1%	45.9%
9,775	FLOYD	3,925	2,071	1,728	126	343 R	52.8%	44.0%	54.5%	45.5%
7,621	FLUVANNA	2,770	1,296	1,415	59	119 D	46.8%	51.1%	47.8%	52.2%
26,858	FRANKLIN COUNTY	10,199	3,532	6,439	228	2,907 D	34.6%	63.1%	35.4%	64.6%
28,893	FREDERICK	8,672	5,162	3,389	121	1,773 R	59.5%	39.1%	60.4%	39.6%
16,741	GILES	6,739	2,731	3,779	229	1,048 D	40.5%	56.1%	42.0%	58.0%
14,059	GLOUCESTER	6,404	3,025	3,156	223	131 D	47.2%	49.3%	48.9%	51.1%
10,069	GOOCHLAND	4,455	2,104	2,259	92	155 D	47.2%	50.7%	48.2%	51.8%
15,439	GRAYSON	6,251	3,021	3,146	84	125 D	48.3%	50.3%	49.0%	51.0%
5,248	GREENE	2,130	1,095	895	140	200 R	51.4%	42.0%	55.0%	45.0%
9,604	GREENSVILLE	3,646	1,137	2,413	96	1,276 D	31.2%	66.2%	32.0%	68.0%
30,076	HALIFAX	8,697	4,045	4,352	300	307 D	46.5%	50.0%	48.2%	51.8%
37,479	HANOVER	17,859	11,559	6,069	231	5,490 R	64.7%	34.0%	65.6%	34.4%
154,364	HENRICO	68,981	45,405	21,729	1,847	23,676 R	65.8%	31.5%	67.6%	32.4%
50,901	HENRY	16,024	5,612	9,680	732	4,068 D	35.0%	60.4%	36.7%	63.3%
2,529	HIGHLAND	1,132	629	493	10	136 R	55.6%	43.6%	56.1%	43.9%
18,285	ISLE OF WIGHT	7,009	2,718	4,145	146	1,427 D	38.8%	59.1%	39.6%	60.4%
17,853	JAMES CITY	6,454	3,186	3,000	268	186 R	49.4%	46.5%	51.5%	48.5%
5,491	KING AND QUEEN	1,992	778	1,111	103	333 D	39.1%	55.8%	41.2%	58.8%
8,039	KING GEORGE	2,958	1,383	1,513	62	130 D	46.8%	51.1%	47.8%	52.2%
7,497	KING WILLIAM	3,156	1,597	1,501	58	96 R	50.6%	47.6%	51.5%	48.5%
9,126	LANCASTER	4,074	2,381	1,581	112	800 R	58.4%	38.8%	60.1%	39.9%
20,321	LEE	10,284	4,679	5,415	190	736 D	45.5%	52.7%	46.4%	53.6%
37,150	LOUDOUN	17,748	9,192	7,995	561	1,197 R	51.8%	45.0%	53.5%	46.5%
14,004	LOUISA	5,135	2,151	2,857	127	706 D	41.9%	55.6%	43.0%	57.0%
11,687	LUNENBURG	3,652	1,816	1,739	97	77 R	49.7%	47.6%	51.1%	48.9%
8,638	MADISON	3,228	1,710	1,466	52	244 R	53.0%	45.4%	53.8%	46.2%
7,168	MATHEWS	3,303	1,908	1,309	86	599 R	57.8%	39.6%	59.3%	40.7%
29,426	MECKLENBURG	8,769	4,423	4,076	270	347 R	50.4%	46.5%	52.0%	48.0%
6,295	MIDDLESEX	3,039	1,608	1,312	119	296 R	52.9%	43.2%	55.1%	44.9%
47,157	MONTGOMERY	15,742	7,971	7,539	232	432 R	50.6%	47.9%	51.4%	48.6%
11,702	NELSON	4,027	1,516	2,426	85	910 D	37.6%	60.2%	38.5%	61.5%
5,300	NEW KENT	2,644	1,259	1,338	47	79 D	47.6%	50.6%	48.5%	51.5%
14,442	NORTHAMPTON	4,735	2,043	2,459	233	416 D	43.1%	51.9%	45.4%	54.6%
9,239	NORTHUMBERLAND	4,126	2,167	1,814	145	353 R	52.5%	44.0%	54.4%	45.6%
14,260	NOTTOWAY	5,222	2,486	2,558	178	72 D	47.6%	49.0%	49.3%	50.7%

VIRGINIA

PRESIDENT 1976

1970 Census Population	County	Total Vote	Republican	Democratic	Other	Rep.-Dem. Plurality	Percentage Total Vote Rep.	Total Vote Dem.	Major Vote Rep.	Major Vote Dem.
13,792	ORANGE	5,161	2,549	2,309	303	240 R	49.4%	44.7%	52.5%	47.5%
16,581	PAGE	7,337	3,780	3,401	156	379 R	51.5%	46.4%	52.6%	47.4%
15,282	PATRICK	5,377	2,349	2,740	288	391 D	43.7%	51.0%	46.2%	53.8%
58,789	PITTSYLVANIA	17,913	9,173	7,929	811	1,244 R	51.2%	44.3%	53.6%	46.4%
7,696	POWHATAN	3,636	2,010	1,528	98	482 R	55.3%	42.0%	56.8%	43.2%
14,379	PRINCE EDWARD	5,429	2,734	2,448	247	286 R	50.4%	45.1%	52.8%	47.2%
29,092	PRINCE GEORGE	4,960	2,254	2,630	76	376 D	45.4%	53.0%	46.2%	53.8%
95,094	PRINCE WILLIAM	31,524	15,446	15,215	863	231 R	49.0%	48.3%	50.4%	49.6%
29,564	PULASKI	10,624	4,764	5,546	314	782 D	44.8%	52.2%	46.2%	53.8%
5,199	RAPPAHANNOCK	1,981	881	1,071	29	190 D	44.5%	54.1%	45.1%	54.9%
5,841	RICHMOND COUNTY	2,288	1,391	864	33	527 R	60.8%	37.8%	61.7%	38.3%
67,339	ROANOKE COUNTY	26,948	13,587	13,120	241	467 R	50.4%	48.7%	50.9%	49.1%
16,637	ROCKBRIDGE	4,940	2,157	2,525	258	368 D	43.7%	51.1%	46.1%	53.9%
47,890	ROCKINGHAM	15,789	9,768	5,349	672	4,419 R	61.9%	33.9%	64.6%	35.4%
24,533	RUSSELL	10,667	4,287	6,014	366	1,727 D	40.2%	56.4%	41.6%	58.4%
24,376	SCOTT	9,494	4,313	4,496	685	183 D	45.4%	47.4%	49.0%	51.0%
22,852	SHENANDOAH	9,830	6,296	3,364	170	2,932 R	64.0%	34.2%	65.2%	34.8%
31,349	SMYTH	10,641	5,032	5,246	363	214 D	47.3%	49.3%	49.0%	51.0%
18,582	SOUTHAMPTON	5,889	2,366	3,399	124	1,033 D	40.2%	57.7%	41.0%	59.0%
16,424	SPOTSYLVANIA	7,560	3,210	4,210	140	1,000 D	42.5%	55.7%	43.3%	56.7%
24,587	STAFFORD	9,502	4,451	4,900	151	449 D	46.8%	51.6%	47.6%	52.4%
5,882	SURRY	2,833	929	1,829	75	900 D	32.8%	64.6%	33.7%	66.3%
11,464	SUSSEX	4,094	1,360	2,497	237	1,137 D	33.2%	61.0%	35.3%	64.7%
39,816	TAZEWELL	13,439	5,565	7,565	309	2,000 D	41.4%	56.3%	42.4%	57.6%
15,301	WARREN	6,517	2,985	3,221	311	236 D	45.8%	49.4%	48.1%	51.9%
40,835	WASHINGTON	14,015	6,865	6,547	603	318 R	49.0%	46.7%	51.2%	48.8%
12,142	WESTMORELAND	4,568	1,909	2,355	304	446 D	41.8%	51.6%	44.8%	55.2%
35,947	WISE	13,351	5,691	7,134	526	1,443 D	42.6%	53.4%	44.4%	55.6%
22,139	WYTHE	8,241	4,231	3,578	432	653 R	51.3%	43.4%	54.2%	45.8%
27,762	YORK	10,451	5,603	4,736	112	867 R	53.6%	45.3%	54.2%	45.8%

VIRGINIA

PRESIDENT 1976

1970 Census Population	City	Total Vote	Republican	Democratic	Other	Rep.-Dem. Plurality	Percentage Total Vote Rep.	Total Vote Dem.	Major Vote Rep.	Major Vote Dem.
110,938	ALEXANDRIA	37,910	16,880	19,858	1,172	2,978 D	44.5%	52.4%	45.9%	54.1%
6,011	BEDFORD	2,294	1,043	1,122	129	79 D	45.5%	48.9%	48.2%	51.8%
14,857	BRISTOL	6,361	2,943	3,343	75	400 D	46.3%	52.6%	46.8%	53.2%
6,425	BUENA VISTA	1,853	771	993	89	222 D	41.6%	53.6%	43.7%	56.3%
38,880	CHARLOTTESVILLE	13,869	6,673	6,846	350	173 D	48.1%	49.4%	49.4%	50.6%
89,580	CHESAPEAKE	32,157	12,851	17,651	1,655	4,800 D	40.0%	54.9%	42.1%	57.9%
5,501	CLIFTON FORGE	1,893	770	993	130	223 D	40.7%	52.5%	43.7%	56.3%
15,097	COLONIAL HEIGHTS	6,934	4,291	2,409	234	1,882 R	61.9%	34.7%	64.0%	36.0%
10,060	COVINGTON	3,165	1,173	1,820	172	647 D	37.1%	57.5%	39.2%	60.8%
46,391	DANVILLE	17,212	10,235	6,425	552	3,810 R	59.5%	37.3%	61.4%	38.6%
5,300	EMPORIA	2,020	1,055	899	66	156 R	52.2%	44.5%	54.0%	46.0%
21,970	FAIRFAX CITY	7,823	4,174	3,464	185	710 R	53.4%	44.3%	54.6%	45.4%
10,772	FALLS CHURCH	4,588	2,323	2,202	63	121 R	50.6%	48.0%	51.3%	48.7%
6,880	FRANKLIN CITY	2,290	1,127	1,116	47	11 R	49.2%	48.7%	50.2%	49.8%
14,450	FREDERICKSBURG	5,150	2,527	2,550	73	23 D	49.1%	49.5%	49.8%	50.2%
6,278	GALAX	2,370	1,128	1,218	24	90 D	47.6%	51.4%	48.1%	51.9%
120,779	HAMPTON	36,048	15,021	19,202	1,825	4,181 D	41.7%	53.3%	43.9%	56.1%
14,605	HARRISONBURG	5,358	3,376	1,803	179	1,573 R	63.0%	33.7%	65.2%	34.8%
23,471	HOPEWELL	7,807	3,764	3,691	352	73 R	48.2%	47.3%	50.5%	49.5%
7,597	LEXINGTON	2,035	1,027	945	63	82 R	50.5%	46.4%	52.1%	47.9%
54,083	LYNCHBURG	23,804	14,564	8,227	1,013	6,337 R	61.2%	34.6%	63.9%	36.1%
9,164	MANASSAS	3,737	1,992	1,646	99	346 R	53.3%	44.0%	54.8%	45.2%
6,844	MANASSAS PARK	1,189	444	709	36	265 D	37.3%	59.6%	38.5%	61.5%
19,653	MARTINSVILLE	6,935	3,147	3,491	297	344 D	45.4%	50.3%	47.4%	52.6%
138,177	NEWPORT NEWS	44,492	20,914	23,058	520	2,144 D	47.0%	51.8%	47.6%	52.4%
307,951	NORFOLK	70,402	28,099	39,295	3,008	11,196 D	39.9%	55.8%	41.7%	58.3%
4,001	NORTON	1,430	577	811	42	234 D	40.3%	56.7%	41.6%	58.4%
36,103	PETERSBURG	13,082	5,041	7,852	189	2,811 D	38.5%	60.0%	39.1%	60.9%
5,441	POQUOSON	2,640	1,461	1,140	39	321 R	55.3%	43.2%	56.2%	43.8%
110,963	PORTSMOUTH	36,246	12,872	22,837	537	9,965 D	35.5%	63.0%	36.0%	64.0%
11,596	RADFORD	4,122	1,844	2,240	38	396 D	44.7%	54.3%	45.2%	54.8%
249,621	RICHMOND CITY	83,110	37,176	44,687	1,247	7,511 D	44.7%	53.8%	45.4%	54.6%
92,115	ROANOKE CITY	35,949	14,738	20,696	515	5,958 D	41.0%	57.6%	41.6%	58.4%
21,982	SALEM	8,690	4,196	4,404	90	208 D	48.3%	50.7%	48.8%	51.2%
6,889	SOUTH BOSTON	2,438	1,389	1,001	48	388 R	57.0%	41.1%	58.1%	41.9%
24,504	STAUNTON	7,863	4,681	2,951	231	1,730 R	59.5%	37.5%	61.3%	38.7%
45,024	SUFFOLK	15,609	6,066	9,246	297	3,180 D	38.9%	59.2%	39.6%	60.4%
172,106	VIRGINIA BEACH	63,518	34,593	25,824	3,101	8,769 R	54.5%	40.7%	57.3%	42.7%
16,707	WAYNESBORO	5,915	3,528	2,209	178	1,319 R	59.6%	37.3%	61.5%	38.5%
9,069	WILLIAMSBURG	3,195	1,654	1,468	73	186 R	51.8%	45.9%	53.0%	47.0%
14,643	WINCHESTER	6,484	4,075	2,346	63	1,729 R	62.8%	36.2%	63.5%	36.5%
4,648,494	TOTAL	1,697,094	836,554	813,896	46,644	22,658 R	49.3%	48.0%	50.7%	49.3%

VIRGINIA

SENATOR 1976

1970 Census Population	County	Total Vote	Independent	Democratic	Other	Ind.-Dem. Plurality	Percentage Total Vote Ind.	Percentage Total Vote Dem.	Percentage Major Vote Ind.	Percentage Major Vote Dem.
29,004	ACCOMACK	8,911	6,023	2,574	314	3,449 I	67.6%	28.9%	70.1%	29.9%
37,780	ALBEMARLE	15,877	9,288	6,074	515	3,214 I	58.5%	38.3%	60.5%	39.5%
12,461	ALLEGHANY	4,190	2,514	1,544	132	970 I	60.0%	36.8%	62.0%	38.0%
7,592	AMELIA	3,164	2,095	978	91	1,117 I	66.2%	30.9%	68.2%	31.8%
26,072	AMHERST	7,289	4,832	2,280	177	2,552 I	66.3%	31.3%	67.9%	32.1%
9,784	APPOMATTOX	3,678	2,649	866	163	1,783 I	72.0%	23.5%	75.4%	24.6%
174,284	ARLINGTON	60,714	27,377	30,619	2,718	3,242 D	45.1%	50.4%	47.2%	52.8%
44,220	AUGUSTA	13,806	8,945	3,880	981	5,065 I	64.8%	28.1%	69.7%	30.3%
5,192	BATH	1,915	1,418	415	82	1,003 I	74.0%	21.7%	77.4%	22.6%
26,728	BEDFORD	8,654	5,207	3,017	430	2,190 I	60.2%	34.9%	63.3%	36.7%
5,423	BLAND	1,926	1,343	468	115	875 I	69.7%	24.3%	74.2%	25.8%
18,193	BOTETOURT	6,999	4,070	2,460	469	1,610 I	58.2%	35.1%	62.3%	37.7%
16,172	BRUNSWICK	5,066	3,228	1,722	116	1,506 I	63.7%	34.0%	65.2%	34.8%
32,071	BUCHANAN	8,483	3,334	4,654	495	1,320 D	39.3%	54.9%	41.7%	58.3%
10,597	BUCKINGHAM	3,520	2,354	1,026	140	1,328 I	66.9%	29.1%	69.6%	30.4%
43,319	CAMPBELL	10,985	3,385	2,274	5,326	1,111 I	30.8%	20.7%	59.8%	40.2%
13,925	CAROLINE	4,327	2,208	1,939	180	269 I	51.0%	44.8%	53.2%	46.8%
23,092	CARROLL	7,209	4,229	2,566	414	1,663 I	58.7%	35.6%	62.2%	37.8%
6,158	CHARLES CITY	1,732	558	1,056	118	498 D	32.2%	61.0%	34.6%	65.4%
11,551	CHARLOTTE	4,169	3,056	980	133	2,076 I	73.3%	23.5%	75.7%	24.3%
76,855	CHESTERFIELD	41,375	29,382	10,778	1,215	18,604 I	71.0%	26.0%	73.2%	26.8%
8,102	CLARKE	2,714	2,093	500	121	1,593 I	77.1%	18.4%	80.7%	19.3%
3,524	CRAIG	1,656	860	747	49	113 I	51.9%	45.1%	53.5%	46.5%
18,218	CULPEPER	6,370	4,343	1,721	306	2,622 I	68.2%	27.0%	71.6%	28.4%
6,179	CUMBERLAND	2,396	1,441	887	68	554 I	60.1%	37.0%	61.9%	38.1%
16,077	DICKENSON	6,868	2,622	3,387	859	765 D	38.2%	49.3%	43.6%	56.4%
25,046	DINWIDDIE	5,882	3,519	2,238	125	1,281 I	59.8%	38.0%	61.1%	38.9%
7,099	ESSEX	2,437	1,692	680	65	1,012 I	69.4%	27.9%	71.3%	28.7%
455,021	FAIRFAX COUNTY	191,615	90,750	89,908	10,957	842 I	47.4%	46.9%	50.2%	49.8%
26,375	FAUQUIER	8,346	5,316	2,585	445	2,731 I	63.7%	31.0%	67.3%	32.7%
9,775	FLOYD	3,361	2,146	1,023	192	1,123 I	63.9%	30.4%	67.7%	32.3%
7,621	FLUVANNA	2,563	1,662	817	84	845 I	64.8%	31.9%	67.0%	33.0%
26,858	FRANKLIN COUNTY	9,212	5,711	3,068	433	2,643 I	62.0%	33.3%	65.1%	34.9%
28,893	FREDERICK	8,512	6,153	1,849	510	4,304 I	72.3%	21.7%	76.9%	23.1%
16,741	GILES	5,922	3,409	2,214	299	1,195 I	57.6%	37.4%	60.6%	39.4%
14,059	GLOUCESTER	5,678	3,765	1,694	219	2,071 I	66.3%	29.8%	69.0%	31.0%
10,069	GOOCHLAND	4,178	2,448	1,651	79	797 I	58.6%	39.5%	59.7%	40.3%
15,439	GRAYSON	4,603	2,272	2,094	237	178 I	49.4%	45.5%	52.0%	48.0%
5,248	GREENE	1,882	1,164	594	124	570 I	61.8%	31.6%	66.2%	33.8%
9,604	GREENSVILLE	3,215	1,701	1,471	43	230 I	52.9%	45.8%	53.6%	46.4%
30,076	HALIFAX	7,574	5,409	1,725	440	3,684 I	71.4%	22.8%	75.8%	24.2%
37,479	HANOVER	17,227	12,547	4,217	463	8,330 I	72.8%	24.5%	74.8%	25.2%
154,364	HENRICO	66,413	46,576	17,724	2,113	28,852 I	70.1%	26.7%	72.4%	27.6%
50,901	HENRY	13,775	7,394	5,798	583	1,596 I	53.7%	42.1%	56.0%	44.0%
2,529	HIGHLAND	1,124	921	160	43	761 I	81.9%	14.2%	85.2%	14.8%
18,285	ISLE OF WIGHT	6,564	3,727	2,683	154	1,044 I	56.8%	40.9%	58.1%	41.9%
17,853	JAMES CITY	5,708	3,329	2,192	187	1,137 I	58.3%	38.4%	60.3%	39.7%
5,491	KING AND QUEEN	1,591	992	525	74	467 I	62.4%	33.0%	65.4%	34.6%
8,039	KING GEORGE	2,722	1,702	845	175	857 I	62.5%	31.0%	66.8%	33.2%
7,497	KING WILLIAM	2,932	1,856	1,012	64	844 I	63.3%	34.5%	64.7%	35.3%
9,126	LANCASTER	3,854	2,700	1,053	101	1,647 I	70.1%	27.3%	71.9%	28.1%
20,321	LEE	8,434	4,424	3,285	725	1,139 I	52.5%	38.9%	57.4%	42.6%
37,150	LOUDOUN	16,567	9,487	6,178	902	3,309 I	57.3%	37.3%	60.6%	39.4%
14,004	LOUISA	4,712	2,830	1,691	191	1,139 I	60.1%	35.9%	62.6%	37.4%
11,687	LUNENBURG	3,501	2,476	893	132	1,583 I	70.7%	25.5%	73.5%	26.5%
8,638	MADISON	3,159	2,196	802	161	1,394 I	69.5%	25.4%	73.2%	26.8%
7,168	MATHEWS	2,998	2,213	691	94	1,522 I	73.8%	23.0%	76.2%	23.8%
29,426	MECKLENBURG	8,063	5,709	2,101	253	3,608 I	70.8%	26.1%	73.1%	26.9%
6,295	MIDDLESEX	2,700	1,880	724	96	1,156 I	69.6%	26.8%	72.2%	27.8%
47,157	MONTGOMERY	14,848	8,774	5,607	467	3,167 I	59.1%	37.8%	61.0%	39.0%
11,702	NELSON	3,725	2,289	1,319	117	970 I	61.4%	35.4%	63.4%	36.6%
5,300	NEW KENT	2,508	1,586	797	125	789 I	63.2%	31.8%	66.6%	33.4%
14,442	NORTHAMPTON	4,178	2,409	1,617	152	792 I	57.7%	38.7%	59.8%	40.2%
9,239	NORTHUMBERLAND	3,706	2,529	1,024	153	1,505 I	68.2%	27.6%	71.2%	28.8%
14,260	NOTTOWAY	4,722	3,106	1,438	178	1,668 I	65.8%	30.5%	68.4%	31.6%

VIRGINIA

SENATOR 1976

1970 Census Population	County	Total Vote	Independent	Democratic	Other	Ind.-Dem. Plurality	Percentage Total Vote Ind.	Percentage Total Vote Dem.	Percentage Major Vote Ind.	Percentage Major Vote Dem.
13,792	ORANGE	4,608	2,965	1,401	242	1,564 I	64.3%	30.4%	67.9%	32.1%
16,581	PAGE	6,484	4,391	1,747	346	2,644 I	67.7%	26.9%	71.5%	28.5%
15,282	PATRICK	4,320	2,831	1,189	300	1,642 I	65.5%	27.5%	70.4%	29.6%
58,789	PITTSYLVANIA	15,325	10,843	3,874	608	6,969 I	70.8%	25.3%	73.7%	26.3%
7,696	POWHATAN	3,427	2,255	1,107	65	1,148 I	65.8%	32.3%	67.1%	32.9%
14,379	PRINCE EDWARD	4,806	3,104	1,488	214	1,616 I	64.6%	31.0%	67.6%	32.4%
29,092	PRINCE GEORGE	4,554	2,718	1,720	116	998 I	59.7%	37.8%	61.2%	38.8%
95,094	PRINCE WILLIAM	28,921	13,531	13,568	1,822	37 D	46.8%	46.9%	49.9%	50.1%
29,564	PULASKI	9,456	5,481	3,569	406	1,912 I	58.0%	37.7%	60.6%	39.4%
5,199	RAPPAHANNOCK	1,991	1,265	608	118	657 I	63.5%	30.5%	67.5%	32.5%
5,841	RICHMOND COUNTY	2,279	1,771	452	56	1,319 I	77.7%	19.8%	79.7%	20.3%
67,339	ROANOKE COUNTY	25,581	16,396	8,134	1,051	8,262 I	64.1%	31.8%	66.8%	33.2%
16,637	ROCKBRIDGE	4,573	3,024	1,396	153	1,628 I	66.1%	30.5%	68.4%	31.6%
47,890	ROCKINGHAM	14,897	10,014	4,034	849	5,980 I	67.2%	27.1%	71.3%	28.7%
24,533	RUSSELL	9,298	4,514	4,415	369	99 I	48.5%	47.5%	50.6%	49.4%
24,376	SCOTT	7,789	4,114	3,231	444	883 I	52.8%	41.5%	56.0%	44.0%
22,852	SHENANDOAH	9,215	6,791	1,942	482	4,849 I	73.7%	21.1%	77.8%	22.2%
31,349	SMYTH	9,455	6,394	2,814	247	3,580 I	67.6%	29.8%	69.4%	30.6%
18,582	SOUTHAMPTON	5,172	3,486	1,567	119	1,919 I	67.4%	30.3%	69.0%	31.0%
16,424	SPOTSYLVANIA	6,939	4,099	2,470	370	1,629 I	59.1%	35.6%	62.4%	37.6%
24,587	STAFFORD	8,985	5,510	2,981	494	2,529 I	61.3%	33.2%	64.9%	35.1%
5,882	SURRY	2,496	1,405	998	93	407 I	56.3%	40.0%	58.5%	41.5%
11,464	SUSSEX	3,761	1,905	1,736	120	169 I	50.7%	46.2%	52.3%	47.7%
39,816	TAZEWELL	11,711	6,186	3,961	1,564	2,225 I	52.8%	33.8%	61.0%	39.0%
15,301	WARREN	6,082	3,607	2,177	298	1,430 I	59.3%	35.8%	62.4%	37.6%
40,835	WASHINGTON	11,979	7,966	3,612	401	4,354 I	66.5%	30.2%	68.8%	31.2%
12,142	WESTMORELAND	3,935	2,241	1,502	192	739 I	57.0%	38.2%	59.9%	40.1%
35,947	WISE	11,315	5,653	5,195	467	458 I	50.0%	45.9%	52.1%	47.9%
22,139	WYTHE	7,238	4,508	2,361	369	2,147 I	62.3%	32.6%	65.6%	34.4%
27,762	YORK	9,732	6,307	3,150	275	3,157 I	64.8%	32.4%	66.7%	33.3%

VIRGINIA

SENATOR 1976

1970 Census Population	City	Total Vote	Independent	Democratic	Other	Ind.-Dem. Plurality	Percentage: Total Vote Ind.	Total Vote Dem.	Major Vote Ind.	Major Vote Dem.
110,938	ALEXANDRIA	34,524	13,250	19,502	1,772	6,252 D	38.4%	56.5%	40.5%	59.5%
6,011	BEDFORD	2,079	1,197	847	35	350 I	57.6%	40.7%	58.6%	41.4%
14,857	BRISTOL	5,676	3,887	1,663	126	2,224 I	68.5%	29.3%	70.0%	30.0%
6,425	BUENA VISTA	1,639	1,058	533	48	525 I	64.6%	32.5%	66.5%	33.5%
38,880	CHARLOTTESVILLE	13,085	6,893	5,849	343	1,044 I	52.7%	44.7%	54.1%	45.9%
89,580	CHESAPEAKE	28,583	16,402	11,214	967	5,188 I	57.4%	39.2%	59.4%	40.6%
5,501	CLIFTON FORGE	1,702	1,039	599	64	440 I	61.0%	35.2%	63.4%	36.6%
15,097	COLONIAL HEIGHTS	6,490	4,504	1,671	315	2,833 I	69.4%	25.7%	72.9%	27.1%
10,060	COVINGTON	2,833	1,523	1,172	138	351 I	53.8%	41.4%	56.5%	43.5%
46,391	DANVILLE	14,245	10,313	3,313	619	7,000 I	72.4%	23.3%	75.7%	24.3%
5,300	EMPORIA	1,815	1,261	530	24	731 I	69.5%	29.2%	70.4%	29.6%
21,970	FAIRFAX CITY	7,458	3,672	3,322	464	350 I	49.2%	44.5%	52.5%	47.5%
10,772	FALLS CHURCH	4,292	2,076	1,992	224	84 I	48.4%	46.4%	51.0%	49.0%
6,880	FRANKLIN CITY	2,053	1,365	635	53	730 I	66.5%	30.9%	68.3%	31.8%
14,450	FREDERICKSBURG	4,797	2,831	1,824	142	1,007 I	59.0%	38.0%	60.8%	39.2%
6,278	GALAX	2,002	1,095	846	61	249 I	54.7%	42.3%	56.4%	43.6%
120,779	HAMPTON	32,667	17,212	14,134	1,321	3,078 I	52.7%	43.3%	54.9%	45.1%
14,605	HARRISONBURG	4,923	3,242	1,418	263	1,824 I	65.9%	28.8%	69.6%	30.4%
23,471	HOPEWELL	7,039	4,124	2,655	260	1,469 I	58.6%	37.7%	60.8%	39.2%
7,597	LEXINGTON	1,905	1,204	671	30	533 I	63.2%	35.2%	64.2%	35.8%
54,083	LYNCHBURG	22,245	14,602	6,850	793	7,752 I	65.6%	30.8%	68.1%	31.9%
9,164	MANASSAS	3,408	1,803	1,412	193	391 I	52.9%	41.4%	56.1%	43.9%
6,844	MANASSAS PARK	1,062	489	517	56	28 D	46.0%	48.7%	48.6%	51.4%
19,653	MARTINSVILLE	6,018	3,478	2,246	294	1,232 I	57.8%	37.3%	60.8%	39.2%
138,177	NEWPORT NEWS	41,070	24,307	15,897	866	8,410 I	59.2%	38.7%	60.5%	39.5%
307,951	NORFOLK	63,549	31,533	29,751	2,265	1,782 I	49.6%	46.8%	51.5%	48.5%
4,001	NORTON	1,258	712	496	50	216 I	56.6%	39.4%	58.9%	41.1%
36,103	PETERSBURG	11,890	5,613	5,988	289	375 D	47.2%	50.4%	48.4%	51.6%
5,441	POQUOSON	2,515	1,991	476	48	1,515 I	79.2%	18.9%	80.7%	19.3%
110,963	PORTSMOUTH	33,569	17,694	15,304	571	2,390 I	52.7%	45.6%	53.6%	46.4%
11,596	RADFORD	3,808	2,092	1,611	105	481 I	54.9%	42.3%	56.5%	43.5%
249,621	RICHMOND CITY	78,080	37,697	38,256	2,127	559 D	48.3%	49.0%	49.6%	50.4%
92,115	ROANOKE CITY	33,579	18,918	13,213	1,448	5,705 I	56.3%	39.3%	58.9%	41.1%
21,982	SALEM	8,105	5,154	2,605	346	2,549 I	63.6%	32.1%	66.4%	33.6%
6,889	SOUTH BOSTON	2,217	1,632	522	63	1,110 I	73.6%	23.5%	75.8%	24.2%
24,504	STAUNTON	7,292	4,504	2,263	525	2,241 I	61.8%	31.0%	66.6%	33.4%
45,024	SUFFOLK	13,974	7,815	5,845	314	1,970 I	55.9%	41.8%	57.2%	42.8%
172,106	VIRGINIA BEACH	58,404	37,621	18,504	2,279	19,117 I	64.4%	31.7%	67.0%	33.0%
16,707	WAYNESBORO	5,573	3,609	1,790	174	1,819 I	64.8%	32.1%	66.8%	33.2%
9,069	WILLIAMSBURG	2,903	1,711	1,110	82	601 I	58.9%	38.2%	60.7%	39.3%
14,643	WINCHESTER	6,146	4,757	1,165	224	3,592 I	77.4%	19.0%	80.3%	19.7%
4,648,494	TOTAL	1,557,500	890,778	596,009	70,713	294,769 I	57.2%	38.3%	59.9%	40.1%

VIRGINIA

CONGRESS

CD	Year	Total Vote	Republican Vote	Republican Candidate	Democratic Vote	Democratic Candidate	Other Vote	Rep.-Dem. Plurality	Percentage Total Vote Rep.	Percentage Total Vote Dem.	Percentage Major Vote Rep.	Percentage Major Vote Dem.
1	1976	147,850	71,789	TRIBLE, PAUL	70,159	QUINN, ROBERT E.	5,902	1,630 R	48.6%	47.5%	50.6%	49.4%
1	1974	58,474			58,338	DOWNING, THOMAS N.	136	58,338 D		99.8%		100.0%
1	1972	129,218	28,310	WELLS, KENNETH D.	100,901	DOWNING, THOMAS N.	7	72,591 D	21.9%	78.1%	21.9%	78.1%
2	1976	120,847	79,381	WHITEHURST, G. W.	41,464	WASHINGTON, ROBERT E.	2	37,917 R	65.7%	34.3%	65.7%	34.3%
2	1974	82,299	49,369	WHITEHURST, G. W.	32,923	RICHARDS, ROBERT R.	7	16,446 R	60.0%	40.0%	60.0%	40.0%
2	1972	108,482	79,672	WHITEHURST, G. W.	28,803	BURLAGE, L. CHARLES	7	50,869 R	73.4%	26.6%	73.4%	26.6%
3	1976	146,788			129,066	SATTERFIELD, DAVID	17,722	129,066 D		87.9%		100.0%
3	1974	72,996			64,627	SATTERFIELD, DAVID	8,369	64,627 D		88.5%		100.0%
3	1972	102,679			102,523	SATTERFIELD, DAVID	156	102,523 D		99.8%		100.0%
4	1976	140,480	74,495	DANIEL, ROBERT W.	65,982	O BRIEN, J. W.	3	8,513 R	53.0%	47.0%	53.0%	47.0%
4	1974	101,748	48,032	DANIEL, ROBERT W.	36,489	SCHLITZ, LESTER E.	17,227	11,543 R	47.2%	35.9%	56.8%	43.2%
4	1972	122,159	57,520	DANIEL, ROBERT W.	45,776	GIBSON, ROBERT E.	18,863	11,744 R	47.1%	37.5%	55.7%	44.3%
5	1976	101,079			101,038	DANIEL, W. C.	41	101,038 D		100.0%		100.0%
5	1974	52,751			52,459	DANIEL, W. C.	292	52,459 D		99.4%		100.0%
5	1972	83,819			83,772	DANIEL, W. C.	47	83,772 D		99.9%		100.0%
6	1976	145,976	90,830	BUTLER, M. CALDWELL			55,146	90,830 R	62.2%		100.0%	
6	1974	101,463	45,805	BUTLER, M. CALDWELL	27,350	PUCKETT, PAUL	28,308	18,455 R	45.1%	27.0%	62.6%	37.4%
6	1972	137,650	75,189	BUTLER, M. CALDWELL	53,928	ANDERSON, WILLIS M.	8,533	21,261 R	54.6%	39.2%	58.2%	41.8%
7	1976	141,482	115,508	ROBINSON, J. KENNETH			25,974	115,508 R	81.6%		100.0%	
7	1974	103,100	54,267	ROBINSON, J. KENNETH	48,611	GILLIAM, GEORGE H.	222	5,656 R	52.6%	47.1%	52.7%	47.3%
7	1972	134,634	89,120	ROBINSON, J. KENNETH	45,513	WILLIAMS, MURAT	1	43,607 R	66.2%	33.8%	66.2%	33.8%
8	1976	161,327	68,729	TATE, JAMES R.	83,245	HARRIS, HERBERT E.	9,353	14,516 D	42.6%	51.6%	45.2%	54.8%
8	1974	92,082	38,997	PARRIS, STANFORD E.	53,074	HARRIS, HERBERT E.	11	14,077 D	42.4%	57.6%	42.4%	57.6%
8	1972	136,099	60,446	PARRIS, STANFORD E.	51,444	HORAN, ROBERT F.	24,209	9,002 R	44.4%	37.8%	54.0%	46.0%
9	1976	167,504	96,052	WAMPLER, WILLIAM C.	71,439	HORNE, CHARLES J.	13	24,613 R	57.3%	42.6%	57.3%	42.7%
9	1974	133,969	68,183	WAMPLER, WILLIAM C.	65,783	HORNE, CHARLES J.	3	2,400 R	50.9%	49.1%	50.9%	49.1%
9	1972	136,470	98,178	WAMPLER, WILLIAM C.	36,000	CHRISTIAN, ZANE DALE	2,292	62,178 R	71.9%	26.4%	73.2%	26.8%
10	1976	189,489	73,616	CALLAHAN, VINCENT F.	103,689	FISHER, JOSEPH L.	12,184	30,073 D	38.8%	54.7%	41.5%	58.5%
10	1974	125,304	56,649	BROYHILL, JOEL T.	67,184	FISHER, JOSEPH L.	1,471	10,535 D	45.2%	53.6%	45.7%	54.3%
10	1972	179,778	101,138	BROYHILL, JOEL T.	78,638	MILLER, HAROLD O.	2	22,500 R	56.3%	43.7%	56.3%	43.7%

VIRGINIA

Under Virginia's local government system a number of urban areas – 39 in 1973, 38 in 1974 and 41 in 1976 – are organized as cities independent of county authority. The number of these cities is subject to change and their boundaries alter from year to year. In 1974 Nansemond city and Suffolk city merged and became the new Suffolk city. In 1975 Manassas and Manassas Park cities were created out of parts of Prince William county and Poquoson city was created out of part of York county. County and city population figures have been adjusted to reflect these changes.

1976 GENERAL ELECTION

President — Other vote was 17,802 Camejo (Socialist Workers); 16,686 Anderson (American); 7,508 LaRouche (U.S. Labor); 4,648 MacBride (Libertarian).

Senator — As there was no Republican candidate in the Senate race, the vote for Byrd (Independent) is carried in the data tables in the first column and the plurality figures are the Byrd Independent/Democratic plurality. Other vote was 70,559 Perper (Independent); 154 scattered. There was a misalignment of the candidates names on the voting machines in Campbell county which resulted in Perper receiving the highest number of votes in that county. Although the error was acknowledged after the election, the State Board of Elections and Senator Byrd (the winning candidate) decided that no further action needed to be taken and the Campbell county returns were certified as reported.

Congress — Other vote was scattered in CD's 2, 4, 5 and 7; 5,887 McClaine (Independent) and 15 scattered in CD 1; 17,503 Ogden (Independent) and 219 scattered in CD 3; 55,115 Saunders (Independent) and 31 scattered in CD 6; 25,731 Hutt (Independent) and 243 scattered in CD 7; 9,292 Cannon (Independent) and 61 scattered in CD 8; 12,124 Rittenhouse (Independent) and 60 scattered in CD 10.

1976 PRIMARIES

JUNE 8 REPUBLICAN

Senator — None. No candidate.

Congress — Candidates unopposed or nominated by convention in six CD's. No candidates in CD's 3 and 5. Contested as follows:

CD 8 — 7,128 James R. Tate; 6,985 Robert L. Thoburn; 1,977 Frank J. Kelly; 1,348 Elizabeth C. McCann; 675 T. Farrell Egge.
CD 10 — 6,496 Vincent F. Callahan; 5,934 Frank R. Wolf; 1,861 Kimon T. Karabatsos.

JUNE 8 DEMOCRATIC

Senator — Elmo R. Zumwalt, unopposed.

Congress — Candidates unopposed or nominated by convention in five CD's. No candidates in CD's 6 and 7. Contested as follows:

CD 1 — 31,170 Robert E. Quinn; 20,113 Jessie M. Rattley; 11,828 George W. Grayson.
CD 2 — 10,388 Robert E. Washington; 4,545 James A. Mulligan.
CD 4 — 14,911 J. W. O'Brien; 11,741 Curtis W. Harris.

WASHINGTON

GOVERNOR

Dixy Lee Ray (D). Elected 1976 to a four-year term.

SENATORS

Henry M. Jackson (D). Re-elected 1976 to a six-year term. Previously elected 1970, 1964, 1958, 1952.

Warren G. Magnuson (D). Re-elected 1974 to a six-year term. Previously elected 1968, 1962, 1956, 1950, 1944.

REPRESENTATIVES

1. Joel Pritchard (R)
2. Lloyd Meeds (D)
3. Don Bonker (D)
4. Mike McCormack (D)
5. Thomas S. Foley (D)
6. Norman D. Dicks (D)
7. Brock Adams (D)

POSTWAR VOTE FOR GOVERNOR

Year	Total Vote	Republican Vote	Republican Candidate	Democratic Vote	Democratic Candidate	Other Vote	Rep.-Dem. Plurality	Percentage Total Vote Rep.	Percentage Total Vote Dem.	Percentage Major Vote Rep.	Percentage Major Vote Dem.
1976	1,546,382	687,039	Spellman, John D.	821,797	Ray, Dixy Lee	37,546	134,758 D	44.4%	53.1%	45.5%	54.5%
1972	1,472,542	747,825	Evans, Daniel J.	630,613	Rosellini, Albert D.	94,104	117,212 R	50.8%	42.8%	54.3%	45.7%
1968	1,265,355	692,378	Evans, Daniel J.	560,262	O'Connell, John J.	12,715	132,116 R	54.7%	44.3%	55.3%	44.7%
1964	1,250,274	697,256	Evans, Daniel J.	548,692	Rosellini, Albert D.	4,326	148,564 R	55.8%	43.9%	56.0%	44.0%
1960	1,215,748	594,122	Andrews, Lloyd J.	611,987	Rosellini, Albert D.	9,639	17,865 D	48.9%	50.3%	49.3%	50.7%
1956	1,128,977	508,041	Anderson, Emmett T.	616,773	Rosellini, Albert D.	4,163	108,732 D	45.0%	54.6%	45.2%	54.8%
1952	1,078,497	567,822	Langlie, Arthur B.	510,675	Mitchell, Hugh B.	–	57,147 R	52.6%	47.4%	52.6%	47.4%
1948	883,141	445,958	Langlie, Arthur B.	417,035	Wallgren, Mon C.	20,148	28,923 R	50.5%	47.2%	51.7%	48.3%

POSTWAR VOTE FOR SENATOR

Year	Total Vote	Republican Vote	Republican Candidate	Democratic Vote	Democratic Candidate	Other Vote	Rep.-Dem. Plurality	Percentage Total Vote Rep.	Percentage Total Vote Dem.	Percentage Major Vote Rep.	Percentage Major Vote Dem.
1976	1,491,111	361,546	Brown, George M.	1,071,219	Jackson, Henry M.	58,346	709,673 D	24.2%	71.8%	25.2%	74.8%
1974	1,007,847	363,626	Metcalf, Jack	611,811	Magnuson, Warren G.	32,410	248,185 D	36.1%	60.7%	37.3%	62.7%
1970	1,066,807	170,790	Elicker, Charles W.	879,385	Jackson, Henry M.	16,632	708,595 D	16.0%	82.4%	16.3%	83.7%
1968	1,236,063	435,894	Metcalf, Jack	796,183	Magnuson, Warren G.	3,986	360,289 D	35.3%	64.4%	35.4%	64.6%
1964	1,213,088	337,138	Andrews, Lloyd J.	875,950	Jackson, Henry M.	–	538,812 D	27.8%	72.2%	27.8%	72.2%
1962	943,229	446,204	Christensen, Richard G.	491,365	Magnuson, Warren G.	5,660	45,161 D	47.3%	52.1%	47.6%	52.4%
1958	886,822	278,271	Bantz, William B.	597,040	Jackson, Henry M.	11,511	318,769 D	31.4%	67.3%	31.8%	68.2%
1956	1,122,217	436,652	Langlie, Arthur B.	685,565	Magnuson, Warren G.	–	248,913 D	38.9%	61.1%	38.9%	61.1%
1952	1,058,735	460,884	Cain, Harry P.	595,288	Jackson, Henry M.	2,563	134,404 D	43.5%	56.2%	43.6%	56.4%
1950	744,783	342,464	Williams, Walter	397,719	Magnuson, Warren G.	4,600	55,255 D	46.0%	53.4%	46.3%	53.7%
1946	660,342	358,847	Cain, Harry P.	298,683	Mitchell, Hugh B.	2,812	60,164 R	54.3%	45.2%	54.6%	45.4%

WASHINGTON

Districts Established April 21, 1972

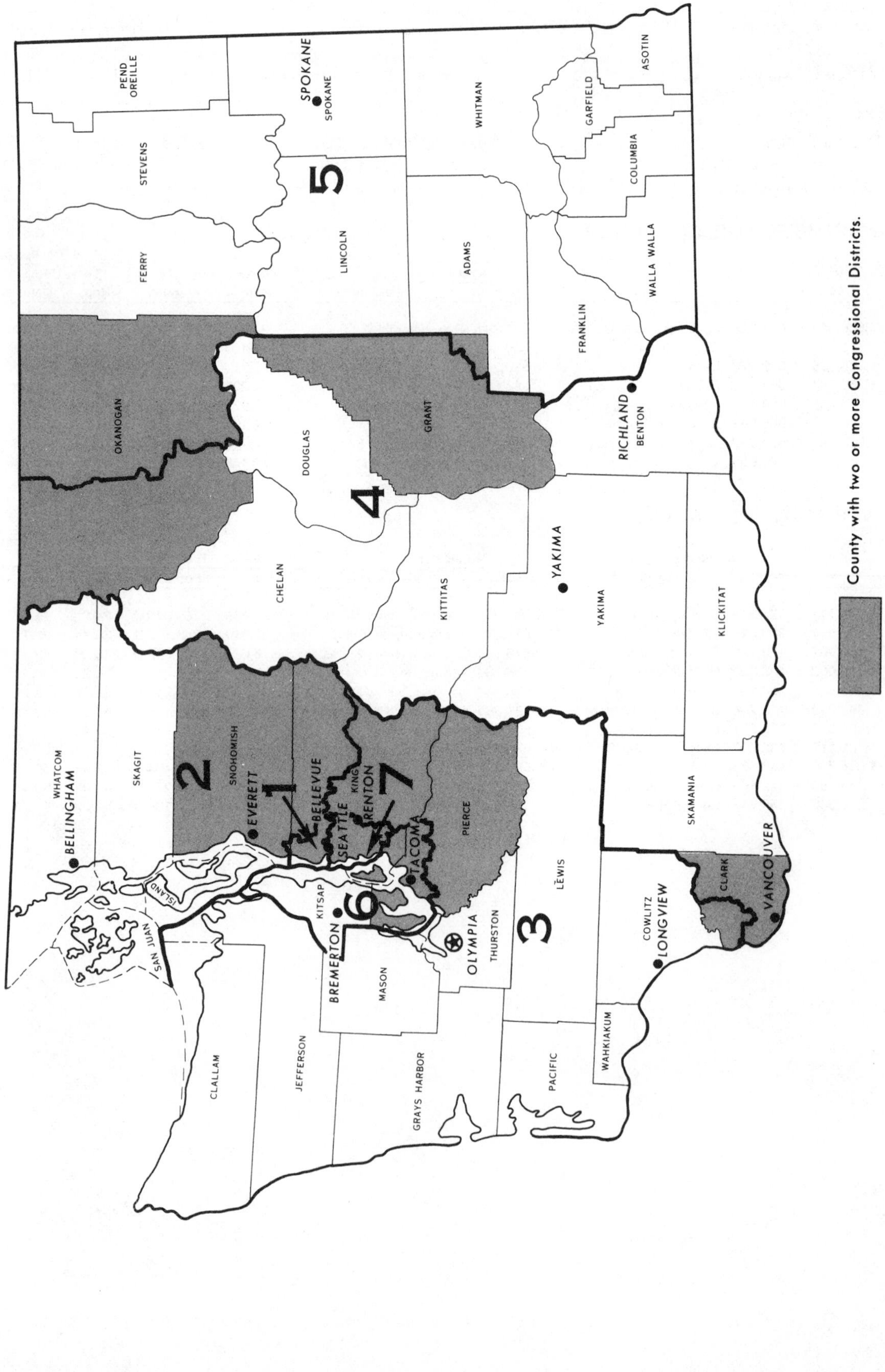

WASHINGTON

PRESIDENT 1976

1970 Census Population	County	Total Vote	Republican	Democratic	Other	Rep.-Dem. Plurality	Percentage Total Vote Rep.	Percentage Total Vote Dem.	Percentage Major Vote Rep.	Percentage Major Vote Dem.
12,014	ADAMS	4,773	2,795	1,790	188	1,005 R	58.6%	37.5%	61.0%	39.0%
13,799	ASOTIN	5,828	2,752	2,898	178	146 D	47.2%	49.7%	48.7%	51.3%
67,540	BENTON	34,611	22,135	11,306	1,170	10,829 R	64.0%	32.7%	66.2%	33.8%
41,355	CHELAN	18,692	10,492	7,623	577	2,869 R	56.1%	40.8%	57.9%	42.1%
34,770	CLALLAM	18,386	9,132	8,268	986	864 R	49.7%	45.0%	52.5%	47.5%
128,454	CLARK	61,201	27,938	31,080	2,183	3,142 D	45.6%	50.8%	47.3%	52.7%
4,439	COLUMBIA	2,034	1,153	829	52	324 R	56.7%	40.8%	58.2%	41.8%
68,616	COWLITZ	28,406	12,531	14,958	917	2,427 D	44.1%	52.7%	45.6%	54.4%
16,787	DOUGLAS	8,564	4,547	3,809	208	738 R	53.1%	44.5%	54.4%	45.6%
3,655	FERRY	1,692	776	814	102	38 D	45.9%	48.1%	48.8%	51.2%
25,816	FRANKLIN	10,403	5,671	4,369	363	1,302 R	54.5%	42.0%	56.5%	43.5%
2,911	GARFIELD	1,560	892	616	52	276 R	57.2%	39.5%	59.2%	40.8%
41,881	GRANT	17,721	9,192	7,777	752	1,415 R	51.9%	43.9%	54.2%	45.8%
59,553	GRAYS HARBOR	23,893	9,464	13,478	951	4,014 D	39.6%	56.4%	41.3%	58.7%
27,011	ISLAND	14,104	7,804	5,859	441	1,945 R	55.3%	41.5%	57.1%	42.9%
10,661	JEFFERSON	6,092	2,794	2,913	385	119 D	45.9%	47.8%	49.0%	51.0%
1,156,633	KING	550,119	279,382	248,743	21,994	30,639 R	50.8%	45.2%	52.9%	47.1%
101,732	KITSAP	50,750	23,124	25,701	1,925	2,577 D	45.6%	50.6%	47.4%	52.6%
25,039	KITTITAS	10,017	4,765	4,858	394	93 D	47.6%	48.5%	49.5%	50.5%
12,138	KLICKITAT	5,719	2,573	2,890	256	317 D	45.0%	50.5%	47.1%	52.9%
45,467	LEWIS	21,167	10,933	9,026	1,208	1,907 R	51.7%	42.6%	54.8%	45.2%
9,572	LINCOLN	5,081	2,925	1,978	178	947 R	57.6%	38.9%	59.7%	40.3%
20,918	MASON	11,291	4,758	6,060	473	1,302 D	42.1%	53.7%	44.0%	56.0%
25,867	OKANOGAN	11,595	5,455	5,543	597	88 D	47.0%	47.8%	49.6%	50.4%
15,796	PACIFIC	7,350	2,781	4,278	291	1,497 D	37.8%	58.2%	39.4%	60.6%
6,025	PEND OREILLE	3,170	1,516	1,533	121	17 D	47.8%	48.4%	49.7%	50.3%
411,027	PIERCE	159,148	74,668	78,238	6,242	3,570 D	46.9%	49.2%	48.8%	51.2%
3,856	SAN JUAN	3,722	1,998	1,467	257	531 R	53.7%	39.4%	57.7%	42.3%
52,381	SKAGIT	26,837	13,060	12,718	1,059	342 R	48.7%	47.4%	50.7%	49.3%
5,845	SKAMANIA	2,652	1,102	1,436	114	334 D	41.6%	54.1%	43.4%	56.6%
265,236	SNOHOMISH	115,488	55,375	55,623	4,490	248 D	47.9%	48.2%	49.9%	50.1%
287,487	SPOKANE	127,954	68,290	55,660	4,004	12,630 R	53.4%	43.5%	55.1%	44.9%
17,405	STEVENS	9,109	4,719	3,824	566	895 R	51.8%	42.0%	55.2%	44.8%
76,894	THURSTON	44,056	21,000	21,247	1,809	247 D	47.7%	48.2%	49.7%	50.3%
3,592	WAHKIAKUM	1,710	704	942	64	238 D	41.2%	55.1%	42.8%	57.2%
42,176	WALLA WALLA	18,400	10,883	7,012	505	3,871 R	59.1%	38.1%	60.8%	39.2%
81,950	WHATCOM	41,679	20,007	19,739	1,933	268 R	48.0%	47.4%	50.3%	49.7%
37,900	WHITMAN	15,068	8,168	6,197	703	1,971 R	54.2%	41.1%	56.9%	43.1%
144,971	YAKIMA	55,492	29,478	24,223	1,791	5,255 R	53.1%	43.7%	54.9%	45.1%
3,409,169	TOTAL	1,555,534	777,732	717,323	60,479	60,409 R	50.0%	46.1%	52.0%	48.0%

WASHINGTON

GOVERNOR 1976

1970 Census Population	County	Total Vote	Republican	Democratic	Other	Rep.-Dem. Plurality	Percentage Total Vote Rep.	Percentage Total Vote Dem.	Percentage Major Vote Rep.	Percentage Major Vote Dem.
12,014	ADAMS	4,799	2,524	2,112	163	412 R	52.6%	44.0%	54.4%	45.6%
13,799	ASOTIN	5,848	3,231	2,493	124	738 R	55.2%	42.6%	56.4%	43.6%
67,540	BENTON	34,867	11,367	23,006	494	11,639 D	32.6%	66.0%	33.1%	66.9%
41,355	CHELAN	18,517	9,926	8,278	313	1,648 R	53.6%	44.7%	54.5%	45.5%
34,770	CLALLAM	18,414	7,514	10,234	666	2,720 D	40.8%	55.6%	42.3%	57.7%
128,454	CLARK	60,863	27,222	32,038	1,603	4,816 D	44.7%	52.6%	45.9%	54.1%
4,439	COLUMBIA	2,024	1,027	965	32	62 R	50.7%	47.7%	51.6%	48.4%
68,616	COWLITZ	27,295	11,501	14,930	864	3,429 D	42.1%	54.7%	43.5%	56.5%
16,787	DOUGLAS	8,504	4,134	4,263	107	129 D	48.6%	50.1%	49.2%	50.8%
3,655	FERRY	1,648	773	805	70	32 D	46.9%	48.8%	49.0%	51.0%
25,816	FRANKLIN	10,174	3,826	6,187	161	2,361 D	37.6%	60.8%	38.2%	61.8%
2,911	GARFIELD	1,547	951	579	17	372 R	61.5%	37.4%	62.2%	37.8%
41,881	GRANT	17,201	8,589	8,148	464	441 R	49.9%	47.4%	51.3%	48.7%
59,553	GRAYS HARBOR	24,400	10,072	13,567	761	3,495 D	41.3%	55.6%	42.6%	57.4%
27,011	ISLAND	13,947	6,358	7,408	181	1,050 D	45.6%	53.1%	46.2%	53.8%
10,661	JEFFERSON	5,970	2,644	3,121	205	477 D	44.3%	52.3%	45.9%	54.1%
1,156,633	KING	545,518	254,945	277,502	13,071	22,557 D	46.7%	50.9%	47.9%	52.1%
101,732	KITSAP	51,251	19,626	30,399	1,226	10,773 D	38.3%	59.3%	39.2%	60.8%
25,039	KITTITAS	9,790	4,733	4,878	179	145 D	48.3%	49.8%	49.2%	50.8%
12,138	KLICKITAT	5,582	2,411	3,016	155	605 D	43.2%	54.0%	44.4%	55.6%
45,467	LEWIS	21,339	7,633	13,109	597	5,476 D	35.8%	61.4%	36.8%	63.2%
9,572	LINCOLN	5,159	2,907	2,153	99	754 R	56.3%	41.7%	57.5%	42.5%
20,918	MASON	11,343	4,052	6,984	307	2,932 D	35.7%	61.6%	36.7%	63.3%
25,867	OKANOGAN	11,389	5,462	5,543	384	81 D	48.0%	48.7%	49.6%	50.4%
15,796	PACIFIC	7,392	2,656	4,474	262	1,818 D	35.9%	60.5%	37.3%	62.7%
6,025	PEND OREILLE	3,154	1,438	1,641	75	203 D	45.6%	52.0%	46.7%	53.3%
411,027	PIERCE	157,312	54,543	99,527	3,242	44,984 D	34.7%	63.3%	35.4%	64.6%
3,856	SAN JUAN	3,667	1,907	1,658	102	249 R	52.0%	45.2%	53.5%	46.5%
52,381	SKAGIT	26,947	11,486	14,750	711	3,264 D	42.6%	54.7%	43.8%	56.2%
5,845	SKAMANIA	2,582	1,126	1,403	53	277 D	43.6%	54.3%	44.5%	55.5%
265,236	SNOHOMISH	115,914	46,946	66,369	2,599	19,423 D	40.5%	57.3%	41.4%	58.6%
287,487	SPOKANE	128,998	64,044	61,494	3,460	2,550 R	49.6%	47.7%	51.0%	49.0%
17,405	STEVENS	9,181	4,556	4,177	448	379 R	49.6%	45.5%	52.2%	47.8%
76,894	THURSTON	44,272	18,984	23,957	1,331	4,973 D	42.9%	54.1%	44.2%	55.8%
3,592	WAHKIAKUM	1,671	692	938	41	246 D	41.4%	56.1%	42.5%	57.5%
42,176	WALLA WALLA	18,036	10,177	7,562	297	2,615 R	56.4%	41.9%	57.4%	42.6%
81,950	WHATCOM	40,506	17,688	21,599	1,219	3,911 D	43.7%	53.3%	45.0%	55.0%
37,900	WHITMAN	15,069	8,679	5,875	515	2,804 R	57.6%	39.0%	59.6%	40.4%
144,971	YAKIMA	54,292	28,689	24,655	948	4,034 R	52.8%	45.4%	53.8%	46.2%
3,409,169	TOTAL	1,546,382	687,039	821,797	37,546	134,758 D	44.4%	53.1%	45.5%	54.5%

WASHINGTON

SENATOR 1976

1970 Census Population	County	Total Vote	Republican	Democratic	Other	Rep.-Dem. Plurality	Percentage: Total Vote Rep.	Total Vote Dem.	Major Vote Rep.	Major Vote Dem.
12,014	ADAMS	4,684	1,816	2,619	249	803 D	38.8%	55.9%	40.9%	59.1%
13,799	ASOTIN	5,698	1,496	3,963	239	2,467 D	26.3%	69.6%	27.4%	72.6%
67,540	BENTON	34,319	7,790	25,579	950	17,789 D	22.7%	74.5%	23.3%	76.7%
41,355	CHELAN	17,513	5,765	11,429	319	5,664 D	32.9%	65.3%	33.5%	66.5%
34,770	CLALLAM	18,124	4,717	12,525	882	7,808 D	26.0%	69.1%	27.4%	72.6%
128,454	CLARK	60,382	13,680	44,401	2,301	30,721 D	22.7%	73.5%	23.6%	76.4%
4,439	COLUMBIA	1,935	672	1,223	40	551 D	34.7%	63.2%	35.5%	64.5%
68,616	COWLITZ	26,484	5,111	20,821	552	15,710 D	19.3%	78.6%	19.7%	80.3%
16,787	DOUGLAS	8,301	2,706	5,460	135	2,754 D	32.6%	65.8%	33.1%	66.9%
3,655	FERRY	1,479	433	969	77	536 D	29.3%	65.5%	30.9%	69.1%
25,816	FRANKLIN	9,780	2,539	6,937	304	4,398 D	26.0%	70.9%	26.8%	73.2%
2,911	GARFIELD	1,489	558	905	26	347 D	37.5%	60.8%	38.1%	61.9%
41,881	GRANT	16,389	5,048	10,635	706	5,587 D	30.8%	64.9%	32.2%	67.8%
59,553	GRAYS HARBOR	20,343	4,242	15,213	888	10,971 D	20.9%	74.8%	21.8%	78.2%
27,011	ISLAND	12,821	3,442	9,147	232	5,705 D	26.8%	71.3%	27.3%	72.7%
10,661	JEFFERSON	5,724	1,485	3,936	303	2,451 D	25.9%	68.8%	27.4%	72.6%
1,156,633	KING	522,198	113,047	386,686	22,465	273,639 D	21.6%	74.0%	22.6%	77.4%
101,732	KITSAP	50,527	8,385	40,342	1,800	31,957 D	16.6%	79.8%	17.2%	82.8%
25,039	KITTITAS	9,261	2,383	6,676	202	4,293 D	25.7%	72.1%	26.3%	73.7%
12,138	KLICKITAT	5,501	1,459	3,844	198	2,385 D	26.5%	69.9%	27.5%	72.5%
45,467	LEWIS	20,901	6,282	13,579	1,040	7,297 D	30.1%	65.0%	31.6%	68.4%
9,572	LINCOLN	5,017	2,326	2,501	190	175 D	46.4%	49.9%	48.2%	51.8%
20,918	MASON	11,199	2,485	8,214	500	5,729 D	22.2%	73.3%	23.2%	76.8%
25,867	OKANOGAN	11,172	3,199	7,324	649	4,125 D	28.6%	65.6%	30.4%	69.6%
15,796	PACIFIC	6,974	1,263	5,411	300	4,148 D	18.1%	77.6%	18.9%	81.1%
6,025	PEND OREILLE	3,071	913	2,097	61	1,184 D	29.7%	68.3%	30.3%	69.7%
411,027	PIERCE	150,397	30,131	114,979	5,287	84,848 D	20.0%	76.5%	20.8%	79.2%
3,856	SAN JUAN	3,255	1,364	1,764	127	400 D	41.9%	54.2%	43.6%	56.4%
52,381	SKAGIT	26,568	8,285	17,330	953	9,045 D	31.2%	65.2%	32.3%	67.7%
5,845	SKAMANIA	2,536	600	1,880	56	1,280 D	23.7%	74.1%	24.2%	75.8%
265,236	SNOHOMISH	114,624	25,603	85,036	3,985	59,433 D	22.3%	74.2%	23.1%	76.9%
287,487	SPOKANE	127,429	41,580	80,762	5,087	39,182 D	32.6%	63.4%	34.0%	66.0%
17,405	STEVENS	9,014	3,058	5,349	607	2,291 D	33.9%	59.3%	36.4%	63.6%
76,894	THURSTON	43,616	10,269	31,425	1,922	21,156 D	23.5%	72.0%	24.6%	75.4%
3,592	WAHKIAKUM	1,539	320	1,197	22	877 D	20.8%	77.8%	21.1%	78.9%
42,176	WALLA WALLA	17,140	5,142	11,568	430	6,426 D	30.0%	67.5%	30.8%	69.2%
81,950	WHATCOM	38,624	12,690	24,130	1,804	11,440 D	32.9%	62.5%	34.5%	65.5%
37,900	WHITMAN	14,734	5,332	8,553	849	3,221 D	36.2%	58.0%	38.4%	61.6%
144,971	YAKIMA	50,349	13,930	34,810	1,609	20,880 D	27.7%	69.1%	28.6%	71.4%
3,409,169	TOTAL	1,491,111	361,546	1,071,219	58,346	709,673 D	24.2%	71.8%	25.2%	74.8%

WASHINGTON

CONGRESS

CD	Year	Total Vote	Republican Vote	Republican Candidate	Democratic Vote	Democratic Candidate	Other Vote	Rep.-Dem. Plurality	Percentage Total Vote Rep.	Percentage Total Vote Dem.	Percentage Major Vote Rep.	Percentage Major Vote Dem.
1	1976	224,561	161,354	PRITCHARD, JOEL	58,006	WOOD, DAVE	5,201	103,348 R	71.9%	25.8%	73.6%	26.4%
1	1974	156,021	108,391	PRITCHARD, JOEL	44,655	KNEDLIK, W. R.	2,975	63,736 R	69.5%	28.6%	70.8%	29.2%
1	1972	213,941	107,581	PRITCHARD, JOEL	104,959	HEMPELMANN, JOHN	1,401	2,622 R	50.3%	49.1%	50.6%	49.4%
2	1976	217,858	106,786	GARNER, JOHN N.	107,328	MEEDS, LLOYD	3,744	542 D	49.0%	49.3%	49.9%	50.1%
2	1974	136,544	53,157	REED, RONALD C.	81,565	MEEDS, LLOYD	1,822	28,408 D	38.9%	59.7%	39.5%	60.5%
2	1972	190,081	75,181	REAMS, BILL	114,900	MEEDS, LLOYD		39,719 D	39.6%	60.4%	39.6%	60.4%
3	1976	205,072	57,517	ELHART, CHUCK	145,198	BONKER, DON	2,357	87,681 D	28.0%	70.8%	28.4%	71.6%
3	1974	154,270	58,774	KRAMER, A. LUDLOW	93,980	BONKER, DON	1,516	35,206 D	38.1%	60.9%	38.5%	61.5%
3	1972	185,497	62,564	MCCONKEY, R. C.	122,933	HANSEN, JULIA BUTLER		60,369 D	33.7%	66.3%	33.7%	66.3%
4	1976	199,664	81,813	GRANGER, DICK	115,364	MCCORMACK, MIKE	2,487	33,551 D	41.0%	57.8%	41.5%	58.5%
4	1974	144,198	59,249	PAXTON, FLOYD	84,949	MCCORMACK, MIKE		25,700 D	41.1%	58.9%	41.1%	58.9%
4	1972	187,405	89,812	BLEDSOE, STEWART	97,593	MCCORMACK, MIKE		7,781 D	47.9%	52.1%	47.9%	52.1%
5	1976	207,571	84,262	ALTON, DUANE	120,415	FOLEY, THOMAS S.	2,894	36,153 D	40.6%	58.0%	41.2%	58.8%
5	1974	136,698	48,739	GAGE, GARY G.	87,959	FOLEY, THOMAS S.		39,220 D	35.7%	64.3%	35.7%	64.3%
5	1972	185,322	34,742	PRIVETTE, CLARICE	150,580	FOLEY, THOMAS S.		115,838 D	18.7%	81.3%	18.7%	81.3%
6	1976	187,754	47,539	REYNOLDS, ROBERT M.	137,964	DICKS, NORMAN D.	2,251	90,425 D	25.3%	73.5%	25.6%	74.4%
6	1974	132,754	37,400	NALLEY, GEORGE M.	95,354	HICKS, FLOYD V.		57,954 D	28.2%	71.8%	28.2%	71.8%
6	1972	175,263	48,914	LOWRY, THOMAS C.	126,349	HICKS, FLOYD V.		77,435 D	27.9%	72.1%	27.9%	72.1%
7	1976	183,122	46,448	PRITCHARD, RAYMOND	133,673	ADAMS, BROCK	3,001	87,225 D	25.4%	73.0%	25.8%	74.2%
7	1974	120,440	34,847	PRITCHARD, RAYMOND	85,593	ADAMS, BROCK		50,746 D	28.9%	71.1%	28.9%	71.1%
7	1972	164,324	19,889	FREEMAN, J. J.	140,307	ADAMS, BROCK	4,128	120,418 D	12.1%	85.4%	12.4%	87.6%

WASHINGTON

1976 GENERAL ELECTION

President Other vote was 36,986 McCarthy (Independent); 8,585 Maddox (American Independent); 5,046 Anderson (American Constitution); 5,042 MacBride (Libertarian); 1,124 Wright (Bicentennial Reality); 905 Camejo (Socialist Workers); 903 LaRouche (U.S. Labor); 817 Hall (Communist); 713 Levin (Socialist Labor); 358 Zeidler (Socialist).

Governor Other vote was 12,406 Manning (American Independent); 12,400 Kelly (Owl); 4,137 Killman (Socialist Labor); 4,133 Willey (Libertarian); 3,106 Bethard (Socialist Workers); 1,364 Olafson (U.S. Labor).

Senator Other vote was 28,182 Smith (American Independent); 19,373 Kenney (Libertarian); 7,402 Bermann (Socialist Workers); 3,389 Wertz (U.S. Labor).

Congress Other vote was 4,230 Gottlieb (Libertarian) and 971 Patrick Ruckert (U.S. Labor) in CD 1; 1,963 Bly (American Constitution) and 1,781 Carol Ruckert (U.S. Labor) in CD 2; Kilber (U.S. Labor) in CD 3; 1,586 Busby (American Constitution) and 901 Andromidas (U.S. Labor) in CD 4; 1,959 Sandahl (Libertarian) and 935 Liebowitz (U.S. Labor) in CD 5; Duane (U.S. Labor) in CD 6; 1,668 Goosman (American Constitution) and 1,333 Wertz (U.S. Labor) in CD 7.

1976 PRIMARIES

SEPTEMBER 21 REPUBLICAN

Governor 185,439 John D. Spellman; 111,957 Harley Hoppe; 4,798 Emmett Watson; 2,636 Carl D. Ricketts; 1,654 John Patrick.

Senator 51,885 George M. Brown; 43,905 Warren Hanson; 28,030 Henry C. Nielsen; 21,639 Wilbur R. Parkin; 16,881 Will Davis; 13,526 Clarice L. R. Privette.

Congress Unopposed in three CD's. Charles Kimball, the unopposed candidate in CD 5, died before the primary and Duane Alton was substituted by the local party committee after the primary. Contested as follows:

CD 3 20,576 Chuck Elhart; 8,320 Richard F. Dideon.
CD 4 20,232 Dick Granger; 15,717 Bruce Cone; 9,384 James C. May.
CD 6 6,511 Robert M. Reynolds; 5,020 George Van Buskirk; 2,787 Jeff G. Prosser.
CD 7 18,988 Raymond Pritchard; 10,331 William M. Champion.

SEPTEMBER 21 DEMOCRATIC

Governor 205,232 Dixy Lee Ray; 198,336 Wes Uhlman; 136,290 Marvin Durning; 5,588 Duke Stockton.

Senator 549,974 Henry M. Jackson; 54,470 Dennis Kelley; 24,559 Paul Gumbel.

Congress Unopposed in three CD's. Contested as follows:

CD 1 22,581 Dave Wood; 11,439 Carl V. Holman.
CD 2 52,964 Lloyd Meeds; 15,773 Don Lenderman.
CD 6 39,613 Norman D. Dicks; 30,036 Mike Parker; 15,332 Eugene W. Wiegman; 14,580 Gordon N. Johnson; 5,195 Jim O'Donnell; 4,560 Jim Nicholls.
CD 7 71,305 Brock Adams; 5,912 Jack May.

WEST VIRGINIA

GOVERNOR

John D. Rockefeller (D). Elected 1976 to a four-year term.

SENATORS

Robert C. Byrd (D). Re-elected 1976 to a six-year term. Previously elected 1970, 1964, 1958.

Jennings Randolph (D). Re-elected 1972 to a six-year term. Previously elected 1966, 1960, and in 1958 to fill out term vacated by the death of Senator Matthew M. Neely.

REPRESENTATIVES

1. Robert H. Mollohan (D)
2. Harley O. Staggers (D)
3. John M. Slack (D)
4. Nick J. Rahall (D)

POSTWAR VOTE FOR GOVERNOR

								Percentage			
	Total	Republican		Democratic		Other	Rep.-Dem.	Total Vote		Major Vote	
Year	Vote	Vote	Candidate	Vote	Candidate	Vote	Plurality	Rep.	Dem.	Rep.	Dem.
1976	749,270	253,420	Underwood, Cecil H.	495,661	Rockefeller, John D.	189	242,241 D	33.8%	66.2%	33.8%	66.2%
1972	774,279	423,817	Moore, Arch A.	350,462	Rockefeller, John D.	–	73,355 R	54.7%	45.3%	54.7%	45.3%
1968	743,845	378,315	Moore, Arch A.	365,530	Sprouse, James M.	–	12,785 R	50.9%	49.1%	50.9%	49.1%
1964	788,582	355,559	Underwood, Cecil H.	433,023	Smith, Hulett C.	–	77,464 D	45.1%	54.9%	45.1%	54.9%
1960	827,420	380,665	Neely, Harold E.	446,755	Barron, W. W.	–	66,090 D	46.0%	54.0%	46.0%	54.0%
1956	817,623	440,502	Underwood, Cecil H.	377,121	Mollohan, Robert H.	–	63,381 R	53.9%	46.1%	53.9%	46.1%
1952	882,527	427,629	Holt, Rush D.	454,898	Marland, William C.	–	27,269 D	48.5%	51.5%	48.5%	51.5%
1948	768,061	329,309	Boreman, Herbert	438,752	Patteson, Okey L.	–	109,443 D	42.9%	57.1%	42.9%	57.1%

POSTWAR VOTE FOR SENATOR

								Percentage			
	Total	Republican		Democratic		Other	Rep.-Dem.	Total Vote		Major Vote	
Year	Vote	Vote	Candidate	Vote	Candidate	Vote	Plurality	Rep.	Dem.	Rep.	Dem.
1976	566,790	–	–	566,423	Byrd, Robert C.	367	566,423 D	–	99.9%	–	100.0%
1972	731,841	245,531	Leonard, Louise	486,310	Randolph, Jennings	–	240,779 D	33.5%	66.5%	33.5%	66.5%
1970	445,623	99,658	Dodson, Elmer H.	345,965	Byrd, Robert C.	–	246,307 D	22.4%	77.6%	22.4%	77.6%
1966	491,216	198,891	Love, Francis J.	292,325	Randolph, Jennings	–	93,434 D	40.5%	59.5%	40.5%	59.5%
1964	761,087	246,072	Benedict, Cooper P.	515,015	Byrd, Robert C.	–	268,943 D	32.3%	67.7%	32.3%	67.7%
1960	828,292	369,935	Underwood, Cecil H.	458,355	Randolph, Jennings	2	88,420 D	44.7%	55.3%	44.7%	55.3%
1958	644,917	263,172	Revercomb, Chapman	381,745	Byrd, Robert C.	–	118,573 D	40.8%	59.2%	40.8%	59.2%
1958s	630,677	256,510	Hoblitzell, John D.	374,167	Randolph, Jennings	–	117,657 D	40.7%	59.3%	40.7%	59.3%
1956s	805,174	432,123	Revercomb, Chapman	373,051	Marland, William C.	–	59,072 R	53.7%	46.3%	53.7%	46.3%
1954	593,329	268,066	Sweeney, Tom	325,263	Neely, Matthew M.	–	57,197 D	45.2%	54.8%	45.2%	54.8%
1952	876,573	406,554	Revercomb, Chapman	470,019	Kilgore, Harley M.	–	63,465 D	46.4%	53.6%	46.4%	53.6%
1948	763,888	328,534	Revercomb, Chapman	435,354	Neely, Matthew M.	–	106,820 D	43.0%	57.0%	43.0%	57.0%
1946	542,768	269,617	Sweeney, Tom	273,151	Kilgore, Harley M.	–	3,534 D	49.7%	50.3%	49.7%	50.3%

One of the elections in 1958 and that in 1956 were for short terms to fill vacancies.

WEST VIRGINIA

Districts Established March 6, 1971

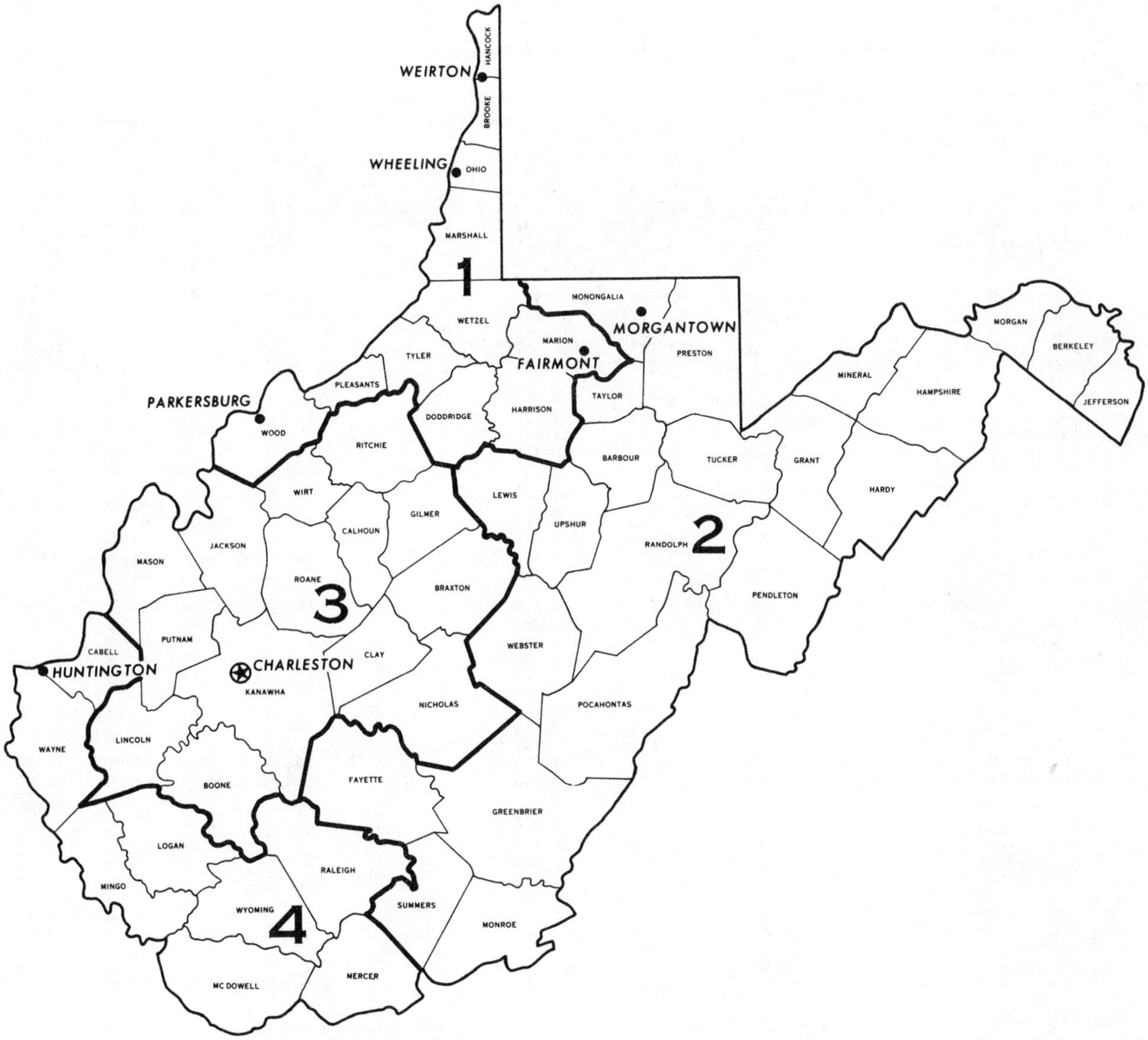

WEST VIRGINIA

PRESIDENT 1976

1970 Census Population	County	Total Vote	Republican	Democratic	Other	Rep.-Dem. Plurality	Percentage Total Vote Rep.	Percentage Total Vote Dem.	Percentage Major Vote Rep.	Percentage Major Vote Dem.
14,030	BARBOUR	6,882	3,235	3,647		412 D	47.0%	53.0%	47.0%	53.0%
36,356	BERKELEY	17,151	8,935	8,216		719 R	52.1%	47.9%	52.1%	47.9%
25,118	BOONE	11,604	3,072	8,528	4	5,456 D	26.5%	73.5%	26.5%	73.5%
12,666	BRAXTON	5,928	1,913	4,012	3	2,099 D	32.3%	67.7%	32.3%	67.7%
29,685	BROOKE	13,007	4,792	8,197	18	3,405 D	36.8%	63.0%	36.9%	63.1%
106,918	CABELL	40,455	19,644	20,811		1,167 D	48.6%	51.4%	48.6%	51.4%
7,046	CALHOUN	3,457	1,283	2,173	1	890 D	37.1%	62.9%	37.1%	62.9%
9,330	CLAY	3,944	1,282	2,662		1,380 D	32.5%	67.5%	32.5%	67.5%
6,389	DODDRIDGE	3,049	1,804	1,245		559 R	59.2%	40.8%	59.2%	40.8%
49,332	FAYETTE	20,955	5,459	15,496		10,037 D	26.1%	73.9%	26.1%	73.9%
7,782	GILMER	3,616	1,371	2,245		874 D	37.9%	62.1%	37.9%	62.1%
8,607	GRANT	4,302	2,976	1,323	3	1,653 R	69.2%	30.8%	69.2%	30.8%
32,090	GREENBRIER	14,153	5,862	8,291		2,429 D	41.4%	58.6%	41.4%	58.6%
11,710	HAMPSHIRE	5,201	2,097	3,104		1,007 D	40.3%	59.7%	40.3%	59.7%
39,749	HANCOCK	17,398	6,771	10,627		3,856 D	38.9%	61.1%	38.9%	61.1%
8,855	HARDY	4,851	1,858	2,993		1,135 D	38.3%	61.7%	38.3%	61.7%
73,028	HARRISON	36,687	15,172	21,467	48	6,295 D	41.4%	58.5%	41.4%	58.6%
20,903	JACKSON	10,694	5,360	5,334		26 R	50.1%	49.9%	50.1%	49.9%
21,280	JEFFERSON	9,030	3,864	5,166		1,302 D	42.8%	57.2%	42.8%	57.2%
229,515	KANAWHA	95,991	42,213	53,602	176	11,389 D	44.0%	55.8%	44.1%	55.9%
17,847	LEWIS	7,696	3,736	3,960		224 D	48.5%	51.5%	48.5%	51.5%
18,912	LINCOLN	8,257	2,997	5,260		2,263 D	36.3%	63.7%	36.3%	63.7%
46,269	LOGAN	17,143	4,021	13,122		9,101 D	23.5%	76.5%	23.5%	76.5%
50,666	MCDOWELL	14,688	4,107	10,557	24	6,450 D	28.0%	71.9%	28.0%	72.0%
61,356	MARION	28,191	10,391	17,800		7,409 D	36.9%	63.1%	36.9%	63.1%
37,598	MARSHALL	15,346	6,705	8,641		1,936 D	43.7%	56.3%	43.7%	56.3%
24,306	MASON	11,974	5,205	6,769		1,564 D	43.5%	56.5%	43.5%	56.5%
63,206	MERCER	25,552	10,791	14,761		3,970 D	42.2%	57.8%	42.2%	57.8%
23,109	MINERAL	11,028	5,130	5,898		768 D	46.5%	53.5%	46.5%	53.5%
32,780	MINGO	11,666	3,010	8,655	1	5,645 D	25.8%	74.2%	25.8%	74.2%
63,714	MONONGALIA	27,990	11,827	16,163		4,336 D	42.3%	57.7%	42.3%	57.7%
11,272	MONROE	6,047	2,750	3,297		547 D	45.5%	54.5%	45.5%	54.5%
8,547	MORGAN	4,298	2,369	1,929		440 R	55.1%	44.9%	55.1%	44.9%
22,552	NICHOLAS	9,697	3,462	6,235		2,773 D	35.7%	64.3%	35.7%	64.3%
64,197	OHIO	24,293	12,476	11,817		659 R	51.4%	48.6%	51.4%	48.6%
7,031	PENDLETON	3,658	1,554	2,104		550 D	42.5%	57.5%	42.5%	57.5%
7,274	PLEASANTS	3,307	1,608	1,699		91 D	48.6%	51.4%	48.6%	51.4%
8,870	POCAHONTAS	4,075	1,740	2,330	5	590 D	42.7%	57.2%	42.8%	57.2%
25,455	PRESTON	11,314	5,719	5,595		124 R	50.5%	49.5%	50.5%	49.5%
27,625	PUTNAM	14,560	6,334	8,226		1,892 D	43.5%	56.5%	43.5%	56.5%
70,080	RALEIGH	30,405	10,637	19,768		9,131 D	35.0%	65.0%	35.0%	65.0%
24,596	RANDOLPH	12,087	4,822	7,265		2,443 D	39.9%	60.1%	39.9%	60.1%
10,145	RITCHIE	4,815	2,874	1,941		933 R	59.7%	40.3%	59.7%	40.3%
14,111	ROANE	6,736	3,216	3,519	1	303 D	47.7%	52.2%	47.8%	52.2%
13,213	SUMMERS	6,197	2,254	3,943		1,689 D	36.4%	63.6%	36.4%	63.6%
13,878	TAYLOR	6,796	2,891	3,905		1,014 D	42.5%	57.5%	42.5%	57.5%
7,447	TUCKER	3,719	1,396	2,323		927 D	37.5%	62.5%	37.5%	62.5%
9,929	TYLER	4,331	2,514	1,817		697 R	58.0%	42.0%	58.0%	42.0%
19,092	UPSHUR	8,302	4,789	3,513		1,276 R	57.7%	42.3%	57.7%	42.3%
37,581	WAYNE	15,967	6,009	9,958		3,949 D	37.6%	62.4%	37.6%	62.4%
9,809	WEBSTER	3,908	971	2,931	6	1,960 D	24.8%	75.0%	24.9%	75.1%
20,314	WETZEL	8,835	3,793	5,042		1,249 D	42.9%	57.1%	42.9%	57.1%
4,154	WIRT	2,213	1,031	1,182		151 D	46.6%	53.4%	46.6%	53.4%
86,818	WOOD	35,457	18,382	17,075		1,307 R	51.8%	48.2%	51.8%	48.2%
30,095	WYOMING	12,061	4,286	7,775		3,489 D	35.5%	64.5%	35.5%	64.5%
1,744,237	TOTAL	750,964	314,760	435,914	290	121,154 D	41.9%	58.0%	41.9%	58.1%

WEST VIRGINIA

GOVERNOR 1976

1970 Census Population	County	Total Vote	Republican	Democratic	Other	Rep.-Dem. Plurality	Percentage Total Vote Rep.	Percentage Total Vote Dem.	Percentage Major Vote Rep.	Percentage Major Vote Dem.
14,030	BARBOUR	6,849	3,103	3,746		643 D	45.3%	54.7%	45.3%	54.7%
36,356	BERKELEY	17,034	8,269	8,765		496 D	48.5%	51.5%	48.5%	51.5%
25,118	BOONE	11,587	2,805	8,779	3	5,974 D	24.2%	75.8%	24.2%	75.8%
12,666	BRAXTON	5,879	1,851	4,028		2,177 D	31.5%	68.5%	31.5%	68.5%
29,685	BROOKE	12,919	3,183	9,735	1	6,552 D	24.6%	75.4%	24.6%	75.4%
106,918	CABELL	39,622	13,525	26,097		12,572 D	34.1%	65.9%	34.1%	65.9%
7,046	CALHOUN	3,433	1,248	2,185		937 D	36.4%	63.6%	36.4%	63.6%
9,330	CLAY	3,930	1,220	2,710		1,490 D	31.0%	69.0%	31.0%	69.0%
6,389	DODDRIDGE	3,060	1,721	1,339		382 R	56.2%	43.8%	56.2%	43.8%
49,332	FAYETTE	20,924	4,911	16,013		11,102 D	23.5%	76.5%	23.5%	76.5%
7,782	GILMER	3,602	1,336	2,266		930 D	37.1%	62.9%	37.1%	62.9%
8,607	GRANT	4,219	2,643	1,576		1,067 R	62.6%	37.4%	62.6%	37.4%
32,090	GREENBRIER	14,070	5,435	8,635		3,200 D	38.6%	61.4%	38.6%	61.4%
11,710	HAMPSHIRE	5,049	1,672	3,377		1,705 D	33.1%	66.9%	33.1%	66.9%
39,749	HANCOCK	16,750	3,928	12,822		8,894 D	23.5%	76.5%	23.5%	76.5%
8,855	HARDY	4,259	1,658	2,601		943 D	38.9%	61.1%	38.9%	61.1%
73,028	HARRISON	36,364	12,334	24,020	10	11,686 D	33.9%	66.1%	33.9%	66.1%
20,903	JACKSON	10,780	4,793	5,987		1,194 D	44.5%	55.5%	44.5%	55.5%
21,280	JEFFERSON	8,819	2,971	5,848		2,877 D	33.7%	66.3%	33.7%	66.3%
229,515	KANAWHA	95,174	33,422	61,709	43	28,287 D	35.1%	64.8%	35.1%	64.9%
17,847	LEWIS	7,650	3,154	4,496		1,342 D	41.2%	58.8%	41.2%	58.8%
18,912	LINCOLN	8,059	2,889	5,170		2,281 D	35.8%	64.2%	35.8%	64.2%
46,269	LOGAN	16,964	3,332	13,632		10,300 D	19.6%	80.4%	19.6%	80.4%
50,666	MCDOWELL	14,449	2,839	11,561	49	8,722 D	19.6%	80.0%	19.7%	80.3%
61,356	MARION	27,929	7,105	20,824		13,719 D	25.4%	74.6%	25.4%	74.6%
37,598	MARSHALL	16,512	5,366	11,146		5,780 D	32.5%	67.5%	32.5%	67.5%
24,306	MASON	11,974	4,478	7,496		3,018 D	37.4%	62.6%	37.4%	62.6%
63,206	MERCER	25,247	8,460	16,787		8,327 D	33.5%	66.5%	33.5%	66.5%
23,109	MINERAL	10,926	4,085	6,841		2,756 D	37.4%	62.6%	37.4%	62.6%
32,780	MINGO	11,436	2,485	8,868	83	6,383 D	21.7%	77.5%	21.9%	78.1%
63,714	MONONGALIA	27,930	8,220	19,710		11,490 D	29.4%	70.6%	29.4%	70.6%
11,272	MONROE	6,013	2,764	3,249		485 D	46.0%	54.0%	46.0%	54.0%
8,547	MORGAN	4,217	2,084	2,133		49 D	49.4%	50.6%	49.4%	50.6%
22,552	NICHOLAS	9,681	3,165	6,516		3,351 D	32.7%	67.3%	32.7%	67.3%
64,197	OHIO	26,451	8,663	17,788		9,125 D	32.8%	67.2%	32.8%	67.2%
7,031	PENDLETON	3,610	1,302	2,308		1,006 D	36.1%	63.9%	36.1%	63.9%
7,274	PLEASANTS	3,320	1,304	2,016		712 D	39.3%	60.7%	39.3%	60.7%
8,870	POCAHONTAS	4,046	1,511	2,535		1,024 D	37.3%	62.7%	37.3%	62.7%
25,455	PRESTON	11,234	4,812	6,422		1,610 D	42.8%	57.2%	42.8%	57.2%
27,625	PUTNAM	14,576	5,154	9,422		4,268 D	35.4%	64.6%	35.4%	64.6%
70,080	RALEIGH	30,221	9,550	20,671		11,121 D	31.6%	68.4%	31.6%	68.4%
24,596	RANDOLPH	11,939	3,473	8,466		4,993 D	29.1%	70.9%	29.1%	70.9%
10,145	RITCHIE	4,845	2,602	2,243		359 R	53.7%	46.3%	53.7%	46.3%
14,111	ROANE	6,693	3,079	3,614		535 D	46.0%	54.0%	46.0%	54.0%
13,213	SUMMERS	6,158	2,183	3,975		1,792 D	35.4%	64.6%	35.4%	64.6%
13,878	TAYLOR	6,767	2,548	4,219		1,671 D	37.7%	62.3%	37.7%	62.3%
7,447	TUCKER	3,705	1,250	2,455		1,205 D	33.7%	66.3%	33.7%	66.3%
9,929	TYLER	4,355	2,177	2,178		1 D	50.0%	50.0%	50.0%	50.0%
19,092	UPSHUR	8,275	3,748	4,527		779 D	45.3%	54.7%	45.3%	54.7%
37,581	WAYNE	15,573	4,729	10,844		6,115 D	30.4%	69.6%	30.4%	69.6%
9,809	WEBSTER	3,872	956	2,916		1,960 D	24.7%	75.3%	24.7%	75.3%
20,314	WETZEL	8,824	2,548	6,276		3,728 D	28.9%	71.1%	28.9%	71.1%
4,154	WIRT	2,229	874	1,355		481 D	39.2%	60.8%	39.2%	60.8%
86,818	WOOD	37,284	14,788	22,496		7,708 D	39.7%	60.3%	39.7%	60.3%
30,095	WYOMING	11,983	3,715	8,268		4,553 D	31.0%	69.0%	31.0%	69.0%
1,744,237	TOTAL	749,270	253,420	495,661	189	242,241 D	33.8%	66.2%	33.8%	66.2%

WEST VIRGINIA

SENATOR 1976

1970 Census Population	County	Total Vote	Republican	Democratic	Other	Rep.-Dem. Plurality	Percentage Total Vote Rep.	Percentage Total Vote Dem.	Percentage Major Vote Rep.	Percentage Major Vote Dem.
14,030	BARBOUR	5,059		5,059		5,059 D		100.0%		100.0%
36,356	BERKELEY	13,177		13,177		13,177 D		100.0%		100.0%
25,118	BOONE	9,882		9,872	10	9,872 D		99.9%		100.0%
12,666	BRAXTON	4,649		4,638	11	4,638 D		99.8%		100.0%
29,685	BROOKE	10,435		10,410	25	10,410 D		99.8%		100.0%
106,918	CABELL	25,618		25,618		25,618 D		100.0%		100.0%
7,046	CALHOUN	2,581		2,578	3	2,578 D		99.9%		100.0%
9,330	CLAY	3,095		3,095		3,095 D		100.0%		100.0%
6,389	DODDRIDGE	1,981		1,981		1,981 D		100.0%		100.0%
49,332	FAYETTE	18,021		18,021		18,021 D		100.0%		100.0%
7,782	GILMER	2,814		2,814		2,814 D		100.0%		100.0%
8,607	GRANT	2,043		2,041	2	2,041 D		99.9%		100.0%
32,090	GREENBRIER	11,044		11,044		11,044 D		100.0%		100.0%
11,710	HAMPSHIRE	4,031		4,031		4,031 D		100.0%		100.0%
39,749	HANCOCK	12,139		12,139		12,139 D		100.0%		100.0%
8,855	HARDY	3,100		3,100		3,100 D		100.0%		100.0%
73,028	HARRISON	28,942		28,787	155	28,787 D		99.5%		100.0%
20,903	JACKSON	7,425		7,425		7,425 D		100.0%		100.0%
21,280	JEFFERSON	7,481		7,481		7,481 D		100.0%		100.0%
229,515	KANAWHA	68,468		68,389	79	68,389 D		99.9%		100.0%
17,847	LEWIS	6,067		6,067		6,067 D		100.0%		100.0%
18,912	LINCOLN	5,810		5,810		5,810 D		100.0%		100.0%
46,269	LOGAN	13,767		13,767		13,767 D		100.0%		100.0%
50,666	MCDOWELL	11,974		11,939	35	11,939 D		99.7%		100.0%
61,356	MARION	21,614		21,614		21,614 D		100.0%		100.0%
37,598	MARSHALL	13,160		13,160		13,160 D		100.0%		100.0%
24,306	MASON	8,429		8,429		8,429 D		100.0%		100.0%
63,206	MERCER	19,835		19,835		19,835 D		100.0%		100.0%
23,109	MINERAL	8,266		8,266		8,266 D		100.0%		100.0%
32,780	MINGO	9,119		9,100	19	9,100 D		99.8%		100.0%
63,714	MONONGALIA	23,360		23,360		23,360 D		100.0%		100.0%
11,272	MONROE	4,185		4,185		4,185 D		100.0%		100.0%
8,547	MORGAN	3,000		3,000		3,000 D		100.0%		100.0%
22,552	NICHOLAS	7,803		7,803		7,803 D		100.0%		100.0%
64,197	OHIO	19,753		19,753		19,753 D		100.0%		100.0%
7,031	PENDLETON	2,531		2,531		2,531 D		100.0%		100.0%
7,274	PLEASANTS	2,477		2,477		2,477 D		100.0%		100.0%
8,870	POCAHONTAS	3,087		3,077	10	3,077 D		99.7%		100.0%
25,455	PRESTON	8,349		8,349		8,349 D		100.0%		100.0%
27,625	PUTNAM	11,223		11,223		11,223 D		100.0%		100.0%
70,080	RALEIGH	23,816		23,816		23,816 D		100.0%		100.0%
24,596	RANDOLPH	9,565		9,565		9,565 D		100.0%		100.0%
10,145	RITCHIE	3,169		3,169		3,169 D		100.0%		100.0%
14,111	ROANE	4,457		4,444	13	4,444 D		99.7%		100.0%
13,213	SUMMERS	4,988		4,988		4,988 D		100.0%		100.0%
13,878	TAYLOR	5,348		5,348		5,348 D		100.0%		100.0%
7,447	TUCKER	2,861		2,861		2,861 D		100.0%		100.0%
9,929	TYLER	2,815		2,815		2,815 D		100.0%		100.0%
19,092	UPSHUR	5,615		5,615		5,615 D		100.0%		100.0%
37,581	WAYNE	10,635		10,635		10,635 D		100.0%		100.0%
9,809	WEBSTER	3,298		3,293	5	3,293 D		99.8%		100.0%
20,314	WETZEL	7,021		7,021		7,021 D		100.0%		100.0%
4,154	WIRT	1,625		1,625		1,625 D		100.0%		100.0%
86,818	WOOD	26,774		26,774		26,774 D		100.0%		100.0%
30,095	WYOMING	9,009		9,009		9,009 D		100.0%		100.0%
1,744,237	TOTAL	566,790		566,423	367	566,423 D		99.9%		100.0%

WEST VIRGINIA

CONGRESS

CD	Year	Total Vote	Republican Vote	Republican Candidate	Democratic Vote	Democratic Candidate	Other Vote	Rep.-Dem. Plurality	Percentage Total Vote Rep.	Percentage Total Vote Dem.	Percentage Major Vote Rep.	Percentage Major Vote Dem.
1	1976	186,263	78,159	MCCUSKEY, JOHN F.	108,103	MOLLOHAN, ROBERT H.	1	29,944 D	42.0%	58.0%	42.0%	58.0%
1	1974	121,423	48,966	LAURITA, JOE	72,457	MOLLOHAN, ROBERT H.		23,491 D	40.3%	59.7%	40.3%	59.7%
1	1972	187,336	57,274	KAPNICKY, GEORGE E.	130,062	MOLLOHAN, ROBERT H.		72,788 D	30.6%	69.4%	30.6%	69.4%
2	1976	186,832	50,079	SLOAN, JIM	136,749	STAGGERS, HARLEY O.	4	86,670 D	26.8%	73.2%	26.8%	73.2%
2	1974	114,462	40,779	LOY, WILLIAM H.	73,683	STAGGERS, HARLEY O.		32,904 D	35.6%	64.4%	35.6%	64.4%
2	1972	183,235	54,949	DIX, DAVID	128,286	STAGGERS, HARLEY O.		73,337 D	30.0%	70.0%	30.0%	70.0%
3	1976	128,479			128,086	SLACK, JOHN M.	393	128,086 D		99.7%		100.0%
3	1974	113,209	35,623	LARCAMP, WILLIAM L.	77,586	SLACK, JOHN M.		41,963 D	31.5%	68.5%	31.5%	68.5%
3	1972	185,787	67,441	HIGGINS, T. DAVID	118,346	SLACK, JOHN M.		50,905 D	36.3%	63.7%	36.3%	63.7%
4	1976	161,520	28,825	GOODMAN, E. S.	73,626	RAHALL, NICK J.	59,069	44,801 D	17.8%	45.6%	28.1%	71.9%
4	1974	66,420			66,420	HECHLER, KEN		66,420 D		100.0%		100.0%
4	1972	164,842	64,242	NEAL, JOE	100,600	HECHLER, KEN		36,358 D	39.0%	61.0%	39.0%	61.0%

WEST VIRGINIA

1976 GENERAL ELECTION

President — Original uncorrected canvass gave the Republican total vote as 314,726 and the Democratic total vote as 435,864. The votes in both the Democratic and Republican totals in Wood county were amended. Other vote was 113 McCarthy (write-in); 17 Anderson (write-in); 16 MacBride (write-in); 12 Maddox (write-in); 5 Hall (write-in); 2 Camejo (write-in); 125 scattered.

Governor — Original canvass was amended twice; uncorrected canvass totals for the Republican vote were 253,398 and 253,423; uncorrected canvass totals for the Democratic vote were 495,600 and 495,659. The votes in both the Democratic and Republican totals in Wood county were amended. Other vote was scattered.

Senator — Original uncorrected canvass gave the Democratic total vote as 566,359. The Wood county vote was amended. Other vote was scattered.

Congress — Original uncorrected canvass gave the Republican vote as 78,134 and the Democratic vote as 108,055 in CD 1. In that CD the Wood county vote was amended. In CD 2 McDowell county was incorrectly listed as being in CD 2 in the original canvass, and the uncorrected totals were Republican 52,230, Democratic 145,405. Other vote was scattered in CD's 1, 2 and 3; 59,067 Hechler (write-in) and 2 scattered. in CD 4.

1976 PRIMARIES

MAY 11 REPUBLICAN

Governor — 97,671 Cecil H. Underwood; 44,393 Ralph D. Albertazzie; 3,408 Melton M. Maloney; 2,593 Larry R. Lunsford; 2,442 John W. Lusher; 1,257 E. E. Cumptan.

Senator — None. No candidate.

Congress — Unopposed in two CD's. No candidate in CD 3. Contested as follows:

CD 1 — 25,748 John F. McCuskey; 11,897 Donald Chaney.

MAY 11 DEMOCRATIC

Governor — 206,732 John D. Rockefeller; 118,707 James M. Sprouse; 52,791 Ken Hechler; 26,222 John G. Hutchinson; 4,249 Ezra H. Graley; 3,536 Powell Lane; 2,345 H. John Rogers; 1,581 Si Allen.

Senator — Robert C. Byrd, unopposed.

Congress — Unopposed in two CD's. Contested as follows:

CD 3 — 70,716 John M. Slack; 10,761 Avis L. Hill.

CD 4 — 33,742 Nick J. Rahall; 21,602 Dan Burleson; 14,999 Bob E. Myers; 11,677 Hawey A. Wells; 8,081 Irvine Damron.

WISCONSIN

GOVERNOR

Martin J. Schreiber (D). Elected as Lieutenant-Governor in 1974 and succeeded upon the resignation of Governor Lucey in July 1977. Next election in 1978.

SENATORS

Gaylord A. Nelson (D). Re-elected 1974 to a six-year term. Previously elected 1968, 1962.

William Proxmire (D). Re-elected 1976 to a six-year term. Previously elected 1970, 1964, 1958, and in August 1957 to fill out term vacated by the death of Senator Joseph R. McCarthy.

REPRESENTATIVES

1. Les Aspin (D)
2. Robert Kastenmeier (D)
3. Alvin Baldus (D)
4. Clement J. Zablocki (D)
5. Henry S. Reuss (D)
6. William A. Steiger (R)
7. David R. Obey (D)
8. Robert J. Cornell (D)
9. Robert W. Kasten (R)

POSTWAR VOTE FOR GOVERNOR

								Percentage			
	Total	Republican		Democratic		Other	Rep.-Dem.	Total Vote		Major Vote	
Year	Vote	Vote	Candidate	Vote	Candidate	Vote	Plurality	Rep.	Dem.	Rep.	Dem.
1974	1,181,976	497,195	Dyke, William D.	628,639	Lucey, Patrick J.	56,142	131,444 D	42.1%	53.2%	44.2%	55.8%
1970	1,343,160	602,617	Olson, Jack B.	728,403	Lucey, Patrick J.	12,140	125,786 D	44.9%	54.2%	45.3%	54.7%
1968	1,689,738	893,463	Knowles, Warren P.	791,100	LaFollette, Bronson C.	5,175	102,363 R	52.9%	46.8%	53.0%	47.0%
1966	1,170,173	626,041	Knowles, Warren P.	539,258	Lucey, Patrick J.	4,874	86,783 R	53.5%	46.1%	53.7%	46.3%
1964	1,694,887	856,779	Knowles, Warren P.	837,901	Reynolds, John W.	207	18,878 R	50.6%	49.4%	50.6%	49.4%
1962	1,265,900	625,536	Kuehn, Philip G.	637,491	Reynolds, John W.	2,873	11,955 D	49.4%	50.4%	49.5%	50.5%
1960	1,728,009	837,123	Kuehn, Philip G.	890,868	Nelson, Gaylord A.	18	53,745 D	48.4%	51.6%	48.4%	51.6%
1958	1,202,219	556,391	Thomson, Vernon W.	644,296	Nelson, Gaylord A.	1,532	87,905 D	46.3%	53.6%	46.3%	53.7%
1956	1,557,788	808,273	Thomson, Vernon W.	749,421	Proxmire, William	94	58,852 R	51.9%	48.1%	51.9%	48.1%
1954	1,158,666	596,158	Kohler, Walter J.	560,747	Proxmire, William	1,761	35,411 R	51.5%	48.4%	51.5%	48.5%
1952	1,615,214	1,009,171	Kohler, Walter J.	601,844	Proxmire, William	4,199	407,327 R	62.4%	37.3%	62.6%	37.4%
1950	1,138,148	605,649	Kohler, Walter J.	525,319	Thompson, Carl W.	7,180	80,330 R	53.2%	46.2%	53.6%	46.4%
1948	1,266,139	684,839	Rennebohm, Oscar	558,497	Thompson, Carl W.	22,803	126,342 R	54.1%	44.1%	55.1%	44.9%
1946	1,040,444	621,970	Goodland, Walter	406,499	Hoan, Daniel W.	11,975	215,471 R	59.8%	39.1%	60.5%	39.5%

The term of office for Wisconsin's Governor was increased from two to four years effective with the 1970 election.

POSTWAR VOTE FOR SENATOR

								Percentage			
	Total	Republican		Democratic		Other	Rep.-Dem.	Total Vote		Major Vote	
Year	Vote	Vote	Candidate	Vote	Candidate	Vote	Plurality	Rep.	Dem.	Rep.	Dem.
1976	1,935,183	521,902	York, Stanley	1,396,970	Proxmire, William	16,311	875,068 D	27.0%	72.2%	27.2%	72.8%
1974	1,199,495	429,327	Petri, Thomas E.	740,700	Nelson, Gaylord A.	29,468	311,373 D	35.8%	61.8%	36.7%	63.3%
1970	1,338,967	381,297	Erickson, John E.	948,445	Proxmire, William	9,225	567,148 D	28.5%	70.8%	28.7%	71.3%
1968	1,654,861	633,910	Leonard, Jerris	1,020,931	Nelson, Gaylord A.	20	387,021 D	38.3%	61.7%	38.3%	61.7%
1964	1,673,776	780,116	Renk, Wilbur N.	892,013	Proxmire, William	1,647	111,897 D	46.6%	53.3%	46.7%	53.3%
1962	1,260,168	594,846	Wiley, Alexander	662,342	Nelson, Gaylord A.	2,980	67,496 D	47.2%	52.6%	47.3%	52.7%
1958	1,194,678	510,398	Steinle, Roland J.	682,440	Proxmire, William	1,840	172,042 D	42.7%	57.1%	42.8%	57.2%
1957s	772,620	312,931	Kohler, Walter J.	435,985	Proxmire, William	23,704	123,054 D	40.5%	56.4%	41.8%	58.2%
1956	1,523,356	892,473	Wiley, Alexander	627,903	Maier, Henry W.	2,980	264,570 R	58.6%	41.2%	58.7%	41.3%
1952	1,605,228	870,444	McCarthy, Joseph R.	731,402	Fairchild, Thomas E.	3,382	139,042 R	54.2%	45.6%	54.3%	45.7%
1950	1,116,135	595,283	Wiley, Alexander	515,539	Fairchild, Thomas E.	5,313	79,744 R	53.3%	46.2%	53.6%	46.4%
1946	1,014,594	620,430	McCarthy, Joseph R.	378,772	McMurray, Howard J.	15,392	241,658 R	61.2%	37.3%	62.1%	37.9%

The 1957 election was held in August for a short term to fill a vacancy.

WISCONSIN

Districts Established November 20, 1971

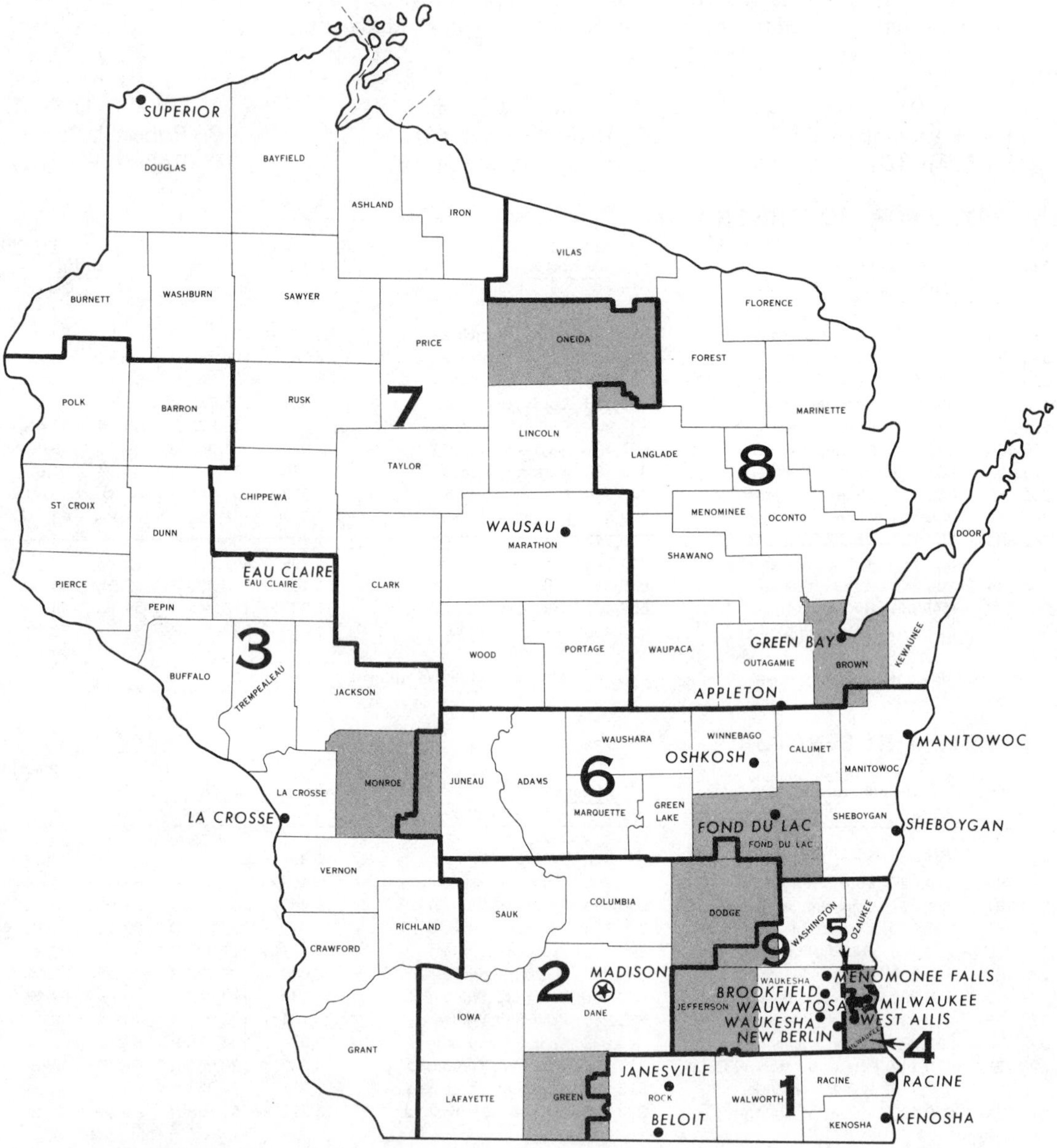

County with two or more Congressional Districts.

WISCONSIN

PRESIDENT 1976

1970 Census Population	County	Total Vote	Republican	Democratic	Other	Rep.-Dem. Plurality	Percentage Total Vote Rep.	Total Vote Dem.	Major Vote Rep.	Major Vote Dem.
9,234	ADAMS	5,594	2,377	3,089	128	712 D	42.5%	55.2%	43.5%	56.5%
16,743	ASHLAND	7,961	3,045	4,688	228	1,643 D	38.2%	58.9%	39.4%	60.6%
33,955	BARRON	16,406	7,393	8,678	335	1,285 D	45.1%	52.9%	46.0%	54.0%
11,683	BAYFIELD	6,706	2,624	3,885	197	1,261 D	39.1%	57.9%	40.3%	59.7%
158,244	BROWN	72,318	36,571	33,572	2,175	2,999 R	50.6%	46.4%	52.1%	47.9%
13,743	BUFFALO	6,441	2,844	3,448	149	604 D	44.2%	53.5%	45.2%	54.8%
9,276	BURNETT	6,469	2,573	3,720	176	1,147 D	39.8%	57.5%	40.9%	59.1%
27,604	CALUMET	13,157	6,589	6,241	327	348 R	50.1%	47.4%	51.4%	48.6%
47,717	CHIPPEWA	20,155	8,137	11,538	480	3,401 D	40.4%	57.2%	41.4%	58.6%
30,361	CLARK	13,784	6,095	7,238	451	1,143 D	44.2%	52.5%	45.7%	54.3%
40,150	COLUMBIA	19,933	10,075	9,457	401	618 R	50.5%	47.4%	51.6%	48.4%
15,252	CRAWFORD	7,226	3,393	3,629	204	236 D	47.0%	50.2%	48.3%	51.7%
290,272	DANE	152,756	63,466	82,321	6,969	18,855 D	41.5%	53.9%	43.5%	56.5%
69,004	DODGE	31,674	17,335	13,643	696	3,692 R	54.7%	43.1%	56.0%	44.0%
20,106	DOOR	11,420	6,557	4,553	310	2,004 R	57.4%	39.9%	59.0%	41.0%
44,657	DOUGLAS	20,989	6,999	13,478	512	6,479 D	33.3%	64.2%	34.2%	65.8%
29,154	DUNN	15,040	6,751	7,882	407	1,131 D	44.9%	52.4%	46.1%	53.9%
67,219	EAU CLAIRE	35,386	16,388	18,263	735	1,875 D	46.3%	51.6%	47.3%	52.7%
3,298	FLORENCE	1,925	922	965	38	43 D	47.9%	50.1%	48.9%	51.1%
84,567	FOND DU LAC	39,895	22,226	16,571	1,098	5,655 R	55.7%	41.5%	57.3%	42.7%
7,691	FOREST	4,245	1,604	2,574	67	970 D	37.8%	60.6%	38.4%	61.6%
48,398	GRANT	22,220	12,016	9,639	565	2,377 R	54.1%	43.4%	55.5%	44.5%
26,714	GREEN	13,076	7,085	5,632	359	1,453 R	54.2%	43.1%	55.7%	44.3%
16,878	GREEN LAKE	8,612	5,020	3,411	181	1,609 R	58.3%	39.6%	59.5%	40.5%
19,306	IOWA	8,685	4,195	4,252	238	57 D	48.3%	49.0%	49.7%	50.3%
6,533	IRON	3,805	1,340	2,399	66	1,059 D	35.2%	63.0%	35.8%	64.2%
15,325	JACKSON	7,276	3,406	3,735	135	329 D	46.8%	51.3%	47.7%	52.3%
60,060	JEFFERSON	28,876	15,528	12,577	771	2,951 R	53.8%	43.6%	55.2%	44.8%
18,455	JUNEAU	9,087	4,242	4,512	333	270 D	46.7%	49.7%	48.5%	51.5%
117,917	KENOSHA	51,338	22,349	27,585	1,404	5,236 D	43.5%	53.7%	44.8%	55.2%
18,961	KEWAUNEE	9,322	4,447	4,607	268	160 D	47.7%	49.4%	49.1%	50.9%
80,468	LA CROSSE	41,704	24,188	16,674	842	7,514 R	58.0%	40.0%	59.2%	40.8%
17,456	LAFAYETTE	8,195	4,131	3,839	225	292 R	50.4%	46.8%	51.8%	48.2%
19,220	LANGLADE	8,936	4,630	4,134	172	496 R	51.8%	46.3%	52.8%	47.2%
23,499	LINCOLN	11,738	5,672	5,800	266	128 D	48.3%	49.4%	49.4%	50.6%
82,294	MANITOWOC	36,798	16,039	19,819	940	3,780 D	43.6%	53.9%	44.7%	55.3%
97,457	MARATHON	48,054	21,898	24,934	1,222	3,036 D	45.6%	51.9%	46.8%	53.2%
35,810	MARINETTE	17,439	8,591	8,482	366	109 R	49.3%	48.6%	50.3%	49.7%
8,865	MARQUETTE	5,217	2,607	2,516	94	91 R	50.0%	48.2%	50.9%	49.1%
2,607	MENOMINEE	1,122	324	766	32	442 D	28.9%	68.3%	29.7%	70.3%
1,054,262	MILWAUKEE	456,545	192,008	249,739	14,798	57,731 D	42.1%	54.7%	43.5%	56.5%
31,610	MONROE	13,998	7,242	6,465	291	777 R	51.7%	46.2%	52.8%	47.2%
25,553	OCONTO	13,048	6,232	6,541	275	309 D	47.8%	50.1%	48.8%	51.2%
24,427	ONEIDA	14,947	7,347	7,216	384	131 R	49.2%	48.3%	50.4%	49.6%
119,356	OUTAGAMIE	52,568	28,363	23,079	1,126	5,284 R	54.0%	43.9%	55.1%	44.9%
54,421	OZAUKEE	31,961	19,817	11,271	873	8,546 R	62.0%	35.3%	63.7%	36.3%
7,319	PEPIN	3,338	1,312	1,955	71	643 D	39.3%	58.6%	40.2%	59.8%
26,652	PIERCE	14,112	5,676	8,039	397	2,363 D	40.2%	57.0%	41.4%	58.6%
26,666	POLK	14,924	6,159	8,485	280	2,326 D	41.3%	56.9%	42.1%	57.9%
47,541	PORTAGE	26,269	9,520	15,912	837	6,392 D	36.2%	60.6%	37.4%	62.6%
14,520	PRICE	7,428	3,204	4,028	196	824 D	43.1%	54.2%	44.3%	55.7%
170,838	RACINE	75,787	37,088	36,740	1,959	348 R	48.9%	48.5%	50.2%	49.8%
17,079	RICHLAND	8,258	4,466	3,634	158	832 R	54.1%	44.0%	55.1%	44.9%
131,970	ROCK	57,860	28,325	28,048	1,487	277 R	49.0%	48.5%	50.2%	49.8%
14,238	RUSK	6,989	2,724	4,050	215	1,326 D	39.0%	57.9%	40.2%	59.8%
34,354	ST. CROIX	18,715	7,685	10,601	429	2,916 D	41.1%	56.6%	42.0%	58.0%
39,057	SAUK	19,220	9,577	9,204	439	373 R	49.8%	47.9%	51.0%	49.0%
9,670	SAWYER	5,918	2,720	3,055	143	335 D	46.0%	51.6%	47.1%	52.9%
32,650	SHAWANO	15,584	8,505	6,751	328	1,754 R	54.6%	43.3%	55.7%	44.3%
96,660	SHEBOYGAN	47,413	22,332	24,226	855	1,894 D	47.1%	51.1%	48.0%	52.0%
16,958	TAYLOR	7,921	3,591	4,101	229	510 D	45.3%	51.8%	46.7%	53.3%
23,344	TREMPEALEAU	11,740	5,341	6,218	181	877 D	45.5%	53.0%	46.2%	53.8%
24,557	VERNON	11,914	6,132	5,534	248	598 R	51.5%	46.4%	52.6%	47.4%
10,958	VILAS	8,350	4,929	3,209	212	1,720 R	59.0%	38.4%	60.6%	39.4%
63,444	WALWORTH	31,365	18,091	12,418	856	5,673 R	57.7%	39.6%	59.3%	40.7%

WISCONSIN

PRESIDENT 1976

1970 Census Population	County	Total Vote	Republican	Democratic	Other	Rep.-Dem. Plurality	Percentage Total Vote Rep.	Total Vote Dem.	Major Vote Rep.	Major Vote Dem.
10,601	WASHBURN	6,467	2,787	3,503	177	716 D	43.1%	54.2%	44.3%	55.7%
63,839	WASHINGTON	34,120	18,798	14,422	900	4,376 R	55.1%	42.3%	56.6%	43.4%
231,365	WAUKESHA	121,133	70,418	47,487	3,228	22,931 R	58.1%	39.2%	59.7%	40.3%
37,780	WAUPACA	18,086	10,849	6,857	380	3,992 R	60.0%	37.9%	61.3%	38.7%
14,795	WAUSHARA	8,098	4,449	3,485	164	964 R	54.9%	43.0%	56.1%	43.9%
129,934	WINNEBAGO	58,127	32,149	24,485	1,493	7,664 R	55.3%	42.1%	56.8%	43.2%
65,362	WOOD	30,992	15,479	14,728	785	751 R	49.9%	47.5%	51.2%	48.8%
4,417,933	TOTAL	2,104,175	1,004,987	1,040,232	58,956	35,245 D	47.8%	49.4%	49.1%	50.9%

WISCONSIN

SENATOR 1976

1970 Census Population	County	Total Vote	Republican	Democratic	Other	Rep.-Dem. Plurality	Percentage Total Vote Rep.	Total Vote Dem.	Major Vote Rep.	Major Vote Dem.
9,234	ADAMS	5,172	1,375	3,787	10	2,412 D	26.6%	73.2%	26.6%	73.4%
16,743	ASHLAND	6,159	1,297	4,834	28	3,537 D	21.1%	78.5%	21.2%	78.8%
33,955	BARRON	14,046	4,295	9,726	25	5,431 D	30.6%	69.2%	30.6%	69.4%
11,683	BAYFIELD	6,233	1,307	4,905	21	3,598 D	21.0%	78.7%	21.0%	79.0%
158,244	BROWN	65,420	15,408	49,427	585	34,019 D	23.6%	75.6%	23.8%	76.2%
13,743	BUFFALO	6,187	1,813	4,374		2,561 D	29.3%	70.7%	29.3%	70.7%
9,276	BURNETT	5,368	1,144	4,192	32	3,048 D	21.3%	78.1%	21.4%	78.6%
27,604	CALUMET	11,564	2,873	8,653	38	5,780 D	24.8%	74.8%	24.9%	75.1%
47,717	CHIPPEWA	19,248	3,578	15,531	139	11,953 D	18.6%	80.7%	18.7%	81.3%
30,361	CLARK	12,460	3,460	8,930	70	5,470 D	27.8%	71.7%	27.9%	72.1%
40,150	COLUMBIA	18,103	6,551	11,506	46	4,955 D	36.2%	63.6%	36.3%	63.7%
15,252	CRAWFORD	5,528	1,574	3,938	16	2,364 D	28.5%	71.2%	28.6%	71.4%
290,272	DANE	141,644	37,572	99,327	4,745	61,755 D	26.5%	70.1%	27.4%	72.6%
69,004	DODGE	29,040	10,470	18,406	164	7,936 D	36.1%	63.4%	36.3%	63.7%
20,106	DOOR	9,852	3,487	6,297	68	2,810 D	35.4%	63.9%	35.6%	64.4%
44,657	DOUGLAS	19,031	2,069	16,764	198	14,695 D	10.9%	88.1%	11.0%	89.0%
29,154	DUNN	13,162	3,045	10,063	54	7,018 D	23.1%	76.5%	23.2%	76.8%
67,219	EAU CLAIRE	32,658	7,243	25,234	181	17,991 D	22.2%	77.3%	22.3%	77.7%
3,298	FLORENCE	1,566	424	1,141	1	717 D	27.1%	72.9%	27.1%	72.9%
84,567	FOND DU LAC	33,874	10,225	23,298	351	13,073 D	30.2%	68.8%	30.5%	69.5%
7,691	FOREST	3,380	640	2,727	13	2,087 D	18.9%	80.7%	19.0%	81.0%
48,398	GRANT	18,582	6,970	11,527	85	4,557 D	37.5%	62.0%	37.7%	62.3%
26,714	GREEN	12,190	4,185	7,970	35	3,785 D	34.3%	65.4%	34.4%	65.6%
16,878	GREEN LAKE	7,928	3,647	4,266	15	619 D	46.0%	53.8%	46.1%	53.9%
19,306	IOWA	7,859	2,572	5,252	35	2,680 D	32.7%	66.8%	32.9%	67.1%
6,533	IRON	3,005	543	2,450	12	1,907 D	18.1%	81.5%	18.1%	81.9%
15,325	JACKSON	6,278	1,428	4,839	11	3,411 D	22.7%	77.1%	22.8%	77.2%
60,060	JEFFERSON	25,874	8,889	16,891	94	8,002 D	34.4%	65.3%	34.5%	65.5%
18,455	JUNEAU	7,989	2,801	5,163	25	2,362 D	35.1%	64.6%	35.2%	64.8%
117,917	KENOSHA	46,125	8,748	36,869	508	28,121 D	19.0%	79.9%	19.2%	80.8%
18,961	KEWAUNEE	7,536	1,483	6,014	39	4,531 D	19.7%	79.8%	19.8%	80.2%
80,468	LA CROSSE	39,314	11,007	28,165	142	17,158 D	28.0%	71.6%	28.1%	71.9%
17,456	LAFAYETTE	6,918	2,071	4,838	9	2,767 D	29.9%	69.9%	30.0%	70.0%
19,220	LANGLADE	7,138	1,704	5,418	16	3,714 D	23.9%	75.9%	23.9%	76.1%
23,499	LINCOLN	10,190	2,872	7,300	18	4,428 D	28.2%	71.6%	28.2%	71.8%
82,294	MANITOWOC	34,272	6,896	27,206	170	20,310 D	20.1%	79.4%	20.2%	79.8%
97,457	MARATHON	41,291	9,308	31,609	374	22,301 D	22.5%	76.6%	22.7%	77.3%
35,810	MARINETTE	15,164	4,069	11,040	55	6,971 D	26.8%	72.8%	26.9%	73.1%
8,865	MARQUETTE	4,774	1,784	2,983	7	1,199 D	37.4%	62.5%	37.4%	62.6%
2,607	MENOMINEE	678	74	592	12	518 D	10.9%	87.3%	11.1%	88.9%
1,054,262	MILWAUKEE	440,152	98,874	336,826	4,452	237,952 D	22.5%	76.5%	22.7%	77.3%
31,610	MONROE	13,142	4,362	8,774	6	4,412 D	33.2%	66.8%	33.2%	66.8%
25,553	OCONTO	12,254	3,703	8,531	20	4,828 D	30.2%	69.6%	30.3%	69.7%
24,427	ONEIDA	12,631	3,376	9,217	38	5,841 D	26.7%	73.0%	26.8%	73.2%
119,356	OUTAGAMIE	48,329	14,414	33,546	369	19,132 D	29.8%	69.4%	30.1%	69.9%
54,421	OZAUKEE	30,756	11,864	18,815	77	6,951 D	38.6%	61.2%	38.7%	61.3%
7,319	PEPIN	2,772	636	2,122	14	1,486 D	22.9%	76.6%	23.1%	76.9%
26,652	PIERCE	13,448	4,019	9,413	16	5,394 D	29.9%	70.0%	29.9%	70.1%
26,666	POLK	12,888	3,191	9,686	11	6,495 D	24.8%	75.2%	24.8%	75.2%
47,541	PORTAGE	24,648	4,912	19,428	308	14,516 D	19.9%	78.8%	20.2%	79.8%
14,520	PRICE	6,754	1,817	4,906	31	3,089 D	26.9%	72.6%	27.0%	73.0%
170,838	RACINE	68,011	16,140	51,472	399	35,332 D	23.7%	75.7%	23.9%	76.1%
17,079	RICHLAND	7,589	3,340	4,232	17	892 D	44.0%	55.8%	44.1%	55.9%
131,970	ROCK	50,961	15,303	35,389	269	20,086 D	30.0%	69.4%	30.2%	69.8%
14,238	RUSK	5,590	1,092	4,468	30	3,376 D	19.5%	79.9%	19.6%	80.4%
34,354	ST. CROIX	17,456	4,145	13,303	8	9,158 D	23.7%	76.2%	23.8%	76.2%
39,057	SAUK	17,623	6,297	11,212	114	4,915 D	35.7%	63.6%	36.0%	64.0%
9,670	SAWYER	4,556	1,598	2,944	14	1,346 D	35.1%	64.6%	35.2%	64.8%
32,650	SHAWANO	13,453	5,270	8,152	31	2,882 D	39.2%	60.6%	39.3%	60.7%
96,660	SHEBOYGAN	45,578	10,773	34,710	95	23,937 D	23.6%	76.2%	23.7%	76.3%
16,958	TAYLOR	6,622	1,690	4,906	26	3,216 D	25.5%	74.1%	25.6%	74.4%
23,344	TREMPEALEAU	10,524	2,512	8,004	8	5,492 D	23.9%	76.1%	23.9%	76.1%
24,557	VERNON	9,851	4,512	5,333	6	821 D	45.8%	54.1%	45.8%	54.2%
10,958	VILAS	6,627	2,344	4,241	42	1,897 D	35.4%	64.0%	35.6%	64.4%
63,444	WALWORTH	28,065	11,135	16,826	104	5,691 D	39.7%	60.0%	39.8%	60.2%

WISCONSIN

SENATOR 1976

1970 Census Population	County	Total Vote	Republican	Democratic	Other	Rep.-Dem. Plurality	Percentage Total Vote Rep.	Percentage Total Vote Dem.	Percentage Major Vote Rep.	Percentage Major Vote Dem.
10,601	WASHBURN	5,066	1,310	3,722	34	2,412 D	25.9%	73.5%	26.0%	74.0%
63,839	WASHINGTON	32,463	10,740	21,608	115	10,868 D	33.1%	66.6%	33.2%	66.8%
231,365	WAUKESHA	115,883	37,690	77,590	603	39,900 D	32.5%	67.0%	32.7%	67.3%
37,780	WAUPACA	16,507	7,627	8,845	35	1,218 D	46.2%	53.6%	46.3%	53.7%
14,795	WAUSHARA	7,489	3,130	4,355	4	1,225 D	41.8%	58.2%	41.8%	58.2%
129,934	WINNEBAGO	56,286	16,222	39,715	349	23,493 D	28.8%	70.6%	29.0%	71.0%
65,362	WOOD	28,409	6,963	21,227	219	14,264 D	24.5%	74.7%	24.7%	75.3%
4,417,933	TOTAL	1,935,183	521,902	1,396,970	16,311	875,068 D	27.0%	72.2%	27.2%	72.8%

WISCONSIN

CONGRESS

			Republican		Democratic				Percentage			
		Total					Other	Rep.-Dem.	Total Vote		Major Vote	
CD	Year	Vote	Vote	Candidate	Vote	Candidate	Vote	Plurality	Rep.	Dem.	Rep.	Dem.
1	1976	209,807	71,427	PETRIE, WILLIAM W.	136,162	ASPIN, LES	2,218	64,735 D	34.0%	64.9%	34.4%	65.6%
1	1974	116,191	34,288	SMITH, LEONARD W.	81,902	ASPIN, LES	1	47,614 D	29.5%	70.5%	29.5%	70.5%
1	1972	190,937	66,665	STALBAUM, MERRILL E.	122,973	ASPIN, LES	1,299	56,308 D	34.9%	64.4%	35.2%	64.8%
2	1976	236,545	81,350	MILLER, ELIZABETH T.	155,158	KASTENMEIER, ROBERT	37	73,808 D	34.4%	65.6%	34.4%	65.6%
2	1974	144,453	50,890	MILLER, ELIZABETH T.	93,561	KASTENMEIER, ROBERT	2	42,671 D	35.2%	64.8%	35.2%	64.8%
2	1972	217,318	68,167	KELLY, J. MICHAEL	148,136	KASTENMEIER, ROBERT	1,015	79,969 D	31.4%	68.2%	31.5%	68.5%
3	1976	239,311	100,218	GUNDERSEN, ADOLF L.	139,083	BALDUS, ALVIN	10	38,865 D	41.9%	58.1%	41.9%	58.1%
3	1974	150,028	71,171	THOMSON, VERNON W.	76,668	BALDUS, ALVIN	2,189	5,497 D	47.4%	51.1%	48.1%	51.9%
3	1972	206,356	112,905	THOMSON, VERNON W.	91,953	THORESEN, WALTER	1,498	20,952 R	54.7%	44.6%	55.1%	44.9%
4	1976	172,243			172,166	ZABLOCKI, CLEMENT J.	77	172,166 D		100.0%		100.0%
4	1974	116,995	27,818	COLLISON, LEWIS D.	84,768	ZABLOCKI, CLEMENT J.	4,409	56,950 D	23.8%	72.5%	24.7%	75.3%
4	1972	197,072	45,003	MROZINSKI, PHILLIP D.	149,078	ZABLOCKI, CLEMENT J.	2,991	104,075 D	22.8%	75.6%	23.2%	76.8%
5	1976	173,511	36,413	HICKS, ROBERT L.	134,935	REUSS, HENRY S.	2,163	98,522 D	21.0%	77.8%	21.3%	78.7%
5	1974	81,361	16,293	MORRIES, MILDRED A.	65,060	REUSS, HENRY S.	8	48,767 D	20.0%	80.0%	20.0%	80.0%
5	1972	164,654	33,627	VAN HECKE, FREDERICK	127,273	REUSS, HENRY S.	3,754	93,646 D	20.4%	77.3%	20.9%	79.1%
6	1976	220,271	139,541	STEIGER, WILLIAM A.	80,715	SMITH, JOSEPH C.	15	58,826 R	63.3%	36.6%	63.4%	36.6%
6	1974	145,660	86,652	STEIGER, WILLIAM A.	51,571	SIMENZ, NANCY J.	7,437	35,081 R	59.5%	35.4%	62.7%	37.3%
6	1972	198,610	130,701	STEIGER, WILLIAM A.	63,643	ADAMS, JAMES A.	4,266	67,058 R	65.8%	32.0%	67.3%	32.7%
7	1976	233,937	60,952	SAVINO, FRANK A.	171,366	OBEY, DAVID R.	1,619	110,414 D	26.1%	73.3%	26.2%	73.8%
7	1974	148,172	43,558	BURGER, JOSEF	104,468	OBEY, DAVID R.	146	60,910 D	29.4%	70.5%	29.4%	70.6%
7	1972	215,612	80,207	O KONSKI, ALVIN E.	135,385	OBEY, DAVID R.	20	55,178 D	37.2%	62.8%	37.2%	62.8%
8	1976	228,106	107,048	FROEHLICH, HAROLD V.	115,996	CORNELL, ROBERT J.	5,062	8,948 D	46.9%	50.9%	48.0%	52.0%
8	1974	146,840	66,889	FROEHLICH, HAROLD V.	79,923	CORNELL, ROBERT J.	28	13,034 D	45.6%	54.4%	45.6%	54.4%
8	1972	201,643	101,634	FROEHLICH, HAROLD V.	97,795	CORNELL, ROBERT J.	2,214	3,839 R	50.4%	48.5%	51.0%	49.0%
9	1976	248,524	163,791	KASTEN, ROBERT W.	84,706	MCDONALD, LYNN M.	27	79,085 R	65.9%	34.1%	65.9%	34.1%
9	1974	146,871	77,733	KASTEN, ROBERT W.	66,071	ADELMAN, LYNN S.	3,067	11,662 R	52.9%	45.0%	54.1%	45.9%
9	1972	208,892	128,230	DAVIS, GLENN R.	76,585	FINE, RALPH A.	4,077	51,645 R	61.4%	36.7%	62.6%	37.4%

WISCONSIN

1976 GENERAL ELECTION

President — Other vote was 34,943 McCarthy (Independent); 8,552 Maddox (American); 4,298 Zeidler (Democratic Socialist); 3,814 MacBride (Libertarian); 1,691 Camejo (Socialist Workers); 943 Wright (People's); 749 Hall (Communist); 738 LaRouche (U.S. Labor); 389 Levin (Socialist Labor); 2,839 scattered.

Senator — Other vote was 7,354 Hart (Democratic Socialist); 4,876 Schwarz (Socialist Workers); 2,148 MacLaurin (U.S. Labor); 1,731 Nordlander (Socialist Labor); 202 scattered.

Congress — Other vote was scattered in CD's 2, 3, 4, 6 and 9; 2,205 Zimmerman (American) and 13 scattered in CD 1; 1,563 Chapman (Independent), 597 Sokoly (Independent) and 3 scattered in CD 5; 1,575 Olishkewych (American) and 44 scattered in CD 7; 5,056 Hoeft (American) and 6 scattered in CD 8.

1976 PRIMARIES

SEPTEMBER 14 REPUBLICAN

Senator — Stanley York, unopposed.

Congress — Unopposed in six CD's. No candidate in CD 4. Contested as follows:

CD 3 — 28,300 Adolph L. Gundersen; 5,815 Timothy L. Bearson.
CD 8 — 16,727 Harold V. Froehlich; 10,008 John R. Byrnes.

SEPTEMBER 14 DEMOCRATIC

Senator — William Proxmire, unopposed.

Congress — Unopposed in six CD's. Contested as follows:

CD 4 — 29,540 Clement J. Zablocki; 5,838 Roman R. Blenski.
CD 5 — 28,670 Henry S. Reuss; 15,782 James C. Newcomb.
CD 8 — 27,083 Robert J. Cornell; 11,049 Demetrio A. Verich.

SEPTEMBER 14 AMERICAN

Senator — None. No candidate.

Congress — Unopposed in the two CD's in which a candidate was nominated.

WYOMING

GOVERNOR

Ed Herschler (D). Elected 1974 to a four-year term.

SENATORS

Clifford P. Hansen (R). Re-elected 1972 to a six-year term. Previously elected 1966.

Malcolm Wallop (R). Elected 1976 to a six-year term.

REPRESENTATIVE

At-Large. Teno Roncalio (D)

POSTWAR VOTE FOR GOVERNOR

									Percentage			
	Total	Republican		Democratic		Other	Rep.-Dem.	Total Vote		Major Vote	
Year	Vote	Vote	Candidate	Vote	Candidate	Vote	Plurality	Rep.	Dem.	Rep.	Dem.
1974	128,386	56,645	Jones, Dick	71,741	Herschler, Ed	–	15,096 D	44.1%	55.9%	44.1%	55.9%
1970	118,257	74,249	Hathaway, Stan	44,008	Rooney, John J.	–	30,241 R	62.8%	37.2%	62.8%	37.2%
1966	120,873	65,624	Hathaway, Stan	55,249	Wilkerson, Ernest	–	10,375 R	54.3%	45.7%	54.3%	45.7%
1962	119,268	64,970	Hansen, Clifford P.	54,298	Gage, Jack R.	–	10,672 R	54.5%	45.5%	54.5%	45.5%
1958	112,537	52,488	Simpson, Milward L.	55,070	Hickey, J. J.	4,979	2,582 D	46.6%	48.9%	48.8%	51.2%
1954	111,438	56,275	Simpson, Milward L.	55,163	Jack, William	–	1,112 R	50.5%	49.5%	50.5%	49.5%
1950	96,959	54,441	Barrett, Frank A.	42,518	McIntyre, John J.	–	11,923 R	56.1%	43.9%	56.1%	43.9%
1946	81,353	38,333	Wright, Earl	43,020	Hunt, Lester C.	–	4,687 D	47.1%	52.9%	47.1%	52.9%

POSTWAR VOTE FOR SENATOR

								Percentage			
	Total	Republican		Democratic		Other	Rep.-Dem.	Total Vote		Major Vote	
Year	Vote	Vote	Candidate	Vote	Candidate	Vote	Plurality	Rep.	Dem.	Rep.	Dem.
1976	155,368	84,810	Wallop, Malcolm	70,558	McGee, Gale	–	14,252 R	54.6%	45.4%	54.6%	45.4%
1972	142,067	101,314	Hansen, Clifford P.	40,753	Vinich, Mike	–	60,561 R	71.3%	28.7%	71.3%	28.7%
1970	120,486	53,279	Wold, John S.	67,207	McGee, Gale	–	13,928 D	44.2%	55.8%	44.2%	55.8%
1966	122,689	63,548	Hansen, Clifford P.	59,141	Roncalio, Teno	–	4,407 R	51.8%	48.2%	51.8%	48.2%
1964	141,670	65,185	Wold, John S.	76,485	McGee, Gale	–	11,300 D	46.0%	54.0%	46.0%	54.0%
1962s	119,372	69,043	Simpson, Milward L.	50,329	Hickey, J. J.	–	18,714 R	57.8%	42.2%	57.8%	42.2%
1960	138,550	78,103	Thomson, E. Keith	60,447	Whitaker, Ray	–	17,656 R	56.4%	43.6%	56.4%	43.6%
1958	114,157	56,122	Barrett, Frank A.	58,035	McGee, Gale	–	1,913 D	49.2%	50.8%	49.2%	50.8%
1954	112,252	54,407	Harrison, William H.	57,845	O'Mahoney, Joseph C.	–	3,438 D	48.5%	51.5%	48.5%	51.5%
1952	130,097	67,176	Barrett, Frank A.	62,921	O'Mahoney, Joseph C.	–	4,255 R	51.6%	48.4%	51.6%	48.4%
1948	101,480	43,527	Robertson, Edward V.	57,953	Hunt, Lester C.	–	14,426 D	42.9%	57.1%	42.9%	57.1%
1946	81,557	35,714	Henderson, Harry B.	45,843	O'Mahoney, Joseph C.	–	10,129 D	43.8%	56.2%	43.8%	56.2%

The election in 1962 was for a short term to fill a vacancy.

WYOMING

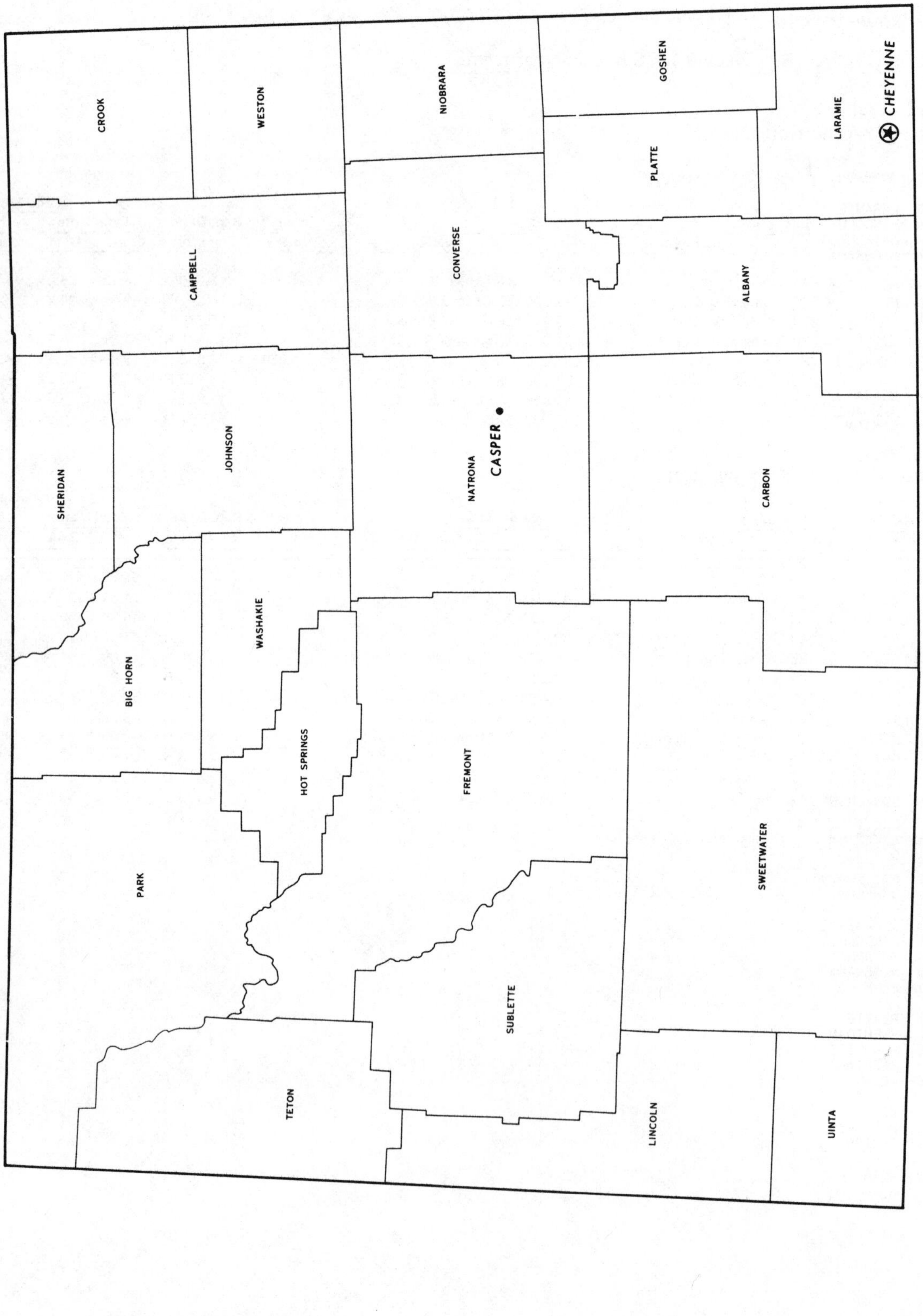
CROOK
WESTON
NIOBRARA
GOSHEN
LARAMIE
CHEYENNE
PLATTE
CAMPBELL
CONVERSE
ALBANY
SHERIDAN
JOHNSON
NATRONA
CASPER
CARBON
BIG HORN
WASHAKIE
HOT SPRINGS
FREMONT
SWEETWATER
PARK
SUBLETTE
TETON
LINCOLN
UINTA

WYOMING

PRESIDENT 1976

1970 Census Population	County	Total Vote	Republican	Democratic	Other	Rep.-Dem. Plurality	Percentage Total Vote Rep.	Percentage Total Vote Dem.	Percentage Major Vote Rep.	Percentage Major Vote Dem.
26,431	ALBANY	11,622	6,734	4,663	225	2,071 R	57.9%	40.1%	59.1%	40.9%
10,202	BIG HORN	4,747	3,117	1,618	12	1,499 R	65.7%	34.1%	65.8%	34.2%
12,957	CAMPBELL	4,995	3,306	1,620	69	1,686 R	66.2%	32.4%	67.1%	32.9%
13,354	CARBON	6,584	3,556	3,010	18	546 R	54.0%	45.7%	54.2%	45.8%
5,938	CONVERSE	3,347	2,188	1,150	9	1,038 R	65.4%	34.4%	65.5%	34.5%
4,535	CROOK	2,139	1,438	653	48	785 R	67.2%	30.5%	68.8%	31.2%
28,352	FREMONT	11,063	6,584	4,423	56	2,161 R	59.5%	40.0%	59.8%	40.2%
10,885	GOSHEN	5,038	2,764	2,262	12	502 R	54.9%	44.9%	55.0%	45.0%
4,952	HOT SPRINGS	2,379	1,413	958	8	455 R	59.4%	40.3%	59.6%	40.4%
5,587	JOHNSON	2,866	2,042	797	27	1,245 R	71.2%	27.8%	71.9%	28.1%
56,360	LARAMIE	26,294	14,061	12,040	193	2,021 R	53.5%	45.8%	53.9%	46.1%
8,640	LINCOLN	4,044	2,464	1,555	25	909 R	60.9%	38.5%	61.3%	38.7%
51,264	NATRONA	22,621	13,761	8,640	220	5,121 R	60.8%	38.2%	61.4%	38.6%
2,924	NIOBRARA	1,477	1,042	427	8	615 R	70.5%	28.9%	70.9%	29.1%
17,752	PARK	8,602	5,878	2,656	68	3,222 R	68.3%	30.9%	68.9%	31.1%
6,486	PLATTE	3,450	1,844	1,593	13	251 R	53.4%	46.2%	53.7%	46.3%
17,852	SHERIDAN	8,652	5,382	3,206	64	2,176 R	62.2%	37.1%	62.7%	37.3%
3,755	SUBLETTE	1,826	1,284	528	14	756 R	70.3%	28.9%	70.9%	29.1%
18,391	SWEETWATER	10,574	4,937	5,575	62	638 D	46.7%	52.7%	47.0%	53.0%
4,823	TETON	3,957	2,667	1,204	86	1,463 R	67.4%	30.4%	68.9%	31.1%
7,100	UINTA	3,811	2,124	1,559	128	565 R	55.7%	40.9%	57.7%	42.3%
7,569	WASHAKIE	3,541	2,361	1,168	12	1,193 R	66.7%	33.0%	66.9%	33.1%
6,307	WESTON	2,714	1,770	934	10	836 R	65.2%	34.4%	65.5%	34.5%
332,416	TOTAL	156,343	92,717	62,239	1,387	30,478 R	59.3%	39.8%	59.8%	40.2%

SENATOR 1976

1970 Census Population	County	Total Vote	Republican	Democratic	Other	Rep.-Dem. Plurality	Percentage Total Vote Rep.	Percentage Total Vote Dem.	Percentage Major Vote Rep.	Percentage Major Vote Dem.
26,431	ALBANY	12,019	6,027	5,992		35 R	50.1%	49.9%	50.1%	49.9%
10,202	BIG HORN	4,706	2,880	1,826		1,054 R	61.2%	38.8%	61.2%	38.8%
12,957	CAMPBELL	4,970	3,397	1,573		1,824 R	68.4%	31.6%	68.4%	31.6%
13,354	CARBON	6,504	2,909	3,595		686 D	44.7%	55.3%	44.7%	55.3%
5,938	CONVERSE	3,321	2,012	1,309		703 R	60.6%	39.4%	60.6%	39.4%
4,535	CROOK	2,110	1,477	633		844 R	70.0%	30.0%	70.0%	30.0%
28,352	FREMONT	10,836	6,282	4,554		1,728 R	58.0%	42.0%	58.0%	42.0%
10,885	GOSHEN	5,035	2,578	2,457		121 R	51.2%	48.8%	51.2%	48.8%
4,952	HOT SPRINGS	2,301	1,176	1,125		51 R	51.1%	48.9%	51.1%	48.9%
5,587	JOHNSON	2,835	1,972	863		1,109 R	69.6%	30.4%	69.6%	30.4%
56,360	LARAMIE	26,129	11,873	14,256		2,383 D	45.4%	54.6%	45.4%	54.6%
8,640	LINCOLN	3,897	2,183	1,714		469 R	56.0%	44.0%	56.0%	44.0%
51,264	NATRONA	22,494	12,283	10,211		2,072 R	54.6%	45.4%	54.6%	45.4%
2,924	NIOBRARA	1,490	1,056	434		622 R	70.9%	29.1%	70.9%	29.1%
17,752	PARK	8,158	5,341	2,817		2,524 R	65.5%	34.5%	65.5%	34.5%
6,486	PLATTE	3,406	1,952	1,454		498 R	57.3%	42.7%	57.3%	42.7%
17,852	SHERIDAN	9,151	5,389	3,762		1,627 R	58.9%	41.1%	58.9%	41.1%
3,755	SUBLETTE	1,806	1,267	539		728 R	70.2%	29.8%	70.2%	29.8%
18,391	SWEETWATER	10,363	4,543	5,820		1,277 D	43.8%	56.2%	43.8%	56.2%
4,823	TETON	3,925	2,582	1,343		1,239 R	65.8%	34.2%	65.8%	34.2%
7,100	UINTA	3,703	1,781	1,922		141 D	48.1%	51.9%	48.1%	51.9%
7,569	WASHAKIE	3,504	2,070	1,434		636 R	59.1%	40.9%	59.1%	40.9%
6,307	WESTON	2,705	1,780	925		855 R	65.8%	34.2%	65.8%	34.2%
332,416	TOTAL	155,368	84,810	70,558		14,252 R	54.6%	45.4%	54.6%	45.4%

WYOMING

CONGRESS

CD	Year	Total Vote	Republican Vote	Republican Candidate	Democratic Vote	Democratic Candidate	Other Vote	Rep.-Dem. Plurality	Percentage Total Vote Rep.	Percentage Total Vote Dem.	Percentage Major Vote Rep.	Percentage Major Vote Dem.
AL	1976	151,868	66,147	HART, LARRY	85,721	RONCALIO, TENO		19,574 D	43.6%	56.4%	43.6%	56.4%
AL	1974	126,933	57,499	STROOCK, TOM	69,434	RONCALIO, TENO		11,935 D	45.3%	54.7%	45.3%	54.7%
AL	1972	146,299	70,667	KIDD, WILLIAM	75,632	RONCALIO, TENO		4,965 D	48.3%	51.7%	48.3%	51.7%
AL	1970	116,304	57,848	ROBERTS, HARRY	58,456	RONCALIO, TENO		608 D	49.7%	50.3%	49.7%	50.3%
AL	1968	123,313	77,363	WOLD, JOHN S.	45,950	LINFORD, VELMA		31,413 R	62.7%	37.3%	62.7%	37.3%
AL	1966	119,426	62,984	HARRISON, WILLIAM H.	56,442	CHRISTIAN, AL		6,542 R	52.7%	47.3%	52.7%	47.3%
AL	1964	139,175	68,482	HARRISON, WILLIAM H.	70,693	RONCALIO, TENO		2,211 D	49.2%	50.8%	49.2%	50.8%
AL	1962	116,474	71,489	HARRISON, WILLIAM H.	44,985	MANKUS, LOUIS A.		26,504 R	61.4%	38.6%	61.4%	38.6%
AL	1960	134,331	70,241	HARRISON, WILLIAM H.	64,090	ARMSTRONG, H. T.		6,151 R	52.3%	47.7%	52.3%	47.7%
AL	1958	111,780	59,894	THOMSON, E. KEITH	51,886	WHITAKER, RAY		8,008 R	53.6%	46.4%	53.6%	46.4%
AL	1956	120,128	69,903	THOMSON, E. KEITH	50,225	O CALLAGHAN, JERRY		19,678 R	58.2%	41.8%	58.2%	41.8%
AL	1954	108,771	61,111	THOMSON, E. KEITH	47,660	TULLY, SAM		13,451 R	56.2%	43.8%	56.2%	43.8%
AL	1952	126,720	76,161	HARRISON, WILLIAM H.	50,559	ROSE, ROBERT R.		25,602 R	60.1%	39.9%	60.1%	39.9%
AL	1950	93,348	50,865	HARRISON, WILLIAM H.	42,483	CLARK, JOHN B.		8,382 R	54.5%	45.5%	54.5%	45.5%
AL	1948	97,464	50,218	BARRETT, FRANK A.	47,246	FLANNERY, L. G.		2,972 R	51.5%	48.5%	51.5%	48.5%
AL	1946	79,438	44,482	BARRETT, FRANK A.	34,956	MCINTYRE, JOHN J.		9,526 R	56.0%	44.0%	56.0%	44.0%

WYOMING

1976 GENERAL ELECTION

President Other vote was 624 McCarthy (write-in); 290 Anderson (write-in); 89 MacBride (write-in); 30 Maddox (write-in); 354 scattered.

Senator

Congress

1976 PRIMARIES

SEPTEMBER 14 REPUBLICAN

Senator 41,445 Malcolm Wallop; 6,965 Nels T. Larson; 5,727 Doyle Henry.

Congress Unopposed at-large.

SEPTEMBER 14 DEMOCRATIC

Senator Gale McGee, unopposed.

Congress Contested as follows:

AL 41,393 Teno Roncalio; 6,751 Al Hamburg.

DISTRICT OF COLUMBIA

GOVERNMENT

The District of Columbia is governed by a Mayor and a City Council of thirteen.

MAYOR

Walter E. Washington (D). Elected 1974 to a four-year term.

DELEGATE

Walter E. Fauntroy (D)

POSTWAR VOTE FOR MAYOR

Year	Total Vote	Republican Vote	Republican Candidate	Democratic Vote	Democratic Candidate	Other Vote	Rep.-Dem. Plurality	Percentage Total Vote Rep.	Percentage Total Vote Dem.	Percentage Major Vote Rep.	Percentage Major Vote Dem.
1974	105,183	3,703	Champion, Jackson R.	84,676	Washington, Walter E.	16,804	80,973 D	3.5%	80.5%	4.2%	95.8%

POSTWAR VOTE FOR DELEGATE

Year	Total Vote	Republican Vote	Republican Candidate	Democratic Vote	Democratic Candidate	Other Vote	Rep.-Dem. Plurality	Percentage Total Vote Rep.	Percentage Total Vote Dem.	Percentage Major Vote Rep.	Percentage Major Vote Dem.
1976	159,790	21,699	Hall, Daniel L.	123,464	Fauntroy, Walter E.	14,627	101,765 D	13.6%	77.3%	14.9%	85.1%
1974	104,014	9,166	Phillips, William R.	66,337	Fauntroy, Walter E.	28,511	57,171 D	8.8%	63.8%	12.1%	87.9%
1972	159,612	39,487	Chin-Lee, William	95,300	Fauntroy, Walter E.	24,825	55,813 D	24.7%	59.7%	29.3%	70.7%
1971	116,635	29,249	Nevius, John A.	68,166	Fauntroy, Walter E.	19,220	38,917 D	25.1%	58.4%	30.0%	70.0%

The 1971 election was for a short term to the end of the 92nd Congress.

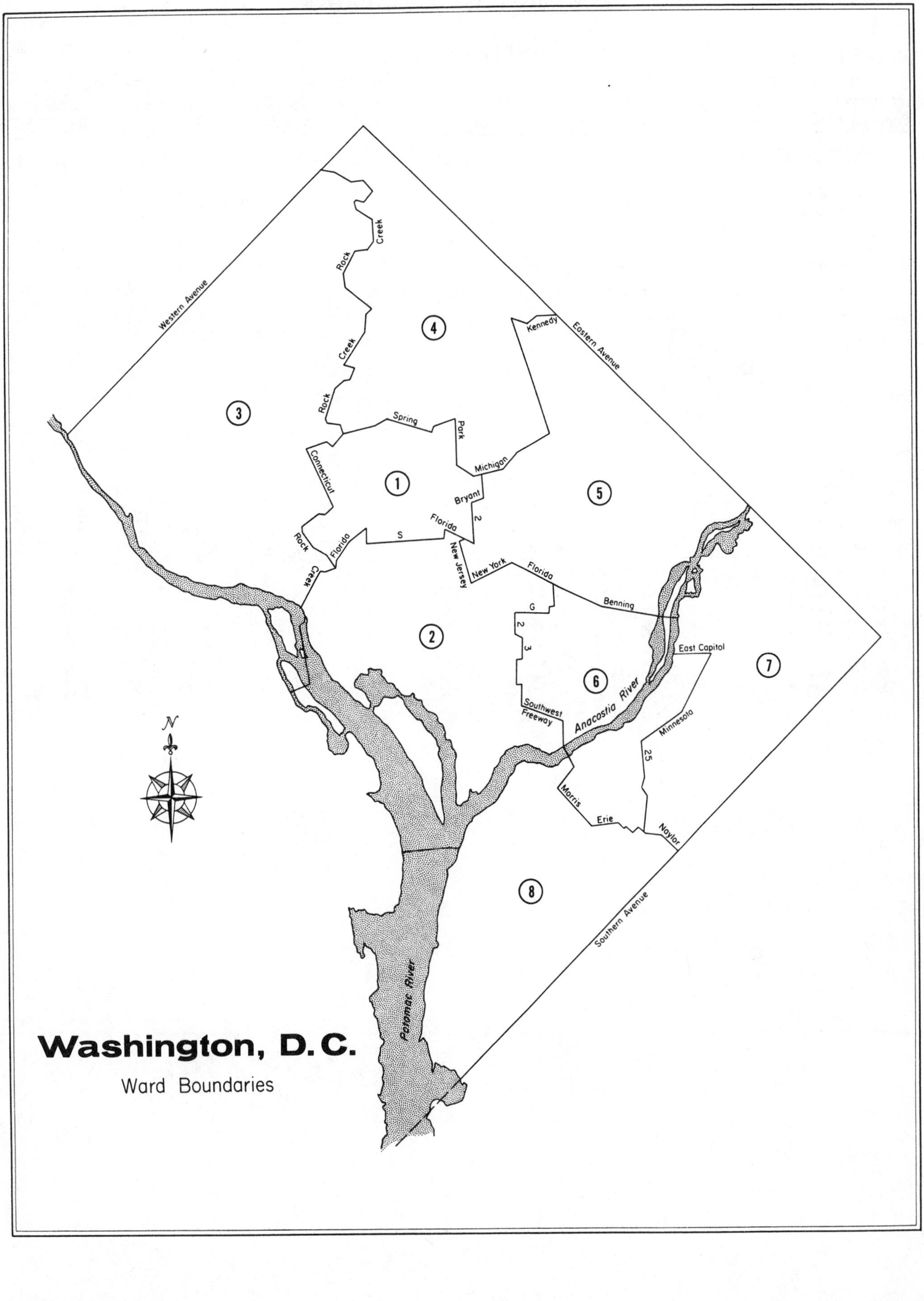
Western Avenue
Rock Creek
Rock Creek
4
3
Kennedy
Eastern Avenue
Spring
Park
Connecticut
1
Michigan
Bryant
5
2
S
Florida
Rock
Creek
New Jersey
New York
Florida
G
Benning
2
3
6
East Capitol
7
Southwest Freeway
Anacostia River
Minnesota
25
Morris
Erie
Naylor
8
Southern Avenue
Potomac River
N
Washington, D.C.
Ward Boundaries

DISTRICT OF COLUMBIA

PRESIDENT 1976

1970 Census Population	Ward	Total Vote	Republican	Democratic	Other	Rep.-Dem. Plurality	Percentage Total Vote Rep.	Percentage Total Vote Dem.	Percentage Major Vote Rep.	Percentage Major Vote Dem.
94,215	WARD 1	16,577	2,064	13,982	531	11,918 D	12.5%	84.3%	12.9%	87.1%
94,076	WARD 2	19,245	4,019	14,638	588	10,619 D	20.9%	76.1%	21.5%	78.5%
94,719	WARD 3	35,729	15,184	19,583	962	4,399 D	42.5%	54.8%	43.7%	56.3%
94,193	WARD 4	26,785	2,064	24,432	289	22,368 D	7.7%	91.2%	7.8%	92.2%
94,679	WARD 5	21,503	1,365	19,932	206	18,567 D	6.3%	92.7%	6.4%	93.6%
95,192	WARD 6	16,947	1,575	15,032	340	13,457 D	9.3%	88.7%	9.5%	90.5%
95,019	WARD 7	20,641	1,136	19,372	133	18,236 D	5.5%	93.9%	5.5%	94.5%
94,417	WARD 8	11,403	466	10,847	90	10,381 D	4.1%	95.1%	4.1%	95.9%
756,510	TOTAL	168,830	27,873	137,818	3,139	109,945 D	16.5%	81.6%	16.8%	83.2%

DELEGATE 1976

1970 Census Population	Ward	Total Vote	Republican	Democratic	Other	Rep.-Dem. Plurality	Percentage Total Vote Rep.	Percentage Total Vote Dem.	Percentage Major Vote Rep.	Percentage Major Vote Dem.
94,215	WARD 1	15,742	1,566	12,149	2,027	10,583 D	9.9%	77.2%	11.4%	88.6%
94,076	WARD 2	18,145	3,063	12,997	2,085	9,934 D	16.9%	71.6%	19.1%	80.9%
94,719	WARD 3	32,613	11,611	16,888	4,114	5,277 D	35.6%	51.8%	40.7%	59.3%
94,193	WARD 4	24,709	1,380	21,407	1,922	20,027 D	5.6%	86.6%	6.1%	93.9%
94,679	WARD 5	21,188	1,126	18,776	1,286	17,650 D	5.3%	88.6%	5.7%	94.3%
95,192	WARD 6	16,272	1,578	13,122	1,572	11,544 D	9.7%	80.6%	10.7%	89.3%
95,019	WARD 7	20,103	969	18,132	1,002	17,163 D	4.8%	90.2%	5.1%	94.9%
94,417	WARD 8	11,018	406	9,993	619	9,587 D	3.7%	90.7%	3.9%	96.1%
756,510	TOTAL	159,790	21,699	123,464	14,627	101,765 D	13.6%	77.3%	14.9%	85.1%

DISTRICT OF COLUMBIA

1976 GENERAL ELECTION

President — Other vote was 545 Camejo (Socialist Workers); 274 MacBridge (Libertarian); 219 Hall (Communist); 157 LaRouche (U.S. Labor); 1,944 scattered.

Delegate — Under legislation enacted in 1970, the District of Columbia elects a single non-voting Delegate to serve in Congress. Other vote was 6,423 Aronica (D.C. Statehood); 3,926 Pennington (U.S. Labor); 3,576 Reavis (Workers); 702 scattered.

1976 PRIMARIES

MAY 4 REPUBLICAN

Delegate — No candidates names appeared on the ballot; of 842 write-in votes, Daniel L. Hall received 201 and was nominated.

MAY 4 DEMOCRATIC

Delegate — Walter E. Fauntroy, unopposed.

MAY 4 D.C. STATEHOOD

Delegate — Louis Aronica, unopposed.